PRENTICE HALL
LITERATURE

GRADE 6

COMMON CORE EDITION

Upper Saddle River, New Jersey

Boston, Massachusetts

Chandler, Arizona

Glenview, Illinois

PEARSON

Cover: (L) ©PBNJ Productions/Blend Images/Getty Images, (TL) ©Robert Yin/Corbis, (TR) ©Georges Antoni/Hemis/Corbis, (C) ©Pawel Libera/Corbis, (BR) ©Arctic-Images/Getty Images, (BC) ©Hannes Hepp/Getty Images

---

Acknowledgments appear on page R58, which constitutes an extension of this copyright page.

ISBN-13: 978-0-13-319552-1
ISBN-10:   0-13-319552-X
2 3 4 5 6 7 8 9 10 VO63 15 14 13 12 11

Master Teacher Board

Contributing Authors

The contributing authors guided the direction and philosophy of Pearson Prentice Hall Literature. *Working with the development team, they helped to build the pedagogical integrity of the program and to ensure its relevance for today's teachers and students.*

Grant Wiggins, Ed.D., is the President of Authentic Education in Hopewell, New Jersey. He earned his Ed.D. from Harvard University and his B.A. from St. John's College in Annapolis. Grant consults with schools, districts, and state education departments on a variety of reform matters; organizes conferences and workshops; and develops print materials and Web resources on curricular change. He is the coauthor, with Jay McTighe, of *Understanding by Design* and *The Understanding by Design Handbook,* the award-winning and highly successful materials on curriculum published by ASCD. His work has been supported by the Pew Charitable Trusts, the Geraldine R. Dodge Foundation, and the National Science Foundation. *The Association for Supervision of Curriculum Development (ASCD), publisher of the "Understanding by Design Handbook" co-authored by Grant Wiggins and registered owner of the trademark "Understanding by Design," has not authorized, approved, or sponsored this work and is in no way affiliated with Pearson or its products.*

Jeff Anderson has worked with struggling writers and readers for almost 20 years. Anderson's specialty is the integration of grammar and editing instruction into the processes of reading and writing. He has published two books, *Mechanically Inclined: Building Grammar, Usage, and Style into Writer's Workshop,* and *Everyday Editing: Inviting Students to Develop Skill and Craft in Writer's Workshop,* as well as a DVD, *The Craft of Grammar.* Anderson's work has appeared in *English Journal.* Anderson won the NCTE Paul and Kate Farmer Award for his *English Journal* article on teaching grammar in context.

Arnetha F. Ball, Ph.D., is a Professor at Stanford University. Her areas of expertise include language and literacy studies of diverse student populations, research on writing instruction, and teacher preparation for working with diverse populations. She is the author of *African American Literacies Unleashed* with Dr. Ted Lardner, and *Multicultural Strategies for Education and Social Change.*

Sheridan Blau is Professor of Education and English at the University of California, Santa Barbara, where he directs the South Coast Writing Project and the Literature Institute for Teachers. He has served in senior advisory roles for such groups as the National Board for Professional Teaching Standards, the College Board, and the American Board for Teacher Education. Blau served for twenty years on the National Writing Project Advisory Board and Task Force, and is a former president of NCTE. Blau is the author of *The Literature Workshop: Teaching Texts and Their Readers,* which was named by the Conference on English Education as the 2004 Richard Meade Award winner for outstanding research in English education.

William G. Brozo, Ph.D., is a Professor of Literacy at George Mason University in Fairfax, Virginia. He has taught reading and language arts in junior and senior high school and is the author of numerous texts on literacy development. Dr. Brozo's work focuses on building capacity among teacher leaders, enriching the literate culture of schools, enhancing the literate lives of boys, and making teaching more responsive to the needs of all students. His recent publications include *Bright Beginnings for Boys: Engaging Young Boys in Active Literacy* and the *Adolescent Literacy Inventory.*

Doug Buehl is a teacher, author, and national literacy consultant. He is the author of *Classroom Strategies for Interactive Learning* and coauthor of *Reading and the High School Student: Strategies to Enhance Literacy;* and *Strategies to Enhance Literacy and Learning in Middle School Content Area Classrooms.*

Jim Cummins, Ph.D., is a professor in the Modern Language Centre at the University of Toronto. He is the author of numerous publications, including *Negotiating Identities: Education for Empowerment in a Diverse Society.* Cummins coined the acronyms BICS and CAPT to help differentiate the type of language ability students need for success.

Harvey Daniels, Ph.D., has been a classroom teacher, writing project director, author, and university professor. "Smokey" serves as an international consultant to schools, districts, and educational agencies. He is known for his work on student-led book clubs, as recounted in *Literature Circles: Voice and Choice in Book Clubs & Reading Groups* and *Mini Lessons for Literature Circles.* Recent works include *Subjects Matter: Every Teacher's Guide to Content-Area Reading* and *Content Area Writing: Every Teacher's Guide.*

Jane Feber taught language arts in Jacksonville, Florida, for 36 years. Her innovative approach to instruction has earned her several awards, including the NMSA Distinguished Educator Award, the NCTE Edwin A. Hoey Award, the Gladys Prior Award for Teaching Excellence, and the Florida Council of Teachers of English Teacher of the Year Award. She is a National Board Certified Teacher, past president of the Florida Council of Teachers of English, and is the author of *Creative Book Reports* and *Active Word Play*.

Danling Fu, Ph.D., is Professor of Language and Culture in the College of Education at the University of Florida. She researches and provides inservice to public schools nationally, focusing on literacy instruction for new immigrant students. Fu's books include *My Trouble is My English* and *An Island of English* addressing English language learners in the secondary schools. She has authored chapters in the *Handbook of Adolescent Literacy Research* and in *Adolescent Literacy: Turning Promise to Practice*.

Kelly Gallagher  is a full-time English teacher at Magnolia High School in Anaheim, California. He is the former co-director of the South Basin Writing Project at California State University, Long Beach. Gallagher wrote *Reading Reasons: Motivational Mini-Lessons for the Middle and High School*, *Deeper Reading: Comprehending Challenging Texts 4-12*, and *Teaching Adolescent Writers*. Gallagher won the Secondary Award of Classroom Excellence from the California Association of Teachers of English—the state's top English teacher honor.

Sharroky Hollie, Ph.D.,  is an assistant professor at California State University, Dominguez Hills, and an urban literacy visiting professor at Webster University, St. Louis. Hollie's work focuses on professional development, African American education, and second language methodology. He is a contributing author in two texts on culturally and linguistically responsive teaching. He is the Executive Director of the Center for Culturally Responsive Teaching and Learning and the co-founding director of the Culture and Language Academy of Success, an independent charter school in Los Angeles.

Dr. Donald J. Leu, Ph.D.,  teaches at the University of Connecticut and holds a joint appointment in Curriculum and Instruction and in Educational Psychology. He directs the New Literacies Research Lab and is a member of the Board of Directors of the International Reading Association. Leu studies the skills required to read, write, and learn with Internet technologies. His research has been funded by groups including the U.S. Department of Education, the National Science Foundation, and the Bill & Melinda Gates Foundation.

Jon Scieszka  founded GUYS READ, a nonprofit literacy initiative for boys, to call attention to the problem of getting boys connected with reading. In 2008, he was named the first U.S. National Ambassador for Young People's Literature by the Library of Congress. Scieszka taught from first grade to eighth grade for ten years in New York City, drawing inspiration from his students to write *The True Story of the 3 Little Pigs!*, *The Stinky Cheese Man*, the *Time Warp Trio* series of chapter books, and the *Trucktown* series of books for beginning readers.

Sharon Vaughn, Ph.D.,  teaches at the University of Texas at Austin. She is the previous Editor-in-Chief of the *Journal of Learning Disabilities* and the co-editor of *Learning Disabilities Research and Practice*. She is the recipient of the American Education Research Association SIG Award for Outstanding Researcher. Vaughn's work focuses on effective practices for enhancing reading outcomes for students with reading difficulties. She is the author of more than 100 articles, and numerous books designed to improve research-based practices in the classroom.

Karen K. Wixson  is Dean of the School of Education at the University of North Carolina, Greensboro. She has published widely in the areas of literacy curriculum, instruction, and assessment. Wixson has been an advisor to the National Research Council and helped develop the National Assessment of Educational Progress (NAEP) reading tests. She is a past member of the IRA Board of Directors and co-chair of the IRA Commission on RTI. Recently, Wixson served on the English Language Arts Work Team that was part of the Common Core State Standards Initiative.

Each unit addresses a BIG Question to enrich exploration of literary concepts and reading strategies.

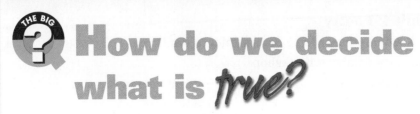

How do we decide what is *true?*

INFORMATIONAL TEXT HIGHLIGHTED

PHLit Online!
www.PHLitOnline.com
Interactive resources provide personalized instruction and activities online.

Skills at a Glance

This page provides a quick look at the skills you will learn and practice in Unit 1.

Reading Skills

Make Predictions

  Use Your Prior Knowledge

  Read Ahead to Check Your Predictions

Fact and Opinion

  Recognize Clues That
    Indicate an Opinion

  Check Facts by Using Resources

Reading for Information

Analyze Structural Features

Make and Support Assertions

Literary Analysis

Theme

Central Idea

Plot

Narrator and Point of View

Comparing Fiction and Nonfiction

Author's Perspective

Tone

Comparing Symbolism

Vocabulary

Big Question Vocabulary

Suffixes: -ation, -able

Prefixes: pre-, be-

Roots: -seque-, -pel-, -pul-, -scrib-,
  -scrip-, -met-, -mens-

Using a Dictionary and Thesaurus

Conventions

Common and Proper Nouns

Singular and Plural Nouns

Revising for Errors With Possessive Nouns

Pronouns (Personal and Possessive)

Pronouns (Interrogative and Indefinite)

Revising for Pronoun-Antecedent Agreement

Writing

Writing About the Big Question

News Report

Autobiographical Narrative

Writing Workshop: Informative Text:
  Descriptive Essay

Dramatic Scene

Personal Anecdote

Timed Writing

Writing Workshop: Narrative Text:
  Autobiographical Narrative

Speaking and Listening

Conversation

Monologue

Following Oral Directions

Research and Technology

Brochure

Poster or Chart

 Common Core State Standards
Addressed in This Unit

Reading Literature RL.6.1, RL.6.2, RL.6.3, RL.6.4, RL.6.6, RL.6.9, RL.6.10

Reading Informational Text RI.6.1, RI.6.2, RI.6.5, RI.6.6, RI.6.7, RI.6.8, RI.6.10

Writing W.6.1.b, W.6.2, W.6.2.a, W.6.2.b, W.6.2.d, W.6.2.e, W.6.2.f, W.6.3, W.6.3.a–3.d, W.6.4, W.6.5, W.6.6, W.6.7, W.6.9.a, W.6.9.b, W.6.10

Speaking and Listening SL.6.1, SL.6.1.c, SL.6.1.d, SL.6.4, SL.6.5, SL.6.6

Language L.6.1, L.6.1.a–1.d, L.6.2, L.6.2.b, L.6.3.a, L.6.3.b, L.6.4, L.6.4.b, L.6.4.c, L.6.5.c, L.6.6

[For the full wording of the standards, see the standards chart in the front of your textbook.]

Is *conflict* always bad?

Structure and Plot
Characterization

Make Inferences
Characterization

Make Inferences
Conflict and Resolution

INFORMATIONAL TEXT HIGHLIGHTED

PHLit Online!
www.PHLitOnline.com
Interactive resources provide personalized instruction and activities online.

Skills at a Glance

This page provides a quick look at the skills you will learn and practice in Unit 2.

Reading Skills

Make Inferences
  Use Details
  Use Prior Knowledge
Draw Conclusions
  Ask Questions
  Use Prior Knowledge

Reading for Information

Use Text Aids and Features
Analyze Compare-and-
  Contrast Organization

Literary Analysis

Structure and Plot
Characterization
Conflict and Resolution
Comparing Characters' Motives
Theme
Setting
Comparing Setting and Theme

Vocabulary

Big Question Vocabulary
Prefixes: *dis-, re-, ex-, in-*
Roots: *-migr-, -clin-, -tempor-*
Word Origins

Conventions

Verbs
Principal Parts of Verbs
Correcting Errors With Verbs
Simple Verb Tenses
Perfect Tenses of Verbs
Revising to Maintain Verb Tense

Writing

Writing About the Big Question
Help-Wanted Ad
Persuasive Speech
Writing Workshop:
  Argumentative Text: Review
Description
Personal Narrative
Timed Writing
Writing Workshop: Narrative Text:
  Short Story

Speaking and Listening

Interview
Evaluating a Persuasive Message

Research and Technology

Compare-and-Contrast Chart
Presentation

**Common Core State Standards
Addressed in This Unit**

Reading Literature RL.6.1, RL.6.2, RL.6.3, RL.6.5,
RL.6.10
Reading Informational Text RI.6.1, RI.6.3, RI.6.10
Writing W.6.1.a, W.6.3, W.6.3.a, W.6.3.e, W.6.4,
W.6.9.a, W.6.10
Speaking and Listening SL.6.1, SL.6.1.c, SL.6.2,
SL.6.3
Language L.6.1, L.6.4.b, L.6.6
[For the full wording of the standards, see the standards
chart in the front of your textbook.]

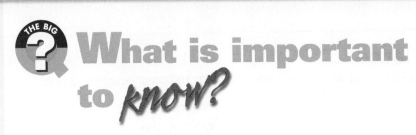

What is important to *know?*

Point of View
and Purpose

Development of Ideas
Word Choice and Tone

Author's Purpose
Autobiographical
Essay

Author's Purpose
Expository Essay

INFORMATIONAL TEXT HIGHLIGHTED

PHLit Online!
www.PHLitOnline.com
Interactive resources provide
personalized instruction and
activities online.

Skills at a Glance

This page provides a quick look at the skills you will learn and practice in Unit 3.

Reading Skills

Author's Purpose
  Learn to Recognize Details
  Ask Questions
Main Idea
  Identifying Key Details
  Distinguish Between Important
  and Unimportant Details

Reading for Information

Evaluate Author's Conclusions
Recognize Propaganda
  Techniques

Literary Analysis

Point of View and Purpose
Development of Ideas
Word Choice and Tone
Autobiographical Essay
Expository Essay
Comparing Biography and Autobiography
Author's Influences
Mood
Comparing Authors' Styles

Vocabulary

Big Question Vocabulary
Suffixes: *-ance, -ity, -ible, -ent*
Prefixes: *sup-, super-, ir-*
Roots: *-volv-, -tort-*
Words With Multiple Meanings

Conventions

Adjectives and Articles
Comparisons With Adjectives
Revising for Correct Use
  of Troublesome Modifiers
Adverbs

Conjunctions and Interjections
Combining Sentences
  Using Coordinating Conjunctions

Writing

Writing About the Big Question
Letter
Persuasive Letter
Writing Workshop: Explanatory Text:
  How-to Essay
Journal Entry
Problem-and-Solution Essay
Timed Writing
Writing Workshop: Argumentative Text:
  Persuasive Essay

Speaking and Listening

Instructional Presentation
Informal Discussion
Problem-Solution Proposal

Research and Technology

Research Project
Informative Presentation

Common Core State Standards Addressed in This Unit

Reading Literature RL.6.10
Reading Informational Text RI.6.1, RI.6.2, RI.6.3, RI.6.4, RI.6.5, RI.6.6, RI.6.8, RI.6.10
Writing W.6.1, W.6.1.a–1.e, W.6.2, W.6.2.a–2.d, W.6.3, W.6.3.b, W.6.4, W.6.5, W.6.8, W.6.9.b, W.6.10
Speaking and Listening SL.6.1, SL.6.1.a, SL.6.1.b, SL.6.1.d, SL.6.4
Language L.6.1, L.6.1.e, L.6.2.b, L.6.3, L.6.4.a, L.6.4.c, L.6.4.d, L.6.6
[For the full wording of the standards, see the standards chart in the front of your textbook.]

Do we need words to *communicate* well?

Figurative and
Connotative Language
Poetic Structure

Context Clues
Rhythm and
Rhyme

Context Clues
Figurative Language

INFORMATIONAL TEXT HIGHLIGHTED

Skills at a Glance

This page provides a quick look at the skills you will learn and practice in Unit 4.

Reading Skills

Context Clues
  Ask Questions
  Reread and Read Ahead
Paraphrasing
  Reread
  Reading Aloud Fluently
    According to Punctuation

Reading for Information

Follow Multiple-Step Instructions
Prepare Applications

Literary Analysis

Figurative and Connotative Language
Poetic Structure
Rhythm and Rhyme
Figurative Language
Comparing Imagery
Forms of Poetry
Sound Devices
Comparing Sensory Language

Vocabulary

Big Question Vocabulary
Roots: *-min-, -mal-*
Suffixes: *-ness, -ant, -less, -ship, -ly, -y*
Connotation and Denotation

Conventions

Simple and Compound Subjects
Sentence Types
Revising for Strong, Functional Sentences
Subject Complements
Predicate Nouns and Predicate
  Adjectives
Revising Choppy Sentences

Writing

Writing About the Big Question
Letter to an Author
Poem
Writing Workshop: Argument:
  Problem-and-Solution Essay
Poem
Prose Description
Timed Writing
Writing Workshop: Informative Text:
  Comparison-and-Contrast Essay

Speaking and Listening

Dramatic Poetry Reading
Delivering a Persuasive Speech

Research and Technology

Presentation of a Poem
Resume

 **Common Core State Standards
Addressed in This Unit**

Reading Literature RL.6.1, RL.6.4, RL.6.5, RL.6.9,
RL.6.10

Reading Informational Text RI.6.1, RI.6.2, RI.6.5,
RI.6.7, RI.6.10

Writing W.6.2, W.6.2.a, W.6.2.b, W.6.2.e, W.6.2.f,
W.6.3.d, W.6.4, W.6.6, W.6.9, W.6.9.a, W.6.10

Speaking and Listening SL.6.1, SL.6.4, SL.6.5, SL.6.6

Language L.6.1, L.6.2.a, L.6.2.b, L.6.3, L.6.3.a, L.6.4,
L.6.4.a, L.6.4.c, L.6.5, L.6.5.a, L.6.5.c, L.6.6

[For the full wording of the standards, see the standards
chart in the front of your textbook.]

How do we decide *who* we are?

INFORMATIONAL TEXT HIGHLIGHTED

PHLit Online!
www.PHLitOnline.com
Interactive resources provide
personalized instruction and
activities online.

Skills at a Glance

This page provides a quick look at the skills you will learn and practice in Unit 5.

Reading Skills

Summarize
  Reread to Identify Main Events
Compare and Contrast
  Picture the Action

Reading for Information

Evaluate Evidence

Literary Analysis

Dramatic Structure
Conflict
Character
Dialogue in Drama
Stage Directions
Comparing Author's Purpose
  Across Genres

Vocabulary

Big Question Vocabulary
Root: -eth-
Prefix: trans-
Borrowed and Foreign Words

Conventions

Prepositions and Appositives
Gerunds and Gerund Phrases
Combining Sentences
  With Participial Phrases
Combining Sentences for Variety

Writing

Writing About the Big Question
Summary
Review

Writing Workshop:
  Argument: Letter
Timed Writing
Explanatory Text: Cause-and-Effect Essay

Speaking and Listening

Debate
Identifying Tone, Mood,
  and Emotion

Research and Technology

Multimedia Presentation

 Common Core State Standards
Addressed in This Unit

Reading Literature RL.6.1, RL.6.2, RL.6.3, RL.6.4, RL.6.5, RL.6.6, RL.6.7, RL.6.9, RL.6.10
Reading Informational Text RI.6.1, RI.6.6, RI.6.8, RI.6.9, RI.6.10
Writing W.6.1, W.6.1.a–1.e, W.6.2, W.6.2.a–2.c, W.6.4, W.6.5, W.6.6, W.6.8, W.6.9, W.6.9.a
Speaking and Listening SL.6.1, SL.6.1.c, SL.6.2
Language L.6.1, L.6.1.b, L.6.2.a, L.6.2.b, L.6.3, L.6.3.a, L.6.4.c, L.6.5.b, L.6.6
[For the full wording of the standards, see the standards chart in the front of your textbook.]

How much do our *communities* shape us?

INFORMATIONAL TEXT HIGHLIGHTED

PHLit
Online!
www.PHLitOnline.com
Interactive resources provide
personalized instruction and
activities online.

Skills at a Glance

This page provides a quick look at the skills you will learn and practice in Unit 6.

Reading Skills

Cause and Effect
  Reread
  Ask Questions
Purpose for Reading
  Preview the Text
  Adjust Your Reading Rate

Reading for Information

Creating Outlines
Connect and Clarify Main Ideas

Literary Analysis

Theme
Structure and Theme
Fables and Folktales
Myths
Comparing Elements of Fantasy
Personification
Universal Theme
Comparing Foreshadowing and Flashback

Vocabulary

Big Question Vocabulary
Suffixes: *-ment, -ous, -ary, -en*
Roots: *-mort-, -splend-, -pen-, -van-*
Idioms

Conventions

Clauses: Independent and Subordinate
Simple, Compound,
  and Complex Sentences
Commas
Punctuating Citations and
  Titles of Reference Works

Writing

Writing About the Big Question
Fable
Compare-and-Contrast Essay
Writing Workshop: Informative Text:
  Multimedia Report
Invitation
Plot Proposal
Timed Writing
Writing Workshop: Informative Text:
  Research Report

Speaking and Listening

Oral Report
Dramatic Reading
Oral Response to Literature

Research and Technology

Annotated Bibliography Entry
Written and Visual Report

 Common Core State Standards
Addressed in This Unit

Reading Literature RL.6.1, RL.6.2, RL.6.4, RL.6.5, RL.6.10

Reading Informational Text RI.6.1, RI.6.2, RI.6.5, RI.6.10

Writing W.6.2, W.6.2.a–2.d, W.6.3.b, W.6.3.c, W.6.3.e, W.6.4, W.6.6, W.6.7, W.6.8, W.6.9.a, W.6.10

Speaking and Listening SL.6.1, SL.6.1.c, SL.6.4, SL.6.5, SL.6.6

Language L.6.1, L.6.2.b, L.6.4.b, L.6.4.d, L.6.5, L.6.5.a, L.6.5.b, L.6.6

[For the full wording of the standards, see the standards chart in the front of your textbook.]

Literature

Informational Text—Literary Nonfiction

▶ **Functional Text**

▶ **Literature in Context—Reading in the Content Areas**

▶ Writing Workshops

▶ Vocabulary Workshops

▶ Communications Workshops

The Common Core State Standards will prepare you to succeed in college and your future career. They are separated into four sections—Reading (Literature and Informational Text), Writing, Speaking and Listening, and Language. Beginning each section, the College and Career Readiness Anchor Standards define what you need to achieve by the end of high school. The grade-specific standards that follow define what you need to know by the end of your current grade level.

©Common Core Reading Standards

College and Career Readiness Anchor Standards

Key Ideas and Details

1. Read closely to determine what the text says explicitly and to make logical inferences from it; cite specific textual evidence when writing or speaking to support conclusions drawn from the text.

2. Determine central ideas or themes of a text and analyze their development; summarize the key supporting details and ideas.

3. Analyze how and why individuals, events, and ideas develop and interact over the course of a text.

Craft and Structure

4. Interpret words and phrases as they are used in a text, including determining technical, connotative, and figurative meanings, and analyze how specific word choices shape meaning or tone.

5. Analyze the structure of texts, including how specific sentences, paragraphs, and larger portions of the text (e.g., a section, chapter, scene, or stanza) relate to each other and the whole.

6. Assess how point of view or purpose shapes the content and style of a text.

Integration of Knowledge and Ideas

7. Integrate and evaluate content presented in diverse formats and media, including visually and quantitatively, as well as in words.

8. Delineate and evaluate the argument and specific claims in a text, including the validity of the reasoning as well as the relevance and sufficiency of the evidence.

9. Analyze how two or more texts address similar themes or topics in order to build knowledge or to compare the approaches the authors take.

Range of Reading and Level of Text Complexity

10. Read and comprehend complex literary and informational texts independently and proficiently.

Grade 6 Reading Standards for Literature

Key Ideas and Details

1. Cite textual evidence to support analysis of what the text says explicitly as well as inferences drawn from the text.

2. Determine a theme or central idea of a text and how it is conveyed through particular details; provide a summary of the text distinct from personal opinions or judgments.

3. Describe how a particular story's or drama's plot unfolds in a series of episodes as well as how the characters respond or change as the plot moves toward a resolution.

Craft and Structure

4. Determine the meaning of words and phrases as they are used in a text, including figurative and connotative meanings; analyze the impact of a specific word choice on meaning and tone.

5. Analyze how a particular sentence, chapter, scene, or stanza fits into the overall structure of a text and contributes to the development of the theme, setting, or plot.

6. Explain how an author develops the point of view of the narrator or speaker in a text.

Integration of Knowledge and Ideas

7. Compare and contrast the experience of reading a story, drama, or poem to listening to or viewing an audio, video, or live version of the text, including contrasting what they "see" and "hear" when reading the text to what they perceive when they listen or watch.

8. (Not applicable to literature)

9. Compare and contrast texts in different forms or genres (e.g., stories and poems; historical novels and fantasy stories) in terms of their approaches to similar themes and topics.

Range of Reading and Level of Text Complexity

10. By the end of the year, read and comprehend literature, including stories, dramas, and poems, in the grades 6–8 text complexity band proficiently, with scaffolding as needed at the high end of the range.

Grade 6 Reading Standards for Informational Text

Key Ideas and Details

1. Cite textual evidence to support analysis of what the text says explicitly as well as inferences drawn from the text.

2. Determine a central idea of a text and how it is conveyed through particular details; provide a summary of the text distinct from personal opinions or judgments.

3. Analyze in detail how a key individual, event, or idea is introduced, illustrated, and elaborated in a text (e.g., through examples or anecdotes).

Craft and Structure

4. Determine the meaning of words and phrases as they are used in a text, including figurative, connotative, and technical meanings.

5. Analyze how a particular sentence, paragraph, chapter, or section fits into the overall structure of a text and contributes to the development of the ideas.

6. Determine an author's point of view or purpose in a text and explain how it is conveyed in the text.

Integration of Knowledge and Ideas

7. Integrate information presented in different media or formats (e.g., visually, quantitatively) as well as in words to develop a coherent understanding of a topic or issue.

8. Trace and evaluate the argument and specific claims in a text, distinguishing claims that are supported by reasons and evidence from claims that are not.

9. Compare and contrast one author's presentation of events with that of another (e.g., a memoir written by and a biography on the same person).

Range of Reading and Level of Text Complexity

10. By the end of the year, read and comprehend literary nonfiction in the grades 6–8 text complexity band proficiently, with scaffolding as needed at the high end of the range.

© Common Core Writing Standards

College and Career Readiness Anchor Standards

Text Types and Purposes

1. Write arguments to support claims in an analysis of substantive topics or texts, using valid reasoning and relevant and sufficient evidence.

2. Write informative/explanatory texts to examine and convey complex ideas and information clearly and accurately through the effective selection, organization, and analysis of content.

3. Write narratives to develop real or imagined experiences or events using effective technique, well-chosen details, and well-structured event sequences.

Production and Distribution of Writing

4. Produce clear and coherent writing in which the development, organization, and style are appropriate to task, purpose, and audience.

5. Develop and strengthen writing as needed by planning, revising, editing, rewriting, or trying a new approach.

6. Use technology, including the Internet, to produce and publish writing and to interact and collaborate with others.

Research to Build and Present Knowledge

7. Conduct short as well as more sustained research projects based on focused questions, demonstrating understanding of the subject under investigation.

8. Gather relevant information from multiple print and digital sources, assess the credibility and accuracy of each source, and integrate the information while avoiding plagiarism.

9. Draw evidence from literary or informational texts to support analysis, reflection, and research.

Range of Writing

10. Write routinely over extended time frames (time for research, reflection, and revision) and shorter time frames (a single sitting or a day or two) for a range of discipline-specific tasks, purposes, and audiences.

Grade 6 Writing Standards

Text Types and Purposes

1. Write arguments to support claims with clear reasons and relevant evidence.

   a. Introduce claim(s) and organize the reasons and evidence clearly.

   b. Support claim(s) with clear reasons and relevant evidence, using credible sources and demonstrating an understanding of the topic or text.

   c. Use words, phrases, and clauses to clarify the relationships among claim(s) and reasons.

   d. Establish and maintain a formal style.

   e. Provide a concluding statement or section that follows from the argument presented.

2. Write informative/explanatory texts to examine a topic and convey ideas, concepts, and information through the selection, organization, and analysis of relevant content.

   a. Introduce a topic; organize ideas, concepts, and information, using strategies such as definition, classification, comparison/contrast, and cause/effect; include formatting (e.g., headings), graphics (e.g., charts, tables), and multimedia when useful to aiding comprehension.

   b. Develop the topic with relevant facts, definitions, concrete details, quotations, or other information and examples.

   c. Use appropriate transitions to clarify the relationships among ideas and concepts.

   d. Use precise language and domain-specific vocabulary to inform about or explain the topic.

   e. Establish and maintain a formal style.

   f. Provide a concluding statement or section that follows from the information or explanation presented.

3. Write narratives to develop real or imagined experiences or events using effective technique, relevant descriptive details, and well-structured event sequences.

   a. Engage and orient the reader by establishing a context and introducing a narrator and/or characters; organize an event sequence that unfolds naturally and logically.

   b. Use narrative techniques, such as dialogue, pacing, and description, to develop experiences, events, and/or characters.

   c. Use a variety of transition words, phrases, and clauses to convey sequence and signal shifts from one time frame or setting to another.

   d. Use precise words and phrases, relevant descriptive details, and sensory language to convey experiences and events.

   e. Provide a conclusion that follows from the narrated experiences or events.

Production and Distribution of Writing

4. Produce clear and coherent writing in which the development, organization, and style are appropriate to task, purpose, and audience.

5. With some guidance and support from peers and adults, develop and strengthen writing as needed by planning, revising, editing, rewriting, or trying a new approach.

6. Use technology, including the Internet, to produce and publish writing as well as to interact and collaborate with others; demonstrate sufficient command of keyboarding skills to type a minimum of three pages in a single sitting.

Research to Build and Present Knowledge

7. Conduct short research projects to answer a question, drawing on several sources and refocusing the inquiry when appropriate.

8. Gather relevant information from multiple print and digital sources; assess the credibility of each source; and quote or paraphrase the data and conclusions of others while avoiding plagiarism and providing basic bibliographic information for sources.

9. Draw evidence from literary or informational texts to support analysis, reflection, and research.

  a. Apply *grade 6 Reading standards* to literature (e.g., "Compare and contrast texts in different forms or genres [e.g., stories and poems; historical novels and fantasy stories] in terms of their approaches to similar themes and topics").

  b. Apply *grade 6 Reading standards* to literary nonfiction (e.g., "Trace and evaluate the argument and specific claims in a text, distinguishing claims that are supported by reasons and evidence from claims that are not").

Range of Writing

10. Write routinely over extended time frames (time for research, reflection, and revision) and shorter time frames (a single sitting or a day or two) for a range of discipline-specific tasks, purposes, and audiences.

ⓒ Common Core
Speaking and Listening Standards

College and Career Readiness Anchor Standards

Comprehension and Collaboration

1. Prepare for and participate effectively in a range of conversations and collaborations with diverse partners, building on others' ideas and expressing their own clearly and persuasively.

2. Integrate and evaluate information presented in diverse media and formats, including visually, quantitatively, and orally.

3. Evaluate a speaker's point of view, reasoning, and use of evidence and rhetoric.

Presentation of Knowledge and Ideas

4. Present information, findings, and supporting evidence such that listeners can follow the line of reasoning and the organization, development, and style are appropriate to task, purpose, and audience.

5. Make strategic use of digital media and visual displays of data to express information and enhance understanding of presentations.

6. Adapt speech to a variety of contexts and communicative tasks, demonstrating command of formal English when indicated or appropriate.

Grade 6 Speaking and Listening Standards

Comprehension and Collaboration

1. Engage effectively in a range of collaborative discussions (one-on-one, in groups, and teacher-led) with diverse partners on *grade 6 topics, texts, and issues,* building on others' ideas and expressing their own clearly.

   a. Come to discussions prepared, having read or studied required material; explicitly draw on that preparation by referring to evidence on the topic, text, or issue to probe and reflect on ideas under discussion.

   b. Follow rules for collegial discussions, set specific goals and deadlines, and define individual roles as needed.

   c. Pose and respond to specific questions with elaboration and detail by making comments that contribute to the topic, text, or issue under discussion.

   d. Review the key ideas expressed and demonstrate understanding of multiple perspectives through reflection and paraphrasing.

2. Interpret information presented in diverse media and formats (e.g., visually, quantitatively, orally) and explain how it contributes to a topic, text, or issue under study.

3. Delineate a speaker's argument and specific claims, distinguishing claims that are supported by reasons and evidence from claims that are not.

Presentation of Knowledge and Ideas

4. Present claims and findings, sequencing ideas logically and using pertinent descriptions, facts, and details to accentuate main ideas or themes; use appropriate eye contact, adequate volume, and clear pronunciation.

5. Include multimedia components (e.g., graphics, images, music, sound) and visual displays in presentations to clarify information.

6. Adapt speech to a variety of contexts and tasks, demonstrating command of formal English when indicated or appropriate. (See grade 6 Language standards 1 and 3 for specific expectations.)

© Common Core Language Standards

College and Career Readiness Anchor Standards

Conventions of Standard English

1. Demonstrate command of the conventions of standard English grammar and usage when writing or speaking.

2. Demonstrate command of the conventions of standard English capitalization, punctuation, and spelling when writing.

Knowledge of Language

3. Apply knowledge of language to understand how language functions in different contexts, to make effective choices for meaning or style, and to comprehend more fully when reading or listening.

Vocabulary Acquisition and Use

4. Determine or clarify the meaning of unknown and multiple-meaning words and phrases by using context clues, analyzing meaningful word parts, and consulting general and specialized reference materials, as appropriate.

5. Demonstrate understanding of figurative language, word relationships, and nuances in word meanings.

6. Acquire and use accurately a range of general academic and domain-specific words and phrases sufficient for reading, writing, speaking, and listening at the college and career readiness level; demonstrate independence in gathering vocabulary knowledge when considering a word or phrase important to comprehension or expression.

Grade 6 Language Standards

Conventions of Standard English

1. Demonstrate command of the conventions of standard English grammar and usage when writing or speaking.
   a. Ensure that pronouns are in the proper case (subjective, objective, possessive).
   b. Use intensive pronouns (e.g., *myself, ourselves*).
   c. Recognize and correct inappropriate shifts in pronoun number and person.
   d. Recognize and correct vague pronouns (i.e., ones with unclear or ambiguous antecedents).
   e. Recognize variations from standard English in their own and others' writing and speaking, and identify and use strategies to improve expression in conventional language.

2. Demonstrate command of the conventions of standard English capitalization, punctuation, and spelling when writing.

    a. Use punctuation (commas, parentheses, dashes) to set off nonrestrictive/ parenthetical elements.

    b. Spell correctly.

Knowledge of Language

3. Use knowledge of language and its conventions when writing, speaking, reading, or listening.

    a. Vary sentence patterns for meaning, reader/listener interest, and style.

    b. Maintain consistency in style and tone.

Vocabulary Acquisition and Use

4. Determine or clarify the meaning of unknown and multiple-meaning words and phrases based on *grade 6 reading and content,* choosing flexibly from a range of strategies.

    a. Use context (e.g., the overall meaning of a sentence or paragraph; a word's position or function in a sentence) as a clue to the meaning of a word or phrase.

    b. Use common, grade-appropriate Greek or Latin affixes and roots as clues to the meaning of a word (e.g., *audience, auditory, audible*).

    c. Consult reference materials (e.g., dictionaries, glossaries, thesauruses), both print and digital, to find the pronunciation of a word or determine or clarify its precise meaning or its part of speech.

    d. Verify the preliminary determination of the meaning of a word or phrase (e.g., by checking the inferred meaning in context or in a dictionary).

5. Demonstrate understanding of figurative language, word relationships, and nuances in word meanings.

    a. Interpret figures of speech (e.g., personification) in context.

    b. Use the relationship between particular words (e.g., cause/effect, part/ whole, item/category) to better understand each of the words.

    c. Distinguish among the connotations (associations) of words with similar denotations (definitions) (e.g., *stingy, scrimping, economical, unwasteful, thrifty*).

6. Acquire and use accurately grade-appropriate general academic and domain-specific words and phrases; gather vocabulary knowledge when considering a word or phrase important to comprehension or expression.

Introductory Unit

© COMMON CORE
Workshops

Building Academic Vocabulary

Writing an Objective Summary

Comprehending Complex Texts

Analyzing Arguments

© Common Core State Standards

Reading Literature 2, 10
Reading Informational Text 2, 8
Writing 1.a, 1.b, 1.e
Language 6

Building Academic Vocabulary

Academic vocabulary is the language you encounter in textbooks and on standardized tests and other assessments. Understanding these words and using them in your classroom discussions and writing will help you communicate your ideas clearly and effectively.

There are two basic types of academic vocabulary: general and domain-specific. **General academic vocabulary** includes words that are not specific to any single course of study. For example, the general academic vocabulary word *analyze* is used in language arts, math, social studies, art, and so on. **Domain-specific academic vocabulary** includes words that are usually encountered in the study of a specific discipline. For example, the words *factor* and *remainder* are most often used in mathematics classrooms and texts.

 Common Core State Standards

Language 6. Acquire and use accurately grade-appropriate general academic and domain-specific words and phrases; gather vocabulary knowledge when considering a word or phrase important to comprehension or expression.

General Academic Vocabulary

Word	Definition	Related Words	Word in Context
abandon (uh BAN duhn) *v.*	leave behind; give something up	abandoned abandoning	Maria decided to abandon the book after reading the first chapter.
accompany (uh KUHM puh nee) *v.*	go along; travel with	accompanied accompanying	I will accompany Jake to school to get his backpack.
accurate (AK yer it) *adj.*	free from error	accurately	Her research proved that her facts were accurate.
achieve (uh CHEEV) *v.*	bring to a successful end; gain	achieved achievement	Through hard work, I will achieve my goal of raising my English grade.
anticipate (an TIS uh peyt) *v.*	expect; foresee	anticipated anticipation	Greta can anticipate winning the spelling bee.
approach (uh PROHCH) *v.*	come near or nearer to	approached approaching	The school bus will approach the parking lot in 300 yards.
argue (AHR gyoo) *v.*	fight using words; debate	argument argumentative	During a debate, you must argue your point clearly.
assess (uh SES) *v.*	estimate the value of; evaluate	assessed assessment	The English test will assess our understanding of the poem.
authority (uh THAWR i tee) *n.*	a person with power or expertise; the power to control	authorities authorize	The teacher has authority over her class.
challenge (CHAL uhnj) *n.*	a dare; a calling into question	challenging challenged	The character set a challenge for his opponent.
common (KOM uhn) *adj.*	ordinary or expected	commonplace uncommon	It is common to have a conflict within a story's plot.

Word	Definition	Related Words	Word in Context
communicate (kuh MYOO nuh kayt) v.	share thoughts or feelings, usually in words	communication communicative	Poets can communicate complex thoughts with very few words.
compile (kuhm PAHYL) v.	put together into one book or work	compiled compilation	The students will compile all their poems into one book.
concept (KON sehpt) n.	general idea or notion	conception	I was able to grasp the broad concept of the news article by skimming.
conclude (kuhn KLOOD) v.	bring to a close; end	conclusion concluded	The story will conclude when the main character has won the race.
confirm (kuhn FURM) v.	support or show to be correct	confirmation confirming	I need to confirm the facts for my research report.
conflict (KON flict) n.	a fight, battle, or struggle	conflicts conflicted	The conflict in the novel was resolved in the end.
consist (kuhn SIST) v.	be made up of or composed of	consisted consistency	The test will consist of multiple-choice and short-answer questions.
context (KON text) n.	the set of circumstances or surrounding words that give a word or phrase its meaning	contexts contextual	We defined the word in its context in the sentence.
contrast (KON trast) v.	show differences between or among	contrasted contrasting	When you contrast two characters, you find the differences between them.
convince (kuhn VIHNS) v.	persuade	convincing convinced	You don't need to convince me that Shakespeare was a brilliant writer!
coordinate (koh AWR dn eyt) v.	show the proper order or relation of things	coordinates coordinating	I had to coordinate my schedule to make time for homework.
correspond (KAWR uh SPOND) v.	agree with or be similar to	correspondence corresponding	My thoughts on the poem did not correspond to my partner's.
crucial (KROO shuhl) adj.	critical; extremely important	crucially	It is crucial that you do well on this test.
defend (dih FEHND) v.	guard from attack; protect	defense defending	The main character was able to defend himself against the bitter cold.
determine (dih TUR muhn) v.	settle; reach a conclusion	determined determination	The author's background can help you determine the author's purpose for writing.
display (dih SPLEY) v.	show or exhibit	displayed displaying	The characters display their traits through their words and actions.

Word	Definition	Related Words	Word in Context
distinguish (dihs TIHNG gwihsh) v.	mark as different; set apart	distinguished distinguishing	It is important to notice traits that distinguish characters.
diverse (duh VURS) adj.	many and different; from different backgrounds	diversity	There were diverse cultures represented in the article.
draft (drahft) n.	a rough or preliminary form of any writing	drafts drafting	We had to hand in the first draft of our report.
encounter (en KOUN ter) v.	come upon or meet with, usually unexpectedly	encountered encountering	The main character will encounter many difficult situations.
establish (ih STAB lish) v.	bring into being; show to be true	established establishment	The author had to establish the reason the character in the book had lied.
evidence (EHV uh duhns) n.	proof in support of a claim or statement	evident	The evidence she used in her essay supports her main idea.
examine (ehg ZAM uhn) v.	study in depth; look at closely	examination examined	To examine a character, look at what he says and also what is said about him.
fact (fakt) n.	idea or thought that is real or true	factual	Be sure something is a fact before you use it to support your argument.
indicate (IN di keyt) v.	be a sign of; show	indicates indication	You must indicate where you found your information.
influence (IHN flu uhns) v.	sway or affect in some other way	influential influenced	One author can often influence the work of another.
interpret (in TUR prit) v.	give or provide the meaning of; explain	interpreting interpretation	We were asked to interpret the poem.
investigate (ihn VEHS tuh gayt) v.	examine thoroughly, as an idea	investigation investigating	The characters went to investigate a mysterious disappearance.
involve (ihn VOLV) v.	include	involving involved	I want the plot of my short story to involve a space expedition.
isolate (I suh layt) v.	set apart	isolated isolation	It is good to isolate each point when using point-by-point organization.
issue (ISH oo) n.	a point about which there is disagreement	issues	We discussed the issue of revenge in class.
judge (juhj) v.	form an opinion of or pass judgment on	judgment judicial	In the story, the main character had to judge who was a true friend.
measure (MEHZH uhr) v.	place a value on	measurement measured	A writer tries to measure many different factors in his or her writing.

Word	Definition	Related Words	Word in Context
modify (MOD uh fahy) *v.*	change the form or quality of	modified modification	We will modify our answers after we finish the book.
motive (MOH tiv) *n.*	something that causes a person to act a certain way	motives, motivation	Her motive for taking my book was that she had lost hers.
observe (uhb ZURV) *v.*	notice or see	observation observed	Observe the shape formed by the lines in this poem.
opinion (uh PIHN yuhn) *n.*	personal view or belief	opinionated	My opinion of the story is very different from that of my friend.
participation (pahr TIHS uh PAY shuhn) *n.*	the act of taking part in an event or activity	participate participant	The teacher appreciated the boy's participation in the group discussion of the novel.
perspective (puhr SPEHK tihv) *n.*	point of view	introspective	I chose to tell my story from the perspective of my family's dog.
pose (pohz) *v.*	display a specific attitude or stance	posture	He might pose as my friend to get my answers to the homework.
process (PROS es) *n.*	a systematic series of actions or changes	processor	Finishing the report was a process of writing and revising.
prove (proov) *v.*	establish the truth of, as in a claim or statement	disprove	I will prove my theory within my report.
purpose (PUR puhs) *n.*	what something is used for	purposeful	The author's purpose for writing became more clear as she read.
quote (kwoht) *v.*	refer to the words of a source	quotation quoted	Quote from a reputable author to add interest to an essay.
refer (rih FUR) *v.*	point back to, as an authority or expert	reference referral	When I write my final draft, I refer to my notes and my outline.
reflect (rih FLEHKT) *v.*	think about or consider	reflection reflecting	The character needed to reflect on what had happened before the conflict could be resolved.
research (REE serch) *n.*	investigation into a subject to find facts	researches researching	The research supported her ideas.

Ordinary Language: She told the story from an interesting angle.

Academic Language: She told the story from an interesting perspective.

Word	Definition	Related Words	Word in Context
resolve (rih ZOLV) v.	settle or bring to an end	resolution resolved	The characters decided to resolve their dispute and became friends.
respond (rih SPOND) v.	reply or answer	response responded	To respond to the essay question, I used evidence, examples, and my own thoughts.
reveal (rih VEEL) v.	show or uncover	revealing revealed	The detective would reveal the truth in the mystery story.
similar (SIHM uh luhr) adj.	alike	similarity similarly	The styles of the two poems are quite similar but the images are very different.
source (sawrs) n.	person or book that provides information	resource outsource	Check the source of that quotation to be sure it is trustworthy.
specific (spi SIF ik) adj.	particular	specify specification	Give specific examples to support your ideas.
structure (STRUHK cher) n.	the way in which parts are arranged to make a whole	structures structured	We studied the structure of the poem.
study (STUHD ee) n.	research or investigation into a claim	studious	I cited a scientific study in my research report that supported my thesis.
study (STUHD ee) v.	look into deeply	studied studying	The two friends in the story liked to study together for English class.
support (suh PAWRT) v.	stand behind or back up	supportive supporting	Details in your essay support your main idea.
suspend (suh SPEND) v.	hang from something above; keep from falling; to bring to a stop	suspenders suspense	In science lab, we have to suspend an object from a rope.
symbolize (SIHM buh lyz) v.	stand for	symbol	What might the flag symbolize in this story?
test (tehst) n.	method or process for proving or disproving a claim	testing tested	After the test, I knew my theory was correct.
unique (yoo NEEK) adj.	one of a kind	uniqueness	My favorite author has a truly unique writing style.
visual (VIHZH u uhl) adj.	able to be seen or understood with the eyes	vision visually	The descriptive passage of the story gives a strong visual image of the scene.

Ordinary Language: The conflict in the story was **brought to an end**.

Academic Language: The conflict in the story was **resolved**.

Practice

Examples of various kinds of domain-specific academic vocabulary appear in the charts below. Some chart rows are not filled in. Look up the definitions of the remaining words, provide one or two related words, and use each word in context on a separate piece of paper.

Social Studies: Domain-Specific Academic Vocabulary

Word	Definition	Related Words	Word in Context
epic (EP ik) *adj.*	huge in size, duration, or importance; heroic	epical	*The Odyssey* tells of an epic journey made by Odysseus.
feudalism (FYOOD l iz uhm) *n.*	social system in the Middle Ages based on land ownership by a privileged class	feudal	Feudalism gave power to lords, or men who owned land.
globalization (GLOH buh lih ZAY shun) *n.*	the inclusion of all parts of the globe	globe, global	Computers have made globalization possible.
interdependence (in ter di PEN dunhnts) *n.*	dependence on one another	interdependent	Interdependence between the two countries keeps the peace.
mobility (moh BIL i tee) *n.*	ability of people to change location or position easily	mobile	Mobility increased with the invention of cars.
archaeologist (ahr kee OL uh jist) *n.*			
civilization (siv uh luh ZAY shuhn) *n.*			
irrigation (ir i GAY shuhn) *n.*			
monarchy (MON er kee) *n.*			
nomadic (noh MAD ik) *adj.*			

Mathematics: Domain-Specific Academic Vocabulary

Word	Definition	Related Words	Word in Context
base (bays) *n.*	a number that is raised to a power by an exponent	bases, basic	In the math problem, the base number was 3 and the exponent was 2.
circumference (ser KUHM fer uhns) *n.*	the length of the boundary of a circle	circumvent	We learned how to find the circumference of a circle.
degree (dih GREE) *n.*	unit of measure for temperature and angles	degrees	The teacher drew a 45-degree angle.
equilateral (ee kwuh LAT er uhl) *adj.*	having sides of the same, or equal, length	equal	On the test, we were asked to draw an equilateral triangle.
prime factorization (prym FAK tuh ri ZAY shun) *n.*	the process of breaking down a number into its prime factors	prime, factor	We used prime factorization to find the factors of 39.
percent (per SENT) *n.*			
power (POU er) *n.*			
sample (SAM puhl) *n.*			
similarity (sim uh LAR i tee) *n.*			
simulation (sim yuh LAY shuhn) *n.*			

Science: Domain-Specific Academic Vocabulary

Word	Definition	Related Words	Word in Context
atmosphere (AT muhs feer) *n.*	the air or gaseous area around the earth or a planet	atmospheric	Earth's atmosphere is different from that of Mars.
atom (AT uhm) *n.*	the smallest part of an element with all the element's properties	atomic	An atom is too small to see with the human eye.
cell (sel) *n.*	the basic unit of living organisms	cellular	A plant cell has a cell membrane.
decomposer (dee kuhm POH zer) *n.*	an organism that feeds on and breaks down dead plant or animal matter	decompose	Decomposers are an important part of the food web.
prey (pray) *n.*	an animal hunted for food	preying	The deer was the hungry lion's prey.

Science: Domain-Specific Academic Vocabulary (*continued*)

Word	Definition	Related Words	Word in Context
climate (KLY mit) *n.*			
crystal (KRIS tl) *n.*			
fungus (FUHNG guhs) *n.*			
gene (jeen) *n.*			
molecule (MOL uh kyool) *n.*			

Art: Domain-Specific Academic Vocabulary

Word	Definition	Related Words	Word in Context
diagonal (dy AG uh nl) *adj.*	on a slant	diagonally	The student used diagonal lines to draw a slanted roof.
horizontal (hawr uh ZON tl) *adj.*	side to side	horizontally	Use horizontal lines to draw the floor and ceiling of a room.
hue (hyoo) *n.*	color; form of a color	hues	She used a purple hue in her painting.
tint (tint) *n.*	refers to a hue plus white	tinted, tinting	The art teacher mixed white with red to create a pink tint.
vertical (VUR ti kuhl) *adj.*	straight up and down	vertically	The painter used vertical lines to paint the walls of a building.
color (KUHL er) *n.*			
curved (kurvd) *adj.*			
edge (ej) *n.*			
line (lyn) *n.*			
shade (shayd) *n.*			

Technology: Domain-Specific Academic Vocabulary

Word	Definition	Related Words	Word in Context
desktop (DESK top) *adj.*	a type of computer that fits on a desk but is not portable	laptop	The classroom had many desktop computers on long tables.
file (fyl) *n.*	an organized collection of data in a single location	files	I saved my report in a file on my computer.
hardware (HAHRD wair) *n.*	electronic devices that make up a computer	software	A computer monitor is an example of hardware.
icon (AHY kon) *n.*	a small picture that stands for a command or file	iconic, icons	Click on the folder icon to open a new file.
monitor (MON i ter) *n.*	the device that displays images and text	monitored, monitoring	A large monitor is handy for showing graphics and photos.
backspace (key) (BAK spays) *n.*			
delete (key) (dih LEET) *n.*			
enter (key) (EN ter) *n.*			
escape (key) (ih SKAYP) *n.*			
online (ON LYN) *adj.*			

Increasing Your Word Knowledge

Increase your word knowledge and chances of success by taking an active role in developing your vocabulary. Here are some tips for you.

To own a word, follow these steps:

Steps to Follow	Model
1. Learn to identify the word and its basic meaning.	The word *examine* means "to look at closely."
2. Take note of the word's spelling.	*Examine* begins and ends with an *e*.
3. Practice pronouncing the word so that you can use it in conversation.	The *e* on the end of the word *examine* is silent. Its second syllable gets the most stress.
4. Visualize the word and illustrate its key meaning.	When I think of the word *examine*, I visualize a doctor checking a patient's health.
5. Learn the various forms of the word and its related words.	*Examination* and *exam* are forms of the word *examine*.
6. Compare the word with similar words.	*Examine*, *peruse*, and *study* are synonyms.
7. Contrast the word with similar words.	*Examine* suggests a more detailed study than *read* or *look at*.
8. Use the word in various contexts.	"I'd like to *examine* the footprints more closely." "I will *examine* the use of imagery in this poem."

Building Your Speaking Vocabulary

Language gives us the ability to express ourselves. The more words you know, the better able you will be to get your points across. There are two main aspects of language: reading and speaking. Using the steps above will help you acquire a rich vocabulary. Follow these steps to help you learn to use this rich vocabulary in discussions, speeches, and conversations.

Steps to Follow	Tip
1. Practice pronouncing the word.	Become familiar with pronunciation guides to allow you to sound out unfamiliar words. Listening to audio books as you read the text will help you learn pronunciations of words.
2. Learn word forms.	Dictionaries often list forms of words following the main word entry. Practice saying word families aloud: "generate," "generated," "generation," "regenerate," "generator."
3. Translate your thoughts.	Restate your own thoughts and ideas in a variety of ways, to inject formality or to change your tone, for example.
4. Hold discussions.	With a classmate, practice using academic vocabulary words in discussions about the text. Choose one term to practice at a time, and see how many statements you can create using that term.
5. Tape-record yourself.	Analyze your word choices by listening to yourself objectively. Note places your word choice could be strengthened or changed.

Writing an Objective Summary

The ability to write objective summaries is key to success in college and in many careers. Writing an effective objective summary involves recording the key ideas of a text as well as demonstrating your understanding.

**Common Core
State Standards**

Reading Literature 2. Determine a theme or central idea of a text and how it is conveyed through particular details; provide a summary of the text distinct from personal opinions or judgements.
Reading Informational Text 2. Determine a central idea of a text and how it is conveyed through particular details; provide a summary of the text distinct from personal opinions or judgments.

What Is an Objective Summary?

An effective objective summary is a short, accurate, and objective overview of a text. Following are key elements of an objective summary:

- A good summary focuses on a text's main points. It includes specific, relevant details that support the main point, but it leaves out unnecessary details.

- A summary should be a restatement of the text's main points, in the order in which they appear in the original text.

- A summary should accurately capture the essence of the longer text it is describing.

What to Avoid in an Objective Summary

- An objective summary is not a collection of sentences or paragraphs copied from the original source.

- It does not include every event, detail, or point in the original text.

- Finally, a good summary does not include evaluative comments, such as the reader's overall opinion of or reaction to the selection.

- An objective summary is not the reader's interpretation or critical analysis of the text.

INFORMATIONAL TEXT

Model Objective Summary

Review the elements of an effective objective summary called out in the sidenotes. Then, write an objective summary of a text you have read. Review your summary. Delete any unnecessary details or opinions.

Summary of "King Midas and the Golden Touch"

"King Midas and the Golden Touch" is a myth that tells the tale of a king who is granted a magical wish.

King Midas, the main character in this ~~popular~~ myth, loved gold. He would go into his dungeon to admire his shiny treasure. However, he did love one thing more than his gold—his daughter Aurelia.

Aurelia loved her father, and every day she would pick a bouquet of colorful, fragrant roses from his garden and bring them to him.

One day the king's guards found an old man asleep in the king's rose garden. Instead of punishing the man, the king invited him to dinner.

After the old man departed, King Midas went to the dungeon to admire his gold. All of a sudden, the glowing figure of a young man appeared. The apparition spoke to the shocked king and explained that he was the old man. To reward Midas for his kindness, the young stranger offered him one wish. King Midas wished that everything he touched would turn to gold.

The next day the king woke up and found that his wish had come true. His bedcovers were spun gold as were his clothes. ~~When he put his glasses on, they, too, turned to gold. That meant he couldn't see through them.~~ Midas rushed out to the garden and excitedly turned his roses into gold.

At breakfast, Aurelia was crying because her roses were made of gold. Midas convinced her to have breakfast with him. Midas lifted a spoonful of porridge to his mouth, but as soon as the porridge touched his lips it turned into a hard golden lump. When Aurelia noticed her father's concern, she went over to comfort him. To the king's horror, Aurelia became a lifeless golden statue at his touch.

As Midas cried, the mysterious stranger suddenly appeared. The stranger told him how to change things back to their original form.

King Midas brought Aurelia and the roses back to life. He did, however, keep one golden rose to remind himself of his experience with the golden touch. ~~Midas learned a good lesson.~~

A one-sentence synopsis highlighting the theme or central idea of the story can be an effective start to a summary.

An adjective describing the story indicates an opinion and should not be included in an objective summary.

Relating the development of the text in chronological order makes a summary easy to follow.

Unnecessary details should be eliminated.

This sentence should be paraphrased rather than copied exactly from the story.

The writer's opinions should not appear in an objective summary.

Comprehending Complex Texts

Common Core State Standards

Reading Literature 10. By the end of the year, read and comprehend literature, including stories, dramas, and poems, in the grades 6–8 text complexity band proficiently, with scaffolding as needed at the high end of the range.

During the coming years in school, you will be required to read increasingly complex texts to prepare you for college and the workplace. A complex text is a text that contains challenging vocabulary; long, complex sentences; figurative language; multiple levels of meaning; or unfamiliar settings and situations. The selections in this textbook include a range of readings, from short stories, to autobiography, poetry, drama, myths, and even science and social studies texts. Some of these texts will fall within your comfort zone; others may be more challenging.

Strategy 1: Multi-draft Reading

Good readers develop the habit of rereading texts in order to comprehend them completely. Just as an actor practices his lines over and over again in order to learn them, good readers return to texts to more fully enjoy and comprehend them. To fully understand a text, try this multi-draft reading strategy:

1st Reading

The first time you read a text, read to gain its basic meaning. If you are reading a narrative text, look for story basics: who the story is about and what happens. If the text is nonfiction, look for main ideas. If you are reading poetry, read first to get an overall impression of the poem.

2nd Reading

During your second reading of a text, focus on ways in which the writer uses language and text structures. Think about why the author chose those words or organizational patterns. Then, examine the author's creative uses of language and the effects of that language. For example, has the author used rhyme, exaggeration, or words with multiple meanings?

3rd Reading

After your third reading, compare and contrast the text with others of its kind you have read. For example, if you have read another myth before, think of ways the myths are alike or different. Evaluate the text's overall effectiveness and its central idea or theme.

INFORMATIONAL TEXT

Independent Practice

As you read this short poem, practice the multi-draft reading strategy by completing a chart like the one below.

"Storm" by H. D. (Hilda Doolittle)

You crash over the trees,
you crack the live branch—
the branch is white,
the green crushed,
each leaf is rent like split wood.

You burden the trees
with black drops,
you swirl and crash—
you have broken off a weighted leaf
in the wind,
it is hurled out,
whirls up and sinks,
a green stone.

Multi-Draft Reading Chart

	My Understanding
1st Reading Look for key ideas and details that unlock basic meaning.	
2nd Reading Read for deeper meanings. Look for ways in which the author used text structures and language to create effects.	
3rd Reading Read to integrate your knowledge and ideas. Connect the text to other texts and to your own experience.	

Strategy 2: Close Read the Text

Complex texts require close reading, a careful analysis of the words, phrases, and sentences. When you close read, use the following tips to comprehend the text:

Tips for Close Reading
1. Break down long sentences into parts. Look for the subject of the sentence and its verb. Then identify which parts of the sentence modify, or give more information about, its subject.
2. Reread passages. When reading complex texts, be sure to reread passages to confirm that you understand their meaning.

3. Look for context clues, such as the types listed below.
 	
  a. Restatement of an idea. For example, in this sentence, "have everlasting life" restates the adjective *immortal*.
    Gilgamesh wanted to be **immortal,** or have everlasting life.
 	
  b. Definition of sophisticated words. In this sentence, the underlined information defines the word *empire*.
    An **empire** is a <u>large territory made up of many different places all under the control of a single ruler.</u>
 	
  c. Examples of concepts and topics.
    Flowers <u>such as nasturtiums, daisies, and marigolds</u> grew along the side of the walk.
 	
  d. Contrasts of ideas and topics. In the following sentence, the phrase "on the other hand" indicates a contrast. You can guess that *loquacious* means the opposite of "not talkative."
    President Coolidge was not talkative; President Clinton, <u>on the other hand,</u> was **loquacious.**

4. Identify pronoun antecedents. If long sentences contain pronouns, reread the text to make sure you know to what the pronouns refer. The pronoun *its* in the following sentence refers to Yellowstone National Part, not the U.S. government. Yellowstone National Park was set aside by the U.S. government for people to enjoy for **its** natural beauty.
5. Look for conjunctions, such as *and*, *or*, and *yet*, to understand relationships between ideas.
6. Paraphrase, or restate in your own words, passages of difficult text in order to check your understanding. Remember that a paraphrase is a word-for-word rephrasing of an original text; it is not a summary.

INFORMATIONAL TEXT

Close-Read Model

As you read this complex document, take note of the sidenotes that model ways to unlock meaning in the text.

---

from "How to Tell a Story" by Mark Twain

. . . The humorous story is American, the comic story is English, the witty story is French. The humorous story depends for its effect upon the manner of the telling; the comic story and the witty story upon the matter. . . .

The humorous story is strictly a work of art—high and delicate art—and only an artist can tell it; but no art is necessary in telling the comic and the witty story; anybody can do it. The art of telling a humorous story—understand, I mean by word of mouth, not print—was created in America, and has remained at home.

The humorous story is told gravely; the teller does his best to conceal the fact that he even dimly suspects that there is anything funny about it; but the teller of the comic story tells you beforehand that it is one of the funniest things he has ever heard, then tells it with eager delight, and is the first person to laugh when he gets through. And sometimes, if he has had good success, he is so glad and happy that he will repeat the "nub" of it and glance around from face to face, collecting applause, and then repeat it again. It is a pathetic thing to see.

Very often, of course, the rambling and disjointed humorous story finishes with a nub, point, snapper, or whatever you like to call it. Then the listener must be alert, for in many cases the teller will divert attention from that nub by dropping it in a carefully casual and indifferent way, with the pretence that he does not know it is a nub.

The word *but* signals a contrast in ideas.

The dashes indicate an interruption of thought. The main part of this sentence appears in yellow highlight. Less important information appears in green.

Context clues that appear in gray highlighting help you understand the meaning of the word *gravely*.

Additional examples and commentary help you get an idea of the meaning of *nub*.

Strategy 3: Ask Questions

Be an attentive reader by asking questions as you read. Throughout this textbook, we have provided questions for you following each selection. These questions are sorted into three basic categories that build in sophistication and lead you to a deeper understanding of the texts you read. Here is an example from this text:

Some questions are about **Key Ideas and Details** in the text. To answer these questions, you will need to locate and cite explicit information in the text or draw inferences from what you have read.

Some questions are about **Craft and Structure** in the text. To answer these questions, you will need to analyze how the author developed and structured the text. You will also look for ways in which the author artfully used language and how those word choices impacted the meaning and tone of the work.

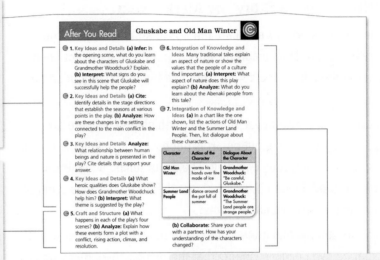

After You Read   Gluskabe and Old Man Winter

1. Key Ideas and Details (a) Infer: In the opening scene, what do you learn about the characters of Gluskabe and Grandmother Woodchuck? Explain. **(b) Interpret:** What signs do you see in this scene that Gluskabe will successfully help the people?

2. Key Ideas and Details (a) Cite: Identify details in the stage directions that establish the seasons at various points in the play. **(b) Analyze:** How are these changes in the setting connected to the main conflict in the play?

3. Key Ideas and Details Analyze: What relationship between human beings and nature is presented in the play? Cite details that support your answer.

4. Key Ideas and Details (a) What heroic qualities does Gluskabe show? How does Grandmother Woodchuck help him? **(b) Interpret:** What theme is suggested by the play?

5. Craft and Structure (a) What happens in each of the play's four scenes? **(b) Analyze:** Explain how these events form a plot with a conflict, rising action, climax, and resolution.

6. Integration of Knowledge and Ideas Many traditional tales explain an aspect of nature or show the values that the people of a culture find important. **(a) Interpret:** What aspect of nature does this play explain? **(b) Analyze:** What do you learn about the Abenaki people from this tale?

7. Integration of Knowledge and Ideas (a) In a chart like the one shown, list the actions of Old Man Winter and the Summer Land People. Then, list dialogue about these characters.

Character	Action of the Character	Dialogue About the Character
Old Man Winter	warms his hands over fire made of ice	Grandmother Woodchuck: "Be careful, Gluskabe."
Summer Land People	dance around the pot full of summer	Grandmother Woodchuck: "The Summer Land people are strange people."

(b) Collaborate: Share your chart with a partner. How has your understanding of the characters changed?

Some questions are about the **Integration of Knowledge and Ideas** in the text. These questions ask you to evaluate a text in many different ways, such as comparing texts, analyzing arguments in the text, and using many other methods of thinking critically about a text's ideas.

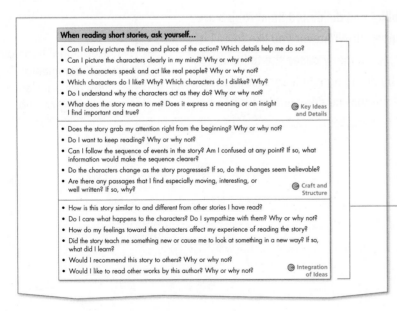

When reading short stories, ask yourself...

- Can I clearly picture the time and place of the action? Which details help me do so?
- Can I picture the characters clearly in my mind? Why or why not?
- Do the characters speak and act like real people? Why or why not?
- Which characters do I like? Why? Which characters do I dislike? Why?
- Do I understand why the characters act as they do? Why or why not?
- What does the story mean to me? Does it express a meaning or an insight I find important and true?

    Key Ideas and Details

- Does the story grab my attention right from the beginning? Why or why not?
- Do I want to keep reading? Why or why not?
- Can I follow the sequence of events in the story? Am I confused at any point? If so, what information would make the sequence clearer?
- Do the characters change as the story progresses? If so, do the changes seem believable?
- Are there any passages that I find especially moving, interesting, or well written? If so, why?

    Craft and Structure

- How is this story similar to and different from other stories I have read?
- Do I care what happens to the characters? Do I sympathize with them? Why or why not?
- How do my feelings toward the characters affect my experience of reading the story?
- Did the story teach me something new or cause me to look at something in a new way? If so, what did I learn?
- Would I recommend this story to others? Why or why not?
- Would I like to read other works by this author? Why or why not?

    Integration of Ideas

As you read independently, ask similar types of questions to ensure that you fully enjoy and comprehend texts you read for school and for pleasure. We have provided sets of questions for you on the Independent Reading pages at the end of each unit.

INFORMATIONAL TEXT

Model

Following is an example of a complex text. The sidenotes show sample questions that an attentive reader might ask while reading.

Sample questions:

from "Rendezvous with Despair" by Thomas E. Dewey

The President has said we have a rendezvous with destiny. We seem to be on our way toward a rendezvous with despair.

Fellow Republicans, as a party, let us turn away from that rendezvous and let us start going in the other direction and start now.

The one ultimate unforgivable crime is to despair of the republic. The one essential to the survival of the republic is to know it will survive and will survive into a future that is always larger, always better. In every era for a century and a half it has been doomed to death by gloomy young theorists and by tired and hopeless elders. And history laughs at them as each time the dynamic forces of a free republic led by free men have given the lie to the defeatists while the system of free economic enterprise has marched onward, sweeping the nation's increased population to full employment and ever higher living standards.

Key Ideas and Details Who is the *we* in these sentences? Who is the *us* in the next sentence?

Craft and Structure In what ways does Dewey use language creatively in this text?

Integration of Knowledge and Ideas Do you agree with Dewey's point of view? Why or why not?

INFORMATIONAL TEXT

Independent Practice

Write three to five questions you might ask yourself as you read this passage from a speech delivered by Herbert Hoover in 1935.

from "The Bill of Rights" by Herbert Hoover

Our Constitution is not alone the working plan of a great Federation of States under representative government. There is embedded in it also the vital principles of the American system of liberty . . . which not even the government may infringe and which we call the Bill of Rights. It does not require a lawyer to interpret those provisions. . . . Among others the freedom of worship, freedom of speech and of the press, the right of peaceable assembly, equality before the law, just trial for crime, freedom from unreasonable search, and security from being deprived of life, liberty, or property without due process of law, are the principles which distinguish our civilization. . . . Herein is the expression of the spirit of men who would be forever free.

Analyzing Arguments

The ability to evaluate an argument, as well as to make one, is an important skill for success in college and in the workplace.

**Common Core
State Standards**

Reading Informational Text 8.
Trace and evaluate the argument and specific claims in a text, distinguishing claims that are supported by reasons and evidence from claims that are not.
Language 6. Acquire and use accurately grade-appropriate general academic and domain-specific words and phrases; gather vocabulary knowledge when considering a word or phrase important to comprehension or expression.

What Is an Argument?

When you think of the word *argument,* you might think of a disagreement between two people. This type of argument involves trading opinions and evidence in a conversation. A formal argument, however, presents one side of a controversial or debatable issue. A good argument is supported by reasoning and evidence.

Purposes of Argument

There are three main purposes for writing a formal argument:

- to change the reader's mind
- to convince the reader to accept what is written
- to motivate the reader to take action, based on what is written

Elements of Argument

Claim (assertion)—what the writer is trying to prove

Example: Local governments should give vouchers (an allow-ance to be used for schooling) to parents who send their chil-dren to private schools.

Grounds (evidence)—the support used to convince the reader

Example: The parents pay taxes to support local schools. Children are required by law to attend school.

Justification—the link between the grounds and the claim; why the grounds are credible

Example: If the children don't attend a public school, they are not getting the benefit of the tax dollars their parents have paid. Local governments should support parents' choices of schools for their children by giving them vouchers.

Evaluating Claims

When reading or listening to a formal argument, critically assess the claims that are made. Which claims are based on fact or can be proved true? Also evaluate evidence that supports the claims. If there is little or no reasoning or evidence provided to support the claims, the argument may not be sound or valid.

INFORMATIONAL TEXT

Model Argument

Nelson Mandela's Address Upon His Release From Prison

...Today the majority of South Africans, black and white, recognize that apartheid has no future. It has to be ended by our own decisive mass action in order to build peace and security. The mass campaign of defiance and other actions of our organization and people can only culminate in the establishment of democracy. The destruction caused by apartheid on our sub-continent is incalculable. The fabric of family life of millions of my people has been shattered. . . . Our economy lies in ruins and our people are embroiled in political strife. . . .

Claim: All South Africans must work together to end apartheid.

Justification: Apartheid has caused problems for the people as well as the country.

The need to unite the people of our country is as important a task now as it always has been. No individual leader is able to take on this enormous task on his own. . . .

Grounds: No one can do the job alone.

Our struggle has reached a decisive moment. We call on our people to seize this moment so that the process towards democracy is rapid and uninterrupted. We have waited too long for our freedom. We can no longer wait. Now is the time to intensify the struggle on all fronts. To relax our efforts now would be a mistake which generations to come will not be able to forgive. The sight of freedom looming on the horizon should encourage us to redouble our efforts.

Grounds: Black South Africans have waited too long for their freedom.

...We call on the international community to continue the campaign to isolate the apartheid regime. To lift sanctions now would be to run the risk of aborting the process towards the complete eradication of apartheid.

Our march to freedom is irreversible. . . . Universal suffrage on a common voters' role in a united democratic and non-racial South Africa is the only way to peace and racial harmony.

Grounds: Universal *suffrage*—the right to vote—is key to peace and racial harmony.

In conclusion I wish to quote my own words during my trial in 1964. They are true today as they were then:

'I have fought against white domination and I have fought against black domination. I have cherished the ideal of a democratic and free society in which all persons live together in harmony and with equal opportunities. It is an ideal which I hope to live for and to achieve. But if needs be, it is an ideal for which I am prepared to die.'

A strong conclusion does more than simply restate the claim.

The Art of Argument: Rhetorical Devices and Persuasive Techniques

Rhetorical Devices

Rhetoric is the art of using language in order to make a point or to persuade listeners. Rhetorical devices such as the ones listed below are accepted elements of argument. Their use is regarded as a key part of an effective argument.

Rhetorical Device	Examples
Repetition The repeated use of certain words, phrases, or sentences	**Vote** for me. **Vote** for honesty. **Vote** for progress.
Parallelism The repeated use of similar grammatical structures	<u>To teach</u> is <u>to inspire</u>. <u>To learn</u> is to <u>explore</u>.
Rhetorical Question Calling attention to the issue by implying an obvious answer	Aren't all people equal under the law?
Sound Devices The use of alliteration, assonance, rhyme, or rhythm	**W**aste **n**ot, **w**ant **n**ot.
Simile and Metaphor Comparing two like things or asserting that one thing is another	The trees surrounded the house <u>like guards on patrol</u>.

Persuasive Techniques

The persuasive techniques below are often found in informal persuasion.

Persuasive Technique	Examples
Bandwagon Approach/Anti-Bandwagon Approach Appeals to a person's desire to belong/ Encourages or celebrates individuality	You have to see that movie; everyone in our class has seen it. Use your best judgment; don't follow the crowd.
Emotional Appeal Capitalizes on people's fear, anger, or desire	Without a sprinkler system, this school building is a fire trap.
Endorsement/Testimony Employs a well-known person to promote a product or idea	Meditation and positive thinking have helped me become president of this company.
Loaded Language Uses words charged with emotion	This medal recognizes the integrity of the brave people who defend our beloved country.
"Plain Folks" Appeal Shows a connection to everyday, ordinary people	I worry about rising gas prices just like you do.
Hyperbole Exaggerates to make a point	If I've heard that complaint once, I've heard it a thousand times.

INFORMATIONAL TEXT

Model Speech

The excerpted speech below includes examples of rhetorical devices and persuasive techniques.

---

from "Speech Celebrating George Washington's Birthday" by Jane Addams

… What is a great man who has made his mark upon history? Every time, if we think far enough, he is a man who has looked through the confusion of the moment and has seen the moral issue involved; he is a man who has refused to have his sense of justice distorted; he has listened to his conscience until conscience becomes a trumpet call to like-minded men, so that they gather about him and together, with mutual purpose and mutual aid, they make a new period in history. . . .

If we go back to George Washington, and ask what he would be doing were he bearing our burdens now, and facing our problems at this moment, we would, of course, have to study his life bit by bit; his life as a soldier, as a statesman, and as a simple Virginia planter.

First, as a soldier. What is it that we admire about the soldier? It certainly is not that he goes into battle; what we admire about the soldier is that he has the power of losing his own life for the life or a larger cause; that he holds his personal suffering of no account; that he flings down in the gage of battle his all, and says, "I will stand or fall with this cause." That, it seems to me, is the glorious thing we most admire, and if we are going to preserve that same spirit of the soldier, we will have to found a similar spirit in the civil life of the people, the same pride in civil warfare, the spirit of courage, and the spirit of self-surrender which lies back of this. . . .

This rhetorical question gives the reader a purpose for reading.

Repeated grammatical structures give the speech rhythm.

The metaphor comparing conscience to a trumpet call emphasizes the importance of the statement.

Sound devices, such as alliteration, emphasize a phrase.

The parallel grammatical structure provides a rhythm, and introduces the organization of the remainder of the speech.

Addams uses parallelism and repetition to emphasize her main points.

Composing an Argument

Common Core
State Standards

Writing 1.a. Introduce claim(s) and organize the reasons and evidence clearly.

1.b. Support claim(s) with clear reasons and relevant evidence, using credible sources and demonstrating an understanding of the topic or text.

1.e. Provide a concluding statement or section that follows from the argument presented.

Choosing a Topic

You should choose a topic that matters to people—and to you. Once you have chosen a topic, you should check to make sure you can make an arguable claim. Ask yourself:

1. What am I trying to prove? What ideas should I express?
2. Are there people who would disagree with my claim? What opinions might they have?
3. Do I have enough relevant evidence to support my claim?

If you are able to put into words what you want to prove and answered "yes" to questions 2 and 3, you have an arguable claim.

Introducing the Claim and Establishing Its Significance

Before you begin writing, think about your audience and how much you think they already know about your chosen topic. Then, provide only as much background information as necessary. Remember that you are not writing a summary of the issue—you are developing an argument. Once you have provided context for your argument, you should clearly state your claim, or thesis. A written argument's claim often, but not always, appears in the first paragraph.

Developing Your Claim with Reasoning and Evidence

Now that you have made your claim, you must support it with evidence, or grounds. A good argument should have at least three solid pieces of evidence to support the claim. Evidence can range from personal experience to researched data or expert opinion. Knowing your audience's knowledge level, concerns, values, and possible biases can help inform your decision on what kind of evidence will have the strongest impact. Make sure your evidence is up to date and comes from a credible source. Don't forget to credit your sources. You should also address the opposing counterclaim within the body of your argument. Consider points you have made or evidence you have provided that a person might challenge. Decide how best to respond to these counterclaims.

Writing a Concluding Statement or Section

Restate your claim in the conclusion of your argument, and synthesize, or pull together, the evidence you have provided. Make your conclusion strong enough to be memorable to the reader; leave him or her with something to think about.

Practice

Complete an outline like the one below to help you plan your own argument.

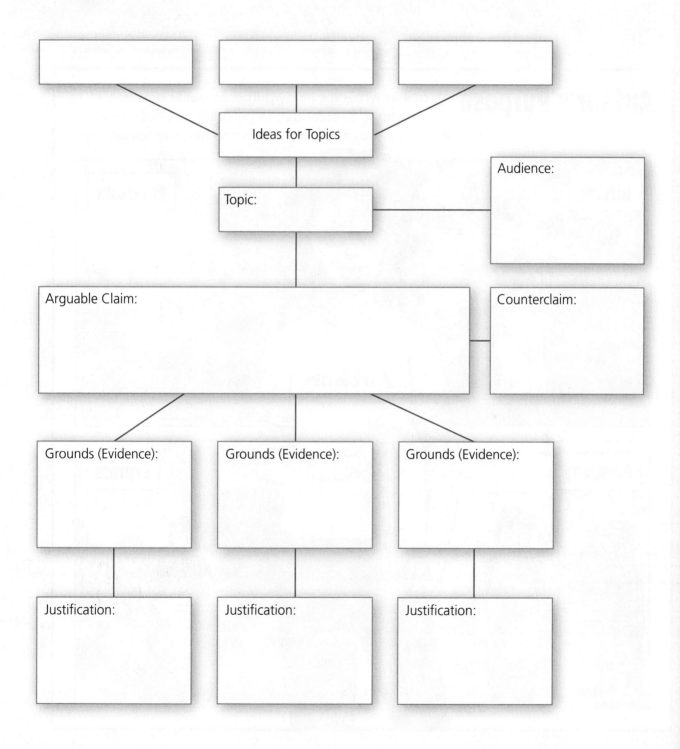

PICTURE IT!

A Comprehension Handbook

Author's Purpose

An author writes for many purposes, some of which are to inform, to entertain, to persuade, or to express. An author may have more than one purpose for writing.

Inform

Entertain

Persuade

Express

Cause and Effect

An effect is something that happens. A cause is why that thing happens. An effect sometimes has more than one cause. A cause sometimes has more than one effect. Clue words such as *because*, *as a result*, *therefore*, and *so that* can signal causes and effects.

Cause

Effect

Compare and Contrast

To compare and contrast is to look for similarities and differences in things. Clue words such as *like* or *as* show similarities. Clue words such as *but* or *unlike* show differences.

Context Clues

You can use context clues—the words and phrases around an unfamiliar word—to determine the meaning of an unfamiliar word.

Draw Conclusions

When we draw conclusions, we make sensible decisions or form reasonable opinions after thinking about the facts and details in what we are reading.

Fact and Opinion

A fact is something that can be proved. Facts are based on evidence.
Opinions express ideas and are based on interpretation of evidence.

Main Idea and Details

Main idea is the most important idea about a topic.

Details are smaller pieces of information that support the main idea.

Making Predictions

To make predictions, use text, graphics, and prior knowledge to predict what might happen in a story or what you might learn from a text. As you read, new information can lead to new or revised predictions.

Making Inferences

When we make inferences, or infer something, we come to a conclusion based on a detail an author provides in the text.

Paraphrasing

Paraphrasing is restating a sentence or an idea in your own words. Paraphrasing can lead to a better understanding of what we read.

Setting a Purpose for Reading

When we set a purpose for reading, we approach a text with a specific goal or question that we would like answered. Setting a purpose for reading guides comprehension by focusing our attention on specific information.

Media Literacy Handbook

INTRODUCTION: Today, messages are transmitted across a variety of media modes, such as film, television, radio, and the Internet. As you interact with these messages each day—in images, advertisements, movies, and an array of different contexts—it is important to consider the potential influence of the medium.

- What is the intention of the message?
- How is it communicated?
- How do specific elements of the medium—such as color, image, or font—help convey the message?
- Why might the creator of the message have selected this medium?

These are the key issues of media literacy, the study of messages in the media and their impact.

Camera Shots and Angles

Filmmakers create camera shots and sequences to help them tell stories. Some shots capture an entire scene; others zoom in on specific characters.

Special Effects

Filmmakers use special effects to create on-screen illusions that bring the imagination to life.

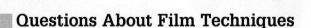

Questions About Film Techniques

- What effect is created by the choice of camera angle shown in the image at left? Choose another camera angle and explain how that shot might convey a different message than the one shown here.

- Study the images above. In what way does the use of special effects make the film better for viewers?

Media Literacy Handbook

Focus and Framing
A sharp focus captures all details in a photographic image. A softer focus lessens the amount of detail that can be seen. The framing of elements within a photograph directs the eye toward a portion of the image.

Lighting and Shadow
Lighting techniques are used in photography to enhance mood and direct the viewer's focus.

from
The Pigman & Me
Paul Zindel

▲ **Critical Viewing**
What are some conflicts among students that might occur in a scene like this one? **[Analyze]**

When trouble came to me, it didn't involve anybody I thought it would. It involved the nice, normal, smart boy by the name of John Quinn. Life does that to us a lot. Just when we think something awful's going to happen one way, it throws you a curve and the something awful happens another way. This happened on the first Friday, during gym period, when we were allowed to play games in the school yard. A boy by the name of Richard Cahill, who lived near an old linoleum factory, asked me if I'd like to play paddle ball with him, and I said, "Yes." Some of the kids played

498 Types of Nonfiction

Special Techniques

Most images you see today have been manipulated or changed in some way. Even a small change—such as an added graphic element or a difference in shading—can alter the mood of an image.

Questions About Graphics and Photos

- What would be the effect if the image above left used a sharp focus instead of a combination of a sharp and soft focus?

- In what way does the use of color and light create mood in the photo below left?

- What special techniques were applied to the original photograph shown above? What effect does the use of special techniques create?

Media Literacy Handbook

Persuasive Techniques

Advertisements use carefully selected visual elements and specific language to appeal to the viewer's emotions.

LEARN THE
TEXAS TWO-STEP

SEE WHERE IT
LEADS YOU.

Boogie on down to the Texas Coast.
The water's great.

Get your FREE Travel Guide

NOW

TEXAS
It's like a whole other country.

TEXAS TRAVEL GUIDE

Text and Graphics

Newspaper and magazine layouts are constructed to capture the eye and quickly convey the important ideas of a story. The use of type fonts, images, and page space direct the eye to portions of the printed page.

Questions About Print Media

- What image or graphic dominates the advertisement at left? In what way does the use of language in the ad enhance its message?

- Which of the above grabs your attention: the image or the captions on the magazine cover? Explain.

- What do you notice first on the magazine cover? What overall effect does the use of type size and fonts create?

How is this book organized?

- There are six units, each focusing on a specific genre.
- Each unit has a Big Question to get you thinking about important ideas and to guide your reading.
- A Literary Analysis Workshop begins each unit, providing instruction and practice for essential skills.

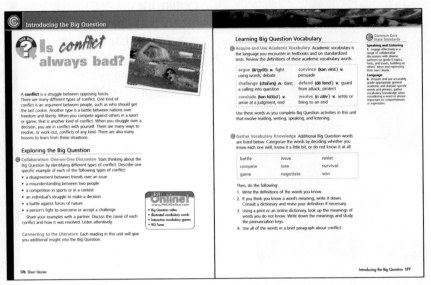

◀ At the beginning of the unit, **Introducing the Big Question** provides a reading focus for the entire unit. Use **academic vocabulary** to think, talk, and write about this question.

A **Literary Analysis Workshop** provides an overview of the unit genre, an in-depth exploration of Common Core State Standards, as well as models and practice opportunities. ▶

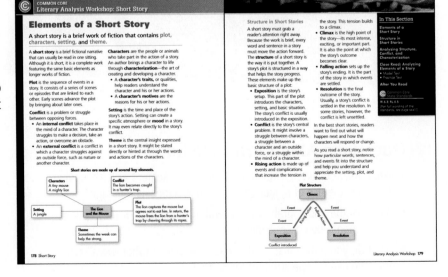

How are the literary selections organized?

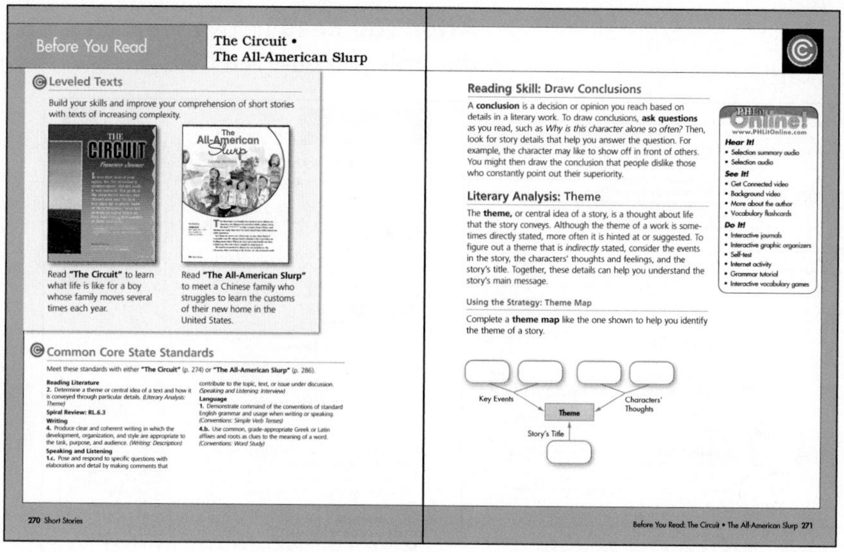

◀ **Before You Read** introduces two selection choices that both teach the same skills. Your teacher will help you choose the selection that is right for you.

Writing About the Big Question is a quick-writing activity that helps you connect the Big Question to the selection you are about to read.

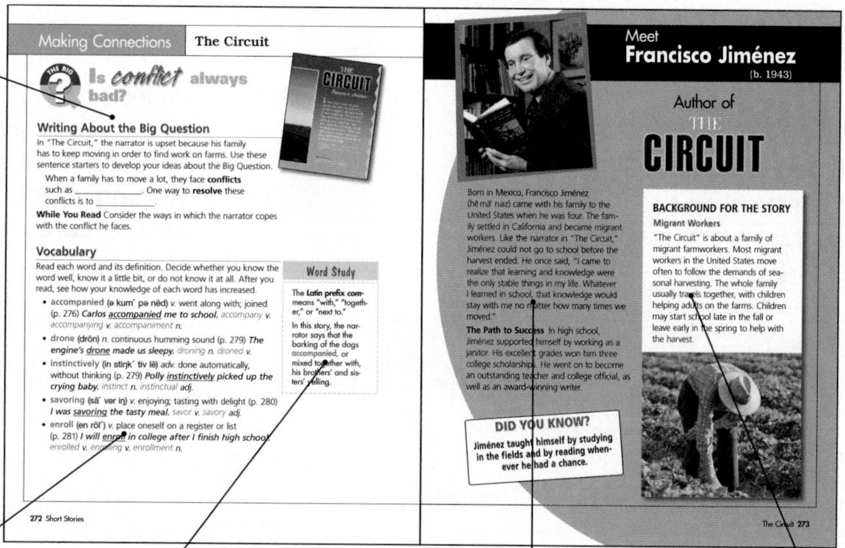

Vocabulary and Word Study introduce important selection vocabulary words and teach you about prefixes, suffixes, and roots.

Meet the Author and Background teach you about the author's life and provide information that will help you understand the selection.

How are the literary selections organized? *(continued)*

After You Read helps you practice the skills you have learned. ▼

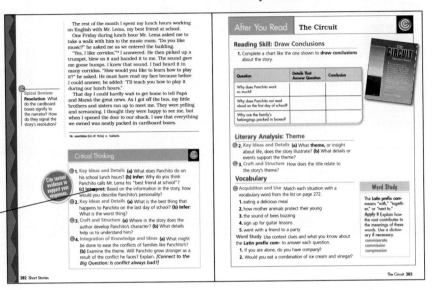

Critical Thinking questions help you reflect on what you have read and apply the Big Question to the selection.

Projects and activities help you deepen your understanding of the selection while strengthening your **writing, listening, speaking, and research skills.**

Integrated Language Skills provides instruction and practice for important grammar skills.

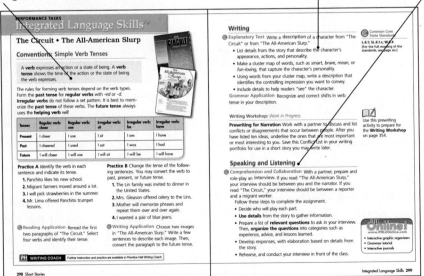

What special features will I find in this book?

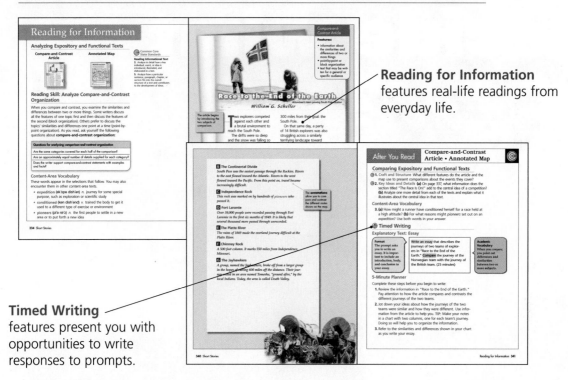

Reading for Information
features real-life readings from everyday life.

Timed Writing
features present you with opportunities to write responses to prompts.

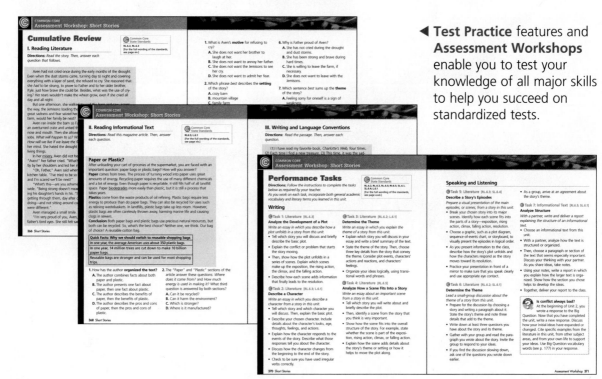

◀ Test Practice features and Assessment Workshops
enable you to test your knowledge of all major skills to help you succeed on standardized tests.

THE BIG ? How do we decide what is *true*?

Fiction and Nonfiction

PHLit Online!
www.PHLitOnline.com

Hear It!
- Selection summary audio
- Selection audio
- BQ Tunes

See It!
- Author videos
- Big Question video
- Get Connected videos
- Background videos
- More about the authors
- Illustrated vocabulary words
- Vocabulary flashcards

Do It!
- Interactive journals
- Interactive graphic organizers
- Grammar tutorials
- Interactive vocabulary games
- Test practice

How do we decide what is *true?*

Something that is true is real, genuine, or reliable. It is fact as opposed to fantasy. Yet, even a fantasy story can have elements of truth, and something that looks realistic can be false. Every day we see and hear information—in books, in newspapers, on television, and on the Internet. Sometimes it is a challenge to determine whether what we are seeing and hearing is true. A variety of different strategies can help us tell fact from fiction.

Exploring the Big Question

Collaboration: One-on-One Discussion Start thinking about the Big Question by identifying situations that require us to decide what is true. Describe one specific example of each of the following situations, based on your own experience or that of others:

- Reading product information to decide which product to buy
- Reading information on a Web site
- Helping to settle an argument between friends
- Making wise food choices by comparing advertisements to nutrition labels
- Reading about an event in history

Share your examples with a partner. Then, discuss why it is important to decide what is true in each case. Build on each other's ideas as you explore each situation. Come to an agreement and share the main points of your discussion with the class as a whole.

Connecting to the Literature Each reading in this unit will give you additional insight into the Big Question.

PHLit Online!
www.PHLitOnline.com

- Big Question video
- Illustrated vocabulary words
- Interactive vocabulary games
- BQ Tunes

Learning Big Question Vocabulary

© Acquire and Use Academic Vocabulary Academic vocabulary is the language you encounter in textbooks and on standardized tests. Review the definitions of these academic vocabulary words.

> **confirm** (kən fʉrm´) **v.** show to be correct; prove to be true or valid; verify
>
> **determine** (dē tʉr´ mən) **v.** find out what is true; reach a conclusion
>
> **evidence** (ev´ə dəns) **n.** proof in support of a claim or statement
>
> **fact** (fakt) **n.** something that is true or that has happened
>
> **investigate** (in ves´ tə gāt´) **v.** look into to learn the facts; examine thoroughly
>
> **opinion** (ə pin´ yən) **n.** personal view or belief
>
> **prove** (pro͞ov) **v.** establish the truth of
>
> **study** (stud´ē) **n.** research or investigation into a subject
>
> **test** (test) **n.** method or process for proving or disproving a claim

Use these words as you complete Big Question activities in this unit that involve reading, writing, speaking, and listening.

© Gather Vocabulary Knowledge Additional Big Question words are listed below. Categorize the words by deciding whether you know each one well, know it a little bit, or do not know it at all.

decision	fiction	true
fantasy	realistic	unbelievable

Then, do the following:

1. Write the definitions of the words you know.
2. For the words you know, consult a dictionary to confirm their meanings. Revise your definitions if necessary.
3. Using a print or an online dictionary, look up the meanings of the words you do not know. Then, write the meanings.
4. Use all of the words in a brief paragraph about truth.

Common Core State Standards

Speaking and Listening
1. Engage effectively in a range of collaborative discussions with diverse partners on *grade 6 topics, texts, and issues,* building on others' ideas and expressing their own clearly.

Language
4.d. Verify the preliminary determination of the meaning of a word or phrase.
6. Acquire and use accurately grade-appropriate general academic and domain-specific words and phrases; gather vocabulary knowledge when considering a word or phrase important to comprehension or expression.

Elements of Fiction and Nonfiction

Fiction and nonfiction are two main types of writing.

Fiction is writing that tells stories about imaginary people, animals, and events. When you read fiction, you enter a world that was made up by an author.

Nonfiction is writing that provides facts about real people, events, and ideas. Authors of nonfiction present information that teaches you about a subject or that tries to convince you to do or to believe something.

Though fiction and nonfiction are different, they sometimes share common elements. For example,

writers of fiction may base imaginary characters on real people. Fiction writers may also set imaginary events in real places.

Likewise, writers of nonfiction may use some of the same storytelling techniques that fiction writers use. For example, nonfiction writers may use vivid descriptions and quote conversations between people in order to make their writing come alive.

The chart below compares and contrasts the main elements of fiction and nonfiction.

Elements of Fiction and Nonfiction

Fiction	Nonfiction
tells about made-up people or animals, called **characters**	tells about real people
describes **conflicts,** or struggles, in a series of made-up events, called the **plot**	describes **conflicts** and events that really happened
is told by a speaker called the **narrator**	is told by the author, who is a real person
takes place in a **setting,** or time and place, that may be real or imaginary	gives facts or ideas about real time periods and places
often suggests a **theme**—a lesson or an insight about life	focuses on a **central idea,** or main point

Forms of Fiction

There are three main forms of fiction.

Short stories are brief works of fiction. They usually focus on one main conflict and just a few characters. In addition, they usually convey a single theme.

Novels are longer works of fiction that are sometimes divided into chapters. A novel usually has a more complicated plot and more characters than a short story has. Novels may be about more than one conflict and may describe many events. A novel may also suggest more than one theme.

Novellas are longer and more complex than short stories but are shorter than novels. They usually focus on fewer characters than novels and have less complicated plots.

Forms of Nonfiction

Nonfiction works come in many forms. Two main categories of nonfiction are functional texts and literary nonfiction.

Functional texts provide information and give directions that help readers accomplish various tasks. These texts often include visuals such as pictures, charts, or diagrams to make the information clear.

Literary nonfiction describes true events and real people but uses elements of literature to do so. For example, literary nonfiction may contain dialogue, conversations, and poetic language.

The chart below gives examples of different types of functional texts and literary nonfiction.

 Common Core State Standards

RL.6.2; RI.6.2
[For the full wording of the standards, see the standards chart in the front of your textbook.]

Examples of Functional Texts	Examples of Literary Nonfiction
Assembly instructions have diagrams and numbered steps that explain how to put something together.	An **autobiography** is an account of a person's life written by that person.
A **brochure** uses words and pictures to give information about places, services, or events.	A **biography** is an account of a person's life written by someone else.
A **recipe** gives step-by-step directions for preparing food.	An **essay** is a brief written work about a particular subject.
A **schedule** lists the intended times for specific events.	A **journal** or **diary** is a record of daily events and the writer's thoughts and feelings about them.
An **application** is a form that you fill out to make a request.	A **letter** is a written form of communication from one person to another.

Determining Themes in Fiction

Common Core State Standards

Reading Literature
2. Determine a theme or central idea of a text and how it is conveyed through particular details.

In fiction, themes are lessons or insights about life.

A **theme** is a central message about life. When you read fiction, remember that the subject and the theme are not the same thing. The subject is what the story is about. The theme is an insight about the subject. The chart below shows the difference between subjects and themes.

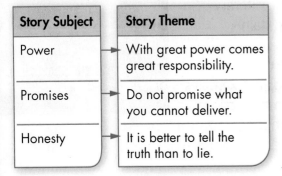

Story Subject	Story Theme
Power	With great power comes great responsibility.
Promises	Do not promise what you cannot deliver.
Honesty	It is better to tell the truth than to lie.

Example:
North Wind and South Wind competed to see who was strong enough to make a traveler remove his cloak. North Wind blew cold, harsh gusts that made the traveler pull his cloak tighter about him. Then, South Wind blew warm, soft breezes. The traveler felt so hot that he removed his cloak.

Possible Themes
- Great force does not guarantee success.
- Gentleness can succeed where force fails.

Stated and Implied Themes
Sometimes, an author directly states the theme of a work. More often, though, the theme is *implied,* or suggested, through the words and experiences of the characters or through the events in a story.

When the theme of a story is unstated, different people may interpret, or understand, the theme in different ways. Consider, for example, the story of North Wind and South Wind.

Notice that both statements of theme are based on events in the story. The best interpretations of theme are based on key details and events.

Universal Themes The story of North Wind and South Wind has a **universal theme**—a message about life that is expressed in many different cultures and time periods. These themes relate to experiences that are common to many people. Look for universal themes when you read fiction, but remember that not all themes are universal.

Determining Central Ideas in Nonfiction

Works of literary nonfiction express central, or main, ideas.

Common Core State Standards

Reading Informational Text
2. Determine a central idea of a text and how it is conveyed through particular details.

The **central, or main, idea** is the key point in a work of literary nonfiction. Sometimes, a central idea is directly stated, then supported, or explained, with details. Other times, a central idea is *implied*, or suggested. You can figure out an implied central idea by identifying what the supporting details have in common.

Many nonfiction works convey only one central idea, which is supported by a main idea in each paragraph. A paragraph's main idea is usually stated in a **topic sentence,** which is often the first sentence of the paragraph.

The outline below shows three paragraphs with topic sentences that support the central idea of the work.

Example: Topic Sentence Outline

I. Central Idea: Daily exercise is good for you.

II. Paragraph 1: Exercise boosts your brain power.

III. Paragraph 2: Exercise helps prevent many diseases.

IV. Paragraph 3: Exercise makes you stronger.

Just as each paragraph supports the central idea of the whole work, key details support the topic sentence of each paragraph. The example below shows a supporting detail for Paragraph 1.

Example: Supporting Detail

Exercise releases a chemical that can enhance brain growth and function.

Author's Purpose and Central Idea

An **author's purpose** is his or her main reason for writing. Three general purposes are to **inform,** to **entertain,** and to **persuade,** or convince.

Nonfiction writers also have specific purposes for writing. For instance, a writer may want to inform readers about a specific topic. The central idea is the point the writer wants to make about that topic.

General Purpose	To inform
Specific Purpose	To inform readers about the history of baseball
Central Idea	Baseball comes from an English sport called rounders.

Close Read: Theme in Fiction

The elements of a story help develop its theme.

In most stories, authors do not directly tell you the theme. Instead, they develop it through their use of various literary elements. Readers use details in these elements as clues to the story's main message. As you read a story, look for key details in the following elements. Think about the message these details suggest.

Clues to Theme	Tips
Plot and Conflict **Plot** is the series of events in the story. **Conflict** is a struggle between opposing forces. It moves the plot forward.	• Think about the reasons for the conflict. • Notice how the characters respond to the conflict. • Determine whether the characters are able to resolve, or end, the conflict. • Identify any lessons that the characters learn from the conflict.
Setting The **setting** is the time and place of the story. In some stories, setting is just a background. In other stories, setting is an important clue to theme.	• Identify the time and place in which the story's action occurs. • Ask yourself whether the setting is important to the characters and events in the story. • Find details that help you picture the setting.
Characters **Characters** are the people or animals in a story.	• Look at words that describe the characters. Think about what the characters think, say, and do. • Notice whether the characters change as a result of their experiences. • Ask yourself whether the characters learn from their experiences or from the experiences of others.
Descriptions and Symbols **Descriptions** tell what something looks like, sounds like, feels like, and so on. A **symbol** is anything that represents something else. For example, a red rose often represents love.	• Notice descriptions that are especially vivid. • Notice descriptions that are repeated throughout the story. • Determine whether certain objects, people, or places have a special meaning to the narrator or a character.

Model

About the Text This story is set in the 1930s in the Deep South. The Logans, an African American family, struggle against poverty and racism, but they have few opportunities to change their situation. Joined by other African American families, the Logans boycott, or refuse to do business with, a local store that had mistreated customers. The families travel farther away to Vicksburg to buy their supplies.

In this excerpt, Cassie, the narrator, tells about a conversation with her father and her older brother, Stacey, after two farmers tell Papa Logan that they can no longer participate in the boycott.

---

from *Roll of Thunder, Hear My Cry*
by Mildred D. Taylor

When the men had left, Stacey snapped, "They got no right pulling out! Just 'cause them Wallaces threaten them one time they go jumping all over themselves to get out like a bunch of scared jackrabbits—"

Papa stood suddenly and grabbed Stacey upward. "You, boy, don't you get so grown you go to talking 'bout more than you know. Them men, they doing what they've gotta do. You got any idea what a risk they took just to go shopping in Vicksburg in the first place? They go on that chain gang and their families got nothing. They'll get kicked off that plot of land they tend and there'll be no place for them to go. You understand that?"

"Y-yessir," said Stacey. Papa released him and stared moodily into the night. "You were born blessed, boy, with land of your own. If you hadn't been, you'd cry out for it while you try to survive ... like Mr. Lanier and Mr. Avery. Maybe even do what they doing now. It's hard on a man to give up, but sometimes it seems there just ain't nothing else he can do."

"I ... I'm sorry, Papa," Stacey muttered.

After a moment, Papa reached out and draped his arm over Stacey's shoulder.

Setting In the Deep South of the 1930s, land ownership was a source of pride for African Americans. However, ownership could also be a source of conflict.

Conflict The dialogue, or conversation, points out that some of the Logans' neighbors have given up the boycott.

EXEMPLAR TEXT

Model continued

Descriptions and Symbols Papa describes the fig tree, which keeps growing and will not give up. The fig tree stands for the Logan family, which also is determined to survive.

Characters Papa's words reveal his strength. His statement "There's a lesson to be learned" is a clue that he will directly state a theme.

Conflict Many people have stopped boycotting the store. Papa does not want to be alone, but he seems determined to go to Vicksburg.

Characters Mama is quiet before she tells Papa to "wait awhile" before going to Vicksburg. She may be frightened, but she shows a quiet courage in advising Papa to wait.

"Papa," I said, standing to join them, "we giving up too?"

Papa looked down at me and brought me closer, then waved his hand toward the drive. "You see that fig tree over yonder, Cassie? Them other trees all around … that oak and walnut, they're a lot bigger and they take up more room and give so much shade they almost overshadow that little ole fig. But that fig tree's got roots that run deep, and it belongs in that yard as much as that oak and walnut. It keeps on blooming, bearing good fruit year after year, knowing all the time it'll never get as big as them other trees. Just keeps on growing and doing what it gotta do. It don't give up. It give up, it'll die. There's a lesson to be learned from that little tree, Cassie girl, 'cause we're like it. We keep doing what we gotta, and we don't give up. We can't."

After Mr. Morrison had retired to his own house and Big Ma, the boys, and I had gone to bed, Papa and Mama remained on the porch, talking in hushed whispers. It was comforting listening to them, Mama's voice a warm, lilting murmur, Papa's a quiet, easy-flowing hum. After a few minutes they left the porch and their voices grew faint. I climbed from the bed, careful not to awaken Big Ma, and went to the window. They were walking slowly across the moon-soaked grass, their arms around each other.

"First thing tomorrow, I'm gonna go 'round and see how many folks are still in this thing," Papa said, stopping under the oak near the house. "I wanna know before we make that trip to Vicksburg."

Mama was quiet a moment. "I don't think you and Mr. Morrison should go to Vicksburg right now, David. Not with the Wallaces threatening people like they are. Wait awhile."

Determining the Theme By thinking about the setting, conflict, symbols, and characters, you might interpret the theme this way: *Never give up, no matter what.*

Independent Practice

About the Selection To write this story, Jane Yolen drew upon Scottish ballads and tales about strange characters called *selchies,* or *silkies*. These are mythical seals that can take on human form by shrugging out of their skins. The wild, beautiful coast described in the story is much like the remote fishing villages and rocky coastlines where seals gather to rest and breed today.

"Greyling" by Jane Yolen

Once on a time when wishes were aplenty, a fisherman and his wife lived by the side of the sea. All that they ate came out of the sea. Their hut was covered with the finest mosses that kept them cool in the summer and warm in the winter. And there was nothing they needed or wanted except a child.

Each morning, when the moon touched down behind the water and the sun rose up behind the plains, the wife would say to the fisherman, "You have your boat and your nets and your lines. But I have no baby to hold in my arms." And again, in the evening, it was the same. She would weep and wail and rock the cradle that stood by the hearth. But year in and year out the cradle stayed empty.

Now the fisherman was also sad that they had no child. But he kept his sorrow to himself so that his wife would not know his grief[1] and thus double her own. Indeed, he would leave the hut each morning with a breath of song and return each night with a whistle on his lips. His nets were full but his heart was empty, yet he never told his wife.

One sunny day, when the beach was a tan thread spun between sea and plain, the fisherman as usual went down to his boat. But this day he found a small grey seal stranded on the sandbar, crying for its own.

The fisherman looked up the beach and down. He looked in front of him and behind. And he looked to the town on the great grey cliffs that sheared[2] off into the sea. But there were no other seals in sight.

Setting What do the words "Once on a time" suggest about the setting of the story?

Plot and Conflict What is the couple's main problem?

---

1. **grief** (grēf) *n.* deep sadness.
2. **sheared** (shird) *v.* cut off sharply.

Practice continued

Characters What do his actions tell you about the fisherman?

So he shrugged his shoulders and took off his shirt. Then he dipped it into the water and wrapped the seal pup carefully in its folds.

"You have no father and you have no mother," he said.

"And I have no child. So you shall come home with me."

And the fisherman did no fishing that day but brought the seal pup, wrapped in his shirt, straight home to his wife.

When she saw him coming home early with no shirt on, the fisherman's wife ran out of the hut, fear riding in her heart. Then she looked wonderingly at the bundle which he held in his arms.

"It's nothing," he said, "but a seal pup I found stranded in the shallows and longing for its own. I thought we could give it love and care until it is old enough to seek its kin."

The fisherman's wife nodded and took the bundle. Then she uncovered the wrapping and gave a loud cry. "Nothing!" she said. "You call this nothing?"

The fisherman looked. Instead of a seal lying in the folds, there was a strange child with great grey eyes and silvery grey hair, smiling up at him.

The fisherman wrung his hands. "It is a selchie," he cried. "I have heard of them. They are men upon the land and seals in the sea. I thought it was but a tale."

"Then he shall remain a man upon the land," said the fisherman's wife, clasping the child in her arms, "for I shall never let him return to the sea."

Conflict Why does the fisherman feel it is wrong not to let the child return to the sea?

"Never," agreed the fisherman, for he knew how his wife had wanted a child. And in his secret heart, he wanted one, too. Yet he felt, somehow, it was wrong.

"We shall call him Greyling," said the fisherman's wife, "for his eyes and hair are the color of a storm-coming sky. Greyling, though he has brought sunlight into our home."

And though they still lived by the side of the water in a hut covered with mosses that kept them warm in the winter and cool in the summer, the boy Greyling was never allowed into the sea.

He grew from a child to a lad. He grew from a lad to a young man. He gathered driftwood for his mother's hearth and searched the tide pools for shells for her mantel. He mended his father's nets and tended his father's boat. But though he often stood by the shore or high in the town on the great grey cliffs, looking and longing and grieving in his heart for what he did not really know, he never went into the sea.

Then one wind-wailing morning just fifteen years from the day that Greyling had been found, a great storm blew up suddenly in the North. It was such a storm as had never been seen before: the sky turned nearly black and even the fish had trouble swimming. The wind pushed huge waves onto the shore. The waters gobbled up the little hut on the beach. And Greyling and the fisherman's wife were forced to flee to the town high on the great grey cliffs. There they looked down at the roiling, boiling, sea. Far from shore they spied the fisherman's boat, its sails flapping like the wings of a wounded gull. And clinging to the broken mast was the fisherman himself, sinking deeper with every wave.

The fisherman's wife gave a terrible cry. "Will no one save him?" she called to the people of the town who had gathered on the edge of the cliff. "Will no one save my own dear husband who is all of life to me?"

Symbols How does the color grey connect the human baby to the baby seal that he was?

Characters What do you think Greyling is longing for, and why?

Conflict What force is the fisherman struggling against?

Practice continued

Conflict How do these events intensify the conflict for the fisherman's wife?

But the townsmen looked away. There was no man there who dared risk his life in that sea, even to save a drowning soul.

"Will no one at all save him?" she cried out again.

"Let the boy go," said one old man, pointing at Greyling with his stick. "He looks strong enough."

But the fisherman's wife clasped Greyling in her arms and held his ears with her hands. She did not want him to go into the sea. She was afraid he would never return.

"Will no one save my own dear heart?" cried the fisherman's wife for a third and last time.

But shaking their heads, the people of the town edged to their houses and shut their doors and locked their windows and set their backs to the ocean and their faces to the fires that glowed in every hearth.

"I will save him, Mother," cried Greyling, "or die as I try."

And before she could tell him no, he broke from her grasp and dived from the top of the great cliffs, down, down, down into the tumbling sea.

"He will surely sink," whispered the women as they ran from their warm fires to watch.

"He will certainly drown," called the men as they took down their spyglasses from the shelves.

They gathered on the cliffs and watched the boy dive down into the sea.

Descriptions and Symbols What might the loss of Greyling's clothes and skin represent?

As Greyling disappeared beneath the waves, little fingers of foam tore at his clothes. They snatched his shirt and his pants and his shoes and sent them bubbling away to the shore. And as Greyling went deeper beneath the waves, even his skin seemed to slough[3] off till he swam, free at last, in the sleek grey coat of a great grey seal.

---

3. slough (sluf) *v.* be cast off; be gotten rid of.

The selchie had returned to the sea.

But the people of the town did not see this. All they saw was the diving boy disappearing under the waves and then, farther out, a large seal swimming toward the boat that wallowed[4] in the sea. The sleek grey seal, with no effort at all, eased the fisherman to the shore though the waves were wild and bright with foam. And then, with a final salute, it turned its back on the land and headed joyously out to sea.

The fisherman's wife hurried down to the sand. And behind her followed the people of the town. They searched up the beach and down, but they did not find the boy.

"A brave son," said the men when they found his shirt, for they thought he was certainly drowned.

"A very brave son," said the women when they found his shoes, for they thought him lost for sure.

"Has he really gone?" asked the fisherman's wife of her husband when at last they were alone.

"Yes, quite gone," the fisherman said to her. "Gone where his heart calls, gone to the great wide sea. And though my heart grieves at his leaving, it tells me this way is best."

The fisherman's wife sighed. And then she cried. But at last she agreed that, perhaps, it was best. "For he is both man and seal," she said. "And though we cared for him for a while, now he must care for himself." And she never cried again. So once more they lived alone by the side of the sea in a new little hut which was covered with mosses to keep them warm in the winter and cool in the summer.

Yet, once a year, a great grey seal is seen at night near the fisherman's home. And the people in town talk of it, and wonder. But seals do come to the shore and men do go to the sea; and so the townfolk do not dwell upon it very long.

But it is no ordinary seal. It is Greyling himself come home—come to tell his parents tales of the lands that lie far beyond the waters, and to sing them songs of the wonders that lie far beneath the sea.

Descriptions What does this description tell you about Greyling's feelings?

Characters What have the fisherman and his wife learned from their experiences?

Theme How would you state the theme of the story? Which details gave you clues to the theme?

---

4. **wallowed** (wäl´ ōd) *v.* rolled and tilted.

Close Read: Central Idea in Nonfiction

Authors often state a central idea early in a work. Supporting details develop that idea.

In works of literary nonfiction, authors provide details that support their central ideas. Each paragraph in a work might express and support its own central idea. Those ideas, in turn, develop the central idea of the entire work.

Stated Central Idea Nonfiction authors often state the central idea early in a work. Look at the example below.

Implied Central Idea Other times, however, authors suggest, or imply, the central idea. In these cases, readers can connect supporting details to determine that idea.

Example: Stated Central Idea

Adopting a grown-up dog is better than adopting a puppy. Grown-up dogs have developed their personalities and need less care and training than puppies.

Example: Implied Central Idea

When you adopt a grown-up dog from a shelter, you know what the dog's personality is like. You can also see how large the dog has grown. In addition, you can tell if the dog has had any training.

This example does not state the central idea. All the sentences, however, state the advantages of adopting a grown-up dog.

Types of Supporting Details

Facts are statements that can be proved true. *Example: There are 17 penguin species.*	**Quotations** are word-for-word reports of what someone said. *Example: The principal said, "We will do our best to meet this challenge."*
Personal experiences are firsthand accounts of events in a person's life. *Example: After the first lesson, I realized that fencing was more difficult than it looked.*	**Descriptions** are details that tell how someone or something looked, felt, sounded, and so on. *Example: She was a remarkably good soccer player—quick, strong, and decisive.*
Examples are specific illustrations of a general idea. *Example: This is the state's most popular race. Each year more than 35,000 runners compete.*	**Comparisons** are statements that point out the similarities or differences between different people, places, or things. *Example: Hacking people's e-mail is like stealing letters from their mailboxes.*

Model

About the Text John Adams wrote this letter in 1822. In the letter, he tells what happened when a committee appointed him and Thomas Jefferson to write a "Declaration of Independence."

from "Letter on Thomas Jefferson" by John Adams

Mr. Jefferson came into Congress, in June, 1775, and brought with him a reputation for literature, science, and a happy talent of composition. Writings of his were handed about, remarkable for the peculiar felicity of expression. Though a silent member in Congress, he was so prompt, frank, explicit, and decisive upon committees and in conversation, not even Samuel Adams was more so, that he soon seized upon my heart; and upon this occasion I gave him my vote, and did all in my power to procure the votes of others. I think he had one more vote than any other, and that placed him at the head of the committee. I had the next highest number, and that placed me second. The committee met, discussed the subject, and then appointed Mr. Jefferson and me to make the draught, I suppose because we were the two first on the list.

The sub-committee met. Jefferson proposed to me to make the draught. I said, "I will not."

"You should do it."

"Oh! no."

"Why will you not? You ought to do it."

"I will not."

"Why?"

"Reasons enough."

"What can be your reasons?"

"Reason first—You are a Virginian, and a Virginian ought to appear at the head of this business. Reason second—I am obnoxious, suspected, and unpopular. You are much otherwise. Reason third— You can write ten times better than I can."

"Well," said Jefferson, "if you are decided, I will do as well as I can."

"Very well. When you have drawn it up, we will have a meeting."

Descriptions Adams says Jefferson was well read and was a good writer. Adams focuses on these qualities to show why Jefferson was chosen to co-write the Declaration of Independence.

Personal Experiences Adams makes it clear that he was present at the meeting and is relating firsthand experiences.

Quotations The conversation between Adams and Jefferson shows what the two men were like and explains how they worked together.

Central Idea Details in the text suggest this central idea: Adams persuaded Jefferson to write the first draft of the Declaration of Independence because Adams thought Jefferson was the best qualified to do so.

Independent Practice

About the Selection Jane Yolen first presented this work as a speech. It describes her love for Scotland.

Personal Experiences
Based on Yolen's statements about her personal experiences, what do you think this speech will be about?

Descriptions How does this description support Yolen's idea that the Highlands are the "home of the heart"?

Facts How do these facts about harling help you understand the place Yolen is describing?

"My Heart Is in the Highlands" by Jane Yolen

I first set foot on Scottish soil in the mid '80s, when my husband and I—between conferences (science fiction for me, computer science for him)—took a trip north from Brighton.

We drove, being used to long road trips and camping vacations with our children, and were predictably stunned by Edinburgh and its looming castle on the hill. None of America, and blessed little of Brighton, had prepared us for such a sight.

But it was when we began our ascent through the Highlands that it became clear to us that here was the home of the heart. . . .

I love the white-washed stone cottages here in Scotland, small cozy homes that seem to have grown rough hewn right up from the land. I love the gray stone mansions and the tall stone tower houses, too.

If you search the histories of any individual town here, or a particular street, you will find that these homes and walled gardens have often been built upon older, vanished buildings. Where a kirk or a tollbooth or a great hall once stood, now a townsman's seven-room house with mod cons squats.[1]

But it is not just the site that has been cannibalized. The very stones have been reused. So in Scotland history lies upon history. As a wonderful little book on the royal burgh of Falkland in the Kingdom of Fife[2] puts it: "Absorbing stones from an old building into the fabric of the later one is . . . a way of holding on to the past."

After the stones have been pulled together and balanced and mortared into place, the walls are harled, or roughcast[3] so as to protect the soft stone and mortar from the winter winds and heavy gales.

Stones, harling, a way of holding on to the past. It's all a perfect metaphor for writing a book, especially books set here in Scotland.

Writers use stones from the past, reshaping and rebuilding with them. And then they protect the soft memories with a harling of technique.

---

1. **kirk** (kʉrk) . . . **mod cons squats** Where churches or other structures were, now there are houses with modern conveniences.
2. **royal burgh** (bʉrg) . . . **Fife** Falkland, once the home of the Earls of Fife, is a Scottish town created by royal charter.
3. **roughcast** (ruf′ kast′) v. covered in coarse stucco, a cement-like substance.

How can it be otherwise? All fiction uses memory. Or re-memory for those of us whose grasp of the past is exceeded by the need to embellish, decorate, deepen, widen and otherwise change what was actual.

As a writer, I am made up of the little building blocks of my own private history, and what I know of the world that has already been rebuilt upon. My infancy told to me so often by my parents in delicious anecdote, my childhood captured in photos and catchlines, my adolescence in letters and journals, my young adulthood in poetry and prose.

I simply take those story-stones and use them again in any new building. Or I thieve from my closest friends and relatives, from my husband's life and my children. They don't just endure such thievery— they expect it. A warning—get to know me well and you will most certainly find yourself enshrined in one of my books.

But even those closest to me sometimes have trouble identifying themselves when next they meet themselves in fiction. For they will have been metamorphosed[4] into a toad or a selchie or a wind blowing in over the wall. Even I don't always know whose bones lie beneath a particular character's skin.

That's because fiction (to mix this metaphor hopelessly) is a magic mirror that gives back a changed self.

Comparisons According to Yolen, how are her memories similar to the old stones used to build things in the Highlands?

Central Idea Based on the details Yolen provides, what do you think is the central idea of this speech? Explain.

---

4. **metamorphosed** (met´ ə môr´ fōzd´) v. changed in form or shape.

After You Read | Greyling • My Heart Is in the Highlands

1. **Key Ideas and Details** What is the main conflict in "Greyling"?

2. **Key Ideas and Details Evaluate:** Should the couple have kept Greyling from the sea? Explain.

3. **Key Ideas and Details** What **theme** about parents and children does "Greyling" present? Explain.

4. **Key Ideas and Details** What do you think is Yolen's **purpose** in writing "My Heart Is in the Highlands"? Explain.

5. **Key Ideas and Details** According to Yolen, how is writing a book like reusing old stones?

6. **Key Ideas and Details (a)** Write an objective summary of "Greyling." Include only key ideas and details, not personal opinions. **(b)** Write an objective summary of "My Heart Is in the Highlands."

7. **Integration of Knowledge and Ideas** Using a chart, list details that show "Greyling" is **fiction.**

Fictional Details	Importance to the Story

© Leveled Texts

Build your skills and improve your comprehension of fiction with texts of increasing complexity.

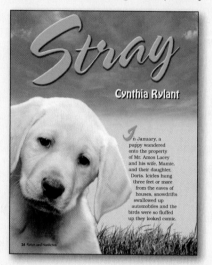

Read **"Stray"** to find out what happens when a girl becomes attached to a wonderful dog that her parents will not let her keep.

Read **"The Homecoming"** to encounter a well-intentioned woodcutter who cannot find the time to chop wood.

© Common Core State Standards

Meet these standards with either **"Stray"** (p. 24) or **"The Homecoming"** (p. 32).

Reading Literature
3. Describe how a particular story's or drama's plot unfolds in a series of episodes as well as how the characters respond or change as the plot moves toward a resolution. (*Literary Analysis: Plot*)

Writing
2.b. Develop the topic with relevant facts, definitions, concrete details, quotations, or other information and examples. **2.e.** Establish and maintain a formal style. (*Writing: News Report*)

4. Produce clear and coherent writing in which the development, organization, and style are appropriate to task, purpose, and audience. (*Writing: News Report*)

7. Conduct short research projects to answer a question, drawing on several sources and refocusing the inquiry when appropriate. (*Research and Technology: Brochure*)

Speaking and Listening
4. Present claims and findings, sequencing ideas logically and using pertinent descriptions, facts, and details to accentuate main ideas or themes. (*Writing: News Report*)

Language
2. Demonstrate command of the conventions of standard English capitalization, punctuation, and spelling when writing. (*Conventions: Common and Proper Nouns*)

4.b. Use common, grade-appropriate Greek or Latin affixes and roots as clues to the meaning of a word. (*Vocabulary: Word Study*)

Reading Skill: Make Predictions

A **prediction** is a developing idea about what will happen next in a story. You can **use your prior knowledge** to help you make predictions. To do this, relate what you already know to details in the story. For example, if you have ever moved to a new neighborhood, you know that making new friends can be difficult. If the story tells you that a character is shy and has moved to a new neighborhood, you can combine what you know with the information in the story to predict that the character will not make friends easily.

Literary Analysis: Plot

One key element of short stories is plot. **Plot** is the arrangement of events in a story. Plot includes the following elements:

- **Exposition:** introduction of setting, characters, and situation
- **Conflict:** the story's central problem
- **Rising Action:** events that increase tension
- **Climax:** high point of the story, when the story's outcome becomes clear and changes in the characters become apparent
- **Falling Action:** events that follow the climax
- **Resolution:** the final outcome

Using the Strategy: Plot Diagram

Use a **plot diagram** like the one below to keep track of important events in the stories that follow.

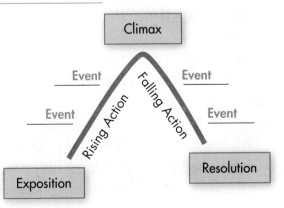

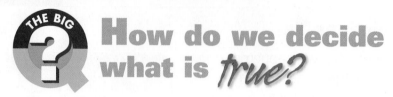

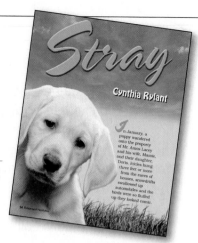

How do we decide what is *true?*

Writing About the Big Question

In "Stray," Doris is upset because her parents tell her they cannot afford to keep the stray dog she found. Is it true that keeping a dog as a pet can be expensive? Use this sentence starter to develop your ideas about the Big Question.

Before you **decide** if you can own a pet you should
determine _____.

While You Read Look for signs that Doris understands her parents' reason for saying no even though she is upset about her parents' decision.

Vocabulary

Read each word and its definition. Decide whether you know the word well, know it a little bit, or do not know it at all. After you read, see how your knowledge of each word has increased.

- **timidly** (tim´ id lē) *adv.* in a way that shows fear or shyness (p. 25) *The little girl <u>timidly</u> asked for a cookie.* timid *adj.* timidity *n.*

- **trudged** (trudj´d) *v.* walked as if tired or with effort. (p. 25) *Larry <u>trudged</u> into the classroom ten minutes late.* trudge *v.* trudging *v.*

- **grudgingly** (gruj´ iŋ lē) *adv.* in an unwilling or resentful way (p. 25) *Peter <u>grudgingly</u> admitted that he was wrong.* grudge *n.*

- **ignore** (ig nôr´) *v.* pay no attention to (p. 26) *I will <u>ignore</u> the noise in the halls as I take my test.* ignored *v.* ignoring *v.*

- **exhausted** (eg zôst´ əd) *adj.* very tired (p. 27) *Cindy was <u>exhausted</u> after cleaning the house.* exhaust *v.* exhaustion *n.*

- **starvation** (stär vā´ shən) *state of extreme hunger (p. 27) I felt like I was suffering from <u>starvation</u> after a full day without eating.* starve *v.* starving *v.*

Word Study

The **Latin suffix -ation** changes a verb to a noun. It means "the condition of being."

In this story, Doris's dad says that Doris should feed the dog or it will die of **starvation**, or the condition of being starved.

Meet
Cynthia Rylant
(b. 1954)

Author of
"*Stray*"

As a child, Cynthia Rylant never imagined that she would be a writer. "I always felt my life was too limited," she says. "Nothing to write about." At age twenty-four, however, she found that her life did in fact contain the seeds of many stories. Her first book, *When I Was Young in the Mountains*, describes her childhood in the hills of West Virginia. Cynthia lived with her grandparents for four years in a tiny house without plumbing. The hardships she experienced are reflected in "Stray." Since the publication of her first book, Rylant has written more than sixty children's books.

BACKGROUND FOR THE STORY
Animal Shelters
Animal shelters take in stray and unwanted animals like the dog in "Stray." Although they can seem crowded, noisy, and smelly, most shelters have the best interests of the animals at heart. In addition to caring for animals, many shelters provide education on the responsibilities of having a pet.

DID YOU KNOW?
Unlike many writers, Rylant does not use a computer to write her stories. Instead, she writes by hand on yellow legal pads.

Stray

Cynthia Rylant

In January, a puppy wandered onto the property of Mr. Amos Lacey and his wife, Mamie, and their daughter, Doris. Icicles hung three feet or more from the eaves of houses, snowdrifts swallowed up automobiles and the birds were so fluffed up they looked comic.

The puppy had been abandoned, and it made its way down the road toward the Laceys' small house, its ears tucked, its tail between its legs, shivering.

Doris, whose school had been called off because of the snow, was out shoveling the cinderblock front steps when she spotted the pup on the road. She set down the shovel.

"Hey! Come on!" she called.

The puppy stopped in the road, wagging its tail *timidly*, trembling with shyness and cold.

Doris *trudged* through the yard, went up the shoveled drive and met the dog.

"Come on, Pooch."

"Where did *that* come from?" Mrs. Lacey asked as soon as Doris put the dog down in the kitchen.

Mr. Lacey was at the table, cleaning his fingernails with his pocketknife. The snow was keeping him home from his job at the warehouse.

"I don't know where it came from," he said mildly, "but I know for sure where it's going."

Doris hugged the puppy hard against her. She said nothing.

Because the roads would be too bad for travel for many days, Mr. Lacey couldn't get out to take the puppy to the pound[1] in the city right away. He agreed to let it sleep in the basement while Mrs. Lacey *grudgingly* let Doris feed it table scraps. The woman was sensitive about throwing out food.

By the looks of it, Doris figured the puppy was about six months old, and on its way to being a big dog. She thought it might have some shepherd in it. •

Four days passed and the puppy did not complain. It never cried in the night or howled at the wind. It didn't tear up everything in the basement. It wouldn't even follow Doris up the basement steps unless it was invited.

It was a good dog.

Several times Doris had opened the door in the kitchen that led to the basement and the puppy had been there, all stretched out, on the top step. Doris knew it had wanted some company and that it had lain against the door,

---

1. **pound** (pound) *n.* animal shelter.

Vocabulary
timidly (tim´ id lē) *adv.* in a way that shows fear or shyness
trudged (trudj´d) *v.* walked as if tired or with effort
grudgingly (gruj´ iŋ lē) *adv.* in an unwilling or resentful way

Make Predictions
Based on what you know about big dogs, do you predict that Mr. Lacey will change his mind?

Plot
What action up until this point in the story suggests a conflict? Explain.

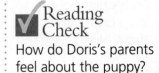

Reading Check
How do Doris's parents feel about the puppy?

▲ **Critical Viewing**
Why might a girl like Doris become attached to a dog like this one? **[Analyze]**

Vocabulary
ignore (ig nôr´) v. pay no attention to

ⓒ
Spiral Review
Character What do Doris's failed efforts to avoid crying tell you about her character?

listening to the talk in the kitchen, smelling the food, being a part of things. It always wagged its tail, eyes all sleepy, when she found it there.

Even after a week had gone by, Doris didn't name the dog. She knew her parents wouldn't let her keep it, that her father made so little money any pets were out of the question, and that the pup would definitely go to the pound when the weather cleared.

Still, she tried talking to them about the dog at dinner one night.

"She's a good dog, isn't she?" Doris said, hoping one of them would agree with her.

Her parents glanced at each other and went on eating.

"She's not much trouble," Doris added. "I like her." She smiled at them, but they continued to ignore her.

"I figure she's real smart," Doris said to her mother. "I could teach her things."

Mrs. Lacey just shook her head and stuffed a forkful of sweet potato in her mouth. Doris fell silent, praying the weather would never clear.

But on Saturday, nine days after the dog had arrived, the sun was shining and the roads were plowed. Mr. Lacey opened up the trunk of his car and came into the house.

Doris was sitting alone in the living room, hugging a pillow and rocking back and forth on the edge of a chair. She was trying not to cry but she was not strong enough. Her face was wet and red, her eyes full of distress.

Mrs. Lacey looked into the room from the doorway.

"Mama," Doris said in a small voice. "Please."

Mrs. Lacey shook her head.

"You know we can't afford a dog, Doris. You try to act more grown-up about this."

Doris pressed her face into the pillow.

Outside, she heard the trunk of the car slam shut, one of the doors open and close, the old engine cough and choke and finally start up.

"Daddy," she whispered. "Please."

She heard the car travel down the road, and, though it was early afternoon, she could do nothing but go to her bed. She cried herself to sleep, and her dreams were full of searching and searching for things lost.

It was nearly night when she finally woke up. Lying there, like stone, still exhausted, she wondered if she would ever in her life have anything. She stared at the wall for a while.

But she started feeling hungry, and she knew she'd have to make herself get out of bed and eat some dinner. She wanted not to go into the kitchen, past the basement door. She wanted not to face her parents.

But she rose up heavily.

Her parents were sitting at the table, dinner over, drinking coffee. They looked at her when she came in, but she kept her head down. No one spoke.

Doris made herself a glass of powdered milk and drank it all down.

Then she picked up a cold biscuit and started out of the room.

"You'd better feed that mutt before it dies of starvation," Mr. Lacey said.

Doris turned around.

"What?"

"I said, you'd better feed your dog. I figure it's looking for you."

Doris put her hand to her mouth.

"You didn't take her?" she asked.

"Oh, I took her all right," her father

"Mama," Doris said in a small voice. "Please."

Reading Check

Why doesn't Doris want to get out of bed to eat?

Stray **27**

Plot
What is surprising about the resolution of the conflict?

answered. "Worst looking place I've ever seen. Ten dogs to a cage. Smell was enough to knock you down. And they give an animal six days to live. Then they kill it with some kind of a shot."

Doris stared at her father.

"I wouldn't leave an ant in that place," he said. "So I brought the dog back."

Mrs. Lacey was smiling at him and shaking her head as if she would never, ever, understand him.

Mr. Lacey sipped his coffee.

"Well," he said, "are you going to feed it or not?"

Critical Thinking

Cite textual evidence to support your responses.

1. **Key Ideas and Details** Why do the Laceys wait before taking the dog to the pound?

2. **Key Ideas and Details** **(a)** What does Doris do when her father first tells her that she cannot keep the dog? **(b) Analyze:** Why does Doris react this way?

3. **Key Ideas and Details** **(a)** In your own words, restate Mr. Lacey's description of the pound. **(b) Analyze:** Why does Mr. Lacey change his mind about keeping the dog?

4. **Integration of Knowledge and Ideas** **(a) Take a Position:** Do you think that Doris should have made a stronger case for keeping the dog? Why or why not? **(b) Speculate:** What could Doris do in the future to show her father that he was right about keeping the dog?

5. **Integration of Knowledge and Ideas** How does the truth about whether or not the family can keep the dog change over the course of the story? Why does it change? *[Connect to the Big Question: How do we decide what is true?]*

Reading Skill: Make Predictions

1. Copy and complete the chart to show how you used prior knowledge and story clues to **predict** the answer to these questions. **(a)** What will Doris's parents say about the puppy? **(b)** What will her father do when the weather finally clears?

Prior Knowledge	Details From Story	Prediction
Puppies are cute.	The puppy is abandoned.	Doris will want to keep it.
(a)		
(b)		

Literary Analysis: Plot

2. **Craft and Structure** What is the **conflict** in the **plot** of this story?

3. **Craft and Structure** What is the **climax,** or high point, in the story? Explain.

Vocabulary

Acquisition and Use Rewrite each sentence. Use a vocabulary word from page 22 to express a meaning similar to the original sentence.

1. The boys pay no attention to the *No Swimming* sign.

2. Kay forces herself to congratulate the winner.

3. Juan blushes as he greets the new teacher.

4. Lucy was very tired after playing soccer for two hours.

5. Betty walked to school with slow, heavy steps.

6. If our boat gets shipwrecked, we will die of not eating.

Word Study Use the context of the sentence and what you know about the **Latin suffix -ation** to explain your answers.

1. What can happen that would cause you *frustration*?

2. A *separation* from a good friend can be difficult. Why?

Word Study

The Latin **suffix -ation** changes a verb to a noun. It means "the condition of being."

Apply It Explain how the suffix contributes to the meaning of these words. Consult a dictionary if necessary.

vacation
elation
violation

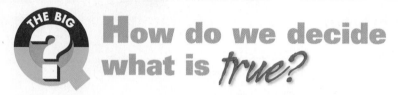

How do we decide what is *true?*

Writing About the Big Question

"The Homecoming" is a fictional story, but it contains a "truth" or a lesson about life. Use this sentence starter to develop your ideas about the Big Question.

Even if a story is **fiction,** I can learn lessons by _____.

While You Read Look for details and events that show this is a *fictional* story. At the same time, look for lessons from which you might learn.

Vocabulary

Read each word and its definition. Decide whether you know the word well, know it a little bit, or do not know it at all. After you read, see how your knowledge of each word has increased.

- **escorting** (es kôrt´ iŋ) *v.* going with, as a companion (p. 33) *My father was <u>escorting</u> the children to the playground. escort n. escorted v.*

- **charitable** (char´i tə bəl) *adj.* kind and generous in giving help to others in need (p. 34) *Cooking a meal for her neighbor was a <u>charitable</u> act. charity n. charitably adv.*

- **distracted** (di strakt´ əd) *adj.* unable to concentrate (p. 34) *I was <u>distracted</u> by the loud music. distract v. distracting adj. distraction n.*

- **murmured** (mʉr´ mərd) *v.* made a low, continuous sound (p. 35) *He <u>murmured</u> appreciatively when he saw the steaming bowl of soup. murmur n. murmuring adj.*

- **fascinated** (fas´ ə nāt´ əd) *adj.* strongly attracted to something interesting or delightful (p. 35) *I am <u>fascinated</u> by the beehive in my yard. fascination n. fascinate v.*

- **recognize** (rek´ əg nīz´) *v.* know and remember (p. 37) *Do you <u>recognize</u> the actor from his television show? recognized v. recognition n.*

Word Study

The **Latin suffix -able** means "having qualities of."

When the woodcutter in this story says he is **charitable** about giving advice, he means that he is showing the quality of *charity,* or generosity.

Meet
Laurence Yep
(b. 1948)

Author of
The Homecoming

Laurence Yep was born and raised in San Francisco, California. A third-generation Chinese American, he began writing in high school and sold his first story when he was just eighteen years old. Since then, he has written many books for young people and has won numerous awards. Much of Yep's subject matter reflects his interest in other worlds. His books of science fiction and fantasy tell of strange events in mysterious lands.

Belonging to Two Cultures As a youth, Yep says, he "wanted to be as American as possible." In his early twenties, he became interested in his Chinese roots. He began researching and writing novels about Chinese immigrants and their descendants. During this time, Yep wrote a book, based on Chinese folk tales, that included "The Homecoming."

BACKGROUND FOR THE STORY
Chess

In "The Homecoming," the main character loses track of time as he watches two men play chess. Chess is a board game that dates back to the sixth century. The object is to *checkmate*, or trap, the opponent's main chess piece, called a *king*. This ancient game of skill can take several hours to complete. The game in the story takes even longer than that!

DID YOU KNOW?
Yep is the author of *Dragonwings* and *Dragon's Gate*. Both were Newbery Honor Books.

The Homecoming

Laurence Yep

Once there was a woodcutter who minded everyone's business but his own. If you were digging a hole, he knew a better way to grip the shovel. If you were cooking a fish, he knew a better recipe. As his village said, he knew a little of everything and most of nothing.

If his wife and children hadn't made palm leaf fans, the family would have starved. Finally his wife got tired of everyone laughing at them. "You're supposed to be a woodcutter. Go up to the hill and cut some firewood."

"Any fool can do that." The woodcutter picked up his hatchet.[1] "In the mountains there's plenty of tall oak. That's what burns best."

His wife pointed out the window. "But there's a stand of pine just over the ridgetop."

Her husband looked pained. "Pine won't sell as well. I'll take my load into town, where folk are too busy to cut their own. Then I'll come back with loads of cash." With a laugh, he shouldered his long pole. After he cut the wood, he would tie it into two big bundles and place each at the end of the pole. Then he would balance the load on his shoulder.

Waving good-bye to his children, he left their house; but his wife walked right with him. "What are you doing?" he asked.

His wife folded her arms as they walked along. "Escorting you."

He slowed down by a boy who was making a kite out of paper and rice paste. "That thing will never fly. You should—"

His wife caught his arm and pulled him along. "Don't be such a busybody."[2]

---

1. **hatchet** (hach´ it) *n.* a short-handled ax.
2. **busybody** (biz´ ē bäd´ ē) *n.* a person who is unusually interested in other people's business.

Plot
What information about the characters and the situation is revealed in the exposition?

Vocabulary
escorting (es kort´ iŋ) *v.* going with, as a companion

Reading Check
Why does the woodcutter refuse to do what his wife suggests?

"If a neighbor's doing something wrong, it's the charitable thing to set that person straight." He tried to stop by a man who was feeding his ducks. "Say, friend. Those ducks'll get fatter if—"

His wife yanked him away and gave him a good shake. "Do I have to blindfold you? We have two children to feed."

"I'm not lazy," he grumbled.

She kept dragging him out of the village. "I never said you were. You can do the work of two people when no one else is around. You're just too easily distracted."

She went with him to the very edge of the fields and sent him on his way. "Remember," she called after him. "Don't talk to anyone." •

He walked with long, steady strides through the wooded hills. "I'll show her. It isn't how often you do something, it's how you do it. I'll cut twice the wood and sell it for double the price and come back in half the time."

Complaining loudly to himself, he moved deep into the mountains. I want just the right sort of oak, he thought to himself. As he walked along, he kept an eye out for a likely tree.

He didn't see the funny old man until he bumped into him. "Oof, watch where you're going," the old man said.

The old man had a head that bulged as big as a melon. He was dressed in a yellow robe embroidered with storks and pine trees.

Playing chess with the old man was another man so fat he could not close his robe. In his hand he had a large fan painted with drinking scenes.

The fat man wagged a finger at the old man. "Don't try to change the subject. I've got you. It's checkmate in two moves."

The funny old man looked back at the chessboard. The lines were a bright red on yellow paper, and the chess pieces were flat disks with words painted in gold on their tops.

"Is it now, is it now?" the funny old man mused.

The woodcutter remembered his wife's warning. But he said to himself, "I'm not actually talking to them. I'm advising them." So he put down his hatchet and pole. "Actually, if you moved that piece"—he jabbed at a disk—"and moved it there"—he pointed at a spot on the board—"you'd have him."

But the old man moved a different disk.

The fat man scratched the top of his bald head. "Now how'd you think of that?"

The woodcutter rubbed his chin. "Yes, how did you think of that?" But then he nodded his head and pointed to one of the fat man's disks. "Still, if you shifted that one, you'd win."

However, the fat man ignored him as he made another move.

"Well," the woodcutter said to the old man, "you've got him now."

But the old man paid him no more mind than the fat man. "Hmmm," he murmured, and set his chin on his fist as he studied the board.

The woodcutter became so caught up in the game that he squatted down. "I know what you have to do. I'll be right here just in case you need to ask."

Neither man said anything to the woodcutter. They just went on playing, and as they played, the woodcutter became more and more fascinated. He forgot about chopping wood. He even forgot about going home. •

When it was night, the funny old man opened a big basket and lifted out a lantern covered with stars. He hung it from a tree and the game went on. Night passed on into day, but the woodcutter was as involved in the game now as the two men.

"Let's take a break." The old man slipped a peach from one big sleeve. The peach was big as the woodcutter's fist, and it filled the woods with a sweet aroma.

"You're just stalling for time," the fat man said. "Move."

"I'm hungry," the old man complained, and took a big bite. However, he shoved a piece along the board. When he held the peach out to the fat man, the fat man bit into it hungrily.

Alternating moves and bites, they went on until there was nothing left of the peach except the peach stone. "I feel

Spiral Review
Character Why do you think the wood-cutter feels the need to call what he is doing "advising" rather than "talking"?

Vocabulary
murmured (mur´ mərd) v. made a low, continuous sound
fascinated (fas´ ə nāt´ əd) v. strongly attracted to something interesting or delightful

Make Predictions
How does your prior knowledge of other stories help you predict that something unusual will happen?

Reading Check
What warning does the woodcutter remember?

much better now," the old man said, and threw the stone over his shoulder.

As the two men had eaten the peach, the woodcutter had discovered that he was famished,[3] but the only thing was the peach stone. "Maybe I can suck on this stone and forget about being hungry. But I wish one of them would ask me for help. We could finish this game a lot quicker."

He tucked the stone into his mouth and tasted some of the peach juices. Instantly, he felt himself filled with energy. Goodness, he thought, I feel like there were lightning bolts zipping around inside me. And he went on watching the game with new energy.

After seven days, the old man stopped and stretched. "I think we're going to have to call this game a draw."

The fat man sighed. "I agree." He began to pick up the pieces.

The woodcutter spat out the stone. "But you could win easily."

The old man finally noticed him. "Are you still here?"

The woodcutter thought that this was his chance now to do a good deed.[4] "It's been a most interesting game. However, if you—"

But the old man made shooing motions with his hands. "You should've gone home long ago."

"But I—" began the woodcutter.

The fat man rose. "Go home. It may already be too late." ●

That's a funny thing to say, the woodcutter thought. He turned around to get his things. But big, fat mushrooms had sprouted among the roots of the trees. A brown carpet surrounded him. He brushed the mushrooms aside until he found a rusty hatchet blade. He couldn't find a trace of the hatchet shaft or of his carrying pole.

Puzzled, he picked up the hatchet blade. "This can't be mine. My hatchet was practically new. Have you two gentlemen seen it?" He turned around again, but the two

"Go home. It may already be too late."

---

3. **famished** (fam′ isht) *adj.* very hungry.
4. **deed** (dēd) *n.* something that is done; an act.

men had disappeared along with the chessboard and chess pieces.

"That's gratitude for you." Picking up the rusty hatchet blade, the woodcutter tried to make his way back through the woods; but he could not find the way he had come up. "It's like someone rearranged all the trees."

Somehow he made his way out of the mountains. However, fields and villages now stood where there had once been wooded hills. "What are you doing here?" he asked a farmer.

"What are you?" the farmer snorted, and went back to working in his field.

The woodcutter thought about telling him that he was swinging his hoe wrong, but he remembered what the two men had said. So he hurried home instead.

The woodcutter followed the river until he reached his own village, but as he walked through the fields, he didn't recognize one person. There was even a pond before the village gates. It had never been there before. He broke into a run, but there was a different house in the spot where his home had been. Even so, he burst into the place.

Two strange children looked up from the table, and a strange woman picked up a broom. "Out!"

The woodcutter raised his arms protectively. "Wait, I live here."

But the woman beat the woodcutter with a broom until he retreated into the street. By now, a crowd had gathered. The woodcutter looked around desperately "What's happened to my village? Doesn't anyone know me?"

The village schoolteacher had come out of the school. He asked the woodcutter his name, and when the woodcutter told him, the schoolteacher pulled at his whiskers. "That

▲ **Critical Viewing**
What advice might the woodcutter have for the different people in this picture? **[Speculate]**

Vocabulary
recognize (rek´ əg nīz´)
v. know and remember

Reading Check

What mistake does the woodcutter make in the woods?

name sounds familiar, but it can't be."

With the crowd following them, he led the woodcutter to the clan temple. "I collect odd, interesting stories." The schoolteacher got out a thick book. "There's a strange incident in the clan book." He leafed through the book toward the beginning and pointed to a name. "A woodcutter left the village and never came back." He added quietly, "But that was several thousand years ago."

"That's impossible," the woodcutter insisted. "I just stayed away to watch two men play a game of chess."

The schoolteacher sighed. "The two men must have been saints. Time doesn't pass for them as it does for us."

And at that moment, the woodcutter remembered his wife's warning.

But it was too late now.

Plot

Why is the schoolteacher important to the resolution of the story?

Critical Thinking

1. **Key Ideas and Details (a)** What do the villagers mean by saying the woodcutter "knew a little of everything and most of nothing"? **(b) Connect:** How do the woodcutter's actions support this statement? **(c) Evaluate:** Why is this description important to the story?

2. **Key Ideas and Details (a)** How do the chess players react to the woodcutter? **(b) Infer:** Why do they treat him this way?

3. **Integration of Knowledge and Ideas (a)** What lesson is expressed in this story? **(b) Take a Position:** Do you agree or disagree with the lesson being taught? Explain.

4. **Integration of Knowledge and Ideas (a)** What details in "The Homecoming" reveal to the reader that this story is not true? **(b)** What true lessons can you learn from the story? **(c)** How are they similar to lessons in other stories you have read? *[Connect to the Big Question: How do we decide what is true?]*

Cite textual evidence to support your responses.

Reading Skill: Make Predictions

1. Copy and complete the chart to show how you made a **prediction** to answer each question. **(a)** What will the woodcutter do when he sees the men playing chess? **(b)** What will happen when he leaves the forest?

Prior Knowledge	Details From Story	Prediction
Busybodies like talking to people.	The woodcutter is a busybody.	The woodcutter will stop to talk.
(a)		
(b)		

Literary Analysis: Plot

2. **Craft and Structure** What is the **conflict** in the **plot** of this story?

3. **Craft and Structure** What is the **climax,** or high point, in the story? Explain.

Vocabulary

Acquisition and Use Rewrite each sentence. Use a vocabulary word from the list on page 30 to express a similar meaning to the original sentence.

1. I was unable to concentrate because of the loud music.
2. Tony will be taking visitors on a tour of the school.
3. Serena could not identify her uncle in the crowd.
4. She answered my question in a soft, low voice.
5. I could not stop studying the ant colony in my backyard.
6. My youth group did a generous deed for the homeless.

Word Study Use what you know about the **Latin suffix -able** to answer each question.

1. If the weather is *changeable,* will it stay the same?
2. If the clock is not *fixable,* should you repair it?

Word Study

The Latin **suffix -able** means "able to be" or "subject to."

Apply It Explain how the suffix contributes to the meaning of these words. Consult a dictionary if necessary.

debatable
dependable
teachable

Integrated Language Skills

Stray • The Homecoming

Conventions:
Common Nouns and Proper Nouns

All nouns are considered either *common* or *proper*. A **common noun** names any one of a group of people, places, or things. A **proper noun** names a particular person, place, or thing.

Proper nouns are always capitalized. **Common nouns** are not capitalized unless they are at the beginning of a sentence or in a title.

Common Nouns	Proper Nouns
That *boy* is the fastest runner.	*Steve* is the fastest runner.
The *girls* enjoyed the ice cream.	*Sue and Alice* enjoyed the ice cream.
Do you want to go to the *city*?	Do you want to go to *Dallas*?
Will you go to *college*?	Will you go to *Brooklyn College*?

Practice A Identify the noun(s) in each sentence and indicate whether they are common nouns or proper nouns.

1. The stray puppy had been abandoned.
2. Mr. Lacey said he would take the puppy to the pound.
3. Doris was upset about what Mama said.
4. The pound was a dismal place.

© **Reading Application** In "Stray," find three proper nouns and three common nouns.

Practice B Identify the common noun in each sentence. Then, rewrite each, substituting a proper noun for each common noun.

1. The woodcutter is fascinated by a boardgame.
2. The woodcutter went to the hills.
3. The old man was too tired to work.
4. A young boy sang a song.

© **Writing Application** In "The Homecoming," identify four places where the author used common nouns instead of proper nouns. Rewrite the examples using proper nouns.

PH WRITING COACH | Further instruction and practice are available in *Prentice Hall Writing Coach*.

Writing

Informative Text Write a **news report** about the story you read. If you read "Stray," write about the family's decision to keep the dog after visiting the animal shelter. If you read "The Homecoming," write about the woodcutter's return to his town.

- Use details from the story to report the action.
- Begin with an effective lead sentence that contains a statistic, a quotation, or another detail to capture the reader's attention. Establish and maintain a formal style.
- Write short, clear sentences that sum up the facts. Include examples and details that support your main point.

Grammar Application If you use proper nouns in your news report, use correct capitalization.

Writing Workshop: *Work in Progress*

Prewriting for Description For a descriptive essay you may write, list the places that are important to you. Choose one place and tell why you like it, what memories you have about it, and why it is special to you. Put this list in your writing portfolio.

Research and Technology

Build and Present Knowledge With a group, create a **brochure** based on the story you read. Make a list of questions about your topic. Then, search the Internet to find information.

If you read "Stray," your brochure will focus on caring for dogs.

- Use key words like these to search the Internet: *feeding a new puppy, training a puppy, puppy care, puppy health.*
- Include the following sections in your brochure: "Feeding Your Puppy," "Puppy Training Tips," "Happy, Healthy Puppies."

If you read "The Homecoming," your brochure will focus on Chinese immortals.

- Use key words like these to search the Internet: *Chinese folk tales and immortals, Chinese folk tales, Chinese immortals.*
- Include the following sections in your brochure: "What Is a Chinese Immortal?," "Common Characteristics of Chinese Immortals," "Folk Tales About Chinese Immortals."

Common Core State Standards

L.6.2; W.6.2.b, W.6.2.e, W.6.4; SL.6.4
[For the full wording of the standards, see page 20.]

Use this prewriting activity to prepare for the **Writing Workshop** on page 86.

PHLit Online!
www.PHLitOnline.com

- Interactive graphic organizers
- Grammar tutorial
- Interactive journals

Ⓒ Leveled Texts

Build your skills and improve your comprehension of literary nonfiction with texts of increasing complexity.

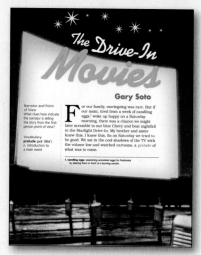

Read **"The Drive-In Movies"** to meet a boy who works very hard to win a special privilege.

Read **"The Market Square Dog"** to find out what happens when a veterinarian and a police officer try to help a stray dog.

Ⓒ Common Core State Standards

Meet these standards with either **"The Drive-In Movies"** (p. 46) or **"The Market Square Dog"** (p. 54).

Reading Literature
6. Explain how an author develops the point of view of the narrator or speaker in a text. (*Literary Analysis: Narrator and Point of View*)

Writing
3. Write narratives to develop real or imagined experiences or events using effective technique, relevant descriptive details, and well-structured event sequences. (*Writing: Autobiographical Narrative*)

Speaking and Listening
6. Adapt speech to a variety of contexts and tasks, demonstrating command of formal English when

indicated or appropriate. (*Speaking and Listening: Conversation*)

Language
1. Demonstrate command of the conventions of standard English grammar and usage when writing or speaking. (*Conventions: Singular and Plural Nouns*)

5.c. Distinguish among the connotations (associations) of words with similar denotations (definitions). (*Vocabulary: Synonyms*)

Reading Skill: Make Predictions

Predictions are developing ideas about what is most likely to happen next. Base your predictions on details in the literature and on your own experience. Keep track of your predictions using a diagram like the one shown. Then, **read ahead to check your prediction.** When you find details that show your original prediction may be wrong, **revise your prediction.** Use these new details to correct and change your ideas.

Using the Strategy: Predictions Chart

Make and revise your predictions using a chart like this.

Literary Analysis: Narrator and Point of View

The **narrator** is the voice that tells a true or imagined story. **Point of view** is the perspective from which the story is told. The author often develops the narrator's point of view using one of the following:

- **First-person point of view:** The narrator takes part in the action of the story and refers to himself or herself as "I." Readers know only what the narrator sees, thinks, and feels.

- **Third-person point of view:** The narrator does not take part in the action. As an outside observer, a third-person narrator can share information that the characters do not know.

Most true stories about a writer's life are told in the first person. As you read, consider how these writers develop point of view.

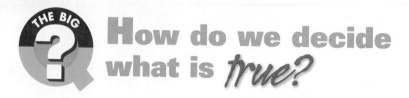

How do we decide what is *true?*

Writing About the Big Question

In "The Drive-In Movies," a boy tries to be extra good in order to please his mother and win a reward. Use these sentence starters to develop your ideas about the Big Question.

A person's **opinion** about a reward will affect _____.

You can **prove** you deserve a reward by _____.

While You Read Look for helpful things the boy does and think about the true reasons he does them.

Vocabulary

Read each word and its definition. Decide whether you know the word well, know it a little bit, or do not know it at all. After you read, see how your knowledge of each word has increased.

- **prelude** (prā´ lo͞od) *n.* introduction to a main event (p. 46) *The orchestra's <u>prelude</u> made me look forward to the concert.*

- **pulsating** (pul´ sāt´ iŋ) *adj.* beating or throbbing in a steady rhythm (p. 48) *The beat was <u>pulsating</u> and made her want to dance.* *pulsate v. pulsated v. pulse n.*

- **migrated** (mī´ grāt əd) *v.* moved from one place to another (p. 48) *The family <u>migrated</u> to the United States from Mexico.* *migrate v. migrating v. migration n.*

- **evident** (ev´ ə dənt) *adj.* easy to see; very clear (p. 49) *The dark clouds made it <u>evident</u> that it would rain.* *evidence n. evidently adv.*

- **winced** (winst) *v.* pulled back slightly as if in pain (p. 49) *Mimi <u>winced</u> when the baseball hit her arm.* *wince v. wincing v.*

- **vigorously** (vig´ ər əs lē) *adv.* forcefully or energetically (p. 49) *He ran <u>vigorously</u> up and down the stairs.* *vigorous adj. vigorousness n. vigor n.*

Word Study

The **Latin prefix** *pre-* means "before."

In this story, the narrator and his siblings begin Saturday mornings by watching television. This activity is a **prelude** to all the activities that they will do later on. It happens *before* the other activities.

Meet
Gary Soto
(b. 1952)

Author of
The Drive-In Movies

As a child, Gary Soto loved the bustle and energy of his Fresno, California, neighborhood. When Soto was six years old, however, a government program changed his neighborhood by replacing many run-down buildings with new ones. "It didn't work in our area," Soto declares today. "The houses were bulldozed, and in their place grew weeds."

As he grew older, Soto continued to feel a sense of loss over his old neighborhood. Today, he believes that his pain and sadness led him to become a writer. Writing helped him to get his feelings down on paper, where he could see them and think about them.

DID YOU KNOW?

Gary Soto is an award-winning author of short stories and poems. Much of his work is based on his own childhood and young-adult experiences.

BACKGROUND FOR THE SELECTION

Drive-In Theaters

A drive-in is an outdoor movie theater where people watch the movies from their cars. The first drive-in theater opened in Camden, New Jersey, in 1933. In the late 1950s, when their popularity was at its peak, there were 5,000 drive-ins in the United States.

The Drive-In Movies

Gary Soto

Narrator and Point of View
What clues here indicate the narrator is telling the story from the first-person point of view?

Vocabulary
prelude (prā´ lōōd´)
n. introduction to a main event

For our family, moviegoing was rare. But if our mom, tired from a week of candling eggs,[1] woke up happy on a Saturday morning, there was a chance we might later scramble to our blue Chevy and beat nightfall to the Starlight Drive-In. My brother and sister knew this. I knew this. So on Saturday we tried to be good. We sat in the cool shadows of the TV with the volume low and watched cartoons, a prelude of what was to come.

---

1. **candling eggs** examining uncooked eggs for freshness by placing them in front of a burning candle.

One Saturday I decided to be extra good. When she came out of the bedroom tying her robe, she yawned a hat-sized yawn and blinked red eyes at the weak brew of coffee I had fixed for her. I made her toast with strawberry jam spread to all the corners and set the three boxes of cereal in front of her. If she didn't care to eat cereal, she could always look at the back of the boxes as she drank her coffee.

I went outside. The lawn was tall but too wet with dew to mow. I picked up a trowel[2] and began to weed the flower bed. The weeds were really bermuda grass, long stringers that ran finger-deep in the ground. I got to work quickly and in no time crescents of earth began rising under my fingernails. I was sweaty hot. My knees hurt from kneeling, and my brain was dull from making the trowel go up and down, dribbling crumbs of earth. I dug for half an hour, then stopped to play with the neighbor's dog and pop ticks from his poor snout.

---

2. **trowel** (trou´ əl) *n.* a small hand tool used by gardeners to weed or dig.

▼ **Critical Viewing**
How is seeing a movie at a drive-in like this one different from seeing it in a regular theater? **[Speculate]**

✓ Reading Check
Why is the narrator being extra good?

Social Studies Connection

Drive-In Movies
The first drive-in theater had three speakers near the screen to project sound. If you parked near the screen, you could hear every word perfectly. If you lived nearby, you heard every word, too. A later system of individual speakers, placed on the car door when the window was rolled down, satisfied angry neighbors.

Connect to the Literature

Why might a trip to the drive-in movies be a reward for the narrator?

Vocabulary
pulsating (pul´ sāt´ iŋ)
adj. beating or throbbing in a steady rhythm
migrated (mī´ grāt əd)
v. moved from one place to another

Spiral Review
Central Idea How do these vivid details contribute to the author's central idea?

I then mowed the lawn, which was still beaded with dew and noisy with bees hovering over clover. This job was less dull because as I pushed the mower over the shaggy lawn, I could see it looked tidier. My brother and sister watched from the window. Their faces were fat with cereal, a third helping. I made a face at them when they asked how come I was working. Rick pointed to part of the lawn. "You missed some over there." I ignored him and kept my attention on the windmill of grassy blades. •

While I was emptying the catcher, a bee stung the bottom of my foot. I danced on one leg and was ready to cry when Mother showed her face at the window. I sat down on the grass and examined my foot: the stinger was **pulsating.** I pulled it out quickly, ran water over the sting and packed it with mud, Grandmother's remedy.

Hobbling, I returned to the flower bed where I pulled more stringers and again played with the dog. More ticks had **migrated** to his snout. I swept the front steps, took out the garbage, cleaned the lint filter to the dryer (easy), plucked hair from the industrial wash basin in the garage (also easy), hosed off the patio, smashed three snails sucking paint from the house (disgusting but fun), tied a bundle of newspapers, put away toys, and, finally, seeing that almost everything was done and the sun was not too high, started waxing the car.

My brother joined me with an old gym sock, and our sister watched us while sucking on a cherry Kool-Aid ice cube. The liquid wax drooled onto the sock, and we began to swirl the white slop on the chrome. My arms ached from

buffing, which though less boring than weeding, was harder. But the beauty was evident. The shine, hurting our eyes and glinting like an armful of dimes, brought Mother out. She looked around the yard and said, "Pretty good." She winced at the grille and returned inside the house.

We began to wax the paint. My brother applied the liquid and I followed him rubbing hard in wide circles as we moved around the car. I began to hurry because my arms were hurting and my stung foot looked like a water balloon. We were working around the trunk when Rick pounded on the bottle of wax. He squeezed the bottle and it sneezed a few more white drops.

We looked at each other. "There's some on the sock," I said. "Let's keep going." •

We polished and buffed, sweat weeping on our brows. We got scared when we noticed that the gym sock was now blue. The paint was coming off. Our sister fit ice cubes into our mouths and we worked harder, more intently, more dedicated to the car and our mother. We ran the sock over the chrome, trying to pick up extra wax. But there wasn't enough to cover the entire car. Only half got waxed, but we thought it was better than nothing and went inside for lunch. After lunch, we returned outside with tasty sandwiches.

Rick and I nearly jumped. The waxed side of the car was foggy white. We took a rag and began to polish vigorously and nearly in tears, but the fog wouldn't come off. I blamed Rick and he blamed me. Debra stood at the window, not wanting to get involved. Now, not only would we not go to the movies, but Mom would surely snap a branch from the plum tree and chase us around the yard.

Vocabulary
evident (ev´ ə dənt)
adj. easy to see; very clear

winced (winst)
v. pulled back slightly, as if in pain

Make Predictions
How do you predict the narrator will feel at the drive-in, after his long day of hard work? Read on to check whether you are correct.

Vocabulary
vigorously (vig´ ər əs lē) *adv.* forcefully or energetically

Mom came out and looked at us with hands on her aproned hips. Finally, she said, "You boys worked so hard." She turned on the garden hose and washed the car. That night we did go to the drive-in. The first feature was about nothing, and the second feature, starring Jerry Lewis, was *Cinderfella*. I tried to stay awake. I kept a wad of homemade popcorn in my cheek and laughed when Jerry Lewis fit golf tees in his nose. I rubbed my watery eyes. I laughed and looked at my mom. I promised myself I would remember that scene with the golf tees and promised myself not to work so hard the coming Saturday. Twenty minutes into the movie, I fell asleep with one hand in the popcorn.

Make Predictions
How does this outcome fit with your prediction about how the narrator would feel after his day of work?

Critical Thinking

Cite textual evidence to support your responses.

1. **Key Ideas and Details (a)** How does Soto persuade his mother to take the family to the drive-in movies? **(b) Draw Conclusions:** Why do you think Soto's mother does not get angry with the children for making a mess with the car wax?

2. **Key Ideas and Details (a)** What two things does Soto promise himself to remember? **(b) Assess:** Do you think he still has fond memories of that day and night? Explain.

3. **Key Ideas and Details (a)** Do you think children should have to do chores before their parents allow them to do something enjoyable? Why or why not? **(b) Discuss:** In a small group, share your responses.

4. **Integration of Knowledge and Ideas (a)** What qualities make a character "extra good"? **(b)** Did the narrator prove himself to be "extra good"? Use details to explain your answer. *[Connect to the Big Question: How do we decide what is true?]*

Reading Skill: Make Predictions

1. **(a)** Did you **predict** that Soto's mother would take the family to the drive-in movies? **(b)** On what details did you base your prediction?

2. As you read, did you change any predictions? Explain.

Literary Analysis: Narrator and Point of View

3. **Craft and Structure** Make a chart to note how the author develops the **point of view.**

Event	Details Provided by Narrator
The narrator is stung by a bee.	The sting hurts.

4. **Craft and Structure** What details about this event would you expect to find if the **narrator** were Soto's mother?

Vocabulary

Acquisition and Use **Synonyms** are words with similar definitions. Their *connotations,* or associations, may be slightly different. For each item, choose a synonym from the vocabulary list on page 44.

1. clear, obvious, _____
2. beginning, introduction, _____
3. shrank back, cringed, _____
4. throbbing, beating, _____
5. actively, energetically, _____
6. traveled, roamed, _____

Word Study Use sentence context and what you know about the **Latin prefix pre-** to explain your answers.

1. How might a movie's *preview* help people decide whether or not to see that movie?

2. Would the *preface* appear at the beginning or the end of a book?

Word Study

The **Latin prefix *pre-*** means "before."

Apply It Explain how the prefix contributes to the meaning of these words. Consult a dictionary if necessary.

precaution
predict
preheat

How do we decide what is *true?*

Writing About the Big Question

In "The Market Square Dog," a stray dog is available for adoption. The veterinarian believes the mixed breed is not wanted because people are looking for a "more elegant" dog. Use this sentence starter to develop your ideas about the Big Question.

To be a **truly** great pet, a dog needs to be _____.

While You Read Look for words that describe why this dog might make a great pet.

Vocabulary

Read each word and its definition. Decide whether you know the word well, know it a little bit, or do not know it at all. After you read, see how your knowledge of each word has increased.

- **devoured** (di vourd) *v.* ate hungrily or greedily (p. 54)
  I devoured my supper and asked for more. devour v. devouring v.

- **trotted** (trät´ əd) *v.* ran in a graceful, light way (p. 55)
  I watched as my horse trotted out of sight.
  trot n. trotting v.

- **anxiously** (aŋk´ shəs lē) *adv.* in a worried or uneasy way (p. 58) *"Am I late?" she asked anxiously. anxious adj. anxiousness n. anxiety n.*

- **classified** (klas´ ə fīd´) *v.* identified as part of a group; designated (p. 58) *The scientists classified the rock as granite. classify v. classifying v.*

- **custody** (kus´ tə dē) *n.* protection or supervision (p. 59) *While the child is in my custody, she will be safe. custodian n. custodial adj.*

- **bewildered** (bē wil´dərd) *adj.* confused by something complicated (p. 59) *Tracy was bewildered by the math problem. bewilder v. bewilderment n. bewildering adj.*

Word Study

The **Anglo Saxon prefix be-** often means "to make."

Wilder is an old word that means "to lose one's way." In this story, the veterinarian is **bewildered,** or lost, by something that the police officer says.

Meet
James Herriot
(1916–1995)

Author of
THE MARKET SQUARE DOG

James Herriot is the pen name of the real-life veterinarian James Alfred Wight. He was born in Scotland and received his veterinary training at Glasgow Veterinary College. After graduating in 1939, Herriot moved to the rural area of Yorkshire, England, and was a veterinarian there for fifty years. As a country doctor, he traveled from farm to farm and village to village, treating animals that needed his care. At age fifty, he began writing, sharing stories based on his experiences as a veterinarian. Despite his fame as a writer, he remained a quiet, modest country doctor throughout his life.

BACKGROUND FOR THE SELECTION

Veterinary Medicine

Veterinarians are doctors who are trained to prevent, diagnose, and treat illnesses in animals. Like doctors who treat humans, veterinarians must attend medical school. Most veterinarians in urban and suburban locations treat household pets. Some veterinarians, like the author of this story, work in the country. They treat cows, horses, and other farm animals in addition to pets.

DID YOU KNOW?

As a veterinarian, James Herriot treated dogs, cats, sheep, cows, horses, and even a troubled "talking" parakeet that refused to talk. As an author, he based many of his stories on those experiences.

THE MARKET SQUARE DOG

James Herriot

On market days when the farmers around Darrowby brought their goods to the little town to sell, I used to take a walk across the cobbled square to meet the farmers who gathered there to chat. One of the farmers was telling me about his sick cow when we saw the little dog among the market stalls. The thing that made us notice the dog was that he was sitting up, begging, in front of the stall selling cakes and biscuits.

"Look at that little chap,"[1] the farmer said. "I wonder where he's come from?"

As he spoke, the stallholder threw him a bun which the dog devoured eagerly, but when the man came round and

---

1. chap (chap) *n.* a fellow or boy.

stretched out a hand the little animal **trotted** away. He stopped, however, at another stall which sold eggs, butter, cheese and scones. Without hesitation, he sat up again in the begging position, rock steady, paws dangling, head pointing expectantly.

I nudged my companion. "There he goes again. I always think a dog looks very appealing sitting up like that."

The farmer nodded. "Yes, he's a bonny[2] little thing, isn't he? What breed would you call him?"

"A cross, I'd say. He's like a small sheepdog, but there's a touch of something else—maybe terrier."

It wasn't long before the dog was munching a biscuit, and this time I walked over to him, and as I drew near I spoke gently. "Here, boy," I said, squatting down in front of him. "Come on, let's have a look at you."

He turned to face me, and for a moment two friendly brown eyes gazed at me from a wonderfully attractive face. The fringed tail waved in response to my words, but as I moved nearer he turned and trotted away among the market-day crowd until he was lost to sight.

I was standing there, trying to see where he had gone, when a young policeman came up to me.

"I've been watching that wee[3] dog begging among the stalls all morning," he said, "but, like you, I haven't been able to get near him."

"Yes, it's strange. You can see he's friendly, but he's also afraid. I wonder who owns him."

"I reckon he's a stray, Mr. Herriot. I'm interested in dogs myself and fancy I know just about all of them around here. But this one is a stranger to me."

I nodded. "I'm sure you're right. Anything could have happened to him. He could have been ill-treated by somebody and run away, or he could have been dumped from a car."

▲ **Critical Viewing**
Why is a market like the one shown here a good place for a hungry dog to look for food? **[Analyze]**

Vocabulary
trotted (trät´ əd) *v.* ran in a graceful, light way

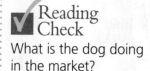

Reading Check
What is the dog doing in the market?

2. **bonny** (bän´ ē) *adj.* attractive, pretty, or handsome.
3. **wee** (wē) *adj.* small; tiny.

Make Predictions
What do you think might happen to the dog? Read ahead to verify your prediction.

Ⓒ

Spiral Review
Central Idea How does this memory help to establish the central idea of the narrative?

"Yes," the policeman replied, "there are some cruel people about. I don't know how anybody can leave a helpless animal to fend for itself like that. I've had a few tries at catching him, but it's no good."

The memory stayed with me for the rest of the day. It is our duty to look after the animals who depend on us and it worried me to think of the little creature wandering about in a strange place, sitting up and asking for help in the only way he knew.

Market day is on a Monday and on the Friday of that week my wife Helen and I had a treat planned for ourselves; we were going to the races in Brawton. Helen was making up a picnic basket with home-made ham-and-egg-pie, chicken sandwiches and a chocolate cake. I was wearing my best suit and I couldn't help feeling very smart[4] because country vets have to work mostly in the fields and cowsheds and I hardly ever got dressed up. Helen, too, had put on her best dress and a fancy hat I had never seen before. As a vet's wife, she too had to work very hard and we weren't able to go out together very often.

We were just about to leave the house when the doorbell rang. It was the young policeman I had been talking to on market day.

"I've got that dog, Mr. Herriot," he said. "You know—the one that was begging in the market square."

"Oh good," I replied, "so you managed to catch him at last."

The policeman paused. "No, not really. One of our men found him lying by the roadside about a mile out of town and brought him in. I'm afraid he's been knocked down. We've got him here in the car."

I went out and looked into the car. The little dog was lying very still on the back seat, but when I stroked the dark coat his tail stirred briefly.

"He can still manage a wag, anyway," I said.

The policeman nodded. "Yes, there's no doubt he's a good-natured wee thing."

---

4. **smart** (smärt) *adj.* stylish; well-dressed.

I tried to examine him as much as possible without touching because I didn't want to hurt him, but I could see that he had cuts all over his body and one hind leg lay in such a way that I knew it must be broken. When I gently lifted his head, I saw that one eyelid was badly torn so that the eye was completely closed. But the other soft brown eye looked at me trustingly.

Narrator and Point of View
Why don't readers learn more about the details of the dog's accident?

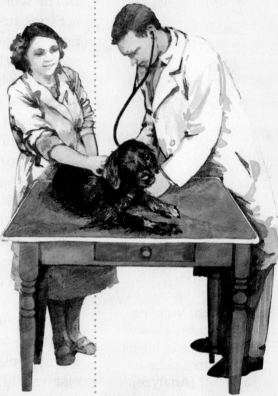

"Can you do anything for him, Mr. Herriot?" asked the policeman. "Can you save him?"

"I'll do my best," I replied.

I carried the little animal into the surgery and laid him on the table.

"There's an hour or two's work here, Helen," I said to my wife. "I'm very sorry, but we won't be able to go to the races."

"Never mind," she replied. "We must do what we can for this fellow."

Rather sadly she took off her fancy hat and I took off my good jacket. Dressed in our white coats we began to work.

Helen was used to helping me and she gave the anaesthetic,[5] then I set the broken leg in plaster and stitched up the wounds. The worst thing was the eye because even after I had stitched the eyelid it was still bruised and tightly closed and I was worried that he might lose the sight in that eye.

By the time we had finished, it was too late to go out anywhere, but Helen was quite cheerful. "We can still have our picnic," she said.

We carried the sleeping dog out to the garden and laid him on a mat on the lawn so that we could watch him as he came round from the anaesthetic.

Out there in the old high-walled garden the sun shone down on the flowers and the apple trees. Helen put on her fancy hat again and I put my smart jacket back on and as we sat there, enjoying the good things from the picnic

Narrator and Point of View
What information might you read here if this part of the story were told from Helen's point of view?

Reading Check

Why does the policeman bring the dog to the narrator's house?

---

5. **anaesthetic** (an´es thet´ik) *n.* British spelling of **anesthetic**: a medicine that makes a patient fall asleep so that surgery can be performed without causing the patient pain.

Vocabulary

anxiously (aŋk´ shəs lē)
adv. in a worried
or uneasy way

classified (klas´ ə fīd)
v. identified as part of
a group; designated

basket, we felt that we were still having a day out. But Helen kept glancing **anxiously** at the little dog and I knew she was thinking the same thing as I was. Would he be all right after all that we had done for him and, even then, what was going to happen to him? Would his owners ever come to claim him, because if they didn't, he had nobody in the world to look after him.

Since he had been found by the police, he was **classified** as a stray and had to go into the kennels at the police station. When I visited him there two days later, he greeted me excitedly, balancing well on his plastered leg, his tail swishing. All his fear seemed to have gone. I was delighted to see that the injured eye was now fully open, and the swelling down.

The young policeman was as pleased as I was. "Look at that!" he exclaimed. "He's nearly as good as new again."

"Yes," I said, "he's done wonderfully well." I hesitated for a moment. "Has anybody enquired about him?"

He shook his head. "Nothing yet, but we'll keep hoping, and in the meantime we'll take good care of him here."

I visited the kennels often, and each time the shaggy little creature jumped up to greet me, laughing into my face, mouth open, eyes shining. But nobody seemed to want him.

After a few more days it was clear that no owner was going to claim him, and my only hope was that somebody else would take him and give him a home.

There were other stray dogs in the kennels, and on one visit I saw a farmer calling to collect his wandering sheepdog.

Then a family was overjoyed at being reunited with their handsome golden retriever.

Finally a little old lady came in and tearfully gathered her tiny Yorkshire terrier into her arms. But nobody came for my little patient.

Various strangers came too, looking for a pet, but nobody seemed to be interested in him. Maybe it was because he was only a mongrel and the people who visited the kennels wanted a more elegant dog—yet I knew that he would make a perfect pet for anybody.

A week passed before I went again to the police station. The little dog's kennel was empty.

"What's happened?" I asked the policeman. "Has somebody taken him?"

The policeman looked very grave. "No," he replied, "I'm afraid he's been arrested."

"Arrested?" I said in astonishment. "What do you mean?"

"Well," he said, "it seems that it's against the law for a dog to go begging in the market square so he has been taken into police custody."

I was bewildered. "What are you talking about? A dog can't be arrested."

The policeman, still very solemn, shrugged his shoulders. "This dog was."

"I still don't know what this is all about," I said. "Where is he now?"

"I'll take you to him," the policeman replied.

We left the police station and walked a short way along the road to a pretty cottage.

We went inside and there, in the sitting-room, curled up in a big new doggy bed was my little friend. Two small girls were sitting by his side, stroking his coat.

The policeman threw back his head and laughed. "I've just been kidding you, Mr. Herriot. This is my house and I've taken him as a pet for my two daughters. They've been wanting a dog for some time and I've got so fond of this wee chap that I thought he'd be just right for them."

A wave of relief swept over me. "Well, that's wonderful," I

said and I looked at his kind face gratefully. "What's your name?" I asked.

"Phelps," he replied. "PC Phelps. And they call me Funny Phelps at the police station because I like playing jokes on people."

"Well, you certainly took me in," I said. "Arrested indeed!"

He laughed again. "Well, you've got to admit he's in the hands of the law now!"

I laughed too. I didn't mind having the joke played on me because, funny Phelps or not, he was obviously a nice Phelps and would be a kind master for my doggy friend.

It was a happy day when I took the plaster off the little dog's leg and found that the break had healed perfectly. All the nasty cuts had healed, too, and when I lifted him down from the table, the small girls held up a beautiful new red collar with a lead to match. Their new pet liked the look of them because he sat up in that position I remembered so well, his paws dangling, his face looking up eagerly. The begging dog had found a home at last.

Make Predictions
Was your prediction about where the police officer would take the narrator correct? Explain.

Critical Thinking

1. **Key Ideas and Details** **(a)** What event leads the narrator to help the dog? **(b) Draw Conclusions:** Why do you think the narrator visits the dog at the police station?

2. **Key Ideas and Details** **(a)** At the beginning of the story, why does the dog run away from people who try to pet him? **(b) Compare and Contrast:** How does this behavior change at the end of the story? **(c) Infer:** Why do you think the dog's behavior changes in this way?

Cite textua
evidence t
support yo
response

3. **Integration of Knowledge and Ideas** If the story were to continue, do you think the veterinarian and the police officer would become great friends? Why or why not?

4. **Integration of Knowledge and Ideas** The police officer says that the dog has been "taken into custody." What is true, and what is untrue, about this statement? *[Connect to the Big Question: How do we decide what is true?]*

Reading Skill: Make Predictions

1. (a) What did you **predict** would happen to the dog?
   (b) On what details did you base your prediction?

2. As you read, did you change any predictions? Explain.

Literary Analysis: Narrator's Point of View

3. Craft and Structure Make a chart to note how the author develops the narrator's **point of view** and how that affects what readers know about events in the story.

Event	Details Provided by Narrator
The dog disappears.	The narrator learns of the dog's new home.

4. Craft and Structure What details would you expect to find if the **narrator** were the police officer?

Vocabulary

Acquisition and Use Synonyms are words with similar definitions. Their *connotations,* or associations, may be slightly different. For each item, choose a synonym from the vocabulary list on page 52.

1. ran, dashed, _____

2. protection, safekeeping, _____

3. nervously, worriedly, _____

4. ate, consumed, _____

5. confused, puzzled, _____

6. categorized, grouped, _____

Word Study Use the context of the sentences and what you know about the **Anglo Saxon prefix *be-*** to explain each answer.

1. Would a lonely boy be sad if someone *befriended* him?

2. If someone is *beloved* by many, is she popular?

Word Study

The **Anglo Saxon prefix *be-*** often means "make."

Apply It Explain how the prefix contributes to the meaning of these words. Consult a dictionary if necessary.

belittle
beside
bemoan

Integrated Language Skills

The Drive-In Movies • The Market Square Dog

Conventions: Singular and Plural Nouns

A **noun** is a word that names a person, place, or thing. **Singular nouns** refer to one person, place, or thing. **Plural nouns** refer to more than one.

The **plural** form of most nouns is formed by adding the letter -s or the letters -es to the end of the word. Other nouns form their plurals differently.

Examples of Singular Nouns	Their Plural Forms
bell	bells
dish	dishes
tray	trays
country	countries
woman	women

Practice A Identify whether each of these nouns is singular or plural. Then, use each word in a sentence.

1. movie
2. cartoons
3. sandwiches
4. grass
5. mice

ⓒ Reading Application In "The Drive-In Movies," find two more singular nouns and two more plural nouns.

Practice B Write the plural form of each singular noun. Then use each plural noun in a sentence.

1. sheepdog
2. stray
3. man
4. dress
5. surgery

ⓒ Writing Application Scan "The Market Square Dog" to find four more nouns. Write both their singular and their plural forms. Then, use each pair of nouns in a sentence.

PH WRITING COACH Further instruction and practice are available in *Prentice Hall Writing Coach*.

Writing

Narrative Text Each of these selections is packed with details about an event in the narrator's life. Write an **autobiographical narrative** about an interesting experience in your life.

Common Core State Standards

L.5.c; W.6.3; SL.6.6
[For the full wording of the standards, see page 42.]

- Think of important events in your life and jot them down.

- Narrow your topic and choose an experience.

- List the events and details of where, when, and with whom the experience took place. Number the order of events.

- Use your notes and numbered list to write your narrative.

Grammar Application Use the correct plural forms and singular forms of the nouns in your narrative.

Writing Workshop: *Work in Progress*

Prewriting for Descriptive Essay Look back at your Place List, and focus on your favorite for your topic. Read the notes you wrote about it. Write complete sentences to describe each sensory detail and save them in your writing portfolio.

Use this prewriting activity to prepare for the **Writing Workshop** on page 86.

Speaking and Listening

Comprehension and Collaboration With a partner, write a **conversation** that the narrator of the story might have had with another character about story events. Then, act out the conversation for the class or a small group.

- If you read "The Drive-In Movies," write a conversation that Soto and his mother might have had the morning after their trip to the drive-in.

- If you read "The Market Square Dog," write a conversation in which Herriot tells his wife about how the police officer adopted the dog.

Follow these steps to complete the assignment.

- Begin by jotting down details from the story, as well as your own creative ideas, to invent an interesting dialogue.

- Ask your partner questions and make observations, keeping each character's traits, goals, and feelings in mind.

- Practice using eye contact when listening and speaking.

- Finally, when you act out your conversation, use expressive tones of voice and gestures to engage your audience.

www.PHLitOnline.com
- Interactive graphic organizers
- Grammar tutorial
- Interactive journals

Test Practice: Reading

Make Predictions

Fiction Selection

Directions: *Read the selection. Then, answer the questions.*

The very first time I baby-sat for Hunter, an adorable 5-year-old boy, things did not go well. I tried to do a good job by following his parents' rules and putting him to bed on time.

As I tucked him in, Hunter said, "Tell me a story, Doug."

I began a story about a little boy who gets a new bunny as a pet. Hunter interrupted and asked me to make the story scary. I did not think it was a good idea, but after he begged and promised to go right to sleep if I told him a scary story, I agreed. I made the bunny turn into a gigantic monster.

After the story, I said good night to Hunter. I planned to go to the kitchen to do my homework.

Hunter clutched my arm. "That was really scary," he said.

1. Which of the following predictions is most logical?
   A. Doug will finish all of his homework.
   B. Hunter will ask for another scary story.
   C. Hunter will not be able to sleep because he is frightened.
   D. Hunter's parents will come home early.

2. From this experience, Doug will learn that he should—
   A. refuse to baby-sit for difficult children.
   B. trust his own judgment.
   C. follow parents' rules while baby-sitting.
   D. not baby-sit anymore.

3. If Doug baby-sits for Hunter again, what will he do differently?
   A. He will let Hunter sleep with the lights on.
   B. He will not bring any homework.
   C. He will put Hunter to bed earlier.
   D. He will not tell Hunter a scary story.

4. Which of the following *best* helps you predict whether Doug will baby-sit for Hunter again?
   A. Hunter's reaction to Doug's scary story
   B. Hunter's ability to follow his parents' rules
   C. Doug's attitude toward homework
   D. a clue in the first sentence

Writing for Assessment

Imagine that Doug is baby-sitting for another child. The child does not like the food that his parents left for dinner and he wants ice cream. In two sentences, predict what Doug will do based on what he learned from his experience with Hunter.

Nonfiction Selection

Directions: *Read the selection. Then, answer the questions.*

Excerpt from "Guide to Being an Awesome Babysitter"

When you baby-sit for a child for the first time, make sure to ask the parents about the rules in their home and write them down. Some things you should know are: the child's bedtime; what snacks are allowed; whether you can take the child for a walk; and whether it is okay to watch television.

There are a few rules that you should follow every time you baby-sit. First, respect the family's privacy and do not snoop in their personal things. Next, do not watch movies, listen to music, or read books that might be too mature for the child you are baby-sitting. Finally, never invite a guest to visit you while you are babysitting unless you have the parents' permission.

1. Based on the passage, which do you pre-
   dict might be the name of the chapter?
   A. "Baby-Sitting Can Be Fun"
   B. "Starting Your Baby-Sitting Business"
   C. "Learn the Rules"
   D. "Dealing With Difficult Children"

2. Predict which advice would be most
   helpful to someone who baby-sits for
   several families.
   A. Write down each family's rules.
   B. Feed the children snacks that are
      allowed.
   C. Do not touch any personal items.
   D. Do not watch scary movies.

3. What words in the second paragraph
   help you predict that the information
   that follows is important?
   A. *some rules*
   B. *every time*
   C. *do not touch*
   D. *parents' permission*

4. The book's next chapter is called "Safety
   First." What advice do you predict it will
   give?
   A. Read the children a bedtime story.
   B. Keep emergency phone numbers.
   C. Bring your homework with you.
   D. Ask when the parents will be home.

Writing for Assessment

Comparing Texts
If Doug had read the rules above before
he baby-sat for Hunter, how might
he have acted differently? In a short
paragraph, support your prediction with
details from both passages.

www.PHLitOnline.com
• Online practice
• Instant feedback

Reading for Information

Analyzing Functional and Expository Texts

Web Site

News Article

Reading Skill: Analyze Structural Features

Web sites and news articles are two important sources of information. When you find a print or an online resource, **analyze its structural features.** To do so, notice how the features connect different parts of the text. Look critically, to make sure the structure is logical. Also, check to see that opinions are supported and that information comes from reliable sources, such as a government agency or a school.

This chart gives examples of structural features.

Structural Features of Online Resources	Structural Features of News Articles
• **URL:** Web address • **home page:** opening page of a Web site • **links:** connections to other pages or sites • **icons:** images or small drawings that often highlight links • **menus:** listings of links	• **headline:** text that provides overview of content • **byline:** line that shows who wrote the article • **dateline:** information that tells where and when the story takes place • **captions:** information about pictures or other visuals

Content-Area Vocabulary

These words appear in the selections that follow. You may also encounter them in other content-area texts.

- **equines** (ē′kwīns′) *n.* horses
- **resuscitation** (ri sus′ə tā′ shən) *n.* the act of being brought back to life or consciousness; the act of being revived
- **inhalation** (in′hə lā′shən) *n.* a breathing in; a drawing in of air, gas, smoke, etc., into the lungs

Common Core
State Standards

Reading Informational Text
5. Analyze how a particular sentence, paragraph, chapter, or section fits into the overall structure of a text and contributes to the development of the ideas.

Language
6. Acquire and use accurately grade-appropriate general academic and domain-specific words and phrases; gather vocabulary knowledge when considering a word or phrase important to comprehension or expression.

This is a recent home page for Animaland®, a Web site published by the American Society for the Prevention of Cruelty to Animals (ASPCA). It is a starting point that will lead you to other pages within the site.

http://www.aspca.org/site/PageServer?pagename=kids_home

Web Site

Features:

- home page with links to other pages
- informative text
- photos or other images
- may include audio or video content

ANIMALAND®

Each of these buttons leads to more information on a topic. By clicking on the button, you will open up a new page of the Web site.

Nose for News | Pet Care | Ask Azula | Animal Careers | Animal ABCs | Real Issues | Cartoons | Activities | Pet of the Week | Home

SPOTLIGHT ON...

THINK YOU'VE GOT HORSE POWER?
Do you know about equines or are you just horsing around? Saddle up and take our quiz!

"MOO"VE OVER!
Meet the 1,500-pound manatee, also known as a sea cow.

SUMMER'S HERE!
How to keep your pets cool when it's hot.

Another way to navigate a Web site is to click on an underlined item, or link. Like buttons, links take you to specific types of information.

ASK AZULA

Why do some frogs have teeth?
— *Tenille*

I'd be *hoppy* to answer your question, Tenille!

Learn More

PET OF THE WEEK

Meet Caya
Submitted by Jaime, age 11

Favorite Trick: "Playing with her kitty fishing pole with a fuzzy mouse on the hook"

Favorite Treat: Tuna

Why I Love Caya: "She's silly and spunky, just like her owner!"

Send in your pet's photo!

PET CARE CARTOON
Learn why it's important to keep your cat indoors!

PLAY ▶

http://www.aspca.org/site/PageServer?pagename=kids_home

This page appears when you click on the button labeled "Pet Care" and then click on "Dog Care."

These buttons are the same as the ones found on the Web site's home page. At any time, you can click on a button to go to a different Web page.

Nose for News | Pet Care | Ask Azula | Animal Careers | Animal ABCs | Real Issues | Cartoons | Activities | Pet of the Week | Home

PET CARE

Dog Care: The 411

Scientific name: *Canis familiaris*

Size: XS, S, M, L, XL!! Dogs range in size from tiny four-pound tea cup poodles to Irish wolfhounds, the tallest dogs at almost three feet high.

Lifespan: As a rule, smaller dogs tend to live longer than larger ones. A compact Chihuahua can live to be 16, while giant breeds like bull mastiffs usually live to be about eight years old. And somewhere in the middle, the average, All-American mixed-breed pooch has a lifespan of about 12 to 14 years.

Colors/varieties: There are more than 400 different breeds of dogs —spotted Dalmatians, shiny black Labrador retrievers, brindle-coated boxers...to name just a few! But the most popular pooches of all are non-pedigree—that includes shaggy dogs, dogs with hairy ears, dogs with all-white socks, dogs with fluffy tails, and everything in between. You may have heard people call these dogs "mutts," but we prefer *one-of-a-kind*!

Parents and teachers, click here [link] for more dog care information to share with your students and children.

LEARN MORE
- The 411
- Chow Time!
- Home Sweet Home
- Fun & Games

Dog Care
Cat Care
Bird Care
Rabbit Care
Fish Care
Gerbil Care
Hamster Care
Guinea Pig Care
Mouse Care
Rat Care

This is a list of links that connect to the different animals that are discussed in the Web site's "Pet Care" guide.

Features:

- text for a general audience
- information about a current event or an issue
- photos and captions

The headline gives you an overview of the article's content.

Rescuers to Carry Oxygen Masks for Pets

By Associated Press
Updated: 9/3/2006

APPLETON, Wis.

The dateline tells you where and when the story takes place.

Pets here will be breathing a little easier now that local rescuers will be carrying oxygen masks designed for animals.

Six Appleton fire trucks and 13 ambulances will be equipped with masks intended for use on dogs, cats and other small animals.

Alderman Richard Thompson initiated the program after he saw a newspaper photograph of a firefighter in Superior giving mouth-to-mouth resuscitation to a cat rescued from a house fire.

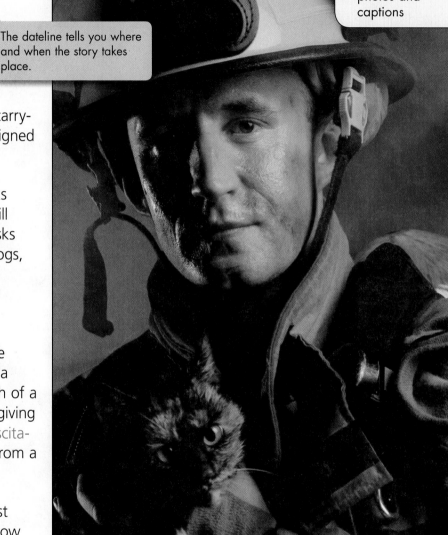

"A pet is family to most people," he said. "I know I wouldn't want to lose Maggie, my collie, or Lucy, my Tabby cat, to a fire, carbon monoxide poisoning or who knows what else."

The money to pay for each $49 mask came from donations by local animal lovers.

"It was something to see," Thompson said. "There was no organized solicitation effort. People and community groups just read or heard about the program and stepped up to the plate."

The masks, which come in three sizes, will be distributed to each of six fire stations and to the Appleton Police Department K-9 unit, he said.

The Madison Fire Department carries similar masks on its seven ambulances, said Lori Wirth, the department's community education officer.

The Madison department also bought its masks with money raised from unsolicited donations, she said. In fact, the department raised so much money it was able to buy mask kits for several neighboring communities.

Wirth said the department's firefighters haven't had to use the masks yet but they're trained and willing.

"What we've done so far is use the masks as a way to remind people to get out of their residence in the event of a fire and don't go searching for pets," she said. "Firefighters will care for any pets we find in the event they suffer from smoke **inhalation**."

A firefighter places an oxygen mask on a cat.

The caption provides information about the photo.

Comparing Functional and Expository Texts

1. Craft and Structure **(a)** In what ways are the **structural features** of the Web site and news article alike and different? **(b)** What does each of these texts help you learn about the care of pets? **(c)** Explain how you might use each of these sources to check the accuracy of information.

Content-Area Vocabulary

2. (a) Explain how a change in suffix alters the meanings and parts of speech of these words: *resuscitation, resuscitate,* and *resuscitator.*
(b) Use each word in a sentence that shows its meaning.

Timed Writing

Explanatory Text: Write a Letter

> **Format and Audience**
> The prompt gives specific directions about what you are writing (a letter) and your audience (a friend).

Review what you have learned about using a Web site. Write a letter to a friend in which you summarize the features of the ASPCA Web site and explain why it can be considered a reliable source of information. (25 minutes)

> **Academic Vocabulary**
> When you *summarize* a text, you give only the most important details. When you *explain* why the Web site is reliable, you tell why its information can be trusted.

5-Minute Planner

Complete these steps before you begin to write:

1. Read the prompt. Look for key words, like the ones highlighted, to help you understand the assignment.

2. List details to include in your explanation. **TIP** Web sites with URLs that end in .edu (educational institution), .gov (government agency), or .org (nonprofit organization) are usually reliable and trustworthy.

3. Identify the organization that posted this Web site. How does this group's involvement affect the Web site's reliability?

4. Use your notes to outline a three-paragraph letter. Include a salutation (a greeting), a body, and an appropriate closing.

Comparing Fiction and Nonfiction

Fiction is writing that tells about imaginary people, animals, and events. Examples of fiction include short stories and folk tales.

Nonfiction is writing that tells about real people, animals, places, events, and ideas. Examples of nonfiction include biographies and newspaper articles.

The selections that follow are both about monkeys. "Why Monkeys Live in Trees" is fiction, and "The Case of the Monkeys That Fell From the Trees" is nonfiction. Authors of fiction and nonfiction approach **similar themes and topics** in different ways. For example, these selections have a similar topic—monkeys. However, the authors have different purposes, or reasons, for writing. In "Why Monkeys Live in Trees," the author tells a fictional story that explains how monkeys came to live in trees. "The Case of the Monkeys That Fell From the Trees" is a nonfiction work in which the author, a scientist, sets out to explain a real-life case of monkeys becoming ill.

As you read the selections, look for ways in which the works are alike and different. Ask yourself the following questions to help in your analysis.

- What is the author's main reason, or purpose, for writing?

- Although written in different genres, or types of literature, both selections offer information about monkeys. What types of details does each work present?

- What type of language does the author use? Is it funny? Serious? Scientific? How do the language choices relate to the author's purpose for writing?

Use a Venn diagram like the one shown to organize your observations.

**Why Monkeys
Live in Trees**

**The Case of the
Monkeys That Fell
From the Trees**

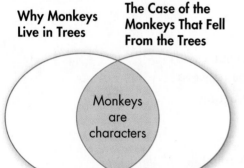

Monkeys
are
characters

 **Common Core
State Standards**

Reading Literature
9. Compare and contrast texts in different forms or genres in terms of their approaches to similar themes and topics.

Reading Informational Text
9. Compare and contrast one author's presentation of events with that of another.

Writing
2.a. Introduce a topic; organize ideas, concepts, and information, using strategies such as definition, classification, comparison/contrast, and cause/effect; include formatting, graphics, and multimedia when useful to aiding comprehension. *(Timed Writing, p. 85)*

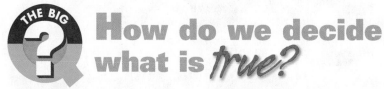
Writing About the Big Question

Think about what you already know about monkeys—where they live, what they eat, and what special abilities they have. Use this sentence starter to develop your ideas about the Big Question.

In **reality,** monkeys who live in trees probably _____ but in a **fictional** story, they might _____.

Meet the Authors

Julius Lester (b. 1939)

Author of "Why Monkeys Live in Trees"

As a teenager, Julius Lester knew exactly what he wanted to be: a musician. "I was not a good writer," he recalls, "and I never dreamed I'd become an award-winning author."

Music, Civil Rights, and Writing After graduating from college, Lester had a successful musical career. He also became active in the civil rights movement of the 1960s and wrote books inspired by his African American heritage.

Susan E. Quinlan (b. 1954)

Author of "The Case of the Monkeys That Fell From the Trees"

Susan E. Quinlan and her husband, Bud Lehnhausen, have worked together for more than twenty-five years, conducting wildlife research and teaching natural history courses.

The Subject Is Nature Quinlan's work is inspired by her love of wildlife. "I write about nature and the work of scientists because I want to share my fascination in these topics with young readers," she says.

WHY MONKEYS LIVE IN TREES

AFRICAN FOLK TALE

JULIUS LESTER

▲ Critical Viewing
Based on this picture, what human characteristics does this monkey seem to have? **[Connect]**

Vocabulary
reflection (ri flek´ shən) *n.* image of one's self, as seen in a mirror

Fiction and Nonfiction
What details here show that this is a work of fiction?

One day Leopard was looking at his reflection in a pool of water. Looking at himself was Leopard's favorite thing in the world to do. Leopard gazed, wanting to be sure that every hair was straight and that all his spots were where they were supposed to be. This took many hours of looking at his reflection, which Leopard did not mind at all.

Finally he was satisfied that nothing was disturbing his handsomeness, and he turned away from the pool of water. At that exact moment, one of Leopard's children ran up to him.

"Daddy! Daddy! Are you going to be in the contest?"

"What contest?" Leopard wanted to know. If it was a beauty contest, of course he was going to be in it.

"I don't know. Crow the Messenger just flew by. She said that King Gorilla said there was going to be a contest."

Without another word, Leopard set off. He went north-by-northeast, made a right turn at the mulberry bush and traveled east-by-south-by-west until he came to a hole in the ground. He went around in a circle five times, and headed north-by-somersault until he came to a big clearing in the middle of the jungle and that's where King Gorilla was.

King Gorilla sat at one end of the clearing on his throne. Opposite him, at the other side of the clearing, all the animals sat in a semicircle. In the middle, between King Gorilla and the animals, was a huge mound of what looked like black dust.

Leopard looked around with calm dignity. Then he strode regally over to his friend, Lion.

"What's that?" he asked, pointing to the mound of black dust.

"Don't know," Lion replied. "King Gorilla said he will give a pot of gold to whoever can eat it in one day. I can eat it in an hour."

Leopard laughed. "I'll eat it in a half hour."

It was Hippopotamus's turn to laugh. "As big as my mouth is, I'll eat that mound in one gulp."

The time came for the contest. King Gorilla had the animals pick numbers to see who would go in what order. To everybody's dismay, Hippopotamus drew Number 1.

Hippopotamus walked over to the mound of black dust. It was bigger than he had thought. It was much too big to eat in one gulp. Nonetheless, Hippopotamus opened his mouth as wide as he could, and that was very wide indeed, and took a mouthful of the black dust.

He started chewing. Suddenly he leaped straight into the air and screamed. He screamed so loudly that it knocked the ears off the chickens and that's why to this day chickens don't have ears.

Hippopotamus screamed and Hippopotamus yelled. Hippopotamus roared and Hippopotamus bellowed. Then he started sneezing and crying and tears rolled down his face like he was standing in the shower. Hippopotamus ran to the river and drank as much water as he could, and that was very much, indeed, to cool his mouth and tongue and throat.

The animals didn't understand what had happened to Hippopotamus, but they didn't care. They were happy because they still had a chance to win the pot of gold. Of course, if they had known that the mound of black dust was really a mound of black pepper, maybe they wouldn't have wanted the gold.

Nobody was more happy than Leopard because he had

Vocabulary
regally (rē´ gə lē) *adv.* in a royal way; like a king or queen

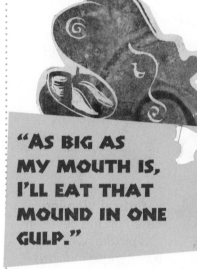

"AS BIG AS MY MOUTH IS, I'LL EAT THAT MOUND IN ONE GULP."

Vocabulary
bellowed (bel´ ōd) *v.* cried out in a low, loud voice

Reading Check
What is Leopard's favorite pastime?

drawn Number 2. He walked up to the black mound and sniffed at it.

"AAAAAAAACHOOOOOOO!" Leopard didn't like that but then he remembered the pot of gold. He opened his mouth wide, took a mouthful and started chewing and swallowing.

Leopard leaped straight into the air, did a back double flip and screamed. He yelled and he roared and he bellowed and, finally, he started sneezing and crying, tears rolling down his face like a waterfall. Leopard ran to the river and washed out his mouth and throat and tongue.

Lion was next, and the same thing happened to him as it did to all the animals. Finally only Monkey remained.

Monkey approached King Gorilla. "I know I can eat all of whatever that is, but after each mouthful, I'll need to lie down in the tall grasses and rest."

King Gorilla said that was okay.

Monkey went to the mound, took a tiny bit of pepper on his tongue, swallowed, and went into the tall grasses. A few minutes later, Monkey came out, took a little more, swallowed it, and went into the tall grasses.

Soon the pile was almost gone. The animals were astonished to see Monkey doing what they had not been able to do. Leopard couldn't believe it either. He climbed a tree and stretched out on a sturdy limb to get a better view. From his limb high in the tree Leopard could see into the tall grasses where Monkey went to rest. Wait a minute! Leopard thought something was suddenly wrong with his eyes because he thought he saw a hundred monkeys hiding in the tall grasses.

He rubbed his eyes and looked another look. There wasn't anything wrong with his eyes. There were a hundred monkeys in the tall grasses and they all looked alike!

Just then, there was the sound of loud applause. King Gorilla

Spiral Review
Theme At this point in the story, how have all the animals reacted to the challenge of eating the pepper? What themes do their reactions suggest?

▼ **Critical Viewing** Based on the details in this picture, why might a writer use monkeys in a tale meant to entertain? **[Analyze]**

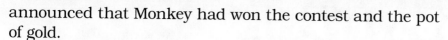

announced that Monkey had won the contest and the pot of gold.

Leopard growled a growl so scary that even King Gorilla was frightened. Leopard wasn't thinking about anybody except the monkeys. He took a long and beautiful leap from the tree right smack into the middle of the tall grasses where the monkeys were hiding.

The monkeys ran in all directions. When the other animals saw monkeys running from the grasses, they realized that the monkeys had tricked them and started chasing them. Even King Gorilla joined in the chase. He wanted his gold back.

The only way the monkeys could escape was to climb to the very tops of the tallest trees where no one else, not even Leopard, could climb.

And that's why monkeys live in trees to this very day.

Fiction and Nonfiction
Identify a detail in this passage that is realistic, even though the story is fiction.

AND THAT'S WHY MONKEYS LIVE IN TREES TO THIS VERY DAY.

Critical Thinking ©

© **1. Key Ideas and Details (a)** What must the animals do in the contest? **(b) Infer:** Why do the animals think it will be easy to win the contest? **(c) Support:** Explain why the contest proves to be more difficult than the animals thought.

© **2. Key Ideas and Details (a)** What does the monkey say he has to do between bites of pepper? **(b) Deduce:** Why is the monkey able to eat all the pepper?

© **3. Key Ideas and Details** What two facts of nature does this tale pretend to explain?

© **4. Key Ideas and Details (a) Assess:** Is King Gorilla's contest a fair one? Explain, citing details from the text.
(b) Make a Judgment: Do the monkeys deserve to win? Why or why not?

© **5. Integration of Knowledge and Ideas (a)** What abilities do the animals in this story have that real animals do not have? **(b)** Do you think the explanation of why monkeys live in trees is based on facts or fantasy? Explain. *[Connect to the Big Question: How do we decide what is true?]*

Cite textual evidence to support your responses.

THE CASE OF THE MONKEYS THAT FELL FROM THE TREES

Susan E. Quinlan

When the incidents began in August 1972, biologist Ken Glander and his wife, Molly, had been studying the eating habits of a troop of howling monkeys in northwestern Costa Rica for nearly three months. Then, over a two-week period, seven monkeys from various troops in the area fell out of trees and died. Another fell but climbed back up.

One morning the Glanders watched a female howling monkey with a ten-day-old baby turn in tight circles on a tree branch. Abruptly, she fell off the branch. For a moment she hung upside down, suspended by her long tail. Then her grip failed and she plunged thirty-five feet to the forest floor. Dazed but still alive, she climbed back up, carrying her clinging infant. She stopped on a thick branch and sat there without eating for the next twenty-four hours.

Normally, howling monkeys are skilled, nimble climbers. They often leap ten feet or more between tree limbs, and they almost never fall. Why were monkeys suddenly falling from trees?

Glander wondered if a disease or parasite[1] might be involved. He asked scientists in the microbiology department at the University of Costa Rica to examine some of the dead monkeys and look for clues. The scientists found no signs of disease or parasites. Nor had the monkeys starved. All had died in apparently healthy condition. Glander began to think they had been poisoned. But who or what would poison wild monkeys? Glander had several green, leafy suspects in mind, all of them tropical forest trees.

Many tropical trees have similar-looking leaves and trunks, so it is difficult to determine their species.[2] But tropical plant expert Paul Opler had identified all the trees in the Glanders' study area. Several poisonous species were present. Suspiciously, some of the monkeys that fell had been feeding in trees known to have poisonous leaves. Yet Glander knew this proved nothing.

All plants produce chemicals called secondary compounds, many of which are poisonous. Plants make these chemicals for a variety of purposes. Some ward

---

1. **parasite** (par´ə sīt) plant, animal, or insect that lives on or in another living thing, called "the host." The parasite gets its food from the blood or tissue of the host.
2. **species** (spē´ sēz) group of plants or animals, scientifically classified because of similar traits.

off plant-eating animals, especially insects. But howling monkeys eat nothing except plants, so they could not survive unless they were able to digest or tolerate plant poisons. Other scientists had observed howlers eating leaves from many kinds of trees, including poisonous species, without any signs of distress. As a result, most scientists assumed that howling monkeys had an unlimited food supply in their lush tropical forest homes. Glander wasn't so sure.

The monkeys that fell from the trees strengthened his belief that howling monkeys could not eat leaves from just any tree. He suspected that certain trees were monkey killers, but he needed evidence before he could point fingers. He and Molly began collecting the data they needed to make a case.

Their days started around 4 or 5 a.m. That's when the monkeys awoke, often greeting the day with roars and growls. The monkeys soon set off, alternating bouts of feeding with periods of crawling, leaping, and climbing through the treetops. Wherever the monkeys went, the Glanders followed on foot.

At midday, the monkeys settled down. Draping themselves over large branches, their arms and legs dangling, the howlers slept with their tails wrapped around branches to anchor them in place. Late in the day, when the air cooled a few degrees, the monkeys stirred. They climbed and fed until settling down for the night at sunset.

For twelve months, the Glanders endured long days, mosquitoes, heavy rains, and temperatures that sometimes soared over 100°F. They did this in order to make their observations of the monkey troop as continuous as possible. Throughout each day, they recorded how many minutes the monkeys spent sleeping, eating, and moving. They recorded which of 1,699 individually numbered trees the monkeys slept in and ate from, and exactly which parts the monkeys ate—leaves, fruits, flowers, or stems.

Each day, the scientists collected samples of leaves from every tree the monkeys fed in that day, and leaves from nearby trees of the same species. The monkeys had visited these trees but did not feed in them. The Glanders tagged the leaves with wire labels, noting the tree, the date, and the time that the sample was collected. Next, they dried the leaves in an oven, then packed them in zippered plastic bags for later study.

The Glanders soon noticed that the howlers ate new leaves whenever they could, only occasionally eating fruits, flowers, or mature leaves. In certain trees, the monkeys plucked off the leaves, then stripped and tossed away the leaf blades. They ate only the remaining leaf stems. Other scientists thought this messy feeding behavior meant that howling monkeys could afford to be wasteful in a forest where food was so abundant. Glander wasn't convinced.

After thousands of hours of field work, including nearly two thousand hours of observing monkeys, Glander reviewed all the records he and Molly had gathered. Their careful data showed that howlers had not eaten leaves from just any trees in the forest. Indeed, the monkeys had rarely eaten leaves from the most common tree species. Instead, they spent most of their feeding time in a few uncommon kinds of trees. All told, the monkeys had eaten from only 331 of the 1,699 trees in the area. More surprisingly, they had spent three-quarters of their feeding time in just 88 trees. The data showed that the monkeys selected only certain tree species for feeding.

Glander discovered something even more surprising. The monkeys had not eaten leaves from all the trees of favored species. Instead, they ate leaves from just a few individual trees of most species. For example, the monkeys traveled through most of the 149 madera negra trees in the area, but they ate mature leaves from only three of these. This pattern fascinated Glander, because the madera negra is one of the most toxic[3] trees in the forest. Its leaves are used to make rat poison.

To learn more, Glander chemically analyzed all the leaves he and Molly had collected from the madera negra trees in the study area during their field studies. The results were startling. The three individual trees from which the monkeys had eaten mature leaves showed no traces of poison alkaloids.[4] But leaves collected from the other madera negras were packed with these poisons. Somehow, the monkeys had picked out those very few trees whose leaves were not poisonous.

---

3. **toxic** (täk´ sik) poisonous.
4. **alkaloids** (al´ kə lɔidz) group of chemical substances, some poisonous, found in plants.

▲ **Critical Viewing**
Why do you think this monkey is called a howler monkey? **[Hypothesize]**

Fiction and Nonfiction
How do the Glanders find answers to their questions?

 Reading Check

For about how long did the Glanders observe the monkeys?

Science Connection

Living Layers

Tropical rainforests cover seven percent of Earth's surface yet are home to fifty percent of the world's species. In the rainforest, the trees form distinct layers. Each layer is like a unique habitat. The chart shows the different species that live in each layer.

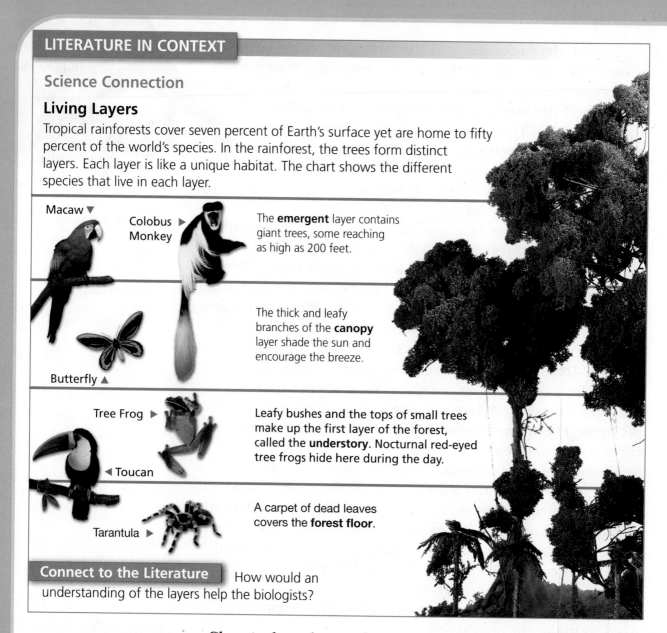

Macaw ▼

Colobus ► Monkey

The **emergent** layer contains giant trees, some reaching as high as 200 feet.

Butterfly ▲

The thick and leafy branches of the **canopy** layer shade the sun and encourage the breeze.

Tree Frog ►

Leafy bushes and the tops of small trees make up the first layer of the forest, called the **understory**. Nocturnal red-eyed tree frogs hide here during the day.

◄ Toucan

A carpet of dead leaves covers the **forest floor**.

Tarantula ►

Connect to the Literature   How would an understanding of the layers help the biologists?

Chemical analyses of mature leaves from other kinds of trees revealed a similar pattern. The howling monkeys had consistently selected the most nutritious, most digestible, and least poisonous leaves available in their patch of forest. Glander noted that howlers ate only the leaf stems in some trees because the stems contained fewer poisons than the leaves. His data showed that instead of being sloppy eaters awash in a sea of food, howling monkeys are cautious, picky eaters in a forest filled with poisons.

But the mystery of the monkeys that fell from the trees was not solved. If howling monkeys can identify and avoid the most toxic leaves, why would they ever become poisoned and fall? Glander uncovered more clues by studying plants and their poisons.

The concentration of poison is not uniform among those plants that produce poisonous secondary compounds. The kinds and amounts of poison present vary widely among plant species, among individual plants of a single species, and even within the parts of a single plant. In fact, individual plants make varying amounts of poisons at different times of year and under different growing conditions. Some plants produce more poisons after their leaves or twigs are eaten by plant-eating animals. These same plants make fewer poisons if they are not damaged by plant-eaters. Due to these constant changes, Glander realized that monkeys could not simply learn which trees had poisonous leaves and which had edible ones. Their task was far more complicated. How did the monkeys do it?

Again, Glander found an answer in his field records. Howlers had fed in 331 of the trees in the study area, but they made only one stop in 104 of these trees. In each case, a solitary adult monkey visited the tree briefly, ate just a little bit, and then moved on. Glander thinks these monkeys were "sampling" the leaves for poisons. If the plant parts were toxic, they probably tasted bad or made the monkey who sampled them feel slightly ill. He suspects that each monkey troop finds out which trees currently have the least poisonous leaves by regularly and carefully sampling from trees throughout the area. By using this technique, the monkeys would avoid eating too many of the most toxic plant poisons.

Considering the ever-changing toxicity of the leaves in a forest, however, Glander reasoned that individual monkeys may sometimes make mistakes. They may eat too many of the wrong leaves. More importantly, when edible leaves are scarce due to unusual conditions, monkeys may be forced to eat leaves they wouldn't otherwise choose. Glander first saw monkeys falling from trees during a severe drought[5] year, when the howlers' food choices were quite limited. Because some poisons produced by tropical plants affect animal muscles and nerves, eating the wrong leaves could certainly cause illness, dizziness, and deadly falls.

---

5. **drought** (drout) period of little or no rain.

Fiction and Nonfiction
Which details in this paragraph are not often included in works of fiction?

Reading Check
According to Glander, how do the monkeys know which leaves are poisonous?

Spiral Review
Central Idea How does this discussion of the monkeys' "pantry" help to convey the author's central idea?

Fiction and Nonfiction Is it a fact that monkeys eat leaves for medicinal purposes? Explain.

Today, after more than thirty years of studying monkeys, Ken Glander is convinced that the falling monkeys he and Molly observed were poisoned by eating leaves from the wrong trees at the wrong time. His work shows that a tropical forest is like a pantry filled with a mixture of foods and poisons. Only the most selective eaters can avoid the poisons and find enough edible food to survive.

However, the monkeys' poison-filled pantry has a silver lining. Poison chemicals used in small amounts often have medicinal value. Many human medicines contain plant poisons, including aspirin, quinine, atropine, morphine, digitoxin (a heart medicine), and cancer-fighting vincristine and paclitaxel. In fact, an estimated one-fourth of all medicines prescribed in the United States today come from plants.

Glander and other researchers have gathered some evidence that howlers and other monkeys sometimes select poisonous leaves for medicinal purposes, such as ridding themselves of parasites. Glander thinks scientists searching for new medicines for people might get some useful tips from howlers. The monkeys' behavior might help scientists select those plants most worth sampling.

Critical Thinking

Cite textual evidence to support your responses.

© 1. **Key Ideas and Details (a)** What mystery do the scientists try to solve? **(b) Cause and Effect:** Why does Glander suspect the monkeys have been poisoned?

© 2. **Key Ideas and Details (a)** Why is Glander fascinated by the monkeys eating madera negra leaves? **(b) Cause and Effect:** What evidence indicates that the monkeys are "cautious, picky eaters"?

© 3. **Key Ideas and Details (a)** What do the Glanders conclude about why some monkeys died, but others did not? **(b) Cause and Effect:** What makes Glander think that howler monkeys may provide useful tips to scientists?

© 4. **Integration of Knowledge and Ideas** Is what happened to the monkeys based on facts or fantasy? Explain. *[Connect to the Big Question: How do we decide what is true?]*

Comparing Fiction and Nonfiction

1. **Key Ideas and Details** **(a)** In a chart like the one shown, explain how two specific details in "Why Monkeys Live in Trees" prove that the selection is **fiction.** One detail is given as an example.

Detail	Why It Is Fiction
Leopard uses his reflection to see how he looks.	Real animals do not check their appearance.

(b) Next, create a new chart to explain how three specific details in "The Case of the Monkeys That Fell From the Trees" prove that the selection is **nonfiction.**

2. **Integration of Knowledge and Ideas** Use an example from each work to support the following:

   • A fictional story may contain details that seem realistic.

   • A nonfiction selection may contain surprising facts.

⏱ Timed Writing

Explanatory Text: Essay

Compare and contrast the monkeys in "Why Monkeys Live in Trees" and in "The Case of the Monkeys That Fell From the Trees." Use details from the selections to support your points. **(30 minutes)**

5-Minute Planner

1. Read the prompt carefully and completely.

2. Organize your ideas by answering these questions:

   • What can the monkeys in "Why Monkeys Live in Trees" do that real monkeys cannot do?

   • What real-life things do the monkeys in "The Case of the Monkeys That Fell From the Trees" do?

   • How are the monkeys in both selections alike and different?

3. Reread the prompt, and then draft your essay.

Writing Workshop

 **Common Core State Standards**

Writing
2.b. Develop the topic with relevant facts, definitions, concrete details, quotations, or other information and examples.
2.d. Use precise language and domain-specific vocabulary to inform about or explain the topic.

Language
4.c. Consult reference materials, both print and digital, to find the pronunciation of a word or determine or clarify its precise meaning or its part of speech.

Write Informative Texts

Description: Descriptive Essay

Defining the Form In **descriptive writing,** the writer creates word pictures that help readers imagine the way something looks, feels, smells, tastes, or sounds. You might use description in many other forms of writing, including informative and persuasive texts.

Assignment Write a descriptive essay to inform readers about a place you know well, such as your grandparents' house or a park. Include these elements:

- ✓ a *main impression* of the setting, supported by details that add specific information
- ✓ rich *sensory details* that appeal to the five senses
- ✓ an *organization* that helps readers picture the setting
- ✓ language that creates *vivid images and comparisons*
- ✓ error-free writing, including *correct use of pronouns*

To preview the criteria on which your descriptive essay may be judged, see the rubric on page 91.

 Writing Workshop: *Work in Progress*

Review the work you did on pages 41 and 63.

Prewriting/Planning Strategy

Gather details. After you have selected the place you wish to describe, use a sensory details chart to help you gather details about the sights, scents, textures, sounds, and tastes associated with your setting. This model shows details related to a campsite.

Sights	Scents	Textures	Sounds	Tastes
tall pine trees	fire smoke	crunchy pine needles	hoot of owls	(none)
campfire flames	spicy pines	underfoot	snap of logs burning	

PHLit Online!
www.PHLitOnline.com
- Illustrated vocabulary words
- Interactive vocabulary games
- Vocabulary flashcards

Creating Vivid Descriptions

Word choice is the specific language a writer uses to create a strong impression. You can paint a vivid picture of the setting you chose to write about by using precise adjectives and verbs. Follow these tips.

Choosing Precise Adjectives Review the chart on the previous page. Notice that it contains both vivid and vague descriptions. *Crunchy pine needles underfoot* is vivid. The adjective *crunchy* will help readers feel and hear the crunch of brittle pine needles. However, *tall pine trees* is not as vivid. Many things are tall. To find a more precise adjective, try one of these strategies:

- Picture the pine trees and jot down all the descriptive words that come to mind.

- Use a dictionary or thesaurus to find synonyms for *tall*.

In a thesaurus, for example, you might find the synonym *towering*. Notice the vividness of this description: *pine trees towering far overhead*.

Choosing Precise Words The chart on page 86 also contains strong verbs such as *hoot* and *snap*. These words describe the sounds exactly. Look over the notations you made on your chart. Ask yourself, *Do the words describe the sensations exactly?* If not, use your own visual images of the scene, and reference sources such as a dictionary or thesaurus, to revise your word choices. You might also use a word web like this to zero in on the most vivid verbs.

| PH | **WRITING COACH** |

Further instruction and practice are available in *Prentice Hall Writing Coach*.

blazing and smoking

campfire flames

burning bright

dancing and flickering

Checking Your Language Once your sensory details chart contains vivid words, begin to draft your descriptive essay. As you do, review your word choices. If any words seem vague or dull, choose stronger ones. Put some power and punch into your description!

Drafting Strategies

Organize the details. Before you write, arrange the details in an order that will help readers picture the setting. Arrange important elements in **spatial order**—left to right, front to back, or outward from the most important feature.

Use figurative language. Figurative language is writing that is not meant to be taken literally. Use figurative language, such as similes and metaphors, to create vivid images and comparisons.

- **Simile:** a comparison using *like* or *as*. For example, "The campfire smoke was as thick as a curtain."

- **Metaphor:** a comparison in which one thing is referred to as if it *were* another. For example, "a curtain of smoke."

Establish a controlling idea. As you draft, weave together your descriptive details to create an overall impression of your subject. Choose details that work together to create a single, strong description.

Revising Strategies

Revise to vary sentence length. Check to make sure your writing flows in a clear and logical sequence. Do not repeat the same sentence structure over and over. Delete sentences that seem repetitive or unclear. Combine short, choppy sentences, or, to emphasize unusual or unique details, break a series of long sentences into shorter ones.

Sentence	Problem	Revision
Though there is so much darkness, there is light from the fire and the fire provides us warmth.	Long, repetitive sentence	The fire provides warmth and light from the cold darkness around our campsite.
The pine trees are tall. The trees smell of pine. The needles are crunchy.	Short, choppy sentences	The pine trees tower overhead. We crunch the pine needles as we walk and smell the fresh pine scent.

Revise to heighten interest. Share your writing with a partner. Have your partner describe the style of your writing and its tone, or emotional attitude. Ask if your style and tone are consistent. If they are not, revise by replacing words that seem out of place or suggest a feeling you do not mean to convey.

**Common Core
State Standards**

Writing

2. Write informative/explanatory texts to examine a topic and convey ideas, concepts, and information through the selection, organization, and analysis of relevant content.

5. With some guidance and support from peers and adults, develop and strengthen writing as needed by planning, revising, editing, rewriting, or trying a new approach.

Language

2. Demonstrate knowledge of the conventions of standard English capitalization, punctuation, and spelling when writing.

3.a. Vary sentence patterns for meaning, reader/listener interest, and style.

3.b. Maintain consistency in style and tone.

Revising for Errors with Possessive Nouns

Possessive nouns are used to show ownership. Most errors occur when apostrophes are left out or placed incorrectly.

Identifying Errors in Possessive Nouns To form the possessive form of most singular nouns, add an apostrophe and an *s*.

▶ **Examples: Mary's** coat; the **boss's** desk

Most plural nouns end in *-s*. To form the possessive form of most plural nouns, simply add an apostrophe.

▶ **Examples:** the **Smiths'** car; the **girls'** basketball team

Some plural nouns do not end in *-s*. To make the possessive form of these nouns, add an apostrophe and an *-s*.

▶ **Examples:** the **children's** toys; the **women's** book club

Type of Noun	Rule for Forming Possessive	Correct Possessive Form
singular noun	Add apostrophe -s.	*cat's* dish
singular noun ending in -s	Add apostrophe -s.	*dress's* hem
plural noun ending in -s	Add apostrophe.	*boys'* desks
plural noun that does not end in -s	Add apostrophe -s.	*mice's* nest

PH WRITING COACH

Further instruction and practice are available in *Prentice Hall Writing Coach*.

Fixing Errors To fix errors related to possessive nouns, follow these steps:

1. Identify each noun that shows ownership.
2. Decide whether the noun is singular or plural.
3. Follow the rules for making possessive nouns to fix any errors.

Grammar in Your Writing

Reread your essay and circle any possessive nouns that you find. Use the rules and examples to make the necessary corrections.

Student Model: Hailley White, Somerset, KY

 Common Core State Standards

Writing
6. Use technology, including the Internet, to produce and publish writing as well as to interact and collaborate with others.
Language
2.b. Spell correctly.

The Night Life

As I sit here on my cold, damp patio in early fall, I look at the dark sky. I see the beautiful, bright stars as they twinkle. I am always in awe as I look up there, and my heart sometimes skips a beat. In such a vast sky, the expanse of it all makes me feel as though I am as small as a tiny ant. Also in the darkness is the moon, the big hunk of cheese. The man in the moon is clearly visible. He is smiling down on all of us, watching our every move.

While staring up, I feel a tug at my pant leg. It is my little chunky dog, Bridget. Her tail starts to wag as I scratch behind her ears. She is a good dog—that is a fact. I hear her barking sometimes when I am sleeping, probably at some cat. Bridget is my guard dog, but I wish I could make more time to spend with her.

I love the sounds of nature at nighttime. The sound of crickets rubbing their little legs together makes the most lovely noise. Then there is the big hoot owl in some distant tree, hooting a lonesome tune. Off in the distance there is the big bullfrog. All of these wonderful sounds are like a luring lullaby that could rock me to sleep.

There are small, medium, and large trees out in the wild. Each one makes the blackness a little more scary. Though there is so much darkness, a tall street light shows off a silvery glow. This is helpful for people who are coming home from a late night shift.

The air smells like freshly cut grass. In the dim light, the grass looks like asphalt, it is so black. When I take a step, it is really damp from the fallen dew, and the wetness gives everything a shimmery look. There is also the smell of decaying leaves. They make a crunching noise underneath my feet. I feel so free just running around my backyard barefoot in the dark. The leaves and the dew feel absolutely refreshing. You should really try it sometime.

House after house surrounds me. One has its lights on, showing that someone is still awake. The other houses' lights are completely out, and everyone is probably snug in their beds. I can see red blinking lights over the hills and valleys. They must be towers for cell phones, so people can communicate—even in the dark.

The sounds are not the same as they are in the daylight. It is really amazing that the world can be so quiet for a few hours. The sounds of nature are really peaceful to me. There is a slight breeze blowing, but that is okay. I wish that I could stand here forever, staring up at the total darkness, except for the light of a few stars.

In the first sentence, Hailley presents the setting she will describe.

The writer creates a vivid image with a simile that compares night sounds to a lullaby.

Hailley brings her setting to life by using images that appeal to smell, sight, touch, and sound.

By organizing her essay to focus on sensory images that surround her, the writer makes readers feel like they are in the setting she describes.

Editing and Proofreading

Correct errors in grammar, spelling, and punctuation.

Focus on comparative and superlative adjectives. Be sure that you have used adjectives correctly.

- **Comparative adjectives compare two things.** The pine tree is *taller* than the oak tree. A sunset is *more beautiful* than a sunrise.

- **Superlative adjectives compare three or more things.** That pine tree is the *tallest* tree in the forest. This sunset is the *most beautiful* one I have ever seen.

Publishing and Presenting

Consider one of the following ways to share your writing:

Record it. Make an audio recording of your description. Ask classmates to imagine the setting as you play the tape.

Mail it. Send your descriptive essay to a friend or relative, enclosed in either a letter or an e-mail message.

Reflecting on Your Writing

Writer's Journal Jot down your answers to these questions:

- *How did gathering details of your setting help you to revisit it?*
- *Which strategy would you use again? Why?*

Rubric for Self-Assessment

Find evidence in your writing to address each category. Then use the rating scale to grade your work.

Spiral Review

Earlier in the unit, you learned about **singular and plural nouns** (p. 62). Review your writing for correct use of singular and plural nouns.

Criteria	Rating Scale
	not very *very*
Focus: How clear is the main impression?	1 2 3 4 5
Organization: How clear is your organization?	1 2 3 4 5
Support/Elaboration: How effectively do you use sensory details in your description?	1 2 3 4 5
Style: How vivid is the language?	1 2 3 4 5
Conventions: How good is your grammar, especially your use of possessive nouns?	1 2 3 4 5

Leveled Texts

Build your skills and improve your comprehension of literary
nonfiction with texts of increasing complexity.

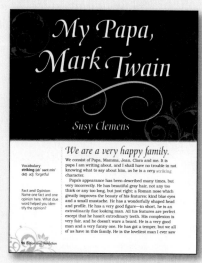

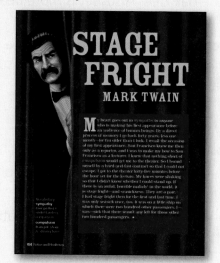

Read **"My Papa, Mark
Twain"** to find out how a girl
describes her father—a very
famous man.

Read **"Stage Fright"** to learn
how a popular humorist
suffered the first time he had
to make a speech.

Common Core State Standards

Meet these standards with either **"My Papa, Mark Twain"** (p. 96) or **"Stage Fright"** (p. 104).

Reading Informational Text
6. Determine an author's point of view or purpose in a
text and explain how it is conveyed in the text. *(Literary
Analysis: Author's Perspective)*

Writing
3. Write narratives to develop real or imagined experiences
or events using effective technique, relevant descriptive
details, and well-structured event sequences. *(Writing:
Dramatic Scene)*

Speaking and Listening
4. Present claims and findings, sequencing ideas logically
and using pertinent descriptions, facts, and details to
accentuate main ideas or themes; use appropriate eye

contact, adequate volume, and clear pronunciation.
(Research and Technology: Poster or Chart)

5. Include multimedia components (e.g., graphics, images,
music, sound) and visual displays in presentations to clarify
information. *(Research and Technology: Poster or Chart)*

Language
1.a. Ensure that pronouns are in the proper case.
(Conventions: Pronouns)

4.b. Use common, grade-appropriate Greek or Latin
affixes and roots as clues to the meaning of a word.
(Vocabulary: Word Study)

Reading Skill: Fact and Opinion

Nonfiction works often include an author's opinion as well as facts. A **fact** is information that can be proved. An **opinion** is a person's judgment or belief. To **recognize clues that indicate an opinion,** do this:

- Look for phrases that indicate an opinion, such as *I believe* or *in my opinion.*
- Look for words that indicate a personal judgment, such as *wonderful* or *terrible.*
- Be aware of words, such as *always, nobody, worst,* and *all,* that might indicate a personal judgment or viewpoint.

Literary Analysis: Author's Perspective

An **author's perspective,** or *author's point of view,* is the viewpoint from which he or she writes. This perspective is based on the author's beliefs and background. The author's perspective reveals his or her own feelings or personal interest in a subject.

Using the Strategy: Perspective Chart

As you read, use a diagram like this to look for details that reveal the author's perspective.

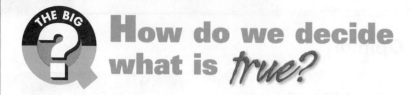

How do we decide what is *true?*

Writing About the Big Question

In "My Papa, Mark Twain," a girl gives a personal view of her father that differs in many ways from the public's image of him. Use these sentence starters to develop your ideas about the Big Question.

To find out what a person is **really** like, you must _____.

You can **confirm** your opinion about a person by _____.

While You Read Look for details that tell what Mark Twain is like at home, where the public cannot see him.

Vocabulary

Read each word and its definition. Decide whether you know the word well, know it a little bit, or do not know it at all. After you read, see how your knowledge of each word has increased.

- **striking** (strī´ kiŋ) *adj.* very noticeable or impressive; unusual (p. 96) *The actor's costume was <u>striking</u>.* strike *v.*

- **absent-minded** (ab´ sənt mīnd´ əd) *adj.* forgetful (p. 96) *I was so <u>absent-minded</u>, I lost my keys three times.* absent-mindedly *adv.* absent-mindedness *n.*

- **incessantly** (in ses´ ənt lē) *adv.* constantly; continuously (p. 97) *The neighbor banged on the drum <u>incessantly</u>.* incessant *adj.*

- **consequently** (kän´ si kwent´ lē) *adv.* as a result (p. 97) *I tripped and <u>consequently</u> spilled the milk.* consequent *adj.* consequence *n.* consequential *adj.*

- **impatient** (im´ pā´ shənt) *adj.* feeling or showing annoyance because of delay (p. 98) *She was <u>impatient</u> as she waited to cross the street.* impatiently *adv.* impatience *n.*

- **peculiar** (pi kyo͞ol´ yər) *adj.* out of the ordinary; odd (p. 98) *The woman's purple hair looked <u>peculiar</u>.* peculiarly *adv.* peculiarity *n.*

Word Study

The **Latin root -sequ-** or **-sec-** means "to follow."

Susy Clemens describes a funny scene in which her father opens a window and, **consequently**, the burglar alarm goes off. The sounding of the alarm *follows* the window opening.

Meet
Susy Clemens
(1872–1896)

Author of
My Papa, Mark Twain

Olivia Susan Clemens, called Susy, was the eldest daughter of American author Mark Twain. She was born in Elmira, New York, and grew up in her family's luxurious home in Hartford, Connecticut. There, her parents entertained famous people of the time—and Susy had the opportunity to meet them. **A Short Life** It is said that Susy was her father's favorite daughter. After she died at age twenty-four, Twain's writing turned darker and more serious.

BACKGROUND FOR THE BIOGRAPHY
Family Biographer

At age thirteen, Susy Clemens decided to secretly write a biography of her father, author Mark Twain. Susy kept her work-in-progress hidden in her bedroom. When her father saw the biography, he was delighted.

DID YOU KNOW?

Susy Clemens's complete biography of her father, *Papa: An Intimate Biography of Mark Twain*, was not published until 1985. The edition preserves her misspellings and punctuation errors.

My Papa, Mark Twain

Susy Clemens

We are a very happy family.

We consist of Papa, Mamma, Jean, Clara and me. It is papa I am writing about, and I shall have no trouble in not knowing what to say about him, as he is a *very* striking character.

Papa's appearance has been described many times, but very incorrectly. He has beautiful gray hair, not any too thick or any too long, but just right; a Roman nose which greatly improves the beauty of his features; kind blue eyes and a small mustache. He has a wonderfully shaped head and profile. He has a very good figure—in short, he is an extrodinarily fine looking man. All his features are perfect except that he hasn't extrodinary teeth. His complexion is very fair, and he doesn't ware a beard. He is a very good man and a very funny one. He has got a temper, but we all of us have in this family. He is the loveliest man I ever saw or ever hope to see—and oh, so absent-minded.

Papa's favorite game is billiards, and when he is tired and wishes to rest himself he stays up all night and plays billiards, it seems to rest his head. He smokes a great deal almost incessantly. He has the mind of an author exactly, some of the simplest things he can't understand. Our burglar alarm is often out of order, and papa had been obliged to take the mahogany room off from the alarm altogether for a time, because the burglar alarm had been in the habit of ringing even when the mahogany-room window was closed. At length he thought that perhaps the burglar alarm might be in order, and he decided to try and see; accordingly he put it on and then went down and opened the window; consequently the alarm bell rang, it would even if the alarm had been in order. Papa went despairingly upstairs and said to mamma, "Livy the mahogany room won't go on. I have just opened the window to see."

Vocabulary
incessantly (in ses´ ənt lē) *adv.* constantly; continually

consequently (kän´ si kwent´ lē) *adv.* as a result

Reading Check
What is the relationship between the writer and her subject?

Author's Perspective
How might Papa's retelling of the burglar alarm incident be different from Susy's version?

Vocabulary
impatient (im′pā′ shənt) *adj.* feeling or showing annoyance because of delay

peculiar (pi kyōōl′ yər) *adj.* out of the ordinary; odd

▼ **Critical Viewing**
What details in this picture show the Clemens family's closeness? **[Analyze]**

"Why, Youth," mamma replied. "If you've opened the window, why of course the alarm will ring!"

"That's what I've opened it for, why I just went down to see if it would ring!"

Mamma tried to explain to papa that when he wanted to go and see whether the alarm would ring while the window was closed he *mustn't go* and open the window— but in vain, papa couldn't understand, and got very impatient with mamma for trying to make him believe an impossible thing true. ●

Papa has a peculiar gait we like, it seems just to suit him, but most people do not; he always walks up and down the room while thinking and between each coarse at meals.

Papa is very fond of animals particularly of cats, we had a dear little gray kitten once that he named "Lazy" (papa always wears gray to match his hair and eyes) and he would carry him around on his shoulder, it was a mighty pretty sight! the gray cat sound asleep against papa's gray coat and hair. The names that he has give our different cats are really remarkably funny, they are named Stray Kit, Abner, Motley, Fraeulein, Lazy, Buffalo Bill, Soapy Sall, Cleveland, Sour Mash, and Pestilence and Famine.

Papa uses very strong language, but I have an idea not nearly so strong as when he first married mamma. A lady acquaintance of his is rather apt to interrupt what one is saying, and papa told mamma he thought he should say to the lady's husband "I am glad your wife wasn't present when the Deity said Let there be light."

Papa said the other day, "I am a mugwump[1] and a mugwump is pure from the marrow out." (Papa knows that I am writing this biography of him, and he said this for it.) He doesn't like to go to church at all, why I never understood, until just now, he told us

---

1. **mugwump** (mug ′ wump′) *n.* Republican who refused to support the party candidates in the 1884 election.

the other day that he couldn't bear to hear anyone talk but himself, but that he could listen to himself talk for hours without getting tired, of course he said this in joke, but I've no dought it was founded on truth.

One of papa's latest books is "The Prince and the Pauper" and it is unquestionably the best book he has ever written, some people want him to keep to his old style, some gentleman wrote him, "I enjoyed Huckleberry Finn immensely and am glad to see that you have returned to your old style." That enoyed me, that enoyed me greatly, because it trobles me to have so few people know papa, I mean realy know him, they think of Mark Twain as a humorist joking at everything; "And with a mop of reddish brown hair which sorely needs the barbar brush, a roman nose, short stubby mustache, a sad care-worn face, with maney crows' feet" etc. That is the way people picture papa, I have wanted papa to write a book that would reveal something of his kind sympathetic nature, and "The Prince and the Pauper" partly does it. The book is full of lovely charming ideas, and oh the language! It is perfect. I think that one of the most touching scenes in it is where the pauper is riding on horseback with his nobles in the "recognition procession" and he sees his mother oh and then what followed! How she runs to his side, when she sees him throw up his hand palm outward, and is rudely pushed off by one of the King's officers, and then how the little pauper's conscience troubles him when he remembers the shameful words that were falling from his lips when she was turned from his side "I know you not woman" and how his grandeurs were stricken valueless and his pride consumed to ashes. It is a wonderfully beautiful and touching little scene, and papa has described it so wonderfully. I never saw a man with so much variety of feeling as papa has; now the "Prince and the Pauper" is full of touching places, but there is always a streak of humor in them somewhere. Papa very seldom writes a passage without some humor in it somewhere and I don't think he ever will.

LITERATURE IN CONTEXT

Humanities Connection

Twain Makes His Mark
At the 1890 stage premiere of *The Prince and the Pauper*, Mark Twain had no idea that it would someday be made into several movies. The first, a 1915 silent film, starred a woman in both lead roles. The second version used identical twin boys.

The popularity of Twain's fiction did not make him wealthy, but at his death in 1910, he left behind a rich literary legacy.

Connect to the Literature

Why does Susy Clemens believe that *The Prince and the Pauper* is her father's best book?

Spiral Review
Central Idea How do the details about *The Prince and the Pauper* contribute to the author's central idea?

Author's Perspective
What details on this page show the author's feelings toward her subject?

BY
MARK TWAIN.

Clara and I are sure that papa played the trick on Grandma about the whipping that is related in "The Adventures of Tom Sawyer": "Hand me that switch." The switch hovered in the air, the peril was desperate—"My, look behind you Aunt!" The old lady whirled around and snatched her skirts out of danger. The lad fled on the instant, scrambling up the high board fence and disappeared over it.

We know papa played "Hookey" all the time. And how readily would papa pretend to be dying so as not to have to go to school! Grandma wouldn't make papa go to school, so she let him go into a printing office to learn the trade. He did so, and gradually picked up enough education to enable him to do about as well as those who were more studious in early life.

Critical Thinking

Cite textual evidence to support your responses.

© **1. Key Ideas and Details** Make a three-column chart. In the first column, write three details that Susy uses to describe her father's appearance. In the second column, list three words Susy would use to describe her father. Finally, in the third column, list three words you would use to describe him.

© **2. Key Ideas and Details (a)** What facts does the author give about her father's education? **(b) Deduce:** How do you think she feels about her father's lack of formal education?

© **3. Craft and Structure** This essay contains many misspelled words. Why do you think it was published without the errors being corrected?

© **4. Integration of Knowledge and Ideas** Susy offers a family member's perspective of Mark Twain. How might Susy's perspective affect the truth of her description? *[Connect to the Big Question: How do we decide what is true?]*

Reading Skill: Fact and Opinion

1. When the author says that *The Prince and the Pauper* is the best book Mark Twain has ever written, is she expressing a **fact** or an **opinion?** Explain.

2. In a chart like this one, list three opinions that Susy gives and the clue words that helped you identify each one.

Opinion	Clue Word

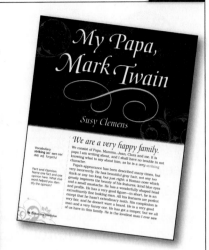

Literary Analysis: Author's Perspective

© **3. Craft and Structure** Identify two details of Susy Clemens's life that show her **perspective.**

© **4. Craft and Structure** How might the author's point of view be different if someone outside Twain's family had written this biography?

Vocabulary

© **Acquisition and Use** Describe each item by writing a sentence that uses a vocabulary word from the list on page 94.

1. a person who never stops talking

2. a cause and a result

3. someone with a bad memory

4. a person whom you greatly admire

5. a strange animal

6. a person who is annoyed because the school bus is late

Word Study Use what you know about the **Latin root -sequ-** to explain your answer to each question.

1. Do the days of the week occur in a *sequence*?

2. When does an author write a *sequel*?

Word Study

The **Latin root -sequ-** or **-sec-** means "to follow."

Apply It Explain how the root contributes to the meaning of these words. Consult a dictionary if necessary.

consecutive

second

consequent

How do we decide what is *true?*

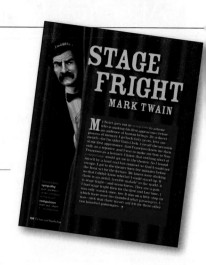

Writing About the Big Question

In "Stage Fright," the author describes having to hide his true feelings. Use this sentence starter to develop your ideas about the Big Question.

A person's behavior (does/does not) always **prove** that he or she is being **truthful** because _____.

While You Read Look for the ways that Mark Twain hides his true feelings.

Vocabulary

Read each word and its definition. Decide whether you know the word well, know it a little bit, or do not know it at all. After you read, see how your knowledge of each word has increased.

- **sympathy** (sim´ pə thē) *n.* understanding; compassion (p. 104) *Lola was filled with* <u>sympathy</u> *for her sister.* *sympathetic adj. sympathize v.*

- **compulsion** (kəm pul´ shən) *n.* driving force (p. 104) *A sudden* <u>compulsion</u> *led her to volunteer her time.* *compulsive adj.*

- **intently** (in tent´ lē) *adv.* purposefully; earnestly (p. 105) *Bruce always worked* <u>intently</u> *on his homework.* *intent adj. intention n.*

- **awed** (ôd) *adj.* filled with feelings of fear and wonder (p. 106) *The tourists were* <u>awed</u> *by the glaciers.* *awe n.*

- **agonizing** (ag´ ə nīz´ iŋ) *adj.* making great efforts or struggling; being in great pain (p. 106) *We were* <u>agonizing</u> *about my future.* *agonize v. agonized v. agony n.*

- **hereditary** (hə red´ i ter´ ē) *adj.* passed down from generation to generation (p. 106) *We learned about* <u>hereditary</u> *diseases in science class.* *heredity n. inherit v.*

Word Study

The **Latin root -pel-** or **-pul-** means "to drive."

Mark Twain describes being afraid to appear before an audience. He says that nothing short of a **compulsion**, or strong driving force, will get him to the theater.

Author of
STAGE FRIGHT

Mark Twain was born with a much longer name—Samuel Langhorn Clemens. Growing up along the Mississippi River, in Hannibal, Missouri, Twain became a riverboat pilot at the age of twenty-three. Later, when he became an author, he adopted the pen name Mark Twain. This name comes from slang used by riverboat pilots and means "two fathoms (six feet) deep."

A Legendary Writer Mark Twain is considered one of the best American writers of the nineteenth century. In addition to writing books, Twain gave humorous lectures around the world. "Stage Fright" is a transcription of a speech he gave after his daughter's first public singing recital.

DID YOU KNOW?

Mark Twain's novel *Tom Sawyer* (1876) is his most popular work, although many people consider *The Adventures of Huckleberry Finn* (1884) to be America's greatest novel.

BACKGROUND FOR THE SPEECH

Stage Fright

Many people experience a physical reaction to the stress of performing in public. Under stress, the heart beats faster, blood pressure rises, blood rushes to the muscles and brain, blood sugar increases for extra energy, sweat glands become active, and the mouth gets dry.

STAGE FRIGHT

MARK TWAIN

My heart goes out in sympathy to anyone who is making his first appearance before an audience of human beings. By a direct process of memory I go back forty years, less one month—for I'm older than I look. I recall the occasion of my first appearance. San Francisco knew me then only as a reporter, and I was to make my bow to San Francisco as a lecturer. I knew that nothing short of compulsion would get me to the theater. So I bound myself by a hard-and-fast contract so that I could not escape. I got to the theater forty-five minutes before the hour set for the lecture. My knees were shaking so that I didn't know whether I could stand up. If there is an awful, horrible malady[1] in the world, it is stage fright—and seasickness. They are a pair. I had stage fright then for the first and last time. I was only seasick once, too. It was on a little ship on which there were two hundred other passengers. I—was—sick. I was so sick that there wasn't any left for those other two hundred passengers. ●

1. **malady** (mal' ə dē) *n.* illness.

It was dark and lonely behind the scenes in that theater, and I peeked through the little peek holes they have in theater curtains and looked into the big auditorium. That was dark and empty, too. By and by it lighted up, and the audience began to arrive.

I had got a number of friends of mine, stalwart[2] men, to sprinkle themselves through the audience armed with big clubs. Every time I said anything they could possibly guess I intended to be funny, they were to pound those clubs on the floor. Then there was a kind lady in a box up there, also a good friend of mine, the wife of the governor. She was to watch me intently, and whenever I glanced toward her she was going to deliver a gubernatorial laugh that would lead the whole audience into applause.

At last I began. I had the manuscript tucked under a United States flag in front of me where I could get at it in case of need. But I managed to get started without it. I walked up and down—I was young in those days and needed the exercise—and talked and talked.

2. **stalwart** (stôl′ wərt) *adj.* strong; sturdy.

Fact and Opinion
Name one fact and one opinion in this paragraph.

Spiral Review
Central Idea How does the humor of this paragraph help to develop Twain's central idea?

Vocabulary
intently (in tent′ lē) *adv.* purposefully; earnestly

▼ **Critical Viewing**
Why might someone feel stage fright in front of an audience like this? **[Analyze]**

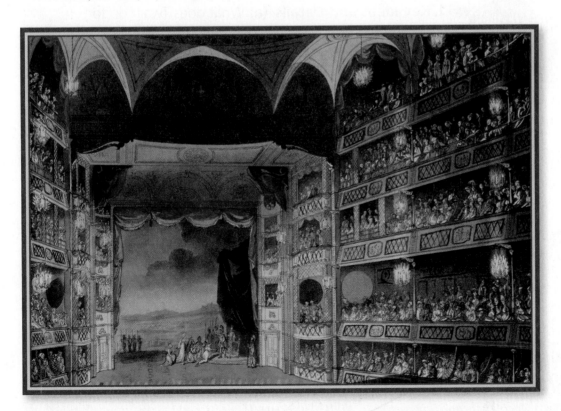

Author's Perspective
How would the story of Twain's first appearance be different if it were written by the governor's wife?

Right in the middle of the speech I had placed a gem. I had put in a moving, pathetic part which was to get at the hearts and souls of my hearers. When I delivered it, they did just what I hoped and expected. They sat silent and awed. I had touched them. Then I happened to glance up at the box where the governor's wife was—you know what happened. •

Well, after the first agonizing five minutes, my stage fright left me, never to return. I know if I was going to be hanged I could get up and make a good showing, and I intend to. But I shall never forget my feelings before the agony left me, and I got up here to thank you for her for helping my daughter, by your kindness, to live through her first appearance. And I want to thank you for your appreciation of her singing, which is, by the way, hereditary.

Critical Thinking

Cite textual evidence to support your responses.

© 1. **Key Ideas and Details (a)** What does Twain do to ensure that he will get a laugh during his first speech? **(b) Evaluate:** Do you think this is a good plan? Why or why not?

© 2. **Key Ideas and Details (a)** What physical reactions does Mark Twain experience before giving his first speech? **(b) Draw Conclusions:** How might a little bit of stage fright help a presenter?

© 3. **Key Ideas and Details (a)** What was the prearranged signal between Twain and the governor's wife? **(b) Speculate:** How do you think Twain felt after he'd delivered the "gem" in his speech?

© 4. **Integration of Knowledge and Ideas (a)** According to the text, how do Twain's feelings about public speaking change? **(b)** If he had been true to his feelings, how do you think he would have felt after his speech? *[Connect to the Big Question: How do we decide what is true?]*

Reading Skill: Fact and Opinion

1. In a chart like this, list three **opinions** that Twain gives and the clue words that helped you identify each one.

Opinion	Clue Word

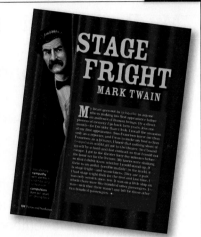

2. What **facts** does Twain give about the theater where he makes his first appearance?

Literary Analysis: Author's Perspective

3. Craft and Structure **(a)** Identify two feelings that Twain has about his first public-speaking engagement. **(b)** How does each detail convey his personal interest?

4. Craft and Structure How might the **author's perspective,** or point of view, have been different if Twain's daughter had written "Stage Fright"?

Vocabulary

Acquisition and Use Describe each item by writing a sentence that uses a word from the list on page 102.

1. an athlete's strong desire to compete

2. a mother's feelings for her sick child

3. the way a fan watches the ending of a close game

4. what a person felt during a powerful storm

5. a trait, like eye color, that a person shares with a parent

6. a painful or embarrassing moment

Word Study Use what you know about the **Latin root -pel-** or **-pul-** to explain your answer to each question.

1. If something *repulses* you, do you want to be near it?

2. Why do most people feel *compelled* to tell the truth?

Word Study

The **Latin root -pel-** or **-pul-** means "to drive."

Apply It Explain how the root contributes to the meaning of these words. Consult a dictionary if you need to.

impulse
repel
compulsory

Integrated Language Skills

My Papa, Mark Twain • Stage Fright

Conventions: Pronouns

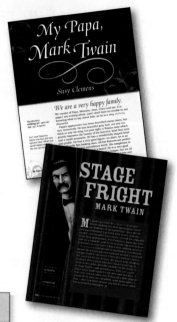

A **pronoun** is a word that takes the place of a noun or another pronoun.

A **personal pronoun** refers to a specific noun that is named elsewhere in the text. A **subjective pronoun** is the subject of the sentence. An **objective pronoun** is the object. It receives the action of the verb. In this sentence, *we* is subjective and *him* is objective: *We waited for him.* **Possessive pronouns** show ownership.

Examples of Personal Pronouns	Examples of Possessive Pronouns
Jan said that *she* would help paint the fence.	Hans rode *his* bike to the park.
Ask Dave and Sally if *they* are going to the play.	Jim and Ramon are eating *their* lunch.

Practice A Identify the pronoun in each sentence. Then, tell whether it is a personal pronoun or a possessive pronoun.

1. Susy Clemens wrote about her father.
2. His professional name was Mark Twain.
3. When did he write his first book?
4. Have you read *Tom Sawyer*?
5. The librarian read a chapter to us.

© **Reading Application** Scan "My Papa, Mark Twain," to find two personal pronouns and two possessive pronouns.

Practice B Identify each of these words as either a personal pronoun or a possessive pronoun. Then, use each one in a sentence.

1. we
2. its
3. your
4. them
5. their

© **Writing Application** Write two sentences with personal and possessive pronouns. (Example: *He was nervous about speaking in front of his peers.*)

PH WRITING COACH Further instruction and practice are available in *Prentice Hall Writing Coach*.

Writing

Narrative Text Turn a passage from either "My Papa, Mark Twain" or "Stage Fright" into a **dramatic scene.** Follow this format:

Papa: I just opened the window to see if the alarm works.

Mamma *(laughing)*: If you've opened the window, why of course the alarm will ring!

- First, decide which characters are present in the scene and what they would say to each other.
- Add stage directions to show the characters' actions.

Grammar Application Use proper forms of personal pronouns and possessive pronouns in your dramatic scene.

Writing Workshop: *Work in Progress*

Prewriting for Narration For an autobiographical narrative you may write, list experiences that taught you how to be happier. Select one experience as your topic. Make an Experience Web to note the events that occurred and the people who shared your experience. Save the Experience Web in your writing portfolio.

Research and Technology

Build and Present Knowledge With a partner, research facts about Mark Twain. Use those facts to make and present a **poster** or **chart.**

- If you read "My Papa, Mark Twain," find facts about some of the main characters in Mark Twain's books.
- If you read "Stage Fright," find facts about stage fright.

Follow these steps to complete the assignment:

- Search for facts in reliable sources. In a library or on the Internet, select encyclopedias and other nonfiction sources.
- From your sources, jot down notes.
- Decide which type of graphic organizer to use in order to present your information clearly.
- Present your poster or chart, summarizing the most important points of your research. As you present your work, speak loudly and clearly enough to be heard and understood.

Common Core State Standards

L.6.1.a; W.6.3; SL.6.4, SL.6.5
[For the full wording of the standards, see page 92.]

Use this prewriting activity to prepare for the **Writing Workshop** on page 154.

PHLit Online!
www.PHLitOnline.com
- Interactive graphic organizers
- Grammar tutorial
- Interactive journals

© Leveled Texts

Build your skills and improve your comprehension of literary nonfiction with texts of increasing complexity.

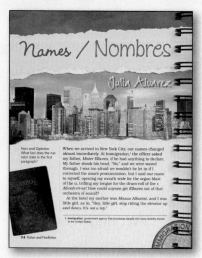

Read **"Names/Nombres"** to find out how language differences affect the relationships between a Latina girl and her classmates at school.

Read **"The Lady and the Spider"** to learn facts that may change your feelings about spiders.

© Common Core State Standards

Meet these standards with either **"Names/Nombres"** (p. 114) or **"The Lady and the Spider"** (p. 124).

Reading Literature
4. Determine the meanings of words and phrases as they are used in a text, including figurative and connotative meanings; analyze the impact of specific word choice on meaning and tone. (*Literary Analysis: Tone*)

Reading Informational Text
8. Trace and evaluate the argument and specific claims in a text, distinguishing claims that are supported by reasons and evidence from claims that are not. (*Reading Skill: Fact and Opinion*)

Writing
3.d. Use precise words and phrases, relevant descriptive details, and sensory language to convey experiences and events. (*Writing: Personal Anecdote*)

Speaking and Listening
6. Adapt speech to a variety of contexts and tasks, demonstrating command of formal English when indicated or appropriate. (*Speaking and Listening: Monologue*)

Language
1. Demonstrate command of the conventions of standard English grammar and usage when writing or speaking.

1.b. Use intensive pronouns. (*Conventions: Pronouns*)

6. Acquire and use accurately grade-appropriate general academic and domain-specific words and phrases; gather vocabulary knowledge when considering a word or phrase important to comprehension or expression. (*Vocabulary: Word Study*)

Reading Skill: Fact and Opinion

To evaluate the author's claims or ideas in a work of nonfiction, you must understand the difference between **fact** and **opinion.** A **fact,** unlike an opinion, can be proved. An **opinion** expresses a judgment that can be supported but not proved. You can **check facts by using resources** such as the following:

- dictionaries
- encyclopedias
- reliable Web sites

Using the Strategy: Fact-Checking Chart

To help you keep track of facts found in a nonfiction work, use a chart like the one shown.

Fact	Reference Source	True	False
Tigers live in only cold climates.	Internet		✓

Literary Analysis: Tone

The **tone** of a literary work is the writer's attitude toward his or her audience and subject. The tone can often be described in one word, such as *playful, serious,* or *humorous.* Factors that contribute to the tone are word choice, sentence structure, and sentence length. Notice how word choice can create a friendly tone, as in this example:

If you plan ahead, I promise you, you'll have the best party ever!

As you read, look for details that convey a certain tone.

How do we decide what is *true?*

Writing About the Big Question

In "Names/Nombres," a girl hesitates to correct people who mispronounce her name, even though it hurts. Use this sentence starter to develop your ideas about the Big Question.

Sometimes it takes courage to show your **true** feelings because

_____.

While You Read Think about what is revealed by the author's true feelings about her name.

Vocabulary

Read each word and its definition. Decide whether you know the word well, know it a little bit, or do not know it at all. After you read, see how your knowledge of each word has increased.

- **mistook** (mis tŏŏk´) *v.* identified incorrectly; misunderstood (p. 115) *She mistook his nod for a yes.* mistake *n.* mistaken *adj.*

- **pursue** (pər sōō´) *v.* be involved in; follow (p. 115) *I will pursue my dream and become a doctor.* pursued *v.* pursuing *v.* pursuit *n.*

- **transport** (trans pôrt´) *v.* carry from one place to another (p. 116) *Harry could not transport the heavy refrigerator by himself.* transported *v.* transporting *v.* transportation *n.*

- **inevitably** (in ev´ i tə blē´) *adv.* unavoidably (p. 117) *Inevitably, the sun shines when we bring an umbrella.* inevitable *adj.* inevitability *n.*

- **chaotic** (kā ät´ ik) *adj.* completely confused (p. 118) *Our house became chaotic because of all the guests.* chaos *n.* chaotically *adv.*

- **inscribed** (in skrībd´) *v.* written on (p. 120) *The watch was inscribed with my initials.* inscribing *v.* inscription *n.*

Word Study

The **Latin root -scrib-** or **-scrip-** means "to write."

In this story, the narrator's family buys a special cake for her graduation party. The cake is **inscribed** with writing that says "Happy Graduation."

Meet
Julia Alvarez
(b. 1950)

Author of
Names / Nombres

Although Julia Alvarez was born in New York City, her family soon returned to the Dominican Republic. After Julia's father worked to overthrow the dictator there, he and his family fled the country. Julia was ten years old when they arrived in the United States.

Name Game From the moment young Julia arrived in New York City, she felt she had to "translate her experiences into English." Sometimes, as she shows in "Names/Nombres," it was the English speakers who did the translating.

BACKGROUND FOR THE ESSAY
Languages

In "Names/Nombres," Julia Alvarez tells how language differences have made her feel like an outsider. For example, in Spanish, the letter *j* is used for the sound English speakers associate with *h*. The letter *r* has a very different sound from its sound in English. Although many Spanish words have found their way into English, some of their pronunciations have changed over time.

DID YOU KNOW?

In high school, Julia Alvarez realized that she wanted to pursue a career as a writer. Today, she says, "I write to find out what I'm thinking."

Names / Nombres

Julia Alvarez

Fact and Opinion
What fact does the narrator state in the first paragraph?

When we arrived in New York City, our names changed almost immediately. At Immigration,[1] the officer asked my father, *Mister Elbures*, if he had anything to declare. My father shook his head, "No," and we were waved through. I was too afraid we wouldn't be let in if I corrected the man's pronunciation, but I said our name to myself, opening my mouth wide for the organ blast of the *a*, trilling my tongue for the drum-roll of the *r*, *All-vah-rrr-es*! How could anyone get *Elbures* out of that orchestra of sound?

At the hotel my mother was *Missus Alburest*, and I was little girl, as in, "Hey, *little girl*, stop riding the elevator up and down. It's *not* a toy."

---

1. Immigration government agency that processes people who have recently moved to the United States.

When we moved into our new apartment building, the super[2] called my father *Mister Alberase*, and the neighbors who became mother's friends pronounced her name *Jew-lee-ah* instead of *Hoo-lee-ah*. I, her namesake, was known as *Hoo-lee-tah* at home. But at school, I was *Judy* or *Judith*, and once an English teacher mistook me for *Juliet*.

It took awhile to get used to my new names. I wondered if I shouldn't correct my teachers and new friends. But my mother argued that it didn't matter. "You know what your friend Shakespeare said, '*A rose by any other name would smell as sweet.*'" My father had gotten into the habit of calling any famous author "my friend" because I had begun to write poems and stories in English class.

By the time I was in high school, I was a popular kid, and it showed in my name. Friends called me *Jules* or *Hey Jude*, and once a group of troublemaking friends my mother forbade me to hang out with called me *Alcatraz*. I was *Hoo-lee-tah* only to Mami and Papi and uncles and aunts who came over to eat *sancocho* on Sunday afternoons—old world folk whom I would just as soon go back to where they came from and leave me to pursue whatever mischief I wanted to in America. JUDY ALCATRAZ: the name on the Wanted Poster would read. Who would ever trace her to me? ●

My older sister had the hardest time getting an American name for herself because *Mauricia* did not translate into English. Ironically, although she had the most foreign-sounding name, she and I were the Americans in the family. We had been born in New York City when our parents had first tried immigration and then gone back "home," too homesick to

---

2. **super** *n.* superintendent; person who manages an apartment building.

Names/Nombres **115**

Vocabulary

transport (trans pôrt´)
v. carry from one
place to another

~~Judy~~

~~Alcatraz~~

Maureen

~~Maudy~~

stay. My mother often
told the story of how she
had almost changed
my sister's name in
the hospital.

After the delivery,
Mami and some
other new mothers
were cooing over
their new baby sons
and daughters and
exchanging names and
weights and delivery
stories. My mother was
embarrassed among the Sallys
and Janes and Georges and
Johns to reveal the rich, noisy
name of *Mauricia*, so when her turn
came to brag, she gave her baby's name
as *Maureen*.

"Why'd ya give her an Irish name with so
many pretty Spanish names to choose from?"
one of the women asked.

My mother blushed and admitted her baby's real
name to the group. Her mother-in-law had recently died,
she apologized, and her husband had insisted that the
first daughter be named after his mother, *Mauran*. My
mother thought it the ugliest name she had ever heard,
and she talked my father into what she believed was
an improvement, a combination of *Mauran* and her own
mother's name, *Felicia*.

"Her name is *Mao-ree-shee-ah*," my mother said to the
group of women.

"Why that's a beautiful name," the new mothers cried.
"*Moor-ee-sha, Moor-ee-sha*," they cooed into the pink
blanket. *Moor-ee-sha* it was when we returned to the States
eleven years later. Sometimes, American tongues found
even that mispronunciation tough to say and called her
Maria or *Marsha* or *Maudy* from her nickname *Maury*.
I pitied her. What an awful name to have to transport
across borders!

My little sister, Ana, had the easiest time of all. She was plain *Anne*—that is, only her name was plain, for she turned out to be the pale, blond "American beauty" in the family. The only Hispanic thing about her was the affectionate nicknames her boyfriends sometimes gave her. *Anita*, or as one goofy guy used to sing to her to the tune of the banana advertisement, *Anita Banana*.[3]

Later, during her college years in the late '60s, there was a push to pronounce Third World names correctly. I remember calling her long distance at her group house and a roommate answering.

"Can I speak to Ana?" I asked, pronouncing her name the American way.

"Ana?" The man's voice hesitated. "Oh! you must mean *Ah-nah!*"

Our first few years in the States, though, ethnicity was not yet "in." Those were the blond, blue-eyed, bobby sock years of junior high and high school before the '60s ushered in peasant blouses, hoop earrings, serapes.[4] My initial desire to be known by my correct Dominican name faded. I just wanted to be Judy and merge with the Sallys and Janes in my class. But inevitably, my accent and coloring gave me away. "So where are you from, Judy?"

"New York," I told my classmates. After all, I had been born blocks away at Columbia Presbyterian Hospital.

"I mean, *originally*."

"From the Caribbean," I answered vaguely, for if I specified, no one was quite sure on what continent our island was located.

"Really? I've been to Bermuda. We went last April for spring vacation. I got the worst sunburn! So, are you from Portoriko?"

"No," I sighed. "From the Dominican Republic."

"Where's that?"

"South of Bermuda."

"Her name is Mao-ree-shee-ah," my mother said to the group of women.

Vocabulary
inevitably
(in ev´ i tə blē) *adv.* unavoidably

Fact and Opinion
How could you check the fact that the narrator was born in Columbia Presbyterian Hospital?

Reading
Check
What other names was Julia known by when she came to the United States?

3. ***Anita Banana*** play on the name *Chiquita Banana*, a character in a company's ad.
4. **serapes** (sə rä´ pēz) *n.* colorful shawls worn in Latin America.

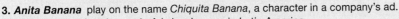

They were just being curious, I knew, but I burned with shame whenever they singled me out as a "foreigner," a rare, exotic friend.

"Say your name in Spanish, oh please say it!" I had made mouths drop one day by rattling off my full name, which according to Dominican custom, included my middle names, Mother's and Father's surnames for four generations back.

"Julia Altagracia María Teresa Álvarez Tavares Perello Espaillat Julia Pérez Rochet González," I pronounced it slowly, a name as **chaotic** with sounds as a Middle Eastern bazaar[5] or market day in a South American village.

My Dominican heritage was never more apparent than when my extended family attended school occasions. For my graduation, they all came, the whole lot of aunts and uncles and the many little cousins who snuck in without tickets. They sat in the first row in order to better understand the Americans' fast-spoken English. But how

---

5. **bazaar** (bə zär´) *n.* marketplace, frequently outdoors.

Vocabulary
chaotic (kā ät´ ik) *adj.* completely confused

Ⓒ

Spiral Review
Central Idea Explain why Alvarez's Spanish name is an important detail in this essay.

could they listen when they were constantly speaking among themselves in florid-sounding phrases, rococo[6] consonants, rich, rhyming vowels?

Introducing them to my friends was a further trial to me. These relatives had such complicated names and there were so many of them, and their relationships to myself were so convoluted. There was my Tía Josefina, who was not really an aunt but a much older cousin. And her daughter, Aida Margarita, who was adopted, *una hija de crianza*. My uncle of affection, Tío José, brought my *madrina* Tía Amelia and her *comadre* Tía Pilar. My friends rarely had more than a "Mom and Dad" to introduce.

After the commencement ceremony my family waited outside in the parking lot while my friends and I signed yearbooks with nicknames which recalled our high school good times: "Beans" and "Pepperoni" and "Alcatraz." We hugged and cried and promised to keep in touch.

---

6. **rococo** (rə kō´ kō) *adj.* fancy style of art of the early eighteenth century.

"Say your name in Spanish, oh please say it!"

Our goodbyes went on too long. I heard my father's voice calling out across the parking lot, "*Hoo-lee-tah! Vamonos!*"

Back home, my *tíos* and *tías* and *primas*, Mami and Papi, and *mis hermanas* had a party for me with *sancocho* and a storebought *pudín*, inscribed with *Happy Graduation, Julie.* There were many gifts—that was a plus to a large family! I got several wallets and a suitcase with my initials and a graduation charm from my godmother and money from my uncles. The biggest gift was a portable typewriter from my parents for writing my stories and poems.

Someday, the family predicted, my name would be well-known throughout the United States. I laughed to myself, wondering which one I would go by.

Critical Thinking

1. Key Ideas and Details (a) How does Julia's family say her name? **(b) Analyze Cause and Effect:** Explain why some English speakers mispronounce her name.

2. Key Ideas and Details (a) How does Julia respond when her classmates ask her where she comes from? **(b) Draw Conclusions:** Why does she respond as she does? **(c) Evaluate:** Would you make the same decision in the same situation? Why or why not?

3. Craft and Structure (a) Explain how the title captures the focus of Alvarez's narrative. **(b) Analyze:** How do Alvarez's feelings about the topic change over time? **(c) Synthesize:** What do names represent for Alvarez and others?

4. Integration of Knowledge and Ideas (a) Do you feel that your name shows your true personality and identity? **(b)** If you could pick a new name, what would it be? **(c)** How might this new name express your true personality and identity? *[Connect to the Big Question: How do we decide what is true?]*

Cite textual evidence to support your responses.

Reading Skill: Fact and Opinion

1. How might you check the fact that Julia Alvarez was born in New York City?

2. Alvarez relates the story of her sister's name by saying, "My mother thought it the ugliest name she had ever heard." Is her mother stating a **fact** or an **opinion?** Explain.

Literary Analysis: Tone

3. Craft and Structure "Names/Nombres" is written in an informal, or friendly, **tone.** In a chart like the one shown, rewrite the two sentences in a more serious, or formal, tone.

Informal Tone	Formal Tone
"It took a while to get used to my new names." "My mother blushed and admitted her baby's real name to the group."	

Vocabulary

Acquisition and Use Explain why each statement is true or false.

1. A *chaotic* place is calm and relaxing.

2. Something etched with initials has been *inscribed*.

3. If you do not study for a test, you will *inevitably* pass.

4. A net is a useful tool if you want to *transport* water.

5. A hospital is a good place to *pursue* a medical career.

6. People commonly *mistook* me for my identical twin.

Word Study Use context and what you know about the **Latin root -scrib-** or **-scrip-** to explain your answers.

1. How would the *script* of a play be helpful to an actor?

2. Why might you get in trouble for *scribbling* in a book?

Word Study

The **Latin root -scrib-** or **-scrip-** means "to write."

Apply It Explain how the root contributes to the meaning of these words. Consult a dictionary if necessary.

prescription
manuscript
scribe

How do we decide what is *true?*

Writing About the Big Question

"The Lady and the Spider" presents both true statements and opinions about spiders. Use these sentence starters to develop your ideas about the Big Question.

Some people fear spiders because _____.

An important **fact** about spiders is _____.

While You Read Look for true statements and common opinions about spiders.

Vocabulary

Read each word and its definition. Decide whether you know the word well, know it a little bit, or do not know it at all. After you have read, see how your knowledge of each word has increased.

- **mode** (mōd) *n.* a way of acting, doing, or being (p. 124) *Mom was in a professional mode for her meeting.*

- **frenzied** (fren´ zēd) *adj.* acting in a wild, uncontrolled way (p. 125) *The dogs were frenzied when they saw the food. frenzy n.*

- **inhabited** (in ha´ bit əd) *adj.* lived in; occupied (p. 126) *The house on the beach is inhabited. inhabit v. habitat n.*

- **equipped** (ē kwipt´) *adj.* having what is needed (p. 127) *The student was well equipped to take the test. equipment n.*

- **dimensions** (də men´ shənz) *n.* measurements; importance. (p. 127) *Painting gave new dimensions to her art.*

- **catastrophe** (kə tas´ trə fē) *n.* disaster or misfortune (p. 128) *The car accident was a catastrophe. catastrophic adj. catastrophically adv.*

Word Study

The **Latin root -met-** or **-mens-** means "to measure."

In this essay, the writer says that if humans were more like spiders, their lives would take on new **dimensions.** He means that their lives would change in so many ways that it would be hard to measure.

Author of
The Lady and the Spider

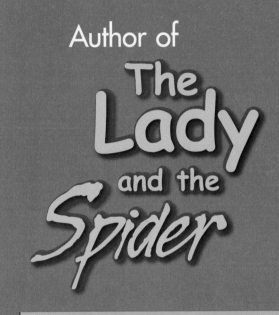

Ask Robert Fulghum what he has learned about life and he might say, "All I really need to know I learned in kindergarten." That is the title of his first bestseller, which includes humorous essays such as "The Lady and the Spider."

Helping Others Fulghum believes in helping others. He raises money for charity by playing in a band called the Rock Bottom Remainders. His fellow musicians include authors Stephen King and Amy Tan, and Matt Groening, the creator of The Simpsons. Fulghum has also donated money from one of his books to a human rights charity. "I don't think the thing is to be well known," he says, "but being worth knowing."

BACKGROUND FOR THE ESSAY

Phobias

The mere mention of certain animals—such as spiders—horrifies some people. An unreasonable fear is known as a *phobia*. The woman in "The Lady and the Spider" suffers from arachnophobia, a fear of spiders.

DID YOU KNOW?

Fulghum did not set out to be a writer. He worked as a ranch hand, a salesman, an art teacher, and a minister before becoming a full-time writer. Fulghum's seven books have sold more than 15 million copies worldwide.

The Lady and the Spider

Robert Fulghum

This is my neighbor. Nice lady.

Vocabulary
mode (mōd) *n.* a way of acting, doing, or being

Coming out her front door, on her way to work and in her "looking good" mode. She's locking the door now and picking up her daily luggage: purse, lunch bag, gym bag for aerobics, and the garbage bucket to take out. She turns, sees me, gives me the big, smiling Hello, takes three steps across her front porch. And goes "AAAAAAAAGGGGGGGGGGHHHHHHHHHH!!!!" (*That's a direct quote.*) At about the level of a fire engine at full cry. Spider web! She has walked full force into a spider web. And the pressing question, of course: Just where is the spider *now*?

She flings her baggage in all directions. And at the same time does a high-kick, jitterbug sort of dance—like a mating stork in crazed heat. Clutches at her face and hair and goes "AAAAAAAGGGGGGGHHHHHHHHH!!!!!" at a new level of intensity. Tries opening the front door without unlocking it. Tries again. Breaks key in the lock. Runs around the house headed for the back door. Doppler effect[1] of "A A A A A G G G H H H H a a g g h . . ."

Now a different view of this scene. Here is the spider. Rather ordinary, medium gray, middle-aged lady spider. She's been up since before dawn working on her web, and all is well. Nice day, no wind, dew point just right to keep things sticky. She's out checking the moorings[2] and thinking about the little gnats she'd like to have for breakfast. Feeling good. Ready for action. All of a sudden—earthquake, tornado, volcano. The web is torn loose and is wrapped around a frenzied moving haystack, and a huge piece of raw-but-painted meat is making a sound the spider never heard before: "AAAAAAA-GGGGGGGGGHHHHHHHHHH!!!!!!" It's too big to wrap up and eat later, and it's moving too much to hold down. Jump for it? Hang on and hope? Dig in?

Human being. She has caught a human being. And the pressing question is, of course: Where is

"AAAAAGGGHHHHaaggh..."

it going and what will it do when it gets there?

The neighbor lady thinks the spider is about the size of a lobster and has big rubber lips and poisonous fangs. The

---

1. **Doppler effect** apparent change in the pitch of a sound, caused by the movement of the source or the listener.
2. **moorings** *n.* lines or cables that hold a ship or something else in place.

Tone
How does the direct quotation from the lady indicate an informal tone?

Vocabulary
frenzied (fren´ zēd) *adj.* acting in a wild, uncontrolled way

Spiral Review
Central Idea What point is the author making with this description of the spider's view of a person?

Reading Check
Why is the speaker's neighbor screaming?

Vocabulary

inhabited (in hab´ it əd)
adj. lived in; occupied

neighbor lady will probably strip to the skin and take a full shower and shampoo just to make sure it's gone—and then put on a whole new outfit to make certain she is not inhabited.

The spider? Well, if she survives all this, she will really have something to talk about—the one that got away that was THIS BIG. "And you should have seen the JAWS on the thing!"

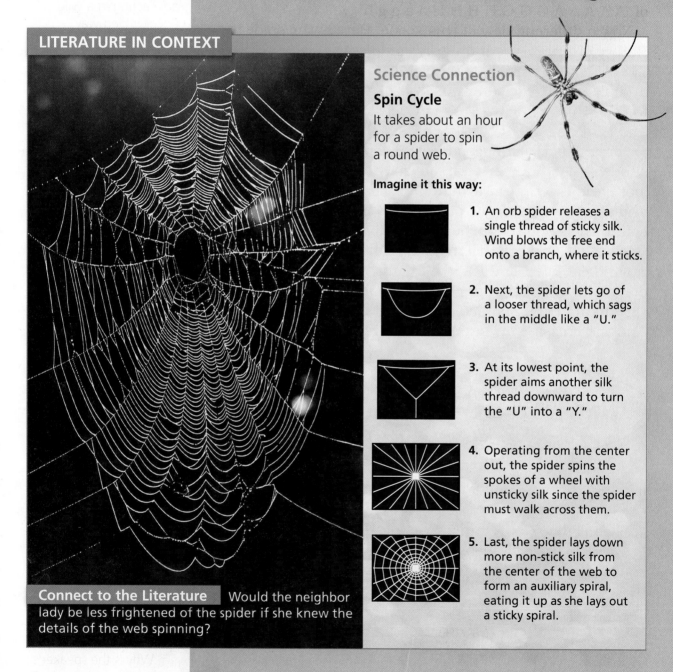

LITERATURE IN CONTEXT

Science Connection

Spin Cycle
It takes about an hour for a spider to spin a round web.

Imagine it this way:

1. An orb spider releases a single thread of sticky silk. Wind blows the free end onto a branch, where it sticks.

2. Next, the spider lets go of a looser thread, which sags in the middle like a "U."

3. At its lowest point, the spider aims another silk thread downward to turn the "U" into a "Y."

4. Operating from the center out, the spider spins the spokes of a wheel with unsticky silk since the spider must walk across them.

5. Last, the spider lays down more non-stick silk from the center of the web to form an auxiliary spiral, eating it up as she lays out a sticky spiral.

Connect to the Literature   Would the neighbor lady be less frightened of the spider if she knew the details of the web spinning?

Spiders. Amazing creatures. Been around maybe 350 million years, so they can cope with about anything. Lots of them, too—sixty or seventy thousand per suburban acre. It's the web thing that I envy. Imagine what it would be like if people were equipped like spiders. If we had this little six-nozzled aperture[3] right at the base of our spine and we could make yards of something like glass fiber with it. Wrapping packages would be a cinch! Mountain climbing would never be the same. Think of the Olympic events. And child rearing would take on new dimensions. Well, you take it from there. It boggles the mind. Cleaning up human-sized webs would be a mess, on the other hand.

All this reminds me of a song I know. And you know, too. And your parents and your children, they know. About the eensy-weensy spider. Went up the waterspout. Down came the rain and washed the spider out. Out came the sun and dried up all the rain. And the eensy-weensy spider went up the spout again. You probably know the motions, too.

What's the deal here? Why do we all know that song? Why do we keep passing it on to our kids? Especially when it puts spiders in such a favorable light? Nobody goes "AAAAAAAGGGGGGGGGHHHHHHHHH!!!!!" when they sing it. Maybe because it puts the life adventure in such clear and simple terms. The small creature is alive and looks for adventure. Here's the drainpipe—a long tunnel going up toward some light. The spider doesn't even think about it— just goes. Disaster befalls it—rain, flood, powerful forces. And the spider is knocked down and out beyond where it started. Does the spider say, "To heck with that"? No. Sun comes out—clears things up—dries off the spider. And the small creature goes over to the drainpipe and looks up and thinks it really wants to know what is up there. It's a little wiser now—checks the sky first, looks for better toeholds, says a spider prayer, and heads up through mystery toward the light and wherever.

---

3. **aperture** (ap´ ər chər) *n.* hole or opening.

"AAAAAGGGGHHHHHaaggh..."

Fact and Opinion
List one fact and one opinion in this paragraph.

Vocabulary
equipped (ē kwipt´) *adj.* having what is needed
dimensions (də men´ shəns) *n.* measurements; importance

Tone
What do these questions suggest about the author's attitude toward the song?

▼ **Critical Viewing**
What details about this spider might make a person feel afraid? **[Analyze]**

Vocabulary

catastrophe
(kə tas´ trə fē) *n.*
disaster or misfortune

Fact and Opinion

How could you check to
see if "spiders tell their
kids" about how to
survive?

Living things have been doing just that for a long, long
time. Through every kind of disaster and setback and
catastrophe. We are survivors. And we teach our kids
about that. And maybe spiders tell their kids about it, too,
in their spider sort of way.

So the neighbor lady will survive and be a little wiser
coming out the door on her way to work. And the spider,
if it lives, will do likewise. And if not, well, there are lots
more spiders, and the word gets around. Especially when
the word is "AAAAAAAGGGGGGGGHHHHHHHHH!!!!"

Critical Thinking

1. Key Ideas and Details **(a)** What does the lady do with
her baggage? **(b) Infer:** How does she feel about spiders?

2. Key Ideas and Details **(a)** What are two thoughts
the woman has about the situation? **(b)** What are two
thoughts the spider has about the situation? **(c) Analyze:**
Why do you think the author tells what both the lady and
the spider are thinking?

3. Key Ideas and Details **(a)** How do you think the
author feels about spiders? **(b) Analyze:** What makes
you think this?

4. Integration of Knowledge and Ideas **(a)** Whose side
are you on—the lady's or the spider's? **(b) Discuss:** In a
small group, discuss. Then, select one response to share
with the class.

5. Integration of Knowledge and Ideas **(a)** How are the
lady's and the author's feelings about spiders alike and different? **(b)** Which feelings seem based on truth, and which
seem based on fears and opinions? *[Connect to the Big
Question: How do we decide what is true?]*

Cite textual
evidence to
support your
responses.

Reading Skill: Fact and Opinion

1. (a) List two details about the lady's fear that the author presents as **facts. (b)** List two details about the lady's fear that the author presents as **opinions.**

2. What are two facts from the essay that you could prove true or false by checking resources on the Internet?

Literary Analysis: Tone

© 3. Craft and Structure The passage in the chart has an informal **tone.** Rewrite it in a more serious, or formal, tone.

Informal Tone	Formal Tone
"Spiders. Amazing creatures. Been around maybe 350 million years, so they can cope with just about anything. Lots of them, too—sixty or seventy thousand per suburban acre. It's the web thing that I envy."	

Vocabulary

© Acquisition and Use Explain why each statement is true or false.

1. Houses cannot be *inhabited*.

2. Your *mode* of dressing is your own unique style.

3. A *frenzied* person is very calm and organized.

4. To win a wonderful prize would be a *catastrophe*.

5. Your teacher can tell you the *dimensions* of a project.

6. The basketball team is *equipped* with bases and bats.

Word Study Use what you know about the **Latin root -met-** or **-mens-** to explain your answer to each question.

1. Why is the *metric* system a useful tool?

2. Is the size of a whale *immense?*

Word Study

The **Latin root -met-** or **-mens-** means "to measure."

Apply It Explain how the root contributes to the meaning of these words. Consult a dictionary if necessary.

diameter
immense
thermometer

Integrated Language Skills

Names/Nombres • The Lady and the Spider

Conventions: Pronouns

A **pronoun** is a word that takes the place of a noun or another pronoun.

Interrogative pronouns are used in questions.

Indefinite pronouns refer to one or more objects or people.

Interrogative Pronouns	Indefinite Pronouns
Who would like an apple?	*Some* of my friends live in Cleveland.
Which of these hats is yours?	*None* of the children are absent.
With *whom* are you going to the party?	Please serve *all* of the cookies.
What is in the basket?	Can *everyone* hear the speaker?

Intensive pronouns add emphasis to another noun or pronoun in the sentence. They are formed by adding *-self* or *selves* to a pronoun, as in *herself* and *ourselves*.

Practice A Identify the pronoun in each sentence as interrogative or indefinite.

1. What were the names of Julia's sisters?
2. Everyone mispronounced Julia's name.
3. Julia's mother met someone there.
4. With whom did the officer speak?
5. Which of Julia's uncles is her favorite?

ⓒ **Reading Application** In "Names/Nombres," find two interrogative pronouns and two indefinite pronouns.

Practice B Identify these words as interrogative, indefinite, or intensive. Use each in a sentence.

1. who
2. any
3. all
4. what
5. myself

ⓒ **Writing Application** Write two sentences containing interrogative pronouns and intensive pronouns.

PH **WRITING COACH**   Further instruction and practice are available in *Prentice Hall Writing Coach.*

Writing

 **Common Core State Standards**

L.6.1, L.6.1.b, L.6.6; W.6.3.d; SL.6.6
[For the full wording of the standards, see page 110.]

Narrative Text These selections relate **personal anecdotes,** or brief, true stories about personal experience. If you read "Names/Nombres," write about a happy experience you had growing up. If you read "The Lady and the Spider," write about an experience with an animal or an object in nature.

- Brainstorm a list of interesting experiences.
- Choose the experience you will most enjoy writing about.
- List vivid details. Use descriptive and sensory language that captures what you saw, heard, and felt.
- Write down your reactions to the experience.
- Use your notes to write your personal anecdote.

Grammar Application Use interrogative and indefinite pronouns in your anecdote.

Writing Workshop: *Work in Progress*

Prewriting for Autobiographical Narrative Look over the Experience Web you created. Make a list of the events, putting them in the order in which they occurred. Then think: *Why did each event occur?* Jot down notes after each event.

Use this prewriting activity to prepare for the **Writing Workshop** on page 154.

Speaking and Listening

Comprehension and Collaboration A **monologue** is a speech in which someone expresses his or her thoughts. Write and deliver a monologue to a partner.

- If you read "Names/Nombres," write a monologue that presents the thoughts of young Julia Alvarez as she hears someone mispronounce her name for the first time.
- If you read "The Lady and the Spider," write a monologue that either the woman or the spider delivers after they collide.

Follow these steps to complete the assignment:

- Jot down words and phrases that express feelings.
- Describe why your character would feel that way.
- Use vocabulary that reflects the character's personality.
- Additionally, be sure to consistently use such pronouns as *I, my, me, we,* and *us.*

www.PHLitOnline.com
- Interactive graphic organizers
- Grammar tutorial
- Interactive journals

Test Practice: Reading

Fact and Opinion

Fiction Selection

Directions: *Read the selection. Then, answer the questions.*

"Be careful," warned the dealer as I picked up a beautiful stamp from the counter. I wanted to own it so I hoped it wasn't too expensive. I asked the dealer to tell me about it.

"That's the most valuable stamp in the shop," he said. "It's the prettiest, too. You'll never see another one of those. There are only five in the world. I found the stamp when I was traveling in North Africa. Stamp collecting is a hobby for the adventurous."

I put back the beautiful stamp very carefully. I knew that I probably wouldn't be able to afford it, but I was thrilled to have seen such an amazing find!

1. Which statement from the passage is a fact?
   A. You'll never see another one of those.
   B. That's the most valuable stamp in the shop.
   C. It's the prettiest, too.
   D. Stamp collecting is a hobby for the adventurous.

2. Which fact can be checked on the internet?
   A. That's the most valuable stamp in the shop.
   B. There are only five in the world.
   C. It's the prettiest, too.
   D. Stamp collecting is a hobby for the adventurous.

3. Which statement is an opinion?
   A. That's the most valuable stamp in the shop.
   B. It's the prettiest, too.
   C. There are only five in the world.
   D. I found the stamp when I was traveling in North Africa.

4. Which statement is an opinion that is based on facts?
   A. You'll never see another one of those.
   B. There are only five in the world.
   C. That's the most valuable stamp in the shop.
   D. I found the stamp when I was traveling in North Africa.

Writing for Assessment

Write a paragraph in which you identify two facts and two opinions that the narrator expresses in this passage.

Nonfiction Selection

Directions: *Read the selection. Then, answer the questions.*

The postage stamp did not exist before 1840. People who received letters paid the delivery cost. This made no sense. Many people refused letters because the delivery cost was too high.

Sir Rowland Hill invented the postage stamp. It was a great invention. Sir Rowland's idea was that the delivery cost should be paid by the person sending a letter. A piece of paper would be stuck on the letter to show that the sender paid. This piece of paper was the postage stamp.

Sir Rowland designed the first stamp. On it was a picture of Queen Victoria. Stamp collectors everywhere should thank Sir Rowland. Without him, the hobby of stamp collecting would not exist.

1. Which statement from the passage is an opinion?
   A. Sir Rowland's idea was that the delivery cost should be paid by the sender.
   B. Sir Rowland designed the first stamp.
   C. Stamp collectors everywhere should thank Sir Rowland.
   D. The postage stamp did not exist before 1840.

2. Which statement is a fact?
   A. This made no sense.
   B. It was a great invention.
   C. Before that, people who received letters paid the delivery cost.
   D. Stamp collectors everywhere should thank Sir Rowland.

3. Which statement *cannot* be checked using an encyclopedia?
   A. Sir Rowland designed the first stamp.
   B. On it was a picture of Queen Victoria.
   C. It was a great invention.
   D. A piece of paper would be stuck on the letter to show the sender paid.

4. Which fact supports the author's opinion that without Sir Rowland, the hobby of stamp collecting would not exist?
   A. Sir Rowland designed the first stamp.
   B. On it was a picture of Queen Victoria.
   C. Many people refused letters.
   D. Stamp collectors everywhere should thank Sir Rowland.

Writing for Assessment

Comparing Texts
Imagine that the stamp dealer in the first passage has found a stamp from 1840 with a picture of Queen Victoria on it. Write a few sentences explaining how his find might change at least one fact and one opinion in the first passage.

PHLit
Online!
www.PHLitOnline.com
- Online practice
- Instant feedback

Reading for Information

Analyzing Functional and Expository Texts

Atlas Entry

Travel Brochure

Common Core State Standards

Reading Informational Text
7. Integrate information presented in different media or formats as well as in words to develop a coherent understanding of a topic or issue.

Writing
2.f. Provide a concluding statement or section that follows from the information or explanation presented.

Language
6. Acquire and use accurately grade-appropriate general academic and domain-specific words and phrases; gather vocabulary knowledge when considering a word or phrase important to comprehension or expression.

Reading Skill: Make and Support Assertions

An **assertion** is a statement, such as, "I like all kinds of animals" or "The crops were harvested." When you respond to a text, you make assertions about what you have read. Reasonable assertions can be supported by examples and details from the text. If the work you are reading contains both printed text and graphics, integrate, or bring together, the information. To do this, read the printed text and study the graphics. Then, combine the information to make assertions about the overall meaning of the text.

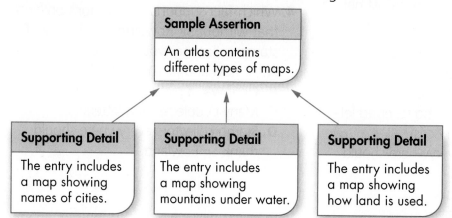

Sample Assertion

An atlas contains different types of maps.

Supporting Detail

The entry includes a map showing names of cities.

Supporting Detail

The entry includes a map showing mountains under water.

Supporting Detail

The entry includes a map showing how land is used.

Content-Area Vocabulary

These words appear in the selections that follow. You may also encounter them in other content-area texts.

- **fertile** (furt´'l) *adj.* able to produce much; able to produce crops easily

- **rejuvenate** (ri jo͞o´ və nāt´) *v.* cause to feel or seem young or vigorous again; bring back youthful qualities

The Caribbean

Atlas Entry

Features:

- alphabetical entries for easy reference
- short articles that convey facts about places
- maps and charts that display regions and their characteristics

The introductory section gives general information about the islands in the Caribbean Sea. The assertions in the text are supported by the map shown here.

The Caribbean Sea is enclosed by an arc of many hundreds of islands, islets, and offshore reefs that reach from Florida in the United States around to Venezuela in South America. From 1492, Spain, France, Britain, and the Netherlands claimed the islands as colonies.

Hispaniola

Monte Cristi · Puerto Plata

Cap-Haïtien

Santiago

Gonaïves

La Vega · San Francisco de Macorís

Île de la Gonâve

HAITI

Pico Duarte 10,417ft

Cordillera Central

SANTO DOMINGO

Jérémie

PORT-AU-PRINCE

La Romana

Isla Saona

Cayes · Jacmel

DOMINICAN REPUBLIC

Isla Beata

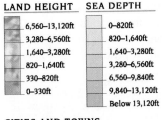

LAND HEIGHT	SEA DEPTH
6,560–13,120ft	0–820ft
3,280–6,560ft	820–1,640ft
1,640–3,280ft	1,640–3,280ft
820–1,640ft	3,280–6,560ft
330–820ft	6,560–9,840ft
0–330ft	9,840–13,120ft
	Below 13,120ft

CITIES AND TOWNS

- ◙ Over 500,000 people
- ◉ 100,000–500,000
- ○ 50,000–100,000
- ○ Less than 50,000

N
W · E
S

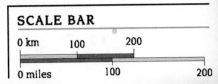

SCALE BAR

0 km   100   200

0 miles   100   200

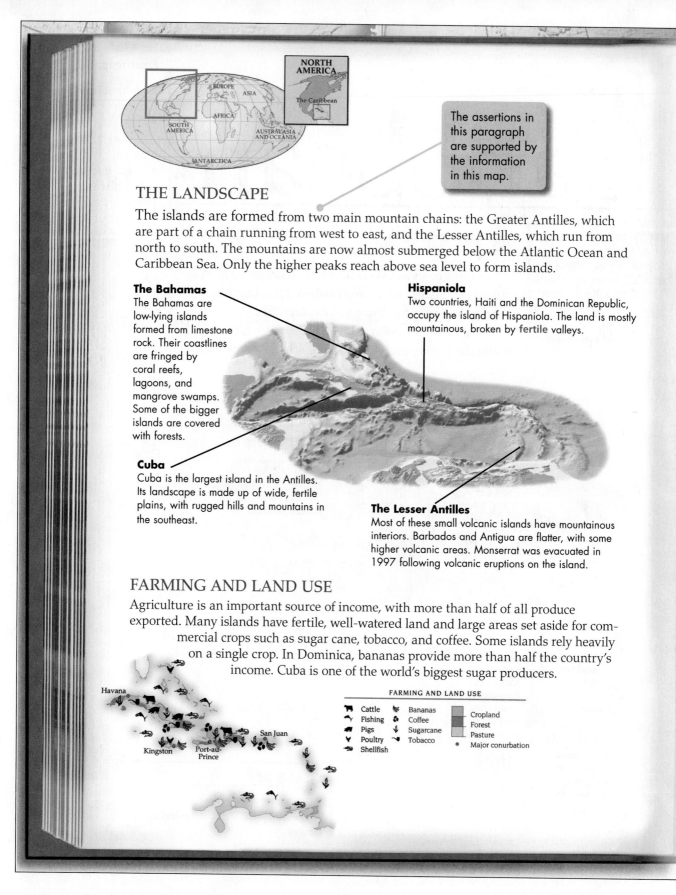

NORTH AMERICA

The Caribbean

> The assertions in this paragraph are supported by the information in this map.

THE LANDSCAPE

The islands are formed from two main mountain chains: the Greater Antilles, which are part of a chain running from west to east, and the Lesser Antilles, which run from north to south. The mountains are now almost submerged below the Atlantic Ocean and Caribbean Sea. Only the higher peaks reach above sea level to form islands.

The Bahamas
The Bahamas are low-lying islands formed from limestone rock. Their coastlines are fringed by coral reefs, lagoons, and mangrove swamps. Some of the bigger islands are covered with forests.

Hispaniola
Two countries, Haiti and the Dominican Republic, occupy the island of Hispaniola. The land is mostly mountainous, broken by **fertile** valleys.

Cuba
Cuba is the largest island in the Antilles. Its landscape is made up of wide, fertile plains, with rugged hills and mountains in the southeast.

The Lesser Antilles
Most of these small volcanic islands have mountainous interiors. Barbados and Antigua are flatter, with some higher volcanic areas. Monserrat was evacuated in 1997 following volcanic eruptions on the island.

FARMING AND LAND USE

Agriculture is an important source of income, with more than half of all produce exported. Many islands have fertile, well-watered land and large areas set aside for commercial crops such as sugar cane, tobacco, and coffee. Some islands rely heavily on a single crop. In Dominica, bananas provide more than half the country's income. Cuba is one of the world's biggest sugar producers.

Havana
San Juan
Kingston
Port-au-Prince

FARMING AND LAND USE

Cattle	Bananas	Cropland
Fishing	Coffee	Forest
Pigs	Sugarcane	Pasture
Poultry	Tobacco	• Major conurbation
Shellfish		

Features:

- glossy, highly designed pages
- short articles meant to engage readers
- text that inspires readers to visit

The **Florida Keys**

The photograph supports the assertion in the text that the Florida Keys are naturally beautiful.

Most people know the Florida Keys and Key West as a great getaway. One of the most unique places on earth. Calm. Serene. Laid back. Just the right setting to recharge your batteries and rejuvenate your spirits.

But a getaway to the Florida Keys and Key West is much more than peace and quiet. And not just because of the legendary fishing and the world's most spectacular dive sites.

The Keys mean history. Art. Theater. Museums. Shopping. Fine dining. Entertainment. And much more. All told, 120 miles of perfect balance between natural beauty and extraordinary excitement. Between relaxation and activities. Between the quaint and the classic.

And you'll find our accommodations just as diverse as our pleasures. From some of the best camping spots in the country to luxurious hotels. From charming bed-and-breakfasts to rustic, family-owned lodgings. In other words, we've got something for everyone.

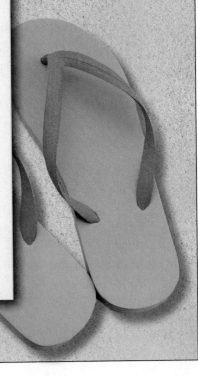

The assertion that Key West is unlike any other place is supported by the photo of a family enjoying a unique vacation.

Key West

Whether you drive or fly into Key West, one thing's for sure: there's simply no place quite like it. An island city of palm-lined streets boasting Victorian homes, gingerbread conch houses and mansions on the National Register.

John Audubon and Ernest Hemingway lived here. One had a passion for preservation. The other, a great zest for living. And that combination gives Key West its unique personality. The moment you get on world-famous Duval Street, in Old Town Key West, you do more than feel the ambiance. You become a part of it.

Key West is unique. And unspoiled. A feast for your heart and your soul. In short, if you're planning on visiting Key West, plan on staying longer than anticipated.

Comparing Functional and Expository Texts

1. Key Ideas and Details **(a)** What information can you find in an atlas that you would not find in a travel brochure? **(b)** What information can you find in a travel brochure that you would not find in an atlas? **(c)** In what situation might each type of text be useful? Why?

Content-Area Vocabulary

2. (a) Add the suffix *–tion* to the base word *rejuvenate*. Explain how the suffix alters the meaning of the base word. **(b)** Do the same with the suffix *–ed.* **(c)** Use each word in a sentence that shows its meaning.

Timed Writing

Informative Text: Description

> **Format**
> The prompt asks you to write a description that contains assertions.

Describe what it might be like to vacation on a typical Caribbean island. In your description, make assertions about what people might experience there. Support your ideas by citing the facts provided in the atlas entry. (20 minutes)

> **Academic Vocabulary**
> *Facts* are statements that can be proved. You can assume that statements made in a reference book, such as an atlas, are facts.

5-Minute Planner

Complete these steps before you begin to write:

1. Review the atlas entry to gather information. **TIP** Read both the print text and the graphics. Combine what you learn to make assertions about the overall meaning of the text.

2. Jot down relevant facts as you reread the atlas entry.

3. Identify assertions you can make based on the facts you have gathered. Jot down your assertions. Make sure that your assertions are based on facts.

4. Use your notes to prepare a quick outline. Plan an interesting introduction and a concluding statement that follows from and supports your main ideas. Refer to the outline as you write your description.

Comparing Symbolism

A **symbol** is anything that stands for something else. In literature, symbols often stand for ideas, such as love or hope. Writers often use **symbolism** to reinforce the theme or message of a story. To interpret symbols, notice items that seem to be of special importance and analyze the details the writer uses to describe them.

As you interpret symbols, keep these points in mind:

- The meaning of a symbol is often open to interpretation by the reader, but it should be based on story events and details.

- A symbol may have more than one meaning.

Both selections that follow use symbolism to represent a larger theme. As you analyze each symbol, notice the words the author uses to describe it. Writers choose words and phrases not just for their literal meanings, but also for the thoughts and emotions that they trigger. The feelings that a word brings to mind are called **connotations.** Authors use words with specific connotations to describe the symbols in their stories. For example, when Ray Bradbury uses the word *gazelles* in the first story, he does not want readers to think only of the animals themselves. He also wants to summon up the qualities connected with gazelles—grace, speed, beauty.

As you read, use a chart like this one to compare the use of symbols in each story.

Common Core State Standards

Reading Literature
2. Determine a theme or central idea of a text and how it is conveyed through particular details; provide a summary of the text distinct from personal opinions or judgments.
4. Determine the meaning of words and phrases as they are used in a text, including figurative and connotative meanings; analyze the impact of a specific word choice on meaning and tone.

Writing
2.a. Introduce a topic; organize ideas, concepts, and information, using strategies such as definition, classification, comparison/contrast, and cause/ effect; include formatting, graphics, and multimedia when useful to aiding comprehension.

	The Sound of Summer Running	Eleven
Symbol	sneakers	red sweater
Descriptive words from story		
Details		
The symbol represents		

PHLit Online!
www.PHLitOnline.com

- Vocabulary flashcards
- Interactive journals
- More about the authors
- Selection audio
- Interactive graphic organizers

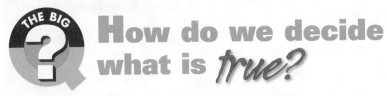

How do we decide what is *true?*

Writing About the Big Question

In these selections, an article of clothing has a symbolic meaning for the main character. Use this sentence starter to develop your ideas about the Big Question:

It (is, is not) **realistic** to believe that certain objects have special meaning because _____.

Meet the Authors

Ray Bradbury (b. 1920)

Author of "The Sound of Summer Running"

As a boy, Ray Bradbury nourished his imagination by attending circuses, watching magicians, and reading science-fiction novels. Bradbury once stated, "My life filled up with these wonderful events and people and images, and they stirred my imagination so that by the time I was twelve, I decided to become a writer. Just like that."

Although he is most famous for his science-fiction tales, his childhood fears and dreams fill the pages of his 1957 novel *Dandelion Wine,* which includes "The Sound of Summer Running."

Sandra Cisneros (b. 1954)

Author of "Eleven"

Sandra Cisneros writes about her life, her family, and her Mexican heritage. "I'm trying to write the stories that haven't been written," Cisneros once said about her own writing. ". . . I'm determined to fill a literary void." Her award-winning collection of short stories, "*The House on Mango Street,*" is about a young Mexican American girl growing up in Chicago. The book was inspired by the stories of the students Cisneros met while she was a teacher.

The Sound of Summer Running

from **Dandelion Wine**

Ray Bradbury

ate that night, going home from the show with his mother and father and his brother Tom, Douglas saw the tennis shoes in the bright store window. He glanced quickly away, but his ankles were seized, his feet suspended, then rushed. The earth spun; the shop awnings slammed their canvas wings overhead with the thrust of his body running. His mother and father and brother walked quietly on both sides of him. Douglas walked backward, watching the tennis shoes in the midnight window left behind.

"It was a nice movie," said Mother.

Douglas murmured, "It was . . ."

It was June and long past time for buying the special shoes that were quiet as a summer rain falling on the walks. June and the earth full of raw power and everything everywhere in motion. The grass was still pouring in from the country, surrounding the sidewalks, stranding the houses. Any moment the town would capsize, go down and leave not a stir in the clover and weeds. And here Douglas stood, trapped on the dead cement and the red-brick streets, hardly able to move.

"Dad!" He blurted it out. "Back there in that window, those Cream-Sponge Para Litefoot Shoes . . ."

His father didn't even turn. "Suppose you tell me why you need a new pair of sneakers. Can you do that?"

"Well . . ."

It was because they felt the way it feels every summer when you take off your shoes for the first time and run in the grass. They felt like it feels sticking your feet out of the hot covers in wintertime to let the cold wind from the open window blow on them suddenly and you let them stay out a long time until you pull them back in under the covers again to feel them, like packed snow. The tennis shoes felt like it always feels the first time every year wading in the slow waters of the creek and seeing your feet below, half an inch further downstream, with refraction, than the real part of you above water.

"Dad," said Douglas, "it's hard to explain."

Somehow the people who made tennis shoes knew what boys needed and wanted. They put marshmallows and coiled springs in the soles and they wove the rest out of grasses bleached and fired in the wilderness. Somewhere deep in the soft loam of the shoes the thin hard sinews of the buck deer were hidden. The people that made the shoes must have watched a lot of winds blow the trees and a lot of rivers going down to the lakes. Whatever it was, it was in the shoes, and it was summer.

Douglas tried to get all this in words.

"Yes," said Father, "but what's wrong with last year's sneakers? Why can't you dig *them* out of the closet?"

Well, he felt sorry for boys who lived in California where they wore tennis shoes all year and never knew what it was to get winter off your feet, peel off the iron leather shoes all full of snow and rain and run barefoot for a day and then lace on the first new tennis shoes of the season, which was better than barefoot. The magic was always in the new pair

Symbolism
How does Douglas feel about the tennis shoes?

Reading Check

Why are the shoes so appealing to Douglas?

of shoes. The magic might die by the first of September, but now in late June there was still plenty of magic, and shoes like these could jump you over trees and rivers and houses. And if you wanted, they could jump you over fences and sidewalks and dogs.

"Don't you see?" said Douglas. "I just *can't* use last year's pair."

For last year's pair were dead inside. They had been fine when he started them out, last year. But by the end of summer, every year, you always found out, you always knew, you couldn't really jump over rivers and trees and houses in them, and they were dead. But this was a new year, and he felt that this time, with this new pair of shoes, he could do anything, anything at all.

They walked up on the steps to their house. "Save your money," said Dad. "In five or six weeks—"

"Summer'll be over!"

Lights out, with Tom asleep, Douglas lay watching his feet, far away down there at the end of the bed in the moonlight, free of the heavy iron shoes, the big chunks of winter fallen away from them.

"Reason. I've got to think of reasons for the shoes."

Well, as anyone knew, the hills around town were wild with friends putting cows to riot, playing barometer[1] to the atmospheric changes, taking sun, peeling like calendars each day to take more sun. To catch those friends, you must run much faster than foxes or squirrels. As for the town, it steamed with enemies grown irritable with heat, so remembering every winter argument and insult. *Find friends, ditch enemies!* That was the Cream-Sponge Para Litefoot motto. *Does the world run too fast? Want to catch up? Want to be alert, stay alert? Litefoot, then! Litefoot!*

He held his coin bank up and heard the faint small tinkling, the airy weight of money there.

Whatever you want, he thought, you got to make your own way. During the night now, let's find that path through the forest. . . .

Downtown, the store lights went out, one by one. A wind blew in the window. It was like a river going downstream and his feet wanting to go with it.

---

1. barometer (bə räm′ ət ər) *n.* device that measures air pressure, to predict weather changes.

Symbolism
How are old tennis shoes like the end of summer?

In his dreams he heard a rabbit running running running in the deep warm grass.

Old Mr. Sanderson moved through his shoe store as the proprietor of a pet shop must move through his shop where are kenneled animals from everywhere in the world, touching each one briefly along the way. Mr. Sanderson brushed his hands over the shoes in the window, and some of them were like cats to him and some were like dogs; he touched each pair with concern, adjusting laces, fixing tongues. Then he stood in the exact center of the carpet and looked around, nodding.

There was a sound of growing thunder.

One moment, the door to Sanderson's Shoe Emporium was empty. The next, Douglas Spaulding stood clumsily there, staring down at his leather shoes as if these heavy things could not be pulled up out of the cement. The thunder had stopped when his shoes stopped. Now, with painful slowness, daring to look only at the money in his cupped hand, Douglas moved out of the bright sunlight of Saturday noon. He made careful stacks of nickels, dimes, and quarters on the counter, like someone playing chess and worried if the next move carried him out into sun or deep into shadow.

"Don't say a word!" said Mr. Sanderson.

Douglas froze.

"First, I know just what you want to buy," said Mr. Sanderson. "Second, I see you every afternoon at my window; you think I don't see? You're wrong. Third, to give it its full name, you want the Royal Crown Cream-Sponge Para Litefoot Tennis Shoes: 'Like Menthol On Your Feet!' Fourth, you want credit."

"No!" cried Douglas, breathing hard, as if he'd run all night in his dreams. "I got something better than credit to offer!" he gasped. "Before I tell, Mr. Sanderson, you got to do me one small favor. Can you remember when was the last time you yourself wore a pair of Litefoot sneakers, sir?"

Mr. Sanderson's face darkened. "Oh, ten, twenty, say, thirty years ago. Why . . . ?"

"Mr. Sanderson, don't you think you owe it to your customers, sir, to at least try the tennis shoes you sell, for just one minute, so you know how they feel? People

Symbolism
How do the descriptions in the first paragraph add other meanings to the shoes?

Spiral Review
Central Idea
Contrast the way Mr. Sanderson talks about the sneakers with the way Douglas thinks and talks about the sneakers.

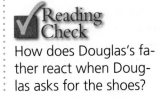

Reading Check
How does Douglas's father react when Douglas asks for the shoes?

The Sound of Summer Running **145**

forget if they don't keep testing things. United Cigar Store man smokes cigars, don't he? Candy-store man samples his own stuff, I should think. So . . ."

"You may have noticed," said the old man, "I'm wearing shoes."

"But not sneakers, sir! How you going to sell sneakers unless you can rave about them and how you going to rave about them unless you know them?"

Mr. Sanderson backed off a little distance from the boy's fever, one hand to his chin. "Well . . ."

"Mr. Sanderson," said Douglas, "you sell me something and I'll sell you something just as valuable."

"Is it absolutely necessary to the sale that I put on a pair of the sneakers, boy?" said the old man.

"I sure wish you could, sir!"

The old man sighed. A minute later, seated panting quietly, he laced the tennis shoes to his long narrow feet. They looked detached and alien[2] down there next to the dark cuffs of his business suit. Mr. Sanderson stood up.

"How do they *feel*?" asked the boy.

"How do they feel, he asks; they feel fine." He started to sit down.

"Please!" Douglas held out his hand. "Mr. Sanderson, now could you kind of rock back and forth a little, sponge around, bounce kind of, while I tell you the rest? It's this: I give you my money, you give me the shoes, I owe you a dollar. But, Mr. Sanderson, *but*—soon as I get those shoes on, you know what *happens*?"

"What?"

"Bang! I deliver your packages, pick up packages, bring you coffee, burn your trash, run to the post office, telegraph office, library! You'll see twelve of me in and out, in and out, every minute. Feel those shoes, Mr. Sanderson, *feel* how

▲ **Critical Viewing**
Do you think that Douglas would be drawn to shoes like these? Why or why not? **[Speculate]**

Symbolism
Why do you think Mr. Sanderson does not have the same reaction to the sneakers as Douglas?

---

2. alien (āl´ yən) *adj.* foreign; unfamiliar.

fast they'd take me? All those springs inside? Feel all the running inside? Feel how they kind of grab hold and can't let you alone and don't like you just *standing* there? Feel how quick I'd be doing the things you'd rather not bother with? You stay in the nice cool store while I'm jumping all around town! But it's not me really, it's the shoes. They're going like mad down alleys, cutting corners, and back! There they go!"

Mr. Sanderson stood amazed with the rush of words. When the words got going the flow carried him; he began to sink deep in the shoes, to flex his toes, limber[3] his arches, test his ankles. He rocked softly, secretly, back and forth in a small breeze from the open door. The tennis shoes silently hushed themselves deep in the carpet, sank as in a jungle grass, in loam and resilient clay. He gave one solemn bounce of his heels in the yeasty dough, in the yielding and welcoming earth. Emotions hurried over his face as if many colored lights had been switched on and off. His mouth hung slightly open. Slowly he gentled and rocked himself to a halt, and the boy's voice faded and they stood there looking at each other in a tremendous and natural silence.

Symbolism
How are Mr. Sanderson's feelings for the shoes similar to Douglas's in this paragraph?

A few people drifted by on the sidewalk outside, in the hot sun.

Still the man and boy stood there, the boy glowing, the man with **revelation** in his face.

"Boy," said the old man at last, "in five years, how would you like a job selling shoes in this emporium?"

"Gosh, thanks, Mr. Sanderson, but I don't know what I'm going to be yet."

Vocabulary
revelation
(rev´ ə lā´ shən) *n.* sudden rush of understanding

"Anything you want to be, son," said the old man, "you'll be. No one will ever stop you."

The old man walked lightly across the store to the wall of ten thousand boxes, came back with some shoes for the boy, and wrote up a list on some paper while the boy was lacing the shoes on his feet and then standing there, waiting.

The old man held out his list. "A dozen things you got to do for me this afternoon. Finish them, we're even Stephen, and you're fired."

"Thanks, Mr. Sanderson!" Douglas bounded away.

"Stop!" cried the old man.

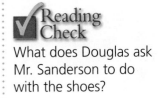

Reading Check
What does Douglas ask Mr. Sanderson to do with the shoes?

---

3. limber (lim´ bər) *v.* loosen up (a muscle or limb); make easy to bend.

Symbolism
What two things in nature are used to describe the new shoes?

Douglas pulled up and turned.

Mr. Sanderson leaned forward. "How do they *feel*?"

The boy looked down at his feet deep in the rivers, in the fields of wheat, in the wind that already was rushing him out of the town. He looked up at the old man, his eyes burning, his mouth moving, but no sound came out.

"Antelopes?" said the old man, looking from the boy's face to his shoes. "Gazelles?"

The boy thought about it, hesitated, and nodded a quick nod. Almost immediately he vanished. He just spun about with a whisper and went off. The door stood empty. The sound of the tennis shoes faded in the jungle heat.

Mr. Sanderson stood in the sun-blazed door, listening. From a long time ago, when he dreamed as a boy, he remembered the sound. Beautiful creatures leaping under the sky, gone through brush, under trees, away, and only the soft echo their running left behind.

"Antelopes," said Mr. Sanderson. "Gazelles."

He bent to pick up the boy's abandoned winter shoes, heavy with forgotten rains and long-melted snows. Moving out of the blazing sun, walking softly, lightly, slowly, he headed back toward civilization. . . .

Critical Thinking

Cite textual evidence to support your responses.

1. **Key Ideas and Details (a)** What are Douglas's feelings about last year's sneakers? **(b) Infer:** Why does he feel this way?

2. **Key Ideas and Details (a)** What is Mr. Sanderson's reaction when Douglas asks him to try on the sneakers? **(b) Deduce:** Why does he react this way? **(c) Analyze:** Explain the change after he tries the sneakers.

3. **Key Ideas and Details (a)** Explain Douglas's plan. Why does he think Mr. Sanderson must try on the sneakers? **(b) Make a Judgment:** Would this plan work on most store owners? Explain.

4. **Integration of Knowledge and Ideas (a)** Based on the writer's description, how does Douglas feel about the sneakers? **(b)** Explain how this idea relates to the story's theme. *[Connect to the Big Question: How do we decide what is true?]*

Eleven

Sandra Cisneros

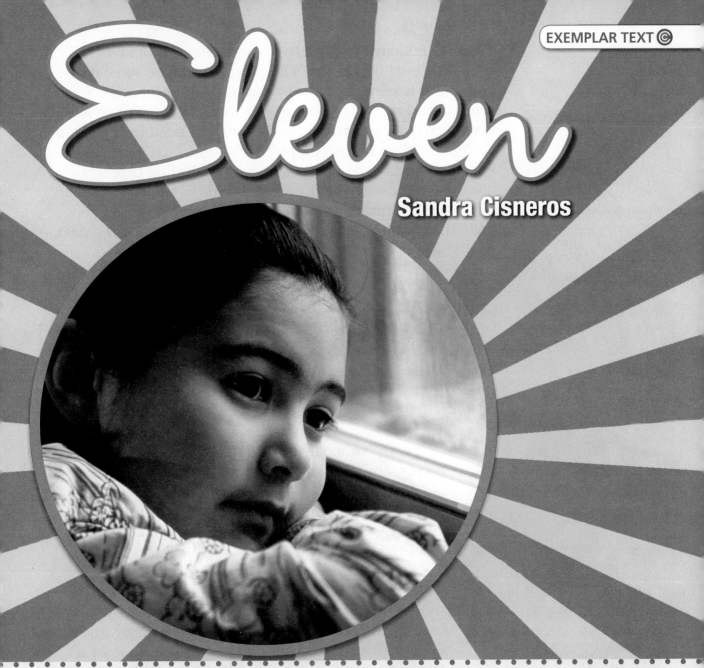

What they don't understand about birthdays and what they never tell you is that when you're eleven, you're also ten, and nine, and eight, and seven, and six, and five, and four, and three, and two, and one. And when you wake up on your eleventh birthday you expect to feel eleven, but you don't. You open your eyes and everything's just like yesterday, only it's today. And you don't feel eleven at all. You feel like you're still ten. And you are—underneath the year that makes you eleven.

Like some days you might say something stupid, and that's the part of you that's still ten. Or maybe some days you might need to sit on your mama's lap because you're scared, and that's the part of you that's five. And one day when you're all grown up maybe you will need to cry like if you're three, and that's okay. That's what I tell Mama when she's sad and needs to cry. Maybe she's feeling three.

Because the way you grow old is kind of like an onion or like the rings inside a tree trunk or like my little wooden dolls that fit one inside the other, each year inside the next one. That's how being eleven years old is.

You don't feel eleven. Not right away. It takes a few days, weeks even, sometimes even months before you say eleven when they ask you. And you don't feel smart eleven, not until you're almost twelve. That's the way it is.

Only today I wish I didn't have just eleven years rattling inside me like pennies in a tin Band-Aid box. Today I wish I was one-hundred-and-two instead of eleven because if I was one-hundred-and-two I'd have known what to say when Mrs. Price put the red sweater on my desk. I would've known how to tell her it wasn't mine instead of just sitting there with that look on my face and nothing coming out of my mouth.

"Whose is this?" Mrs. Price says, and she holds the red sweater up in the air for all the class to see. "Whose? It's been sitting in the coatroom for a month."

"Not mine," says everybody. "Not me."

"It has to belong to somebody," Mrs. Price keeps saying, but nobody can remember. It's an ugly sweater with red plastic buttons and a collar and sleeves all stretched out like you could use it for a jump rope. It's maybe a thousand years old and even if it belonged to me I wouldn't say so.

Maybe because I'm skinny, maybe because she doesn't like me, that stupid Felice Garcia says, "I think it belongs to Rachel." An ugly sweater like that, all raggedy and old, but Mrs. Price believes her. Mrs. Price takes the sweater and puts it right on my desk, but when I open my mouth nothing comes out.

"That's not, I don't, you're not . . . not mine," I finally say in a little voice that was maybe me when I was four.

"Of course it's yours," Mrs. Price says, "I remember you

Vocabulary
raggedy (rag´ i dē)
adj. torn from wear

wearing it once." Because she's older and the teacher, she's right and I'm not.

Not mine, not mine, not mine, but Mrs. Price is already turning to page 32, and math problem number four. I don't know why but all of a sudden I'm feeling sick inside, like the part of me that's three wants to come out of my eyes, only I squeeze them shut tight and bite down on my teeth real hard and try to remember today I am eleven, eleven. Mama is making a cake for me for tonight, and when Papa comes home everybody will sing happy birthday, happy birthday to you.

But when the sick feeling goes away and I open my eyes, the red sweater's still sitting there like a big red mountain. I move the red sweater to the corner of my desk with my ruler. I move my pencil and books and eraser as far from it as possible. I even move my chair a little to the right. Not mine, not mine, not mine.

In my head I'm thinking how long till lunch time, how long till I can take the red sweater and throw it over the schoolyard fence, or leave it hanging on a parking meter, or bunch it up into a little ball and toss it in the alley. Except when math period ends Mrs. Price says loud and in front of everybody, "Now, Rachel, that's enough," because she sees I've shoved the red sweater to the tippy-tip corner of my desk and it's hanging all over the edge like a waterfall, but I don't care.

"Rachel," Mrs. Price says. She says it like she's getting mad. "You put that sweater on right now and no more nonsense."

"But it's not . . ."

"Now!" Mrs. Price says.

This is when I wish I wasn't eleven, because all the years inside of me—ten, nine, eight, seven, six, five, four, three, two, and one—are all pushing at the back of my eyes when I put one arm through one sleeve of the sweater that smells like cottage cheese, and then the other arm through the other and stand there with my arms apart as if the sweater hurts me and it does, all itchy and full of germs that aren't even mine.

That's when everything I've been holding in since this morning, since when Mrs. Price put the sweater on my desk, finally lets go, and all of a sudden I'm crying in front of everybody. I wish I was invisible but I'm not. I'm eleven and it's my birthday today and I'm crying like I'm three in

Symbolism
How do Rachel's actions in this paragraph build the importance of the sweater?

Spiral Review
Central Idea How does Rachel's description of the sweater as a "big red mountain" connect with the idea of an unwanted thing?

Vocabulary
alley (al′ ē) *n.* narrow street between or behind buildings

Vocabulary
invisible (in viz′ə bəl) *adj.* not able to be seen

Reading Check
How does the narrator feel about her eleventh birthday?

Symbolism
How are the red sweater and turning eleven years old alike for Rachel?

front of everybody. I put my head down on the desk and bury my face in my stupid clown sweater arms. My face all hot and spit coming out of my mouth because I can't stop the little animal noises from coming out of me, until there aren't any more tears left in my eyes, and it's just my body shaking like when you have the hiccups, and my whole head hurts like when you drink milk too fast.

But the worst part is right before the bell rings for lunch. That stupid Phyllis Lopez, who is even dumber than Felice Garcia, says she remembers the red sweater is hers! I take it off right away and give it to her, only Mrs. Price pretends like everything's okay.

Today I'm eleven. There's a cake Mama's making for tonight, and when Papa comes home from work we'll eat it. There'll be candles and presents and everybody will sing happy birthday, happy birthday to you, Rachel, only it's too late.

I'm eleven today. I'm eleven, ten, nine, eight, seven, six, five, four, three, two, and one, but I wish I was one-hundred-and-two. I wish I was anything but eleven, because I want today to be far away already, far away like a tiny kite in the sky, so tiny-tiny you have to close your eyes to see it.

Critical Thinking

1. **Key Ideas and Details (a)** What is special about the day? **(b) Analyze:** Explain how Rachel can be eleven and all her younger ages, too.

2. **Key Ideas and Details (a)** Why does Rachel wish she were "anything but eleven"? **(b) Connect:** How do the story's events suggest that Rachel's theory about ages has some truth to it?

Cite textual evidence to support your responses.

3. **Integration of Knowledge and Ideas (a)** What are some advantages and disadvantages to "growing up"? **(b) Apply:** What disadvantages to growing up do Rachel's experiences illustrate?

4. **Integration of Knowledge and Ideas** How do Rachel's feelings compare to Douglas's feelings about the shoes in the previous selection? Are they based more on fact or emotion? Explain. *[Connect to the Big Question: How do we decide what is true?]*

Comparing Symbolism

© **1. Key Ideas and Details (a)** Explain what the new shoes symbolize for Douglas. **(b)** Use details and words from the story to explain your interpretation.

© **2. Key Ideas and Details (a)** Explain what the red sweater symbolizes for Rachel in "Eleven." **(b)** What details and words from the story support your ideas?

© **3. Key Ideas and Details** How is the emotion of each symbol different for Rachel and Douglas?

⏱ Timed Writing

Explanatory Text: Essay

Compare and contrast the ways symbols can be positive and negative. Complete a chart like the one shown. Then, use your information to explain in a short essay how the symbols in these stories help the authors express positive or negative feelings. **(30 minutes)**

Story	Symbol	+ or – ?		Evidence
		☐	☐	
		☐	☐	

5-Minute Planner

1. Read the prompt carefully.

2. Gather your answers to the questions above and the information from your graphic organizer on page 140.

3. Take special note of words and phrases from the story that contribute directly to the symbol's meaning, like *ugly*. In your essay, be sure to analyze the positive or negative connotations of the words used to describe the sneakers and the sweater.

4. Reread the prompt, and then draft your essay.

Writing Workshop

Common Core State Standards

Writing

3. Write narratives to develop real or imagined experiences or events using effective technique, relevant descriptive details, and well-structured event sequences.

3.a. Engage and orient the reader by establishing a context and introducing a narrator and/or characters; organize an event sequence that unfolds naturally and logically.

5. With some guidance and support from peers and adults, develop and strengthen writing as needed by planning, revising, editing, rewriting, or trying a new approach.

Write a Narrative

Narration: Autobiographical Narrative

Defining the Form Some of the best stories revolve around real events in writers' lives. These types of stories are called **autobiographical narratives.** Elements of this type of writing appear in letters, journals, persuasive essays, and anecdotes.

Assignment Write an autobiographical narrative about an event that caused you to change. Include these elements:

- ✓ *setting* revealed through *description*
- ✓ a clear, logical *sequence of events*
- ✓ a *central problem or conflict* that you or someone else resolves
- ✓ *vivid sensory details* that develop plot and character and show your point of view
- ✓ narrative techniques, including *dialogue and pacing*
- ✓ *correct use of pronouns and antecedents*

To preview the criteria on which your autobiographical narrative may be judged, see the rubric on page 161.

 Writing Workshop: *Work in Progress*

Review the work you did on pages 109 and 131.

WRITE GUY
Jeff Anderson, M.Ed.

What Do You Notice?

Structure and Style

The following sentence is from Robert Fulghum's essay "The Lady and the Spider." Read the sentence several times.

The web is torn loose and is wrapped around a frenzied moving haystack, and a huge piece of raw-but-painted meat is making a sound the spider never heard before: "AAAAAAAGGGGGGGGGGGHHHHHHHHHH!!!!!!"

With a partner, discuss the qualities that make this sentence interesting. For example, you may want to talk about the writer's use of word choice, sentence structure, and imagery. Now, think about ways you might use similar elements in your narrative.

Reading-Writing Connection

To get the feel for narrative nonfiction, read "Names/Nombres" by Julia Alvarez on page 114.

Prewriting/Planning Strategies

List special events. To find the right topic for your autobio-graphical narrative, consider events that were special for you. These strategies will help:

PHLit Online!
www.PHLitOnline.com
- Author video: Writing Process
- Author video: Rewards of Writing

- **Freewrite.** Write whatever thoughts occur to you about a general topic, such as *holidays, adventures,* or *a problem solved.* Focus more on getting your ideas down than on writing correctly. After five minutes, read over your thoughts, and choose a topic from among them.

- **Make a memory checklist.** In the first column of a three-column chart, list special people, unique places, and memorable events. In the next column, describe each one. In the last column, give an example to support each description. Choose one memory as your topic.

Consider relationships. Take a few moments to reflect on your relationships with people at school and at home. Jot down your thoughts about how your interactions with others affect your life.

Zero in and focus. Once you have chosen a topic, narrow it by focusing on one significant part: a surprise, a problem, or some other aspect of the experience that makes it stand out in your mind.

Make a timeline. Begin to gather the details that you will use to develop your narrative. List the events and supporting details in the correct order on a timeline like the one shown.

Timeline

Event 1: I decided to take the canoe out after dark by myself.

Event 2: As I paddled to the far side of the lake, I heard thunder.

Event 3: The first bolt of lightning hit in the forest.

It was a calm night, so I thought my grandfather was wrong about a storm.

The thunder came in low rumbles at first, then louder and louder.

Suddenly, I was terrified! I had to seek shelter.

Drafting Strategies

 **Common Core State Standards**

Writing

3.a. Engage and orient the reader by establishing a context and introducing a narrator and/ or characters; organize an event sequence that unfolds naturally and logically.

3.b. Use narrative techniques, such as dialogue, pacing, and description, to develop experiences, events, and/or characters.

3.d. Use precise words and phrases, relevant descriptive details, and sensory language to convey experiences and events.

Decide on the order of events. Review your timeline. Then, make a decision about the order in which you will present events.

- **Chronological order:** Many stories start with the first event and then add the others in the order in which they occurred.

- **Chronological order with flashback:** Some stories begin at the end and flash back to the beginning. Then, through flashback, the writer tells the rest of the story in chronological order.

Plan to present your conflict. On a conflict map like this one, list each event that builds toward the **climax,** the story's highest point of tension. Then, list the events that reduce the tension until the last scene, or resolution, takes place. Use your conflict map as you draft.

Use sensory language. Add interest to your description with vivid verbs, concrete nouns, and adjectives that develop the action and setting.

Dull: As I went across the lake, I heard noises far away.

Vivid: As I paddled across the peaceful lake, I was suddenly aware of low rumbles of thunder rolling toward me.

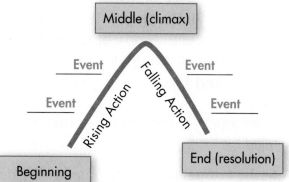

Use dialogue and pacing. Instead of describing a situation, use dialogue, or the words of conversations, to show characters' feelings and reactions. In addition, vary the speed, or pacing, of your story. Decide when to slow the pace by adding details and when to speed up to create tension. This will help build suspense to make readers want to know what will happen next.

Model: "Kate," Granddad said. "Where are you going?"

"Out in the canoe," I said.

"But it's dark, and there's a storm coming," he warned. "The weather's going to turn nasty!"

"Aw, Grandad," I replied, feeling independent.

"The water's as flat as a mirror. I'll be fine!"

Develop your point of view. Use language to show your thoughts and feelings about the event as you experienced it.

Writers on Writing

Jane Yolen On Writing Narratives

Jane Yolen is the author of "Greyling" (p. 9) and "My Heart Is in the Highlands" (p. 17).

I loved stories about King Arthur and Merlin since I was a child, so of course I wanted to write about them when I grew up. *Passager* and the two books after it that make up the Young Merlin Trilogy each begin with a short story. Now, short stories can focus on a moment in time or a moment of emotion. A novel needs a longer narrative or story, in which a character grows, changes, or "gets wisdom."

"I write with both my head and my heart."
—Jane Yolen

Professional Model:

from *Passager*, Book 1 of The Young Merlin Trilogy

The whole time he had lived alone in the woods came to one easy winter, one very wet spring, one mild summer, and one brilliant fall.

A year.

But for an eight-year-old that is a good portion of a lifetime. He remembered all of that year. What he could not recall clearly was how he had come to the woods, how he had come to be alone. What he could recall made him uneasy. He remembered it mostly at night. And in dreams.

He remembered a large, smoky hearth and the smell of meat drippings. A hand slapped his—he remembered this, though he could not remember who had slapped him or why. That was not one of the bad dreams, though. He could clearly recall the taste of the meat before the slap, and it was good.

In the old tales, Merlin went mad as an adult and ran off into the woods for a year. But I thought having him be a child was more interesting.

My Merlin is a reader of dreams, which we find out in the second book. This is called foreshadowing, where the author puts down clues for later on in the story.

Authors write with a particular style or voice. In this kind of fantasy, I use a bardic (like the old bards or poet-singers) or Biblical voice. The phrase "and it was good" appears often in the beginning of the Bible.

Revising Strategies

 Common Core
State Standards

Writing

3.c. Use a variety of transition words, phrases, and clauses to convey sequence and signal shifts from one time frame or setting to another.

3.d. Use precise words and phrases, relevant descriptive details, and sensory language to convey experiences and events.

Language

1.c. Recognize and correct inappropriate shifts in pronoun number and person.

1.d. Recognize and correct vague pronouns.

Identify and strengthen transitions. Draw an arrow from one paragraph to the next and explain the relationship between the paragraphs it links. Then, ask yourself these questions:

- Do events in one paragraph cause those in the next?
- Does one paragraph give information that a reader needs in order to understand the next paragraph?
- Does one paragraph create curiosity or suspense about what might happen in the next paragraph?

If a paragraph is not related to the ones before and after it, rewrite or move it. Use transitions to clarify shifts in time or ideas. Transitional words and phrases, such as *next, afterward, in the meantime,* and *the next day* can clarify the connections between sentences or paragraphs.

Pack some punch into your lead. The first sentence of your autobiographical narrative is the **lead.** It should be an attention grabber that makes your readers curious and committed to reading on to find out what happens. These ideas might help you to pack more power into that all-important sentence:

Start with...	Example
An exciting action	Crash! A bolt of lightning hit somewhere on the island, with ear-splitting, terrifying power.
A hint about a potential problem	The sky darkened unexpectedly with storm clouds.
Dramatic dialogue	"Don't go out on that lake alone!" Granddad warned.

Add vivid details. Scan your draft and circle vague words such as *nice* and *great*. Replace those words with more vivid choices that appeal to the senses of sight, sound, touch, taste, and smell.

Peer Review

Work with a partner to discuss your use of sensory details and concrete language, and revise if necessary.

Revising for Pronoun/Antecedent Agreement

A **pronoun** takes the place of a noun. The noun that is referred to by the pronoun is called the **antecedent.**

Identifying Errors in Agreement A pronoun and its antecedent must agree in number. Use a singular pronoun with a singular antecedent. Use a plural pronoun with a plural antecedent.

Singular Pronoun and Antecedent
California is a popular vacation spot because **it** has many beautiful beaches.

Plural Pronoun and Antecedent
My **parents** said that **they** would attend my play.

Sometimes, the antecedent is not a noun, but an indefinite pronoun such as *anyone, everything,* or *nothing.* Most errors in pronoun/antecedent agreement occur when the antecedent is a singular indefinite pronoun. Be sure to use the correct pronoun depending on how it is used in the sentence (subject, object, possessive).

PH **WRITING COACH**

Further instruction and practice are available in *Prentice Hall Writing Coach.*

Singular Indefinite Pronoun and Antecedent
Somebody on the boys' team left **his** catcher's mitt on the bus.

Plural Indefinite Pronoun and Antecedent
Many of the students brought **their** reports in on Thursday.

A vague or ambiguous pronoun is one that does not refer clearly to a specific noun.

Fixing Errors To find and fix errors related to pronoun use, follow these steps:

1. Identify each pronoun/antecedent pair that you used.
2. Decide whether the antecedent is singular or plural.
3. Follow the rules of agreement to fix any errors.
4. Make sure pronouns refer to specific antecedents.

Grammar in Your Writing
Reread your autobiographical narrative. Look for pronouns and antecedents. Then, use the rules above to make corrections.

A Time to Heal

My knee had been bothering me for quite a while. At first my parents weren't concerned. My mom said, "It's probably just growing pains." The pain continued, so my parents took me to the doctor. The doctor took X-rays, bone scans, and MRI's. When we went back to the doctor for the results of the tests, the doctor entered the examining room, looking very serious. "Kyle," he said, "you have a rare condition called Osteochondritis Dissecans. It means that part of your lower femur has died because there is no longer a blood supply to that area." He explained that this could be a very serious condition. My parents and I were in shock! I was very afraid.

The doctor gave me two options. He said, "You can have six months of complete rest—except walking or swimming—or you can have surgery to regenerate the blood supply to that area of the bone." The surgery involves drilling microscopic holes in the bone. I wasn't thrilled with either choice.

Faced with that decision, my parents and I decided to try resting before having the surgery. I couldn't finish my baseball season and was forced to sit out the football and basketball seasons also. It was really hard for me when friends asked me why I hadn't tried out for the teams.

After six months of rest, I had more bad news—my leg had not gotten better, so the doctor said, "Kyle, we have no other choice but to move forward with the surgery." The surgery will take about three months to heal. My recovery will require me to be on crutches for a month, then gradually over the next two months start putting weight back on my leg. At the end of three months I will be back on my feet in time for spring baseball.

"Hey, Kyle," my friend Alex asked, "isn't it hard not to play sports?"

"Alex," I said, "the thing I miss the most is just being around you guys. It's been really lonely. I can't wait to get back into it again."

I realize how fortunate I am. During my doctor visits I have met some really incredible people. I met a little girl who had to have her foot amputated because of a birth defect. She walks around as if she were no different than anyone else. She will be receiving a prosthetic foot when she is older so that she has better balance and can wear a shoe. I have been in the waiting area with kids who have cancer and other incurable diseases. Mine is an injury that can be corrected with surgery. I feel very lucky because I have an excellent chance of a complete recovery. A year off from sports taught me to appreciate what I took for granted, like friends and being a part of a team.

This straightforward lead makes readers want to find out why Kyle's knee was bothering him.

Here, Kyle introduces the central problem that is the focus of his autobiographical narrative.

Transitions such as *before* and *after* help readers follow the chronological order of events.

Vivid details add impact. They support the closing sentence of the narrative.

Editing and Proofreading

Review your draft to correct errors in grammar, spelling, and punctuation.

Focus on punctuating dialogue. If you include conversations in your writing, follow the proper formatting rules.

- Enclose all direct quotations in quotation marks. *"You were right," I said to Jim.*
- Place a comma after the words that introduce the speaker. *Jim replied, "Well, you learned a lesson today."*
- Use commas and quotation marks before and after any interrupting words. *"Next time," I said, "I guess I'll listen."*

Publishing and Presenting

Consider one of the following ways to share your writing:

Deliver a speech. Use your autobiographical narrative as the basis for a dramatic presentation.

Get it published. Mail your narrative to a magazine that publishes student writing. Include a letter introducing your essay.

Reflecting on Your Writing

Writer's Journal Jot down your answer to this question: *What new insights did you gain about this experience?*

Rubric for Self-Assessment

Find evidence in your writing to address each category. Then use the rating scale to grade your work.

Spiral Review

Earlier in the unit, you learned about **personal and possessive pronouns** (p. 108) and **interrogative and indefinite pronouns** (p. 130). Check your use of pronouns in your narrative to make sure that all pronouns agree with their antecedents in gender, case, and number.

PH WRITING COACH

Further instruction and practice are available in *Prentice Hall Writing Coach.*

Criteria	Rating Scale
	not very very
Focus: How clearly does the narrative present the problem or conflict?	1 2 3 4 5
Organization: How clearly is the sequence of events presented?	1 2 3 4 5
Support/Elaboration: How effective are the sensory details in describing people, places, and events?	1 2 3 4 5
Style: How well does the language reflect an appropriate point of view?	1 2 3 4 5
Conventions: How correct is your grammar, especially your use of pronouns and antecedents?	1 2 3 4 5

Vocabulary Workshop

Using a Dictionary and Thesaurus

Common Core
State Standards

Language
4.c. Consult reference materials, both print and digital, to find the pronunciation of a word or determine or clarify its precise meaning or its part of speech.
5.c. Distinguish among the connotations (associations) of words with similar denotations (definitions).

A **dictionary** provides the meaning, pronunciation, and part of speech of words in the English language. It also gives a word's **etymology,** or origins. A word's etymology explains how words change, how they are borrowed from other languages, and how new words are invented, or "coined." Notice what this dictionary entry reveals about the word *athlete*.

athlete (ath' lēt') *n.* [L *athleta* < Gr athlētēs, contestant in the games] a person trained in exercises, games, or contests requiring such qualities as physical strength, skills, and speed.

A **thesaurus** provides synonyms, or words with similar meanings, for many words in the English language. A thesaurus can help you find a word that means exactly what you want to say. The thesaurus entry shown gives several synonyms for *athlete*. Notice how each word has a slightly different meaning.

athlete *n.* acrobat, gymnast, player, contestant, champion, sportsman, contender, challenger.

Follow these steps to use a thesaurus effectively:

- Identify a word in your writing that could be more precise.
- Read through the words that your thesaurus lists as synonyms.
- Choose the word that best expresses your intended meaning.
- Use a dictionary to make sure you are using the word correctly.

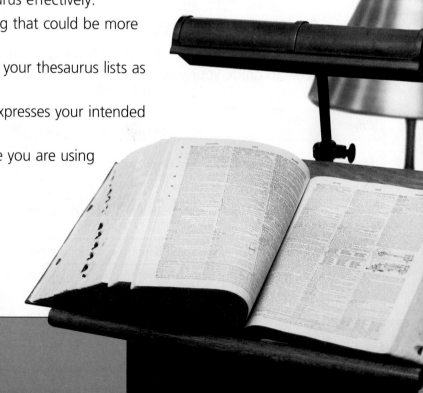

Where to Find a Dictionary and Thesaurus You can find these resources in book form at your school or library. You can also find them in electronic form on the Internet. Ask your teacher to recommend the best online word-study resources.

Practice A Find these words in a dictionary. Show how each one breaks into syllables, and which syllable is stressed. Then, write each word's definition. Finally, use each word in a sentence that shows its meaning.

1. estimate   **2.** intuition   **3.** temporary   **4.** distinguish

Practice B Find each word in a thesaurus. Select two synonyms for the word. Explain how the meaning of each synonym is different from the meaning of the original word. Then, use each synonym in a sentence that shows its exact meaning. Remember to use a dictionary to check the meanings of your synonyms.

1. laugh (verb)   **2.** large (adjective)   **3.** story (noun)

Activity Create a quick-reference thesaurus of some commonly used words. Make notecards like the one shown for the words *strong*, *happy*, and *smart*. Share your words with classmates, collecting more synonyms. Then, with a partner, discuss the shades of meaning that each word conveys. You can use quick-reference cards like these to help you find precise words when you write.

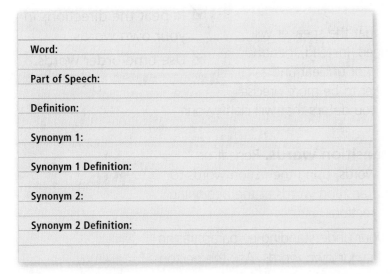

Word:

Part of Speech:

Definition:

Synonym 1:

Synonym 1 Definition:

Synonym 2:

Synonym 2 Definition:

Comprehension and Collaboration

With a small group, take turns suggesting synonyms for the following words. Use a dictionary and a thesaurus to check your answers and to find additional synonyms.

look (verb)

speak (verb)

nervous (adjective)

Communications Workshop

Following Oral Directions

To understand and carry out **multistep oral directions,** or spoken directions with several steps, listen carefully to the speaker. Then, write down or restate the directions in the correct sequence. The following strategies will help you demonstrate effective listening skills.

Learn the Skills

Follow these guidelines to understand and apply oral directions.

Focus your attention. As you listen to directions, pay close attention to the speaker. Try to avoid or ignore distractions and focus on what is being said.

Notice action words and time-order words. Listen for the key action word in each step. These words tell you what to do. In these directions for a fire drill, the action words are underlined:

▶ **Example:** First, <u>close</u> the doors and windows. Then, <u>walk</u> to the nearest exit. When you are outside, <u>stand</u> with your class while the teacher counts the people in the group.

Most directions are stated in chronological order, or the sequence in which they are meant to occur. For this reason, they usually include time-order words, such as *first, then, next,* and *last.*

Ask questions. Do not assume that the speaker will give you all the information you need. Instead, identify any information you think is missing or unclear and ask questions. You may need the speaker to be more precise in his or her description or to give you details that will clarify your understanding.

Use the action words and transition words. Repeat or restate the directions in your own words, using the action words to recall the action required. Use the transition words at the beginning of each step to restate multistep directions.

Paraphrase directions. Clarify your understanding by paraphrasing the directions, or repeating them in your own words. Ask the person giving the directions to correct any misunderstanding.

Common Core State Standards

Speaking and Listening

1.c. Pose and respond to specific questions with elaboration and detail by making comments that contribute to the topic, text, or issue under discussion.

1.d. Review the key ideas expressed and demonstrate understanding of multiple perspectives through reflection and paraphrasing.

Checklist

Listen Carefully

☑ Focus on the speaker. Listen for main ideas.

☑ Notice the action word in each step.

☑ Notice time-order words.

☑ Ask questions.

Restate Carefully

☑ Repeat the directions in your own words.

☑ Use time-order words.

Practice the Skills

ⓒ Presentation of Knowledge and Ideas Use what you have learned in the workshop to perform the following activity.

ACTIVITY: Giving and Following Oral Directions

Work with a partner to take turns giving and following oral directions.

- Choose a multi-step task that you can complete in your classroom, such as addressing an envelope, formatting a document, or taking and editing a picture.
- Break the task into time-ordered steps, including transition words that show sequence.
- Keep the steps clear and simple so that your partner can complete the task correctly. Answer any questions your partner may have.
- Deliver the directions clearly, without rushing.
- When it is your turn to follow directions, listen carefully and restate them, using each step in the checklist on the left page.
- Finally, carry out your partner's instructions and complete the task.

Use a guide for following directions like the one shown to take notes on your partner's presentation.

Guide for Following Oral Directions

Steps
Record each step in chronological order. Write the action verb first.

Step 1: _____

Step 2: _____

Step 3: _____

Step 4: _____

Step 5: _____

Step 6: _____

Areas of Confusion
Which steps are confusing?
Do any terms need to be defined?

Summarize
My restatement, or paraphrase, of the directions:
Does my restatement of the directions match those intended by my partner?
Can I successfully carry out these directions?

ⓒ Comprehension and Collaboration With your classmates, discuss which steps made following oral directions easy and which steps made following oral directions difficult.

Cumulative Review

 **Common Core**
State Standards

RL.6.3, RL.6.4
[For the full wording of the standards, see the standards chart in the front of your textbook.]

I. Reading Literature

Directions: *Read the story. Then, answer each question that follows.*

First, there's the gleaming white hat. Then, the lean, tough figure under the hat. Of course, there's also the graceful animal under the figure—and the *thwomping* of hooves across a valley floor as the good guy comes in to save the day. What kid, watching these images on TV, *hasn't* longed to be a cowboy?

Day and night I dreamed the cowboy dream. Finally, when I was nearly thirteen, my parents arranged for me to visit Uncle Cody's ranch for three weeks. At long last, my dream would come true.

On my first day at the ranch, I met Joe Bill, the head wrangler. A wrangler handles all the saddle horses. His job was to teach me to ride, a skill as necessary to being a cowboy as swimming is to being a salmon. Joe Bill wore not a hero's white hat but a black hat. That should have been my first clue.

"Come on, boy!" Joe Bill said, cupping his hands to boost me onto an enormous gray horse. "Don't worry, son—this mare's as gentle as they come." Joe Bill must have mistaken my quivering legs for a sign of fear. I think that's the moment I began to dislike him. I imagined that he felt <u>disdain</u> for this soft, awkward city boy in his cotton baseball cap and sneakers.

Joe Bill told me how to sit in the saddle and hold the reins. Guiding the mare, he walked the horse around the corral. I felt like a three-year-old. I felt clumsy. My cowboy dream hadn't included this uneasy feeling on the back of a horse. "Let me try her by myself," I finally said impatiently.

Joe Bill looked up at me with a wide grin under his thick mustache. "All rightie!" he said, and backed away from the horse, still grinning. "Give 'er a little nudge."

I gave her more than a little nudge, I guess. All I remember was flapping at the horse's sides with my feet and shaking the reins with both hands. The next thing I knew, I was on my back on the ground. My mouth was full of dirt. Joe Bill was helping me up. Right then, as I struggled to my feet, I could feel my cowboy dream dissolving.

1. What information about the narrator is revealed in the **exposition?**
   A. He is afraid to ride a horse.
   B. He does not like Joe Bill.
   C. He has always dreamed of being a cowboy.
   D. He does not like to be treated like a child.

2. What clue indicates that the story is told from the **first-person point of view?**
   A. The characters are referred to as "he" and "him."
   B. The narrator shares information that the characters do not know.
   C. The narrator is an outside observer of the action in the story.
   D. The narrator participates in the action of the story.

3. What event is the **climax** of the narrative?
   A. The main character goes to Uncle Cody's ranch.
   B. The main character meets Joe Bill.
   C. The main character rides a horse.
   D. The main character falls off the horse.

4. Which of the following is a **symbol** for "bad guys" in cowboy movies?
   A. a black hat
   B. a white hat
   C. a gray horse
   D. a thick mustache

5. Which phrase is a clue that this sentence from the text states an **opinion?** *I think that's the moment I began to dislike him*.
   A. I think
   B. that's the moment
   C. I began
   D. to dislike him

6. Which sentence states a **fact?**
   A. What kid *hasn't* longed to be a cowboy?
   B. At long last, my dream would come true.
   C. A wrangler handles all the saddle horses.
   D. I felt like a three-year-old.

7. **Vocabulary** Which word is closest in meaning to the underlined word *disdain*?
   A. pity
   B. friendliness
   C. dislike
   D. disappointment

8. What does the narrator most likely mean when he says "I could feel my cowboy dream dissolving"?
   A. He has lost respect for cowboys.
   B. He feels ashamed of himself.
   C. He is determined to learn to ride a horse.
   D. He no longer wants to be a cowboy.

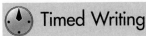 Timed Writing

9. **Explain** the internal conflict faced by the narrator. **Support** your ideas with evidence from the text.

 **GO ON**

II. Reading Informational Text

Directions: *Read the excerpt from an online article. Then, answer each question that follows.*

Common Core State Standards

RI.6.5; W.6.3.d, W.6.5; L.6.1.
[For the full wording of the standards, see the standards chart in the front of your textbook.]

How to Ride a Horse

These steps outline the basics of riding.

Before You Ride: Safety First

When you are first learning to ride a horse, it is important to have an experienced rider with you. Riding a horse can be dangerous. Always wear a helmet and riding boots.

Steady Now: Mounting the Horse

The experienced rider will help by holding your horse steady. First, stand on the left side of the horse and take the reins in your left hand. Then grab the saddle horn. Place your left foot in the stirrup. Next, pull yourself up. Lower yourself into the saddle, placing your right foot in the right stirrup. Use the reins to tell your horse which way to go. Pull to the left to go left. Pull back to stop your horse.

Take It Easy: Go Slowly at First

Begin by learning how to keep your balance on a horse. Practice starting, stopping, and turning the horse to the left or right. When you gain more confidence, you can ride the horse at a trot, then at a <u>canter</u>, and finally at a gallop.

1. What type of **organization** is used in the section "Steady Now: Mounting the Horse"?
   A. cause and effect
   B. step by step
   C. comparison and contrast
   D. problem and solution

2. Which **organizational feature** does the author use to help the reader understand the information in the article?
   A. subheadings
   B. captions
   C. sensory details
   D. definitions

3. Which statement is an **assertion?**
   A. Riding a horse can be dangerous.
   B. Always wear a helmet and riding boots.
   C. Place your left foot in the stirrup.
   D. If you pull the reins back, your horse will stop.

4. **Vocabulary** Which phrase is closest in meaning to the underlined word *canter*?
   A. slow walk
   B. fast run
   C. medium-paced movement
   D. movement at top speed

III. Writing and Language Conventions

Directions: *Read the passage. Then, answer each question that follows.*

(1) Suddenly, Poppa stopped the car. (2) He wanted to show us something. (3) In my minds eye, I tried to picture what it might be. (4) Outside, the air was cool and damp. (5) I breathed in the rich, spicy odor of pine. (6) We hiked along, our feet padding on the soft, moist ground. (7) Fern leaf surrounded the trail. (8) Beauty surrounded us completely. (9) Then I heard water splashing onto water. (10) A small sign pointed north to angel falls. (11) Suddenly, there it was: a long white strip of water rushing over a tall cliff and plunging into a blue pool below.

1. Which sentence best adds to the writer's **main impression** of the experience?
   A. My Poppa always enjoyed surprising us.
   B. This was the place where my sister and I learned to swim.
   C. The cool mist from the falling water tickled our faces.
   D. I was relieved when we finally arrived at the waterfall.

2. Which revision to sentence 10 uses correct capitalization of **proper nouns?**
   A. A small sign pointed North to Angel Falls.
   B. A small sign pointed north to Angel falls.
   C. A small sign pointed North to angel falls.
   D. A small sign pointed north to Angel Falls.

3. How could sentence 7 be revised to add a **sensory detail** that appeals to the sense of touch?
   A. Pungent fern leaf surrounded the trail.
   B. Fern leaf crept along the trail.
   C. Bright green fern leaf surrounded the trail.
   D. Soft, downy fern leaf surrounded the trail.

4. Which synonym is the *best* replacement for the word *strip*, in sentence 11?
   A. ribbon
   B. length
   C. piece
   D. stripe

5. In sentence 3, what is the correct way to rewrite the **possessive noun** in the phrase "minds eye"?
   A. minds' eye
   B. mind's eye
   C. minds's eye
   D. mindes' eye

Performance Tasks

Directions: *Follow the instructions to complete the tasks below as required by your teacher.*

As you work on each task, incorporate both general academic vocabulary and literary terms you learned in this unit.

Common Core State Standards

RL.6.2, RL.6.3, RL.6.9; RI.6.2, RI.6.5, RI.6.6; W.6.2, W.6.2.a; SL.6.1.a, SL.6.1.d, SL.6.5, SL.6.6; L.6.1.a, L.6.2.b
[For the full wording of the standards, see the standards chart in the front of your textbook.]

Writing

Task 1: Literature [RL.6.2; L.6.1.a]

Determine a Theme

Write an essay in which you explain the theme of a work of fiction from this unit.

- Tell which work you have chosen and why you chose it.
- State your interpretation of the theme.
- Identify at least three specific details from the story that help to convey that theme. Consider whether the details show connections, differences, or similarities.
- To make sure readers understand your interpretation, include a brief summary of the story.
- Edit to make sure pronouns are in the proper case.

Task 2: Informational Text [RI.6.2; L.6.2.b]

Determine a Central Idea

Write an essay in which you explain the central idea conveyed in a work of literary nonfiction from this unit.

- Tell which work you have chosen and why you chose it.
- Explain the author's purpose for writing the work, and identify the central idea he or she expresses.
- Discuss at least three specific details from the work that help to convey the central idea. Explain whether the details add facts, provide examples, or fulfill another purpose.
- To make sure readers understand your analysis, include a brief summary of the work.
- Edit your writing for correct spelling.

Task 3: Literature [RL.6.9; W.6.2, W.6.2.a]

Compare Genres

Write an essay in in which you compare and contrast two selections in this unit that address similar topics but represent two different genres. One should be fiction and one should be nonfiction.

- Tell which works you chose. Explain the topic the two works share.
- Describe how each author presents the topic. For example, explain whether the author tells a story or presents information.
- Identify at least three points of similarity or difference in the ways each work presents the topic.
- Organize ideas clearly, using appropriate transitions to show relationships among ideas.
- Develop and support your ideas by using quotations from the texts.

Speaking and Listening

Task 4: Informational Text
[RI.6.6; SL.6.1.a, SL.6.1.d]

Analyze an Author's Point of View

Lead a small group discussion about the author's point of view in a nonfiction work from this unit.

- Before you meet with your group, choose a work in which the author expresses a clear point of view. Ask your group members to read the work you chose.
- Review the work and make notes about the author's point of view. Identify at least three details from the text that help to convey the point of view.
- Start the discussion by explaining your ideas. Then, invite group members to offer their comments and ideas.
- Review the ideas group members express and paraphrase to demonstrate your understanding. Then, share your group's ideas with the whole class.

Task 5: Literature [RL.6.3; SL.6.5]

Analyze the Structure of a Story

Write and deliver a presentation in which you analyze the structure of a story from this unit.

- Explain which story you chose and summarize the plot.
- Identify the scenes or episodes that make up the plot. Explain what each scene tells you about the events or characters.
- Explain how the characters respond or change in each scene or episode.
- Using your analysis, create storyboards, or illustrations, of the story's main episodes.

Display the storyboard or illustrations as you present your analysis of the story to the class.

Task 6: Informational Text [RI.6.5; SL.6.6]

Analyze the Structure of a Nonfiction Text

Write and present a detailed outline that shows the structure of a work of literary nonfiction from this unit.

- Identify the ideas and information expressed in each paragraph of the work.
- Consider how individual paragraphs relate to each other and whether the work has distinct sections.
- Note whether each paragraph presents additional details about an idea or introduces a new idea.
- Organize the outline into a graphic that clearly shows the structure of the work.
- Explain your outline to the class. Speak clearly, using academic language appropriate to a classroom setting.

THE BIG ?

How do we decide what is true?

At the beginning of Unit 1, you wrote a response to the Big Question. Now that you have completed the unit, write a new response. Discuss how your initial ideas have expanded or changed. Cite specific examples from the literature in this unit, from other subject areas, and from your own life to support your ideas. Use Big Question vocabulary words (p. 3) in your response.

Featured Titles

In this unit, you have read a variety of fiction and literary nonfiction. Continue to read on your own. Select books that you enjoy, but challenge yourself to explore new topics, new authors, and works of increasing depth and complexity. The titles suggested below will help you get started.

Literature

Woman Hollering Creek and Other Stories
by Sandra Cisneros
Vintage, 1992   EXEMPLAR TEXT

 In this collection of **short stories,** Cisneros writes about Mexican Americans living in border towns— their lives, their dreams, and their families. The collection includes the story "Eleven."

Roll of Thunder, Hear My Cry
by Mildred D. Taylor   EXEMPLAR TEXT

 This award-winning **novel,** set in the southern United States in the 1930s, tells the story of one African American family as they face the brutality of poverty and racism with strength and pride.

Alice's Adventures in Wonderland and Through the Looking Glass
by Lewis Carroll
Signet Classic, 2000   EXEMPLAR TEXT

 In these two beloved works of **fiction,** you will travel with Alice down the rabbit hole and through the looking glass. There, in a world of fantasy, you will meet the Mad Hatter, the Queen of Hearts, and other delightful characters. The classic poem "Jabberwocky" is included.

Informational Texts

Free at Last! The Story of Martin Luther King, Jr.
by Angela Bull

 This **biography** provides facts on how the slain civil rights leader raised the American social conscience about equality and nonviolence. Read about King's struggle to deliver a message of peace.

Tiger Tales
by Deborah Chancellor

 This **nonfiction** book uncovers the truth about how the number of wild tigers and other animal populations are decreasing because of hunting.

The Circuit
by Francisco Jiménez

 In this **autobiography,** Jiménez tells of his difficult early years as part of a family of migrant farm workers. To him, life consisted of constant moving around and work, with school wedged in around harvesting jobs.

Preparing to Read Complex Texts

Attentive Reading As you read on your own, ask yourself questions about the text. The questions shown below and others that you ask as you read will help you learn and enjoy literature even more.

Common Core State Standards

Reading Literature/Informational Text 10. By the end of the year, read and comprehend literature, including stories, dramas, and poems, and literary nonfiction in the grades 6–8 text complexity band proficiently, with scaffolding as needed at the high end of the range.

When reading fiction, ask yourself...

- Whose "voice" is telling the story? Do I like that voice?
- Does the story offer a message that I think is important and true? Why or why not?

Ⓒ **Key Ideas and Details**

- Does the author describe places in a way that helps me picture them clearly? Why or why not?
- Do any details seem wrong? If so, which ones, and why?
- Do I understand why characters act and feel as they do? Do their thoughts and actions seem real? Why or why not?

Ⓒ **Craft and Structure**

- Do I care what happens in the story? Why or why not?
- Does the story remind me of others I have read? If so, how?

Ⓒ **Integration of Ideas**

When reading nonfiction, ask yourself...

- Who is the author? Why did he or she write the work?
- Has the author made me care about the subject? Why or why not?

Ⓒ **Key Ideas and Details**

- Does the author organize ideas well, or is the text hard to follow?
- Does the author use evidence that helps me understand the ideas?
- Does the author support his or her claims with solid evidence?

Ⓒ **Craft and Structure**

- Does the author leave out ideas I think are important?
- Do I agree with some of the author's ideas but not with others? If so, why?
- What else have I read about this topic? How is this work similar to or different from those other works?
- What have I learned from this text?

Ⓒ **Integration of Ideas**

THE BIG Q

Is *conflict* always bad?

Short Stories

PHLit
Online!
www.PHLitOnline.com

Hear It!
• Selection summary audio
• Selection audio
• BQ Tunes

See It!
• Author videos
• Big Question video
• Get Connected videos
• Background videos
• More about the authors
• Illustrated vocabulary words
• Vocabulary flashcards

Do It!
• Interactive journals
• Interactive graphic organizers
• Grammar tutorials
• Interactive vocabulary games
• Test practice

THE BIG ? Is *conflict* always bad?

A **conflict** is a struggle between opposing forces. There are many different types of conflict. One kind of conflict is an argument between people, such as who should get the last cookie. Another type is a battle between nations over freedom and liberty. When you compete against others in a sport or game, that is another kind of conflict. When you struggle over a decision, you are in conflict with yourself. There are many ways to resolve, or work out, conflicts of any kind. There are also many lessons to learn from these situations.

Exploring the Big Question

© **Collaboration: One-on-One Discussion** Start thinking about the Big Question by identifying different types of conflict. Describe one specific example of each of the following types of conflict:

- a disagreement between friends over an issue
- a misunderstanding between two people
- a competition in sports or in a contest
- an individual's struggle to make a decision
- a battle against forces of nature
- a person's fight to overcome or accept a challenge

    Share your examples with a partner. Discuss the cause of each conflict and how it was resolved. Listen attentively.

Connecting to the Literature Each reading in this unit will give you additional insight into the Big Question.

PHLit Online!
www.PHLitOnline.com
- Big Question video
- Illustrated vocabulary words
- Interactive vocabulary games
- BQ Tunes

Learning Big Question Vocabulary

Acquire and Use Academic Vocabulary Academic vocabulary is the language you encounter in textbooks and on standardized tests. Review the definitions of these academic vocabulary words.

argue (är′gyŏŏ) *v.* fight using words; debate

challenge (chal′ənj) *n.* dare; a calling into question

conclude (kən klŏŏd′) *v.* arrive at a judgment; end

convince (kən vins′) *v.* persuade

defend (dē fend′) *v.* guard from attack; protect

resolve (ri zälv′) *v.* settle; bring to an end

Use these words as you complete Big Question activities in this unit that involve reading, writing, speaking, and listening.

Gather Vocabulary Knowledge Additional Big Question words are listed below. Categorize the words by deciding whether you know each one well, know it a little bit, or do not know it at all.

battle	issue	resist
compete	lose	survival
game	negotiate	win

Then, do the following:

1. Write the definitions of the words you know.

2. If you think you know a word's meaning, write it down. Consult a dictionary and revise your definition if necessary.

3. Using a print or an online dictionary, look up the meanings of words you do not know. Write down the meanings and study the pronunciations.

4. Use all of the words in two brief paragraphs. In the first paragraph, write about a conflict that had positive results. In the second, discuss a conflict that had negative results.

Common Core State Standards

Speaking and Listening
1. Engage effectively in a range of collaborative discussions with diverse partners on grade 6 topics, texts, and issues, building on others' ideas and expressing their own clearly.

Language
6. Acquire and use accurately grade-appropriate general academic and domain-specific words and phrases; gather vocabulary knowledge when considering a word or phrase important to comprehension or expression.

Elements of a Short Story

A short story is a brief work of fiction that contains plot, characters, setting, and theme.

A **short story** is a brief fictional narrative that can usually be read in one sitting. Although it is short, it is a complete work featuring the same basic elements as longer works of fiction.

Plot is the sequence of events in a story. It consists of a series of scenes or episodes that are linked to each other. Early scenes advance the plot by bringing about later ones.

Conflict is a problem or struggle between opposing forces.
- An **internal conflict** takes place in the mind of a character. The character struggles to make a decision, take an action, or overcome an obstacle.
- An **external conflict** is a conflict in which a character struggles against an outside force, such as nature or another character.

Characters are the people or animals who take part in the action of a story. An author brings a character to life through **characterization**—the art of creating and developing a character.
- A **character's traits,** or qualities, help readers understand the character and his or her actions.
- A **character's motives** are the reasons for his or her actions.

Setting is the time and place of the story's action. Setting can create a specific atmosphere or **mood** in a story. It may even relate directly to the story's conflict.

Theme is the central insight expressed in a short story. It might be stated directly or hinted at through the words and actions of the characters.

Short stories are made up of several key elements.

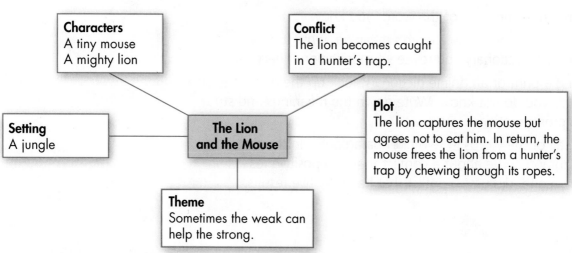

Characters
A tiny mouse
A mighty lion

Conflict
The lion becomes caught in a hunter's trap.

Setting
A jungle

The Lion and the Mouse

Plot
The lion captures the mouse but agrees not to eat him. In return, the mouse frees the lion from a hunter's trap by chewing through its ropes.

Theme
Sometimes the weak can help the strong.

Structure in Short Stories

A short story must grab a reader's attention right away. Because the work is brief, every part of the story must move the action forward. The **structure** of a short story is the way it is put together. A story's plot is structured in a way that helps the story progress. These elements make up the basic structure of a plot:

- **Exposition** is the story's setup. This part of the plot introduces the characters, setting, and basic situation. The story's conflict is usually introduced in the exposition.
- **Conflict** is the story's central problem. It might involve a struggle between characters, a struggle between a character and an outside force, or a struggle within the mind of a character.
- **Rising action** is made up of events and complications that increase the tension in the story. This tension builds to a climax.

- **Climax** is the high point of the story—its most intense, exciting, or important part. It is also the point at which the story's outcome becomes clear.
- **Falling action** sets up the story's ending. It is the part of the story in which events are settled.
- **Resolution** is the final outcome of the story. Usually, a story's conflict is settled in the resolution. In some stories, however, the conflict is left unsettled.

In the best short stories, readers want to find out what will happen next and how the characters will respond or change.

As you read a short story, notice how particular words, sentences, and events fit into the structure and help you understand the setting, plot, and theme.

In This Section

Elements of a Short Story

Structure in Short Stories

Analyzing Structure, Conflict, and Characterization

Close Read: Analyzing Elements of a Story
- Model Text
- Practice Text

After You Read

 Common Core State Standards

RL.6.3; RL.6.5
[For full wording of the standards, see the standards chart in the front of your textbook.]

Plot Structure

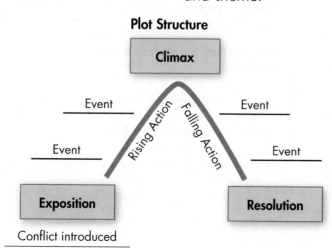

Analyzing Structure, Conflict, and Characterization

Characters respond and change as a short story's plot unfolds.

Common Core State Standards

Reading Literature

3. Describe how a particular story's plot unfolds in a series of episodes as well as how the characters respond or change as the plot moves toward a resolution.

5. Analyze how a particular sentence, chapter, or scene fits into the overall structure of a text and contributes to the development of the theme, setting, or plot.

The best short stories are **structured,** or put together, in ways that build readers' interest and move the action forward. In a good short story, each scene or episode has a purpose and contributes to the overall impact of the story. For example, the details in a specific scene can develop a key element, such as **setting.**

> **Example: Scene Developing Setting**
> The long, narrow hallway was completely deserted. I squinted in the dim light, struggling to see the door at the far end. The musty dampness sent a shiver through my body as I put one unsteady foot in front of the other.

In the example above, the words and sentences work together to develop the setting: a damp, dark, empty hallway. This scene also introduces another key story element. Notice that the narrator is *unsteady.* This detail indicates a possible **conflict,** or problem. Further details in the story will establish what specific conflict the narrator faces. Conflict moves a story forward because a reader must keep reading to find out what the problem is and how it affects the characters.

Types of Conflict As a short story progresses, scenes or events in the plot contribute to the conflict and its **resolution**—the way in which the conflict is settled. Conflicts may be *internal* or *external.* There are different types of external conflict, such as conflict with nature and conflict with society. Review the examples in the chart below. As you read a variety of short stories, you will find that some stories have several conflicts, which are usually related to each other.

> **Types of Conflict**
>
> **Internal Conflict:** a problem that takes place in a character's mind
> **Examples:**
> - an effort to overcome a feeling, like insecurity
> - a struggle to do the right thing
> - a struggle to choose between two courses of action
>
> **External Conflict:** a struggle against an outside force
> **Examples:**
> - a fight or argument between two people
> - a struggle against a natural force, such as an earthquake
> - a struggle against a social institution, such as a law or a tradition

Characterization A key part of the experience of reading a short story is getting to know the characters and finding out how they respond to the conflicts they face. Characterization is the method an author uses to develop characters and reveal their **traits,** or qualities.

There are two types of characterization. With **direct characterization,** the author makes statements that directly describe what the character is like.

> **Example: Direct Characterization**
>
> Mariah is the bravest girl in the sixth grade. She may be pale and tiny, but nothing scares her—not spiders, not huge barking dogs, not even mean old Mr. Jonas down the block.

With **indirect characterization,** the author reveals a character through that character's words and actions or through the words and actions of other characters.

> **Example: Indirect Characterization**
>
> I don't care what those young fools say; I will not leave this place. I have lived on this mountain since that roaring highway was a dirt road. My body may be bent, but I will stand firm.

Characters and Conflict As characters react to the conflicts in a story, their responses help advance the plot, as well as fuel their own growth and development as characters. The example that follows describes a story about a young boy. Notice how each of the boy's actions

brings about a new development in the plot. In turn, each new development causes a change in the boy's actions or attitude.

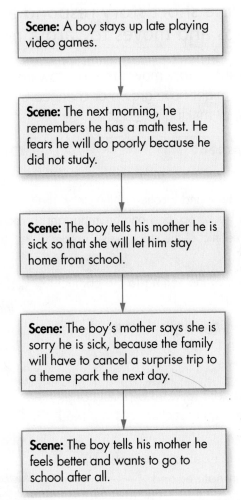

Scene: A boy stays up late playing video games.

Scene: The next morning, he remembers he has a math test. He fears he will do poorly because he did not study.

Scene: The boy tells his mother he is sick so that she will let him stay home from school.

Scene: The boy's mother says she is sorry he is sick, because the family will have to cancel a surprise trip to a theme park the next day.

Scene: The boy tells his mother he feels better and wants to go to school after all.

Characters and Theme Often, the changes a character undergoes are clues to the story's theme, or the insight the story conveys. For instance, in the example above, the story's theme might be stated like this: *It is always best to tell the truth.* As you read, pay close attention to clues in dialogue or description that might provide a window into a story's theme.

Close Read: Elements of a Short Story

Characters in a short story respond and change as the plot develops and moves toward a resolution.

Each event in a short story moves the plot toward the resolution. By the story's end, a character might have grown or changed by having a new insight, learning something new, or making a decision.

Plot Development	Character Development
Setting The setting is the time and location of the story. The setting can be a backdrop, or it can be important to the action or conflict of the story. As you read, think about • the importance of the setting to the conflict and events; and • whether the setting affects what the characters say and do.	**Character Traits** A character's traits are his or her qualities. As you read, be aware of • whether the author describes the character directly through *direct characterization;* • whether you learn about the character through *indirect characterization*—his or her words and actions or the words and actions of other characters; • what the character looks like, thinks, and does; • what the character says and how he or she says it; and • how others respond to the character.
Conflict Conflict moves a story forward by influencing characters' actions and reactions. As you read, notice • if the struggle is external, internal, with society, or with nature; and • what the characters say and do in response to the conflict.	**Character's Actions** As characters respond to events in a story, their actions cause other events to occur. As you read, identify • the events that cause a character to take an action; • details that show what the character says, does, and feels; and • ways that a character's actions influence the plot or give clues about the theme of the story.
Theme The theme of the story is the insight about life that the story conveys. You can often figure out the theme by noticing what happens to characters in the story. As you read, • think about what the characters learn about themselves or the world around them; and • consider how the characters change by the end of the story.	

Model

About the Text Leo Tolstoy was born in Russia in 1828. Although he was born into a wealthy family, Tolstoy wrote many short stories about struggling Russian farmers.

"The Old Grandfather and His Little Grandson" by Leo Tolstoy

The grandfather had become very old. His legs would not carry him, his eyes could not see, his ears could not hear, and he was toothless. When he ate, bits of food sometimes dropped out of his mouth. His son and his son's wife no longer allowed him to eat with them at the table. He had to eat his meals in a corner near the stove.

One day they gave him his food in a bowl. He tried to move the bowl closer; it fell to the floor and broke. His daughter-in-law scolded him. She told him that he spoiled everything in the house and broke their dishes, and she said that from now on he would get his food in a wooden dish. The old man sighed and said nothing.

A few days later, the old man's son and his wife were sitting in their hut, resting and watching their little boy playing on the floor. They saw him putting together something out of small pieces of wood. His father asked him, "What are you making, Misha?"

The little grandson said, "I'm making a wooden bucket. When you and Mamma get old, I'll feed you out of this wooden dish."

The young peasant and his wife looked at each other, and tears filled their eyes. They were ashamed because they had treated the old grandfather so meanly, and from that day they again let the old man eat with them at the table and took better care of him.

Character Traits The author uses direct characterization to describe what the grandfather looks like and how he acts. The reader feels the sadness of the grandfather's life.

Conflict There is conflict between the grandfather and his daughter-in-law. She wants her home to be neat and orderly, but the old, frail grandfather cannot help breaking things and making a mess.

Character's Actions The grandson's words and actions move the plot to its climax—the turning point that leads to the resolution. The son and his wife are forced to consider what it would feel like to be treated poorly.

Theme The author directly describes how the characters change their behavior. This information points to an insight, or theme: *Treat others the way you want to be treated.*

Independent Practice

About the Selection In 1970, Jean Craighead George flew to Alaska to learn about wolves. She spent ten days in Denali National Park to gather details for the setting and characters in this short story.

Setting What challenges might a wounded wolf face in a setting like this?

Character Traits What does this action tell you about Roko?

Conflict What conflict does Roko face? How does the setting contribute to the conflict?

"The Wounded Wolf" by Jean Craighead George

A wounded wolf climbs Toklat Ridge,[1] a massive spine of rock and ice. As he limps, dawn strikes the ridge and lights it up with sparks and stars. Roko, the wounded wolf, blinks in the ice fire, then stops to rest and watch his pack run the thawing Arctic valley.

They plunge and turn. They fight the mighty caribou that struck young Roko with his hoof and wounded him. He jumped between the beast and Kiglo, leader of the Toklat pack. Young Roko spun and fell. Hooves, paws, and teeth roared over him. And then his pack and the beast were gone.

Gravely injured, Roko pulls himself toward the shelter rock. Weakness overcomes him. He stops. He and his pack are thin and hungry. This is the season of starvation. The winter's harvest has been taken. The produce of spring has not begun.

Young Roko glances down the valley. He droops his head and stiffens his tail to signal to his pack that he is badly hurt. Winds wail. A frigid blast picks up long shawls of snow and drapes them between young Roko and his pack. And so his message is not read.

A raven scouting Toklat Ridge sees Roko's signal. "Kong, kong, kong," he bells—death is coming to the ridge; there will be flesh and bone for all. His voice rolls out across the valley. It penetrates the rocky cracks where the Toklat ravens rest. One by one they hear and spread their wings. They beat their way to Toklat Ridge. They alight upon the snow and walk behind the wounded wolf.

"Kong," they toll[2] with keen excitement, for the raven clan is hungry, too. "Kong, kong"—there will be flesh and bone for all.

Roko snarls and hurries toward the shelter rock. A cloud of snow envelops him. He limps in blinding whiteness now.

---

1. **Toklat Ridge** the top of a mountain located in Alaska's Denali National Park and Preserve.
2. **toll** (tōl) *v.* announce.

A ghostly presence flits around. "Hahahahahahaha," the white fox states—death is coming to the Ridge. Roko smells the fox tagging at his heels.

The cloud whirls off. Two golden eyes look up at Roko. The snowy owl has heard the ravens and joined the deathwatch.

Roko limps along. The ravens walk. The white fox leaps. The snowy owl flies and hops along the rim of Toklat Ridge. Roko stops. Below the ledge out on the flats the musk-ox herd is circling. They form a ring and all face out, a fort of heads and horns and fur that sweeps down to their hooves. Their circle means to Roko that an enemy is present. He squints and smells the wind. It carries scents of thawing ice, broken grass—and earth. The grizzly bear is up! He has awakened from his winter's sleep. A craving need for flesh will drive him.

Roko sees the shelter rock. He strains to reach it. He stumbles. The ravens move in closer. The white fox boldly walks beside him. "Hahaha," he yaps. The snowy owl flies ahead, alights, and waits.

The grizzly hears the eager fox and rises on his flat hind feet. He twists his powerful neck and head. His great paws dangle at his chest. He sees the animal procession and hears the ravens' knell[3] of death. Dropping to all fours, he joins the march up Toklat Ridge.

Roko stops; his breath comes hard. A raven alights upon his back and picks the open wound. Roko snaps. The raven flies and circles back. The white fox nips at Roko's toes. The snowy owl inches closer. The grizzly bear, still dulled by sleep, stumbles onto Toklat Ridge.

Only yards from the shelter rock, Roko falls.

Instantly the ravens mob him. They scream and peck and stab at his eyes. The white fox leaps upon his wound. The snowy owl sits and waits.

Young Roko struggles to his feet. He bites the ravens. Snaps the fox. And lunges at the stoic[4] owl. He turns and warns the grizzly bear. Then he bursts into a run and falls against the shelter rock. The wounded wolf wedges down between the rock and barren ground. Now protected on three sides, he turns and faces all his foes.

Character's Actions
How do Roko's actions in this scene influence the behavior of the other animals on Toklat Ridge?

Character Traits
What type of characterization does the author use here? Describe Roko, based on this passage.

---

3. **knell** (nel) *n.* mournful sound, like a slowly ringing bell—usually indicating a death.
4. **stoic** (stō ik) *adj.* calm and unaffected by hardship.

Practice continued

The ravens step a few feet closer. The fox slides toward him on his belly. The snowy owl blinks and waits, and on the ridge rim roars the hungry grizzly bear.

Roko growls.

The sun comes up. Far across the Toklat Valley, Roko hears his pack's "hunt's end" song. The music wails and sobs, wilder than the bleating wind. The hunt song ends. Next comes the roll call. Each member of the Toklat pack barks to say that he is home and well.

"Kiglo here," Roko hears his leader bark. There is a pause. It is young Roko's turn. He cannot lift his head to answer: the pack is silent. The leader starts the count once more. "Kiglo here."—A pause. Roko cannot answer.

Character's Actions Why is the raven's action important to the plot of the story?

The wounded wolf whimpers softly. A mindful raven hears. "Kong, kong, kong," he tolls—this is the end. His booming sounds across the valley. The wolf pack hears the raven's message that something is dying. They know it is Roko, who has not answered roll call.

Setting This is the climax of the story. What details of the setting increase the tension?

The hours pass. The wind slams snow on Toklat Ridge. Massive clouds blot out the sun. In their gloom Roko sees the deathwatch move in closer. Suddenly he hears the musk-oxen thundering into their circle. The ice cracks as the grizzly leaves. The ravens burst into the air. The white fox runs. The snowy owl flaps to the top of the shelter rock. And Kiglo rounds the knoll.

In his mouth he carries meat. He drops it close to Roko's head and wags his tail excitedly. Roko licks Kiglo's chin to honor him. Then Kiglo puts his mouth around Roko's nose. This gesture says "I am your leader." And by mouthing Roko, he binds him and all the wolves together.

The wounded wolf wags his tail. Kiglo trots away.

Already Roko's wound feels better. He gulps the food and feels his strength return. He shatters bone, flesh, and gristle and shakes the scraps out on the snow. The hungry ravens swoop upon them. The white fox snatches up a bone. The snowy owl gulps down flesh and fur. And Roko wags his tail and watches.

For days Kiglo brings young Roko food. He gnashes, gorges, and shatters bits upon the snow.

A purple sandpiper winging north sees ravens, owl, and fox. And he drops in upon the feast. The long-tailed jaeger gull flies down and joins the crowd on Toklat Ridge. Roko wags his tail.

One dawn he moves his wounded leg. He stretches it and pulls himself into the sunlight. He walks—he romps. He runs in circles. He leaps and plays with chunks of ice. Suddenly he stops. The "hunt's end" song rings out. Next comes the roll call.

"Kiglo here."

"Roko here," he barks out strongly.

The pack is silent.

"Kiglo here," the leader repeats.

"Roko here."

Across the distance comes the sound of whoops and yips and barks and howls. They fill the dawn with celebration. And Roko prances down the Ridge.

Theme Think about the ways the wolves help each other in this story. What insight can you gain from their behavior?

After You Read | The Wounded Wolf

1. Key Ideas and Details (a) How was Roko injured? **(b) Analyze:** What action does Roko take to save himself?

2. Key Ideas and Details (a) How does Kiglo learn that Roko is hurt? **(b) Infer:** What does Kiglo's behavior show about how wolves take care of pack members?

3. Integration of Knowledge and Ideas (a) What is the conflict in this story? **(b) Synthesize:** Does the conflict teach a lesson? Use details from the story to explain your answer.

4. Integration of Knowledge and Ideas (a) In the first column of a chart like the one shown, identify details that help you picture the setting. **(b) Connect:** In the second column, tell what those details mean in the struggle for survival. **(c) Collaborate:** With a partner, complete the third column with information that explains why the setting is important to the story.

Setting		
What it says	What it means	Why it is important

ⓒ Leveled Texts

Build your skills and improve your comprehension of short stories with texts of increasing complexity.

Read **"The Tail"** to meet a girl who learns that baby-sitting her little brother is not as terrible as she thought.

Read **"Dragon, Dragon"** to enjoy a funny take on a typical fairy-tale problem—a dragon who overruns a kingdom.

ⓒ Common Core State Standards

Meet these standards with either **"The Tail"** (p. 192) or **"Dragon, Dragon"** (p. 206).

Reading Literature

1. Cite textual evidence to support analysis of what the text says explicitly as well as inferences drawn from the text. *(Reading Skill: Make Inferences)*

3. Describe how the characters respond or change as the plot moves toward a resolution. *(Literary Analysis: Characterization)*

Spiral Review: RL.6.5

Writing

4. Produce clear and coherent writing in which the development, organization, and style are appropriate to task, purpose, and audience. *(Writing: Help-Wanted Ad)*

Speaking and Listening

2. Interpret information presented in diverse media and formats and explain how it contributes to a topic, text, or issue under study. *(Research and Technology: Compare-and-Contrast Chart)*

Language

1. Demonstrate command of the conventions of standard English grammar and usage when writing or speaking. *(Conventions: Verbs)*

Language

6. Acquire and use accurately grade-appropriate general academic and domain-specific words and phrases; gather vocabulary knowledge when considering a word or phrase important to comprehension or expression. *(Vocabulary: Word Study)*

Reading Skill: Make Inferences

When you **make inferences,** you make logical assumptions about something not directly stated in the text. To make inferences, **use details** that the writer provides.

Example: Arnie *ran* to the mailbox to see if Jim's letter had *finally* arrived.

- You can infer from the word *finally* that Arnie has been waiting to hear from Jim.
- You can infer from *ran* that he is eager to get the letter.

Literary Analysis: Characterization

Characterization is the way writers develop characters and reveal their traits, or qualities.

- With **direct characterization,** writers make straightforward statements about a character. For example, "Ron is honest."
- With **indirect characterization,** writers present a character's thoughts, words, and actions and reveal what others say and think about the character.

Once you analyze the qualities of a story's main characters, think about ways in which those qualities affect the plot of the story and its outcome. For example, a character's stubbornness may cause him to come into conflict with others in a story.

Using the Strategy: Character Map

Use a **character map** like this one to record character traits.

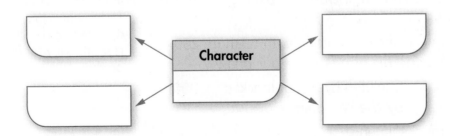

Is *conflict* always bad?

Writing About the Big Question

In "The Tail," a 13-year-old girl is upset when her mother says she has to babysit her brother all summer. Use these sentence starters to develop your ideas about the Big Question.

Arguments between children and their parents can start when _____.

Arguments can have positive **conclusions** when _____.

While You Read Look for positive outcomes of the conflicts between Tasha and her family members.

Vocabulary

Read each word and its definition. Decide whether you know the word well, know it a little bit, or do not know it at all. After you read, see how your knowledge of each word has increased.

- **vow** (vou) *n.* promise or pledge (p. 194) *I will keep my vow, no matter what happens!* *vowed v. avow v.*

- **anxious** (aŋk´ shəs) *adj.* eager (p. 195) *Peggy was anxious to get to the dance on time.* *anxiously adv. anxiousness n. anxiety n.*

- **routine** (ro͞o tēn´) *n.* usual way in which something is done (p. 197) *My morning routine includes brushing my teeth.* *routinely adv. route n.*

- **gnawing** (nô´ iŋ) *v.* biting and cutting with teeth (p. 200) *The dog was gnawing his bone.* *gnawed v. gnaw v.*

- **mauled** (môld) *v.* badly injured by being attacked (p. 200) *The doll was mauled by the cat.* *maul v. mauling v.*

- **spasm** (spaz´ əm) *n.* sudden short burst of energy or activity (p. 201) *His coughing spasm seemed to last forever.* *spastic adj.*

Word Study

The **Latin prefix dis-** often changes a word's meaning to its opposite.

For example, **vow** and **avow** mean "to declare" or "admit something openly."

In this short story, Tasha wants to **disavow**, or deny, responsibility for her brother.

Meet
Joyce Hansen
(b. 1942)

Author of

The Tail

Award-winning author Joyce Hansen was born and raised in New York City and went to college there. She then spent twenty-two years teaching in the city's public schools. Her first three novels—*The Gift-Giver, Yellow Bird and Me,* and *Home Boy*—are all set in New York and focus on the lives of young people. Hansen, now a full-time writer, believes that writing for young people carries "a special responsibility."

A Writer's Influences "I write about what I know and what moves me deeply," she says. "My characters are greatly influenced by my childhood and my students." Hansen learned the art of storytelling from her father. She explains, "My father entertained my brothers and me with stories about his boyhood in the West Indies and his experiences as a young man in the Harlem of the 1920s and 1930s."

DID YOU KNOW?
Four of Hansen's historical novels have earned the Coretta Scott King Honor Book Award.

BACKGROUND FOR THE STORY
Baby-sitting
When parents go out and need someone to watch their young children, they may hire a baby sitter. In many communities, police departments and other service organizations offer courses for future baby sitters. These courses teach first aid, fire safety, and poison control. In some families, however, an older brother or sister may be responsible for "baby-sitting" a younger brother or sister. "The Tail" centers on the thoughts and actions of a teenage girl baby-sitting her brother.

The Tail

Joyce Hansen

▲ **Critical Viewing**
What can you infer about the relationship between these two characters? Explain. **[Infer]**

It began as the worst summer of my life.

The evening before the first day of summer vacation, my mother broke the bad news to me. I was in the kitchen washing dishes and dreaming about the wonderful things my friends and I would be doing for two whole months—practicing for the annual double-dutch[1] contest, which we would definitely win; going to the roller skating rink, the swimming pool, the beach; and sleeping as late in the morning as I wanted to.

_____

1. **double-dutch** a jump-rope game in which two ropes are used at the same time.

"Tasha," my ma broke into my happy thoughts, "your father and I decided that you're old enough now to take on certain responsibilities."

My heart came to a sudden halt. "Responsibilities?"

"Yes. You do know what that word means, don't you?"

I nodded, watching her dice an onion into small, perfect pieces.

"You're thirteen going on fourteen and your father and I decided that you're old enough to watch Junior this summer, because I'm going to start working again."

"Oh, no!" I broke the dish with a crash. "Not that, Mama." Junior is my seven-year-old brother and has been following me like a tail ever since he learned how to walk. And to make matters worse, there are no kids Junior's age on our block. Everyone is either older or younger than he is.

I'd rather be in school than minding Junior all day. I could've cried.

"Natasha! There won't be a dish left in this house. You're not going to spend all summer ripping and roaring. You'll baby-sit Junior."

"But, Ma," I said, "it'll be miserable. That's not fair. All summer with Junior. I won't be able to play with my friends."

She wiped her hands on her apron. "Life ain't always fair." I knew she'd say that.

"You'll still be able to play with your friends," she continued, "but Junior comes first. He is your responsibility. We're a family and we all have to help out." ●

Mama went to work that next morning. Junior and I both stood by the door as she gave her last-minute instructions. Junior held her hand and stared up at her with an innocent look in his bright brown eyes, which everyone thought were so cute. Dimples decorated his round cheeks as he smiled and nodded at me every time Ma gave me an order. I knew he was just waiting for her to leave so he could torment me.

"Tasha, I'm depending on you. Don't leave the block."

"Yes, Ma."

"No company."

"Not even Naomi? She's my best friend."

Make Inferences
Based on her words and actions, how does Tasha feel about baby-sitting her brother?

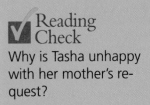

Reading Check
Why is Tasha unhappy with her mother's request?

"No company when your father and I are not home."

"Yes, Ma."

"Don't let Junior hike in the park."

"Yes, Ma."

"Make yourself and Junior a sandwich for lunch."

"Yes, Ma."

"I'll be calling you at twelve, so you'd better be in here fixing lunch. I don't want you all eating junk food all day long."

"Yes, Ma."

"Don't ignore Junior."

"Yes, Ma."

"Clean the breakfast dishes."

"Yes, Ma."

"Don't open the door to strangers."

"Yes, Ma."

Then she turned to Junior. "Now you, young man. You are to listen to your sister."

"Yes, Mommy," he sang out.

"Don't give her a hard time. Show me what a big boy you can be."

"Mommy, I'll do whatever Tasha say."

She kissed us both good-bye and left. I wanted to cry. A whole summer with Junior.

Junior turned to me and raised his right hand. "This is a **vow** of obedience." He looked up at the ceiling. "I promise to do whatever Tasha says."

"What do you know about vows?" I asked.

"I saw it on television. A man—"

"Shut up, Junior. I don't feel like hearing about some television show. It's too early in the morning."

I went into the kitchen to start cleaning, when the downstairs bell rang. "Answer the intercom,[2] Junior. If it's Naomi, tell her to wait for me on the stoop," I called out. I knew that it was Naomi, ready to start our big, fun summer. After a few minutes the bell rang again.

"Junior!" I yelled. "Answer the intercom."

The bell rang again and I ran into the living room. Junior was sitting on the couch, looking at cartoons. "What's wrong with you? Why won't you answer the bell?"

Characterization
Based on this dialogue, how would you describe Tasha's mother? Explain.

Vocabulary
vow (vou) *n.* promise or pledge

---

2. **intercom** *n.* a communication system used in apartment buildings.

He looked at me as if I were crazy. "You told me to shut up. I told you I'd do everything you say."

I pulled my hair. "See, you're bugging me already. Do something to help around here."

I pressed the intercom on the wall. "That you, Naomi?"

"Yeah."

"I'll be down in a minute. Wait for me out front."

"Okay."

I quickly washed the dishes. I couldn't believe how messed up my plans were. Suddenly there was a loud blast from the living room. I was so startled that I dropped a plate and it smashed to smithereens. Ma will kill me, I thought as I ran to the living room. It sounded like whole pieces of furniture were being sucked into the vacuum cleaner.

"Junior," I screamed over the racket, "you have it on too high."

He couldn't even hear me. I turned it off myself.

"What's wrong?"

"Ma vacuumed the living room last night. It doesn't need cleaning."

"You told me to do something to help," he whined.

I finished the dishes in a hurry so that I could leave the apartment before Junior bugged out again.

I was so anxious to get outside that we ran down the four flights of stairs instead of waiting for the elevator. Junior clutched some comic books and his checkers game. He put his Mets baseball cap on backward as usual. Naomi sat on the stoop and Junior plopped right next to her like they were the best of friends.

"Hi, cutey." She smiled at him, turning his cap to the front of his head the way it was supposed to be.

"What are we going to do today, Naomi?" he asked.

Make Inferences
Why do you think Tasha pulls her hair?

Vocabulary
anxious (aŋk´ shəs) *adj.* eager

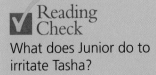
Reading Check
What does Junior do to irritate Tasha?

The Tail **195**

"Junior, you're not going to be in our faces all day," I snapped at him.

"Mama said you have to watch me. So I have to be in your face."

"You're baby-sitting, Tasha?" Naomi asked.

"Yeah." I told her the whole story.

"Aw, that's not so bad. At least you don't have to stay in the house. Junior will be good. Right, cutey?"

He grinned as she pinched his cheeks.

"See, you think he's cute because you don't have no pesty little brother or sister to watch," I grumbled.

"You ready for double-dutch practice?" she asked. "Yvonne and Keisha are going to meet us in the playground."

"Mama said we have to stay on the block," Junior answered before I could even open my mouth.

"No one's talking to you, Junior." I pulled Naomi up off the stoop. "I promised my mother we'd stay on the block, but the playground is just across the street. I can see the block from there."

"It's still not the block," Junior mumbled as we raced across the street.

We always went over to the playground to jump rope. The playground was just by the entrance to the park. There was a lot of space for us to do our fancy steps. The park was like a big green mountain in the middle of Broadway.

I'd figure out a way to keep Junior from telling that we really didn't stay on the block. "Hey, Tasha, can I go inside the park and look for caves?" People said that if you went deep inside the park, there were caves that had been used centuries ago when Native Americans still lived in northern Manhattan.

"No, Ma said no hiking in the park."

"She said no leaving the block, too, and you left the block."

"Look how close we are to the block. I mean, we can even see it. You could get lost inside the park."

"I'm going to tell Ma you didn't stay on the block."

Characterization
What character trait does Tasha show by deciding to go to the playground?

> **Mama said you have to watch me.**

"Okay, me and Naomi will hike with you up to the Cloisters later." That's a museum that sits at the top of the park, overlooking the Hudson River. "Now read your comic books."

"Will you play checkers with me too?"

"You know I hate checkers. Leave me alone." I spotted Keisha and Yvonne walking into the playground. All of us wore shorts and sneakers.

Junior tagged behind me and Naomi as we went to meet them. "Remember you're supposed to be watching me," he said.

"How could I forget."

The playground was crowded. Swings were all taken and the older boys played stickball. Some little kids played in the sandboxes.

Keisha and Yvonne turned and Naomi and I jumped together, practicing a new routine. We were so good that some of the boys in the stickball game watched us. A few elderly people stopped to look at us too. We had an audience, so I really showed off—spinning and doing a lot of fancy footwork.

Suddenly Junior jumped in the ropes with us and people laughed and clapped.

"Junior!" I screamed. "Get out of here!"

Vocabulary
routine (rōō tēn´) *n.* usual way in which something is done

Make Inferences
What are Tasha's feelings as the girls begin to jump?

☑ Reading Check
What does Junior threaten to tell his mother?

◄ **Critical Viewing**
Why might Tasha want to spend her summer in a park like this one? **[Analyze]**

Pet Precautions Americans love their pets and often think of their dogs and cats as members of their families. However, not all animals are safe to approach. If you confront a stray dog, consider it dangerous until you know better. Follow these safety guidelines:

• Approach the dog slowly and gently and keep your face away from its face.

• If a dog is chasing you, stop running because it encourages the animal to chase you.

• Do not touch a dog that is growling, showing its teeth, or barking excitedly.

• Do not look an aggressive dog in the eye. Instead, back away slowly.

Connect to the Literature

Why might Tasha forget these rules as she searches for Junior?

"Remember, your job is to watch me." He grinned. My foot slipped and all three of us got tangled in the ropes and fell.

"Your feet are too big!" Junior yelled.

Everybody roared. I was too embarrassed. I tried to grab him, but he got away from me. "Get lost," I hollered after him as he ran toward the swings.

I tried to forget how stupid I must've looked and went back to the ropes. I don't know how long we'd been jumping when suddenly a little kid ran by us yelling, "There's a wild dog loose up there!" He pointed to the steps that led deep inside the park.

People had been saying for years that a pack of abandoned dogs who'd turned wild lived in the park, but no one ever really saw them.

We forgot about the kid and kept jumping. Then one of the boys our age who'd been playing stickball came over to us. "We're getting out of here," he said. "A big yellow dog with red eyes just bit a kid."

I took the rope from Yvonne. It was time for me and Naomi to turn. "That's ridiculous. Who ever heard of a yellow dog with red eyes?"

Naomi stopped turning. "Dogs look all kind of ways. Especially wild dogs. I'm leaving."

"Me too," Yvonne said.

Keisha was already gone. No one was in the swings or the sandboxes. I didn't even see the old men who usually sat on the benches. "Guess we'd better get out of here too," I said. Then I realized that I didn't see Junior anywhere.

"Junior!" I shouted.

"Maybe he went home," Naomi said.

We dashed across the street. Our block was empty. Yvonne ran ahead of us and didn't stop until she reached her stoop. When I got to my stoop I expected to see Junior there, but no Junior.

"Maybe he went upstairs," Naomi said.

"I have the key. He can't get in the house."

"Maybe he went to the candy store?"

"He doesn't have any money, I don't think. But let's look."

We ran around the corner to the candy store, but no Junior.

As we walked back to the block, I remembered something.

"Oh, no, Naomi, I told him to get lost. And that's just what he did."

"He's probably hiding from us somewhere. You know how he likes to tease." She looked around as we walked up our block. "He might be hiding and watching us right now looking for him." She peeped behind parked cars, in doorways, and even opened the lid of a trash can.

"Junior," I called. "Junior!"

No answer. Only the sounds of birds and cars, sirens and a distant radio. I looked at the empty stoop where Junior should have been sitting. A part of me was gone and I had to find it. And another part of me would be gone if my mother found out I'd lost Junior.

I ran back toward the playground and Naomi followed me. "He's got to be somewhere right around here," she panted.

I ran past the playground and into the park. "Tasha, you're not going in there, are you? The dog."

I didn't answer her and began climbing the stone steps that wound around and through the park. Naomi's eyes stretched all over her face and she grabbed my arm. "It's dangerous up here!"

I turned around. "If you're scared, don't come. Junior's my only baby brother. Dear God," I said out loud, "please let me find him. I will play any kind of game he wants. I'll never yell at him again. I promise never to be mean to him again in my life!"

Naomi breathed heavily behind me. "I don't think Junior would go this far by himself."

I stopped and caught my breath. The trees were thick and the city street sounds were far away now.

"I know Junior. He's somewhere up here making believe he's the king of this mountain. Hey, Junior," I called, "I was just kidding. Don't get lost." We heard a rustling in the

Spiral Review
Setting Which details on this page contribute to the development of the setting? What feeling do they convey?

Make Inferences
How does Tasha feel about Junior's disappearance? How can you tell?

"Oh, no, Naomi, I told him to get lost. And that's just what he did."

Reading Check
Why is Tasha suddenly worried about Junior?

Vocabulary
gnawing (nô´ iŋ) *v.*
biting and cutting
with the teeth

bushes and grabbed each other. "Probably just a bird," I said, trying to sound brave.

As we climbed some more, I tried not to imagine a huge yellow dog with red eyes gnawing at my heels.

The steps turned a corner and ended. Naomi screamed and pointed up ahead. "What's that?"

I saw a big brown and gray monstrous thing with tentacles reaching toward the sky, jutting out of the curve in the path. I screamed and almost ran.

"What is that, Naomi?"

"I don't know."

"This is a park in the middle of Manhattan. It can't be a bear or anything." I screamed to the top of my lungs, "Junior!" Some birds flew out of a tree, but the thing never moved.

All Naomi could say was, "Dogs, Tasha."

I found a stick. "I'm going up. You wait here. If you hear growling and screaming, run and get some help." I couldn't believe how brave I was. Anyway, that thing, whatever it was, couldn't hurt me any more than my mother would if I didn't find Junior.

"You sure, Tasha?"

Vocabulary
mauled (môld) *v.*
badly injured by
being attacked

"No sense in both of us being mauled," I said.

I tipped lightly up the steps, holding the stick like a club. When I was a few feet away from the thing, I crumpled to the ground and laughed so hard that Naomi ran to me. "Naomi, look at what scared us."

She laughed too. "A dead tree trunk."

We both laughed until we cried. Then I saw one of Junior's comic books near a bush. I picked it up and started to cry. "See, he was here. And that animal probably tore him to pieces." Naomi patted my shaking shoulders.

Make Inferences
What can you infer
from Tasha's reaction
to discovering Junior's
comic book?

Suddenly, there was an unbelievable growl. My legs turned to air as I flew down the steps. Naomi was ahead of me. Her two braids stuck out like propellers. My feet didn't even touch the ground. We screamed all the way down the steps. I tripped on the last step and was sprawled out on the ground. Two women passing by bent over me. "Child, are you hurt?" one of them asked.

Then I heard a familiar laugh above me and looked up into Junior's dimpled face. He laughed so hard, he held his stomach with one hand. His checkers game was in the other. A little tan, mangy[3] dog stood next to him, wagging its tail.

I got up slowly. "Junior, I'm going to choke you."

He doubled over with squeals and chuckles. I wiped my filthy shorts with one hand and stretched out the other to snatch Junior's neck. The stupid little dog had the nerve to growl.

"Me and Thunder hid in the bushes. We followed you." He continued laughing. Then he turned to the dog. "Thunder, didn't Tasha look funny holding that stick like she was going to beat up the tree trunk?"

I put my hands around Junior's neck. "This is the end of the tail," I said.

Junior grinned. "You promised. 'I'll play any game he wants. I'll never yell at him again. I promise never to be mean to him again in my life.' "

Naomi giggled. "That's what you said, Tasha." The mutt barked at me. Guess he called himself Junior's protector. I took my hands off Junior's neck.

Then Naomi had a laughing spasm. She pointed at the dog. "Is that what everyone was running from?"

"This is my trusted guard. People say he's wild. He just wants a friend."

"Thunder looks like he's already got a lot of friends living inside his fur," I said. We walked back to the block with the dog trotting right by Junior's side.

I checked my watch when we got to my building. "It's ten to twelve. I have to make lunch for Junior," I told Naomi. "But I'll be back out later."

The dog whined after Junior as we entered the building. "I'll be back soon, Thunder," he said, "after I beat my sister in five games of checkers."

Now he was going to blackmail me.

I heard Naomi giggling as Junior and I walked into the building. The phone rang just as we entered the apartment. I knew it was Ma.

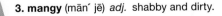

3. **mangy** (mān´ jē) *adj.* shabby and dirty.

Vocabulary
spasm (spaz´ əm) *n.* sudden short burst of energy or activity

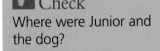
Reading Check

Where were Junior and the dog?

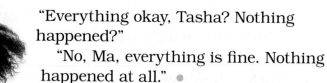

"Everything okay, Tasha? Nothing happened?"

"No, Ma, everything is fine. Nothing happened at all." •

Well, the summer didn't turn out to be so terrible after all. My parents got Thunder cleaned up and let Junior keep him for a pet. Me and my friends practiced for the double-dutch contest right in front of my building, so I didn't have to leave the block. After lunch when it was too hot to jump rope, I'd play a game of checkers with Junior or read him a story. He wasn't as pesty as he used to be, because now he had Thunder. We won the double-dutch contest. And Junior never told my parents that I'd lost him. I found out that you never miss a tail until you almost lose it.

Critical Thinking

Cite textual evidence to support your responses.

© 1. **Key Ideas and Details** **(a)** What information are Tasha and her friends given about a danger in the park? **(b) Draw Conclusions:** Why does this information suddenly cause Tasha great worry?

© 2. **Key Ideas and Details** **(a)** What does Tasha mean when she says, "I found out that you never miss a tail until you almost lose it"? **(b) Analyze:** How does Tasha's statement show a change in her attitude?

© 3. **Integration of Knowledge and Ideas** **Discuss:** Tasha learns some important lessons from her experience. Discuss which lesson might help teenagers you know.

© 4. **Integration of Knowledge and Ideas** Junior makes a vow to always listen to Tasha. **(a)** How does his vow lead to conflict? **(b)** What can Tasha learn from the conflict? *[Connect to the Big Question: Is conflict always bad?]*

Reading Skill: Make Inferences

1. Using a chart like the one shown, list the details from the story that helped you to **make an inference** about Tasha. One example is provided. Give at least two more examples.

Details		Inferences
Tasha tells Naomi, "If you're scared, don't come. Junior's my only baby brother."	→	Tasha is worried and is determined to find Junior, with or without Naomi's help.
	→	

Literary Analysis: Characterization

© **2. Key Ideas and Details** List two examples of **direct characterization** from the story.

© **3. Key Ideas and Details** **(a)** Identify two of Tasha's actions or thoughts. What character traits, or qualities, are revealed in these examples of **indirect characterization? (b)** How has Tasha changed by the story's resolution?

Vocabulary

© **Acquisition and Use** Answer each question, then explain your answer.

1. Would having a back <u>spasm</u> be pleasant?

2. Would a dog enjoy <u>gnawing</u> on a bone?

3. Should lion trainers be afraid of getting <u>mauled</u>?

4. Would you <u>vow</u> to do everything a friend tells you to do?

5. Are you <u>anxious</u> about your next dentist appointment?

6. Do you know what to expect when you follow your daily <u>routine</u>?

Word Study Use what you know about the **Latin prefix dis-** to explain your answer to each question.

1. Do you usually invite people you *dislike* to a party?

2. How would it feel to *dislocate* your shoulder?

Word Study

The **Latin prefix dis-** often changes a word's meaning to its opposite.

Apply It Explain how the prefix contributes to the meaning of these words. Consult a dictionary if necessary.

dissatisfied
disinfect
disallow

Is *conflict* always bad?

Writing About the Big Question

In "Dragon, Dragon," a king is determined to stop a dragon from terrorizing his kingdom. Use this sentence starter to develop your ideas about the Big Question.

To **defend** his or her home, a person might

_____.

While You Read Think about the different ways that defeating the dragon would benefit the entire kingdom.

Vocabulary

Read each word and its definition. Decide whether you know the word well, know it a little bit, or do not know it at all. After you read, see how your knowledge of each word has increased.

- **plagued** (plāgd) *v.* troubled or deeply annoyed (p. 206) *My poison ivy plagued me all day.* plague *n.* plaguing *v.*

- **ravaged** (rav´ ijd) *v.* violently destroyed; ruined (p. 206) *Earthquakes ravaged the country.* ravaging *v.* ravage *v.*

- **tyrant** (tī´ rənt) *n.* harsh, cruel ruler (p. 208) *The tyrant was feared by all.* tyranny *n.* tyrannical *adj.*

- **enviously** (en´ vē əs lē) *adv.* with jealousy (p. 209) *I enviously admired the pearl necklace that Kate wore.* envy *n.* envied *v.* enviable *adj.*

- **reflecting** (ri flekt´ iŋ) *v.* thinking seriously (p. 212) *I was reflecting on all of the different characters in the book.* reflect *v.* reflected *v.* reflection *n.*

- **craned** (krānd) *v.* stretched out for a better look (p. 212) *He craned his neck to see the birds.* crane *v.* crane *n.*

Word Study

The **Latin prefix re-** means "back," "return," or "anew."

After **reflecting**, or realizing after thought, that patience is a good thing, the dragon in this story decides to wait calmly.

Author of
Dragon, Dragon

John Gardner loved old tales about dragons and other monsters. His first successful novel, *Grendel*, retells the Old English story of Beowulf, a famous monster-slaying hero. In an unusual twist, Gardner presents the monster's side of the story in *Grendel.*

Birthday Stories "I had two children," Gardner once said, "and from the time they were about four, on every birthday and every Christmas, I would write them a story, one for each of them."

DID YOU KNOW?
John Gardner always worked on several book projects at a time.

BACKGROUND FOR THE STORY
Dragon Stories

Since ancient times, dragon stories have been told all over the world. Different cultures have different beliefs about these imaginary creatures. Although Asian dragons are believed to be wise and good, in other cultures dragons are thought to be greedy, evil creatures. In most European folklore, the hero who kills a dragon is a brave, strong warrior.

Dragon, Dragon

John Gardner

Vocabulary
plagued (plāgd) v. troubled or deeply annoyed

There was once a king whose kingdom was plagued by a dragon. The king did not know which way to turn. The king's knights were all cowards who hid under their beds whenever the dragon came in sight, so they were of no use to the king at all. And the king's wizard could not help either because, being old, he had forgotten his magic spells. Nor could the wizard look up the spells that had slipped his mind, for he had unfortunately misplaced his wizard's book many years before. The king was at his wit's end.

Vocabulary
ravaged (rav´ ijd) v. violently destroyed; ruined

Every time there was a full moon the dragon came out of his lair and ravaged the countryside. He frightened maidens and stopped up chimneys and broke store windows and set people's clocks back and made dogs bark until no one could hear himself think.

Characterization
Based on his actions, what words would you use to describe the dragon?

He tipped over fences and robbed graves and put frogs in people's drinking water and tore the last chapters out of novels and changed house numbers around so that people crawled into bed with their neighbors.

He stole spark plugs out of people's cars and put firecrackers in people's

◀ **Critical Viewing**
Why would the people of the kingdom fear a dragon like this one? **[Speculate]**

cigars and stole the clappers from all the church bells and sprung every bear trap for miles around so the bears could wander wherever they pleased.

And to top it all off, he changed around all the roads in the kingdom so that people could not get anywhere except by starting out in the wrong direction.

"That," said the king in a fury, "is enough!" And he called a meeting of everyone in the kingdom.

Now it happened that there lived in the kingdom a wise old cobbler who had a wife and three sons. The cobbler and his family came to the king's meeting and stood way in back by the door, for the cobbler had a feeling that since he was nobody important there had probably been some mistake, and no doubt the king had intended the meeting for everyone in the kingdom except his family and him.

Make Inferences
How does the cobbler think he is different from most people in the kingdom?

"Ladies and gentlemen," said the king when everyone was present, "I've put up with that dragon as long as I can. He has got to be stopped."

All the people whispered amongst themselves, and the king smiled, pleased with the impression he had made.

But the wise cobbler said gloomily, "It's all very well to talk about it—but how are you going to do it?"

And now all the people smiled and winked as if to say, "Well, King, he's got you there!"

The king frowned.

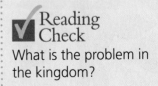
Reading Check

What is the problem in the kingdom?

Vocabulary
tyrant (tī´ rənt) *n.*
harsh, cruel ruler

Characterization
Based on his actions
and words, how would
you describe the
wizard?

"It's not that His Majesty hasn't tried," the queen spoke up loyally.

"Yes," said the king, "I've told my knights again and again that they ought to slay that dragon. But I can't force them to go. I'm not a tyrant."

"Why doesn't the wizard say a magic spell?" asked the cobbler.

"He's done the best he can," said the king.

The wizard blushed and everyone looked embarrassed. "I used to do all sorts of spells and chants when I was younger," the wizard explained. "But I've lost my spell book, and I begin to fear I'm losing my memory too. For instance, I've been trying for days to recall one spell I used to do. I forget, just now, what the deuce it was for. It went something like—

> *Bimble,*
> *Wimble,*
> *Cha, cha*
> CHOOMPF!

Suddenly, to everyone's surprise, the queen turned into a rosebush.

"Oh dear," said the wizard.

"Now you've done it," groaned the king.

"Poor Mother," said the princess.

"I don't know what can have happened," the wizard said nervously, "but don't worry, I'll have her changed back in a jiffy." He shut his eyes and racked his brain for a spell that would change her back.

But the king said quickly, "You'd better leave well enough alone. If you change her into a rattlesnake we'll have to chop off her head."

Meanwhile the cobbler stood with his hands in his pockets, sighing at the waste of time. "About the dragon . . . " he began.

"Oh yes," said the king. "I'll tell you what I'll do. I'll give the princess's hand in marriage to anyone who can make the dragon stop."

"It's not enough," said the cobbler. "She's a nice enough girl, you understand. But how would an ordinary person support her? Also, what about those of us that are already married?"

"In that case," said the king, "I'll offer the princess's hand or half the kingdom or both—whichever is most convenient."

The cobbler scratched his chin and considered it. "It's not enough," he said at last. "It's a good enough kingdom, you understand, but it's too much responsibility."

"Take it or leave it," the king said.

"I'll leave it," said the cobbler. And he shrugged and went home.

But the cobbler's eldest son thought the bargain was a good one, for the princess was very beautiful and he liked the idea of having half the kingdom to run as he pleased. So he said to the king, "I'll accept those terms, Your Majesty. By tomorrow morning the dragon will be slain."

"Bless you!" cried the king.

"Hooray, hooray, hooray!" cried all the people, throwing their hats in the air.

The cobbler's eldest son beamed with pride, and the second eldest looked at him **enviously**. The youngest son said timidly, "Excuse me, Your Majesty, but don't you think the queen looks a little unwell? If I were you I think I'd water her."

"Good heavens," cried the king, glancing at the queen who had been changed into a rosebush, "I'm glad you mentioned it!" ●

Now the cobbler's eldest son was very clever and was known far and wide for how quickly he could multiply fractions in his head. He was perfectly sure he could slay the dragon by somehow or other playing a trick on him, and he didn't feel that he needed his wise old father's advice. But he thought it was only polite to ask, and so he went to his father, who was working as usual at his cobbler's bench, and said, "Well, Father, I'm off to slay the dragon. Have you any advice to give me?"

The cobbler thought a moment and replied, "When and if you come to the dragon's lair, recite the following poem:

Dragon, dragon, how do you do?
I've come from the king to murder you.

Say it very loudly and firmly and the dragon will fall, God willing, at your feet."

"How curious!" said the eldest son. And he thought to himself, "The old man is not as wise as I thought. If I say something like that to the dragon, he will eat me up in an instant. The way to kill a dragon is to out-fox him." And keeping his opinion to himself, the eldest son set forth on his quest.

Make Inferences
What details support the inference that the cobbler is practical and has common sense?

Vocabulary
enviously
(en´ vē əs lē) *adv.*
with jealousy

Characterization
Does the sentence starting "Now the cobbler's eldest son . . ." use direct or indirect characterization? Explain.

Reading Check
Why is the wizard unable to get rid of the dragon?

When he came at last to the dragon's lair, which was a cave, the eldest son slyly disguised himself as a peddler and knocked on the door and called out, "Hello there!"

"There's nobody home!" roared a voice.

The voice was as loud as an earthquake, and the eldest son's knees knocked together in terror.

"I don't come to trouble you," the eldest son said meekly. "I merely thought you might be interested in looking at some of our brushes. Or if you'd prefer," he added quickly, "I could leave our catalogue with you and I could drop by again, say, early next week."

"I don't want any brushes," the voice roared, "and I especially don't want any brushes next week."

"Oh," said the eldest son. By now his knees were knocking together so badly that he had to sit down.

Suddenly a great shadow fell over him, and the eldest son looked up. It was the dragon. The eldest son drew his sword, but the dragon lunged and swallowed him in a single gulp, sword and all, and the eldest son found himself in the dark of the dragon's belly. "What a fool I was not to listen to my wise old father!" thought the eldest son. And he began to weep bitterly. ●

"Well," sighed the king the next morning, "I see the dragon has not been slain yet."

"I'm just as glad, personally," said the princess, sprinkling the queen. "I would have had to marry that eldest son, and he had warts."

Now the cobbler's middle son decided it was his turn to try. The middle son was very strong and he was known far and wide for being able to lift up the corner of a church. He felt perfectly sure he could slay the dragon by simply laying into him, but he thought it would be only polite to ask his father's advice. So he went to his father and said to him, "Well, Father, I'm off to slay the dragon. Have you any advice for me?"

The cobbler told the middle son exactly what he'd told the eldest.

"When and if you come to the dragon's lair, recite the following poem:

Dragon, dragon, how do you do?
I've come from the king to murder you.

Make Inferences
What details support the inference that this is a humorous tale rather than a realistic or scary one?

Characterization
What new details about the eldest son's character do you learn in this paragraph?

Say it very loudly and firmly, and the dragon will fall, God willing, at your feet."

"What an odd thing to say," thought the middle son. "The old man is not as wise as I thought. You have to take these dragons by surprise." But he kept his opinion to himself and set forth.

When he came in sight of the dragon's lair, the middle son spurred his horse to a gallop and thundered into the entrance swinging his sword with all his might.

But the dragon had seen him while he was still a long way off, and being very clever, the dragon had crawled up on top of the door so that when the son came charging in he went under the dragon and on to the back of the cave and slammed into the wall. Then the dragon chuckled and got down off the door, taking his time, and strolled back to where the man and the horse lay unconscious from the terrific blow. Opening his mouth as if for a yawn, the dragon swallowed the middle son in a single gulp and put the horse in the freezer to eat another day.

"What a fool I was not to listen to my wise old father," thought the middle son when he came to in the dragon's belly. And he too began to weep bitterly.

That night there was a full moon, and the dragon ravaged the countryside so terribly that several families moved to another kingdom.

"Well," sighed the king in the morning, "still no luck in this dragon business, I see."

"I'm just as glad, myself," said the princess, moving her mother, pot and all, to the window where the sun could get at her. "The cobbler's middle son was a kind of humpback." ●

Now the cobbler's youngest son saw that his turn had come. He was very upset and nervous, and he wished he had never been born. He was not clever, like his eldest brother, and he was not strong, like his second-eldest brother. He was a decent, honest boy who always minded his elders.

He borrowed a suit of armor from a friend of his who was a knight, and when the youngest son put the armor on it was so heavy he could hardly walk. From another knight he borrowed a sword, and that was so heavy that the only

Make Inferences
How is the middle son different from the eldest son? Support your answer.

▼ **Critical Viewing**
Does the boy in this picture look like a dragon slayer? Explain. **[Evaluate]**

☑ Reading Check
What does the father tell his middle son to do when he gets to the dragon's lair?

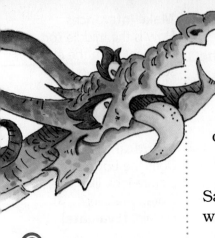

way the youngest son could get it to the dragon's lair was to drag it along behind his horse like a plow.

When everything was in readiness, the youngest son went for a last conversation with his father.

"Father, have you any advice to give me?" he asked.

"Only this," said the cobbler. "When and if you come to the dragon's lair, recite the following poem:

Dragon, dragon, how do you do?
I've come from the king to murder you.

Say it very loudly and firmly, and the dragon will fall, God willing, at your feet."

"Are you certain?" asked the youngest son uneasily.

"As certain as one can ever be in these matters," said the wise old cobbler.

And so the youngest son set forth on his quest. He traveled over hill and dale and at last came to the dragon's cave.

The dragon, who had seen the cobbler's youngest son while he was still a long way off, was seated up above the door, inside the cave, waiting and smiling to himself. But minutes passed and no one came thundering in. The dragon frowned, puzzled, and was tempted to peek out. However, reflecting that patience seldom goes unrewarded, the dragon kept his head up out of sight and went on waiting. At last, when he could stand it no longer, the dragon craned his neck and looked. There at the entrance of the cave stood a trembling young man in a suit of armor twice his size, struggling with a sword so heavy he could lift only one end of it at a time.

At sight of the dragon, the cobbler's youngest son began to tremble so violently that his armor rattled like a house caving in. He heaved with all his might at the sword and got the handle up level with his chest, but even now the point was down in the dirt. As loudly and firmly as he could manage, the youngest son cried—

Dragon, dragon, how do you do?
I've come from the king to murder you.

"What?" cried the dragon, flabbergasted. *"You? You? Murder Me???"* All at once he began to laugh, pointing at the little cobbler's son. *"He he he ho ha!"* he roared, shaking all over, and tears filled his eyes. *"He he he ho ho ho ha ha!*" laughed the dragon. He was laughing so hard he had to hang onto his sides, and he fell off the door and landed on his back, still laughing, kicking his legs helplessly, rolling from side to side, laughing and laughing and laughing.

The cobbler's son was annoyed. "I *do* come from the king to murder you," he said. "A person doesn't like to be laughed at for a thing like that."

"He he he!" wailed the dragon, almost sobbing, gasping for breath. "Of course not, poor dear boy! But really, *he he*, the *idea* of it, *ha, ha, ha!* And that simply ridiculous *poem!*" Tears streamed from the dragon's eyes and he lay on his back perfectly helpless with laughter.

"It's a good poem," said the cobbler's youngest son loyally. "My father made it up." And growing angrier he shouted, "I want you to stop that laughing, or I'll—I'll—" But the dragon could not stop for the life of him. And suddenly, in a terrific rage, the cobbler's son began flopping the sword end over end in the direction of the dragon. Sweat ran off the youngest son's forehead, but he labored on, blistering mad, and at last, with one supreme heave, he had the sword standing on its handle a foot from the dragon's throat. Of its own weight the sword fell, slicing the dragon's head off.

"He he ho huk," went the dragon—and then he lay dead. •

The two older brothers crawled out and thanked their younger brother for saving their lives. "We have learned our lesson," they said.

Then the three brothers gathered all the treasures from the dragon's cave and tied them to the back end of the youngest brother's horse, and tied the dragon's head on behind the treasures, and started home. "I'm glad I listened to my father," the youngest son thought. "Now I'll be the richest man in the kingdom."

There were hand-carved picture frames and silver spoons and boxes of jewels and chests of money and silver compasses and maps telling where there were more treasures buried when these ran out. There was also a

LITERATURE IN CONTEXT

Literature Connection

Traditional Dragon Stories
Much of the humor in "Dragon, Dragon" comes from the way it turns traditional dragon stories upside down. For example, in *Beowulf,* one of the most famous dragon stories of all time, the king is a wise and noble man. A terrible dragon has been attacking his hall and killing his warriors. When brave Beowulf, a true hero, learns that the king needs help, he sails quickly to the rescue, humbly yet bravely presenting himself as the man for the job.

Connect to the Literature

Which of the cobbler's sons is most like Beowulf? Explain.

Reading Check
What happens to the youngest son when he arrives at the dragon's cave?

curious old book with a picture of an owl on the cover, and inside, poems and odd sentences and recipes that seemed to make no sense.

When they reached the king's castle the people all leaped for joy to see that the dragon was dead, and the princess ran out and kissed the youngest brother on the forehead, for secretly she had hoped it would be him.

"Well," said the king, "which half of the kingdom do you want?"

"My wizard's book!" exclaimed the wizard. "He's found my wizard's book!" He opened the book and ran his finger along under the words and then said in a loud voice, "Glmuzk, shkzmlp, blam!"

Instantly the queen stood before them in her natural shape, except she was soaking wet from being sprinkled too often. She glared at the king.

"Oh dear," said the king, hurrying toward the door.

Critical Thinking

Cite textual evidence to support your responses.

1. Key Ideas and Details (a) What advice does the cobbler give to his sons? **(b) Connect:** Why do the sons doubt his advice?

2. Key Ideas and Details (a) What happens to the two elder sons when they attempt to slay the dragon? **(b) Interpret:** What might their fate say about people who do not listen to advice?

3. Key Ideas and Details (a) How does the youngest son succeed in slaying the dragon? **(b) Analyze:** Why is the youngest son successful? **(c) Deduce:** What does the cobbler seem to know all along about his sons and about the dragon?

4. Integration of Knowledge and Ideas In this story, a dragon terrorizes a kingdom. Does anything good result within the community as they respond to the dragon's actions? Explain. Which choice leads to conflict? *[Connect to the Big Question: Is conflict always bad?]*

Reading Skill: Make Inferences

1. Using a chart like the one shown, list the details that led you to **make an inference** about the youngest son. One example is provided. Give at least two more examples.

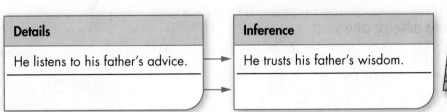

Details
He listens to his father's advice.

Inference
He trusts his father's wisdom.

Literary Analysis: Characterization

2. Craft and Structure List two examples of **direct characterization** from the story.

3. Craft and Structure Identify two actions or thoughts of the youngest son. **(a)** What character traits, or qualities, are revealed in these examples of **indirect characterization? (b)** How have the other brothers changed by the story's resolution?

Vocabulary

Acquisition and Use Answer each question containing a word from the list on page 204. Explain your answer.

1. Does <u>reflecting</u> on a book lead to better understanding?

2. Does a house that a storm has <u>ravaged</u> need repairs?

3. If a turtle <u>craned</u> his neck, was he hiding his head?

4. If a picnic is <u>plagued</u> by mosquitoes, is it fun?

5. Does a <u>tyrant</u> care about what the people want?

6. If you <u>enviously</u> look at a friend's toy, do you like it?

Word Study Use the context of the sentence and your knowledge of the **Latin prefix re-** to explain your answers.

1. If students *reappoint* their class president, are they electing someone new?

2. Would you *reattempt* to do something for the first time?

Word Study

The **Latin prefix re-** means "back," "return," or "anew."

Apply It Explain how the prefix contributes to the meaning of these words. Consult a dictionary if necessary.

revisit
reattach
reawaken

Integrated Language Skills

The Tail • Dragon, Dragon

Conventions: Verbs

A **verb** expresses an action or a state of being. Every complete sentence includes at least one verb.

An **action verb** such as *jump* or *dance* names an action of a person or thing.

A **linking verb** such as *is* or *feels*, connects a noun or pronoun to a word that identifies, renames, or describes the noun or pronoun. Other common linking verbs are *seem*, *look*, and *become*.

Action Verbs	Linking Verbs
Bobby *jumped* over the rocks. (The action is *jumping*.) The tomato plant *grew* taller. (The action is *growing*.)	Katie *is* an artist. (*Is* links *Katie* to *artist*. *Artist* renames *Katie*.) The blanket *feels* soft. (*Feels* links *blanket* to *soft*. *Soft* describes the blanket.)

Practice A Identify the verb(s) in each sentence and indicate whether they are action verbs or linking verbs.

1. Mother told Tasha the bad news in the kitchen.
2. Tasha broke another plate.
3. Junior was a difficult brother.
4. Junior kept his vow.
5. Tasha was worried when Junior disappeared.

Ⓒ **Reading Application** In "The Tail," find one sentence that includes both an action verb and a linking verb.

Practice B Rewrite each sentence so that it contains an action verb instead of a linking verb.

1. The dragon was a pest to the kingdom.
2. The wizard is forgetful.
3. The king was weak and ineffective.
4. Which son was the most intelligent?
5. The dragon had been a problem.

Ⓒ **Writing Application** Review the images that accompany "Dragon, Dragon." Write two sentences describing one image. In one sentence, use action verbs. In the other, use linking verbs. Explain which sentence is more powerful.

PH **WRITING COACH** Further instruction and practice are available in *Prentice Hall Writing Coach*.

Writing

Explanatory Text Write a **help-wanted ad.** If you read "The Tail," write an ad to find a baby sitter. If you read "Dragon, Dragon," write an ad to find a dragon slayer. Address your audience and purpose by following these steps:

- Briefly describe the job's responsibilities or challenges.
- List the qualities and skills you are looking for in an applicant.
- Explain how much you will pay or what reward you will give.
- Organize information according to the categories above.

Grammar Application Review your help-wanted ad to be sure you have used action and linking verbs correctly.

Writing Workshop: *Work in Progress*

Prewriting for Response to Literature To prepare for a literary review you may write, think of a short story you have read recently. List events and ideas in the story that you found most interesting. Save this Ideas List in your writing portfolio.

Research and Technology

Presentation of Ideas Make a **compare-and-contrast chart** about one of these topics. Consult different media sources, such as print materials and online databases.

If you read "The Tail," research two or three games that children can play outdoors. In your chart, categorize the games based on level of difficulty, age-appropriateness, and number of players.

If you read "Dragon, Dragon," search for information about dragon tales in various cultures. In your chart, categorize the tales based on the dragons' physical features; their potential for good and evil; and the types of tales (myth, legend, folk tale) in which they appear.

Follow these steps to complete the assignment:

- Take logical and complete notes on your topic.
- Keep track of all similarities and differences.
- Be sure to note all of your source materials, or the resources you have consulted.
- Use headings to make your chart as clear as possible.
- Present your findings to your classmates in a brief oral report.

Common Core State Standards

L.6.1; W.6.4; SL.6.2
[For the full wording of the standards, see page 188.]

Use this prewriting activity to prepare for the **Writing Workshop** on page 264.

PHLit
Online!
www.PHLitOnline.com

- Interactive graphic organizers
- Grammar tutorial
- Interactive journals

Leveled Texts

Build your skills and improve your comprehension of short stories with texts of increasing complexity.

Read **"Zlateh the Goat"** to find out what happens when a boy and his goat become lost in a fierce winter storm.

Read **"The Old Woman Who Lived With the Wolves"** to learn about a bond of trust that forms between a young woman and a pack of wolves.

Common Core State Standards

Meet these standards with either **"Zlateh the Goat"** (p. 222) or **"The Old Woman Who Lived With the Wolves"** (p. 234).

Reading Literature

1. Cite textual evidence to support analysis of what the text says explicitly as well as inferences drawn from the text. *(Reading Skill: Make Inferences)*

3. Describe how a particular story's or drama's plot unfolds in a series of episodes as well as how the characters respond or change as the plot moves toward a resolution. *(Literary Analysis: Conflict and Resolution)*

Writing

1. Write arguments to support claims with clear reasons and relevant evidence. *(Writing: Persuasive Speech)*

Speaking and Listening

4. Present claims and findings, sequencing ideas logically and using pertinent descriptions, facts, and details to accentuate main ideas or themes; use appropriate eye contact, adequate volume, and clear pronunciation. *(Writing: Persuasive Speech; Research and Technology: Compare-and-Contrast Chart)*

5. Include multimedia components (e.g., graphics) and visual displays in presentations to clarify information. *(Research and Technology: Compare-and-Contrast Chart)*

Language

1. Demonstrate command of the conventions of standard English grammar and usage when writing or speaking. *(Conventions: Principal Parts of Verbs)*

Reading Skill: Make Inferences

An **inference** is a logical assumption you develop about information that is not directly stated. To make an inference, combine text clues with your **prior knowledge,** or what you already know. For example, from the sentence "Tina smiled when she saw the snow," you might infer that Tina is happy. This inference is based on your prior knowledge that people smile when they are happy. Because the text states that Tina is smiling at the snow, you can infer that the snow is the reason she is happy.

Using the Strategy: Inference Chart

Use a chart like this one to make inferences as you read.

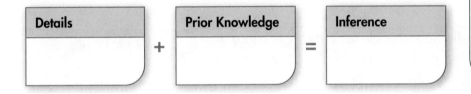

Details		Prior Knowledge		Inference
	+		=	

Literary Analysis: Conflict and Resolution

A **conflict** is a struggle between opposing forces. In a short story, the conflict drives the action. Events in the story contribute to the conflict or to the **resolution**—the way in which the conflict is settled. A conflict can be *external* or *internal.*

- **External conflict:** a character struggles against an outside force, such as another person or an element of nature.
- **Internal conflict:** a character struggles within himself or herself to make a choice, take an action, or overcome a feeling.

A story may have several conflicts, which may be related. As you read, think about the types of conflict that characters face and how they change through their experiences.

Is *conflict* always bad?

Writing About the Big Question

In "Zlateh the Goat," a boy struggles to save his own life—and the life of his family's goat—during a terrible snowstorm. Use this sentence starter to develop your ideas about the Big Question.

A shared struggle for **survival** (does/does not) bring friends closer together because _____.

While You Read Look for ways that Aaron benefits from his experiences during the blizzard.

Vocabulary

Read each word and its definition. Decide whether you know the word well, know it a little bit, or do not know it at all. After you read, see how your knowledge of each word has increased.

- **bound** (bound) *v.* tied (p. 223) *They bound the lifeboat to the ship.* bind *v.* binding *v.* boundary *n.*

- **astray** (ə strā´) *adv.* away from the correct path (p. 224) *The children had gone astray and were lost.* stray *n.* strayed *v.*

- **exuded** (eg zyo͞od´ əd) *v.* gave off; oozed (p. 226) *Penny exuded charm, which made her very popular.* exude *v.* exuding *v.*

- **splendor** (splen´ dər) *n.* gorgeous appearance; magnificence (p. 228) *James loved the splendor of spring.* splendid *adj.*

- **trace** (trās) *n.* mark left behind by something (p. 229) *Her mother said, "Leave no trace of cookie crumbs."* traced *v.* tracing *v.*

- **flickering** (flik´ ər iŋ) *v.* burning unsteadily (p. 229) *The candles' flames were flickering in the breeze.* flicker *v.* flickered *v.*

Word Study

The **Latin prefix *ex-*** means "out," "from," or "beyond."

In this story, dried hay, grass, and flowers **exuded** the sun's warmth, or sent out the warmth of the sun.

Author of
Zlateh the Goat

Isaac Bashevis Singer lived in the United States for more than half his life, but he never forgot the Polish villages of his youth. Singer brought those neighborhoods to life again and again in the stories and novels he wrote during his career.

Keeper of the Culture Prejudice against Jews prompted Singer to leave Poland for New York in 1935. Soon after, World War II devastated the Jewish neighborhoods of Eastern Europe. Yet Singer kept writing stories about the vanished world he remembered. Throughout his life, Singer wrote in his native language of Yiddish, translating many of his stories into English afterward. He explained, "I always knew that a writer has to write in his own language or not at all."

DID YOU KNOW?

In 1978 Singer won the Nobel Prize for Literature, the first Yiddish-language author to be so honored.

BACKGROUND FOR THE STORY

Hypothermia

In "Zlateh the Goat," a young boy is lost outdoors in a winter storm. He runs the risk of frostbite and *hypothermia*. When hypothermia occurs, the body temperature drops below normal and breathing slows. If the victim is not warmed, he or she becomes unconscious.

Zlateh the Goat

Isaac Bashevis Singer

Conflict and Resolution

What conflict is resolved by Reuven's decision to sell Zlateh?

At Hanukkah[1] time the road from the village to the town is usually covered with snow, but this year the winter had been a mild one. Hanukkah had almost come, yet little snow had fallen. The sun shone most of the time. The peasants complained that because of the dry weather there would be a poor harvest of winter grain. New grass sprouted, and the peasants sent their cattle out to pasture.

For Reuven the furrier it was a bad year, and after long hesitation he decided to sell Zlateh the goat. She was old and gave little milk. Feivel the town butcher had offered eight gulden[2] for her. Such a sum would buy Hanukkah candles, potatoes and oil for pancakes, gifts for the children, and other holiday necessaries for the house. Reuven told his oldest boy Aaron to take the goat to town.

---

1. **Hanukkah** (khä´ nʊ kä) Jewish festival celebrated for eight days in early winter. Hanukkah is also called the "festival of lights" because a candle is lit on each of the eight days.
2. **gulden** (gʊl´ dən) *n.* unit of money.

Illustrations copyright © 1966 by Maurice Sendak, copyright renewed 1994 by Maurice Sendak.
Printed with permission from HarperCollins Publishers.

◀ **Critical Viewing**
What do you think life is like in a village like the one in this picture? **[Speculate]**

Aaron understood what taking the goat to Feivel meant, but had to obey his father. Leah, his mother, wiped the tears from her eyes when she heard the news. Aaron's younger sisters, Anna and Miriam, cried loudly. Aaron put on his quilted jacket and a cap with earmuffs, bound a rope around Zlateh's neck, and took along two slices of bread with cheese to eat on the road. Aaron was supposed

Vocabulary
bound (bound)
v. tied

Reading
Check
Why is Aaron taking the goat to Feivel?

Spiral Review
Character How do Zlateh's natural personality traits intensify the conflict at the beginning of the story?

Conflict and Resolution
In what two ways are the snow and wind in conflict with Aaron?

to deliver the goat by evening, spend the night at the butcher's, and return the next day with the money.

While the family said goodbye to the goat, and Aaron placed the rope around her neck, Zlateh stood as patiently and good-naturedly as ever. She licked Reuven's hand. She shook her small white beard. Zlateh trusted human beings. She knew that they always fed her and never did her any harm.

When Aaron brought her out on the road to town, she seemed somewhat astonished. She'd never been led in that direction before. She looked back at him questioningly, as if to say, "Where are you taking me?" But after a while she seemed to come to the conclusion that a goat shouldn't ask questions. Still, the road was different. They passed new fields, pastures, and huts with thatched roofs. Here and there a dog barked and came running after them, but Aaron chased it away with his stick.

The sun was shining when Aaron left the village. Suddenly the weather changed. A large black cloud with a bluish center appeared in the east and spread itself rapidly over the sky. A cold wind blew in with it. The crows flew low, croaking. At first it looked as if it would rain, but instead it began to hail as in summer. It was early in the day, but it became dark as dusk. After a while the hail turned to snow.

In his twelve years Aaron had seen all kinds of weather, but he had never experienced a snow like this one. It was so dense it shut out the light of the day. In a short time their path was completely covered. The wind became as cold as ice. The road to town was narrow and winding. Aaron no longer knew where he was. He could not see through the snow. The cold soon penetrated his quilted jacket.

At first Zlateh didn't seem to mind the change in weather. She, too, was twelve years old and knew what winter meant. But when her legs sank deeper and deeper into the snow, she began to turn her head and look at Aaron in wonderment. Her mild eyes seemed to ask, "Why are we out in such a storm?" Aaron hoped that a peasant would come along with his cart, but no one passed by.

The snow grew thicker, falling to the ground in large, whirling flakes. Beneath it Aaron's boots touched the softness of a plowed field. He realized that he was no longer on the road. He had gone astray. He could no longer figure out which was east or west, which way was the village, the town. The wind whistled, howled, whirled the snow about in eddies.[3] It looked as if white imps were playing tag on the fields. A white dust rose above the ground. Zlateh stopped. She could walk no longer. Stubbornly she anchored her cleft hooves in the earth and bleated as if pleading to be taken home. Icicles hung from her white beard, and her horns were glazed with frost.

Aaron did not want to admit the danger, but he knew just the same that if they did not find shelter they would freeze to death. This was no ordinary storm. It was a mighty blizzard. The snow had reached his knees. His hands were numb, and he could no longer feel his toes. He choked when he breathed. His nose felt like wood, and he rubbed it with snow. Zlateh's bleating began to sound like crying. Those humans in whom

Illustrations copyright © 1966 by Maurice Sendak, copyright renewed 1994 by Maurice Sendak. Printed with permission from HarperCollins Publishers.

Vocabulary
astray (ə strā′)
adv. away from the correct path

Reading
Check

What surprises Zlateh when she and Aaron reach the road?

---

3. eddies (ed′ ēz) *n.* currents of air moving in circular motions like little whirlwinds.

she had so much confidence had dragged her into a trap. Aaron began to pray to God for himself and for the innocent animal.

Suddenly he made out the shape of a hill. He wondered what it could be. Who had piled snow into such a huge heap? He moved toward it, dragging Zlateh after him. When he came near it, he realized that it was a large haystack which the snow had blanketed.

Aaron realized immediately that they were saved. With great effort he dug his way through the snow. He was a village boy and knew what to do. When he reached the hay, he hollowed out a nest for himself and the goat. No matter how cold it may be outside, in the hay it is always warm. And hay was food for Zlateh. The moment she smelled it she became contented and began to eat. Outside, the snow continued to fall. It quickly covered the passageway Aaron had dug. But a boy and an animal need to breathe, and there was hardly any air in their hideout. Aaron bored a kind of a window through the hay and snow and carefully kept the passage clear.

Zlateh, having eaten her fill, sat down on her hind legs and seemed to have regained her confidence in man. Aaron ate his two slices of bread and cheese, but after the difficult journey he was still hungry. He looked at Zlateh and noticed her udders were full. He lay down next to her, placing himself so that when he milked her he could squirt the milk into his mouth. It was rich and sweet. Zlateh was not accustomed to being milked that way, but she did not resist. On the contrary, she seemed eager to reward Aaron for bringing her to a shelter whose very walls, floor, and ceiling were made of food. •

Through the window Aaron could catch a glimpse of the chaos outside. The wind carried before it whole drifts of snow. It was completely dark, and he did not know whether night had already come or whether it was the darkness of the storm. Thank God that in the hay it was not cold. The dried hay, grass, and field flowers exuded the warmth of the summer sun. Zlateh ate frequently; she

Conflict and Resolution
How has the discovery of the haystack temporarily resolved Aaron's problem?

Vocabulary
exuded (eg zyo͞od´ əd)
v. gave off; oozed

nibbled from above, below, from the left and right. Her body gave forth an animal warmth, and Aaron cuddled up to her. He had always loved Zlateh, but now she was like a sister. He was alone, cut off from his family, and wanted to talk. He began to talk to Zlateh. "Zlateh, what do you think about what has happened to us?" he asked.

"Maaaa," Zlateh answered.

"If we hadn't found this stack of hay, we would both be frozen stiff by now," Aaron said.

"Maaaa," was the goat's reply.

"If the snow keeps on falling like this, we may have to stay here for days," Aaron explained.

"Maaaa," Zlateh bleated.

"What does 'Maaaa' mean?" Aaron asked. "You'd better speak up clearly."

"Maaaa, Maaaa," Zlateh tried.

"Well, let it be 'Maaaa' then," Aaron said patiently. "You can't speak, but I know you understand. I need you and you need me. Isn't that right?"

"Maaaa."

Aaron became sleepy. He made a pillow out of some hay, leaned his head on it, and dozed off. Zlateh, too, fell asleep.

When Aaron opened his eyes, he didn't know whether it was morning or night. The snow had blocked up his window. He tried

Illustrations copyright © 1966 by Maurice Sendak, copyright renewed 1994 by Maurice Sendak. Printed with permission from HarperCollins Publishers.

▲ **Critical Viewing**
Why does Aaron look sad here? **[Connect]**

Reading Check

What shelter do Aaron and Zlateh find?

Conflict and Resolution
In what way are Aaron and Zlateh still in danger from the storm?

to clear it, but when he had bored through to the length of his arm, he still hadn't reached the outside. Luckily he had his stick with him and was able to break through to the open air. It was still dark outside. The snow continued to fall and the wind wailed, first with one voice and then with many. Sometimes it had the sound of devilish laughter. Zlateh, too, awoke, and when Aaron greeted her, she answered, "Maaaa." Yes, Zlateh's language consisted of only one word, but it meant many things. Now she was saying, "We must accept all that God gives us—heat, cold, hunger, satisfaction, light, and darkness." •

Aaron had awakened hungry. He had eaten up his food, but Zlateh had plenty of milk.

For three days Aaron and Zlateh stayed in the haystack. Aaron had always loved Zlateh, but in these three days he loved her more and more. She fed him with her milk and helped him keep warm. She comforted him with her patience. He told her many stories, and she always cocked her ears and listened. When he patted her, she licked his hand and his face. Then she said, "Maaaa," and he knew it meant, I love you, too.

Make Inferences
Using your own experience, what inference can you make about how Aaron feels, based on the details in this passage?

The snow fell for three days, though after the first day it was not as thick and the wind quieted down. Sometimes Aaron felt that there could never have been a summer, that the snow had always fallen, ever since he could remember. He, Aaron, never had a father or mother or sisters. He was a snow child, born of the snow, and so was Zlateh. It was so quiet in the hay that his ears rang in the stillness. Aaron and Zlateh slept all night and a good part of the day. As for Aaron's dreams, they were all about warm weather. He dreamed of green fields, trees covered with blossoms, clear brooks, and singing birds. By the third night the snow had stopped, but Aaron did not dare to find his way home in the darkness. The sky became clear and the moon shone, casting silvery nets on the snow. Aaron dug his way out and looked at the world. It was all white, quiet, dreaming dreams of heavenly splendor. The stars were large and close. The moon swam in the sky as in a sea.

Vocabulary
splendor (splen´dər)
n. gorgeous appearance; magnificence

On the morning of the fourth day Aaron heard the ringing of sleigh bells. The haystack was not far from the road. The peasant who drove the sleigh pointed out the way to him—not to the town and Feivel the butcher, but home to the village. Aaron had decided in the haystack that he would never part with Zlateh.

Aaron's family and their neighbors had searched for the boy and the goat but had found no trace of them during the storm. They feared they were lost. Aaron's mother and sisters cried for him; his father remained silent and gloomy. Suddenly one of the neighbors came running to their house with the news that Aaron and Zlateh were coming up the road. •

There was great joy in the family. Aaron told them how he had found the stack of hay and how Zlateh had fed him with her milk. Aaron's sisters kissed and hugged Zlateh and gave her a special treat of chopped carrots and potato peels, which Zlateh gobbled up hungrily.

Nobody ever again thought of selling Zlateh, and now that the cold weather had finally set in, the villagers needed the services of Reuven the furrier once more. When Hanukkah came, Aaron's mother was able to fry pancakes every evening, and Zlateh got her portion, too. Even though Zlateh had her own pen, she often came to the kitchen, knocking on the door with her horns to indicate that she was ready to visit, and she was always admitted. In the evening Aaron, Miriam, and Anna played dreidel.[4] Zlateh sat near the stove watching the children and the flickering of the Hanukkah candles.

Once in a while Aaron would ask her, "Zlateh, do you remember the three days we spent together?"

And Zlateh would scratch her neck with a horn, shake her white bearded head, and come out with the single sound which expressed all her thoughts, and all her love.

---

4. dreidel (drā´ dəl) *n.* small top with Hebrew letters on each of four sides, spun in a game played by children.

Vocabulary
trace (trās) *n.* mark left behind by something

Vocabulary
flickering (flik´ər iŋ) *v.* burning unsteadily

Conflict and Resolution
How is the family's conflict over selling Zlateh resolved?

Illustrations copyright © 1966 by Maurice Sendak, copyright renewed 1994 by Maurice Sendak. Printed with permission from HarperCollins Publishers.

Critical Thinking

1. **Key Ideas and Details** **(a)** What happens to Aaron and Zlateh on the way to town? **(b) Deduce:** Why is their situation dangerous?

2. **Key Ideas and Details** **(a) Draw Conclusions:** Why does the stay in the haystack change Aaron's mind about selling Zlateh? **(b) Apply:** What is the story's message about friendship and trust?

3. **Integration of Knowledge and Ideas** **(a)** What does Aaron learn about himself during his struggle to survive the snowstorm? **(b)** What does he learn about Zlateh during this time? *[Connect to the Big Question: Is conflict always bad?]*

Reading Skill: Make Inferences

1. Aaron's mother and sisters cry over selling Zlateh. What **inference** can you make about their feelings for the goat?

2. What evidence in the story supports the inference that Aaron is quick-thinking and brave?

Literary Analysis: Conflict and Resolution

3. Craft and Structure For each **conflict** listed, tell whether it is internal or external and explain how it was resolved.

Conflict	What Kind?	Resolution
Reuven needs the money he could get for Zlateh, but he loves Zlateh.		
Aaron and Zlateh need food and shelter but are caught in a blizzard.		

4. Craft and Structure Explain how the **resolution** of the first conflict is connected to the second conflict.

Vocabulary

Acquisition and Use Answer each question using a word from page 220.

1. Which word could describe footprints left in the snow?

2. How else can you say that you tied two things together?

3. How can you describe losing your way?

4. How might you describe the light from a star?

5. Which word can describe a place of great beauty?

6. How might you say that a stove gave off heat?

Word Study Use context and what you know about the **Latin prefix ex-** to explain your answer to each question.

1. What happens when you *exhale* a lot of air?

2. Would you vote to *extend* a school holiday?

Word Study

The **Latin prefix ex-** means "out," "from," or "beyond."

Apply It Explain how the prefix **ex-** contributes to the meanings of these words. Consult a dictionary if necessary.

exceed

expand

expose

Is *conflict* always bad?

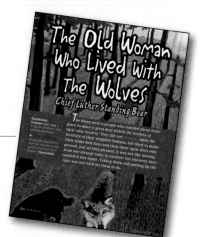

Writing About the Big Question

In "The Old Woman Who Lived With the Wolves," a young girl loses her way during a blizzard and must trust a pack of wolves for her survival. Use this sentence starter to develop your ideas about the Big Question.

Sometimes, when we **convince** ourselves to trust instead of fear something, it may help us _____.

While You Read Look for moments in the story that Marpiyawin feels trust rather than fear.

Vocabulary

Read each word and its definition. Decide whether you know the word well, know it a little bit, or do not know it at all. After you have read, see how your knowledge of each word has increased.

- **trespass** (tres´ pəs) *v.* to go on another's land without permission (p. 234) *Do not __trespass__ across my lawn!* *trespassed v. trespassing v.*

- **coaxed** (kōkst) *v.* persuaded by gentle urging (p. 235) *Lisa __coaxed__ her dog to go through the door.* *coax v. coaxing v.*

- **traversed** (trə vʉrst´) *v.* went across (p. 237) *The horse __traversed__ the stream.* *traverse v. traversing v.*

- **scarce** (skərs) *adj.* not enough to satisfy need (p. 237) *Water is __scarce__ in the desert.* *scarcity n. scarcely adv.*

- **mystified** (mist´ tə fīd´) *v.* perplexed; bewildered (p. 237) *They were __mystified__ by the vague clue.* *mystifying v. mystic adj. mystery n.*

- **offensive** (ə fen´ siv) *adj.* unpleasant (p. 237) *An __offensive__ odor filled the room.* *offensively adv. offensive n.*

Word Study

The **Latin prefix** *in-* can mean "not."

In this story, a character realizes that human odor can be unpleasant, or **offensive**, to animals. To animals, however, the odor of their fellow creatures is **inoffensive**, or not unpleasant.

Meet
Chief Luther Standing Bear
(1868–1939)

Author of

The Old Woman Who Lived With the Wolves

A member of the Oglala Sioux, Chief Standing Bear was originally named **Ota K'Te** (Plenty Kill). He later called himself Standing Bear because it was his father's name. He graduated from the Carlisle Indian School in Pennsylvania and became a writer who fought for Native American rights. In his work, Chief Standing Bear describes the customs and beliefs of the Sioux, including their special relationship with nature. In *Land of the Spotted Eagle,* he wrote, "Earth was bountiful and we were surrounded with the blessings of the great mystery."

DID YOU KNOW?

In addition to being a writer, Luther Standing Bear was an actor and a leader of his people.

BACKGROUND FOR THE STORY

The Sioux

This story comes from the Sioux, a Native American people of the northern plains. The Sioux moved frequently from place to place, settling where they could find good supplies of fresh water and buffalo, their main source of food. Their lives were linked to the cycles of the natural world, so they had a special understanding of the animals in their world.

The Old Woman Who Lived With The Wolves

Chief Luther Standing Bear

The Sioux were a people who traveled about from place to place a great deal within the borders of their own country. They did not trespass upon the territory of their neighbor Indians, but liked to make their home first here and then there upon their own ground, just as they pleased. It was not like moving from one strange town to another, but wherever they settled it was home. Taking down and putting up the tipis was not hard for them to do.

Vocabulary
trespass (tres´ pəs) *v.*
to go on another's land without permission

▼ **Critical Viewing**
Would you approach a wolf like the one in this painting without fear? Explain. **[Speculate]**

The reasons for their moving were many. Perhaps the grass for their ponies ran short, or the water in the creek became low. Maybe the game had gone elsewhere, and maybe the people just moved the camp to a fresh green spot, for the Sioux loved pure water, pure air, and a clean place on which to put their tipis.

One day, long ago, a Sioux village was on the march. There were many people in the party, and many children. A great number of horses carried the tipis, and herds of racing and war horses were being taken care of by the young men. In this crowd was a young woman who carried with her a pet dog. The dog was young and playful, just past the puppy age. The young woman was very fond of her pet, as she had cared for it since it was a wee little thing with eyes still closed. She romped along with the pup, and the way seemed short because she played with it and with the young folks when not busy helping her mother with the packing and unpacking.

One evening Marpiyawin missed her dog. She looked and she called, but he was not to be found. Perhaps someone liked her playful pet and was keeping him concealed, but after a search she became satisfied that no one in camp was hiding him. Then she thought that perhaps he had lain down to sleep somewhere along the way and had been left behind. Then, lastly, she thought that the wolves had enticed him to join their pack. For oftentimes the Sioux dogs were coaxed away and ran with the wolf-pack, always returning, however, in a few days or weeks to the village. ●

So Marpiyawin, thinking the matter over, decided that she would go back over the way her people had journeyed and that somewhere she would find her dog. She would then bring him back to camp with her. Without a word to anyone, she turned back, for she had no fear of becoming lost. Nothing could befall her, so why should she fear? As she walked back, she came to the foothills at the base of the mountains where her village people had spent the summer. As she slept that night, the first snowfall of the autumn came so silently that it did not awaken her. In the morning everything was white with snow, but it was not far to the place where the village had been in camp and so determined was she to find her dog that she decided to keep

Make Inferences
Explain how the details in these paragraphs support the inference that the Sioux enjoy traveling.

Make Inferences
What do these details tell you about how the Sioux feel about animals? Explain.

Vocabulary
coaxed (kōkst) *v.* persuaded by gentle urging

Conflict and Resolution
What conflict is developed here?

Reading Check
Why does Marpiyawin get separated from the rest of her tribe?

Social Studies Connections

Home on the Range
Tipi (or teepee) is the Sioux word for "dwelling place." Tipis were about fourteen feet tall and faced east to greet the rising sun.

Assembling a tipi took about fifteen minutes, a job performed by the tribe's women, who also owned the tipis. ▶

The poles supporting the hides were usually made of lodgepole pine because the wood was tall, thin, and tough. ▶

Moving the tipis was relatively easy. Horses or dogs would drag the tipi poles with the rest of the tribe's belongings. ▼

Connect to the Literature
What features of tipis made them useful and practical homes for the Sioux?

Conflict and Resolution
How has the snow increased the conflict in the story?

going. Marpiyawin now felt that her pet had gone back to the old camping-ground, as dogs often do, and was now there howling and crying to be found.

That afternoon the snow fell thicker and faster and Marpiyawin was forced to seek shelter in a cave, which was rather dark, but warm and comfortable. She was not hungry, for in her little rawhide[1] bag was still some wasna.[2] She was tired, however, so it was not long till she fell asleep, and while she slept she had a most wonderful vision. In her dream the wolves talked to her and she understood them, and when she talked to them they understood her too. They told her that she had lost her way, but that she should trust them and they would not see her suffer from cold or hunger. She replied that she would not worry, and when she awoke it was without fear, even though in the cave with her were the wolves sitting about in a friendly manner.

---

1. **rawhide** (rô´ hīd) *n.* rough leather.
2. **wasna** (wäs´ nuh) *n.* meat and berries pounded and pressed together in flat strips to make a nutritious food that is easy to carry.

The blizzard raged outside for many days, still she was contented, for she was neither cold nor hungry. For meat the wolves supplied her with tender rabbits and at night they kept her body warm with their shaggy coats of fur. As the days wore on, she and the wolves became fast friends.

But clear days finally came and the wolves offered to lead her back to her people, so they set out. They traversed many little valleys and crossed many creeks and streams; they walked up hills and down hills, and at last came to one from which she could look down upon the camp of her people. Here she must say "Good-bye" to her friends and companions—the wolves. This made her feel very sad, though she wanted to see her people again. Marpiyawin thanked all the wolves for their kindness to her and asked what she might do for them. All they asked was that, when the long winter months came and food was scarce, she bring to the top of the hill some nice fat meat for them to eat. This she gladly promised to do and went down the hill toward the camp of her people.

As Marpiyawin neared the village, she smelled a very unpleasant odor. At first it mystified her, then she realized it was the smell of human beings. At once the knowledge came to her that the smell of humans was very different from the smell of animals. This was why she now knew that animals so readily track human beings and why the odor of man is oftentimes so offensive to them. She had been with the wolves so long that she had lost the odor of her people and now was able to see that, while man often considers the animal offensive, so do animals find man offensive. ●

Marpiyawin came to the camp of her people and they were happy to see her, for they had considered her lost and thought she had been taken by an enemy tribe. But she pointed to the top of the hill in the distance, and there sat her friends, their forms black against the sky. In great surprise her people looked, not knowing what to say. They thought she must have just escaped a great danger. So she explained to them that she had been lost and would have perished had not the wolves saved her life. She asked them to give her some of their fat meat that she might carry it to the top of the hill. Her people were so grateful and happy

Vocabulary
traversed (trə vʉrst′) *v.* went across

scarce (skərs) *adj.* not enough to satisfy need

Vocabulary
mystified (mist′ tə fīd′) *v.* perplexed; bewildered

offensive (ə fen′ siv) *adj.* unpleasant

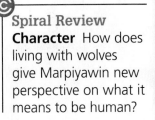

Spiral Review
Character How does living with wolves give Marpiyawin new perspective on what it means to be human?

Reading Check
How is Marpiyawin able to survive in such harsh conditions?

that a young man was sent about the camp telling of the safe return of Marpiyawin and collecting meat from each tipi. Marpiyawin took the meat, placed the bundle on her back, and went up the hill, while the village people looked on in wonder. When she reached the hilltop she spread the meat on the ground and the wolves ate it.

Ever after that, when the long winter months came and food was scarce, and hard to find, Marpiyawin took meat to her friends the wolves. She never forgot their language and oftentimes in the winter their voices calling to her would be heard throughout the village. Then the people would ask the old woman what the wolves were saying. Their calls would be warnings that a blizzard was coming, or that the enemy was passing close, and to send out a scout or to let the old woman know that they were watching her with care.

And so Marpiyawin came to be known to the tribe as "The Old Woman Who Lived with the Wolves," or, in the Sioux language as, "Win yan wan si k'ma nitu ompi ti."

Make Inferences
How do the Sioux feel about wolves, based on their reaction to Marpiyawin's story?

Cite textual evidence to support your responses.

Critical Thinking

© 1. **Key Ideas and Details** **(a)** How did Marpiyawin come to spend time living with the wolves? **(b) Analyze:** Why do you think she is not afraid of the wolves?

© 2. **Key Ideas and Details** **(a)** Would Marpiyawin have survived without the wolves? Support your answer.

© 3. **Integration of Knowledge and Ideas** What does Marpiyawin's experience suggest about the relationship of the Sioux people to nature?

© 4. **Craft and Structure** **(a)** What are two moments in which Marpiyawin experiences trust rather than fear during a conflict? **(b)** How does trust play a part in resolving a conflict? *[Connect to the Big Question: Is conflict always bad?]*

Reading Skill: Make Inferences

1. (a) Think of a time when you lost something. Make an **inference** about how Marpiyawin feels as she sets out to find her dog. **(b)** Explain how your prior knowledge helped you make your inference.

Literary Analysis: Conflict and Resolution

2. Craft and Structure For each **conflict** listed, tell whether it is internal or external and explain how it was resolved.

Conflict	What Kind?	Resolution
Marpiyawin needs food and shelter, but she is lost.		
She is sad to leave the wolves but misses her people.		

3. Craft and Structure Explain how the **resolution** of the first conflict leads to the second conflict.

Vocabulary

Acquisition and Use Answer each question using a word from page 232.

1. Which word could describe a skunk's odor?

2. If there is not enough of something, how could you describe it?

3. How might you say you persuaded someone to do something?

4. How does one feel when something is unclear?

5. How could you say that you crossed the desert?

6. What word applies to sneaking into someone's yard?

Word Study Use context and what you know about the **Latin prefix in-** to explain your answer to each question.

1. Could the flu cause an athlete to be *inactive*?

2. Will an *incomplete* answer affect your score on a test?

Word Study

The **Latin prefix *in-*** can mean "not."

Apply It Explain how the prefix *in-* contributes to the meanings of these words. Consult a dictionary if necessary.

inaccurate
independent
insincere

Integrated Language Skills

Zlateh the Goat • The Old Woman Who Lived With the Wolves

Conventions: Principal Parts of Verbs

Every **verb** has four main forms, or **principal parts.** These parts are used to form verb tenses that show time.

Regular verbs form their past tense and past participles by adding -*ed* or -*d*.

Irregular verbs, such as *be*, form their past tense and past participles in different ways.

Present	talk
Present Participle	(am) talking
Past	talked
Past Participle	(have) talked

Practice A Identify the verb or verbs in each sentence. For each, indicate which of the four principal parts is used.

1. Aaron is taking Zlateh to Feivel.
2. Zlateh had lived with Aaron's family.
3. The sisters gave Zlateh a special meal.
4. Aaron reminds Zlateh of their three days in the haystack.

© **Reading Application** In "Zlateh the Goat," find one sentence with a verb in the past tense and one sentence with a verb in the past participle form.

Practice B Rewrite each sentence, replacing the italicized verb with the principal part indicated in parentheses.

1. The Sioux people *travel* from place to place. (present participle)
2. Marpiyawin *searches* for her dog. (past)
3. The wolves *wait* on the hill. (past)
4. The young man *collects* meat for the wolves. (past participle)

© **Writing Application** Find two sentences in "The Old Woman Who Lived With the Wolves" that use verbs in the past tense. Rewrite the sentences to use the past participle form.

PH **WRITING COACH**　　Further instruction and practice are available in *Prentice Hall Writing Coach.*

Writing

 **Common Core State Standards**

L.6.1; W.6.1; SL.6.4, 6.5
[For the full wording of the standards, see page 218.]

Argument Write and present a short **persuasive speech** that Aaron might give to urge his father to keep Zlateh, or that Marpiyawin might give to urge her people to help the wolves.

- Choose a character and state your position clearly.
- Present at least two reasons that support your position.
- Consider the audience's concerns and counterarguments. Include information to overcome these issues.
- Conclude your speech by summarizing your position.
- Revise your speech to remove less-persuasive details.

Grammar Application Read over your speech and be sure you have used all irregular verbs properly.

Writing Workshop: *Work in Progress*

Prewriting for Response to Literature Review your Ideas List and freewrite about the story you chose. As you write, include as many of your responses as possible. Choose the idea you think best captures your response and put it in your writing portfolio.

Use this prewriting activity to prepare for the **Writing Workshop** on page 264.

Research and Technology

Presentation of Ideas Make and present a **compare-and-contrast chart.**

- If you read "Zlateh the Goat," compare and contrast your hometown to a *shtetl*, a Jewish village like the one in which Aaron and his family live.
- If you read "The Old Woman Who Lived With the Wolves," compare and contrast your hometown to a Sioux settlement, like that of Marpiyawin and her tribe.

Follow these steps to complete the assignment.

- Use key words to search online databases for information.
- Organize the information according to categories such as population, resources, and so on.
- Fill in the chart with information for each category.
- Analyze the information to draw conclusions about the similarities and differences in the communities you studied.
- Write a statement in which you summarize the information in the chart. Explain your ideas aloud. Speak clearly.

PHLit Online!
www.PHLitOnline.com

- Interactive graphic organizers
- Grammar tutorial
- Interactive journals

Test Practice: Reading

Make Inferences

Fiction Selection

Directions: *Read the selection. Then, answer the questions.*

By the time Kim heard the director call her name, her heart was galloping and her knees were shaking. In spite of this, Kim smiled bravely. She had worked too hard to let the jitters get in her way. She owed it to her parents and her singing coach—but especially to herself—to do her best. Kim cleared her throat and nodded to the piano player. She took a deep breath, let it out, and took another. Kim's knees no longer shook. As her singing voice filled the auditorium, the director's eyes grew wide. "Wow!" he said to his assistant. "We don't need to hear any more singers."

1. Why do you think Kim's heart is "galloping" at the start of the passage?
   A. She has run onto the stage.
   B. She is nervous and scared.
   C. She suddenly feels ill.
   D. She is angry with the director.

2. Which inference is *best* supported by the passage?
   A. The piano player is Kim's best friend.
   B. The director is Kim's singing coach.
   C. Kim wrote the song she will sing.
   D. Kim is trying out for a musical.

3. What can you infer about Kim?
   A. She feels more nervous as she sings.
   B. She calms herself before singing.
   C. She has forgotten the words to the song.
   D. She does not enjoy singing.

4. What can you infer about Kim's parents?
   A. They are singers, too.
   B. They are the director's friends.
   C. They have spent money on Kim's singing lessons.
   D. They have left the country.

5. What do the director's words and actions suggest?
   A. He is tired of listening to singers.
   B. He does not like Kim's voice.
   C. He wants Kim to be in the musical.
   D. He thinks Kim is brave.

Writing for Assessment

Use details from the passage to write a short paragraph explaining why Kim is determined to do her best at the tryout.

Nonfiction Selection

Directions: *Read the selection. Then, answer the questions.*

Your palms are sweaty. Your mouth feels dry. You can't think clearly. Your chest feels tight. What's happening? It's your turn to give a science report, and you've got stage fright. This response is common among people who perform in front of audiences. Actors, athletes, musicians, students, and others can suffer from stage fright. It comes from thoughts such as "What if I make a fool of myself?" or "I'll *never* get through this!" These thoughts set off a reaction in the body. Dizziness, shakiness, shortness of breath, and a pounding heart can also be signs of stage fright. What are some ways to decrease this reaction? First, accept that it's not unusual to feel nervous. Take deep breaths. Clench your fists tightly, and then stretch out your fingers. Finally, focus on your task, and try to have fun.

1. Based on details in the text, which type of stage fright is described at the beginning of the passage?
 A. fear of heights
 B. fear of spiders
 C. fear of flying
 D. fear of public speaking

2. Based on the information in the passage, in which job might a person most likely experience stage fright?
 A. singer in a band
 B. children's doctor
 C. clerk at a supermarket
 D. school bus driver

3. Which detail helps you infer that proper breathing can help lessen stage fright?
 A. Accept that stage fright is normal.
 B. Try to have fun.
 C. Take a few deep breaths.
 D. Focus on your task.

4. What inference is *best* supported by the passage?
 A. Stage fright occurs when a person is poorly prepared.
 B. Stage fright most often occurs before a public performance.
 C. Experienced performers do not suffer from stage fright.
 D. Exercise can help prevent stage fright.

Writing for Assessment

Comparing Texts

How is Kim's experience in the first passage similar to or different from the experiences described in the second passage? Which techniques in the second passage does Kim use to calm herself? Write two well-developed paragraphs using details from both passages.

www.PHLitOnline.com
- Online practice
- Instant feedback

Reading for Information

Analyzing Expository Texts

Online Almanac

Textbook Article

Common Core State Standards

Reading Informational Text

5. Analyze how a particular sentence, paragraph, chapter, or section fits into the overall structure of a text and contributes to the development of the ideas.

7. Integrate information presented in different media or formats as well as in words to develop a coherent understanding of a topic or issue.

Writing

1. Write arguments to support claims with clear reasons and relevant evidence.

Language

6. Acquire and use accurately grade-appropriate general academic and domain-specific words and phrases; gather vocabulary knowledge when considering a word or phrase important to comprehension or expression.

Reading Skill: Use Text Aids and Features

Text aids and features organize details in a text and highlight important information, including the writer's central ideas. Identify these structural features as you read to help locate and understand the information in a text. These features also help you to see relationships among the ideas being presented. The following chart gives examples of text aids and features.

Text Aids	Text Features
• chapter titles • main headings and subheadings • highlighted vocabulary and key terms	• maps, graphs, and charts • photographs, drawings, and diagrams with captions

Content-Area Vocabulary

These words appear in the selections that follow. You may also encounter them in other content-area texts.

- **archaeologists** (är′kē äl′ə jists) *n.* people who study human history by finding and analyzing ancient objects and other remains

- **architect** (är′ kə tekt) *n.* person who designs buildings

- **colossal** (kə läs′əl) *adj.* extremely large

Features:

- factual information on a variety of subjects
- text written for a general audience
- references to other sources and related topics
- photographs, illustrations, or other visuals
- interactive features
- references to other sources and related topics

The **main heading** shows the general topic of the almanac entry.

THE SEVEN WONDERS OF THE WORLD

from *Infoplease*®

Since ancient times, numerous "seven wonders" lists have been created. The content of these lists tends to vary and none is definitive. The seven wonders that are most widely agreed upon as being in the original list are the Seven Wonders of the Ancient World, which was compiled by ancient Greek historians and is thus confined to the most magnificent structures known to the ancient Greek world. Of all the Ancient Wonders, the pyramids alone survive.

The Pyramids of Egypt are three pyramids at Giza, outside modern Cairo. The largest pyramid, built by Khufu (Cheops), a king of the fourth dynasty, had an original estimated height of 482 feet (now approximately 450 feet). The base has sides 755 feet long. It contains 2,300,000 blocks; the average weight of each is 2.5 tons. The estimated date of completion is 2680 B.C.

The **subheadings** serve as a list of the Seven Wonders of The Ancient World.

The Hanging Gardens of Babylon were supposedly built by Nebuchadnezzar around 600 B.C. to please his queen, Amuhia. They are also associated with the mythical Assyrian queen Semiramis. **Archaeologists** surmise that the gardens were laid out atop a vaulted building, with provisions for raising water. The terraces were said to rise from 75 to 300 feet.

The Statue of Zeus (Jupiter) at Olympia was made of gold and ivory by the Greek sculptor Phidias (5th century B.C.). Reputed to be 40 feet high, the statue has been lost without a trace, except for reproductions on coins.

Illustrations help you picture how the Seven Wonders once appeared.

The Temple of Artemis (Diana) at Ephesus was begun about 350 B.C., in honor of a non-Hellenic goddess who later became identified with the Greek goddess of the same name. The temple, with Ionic columns 60 feet high, was destroyed by invading Goths in A.D. 262.

The Mausoleum at Halicarnassus was erected by Queen Artemisia in memory of her husband, King Mausolus of Caria in Asia Minor, who died in 353 B.C. Some remains of the structure are in the British Museum. This shrine is the source of the modern word mausoleum.

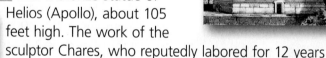

The Colossus at Rhodes was a bronze statue of Helios (Apollo), about 105 feet high. The work of the sculptor Chares, who reputedly labored for 12 years before completing it in 280 B.C., it was destroyed during an earthquake in 224 B.C.

The Pharos (Lighthouse) of Alexandria was built by Sostratus of Cnidus during the 3rd century B.C. on the island of Pharos off the coast of Egypt. It was destroyed by an earthquake in the 13th century.

The **online almanac** entry includes a link to a related topic.

(Some lists include the Walls of Babylon in place of the second or seventh wonder.)

See also The Seven Wonders of the Modern World.

Features:

- factual information about a specific topic
- organization into parts such as units, chapters, and sections
- text written for students of a particular subject
- diagrams, illustrations, and other visual aids

Section 5

Art, Architecture, and Learning in Egypt

from *Prentice Hall Ancient Civilizations*

The **section title** gives an overview of the content that will be discussed.

Homes for the Dead

One of the most important types of Egyptian buildings were temples. Most were built of mud or from stone that was quarried, or mined, far away, and then transported over long distances. The Egyptians created temples for their gods and tombs for their pharaohs.

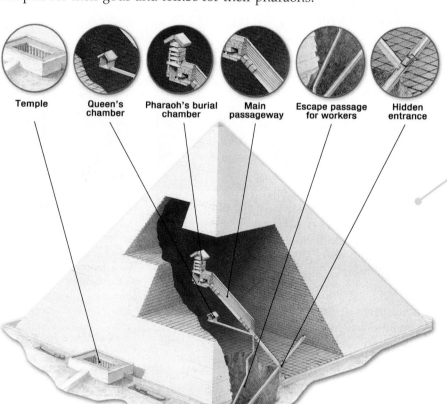

| Temple | Queen's chamber | Pharaoh's burial chamber | Main passageway | Escape passage for workers | Hidden entrance |

The **diagram and captions** illustrate information in the text and provide additional details.

Tombs for the Pharaohs

Tombs of early rulers were underground chambers, or rooms. The burial chamber contained items that the ruler might want in the afterlife.

An **architect** named **Imhotep** designed a new kind of tomb for his pharaoh, with six stone mounds, one on top of the other. The result is known as the Step Pyramid. Later architects made the sides smoother to create a true pyramid.

Three enormous pyramids were built at Giza by **King Khufu**, his son Khafre, and his grandson Menkaure. The tallest of these is the Great Pyramid of Khufu. For more than 4,000 years, this pyramid was the world's tallest building. Nearby stands the famous statue known as the Sphinx. The Sphinx guarded the road to Khafre's pyramid.

The great age of pyramid building ended about 2200 B.C. Pharaohs who ruled after that time carved tombs from the cliffs in the Valley of the Kings and the Valley of the Queens.

Painting and Sculpture Egyptians were skilled artists as well as builders. Much of what we know about life in Egypt comes from paintings found on the walls of tombs. Although these paintings show Egyptians at work and at play, their purpose was not decoration. The paintings were created to provide the person buried in the tomb with all of the objects and pleasures shown on the walls.

Egyptian artists also created wonderful sculptures. A **sculpture** is a statue made of clay, stone, or other materials. Most Egyptian sculptures were statues of people or gods. **Colossal** statues of gods stood in temples. Smaller statues of once-living Egyptians were placed in tombs along with their **mummies**. If the person's mummy was destroyed, the statue could replace it as a home for the dead person's spirit.

Subheadings introduce specific topics within the section's main topic.

Egyptian Pyramids
The pyramids of Egypt are the most famous buildings of the ancient world. These pyramids were built as the tomb of a powerful pharaoh.

Boldface text highlights key terms.

Comparing Expository Texts

1. Craft and Structure **(a)** Identify a text aid or structural feature that you would find in both an online almanac and a textbook. **(b)** Identify a text aid or structural feature that you would find in an online almanac, but not in a textbook. **(c)** Which text makes it easier to find specific information? Explain.

Content-Area Vocabulary

2. Use *archaeologists, architect,* and *colossal* in a brief paragraph that shows you understand the meaning of each word.

⏱ Timed Writing

Argument: Position Statement

> **Format**
> The prompt gives clear directions about the topic and how you should address it.

Throughout history, there have been different lists of the Seven Wonders of the World. Take a position on whether the Egyptian Pyramids should be one of the Seven Wonders of the World. Write a statement of your position and support it with details from the texts you have read.

> **Academic Vocabulary**
> When you *take a position*, you state what you believe about an issue. When you *support* your position, you use details that give reasons for your opinion.

5-Minute Planner

Complete these steps before you begin to write:

1. Read the prompt carefully and completely. Note that the prompt asks you to take a position based on what you have read.

2. Review the two texts. Use text aids and features to locate information about your topic. **TIP:** Relying on text aids and text features alone may lead you to incorrect conclusions. Be sure to review the text completely.

3. Compare the information that is presented in the two texts to connect and clarify main ideas.

4. Jot down your opinion, and make notes about the facts you will use to support your position.

5. Use your notes to prepare a quick outline. Then, use your outline to help you organize your response.

Comparing Characters' Motives

The qualities that make up a character are **character traits.** Character traits can include intelligence, pride, or dishonesty. Authors can directly describe character traits, or they might indirectly reveal them through a character's words and actions or through the words and actions of others. Recognizing character traits helps readers understand a character's actions.

The reasons for a character's actions are called **character motives.** These motives include a character's thoughts, feelings, or desires. Motives can be based on internal or external factors.

- **Internal factors** include thoughts and feelings, such as jealousy, pride, or love.

- **External factors** are events or actions, such as trying to find a lost dog or attempting to win money.

In a short story, the characters' motives and actions affect the direction of the plot. Ultimately, a story's resolution is determined by the actions of its characters. As you read, identify places in each story where a change in a character's motives or actions impacts the conflict and its resolution.

Use a chart like the one shown to compare and contrast the traits and motives of the two girls in the selections that follow.

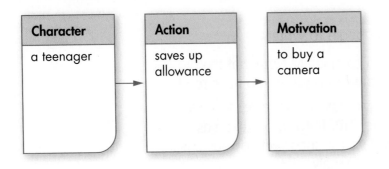

Character	Action	Motivation
a teenager	saves up allowance	to buy a camera

Common Core State Standards

Reading Literature

3. Describe how a particular story's or drama's plot unfolds in a series of episodes as well as how the characters respond or change as the plot moves toward a resolution.

Writing

2. Write informative/explanatory texts to examine a topic and convey ideas, concepts, and information through the selection, organization, and analysis of relevant content.

www.PHLitOnline.com

- Vocabulary flashcards
- Interactive journals
- More about the authors
- Selection audio
- Interactive graphic organizers

Is *conflict* always bad?

Writing About the Big Question

In these stories, each main character thinks of a clever way to get what she wants. Use this sentence starter to develop your ideas.

Negotiation can be helpful when _____.

Meet the Authors

James Berry (b. 1925)

Author of "Becky and the Wheels-and-Brake Boys"

In his writing, James Berry often celebrates the richness of his Jamaican heritage.

Inspiration Berry once explained the inspiration for his writing this way: "[The stories] were straight out of my own childhood and later observations. . . . No one has reported our stories, or the way we saw things. It's the function of writers and poets to bring in the left-out side of the human family."

Judith Viorst (b. 1931)

Author of "The Southpaw"

Born in Newark, New Jersey, Judith Viorst knew as a child that she wanted to be a writer. She kept writing, and eventually found success with her stories and poetry.

Family Characters Viorst's three sons are sometimes characters in her books. When she saw a musical based on her book *Alexander and the Terrible, Horrible, No Good, Very Bad Day,* Viorst said the experience of seeing her family and friends come to life through seven actors was a "truly weird and thrilling thing."

Becky

and the Wheels -and- Brake Boys

James Berry

Even my own cousin Ben was there—riding away, in the ringing of bicycle bells down the road. Every time I came to watch them—see them riding round and round enjoying themselves—they scooted off like crazy on their bikes.

They can't keep doing that. They'll see!

I only want to be with Nat, Aldo, Jimmy, and Ben. It's no fair reason they don't want to be with me. Anybody could go off their head for that. Anybody! A girl can not, not, let boys get away with it all the time.

Bother! I have to walk back home, alone.

I know total-total that if I had my own bike, the Wheels-and-Brake Boys wouldn't treat me like that. I'd just ride away with them, wouldn't I?

Over and over I told my mum I wanted a bike. Over and over she looked at me as if I was crazy. "Becky, d'you think you're a boy? Eh? D'you think you're a boy? In any case, where's the money to come from? Eh?"

Of course I know I'm not a boy. Of course I know I'm not crazy. Of course I know all that's no reason why I can't have a bike. No reason! As soon as I get indoors I'll just have to ask again—ask Mum once more.

At home, indoors, I didn't ask my mum.

It was evening time, but sunshine was still big patches in yards and on housetops. My two younger brothers, Lenny and Vin, played marbles in the road. Mum was taking measurements of a boy I knew, for his new trousers and shirt. Mum made clothes for people. Meggie, my sister two years younger than me, was helping Mum on the veranda. Nobody would be pleased with me not helping. I began to help.

Granny-Liz would always stop fanning herself to drink up a glass of ice water. I gave my granny a glass of ice water, there in her rocking chair. I looked in the kitchen to find shelled coconut pieces to cut into small cubes for the fowls' morning feed. But Granny-Liz had done it. I came and started tidying up bits and pieces of cut-off material around my mum on the floor. My sister got nasty, saying she was already helping Mum. Not a single good thing was happening for me.

With me even being all so thoughtful of Granny's need of a cool drink, she started up some botheration[1] against me.

---

1. **botheration** (bäth´ ər ā´ shən) *n.* trouble.

Characters' Motives
Why does Becky want a bike?

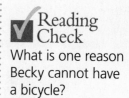
Reading Check
What is one reason Becky cannot have a bicycle?

Vocabulary
menace (men´ əs) *n.*
threat; danger

Listen to Granny-Liz: "Becky, with you moving about me here on the veranda, I hope you dohn have any centipedes or scorpions[2] in a jam jar in your pocket."

"No, mam," I said sighing, trying to be calm. "Granny-Liz," I went on, "you forgot. My centipede and scorpion died." All the same, storm broke against me.

"Becky," my mum said. "You know I don't like you wandering off after dinner. Haven't I told you I don't want you keeping company with those awful riding-about bicycle boys? Eh?"

"Yes, mam."

"Those boys are a menace. Riding bicycles on sidewalks and narrow paths together, ringing bicycle bells and braking at people's feet like wild bulls charging anybody, they're heading for trouble."

"They're the Wheels-and-Brake Boys, mam."

"The what?"

"The Wheels-and-Brake Boys."

"Oh! Given themselves a name as well, have they? Well, Becky, answer this. How d'you always manage to look like you just escaped from a hair-pulling battle? Eh? And don't I tell you not to break the backs down and wear your canvas shoes like slippers? Don't you ever hear what I say?"

"Yes, mam."

"D'you want to end up a field laborer? Like where your father used to be overseer?"[3]

"No, mam."

"Well, Becky, will you please go off and do your homework?"

Everybody did everything to stop me. I was allowed no chance whatsoever. No chance to talk to Mum about the bike I dream of day and night! And I knew exactly the bike I wanted. I wanted a bike like Ben's bike. Oh, I wished I still had even my scorpion on a string to run up and down somebody's back!

I answered my mum. "Yes, mam." I went off into Meg's and my bedroom.

I sat down at the little table, as well as I might. Could homework stay in anybody's head in broad daylight

Characters' Motives
Is Becky's dream of having a bike an internal or external motivation? Explain.

---

2. **scorpions** (skôr´ pē ənz) *n.* close relatives of spiders, with a poisonous stinger at the end of their tails; scorpions are found in warm regions.
3. **overseer** (ō´ vər sē´ ər) *n.* supervisor of workers.

outside? No. Could I keep a bike like Ben's out of my head? Not one bit. That bike took me all over the place. My beautiful bike jumped every log, every rock, every fence. My beautiful bike did everything cleverer than a clever cowboy's horse, with me in the saddle. And the bell, the bell was such a glorious gong of a ring!

If Dad was alive, I could talk to him. If Dad was alive, he'd give me money for the bike like a shot.

I sighed. It was amazing what a sigh could do. I sighed and tumbled on a great idea. Tomorrow evening I'd get Shirnette to come with me. Both of us together would be sure to get the boys interested to teach us to ride. Wow! With Shirnette they can't just ride away!

Next day at school, everything went sour. For the first time, Shirnette and me had a real fight, because of what I hated most.

Shirnette brought a cockroach to school in a shoe-polish tin. At playtime she opened the tin and let the cockroach fly into my blouse. Pure panic and disgust nearly killed me. I crushed up the cockroach in my clothes and practically ripped my blouse off, there in open sunlight. Oh, the smell of a cockroach is the nastiest ever to block your nose! I

▲ **Critical Viewing**
How do the boys in this picture compare to those in the story? **[Connect]**

Reading Check

How does Becky's mother feel about the Wheels-and-Brake Boys?

started running with my blouse to go and wash it. Twice I had to stop and be sick.

I washed away the crushed cockroach stain from my blouse. Then the stupid Shirnette had to come into the toilet, falling about laughing. All right, I knew the cockroach treatment was for the time when I made my centipede on a string crawl up Shirnette's back. But you put fair-is-fair aside. I just barged into Shirnette.

When it was all over, I had on a wet blouse, but Shirnette had one on, too.

Then, going home with the noisy flock of children from school, I had such a new, new idea. If Mum thought I was scruffy, Nat, Aldo, Jimmy, and Ben might think so, too. I didn't like that.

Characters' Motives
What is Becky's motivation for fixing her hair?

After dinner I combed my hair in the bedroom. Mum did her machining[4] on the veranda. Meggie helped Mum. Granny sat there, wishing she could take on any job, as usual.

I told Mum I was going to make up a quarrel with Shirnette. I went, but my friend wouldn't speak to me, let alone come out to keep my company. I stood alone and watched the Wheels-and-Brake Boys again.

This time the boys didn't race away past me. I stood leaning against the tall coconut palm tree. People passed up and down. The nearby main road was busy with traffic. But I didn't mind. I watched the boys. Riding round and round the big flame tree, Nat, Aldo, Jimmy, and Ben looked marvelous.

At first each boy rode round the tree alone. Then each boy raced each other round the tree, going round three times. As he won, the winner rang his bell on and on, till he stopped panting and could laugh and talk properly.

Vocabulary
reckless (rek′ lis) *adj.* not careful; taking chances

Next, most reckless and fierce, all the boys raced against each other. And, leaning against their bicycles, talking and joking, the boys popped soft drinks open, drank, and ate chipped bananas.

I walked up to Nat, Aldo, Jimmy, and Ben and said, "Can somebody teach me to ride?"

"Why don't you stay indoors and learn to cook and sew and wash clothes?" Jimmy said.

---

4. **machining** (mə shēn′ in) *n.* sewing.

I grinned. "I know all that already," I said. "And one day perhaps I'll even be mum to a boy child, like all of you. Can you cook and sew and wash clothes, Jimmy? All I want is to learn to ride. I want you to teach me."

I didn't know why I said what I said. But everybody went silent and serious.

One after the other, Nat, Aldo, Jimmy, and Ben got on their bikes and rode off. I wasn't at all cross with them. I only wanted to be riding out of the playground with them. I knew they'd be heading into the town to have ice cream and things and talk and laugh.

Mum was sitting alone on the veranda. She sewed buttons onto a white shirt she'd made. I sat down next to Mum. Straightaway, "Mum," I said, "I still want to have a bike badly."

"Oh, Becky, you still have that foolishness in your head? What am I going to do?"

Mum talked with some sympathy. Mum knew I was honest. "I can't get rid of it, mam," I said.

Mum stopped sewing. "Becky," she said, staring in my face, "how many girls around here do you see with bicycles?"

"Janice Gordon has a bike," I reminded her.

"Janice Gordon's dad has acres and acres of coconuts and bananas, with a business in the town as well."

I knew Mum was just about to give in. Then my granny had to come out onto the veranda and interfere. Listen to that Granny-Liz. "Becky, I heard your mother tell you over and over she cahn[5] afford to buy you a bike. Yet you keep on and on. Child, you're a girl."

"But I don't want a bike because I'm a girl."

"D'you want it because you feel like a bwoy?" Granny said.

"No. I only want a bike because I want it and want it and want it."

Granny just carried on. "A tomboy's like a whistling woman and a crowing hen, who can only come to a bad end. D'you understand?"

I didn't want to understand. I knew Granny's speech was an awful speech. I went and sat down with Lenny and Vin, who were making a kite.

---

5. **cahn** can't.

© Spiral Review
Setting What cultural attitudes about appropriate roles for girls serve as the background for this story?

Characters' Motives How does Becky feel about Granny-Liz's ideas?

Reading Check
Why do Becky and Shirnette have a fight?

By Saturday morning I felt real sorry for Mum. I could see Mum really had it hard for money. I had to try and help. I knew anything of Dad's—anything—would be worth a great mighty hundred dollars.

I found myself in the center of town, going through the busy Saturday crowd. I hoped Mum wouldn't be too cross. I went into the fire station. With lots of luck I came face to face with a round-faced man in uniform. He talked to me. "Little miss, can I help you?"

I told him I'd like to talk to the head man. He took me into the office and gave me a chair. I sat down. I opened out my brown paper parcel. I showed him my dad's sun helmet. I told him I thought it would make a good fireman's hat. I wanted to sell the helmet for some money toward a bike, I told him.

The fireman laughed a lot. I began to laugh, too. The fireman put me in a car and drove me back home.

Mum's eyes popped to see me bringing home the fireman. The round-faced fireman laughed at my adventure. Mum laughed, too, which was really good. The fireman gave Mum my dad's hat back. Then—mystery, mystery—Mum sent me outside while they talked.

Characters' Motives
What two possible motives does Becky have for trying to sell her father's helmet?

My mum was only a little cross with me. Then—mystery and more mystery—my mum took me with the fireman in his car to his house.

The fireman brought out what? A bicycle! A beautiful, shining bicycle! His nephew's bike. His nephew had been taken away, all the way to America. The bike had been left with the fireman-uncle for him to sell it. And the good, kind fireman-uncle decided we could have the bike—on small payments. My mum looked uncertain. But in a big, big way, the fireman knew it was all right. And Mum smiled a little. My mum had good sense to know it was all right. My mum took the bike from the fireman Mr. Dean.

And guess what? Seeing my bike much, much newer than his, my cousin Ben's eyes popped with envy. But he took on the big job. He taught me to ride. Then he taught Shirnette.

I ride into town with the Wheels-and-Brake Boys now. When she can borrow a bike, Shirnette comes too. We all sit together. We have patties and ice cream and drink drinks together. We talk and joke. We ride about, all over the place.

And, again, guess what? Fireman Mr. Dean became our best friend, and Mum's especially. He started coming around almost every day.

Characters' Motives
What motivates the fireman to sell the bicycle to Becky?

Vocabulary
envy (en´ vē) *n.* desire for what another has

Critical Thinking

1. Key Ideas and Details (a) Why don't Becky's mother and grandmother want her to join the Wheels-and-Brake Boys? **(b) Analyze:** What other reasons keep Becky from getting a bike?

2. Key Ideas and Details (a) What conflict do Becky and Shirnette have? **(b) Infer:** By the end of the story, how are the girls getting along? **(c) Support:** What examples from the story indicate this?

3. Key Ideas and Details (a) What are two of Becky's main character traits? **(b) Analyze:** How do these traits help Becky achieve her goal?

4. Integration of Knowledge and Ideas What lesson does Becky learn from the conflict with her mother and her grandmother? Explain how she changes. *[Connect to the Big Question: Is conflict always bad?]*

Cite textual evidence to support your responses.

The Southpaw

Judith Viorst

▲ **Critical Viewing**
What details in this picture show team spirit? **[Analyze]**

Vocabulary
former (fôr´ mər) *adj.* existing in an earlier time; past

Dear Richard,

    Don't invite me to your birthday party because I'm not coming. And give back the Disneyland sweatshirt I said you could wear.

    If I'm not good enough to play on your team, I'm not good enough to be friends with.

    Your former friend,
    Janet

P.S. I hope when you go to the dentist he finds 20 cavities.

Dear Janet,

    Here is your stupid Disneyland sweatshirt, if that's how you're going to be. I want my comic books now— finished or not. No girl had ever played on the Mapes Street baseball team, and as long as I'm captain, no girl ever will.

    Your former friend,
    Richard

P.S. I hope when you go for your checkup you need a tetanus shot.

Characters' Motives
What motivates Richard to say he would not save Janet a seat on the bus?

Dear Richard,

    I'm changing my goldfish's name from Richard to Stanley. Don't count on my vote for class president next year. Just because I'm a member of the ballet club doesn't mean I'm not a terrific ballplayer.

    Your former friend,
    Janet

P.S. I see you lost your first game 28-0.

Dear Janet,

    I'm not saving any more seats for you on the bus. For all I care you can stand the whole way to school. Why don't you just forget about baseball and learn something nice like knitting?

    Your former friend,
    Richard

P.S. Wait until Wednesday.

Dear Richard,

My father said I could call someone to go with us for a ride and hot-fudge sundaes. In case you didn't notice, I didn't call you.

Your former friend,
Janet

P.S. I see you lost your second game, 34-0.

Dear Janet,

Remember when I took the laces out of my blue-and-white sneakers and gave them to you? I want them back.

Your former friend,
Richard

P.S. Wait until Friday.

Dear Richard,

Congratulations on your un-broken record. Eight straight loses, wow! I understand you're the laughingstock of New Jersey.

Your former friend,
Janet

P.S. Why don't you and your team forget about baseball and learn something nice like knitting maybe?

Dear Janet,

Here's the silver horseback riding trophy that you gave me. I don't think I want to keep it anymore.

Your former friend,
Richard

P.S. I didn't think you'd be the kind who'd kick a man when he's down.

Dear Richard,

I wasn't kicking exactly. I was kicking back.

Your former friend,
Janet

P.S. In case you were wondering, my batting average is .345.

Dear Janet,

Alfie is having his tonsils out tomorrow. We might be able to let you catch next week.

Richard

Dear Richard,

I pitch.

Janet

Dear Janet,

Joel is moving to Kansas and Danny sprained his wrist. How about a permanent place in the outfield?

Richard

Characters' Motives
Is Janet's motivation for writing to Richard external or internal? Explain.

✓ Reading Check

What are Richard and Janet fighting about?

Characters' Motives
What motivations do
Janet and Richard share?

Spiral Review
**Structure and
Setting** How are the
structure and setting
of this story unusual?

Vocabulary
unreasonable
(un rē´ zən ə bəl)
adj. not fair;
not sensible

Dear Richard,
    I pitch.
Janet

Dear Richard,
    Susan Reilly plays first
base, Marilyn Jackson
catches, Ethel Kahn plays
center field, I pitch. It's a
package deal.
    Janet

P.S. Sorry about your 12-
game losing streak.

Dear Richard,
    Nobody ever said that I was
unreasonable. How about Lizzie
Martindale instead?
    Janet

Dear Janet,
    Ronnie caught the chicken pox
and Leo broke his toe and Elwood
has these stupid violin lessons. I'll
give you first base, and that's my
final offer.
    Richard

Dear Janet,
    Please! Not Marilyn
Jackson.
Richard

Dear Janet,
    At least could you call your
goldfish Richard again?
Your friend,
    Richard

Critical Thinking

Cite textual
evidence to
support your
responses.

1. **Key Ideas and Details** **(a)** Why is Janet angry with
   Richard? **(b) Analyze:** What traits are revealed in the
   notes the two characters write each other?

2. **Key Ideas and Details** **(a)** What position does Janet
   want to play? **(b) Infer:** What agreement do Janet and
   Richard reach? **(c) Evaluate:** Does this arrangement suit
   both of them? Explain.

3. **Key Ideas and Details** **(a)** Do you think that Richard's
   baseball team will finally win a game? **(b) Support:**
   What examples from the story indicate this?

4. **Integration of Knowledge and Ideas** **(a)** What
   character traits help Janet resolve her conflict with
   Richard? **(b)** What might Janet learn from this conlict?
   [Connect to the Big Question: Is conflict always bad?]

Comparing Characters' Motives

1. Key Ideas and Details Identify one of Becky's and one of Janet's character traits. Then, give an example from the story of how the author indirectly shows the trait.

2. Key Ideas and Details Use a graphic organizer like the one shown to compare the motives of each girl.

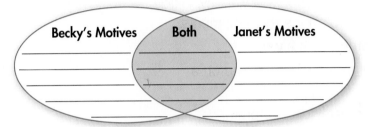

Becky's Motives | Both | Janet's Motives

3. Integration of Knowledge and Ideas (a) What internal motivation do Becky and Janet share? **(b)** How does this affect the events in each story?

⏱ Timed Writing

Explanatory Text: Essay

Compare and contrast the traits and motives of Becky and Janet. In a brief essay, draw conclusions about how each girl's character traits support her motivation to get what she wants. **(35 minutes)**

5-Minute Planner

1. Read the prompt carefully and completely.

2. Gather your ideas by jotting down the answers to these questions:
   - What does each girl want? Why?
   - What character traits help each girl achieve her goal?

3. To organize your responses, record them in a two-column chart. Put Becky's name at the top of Column 1 and Janet's name at the top of Column 2. Circle any similarities you find between the two girls.

4. Reread the prompt, and then draft your essay.

Writing Workshop

**Common Core
State Standards**

Writing
1. Write arguments to support claims with clear reasons and relevant evidence.
1.a. Introduce claim(s) and organize the reasons and evidence clearly.

Language
3.b. Maintain consistency in style and tone.

Write an Argument

Response to Literature: Review

Defining the Form When you read a literary work, the characters, the plot, and the writing itself can spark a reaction in you. In a **response to literature** or a **review,** you share this reaction and present an argument that states and supports your opinion.

Assignment Write a review of a book, short story, essay, article, or poem that you have read recently. Include these elements:

✔ a *summary* of important features of the work

✔ a strong, interesting *focus* or interpretation based on a careful reading of the work

✔ *clear organization* based on several ideas or premises

✔ *supporting details* and examples for each main idea

✔ your own insights about or *judgment* of the work

✔ error-free grammar, including *correct use of troublesome verbs*

To preview the criteria on which your review may be judged, see the rubric on page 269.

 Writing Workshop: *Work in Progress*

Review the work you did on pages 217 and 241.

Prewriting/Planning Strategy

Jot down details to support your position. Choose a literary work that sparks a response in you. Then, think about the details that support your response. For example, consider the plot, characters, or message. Reread the work, noting ideas, examples, and evidence that supports a single idea, or claim, you want to develop. Use a web like the one shown.

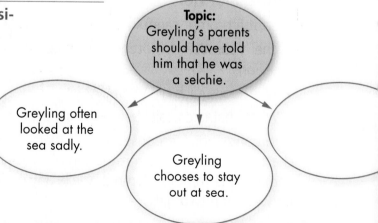

Topic: Greyling's parents should have told him that he was a selchie.

Greyling often looked at the sea sadly.

Greyling chooses to stay out at sea.

Let Your Voice Be Heard

Voice is the personality behind your writing. When your voice comes through in your writing, readers can almost hear you speaking to them. Your voice gives a sense of who you are.

Adapting Your Voice Your voice should be a reflection of you—it should allow your personality to shine through. Remember, though, that there are many sides of your personality. These may include: serious, playful, funny, smart, entertaining, understanding, stubborn, and more.

In addition to reflecting aspects of your personality, your voice changes with your subject matter, attitude toward your reader, purpose, and mood. Consider the following when deciding on the voice of your response to the literary work:

> **PH WRITING COACH**
> Further instruction and practice are available in *Prentice Hall Writing Coach*.

Your subject matter	Evaluate the subject matter of your writing. What are you writing about? Is the subject serious? Funny? Controversial? Are you the expert?	When you write a literary response, you are giving your opinion. That makes you the expert. Nobody knows your opinion but you! So, don't be afraid to give your opinion in a definite way.
Your audience	Your voice changes as your audience changes. For some audiences, you may choose a more formal tone and for others a more casual tone.	Who will be reading your response to the literary work? If your audience is made up of students your age, your voice might be different than if your audience is composed of adults.
Your purpose	What is the purpose of your work? Are you trying to persuade? Entertain? Inform? Your voice changes as your purpose changes.	Are you trying to entertain others with your opinion of the literary work? Are you trying to convince them that the work is worth their time?
Consider different angles	You get to decide whether to present your topic with humor, seriousness, irony, or any mood you choose that is appropriate for the subject matter, purpose, and audience.	Decide what mood you would like to convey to the reader of your response to the literary work.

Evaluating Your Voice After you have drafted your response to a literary work, read it aloud. Does your response reflect your personality? Does it come across the way you want it to?

Drafting Strategies

 Common Core
State Standards

Writing

1.a. Introduce claim(s) and organize the reasons and evidence clearly.

1.b. Support claim(s) with clear reasons and relevant evidence, using credible sources and demonstrating an understanding of the topic or text.

1.e. Provide a concluding statement or section that follows from the argument presented.

Language

3. Use knowledge of language and its conventions when writing, speaking, reading, or listening.

Organize your response. A well-organized draft has these connected parts, as the graphic shows:

Introduction	Body	Conclusion
Identify your response.	*Support your response.*	*Summarize your ideas and make a recommendation.*

- The **introduction** presents your main claims about the work in the form of a statement that captures your response. It also includes a brief summary of the details in the work that support your response.

- The **body** offers evidence to support your claims, including quotations, examples, and specific references to the text.

- Finally, the **conclusion** restates your feelings and opinions about the work. You might explain whether this work has made a lasting impression on you or whether you would recommend it to other readers.

Justify your response. Elaborate on your general ideas by including details that support your claims.

General Idea:	This story is full of suspense.
Specific Support:	Every time the clock chimes, the reader knows the hour of decision is closer.

Revising Strategies

Color-code related details. Review your draft to make sure you have supported each point you have made. Circle each of your main claims in a different color. Use the color of each main claim to underline its supporting points. If a paragraph contains a few different colors, revise by moving sentences to the paragraph they support. If a sentence is neither circled nor underlined, delete it or use it in a new paragraph.

Add a quotation or two. Review the work to search for quotations that support the claims you make. The quotations you choose should elaborate on your ideas, not only repeat them.

Correcting Errors With Verbs

Irregular verbs are those in which the past tense and past participle are not formed by adding *-ed* or *-d* to the present tense. **Troublesome verbs** are verb pairs that are easily confused.

Identifying Incorrect Forms of Irregular Verbs Memorize these verb forms that occur frequently in reading and writing.

Examples of Irregular Verbs			
Present	**Present Participle**	**Past**	**Past Participle**
drink	(am) drinking	drank	(have) drunk
do	(am) doing	did	(have) done
bring	(am) bringing	brought	(have) brought

Identifying Incorrect Forms of Troublesome Verbs The two verbs in each of these pairs are often confused:

> **Lay/Lie** *Lay* means "to put or place something." It takes a direct object. Example: *Shelly will lay the guitar on the table.* *Lie* means "to rest in a reclining position" or "to be situated." Example: *I like to lie in the hammock.*

> **Raise/Rise** *Raise* means "to lift up" or "to cause to rise." It takes a direct object. Example: *Please raise the curtain.*

> *Rise* means "to get up" or "to go up." It does not take a direct object. Example: *My neighbors rise early in the morning.*

PH WRITING COACH

Further instruction and practice are available in *Prentice Hall Writing Coach*.

Fixing Errors To fix incorrect irregular verbs, identify which principal part of the verb is needed.

1. Recall the correct use from the chart of principal parts.
2. Use a dictionary to determine the correct form.

To fix an incorrectly used troublesome verb:

1. Remember the meaning of the verb.
2. Use a dictionary to determine which verb to use.

Grammar in Your Writing

Circle the verbs used in your essay. If any verbs are used incorrectly, fix them using the methods above.

Student Model: Chris Harshfield, Louisville, KY

 **Common Core State Standards**

Language
2. Demonstrate command of the conventions of standard English capitalization, punctuation, and spelling when writing.

Response to *Tuck Everlasting*

Imagine finding a way to stay young forever! That's what the characters in *Tuck Everlasting*, a novel by Natalie Babbitt, do. The novel makes the idea especially interesting by presenting it in a story that makes a realistic situation out of a very unrealistic idea.

Winnie, the main character, meets a strange family, the Tucks. She soon discovers that they have a secret: All of them have drunk from a spring of water that makes them live forever. Because Winnie has a crush on Jesse, one of the Tucks, she is tempted to drink from the spring, too, when she is old enough to marry him. Based on things the characters say and do, we know that this will not be an easy decision for Winnie. The question is very important to readers.

Should Winnie drink from the spring? The theme of this story is not a new one, but the way it is presented is better than in other stories. Like most of the other writers, Babbitt suggests that living forever is not a good idea. Unlike other stories I have read about this theme, however, *Tuck Everlasting* really convinced me by showing examples I could understand. The novel also helped show the theme through characters who seem like real people. Even though I know there is no spring like the one in the book, the book made it seem real enough to get me thinking about the problem Winnie faces.

The final outcome of the story settles the question as far as Winnie is concerned. When Jesse returns years later, he finds her marker in the cemetery. Because she is dead, we know that she decided to not drink from the spring. The words on her marker suggest that she had a happy life, and that she got over Jesse. For Winnie, in any case, Mr. Tuck's memorable and mysterious words prove true: ". . . the stream keeps moving on, taking it all back again" (Babbitt 31).

I was glad to see the mystery of Winnie's life solved for readers. However, the questions that do not get answered left me a little disappointed. I would have preferred to know how Winnie reached her decision, not just what she decided. Overall, though, *Tuck Everlasting* tells a good story and raises interesting questions. In the end, Tuck gives the answer, "Life. Moving, growing, changing, never the same two minutes together" (Babbitt 30).

In the introduction, Chris indicates the focus of his response.

Chris provides a brief summary so that readers can better understand his response.

The response is organized mainly around the theme.

Here, Chris gives his interpretation of the theme and supports it with an example from the novel.

In the conclusion, Chris shares his own feelings and judgments. He finishes with a general impression and a quotation from the novel.

Editing and Proofreading

Check your essay for errors in spelling, punctuation, and grammar.

Focus on punctuating quotations. Check any quotations against the original text to make sure that you have copied the words exactly. Use quotation marks and commas to separate a quotation from the rest of the sentences.

Publishing and Presenting

Consider one of the following ways to share your writing:

Organize a literature discussion day. Arrange a day for you and your classmates to present and discuss your responses to literature.

Write a letter to an author. Turn your review into a letter to the author. Tell what you liked about the work and ask questions about his or her writing, using examples from the book. Share your letter and any response to it with your classmates.

Reflecting on Your Writing

Writer's Journal Jot down your answers to these questions:

- *In what way is jotting down notes while reading helpful in preparing a response to literature?*
- *As you wrote your review, what new insights into the work did you have?*

Spiral Review

Earlier in this unit, you learned about **verbs** (p. 216) and **principal parts of verbs** (p. 240). Review your response to make sure you have used verbs correctly.

PH WRITING COACH

Further instruction and practice are available in *Prentice Hall Writing Coach*.

Rubric for Self-Assessment

Find evidence in your writing to address each category. Then, use the rating scale to grade your work.

Criteria	Rating Scale *not very* → *very*				
Focus: How clearly have you focused on an interesting aspect of the story?	1	2	3	4	5
Organization: How well are ideas, patterns, or images organized?	1	2	3	4	5
Support/Elaboration: How convincing are the supporting details for each main idea?	1	2	3	4	5
Style: How well have you stated your feelings or judgments?	1	2	3	4	5
Conventions: How correct is your grammar, especially your use of irregular verbs?	1	2	3	4	5
Voice: Does your personality come through in your writing?	1	2	3	4	5

⊚ Leveled Texts

Build your skills and improve your comprehension of short stories with texts of increasing complexity.

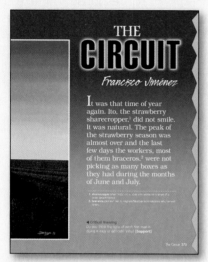

Read **"The Circuit"** to learn what life is like for a boy whose family moves several times each year.

Read **"The All-American Slurp"** to meet a Chinese family who struggles to learn the customs of their new home in the United States.

Common Core State Standards

Meet these standards with either **"The Circuit"** (p. 274) or **"The All-American Slurp"** (p. 286).

Reading Literature
2. Determine a theme or central idea of a text and how it is conveyed through particular details. *(Literary Analysis: Theme)*

Spiral Review: RL.6.3

Writing
4. Produce clear and coherent writing in which the development, organization, and style are appropriate to task, purpose, and audience. *(Writing: Description)*

Speaking and Listening
1.c. Pose and respond to specific questions with elaboration and detail by making comments that

contribute to the topic, text, or issue under discussion. *(Speaking and Listening: Interview)*

Language
1. Demonstrate command of the conventions of standard English grammar and usage when writing or speaking. *(Conventions: Simple Verb Tenses)*

4.b. Use common, grade-appropriate Greek or Latin affixes and roots as clues to the meaning of a word. *(Vocabulary: Word Study)*

Reading Skill: Draw Conclusions

A **conclusion** is a decision or opinion you reach based on details in a literary work. To draw conclusions, **ask questions** as you read, such as *Why is this character alone so often?* Then, look for story details that help you answer the question. For example, the character may like to show off in front of others. You might then draw the conclusion that people dislike those who constantly point out their superiority.

Literary Analysis: Theme

The **theme,** or central idea of a story, is a thought about life that the story conveys. Although the theme of a work is some-times directly stated, more often it is hinted at or suggested. To figure out a theme that is *indirectly* stated, consider the events in the story, the characters' thoughts and feelings, and the story's title. Together, these details can help you understand the story's main message.

PHLit Online!
www.PHLitOnline.com

Hear It!
• Selection summary audio
• Selection audio

See It!
• Get Connected video
• Background video
• More about the author
• Vocabulary flashcards

Do It!
• Interactive journals
• Interactive graphic organizers
• Self-test
• Internet activity
• Grammar tutorial
• Interactive vocabulary games

Using the Strategy: Theme Map

Complete a **theme map** like the one shown to help you identify the theme of a story.

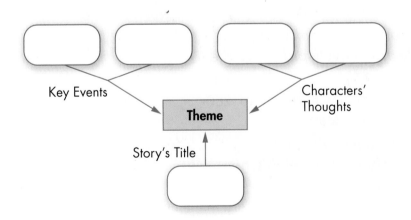

Is _conflict_ always bad?

Writing About the Big Question

In "The Circuit," the narrator is upset because his family has to keep moving in order to find work on farms. Use these sentence starters to develop your ideas about the Big Question.

> When a family has to move a lot, they face **conflicts** such as _____. One way to **resolve** these conflicts is to _____.

While You Read Consider the ways in which the narrator copes with the conflict he faces.

Vocabulary

Read each word and its definition. Decide whether you know the word well, know it a little bit, or do not know it at all. After you read, see how your knowledge of each word has increased.

- **accompanied** (ə kum´ pə nēd) v. went along with; joined (p. 276) *Carlos accompanied me to school.* accompany v. accompanying v. accompaniment n.

- **drone** (drōn) n. continuous humming sound (p. 279) *The engine's drone made us sleepy.* droning n. droned v.

- **instinctively** (in stiŋk´ tiv lē) adv. done automatically, without thinking (p. 279) *Polly instinctively picked up the crying baby.* instinct n. instinctual adj.

- **savoring** (sā´ vər iŋ) v. enjoying; tasting with delight (p. 280) *I was savoring the tasty meal.* savor v. savory adj.

- **enroll** (en rōl´) v. place oneself on a register or list (p. 281) *I will enroll in college after I finish high school.* enrolled v. enrolling v. enrollment n.

Word Study

The **Latin prefix com-** means "with," "together," or "next to."

In this story, the narrator says that the barking of the dogs **accompanied**, or mixed together with, his brothers' and sisters' yelling.

Meet
Francisco Jiménez
(b. 1943)

Author of
THE
CIRCUIT

Born in Mexico, Francisco Jiménez (hē mā′ nəz) came with his family to the United States when he was four. The family settled in California and became migrant workers. Like the narrator in "The Circuit," Jiménez could not go to school before the harvest ended. He once said, "I came to realize that learning and knowledge were the only stable things in my life. Whatever I learned in school, that knowledge would stay with me no matter how many times we moved."

The Path to Success In high school, Jiménez supported himself by working as a janitor. His excellent grades won him three college scholarships. He went on to become an outstanding teacher and college official, as well as an award-winning writer.

DID YOU KNOW?
Jiménez taught himself by studying in the fields and by reading whenever he had a chance.

BACKGROUND FOR THE STORY
Migrant Workers

"The Circuit" is about a family of migrant farmworkers. Most migrant workers in the United States move often to follow the demands of seasonal harvesting. The whole family usually travels together, with children helping adults on the farms. Children may start school late in the fall or leave early in the spring to help with the harvest.

THE CIRCUIT

Francisco Jiménez

It was that time of year again. Ito, the strawberry sharecropper,[1] did not smile. It was natural. The peak of the strawberry season was almost over and the last few days the workers, most of them braceros,[2] were not picking as many boxes as they had during the months of June and July.

---

1. **sharecropper** (sher′ kräp′ ər) *n.* one who works for a share of a crop; tenant farmer.
2. **braceros** (brä ser′ os) *n.* migrant Mexican farm laborers who harvest crops.

◀ **Critical Viewing**
Do you think the type of work this man is doing is easy or difficult? Why? **[Support]**

As the last days of August disappeared, so did the number of *braceros*. Sunday, only one—the best picker—came to work. I liked him. Sometimes we talked during our half-hour lunch break. That is how I found out he was from Jalisco, the same state in Mexico my family was from. That Sunday was the last time I saw him.

When the sun had tired and sunk behind the mountains, Ito signaled us that it was time to go home. "*Ya esora*,"[3] he yelled in his broken Spanish. Those were the words I waited for twelve hours a day, every day, seven days a week, week after week. And the thought of not hearing them again saddened me.

As we drove home Papá did not say a word. With both hands on the wheel, he stared at the dirt road. My older brother, Roberto, was also silent. He leaned his head back and closed his eyes. Once in a while he cleared from his throat the dust that blew in from outside.

Yes, it was that time of year. When I opened the front door to the shack, I stopped. Everything we owned was neatly packed in cardboard boxes. Suddenly I felt even more the weight of hours, days, weeks, and months of work. I sat down on a box. The thought of having to move to Fresno[4] and knowing what was in store for me there brought tears to my eyes.

That night I could not sleep. I lay in bed thinking about how much I hated this move.

A little before five o'clock in the morning, Papá woke everyone up. A few minutes later, the yelling and screaming of my little brothers and sisters, for whom the move was a great adventure, broke the silence of dawn. Shortly, the barking of the dogs accompanied them.

While we packed the breakfast dishes, Papá went outside to start the "Carcanchita."[5] That was the name Papá gave his old '38 black Plymouth. He bought it in a used-car lot in Santa Rosa in the winter of 1949. Papá was very proud of his little jalopy. He had a right to be

---

3. *Ya esora* (yä es ô rä) Spanish for "It's time" (*Ya es hora*).
4. **Fresno** (frez´ nō) *n.* city in central California.
5. **Carcanchita** (kär kän chē´ tä) affectionate name for the car.

Theme
What clues do this event and the narrator's actions give you about the story's theme?

Vocabulary
accompanied (ə kum´ pə nēd) *v.* went along with; joined

proud of it. He spent a lot of time looking at other cars before buying this one. When he finally chose the "Carcanchita," he checked it thoroughly before driving it out of the car lot. He examined every inch of the car. He listened to the motor, tilting his head from side to side like a parrot, trying to detect any noises that spelled car trouble. After being satisfied with the looks and sounds of the car, Papá then insisted on knowing who the

The grinder (La molendera), 1926, Diego Rivera, Museo Nacional de Arte Moderno, Instituto Nacional de Bellas Artes, Mexico City, D.F., Mexico. ©Banco de Mexico Diego Rivera & Frida Kahlo Museums Trust. Av. Cinco de Mayo No. 2, Col. Centro, Del. Cuauhtemoc 06059, Mexico, D.F. Reproduction authorized by the Instituto Nacional de Bellas Artes y Literatura.

original owner was. He never did find out from the car salesman, but he bought the car anyway. Papá figured the original owner must have been an important man because behind the rear seat of the car he found a blue necktie.

Papá parked the car out in front and left the motor running. "*Listo,*"[6] he yelled. Without saying a word, Roberto and I began to carry the boxes out to the car. Roberto carried the two big boxes and I carried the two smaller ones. Papá then threw the mattress on top of the car roof and tied it with ropes to the front and rear bumpers.

Everything was packed except Mamá's pot. It was an old large galvanized[7] pot she had picked up at an army surplus store in Santa María the year I was born. The pot had many dents and nicks, and the more dents and nicks it acquired the more Mamá liked it. "*Mi olla,*"[8] she used to say proudly.

I held the front door open as Mamá carefully carried out her pot by both handles, making sure not to spill

---

6. ***Listo*** (lēs´ tō) Spanish for "Ready."
7. **galvanized** (gal´ və nīzd) *adj.* coated with zinc to prevent rusting.
8. ***Mi olla*** (mē ō´ yä) Spanish for "My pot."

▲ **Critical Viewing**
What are three words that describe the woman in this painting? **[Analyze]**

Draw Conclusions
What do the details so far tell you about the family's attitude toward moving again?

Reading Check
Why is Papá proud of "Carcanchita"?

Geography Connection

Agricultural Seasons

With sunny weather and a favorable climate, California produces more crops than any other state. At every point in the year, there is a different crop ready to be harvested in some part of the state. Migrant workers, such as Panchito's family, migrate from place to place to harvest the available crop. Grapes are picked in the summer and fall in the lush valleys of central and northern California. Peak strawberry season hits the southern coastal regions in the spring. Cotton is harvested in the dry valleys of central and southern California during the winter.

Connect to the Literature

Identify two ways the agricultural seasons affect the characters in this story.

the cooked beans. When she got to the car, Papá reached out to help her with it. Roberto opened the rear car door and Papá gently placed it on the floor behind the front seat. All of us then climbed in. Papá sighed, wiped the sweat off his forehead with his sleeve, and said wearily: "*Es todo.*"[9]

As we drove away, I felt a lump in my throat. I turned around and looked at our little shack for the last time. •

At sunset we drove into a labor camp near Fresno. Since Papá did not speak English, Mamá asked the camp foreman if he needed any more workers. "We don't need no more," said the foreman, scratching his head. "Check with Sullivan down the road. Can't miss him. He lives in a big white house with a fence around it."

When we got there, Mamá walked up to the house. She went through a white gate, past a row of rose bushes, up the stairs to the front door. She rang the doorbell. The porch light went on and a tall husky man came out. They exchanged a few words. After the man went in, Mamá clasped her hands and hurried back to the car. "We have work! Mr. Sullivan said we can stay there the whole season," she said, gasping and pointing to an old garage near the stables.

The garage was worn out by the years. It had no windows. The walls, eaten by termites, strained to support the roof full of holes. The dirt floor, populated by earthworms, looked like a gray road map.

That night, by the light of a kerosene lamp, we unpacked and cleaned our new home. Roberto swept away the loose dirt, leaving the hard ground. Papá plugged the holes in the walls with old newspapers and tin can tops.

---

9. *Es todo* (es tō′ thō) Spanish for "That's everything."

Mamá fed my little brothers and sisters. Papá and Roberto then brought in the mattress and placed it on the far corner of the garage. "Mamá, you and the little ones sleep on the mattress. Roberto, Panchito, and I will sleep outside under the trees," Papá said.

Early next morning Mr. Sullivan showed us where his crop was, and after breakfast, Papá, Roberto, and I headed for the vineyard to pick.

Around nine o'clock the temperature had risen to almost one hundred degrees. I was completely soaked in sweat and my mouth felt as if I had been chewing on a handkerchief. I walked over to the end of the row, picked up the jug of water we had brought, and began drinking. "Don't drink too much; you'll get sick," Roberto shouted. No sooner had he said that than I felt sick to my stomach. I dropped to my knees and let the jug roll off my hands. I remained motionless with my eyes glued on the hot sandy ground. All I could hear was the drone of insects. Slowly I began to recover. I poured water over my face and neck and watched the dirty water run down my arms to the ground.

I still felt a little dizzy when we took a break to eat lunch. It was past two o'clock and we sat underneath a large walnut tree that was on the side of the road. While we ate, Papá jotted down the number of boxes we had picked. Roberto drew designs on the ground with a stick. Suddenly I noticed Papá's face turn pale as he looked down the road. "Here comes the school bus," he whispered loudly in alarm. Instinctively, Roberto and I ran and hid in the vineyards. We did not want to get in trouble for not going to school. The neatly dressed boys about my age got off. They carried books under their arms. After they crossed the street, the bus drove away. Roberto and I came out from hiding and joined Papá. "*Tienen que tener cuidado*,"[10] he warned us.

After lunch we went back to work. The sun kept beating down. The buzzing insects, the wet sweat, and the hot dry dust made the afternoon seem to last forever. Finally the mountains around the valley reached out and swallowed the sun. Within an hour it was too dark to continue

"That night, by the light of a kerosene lamp, we unpacked and cleaned our new home."

Vocabulary
drone (drōn) *n.* continuous humming sound
instinctively (in stiŋk´ tiv lē) *adv.* done automatically, without thinking

Reading Check
What makes work in the vineyard hard for Panchito?

---

10. *Tienen que tener cuidado* (tē en´ en kā ten er´ kwē thä´ thō) Spanish for "You have to be careful."

picking. The vines blanketed the grapes, making it difficult to see the bunches. "*Vámonos,*"[11] said Papá, signaling to us that it was time to quit work. Papá then took out a pencil and began to figure out how much we had earned our first day. He wrote down numbers, crossed some out, wrote down some more. "*Quince,*"[12] he murmured.

When we arrived home, we took a cold shower underneath a waterhose. We then sat down to eat dinner around some wooden crates that served as a table. Mamá had cooked a special meal for us. We had rice and tortillas with "*carne con chile,*"[13] my favorite dish.

The next morning I could hardly move. My body ached all over. I felt little control over my arms and legs. This feeling went on every morning for days until my muscles finally got used to the work. ●

It was Monday, the first week of November. The grape season was over and I could now go to school. I woke up early that morning and lay in bed, looking at the stars and savoring the thought of not going to work and of starting sixth grade for the first time that year. Since I could not sleep, I decided to get up and join Papá and Roberto at breakfast. I sat at the table across from Roberto, but I kept my head down. I did not want to look up and face him. I knew he was sad. He was not going to school today. He was not going tomorrow, or next week, or next month. He would not go until the cotton season was over, and that was sometime in February. I rubbed my hands together and watched the dry, acid stained skin fall to the floor in little rolls.

When Papá and Roberto left for work, I felt relief. I walked to the top of a small grade next to the shack and watched the "Carcanchita" disappear in the distance in a cloud of dust.

Two hours later, around eight o'clock, I stood by the side of the road waiting for school bus number twenty. When it arrived I climbed in. Everyone was busy either talking or yelling. I sat in an empty seat in the back.

When the bus stopped in front of the school, I felt very nervous. I looked out the bus window and saw boys

Vocabulary
savoring (sā´ vər iŋ)
v. enjoying; tasting with delight

Theme
How does the sentence that begins "He would not go" suggest that the family's life follows a cycle? How might this relate to the story's theme?

---

11. *Vámonos* (vä´ mō nōs) Spanish for "Let's go."
12. *Quince* (kēn´ sā) Spanish for "Fifteen."
13. "*carne con chile*" (kär´ nā kən chil´ ā) dish of ground meat, hot peppers, beans, and tomatoes.

and girls carrying books under their arms. I put my hands in my pant pockets and walked to the principal's office. When I entered I heard a woman's voice say: "May I help you?" I was startled. I had not heard English for months. For a few seconds I remained speechless. I looked at the lady who waited for my answer. My first instinct was to answer her in Spanish, but I held back. Finally, after struggling for English words, I managed to tell her that I wanted to enroll in the sixth grade. After answering many questions, I was led to the classroom.

Mr. Lema, the sixth-grade teacher, greeted me and assigned me a desk. He then introduced me to the class. I was so nervous and scared at that moment when everyone's eyes were on me that I wished I were with Papá and Roberto picking cotton. After taking roll, Mr. Lema gave the class the assignment for the first hour. "The first thing we have to do this morning is finish reading the story we began yesterday," he said enthusiastically. He walked up to me, handed me an English book, and asked me to read. "We are on page 125," he said politely. When I heard this, I felt my blood rush to my head; I felt dizzy. "Would you like to read?" he asked hesitantly. I opened the book to page 125. My mouth was dry. My eyes began to water. I could not begin. "You can read later," Mr. Lema said understandingly.

For the rest of the reading period I kept getting angrier and angrier at myself. I should have read, I thought to myself.

During recess I went into the restroom and opened my English book to page 125. I began to read in a low voice, pretending I was in class. There were many words I did not know. I closed the book and headed back to the classroom.

Mr. Lema was sitting at his desk correcting papers. When I entered he looked up at me and smiled. I felt better. I walked up to him and asked if he could help me with the new words. "Gladly," he said.

Vocabulary
enroll (en rōl′) v. place oneself on a register or list

Draw Conclusions
What do the details in this paragraph lead you to conclude about Mr. Lema's character?

Reading Check
Why is Roberto unable to go back to school?

The rest of the month I spent my lunch hours working on English with Mr. Lema, my best friend at school.

One Friday during lunch hour Mr. Lema asked me to take a walk with him to the music room. "Do you like music?" he asked me as we entered the building.

"Yes, I like *corridos*,"[14] I answered. He then picked up a trumpet, blew on it and handed it to me. The sound gave me goose bumps. I knew that sound. I had heard it in many corridos. "How would you like to learn how to play it?" he asked. He must have read my face because before I could answer, he added: "I'll teach you how to play it during our lunch hours."

That day I could hardly wait to get home to tell Papá and Mamá the great news. As I got off the bus, my little brothers and sisters ran up to meet me. They were yelling and screaming. I thought they were happy to see me, but when I opened the door to our shack, I saw that everything we owned was neatly packed in cardboard boxes.

---

14. *corridos* (kō rē´ thōs) *n.* ballads.

Spiral Review
Resolution What do the cardboard boxes signify to the narrator? How do they signal the story's resolution?

Critical Thinking

Cite textual evidence to support your responses.

1. **Key Ideas and Details (a)** What does Panchito do on his school lunch hours? **(b) Infer:** Why do you think Panchito calls Mr. Lema his "best friend at school"? **(c) Interpret:** Based on the information in the story, how would you describe Panchito's personality?

2. **Key Ideas and Details (a)** What is the best thing that happens to Panchito on the last day of school? **(b) Infer:** What is the worst thing?

3. **Craft and Structure (a)** Where in the story does the author develop Panchito's character? **(b)** What details help us to understand Panchito?

4. **Integration of Knowledge and Ideas (a)** What might be done to ease the conflicts of families like Panchito's? **(b)** Examine the theme. Will Panchito grow stronger as a result of the conflict he faces? Explain. *[Connect to the Big Question: Is conflict always bad?]*

Reading Skill: Draw Conclusions

1. Complete a chart like the one shown to **draw conclusions** about the story.

Question	Details That Answer Question	Conclusion
Why does Panchito work so much?		
Why does Panchito not read aloud on the first day of school?		
Why are the family's belongings packed in boxes?		

Literary Analysis: Theme

2. Key Ideas and Details (a) What **theme,** or insight about life, does the story illustrate? **(b)** What details or events support the theme?

3. Craft and Structure How does the title relate to the story's theme?

Vocabulary

Acquisition and Use Match each situation with a vocabulary word from the list on page 272.

1. eating a delicious meal

2. how mother animals protect their young

3. the sound of bees buzzing

4. sign up for guitar lessons

5. went with a friend to a party

Word Study Use context clues and what you know about the **Latin prefix com-** to answer each question.

1. If you are alone, do you have *company*?

2. Would you eat a *combination* of ice cream and vinegar?

Word Study

The **Latin prefix com-** means "with," "together," or "next to."

Apply It Explain how the root contributes to the meanings of these words. Use a dictionary if necessary.

commiserate

commission

compression

Is *conflict* always bad?

Writing About the Big Question

In "The All-American Slurp," the narrator feels conflicted when her family's Chinese customs differ from the American customs of her neighbors. Use these sentence starters to develop your ideas about the Big Question.

Some **issues** you might face if you move to a new country are _____. To resolve these issues, you could _____.

While You Read Look for details that show how the narrator might find a happy solution to her conflict.

Vocabulary

Read each word and its definition. Decide whether you know the word well, know it a little bit, or do not know it at all. After you read, see how your knowledge of each word has increased.

- **emigrated** (em´ i grāt´ əd) *v.* left one country to settle in another (p. 286) *Our neighbors emigrated to the United States from China.* emigrate *v.* emigration *n.* migrate *v.*

- **acquainted** (ə kwānt´ əd) *v.* familiar (p. 288) *I became acquainted with Joe at school.* acquaint *v.* aquaintance *n.*

- **smugly** (smug´ lē) *adv.* in a way that shows too much pride or satisfaction with oneself (p. 289) *We groaned when she smugly told us she had won first prize.* smug *adj.* smugness *n.*

- **systematic** (sis´ tə mat´ ik) *adj.* orderly (p. 291) *He liked the systematic arrangement of the CDs.* systematically *adv.* system *n.*

- **etiquette** (et´ i kit) *n.* acceptable social manners (p. 292) *Saying please is proper etiquette.*

- **consumption** (kən sump´ shen) *n.* eating; drinking; using up (p. 292) *Water consumption increases on hot days.* consume *v.* consumed *v.*

Word Study

The **Latin root -migr-** means "to move" or "to wander."

This story is about the Lin family who **emigrated,** or moved, from China to the United States.

Meet
Lensey Namioka
(b. 1929)

Author of
The
All-American
Slurp

Authors often write about their own experiences. In "The All-American Slurp," Lensey Namioka based the main character on herself. Like her character, Namioka discovered big differences between Chinese and American eating habits.

Writing for Herself Namioka completed her first book, *Princess with a Bamboo Sword,* at the age of eight. As an adult, Namioka began writing the kind of stories she herself enjoyed reading, rather than writing specifically for young people. "Maybe I write these books because I never really grew up," she says.

DID YOU KNOW?

Namioka is Chinese but has her husband's Japanese last name. She has written books about Japan and China.

BACKGROUND FOR THE STORY

Chinese Customs

Every culture has unique customs and rituals surrounding food and meals. In this story, the habits of a Chinese family newly arrived in the United States surprise their neighbors. According to Chinese customs, food is often served on large platters in the center of the table and handled with slender sticks called chopsticks.

The All-American Slurp

Lensey Namioka

Vocabulary

emigrated

(em´ i grāt´ əd) *v.* left one country to settle in another

The first time our family was invited out to dinner in America, we disgraced ourselves while eating celery. We had emigrated to this country from China, and during our early days here we had a hard time with American table manners.

In China we never ate celery raw, or any other kind of vegetable raw. We always had to disinfect the vegetables in boiling water first. When we were presented with our first relish tray, the raw celery caught us unprepared.

We had been invited to dinner by our neighbors, the Gleasons. After arriving at the house, we shook hands with our hosts and packed ourselves into a sofa. As our family of four sat stiffly in a row, my younger brother and I stole glances at our parents for a clue as to what to do next.

Mrs. Gleason offered the relish tray to Mother. The tray looked pretty, with its tiny red radishes, curly sticks of carrots, and long, slender stalks of pale green celery. "Do try some of the celery, Mrs. Lin," she said. "It's from a local farmer, and it's sweet."

Mother picked up one of the green stalks, and Father followed suit. Then I picked up a stalk, and my brother did too. So there we sat, each with a stalk of celery in our right hand.

Mrs. Gleason kept smiling. "Would you like to try some of the dip, Mrs. Lin? It's my own recipe: sour cream and onion flakes, with a dash of Tabasco sauce."

Draw Conclusions
How do you think the narrator feels at this point in the dinner? Explain.

Most Chinese don't care for dairy products, and in those days I wasn't even ready to drink fresh milk. Sour cream sounded perfectly revolting. Our family shook our heads in unison.

Mrs. Gleason went off with the relish tray to the other guests, and we carefully watched to see what they did. Everyone seemed to eat the raw vegetables quite happily.

Mother took a bite of her celery. *Crunch.* "It's not bad!" she whispered.

Father took a bite of his celery. *Crunch.* "Yes, it is good," he said, looking surprised.

I took a bite, and then my brother. *Crunch, crunch.* It was more than good; it was delicious. Raw celery has a slight sparkle, a zingy taste that you don't get in cooked celery. When Mrs. Gleason came around with the relish tray, we each took another stalk of celery, except my brother. He took two.

There was only one problem: long strings ran through the length of the stalk, and they got caught in my teeth. When I help my mother in the kitchen, I always pull the string out before slicing celery.

I pulled the strings out of my stalk. *Z-z-zip, z-z-zip.* My brother followed suit. *Z-z-zip, z-z-zip, z-z-zip.* To my left, my parents were taking care of their own stalks. *Z-z-zip, z-z-zip, z-z-zip.*

Suddenly I realized that there was dead silence except for our zipping. Looking up, I saw that the eyes of everyone in

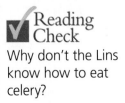
Reading Check
Why don't the Lins know how to eat celery?

the room were on our family. Mr. and Mrs. Gleason, their daughter Meg, who was my friend, and their neighbors the Badels—they were all staring at us as we busily pulled the strings of our celery.

That wasn't the end of it. Mrs. Gleason announced that dinner was served and invited us to the dining table. It was lavishly covered with platters of food, but we couldn't see any chairs around the table. So we helpfully carried over some dining chairs and sat down. All the other guests just stood there.

Mrs. Gleason bent down and whispered to us, "This is a buffet dinner. You help yourselves to some food and eat it in the living room."

Our family beat a retreat back to the sofa as if chased by enemy soldiers. For the rest of the evening, too mortified to go back to the dining table, I nursed a bit of potato salad on my plate.

Next day Meg and I got on the school bus together. I wasn't sure how she would feel about me after the spectacle our family made at the party. But she was just the same as usual, and the only reference she made to the party was, "Hope you and your folks got enough to eat last night. You certainly didn't take very much. Mom never tries to figure out how much food to prepare. She just puts everything on the table and hopes for the best."

I began to relax. The Gleasons' dinner party wasn't so different from a Chinese meal after all. My mother also puts everything on the table and hopes for the best. •

Meg was the first friend I had made after we came to America. I eventually got acquainted with a few other kids in school, but Meg was still the only real friend I had.

My brother didn't have any problems making friends. He spent all his time with some boys who were teaching him baseball, and in no time he could speak English much faster than I could—not better, but faster.

I worried more about making mistakes, and I spoke carefully, making sure I could say everything right before

Draw Conclusions
What can you conclude about the narrator, based on this paragraph?

Vocabulary
acquainted
(ə kwānt´ əd) v. familiar

opening my mouth. At least I had a better accent than my parents, who never really got rid of their Chinese accent, even years later. My parents had both studied English in school before coming to America, but what they had studied was mostly written English, not spoken.

Father's approach to English was a scientific one. Since Chinese verbs have no tense, he was fascinated by the way English verbs changed form according to whether they were in the present, past imperfect, perfect, pluperfect,[1] future, or future perfect tense. He was always making diagrams of verbs and their inflections,[2] and he looked for opportunities to show off his mastery of the pluperfect and future perfect tenses, his two favorites. "I shall have finished my project by Monday," he would say smugly.

Mother's approach was to memorize lists of polite phrases that would cover all possible social situations. She was constantly muttering things like "I'm fine, thank you. And you?" Once she accidentally stepped on someone's foot, and hurriedly blurted, "Oh, that's quite all right!" Embarrassed by her slip, she resolved to do better next time. So when someone stepped on *her* foot, she cried, "You're welcome!"

In our own different ways, we made progress in learning English. But I had another worry, and that was my appearance. My brother didn't have to worry, since Mother bought him blue jeans for school, and he dressed like all the other boys. But she insisted that girls had to wear skirts. By the time she saw that Meg and the other girls were wearing jeans, it was too late. My school clothes were bought already, and we didn't have money left to buy new outfits for me. We had too many other things to buy first, like furniture, pots, and pans.

The first time I visited Meg's house, she took me upstairs to her room, and I wound up trying on her clothes. We were pretty much the same size, since Meg was shorter and thinner than average. Maybe that's how we became friends in the first place. Wearing Meg's jeans and T-shirt, I looked at myself in the mirror. I could almost pass for an American—from the back, anyway. At least the kids in

Vocabulary
smugly (smug´ lē) *adv.* in a way that shows too much pride or satisfaction with oneself

Reading Check
Why is the narrator worried about her appearance?

---

1. **pluperfect** (ploo´ pʉr´ fikt) *adj.* the past perfect tense of verbs in English.
2. **inflections** (in flek´ shəns) *n.* changes in the forms of words to show different tenses.

school wouldn't stop and stare at me in my white blouse and navy blue skirt that went a couple of inches below the knees.

When Meg came to my house, I invited her to try on my Chinese dresses, the ones with a high collar and slits up the sides. Meg's eyes were bright as she looked at herself in the mirror. She struck several sultry poses, and we nearly fell over laughing.

The dinner party at the Gleasons' didn't stop my growing friendship with Meg. Things were getting better for me in other ways too. Mother finally bought me some jeans at the end of the month, when Father got his paycheck. She wasn't in any hurry about buying them at first, until I worked on her. This is what I did. Since we didn't have a car in those days, I often ran down to the neighborhood store to pick up things for her. The groceries cost less at a big supermarket, but the closest one was many blocks away. One day, when she ran out of flour, I offered to borrow a bike from our neighbor's son and buy a ten-pound bag of flour at the supermarket. I mounted the boy's bike and waved to Mother. "I'll be back in five minutes!"

Before I started pedaling, I heard her voice behind me. "You can't go out in public like that! People can see all the way up to your thighs!"

"I'm sorry," I said innocently. "I thought you were in a hurry to get the flour." For dinner we were going to have pot-stickers (fried Chinese dumplings), and we needed a lot of flour.

"Couldn't you borrow a girl's bicycle?" complained Mother. "That way your skirt won't be pushed up."

"There aren't too many of those around," I said. "Almost all the girls wear jeans while riding a bike, so they don't see any point buying a girl's bike."

We didn't eat pot-stickers that evening, and Mother was thoughtful. Next day we took the bus downtown and she bought me a pair of jeans. In the same week, my brother made the baseball team of his junior high school, Father started taking driving lessons, and Mother discovered rummage sales.

We soon got all the furniture we needed, plus a dart

Draw Conclusions
What can you conclude about the narrator based on why she helps her mother?

Theme
How might the activities listed here relate to the story's theme?

board and a 1,000-piece jigsaw puzzle (fourteen hours later, we discovered that it was a 999-piece jigsaw puzzle). There was hope that the Lins might become a normal American family after all. •

Then came our dinner at the Lakeview restaurant.

The Lakeview was an expensive restaurant, one of those places where a headwaiter dressed in tails conducted you to your seat, and the only light came from candles and flaming desserts. In one corner of the room a lady harpist played tinkling melodies.

Father wanted to celebrate, because he had just been promoted. He worked for an electronics company, and after his English started improving, his superiors decided to appoint him to a position more suited to his training. The promotion not only brought a higher salary but was also a tremendous boost to his pride.

Up to then we had eaten only in Chinese restaurants. Although my brother and I were becoming fond of hamburgers, my parents didn't care much for western food, other than chow mein.[3] But this was a special occasion, and Father asked his coworkers to recommend a really elegant restaurant. So there we were at the Lakeview, stumbling after the headwaiter in the murky dining room.

At our table we were handed our menus, and they were so big that to read mine I almost had to stand up again. But why bother? It was mostly in French, anyway.

Father, being an engineer, was always **systematic**. He took out a pocket French dictionary. "They told me that most of the items would be in French, so I came prepared." He even had a pocket flashlight, the size of a marking pen. While Mother held the flashlight over the menu, he looked up the items that were in French.

"*Pâté en croûte,*" (pä tā´ än krōōt) he muttered. "Let's see . . . *pâté* is paste . . . *croûte* is crust . . . hmm . . . a paste in crust."

Vocabulary
systematic
(sis´ tə mat´ ik) *adj.*
orderly

✔ Reading
  Check
Why does Mr. Lin take his family to a fancy restaurant?

---

3. chow mein (chou´ mān´) *n.* thick stew of meat, celery, and Chinese vegetables.

The All-American Slurp **291**

The waiter stood looking patient. I squirmed and died at least fifty times.

At long last Father gave up. "Why don't we just order four complete dinners at random?" he suggested.

"Isn't that risky?" asked Mother. "The French eat some rather peculiar things, I've heard."

"A Chinese can eat anything a Frenchman can eat," Father declared.

The soup arrived in a plate. How do you get soup up from a plate? I glanced at the other diners, but the ones at the nearby tables were not on their soup course, while the more distant ones were invisible in the darkness.

Fortunately my parents had studied books on western etiquette before they came to America. "Tilt your plate," whispered my mother. "It's easier to spoon the soup up that way."

She was right. Tilting the plate did the trick. But the etiquette book didn't say anything about what you did after the soup reached your lips. As any respectable Chinese knows, the correct way to eat your soup is to slurp. This helps to cool the liquid and prevent you from burning your lips. It also shows your appreciation.

We showed our appreciation. *Shloop*, went my father. *Shloop* went my mother. *Shloop, shloop*, went my brother, who was the hungriest.

The lady harpist stopped playing to take a rest. And in the silence, our family's consumption of soup suddenly seemed unnaturally loud. You know how it sounds on a rocky beach when the tide goes out and the water drains from all those little pools? They go *shloop, shloop, shloop.* That was the Lin family, eating soup.

At the next table a waiter was pouring wine. When a large *shloop* reached him, he froze. The bottle continued to pour, and red wine flooded the tabletop and into the lap of a customer. Even the customer didn't notice anything at first, being also hypnotized by the

shloop, shloop, shloop.

It was too much. "I need to go to the toilet," I mumbled, jumping to my feet. A waiter, sensing my urgency, quickly directed me to the ladies' room.

I splashed cold water on my burning face, and as I dried myself with a paper towel, I stared into the mirror. In this perfumed ladies' room, with its pink-and-silver wallpaper and marbled sinks, I looked completely out of place. What was I doing here? What was our family doing in the Lakeview restaurant? In America?

The door to the ladies' room opened. A woman came in and glanced curiously at me. I retreated into one of the toilet cubicles and latched the door.

Time passed—maybe half an hour, maybe an hour. Then I heard the door open again, and my mother's voice. "Are you in there? You're not sick, are you?"

There was real concern in her voice. A girl can't leave her family just because they slurp their soup. Besides, the toilet cubicle had a few drawbacks as a permanent residence. "I'm all right," I said, undoing the latch.

Mother didn't tell me how the rest of the dinner went, and I didn't want to know. In the weeks following, I managed to push the whole thing into the back of my mind, where it jumped out at me only a few times a day. Even now, I turn hot all over when I think of the Lakeview restaurant.

But by the time we had been in this country for three months, our family was definitely making progress toward becoming Americanized. I remember my parents' first PTA meeting. Father wore a neat suit and tie, and Mother put on her first pair of high heels. She stumbled only once. They met my homeroom teacher and beamed as she told them that I would make honor roll soon at the rate I was going. Of course Chinese etiquette forced Father to say that I was a very stupid girl and Mother to protest that the teacher was showing favoritism toward me. But I could tell they were both very proud. •

The day came when my parents announced that they wanted to give a dinner party. We had invited Chinese friends to eat with us before, but this dinner was going to

Draw Conclusions
How does this information about slurping help you understand the story's central problem?

Draw Conclusions
What details support the conclusion that fitting in is important to the narrator?

Reading Check
Why do the Lins slurp their soup?

be different. In addition to a Chinese-American family, we were going to invite the Gleasons.

"Gee, I can hardly wait to have dinner at your house," Meg said to me. "I just *love* Chinese food."

That was a relief. Mother was a good cook, but I wasn't sure if people who ate sour cream would also eat chicken gizzards stewed in soy sauce.

Mother decided not to take a chance with chicken gizzards. Since we had western guests, she set the table with large dinner plates, which we never used in Chinese meals. In fact we didn't use individual plates at all, but picked up food from the platters in the middle of the table and brought it directly to our rice bowls. Following the practice of Chinese-American restaurants, Mother also placed large serving spoons on the platters.

The dinner started well. Mrs. Gleason exclaimed at the beautifully arranged dishes of food: the colorful candied fruit in the sweet-and-sour pork dish, the noodle-thin shreds of chicken meat stir-fried with tiny peas, and the glistening pink prawns in a ginger sauce.

At first I was too busy enjoying my food to notice how the guests were doing. But soon I remembered my duties. Sometimes guests were too polite to help themselves and you had to serve them with more food.

I glanced at Meg, to see if she needed more food, and my eyes nearly popped out at the sight of her plate. It was piled with food: the sweet-and-sour meat pushed right against the

Theme
In what way does Mother's dinner plan show that the family has adjusted to life in America?

chicken shreds, and the chicken sauce ran into the prawns. She had been taking food from a second dish before she finished eating her helping from the first!

Horrified, I turned to look at Mrs. Gleason. She was dumping rice out of her bowl and putting it on her dinner plate. Then she ladled prawns and gravy on top of the rice and mixed everything together, the way you mix sand, gravel, and cement to make concrete.

I couldn't bear to look any longer, and I turned to Mr. Gleason. He was chasing a pea around his plate. Several times he got it to the edge, but when he tried to pick it up with his chopsticks, it rolled back toward the center of the plate again. Finally he put down his chopsticks and picked up the pea with his fingers. He really did! A grown man!

All of us, our family and the Chinese guests, stopped eating to watch the activities of the Gleasons. I wanted to giggle. Then I caught my mother's eyes on me. She frowned and shook her head slightly, and I understood the message: the Gleasons were not used to Chinese ways, and they were just coping the best they could. For some reason I thought of celery strings.

When the main courses were finished, Mother brought out a platter of fruit. "I hope you weren't expecting a sweet dessert," she said. "Since the Chinese don't eat dessert, I didn't think to prepare any."

"Oh, I couldn't possibly eat dessert!" cried Mrs. Gleason. "I'm simply stuffed!"

Meg had different ideas. When the table was cleared, she announced that she and I were going for a walk. "I don't know

Draw Conclusions
What can you conclude about the Lins' eating customs from the narrator's reactions to what the Gleasons do?

Theme
What lesson is the narrator learning about people's experiences?

The All-American Slurp **295**

about you, but I feel like dessert," she told me, when we were outside. "Come on, there's a Dairy Queen down the street. I could use a big chocolate milkshake!"

Although I didn't really want anything more to eat, I insisted on paying for the milkshakes. After all, I was still hostess.

Meg got her large chocolate milkshake and I had a small one. Even so, she was finishing hers while I was only half done. Toward the end she pulled hard on her straws and went *shloop, shloop.*

"Do you always slurp when you eat a milkshake?" I asked, before I could stop myself.

Meg grinned. "Sure. All Americans slurp."

Spiral Review
Resolution How does Meg's ending comment echo an earlier episode of conflict?

Critical Thinking

Cite textual evidence to support your responses.

1. **Key Ideas and Details (a)** Describe the way each Lin family member learns English. **(b) Infer:** What does each person's way of learning English show about his or her personality?

2. **Key Ideas and Details (a)** How do the Lins embarrass themselves at the restaurant? **(b)** In what ways are the Gleasons' actions at the Lins' house similar to those of the Lins at the Gleasons' house?

3. **Craft and Structure (a)** How many plot events in this story take place while the characters are dining? **(b) Infer:** Why might the author have chosen to structure the story this way?

4. **Integration of Knowledge and Ideas** In this story, the narrator hides in the bathroom when her family embarrasses her. Would discussing the conflict with her family have been a positive or negative action? Explain. *[Connect to the Big Question: Is conflict always bad?]*

Reading Skill: Draw Conclusions

1. Complete a chart like the one shown to **draw conclusions** about the story.

Question	Details That Answer Question	Conclusion
Why do the Gleasons stare as the Lins pull celery strings?		
Why do people in the restaurant stare when the Lins slurp their soup?		
What makes the narrator uneasy when the Gleasons come to dinner?		

Literary Analysis: Theme

2. Key Ideas and Details **(a)** What **theme** about cultural differences does the story illustrate? **(b)** What details support the theme?

3. Craft and Structure How does the title relate to the story's theme?

Vocabulary

Acquisition and Use Match each situation with the most appropriate word from the vocabulary list on page 284.

1. got to know someone

2. how a winner might talk

3. moved from Peru to Egypt

4. behaved well

5. feasting on a meal

6. neatly organized CDs

Word Study Use the context of the sentence and what you know about the **Latin root -migr-** to explain your answers.

1. Was an *immigrant* to the United States born here?

2. Do *migratory* birds stay in one location?

Word Study

The **Latin root -migr-** means "to move" or "to wander."

Apply It Explain how the root contributes to the meaning of these words. Consult a dictionary if necessary.

migrant
immigrate
migration

Integrated Language Skills

The Circuit • The All-American Slurp

Conventions: Simple Verb Tenses

A **verb** expresses an action or a state of being. A **verb tense** shows the time of the action or the state of being the verb expresses.

The rules for forming verb tenses depend on the verb types. Form the **past tense** for **regular verbs** with -ed or -d. **Irregular verbs** do not follow a set pattern. It is best to memorize the **past tense** of these verbs. The **future tense** always uses the **helping verb** will.

Tenses	Regular verb: cheer	Regular verb: use	Irregular verb: sit	Irregular verb: be	Irregular verb: have
Present	I cheer	I use	I sit	I am	I have
Past	I cheered	I used	I sat	I was	I had
Future	I will cheer	I will use	I will sit	I will be	I will have

Practice A Identify the verb in each sentence and indicate its tense.

1. Panchito likes his new school.
2. Migrant farmers moved around a lot.
3. I will pick strawberries in the summer.
4. Mr. Lima offered Panchito trumpet lessons.

Reading Application Reread the first two paragraphs of "The Circuit." Select four verbs and identify their tense.

Practice B Change the tense of the following sentences. You may convert the verb to past, present, or future tense.

1. The Lin family was invited to dinner in the United States.
2. Mrs. Gleason offered celery to the Lins.
3. Mother will memorize phrases and repeat them over and over again.
4. I wanted a pair of blue jeans.

Writing Application Choose two images in "The All-American Slurp." Write a few sentences to describe each image. Then, convert the paragraph to the future tense.

PH WRITING COACH Further instruction and practice are available in *Prentice Hall Writing Coach*.

Writing

Explanatory Text Write a **description** of a character from "The Circuit" or from "The All-American Slurp."

- List details from the story that describe the character's appearance, actions, and personality.
- Make a cluster map of words, such as *smart*, *brave*, *mean*, or *fun-loving*, that capture the character's personality.
- Using words from your cluster map, write a description that identifies the controlling impression you want to convey.
- Include details to help readers "see" the character.

Grammar Application Recognize and correct shifts in verb tense in your description.

Writing Workshop: *Work in Progress*

Prewriting for Narration Work with a partner to discuss and list conflicts or disagreements that occur between people. After you have listed ten ideas, underline the ones that are most important or most interesting to you. Save this Conflict List in your writing portfolio for use in a short story you may write later.

Speaking and Listening

Comprehension and Collaboration With a partner, prepare and role-play an **interview.** If you read "The All-American Slurp," your interview should be between you and the narrator. If you read "The Circuit," your interview should be between a reporter and a migrant worker.

Follow these steps to complete the assignment.

- Decide who will play each part.
- **Use details** from the story to gather information.
- Prepare a list of **relevant questions** to ask in your interview. Then, **organize the questions** into categories such as experience, advice, and lessons learned.
- Develop responses, with elaboration based on details from the story.
- Rehearse, and conduct your interview in front of the class.

Common Core State Standards

L.6.1; W.6.4; SL.6.1.c
[For the full wording of the standards, see page 270.]

Use this prewriting activity to prepare for the **Writing Workshop** on page 354.

www.PHLitOnline.com
- Interactive graphic organizers
- Grammar tutorial
- Interactive journals

Ⓒ Leveled Texts

Build your skills and improve your comprehension of short stories with texts of increasing complexity.

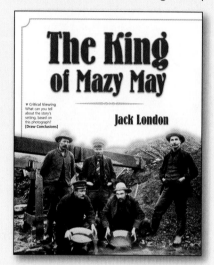

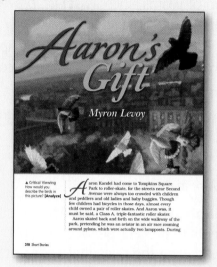

Read **"The King of Mazy May"** to meet a boy who goes on a great adventure and becomes a hero.

Read **"Aaron's Gift"** to learn the true meaning of a gift from a boy to his grandmother.

Ⓒ Common Core State Standards

Meet these standards with either **"The King of Mazy May"** (p. 304) or **"Aaron's Gift"** (p. 318).

Reading Literature
5. Analyze how a particular sentence, chapter, scene, or stanza fits into the overall structure of a text and contributes to the development of the theme, setting, or plot. *(Literary Analysis: Setting)*

Spiral Review: RL.6.3

Writing
3. Write narratives to develop real or imagined experiences or events using effective technique, relevant descriptive details, and well-structured event sequences. *(Writing: Personal Narrative)*

Speaking and Listening
2. Interpret information presented in diverse media and formats and explain how it contributes to a topic, text, or issue under study. *(Research and Technology: Presentation)*

Language
1. Demonstrate command of the conventions of standard English grammar and usage when writing or speaking. *(Conventions: Perfect Tenses of Verbs)*

6. Acquire and use accurately grade-appropriate general academic and domain-specific words and phrases; gather vocabulary knowledge when considering a word or phrase important to comprehension or expression. *(Vocabulary: Word Study)*

Reading Skill: Draw Conclusions

When you form an opinion about what you read, you are **drawing a conclusion.** When reading literature, base your conclusions on details in the text and on your own **prior knowledge**—things you know from your own experience. For example, if a character stares sadly out a window at the pouring rain, you might conclude that the rain is preventing the character from doing something.

Using the Strategy: Conclusions Chart

As you read, use a graphic organizer like the one shown to record the conclusions you draw from the text. Check to see that your conclusions make sense. If they do not, develop new conclusions based on your notes.

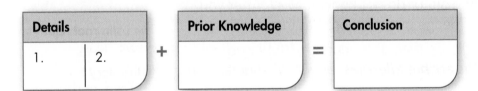

Literary Analysis: Setting

The **setting** of a literary work is the time and place of the action. The time may be a historical era, the present or future, the season of the year, or the hour of the day. The place can be as general as outer space or as specific as a particular street.

Writers may describe the setting of a story in a single sentence or over the course of several paragraphs. In many stories, the setting changes as characters move from place to place or move through time. As you read, notice the development of the setting and its impact on characters and events in a story.

Is *conflict* always bad?

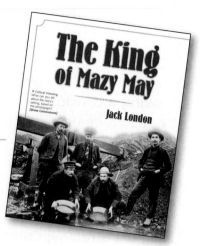

Writing About the Big Question

"The King of Mazy May" is about a boy named Walt who goes to great lengths to protect his friend's gold from thieves. Use this sentence starter to develop your ideas about the Big Question.

To **defend** a friend's property, a person could _____.

While You Read Think about the possible outcomes, both good and bad, that may result from the conflict.

Vocabulary

Read each word and its definition. Decide whether you know the word well, know it a little bit, or do not know it at all. After you read, see how your knowledge of each word has increased.

- **endured** (en dѵrd´) *v.* suffered through (p. 305) *I endured a whole year with terrible allergies.* endure *v.* endurance *n.* duration *n.*

- **liable** (lī´ ə bəl) *adj.* likely to do something or to happen (p. 306) *I was liable to forget my lunch.* liability *n.* reliable *adj.*

- **declined** (dē klīnd´) *v.* refused (p. 310) *I declined the offer of a new hat.* decline *v.* declining *v.* incline *n.*

- **pursuers** (pər sŵ´ ərz) *n.* those who follow in an effort to capture (p. 310) *When I turned the corner, I finally lost my pursuers!* pursue *v.* pursuit *n.* pursued *v.* pursuing *v.*

- **abruptly** (ə brupt´ lē) *adv.* suddenly; unexpectedly (p. 311) *Robert abruptly turned to leave.* abrupt *adj.* abruptness *n.*

- **summit** (sum´ it) *n.* highest part (p. 312) *We were happy to get to the mountain's summit.*

Word Study

The **Latin root -clin-** means "lean."

In this story travelers **declined,** or decided against, going the long way on the Mazy May. The root suggests they leaned away from the idea.

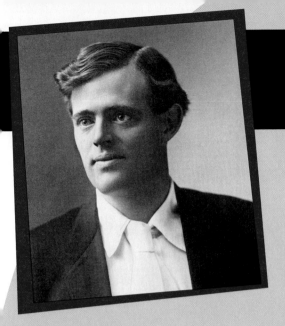

Author of
The King
of Mazy May

Jack London lived an adventurous life. Before this Californian was out of his teens, he had worked in a factory, traveled as a hobo, captained a pirate ship, and searched for gold. London's love of reading and his own adventures inspired him to write.

The Story Behind the Story In 1897, London went to northwestern Canada, where gold had just been discovered. He did not find any gold, but he did have adventures on the way to Dawson, a town in the area. Once, for instance, he made a boat from trees and ran the dangerous White Horse rapids. In "The King of Mazy May," London writes about a young miner who also has a thrilling trip to Dawson.

BACKGROUND FOR THE STORY

Klondike Gold

In 1896, George Carmack found gold in the Klondike region of northwestern Canada. His find began with a quarter ounce of the precious metal—equal in value to what an average worker could earn in a week! Thousands of other prospectors followed Carmack. Most found hardship, but no gold.

DID YOU KNOW?

London wrote more than fifty books, including *The Call of the Wild* and *White Fang.*

The King
of Mazy May

Jack London

▼ **Critical Viewing**
What can you tell about the story's setting, based on this photograph? **[Draw Conclusions]**

Walt Masters is not a very large boy, but there is manliness in his make-up, and he himself, although he does not know a great deal that most boys know, knows much that other boys do not know. He has never seen a train of cars nor an elevator in his life, and for that matter he has never once looked upon a cornfield, a plow, a cow, or even a chicken. He has never had a pair of shoes on his feet, nor gone to a picnic or a party, nor talked to a girl. But he has seen the sun at midnight, watched the ice jams on one of the mightiest of rivers, and played beneath the northern lights,[1] the one white child in thousands of square miles of frozen wilderness.

Walt has walked all the fourteen years of his life in suntanned, moose-hide moccasins, and he can go to the Indian camps and "talk big" with the men, and trade calico and beads with them for their precious furs. He can make bread without baking powder, yeast, or hops, shoot a moose at three hundred yards, and drive the wild wolf dogs fifty miles a day on the packed trail.

Last of all, he has a good heart, and is not afraid of the darkness and loneliness, of man or beast or thing. His father is a good man, strong and brave, and Walt is growing up like him.

Walt was born a thousand miles or so down the Yukon,[2] in a trading post below the Ramparts. After his mother died, his father and he came up on the river, step by step, from camp to camp, till now they are settled down on the Mazy May Creek in the Klondike country. Last year they and several others had spent much toil and time on the Mazy May, and **endured** great hardships; the creek, in turn, was just beginning to show up its richness and to reward them for their heavy labor. But with the news of their discoveries, strange men began to come and go through the short days and long nights, and many unjust things they did to the men who had worked so long upon the creek.

---

1. **northern lights** glowing bands or streamers of light, sometimes appearing in the night sky of the Northern Hemisphere.
2. **Yukon** (yōō′ kän) river flowing through the Yukon Territory of northwest Canada.

Setting
What does the setting of frozen wilderness tell you about Walt's life?

Vocabulary
endured (en dôord′)
v. suffered through

Reading Check
Where does Walt live?

Si Hartman had gone away on a moose hunt, to return and find new stakes driven and his claim jumped.[3] George Lukens and his brother had lost their claims in a like manner, having delayed too long on the way to Dawson to record them. In short, it was the old story, and quite a number of the earnest, industrious prospectors had suffered similar losses.

But Walt Masters's father had recorded his claim at the start, so Walt had nothing to fear now that his father had gone on a short trip up the White River prospecting for quartz. Walt was well able to stay by himself in the cabin, cook his three meals a day, and look after things. Not only did he look after his father's claim, but he had agreed to keep an eye on the adjoining one of Loren Hall, who had started for Dawson to record it.

Loren Hall was an old man, and he had no dogs, so he had to travel very slowly. After he had been gone some time, word came up the river that he had broken through the ice at Rosebud Creek and frozen his feet so badly that he would not be able to travel for a couple of weeks. Then Walt Masters received the news that old Loren was nearly all right again, and about to move on afoot for Dawson as fast as a weakened man could.

Walt was worried, however; the claim was **liable** to be jumped at any moment because of this delay, and a fresh stampede had started in on the Mazy May. He did not like the looks of the newcomers, and one day, when five of them came by with crack dog teams and the lightest of camping outfits, he could see that they were prepared to make speed, and resolved to keep an eye on them. So he locked up the cabin and followed them, being at the same time careful to remain hidden.

He had not watched them long before he was sure that they were professional stampeders, bent on jumping all the claims in sight. Walt crept along the snow at the rim of the creek and saw them change many stakes, destroy old ones, and set up new ones.

In the afternoon, with Walt always trailing on their heels, they came back down the creek, unharnessed their

Setting
How does the time of the story affect travel and communications?

Vocabulary
liable (līʹ ə bəl) *adj.* likely to do something or to happen

Draw Conclusions
What does Walt's behavior tell you about his attitude toward the men?

---

3. **claim jumped** A claim is a piece of land marked by a miner with stakes to show where the borders are. A claim that is jumped is stolen by someone else.

dogs, and went into camp within two claims of his cabin. When he saw them make preparations to cook, he hurried home to get something to eat himself, and then hurried back. He crept so close that he could hear them talking quite plainly, and by pushing the underbrush aside he could catch occasional glimpses of them. They had finished eating and were smoking around the fire.

"The creek is all right, boys," a large, black-bearded man, evidently the leader, said, "and I think the best thing we can do is to pull out tonight. The dogs can follow the trail; besides, it's going to be moonlight. What say you?"

"But it's going to be beastly cold," objected one of the party. "It's forty below zero now."

"An' sure, can't ye keep warm by jumpin' off the sleds an' runnin' after the dogs?" cried an Irishman. "An' who wouldn't? The creek's as rich as a United States mint! Faith, it's an ilegant chanst to be gettin' a run fer yer money! An' if ye don't run, it's mebbe you'll not get the money at all, at all."

"That's it," said the leader. "If we can get to Dawson and record, we're rich men; and there's no telling who's been

▼ **Critical Viewing** What details in this picture show how difficult life was in the Yukon at this time? **[Analyze]**

Spiral Review
**Character and
Conflict** When Walt
overhears the dishonest
strangers, what conflict
is set in motion?

Draw Conclusions
Why is the leader inter-
ested in the unrecorded
claim?

Draw Conclusions
Why would it be impos-
sible to travel seventy
miles to Dawson with-
out dogs?

sneaking along in our tracks, watching us, and perhaps now off to give the alarm. The thing for us to do is to rest the dogs a bit, and then hit the trail as hard as we can. What do you say?"

Evidently the men had agreed with their leader, for Walt Masters could hear nothing but the rattle of the tin dishes which were being washed. Peering out cautiously, he could see the leader studying a piece of paper. Walt knew what it was at a glance—a list of all the unrecorded claims on Mazy May. Any man could get these lists by applying to the gold commissioner at Dawson.

"Thirty-two," the leader said, lifting his face to the men. "Thirty-two isn't recorded, and this is thirty-three. Come on; let's take a look at it. I saw somebody had been working on it when we came up this morning."

Three of the men went with him, leaving one to remain in camp. Walt crept carefully after them till they came to Loren Hall's shaft. One of the men went down and built a fire on the bottom to thaw out the frozen gravel, while the others built another fire on the dump and melted water in a couple of gold pans. This they poured into a piece of canvas stretched between two logs, used by Loren Hall in which to wash his gold.

In a short time a couple of buckets of dirt were sent up by the man in the shaft, and Walt could see the others grouped anxiously about their leader as he proceeded to wash it. When this was finished, they stared at the broad streak of black sand and yellow gold grains on the bottom of the pan, and one of them called excitedly for the man who had remained in camp to come. Loren Hall had struck it rich and his claim was not yet recorded. It was plain that they were going to jump it.

Walt lay in the snow, thinking rapidly. He was only a boy, but in the face of the threatened injustice to old lame Loren Hall he felt that he must do something. He waited and watched, with his mind made up, till he saw the men begin to square up new stakes. Then he crawled away till out of hearing, and broke into a run for the camp of the stampeders. Walt's father had taken their own dogs with him prospecting, and the boy knew how impossible it was for him to undertake the seventy miles to Dawson without the aid of dogs.

Geography Connection

"Cold" Rush

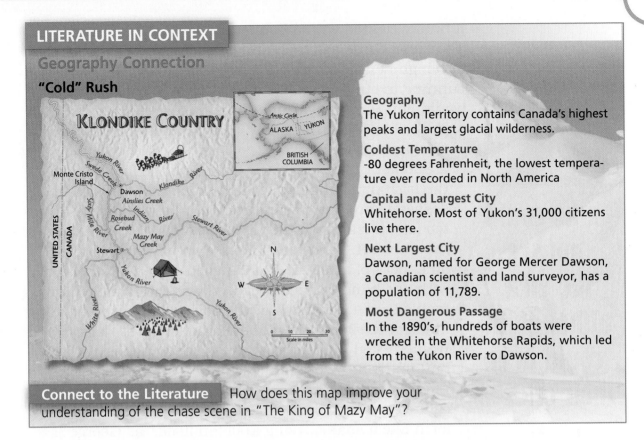

KLONDIKE COUNTRY

Geography
The Yukon Territory contains Canada's highest peaks and largest glacial wilderness.

Coldest Temperature
-80 degrees Fahrenheit, the lowest temperature ever recorded in North America

Capital and Largest City
Whitehorse. Most of Yukon's 31,000 citizens live there.

Next Largest City
Dawson, named for George Mercer Dawson, a Canadian scientist and land surveyor, has a population of 11,789.

Most Dangerous Passage
In the 1890's, hundreds of boats were wrecked in the Whitehorse Rapids, which led from the Yukon River to Dawson.

Connect to the Literature How does this map improve your understanding of the chase scene in "The King of Mazy May"?

Gaining the camp, he picked out, with an experienced eye, the easiest running sled and started to harness up the stampeders' dogs. There were three teams of six each, and from these he chose ten of the best. Realizing how necessary it was to have a good head dog, he strove to discover a leader amongst them; but he had little time in which to do it, for he could hear the voices of the returning men. By the time the team was in shape and everything ready, the claim-jumpers came into sight in an open place not more than a hundred yards from the trail, which ran down the bed of the creek. They cried out to Walt, but instead of giving heed to them he grabbed up one of their fur sleeping robes, which lay loosely in the snow, and leaped upon the sled.

"Mush! Hi! Mush on!" he cried to the animals, snapping the keen-lashed whip among them. •

The dogs sprang against the yoke straps, and the sled jerked under way so suddenly as to almost throw him off. Then it curved into the creek, poising perilously on the runner. He was almost breathless with suspense, when

Setting
What conditions make it difficult for Walt to get to Dawson?

Reading Check
What does Walt decide he must do after overhearing the men?

The King of Mazy May **309**

it finally righted with a bound and sprang ahead again. The creek bank was high and he could not see the men, although he could hear their cries and knew they were running to cut him off. He did not dare to think what would happen if they caught him; he just clung to the sled, his heart beating wildly, and watched the snow rim of the bank above him.

Suddenly, over this snow rim came the flying body of the Irishman, who had leaped straight for the sled in a desperate attempt to capture it; but he was an instant too late. Striking on the very rear of it, he was thrown from his feet, backward, into the snow. Yet, with the quickness of a cat, he had clutched the end of the sled with one hand, turned over, and was dragging behind on his breast, swearing at the boy and threatening all kinds of terrible things if he did not stop the dogs; but Walt cracked him sharply across the knuckles with the butt of the dog whip till he let go.

It was eight miles from Walt's claim to the Yukon— eight very crooked miles, for the creek wound back and forth like a snake, "tying knots in itself," as George Lukens said. And because it was so crooked the dogs could not get up their best speed, while the sled ground heavily on its side against the curves, now to the right, now to the left.

Travelers who had come up and down the Mazy May on foot, with packs on their backs, had declined to go round all the bends, and instead had made shortcuts across the narrow necks of creek bottom. Two of his pursuers had gone back to harness the remaining dogs, but the others took advantage of these shortcuts, running on foot, and before he knew it they had almost overtaken him.

"Halt!" they cried after him. "Stop, or we'll shoot!"

But Walt only yelled the harder at the dogs, and dashed around the bend with a couple of revolver bullets singing after him. At the next bend they had drawn up closer still, and the bullets struck uncomfortably near him but at this point the Mazy May straightened out and ran for half a mile as the crow flies. Here the dogs stretched out in their long wolf swing, and the stampeders, quickly winded, slowed down and waited for their own sled to come up.

> ... he could not see the men, although he could hear their cries ...

Vocabulary
declined (dē klīnd´) *v.* refused

pursuers (pər sōō´ ərz) *n.* those who follow in an effort to capture

Looking over his shoulder, Walt reasoned that they had not given up the chase for good, and that they would soon be after him again. So he wrapped the fur robe about him to shut out the stinging air, and lay flat on the empty sled, encouraging the dogs, as he well knew how.

At last, twisting *abruptly* between two river islands, he came upon the mighty Yukon sweeping grandly to the north. He could not see from bank to bank, and in the quick-falling twilight it loomed a great white sea of frozen stillness. There was not a sound, save the breathing of the dogs, and the churn of the steel-shod sled.

No snow had fallen for several weeks, and the traffic had packed the main river trail till it was hard and glassy as glare ice. Over this the sled flew along, and the dogs kept the trail fairly well, although Walt quickly discovered that he had made a mistake in choosing the leader. As they were driven in single file, without reins, he had to guide them by his voice, and it was evident the head dog had never learned the meaning of "gee" and "haw."[4] He hugged the inside of the curves too closely, often forcing his comrades behind him into the soft snow, while several times he thus capsized[5] the sled.

There was no wind, but the speed at which he traveled created a bitter blast, and with the thermometer down to forty below, this bit through fur and flesh to the very bones. Aware that if he remained constantly upon the sled he would freeze to death, and knowing the practice of Arctic travelers, Walt shortened up one of the lashing thongs, and whenever he felt chilled, seized hold of it, jumped off, and ran behind till warmth was restored. Then he would climb on and rest till the process had to be repeated.

Looking back he could see the sled of his pursuers, drawn by eight dogs, rising and falling over the ice hummocks like a boat in a seaway. The Irishman and the black-bearded leader were with it, taking turns in running and riding.

Night fell, and in the blackness of the first hour or so Walt toiled desperately with his dogs. On account of the

4. **"gee" and "haw"** (jē) and (hô) commands used to tell an animal to turn to the right or the left.
5. **capsized** (kap´ sīzd´) *v.* overturned.

Vocabulary
abruptly (ə brupt´ lē) *adv.* suddenly; unexpectedly

Setting
Why is it good for Walt that it hasn't snowed recently?

Draw Conclusions
What do Walt's actions to stay warm tell you about his determination?

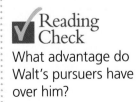

Reading Check
What advantage do Walt's pursuers have over him?

poor lead dog, they were continually floundering off the beaten track into the soft snow, and the sled was as often riding on its side or top as it was in the proper way. This work and strain tried his strength sorely. Had he not been in such haste he could have avoided much of it, but he feared the stampeders would creep up in the darkness and overtake him. However, he could hear them yelling to their dogs, and knew from the sounds they were coming up very slowly. •

When the moon rose he was off Sixty Mile, and Dawson was only fifty miles away. He was almost exhausted, and breathed a sigh of relief as he climbed on the sled again. Looking back, he saw his enemies had crawled up within four hundred yards. At this space they remained, a black speck of motion on the white river breast. Strive as they would, they could not shorten this distance, and strive as he would, he could not increase it.

Draw Conclusions
How would having the proper lead dog help Walt?

Walt had now discovered the proper lead dog, and he knew he could easily run away from them if he could only change the bad leader for the good one. But this was impossible, for a moment's delay, at the speed they were running, would bring the men behind upon him.

When he was off the mouth of Rosebud Creek, just as he was topping a rise, the report of a gun and the ping of a bullet on the ice beside him told him that they were this time shooting at him with a rifle. And from then on, as he cleared the **summit** of each ice jam, he stretched flat on the leaping sled till the rifle shot from the rear warned him that he was safe till the next ice jam was reached.

Vocabulary
summit (sum´ it) *n.* highest part

Now it is very hard to lie on a moving sled, jumping and plunging and yawing[6] like a boat before the wind, and to shoot through the deceiving moonlight at an object four hundred yards away on another moving sled performing equally wild antics. So it is not to be wondered at that the black-bearded leader did not hit him.

After several hours of this, during which, perhaps, a score of bullets had struck about him, their ammunition began to give out and their fire slackened. They took greater care, and shot at him at the most favorable opportunities. He was also leaving them behind, the

---

6. **yawing** (yô´ iŋ) *adj.* swinging from side to side.

distance slowly increasing to six hundred yards.

Lifting clear on the crest of a great jam off Indian River, Walt Masters met with his first accident. A bullet sang past his ears, and struck the bad lead dog.

The poor brute plunged in a heap, with the rest of the team on top of him.

Like a flash Walt was by the leader. Cutting the traces with his hunting knife, he dragged the dying animal to one side and straightened out the team.

He glanced back. The other sled was coming up like an express train. With half the dogs still over their traces, he cried "Mush on!" and leaped upon the sled just as the pursuers dashed abreast[7] of him.

The Irishman was preparing to spring for him—they were so sure they had him that they did not shoot—when Walt turned fiercely upon them with his whip.

He struck at their faces, and men must save their faces with their hands. So there was no shooting just then. Before they could recover from the hot rain of blows, Walt reached out from his sled, catching their wheel dog by the forelegs in midspring, and throwing him heavily. This snarled the team, capsizing the sled and tangling his enemies up beautifully.

---

7. **abreast** (ə brest´) *adv.* alongside.

Draw Conclusions
Based on your own experiences, what do you think gives Walt the strength to continue?

Away Walt flew, the runners of his sled fairly screaming as they bounded over the frozen surface. And what had seemed an accident proved to be a blessing in disguise. The proper lead dog was now to the fore, and he stretched low and whined with joy as he jerked his comrades along. ●

By the time he reached Ainslie's Creek, seventeen miles from Dawson, Walt had left his pursuers, a tiny speck, far behind. At Monte Cristo Island he could no longer see them. And at Swede Creek, just as daylight was silvering the pines, he ran plump into the camp of old Loren Hall.

Almost as quick as it takes to tell it, Loren had his sleeping furs rolled up, and had joined Walt on the sled. They permitted the dogs to travel more slowly, as there was no sign of the chase in the rear, and just as they pulled up at the gold commissioner's office in Dawson, Walt, who had kept his eyes open to the last, fell asleep.

And because of what Walt Masters did on this night, the men of the Yukon have become proud of him, and speak of him now as the King of Mazy May.

Draw Conclusions
Why does Walt fall asleep when the sled pulls into Dawson?

Critical Thinking

© 1. **Key Ideas and Details** **(a)** What are Walt's responsibilities while his father is away? **(b) Compare and Contrast:** How are Walt's responsibilities different from those of other children his age?

© 2. **Key Ideas and Details** **Evaluate:** This story suggests that "manliness" is based on strength and bravery. Explain why you agree or disagree.

© 3. **Integration of Knowledge and Ideas** **(a)** The discovery of gold in the Klondike brought out the best and the worst in people. Why do you think that the discovery of gold had such a major impact? **(b) Apply:** If you had lived during that time, would you have traveled to the Klondike in search of gold? Explain.

Cite textual evidence to support your responses.

© 4. **Integration of Knowledge and Ideas** Does any good result from the conflict between Walt and the thieves? Explain. *[Connect to the Big Question: Is conflict always bad?]*

Reading Skill: Draw Conclusions

1. List three details from the story that support the following **conclusion:** *At the time of this story, life in the Klondike was dangerous and challenging.*

2. Based on your prior knowledge, how do you think Walt feels when people call him the "King of Mazy May"?

Literary Analysis: Setting

3. **Key Ideas and Details (a)** Describe the **setting** of "The King of Mazy May." **(b)** Why is the setting important to the story?

4. **Key Ideas and Details (a)** Use a chart like the one shown to list ways in which details of the setting affect events in the story. **(b)** With a partner, explain your responses.

Details of Setting		Story Events
Time		
Place		

Vocabulary

Acquisition and Use Write a sentence to respond to each item using a word from the vocabulary list on page 302.

1. Explain why Klondike claims were likely to be jumped.
2. Suggest the placement for a lookout tower in a hilly region.
3. Describe an offer that has been refused.
4. Tell how you would react if thieves chased you.
5. Describe the people that are chasing you.
6. Explain how you felt when you finished a difficult week.

Word Study Use the context of the sentence and what you know about the **Latin root -*clin*-** to explain your answers.

1. If you were *reclining*, how would you be sitting?
2. Are you *inclined* to eat worms?

Word Study

The **Latin root -*clin*-** means "lean."

Apply It Explain how the root contributes to the meanings of these words. Use a dictionary if necessary.

inclination
recline

Is *conflict* always bad?

Writing About the Big Question

In "Aaron's Gift," Aaron doesn't listen to his mother when she tells him to stay away from a gang of boys and, as a result, Aaron gets hurt. Use this sentence starter to develop your ideas about the Big Question.

Children might **oppose** their parents, but very often they _____

_____.

While You Read Notice how Aaron's mother helps him deal with the other conflicts he faces in the story.

Vocabulary

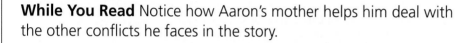

Read each word and its definition. Decide whether you know the word well, know it a little bit, or do not know it at all. After you read, see how your knowledge of each word has increased.

- **thrashing** (thrash´ iŋ) *n.* wild movements (p. 320) *The fish's thrashing broke the fisherman's line.* thrashing *v.* thrash *v.*

- **temporarily** (tem´ pər rer´ ə lē) *adv.* not permanently (p. 322) *I was only allowed to keep the class pet temporarily.* temporary *adj.*

- **pleaded** (plēd´ əd) *v.* begged (p. 323) *Jason pleaded with his parents for a new skateboard.* plead *v.* plea *n.*

- **coaxed** (kōkst) *v.* persuaded by pleading (p. 323) *He coaxed me into going to the party.* coax *v.* coaxing *v.*

- **consoled** (kən sōld´) *v.* comforted (p. 325) *I was consoled by her kind words.* console *v.* consolation *n.* solace *n.*

- **hesitated** (hez´ i tāt´ əd) *v.* stopped because of indecision (p. 326) *Maria hesitated before jumping into the lake.* hesitant *adj.* hesitate *v.* hesitating *v.* hesitation *n.*

Word Study

The **Latin root** *-tempor-* means "time."

In this story, Aaron's mother says he can only have a pet **temporarily**, or for a limited time.

Meet
Myron Levoy
(b. 1930)

Author of
Aaron's Gift

Myron Levoy has loved reading and writing ever since he was a boy growing up in New York City. In a passage about his childhood, he wrote, "Times were hard and toys were few, but I remember from a very early age constant trips to the library with my mother and brother, and the smell and feel of books."

Inspiration Strikes The New York Public Library never lost its appeal for Levoy. When he was sixteen, he got a summer job there. One day Levoy viewed an exhibit of handwritten poems by Edward Arlington Robinson. Seeing poems before him in paper and ink had a strong impact. "Such power, an entire world, on that one small sheet!" Levoy says. "It was absolute and final: yes, I would become a writer above all else!"

DID YOU KNOW?

One of Levoy's most renowned books, *Alan and Naomi*, was nominated for the American Book Award for Children's Literature and was an honor book for the Boston Globe-Horn Book Award.

BACKGROUND FOR THE STORY
Carrier Pigeons

Today, carrier pigeons like the one in "Aaron's Gift" may seem unusual. Carrier pigeons, however, have been used throughout history to carry messages over long distances. The ancient Romans used them to report chariot race results. Pigeons also carried vital messages during World War I.

Aaron's Gift

Myron Levoy

▲ Critical Viewing
How would you describe the birds in this picture? [Analyze]

Aaron Kandel had come to Tompkins Square Park to roller-skate, for the streets near Second Avenue were always too crowded with children and peddlers and old ladies and baby buggies. Though few children had bicycles in those days, almost every child owned a pair of roller skates. And Aaron was, it must be said, a Class A, triple-fantastic roller skater.

Aaron skated back and forth on the wide walkway of the park, pretending he was an aviator in an air race zooming around pylons, which were actually two lampposts. During

his third lap around the racecourse, he noticed a pigeon on the grass, behaving very strangely. Aaron skated to the line of benches, then climbed over onto the lawn.

The pigeon was trying to fly, but all it could manage was to flutter and turn round and round in a large circle, as if it were performing a frenzied dance. The left wing was only half open and was beating in a clumsy, jerking fashion; it was clearly broken.

Luckily, Aaron hadn't eaten the cookies he'd stuffed into his pocket before he'd gone clacking down the three flights

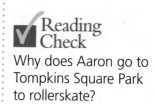

Reading Check

Why does Aaron go to Tompkins Square Park to rollerskate?

Vocabulary
thrashing (thrash´ iŋ) *n.*
wild movements

of stairs from his apartment, his skates already on. He broke a cookie into small crumbs and tossed some toward the pigeon. "Here pidge, here pidge," he called. The pigeon spotted the cookie crumbs and, after a moment, stopped thrashing about. It folded its wings as best it could, but the broken wing still stuck half out. Then it strutted over to the crumbs, its head bobbing forth-back, forth-back, as if it were marching a little in front of the rest of the body—perfectly normal, except for that half-open wing which seemed to make the bird stagger sideways every so often.

The pigeon began eating the crumbs as Aaron quickly unbuttoned his shirt and pulled it off. Very slowly, he edged toward the bird, making little kissing sounds like the ones he heard his grandmother make when she fed the sparrows on the back fire escape.

Then suddenly Aaron plunged. The shirt, in both hands, came down like a torn parachute. The pigeon beat its wings, but Aaron held the shirt to the ground, and the bird couldn't escape. Aaron felt under the shirt, gently, and gently took hold of the wounded pigeon.

"Yes, yes, pidge," he said, very softly. "There's a good boy. Good pigeon, good."

Draw Conclusions
Do you think Aaron would be a good friend? Why or why not?

The pigeon struggled in his hands, but little by little Aaron managed to soothe it. "Good boy, pidge. That's your new name. Pidge. I'm gonna take you home, Pidge. Yes, yes, *ssh*. Good boy. I'm gonna fix you up. Easy, Pidge, easy does it. Easy, boy."

Aaron squeezed through an opening between the row of benches and skated slowly out of the park, while holding the pigeon carefully with both hands as if it were one of his mother's rare, precious cups from the old country. How fast the pigeon's heart was beating! Was he afraid? Or did all pigeons' hearts beat fast?

It was fortunate that Aaron was an excellent skater, for he had to skate six blocks to his apartment, over broken pavement and sudden gratings and curbs and cobblestones. But when he reached home, he asked Noreen Callahan, who was playing on the stoop, to take off his skates for him. He would not chance going up three flights on roller skates this time.

"Is he sick?" asked Noreen.

"Broken wing," said Aaron. "I'm gonna fix him up and make him into a carrier pigeon or something."

"Can I watch?" asked Noreen.

"Watch what?"

"The operation. I'm gonna be a nurse when I grow up."

"OK," said Aaron. "You can even help. You can help hold him while I fix him up."

Aaron wasn't quite certain what his mother would say about his new-found pet, but he was pretty sure he knew what his grandmother would think. His grandmother had lived with them ever since his grandfather had died three years ago. And she fed the sparrows and jays and crows and robins on the back fire escape with every spare crumb she could find. In fact, Aaron noticed that she sometimes created crumbs where they didn't exist, by squeezing and tearing pieces of her breakfast roll when his mother wasn't looking.

Aaron didn't really understand his grandmother, for he often saw her by the window having long conversations with the birds, telling them about her days as a little girl in the Ukraine.[1] And once he saw her take her mirror from

Setting
List three details that show the setting.

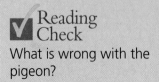

Reading Check
What is wrong with the pigeon?

---

1. **Ukraine** (yo͞o krān´) country located in Eastern Europe. From 1924 to 1991, Ukraine was part of the Soviet Union.

Draw Conclusions
Why does Aaron's grandmother feed the birds?

Vocabulary
temporarily (tem´ pər rer´ ə lē) adv.
not permanently

Draw Conclusions
Based on your own experience and Mr. Kandel's statement, how does Mr. Kandel feel about Aaron?

her handbag and hold it out toward the birds. She told Aaron that she wanted them to see how beautiful they were. Very strange. But Aaron did know that she would love Pidge, because she loved everything.

To his surprise, his mother said he could keep the pigeon, temporarily, because it was sick, and we were all strangers in the land of Egypt,[2] and it might not be bad for Aaron to have a pet. *Temporarily.*

The wing was surprisingly easy to fix, for the break showed clearly and Pidge was remarkably patient and still, as if he knew he was being helped. Or perhaps he was just exhausted from all the thrashing about he had done. Two Popsicle sticks served as splints, and strips from an old undershirt were used to tie them in place. Another strip held the wing to the bird's body.

Aaron's father arrived home and stared at the pigeon. Aaron waited for the expected storm. But instead, Mr. Kandel asked, "Who *did* this?"

"Me," said Aaron. "And Noreen Callahan."

"Sophie!" he called to his wife. "Did you see this! Ten years old and it's better than Dr. Belasco could do. He's a genius!"

As the days passed, Aaron began training Pidge to be a carrier pigeon. He tied a little cardboard tube to Pidge's left leg and stuck tiny rolled-up sheets of paper with secret messages into it: The enemy is attacking at dawn. Or: The guns are hidden in the trunk of the car. Or: Vincent DeMarco is a British spy. Then Aaron would set Pidge down at one end of the living room and put some popcorn at the other end. And Pidge would waddle slowly across the room, cooing softly, while the ends of his bandages trailed along the floor.

At the other end of the room, one of Aaron's friends would take out the message, stick a new one in, turn Pidge around, and aim him at the popcorn that Aaron put down on his side of the room.

And Pidge grew fat and contented on all the popcorn and crumbs and corn and crackers and Aaron's grandmother's breakfast rolls.

---

2. **we were all . . . land of Egypt** a reference to the biblical story of the enslavement of the Hebrew people in Egypt. Around 1300 B.C., the Hebrews were led out of Egypt by Moses.

Aaron had told all the children about Pidge, but he only let his very best friends come up and play carrier-pigeon with him. But telling everyone had been a mistake. A group of older boys from down the block had a club—Aaron's mother called it a gang—and Aaron had longed to join as he had never longed for anything else. To be with them and share their secrets, the secrets of older boys. To be able to enter their clubhouse shack on the empty lot on the next street. To know the password and swear the secret oath. To belong.

About a month after Aaron had brought the pigeon home, Carl, the gang leader, walked over to Aaron in the street and told him he could be a member if he'd bring the pigeon down to be the club mascot.[3] Aaron couldn't believe it; he immediately raced home to get Pidge. But his mother told Aaron to stay away from those boys, or else. And Aaron, miserable, argued with his mother and pleaded and cried and coaxed. It was no use. Not with those boys. No.

Aaron's mother tried to change the subject. She told him that it would soon be his grandmother's sixtieth birthday, a very special birthday indeed, and all the family from Brooklyn and the East Side would be coming to their apartment for a dinner and celebration. Would Aaron try to build something or make something for Grandma? A present made with his own hands would be nice. A decorated box for her hairpins or a crayon picture for her room or anything he liked.

In a flash Aaron knew what to give her: Pidge! Pidge would be her present! Pidge with his wing healed, who might be able to carry messages for her to the doctor or his Aunt Rachel or other people his grandmother seemed to go to a lot. It would be a surprise for everyone. And Pidge would make up for what had happened to Grandma when she'd been a little girl in the Ukraine, wherever that was. Often, in the evening, Aaron's grandmother would talk

---

3. **mascot** (mas´ kät´) *n.* person or animal adopted by a group for good luck.

LITERATURE IN CONTEXT

History Connection

Cossacks Aaron's grandmother has a memory of Cossacks destroying her village. Cossacks were soldiers on horseback. At the time when Aaron's grandmother lived in Ukraine, Cossacks held a special and privileged status. The Russian army used these soldiers to put down revolutionary activities. Sometimes, the Cossacks took the law into their own hands and attacked innocent people.

Connect to the Literature

Why did Aaron's grandmother come to America?

Vocabulary
pleaded (plēd´ əd) *v.* begged
coaxed (kōkst) *v.* persuaded by pleading

Setting
In your own words, describe the setting of Aaron's grandmother's childhood.

▼ **Critical Viewing**
What details in this painting suggest freedom? **[Interpret]**

about the old days long ago in the Ukraine, in the same way that she talked to the birds on the back fire escape. She had lived in a village near a place called Kishinev with hundreds of other poor peasant families like her own. Things hadn't been too bad under someone called Czar Alexander the Second,[4] whom Aaron always pictured as a tall handsome man in a gold uniform. But Alexander the Second was assassinated, and Alexander the Third, whom Aaron pictured as an ugly man in a black cape, became the Czar. And the Jewish people of the Ukraine had no peace anymore.

One day, a thundering of horses was heard coming toward the village from the direction of Kishinev. *The Cossacks! The Cossacks!* someone had shouted. The Czar's horsemen! Quickly, quickly, everyone in Aaron's grandmother's family had climbed down to the cellar through a little trapdoor hidden under a mat in the big central room of their shack. But his grandmother's pet goat, whom she'd loved as much as Aaron loved Pidge and more, had to be left above, because if it had made a sound in the cellar, they would never have lived to see the next morning. They all hid under the wood in the woodbin and waited, hardly breathing.

Suddenly, from above, they heard shouts and calls and screams at a distance. And then the noise was in

---

4. **Czar Alexander the Second** leader of Russia from 1855 to 1881.

their house. Boots pounding on the floor, and everything breaking and crashing overhead. The smell of smoke and the shouts of a dozen men.

The terror went on for an hour and then the sound of horses' hooves faded into the distance. They waited another hour to make sure, and then the father went up out of the cellar and the rest of the family followed. The door to the house had been torn from its hinges and every piece of furniture was broken. Every window, every dish, every stitch of clothing was totally destroyed, and one wall had been completely bashed in. And on the floor was the goat, lying quietly. Aaron's grandmother, who was just a little girl of eight at the time, had wept over the goat all day and all night and could not be consoled.

But they had been lucky. For other houses had been burned to the ground. And everywhere, not goats alone, nor sheep, but men and women and children lay quietly on the ground. The word for this sort of massacre, Aaron had learned, was *pogrom*. It had been a pogrom. And the men on the horses were Cossacks. Hated word. Cossacks.

And so Pidge would replace that goat of long ago. A pigeon on Second Avenue where no one needed trapdoors or secret escape passages or woodpiles to hide under. A pigeon for his grandmother's sixtieth birthday. *Oh wing, heal quickly so my grandmother can send you flying to everywhere she wants!*

But a few days later, Aaron met Carl in the street again. And Carl told Aaron that there was going to be a meeting that afternoon in which a map was going to be drawn up to show where a secret treasure lay buried on the empty lot. "Bring the pigeon and you can come into the shack. We got a badge for you. A new kinda membership badge with a secret code on the back."

Aaron ran home, his heart pounding almost as fast as the pigeon's. He took Pidge in his hands and carried him out the door while his mother was busy in the kitchen making stuffed cabbage, his father's favorite dish. And by the time he reached the street, Aaron had decided to take the bandages off. Pidge would look like a real pigeon again, and none of the older boys would laugh or call him a bundle of rags.

Vocabulary
consoled (kən sōld) *v.* comforted

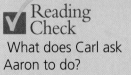
Reading Check

What does Carl ask Aaron to do?

Vocabulary
hesitated (hez´ i tāt´ əd)
v. stopped because of
indecision

Gently, gently he removed the bandages and the splints and put them in his pocket in case he should need them again. But Pidge seemed to hold his wing properly in place.

When he reached the empty lot, Aaron walked up to the shack, then hesitated. Four bigger boys were there. After a moment, Carl came out and commanded Aaron to hand Pidge over.

"Be careful," said Aaron. "I just took the bandages off."

"Oh sure, don't worry," said Carl. By now Pidge was used to people holding him, and he remained calm in Carl's hands.

"OK," said Carl. "Give him the badge." And one of the older boys handed Aaron his badge with the code on the back. "Now light the fire," said Carl.

"What . . . what fire?" asked Aaron.

"The fire. You'll see," Carl answered.

"You didn't say nothing about a fire," said Aaron. "You didn't say nothing to—"

"Hey!" said Carl. "I'm the leader here. And you don't talk unless I tell you that you have p'mission. Light the fire, Al."

The boy named Al went out to the side of the shack, where some wood and cardboard and old newspapers had been piled into a huge mound. He struck a match and held it to the newspapers.

"OK," said Carl. "Let's get 'er good and hot. Blow on it. Everybody blow."

Aaron's eyes stung from the smoke, but he blew alongside the others, going from side to side as the smoke shifted toward them and away.

"Let's fan it," said Al.

In a few minutes, the fire was crackling and glowing with a bright yellow-orange flame.

"Get me the rope," said Carl.

One of the boys brought Carl some cord and Carl, without a word, wound it twice around the pigeon, so that its wings were tight against its body.

"What . . . what are you *doing*!" shouted Aaron. "You're hurting his wing!"

"Don't worry about his wing," said Carl. "We're gonna throw him into the fire. And when we do, we're gonna swear an oath of loyalty to—"

"No! *No!*" shouted Aaron, moving toward Carl.

"Grab him!" called Carl. "Don't let him get the pigeon!"

But Aaron had leaped right across the fire at Carl, taking him completely by surprise. He threw Carl back against the shack and hit out at his face with both fists. Carl slid down to the ground and the pigeon rolled out of his hands. Aaron scooped up the pigeon and ran, pretending he was on roller skates so that he would go faster and faster. And as he ran across the lot he pulled the cord off Pidge and tried to find a place, *any* place, to hide him. But the boys were on top of him, and the pigeon slipped from Aaron's hands.

"Get him!" shouted Carl.

Aaron thought of the worst, the most horrible thing he could shout at the boys. "Cossacks!" he screamed. "You're all Cossacks!"

Two boys held Aaron back while the others tried to catch the pigeon. Pidge fluttered along the ground just out of reach, skittering one way and then the other. Then the boys came at him from two directions. But suddenly Pidge beat his wings in rhythm, and rose up, up over the roof of the nearest tenement, up over Second Avenue toward the park.

With the pigeon gone, the boys turned toward Aaron and tackled him to the ground and punched him and tore his clothes and punched him some more. Aaron twisted and turned and kicked and punched back, shouting "Cossacks! Cossacks!" And somehow the word gave him the strength to tear away from them.

When Aaron reached home, he tried to go past the kitchen quickly so his mother wouldn't see his bloody face and torn clothing. But it was no use; his father was home from work early that night and was seated in the living room. In a moment Aaron was surrounded by his mother, father, and grandmother, and in another moment he had told them everything that had happened, the words tumbling out between his broken sobs. Told them of the present he had planned, of the pigeon for a goat, of the gang, of the badge with the secret code on the back, of the shack, and the fire, and the pigeon's flight over the tenement roof.

And Aaron's grandmother kissed him and thanked him for his present which was even better than the pigeon.

Draw Conclusions
What can you conclude about Aaron from his actions to save Pidge?

Spiral Review
Character and Conflict How do Aaron's actions illustrate a change in his response to the events around him?

Setting
How might Pidge see the difference between the tenement yard and the open sky?

Draw Conclusions
What conclusion can you draw about Aaron based on his desire to replace his grandmother's beloved goat?

"What present?" asked Aaron, trying to stop the series of sobs.

And his grandmother opened her pocketbook and handed Aaron her mirror and asked him to look. But all Aaron saw was his dirty, bruised face and his torn shirt.

Aaron thought he understood and then, again, he thought he didn't. How could she be so happy when there really was no present? And why pretend that there was?

Later that night, just before he fell asleep, Aaron tried to imagine what his grandmother might have done with the pigeon. She would have fed it, and she certainly would have talked to it, as she did to all the birds, and . . . and then she would have let it go free. Yes, of course. Pidge's flight to freedom must have been the gift that had made his grandmother so happy. Her goat has escaped from the Cossacks at last, Aaron thought, half dreaming. And he fell asleep with a smile.

Critical Thinking

Cite textual evidence to support your responses.

1. **Key Ideas and Details (a)** What happened to Aaron's grandmother as a child? **(b) Analyze Cause and Effect:** How does her experience help Aaron decide what to give her for her birthday?

2. **Key Ideas and Details (a)** What does Carl want to do with Pidge? **(b) Compare and Contrast:** How are Carl and the boys like the Cossacks?

3. **Key Ideas and Details (a)** Which is the better gift for Aaron's grandmother: the pigeon or the pigeon's freedom? Explain. **(b) Apply:** What are two other "gifts" that are not physical objects that one person can give another? Explain.

4. **Integration of Knowledge and Ideas** In this story, Aaron gets into a conflict with a gang of boys. Was there anything positive about this conflict or was it best avoided? Explain. *[Connect to the Big Question: Is conflict always bad?]*

Reading Skill: Drawing Conclusions

1. List three story details that support the following **conclusion:** *Aaron is a sensitive and thoughtful boy.*

2. Based on your prior knowledge, why do you think Aaron's mother forbids him to play with Carl and the other boys?

Literary Analysis: Setting

© 3. Key Ideas and Details (a) Describe the **setting** of "Aaron's Gift." **(b)** Why is the setting important to the story?

© 4. Craft and Structure (a) Use a chart like the one shown to list ways in which details of the setting affect events in the story. **(b)** With a partner, explain your responses.

Details of Setting		Story Events
Time		
Place		

Vocabulary

© Acquisition and Use Write a sentence for each item using a word from the "Aaron's Gift" vocabulary list on page 316.

1. Describe how someone got a puppy into its crate.

2. Explain how you responded to a friend whose pet died.

3. Describe a bird that tries to escape from a cage.

4. Describe a shy person who enters a new classroom.

5. Tell how a parent might have begged a child to behave.

6. Describe something you have borrowed.

Word Study Use sentence context and what you know about the **Latin root -*tempor*-** to explain your answers.

1. Would a bandleader expect musicians to play at the same *tempo*?

2. Does Top-40 music sound *contemporary*?

Word Study

The **Latin root -*tempor*-** means "time."

Apply It Explain how the root contributes to the meanings of these words. Consult a dictionary if necessary.

temporary
temporal
contemporaneous

Integrated Language Skills

The King of Mazy May • Aaron's Gift

Conventions: Perfect Tenses of Verbs

The **perfect tenses** of verbs combine a form of *have* with the past participle of the verb.

- The **present perfect tense** shows an action that began in the past and continues in the present.
- The **past perfect tense** shows a past action or condition that ended before another past action began.
- The **future perfect tense** shows a future action or condition that will have ended before another begins.

Present Perfect	Past Perfect	Future Perfect
have, has + past participle	had + past participle	will have + past participle
They *have voted* in this city for seventeen years.	They *had voted* by the time we arrived.	The council *will have voted* by summer.

Practice A Identify the tense in each of the sentences. Indicate whether it is present perfect, past perfect, or future perfect.

1. Walt had never been on his own.
2. Walt had saved the gold.
3. The thieves will have laid their claim before morning.
4. The men of the Yukon have worked hard to find gold.

© Reading Application Review either of the selections and identify examples of the present perfect, past perfect, and future perfect tenses.

Practice B Rewrite each sentence using the tense in parentheses.

1. Aaron had plunged himself onto the pigeon. (present perfect)
2. Grandma will have enjoyed her birthday and gone to sleep. (past perfect)
3. Aaron trained a pigeon. (future perfect)
4. The gang members will have learned their lesson. (present perfect)

© Writing Application Write three sentences describing a day in the future life of a character in one of these selections. In each sentence, use one of the perfect tenses.

PH WRITING COACH | Further instruction and practice are available in *Prentice Hall Writing Coach.*

Writing

Common Core
State Standards

L.6.1; W.6.3; SL.6.2
[For the full wording of the standards, see page 300.]

Narrative Text In both selections, the main characters struggle to meet a goal. Write a brief **personal narrative** describing your experiences as you struggled to meet a goal of your own.

- Jot down the relevant details of your experience.
- Organize your notes into a timeline of events. You can refer to your timeline as you write your narrative.
- Include sensory details as you draft.
- Describe how your feelings changed as a result of your experiences.
- Wrap up your narrative by telling how you felt in the end.

Grammar Application Check your writing to be sure you have used consistent verb tense.

Writing Workshop: *Work in Progress*

Prewriting for Short Story Select a conflict from your Conflict List. Create characters that may be involved in this conflict. For each character, write key words that describe his or her personality. Save this Character Description Profile in your writing portfolio.

Use this prewriting activity to prepare for the **Writing Workshop** on page 354.

Research and Technology

Build and Present Knowledge Prepare a **presentation** with a small group of students.

- If you and your group read "The King of Mazy May," prepare a presentation on the history of gold mining in Canada.
- If you and your group read "Aaron's Gift," prepare a presentation on carrier pigeons in history.

Follow these steps to complete the assignment.

- To research your topic, use **resources** at the library or on the Internet. If you go online, use **keyword searches.**
- Interpret the information you find and decide what information best suits your presentation.
- Create a simple, attractive **visual timeline** that shows important events in time order.
- Practice presenting the information with your group, using your timeline as a guide.
- Present the information to your class.

PHLit Online!
www.PHLitOnline.com
- Interactive graphic organizers
- Grammar tutorial
- Interactive journals

Test Practice: Reading

Draw Conclusions

Fiction Selection

Directions: *Read the selection. Then, answer the questions.*

Andrés and Pedro had always enjoyed taking apart clocks and putting them back together. They had also built radios and repaired the toaster and CD player. Recently, they created a robot. The robot was supposed to ward off burglars by barking like a fierce dog at the sound of the doorbell. It was also supposed to sweep the kitchen floor. But when their parents gathered to watch the robot's first demonstration, things did not go well. Pedro rang the doorbell. The robot sounded more like a quacking duck than a barking dog. The robot *did* sweep the floor for a while. Then, it stepped on the cat's tail, knocked over an umbrella stand, and began spinning in circles. "Back to the drawing board," said Andrés, switching off the robot.

1. What conclusion can you draw from this passage about the relationship between Andrés and Pedro?
  A. They are cousins.
  B. They are neighbors.
  C. They are friends.
  D. They are brothers.

2. You can also conclude that the boys—
  A. enjoy making mischief.
  B. are curious about how things work.
  C. do not like school.
  D. like to compete with each other.

3. Which conclusion is *best* supported by the passage?
  A. The boys will try to fix the robot.
  B. The parents love the robot.
  C. The robot is successful at scaring burglars.
  D. The boys do not work together well.

4. Which detail supports your answer to question 3?
  A. Andrés and Pedro had always enjoyed taking apart clocks.
  B. The robot was supposed to ward off burglars.
  C. The robot *did* sweep the floor for a while.
  D. "Back to the drawing board," said Andrés.

Writing for Assessment

Write two or three sentences telling what you think Andrés and Pedro will do next. Support your conclusion with details from the passage.

Nonfiction Selection

Directions: *Read the selection. Then, answer the questions.*

For years, people have dreamed of having robots to do household chores such as cooking, cleaning, and washing dishes. While this dream is still decades away from coming true, robots are doing important jobs. Surgeons use robots to make precise movements that are difficult for a human hand. Robots pick apples from treetops. They help assemble new cars. Scientists have used robots to explore dangerous places, such as inside active volcanoes and the surface of Mars.

1. What conclusion can you draw from the first sentence of the passage?
   A. Some people enjoy doing household chores.
   B. Some household chores can be dangerous.
   C. Robots cannot do household chores as fast as humans.
   D. Many people find household chores tedious and boring.

2. Which conclusion is most logical?
   A. Robots are cheaper than human surgeons.
   B. Robots can survive higher temperatures than humans.
   C. Robots are not as reliable as humans.
   D. Robots are used only by scientists.

3. What can you conclude about the future of robots?
   A. Robots will no longer be useful to humans.
   B. Robots will become more expensive to use.
   C. Robots will someday be even more useful and efficient.
   D. Robots will no longer exist.

4. Which word *best* describes robots, as they are presented in this passage?
   A. difficult
   B. frightening
   C. dangerous
   D. useful

Writing for Assessment

Comparing Texts

Use details from both passages to write a paragraph describing two advantages and two disadvantages of using robots.

www.PHLitOnline.com
- Online practice
- Instant feedback

Reading for Information

Analyzing Expository and Functional Texts

Compare-and-Contrast Article

Annotated Map

 **Common Core State Standards**

Reading Informational Text

3. Analyze in detail how a key individual, event, or idea is introduced, illustrated, and elaborated in a text.

5. Analyze how a particular sentence, paragraph, chapter, or section fits into the overall structure of a text and contributes to the development of ideas.

Reading Skill: Analyze Compare-and-Contrast Organization

When you compare and contrast, you examine the similarities and differences between two or more things. Some writers discuss all the features of one topic first and then discuss the features of the second (block organization). Others prefer to discuss the topics' similarities and differences one point at a time (point-by-point organization). As you read, ask yourself the following questions about **compare-and-contrast organization:**

Questions for analyzing comparison-and-contrast organization
Are the same categories covered for each half of the comparison?
Are an approximately equal number of details supplied for each category?
Does the writer support compare-and-contrast statements with examples and facts?

Content-Area Vocabulary

These words appear in the selections that follow. You may also encounter them in other content-area texts.

- **expedition** (eks′pə dish′ən) *n.* journey for some special purpose, such as exploration or scientific study

- **conditioned** (kən dish′ənd) *v.* trained the body to get it used to a different type of exercise or environment

- **pioneers** (pī′ə nir′z) *n.* the first people to settle in a new area or to put forth a new idea

Features:

- information about the similarities and differences of two or more things
- point-by-point or block organization
- text that may be written for a general or specific audience

Race to the End of the Earth

Amundsen's team proving South Pole location

William G. Scheller

The article begins by introducing the two subjects of comparison.

Two explorers competed against each other and a brutal environment to reach the South Pole.

The drifts were so deep and the snow was falling so heavily that the team of five Norwegian explorers could hardly see their sled dogs a few feet ahead of them. Behind rose a monstrous mountain barrier. The men had been the first to cross it. But now they and their dogs were stumbling toward a stark and desolate plateau continually blasted by blizzards. The landscape was broken only by the towering peaks of mountains that lay buried beneath a mile of ancient ice. Led by Roald Amundsen, the men were still 300 miles from their goal: the South Pole.

On that same day, a party of 14 British explorers was also struggling across a similarly terrifying landscape toward the same destination. But they were almost twice as far from success. Their commander was Capt. Robert Falcon Scott, a naval officer. Amundsen was Scott's rival.

Preparation Both **expedition** leaders had long been preparing for their race to the South Pole. Amundsen came from a family of hardy sailors, and he had decided at the age of 15 to become a polar explorer. He **conditioned** himself by taking long ski trips across the Norwegian countryside and

The **heading** signals that the writer will compare the subjects' methods of preparation.

by sleeping with his windows open in winter.

By the time of his South Pole attempt, Amundsen was an experienced explorer. He had sailed as a naval officer on an expedition in 1897 that charted sections of the Antarctic coast. Between 1903 and 1906 he commanded the ship that made the first voyage through the Northwest Passage, the icy route that threads its way through the Canadian islands separating the Atlantic and Pacific Oceans. During that long journey Amundsen learned how the native people of the Arctic dress and eat to survive in extreme cold. He also learned that the dogsled was the most efficient method of polar transportation. These lessons would serve him well at

Earth's frozen southern end.

Robert Scott was an officer in the British Navy. He had decided that leading a daring expedition of discovery would be an immediate route to higher rank. He heard that Great Britain's Royal Geographical Society was organizing such an exploration, and he volunteered in 1899 to be its commander. Now he was in command again.

The two expedition leaders had different styles. Scott followed a British tradition of brave sacrifice. He felt that he and his men should be able to reach the South Pole with as little help as possible from sled dogs and special equipment. He did bring dogs to Antarctica, as well as 19 ponies and three gasoline-powered sledges, or sturdy sleds. But his plan was for his team to "man-haul," or carry, all of their own supplies along the final portion of the route.

Roald Amundsen had spent much time in the far north, and he was a practical man. He'd seen how useful dogs were to Arctic inhabitants. He would be traveling in one of

Here, the writer analyzes the differences that affected the outcome of the race.

the most dangerous places on Earth, and he knew that sled dogs would be able to get his party all the way to the South Pole and make a safe return. Amundsen also placed great faith in skis, which he and his Norwegian team members had used since childhood. The British explorers had rarely used skis before this expedition and did not understand their great value.

The two leaders even had different ideas about diet. Scott's men would rely on canned meat. But Amundsen's plan made more sense. He and his men would eat plenty of fresh seal meat. Amundsen may not have fully understood the importance of vitamins, but fresh meat is a better source of vitamin C, which prevents scurvy, a painful and sometimes deadly disease.

The Race Is On! After making long sea voyages from Europe, Scott and Amundsen set up base camps in January on opposite edges of the Ross Ice Shelf. Each team spent the dark winter months making preparations to push on to the Pole when spring would arrive in Antarctica.

Amundsen left base camp on October 20, 1911, with a party of four. Scott, accompanied by nine men, set off from his camp 11 days later. Four others had already gone ahead on the motorized sledges.

Scott's Final Diary Entry

Things went wrong for Scott from the beginning. The sledges broke down and had to be abandoned. Scott and his men soon met up with the drivers, who were traveling on foot. Blizzards then struck and lasted several weeks into December. Scott's ponies were proving to be a poor choice for Antarctic travel as well. Their hooves sank deep into the snow, and their perspiration froze on their bodies, forming sheets of ice. (Dogs do not perspire; they pant.) On December 9, the men shot the last of the surviving weak and frozen ponies. Two days later Scott sent his remaining dogs back to base camp along with several members of the expedition. Over the next month, most of the men

This paragraph ends with a **point-by-point comparison** of the teams' attitudes toward skis.

Each **heading** begins a new section that highlights more similarities and differences.

returned to the camp. Scott's plan from here on was for the five men remaining to manhaul supplies the rest of the way to the Pole and back.

For Scott and his men, the journey was long and brutal. To cover only ten miles each day, the team toiled like dogs—like the dogs they no longer had. Food and fuel were in short supply, so the men lacked the energy they needed for such a crushing task.

Roald Amundsen's careful planning and Arctic experience were paying off. Even so, there's no such thing as easy travel by land in Antarctica. To the men who had just crossed those terrible mountains, the Polar Plateau might have looked easy. But Amundsen's team still had to cross a long stretch they later named the "Devil's Ballroom." It was a thin crust of ice that concealed crevasses, or deep gaps, that could swallow men, sleds, and dogs. Stumbling into one crevasse, a team of dogs dangled by their harnesses until the men could pull them up to safety.

Reaching the Goal On skis, with the "ballroom" behind them and well-fed dogs pulling their supply sleds, Amundsen and his men swept across the ice. The going was smooth for them, and the weather was fine. The Norwegians' only worry was that they'd find Scott had gotten to the Pole first. On the afternoon of December 14, 1911, it was plain that no one was ahead of them. At three o'clock, Amundsen skied in front of the team's sleds, then stopped to look at his navigation instruments. There was no point further south. He was at the South Pole!

This **paragraph** shows that the two teams suffered similar problems.

Gold Rush: The Journey by Land

from *The Sacramento Bee*

Most overlanders began their journey on the Mormon or Oregon trails. The major trailheads for these routes were in Council Bluffs, Iowa, St. Joseph, Missouri, or Independence, Missouri. The overland trip typically took five to six months. Ten to 15 miles of travel in one day would be a good day.

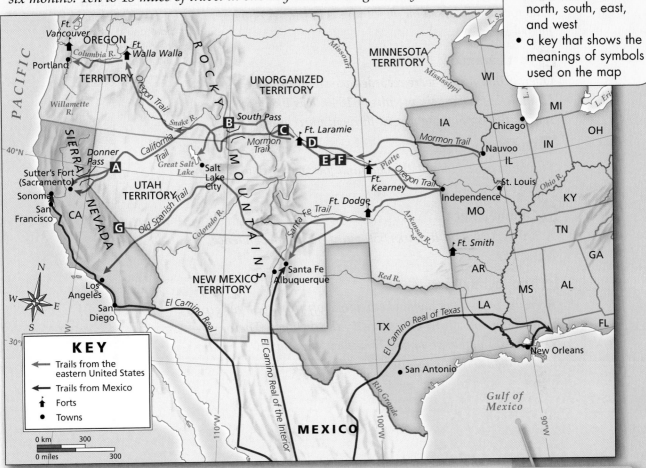

KEY

→ Trails from the eastern United States
← Trails from Mexico
↑ Forts
• Towns

0 km 300
0 miles 300

The **map** helps you to see the differences and similarities of the routes taken.

The routes taken

People often traveled by steamboat up the Ohio River or the Mississippi to reach the major trailheads. The Oregon Trail was created earlier by fur trappers.

A The Humboldt Basin

The dreaded 40-mile stretch of Humboldt Basin promised severe heat, sand deep enough to trap oxen, and no food or water.

B The Continental Divide

South Pass was the easiest passage through the Rockies. Rivers to the east flowed toward the Atlantic. Rivers to the west flowed toward the Pacific. From this point on, travel became increasingly difficult.

C Independence Rock

This rock was marked on by hundreds of pioneers who passed it.

D Fort Laramie

Over 39,000 people were recorded passing through Fort Laramie in the first six months of 1849. It is likely that several thousand more passed through unrecorded.

E The Platte River

The rains of 1849 made the overland journey difficult at the Platte River.

F Chimney Rock

A 500 foot column. It marks 550 miles from Independence, Missouri.

G The Jayhawkers

A group, named the Jayhawkers, broke off from a larger group in the hopes of cutting 600 miles off the distance. Their journey ended in an area named Tomesha, "ground afire," by the local Indians. Today, the area is called Death Valley.

The **annotations** allow you to compare and contrast the different routes shown on the map.

Comparing Expository and Functional Texts

1. Craft and Structure What different features do the article and the map use to present comparisons about the events they cover?

2. Key Ideas and Details (a) On page 337, what information does the section titled "The Race Is On!" add to the central idea of a competition? **(b)** Analyze one more detail from each of the texts and explain what it illustrates about the central idea in that text.

Content-Area Vocabulary

3. (a) How might a runner have *conditioned* herself for a race held at a high altitude? **(b)** For what reasons might *pioneers* set out on an *expedition*? Use both words in your answer.

Timed Writing

Explanatory Text: Essay

Format
The prompt asks you to write an essay. It is important to include an introduction, body, and conclusion in your essay.

Write an essay that describes the journeys of two teams of explorers in "Race to the End of the Earth." Compare the journey of the Norwegian team with the journey of the British team. (25 minutes)

Academic Vocabulary
When you *compare*, you point out differences and similarities between two or more subjects.

5-Minute Planner

Complete these steps before you begin to write:

1. Review the information in "Race to the End of the Earth." Pay attention to how the article compares and contrasts the different journeys of the two teams.

2. Jot down your ideas about how the journeys of the two teams were similar and how they were different. Use information from the article to help you. **TIP:** Make your notes in a chart with two columns, one for each team's journey. Doing so will help you to organize the information.

3. Refer to the similarities and differences shown in your chart as you write your essay.

Comparing Setting and Theme

Setting is the time and place of a story's action. In most stories, the setting serves as a background for the plot and creates atmosphere. Setting can be real or make-believe. Details of setting can include the year, the time of day, or even the weather.

In some stories, the setting has a strong impact on the **theme,** or central lesson about life in the story. A theme may be stated or implied.

- A **stated theme** is expressed directly by the author.
- An **implied theme** is revealed indirectly—through the events, the characters' thoughts and feelings, and often the story's title.

In "The Fun They Had" and "Feathered Friend," notice the impact of the setting on characters and events in the story. Look for clues that reveal the theme of each story. As you read, complete a chart like the one shown.

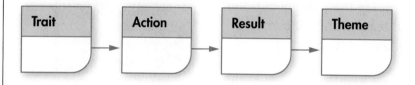

The **historical and cultural setting** of a story refers to the time period in which the characters live and the customs, values, and beliefs of that time and place. The time period during which the author wrote can often influence the historical and cultural setting.

Both of these stories were written during the 1950s—a time of growth and technological advancement in the United States. For example, in 1958, the first U.S. satellite successfully orbited Earth. As you read, consider how real events of the time period may have influenced the settings of these stories.

Common Core State Standards

Reading Literature
2. Determine a theme or central idea of a text and how it is conveyed through particular details; provide a summary of the text distinct from personal opinions or judgments.
5. Analyze how a particular sentence, chapter, scene, or stanza fits into the overall structure of a text and contributes to the development of the theme, setting, or plot.

Writing
2. Write informative/explanatory texts to examine a topic and convey ideas, concepts, and information through the selection, organization, and analysis of relevant content.

www.PHLitOnline.com

- Vocabulary flashcards
- Interactive journals
- More about the authors
- Selection audio
- Interactive graphic organizers

Is *conflict* always bad?

Writing About the Big Question

In one of these stories, a small bird saves the lives of the crew on a space station. In the other, a computer does the work of a teacher. Use this sentence starter to develop your ideas:
An **issue** that might arise when humans rely on animals or computers to do their work is _____.

Meet the Authors

Isaac Asimov (1920–1992)

Author of "The Fun They Had"

Check any section of a library and you will probably find a book by Isaac Asimov. He wrote fiction, medical books, humor, autobiography, essays, a guide to Shakespeare, and science books—more than 400 books in all.

Master of Science Fiction Asimov is best known for his science-fiction writing. During his writing career, Asimov won every major award for this type of writing. He first became interested in the genre as a boy, when he noticed science-fiction magazines on the shelves of his family's candy store. "The Fun They Had," written in 1951, became one of Asimov's most popular science-fiction stories for children.

Arthur C. Clarke (1917–2008)

Author of "Feathered Friend"

Arthur C. Clarke was born in Somerset, England. He became interested in science at an early age and built his first telescope at age thirteen. His first science-fiction story was published in 1946 in the magazine *Astounding Science*.

Television Firsts Clarke became the first television owner on Sri Lanka, the island off India where he lived. He holds another, more important television "first." He was the first to think of sending television and radio signals around the world by bouncing them off satellites.

The Fun They Had

Isaac Asimov

Setting and Theme
What do you already know about the setting from the first paragraph?

*M*argie even wrote about it that night in her diary. On the page headed May 17, 2155, she wrote, "Today Tommy found a real book."

It was a very old book. Margie's grandfather once said that when he was a little boy, his grandfather told him that there was a time when all stories were printed on paper.

They turned the pages, which were yellow and crinkly, and it was awfully funny to read words that stood still instead of moving the way they were supposed to—on a screen, you know. And then, when they turned back to the page before, it had the same words on it that it had had when they read it the first time.

"Gee," said Tommy, "what a waste. When you're through with the book, you just throw it away, I guess. Our television screen must have had a million books on it and it's good for plenty more. I wouldn't throw it away."

"Same with mine," said Margie. She was eleven and hadn't seen as many telebooks as Tommy had. He was thirteen.

She said, "Where did you find it?"

"In my house." He pointed without looking, because he was busy reading. "In the attic."

"What's it about?"

"School."

Margie was scornful. "School? What's there to write about school? I hate school." Margie always hated school, but now she hated it more than ever. The mechanical teacher had been giving her test after test in geography, and she had been doing worse and worse until her mother had shaken her head sorrowfully and sent for the county inspector.

He was a round little man with a red face and a whole box of tools with dials and wires. He smiled at her and gave her an apple, then took the teacher apart. Margie had hoped he wouldn't know how to put it together again, but he knew how all right, and after an hour or so, there it was again, large and ugly, with a big screen on which all the lessons were shown and the questions were asked. That wasn't so bad. The part she hated most was the slot where she had to put homework and test papers. She always had to write them out in a punch code they made her learn when she was six years old, and the mechanical teacher calculated the mark in no time.

The inspector had smiled after he was finished and patted her head. He said to her mother, "It's not the little girl's fault, Mrs. Jones. I think the geography sector was geared a little too quick. Those things happen sometimes. I've slowed it up to an average ten-year level. Actually, the overall pattern of her progress is quite satisfactory." And he patted Margie's head again.

Margie was disappointed. She had been hoping they would take the teacher away altogether. They had once taken Tommy's teacher away for nearly a month because the history sector had blanked out completely.

So she said to Tommy, "Why would anyone write about school?"

Vocabulary
calculated (kal´ kyо̄о lāt´ əd) v. found the answer mathematically

✓ Reading Check
What does Tommy find in his attic?

Vocabulary
loftily (lôft´ i lē) *adv.*
in a proud manner
nonchalantly (nän´ shə
länt lē) *adv.* in a con-
fident and easy way

Setting and Theme
How does the author
indirectly reveal details
about the theme?

Tommy looked at her with very superior eyes. "Because it's not our kind of school, stupid. This is the old kind of school that they had hundreds and hundreds of years ago." He added loftily, pronouncing the word carefully, "*Centuries* ago."

Margie was hurt. "Well, I don't know what kind of school they had all that time ago." She read the book over his shoulder for a while, then said, "Anyway, they had a teacher."

"Sure they had a teacher, but it wasn't a *regular* teacher. It was a man."

"A man? How could a man be a teacher?"

"Well, he just told the boys and girls things and gave them homework and asked them questions."

"A man isn't smart enough."

"Sure he is. My father knows as much as my teacher."

"He can't. A man can't know as much as a teacher."

"He knows almost as much I betcha."

Margie wasn't prepared to dispute that. She said, "I wouldn't want a strange man in my house to teach me."

Tommy screamed with laughter. "You don't know much, Margie. The teachers didn't live in the house. They had a special building and all the kids went there."

"And all the kids learned the same thing?"

"Sure, if they were the same age."

"But my mother says a teacher has to be adjusted to fit the mind of each boy and girl it teaches and that each kid has to be taught differently."

"Just the same, they didn't do it that way then. If you don't like it, you don't have to read the book."

"I didn't say I didn't like it," Margie said quickly. She wanted to read about those funny schools.

They weren't even half finished when Margie's mother called, "Margie! School!"

Margie looked up. "Not yet, Mamma."

"Now," said Mrs. Jones. "And it's probably time for Tommy, too."

Margie said to Tommy, "Can I read the book some more with you after school?"

"Maybe," he said, nonchalantly. He walked away whistling, the dusty old book tucked beneath his arm.

Margie went into the schoolroom. It was right next to her bedroom, and the mechanical teacher was on and waiting for her. It was always on at the same time every day except Saturday and Sunday, because her mother said little girls learned better if they learned at regular hours.

The screen was lit up, and it said: "Today's arithmetic lesson is on the addition of proper fractions. Please insert yesterday's homework in the proper slot."

Margie did so with a sigh. She was thinking about the old schools they had when her grandfather's grandfather was a little boy. All the kids from the whole neighborhood came, laughing and shouting in the schoolyard, sitting together in the schoolroom, going home together at the end of the day. They learned the same things so they could help one another on the homework and talk about it.

And the teachers were people. . . .

The mechanical teacher was flashing on the screen: "When we add the fractions ½ and ¼ . . ."

Margie was thinking about how the kids must have loved it in the old days. She was thinking about the fun they had.

© Spiral Review
Plot Find two sentences that show the historical and cultural setting of the story. Explain why the information in each sentence is important to the plot.

Critical Thinking ©

© 1. **Key Ideas and Details** **(a)** What does Margie write in her diary about the book Tommy found? **(b) Interpret:** Why is the book unusual?

© 2. **Key Ideas and Details** **(a)** What type of teacher does Margie have? **(b) Draw Conclusions:** What problem was the teacher causing for Margie before it was fixed? **(c) Speculate:** How are teachers programmed for individual students?

© 3. **Key Ideas and Details** **(a)** Where is Margie's schoolroom? **(b) Analyze:** What aspects of "old schools" does Margie most admire?

© 4. **Integration of Knowledge and Ideas** What conflict is created by Tommy's discovery of the book? What is something good that comes from this discovery? *[Connect to the Big Question: Is conflict always bad?]*

Cite textual evidence to support your responses.

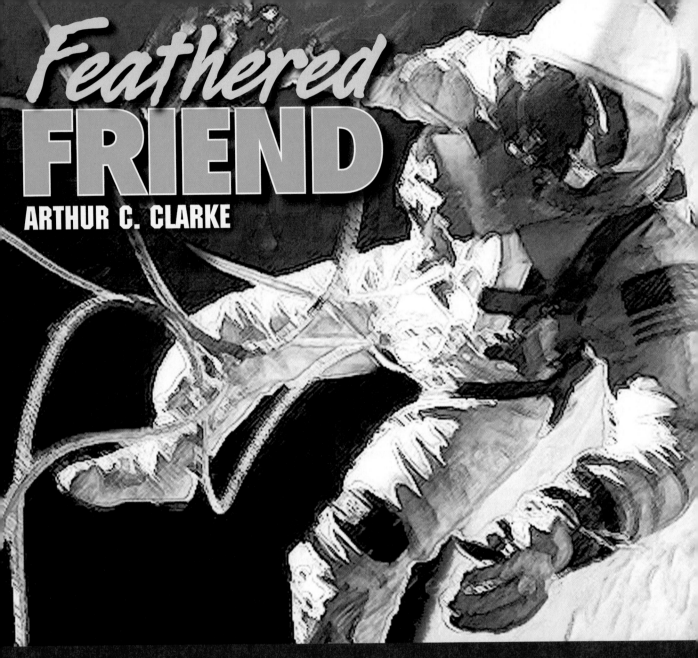

Feathered FRIEND

ARTHUR C. CLARKE

TO THE BEST OF MY KNOWLEDGE, there's never been a regulation that forbids one to keep pets in a space station. No one ever thought it was necessary— and even had such a rule existed, I am quite certain that Sven Olsen would have ignored it.

With a name like that, you will picture Sven at once as a six-foot-six Nordic giant, built like a bull and with a voice to match. Had this been so, his chances of getting a job in space would have been very slim. Actually he was a wiry little fellow, like most of the early spacers, and managed to qualify easily for the 150-pound bonus[1] that kept so many of us on a reducing diet.

Sven was one of our best construction men, and excelled at the tricky and specialized work of collecting assorted girders[2] as they floated around in free fall, making them do the slow-motion, three-dimensional ballet that would get them into their right positions, and **fusing** the pieces together when they were precisely dovetailed into the intended pattern: it was a skilled and difficult job, for a space suit is not the most convenient of garbs in which to work. However, Sven's team had one great advantage over the construction gangs you see putting up skyscrapers down on Earth. They could step back and admire their handiwork without being abruptly parted from it by gravity. . . .

Don't ask me why Sven wanted a pet, or why he chose the one he did. I'm not a psychologist, but I must admit that his selection was very sensible. Claribel weighed practically nothing, her food requirements were tiny—and she was not worried, as most animals would have been, by the absence of gravity.

I first became aware that Claribel was aboard when I was sitting in the little cubbyhole laughingly called my office, checking through my lists of technical stores to decide what items we'd be running out of next. When I heard the musical whistle beside my ear, I assumed that it had come over the station intercom, and waited for an announcement to follow. It didn't; instead, there was a long and involved pattern of melody that made me look up with such a start that I forgot all about the angle beam just behind my head. When the stars had **ceased** to explode before my eyes, I had my first view of Claribel.

She was a small yellow canary, hanging in the air as motionless as a hummingbird—and with much less effort, for her wings were quietly folded along her sides. We stared

Vocabulary
fusing (fyoo´ zin) *n.*
joining permanently

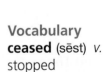

Vocabulary
ceased (sēst) *v.*
stopped

Reading
Check
Where does Sven do his construction work?

---

1. 150-pound bonus extra money for being lightweight.
2. girders (gʉr´ dərz) *n.* long, thick pieces of metal.

at each other for a minute; then, before I had quite recovered my wits, she did a curious kind of backward loop I'm sure no earthbound canary had ever managed, and departed with a few leisurely flicks. It was quite obvious that she'd already learned how to operate in the absence of gravity, and did not believe in doing unnecessary work.

Sven didn't confess to her ownership for several days, and by that time it no longer mattered, because Claribel was a general pet. He had smuggled her up on the last ferry from Earth, when he came back from leave—partly, he claimed, out of sheer scientific curiosity. He wanted to see just how a bird would operate when it had no weight but could still use its wings.

Claribel thrived and grew fat. On the whole, we had little trouble concealing our guest when VIP's from Earth came visiting. A space station has more hiding places than you can count; the only problem was that Claribel got rather noisy when she was upset, and we sometimes had to think fast to explain the curious peeps and whistles that came from ventilating shafts and storage bulkheads. There were a couple of narrow escapes—but then who would dream of looking for a canary in a space station?

We were now on twelve-hour watches, which was not as bad as it sounds, since you need little sleep in space. Though of course there is no "day" and "night" when you are floating in permanent sunlight, it was still convenient to stick to the terms. Certainly when I woke that "morning" it felt like 6:00 a.m. on Earth. I had a nagging headache, and vague memories of fitful, disturbed dreams. It took me ages to undo my bunk straps, and I was still only half awake when I joined the remainder of the duty crew in the mess. Breakfast was unusually quiet, and there was one seat vacant.

"Where's Sven?" I asked, not very much caring.

Critical Viewing
How do you think a canary would act aboard a space station like this? Explain. [Infer]

Setting and Theme
What do the details of setting reveal about the challenges of living in space?

"He's looking for Claribel," someone answered. "Says he can't find her anywhere. She usually wakes him up."

Before I could retort that she usually woke me up, too, Sven came in through the doorway, and we could see at once that something was wrong. He slowly opened his hand, and there lay a tiny bundle of yellow feathers, with two clenched claws sticking pathetically up into the air.

"What happened?" we asked, all equally distressed.

"I don't know," said Sven mournfully. "I just found her like this."

"Let's have a look at her," said Jock Duncan, our cook-doctor-dietitian. We all waited in hushed silence while he held Claribel against his ear in an attempt to detect any heartbeat.

Presently he shook his head. "I can't hear anything, but that doesn't prove she's dead. I've never listened to a canary's heart," he added rather apologetically.

"Give her a shot of oxygen," suggested somebody, pointing to the green-banded emergency cylinder in its recess beside the door. Everyone agreed that this was an excellent idea, and Claribel was tucked snugly into a face mask that was large enough to serve as a complete oxygen tent for her.

To our delighted surprise, she revived at once. Beaming broadly, Sven removed the mask, and she hopped onto his finger. She gave her series of "Come to the cookhouse, boys" trills—then promptly keeled over again.

"I don't get it," lamented Sven. "What's wrong with her? She's never done this before."

For the last few minutes, something had been tugging at my memory. My mind seemed to be very sluggish that morning, as if I was still unable to cast off the burden of sleep. I felt that I could do with some of that oxygen—but before I could reach the mask, understanding exploded in my brain. I whirled on the duty engineer and said urgently:

"Jim! There's something wrong with the air! That's why Claribel's passed out. I've just remembered that miners used to carry canaries down to warn them of gas."

"Nonsense!" said Jim. "The alarms would have gone off. We've got duplicate circuits, operating independently."

"Er—the second alarm circuit isn't connected up yet," his assistant reminded him. That shook Jim; he left without

Spiral Review

Plot Find a paragraph you have read so far that shows the historical and cultural setting of the story. Explain why the information in this paragraph is important to the plot.

Setting and Theme
What do the words and actions of the crew members reveal about their attitude toward Claribel?

Reading Check

What do the crew members do to wake up Claribel?

a word, while we stood arguing and passing the oxygen bottle around like a pipe of peace.

He came back ten minutes later with a sheepish expression. It was one of those accidents that couldn't possibly happen; we'd had one of our rare eclipses by Earth's shadow that night; part of the air purifier had frozen up, and the single alarm in the circuit had failed to go off. Half a million dollars' worth of chemical and electronic engineering had let us down completely. Without Claribel, we should soon have been slightly dead.

So now, if you visit any space station, don't be surprised if you hear an inexplicable snatch of birdsong. There's no need to be alarmed; on the contrary, in fact. It will mean that you're being doubly safeguarded, at practically no extra expense.

Critical Thinking

1. **Key Ideas and Details** **(a)** Where does the story take place? **(b) Compare and Contrast:** Name two features of life in the story that differ from life on Earth.

2. **Integration of Knowledge and Ideas** **(a) Synthesize:** Explain three factors that help the narrator figure out that something is wrong. **(b) Make a Judgment:** Who is responsible for saving the crew's lives: Claribel or the narrator? Explain.

3. **Integration of Knowledge and Ideas** **(a)** What prevented the alarm from warning the crew? **(b) Speculate:** What are some potential problems with using a canary instead of an electric alarm? **(c) Evaluate:** Which do you think is the better alarm? Why?

4. **Integration of Knowledge and Ideas** Do you think it would be good for humans to have pets living with them in space stations? Why or why not? What difficulties might they present? *[Connect to the Big Question: Is conflict always bad?]*

Cite textual evidence to support your responses.

Comparing Setting and Theme

1. Key Ideas and Details Complete a Venn diagram like the one below to show how the settings of "The Fun They Had" and "Feathered Friend" are alike and how they are different.

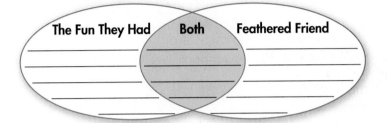

The Fun They Had   Both   Feathered Friend

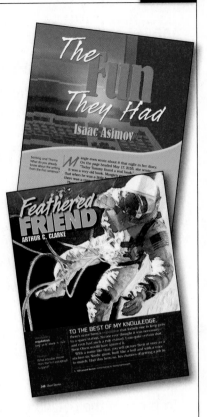

2. Key Ideas and Details (a) How is the mechanical teacher in "The Fun They Had" useful? **(b)** How is the bird in "Feathered Friend" useful?

3. Integration of Knowledge and Ideas (a) What theme about change and progress does "The Fun They Had" convey? Explain. **(b)** What theme about relying on others does "Feathered Friend" convey? Explain.

Timed Writing

Explanatory Text: Essay

Both Isaac Asimov and Arthur C. Clarke imagined a distant future. Write an essay in which you compare and contrast the historical and cultural settings of these stories. Support your ideas with evidence from the texts. **(40 minutes)**

5-Minute Planner

1. Read the prompt carefully and completely.
2. Refer to the chart you created on page 342 and your Venn diagram to help you gather your ideas.
3. Create an outline to organize your response.
4. Reread the prompt, and then draft your essay.

Writing Workshop

 **Common Core State Standards**

Writing

3. Write narratives to develop real or imagined experiences or events using effective technique, relevant descriptive details, and well-structured event sequences.

3.a. Engage and orient the reader by establishing a context and introducing a narrator and/or characters; organize an event sequence that unfolds naturally and logically.

Write a Narrative

Narration: Short Story

Defining the Form **Short stories** are brief works of fiction meant to entertain, to explore ideas, or to tell truths about life. They often feature a conflict, or a problem, faced by one or more characters. You might use elements of a short story in letters, scripts, and screenplays.

Assignment Write a short story about a person who faces a difficult challenge. Your short story should feature these elements:

✔ one or more *well-developed characters*

✔ an *interesting conflict* or problem

✔ a *plot* that moves toward the resolution of the conflict

✔ a clear and accurate *point of view,* or perspective

✔ concrete and sensory details that establish the *setting*

✔ *dialogue,* or conversations between characters

✔ error-free grammar, including the use of *consistent verb tenses*

To preview the criteria on which your short story may be judged, see the rubric on page 361.

 Writing Workshop: *Work in Progress*

Review the work you did on pages 299 and 331.

WRITE GUY
Jeff Anderson, M.Ed.

What Do You Notice?

Descriptive Details

The following sentences are from Francisco Jimenez's short story "The Circuit." Read the sentences several times.

The sun kept beating down. The buzzing insects, the wet sweat, and the hot dry dust made the afternoon seem to last forever. Finally the mountains around the valley reached out and swallowed the sun.

With a partner, discuss the qualities that make these sentences interesting. For example, you may want to talk about the writer's use of imagery, sensory details, and word choice. Now, think about ways you might use similar elements in your short story.

Reading-Writing Connection

To get a feel for short stories, read "Stray" by Cynthia Rylant on page 24.

Prewriting/Planning Strategies

Freewrite. Set a timer and freewrite for five minutes. Start with an image—a person in a boat in the middle of the ocean—or a feeling: curiosity, fear, or loneliness. During freewriting, focus more on the flow of ideas than on spelling or grammar. After five minutes, review your freewriting. Circle ideas to use in your story.

Review art and photos. Look at several pieces of fine art or photography in your textbooks or other sources. For each, imagine a story based on what the image suggests. Choose one of these ideas as the basis of your story.

Identify the conflict. Once you have a general idea of the story you will tell, get a better idea of its conflict—the struggle between two opposing forces. To develop the conflict, ask yourself these questions:

- What does my main character want?
- Who or what is getting in the way?
- What will the character do to overcome this obstacle?

Create your main character. Fill in a web like the one shown to help you get to know your main character.

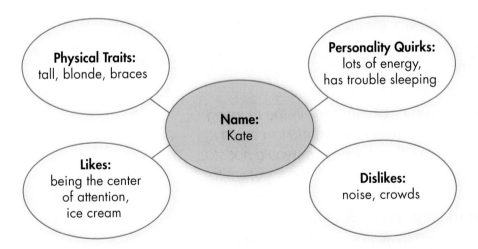

Title your story. With a clear idea of your topic and your main character, list possible titles for your story. Scan your list and choose the title that best captures the essence of what your story will convey.

Drafting Strategies

Develop your plot. Use a plot diagram like the one shown to organize the sequence of events in your short story. Plot often follows this pattern:

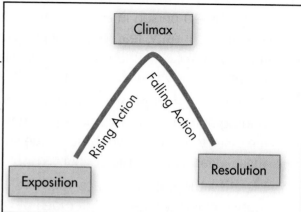

- **Exposition** introduces the characters and situation, including the conflict.
- The **conflict** develops during the **rising action**, which leads to the climax of the story.
- The **climax** is the point of greatest tension in the story.
- In the **falling action,** events and emotions wind down.
- In the **resolution,** the conflict is resolved and loose ends are tied up.

Use sensory details. As you draft your story, make your characters and setting come to life by including **sensory details**—language that describes how things look, sound, feel, taste, and smell. This will help you to develop a setting that the reader can visualize.

Dull: The sky *looked stormy.*

Vivid: The sky *boiled with black clouds and loud thunder.*

Write from a specific point of view. Tell your story from a single point of view, either as a participant (first-person point of view) or an observer (third-person point of view).

First-person point of view: *I woke up early in the morning to the sound of thunder. I couldn't believe it! How could it rain on my big day? I worried that the storm would not stop before noon. I pulled on my clothes and ran downstairs to talk to my mom.*

Third-person point of view: *Harry woke up early in the morning to the sound of thunder. He couldn't believe it! How could it rain on his big day? Harry's face revealed signs of worry and frustration. After dressing, he ran downstairs to talk to his mom.*

Common Core State Standards

Writing

3.a. Engage and orient the reader by establishing a context and introducing a narrator and/or characters; organize an event sequence that unfolds naturally and logically.

3.d. Use precise words and phrases, relevant descriptive details, and sensory language to convey experiences and events.

3.e. Provide a conclusion that follows from the narrated experiences or events.

Writers on Writing

Jean Craighead George
On Revising a Story

Jean Craighead George is the author of "The Wounded Wolf" (p. 184).

My Side of the Mountain is the story of Sam, who leaves a very crowded city home to live off the land and survive in the wilds of the Catskill Mountains, New York. I wrote the book in two weeks. When it was done, I started writing the story all over again. What follows is a look at my changes to the second manuscript. Sam is in his home in a big hemlock tree reading a journal entry from the previous winter. The entry is shown in quotation marks, and "The Baron" is a weasel.

"Live, note all things around you, and write out of love."
—Jean Craighead George

Professional Model:

from *My Side of the Mountain*

"Tomorrow I hope The Baron and I can tunnel out into the sunlight. I wonder if I should dig ~~it~~ the snow. But that would mean I would have to put it somewhere, and the only place to put it is in my nice snug tree. Maybe I can pack it with my hands as I go. I've always dug into the snow from the top, never up from under ~~the snow.~~

"The Baron must dig up from under the snow. I wonder where he puts what he digs ~~the extra.~~ Well, I guess I'll know in the morning."

When I wrote that last winter, I was scared and thought maybe I'd never get out of my tree. I had been scared for two days—ever since the first ~~that~~ blizzard hit the Catskill Mountains—~~but~~ When I came up to the sunlight, which I did by simply poking my head into the soft snow and standing up, I laughed at my dark fears.

In the first version, the book began with Sam telling his Dad goodbye. I thought a flashback to an earlier time, with the journal entry, was much more exciting.

I am Sam now, finding consolation in my wild friend, The Baron Weasel.

I realized that "I wonder where he puts the extra" was not on scene enough for my style of writing so inserted "what he digs." Now I could visualize pawsful of snow and wonder where I would put them if I were Sam.

Revising Strategies

Create logical connections between events. Use a bead chart to make sure that events in your plot are logically connected.

- Underline the major events in your story.
- Summarize each event in a "bead" on a chart like the one shown.
- Show the connections between events by writing a word or phrase in the connector string. Make sure that these ideas have been developed in your story.
- If most of your connectors say *next*, review your story. If you cannot think of a good connection between events, delete or reshape one of the events.
- Transitional words, phrases, and clauses such as *meanwhile, back in town, while Mike waited,* can help you show a shift in time or setting.

Troy doesn't hear any response from Leonard. he starts to worry

Troy starts wondering where Leonard is. he's curious, annoyed

Troy yells to Leonard to stop searching. next

Troy goes into woods to look for Leonard.

- Consider using literary devices such as suspense, foreshadowing, or flashback to add variety to your "string" of events.

Evaluate point of view. Check that the point of view in your story remains the same throughout the story. For example, if the story begins with the point of view of a young boy named Daniel, it should not end with the point of view of Daniel's mother.

Use dialogue to give characters a voice. Review your draft for places to bring your story to life with dialogue. Keep in mind that realistic characters may use slang and interrupt each other.

Vary your sentences and word choices. Revise your story to include a variety of words and sentence lengths. Be sure to use a thesaurus to make descriptions more vivid. Look for a balance of short and long sentences. Providing a variety of sentences will improve your story's flow.

Common Core State Standards

Writing
3.b. Use narrative techniques, such as dialogue, pacing, and description, to develop experiences, events, and/or characters.

3.c. Use a variety of transition words, phrases, and clauses to convey sequence and signal shifts from one time frame or setting to another.

Language
1.e. Recognize variations from standard English in their own and others' writing and speaking, and identify and use strategies to improve expression in conventional language.

Revising to Maintain Verb Tense

A **verb tense** tells the time—past, present, or future—of an action or a state of being. Using different verb tenses in a story can help explain causes and effects, but it can also lead to errors.

Present tense indicates an action or a condition in the present. It may also indicate an action or a condition that occurs regularly.

Ian *is helping* his uncle build a deck. Carla *teaches* swimming.

Past tense tells that an action took place in the past.

The Lanfords *traveled* to Turkey last March.

Future tense tells that an action will take place in the future.

I *will rearrange* my bedroom furniture this weekend.

Identifying Errors Jumping from one verb tense to another can confuse readers. Look at these examples:

Incorrect use of verb tenses:

PAST PRESENT
As Carlos *waited* outside the gym, he *sees* his friend Raul.

Correction:

As Carlos *waited* outside the gym, he *saw* his friend Raul.

Correct use of different tenses to show sequence of events:

PAST FUTURE
Because Amy *finished* her report early, she *will attend* the concert.

> **PH** **WRITING COACH**
> Further instruction and practice are available in *Prentice Hall Writing Coach.*

Fixing Errors Follow these steps to fix errors in verb tenses:

1. **Review your story, noting shifts in verb tenses within a sentence or paragraph.**

2. **Make sure that you have used changes in verb tenses for a good reason.** You may have chosen to show a relationship between ideas or to show the order of events.

3. **Rewrite sentences that contain incorrect shifts in tenses.**

Grammar in Your Writing

With a partner, circle the verbs in each sentence of your drafts and review the vocabulary. If you find any incorrect shifts in verb tenses, fix them using the methods described above.

Student Model: Karina McCorkle, Raleigh, NC

 Common Core
State Standards

Language
2.b. Spell correctly.

Math Mackerel

I sat staring blankly at the sheet of notebook paper in front of me. My teacher had just finished explaining how to divide fractions. I didn't understand it at all. I hated math, and now in sixth grade, math was much harder.

"I wish someone could help me understand math." I whispered.

Suddenly, a fish appeared out of thin air. I stared at him. He was standing on his tail with a flowing red cape and on his chest he had a yellow emblem with the red letters "MM."

"W-who are you?" I stammered.

"I am Math Mackerel. I thought I heard someone asking for help with math," the fish stated proudly.

"Oh, that was me," I said.

"I'll see you at recess." Math Mackerel said as he disappeared with a swish of his tail. And a flick of fins.

My teacher called out, "Time to put your math in your notebooks." I realized I hadn't written down a single problem on my paper.

"Drat!" I thought and put away my paper.

Outside, I sat in a secluded spot behind a bush and waited. Suddenly, Math Mackerel appeared.

"Greetings," said Math Mackerel happily. "I am here to help you with math."

"Are you going to give me all the knowledge I need?" I asked curiously.

"I could do that, but that would be cheating," scoffed Math Mackerel. He whipped out a deck of cards. I raised my eyebrows at him. I couldn't see how a deck of cards could help me with math.

"Do you know how to play Go Fish?" asked Math Mackerel.

"Yes, but how is…" I tried to ask.

"Good, I'll go first." And he began to deal the cards with his fins. Twenty minutes later, we were still playing a hearty game of Go Fish.

"Got any nines?" I asked, peering over my cards.

"Yes, what is one and seven ninths divided by two thirds?" he asked.

"Two and two thirds," I answered.

"Good job!" Math Mackerel said as he slammed his nines on the ground. Suddenly I heard my teacher's whistle. It was time to go inside.

"I will see you tomorrow," Math Mackerel called as he disappeared.

Math Mackerel and I played Go Fish for three weeks, and I got better and better at math. Then one day, my teacher announced a math test to review what we had learned. Suddenly, all my confidence evaporated. Playing with Math Mackerel was something I could handle easily, but a test was a different matter.

At recess, Math Mackerel was already waiting for me.

"Time to continue yesterday's game," Math Mackerel said happily.

"There is going to be a math test on Friday! You have to be there!" I gasped.

"Just remember Go Fish, and you'll be fine." And he disappeared, as his cape swirled around him.

All week, I dreaded Friday. I gulped as the teacher passed out the papers. I worked through the problems and found them easy as I thought about Go Fish. My teacher returned the tests on Monday. I picked mine up and saw an A!

Karina introduces the conflict in the first paragraph of her story.

Karina chooses to write her story from the first-person point of view.

Karina creates dialogue between two central characters.

Here, Karina moves the plot forward to its climax.

Karina includes an exciting climax and ends with the resolution.

Editing and Proofreading

Revise to correct errors in grammar, spelling, and punctuation.

Focus on spelling. **Homophones** are words that sound the same and have similar spellings, but have very different meanings. A spell checker will not find an error if a word is spelled correctly, but is the wrong word choice; therefore, proofread carefully. Here are just a few examples of easily confused words: *our/are, than/then, know/now, lose/loose, accept/except, it's/its*

Publishing and Presenting

Consider one of the following ways to share your writing:

Submit your story. Submit your story to your school's literary magazine, a national magazine, or an e-zine, or enter a contest that publishes student writing. Ask your teacher for suggestions.

Give a reading. Get together with a group of classmates and present a literary reading for an audience at your school.

Reflecting on Your Writing

Writer's Journal Jot down your answer to this question:

The next time you write a story, what do you think you might do differently as a result of this writing experience?

Rubric for Self-Assessment

Find evidence in your writing to address each category. Then use the rating scale to grade your work.

Spiral Review

Earlier in this unit, you learned about **simple verb tenses** (p. 298) and **perfect tenses of verbs** (p. 330). As you review your short story, be sure you have used verbs correctly.

PH WRITING COACH

Further instruction and practice are available in *Prentice Hall Writing Coach.*

Criteria	Rating Scale
	not very very
Focus: How well drawn are the characters?	1 2 3 4 5
Organization: How clearly organized is the story's plot?	1 2 3 4 5
Support/Elaboration: How well do the details and language establish the setting?	1 2 3 4 5
Style: How consistently have you used point of view?	1 2 3 4 5
Conventions: How correct is your grammar, especially your use of verb tenses?	1 2 3 4 5

Vocabulary Workshop

Word Origins

Common Core
State Standards

Language
4.c. Consult reference materials, both print and digital, to find the pronunciation of a word or determine or clarify its precise meaning or its part of speech.

The English language continues to grow and change. New words enter the language from many sources. A word's **origin** and **development,** or **etymology,** are its history. A word's etymology identifies the language in which the word first appeared. It also tells how the word's spelling and meaning have changed over time.

Many English words come from ancient Latin or Greek words or word roots. Others are **allusions,** references to well-known characters, places, or events in history, art, or literature. This chart shows some examples.

Word	Origin	Definition	Example Sentence
prove	Latin word *probare,* which means "test"	to show that something is true	This experiment will prove that light travels faster than sound.
biography	Greek words *bios* ("life") and *graphein* ("to write")	the story of a person's life	The biography of George Washington includes many facts about the American Revolution.
herculean	allusion to Hercules, a hero in ancient Greek myths, known for his great strength	requiring great strength	Moving the heavy box was a herculean task.

Practice A Find each of the following words in a dictionary. Define each word and explain its origin.

1. solo   **2.** martial   **3.** skill

4. marathon   **5.** edict   **6.** mentor

Practice B Each question contains a word that has come into the English language from the Greek or Latin language or from mythology. Use a dictionary to find each italicized word's origin and meaning. Then, use that information to answer each question.

1. What special ability does an *ambidextrous* person have?
2. How did *cereal* get its name?
3. Where will you go if you *circumnavigate* our planet?
4. What does a *dermatologist* treat?
5. Why is the word "goat" a *tetragram*?
6. Why is the word *colossal* used to describe something that is very big?
7. Why is a kangaroo considered a *marsupial*?
8. How would you describe the personality of someone who is *jovial*?

Activity Identify the source of each of the following English words. Then, use a graphic organizer like the one shown to explain how the English word and the source word are related. The first item has been completed as an example.

1. stampede   2. mercurial   3. kindergarten   4. phobia

Source Word	Connection	English Word
the Spanish word *estampar*, which means "to stamp"	When a herd of animals rushes suddenly, the animals *stamp* their feet on the ground.	*stampede*, which means "a sudden rush of a herd of animals"

Comprehension and Collaboration

With a partner, research the following characters from Greek mythology. Then, use a dictionary to find an English word that is based on the character's name. Finally, write a few sentences that explain how the word's meaning relates to the character.

Helios
Pan
Arachne

Communications Workshop

Evaluating a Persuasive Message

Common Core State Standards

A persuasive message encourages the audience to think or act in a certain way.

Learn the Skills

Use the strategies to complete the activity on page 365.

Identify the source of the message. Think about who is delivering the "information" and why. Facts supplied by the person or group may be slanted to favor a point of view.

Evaluate the content of the message. A *fact* is something that can be proved or demonstrated. An *opinion* can be supported but not proved. Notice whether or not the claims in a persuasive message are supported by facts and evidence.

Recognize propaganda. When the information is completely one-sided, it is called *propaganda*. Propaganda is the spreading of misleading ideas. The chart below shows three types of propaganda. These are persuasive techniques that are used in place of factual information.

Speaking and Listening
2. Interpret information presented in diverse media and formats and explain how it contributes to a topic, text, or issue under study.
3. Delineate a speaker's argument and specific claims, distinguishing claims that are supported by reasons and evidence from claims that are not.

Technique	Example
Bandwagon appeals rely on the idea that people make choices to be part of a crowd.	Every sixth-grader thinks this, so you should too.
Testimonials portray famous people giving their opinions or behaving in a certain way.	Sara Superstar uses this product, so it must be good.
Emotional appeals influence an audience through use of loaded language that appeals to feelings rather than logic.	Following this plan will make you a hero.

Evaluate the delivery of the message. Persuasive messages can be delivered in a variety of formats—writing, radio, television, film, or billboards. Ask yourself if the words, sounds, and pictures are meant to make you *feel* a certain way or *think* a certain way.

Practice the Skills

Presentation of Knowledge and Ideas Use what you've learned in this workshop to perform the following task.

ACTIVITY: Evaluate a Persuasive Message

Evaluate a television commercial by following these steps:

- Identify and explain the commercial's message.
- Analyze the propaganda used in the message.
- Decide whether or not the claims in the commercial are supported by evidence.
- Explain how propaganda in the commercial influences your emotions.

Use the Interpretation Guide below to help you evaluate the commercial.

Interpretation Guide

Message
What is the source and content of the message?
Explain the message and its purpose.

Propaganda and Persuasive Techniques
What persuasive techniques are used to influence the viewer? Briefly explain each one used.

❏ Bandwagon appeal
❏ Testimonial
❏ Emotional appeal

Influence on Emotion
How does each technique make you feel? Briefly explain your reasons.
    The message made me want to

❏ buy the product.
❏ not buy the product.
❏ Other (explain).

Conclusion
What claims in the commercial are supported by evidence?
What claims are supported by propaganda?
Is the commercial effective? Why?

Technique(s) Used

Effect of the Message

Comprehension and Collaboration For three days, view several types of advertisements. Take notes on the propaganda used in each one. Also note whether or not the claims in the ads are supported by facts. Compare your findings with a partner.

Cumulative Review

I. Reading Literature

Directions: *Read the story. Then, answer each question that follows.*

 **Common Core
State Standards**

RL.6.2, RL.6.3, RL.6.4; W.6.2
[For the full wording of the standards, see the standards chart in the front of your textbook.]

Aven had not cried once during the early months of the drought. Even when the dust storms came, turning day to night and covering everything with a layer of sand, she refused to cry. She reasoned that she *had* to be strong, to prove to Father and to her older brother, Kyle, just how brave she could be. Besides, what was the use of crying? Her tears wouldn't make the wheat grow, even if she cried all day and all night.

But one afternoon, she walked toward the barn and saw, across the way, the Jemisons loading their wagon with their belongings. A great sadness and fear seized her. If the Jemisons were leaving their farm, would her family be next?

Aven ran inside the barn so Father would not see her. She sat on an overturned crate and untied the bandana that kept dust out of her nose and mouth. Then she allowed the tears to come at last, in great sobs. *What will happen to us? What will happen to the animals? How will we live if we leave the farm?* These questions raced through her mind. She hated the drought and the dust storms as if they were living things.

In her <u>misery</u>, Aven did not hear Father come into the barn. "Aven!" her father cried. "What's wrong, child?" He lifted Aven gently by her shoulders and led her inside the house.

"Oh, Father," Aven said when they were both seated at the kitchen table. "I've tried to be so strong. But the Jemisons are leaving, and I'm scared we'll be next!"

"What's this—are you ashamed of crying?" Father asked, his eyes wide. "Being strong doesn't mean holding back tears," he said, taking his daughter's hands in his. "It means facing the hardships and getting through them, day after day—just like you and Kyle are doing—and not sitting around complaining or wishing that things were different."

Aven managed a small smile.

"I'm very proud of you, Aven," said Father. Aven looked into her father's tired eyes. She still felt sadness. But she was no longer afraid.

1. What is Aven's **motive** for refusing to cry?
   A. She does not want her brother to laugh at her.
   B. She does not want to annoy her father.
   C. She does not want the Jemisons to see her cry.
   D. She does not want to admit her fear.

2. Which phrase *best* describes the **setting** of the story?
   A. cozy barn
   B. mountain village
   C. family farm
   D. small town

3. Which of the following suggests that the **setting** of the story is many years ago?
   A. The Jemisons are leaving in a wagon.
   B. Aven runs to the family's barn.
   C. A drought has ruined the crops.
   D. The family is trying to grow wheat.

4. With which of these does Aven experience an **external conflict?**
   A. the drought and dust storms
   B. her brother Kyle
   C. the Jemisons
   D. her wish to be brave

5. Based on the writer's **characterization,** which word best describes Father?
   A. angry
   B. afraid
   C. kind
   D. hopeful

6. Why is Father proud of Aven?
   A. She has not cried during the drought and dust storms.
   B. She has been strong and brave during hard times.
   C. She is willing to leave the farm, if necessary.
   D. She does not want to leave with the Jemisons.

7. Which sentence *best* sums up the **theme** of the story?
   A. Feeling sorry for oneself is a sign of weakness.
   B. Life can be unfair.
   C. Droughts can cause people to move.
   D. Facing problems directly shows real strength.

8. **Vocabulary** Which word is closest in meaning to the underlined word *misery*?
   A. embarrassment
   B. sorrow
   C. confusion
   D. anger

 Timed Writing

9. In an essay, explain how the writer uses **indirect characterization** to develop Aven's personality as the plot unfolds. **Support** your response with details from the passage.

 GO ON

II. Reading Informational Text

Directions: *Read this magazine article. Then, answer each question.*

Common Core
State Standards

RI.6.5; L.6.1
[For the full wording of the standards, see the standards chart in the front of your textbook.]

Paper or Plastic?

After unloading your cart of groceries at the supermarket, you are faced with an important question: paper bags or plastic bags? How will you answer?

Paper comes from trees. The process of turning wood into paper uses great amounts of energy. Recycling paper requires the use of many different chemicals and a lot of energy. Even though paper is recyclable, it still fills half of all landfill space. Paper <u>biodegrades</u> more easily than plastic, but it is still a process that takes years.

Plastics come from the waste products of oil refining. Plastic bags require less energy to produce than do paper bags. They can also be recycled for uses such as relining wastebaskets. In landfills, plastic bags take up less room. However, plastic bags are often carelessly thrown away, harming marine life and causing clogs in sewers.

Conclusion Both paper bags and plastic bags use precious natural resources, but both can be recycled. So, what's the best choice? Neither one, we think. Our bag of choice? A reusable cotton bag.

Quick Facts: Why we should switch to reusable shopping bags
In one year, the average American uses about 350 plastic bags.
In one year, 14 million trees are cut down to make 10 billion paper bags.
Reusable bags are stronger and can be used for most shopping trips.

1. How has the author **organized the text?**
   A. The author combines facts about both paper and plastic.
   B. The author presents one fact about paper, then one fact about plastic.
   C. The author describes the benefits of paper, then the benefits of plastic.
   D. The author describes the pros and cons of paper, then the pros and cons of plastic.

2. The "Paper" and "Plastic" sections of the article answer these questions: *Where does it come from?* and *How much energy is used in making it?* What third question is answered by both sections?
   A. Can it be recycled?
   B. Can it harm the environment?
   C. Which is stronger?
   D. Where is it manufactured?

III. Writing and Language Conventions

Directions: *Read the passage. Then, answer each question.*

> (1) I have read my favorite book, *Charlotte's Web,* four times. (2) Each time I find a new treasure. (3) This time, it was the sadness and beauty of growing up. (4) Fern, a young girl, rescues Wilbur the pig. (5) She is devoted to Wilbur, even when he leaves her farm. (6) Charlotte the spider soon becomes Wilbur's friend. (7) Later, though, Fern's interests change. (8) She is more interested in her friends than in the farm animals. (9) Through these changes, Fern shows what lays ahead for all of us. (10) When leaving childhood, we gain much, but we lose much, too.

1. Which words in sentences 1 and 2 best support the writer's **opinion?**

A. book, four
B. favorite, treasure
C. read, treasure
D. favorite, new

2. Which sentence should the writer remove from the passage to maintain **focus?**

A. sentence 1
B. sentence 3
C. sentence 6
D. sentence 8

3. Which **verb tense** does the writer use in sentence 1?

A. present
B. present perfect
C. past
D. past perfect

4. How could the writer revise sentence 2 to **maintain the verb tense** of sentence 1?

A. Each time I have found a new treasure.
B. Each time I am finding a new treasure.
C. Each time I was finding a new treasure.
D. Each time I had found a new treasure.

5. Which **linking verb** would best replace the word *is* in sentence 8?

A. was
B. looks
C. felt
D. becomes

6. What is the correct way to rewrite sentence 9 to fix the **troublesome verb?**

A. Through these changes, Fern shows what lay ahead for all of us.
B. Through these changes, Fern shows what laid ahead for all of us.
C. Through these changes, Fern shows what will lay ahead for all of us.
D. Through these changes, Fern shows what lies ahead for all of us.

Performance Tasks

Directions: *Follow the instructions to complete the tasks below as required by your teacher.*

As you work on each task, incorporate both general academic vocabulary and literary terms you learned in this unit.

Common Core State Standards

RL.6.2, RL.6.3, RL.6.5; RI.6.5; SL.6.1, SL.6.4; L.6.1
[For the full wording of the standards, see the standards chart in the front of your textbook.]

Writing

Task 1: Literature [RL.6.3]
Analyze the Development of a Plot

Write an essay in which you describe how a plot unfolds in a story from this unit.

- Tell which story you will discuss and briefly describe the basic plot.

- Explain the conflict or problem that starts the story moving.

- Then, show how the plot unfolds in a series of scenes. Explain which scenes make up the exposition, the rising action, the climax, and the falling action.

- Describe how each scene adds information that finally leads to the resolution.

Task 2: Literature [RL.6.3; L.6.1]
Describe a Character

Write an essay in which you describe a character from a story in this unit.

- Tell which story and which character you will discuss. Then, explain the basic plot.

- Describe your chosen character. Include details about the character's looks, age, thoughts, feelings, and actions.

- Explain how the character responds to the events of the story. Describe what those responses tell you about the character.

- Discuss how the character changes from the beginning to the end of the story.

- Check to be sure you have used irregular verbs correctly.

Task 3: Literature [RL.6.2; L.6.1]
Determine the Theme

Write an essay in which you explain the theme of a story from this unit.

- Explain which story you will discuss in your essay and write a brief summary of the text.

- State the theme of the story. Then, choose three key details from the story that convey the theme. Consider plot events, characters' actions and reactions, and characters' feelings.

- Organize your ideas logically, using transitional words and phrases.

Task 4: Literature [RL.6.5]
Analyze How a Scene Fits Into a Story

Write an essay about an important scene from a story in this unit.

- Tell which story you will write about and briefly describe the plot.

- Then, identify a scene from the story that you think is very important. Explain the significance of the scene.

- Show how the scene fits into the overall structure of the story. For example, state whether the scene is part of the exposition, rising action, climax, or falling action.

- Explain how the scene adds details about the story's theme or setting or how it helps to move the plot along.

Speaking and Listening

ⓒ Task 5: Literature [RL.6.3; SL.6.4]
Describe a Story's Episodes

Prepare a visual presentation of the main episodes, or scenes, from a story in this unit.

- Break your chosen story into its major scenes. Identify how each scene fits into the parts of a story—exposition, rising action, climax, falling action, resolution.
- Choose a graphic, such as a plot diagram, sequence-of-events chart, or storyboard, to visually present the episodes in logical order.
- As you present information to the class, describe how the story's plot unfolds and how the characters respond as the story moves toward its resolution.
- Practice your presentation in front of a mirror to make sure that you speak clearly and use appropriate eye contact.

ⓒ Task 6: Literature [RL.6.2; SL.6.1]
Determine the Theme

Lead a small-group discussion about the theme of a story from this unit.

- Prepare for the discussion by choosing a story and writing a paragraph about it. State the story's theme and note three details that add to the theme.
- Write down at least three questions you have about the story and its theme.
- Gather with your group and read the paragraph you wrote about the story. Invite the group to respond to your ideas.
- If you find the discussion slowing down, ask one of the questions you wrote down earlier.

- As a group, arrive at an agreement about the story's theme.

ⓒ Task 7: Informational Text [RI.6.5; SL.6.1]
Analyze Structure

With a partner, write and deliver a report explaining the structure of an informational text.

- Choose an informational text from this unit.
- With a partner, analyze how the text is structured or organized.
- Then, choose a paragraph or section of the text that seems especially important. Discuss your thinking with your partner. As you share ideas, take notes.
- Using your notes, write a report in which you explain how the larger text is organized. Show how the section you chose helps to develop the ideas.
- Together, deliver your report to the class.

Is conflict always bad?
At the beginning of Unit 2, you wrote a response to the Big Question. Now that you have completed the unit, write a new response. Discuss how your initial ideas have expanded or changed. Cite specific examples from the literature in this unit, from other subject areas, and from your own life to support your ideas. Use Big Question vocabulary words (see p. 177) in your response.

Featured Titles

In this unit, you have read a variety of short stories. Continue to read on your own. Select works that you enjoy, but challenge yourself to explore new authors and works of increasing depth and complexity. These titles will help you get started.

Literature

The Sherlock Holmes Mysteries
by Sir Arthur Conan Doyle
Signet, 1985

Sherlock Holmes is considered one of the greatest fictional detectives of all time. In this **short story** collection, the brilliant Holmes solves baffling crimes with the help of his partner, Dr. Watson.

An Island Like You: Stories of the Barrio
by Judith Ortiz Cofer
Orchard Books, 1995

In this collection of **short stories,** teenagers deal with conflicts between their American culture and their parents' Puerto Rican heritage.

My Side of the Mountain
by Jean Craighead George
Scholastic Book Services, 1988

In this gripping adventure **novel,** Sam Gribley leaves his comfortable home in New York City, bound for the Catskill Mountains. Read how he bravely endures a harsh year in the wilderness.

Come Sing, Jimmy Jo
by Katherine Paterson
Dutton, 1985

Eleven-year-old James Johnson is the lead singer in his family's country-western band. This **novel** explores the conflicts he faces as the band becomes famous.

The Book of Questions
by Pablo Neruda   EXEMPLAR TEXT

Pablo Neruda wrote this collection of **poems** near the end of his life. Each poem is a thought-provoking question, or series of questions, about nature, life, or death.

Informational Text

All Creatures Great and Small
by James Herriot

James Herriot describes his first years as a veterinarian in this collection of **narrative nonfiction.** His tales of helping animals in the English countryside have delighted readers for over 25 years.

Discoveries: Trouble Ahead

The **essays** in this collection cover topics that range from ancient Greece to baseball. Each one features a conflict that the participants turn into an advantage.

Cathedral: The Story of Its Construction
by David Macaulay   EXEMPLAR TEXT

In this illustrated **informational text,** David Macaulay uses detailed pen-and-ink drawings to show how a magnificent cathedral would have been built in the year 1252.

Preparing to Read Complex Texts

Common Core State Standards

Attentive Reading As you read on your own, ask yourself questions about the text. The questions shown below, and others that you ask as you read, will help you learn and enjoy literature even more.

Reading Literature/Informational Text 10. By the end of the year, read and comprehend literature, including stories, dramas, and poems, and literary nonfiction in the grades 6–8 text complexity band proficiently, with scaffolding as needed at the high end of the range.

When reading short stories, ask yourself...

- Can I clearly picture the time and place of the action? Which details help me do so?
- Can I picture the characters clearly in my mind? Why or why not?
- Do the characters speak and act like real people? Why or why not?
- Which characters do I like? Why? Which characters do I dislike? Why?
- Do I understand why the characters act as they do? Why or why not?
- What does the story mean to me? Does it express a meaning or an insight I find important and true?

 Key Ideas and Details

- Does the story grab my attention right from the beginning? Why or why not?
- Do I want to keep reading? Why or why not?
- Can I follow the sequence of events in the story? Am I confused at any point? If so, what information would make the sequence clearer?
- Do the characters change as the story progresses? If so, do the changes seem believable?
- Are there any passages that I find especially moving, interesting, or well written? If so, why?

Craft and Structure

- How is this story similar to and different from other stories I have read?
- Do I care what happens to the characters? Do I sympathize with them? Why or why not?
- How do my feelings toward the characters affect my experience of reading the story?
- Did the story teach me something new or cause me to look at something in a new way? If so, what did I learn?
- Would I recommend this story to others? Why or why not?
- Would I like to read other works by this author? Why or why not?

 Integration of Ideas

THE BIG ? What is important to *know*?

Types of Nonfiction

PHLit
Online!
www.PHLitOnline.com

Hear It!
• Selection summary audio
• Selection audio
• BQ Tunes

See It!
• Author videos
• Big Question video
• Get Connected videos
• Background videos
• More about the authors
• Illustrated vocabulary words
• Vocabulary flashcards

Do It!
• Interactive journals
• Interactive graphic organizers
• Grammar tutorials
• Interactive vocabulary games
• Test practice

What is important to *know?*

Knowledge does not come only from books and the Internet. It also comes from participating in life. You gain knowledge from your daily experience—when you observe what happens around you and when you examine the ideas and events that spark your curiosity. On the one hand, there is no limit to what you can know. Yet, on the other hand, you cannot know everything.

With all the information that is available to you, it is helpful to decide what you think is most important to know.

Exploring the Big Question

Collaboration: One-on-One Discussion Start thinking about the Big Question by exploring what you already know and what you would like to learn. Begin by making a list. Give at least two examples of things that you think are important to know in each of these situations:

- Getting along with family members
- Doing well in school
- Making new friends
- Learning about the world around you
- Facing challenges

Share your examples with a partner. Discuss why you believe the examples on your list are important. Work together to decide which information seems important. Use the Big Question vocabulary in your discussion.

Connecting to the Literature Each reading in this unit will give you additional insight into the Big Question.

PHLit Online!
www.PHLitOnline.com
- Big Question video
- Illustrated vocabulary words
- Interactive vocabulary games
- BQ Tunes

Learning Big Question Vocabulary

Common Core
State Standards

Speaking and Listening
1. Engage effectively in a range of collaborative discussions with diverse partners on grade 6 topics, texts, and issues, building on others' ideas and expressing their own clearly.

Language
4.d. Verify the preliminary determination of the meaning of a word or phrase.
6. Acquire and use accurately grade-appropriate general academic and domain-specific words and phrases; gather vocabulary knowledge when considering a word or phrase important to comprehension or expression.

Acquire and Use Academic Vocabulary Academic vocabulary is the language you encounter in textbooks and on standardized tests. Review the definitions of these academic vocabulary words.

concept (kän´ sept´) *n.* general idea or notion

distinguish (di stiŋ´ gwish) *v.* mark as different; set apart

examine (eg zam´ ən) *v.* study or look at closely

judge (juj) *v.* form an opinion about; decide on

measure (mezh´ ər) *v.* find the value of

observe (əb zʉrv´) *v.* see or notice

purpose (pʉr´ pəs) *n.* use

question (kwes´ chən) *v.* doubt; wonder about

refer (ri fʉr´) *v.* turn to for information such as to a book or an expert

source (sôrs) *n.* something that gives information, such as a book, Web site, or person

study (stud´ ē) *v.* look into deeply

Use these words as you complete Big Question activities in this unit that involve reading, writing, speaking, and listening.

Gather Vocabulary Knowledge Additional Big Question words are listed below. Categorize the words by deciding whether you know each one well, know it a little bit, or do not know it at all.

guess	**limit**
knowledge	**narrow**

Then, do the following:

1. Write the definitions of the words you know.
2. Consult a dictionary to confirm the meaning of the words you know. Revise your definition if necessary.
3. Next, use a print or an online dictionary to look up the meanings of the words you do not know. Then, write the meanings.
4. Use all of the words in a brief paragraph about knowledge.

Elements of Nonfiction

Nonfiction writing tells about real people, places, objects, or events.

Nonfiction writing is about real life. Some forms of nonfiction, such as histories, have been around since ancient times. Others, such as blogs and Web pages, came into being more recently. Nonfiction writing changes with people and technology. It is a large, ever-developing category of literature. Still, all forms of nonfiction have certain basic elements.

- They are written for one or more **purposes,** or reasons.
- They express the writer's unique **point of view,** or perspective, about a subject.
- They use words and phrases that project a certain **tone,** or attitude.
- They **develop or explain ideas** in a logical, organized way.

Informative Texts Many nonfiction texts—like this textbook—are informative. Their main purpose is to inform, or give information to the reader. Newspaper reports, encyclopedia articles, and science books are examples of informative texts.

Narrative Nonfiction Narrative nonfiction tells the story of real people, places, things, and events. These texts usually aim to entertain *and* inform the reader. They might tell the story of a single person's life or the story of an entire group of people. They might describe a dramatic, real-life event.

Literary Nonfiction Authors of literary nonfiction use elements of literature, such as language, in creative ways. They choose words that stir up feelings in the reader. These writers may also use the kinds of comparisons you might find in a poem, or they may include vivid details to make their writing rich and interesting.

The best nonfiction writing opens new windows on the world for the reader. It says, "This is what I see, from the place where I happen to be."

Nonfiction texts . . .	This element of nonfiction is called . . .
Are written from the unique perspective of the author.	Point of View
Are written for one or more reasons.	Author's Purpose
Use specific words to convey specific meanings.	Word Choice
Use vivid details that appeal to the five senses: sight, sound, touch, taste, and smell.	Imagery
Organize ideas in ways that are easy for readers to follow.	Organization

Forms of Nonfiction

There are many forms of nonfiction.

An **autobiography** is a story about the writer's own life, told by the writer. Autobiographies take many different forms.

- A **memoir** describes one or more meaningful events and may express strong feelings.
- A **diary** is a personal record of events and experiences. Most diaries are updated regularly.
- An **autobiographical sketch** is a brief description of the high points of a person's life.

An **essay** is a short work about a single subject. Essays are written for many purposes.

- A **persuasive essay, or argument,** is meant to convince readers to adopt a particular point of view or take a certain action.
- A **narrative essay** tells the story of an event that happened in real life, often one that the writer witnessed, or saw.
- An **expository essay** presents facts, ideas, and explanations.
- A **reflective essay** presents the writer's thoughts and beliefs about a subject or an event.

A **speech** is an oral, or spoken, presentation of a speaker's ideas and beliefs.

- **Persuasive speeches** urge listeners to adopt certain beliefs or take certain actions.
- An **address** is a formal speech to a specific group of people. It may offer deep thoughts on an important occasion.
- A **talk** is an informal presentation in which the speaker shares his or her knowledge on a subject.

In This Section

Elements of Nonfiction

Determining Author's Purpose and Point of View

Analyzing the Development of Key Ideas

Close Read: Author's Purpose
- Model Text
- Practice Text

After You Read

 Common Core
State Standards

RI.6.3, RI.6.4, RI.6.5, RI.6.6
[For the full wording of the standards, see the standards chart in the front of your textbook.]

Other Forms of Nonfiction

Advertisement	Letter	Editorial	Functional Text
• Written for a target audience who might be interested in a product or service • Often includes visuals • Aims to persuade	• Addressed to a specific individual or group • May be personal or formal • Aims to share thoughts, describe events, or request action or information	• States the writer's position on an issue • Featured in newspapers or magazines • Aims to persuade	• Presents facts in an easy-to-read form • Examples include schedules, menus, and charts • Aims to inform

Determining Author's Purpose and Point of View

 **Common Core State Standards**

Reading Informational Text 4. Determine the meaning of words and phrases as they are used in a text, including the figurative, connotative, and technical meanings.

Reading Informational Text 6. Determine an author's point of view or purpose in a text and explain how it is conveyed in the text.

A nonfiction text is written for specific **purposes** and expresses the author's unique **point of view**.

Author's Purpose An author's purpose is his or her main reason for writing. Nonfiction texts are often written to **inform, persuade, entertain, describe,** or **express feelings.** In many cases, an author has more than one reason for writing. For example, an author might write an essay about the impacts of an oil spill to describe and to persuade.

Point of View Every writer views his or her subject through a certain lens, or **point of view,** that is shaped by the writer's values and beliefs.

Example: Graduation Speech

Today we celebrate your goals and accomplishments. We also celebrate your past and future failures—and the lessons that you have learned and will learn from them.

Point of View

The author respects the students, values the marking of occasions, and views life as a learning process.

Word Choice Looking closely at an author's word choice can help you understand his or her point of view. Authors choose specific words and phrases to stir up positive or negative feelings, or **connotations.**

Idea: "Love your neighbor"	Author's Point of View
Positive Connotation: We all know the **timeless truth** "Love your neighbor."	The author values the saying.
Negative Connotation: We have all heard the **tired cliché** "Love your neighbor."	The author finds the saying meaningless.

Tone Tone is the feeling or attitude that you can "hear" in the lines of a work. Tone can usually be summed up in a single word. The tone of the first sentence in the chart shown above might be described as approving. The tone of the second sentence might be described as critical.

Analyzing the Development of Key Ideas

Works of nonfiction express and develop key ideas.

 **Common Core State Standards**

Reading Informational Text 3. Analyze in detail how a key individual, event, or idea is introduced, illustrated, and elaborated in a text.

Reading Informational Text 5. Analyze how a particular sentence, paragraph, chapter, or section fits into the overall structure of a text and contributes to the development of the ideas.

Key Idea All nonfiction texts center on one or more **key ideas.** A key idea is the central idea a writer wishes to convey. Key ideas are usually linked to an author's purpose and the type of text he or she is writing.

- In a persuasive speech meant to convince listeners to vote, the key idea might be: Voting is an important right and responsibility for Americans.
- In an essay meant to reflect on sports in society, the key idea might be: Athletes should be role models.

Key ideas are sometimes stated directly; other times, they are *implied,* or suggested. To understand implied ideas, examine all the parts and details of the text to see what they have in common. Look for the key idea of each paragraph and see how it relates to the overall key idea of the text.

Developing and Supporting the Key Idea Whether stated or unstated, a key idea must be developed and supported. Writers use different types of details to elaborate a key idea.

Type of Support	Example
Anecdotes: brief stories used to make a point	"When I was a boy," Uncle Ramos began . . .
Facts: pieces of data that can be proven	4,000 tons of cans have been recycled.
Figurative language: colorful comparisons	Rivers are the bloodstreams of the world.
Examples: specific cases that illustrate ideas	Boots are "in." Cowboy boots are the most popular.
Quotations: the exact words of a key person	"I have a dream," said Dr. Martin Luther King, Jr.

Writers arrange supporting details in logical, artful ways.

- Writers may introduce the key idea with an anecdote or example at the beginning of a work.
- Writers develop the key idea with blocks of supporting ideas. They group related **sentences** into **paragraphs** and may divide long works into **chapters** or **sections.**
- Writers give their piece an **overall structure.** If the work tells a story, for example, a writer may arrange the events in time order.

Close Read: Author's Purpose

All elements of a nonfiction text point to the purpose.

When you read a nonfiction text, start by looking at the title of the work. It may give you a clue about the author's purpose or the key idea. As you begin to read, look for a stated key idea. If you do not find one, pay attention to the author's use of supporting details. Watch for repeated ideas and notice word choice and tone. Think about the author's point of view. Ask yourself, "What does this author want me to know, do, or feel?"

Clues to the Author's Purpose

Title Look at the **title.** Does it give you a clue about the author's purpose or key idea?	**Ideas** Notice how the author **develops ideas.** How is the writing organized? What types of supporting details are used?
Key Idea Look for a **key idea.** Does the author state it directly? If not, look for repeated ideas.	Find examples of: • **figurative language,** or creative comparison • words with positive or negative **connotations,** or emotional associations
Point of View Identify the **author's point of view,** or perspective. What lens does the author look through? How does this affect what he or she says?	• **anecdotes,** or stories that make a point • **examples,** or specific items in a general category
Tone Think about the **tone** of the text. What is the author's attitude, or main feeling, about his or her subject?	• **facts,** or pieces of information that can be proved true • **quotations,** or someone's exact words

Author's Purpose
What is the **author's purpose?** What does the author want readers to know, feel, or do?

© EXEMPLAR TEXT

Model

About the Text This text is from a biography of American folk singer Woody Guthrie (1912–1967). Guthrie became famous as a traveling musician during the Great Depression of the 1930s. His song "This Land Is Your Land" became widely known in the 1960s and remains his most popular song today.

---

from "Rambling 'Round" from *This Land Was Made for You and Me* by Elizabeth Partridge

"I hate a song that makes you think that you're not any good. I hate a song that makes you think you are just born to lose. I am out to fight those kind of songs to my very last breath of air and my last drop of blood."

Woody Guthrie could never cure himself of wandering off. One minute he'd be there, the next he'd be gone, vanishing without a word to anyone, abandoning those he loved best. He'd throw on a few extra shirts, one on top of the other, sling his guitar over his shoulder, and hit the road. He'd stick out his thumb and hitchhike, swing onto moving freight trains, and hunker down with other traveling men in flophouses, hobo jungles, and Hoovervilles across Depression America.

He moved restlessly from state to state, soaking up songs: work songs, mountain and cowboy songs, sea chanteys, songs from the southern chain gangs. He added them to the dozens he already knew from his childhood until he was bursting with American folk songs. Playing the guitar and singing, he started making up new ones: hard-bitten, rough-edged songs that told it like it was, full of anger and hardship and hope and love.

Woody said the best songs came to him when he was walking down a road. He always had fifteen or twenty songs running around in his mind, just waiting to be put together. Sometimes he knew the words, but not the melody. Usually he'd borrow a tune that was already well known—the simpler the better. As he walked along, he tried to catch a good, easy song that people could sing the first time they heard it, remember, and sing again later.

Title "Rambling 'Round" suggests that this work will be about a person on the move.

Quotation The author introduces her subject with the words of Woody Guthrie himself.

Key Idea The first sentence states the author's key idea— Woody Guthrie was always on the move.

Examples The author names specific kinds of songs to give the reader a flavor for the era.

Author's Purpose This upbeat anecdote matches the author's tone. She wants the reader to learn about Guthrie and to like him.

Independent Practice

About the Selection This nonfiction text was written by Zlata Filipović. When she was a girl, Filipović lived in Sarajevo (sär´ ə yä´ vō), a city in southeastern Europe. Between 1992 and 1996, Sarajevo was under attack during a civil war.

from *Zlata's Diary* by Zlata Filipović

Monday, March 30, 1992

Hey, Diary! You know what I think? Since Anne Frank[1] called her diary Kitty, maybe I could give you a name too. What about:

ASFALTINA PIDZAMETA
SEFIKA HIKMETA
SEVALA MIMMY

or something else???

I'm thinking, thinking . . .
I've decided! I'm going to call you
MIMMY
All right, then, let's start.

Dear Mimmy,

It's almost half-term. We're all studying for our tests. Tomorrow we're supposed to go to a classical music concert at the Skenderija Hall. Our teacher says we shouldn't go because there will be 10,000 people, pardon me, children, there, and somebody might take us as hostages or plant a bomb in the concert hall. Mommy says I shouldn't go. So I won't.

Hey! You know who won the Yugovision Song Contest?! EXTRA NENA!!!???

I'm afraid to say this next thing. Melica says she heard at the hairdresser's that on Saturday, April 4, 1992, there's going to be BOOM—BOOM, BANG—BANG, CRASH Sarajevo. Translation: they're going to bomb Sarajevo.

Love,
Zlata

---

1. **Anne Frank** In 1942, 13-year-old Anne Frank began a diary that she kept for the two years she and her family and some others hid from the Nazis in an attic in Amsterdam. Anne died in a concentration camp in 1945. Her father published parts of the diary in 1947, and it has since become a classic.

Sunday, April 12, 1992

Dear Mimmy,

The new sections of town—Dobrinja, Mojmilo, Vojnicko polje—are being badly shelled. Everything is being destroyed, burned, the people are in shelters. Here in the middle of town, where we live, it's different. It's quiet.

People go out. It was a nice warm spring day today. We went out too. Vaso Miskin Street was full of people, children. It looked like a peace march. People came out to be together, they don't want war. They want to live and enjoy themselves the way they used to. That's only natural, isn't it? Who likes or wants war, when it's the worst thing in the world?

I keep thinking about the march I joined today. It's bigger and stronger than war. That's why it will win. The people must be the ones to win, not the war, because war has nothing to do with humanity. War is something inhuman.

Zlata

Figurative Language
To what does Zlata compare the crowd of people? Why does she say it will "win"?

Tuesday, April 14, 1992

Dear Mimmy,

People are leaving Sarajevo. The airport, train and bus stations are packed. I saw sad pictures on TV of people parting. Families, friends separating. Some are leaving, others staying. It's so sad. Why? These people and children aren't guilty of anything. Keka and Braco[2] came early this morning. They're in the kitchen with Mommy and Daddy, whispering. Keka and Mommy are crying. I don't think they know what to do—whether to stay or to go. Neither way is good.

Zlata

Key Idea What fact does Zlata offer at the beginning of this entry? What stated idea about war does this fact support?

---

2. **Keka and Braco** nicknames of a husband and wife who are friends of Zlata's parents.

Practice continued

Saturday, May 2, 1992

Author's Purpose
Compare this entry to
the first one. How has
Zlata's purpose for
writing changed?

Dear Mimmy,

Today was truly, absolutely the worst day ever in Sarajevo. The shooting started around noon. Mommy and I moved into the hall. Daddy was in his office, under our apartment, at the time. We told him on the intercom to run quickly to the downstairs lobby where we'd meet him. We brought Cicko[3] with us. The gunfire was getting worse, and we couldn't get over the wall to the Bobars',[4] so we ran down to our own cellar.

The cellar is ugly, dark, smelly. Mommy, who's terrified of mice, had two fears to cope with. The three of us were in the same corner as the other day. We listened to the pounding shells, the shooting, the thundering noise overhead. We even heard planes. At one moment I realized that this awful cellar was the only place that could save our lives. Suddenly, it started to look almost warm and nice. It was the only way we could defend ourselves against all this terrible shooting. We heard glass shattering in our street. Horrible. I put my fingers in my ears to block out the terrible sounds. I was worried about Cicko. We had left him behind in the lobby. Would he catch cold there? Would something hit him? I was terribly hungry and thirsty. We had left our half-cooked lunch in the kitchen.

When the shooting died down a bit, Daddy ran over to our apartment and brought us back some sandwiches. He said he could smell something burning and that the phones weren't working. He brought our TV set down to the cellar. That's when we learned that the main post office (near us) was on fire and that they had kidnapped our President. At around 8:00 we went back up to our apartment. Almost every window in our street was broken. Ours were all right, thank God. I saw the post office in flames. A terrible sight. The fire-fighters battled with the raging fire. Daddy took a few photos of the post office being devoured by the flames. He said they wouldn't come out because I had been fiddling with something on the camera. I was sorry. The whole apartment smelled of the burning fire. God, and I used to pass by there every day. It had just been done up. It was huge and beautiful, and now it was being swallowed up by the flames. It was disappearing. That's what this neighborhood of mine looks like, my Mimmy.

Connotations Which
word in this sentence
has strong negative
connotations? What
does this word make
you see or feel?

Tone How would you
describe the tone of
these sentences?

---

3. **Cicko** (chēk´ ō) Zlata's canary.
4. **Bobars'** (Bō´ bërs) next-door neighbors.

I wonder what it's like in other parts of town? I heard on the radio that it was awful around the Eternal Flame.[5] The place is knee-deep in glass. We're worried about Grandma and Granddad. They live there. Tomorrow, if we can go out, we'll see how they are. A terrible day. This has been the worst, most awful day in my eleven-year-old life. I hope it will be the only one. Mommy and Daddy are very edgy. I have to go to bed.

Ciao![6]
Zlata

Tuesday, May 5, 1992

Dear Mimmy,
The shooting seems to be dying down. I guess they've caused enough misery, although I don't know why. It has something to do with politics. I just hope the "kids" come to some agreement. Oh, if only they would, so we could live and breathe as human beings again. The things that have happened here these past few days are terrible. I want it to stop forever. PEACE! PEACE!

I didn't tell you, Mimmy, that we've rearranged things in the apartment. My room and Mommy and Daddy's are too dangerous to be in. They face the hills, which is where they're shooting from. If only you knew how scared I am to go near the windows and into those rooms. So, we turned a safe corner of the sitting room into a "bedroom." We sleep on mattresses on the floor. It's strange and awful. But, it's safer that way. We've turned everything around for safety. We put Cicko in the kitchen. He's safe there, although once the shooting starts there's nowhere safe except the cellar. I suppose all this will stop and we'll all go back to our usual places.

Ciao!
Zlata

Key Idea Zlata has begun to repeat a certain idea. State it in your own words.

Author's Point of View Do you think Zlata is being realistic about the situation she and her family are in? Explain.

---

5. **Eternal Flame** Sarajevo landmark that honors those who died resisting the Nazi occupation during World War II.
6. **Ciao!** (chou) *interj.* hello or goodbye.

Practice continued

Anecdote How does this sentence help Zlata express what she is experiencing?

Tone What feeling does Zlata convey by capitalizing these words?

Thursday, May 7, 1992

Dear Mimmy,

I was almost positive the war would stop, but today . . . Today a shell fell on the park in front of my house, the park where I used to play and sit with my girlfriends. A lot of people were hurt. From what I hear Jaca, Jaca's mother, Selma, Nina, our neighbor Dado and who knows how many other people who happened to be there were wounded. Dado, Jaca and her mother have come home from the hospital, Selma lost a kidney but I don't know how she is, because she's still in the hospital. AND NINA IS DEAD. A piece of shrapnel lodged in her brain and she died. She was such a sweet, nice little girl. We went to kindergarten together, and we used to play together in the park. Is it possible I'll never see Nina again? Nina, an innocent eleven-year-old little girl—the victim of a stupid war. I feel sad. I cry and wonder why? She didn't do anything. A disgusting war has destroyed a young child's life. Nina. I'll always remember you as a wonderful little girl.

Love, Mimmy,
Zlata

Monday, June 29, 1992

Dear Mimmy,

BOREDOM!!! SHOOTING!!! SHELLING!!! PEOPLE BEING KILLED!!! DESPAIR!!! HUNGER!!! MISERY!!! FEAR!!!

That's my life! The life of an innocent eleven-year-old schoolgirl!! A schoolgirl without a school, without the fun and excitement of school. A child without games, without friends, without the sun, without birds, without nature, without fruit, without chocolate or sweets, with just a little powdered milk. In short, a child without a childhood. A wartime child. I now realize that I am really living through a war, I am witnessing an ugly, disgusting war. I and thousands of other children in this town that is being destroyed, that is crying, weeping, seeking help, but getting none. God, will this ever stop, will I ever be a schoolgirl again, will I ever enjoy my childhood again? I once heard that childhood is the most wonderful time of your life. And it is. I loved it, and now an ugly war is taking it all away from me. Why? I feel sad. I feel like crying. I am crying.

Your Zlata

Thursday, October 29, 1992

Dear Mimmy,

Mommy and Auntie Ivanka (from her office) have received grants to specialize in Holland. They have letters of guarantee,[7] and there's even one for me. But Mommy can't decide. If she accepts, she leaves behind Daddy, her parents, her brother. I think it's a hard decision to make. One minute I think—no, I'm against it. But then I remember the war, winter, hunger, my stolen childhood and I feel like going. Then I think of Daddy, Grandma and Granddad, and I don't want to go. It's hard to know what to do. I'm really on edge, Mimmy, I can't write anymore.

Your Zlata

Monday, November 2, 1992

Dear Mimmy,

Mommy thought it over, talked to Daddy, Grandma and Granddad, and to me, and she's decided to go. The reason for her decision is—ME. What's happening in Sarajevo is already too much for me, and the coming winter will make it even harder. All right. But . . . well, I suppose it's better for me to go. I really can't stand it here anymore. I talked to Auntie Ivanka today and she told me that this war is hardest on the children, and that the children should be got out of the city. Daddy will manage, maybe he'll even get to come with us.

Ciao!
Zlata

Anecdote These two entries tell a story. What makes the story suspenseful? What key idea does the story support?

---

7. **letters of guarantee** letters from people or companies promising to help individuals who wanted to leave the country during the war.

Practice continued

Dear Mimmy,

Today is my birthday. My first wartime birthday. Twelve years old. Congratulations. Happy birthday to me!

The day started off with kisses and congratulations. First Mommy and Daddy, then everyone else. Mommy and Daddy gave me three Chinese vanity cases—with flowers on them!

As usual there was no electricity. Auntie Melica came with her family (Kenan, Naida, Nihad) and gave me a book. And Braco Lajtner came, of course. The whole neighborhood got together in the evening. I got chocolate, vitamins, a heart-shaped soap (small, orange), a key chain with a picture of Maja and Bojana, a pendant made of a stone from Cyprus, a ring (silver) and earrings (bingo!).

The table was nicely laid, with little rolls, fish and rice salad, cream cheese (with Feta), canned corned beef, a pie, and, of course—a birthday cake. Not how it used to be, but there's a war on. Luckily there was no shooting, so we could celebrate.

It was nice, but something was missing. It's called peace!

Your Zlata

Development of Ideas What kind of supporting details does Zlata provide here?

Key Idea How do all the examples given above strengthen Zlata's key idea?

Tuesday, July 27, 1993

Dear Mimmy,

Journalists, reporters, TV and radio crews from all over the world (even Japan). They're interested in you, Mimmy, and ask me about you, but also about me. It's exciting. Nice. Unusual for a wartime child.

My days have changed a little. They're more interesting now. It takes my mind off things. When I go to bed at night I think about the day behind me. Nice, as though it weren't wartime, and with such thoughts I happily fall asleep.

But in the morning, when the wheels of the water carts wake me up, I realize that there's a war on, that mine is a wartime life. SHOOTING, NO ELECTRICITY, NO WATER, NO GAS, NO FOOD. Almost no life.

Zlata

Point of View Why does Zlata find the journalists' attention "unusual"?

Thursday, October 7, 1993

Dear Mimmy,

Things are the way they used to be, lately. There's no shooting (thank God), I go to school, read, play the piano . . .

Winter is approaching, but we have nothing to heat with.

I look at the calendar and it seems as though this year of 1993 will again be marked by war. God, we've lost two years listening to gunfire, battling with electricity, water, food, and waiting for peace.

I look at Mommy and Daddy. In two years they've aged ten. And me? I haven't aged, but I've grown, although I honestly don't know how. I don't eat fruit or vegetables, I don't drink juices, I don't eat meat . . . I am a child of rice, peas and spaghetti. There I am talking about food again. I often catch myself dreaming about chicken, a good cutlet, pizza, lasagna . . . Oh, enough of that.

Zlata

Tone Zlata says her family "battled" with the electricity. What attitude toward life does this word suggest?

Practice continued

Tone What is Zlata's tone in this entry? Why?

Tuesday, October 12, 1993

Dear Mimmy,

I don't remember whether I told you that last summer I sent a letter through school to a pen-pal in America. It was a letter for an American girl or boy.

Today I got an answer. A boy wrote to me. His name is Brandon, he's twelve like me, and lives in Harrisburg, Pennsylvania. It really made me happy.

I don't know who invented the mail and letters, but thank you whoever you are. I now have a friend in America, and Brandon has a friend in Sarajevo. This is my first letter from across the Atlantic. And in it is a reply envelope, and a lovely pencil.

A Canadian TV crew and journalist from *The Sunday Times* (Janine) came to our gym class today. They brought me two chocolate bars. What a treat. It's been a long time since I've had sweets.

Love,
Zlata

December 1993

Dear Mimmy,

PARIS. There's electricity, there's water, there's gas. There's, there's . . . life, Mimmy. Yes, life; bright lights, traffic, people, food . . . Don't think I've gone nuts, Mimmy. Hey, listen to me, Paris!? No, I'm not crazy, I'm not kidding, it really is Paris and (can you believe it?) me in it. Me, my Mommy and my Daddy. At last. You're 100% sure I'm crazy, but I'm serious, I'm telling you, dear Mimmy, that I have arrived in Paris. I've come to be with you. You're mine again now and together we're moving into the light. The darkness has played out its part. The darkness is behind us; now we're bathed in light lit by good people. Remember that—good people. Bulb by bulb, not candles, but bulb by bulb, and me bathing in the lights of Paris. Yes, Paris. Incredible. You don't understand. You know, I don't think I understand either. I feel as though I must be crazy, dreaming, as though it's a fairy tale, but it's all TRUE.

Key Idea How does the key idea of this entry differ from earlier ones?

Author's Purpose What does Zlata want her readers—and herself—to believe is true?

After You Read

from Zlata's Diary

1. **Key Ideas and Details (a)** What hardships did Zlata and her family endure during the war? **(b) Infer:** How did these hardships change Zlata's life? **(c) Analyze:** Why did Zlata have mixed feelings about leaving Sarajevo?

2. **Key Ideas and Details** Zlata describes the horrors of war from a specific **point of view.** How might her perspective differ from that of her parents?

3. **Key Ideas and Details (a)** What is Zlata's **purpose** for starting a diary? **(b)** How does this purpose change over time?

4. **Key Ideas and Details (a)** With what **key idea** does the diary conclude? **(b)** What is the **tone** of the diary's last entry? What words or phrases project this tone?

5. **Craft and Structure (a)** What makes this diary an example of **nonfiction? (b)** What makes this diary a type of **autobiography?**

6. **Craft and Structure (a)** Why do you think people around the world read Zlata's diary? **(b)** Why do you think Zlata believed her experiences during the war were important?

7. **Integration of Knowledge and Ideas (a)** Using a chart like the one shown below, find and jot down examples of specific types of **nonfiction** writing in Zlata's diary.

	Examples of Nonfiction Writing
Narration	
Description	

(b) Collaboration: Compare your responses with those of a partner. Then, discuss how the examples you have cited add to the impact and meaning of Zlata's diary.

Leveled Texts

Build your skills and improve your comprehension of nonfiction with texts of increasing complexity.

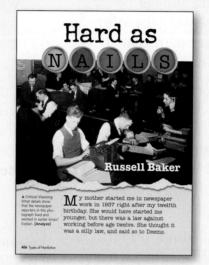

Read **"Water"** to find out how young Helen Keller, who was blind and deaf, first discovered how to communicate with words.

Read **"Hard as Nails"** to learn about the boyhood triumphs and challenges Russell Baker experienced delivering newspapers.

Common Core State Standards

Meet these standards with either **"Water"** (p. 398) or **"Hard as Nails"** (p. 406).

Reading Informational Text
6. Determine an author's point of view or purpose in a text and explain how it is conveyed in the text. *(Reading Skill: Author's Purpose)*

Writing
3. Write narratives to develop real or imagined experiences or events using effective technique, relevant descriptive details, and well-structured event sequences. *(Writing: Letter)*

8. Gather relevant information from multiple print and digital sources; assess the credibility of each source. *(Research and Technology: Research Project)*

Speaking and Listening
1. Engage effectively in a range of collaborative discussions with diverse partners on *grade 6 topics, texts, and issues,*
building on others' ideas and expressing their own clearly. *(Research and Technology: Research Project)*

Language
1. Demonstrate command of the conventions of standard English grammar and usage when writing or speaking. *(Conventions: Adjectives and Articles)*

6. Acquire and use accurately grade-appropriate general academic and domain-specific words and phrases; gather vocabulary knowledge when considering a word or phrase important to comprehension or expression. *(Vocabulary: Word Study)*

Reading Skill: Author's Purpose

An **author's purpose** is the main reason the author writes a literary work. When writing nonfiction, an author can have more than one purpose. For example, in an article about trees, the author's purposes may be to inform readers about fir trees and to persuade readers that fir trees should be protected.

Learn to recognize details that may indicate the author's purpose:

- Facts and statistics are used to *inform* or *persuade.*
- Stories about experiences are used to *entertain.*
- Opinions and thoughts are used to *reflect* on an experience.

Using the Strategy: Author's Purpose Chart

As you read, use a chart such as the one shown to record details from the texts that convey author's purpose.

Topic of Essay	Details About Topic	Author's Specific Purpose

Literary Analysis: Autobiographical Essay

An **autobiographical essay** tells about an event or a time in the author's own life and is written in the first person. The author may include his or her own thoughts, feelings, and reactions.

Authors also include specific details to achieve a purpose. For example, authors may share lessons they have learned from the mistakes they have made.

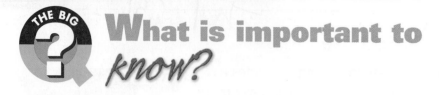

What is important to *know?*

Writing About the Big Question

In "Water," Helen Keller's teacher helps her to begin to communicate using words. Use this sentence starter to develop your ideas about the Big Question.

One important **purpose** of communicating clearly with others is _____.

While You Read Look for details that show how learning to communicate changed Helen Keller's outlook on life.

Vocabulary

Read each word and its definition. Decide whether you know the word well, know it a little bit, or do not know it at all. After you read, see how your knowledge of each word has increased.

- **imitate** (im´ i tāt´) *v.* copy; mimic (p. 399) *We whistle to imitate the sounds of birds.* *imitating v. imitation n.*

- **persisted** (pər sist´ əd) *v.* refused to give up (p. 400) *Juan persisted in calling me until I answered.* *persistently adv. persistent adj. persistence n.*

- **fragments** (frag´ mənts) *n.* small, broken-off parts (p. 400) *Fragments of glass littered the street.* *fragmented v. fragmenting v. fragmentation n.*

- **sentiment** (sen´ tə mənt) *n.* a tender feeling or emotion (p. 400) *The heartfelt sentiment in her letter made me cry.* *sentimental adj.*

- **barriers** (bar´ ē ərz) *n.* things that make progress difficult; obstacles (p. 401) *The language barriers between us made it hard to communicate.* *barrier n.*

- **repentance** (ri pen´ təns) *n.* deep sorrow and regret (p. 401) *Her tears made her repentance seem sincere.* *repent v. repented v.*

Word Study

The **Latin suffix -ance** means "the act or process of doing, being, or feeling." It is used to turn a verb into a noun.

In this narrative essay, Helen Keller feels a sense of sorrow, or **repentance,** for breaking her doll.

Helen Keller
(1880–1968)

Author of
Water

A serious illness left Helen Keller blind and deaf before she was two years old. Helen Keller's family eventually hired Anne Sullivan, a teacher from the Perkins Institution for the Blind, to help her learn to communicate.

Early Lessons In "Water," an excerpt from her autobiography, Keller describes her early lessons with Sullivan. Eventually, Keller learned to read by using Braille (raised dots that stand for letters), to type, and to speak. Keller and Sullivan developed a remarkable teacher and student relationship as well as a unique friendship.

BACKGROUND FOR THE ESSAY

Helen Keller and Anne Sullivan

When teacher Anne Sullivan entered her life, seven-year-old Helen Keller did not even know what words were. She did not understand that objects and ideas have "names." Sullivan herself had lost almost all of her sight and became a student at the Perkins Institute. Although surgery restored some of Sullivan's sight, her experience inspired her to bring language to Keller.

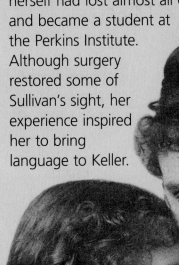

DID YOU KNOW?

After gaining fame for being the first deaf and blind person to graduate from college, Helen Keller wrote several books about her challenging and rewarding relationship with Anne Sullivan.

Water

Helen Keller

*T*he morning after my teacher came she led me into her room and gave me a doll. The little blind children at the Perkins Institution had sent it and Laura Bridgman had dressed it; but I did not know this until afterward. When I had played with it a little while, Miss Sullivan slowly spelled into my hand the word "d-o-l-l." I was at once interested in this finger play and tried to imitate it. When I finally succeeded in making the letters correctly I was flushed with childish pleasure and pride. Running downstairs to my mother I held up my hand and made the letters for doll. I did not know that I was spelling a word or even that words existed; I was simply making my fingers go in monkey-like imitation. In the days that

Spiral Review
Word Choice Why do you think the author chose to spell "d-o-l-l" as she did?

Vocabulary
imitate (im′ i tāt′) *v.* copy; mimic

Autobiographical Essay
What details so far indicate that this is a narrative essay?

Vocabulary
persisted (pər sist′ əd) *v.* refused to give up

fragments (frag′ mənts) *n.* small, broken-off parts

sentiment (sen′ tə mənt) *n.* a tender feeling or emotion

followed I learned to spell in this uncomprehending way a great many words, among them *pin, hat, cup* and a few verbs like *sit, stand* and *walk*. But my teacher had been with me several weeks before I understood that everything has a name. •

One day, while I was playing with my new doll, Miss Sullivan put my big rag doll into my lap also, spelled "d-o-l-l" and tried to make me understand that "d-o-l-l" applied to both. Earlier in the day we had had a tussle over the words "m-u-g" and "w-a-t-e-r." Miss Sullivan had tried to impress it upon me that "m-u-g" is *mug* and that "w-a-t-e-r" is *water*, but I persisted in confounding the two. In despair she had dropped the subject for the time, only to renew it at the first opportunity. I became impatient at her repeated attempts and, seizing the new doll, I dashed it upon the floor. I was keenly delighted when I felt the fragments of the broken doll at my feet. Neither sorrow nor regret followed my passionate outburst. I had not loved the doll. In the still, dark world in which I lived there was no strong sentiment or tenderness. I felt my teacher sweep the fragments to one side of the hearth,[1] and I had a sense of satisfaction that the cause of my discomfort was removed. She brought me my hat, and I knew I was going

---

1. hearth (härth) *n.* the stone or brick floor of a fireplace, sometimes extending into the room.

◀ **Critical Viewing**
What details in this picture show the relationship between Miss Sullivan and Helen? **[Analyze]**

out into the warm sunshine. This thought, if a wordless sensation may be called a thought, made me hop and skip with pleasure. •

We walked down the path to the well-house, attracted by the fragrance of the honeysuckle with which it was covered. Some one was drawing water and my teacher placed my hand under the spout. As the cool stream gushed over one hand she spelled into the other the word *water*, first slowly, then rapidly. I stood still, my whole attention fixed upon the motions of her fingers. Suddenly I felt a misty consciousness as of something forgotten—a thrill of returning thought; and somehow the mystery of language was revealed to me. I knew then that "w-a-t-e-r" meant the wonderful cool something that was flowing over my hand. That living word awakened my soul, gave it light, hope, joy, set it free! There were barriers still, it is true, but barriers that could in time be swept away.

I left the well-house eager to learn. Everything had a name, and each name gave birth to a new thought. As we returned to the house every object which I touched seemed to quiver with life. That was because I saw everything with the strange, new sight that had come to me. On entering the door I remembered the doll I had broken. I felt my way to the hearth and picked up the pieces. I tried vainly to put them together. Then my eyes filled with tears; for I realized what I had done, and for the first time I felt repentance and sorrow. •

Author's Purpose
Based on these details, what do you think is Keller's purpose for writing? Explain.

Vocabulary
barriers (bar´ ē ərz) *n.* things that make progress difficult; obstacles
repentance (ri pen´ təns) *n.* deep sorrow and regret

 Reading Check

How does Helen learn the meaning of the word *water*?

I learned a great many new words that day. I do not remember what they all were; but I do know that *mother, father, sister, teacher* were among them—words that were to make the world blossom for me, "like Aaron's rod, with flowers." It would have been difficult to find a happier child than I was as I lay in my crib at the close of that eventful day and lived over the joys it had brought me, and for the first time longed for a new day to come.

Author's Purpose
What purpose do the details in this paragraph best support?

Critical Thinking

©1. Key Ideas and Details (a) Which event helps Helen to recognize the meaning of *w-a-t-e-r?* **(b) Compare and Contrast:** Explain how water from the pump is the same as and different from water in the mug.

©2. Key Ideas and Details (a) How does Keller feel when she goes to bed on the night she learned about *w-a-t-e-r?* **(b) Infer:** Why does she feel that way? **(c) Draw Conclusions:** What will Keller want to do when she wakes up? Support your conclusion.

©3. Key Ideas and Details (a) What do you think is the most valuable part of being able to communicate? **(b) Discuss:** In a small group, share your responses. Then, as a group, share one response with the class.

©4. Integration of Knowledge and Ideas (a) How might Keller's life have changed after this episode? **(b)** What do you think is the most important communication skill for children to master? Explain. *[Connect to the Big Question: What is important to know?]*

Cite textual evidence to support your responses.

Reading Skill: Author's Purpose

1. What are two **purposes** Keller may have had for writing?

2. What details from the essay indicate each purpose?

Literary Analysis: Autobiographical Essay

3. Craft and Structure Complete a chart like this one to help you see why Keller included particular events in her **autobiographical narrative.**

Event From Narrative	Author's Thoughts and Feelings	Why Is it Included?
Helen breaks her doll.		
Helen connects the word *w-a-t-e-r* with water from the pump.		

4. Key Ideas and Details What do you know about the doll breaking that you would not have known if Anne Sullivan had told the story?

Vocabulary

Acquisition and Use Use words from the vocabulary list on page 396 to write a sentence for each item.

1. Explain why a person would send flowers to a loved one.

2. Describe a person who called every day about a job opportunity.

3. Tell an actor to act like a bird.

4. Explain to a child how to pick up broken glass safely.

5. Describe the functions of fences and stone walls.

6. Tell how you would feel if you lost a friend's belongings.

Word Study Use context and what you know about the **Latin suffix -ance** to explain your answer to each question.

1. How might a scrapbook serve as a *remembrance*?

2. What *utterance* might you offer after receiving a gift?

Word Study

The **Latin suffix -ance** means "the act or process of doing, being, or feeling."

Apply It Explain how the suffix -ance contributes to the meaning of these words. Consult a dictionary if necessary.

continuance
importance
resistance

What is important to *know?*

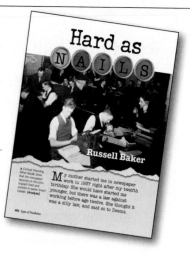

Writing About the Big Question

In "Hard as Nails," Russell Baker must learn skills in order to do a job well. Use this sentence starter to develop your ideas about the Big Question.

Before you start a new job, you should have **knowledge** about _____.

While You Read Look for details about the actions and attitudes that helped Russell Baker succeed at his job.

Vocabulary

Read each word and its definition. Decide whether you know the word well, know it a little bit, or do not know it at all. After you read, see how your knowledge of each word has increased.

- **idle** (īd´ ´l) *adj.* not working or active; doing nothing (p. 407) *The strike left workers idle for many days.* idly *adv.* idleness *n.*

- **embedded** (em bed´ əd) *adj.* firmly fixed in surrounding material (p. 407) *Jewels were embedded in the gold bracelet.* embed *v.* embedding *v.*

- **fulfilling** (fŏŏl fil´ iŋ) *v.* carrying out a promise; satisfying an obligation (p. 408) *By greeting the guests, I was fulfilling my job as hostess.* fulfill *v.* fulfilled *v.* fullfillment *n.*

- **exhaust** (ig zôst´) *v.* use up (p. 408) *Running will exhaust my energy.* exhausted *adj.* exhausting *adj.* exhaustion *n.* exhaust *n.*

- **sublime** (sə blīm´) *adj.* majestic; impressive because of great beauty (p. 409) *The rainbow was sublime.* sublimely *adv.*

- **immense** (i mens´) *adj.* huge (p. 413) *The immense truck blocked the driveway.* immensely *adv.* immenseness *n.*

Word Study

The **Latin suffix -ity** means "the state or condition of." It usually indicates that a word is a noun.

In this essay, Russell Baker describes the **immensity,** or hugeness, of the process of newspaper production.

Author of
Hard as

N A I L S

Russell Baker was born in rural Virginia in 1925. After the death of his father in 1931, Baker's mother moved the family to New Jersey. Six years later, Baker and his family settled in Baltimore, Maryland, where he became a newspaper delivery boy. From then on, Baker worked mainly in the newspaper business. He became a reporter and then a columnist at *The New York Times.*

Career Goals Baker was determined to become a writer as far back as the seventh grade, when he decided that "making up stories must surely be almost as fun as reading them." His essay "Hard as Nails" comes from his book *Growing Up,* which has been called "a wondrous book, funny, sad, and strong." Baker won a Pulitzer Prize both for his newspaper "Observer" column in the *Times* and for *Growing Up.*

BACKGROUND FOR THE ESSAY
Newspaper Boys
Like the writer of "Hard as Nails," newspaper delivery boys working in cities in the 1930s had routes that covered many blocks. At that time, a daily newspaper cost only a few cents. Paperboys might make a dime a week for each subscriber and a penny for each paper they sold on the street.

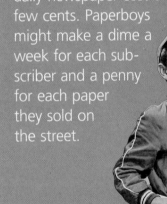

DID YOU KNOW?
Russell Baker was the regular host of the PBS television series *Masterpiece Theatre* from 1992 to 2004.

Hard as NAILS

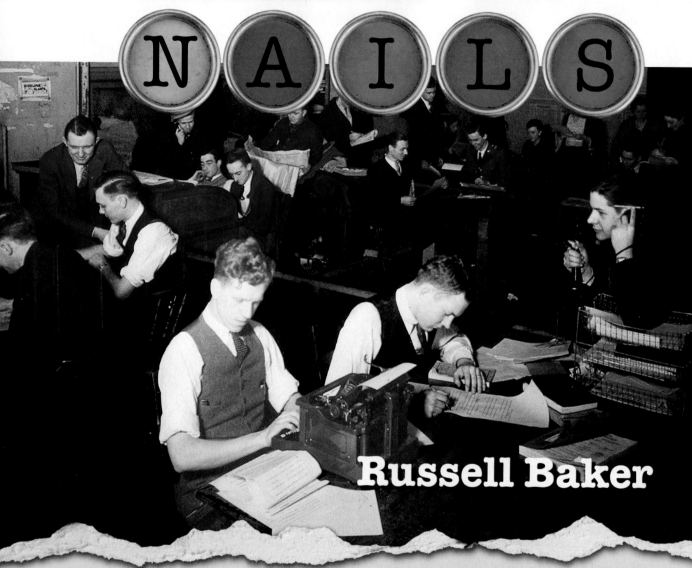

Russell Baker

▲ Critical Viewing
What details show that the newspaper reporters in this photograph lived and worked in earlier times? [Analyze]

My mother started me in newspaper work in 1937 right after my twelfth birthday. She would have started me younger, but there was a law against working before age twelve. She thought it was a silly law, and said so to Deems.

Deems was boss of a group of boys who worked home delivery routes for the *Baltimore News-Post*. She found out about him a few weeks after we got to Baltimore. She just went out on the street, stopped a paperboy, and asked how he'd got his job.

"There's this man Deems . . ."

Deems was short and plump and had curly brown hair. He owned a car and a light gray suit and always wore a necktie and white shirt. A real businessman, I thought the first time I saw him. My mother was talking to him on the sidewalk in front of the Union Square Methodist Church and I was standing as tall as I could, just out of earshot.

"Now, Buddy, when we get down there keep your shoulders back and stand up real straight," she had cautioned me after making sure my necktie was all right and my shirt clean.

Watching the two of them in conversation, with Deems glancing at me now and then, I kept my shoulders drawn back in the painful military style I'd seen in movies, trying to look a foot taller than I really was.

"Come over here, Russ, and meet Mister Deems," she finally said, and I did, managing to answer his greeting by saying, "The pleasure's all mine," which I'd heard people say in the movies. I probably blushed while saying it, because meeting strangers was painfully embarrassing to me.

"If that's the rule, it's the rule," my mother was telling Deems, "and we'll just have to put up with it, but it still doesn't make any sense to me."

As we walked back to the house she said I couldn't have a paper route until I was twelve. And all because of some foolish rule they had down here in Baltimore. You'd think if a boy wanted to work they would encourage him instead of making him stay idle so long that laziness got embedded in his bones. •

That was April. We had barely finished the birthday cake in August before Deems came by the apartment and gave me the tools of the newspaper trade: an account book for keeping track of the customers' bills and a long, brown web belt. Slung around one shoulder and across the chest, the belt made it easy to balance fifteen or twenty pounds of papers against the hip. I had to buy my own wire cutters

Autobiographical Essay
What details so far indicate that this is a narrative essay? Explain.

Vocabulary
idle (īd′ 'l) *adj.* not working or active; doing nothing

embedded (em bed′ əd) *adj.* firmly fixed in surrounding material

Reading Check
Why is Russ's mother so concerned about how Russ looks and stands?

for opening the newspaper bundles the trucks dropped at Wisengoff's store on the corner of Stricker and West Lombard streets.

In February my mother had moved us down from New Jersey, where we had been living with her brother Allen ever since my father died in 1930. This move of hers to Baltimore was a step toward fulfilling a dream. More than almost anything else in the world, she wanted "a home of our own." I'd heard her talk of that "home of our own" all through those endless Depression years when we lived as poor relatives dependent on Uncle Allen's goodness. "A home of our own. One of these days, Buddy, we'll have a home of our own."

That winter she had finally saved just enough to make her move, and she came to Baltimore. There were several reasons for Baltimore. For one, there were people she knew in Baltimore, people she could go to if things got desperate. And desperation was possible, because the moving would exhaust her savings, and the apartment rent was twenty-four dollars a month. She would have to find a job quickly. My sister Doris was only nine, but I was old enough for an after-school job that could bring home a few dollars a week. So as soon as it was legal I went into newspaper work.

The romance of it was almost unbearable on my first day as I trudged west along Lombard Street, then south along Gilmor, and east down Pratt Street with the bundle of newspapers strapped to my hip. I imagined people pausing to admire me as I performed this important

work, spreading the news of the world, the city, and the racetracks onto doorsteps, through mail slots, and under door jambs. I had often gazed with envy at paperboys; to be one of them at last was happiness sublime.

Very soon, though, I discovered drawbacks. The worst of these was Deems. Though I had only forty customers, Deems sent papers for forty-five. Since I was billed for every paper left on Wisengoff's corner, I had to pay for the five extra copies out of income or try to hustle them on the street. I hated standing at streetcar stops yelling, "Paper! Paper!" at people getting off trolleys.[1] Usually, if my mother wasn't around to catch me, I stuck the extras in a dark closet and took the loss.

Deems was constantly baiting new traps to dump more papers on me. When I solved the problem of the five extras by getting five new subscribers for home delivery, Deems announced a competition with mouth-watering prizes for the newsboys who got the most new subscribers. Too innocent to cope with this sly master of private enterprise,[2] I took the bait.

"Look at these prizes I can get for signing up new customers," I told my mother. "A balloon-tire bicycle. A free pass to the movies for a whole year."

The temptation was too much. I reported my five new subscribers to help me in the competition.

Whereupon Deems promptly raised my order from forty-five to fifty papers, leaving me again with the choice of hustling to unload the five extras or losing money.

I won a free pass to the movies, though. It was good for a whole year. And to the magnificent Loew's Century located downtown on Lexington Street. The passes were good only for nights in the middle of the week when I usually had too much homework to allow for movies. Still, in the summer with school out, it was thrilling to go all the way downtown at night to sit in the Century's damask[3] and velvet splendor and see

Vocabulary
sublime (sə blīm´) *adj.* majestic; impressive because of great beauty

Spiral Review
Word Choice What does the author's choice of using the words "magnificent" and "thrilling" in the last paragraph on this page tell you about how he feels about the movie theater?

Reading Check
Why does Baker say that Deems was the worst drawback to being a paperboy?

---

1. **trolleys** (träl´ ēz) *n.* electric passenger trains, also called streetcars, running on rails in the city streets. These were discontinued in most American cities in the mid-1930s.
2. **private enterprise** *n.* business run for profit.
3. **damask** (dam´ əsk) *adj.* made of damask, a shiny cloth often curtains for and used to cover seat cushions in old-time movie theaters.

▲ **Critical Viewing**
Why might it be hard
to concentrate in a
newspaper office like
this one? **[Infer]**

Author's Purpose
Why might Baker
have included these
details about his feel-
ings before going to the
banquet?

**Autobiographical
Essay**
What real event from
the author's life is de-
scribed here?

MGM's glamorous stars in their latest movies.

To collect my prize I had to go to a banquet the paper gave
for its "honor carriers" at the Emerson Hotel. There were
fifty of us, and I was sure the other forty-nine would all turn
out to be slicksters wised up to the ways of the world, who
would laugh at my doltish ignorance of how to eat at a great
hotel banquet. My fear of looking foolish at the banquet
made me lie awake nights dreading it and imagining all the
humiliating mistakes I could make. ●

I had seen banquets in movies. Every plate was surrounded
by a baffling array of knives, forks, and spoons. I knew it
would be the same at the Emerson Hotel. The Emerson was
one of the swankiest hotels in Baltimore. It was not likely to
hold down on the silverware. I talked to my mother.

"How will I know what to eat what with?"

The question did not interest her.

"Just watch what everybody else does, and enjoy
yourself," she said.

I came back to the problem again and again.

"Do you use the same spoon for your coffee as you do
for dessert?"

"Don't worry about it. Everybody isn't going to be staring
at you."

"Is it all right to butter your bread with the same knife you use to cut the meat?"

"Just go and have a good time."

Close to panic, I showed up at the Emerson, found my way to the banquet, and was horrified to find that I had to sit beside Deems throughout the meal. We probably talked about something, but I was so busy sweating with terror and rolling my eyeballs sidewise to see what silverware Deems was using to eat with that I didn't hear a word all night. The following week, Deems started sending me another five extras.

Now and then he also provided a treat. One day in 1938 he asked if I would like to join a small group of boys he was taking to visit the *News-Post* newsroom. My mother, in spite of believing that nothing came before homework at night, wasn't coldhearted enough to deny me a chance to see the city room[4] of a great metropolitan newspaper. I had seen plenty of city rooms in the movies. They were glamorous places full of exciting people like Lee Tracey, Edmund Lowe, and Adolphe Menjou[5] trading wisecracks and making mayors and cops look like saps. To see such a place, to stand, actually stand, in the city room of a great newspaper and look at reporters who were in touch every day with killers and professional baseball players—that was a thrilling prospect.

Because the *News-Post* was an afternoon paper, almost everybody had left for the day when we got there that night. The building, located downtown near the harbor, was disappointing. It looked like a factory, and not a very big factory either. Inside there was a smell compounded of ink, pulp, chemicals, paste, oil, gasoline, greasy rags, and hot metal. We took an elevator up and came into a long room filled with dilapidated[6] desks, battered telephones, and big blocky typewriters. Almost nobody there, just two or three men in shirt-sleeves. It was the first time I'd ever seen Deems look awed.

"Boys, this is the nerve center of the newspaper," he said, his voice heavy and solemn like the voice of Westbrook

Author's Purpose
Why might Baker have included the contrast between newspaper city rooms in movies and the real city room he visits?

✓ Reading Check
What does Baker expect the *News-Post* building to look like on the inside?

---

4. **city room** the office at a newspaper used by those who report on city events.

5. **Lee Tracey, Edmund Lowe, and Adolphe Menjou** actors in movies of the time.

6. **dilapidated** (də lap´ ə dāt´ id) *adj.* rundown; in poor condition.

Hard as Nails **411**

med to be, in the opinion | The *Monitor* undoubtedly reached Fortress Monroe | impossible to say.
Point, aground. The *Mi* ... clo 'k, and may have immediately gone into | Lieut. J ... *orden*, who commanded the *Monitor*,
r or from necessity, an ... ... she would be ready to take ... ... at skill, as ... Chief Engl-
bout a ... ... y.

LITERATURE IN CONTEXT

Culture Connection

Journalism Journalism is an important profession, responsible for informing people about local and world events. Journalists gather, write, and edit material for news stories. They work for newspapers, news services, magazines, radio, or television. In democracies such as the United States, journalists are free to report news without government interference. Reporters are responsible for accuracy and telling all sides of a news story. Editorial writers, meanwhile, express a news organization's views on issues.

Connect to the Literature

How do young Russ's ideas about being a journalist compare with what a journalist actually does?

Van Voorhis, the *March of Time*[7] man, when he said, "Time marches on."

I was confused. I had expected the newsroom to have glamour, but this place had nothing but squalor. The walls hadn't been painted for years. The windows were filthy. Desks were heaped with mounds of crumpled paper, torn sheets of newspaper, overturned paste pots, dog-eared telephone directories. The floor was ankle deep in newsprint, carbon paper, and crushed cigarette packages. Waist-high cans overflowed with trash. Ashtrays were buried under cigarette ashes and butts. Ugly old wooden chairs looked ready for the junk shop.

It looked to me like a place that probably had more cockroaches than we had back home on Lombard Street, but Deems was seeing it through rose-colored glasses.[8] As we stood looking around at the ruins, he started telling us how lucky we were to be newsboys. Lucky to have a foot on the upward ladder so early in life. If we worked hard and kept expanding our paper routes we could make the men who ran this paper sit up and notice us. And when men like that noticed you, great things could happen, because they were important men, the most important of all being the man who owned our paper: Mr. Hearst Himself, William Randolph Hearst, founder of the greatest newspaper organization in America. A great man, Mr. Hearst, but not so great that he didn't appreciate his newsboys, who were the backbone of the business. Many of whom would someday grow up and work at big jobs on this paper. Did we realize that any of us, maybe all of us, could end up one of these days sitting right here in this vitally important room, the newsroom, the nerve center of the newspaper? •

---

7. the *March of Time* a newsreel series that ran from 1935 to 1951, showing current news events along with interviews. Newsreels were shown between feature films at movie theaters.
8. **seeing it through rose-colored glasses** ignoring its unappealing features or drawbacks.

Yes, Deems was right. Riding home on the streetcar that night, I realized I was a lucky boy to be getting such an early start up the ladder of journalism. It was childish to feel let down because the city room looked like such a dump instead of like city rooms in the movies. Deems might be a slave driver, but he was doing it for my own good, and I ought to be grateful. In *News Selling,* the four-page special paper Mr. Hearst published just for his newsboys, they'd run a piece that put it almost as beautifully as Deems had.

YOU'RE A MEMBER OF THE FOURTH ESTATE was the headline on it. I was so impressed that I put the paper away in a safe place and often took it out to read when I needed inspiration. It told how "a great English orator" named Edmund Burke "started a new name for a new profession— the Fourth Estate[9] . . . the press . . . NEWSPAPER MEN."

And it went on to say:

"The Fourth Estate was then . . . and IS now . . . a great estate for HE-men . . . workers . . . those who are proud of the business they're in!"

(Mr. Hearst always liked plenty of exclamation marks, dots, and capital letters.)

"Get that kick of pride that comes from knowing you are a newspaper man. That means something!

"A newspaper man never ducks a dare. YOU are a newspaper man. A salesman of newspapers . . . the final cog[10] in the immense machine of newspaper production—a SERVICE for any man to be proud of.

"So throw back the chest. Hit the route hard each day. Deliver fast and properly. Sell every day. Add to your route because you add to the NEWSPAPER field when you do. And YOU MAKE MONEY DOING IT. It is a great life—a grand opportunity. Don't boot it—build it up. Leave it better than when you came into it."

"It is a great life." I kept coming back to that sentence as I read and reread the thing. No matter how awful it got, and it sometimes got terrible, I never quit believing it was

Autobiographical Essay
William Randolph Hearst was a powerful publisher who owned many newspapers. What details about this real person does Baker include?

Vocabulary
immense (i mens´) *adj.* huge

Reading Check
How does Deems feel about Hearst?

---

9. **Edmund Burke . . . Fourth Estate** Edmund Burke (1729–1797) was an English political figure famous for his speeches and essays. He called the press the "Fourth Estate," meaning it was a base of political power just as were the three social classes in England during that period.

10. **cog** (cäg) *n.* gear.

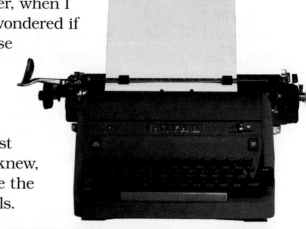

Author's Purpose
Why do you think Baker quotes parts of Hearst's special paper for news-boys?

a great life. I kept at it until I was almost sixteen, chest thrown back, delivering fast and properly, selling every day and adding to my route. At the end I'd doubled its size and was making as much as four dollars a week from it.

A few months after he took us down to see the city room, Deems quit. My mother said he'd found a better job. Later, when I thought about him, I wondered if maybe it wasn't because he hated himself for having to make life hell for boys. I hoped that wasn't the reason because he was the first newspaperman I ever knew, and I wanted him to be the real thing. Hard as nails.

Critical Thinking

Cite textual evidence to support your responses.

1. Key Ideas and Details (a) At the beginning of the selection, what does Baker's mother want him to do? **(b) Compare and Contrast:** How are Baker's dreams for himself similar to and different from his mother's dreams for him?

2. Key Ideas and Details (a) What does Deems do when Russ sells all his papers? **(b) Infer:** What lesson do you think Deems is teaching Russ? **(c) Draw Conclusions:** In the end, why does Russ want to believe that Deems really was "hard as nails"?

3. Key Ideas and Details (a) Does Deems treat the news-boys fairly or unfairly? **(b) Discuss:** In a small group, share your responses. Then, share one response with the class.

4. Integration of Knowledge and Ideas Explain what these words tell us about Baker's attitude: "No matter how awful it got, and it sometimes got terrible, I never quit believing it was a great life." *[Connect to the Big Question: What is important to know?]*

Reading Skill: Author's Purpose

1. What are two **purposes** Baker may have had for writing?

2. What details from the essay indicate each purpose?

Literary Analysis: Autobiographical Essay

© **3. Craft and Structure** Complete a chart like this one to explain why Baker includes certain events in his **autobiographical narrative.**

Hard as NAILS

Russell Baker

My mother started me in newspaper work in 1937 right after my twelfth birthday. She would have started me younger, but there was a law against working before age twelve. She thought it was a silly law, and said so to Deems.

Event From Narrative	Author's Thoughts and Feelings	Why Is it Included?
Baker and his family move to Baltimore.		
Baker goes to the banquet.		

© **4. Key Ideas and Details** What details about the banquet would you not know if Deems had told the story?

Vocabulary

© **Acquisition and Use** Use words from the vocabulary list on page 404 to write sentences for each item.

1. Tell about something that is too big for you to carry.

2. Describe a situation in which something gets used up.

3. Tell about a necklace with many diamonds.

4. Describe the condition of having nothing to do.

5. Tell about what it feels like to achieve a goal.

6. Describe something that makes you very happy.

Word Study Use context and what you know about the **Latin suffix -ity** to answer each question.

1. What conditions might indicate a *possibility* for rain?

2. What is the *nationality* of your favorite actor?

Word Study

The **Latin suffix -ity** means "the state or condition of."

Apply It Explain how the suffix -ity contributes to the meaning of these words. Consult a dictionary if necessary.

neutrality
community
purity

Water • Hard as Nails

Conventions: Adjectives and Articles

An **adjective** is a word that describes a person, place, or thing. Adjectives are often called modifiers because they modify, or make clearer, the meaning of a noun or pronoun.

In these samples, adjectives are italicized.

EXAMPLES: The *little* **kittens** are *black*.
noun

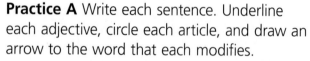

They are *cute*.
pronoun

Adjectives answer one of the following questions: *What kind? Which one? How many? How much?*

Articles are special adjectives: *a, an,* and *the.*

Practice A Write each sentence. Underline each adjective, circle each article, and draw an arrow to the word that each modifies.

1. The teacher gave Helen a pretty doll.
2. Helen felt flushed with childish pleasure.
3. She felt impatient when she could not give an answer.
4. It would have been difficult to find a happier child.
5. She looked forward to a new day.

Ⓒ **Reading Application** In "Water," find a sentence that contains an adjective and an article.

Practice B Identify the word in each item as an article or an adjective. Then, use the question in italics to use the word in a sentence about someone who starts a new job.

1. several (*How many?*)
2. the (*Which one?*)
3. immense (*What kind?*)
4. best (*Which one?*)
5. enough (*How much?*)

Ⓒ **Writing Application** Rewrite this sentence four times by replacing the adjective to change its meaning: *It was a big responsibility.*

| **PH** **WRITING COACH** | Further instruction and practice are available in *Prentice Hall Writing Coach*. |

Writing

 Narrative Text Write a **letter** from the point of view of a main character in the selection you read. In your letter, describe an event that happened in the narrative. Follow these steps:

- Take notes on the event you will describe in your letter.
- Organize the details into a logical sequence.
- Develop events with observations and descriptions.
- Use your notes to write your letter. To review the standard form for personal letters, see page R26.

Grammar Application Check your writing to be sure that you have used adjectives and articles correctly.

Writing Workshop: *Work in Progress*

Prewriting for Exposition: For a how-to essay you may write, list tasks that you know how to do. Consider sports, crafts, and other skills you know well. Give yourself four minutes to make this list. Save this Task List in your writing portfolio.

Research and Technology

 Build and Present Knowledge In a small group, prepare a research **project,** such as a brochure, a poster, or a newspaper article.

- If you read "Water," research careers in the education of people who are blind.
- If you read "Hard as Nails," research jobs in print journalism, such as reporting, editing, photographing, and cartooning.

Follow these steps to complete the assignment.

- Use a variety of sources, such as newspapers, magazines, encyclopedias, and reliable Web sites. Jot down notes and keep them organized.
- Meet with your group to share information. Choose the project format that best suits your topic. Divide the project so that each member has a specific part to complete.
- Use your notes to draft your portion. Then, work together to create the final version.
- Finally, present your project to the class.

Common Core State Standards

L.6.1, L.6.6; W.6.3, W.6.8; SL.6.1
[For the full wording of the standards, see page 394.]

Use this prewriting activity to prepare for the **Writing Workshop** on page 462.

www.PHLitOnline.com
- Interactive graphic organizers
- Grammar tutorial
- Interactive journals

© Leveled Texts

Build your skills and improve your comprehension of nonfiction with texts of increasing complexity.

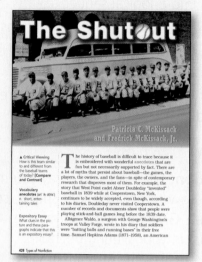

Read **"Jackie Robinson: Justice at Last"** to find out about the important "first" that Jackie Robinson accomplished.

Read **"The Shutout"** to learn about how African American players formed their own baseball leagues.

© Common Core State Standards

Meet these standards with either **"Jackie Robinson: Justice at Last"** (p. 422) or **"The Shutout"** (p. 428).

Reading Informational Text
6. Determine an author's point of view or purpose in a text and explain how it is conveyed in the text. *(Reading Skill: Author's Purpose)*

Writing
1. Write arguments to support claims with clear reasons and relevant evidence. *(Writing: Letter)*

4. Produce clear and coherent writing in which the development, organization, and style are appropriate to task, purpose, and audience. *(Writing: Letter)*

Speaking and Listening
1. Engage effectively in a range of collaborative discussions with diverse partners on grade 6 topics, texts, and issues, building on others' ideas and expressing their own clearly.

1.b. Follow rules for collegial discussions, set specific goals and deadlines, and define individual roles as needed. *(Speaking and Listening: Instructional Presentation)*

Language
1. Demonstrate command of the conventions of standard English grammar and usage when writing or speaking. *(Conventions: Comparisons with Adjectives)*

Language
6. Acquire and use accurately grade-appropriate general academic and domain-specific words and phrases; gather vocabulary knowledge when considering a word or phrase important to comprehension or expression. *(Vocabulary: Word Study)*

Reading Skill: Author's Purpose

An **author's purpose** is his or her reason, or reasons, for writing. There are three general purposes for writing—to inform, to persuade, and to entertain. An author's specific purpose is his or her particular reason for writing. For instance, an author might write to persuade people to vote in a certain election. To understand an author's specific purpose, **ask questions.**

- What kinds of details am I given?
- How are the details presented?
- Why does the author present these details in this way?

The chart below shows the answers to these questions for two different works about building a doghouse. Although both works are on the same topic, the answers to the questions reveal that they have different general purposes.

Using the Strategy: Author's Purpose Chart

Fill in a chart like this one as you read.

What Kinds of Details?	How Presented?	Why?	Purpose
Directions for building a doghouse	Numbered steps	To make the directions easy to follow	To inform
Author tries to build a doghouse	Exaggerated stories	To make the situation funny	To entertain

Literary Analysis: Expository Essay

An **essay** is a short piece of nonfiction about a specific subject. An **expository essay** has one or more of these general purposes:

- providing information
- discussing ideas and opinions
- explaining how to do or make something

As you read an expository essay, notice how the subject of the essay gives a focus to one or more of these general purposes.

What is important to *know?*

▲ Critical Viewing
What details in this 1948 picture of the Negro League East All-Stars indicate their desire to compete? **[Analyze]**

Vocabulary
integrate (in´ tə grāt´) *v.* remove all barriers and allow access to all

Writing About the Big Question

"Jackie Robinson: Justice at Last" describes a baseball star who showed strength and bravery, even when he was treated unfairly. Use this sentence starter to develop your ideas about the Big Question.

If people are unfair to you, it is important to **limit** your reactions, such as _____, because _____.

While You Read Look for the advice that Robinson gets from others and notice how he deals with this information.

Vocabulary

Read each word and its definition. Decide whether you know the word well, know it a little bit, or do not know it at all. After you read, see how your knowledge of each word has increased.

- **integrate** (in´ tə grāt) *v.* remove all barriers and allow free association; bring together as a whole (p. 422) *I would like to <u>integrate</u> all the students into one class.* *integration n.*

- **prejudiced** (prej´ ə dist) *adj.* having unfair feelings of dislike for a specific group (p. 422) *The book's villain has <u>prejudiced</u> feelings for many groups.* *prejudice n.*

- **superb** (sə pʉrb´) *adj.* extremely fine; excellent (p. 423) *The chef's food was <u>superb</u>.* *superbly adv.*

- **petition** (pə tish´ ən) *n.* document that people sign to express demands (p. 423) *Shoppers signed a <u>petition</u> asking for safer parking lots.* *petitioned v. petitioning v.*

- **retaliated** (ri tal´ ē āt´ əd) *v.* punished in return for an injury or wrong done (p. 424) *Mrs. Jones <u>retaliated</u> by refusing to go back to the theater.* *retaliate v. retaliating v.*

- **dignity** (dig´ nə tē) *n.* behaving in a way that makes people respect you (p. 424) *Ana accepted the award with <u>dignity</u>.* *dignify v.*

Word Study

The **Latin prefix** *sup-* or *super-* means "greater than normal."

Jackie Robinson proved himself to be a **superb** athlete because his skills made him far greater than most ballplayers.

Jackie Robinson
JUSTICE AT LAST

Geoffrey C. Ward (b. 1940)

The author of many award-winning books, Geoffrey C. Ward is also a screenwriter and a former editor of *American Heritage* magazine. For more than twenty years, Ward has worked with Ken Burns, writing award-winning television documentaries, including *Baseball*, *The Civil War*, and *The West*.

Ken Burns (b. 1953)

Ken Burns has co-written, produced, and directed several television documentaries and miniseries and has directed movies that have been nominated for Academy Awards. "Jackie Robinson: Justice at Last" is from a book based on Ward and Burns's 1994 television documentary *Baseball*. This documentary won numerous awards, including an Emmy.

BACKGROUND FOR THE ESSAY

"Jackie Robinson: Justice at Last"

In the early 1900s, major league baseball excluded African American players. As a result, these players formed their own teams, and in the 1920s organized the Negro Leagues. Although they did not become as widely known as their white counterparts, some of the best players in baseball history played in the Negro Leagues. Jackie Robinson, the subject of the following essay, began his professional baseball career on the Negro Leagues team the Kansas City Monarchs.

DID YOU KNOW?

Ward and Burns use many original prints and photographs in their documentaries, giving the films a unique, authentic style.

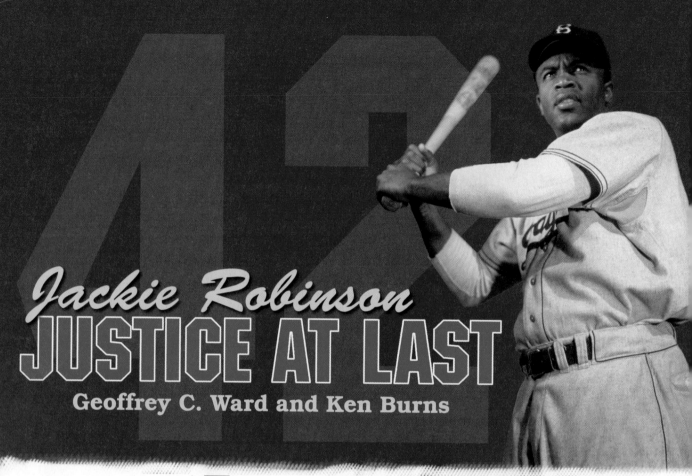

Jackie Robinson
JUSTICE AT LAST

Geoffrey C. Ward and Ken Burns

▲ **Critical Viewing**
What might be the significance of the number 42 in the background of this picture? **[Use Prior Knowledge]**

Vocabulary
integrate (in´ tə grāt) *v.* remove all barriers and allow free association; bring together as a whole

prejudiced (prej´ ə dist) *adj.* having unfair feelings of dislike for a specific group

It was 1945, and World War II had ended. Americans of all races had died for their country. Yet black men were still not allowed in the major leagues. The national pastime was loved by all America, but the major leagues were for white men only.

Branch Rickey of the Brooklyn Dodgers thought that was wrong. He was the only team owner who believed blacks and whites should play together. Baseball, he felt, would become even more thrilling, and fans of all colors would swarm to his ballpark.

Rickey decided his team would be the first to integrate. There were plenty of brilliant Negro league players, but he knew the first black major leaguer would need much more than athletic ability.

Many fans and players were prejudiced—they didn't want the races to play together. Rickey knew the first black player would be cursed and booed. Pitchers would throw at him; runners would spike him. Even his own teammates might try to pick a fight.

But somehow this man had to rise above that. No matter what happened, he must never lose his temper. No matter what was said to him, he must never answer back. If he had even one fight, people might say integration wouldn't work.

When Rickey met Jackie Robinson, he thought he'd found the right man. Robinson was 28 years old, and a superb athlete. In his first season in the Negro leagues, he hit .387. But just as importantly, he had great intelligence and sensitivity. Robinson was college-educated, and knew what joining the majors would mean for blacks. The grandson of a slave, he was proud of his race and wanted others to feel the same.

In the past, Robinson had always stood up for his rights. But now Rickey told him he would have to stop. The Dodgers needed "a man that will take abuse." ●

At first Robinson thought Rickey wanted someone who was afraid to defend himself. But as they talked, he realized that in this case a truly brave man would have to avoid fighting. He thought for a while, then promised Rickey he would not fight back.

Robinson signed with the Dodgers and went to play in the minors in 1946. Rickey was right—fans insulted him, and so did players. But he performed brilliantly and avoided fights. Then, in 1947, he came to the majors.

Many Dodgers were angry. Some signed a petition demanding to be traded. But Robinson and Rickey were determined to make their experiment work.

On April 15—Opening Day—26,623 fans came out to Ebbets Field. More than half of them were black—Robinson was already their hero. Now he was making history just by being on the field.

The afternoon was cold and wet, but no one left the ballpark. The Dodgers beat the Boston Braves, 5–3. Robinson went hitless, but the hometown fans didn't seem to care—they cheered his every move.

Robinson's first season was difficult. Fans threatened to kill him; players tried to hurt him. The St. Louis Cardinals said they would strike if he took the field. And because of laws separating the races in certain states, he often couldn't eat or sleep in the same places as his teammates.

Vocabulary
retaliated (ri tal´ ē
āt´ əd) *v.* punished in
return for an injury
or a wrong done
dignity (dig´ nə
tē) *n.* behaving in
a way that makes
people respect you

Yet through it all, he kept his promise to Rickey. No matter who insulted him, he never retaliated.

Robinson's dignity paid off. Thousands of fans jammed stadiums to see him play. The Dodgers set attendance records in a number of cities.

Slowly his teammates accepted him, realizing that he was the spark that made them a winning team. No one was more daring on the base paths or better with the glove. At the plate, he had great bat control—he could hit the ball anywhere. That season, he was named baseball's first Rookie of the Year.

Jackie Robinson went on to a glorious career. But he did more than play the game well—his bravery taught Americans a lesson. Branch Rickey opened a door, and Jackie Robinson stepped through it, making sure it could never be closed again. Something wonderful happened to baseball—and America—the day Jackie Robinson joined the Dodgers.

Authors' Purpose
How does the final sentence help you understand the authors' specific purpose in writing this essay?

Critical Thinking

Cite textual evidence to support your responses.

1. **Key Ideas and Details (a)** Who was Branch Rickey? **(b) Analyze:** Why is Rickey given a great deal of credit in this essay?

2. **Key Ideas and Details (a)** Name three difficult situations that Jackie Robinson faced. **(b) Analyze:** How did he overcome them?

3. **Key Ideas and Details (a)** What important advice did Branch Rickey give to Jackie Robinson? **(b)** Why was it important for Robinson to keep this advice in mind? *[Connect to the Big Question: What is important to know?]*

Reading Skill: Author's Purpose

1. **(a)** What kinds of details are included in the **essay**?
   (b) In what style are those details presented? Explain.

2. **(a)** What is the general **purpose** of the essay?
   (b) What is its specific purpose?

Literary Analysis: Expository Essay

ⓒ 3. **Key Ideas and Details** Fill in a chart to show the authors' purpose for focusing on the topic of this **expository essay.**

Topic of Essay	Details About Topic	Author's Specific Purpose

Vocabulary

ⓒ **Acquisition and Use** Explain why each of these statements is true or false.

1. Branch Rickey did not want to <u>integrate</u> baseball.
2. People have never <u>retaliated</u> against social injustices.
3. One way to get something done is to sign a <u>petition</u>.
4. At first, the fans and other players were not <u>prejudiced</u> regarding Jackie Robinson.
5. By not fighting back, Robinson showed both courage and <u>dignity</u>.
6. Branch Rickey's choice of Jackie Robinson as the first African American player proved to be a <u>superb</u> decision.

Word Study Use the context of the sentences and what you know about the **Latin prefix sup-** or **super-** to explain your answer to each question.

1. How does a *supermarket* differ from other food stores?
2. What qualities make *Superman* different from others?

Word Study

The **Latin prefix sup-** or **super-** means "greater than normal."

Apply It Explain how the prefix *sup-* or *super-* contributes to the meaning of these words. Consult a dictionary if necessary.

superior
supervise
superpower

What is important to know?

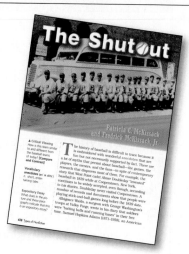

Writing About the Big Question

"The Shutout" describes ways that African American baseball players solved the problem of being prevented from playing in the major leagues. Use this sentence starter to develop your ideas about the Big Question.

Knowing different ways to solve problems is important because _____.

While You Read Look for details that explain the kind of information that is known—or not widely known—about the Negro Leagues.

Vocabulary

Read each word and its definition. Decide whether you know the word well, know it a little bit, or do not know it at all. After you read, see how your knowledge of each word has increased.

- **anecdotes** (an´ ik dōts) *n.* short, entertaining tales (p. 428) *Anecdotes about actors always interest my uncle Sal. anecdotal adj.*

- **evolved** (ē vôlvd´) *v.* grew gradually; developed (p. 429) *Many modern stories have evolved from ancient myths and legends. evolving v. evolve v. devolve v.*

- **diverse** (də vʉrs´) *adj.* various; with differing characteristics (p. 429) *The diverse student body makes my school special. diversity n. diversify v.*

- **composed** (kəm pōzd´) *v.* made up (p. 431) *The book was composed of several essays. compose v. composer n.*

- **irrational** (ir rash´ ə nəl) *adj.* unreasonable (p. 431) *His fear of spiders is irrational. irrationally adv. rational adj.*

- **infamous** (in´ fə məs) *adj.* having a bad reputation (p. 432) *Jim was infamous for being late. infamously adv. famous adj. infamy n.*

Word Study

The **Latin prefix *ir-*** often means "not."

This essay describes the racial prejudices that once kept African American players out of major league baseball. These prejudices were **irrational** because they were not based on rational, or reasonable, thought.

The Shutout

Patricia C. McKissack (b. 1944)
Fredrick McKissack, Jr. (b. 1965)

Authors of "The Shutout"

Patricia McKissack began her career first as an English teacher and then as an editor of children's books. While working as an editor, she decided to become a writer. "I write because there's a need to have books for, by, and about the African American experience and how we helped to develop this country," says McKissack. She is now author of more than seventy-five books for children and young adults.

The Family Business McKissack co-wrote many of her books with her husband, Fredrick McKissack. Together, the couple has won countless awards. Their son, Fredrick McKissack, Jr., is also a writer. With her son, Patricia McKissack wrote *Black Diamond: The Story of the Negro Baseball Leagues,* from which "The Shutout" was taken. *Black Diamond* focuses on the talents and triumphs of leading Negro League baseball players. The book brings to life an important period in the history of baseball.

BACKGROUND FOR THE ESSAY

"The Shutout"

In the earliest days of baseball, African American and white players played side by side. Eventually, however, baseball became segregated, or separated, into teams of "blacks" and "whites." As this essay shows, however, segregation could not "shut out" African Americans from playing the game and creating baseball legends as amazing as those of their white counterparts.

DID YOU KNOW?

Patricia and Fredrick McKissack usually have four or five books in progress at any time.

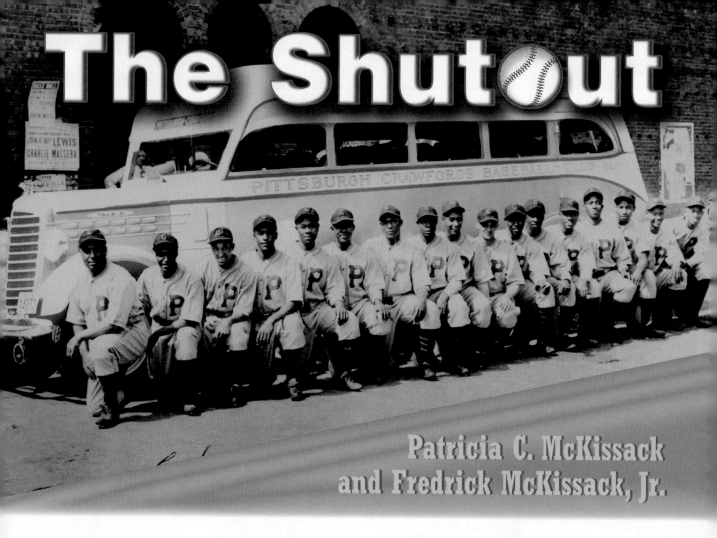

The Shutout

**Patricia C. McKissack
and Fredrick McKissack, Jr.**

The history of baseball is difficult to trace because it is embroidered with wonderful anecdotes that are fun but not necessarily supported by fact. There are a lot of myths that persist about baseball—the games, the players, the owners, and the fans—in spite of contemporary research that disproves most of them. For example, the story that West Point cadet Abner Doubleday "invented" baseball in 1839 while at Cooperstown, New York, continues to be widely accepted, even though, according to his diaries, Doubleday never visited Cooperstown. A number of records and documents show that people were playing stick-and-ball games long before the 1839 date.

Albigence Waldo, a surgeon with George Washington's troops at Valley Forge, wrote in his diary that soldiers were "batting balls and running bases" in their free time. Samuel Hopkins Adams (1871–1958), an American historical novelist, stated that his grandfather "played baseball on Mr. Mumford's pasture" in the 1820's.

Although baseball is a uniquely American sport, it was not invented by a single person. Probably the game evolved from a variety of stick-and-ball games that were played in Europe, Asia, Africa, and the Americas for centuries and brought to the colonies by the most diverse group of people ever to populate a continent. More specifically, some historians believe baseball is an outgrowth of its first cousin, *rounders*, an English game. Robin Carver wrote in his *Book of Sports* (1834) that "an American version of rounders called *goal ball* was rivaling cricket in popularity."

It is generally accepted that by 1845, baseball, as it is recognized today, was becoming popular, especially in New York. In that year a group of baseball enthusiasts organized the New York Knickerbocker Club. They tried to standardize the game by establishing guidelines for "proper play."

The Knickerbockers' rules set the playing field—a diamond-shaped infield with four bases (first, second, third, and home) placed ninety feet apart. At that time, the pitching distance was forty-five feet from home base and the "pitch" was thrown under-handed. The three-strikes-out rule, the three-out inning, and the ways in which a player could be called out were also specified. However, the nine-man team and nine-inning game were not established until later. Over the years, the Knickerbockers' basic rules of play haven't changed much. •

In 1857–1858, the newly organized National Association of Base Ball Players was formed, and baseball became a business. Twenty-five clubs—mostly from eastern states—formed the Association for the purpose of setting rules and guidelines for club and team competition. The Association defined a professional player as a person who "played for money, place or emolument (profit)." The Association also

Vocabulary

evolved (ē välvd´) *v.* grew gradually; developed

diverse (də vɨrs´) *adj.* various; with differing characteristics

✓ Reading Check
Who set early guidelines for playing baseball?

authorized an admission fee for one of the first "all-star" games between Brooklyn and New York. Fifteen hundred people paid fifty cents to see that game. Baseball was on its way to becoming the nation's number-one sport.

By 1860, the same year South Carolina seceded from the Union, there were about sixty teams in the Association. For obvious reasons none of them were from the South. Baseball's development was slow during the Civil War years, but teams continued to compete, and military records show that, sometimes between battles, Union soldiers chose up teams and played baseball games. It was during this time that records began mentioning African-American players. One war journalist noted that black players were "sought after as teammates because of their skill as ball handlers."

Information about the role of African Americans in the early stages of baseball development is slight. Several West African cultures had stick-and-ball and running games, so at least some blacks were familiar with the concept of baseball. Baseball, however, was not a popular southern sport, never equal to boxing, wrestling, footracing, or horse racing among the privileged landowners. •

Slave owners preferred these individual sports because they could enter their slaves in competitions, watch the event from a safe distance, pocket the winnings, and personally never raise a sweat. There are documents to show that slave masters made a great deal of money from the athletic skills of their slaves.

Free blacks, on the other hand, played on and against integrated[1] teams in large eastern cities and in small midwestern hamlets. It is believed that some of the emancipated[2] slaves and runaways who served in the Union Army learned how to play baseball from northern blacks and whites who had been playing together for years.

After the Civil War, returning soldiers helped to inspire a new interest in baseball all over the country. Teams sprung up in northern and midwestern cities, and naturally African Americans were interested in joining some of these clubs. But the National Association of Base Ball Players had other ideas. They voted in December 1867 not to admit

Spiral Review
Development of Ideas What key idea about baseball history do the facts presented in this paragraph develop?

Expository Essay What details in this paragraph provide focus for the topic of the essay?

Authors' Purpose Based on what you have read so far, what is the authors' general purpose for writing this essay? What is the authors' specific purpose?

---

1. integrated (in´ tə grāt´ id) *adj.* open to both African Americans and whites.
2. emancipated (ē man´ sə pāt´ id) *adj.* freed from slavery.

any team for membership that "may be composed of one or more colored persons." Their reasoning was as irrational as the racism that shaped it: "If colored clubs were admitted," the Association stated, "there would be in all probability some division of feeling whereas, by excluding them no injury could result to anyone . . . and [we wish] to keep out of the convention the discussion of any subjects having a political bearing as this [admission of blacks on the Association teams] undoubtedly would."

So, from the start, organized baseball tried to limit or exclude African-American participation. In the early days a few black ball players managed to play on integrated minor league teams. A few even made it to the majors, but by the turn of the century, black players were shut out of the major leagues until after World War II. That doesn't mean African Americans didn't play the game. They did. ●

Black people organized their own teams, formed leagues, and competed for championships. The history of the old "Negro Leagues" and the players who barnstormed[3] on black diamonds is one of baseball's most interesting chapters, but the story is a researcher's nightmare. Black baseball was outside the mainstream of the major leagues, so team and player records weren't well kept, and for the

---

3. barnstormed *v.* went from one small town to another, putting on exhibitions.

most part, the white press ignored black clubs or portrayed them as clowns. And for a long time the Baseball Hall of Fame didn't recognize any of the Negro League players. Because of the lack of documentation, many people thought the Negro Leagues' stories were nothing more than myths and yarns, but that is not the case. The history of the Negro Leagues is a patchwork of human drama and comedy, filled with legendary heroes, infamous owners, triple-headers, low pay, and long bus rides home—not unlike the majors.

Critical Thinking

Cite textual evidence to support your responses.

© 1. **Key Ideas and Details** **(a)** When did baseball become popular, and who created the playing rules? **(b) Analyze:** Give specific examples of the changes that occurred following the creation of baseball as a professional sport. **(c) Generalize:** What is one reason baseball rules and regulations were created?

© 2. **Key Ideas and Details** **(a)** What were the team owners' reasons for not letting African Americans play? **(b) Identify Cause and Effect:** What effect did this exclusion have on the history of baseball? **(c) Connect:** What attitudes and conditions contributed to this exclusion?

© 3. **Key Ideas and Details** **Make a Judgment:** Are sports today segregated in any way? Explain.

© 4. **Craft and Structure** The authors state that because few records were kept, "many people thought the Negro Leagues' stories were nothing more than myths and yarns." Why would more widespread knowledge of the history of the Negro Leagues have been valuable? *[Connect to the Big Question: What is important to know?]*

Reading Skill: Author's Purpose

1. (a) What kinds of details are included in the essay?
(b) In what style are those details presented? Explain.

2. (a) What is the general **purpose** of the essay?
(b) What is its specific purpose?

Literary Analysis: Expository Essay

3. Key Ideas and Details Fill in a chart like this one to show the authors' specific purpose for focusing on the topic of this **expository essay.** Include the details they use to develop ideas.

Topic of Essay	Details About Topic	Author's Specific Purpose

Vocabulary

Acquisition and Use Explain why these statements are true or false. Do not include the underlined words in your answers.

1. Golf <u>evolved</u> from bowling.

2. Canines do not comprise a <u>diverse</u> group of dogs.

3. The belief that rocks can think is totally <u>irrational</u>.

4. <u>Anecdotes</u> explain how water turns into ice.

5. Scientists become <u>infamous</u> for their great discoveries.

6. Newspapers are often <u>composed</u> of both facts and opinions.

Word Study Use the context of the sentences and what you know about the **Latin prefix ir-** to explain answers.

1. Would an *irresponsible* person make a good babysitter?

2. How might an *irremovable* stain ruin a favorite shirt?

Word Study

The **Latin prefix *ir-***
often means "not."

Apply It Explain how the prefix *ir-* contributes to the meaning of these words. Consult a dictionary if necessary.

irreversible
irresistible
irregular

Jackie Robinson: Justice at Last • The Shutout

Conventions: Comparisons With Adjectives

An **adjective** is a word that describes a person, place, or thing.

Positive Adjectives	Comparative Adjectives	Superlative Adjectives
used to describe people, places, or things; not used to compare	used to compare two people, places, or things	used to compare three or more people, places, or things

Comparative and **superlative adjectives** are formed from **positive adjectives.** Follow these rules:

1. If a positive adjective contains one or two syllables, add the ending -*er* or -*est*.

2. If a positive adjective contains three or more syllables, usually use the words *more* or *most.*

Practice A Write an original sentence about the selection you read using the comparative or superlative adjective listed below.

1. older

2. more expensive

3. most popular

4. easiest

5. more interesting

©**Reading Application** Reread each sentence you wrote in Practice A, and then tell how many people, places, or things are being compared.

Practice B Identify whether each of the following adjectives is comparative or superlative. Then, write a sentence about the selection you read, using that adjective.

1. wisest

2. stronger

3. greatest

4. more talented

5. most remarkable

©**Writing Application** Write two more sentences. Use a comparative adjective in the first sentence and a superlative adjective in the second sentence.

PH **WRITING COACH** Further instruction and practice are available in *Prentice Hall Writing Coach.*

Writing

 **Common Core State Standards**

L.6.1; W.6.1, W.6.4; SL.6.1, SL.6.1.b
[For the full wording of the standards, see page 418.]

Argument Write a **letter** to a friend, persuading him or her to read the expository essay that you read.

- Take notes on the most interesting details and events.
- Use your notes to draft your letter, clearly stating your reasons for recommending the essay.
- Revise your letter, strengthening your persuasive language and tightening the organization of the reasons and evidence that you present.
- Write a final copy, using the letter format on p. R26.

Grammar Application Check your letter to be sure that any comparisons using adjectives follow the rules on page 434.

Writing Workshop: *Work in Progress*

Prewriting for Exposition Reread the Task List in your writing portfolio. Choose a task and jot down the steps that a reader must take to complete it. Put this list in your portfolio.

Use this prewriting activity to prepare for the **Writing Workshop** on page 462.

Speaking and Listening

Comprehension and Collaboration Invite a coach to discuss baseball basics. Then, in a small group, prepare an **instructional presentation** for younger students.

Follow these steps to complete the assignment:

- While listening to the coach's presentation, take notes to summarize the main ideas and tips.
- Meet with your group to discuss the project, set deadlines, and assign specific topics for your presentation. Use effective speaking and listening skills as you discuss and plan each group member's responsibility.
- Based on notes and discussion, draft your portion of the project. Include a summary of the coach's ideas, a demonstration of a skill, and an explanation of key terms.
- Meet with your group to review each other's work. Ask group members questions and make observations about the work. Then, revise your draft, making sure that your language is appropriate for a younger audience.
- Work with your group to create your final version of the project. Then, present it to your audience.

Test Practice: Reading

Author's Purpose

Fiction Selection

Directions: *Read the selection. Then, answer the questions.*

The day after we arrived in Chicago, Uncle Ray surprised us with tickets for a Cubs game. I was excited. I had never seen a live baseball game before. We took a crowded train to Wrigley Field. When we got there, we shoved our way through about a million humans to get to our seats. The game had already begun. The players on the field seemed remote, the game unreal. More real to me was the scene in the stands: people laughing and eating, the vendors tossing bags of peanuts above our heads. The smell of hot dogs and popcorn hung in the air. I couldn't take my eyes off the show around me. When the game ended, we squeezed our way out of the stadium and back onto a train. Maybe the next time I go to a baseball game, I'll actually watch the game.

1. What is the author's general purpose for writing this passage?
   A. to inform
   B. to entertain
   C. to persuade
   D. to warn

2. What is the author's specific purpose?
   A. to share the excitement of going to a baseball game
   B. to describe historic Wrigley Field
   C. to provide facts about the city of Chicago
   D. to analyze a baseball game

3. Which elements do *not* contribute to the author's specific purpose?
   A. the use of the past tense
   B. the use of chronological order
   C. sensory details
   D. the humorous tone

4. What kinds of details does the writer emphasize in order to achieve a specific purpose?
   A. the actions of the baseball players
   B. the thoughts of Uncle Ray
   C. the crowd's reaction to the game
   D. a spectator's impressions of the scene

Writing for Assessment

In a paragraph, give three pieces of advice to explain how writers can achieve their purpose for writing. Use this passage as an example text.

Nonfiction Selection

Directions: *Read the selection. Then, answer the questions.*

Fenway Park, the home of the Boston Red Sox, is the oldest professional baseball stadium in the United States. The stadium opened on April 20, 1912. On that day, the Red Sox defeated the New York Highlanders, the team that later became the Yankees. The stadium is named for its location in the Fenway section of Boston, and it is the second home field for the Red Sox. The team was established in 1901, with a different name—the Boston Americans—and a different home field. In 1904, General Charles Henry Taylor, a Civil War veteran, bought the team. He changed the team name to the Red Sox in 1907. Three years later, construction of a new ballpark, Fenway Park, began.

1. What is the topic of this passage?
  A. Fenway Park
  B. the Red Sox
  C. the Yankees
  D. Stadiums

2. What is the author's general purpose for writing the passage?
  A. to persuade
  B. to give directions
  C. to inform
  D. to entertain

3. What is the author's specific purpose for writing the passage?
  A. to teach the rules of baseball
  B. to give directions to Fenway Park
  C. to give a brief history of Fenway Park
  D. to describe the construction of Fenway Park

4. Which phrase from the passage most clearly indicates the author's purpose?
  A. "oldest professional baseball stadium"
  B. "that later became the Yankees"
  C. "the Boston Americans"
  D. "a Civil War veteran"

Writing for Assessment

Connecting Across Texts

In a paragraph, compare the types of details used in the two passages and note how those details help the authors achieve their purposes. In your writing, propose a title for each passage that helps make its purpose more apparent.

PHLit Online!
www.PHLitOnline.com
- Online practice
- Instant feedback

Reading for Information

Analyzing Arguments

Persuasive Speech

Editorial

 **Common Core State Standards**

Reading Informational Text

3. Analyze in detail how a key individual, event, or idea is introduced, illustrated, and elaborated in a text.

8. Trace and evaluate the argument and specific claims in a text, distinguishing claims that are supported by reasons and evidence from claims that are not.

Writing

1.a. Introduce claim(s) and organize the reasons and evidence clearly.

1.b. Support claim(s) with clear reasons and relevant evidence, using credible sources and demonstrating an understanding of the topic or text. (Timed Writing)

Language

6. Acquire and use accurately grade-appropriate general academic and domain-specific words and phrases; gather vocabulary knowledge when considering a word or phrase important to comprehension or expression.

Reading Skill: Evaluate Author's Conclusions

The purpose of a persuasive speech or editorial is to convince readers to think or act in a certain way. In effective persuasive writing, the author presents evidence to support his or her conclusions. When you read persuasive writing, **evaluate the author's conclusions.** Determine whether his or her arguments are supported by evidence, such as facts, examples, and statistics. Then, decide whether you agree with the conclusions. Use a checklist like the one shown to help you.

Checklist for Evaluating an Author's Conclusions

☐ Does the author present a clear argument?

☐ Is the argument supported by evidence?

☐ Is the evidence believable?

☐ Does the author use sound reasoning to develop the argument?

☐ Do I agree with the conclusions? Why or why not?

Content-Area Vocabulary

These words appear in the selections that follow. You may also encounter them in other content-area texts.

- **extinction** (ek stiŋk´ shən) *n.* act of bringing to an end; wiping out; destruction

- **amendment** (ə mend´ mənt) *n.* change made to a law or bill by adding, deleting, or altering its language

- **collaboration** (kə lab´ ə rā´ shən) *n.* act of working together

Features:

- a clear statement of the speaker's position on an issue
- facts, statistics, and reasons that support the speaker's position
- powerful language intended to persuade and grab listeners' attention
- text spoken aloud to an audience

Preserving a Great American Symbol

Richard Durbin

Congressman Richard Durbin gave the following humorous speech in the House of Representatives on July 26, 1989. While most speeches to Congress are serious, Durbin's is humorous yet persuasive and "drives home" the point that wooden baseball bats should not be replaced with metal ones.

In his introduction, Durbin clearly states his position on an issue.

Mr. Speaker, I rise to condemn the desecration of a great American symbol. No, I am not referring to flagburning; I am referring to the baseball bat.

Several experts tell us that the wooden baseball bat is doomed to **extinction**, that major league baseball players will soon be standing at home plate with aluminum bats in their hands.

Baseball fans have been forced to endure countless indignities by those who just cannot leave well enough alone: designated hitters,[1] plastic grass, uniforms that look like pajamas, chicken clowns dancing on the base lines, and, of course, the most heinous sacrilege, lights in Wrigley Field.[2]

> Durbin uses humor to enhance his argument.

Are we willing to hear the crack of a bat replaced by the dinky ping? Are we ready to see the Louisville Slugger replaced by the aluminum ping dinger? Is nothing sacred?

Please do not tell me that wooden bats are too expensive, when players who cannot hit their weight are being paid more money than the President of the United States.

Please do not try to sell me on the notion that these metal clubs will make better hitters.

What will be next? Teflon baseballs? Radar-enhanced gloves? I ask you.

I do not want to hear about saving trees. Any tree in America would gladly give its life for the glory of a day at home plate.

> Durbin closes the speech by stating his main conclusion on the issue.

I do not know if it will take a constitutional **amendment** to keep our baseball traditions alive, but if we forsake the great Americana of broken-bat singles and pine tar,[3] we will have certainly lost our way as a nation.

---

1. **designated hitter** player who bats in place of the pitcher and does not play any other position. The position was created in 1973 in the American League. Some fans argue that it has changed the game for the worse.
2. **Wrigley Field** historic baseball field in Chicago. It did not have lights for night games until 1988. Some fans regretted the change.
3. **broken-bat singles . . . pine tar** two references to quirks of the game of baseball. When a batter breaks a wooden bat while hitting the ball and makes it to first base, it is a notable event in a baseball game. Pine tar is a substance used to improve the batter's grip on a wooden bat.

Features:

- text featured in newspapers or magazines
- a statement of the writer's position on an issue
- facts, statistics, and reasons that support the writer's position

The photograph of a young athlete supports the author's purpose, which is to convince readers that baseball is important to young people.

Jake Wood Baseball
is the start of something special

This part of the title supports the author's conclusion that Jake Wood baseball should be highly valued.

Reginald T. Dogan

On April 15, 1947, Jackie Robinson cleared a path for desegregation by becoming the first black man to play Major League Baseball.

He changed the game—and the country—in the process.

On a warm and sunny Saturday morning, one week after the 60th anniversary and the celebration of Robinson breaking the color line, the Jake Wood Inner City Baseball League brought youth baseball back to the inner city.

This new league won't change the game or the country, but it did bring together county and city, boys and girls, moms and dads to make a field of dreams a reality.

When I arrived at Raymond Riddle Park on T Street, cars lined the field behind the fire station. The stands were filled and brimming with excitement, as young boys and girls donning spanking-new uniforms representing Major League teams, stood on the chalk-lined infield awaiting the opening day ceremony.

Before football and basketball stole the hearts and minds of our youth, baseball was the first choice of every kid in the inner city because it was passed down by the generations.

Today, many young boys no longer dream of, much less play, baseball. Unlike football and basketball, baseball seems less contemporary for inner-city kids.

The credit for the Jake Wood League goes to a unique collaboration among the City of Pensacola, Escambia County, the West Pensacola Youth Association, as well as the community and individual sponsorship and support.

Die-hard baseball proponents like Jake Wood, Johnny Blackmon, Lumon May, Buddy Connelly, Kevin Briesky, and Dave Flaherty, to name a few, deserve the highest praise for their hard work behind the scene.

They are a diverse group of adults who haven't forgotten the joy of competing and the life lessons instilled on the diamond.

Naming the new league in honor of Pensacola resident Jake Wood, a former professional baseball player with the Detroit Tigers and Cincinnati Reds, gives it instant name recognition and credibility.

The league consists of 11 teams—five from the West Pensacola Youth Association, five from the Southern Youth Sports Association, and one from the Fricker Center.

The teams—Tee Ball (ages 4–7), Coach Pitch (ages 8–9), and Little League (ages 10–12)—are scheduled to play 10 games each. The games will be played on Mondays, Thursdays, and Saturdays.

From what I witnessed Saturday, the Jake Wood League is the start of something special.

The final scores meant little compared to the lifetime of memories. The outcome of the games was not nearly as important as the input and excitement generated by fans, family, and players.

Baseball, or any sport for that matter, is so very important for our young people. It teaches them teamwork, sportsmanship, and discipline. It provides exercise and excitement under adult guidance and supervision. It keeps children actively involved on the field and off the streets.

Over the years, I've discovered that there are three kinds of people in the world: those who make things happen, those who watch things happen, and those who wonder what happened.

If you're the kind of person who wonders or watches what happens, go to Raymond Riddle Park and see people who know how to make things happen.

The author concludes with a dramatic sentence to strengthen the impact of the editorial.

Comparing Arguments

1. Key Ideas and Details **(a)** Does Durbin provide enough evidence for you to draw a **conclusion** about his topic? Explain. **(b)** Do you agree or disagree with his position? Why? **(c)** Which author is more effective in supporting his claims with evidence and reasons? Explain.

Content-Area Vocabulary

2. (a) Is Durbin's use of *extinction* in reference to wooden bats meant to be humorous or serious on page 440? Explain. **(b)** Use all three vocabulary words from page 438 in a paragraph about the Endangered Species Act.

Timed Writing

Argument: Editorial

> **Format**
> The prompt directs you to write an editorial. Therefore, your writing must be persuasive.

Write an editorial in response to Durbin's speech. Take a position on the other side of the issue. Make assertions to convince your audience that major league baseball should allow aluminum bats. (30 minutes)

> **Academic Vocabulary**
> When you *take a position* on an issue, you form an opinion about it, based on evidence.

5-Minute Planner

Complete these steps before you begin to write:

1. Read the prompt, looking for highlighted words.
2. Reread Durbin's speech and evaluate his argument. What evidence does the author give to support his conclusions?
3. Identify weak points in the author's argument, such as claims that are not supported by evidence.
4. Jot down your position, including valid reasons and evidence that support it.
5. Use your notes to develop a quick outline. Then, use the outline to help you organize your editorial.

Comparing Biography and Autobiography

Biography is a form of nonfiction in which a writer tells the life story of another person. Biographies often present the experiences and actions of famous people, but they can also be written about ordinary people.

In contrast, an **autobiography** is a form of nonfiction in which a person narrates his or her own life story. In autobiographies, writers may explain their actions, offer their feelings about events, or reveal the private side of public events. Biography and autobiography have these differences:

- Biography is written in the third person (using pronouns *he* and *she*), is based on research, and may be a more objective work.

- Autobiography is written in the first person (using the pronoun *I*), is based on firsthand thoughts, and is a more personal presentation.

Writers of both forms, however, give a wide array of facts and events. As you read, note the details about each subject on a chart like this.

**Common Core
State Standards**

Reading Informational Text
6. Determine an author's point of view or purpose in a text and explain how it is conveyed in the text.

Writing
2. Write informative/explanatory texts to examine a topic and convey ideas, concepts, and information through the selection, organization, and analysis of relevant content. *(Timed Writing)*

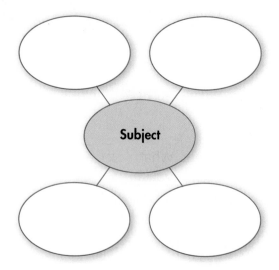

Subject

What is important to know?

Writing About the Big Question

The selections that follow are both nonfiction accounts but each give very different types of information. Use the following sentence starter to help you develop your ideas.

Some **observations** I have about nonfiction are _____.

Meet the Authors

Julia Alvarez (b. 1950)
Author of *Something to Declare*

Although born in New York City, Julia Alvarez was raised until age ten in the Dominican Republic. She is the author of novels, short stories, poems, and nonfiction.

Play on Words The title *Something to Declare* is a play on a question Alvarez, as a child, heard officials ask people entering the United States: "Do you have anything to declare?" The question means "Are you bringing in any items that we need to know about?" The verb *declare* also means "say forcefully." The following selection, the introduction to Alvarez's book of essays, is her answer.

Russell Freedman (b. 1929)
Author of "A Backwoods Boy"

Russell Freedman developed research skills as a reporter and went on to write more than thirty nonfiction books. "A Backwoods Boy" is from *Lincoln: A Photobiography*.

Highlighting History Freedman began writing books about history for young readers because his own children were not interested in the past. He is committed to making actual events come alive through vivid, revealing writing and fascinating, authentic photos.

2 from Something to Declare

Julia Alvarez

Vocabulary
concludes (kən kloodz´) *v.* comes to an end

perplexities
(pər plek´ sə tēz) *n.* things that confuse or puzzle

The first time I received a letter from one of my readers, I was surprised. I had just published my first book of poems, *Homecoming*, which concludes with a sonnet sequence titled "33." My reader wanted to know why I had included forty-one sonnets when the title of the sequence was "33."

I considered not answering. Often, it is the little perplexities and curiosities and quandaries that remain after I have finished reading a book that send me to buy another book by that author. If I want to know more, the best way to find out is to read all the books that the author has written.

In the end, though, I couldn't resist. I wrote back, explaining how thirty-three represented my age at the time I wrote the sequence, how I had meant to include only thirty-three sonnets but I kept writing them and writing them, how the sonnets were not sonnets in the traditional sense. . . . Before I knew it, I had written my reader not just a note on my sonnet sequence but a short essay.

Biography and Autobiography
Which of her own actions is Alvarez explaining?

Many of the essays in this book began in just that way— as answers to such queries. Jessica Peet, a high-school student, read my first novel, *How the García Girls Lost Their Accents*, in her Vermont Authors class and wanted to know if I considered myself a Vermonter. The Lane Series, our local arts and entertainment series, wanted to know what I might have to say about opera. Share Our Strength was putting together a fund-raising anthology. Did I have anything at all to declare about food?

I could not really say to any of them, "Read my novels or my poems or my stories." These folks wanted what my boarding-school housemother used to call a straight answer. Which is where essays start. Not that they obey housemothers. Not that they list everything you are supposed to list on that Customs Declaration form. (How could the wild, multitudinous, daily things in anyone's head be inventoried in a form?) But that is the pretext of essays: *we have something to declare.*

And so this essay book is dedicated to you, my readers, who have asked me so many good questions and who want to know more than I have told you in my novels and poems. About my experience of immigration, about switching languages, about the writing life, the teaching life, the family life, about all of those combined.

Your many questions boil down finally to this one question: Do you have anything more to declare? Yes, I do.

Biography and Autobiography
What do you know about Alvarez's life based on the many organizations listed in this essay?

Spiral Review
Word Choice
Alvarez addresses readers directly as "you." What effect does her word choice have on readers?

Critical Thinking

1. **Key Ideas and Details (a)** Why does Alvarez consider not answering the reader's question about the sonnets in *Homecoming*? **(b) Infer:** What do her reasons reveal about her?

2. **Key Ideas and Details (a)** What does Alvarez realize about her readers and their questions about her? **(b) Connect:** Where does this realization lead Alvarez?

3. **Integration of Knowledge and Ideas (a)** How is the book *Something to Declare* different from Alvarez's other books? **(b) Speculate:** Do you think Alvarez enjoys writing essays more than she enjoys writing novels or poems? Explain.

4. **Integration of Knowledge and Ideas (a)** What question would you like to ask Alvarez? **(b)** Why is this information important to you? Would Alvarez be the appropriate person to ask? *[Connect to the Big Question: What is important to know?]*

Cite textual evidence to support your responses.

A Backwoods Boy

Russell Freedman

"It is a great piece of folly to attempt to make anything out of my early life. It can all be condensed into a simple sentence, and that sentence you will find in Gray's Elegy[1]—'the short and simple annals[2] of the poor.' That's my life, and that's all you or anyone else can make out of it."[3]

Abraham Lincoln never liked to talk much about his early life. A poor backwoods farm boy, he grew up swinging an ax on frontier homesteads in Kentucky, Indiana, and Illinois.

He was born near Hodgenville, Kentucky, on February 12, 1809, in a log cabin with one window, one door, a chimney, and a hardpacked dirt floor. His parents named him after his pioneer grandfather. The first Abraham Lincoln had been shot dead by hostile Indians in 1786, while planting a field of corn in the Kentucky wilderness.

Young Abraham was still a toddler when his family packed their belongings and moved to another log-cabin farm a few miles north, on Knob Creek. That was the first home he could remember, the place where he ran and played as a barefoot boy.

He remembered the bright waters of Knob Creek as it tumbled past the Lincoln cabin and disappeared into the Kentucky hills. Once he fell into the rushing creek and almost drowned before he was pulled out by a neighbor boy. Another time he caught a fish and gave it to a passing soldier.

Lincoln never forgot the names of his first teachers— Zachariah Riney followed by Caleb Hazel—who ran a windowless log schoolhouse two miles away. It was called a "blab school." Pupils of all ages sat on rough wooden benches and bawled out their lessons aloud. Abraham went there with his sister Sarah, who was two years older, when they could be spared from their chores at home. Holding hands, they would walk through scrub trees and across creek bottoms to the schoolhouse door. They learned their numbers from one to ten, and a smattering of reading, writing, and spelling.

---

1. **elegy** (el´ ə jē) *n.* poem praising someone who has died.
2. **annals** (an´ əlz) *n.* historical records.
3. **"It is a great . . . out of it"** This is a quotation from Lincoln.

◀ **Critical Viewing**
Is it surprising that a president of the United States did hard labor like this? Why or why not? **[Assess]**

Biography and Autobiography
Which words here indicate that Freedman is using the third-person point of view?

Biography and Autobiography
Why might Freedman have included facts about the fish and about Lincoln's school memories?

Reading Check
What prevented Abraham Lincoln from attending school every day?

▲ Lincoln as a boy.

Their parents couldn't read or write at all. Abraham's mother, Nancy, signed her name by making a shakily drawn mark. He would remember her as a thin, sad-eyed woman who labored beside her husband in the fields. She liked to gather the children around her in the evening to recite prayers and Bible stories she had memorized.

His father, Thomas, was a burly, barrel-chested farmer and carpenter who had worked hard at homesteading since marrying Nancy Hanks in 1806. A sociable fellow, his greatest pleasure was to crack jokes and swap stories with his chums. With painful effort, Thomas Lincoln could scrawl his name. Like his wife, he had grown up without education, but that wasn't unusual in those days. He supported his family by living off his own land, and he watched for a chance to better himself.

In 1816, Thomas decided to pull up stakes again and move north to Indiana, which was about to join the Union as the nation's nineteenth state. Abraham was seven. He remembered the one-hundred-mile journey as the hardest experience of his life. The family set out on a cold morning in December, loading all their possessions on two horses. They crossed the Ohio River on a makeshift ferry, traveled through towering forests, then hacked a path through tangled underbrush until they reached their new homesite near the backwoods community of Little Pigeon Creek.

Thomas put up a temporary winter shelter—a crude, three-sided lean-to of logs and branches. At the open end, he kept a fire burning to take the edge off the cold and scare off the wild animals. At night, wrapped in bearskins and huddled by the fire, Abraham and Sarah listened to wolves howl and panthers scream.

Abraham passed his eighth birthday in the lean-to. He was big for his age, "a tall spider of a boy," and old enough to handle an ax. He helped his father clear the land. They planted corn and pumpkin seeds between the tree stumps. And they built a new log cabin, the biggest one yet, where Abraham climbed a ladder and slept in a loft beneath the roof.

Soon after the cabin was finished, some of Nancy's kinfolk arrived. Her aunt and uncle with their adopted son Dennis had decided to follow the Lincolns to Indiana. Dennis Hanks became an extra hand to Thomas and a big brother to Abraham, someone to run and wrestle with.

A year later, Nancy's aunt and uncle lay dead, victims of the dreaded "milk sickness" (now known to be caused by a poisonous plant called white snake root). An epidemic of the disease swept through the Indiana woods in the summer of 1818. Nancy had nursed her relatives until the end, and then she too came down with the disease. Abraham watched his mother toss in bed with chills, fever, and pain for seven days before she died at the age of thirty-four. "She knew she was going to die," Dennis Hanks recalled. "She called up the children to her dying side and told them to be good and kind to their father, to one another, and to the world."

Thomas built a coffin from black cherry wood, and nine-year-old Abraham whittled the pegs that held the wooden planks together. They buried Nancy on a windswept hill, next to her aunt and uncle. Sarah, now eleven, took her mother's place, cooking, cleaning, and mending clothes for her father, brother, and cousin Dennis in the forlorn and lonely cabin.

Thomas Lincoln waited for a year. Then he went back to Kentucky to find himself a new wife. He returned in a

Biography and Autobiography
What do these details about the temporary home tell you about Lincoln's childhood?

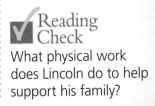

Reading Check
What physical work does Lincoln do to help support his family?

four-horse wagon with a widow named Sarah Bush Johnston, her three children, and all her household goods. Abraham and his sister were fortunate, for their stepmother was a warm and loving person. She took the motherless children to her heart and raised them as her own. She also spruced up the neglected Lincoln cabin, now shared by eight people who lived, ate, and slept in a single smoky room with a loft.

Abraham was growing fast, shooting up like a sunflower, a spindly youngster with big bony hands, unruly black hair, a dark complexion, and luminous gray eyes. He became an expert with the ax, working alongside his father, who also hired him out to work for others. For twenty-five cents a day, the boy dug wells, built pigpens, split fence rails, felled trees. "My how he could chop!" exclaimed a friend. "His ax would flash and bite into a sugar tree or a sycamore, and down it would come. If you heard him felling trees in a clearing, you would say there were three men at work, the way the trees fell."

Meanwhile, he went to school "by littles," a few weeks one winter, maybe a month the next. Lincoln said later that all his schooling together "did not amount to one year." Some fragments of his schoolwork still survive, including a verse that he wrote in his homemade arithmetic book: "Abraham Lincoln/his hand and pen/he will be good but/god knows When."

Mostly, he educated himself by borrowing books and newspapers. There are many stories about Lincoln's efforts to find enough books to satisfy him in that backwoods country. Those he liked he read again and again, losing himself in the adventures of *Robinson Crusoe* or the magical tales of *The Arabian Nights*. He was thrilled by a biography of George Washington, with its stirring account of the Revolutionary War. And he came to love the rhyme and rhythm of poetry, reciting passages from Shakespeare or the Scottish poet Robert Burns at the drop of a hat. He would carry a book out to the field with him, so he could read at the end of each plow furrow, while the horse was getting its breath. When noon came, he would sit under a tree and read while he ate. "I never saw Abe after he was twelve that he didn't have a book in his hand or in his pocket," Dennis Hanks remembered. "It didn't seem natural to see a feller read like that."

By the time he was sixteen, Abraham was six feet tall—"the gangliest awkwardest feller . . . he appeared to be all joints," said a neighbor. He may have looked awkward, but hard physical labor had given him a tough, lean body with muscular arms like steel cables. He could grab a woodsman's ax by the handle and hold it straight out at arm's length. And he was one of the best wrestlers and runners around.

He also had a reputation as a comic and storyteller. Like his father, Abraham was fond of talking and listening to talk. About this time he had found a book called *Lessons in Elocution*, which offered advice on public speaking. He practiced before his friends, standing on a tree stump as he entertained them with fiery imitations of the roving preachers and politicians who often visited Little Pigeon Creek.

Folks liked young Lincoln. They regarded him as a good-humored, easy-going boy—a bookworm maybe, but smart and willing to oblige. Yet even then, people noticed that he could be moody and withdrawn. As a friend put it, he was "witty, sad, and reflective by turns."

At the age of seventeen, Abraham left home for a few months to work as a ferryman's helper on the Ohio River. He was eighteen when his sister Sarah died early in 1828, while giving birth to her first child.

That spring, Abraham had a chance to get away from the backwoods and see something of the world. A local merchant named James Gentry hired Lincoln to accompany his son Allen on a twelve-hundred-mile flatboat voyage to New Orleans. With their cargo of country

Biography and Autobiography
What impression of Lincoln does the writer convey with this information?

Vocabulary
regarded (ri gärd´ əd) *v.* thought of; considered

Reading Check
Why does Lincoln leave the prairie?

produce, the two boys floated down the Ohio River and into the Mississippi, maneuvering with long poles to avoid snags and sandbars, and to navigate in the busy river traffic.

New Orleans was the first real city they had ever seen. Their eyes must have popped as the great harbor came into view, jammed with the masts of sailing ships from distant ports all over the world. The city's cobblestone streets teemed with sailors, traders, and adventurers speaking strange languages. And there were gangs of slaves everywhere. Lincoln would never forget the sight of black men, women, and children being driven along in chains and auctioned off like cattle. In those days, New Orleans had more than two hundred slave dealers.

The boys sold their cargo and their flatboat and returned up river by steamboat. Abraham earned twenty-four dollars—a good bit of money at the time—for the three-month trip. He handed the money over to his father, according to law and custom.

Thomas Lincoln was thinking about moving on again. Lately he had heard glowing reports about Illinois, where instead of forests there were endless prairies with plenty of rich black soil. Early in 1830, Thomas sold his Indiana farm. The Lincolns piled everything they owned into two ox-drawn wagons and set out over muddy roads, with Abraham, just turned twenty-one, driving one of the wagons himself. They traveled west to their new homesite in central Illinois, not far from Decatur. Once again, Abraham helped his father build a cabin and start a new farm.

He stayed with his family through their first prairie winter, but he was getting restless. He had met an enterprising fellow named Denton Offutt, who wanted him to

Biography and Autobiography
Which details tell why Lincoln's eyes "must have popped" in New Orleans?

take another boatload of cargo down the river to New Orleans. Abraham agreed to make the trip with his stepbrother, John Johnston, and a cousin, John Hanks.

When he returned to Illinois three months later, he paid a quick farewell visit to his father and stepmother. Abraham was twenty-two now, of legal age, free to do what he wanted. His parents were settled and could get along without him. Denton Offutt was planning to open a general store in the flourishing village of New Salem, Illinois, and he had promised Lincoln a steady job.

Lincoln arrived in New Salem in July 1831 wearing a faded cotton shirt and blue jeans too short for his long legs—a "friendless, uneducated, penniless boy," as he later described himself. He tended the counter at Denton Offutt's store and slept in a room at the back.

The village stood in a wooded grove on a bluff above the Sangamon River. Founded just two years earlier, it had about one hundred people living in one- and two-room log houses. Cattle grazed behind split-rail fences, hogs snuffled along dusty lanes, and chickens and geese flapped about underfoot.

Biography and Autobiography
How do his experiences in New Orleans and cargo-boating change Lincoln's life?

✔ Reading Check
Why does Lincoln go to New Salem, Illinois?

LITERATURE IN CONTEXT

History Connection

Making History
President Abraham Lincoln delivered the Gettysburg Address on November 19, 1863, at the dedication of the national cemetery on the Civil War battlefield in Gettysburg, Pennsylvania.

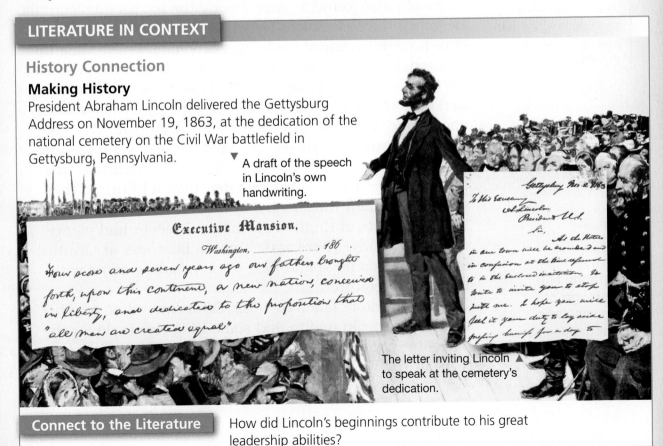

▼ A draft of the speech in Lincoln's own handwriting.

The letter inviting Lincoln ▲ to speak at the cemetery's dedication.

Connect to the Literature   How did Lincoln's beginnings contribute to his great leadership abilities?

New Salem was still a small place, but it was growing. The settlers expected it to become a frontier boom town.

With his gifts for swapping stories and making friends, Lincoln fit easily into the life of the village. He showed off his skill with an ax, competed in footraces, and got along with everyone from Mentor Graham, the schoolmaster, to Jack Armstrong, the leader of a rowdy gang called the Clary's Grove boys. Armstrong was the wrestling champion of New Salem. He quickly challenged Lincoln to a match.

Biography and Autobiography
What does this anecdote about wrestling reveal about Lincoln?

On the appointed day, an excited crowd gathered down by the river, placing bets as the wrestlers stripped to the waist for combat. They circled each other, then came to grips, twisting and tugging until they crashed to the ground with Lincoln on top. As he pinned Armstrong's shoulders to the ground, the other Clary's Grove boys dived in to join the scuffle. Lincoln broke away, backed against a cliff, and defiantly offered to take them all on—one at a time. Impressed, Armstrong jumped to his feet and offered Lincoln his hand, declaring the match a draw. After that, they were fast friends.

Spiral Review
Word Choice
What effect do the transitions *after that* and *also* have on the flow of ideas?

Lincoln also found a place among the town's intellectuals. He joined the New Salem Debating Society, which met once a week in James Rutledge's tavern. The first time he debated, he seemed nervous. But as he began to speak in his high, reedy voice, he surprised everyone with the force and logic of his argument. "He was already a fine speaker," one debater recalled. "All he lacked was culture."

Lincoln was self-conscious about his meager education, and ambitious to improve himself. Mentor Graham, the schoolmaster and a fellow debater, took a liking to the young man, lent him books, and offered to coach him in the fine points of English grammar. Lincoln had plenty of time to study. There wasn't much business at Offutt's store, so he could spend long hours reading as he sat behind the counter.

Biography and Autobiography
What important career decision does the author relate here?

When the store failed in 1832, Offutt moved on to other schemes. Lincoln had to find something else to do. At the age of twenty-three, he decided to run for the Illinois state legislature. Why not? He knew everyone in town, people

◀ **Critical Viewing**
Which side of
Lincoln's life does this
portrait illustrate?
[Interpret]

liked him, and he was rapidly gaining confidence as a
public speaker. His friends urged him to run, saying that
a bright young man could go far in politics. So Lincoln
announced his candidacy and his political platform. He
was in favor of local improvements, like better roads and
canals. He had made a study of the Sangamon River, and
he proposed that it be dredged and cleared so steamboats
could call at New Salem—insuring a glorious future for
the town.

Before he could start his campaign, an Indian war flared
up in northern Illinois. Chief Black Hawk of the Sauk and
Fox tribes had crossed the Mississippi, intending, he said,
to raise corn on land that had been taken from his people
thirty years earlier. The white settlers were alarmed, and
the governor called for volunteers to stop the invasion.
Lincoln enlisted in a militia company made up of his friends
and neighbors. He was surprised and pleased when the men
elected him as their captain, with Jack Armstrong as first
sergeant. His troops drilled and marched, but they never
did sight any hostile Indians. Years later, Lincoln would joke
about his three-month stint as a military man, telling how

Reading
Check

How does Lincoln
improve his public
speaking skills?

he survived "a good many bloody battles with mosquitoes."

By the time he returned to New Salem, election day was just two weeks off. He jumped into the campaign—pitching horseshoes with voters, speaking at barbecues, chatting with farmers in the fields, joking with customers at country stores. He lost, finishing eighth in a field of thirteen. But in his own precinct,[4] where folks knew him, he received 227 votes out of 300 cast.

Biography and Autobiography
Which character traits does this information about campaigning show?

Defeated as a politician, he decided to try his luck as a frontier merchant. With a fellow named William Berry as his partner, Lincoln operated a general store that sold everything from axes to beeswax. But the two men showed little aptitude for business, and their store finally "winked out," as Lincoln put it. Then Berry died, leaving Lincoln saddled with a $1,100 debt—a gigantic amount for someone who had never earned more than a few dollars a month. Lincoln called it "the National Debt," but he vowed to repay every cent. He spent the next fifteen years doing so.

To support himself, he worked at all sorts of odd jobs. He split fence rails, hired himself out as a farmhand, helped at the local gristmill.[5] With the help of friends, he was appointed postmaster of New Salem, a part-time job that paid about fifty dollars a year. Then

Biography and Autobiography
What do the facts here suggest about Lincoln's attitude toward work?

he was offered a chance to become deputy to the local surveyor.[6] He knew nothing about surveying, so he bought a compass, a chain, and a couple of textbooks on the subject. Within six weeks, he had taught himself enough to start work—laying out roads and townsites, and marking off property boundaries.

As he traveled about the county, making surveys and delivering mail to faraway farms, people came to know him as an honest and dependable fellow. Lincoln could be counted on to witness a contract, settle a boundary

---

4. **precinct** (prē′ siŋkt) *n.* election district.
5. **gristmill** (grist′ mil′) *n.* place where grain is ground into flour.
6. **surveyor** (sər vā′ ər) *n.* person who identifies or marks the boundaries of land.

dispute, or compose a letter for folks who couldn't write much themselves. For the first time, his neighbors began to call him "Abe."

In 1834, Lincoln ran for the state legislature again. This time he placed second in a field of thirteen candidates, and was one of four men elected to the Illinois House of Representatives from Sangamon County. In November, wearing a sixty-dollar tailor-made suit he had bought on credit, the first suit he had ever owned, the twenty-five-year-old legislator climbed into a stagecoach and set out for the state capital in Vandalia.

In those days, Illinois lawmakers were paid three dollars a day to cover their expenses, but only while the legislature was in session. Lincoln still had to earn a living. One of his fellow representatives, a rising young attorney named John Todd Stuart, urged Lincoln to take up the study of law. As Stuart pointed out, it was an ideal profession for anyone with political ambitions.

And in fact, Lincoln had been toying with the idea of becoming a lawyer. For years he had hung around frontier courthouses, watching country lawyers bluster and strut as they cross-examined witnesses and delivered impassioned speeches before juries. He had sat on juries himself, appeared as a witness, drawn up legal documents for his neighbors. He had even argued a few cases before the local justice of the peace.

Yes, the law intrigued him. It would give him a chance to rise in the world, to earn a respected place in the community, to live by his wits instead of by hard physical labor.

Yet Lincoln hesitated, unsure of himself because he had so little formal education. That was no great obstacle, his friend Stuart kept telling him. In the 1830's, few American lawyers had ever seen the inside of a law school. Instead, they "read law" in the office of a practicing attorney until they knew enough to pass their exams.

Lincoln decided to study entirely on his own. He borrowed some law books from Stuart, bought others at an auction, and began to read and memorize legal codes[7] and precedents.[8] Back in New Salem, folks would see him

Vocabulary
intrigued (in trēgd´) *v.* fascinated

Biography and Autobiography
How would you describe Lincoln's attitude toward becoming a lawyer?

---

7. legal codes body of law, as for a nation or a city, arranged systematically.
8. precedents (pres´ ə dents) *n.* legal cases that may serve as a reference.

walking down the road, reciting aloud from one of his law books, or lying under a tree as he read, his long legs stretched up the trunk. He studied for nearly three years before passing his exams and being admitted to practice on March 1, 1837.

By then, the state legislature was planning to move from Vandalia to Springfield, which had been named the new capital of Illinois. Lincoln had been elected to a second term in the legislature. And he had accepted a job as junior partner in John Todd Stuart's Springfield law office.

In April, he went back to New Salem for the last time to pack his belongings and say goodbye to his friends. The little village was declining now. Its hopes for growth and prosperity had vanished when the Sangamon River proved too treacherous for steamboat travel. Settlers were moving away, seeking brighter prospects elsewhere.

By 1840, New Salem was a ghost town. It would have been forgotten completely if Abraham Lincoln hadn't gone there to live when he was young, penniless, and ambitious.

Critical Thinking

Cite textual evidence to support your responses.

1. **Key Ideas and Details (a)** Identify two facts about Lincoln between the ages of eight and twenty-one. **(b) Generalize:** What words would you use to describe Lincoln at that time in his life?

2. **Key Ideas and Details (a) Analyze:** In what ways did Lincoln's life change in New Salem? **(b) Connect:** How is the Lincoln of New Salem similar to or different from the Lincoln whom most people know in American history?

3. **Key Ideas and Details (a)** How did Lincoln continue to develop and change after he was elected to office? **(b) Speculate:** In what ways did these experiences help him become a leader?

4. **Integration of Knowledge and Ideas (a)** What important information about Lincoln is missing from "A Backwoods Boy"? **(b)** Why is this missing information important to know? *[Connect to the Big Question: What is important to know?]*

Comparing Biography and Autobiography

1. Key Ideas and Details (a) What facts about her writing life does Julia Alvarez include in the selection from *Something to Declare?* **(b)** How does she feel about these experiences? Explain.

2. Key Ideas and Details (a) What details in "A Backwoods Boy" help Freedman show that Lincoln had a difficult childhood? **(b)** What details show that Lincoln chose his own path to build success for himself?

3. Craft and Structure (a) What might be "missing" from Alvarez's story if it were written by a biographer? **(b)** How would the presentation of events differ if Lincoln himself had narrated "A Backwoods Boy"? Explain.

⏱ Timed Writing

Explanatory Text: Essay

Compare and contrast what you learned about Julia Alvarez and what you learned about Abraham Lincoln. In an essay, discuss how the autobiography and biography helped you to get to know these people. In your writing, compare one author's presentation of events with the other's. **(25 minutes)**

5-Minute Planner

1. Read the prompt carefully and completely.

2. Gather your thoughts by creating a two-column chart in which you list specific details that you have learned about each person. Also, record further questions you have about each person.

3. Use your notes, the chart you created on p. 444, and the chart you just created to plan your response.

4. Reread the prompt, and then draft your essay.

Writing Workshop

 **Common Core State Standards**

Writing

2. Write informative/explanatory texts to examine a topic and convey ideas, concepts, and information through the selection, organization, and analysis of relevant content.

2.a. Introduce a topic; organize ideas, concepts, and information, using strategies such as definition, classification, comparison/ contrast, and cause/effect; include formatting, graphics, and multimedia when useful to aiding comprehension.

2.d. Use precise language and domain-specific vocabulary to inform about or explain the topic.

4. Produce clear and coherent writing in which the development, organization, and style are appropriate to task, purpose, and audience.

Write an Explanatory Text

Exposition: How-to Essay

Defining the Form Expository writing is writing that explains or informs. In a **how-to essay,** you explain how to do or make something. You might use elements of a how-to essay when you write recipes, step-by-step instructions, or travel directions.

Assignment Write a how-to essay to explain a process. Include these elements:

- ✔ a *specific, achievable result*
- ✔ a *list of all materials* needed
- ✔ a clear *sequence of steps,* presented in exact order
- ✔ *transitional words and phrases* to make the order clear
- ✔ *illustrations or diagrams,* as needed, to provide further explanation of any complicated steps
- ✔ a clear *organizational format*
- ✔ error-free writing, especially the *correct use of modifiers*

To preview the criteria on which your how-to essay may be judged, see the rubric on page 467.

 Writing Workshop: *Work in Progress*

Review the work you did on pages 417 and 435.

Prewriting/Planning Strategy

Brainstorm to gather details. Make a list of activities you enjoy, and choose one to be your topic. Use a two-column chart like the one shown to gather important details about your topic.

How to Make Spaghetti	
STEPS:	**MATERIALS:**
1. Fill pot with water.	1. large pot with lid
2. Add salt.	2. spaghetti
3. Bring water to boil.	3. teaspoon of salt
4.	4.

Making Each Step Clear

The **organization** of a how-to essay is extremely important. After all, your purpose is to explain how to do something. To explain a process effectively, make sure that the steps appear in the correct order and that each one is written clearly and precisely. The following tips will help you write clear, well-organized directions.

Visualizing the Steps Picture yourself following the steps in your prewriting chart. Doing so will help you make sure that you have not left out any steps and that the steps appear logically. Be sure every material, ingredient, and tool is noted on your chart. List the materials in the order in which they will be needed so that your reader can organize his or her workspace. Make any corrections or additions needed.

Identifying Your Audience Think about who will be reading your how-to essay—classmates, adults, or young children. Think about what your audience already knows about your topic or similar processes and what further information they might need in order to follow your directions successfully. Create a chart similar to the one below.

Audience:	
To achieve this goal:	**Answer these questions:**
Provide enough explanation so that readers can follow each step successfully.	1. Which steps might need further explanation? 2. What words might be too difficult for my audience? What substitutions should I make?
Provide enough information about the materials.	3. Which materials or recipe ingredients might be unfamiliar to my readers? 4. What additional information might be helpful? 5. If any materials might be difficult for them to find, what substitutions might they use?
Draw on your readers' experience to make the directions clearer.	6. What similar tasks or processes might be familiar to my readers? 7. What comparisons might I make in order to clarify my directions?

Drafting Strategies

Plan your draft so that it has a clear beginning, middle, and end.

Include a catchy introduction. First, identify the task and build your reader's interest. Then, transition into the topic and purpose of your essay by introducing the steps of the process.

Present a step-by-step guide. Next, list the materials in the order in which they will be used. Present the steps in exact order, adding details and illustrations as needed. Use transitional words and phrases such as *first, next, after, then,* and *finally* to keep the order of the steps clear.

Finish with a summary and a send-off. Sum up the process and encourage your readers to enjoy the finished product.

Plan and sketch your illustrations and diagrams. Decide which steps your audience might find especially complicated. Illustrations or diagrams can help you clarify those steps. Plan and sketch any visual aids. Then, assign each sketch a number that corresponds to the related process step. When you create your final draft, place the visuals next to the appropriate steps.

Revising Strategies

Strengthen your opening. To evaluate and strengthen your introduction, ask yourself these questions:

- Does it clearly define the task?
- Does it make the readers want to keep reading?
- Does it make a transition into the steps of the process?

Use your answers to these questions to guide your revision.

Check your use of transitions. In a how-to essay, transitional words and phrases help readers follow the steps. As you review your draft, add transitions where necessary to clarify the order of steps. Consult the list of common transitions shown here.

Useful Chronological Transitions	
first	once you have…
next	at the same time
then	while you…
after you have…	finally

Common Core State Standards

Writing

2.a. Introduce a topic; organize ideas, concepts, and information, using strategies such as definition, classification, comparison/contrast, and cause/effect; include formatting, graphics, and multimedia when useful to aiding comprehension.

2.b. Develop the topic with relevant facts, definitions, concrete details, quotations, or other information and examples.

2.c. Use appropriate transitions to clarify the relationships among ideas and concepts.

Revising for Correct Use of Troublesome Modifiers

Modifiers are adjectives and adverbs that add details and description to your writing. Errors can occur when writers mistake adjectives for adverbs.

- **Adjectives:** Use adjectives to modify nouns or pronouns.
  Examples: *This is a <u>tasty</u> meal. It was <u>easy</u> to prepare.*

- **Adverbs:** Use adverbs to modify action verbs.
  Example: *They set the table <u>perfectly</u>.*

Errors Involving *Good* and *Well* To identify and fix errors related to the modifiers *good* and *well*, review these rules:

- ***Good*** is an adjective that modifies only nouns and pronouns.
  Example: *This meal is <u>good</u>. (Good* modifies <u>meal</u>.)

- ***Well*** is an adverb that modifies action verbs.
  Example: *Stir the spaghetti <u>well</u>. (Well* modifies <u>stir</u>.)

Errors Involving *Better* and *Best* To identify and fix errors related to the modifiers *better* and *best*, determine the number of things or actions.

- Use ***better*** when two things or actions are being compared.
  Example: *I think spaghetti is <u>better</u> than rice.*

- Use ***best*** when three or more things or actions are being compared.
  Example: *I think spaghetti is the <u>best</u> food of all.*

Fixing Errors Follow these steps to correct modifier errors.

1. Find the modifiers in your writing.

2. For *good* and *well,* determine whether the words are used as adjectives or adverbs. Using the rules on this page, replace words you have used incorrectly.

3. For *better* and *best,* choose the modifier that suits the number of items being compared.

Grammar in Your Writing

Reread your draft and circle the modifiers *good, well, better,* and *best.* Use the rules above to make all necessary corrections.

> **PH WRITING COACH**
>
> Further instruction and practice are available in *Prentice Hall Writing Coach*.

Student Model: Sara Noē, La Porte, IN

 **Common Core State Standards**

Language
2.b. Spell correctly.

How to Write a Poem

The technique of writing poetry varies among different poets. My format depends on the mood I'm in, the environment around me, and what my inspiration is. I can't think of a poem whenever I want to; I have to let it come to me on its own. However, there are many other ways to write poems that rhyme. The most common process I've seen follows these steps:

1. picking a topic you're good at or having knowledge about the subject
2. brainstorming for words that relate to your topic
3. thinking up more words that rhyme with your first list and that also describe your topic
4. creating phrases that include your rhyming words at the end. Finally, combining your phrases into one and trying to get the words to flow together

> Sara numbers her steps to show their clear sequence.

If you choose a topic you don't like or don't know a lot about, your poem may end up being dull or boring. Sometimes there's a topic you can't get off your mind, and research may help you find out enough to write about it. Word webs and lists are the best way to brainstorm for words. If another way helps you more, go for it!

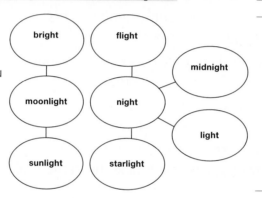

> She uses a diagram to explain the use of a word web.

Remember to make sure your words relate to your topic. For rhyming words, just go through the alphabet until you have plenty. Once you have your list done, sit down in a quiet place and begin organizing the words into phrases. The rhyming words from your list should be at the end of each phrase. Here is where the words and ideas need to flow together. Finally, put all of your phrases together. When you are finished, your words should blend together in one smooth poem.

Those are the steps for rhyming poems, but free-form poems don't rhyme. For these, the best I can tell you is to use your imagination. A thesaurus might help you with finding majestic words or just the right ones for your needs. Poetry is very cheap; the only materials you need are paper, a pencil, and your imagination. Pretty much anybody can write poetry, but it takes dedication and a lot of determination to make it a good poem. Some people write poetry for competition, while others just write in their spare time. Some people, like me, do both. Competition is fun occasionally, but if that's the only reason you write poems, then that may take all the excitement out of it. Poetry is my hobby, and it can easily be yours. Just do your best, and be proud of what you accomplish. Go for it!

> Sara lists all of the materials needed for the process she is explaining.

> She describes a specific result of following the directions in her essay.

Editing and Proofreading

Revise your draft to correct errors in grammar, spelling, and punctuation.

Focus on easily confused words. Some frequently used words are sometimes confused with other words that sound almost the same or that have similar meanings. Double-check your essay for commonly mistaken words, and make any necessary corrections. Here are some examples:

accept, except	than, then	loose, lose
are, our	their, there, they're	your, you're

Spiral Review

Earlier in the unit, you learned about **adjectives and articles** (p. 416) and **comparisons with adjectives** (p. 434). Review your how-to essay to be sure that you have used all adjectives and articles correctly.

Publishing and Presenting

Consider the following possibilities for sharing your work:

Give a demonstration. Using the information in your essay, give a demonstration. Make visual aids such as posters, diagrams, and photographs to use with your presentation.

Create a "how-to" Web page. Work with a teacher to design a Web page presenting the how-to essays of your class.

Reflecting on Your Writing

Writer's Journal Jot down your answers to these questions:

- *What did you learn about the process you were explaining?*
- *Do you think that the part of the activity that was hardest to explain is the hardest to do? Explain your answer.*

PH WRITING COACH

Further instruction and practice are available in *Prentice Hall Writing Coach*.

Rubric for Self-Assessment

Find evidence in your writing to address each category. Then use the rating scale to grade your work.

Criteria	Rating Scale
	not very *very*
Focus: How well have you focused your topic?	1 2 3 4 5
Organization: How organized is the sequence of steps and list of materials?	1 2 3 4 5
Style: How well do you use transitions to make the steps clear?	1 2 3 4 5
Conventions: How good is your grammar, especially your use of modifiers?	1 2 3 4 5
Support/Elaboration: How helpful are illustrations or diagrams?	1 2 3 4 5

Leveled Texts

Build your skills and improve your comprehension of nonfiction with texts of increasing complexity.

Read **"Turkeys"** to meet a girl who wakes up to a surprise she will never forget.

Read **"Langston Terrace"** to learn about the author's childhood home.

Common Core State Standards

Meet these standards with either **"Turkeys"** (p. 472) or **"Langston Terrace"** (p. 480).

Reading Informational Text
2. Determine a central idea of a text and how it is conveyed through particular details; provide a summary of the text distinct from personal opinions or judgments. *(Reading Skill: Main Idea)*

Writing
3. Write narratives to develop real or imagined experiences or events using effective technique, relevant descriptive details, and well-structured event sequences.
3.b. Use narrative techniques, such as dialogue, pacing, and description, to develop experiences, events, and/or characters. *(Writing: Journal Entry)*

8. Gather relevant information from multiple print and digital sources; assess the credibility of each source. *(Research and Technology: Informative Presentation)*

Speaking and Listening
4. Present claims and findings, sequencing ideas logically and using pertinent descriptions, facts, and details to accentuate main ideas or themes; use appropriate eye contact, adequate volume, and clear pronunciation. *(Research and Technology: Informative Presentation)*

Language
1. Demonstrate command of the conventions of standard English grammar and usage when writing or speaking. *(Conventions: Adverbs)*

6. Acquire and use accurately grade-appropriate general academic and domain-specific words and phrases; gather vocabulary knowledge when considering a word or phrase important to comprehension or expression. *(Vocabulary: Word Study)*

Reading Skill: Main Idea

The **main idea** is the most important point in a literary work. Sometimes the main idea is stated directly. At other times, you must figure it out by **identifying key details** in the text.

- Key details often reveal what a work is about.
- They are sometimes repeated throughout a work.
- They are related to other details in a work.
- Together, the key details support the main idea.

Using the Strategy: Main Idea Map

As you read, use a graphic organizer like the one shown to record key details. Then use those details to determine the main idea.

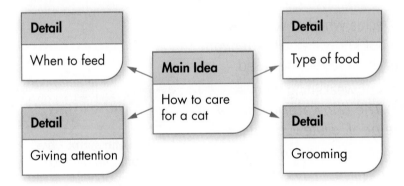

Literary Analysis: Author's Influences

An **author's influences** are the factors that affect his or her writing. These influences may include historical factors, such as world events that happened during the author's lifetime. For example, the gold rush of 1849 might have influenced the ideas of an author who grew up in California in the 1850s. Authors are also influenced by cultural factors, such as the way they live and what they think is important. As you read, look for details that indicate an author's influences.

What is important to *know?*

Writing About the Big Question

In "Turkeys," a girl helps save wild turkeys from disappearing, or becoming extinct. Use these sentence starters to help you develop your ideas about the Big Question.

People who work to save animals from extinction must **examine** _____. The **knowledge** they gain from their studies can be used to _____.

While You Read Ask yourself these questions about the people who study the birds: How much knowledge do they have about wild turkeys? What knowledge might they be missing?

Vocabulary

Read each word and its definition. Decide whether you know the word well, know it a little bit, or do not know it at all. After you read, see how your knowledge of each word has increased.

- **dilution** (di loo´ shən) *n.* process of weakening by mixing with something else (p. 472) *The rainwater caused a dilution of the chlorine in the pool.* dilute *v.* diluted *v.*

- **demise** (di mīz´) *n.* end of existence; death (p. 472) *A laser beam caused the superhero's demise.* demised *v.*

- **methods** (meth´ ədz) *n.* ways of doing something (p. 473) *The artist's methods were new to the school.* methodical *adj.*

- **sensible** (sen´ sə bəl) *adj.* logical; practical; intelligent (p. 475) *She was sensible not to wear her new shoes on a rainy day.* sensibly *adv.* sensibility *n.*

- **descendants** (dē sen´ dənts) *n.* a person's children, grandchildren, great-grandchildren, and so on (p. 476) *I am one of Granny's descendants.* descendant *n.* descend *v.* descent *n.*

- **vigilance** (vij´ ə ləns) *n.* watchfulness (p. 476) *The officer's vigilance prevented a crime.* vigilant *adj.* vigil *n.*

Word Study

The **Latin suffix *-ible*** means "tending to" or "capable of." It always forms an adjective.

In this story, the narrator describes herself as **sensible**, which means that she tends to have good sense.

Meet
Bailey White
(b. 1950)

Author of
Turkeys

Bailey White's father, Robb, was a writer of children's stories and television and movie scripts. Inspired by her father's love of words, White began writing in her teen years. Her mother, Rosalie, was a farmer. Through her mother, White gained an admiration for nature.

Letting the Story Roll As a teacher in Thomasville, Georgia, White did not expect to become famous. However, as an essayist on National Public Radio, she shared her observations with listeners across the country. About fiction, White states, "I liked the idea of starting with just anything . . . and being free to just let the story roll out from there."

DID YOU KNOW?

White's collection of essays, *Mama Makes up her Mind and Other Dangers of Southern Living*, was on the bestseller list for 55 weeks.

BACKGROUND FOR THE ESSAY

Conservation

"Turkeys" describes the efforts of conservationists to preserve a population of wild turkeys. Conservation became an issue in the United States in the early 1900s when President Theodore Roosevelt established the first wildlife refuge at Pelican Island, Florida. He later set aside more than 140 million acres nationwide as forest reserves.

Turkeys

Bailey White

▲ **Critical Viewing**
Why might scientists be interested in studying turkeys? **[Speculate]**

Vocabulary
dilution (di lōō´ shən) *n.* process of weakening by mixing with something else
demise (di mīz´) *n.* end of existence; death

Something about my mother attracts ornithologists.[1] It all started years ago when a couple of them discovered she had a rare species of woodpecker coming to her bird feeder. They came in the house and sat around the window, exclaiming and taking pictures with big fancy cameras. But long after the red cockaded woodpeckers had gone to roost, the ornithologists were still there. There always seemed to be three or four of them wandering around our place and staying for supper.

In those days, during the 1950's, the big concern of ornithologists in our area was the wild turkey. They were rare, and the pure-strain wild turkeys had begun to interbreed with farmers' domestic stock. The species was being degraded. It was extinction by dilution, and to the ornithologists it was just as tragic as the more dramatic demise of the passenger pigeon or the Carolina parakeet. ●

---

1. **ornithologists** (ôr´ nə thäl´ ə jists) *n.* people who study birds.

One ornithologist had devised a formula to compute the ratio of domestic to pure-strain wild turkey in an individual bird by comparing the angle of flight at takeoff and the rate of acceleration. And in those sad days, the turkeys were flying low and slow.

It was during that time, the spring when I was six years old, that I caught the measles. I had a high fever, and my mother was worried about me. She kept the house quiet and dark and crept around silently, trying different methods of cooling me down.

Even the ornithologists stayed away—but not out of fear of the measles or respect for a household with sickness. The fact was, they had discovered a wild turkey nest. According to the formula, the hen was pure-strain wild—not a taint of the sluggish domestic bird in her blood—and the ornithologists were camping in the woods, protecting her nest from predators and taking pictures.

One night our phone rang. It was one of the ornithologists. "Does your little girl still have measles?" he asked.

Main Idea
How do these details support the main idea that the wild turkeys are becoming rare?

Vocabulary
methods (meth´ ədz) *n.* ways of doing something

Reading Check
Why are the ornithologists concerned?

Science Connection

Leaving the Nest

▼ Ostrich egg

Most bird's eggs need to be kept at a regular temperature between 99 and 102 degrees Fahrenheit in order to hatch. For most birds, this means incubating, or warming, the eggs, usually by sitting on them. For some birds in extremely hot climates, though, the parent bird may actually have to cool the egg to keep it at the correct temperature. The parent bird cools the egg by shading it or dripping water on it.

	Wild Turkey	Ruby-throated Hummingbird	Ostrich
Nest	Rough pile of leaves, twigs, brush on ground	Cup made of moss, fluff, and spiderwebs in a tree	Shallow hole in ground
Incubation time	28 days	14 days	42 days
Egg size	2½ to 3 inches wide—less than a pound (a little larger than a chicken's egg)	Size of a bean	6 inches—3 lbs. (the equivalent of two dozen chicken eggs)
Young leave nest and feed themselves	12–24 hours after hatching	3 weeks after hatching	Almost immediately
Fledged (having all the feathers needed to fly)	10 days old	2–3 weeks old	Ostriches never fly, but they have all their feathers when they hatch.

▼ Chicken egg

Young turkeys are called "poults." Although they can walk and feed themselves, they stay with the parent birds until they can fly and escape on their own from predators. Even then, they may continue to travel as a group.

Connect to the Literature

Why are the scientists able to hatch and raise the baby turkeys without the mother bird? Which would it be easier for them to hatch in the same way—hummingbirds or ostriches? Explain.

▼ Hummingbird egg

Spiral Review
Development of Ideas What results from the author's high temperature?

"Yes," said my mother. "She's very sick. Her temperature is 102."

"I'll be right over," said the ornithologist.

In five minutes a whole carload of them arrived. They marched solemnly into the house, carrying a cardboard box. "A hundred and two, did you say? Where is she?" they asked my mother.

They crept into my room and set the box down on the bed. I was barely conscious, and when I opened my eyes, their worried faces hovering over me seemed to float out of the darkness like giant, glowing eggs. They snatched the covers off me and felt me all over. They consulted in whispers.

"Feels just right, I'd say."

"A hundred two—can't miss if we tuck them up close and she lies still."

I closed my eyes then, and after a while the ornithologists drifted away, their pale faces bobbing up and down on the black wave of fever. •

The next morning I was better. For the first time in days I could think. The memory of the ornithologists with their whispered voices was like a dream from another life. But when I pulled down the covers, there staring up at me with googly eyes and wide mouths were sixteen fuzzy baby turkeys, and the cracked chips and caps of sixteen brown speckled eggs.

I was a sensible child. I gently stretched myself out. The eggshells crackled, and the turkey babies fluttered and cheeped and snuggled against me. I laid my aching head back on the pillow and closed my eyes. "The ornithologists," I whispered. "The ornithologists have been here."

It seems the turkey hen had been so disturbed by the elaborate protective measures that had been undertaken on her behalf that she had abandoned her nest on the night the eggs were due to hatch. It was a cold night. The ornithologists, not having an incubator on hand, used their heads and came up with the next best thing.

The baby turkeys and I gained our strength together. When I was finally able to get out of bed and feebly creep around the house, the turkeys peeped and cheeped around my ankles, scrambling to keep up with me and tripping over their own big spraddle-toed feet. When I went outside for the first time, the turkeys tumbled after me down the steps and scratched around in the yard while I sat in the sun. •

Main Idea
What key detail do you learn here that is important to the ornithologists' plan?

Vocabulary
sensible (sen´ sə bəl) *adj.* logical; practical; intelligent

Reading Check
What happened to the author when she was six years old?

Finally, in late summer, the day came when they were ready to fly for the first time as adult birds. The ornithologists gathered. I ran down the hill, and the turkeys ran too. Then, one by one, they took off. They flew high and fast. The ornithologists made Vs with their thumbs and forefingers, measuring angles. They consulted their stopwatches and paced off distances. They scribbled in their tiny notebooks. Finally they looked at each other. They sighed. They smiled. They jumped up and down and hugged each other. "One hundred percent pure wild turkey!" they said.

Nearly forty years have passed since then. Now there's a vaccine for measles. And the woods where I live are full of pure wild turkeys. I like to think they are all descendants of those sixteen birds I saved from the vigilance of the ornithologists.

Vocabulary
descendants (dē sen´dənts) *n.* a person's children, grandchildren, great grandchildren and so on

vigilance (vij´ ə ləns) *n.* watchfulness

Critical Thinking

1. **Key Ideas and Details** **(a)** Where do the events in "Turkeys" take place? **(b) Analyze:** What problem threatens the wild turkey at this time?

2. **Key Ideas and Details** **(a)** Why are the ornithologists around the author's home? **(b) Interpret:** At the beginning of the essay, what is the relationship between the author and the ornithologists?

3. **Key Ideas and Details** **(a)** What event brings the wild turkey and the author together? **(b) Evaluate:** Why is the author's fever important to the ornithologists? **(c) Analyze:** What is amusing about the solution to the ornithologists' problem?

4. **Key Ideas and Details** **(a)** Do you think the actions of the ornithologists in this narrative are important? Why or why not? **(b) Interpret:** How do you think White feels when she watches the turkeys take off? Explain.

5. **Integration of Knowledge and Ideas** What important discovery about wild turkeys do the ornithologists learn that might affect their future research? *[Connect to the Big Question: What is important to know?]*

Cite textu
evidence
support y
respons

Reading Skill: Main Idea

1. Bailey White's thoughts and feelings about the ornithologists make up the main idea of this essay. List four **key details** that show White's thoughts and feelings.

2. In your own words, state the **main idea** of this essay.

Literary Analysis: Author's Influences

3. Key Ideas and Details In a chart like the one shown, list cultural and historical factors that may have **influenced** White's writing of "Turkeys."

Time and Place	Cultural Background	World Events

4. Key Ideas and Details Which factors on your completed chart do you think influenced the author's writing the most? Explain.

Vocabulary

Acquisition and Use Answer each of the following questions with either *yes* or *no*. Then, explain your answer.

1. Is a <u>dilution</u> of bleach stronger than plain bleach?

2. Are there many <u>methods</u> in the study of science?

3. Is it <u>sensible</u> to wear flip-flops when mountain climbing?

4. Can a flood cause the <u>demise</u> of a bug?

5. Will a town's <u>vigilance</u> increase the crime rate?

6. Are you a <u>descendant</u> of your great-grandparents?

Word Study Use the context of the sentence and what you know about the **Latin suffix -ible** to explain your answer to each question.

1. Is plastic *edible*?

2. Is air *visible*?

Word Study

The **Latin suffix -ible** means "tending to," or "capable of." It always forms an adjective.

Apply It Explain how the suffix -ible contributes to the meaning of these words. Consult a dictionary if necessary.

terrible
permissible
possible

What is important to *know?*

Writing About the Big Question

In "Langston Terrace," the narrator and her family move to a new neighborhood. Use the following sentence starter to help you develop your ideas about the Big Question.

Knowledge you might like to have about your future neighborhood includes _____.

While You Read Notice which features of Langston Terrace are important to the narrator because they help her to feel at home.

Vocabulary

Read each word and its definition. Decide whether you know the word well, know it a little bit, or do not know it at all. After you have read, see how your knowledge of each word has increased.

- **applications** (ap´ li kā´ shənz) *n.* forms filled out to make a request (p. 480) *I had to fill out applications for camp.* apply *v.* applying *v.* applicant *n.*

- **community** (kə myoo´ nə tē) *n.* group of people living in the same area (p. 482) *Our community is very diverse.*

- **resident** (rez´ i dənt) *adj.* living in a particular place (p. 482) *Resident students live on campus.* reside *v.* resident *n.* residential *adj.* residence *n.*

- **choral** (kôr´ əl) *adj.* relating to a singing group or choir (p. 482) *The choral music was written by a famous composer.* chorus *n.* choir *n.*

- **reunion** (rē yoon´ yən) *n.* a gathering of people who have been separated (p. 484) *The picnic is a family reunion.* reunite *v.* reuniting *v.*

- **homey** (hōm´ ē) *adj.* comfortable; having a feeling of home (p. 484) *The empty house did not feel homey.* hominess *n.*

Word Study

The **Latin suffix -ent** can form an adjective or a noun. As a word part, it means "has," "shows," or "does."

In this story, the narrator is a **resident** of Langston Terrace, which means she has a residence, or home, there.

Meet
Eloise Greenfield
(b. 1929)

Author of
Langston Terrace

Eloise Greenfield spent many hours reading in the library, which was a two-minute walk from her home. Although she loved books, she did not enjoy writing.

A Love of Words One day, however, Greenfield sat down and began to write. Since then, she has published more than thirty books, including picture books, collections of poetry, and biographies. Greenfield once said, "I love words . . . sometimes they make me laugh. Other times, I feel a kind of pain in struggling to find the right ones. But I keep struggling, because I want to do my best, and because I want children to have the best."

BACKGROUND FOR THE ESSAY

Langston Terrace

Langston Terrace was the first public housing project in Washington, D.C., and the second in the nation. Built in 1938, it housed 274 African American working-class families. Eloise Greenfield's family was among the first to move in. Today, Langston Terrace is a national historic landmark.

DID YOU KNOW?

"Langston Terrace" comes from the book *Childtimes,* which tells the story of Greenfield's family. Greenfield wrote *Childtimes* with her mother, Lessie Jones Little.

Langston Terrace

Eloise Greenfield

Builders in the City, 1993, Jacob Lawrence, The Jacob and Gwendolyn Lawrence Foundation/© Artists Rights Society (ARS), New York

▲ **Critical Viewing**
What do you think these men are building? Why do you think so? **[Speculate]**

Vocabulary
applications (ap′ li kā′ shənz) *n.* forms filled out to make a request

I fell in love with Langston Terrace the very first time I saw it. Our family had been living in two rooms of a three-story house when Mama and Daddy saw the newspaper article telling of the plans to build it. It was going to be a low-rent housing project in northeast Washington, and it would be named in honor of John Mercer Langston, the famous black lawyer, educator, and congressman.

So many people needed housing and wanted to live there, many more than there would be room for. They were all filling out applications, hoping to be one of the 274 families chosen. My parents filled out one, too.

I didn't want to move. I knew our house was crowded—there were eleven of us, six adults and five children—but I didn't want to leave my friends, and I didn't want to go

480 Types of Nonfiction

to a strange place and be the new person in a neighborhood and a school where most of the other children already knew each other. I was eight years old, and I had been to three schools. We had moved five times since we'd been in Washington, each time trying to get more space and a better place to live. But rent was high so we'd always lived in a house with relatives and friends, and shared the rent.

One of the people in our big household was Lillie, Daddy's cousin and Mama's best friend. She and her husband also applied for a place in the new project, and during the months that it was being built, Lillie and Mama would sometimes walk fifteen blocks just to stand and watch the workmen digging holes and laying bricks. They'd just stand there watching and wishing. And at home, that was all they could talk about. "When we get our new place . . ." "If we get our new place . . ."

Lillie got her good news first. I can still see her and Mama standing at the bottom of the hall steps, hugging and laughing and crying, happy for Lillie, then sitting on the steps, worrying and wishing again for Mama.

Finally, one evening, a woman came to the house with our good news, and Mama and Daddy went over and picked out the house they wanted. We moved on my ninth birthday. Wilbur, Gerald, and I went to school that morning from one house, and when Daddy came to pick us up, he took us home to another one. All the furniture had been moved while we were in school.

Langston Terrace was a lovely birthday present. It was built on a hill, a group of tan brick houses and apartments with a playground as its center. The red mud surrounding the concrete walks had not yet been covered with black soil and grass seed, and the holes that would soon be homes for young trees were filled with rainwater. But it still looked beautiful to me.

We had a whole house all to ourselves. Upstairs and downstairs. Two bedrooms, and the living room would be my bedroom at night. Best of all, I wasn't the only new

LITERATURE IN CONTEXT

Biography Connection

The Man Langston Terrace Honors

John Mercer Langston (1829–1897) became Ohio's first African American lawyer in 1854. Langston helped runaway slaves escape along the Ohio part of the Underground Railroad. In 1868, he started the law department at Howard University in Washington, D.C., becoming the department's dean and later the university's acting president. Langston became the first African American congressman from Virginia when he was elected to the U.S. House of Representatives in 1888.

Connect to the Literature

Does this information support Eloise Greenfield's description of Langston? Why or why not?

✓ **Reading Check**

Why is the move to Langston Terrace exciting for the whole family?

person. Everybody was new to this new little community, and by the time school opened in the fall, we had gotten used to each other and had made friends with other children in the neighborhood, too.

I guess most of the parents thought of the new place as an in-between place. They were glad to be there, but their dream was to save enough money to pay for a house that would be their own. Saving was hard, though, and slow, because each time somebody in a family got a raise on the job, it had to be reported to the manager of the project so that the rent could be raised, too. Most people stayed years longer than they had planned to, but they didn't let that stop them from enjoying life.

They formed a resident council to look into any neighborhood problems that might come up. They started a choral group and presented music and poetry programs on Sunday evenings in the social room or on the playground. On weekends, they played horseshoes and softball and other games. They had a reading club that met once a week at the Langston branch of the public library, after it opened in the basement of one of the apartment buildings.

Students with Books, 1966, Jacob Lawrence, The Jacob and Gwendolyn Lawrence Foundation/© Artists Rights Society (ARS), New York

Street Scene (Boy with Kite), 1962, Jacob Lawrence, The Jacob and Gwendolyn Lawrence Foundation/© Artists Rights Society (ARS), New York.

◄ **Critical Viewing**
What details in this painting would appeal to children? Why? **[Connect]**

The library was very close to my house. I could leave by my back door and be there in two minutes. The playground was right in front of my house, and after my sister Vedie was born and we moved a few doors down to a three-bedroom house, I could just look out of my bedroom window to see if any of my friends were out playing.

There were so many games to play and things to do. We played hide-and-seek at the lamppost, paddle tennis and shuffleboard, dodge ball and jacks. We danced in fireplug showers, jumped rope to rhymes, played "Bouncy, Bouncy, Bally," swinging one leg over a bouncing ball, played baseball on a nearby field, had parties in the social room and bus trips to the beach. In the playroom, we played Ping-Pong and pool, learned to sew and embroider and crochet.

For us, Langston Terrace wasn't an in-between place. It was a growing-up place, a good growing-up place. Neighbors who cared, family and friends, and a lot of fun. Life was good. Not perfect, but good. We knew about problems, heard about them, saw them, lived through some hard ones ourselves, but our community wrapped itself around us, put itself between us and the hard knocks, to cushion the blows. ●

It's been many years since I moved away, but every once in a long while I go back, just to look at things and

© **Spiral Review**
Development of Ideas How important are memories to the author?

Author's Influences
How do the author's childhood experiences influence her attitude about the importance of family and friends?

Langston Terrace **483**

remember. The large stone animals that decorated the playground are still there. A walrus, a hippo, a frog, and two horses. They've started to crack now, but I remember when they first came to live with us. They were friends, to climb on or to lean against, or to gather around in the evening. You could sit on the frog's head and look way out over the city at the tall trees and rooftops.

Nowadays, whenever I run into old friends, mostly at a funeral, or maybe a wedding, after we've talked about how we've been and what we've been doing, and how old our children are, we always end up talking about our childtime in our old neighborhood. And somebody will say, "One of these days we ought to have a Langston reunion." That's what we always called it, just "Langston," without the "Terrace." I guess because it sounded more homey. And that's what Langston was. It was home.

Critical Thinking

Cite textual evidence to support your responses.

1. **Key Ideas and Details (a)** Why does Eloise's family move many times before moving to Langston Terrace? **(b) Compare and Contrast:** How is the family's new home similar to the old home? How is it different?

2. **Key Ideas and Details (a)** On what day does Eloise's family move to Langston Terrace? **(b) Draw Conclusions:** How does Eloise feel on this day? Explain.

3. **Key Ideas and Details (a)** Why do some of the parents think of Langston Terrace as an "in-between place"? **(b) Speculate:** How might the author's story have been different if Langston Terrace had been an in-between place?

4. **Key Ideas and Details (a)** As an adult, how does Eloise Greenfield feel about Langston Terrace? **(b) Speculate:** Why might former residents of Langston Terrace want to have a reunion? Explain.

5. **Integration of Knowledge and Ideas (a)** What made Langston Terrace feel like home to Eloise and her family? **(b)** Why is it important for a community to make newcomers feel comfortable? *[Connect to the Big Question: What is important to know?]*

Reading Skill: Main Idea

1. Eloise Greenfield's thoughts and feelings about Langston Terrace make up the main idea of this essay. List four **key details** that show Greenfield's thoughts and feelings.

2. In your own words, state the **main idea** of this essay.

Literary Analysis: Author's Influences

3. Key Ideas and Details In a chart like the one shown, list cultural and historical factors that may have **influenced** Greenfield's writing of "Langston Terrace."

Time and Place	Cultural Background	World Events

4. Key Ideas and Details Which factors on your completed chart do you think influenced the author's writing the most? Explain.

Vocabulary

Acquisition and Use Answer each question with either *yes* or *no*. Then explain your answer.

1. If someone wants a job, should he or she fill out an <u>application</u>?

2. Can a <u>community</u> help someone in need?

3. Does an apartment <u>resident</u> need a place to live?

4. To see an old friend, should you go to a <u>reunion</u>?

5. If you hate to sing, should you join a <u>choral</u> group?

6. Does your school feel <u>homey</u>?

Word Study Use the context of the sentence and what you know about the **Latin suffix -ent** to explain your answers.

1. Are you *patient* when you cannot wait for something?

2. If you really want something, should you be *insistent*?

Word Study

The **Latin suffix -ent** forms adjectives and nouns. It means "has," "shows," or "does."

Apply It Explain how the suffix -ent contributes to the meaning of these words. Consult a dictionary if necessary.

persistent
different
complacent

Integrated Language Skills

Turkeys • Langston Terrace

Conventions: Adverbs

An **adverb** is a word that modifies—or describes—a verb, an adjective, or another adverb.

Many adverbs end in -ly. All adverbs answer the following questions: *Where? When? How? To what extent?*

Adverb	Function	Question Answered
He ran <u>slowly</u>.	modifies *ran*	*How* did he run?
She walked <u>extremely</u> slowly.	modifies *slowly*	*To what extent* did she walk slowly?
Maples are <u>very</u> tall trees.	modifies *tall*	*To what extent* are they tall?
We went <u>home</u>.	modifies *went*	*Where* did we go?

Practice A Write the adverb that modifies the underlined word in each sentence, and then explain what question it answers.

1. The ornithologists <u>spoke</u> quietly.
2. Bailey <u>slept</u> fitfully.
3. They <u>tucked</u> the eggs close to Bailey's feverish body.
4. The turkeys softly <u>peeped</u> in the bed.
5. The ornithologists' faces <u>drifted</u> away as Bailey fell asleep.

© **Reading Application** Find four adverbs in "Turkeys." Identify each modified word.

Practice B Add adverbs to the following sentences to modify the underlined words.

1. Eloise Greenfield's house was <u>noisy</u>.
2. The house they moved into was <u>big</u>.
3. Eloise's mom <u>filled out</u> the application.
4. The children in the neighborhood <u>played</u> together.
5. Eloise <u>remembers</u> Langston Terrace.

© **Writing Application** Jot down at least four adverbs that could complete the following sentence: A neighborhood can _____ make you feel welcome.

PH **WRITING COACH** | Further instruction and practice are available in *Prentice Hall Writing Coach*.

Writing

Common Core State Standards

L.6.1, L.6.6; W.6.3, W.6.3.b, W.6.8; SL.4
[For the full wording of the standards, see page 468.]

Narrative Text Write a **journal entry** as the narrator from either "Turkeys" or "Langston Terrace."

- Choose an event that interests you in the essay you read.
- Jot down notes about the narrator's reaction to the event.
- Write an entry from the point of view of the narrator.
- Remember to include the thoughts, feelings, and reactions you think the narrator might feel.

Grammar Application Check your writing to be sure that you have used adverbs correctly.

Writing Workshop: *Work in Progress*

Prewriting for Exposition For a persuasive essay you might write, work with a small group to list five ideas for positive changes in your community. You might list solutions to problems or ideas for improvements. Write one sentence that clearly states each idea. Save this List in your writing portfolio.

Use this prewriting activity to prepare for the **Writing Workshop** on page 526.

Research and Technology

Build and Present Knowledge In a group, use Internet or library resources to prepare an **informative presentation.**

- If you read "Turkeys," your presentation should focus on the importance of conservation.
- If you read "Langston Terrace," your presentation should focus on the importance of community.

Follow these steps to complete the assignment.

- Choose your topic and narrow your focus.
- Research your topic using various resource materials, including books as well as reputable online sources.
- Prepare a poster that highlights the most important facts about your topic. Use art or photographs to engage viewers.
- Present your work to the class. Have each group member discuss a different aspect of your topic.

www.PHLitOnline.com
- Interactive graphic organizers
- Grammar tutorial
- Interactive journals

© Leveled Texts

Build your skills and improve your comprehension of nonfiction with texts of increasing complexity.

Read **"La Leña Buena"** to understand why the wood of the mesquite tree was important to the author's uncle.

Read the excerpt from **"The Pigman & Me"** to find out what happens when a boy unknowingly breaks a school rule.

© Common Core State Standards

Meet these standards with either **"La Leña Buena"** (p. 492) or *from* **"The Pigman & Me"** (p. 498).

Reading Informational Texts
2. Determine a central idea of a text and how it is conveyed through particular details; provide a summary of the text distinct from personal opinions or judgments. *(Reading Skill: Main Idea)*
4. Determine the meaning of words and phrases as they are used in a text, including figurative meanings. *(Literary Analysis: Spiral Review)*

Writing
2.a. Introduce a topic; organize ideas, concepts, and information, using strategies such as definition, classification, comparison/contrast, and cause/effect.
2.b. Develop the topic with relevant facts, definitions, concrete details, quotations, or other information and examples. *(Writing: Problem-and-Solution Essay)*

Speaking and Listening
1.a. Come to discussions prepared, having read or studied required material; explicitly draw on that preparation by referring to evidence on the topic, text, or issue to probe and reflect on ideas under discussion. **1.b.** Follow rules for collegial discussions. **1.d.** Review the key ideas expressed and demonstrate understanding of multiple perspectives through reflection and paraphrasing. *(Speaking and Listening: Informal Discussion)*

Language
1. Demonstrate command of the conventions of standard English grammar and usage when writing or speaking.
3. Use knowledge of language and its conventions when writing, speaking, reading, or listening. *(Conventions: Conjunctions and Interjections)*

Reading Skill: Main Idea

The **main idea** is the most important point in a literary work. Individual paragraphs or sections may also have a central idea that supports the main idea of the work. To determine the main idea, **distinguish between important and unimportant details.** Important details are pieces of information that tell more about the main idea. They are also called *supporting details.*

- Ask yourself questions such as these about details in a literary work: *Why did the author include this detail? Does this detail help readers understand the main idea of the work?*
- Keep in mind that not all details support the main idea.

Using the Strategy: Main Idea Checklist

To track details as you read, use a chart like the one shown.

Selection: "The 1980 Miracle On Ice"				
Detail	In hockey, Maltsev scored to make the score 3–2 for the U.S.S.R.	The final score was 4–3 in favor of the U.S.	Mike Eruzione scored the winning goal.	Sweden took the bronze medal.
Important?		✓	✓	

Main Idea: The United States beat the heavily-favored Soviet Union in the 1980 Winter Olympics.

Literary Analysis: Mood

Mood is the overall feeling a literary work produces in a reader. For example, the mood of a work may be happy, sad, scary, or hopeful. To create a particular mood, writers carefully choose words and create word pictures that appeal to the reader's senses.

Some literary works present a single mood throughout the piece. In other works, the mood changes within the selection.

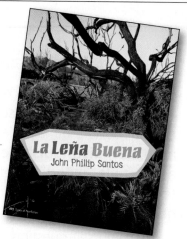

La Leña Buena
John Phillip Santos

What is important to *know?*

Writing About the Big Question

In "La Leña Buena," the author explains that his uncle was an expert at making a special kind of charcoal. Use this sentence starter to help you develop your ideas about the Big Question.

One way to **distinguish** an expert from someone who has basic **knowledge** about a topic is _____.

While You Read Look for details that tell you that Tío Abran was an expert in his field.

Vocabulary

Read each word and its definition. Decide whether you know the word well, know it a little bit, or do not know it at all. After you read, see how your knowledge of each word has increased.

- **engulfing** (en gulf´ iŋ) *adj.* swallowing up; overwhelming (p. 493) *Before we knew it, the waves were engulfing the sand toys. engulf v. engulfed v.*

- **fragrant** (frā´ grənt) *adj.* having a pleasant odor (p. 493) *The fragrant roses lifted my mood. fragrance n. fragrantly adv.*

- **treacheries** (trech´ ər ēz) *n.* acts of betrayal (p. 493) *Examples of treacheries include lying, cheating, and stealing. treacherous adj. treacherousness n.*

- **revolution** (rev´ ə loo´ shən) *n.* complete or radical change of any kind (p. 493) *After the revolution, the crime rate fell. revolutionary adj. revolutionize v. revolutionist n.*

- **confiscated** (kän´ fis kāt´ əd) *v.* seized, often by a governmental authority (p. 493) *Police confiscated the illegally parked car. confiscate v. confiscating v.*

- **reluctantly** (ri luk´ tənt lē) *adv.* unwillingly; unenthusiastically (p. 494) *Lucy reluctantly left the party. reluctant adj. reluctance n.*

Word Study

The **Latin root -*volv*-** means "roll" or "turn."

In this essay, there is a **revolution** in Mexico, or a turning over of the government from one group to another.

Meet
John Phillip Santos
(b. 1957)

Author of
La Leña Buena

John Phillip Santos began writing poetry when he was young and developed a love of words. He went on to become a writer, journalist, filmmaker, and producer.

Stories To Tell In speaking to students, Santos reminds them that the United States is home to people from all over the world and that all these people have stories to tell. He encourages young people to find their own stories by studying their past.

BACKGROUND FOR THE ESSAY

Mexico in the Early 1900s

"La Leña Buena" tells why some Mexicans left Mexico in the early 1900s. The Mexican Revolution, a violent civil war, lasted from 1910 to 1920 and left the country in a condition that was difficult for all but the wealthiest citizens. Most urban workers, farmers, and peasants were very poor. Large numbers of Mexicans, eager for better opportunities, crossed the border into the United States.

La Leña Buena

John Phillip Santos

Background You can burn a mesquite tree for heat, turn it into fragrant charcoal for grilling, fashion furniture from it, eat its bean pods, and make medicine from its bark. In Texas, though, some cattlemen are not members of the mesquite fan club. They call the trees "range weeds" because they crowd into grasslands. In the past, Texans eliminated the trees with fire. Now, because of controls on the use of fire, mesquite trees have multiplied. Depending on your perspective, this tree is awesome or awful.

Good wood is like a jewel, Tío Abrán, my great-grandfather Jacobo's twin brother, used to say. Huisache burns fast, in twisting yellow flames, engulfing the log in a cocoon of fire. It burns brightly, so it is sought after for Easter bonfires. But it does not burn hot, so it's poor wood for home fires. On a cold morning in the sierra, you can burn a whole tree by noon. Mesquite, and even better, cedar—these are noble, hard woods. They burn hot and long. Their smoke is fragrant. And if you know how to do it, they make exquisite charcoal.

"*La leña buena es como una joya*"

Good wood is like a jewel. And old Tío Abrán knew wood the way a jeweler knows stones, and in northern Coahuila, from Múzquiz to Rosita, his charcoal was highly regarded for its sweet, long-burning fire.

Abrán was one of the last of the Garcias to come north. Somewhere around 1920, he finally had to come across the border with his family. He was weary of the treacheries along the roads that had become a part of life in the sierra towns since the beginning of the revolution ten years earlier. Most of the land near town had been deforested and the only wood he could find around Palaú was huisache. To find any of the few pastures left with arbors of mesquite trees, he had to take the unpaved mountain road west from Múzquiz, along a route where many of the militantes[1] had their camps. Out by the old Villa las Rusias, in a valley far off the road, there were mesquite trees in every direction as far as you could see. He made an arrangement with the owner of the villa to give him a cut from the sale of charcoal he made from the mesquite. But many times, the revolucionarios confiscated his day's load of wood, leaving

---

1. **militantes** (mil´ ē tan´ tās) *n.* Spanish for "militants"—people who fight or are willing to fight.

Spiral Review
Figurative Language Identify the simile in the first sentence. How does it reveal the author's attitude?

Vocabulary
engulfing (en gulf´ iŋ) *adj.* swallowing up; overwhelming

fragrant (frā´ grənt) *adj.* having a pleasant odor

Main Idea
What details in the first paragraph give clues about the main idea of the selection?

Vocabulary
treacheries (trech´ ər ēz) *n.* acts of betrayal
revolution (rev´ ə lōō´ shən) *n.* complete or radical change of any kind
confiscated (kän´ fis kāt´ əd) *v.* seized, often by a governmental authority

him to return home, humiliated, with an empty wagon.

Aside from Tía Pepa and Tío Anacleto, who had returned to Mexico by then, he had been the last of the Garcias left in Mexico, and he had left reluctantly. On the day he arrived in San Antonio with his family, he had told his brother Abuelo Jacobo, "If there was still any mesquite that was easy to get to, we would've stayed."

Vocabulary
reluctantly (ri luk´ tənt lē) *adv.* unwillingly; unenthusiastically

Critical Thinking

Cite textual evidence to support your responses.

1. **Key Ideas and Details** **(a)** How does Tío Abrán earn his living in Mexico? **(b) Connect:** What are the "treacheries" that the author mentions in this work? **(c) Infer:** Why do you think the revolutionaries take Tío Abrán's wood?

2. **Key Ideas and Details** **(a)** Where were most members of the Garcia family living while Tío Abrán was still in Mexico? **(b) Interpret:** What role do trees play in Tío Abrán's decision to stay and then to leave Mexico? **(c) Speculate:** Do you think that he continues in the same line of work after he moves? Explain.

3. **Key Ideas and Details** **(a)** What does Tío Abrán say on the day of his arrival in San Antonio, Texas? **(b) Infer:** What does this remark tell you about his feelings toward Mexico?

4. **Key Ideas and Details** **(a)** Do you think that Tío Abrán's decision to leave Mexico was a wise one for his family? Explain. **(b) Speculate:** How do you think the author has been affected by his great-uncle's decision? **(c) Discuss:** Share your response with a partner. Then, discuss whether someone else's response affected your thinking.

5. **Integration of Knowledge and Ideas** **(a)** What details in the story reveal that Tío Abrán was an expert in his field? **(b)** How do you think he became an expert? *[Connect to the Big Question: What is important to know?]*

Reading Skill: Main Idea

1. What is the **main idea** of this essay?

2. Which important **details** support the main idea?

3. (a) What is one **unimportant detail? (b)** Explain.

Literary Analysis: Mood

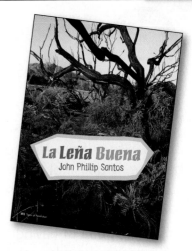

4. Craft and Structure What is one **mood** suggested by specific words and phrases in this essay?

5. Craft and Structure Complete a chart like the one shown to analyze which words and images create the mood in "La Leña Buena."

Words	Images	Mood

Vocabulary

Acquisition and Use Write sentences that correctly use each word pair.

1. confiscated; cameras

2. fragrant; laundry

3. engulfing; crowd

4. revolution; change

5. treacheries; enemy

6. reluctantly; spoke

Word Study Use the context of the sentence and what you know about **Latin root -volv-** to explain your answers.

1. Can you go straight through a *revolving* door?

2. Describe the earth's *revolution* around the sun.

Word Study

The **Latin root -volv-** means "roll" or "turn."

Apply It Explain how the root -volv- contributes to the meaning of these words. Consult a dictionary if necessary.

evolve

involve

volume

What is important to *know?*

Writing About the Big Question

In this excerpt from *The Pigman & Me*, a boy gets into trouble because he does not know the rules in gym class at his new school. Use the following sentence starters to help you develop your ideas about the Big Question.

The **purpose** of having rules at school is _____.

Knowing the rules can help you _____.

While You Read Look for instances in which knowing and following the rules would have helped the author.

Vocabulary

Read each word and its definition. Decide whether you know the word well, know it a little bit, or do not know it at all. After you read, see how your knowledge of each word has increased.

- **exact** (eg zakt´) *v.* demand with force or authority (p. 499) *The detective will <u>exact</u> the information from him.*

- **demented** (dē ment´ əd) *adj.* insane; mad (p. 501) *The actor played that <u>demented</u> character so well, we thought he was really crazy! dement v. dementedly adv.*

- **observant** (əb zurv´ ənt) *adj.* quick to notice; alert (p. 502) *An <u>observant</u> person will notice even small details. observe v. observantly adv. observation n.*

- **undulating** (un´ jə lāt´ iŋ) *adj.* moving in waves, like a snake (p. 504) *The banner was <u>undulating</u> in the breeze. undulate v. undulated v.*

- **distorted** (di stôrt´ əd) *adj.* twisted out of normal shape (p. 504) *The <u>distorted</u> photos looked odd. distortion n.*

- **condemnation** (kän´ dem nā´ shən) *n.* expression of strong disapproval (p. 505) *She showed her <u>condemnation</u> of our proposal by shaking her head and frowning. condemn v.*

Word Study

The **Latin root -*tort*-** means "twist out of shape."

In this story, the author describes his class-mates' faces as being **distorted**, or twisted out of normal shape.

Meet
Paul Zindel
(1936–2003)

Author of
The Pigman & Me

As a teenager, Paul Zindel lived for a while on Staten Island, New York, with his mother and sister. Before he wrote the novel *The Pigman & Me*, Zindel taught high school science while writing in his spare time. After the success of *The Pigman & Me*, Zindel started writing full time.

Writing for Teens "I felt I could do more for teenagers by writing for them," he once said. He discovered that most young adult books did not relate to the teenagers he knew. Zindel made a list of pointers and then wrote another novel, following his own advice.

BACKGROUND FOR THE ESSAY

Ground Rules

Every place and situation has its own set of rules. Some of these rules are formal and printed. Sometimes, though, the unwritten rules may be just as important as the written ones. For example, an unwritten rule is to support your friends. In this excerpt, the author recalls a time when he had to figure out how to manage unwritten rules.

from The Pigman & Me

Paul Zindel

▲ **Critical Viewing**
What are some conflicts among students that might occur in a scene like this one? **[Analyze]**

When trouble came to me, it didn't involve anybody I thought it would. It involved the nice, normal, smart boy by the name of John Quinn. Life does that to us a lot. Just when we think something awful's going to happen one way, it throws you a curve and the something awful happens another way. This happened on the first Friday, during gym period, when we were allowed to play games in the school yard. A boy by the name of Richard Cahill, who lived near an old linoleum factory, asked me if I'd like to play paddle ball with him, and I said, "Yes." Some of the kids played softball, some played warball, and there were a few other games where you could sign out equipment and do what you wanted. What I didn't know was that you were allowed to sign out the paddles for only fifteen minutes per period so more kids could get a chance to use them. I just didn't happen to know that little rule, and Richard Cahill didn't think to tell me about it. Richard was getting a drink from the water fountain when John Quinn came up to me and told me I had to give him my paddle.

"No," I said, being a little paranoid about being the new kid and thinking everyone was going to try to take advantage of me.

"Look, you *have* to give it to me," John Quinn insisted.

That was when I did something berserk. I was so wound up and frightened that I didn't think, and I struck out at him with my right fist. I had forgotten I was holding the paddle, and it smacked into his face, giving him an instant black eye. John was shocked. I was shocked. Richard Cahill came running back and he was shocked.

"What's going on here?" Mr. Trellis, the gym teacher, growled.

"He hit me with the paddle," John moaned, holding his eye. He was red as a beet, as Little Frankfurter, Conehead, Moose, and lots of the others gathered around.

"He tried to take the paddle away from me!" I complained.

"His time was up," John said.

Mr. Trellis set me wise to the rules as he took John over to a supply locker and pulled out a first-aid kit.

"I'm sorry," I said, over and over again.

Then the bell rang, and all John Quinn whispered to me was that he was going to get even. He didn't say it like a nasty rotten kid, just more like an all-American boy who knew he'd have to regain his dignity about having to walk around school with a black eye. Before the end of school, Jennifer came running up to me in the halls and told me John Quinn had announced to everyone he was going to exact revenge on me after school on Monday. That was the note of disaster my first week at school ended on, and I was terrified because I didn't know how to fight. I had never even been in a fight. What had happened was all an accident. It really was. ●

Main Idea
What details support the main idea that Paul did not expect or intend to injure John?

Vocabulary
exact (eg zakt´) *v.* demand with force or authority

Reading Check
What misunderstanding takes place in the school yard?

Main Idea
Is the detail about "the twins, being such copycats" important to the main idea of the paragraph? Explain.

Mood
What words create a threatening mood in this paragraph?

When Nonno Frankie arrived on Saturday morning, he found me sitting in the apple tree alone. Mom had told him it was O.K. to walk around the whole yard now, as long as he didn't do any diggings or mutilations other than weed-pulling on her side. I was expecting him to notice right off the bat that I was white with fear, but instead he stood looking at the carvings Jennifer and I had made in the trunk of the tree. I thought he was just intensely curious about what "ESCAPE! PAUL & JENNIFER!" meant. Of course, the twins, being such copycats, had already added their names so the full carving away of the bark now read, "ESCAPE! PAUL & JENNIFER! & NICKY & JOEY!" And the letters circled halfway around the tree.

"You're killing it," Nonno Frankie said sadly.

"What?" I jumped down to his side.

"The tree will die if you cut any more."

I thought he was kidding, because all we had done was carve off the outer pieces of bark. We hadn't carved deep into the tree, not into the *heart* of the tree. The tree was too important to us. It was the most crucial place to me and Jennifer, and the last thing we'd want to do was hurt it.

"The heart of a tree isn't deep inside of it. Its heart and blood are on the *outside*, just under the bark," Nonno Frankie explained. "That's the living part of a tree. If you carve in a circle all around the trunk, it's like slitting its throat. The water and juices and life of the tree can't move up from the roots!" I knew about the living layer of a tree, but I didn't know exposing it would kill the whole tree. I just never thought about it, or I figured trees patched themselves up.

"Now it can feed itself from only half its trunk," Nonno Frankie explained. "You must not cut any more."

"I won't," I promised. Then I felt worse than ever. Not only was I scheduled to get beat up by John Quinn after school on Monday, I was also a near tree-killer. Nonno Frankie finally looked closely at me.

"Your first week at school wasn't all juicy meatballs?" he asked.

That was all he had to say, and I spilled out each and every horrifying detail. Nonno Frankie let me babble on and on. He looked as if he understood exactly how I felt and wasn't going to call me stupid or demented or a big yellow coward. When I didn't have another word left in me, I just shut up and stared down at the ground.

"Stab nail at ill Italian bats!" Nonno Frankie finally said.

"What?"

He repeated the weird sentence and asked me what was special about it. I guessed, "It reads the same backward as forward?"

"Right! Ho! Ho! Ho! See, you learn! You remember things I teach you. So today I will teach you how to fight, and you will smack this John Quinn around like floured pizza dough."

"But I can't fight."

"I'll show you Sicilian combat tactics."

"Like what?"

"Everything about Italian fighting. It has to do with your mind and body. Things you have to know so you don't have to be afraid of bullies. Street smarts my father taught me. Like 'Never miss a good chance to shut up!'"

VAROOOOOOOOOOOM!

A plane took off over our heads. We walked out beyond the yard to the great field overlooking the airport.

Nonno Frankie suddenly let out a yell. "Aaeeeeeyaaaayeeeeeh!" It was so blood-curdlingly weird, I decided to wait until he felt like explaining it.

"Aaeeeeeyaaaayeeeeeh!" he bellowed again. "It's good to be able to yell like Tarzan!" he said. "This confuses your enemy, and you can also yell it if you have to retreat. You run away roaring and everyone thinks you at least have guts! It confuses everybody!"

"Is that all I need to know?" I asked, now more afraid than ever of facing John Quinn in front of all the kids.

"No. Tonight I will cut your hair."

"Cut it?"

"Yes. It's too long!"

"It is?"

"Ah," Nonno Frankie said, "you'd be surprised how many kids lose fights because of their hair. Alexander the Great always ordered his entire army to shave their heads. Long hair makes it easy for an enemy to grab it and cut off your head."

Vocabulary
demented (dē
ment´ əd) *adj.*
insane; mad

Reading
Check
What advice does Paul get from Nonno Frankie?

Main Idea
What details support the main idea that Nonno Frankie is an unusual character?

Mood
How does the author create a humorous mood?

Vocabulary
observant (əb zʉrv´ ənt) *adj.* quick to notice; alert

"John Quinn just wants to beat me up!"

"You can never be too sure. This boy might have the spirit of Genghis Khan!"

"Who was Genghis Khan?"

"Who? He once killed two million enemies in one hour. Some of them he killed with yo-yos."

"Yo-yos?"

"See, these are the things you need to know. The yo-yo was first invented as a weapon. Of course, they were as heavy as steel pipes and had long rope cords, but they were still yo-yos!"

"I didn't know that," I admitted.

"That's why I'm telling you. You should always ask about the rules when you go to a new place."

"I didn't think there'd be a time limit on handball paddles."

"That's why you must ask."

"I can't ask everything," I complained.

"Then you *read*. You need to know all the rules wherever you go. Did you know it's illegal to hunt camels in Arizona?"

"No."

"See? These are little facts you pick up from books and teachers and parents as you grow older. Some facts and rules come in handy, some don't. You've got to be observant. Did you know that Mickey Mouse has only *four* fingers on each hand?"

"No."

"All you have to do is look. And rules change! You've got to remember that. In ancient Rome, my ancestors worshipped a god who ruled over mildew. Nobody does anymore, but it's an interesting thing to know. You have to be connected to the past and present and future. At NBC, when they put in a new cookie-cutting machine, I had to have an open mind. I had to prepare and draw upon everything I knew so that I didn't get hurt."

Nonno Frankie must have seen my mouth was open so wide a baseball could have flown into my throat and choked me to death. He stopped at the highest point in the rise of land above the airport. "I can see you want some meat and potatoes. You want to know exactly how to beat this vicious John Quinn."

"He's not vicious."

"Make believe he is. It'll give you more energy for the fight. When he comes at you, don't underestimate the power of negative thinking! You must have only positive thoughts in your heart that you're going to cripple this monster. Stick a piece of garlic in your pocket for good luck. A woman my mother knew in Palermo did this, and she was able to fight off a dozen three-foot-tall muscular Greeks who landed and tried to eat her. You think this is not true, but half her town saw it. The Greeks all had rough skin and wore backpacks and one-piece clothes. You have to go with what you feel in your heart. One of my teachers in Sicily believed the Portuguese man-of-war jellyfish originally came from England. He felt that in his heart, and he eventually proved it. He later went on to be awarded a government grant to study tourist swooning sickness in Florence."

"But how do I hold my hands to fight? How do I hold my fists?" I wanted to know.

"Like this!" Nonno Frankie demonstrated, taking a boxing stance with his left foot and fist forward.

"And then I just swing my right fist forward as hard as I can?"

"No. First you curse him."

"Curse him?"

"Yes, you curse this John Quinn. You tell him, 'May your left ear wither and fall into your right pocket!' And you tell him he looks like a fugitive from a brain gang! And tell him he has a face like a mattress! And that an espresso coffee cup would fit on his head like a sombrero. And then you just give him the big Sicilian surprise!"

"What?"

"You kick him in the shins!" •

By the time Monday morning came, I was a nervous wreck. Nonno Frankie had gone back to New York the night before, but had left me a special bowl of pasta and steamed octopus that he said I should eat for breakfast so I'd have "gusto" for combat. I had asked him not to discuss my upcoming bout with my mother or sister, and Betty didn't say anything so I assumed she hadn't heard about it.

Jennifer had offered to get one of her older brothers to protect me, and, if I wanted, she was willing to tell Miss

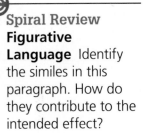

Main Idea
What is the main idea of this paragraph?

Spiral Review
Figurative Language Identify the similes in this paragraph. How do they contribute to the intended effect?

Reading Check

Why does Nonno Frankie insist that Paul always know the rules?

Mood
How does the author create a different mood in this passage?

Vocabulary
undulating (un´ jə lā tiŋ) *adj.* moving in waves, like a snake

distorted (di stôrt´ əd) *adj.* twisted out of normal shape

Haines so she could stop anything from happening. I told her, "No." I thought there was a chance John Quinn would have even forgotten the whole incident and wouldn't make good on his revenge threat. Nevertheless, my mind was numb with fear all day at school. In every class I went to, it seemed there were a dozen different kids coming over to me and telling me they heard John Quinn was going to beat me up after school.

At 3 P.M. sharp, the bell rang.

All the kids started to leave school.

I dawdled.

I cleaned my desk and took time packing up my books. Jennifer was at my side as we left the main exit of the building. There, across the street in a field behind Ronkewitz's Candy Store, was a crowd of about 300 kids standing around like a big, undulating horseshoe, with John Quinn standing at the center bend glaring at me.

"You could run," Jennifer suggested, tossing her hair all to the left side of her face. She looked much more than pretty now. She looked loyal to the bone.

"No," I said. I just walked forward toward my fate, with the blood in my temples pounding so hard I thought I was going to pass out. Moose and Leon and Mike and Conehead and Little Frankfurter were sprinkled out in front of me, goading me forward. I didn't even hear what they said. I saw only their faces distorted in ecstasy and expectation. They looked like the mob I had seen in a sixteenth-century etching where folks in London had bought tickets to watch bulldogs attacking water buffalo.

John stood with his black eye, and his fists up.

I stopped a few feet from him and put my fists up. A lot of kids in the crowd started to shout, "Kill him, Johnny!" but I may have imagined that part.

John came closer. He started to dance on his feet like all father-trained fighters do. I danced, too, as best I could. The crowd began to scream for blood. Jennifer kept shouting, "Hey, there's no need to fight! You don't have to fight, guys!"

But John came in for the kill. He was close enough now so any punch he threw could hit me. All I thought of was Nonno Frankie, but I couldn't remember half of what he told me and I didn't think any of it would work anyway.

"*Aaeeeeeyaaaayeeeeeh!*" I suddenly screamed at John. He stopped in his tracks and the crowd froze in amazed silence. Instantly, I brought back my right foot, and shot it forward to kick John in his left shin. The crowd was shocked, and booed me with mass condemnation for my Sicilian fighting technique. I missed John's shin, and kicked vainly again. He threw a punch at me. It barely touched me, but I was so busy kicking, I tripped myself and fell down. The crowd cheered. I realized everyone including John thought his punch had floored me. I decided to go along with it. I groveled in the dirt for a few moments, and then stood up slowly holding my head as though I'd received a death blow. John put his fists down. He was satisfied justice had been done and his black eye had been avenged. He turned to leave, but Moose wasn't happy.

"Hey, ya didn't punch him enough," Moose complained to John.

"It's over," John said, like the decent kid he was.

"No, it's not," Moose yelled, and the crowd began to call for more blood. Now it was Moose coming toward me, and I figured I was dead meat. He came closer and closer. Jennifer shouted for him to stop and threatened to pull his eyeballs out, but he kept coming. And that was when something amazing happened. I was aware of a figure taller than me, running, charging. The figure had long blond hair, and it struck Moose from behind. I could see it was a girl and she had her hands right around Moose's neck,

▲ **Critical Viewing**
How are these boys similar to John and Paul? **[Compare]**

Vocabulary
condemnation
(kän′ dem nā′ shən)
n. expression of strong disapproval

Reading Check
How has Paul been feeling about this fight?

from The Pigman & Me **505**

choking him. When she let him go, she threw him about ten feet, accidentally tearing off a religious medal from around his neck. Everyone stopped dead in their tracks, and I could see my savior was my sister.

"If any of you tries to hurt my brother again, I'll rip your guts out," she announced.

Moose was not happy. Conehead and Little Frankfurter were not happy. But the crowd broke up fast and everyone headed home. I guess that was the first day everybody learned that if nothing else, the Zindel kids stick together. As for Nonno Frankie's Sicilian fighting technique, I came to realize he was ahead of his time. In fact, these days it's called karate.

Critical Thinking

Cite textual evidence to support your responses.

1. **Key Ideas and Details (a)** Identify two pieces of advice that Nonno Frankie gives Paul. **(b) Analyze:** Does Frankie's advice apply to more than the fight itself? Explain.

2. **Key Ideas and Details (a)** What does Paul do after he falls down during the fight? **(b) Infer:** Why does he do this? **(c) Analyze:** Is his strategy a good one? Explain.

3. **Key Ideas and Details (a)** Explain the difference between John's attitude and the attitude of the other students after Paul falls down. **(b) Analyze:** What problems does the attitude of the other students create for John and for Paul?

4. **Integration of Knowledge and Ideas (a)** How did a lack of knowledge cause trouble for Paul? **(b)** Was Nonno Frankie's advice helpful to Paul in his fight with John Quinn? Explain. **(c)** Will any of Nonno Frankie's advice be helpful to Paul in the future? Explain. *[Connect to the Big Question: What is important to know?]*

Reading Skill: Main Idea

1. What is the **main idea** of this selection?
2. What are two **important details** in the selection that support this main idea?
3. What is one **unimportant detail** that does not support the main idea?

Literary Analysis: Mood

4. **Craft and Structure** What is one **mood,** or overall feeling, that the author creates in this essay?
5. **Craft and Structure** Complete a chart like the one shown to analyze which words and images create the mood in "The Pigman & Me."

| Words | Images | Mood |

Vocabulary

Acquisition and Use Write sentences that correctly use each word pair.

1. exact (as a verb); payment
2. undulating; necklace
3. distorted; ideas
4. demented; stranger
5. observant; spy
6. condemnation; thieves

Word Study Use the context of the sentence and what you know about the **Latin root *-tort-*** to explain your answers.

1. What can a *contortionist* do?
2. Can you watch television if the screen has a *distortion*?

Word Study

The **Latin root *-tort-*** means "twist out of shape."

Apply It Explain how the root *-tort-* contributes to the meaning of these words. Consult a dictionary if necessary.

retort
contort
torturous

Integrated Language Skills

La Leña Buena • *from* The Pigman & Me

Conventions: Conjunctions and Interjections

Conjunctions connect sentence parts and help show the relationship between those parts. **Interjections** express feelings. The use of conjunctions helps to improve the flow of your writing. Interjections add liveliness to dialogue and narration.

Examples of Conjunctions	Examples of Interjections
and, or, but, nor, for, yet, and *so*	*ah, aha, golly, hey, oh, oops, shh,* and *whew*

Practice A Fill in the blanks with a conjunction or interjection that fits the sentence.

1. Huisache burns brightly, _____ it is used for Easter bonfires.
2. Mesquite burns hot _____ long.
3. "_____ ! I've had a long day."
4. "_____, now I understand the difference between huisache _____ mesquite."
5. Neither Tío Abrán _____ Tío Pepa stayed.

Ⓒ **Reading Application** Find three conjunctions in "La Leña Buena." In a few sentences, explain the relationship between the words, phrases, or clauses that are connected by the conjunctions.

Practice B Improve these sentences by combining them, if necessary, and adding a conjunction or interjection.

1. Sometimes the kids played softball. Other times they played baseball.
2. Paul was frightened. He could not think. He hit John Quinn with the paddle.
3. "There they are. You better run!"
4. "It hurts," John yelled.
5. Jennifer was pretty. She was also loyal.

Ⓒ **Writing Application** Write a paragraph about a gym class, using four conjunctions and two interjections. Circle the conjunctions and underline the interjections.

PH WRITING COACH   Further instruction and practice are available in *Prentice Hall Writing Coach*.

Writing

Common Core State Standards

L.6.1, L.6.3; W.6.2.a, W.6.2.b; SL.6.1.a, SL.6.1.b, SL.6.1.d
[For the full wording of the standards, see page 488.]

Explanatory Text Write a **problem-and-solution essay** based on the selection you read. Your essay should help a newcomer adjust to either a new school or a new country.

- Clearly state the problem that the newcomer might face.
- Provide step-by-step solutions to the problem.
- Explain why your solutions will help solve the problem.
- Support your suggested solutions with concrete details, examples, or anecdotes.

Grammar Application Check your writing to be sure that you have used conjunctions and interjections correctly.

Writing Workshop: *Work in Progress*

Prewriting for Exposition Select one item from your Change List and list two facts that support the idea. Then, jot down one way you can appeal to the emotions of your audience to convince them that this change should be made. Save this Support for a Change in your writing portfolio.

Use this prewriting activity to prepare for the **Writing Workshop** on page 526.

Speaking and Listening

Comprehension and Collaboration In a small group, hold an **informal discussion** based on the selection you read:

- If you read "La Leña Buena," discuss the pros and cons of having relatives living near you.
- If you read the excerpt from *The Pigman & Me,* discuss how students should act in order to make friends at a new school.

Follow these steps to complete the assignment:

- Gather in a group and confirm the topic of discussion.
- Allow each person in the group an opportunity to offer opinions about the topic.
- Support opinions with facts and examples.
- Use good listening skills when others are talking.
- At the end of the discussion, reflect on the group's responses and paraphrase the group's ideas.
- Share your paraphrase with the rest of the class.

PHLit **Online!**

www.PHLitOnline.com
- Interactive graphic organizers
- Grammar tutorial
- Interactive journals

Test Practice: Reading

Main Idea

Fiction Selection

Directions: *Read the selection. Then, answer the questions.*

On the first morning of his new life—a Saturday—Freddie awoke at 5:30. He laced on his running shoes, slipped out the back door, and jogged to the running track near his house. After an hour's run, Freddie returned home and got on his bike. He rode to Sunny Grove and back, a three-hour ride. His legs were beginning to ache, but Freddie was unstoppable. Next, he walked two miles to the public swimming pool, where he swam laps for an hour and then walked home. By the end of the day, Freddie could hardly move. Freddie's sister, Elena, said to Freddie, "You can't go from no exercise to six hours of it the first day! You have to add a little at a time, so your body can adjust." Freddie knew that Elena was right. He promised to start another new life tomorrow, this time a little more slowly.

1. What part of the passage contains the main idea?
- **A.** the first sentence
- **B.** the second sentence
- **C.** the middle of the passage
- **D.** the last two sentences

2. What is the main idea of the passage?
- **A.** Freddie wakes up early every Saturday morning.
- **B.** Freddie enjoys many different types of exercise.
- **C.** Freddie learns to not do too much exercise too soon.
- **D.** Freddie wants to become a famous athlete.

3. What detail supports the idea that Freddie needs to make a change?
- **A.** Freddie can hardly move.
- **B.** Freddie wakes up too early.
- **C.** Freddie exercises nonstop.
- **D.** Elena gives Freddie some good advice.

4. Which of these details supports the main idea of the passage?
- **A.** Freddie laces on his running shoes.
- **B.** Freddie rides to Sunny Grove.
- **C.** Freddie had done no exercise before Saturday.
- **D.** Freddie walks to the swimming pool.

Writing for Assessment

List the details in this passage that support the main idea.

Nonfiction Selection

Directions: *Read the selection. Then, answer the questions.*

What's the best way to get healthy and stay healthy? The answer is simple. Eat the right foods and get plenty of exercise. Put healthful foods into your body, and your body will reward you by giving you energy and strength. Healthful foods include fresh fruit and fresh vegetables. These supply vitamins and minerals that your body needs to stay in tip-top shape. For example, your body needs Vitamin C. Oranges and tomatoes are a good source of this important vitamin. As with smart eating, regular exercise helps your muscles stay strong. Don't forget that your heart is a muscle, too. Exercise also makes you feel great! Running, fast-walking, biking, and swimming offer excellent workouts, if you do them for at least thirty minutes at a time. Staying healthy is not always easy, but the formula is simple. Eat right and keep moving!

1. What is the main idea of the passage?
   A. Healthful foods give your body energy.
   B. Your body needs vitamins and minerals.
   C. A good diet and exercise lead to good health.
   D. Staying healthy is not always easy.

2. Which of these details supports the idea that eating right is important?
   A. Fruits and vegetables promote health.
   B. Oranges are a source of Vitamin C.
   C. Your heart is a muscle.
   D. Exercise for thirty minutes at a time.

3. According to the passage, why is exercise important?
   A. It provides you with vitamins.
   B. It helps you run fast.
   C. It helps you eat right.
   D. It helps keep your muscles strong.

4. Which detail does *not* directly support the main idea?
   A. Proper diet and exercise keep you healthy.
   B. Fruits and vegetables are healthful foods.
   C. Running and biking are good forms of exercise.
   D. Staying healthy is not always easy.

Writing for Assessment

Connecting Across Texts

Write a paragraph that combines key details from both reading passages. Then, write the main idea of your paragraph.

www.PHLitOnline.com
- Online practice
- Instant feedback

Reading for Information

Analyzing Argumentative Texts

Advertisement

Advertisement

Ⓒ **Common Core State Standards**

Reading Informational Text
5. Analyze how a particular sentence, paragraph, chapter, or section fits into the overall structure of a text and contributes to the development of the ideas.

Language
4.c. Consult reference materials, both print and digital, to find the pronunciation of a word or determine or clarify its precise meaning or its part of speech.

Reading Skill: Recognize Propaganda

The goal of an advertisement is to persuade readers to purchase a product or service. To avoid drawing false conclusions from an advertisement, learn to **recognize propaganda.** Propaganda is information that is one-sided or misleading. As you read, use the following chart to help you identify propaganda techniques.

Propaganda Technique	Explanation	Example
Broad generalizations	Sweeping claims that cannot be proved	"There's nothing like it in the world!"
Hidden messages	Pictures or words that convey an idea without stating it directly	A photo of an Olympic runner, suggesting you'll be a winner if you buy a certain brand of sneakers
Loaded language	Words that appeal to our emotions	"It's a miracle product!"
Bandwagon appeals	Implying that "everyone else" uses a certain product	"Thousands of allergy sufferers use Sneeze-Free."
Faulty reasoning	Using unrelated or unconnected details as support	More people have cats than dogs, so cats must be easier to take care of.

Content-Area Vocabulary

These words appear in the selections that follow. You may also encounter them in other content-area texts.

- **soles** (sōlz) *n.* the bottoms of feet, shoes, slippers, etc.
- **platform** (plat′ fôrm′) *n.* a raised level surface

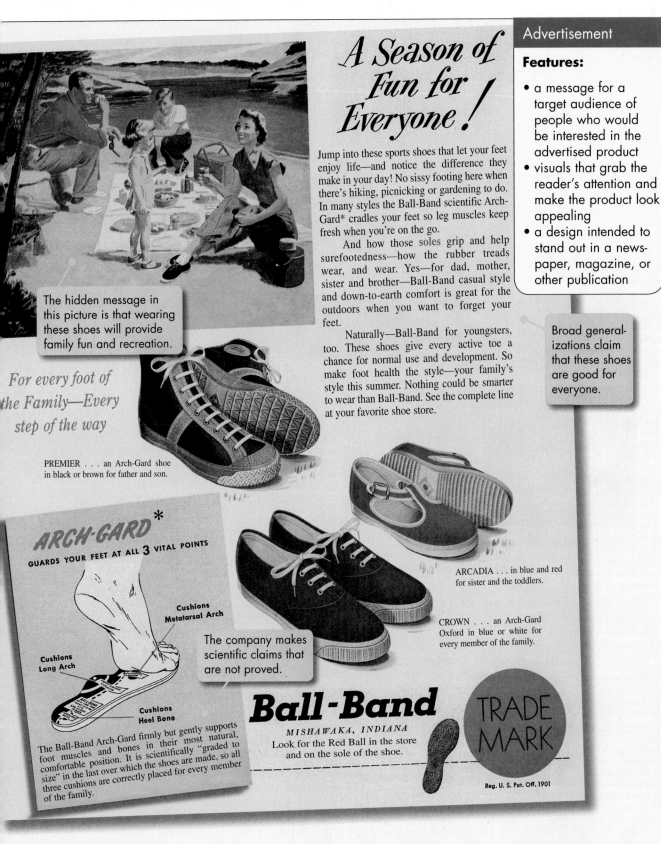

A Season of Fun for Everyone!

Jump into these sports shoes that let your feet enjoy life—and notice the difference they make in your day! No sissy footing here when there's hiking, picnicking or gardening to do. In many styles the Ball-Band scientific Arch-Gard* cradles your feet so leg muscles keep fresh when you're on the go.

And how those soles grip and help surefootedness—how the rubber treads wear, and wear. Yes—for dad, mother, sister and brother—Ball-Band casual style and down-to-earth comfort is great for the outdoors when you want to forget your feet.

Naturally—Ball-Band for youngsters, too. These shoes give every active toe a chance for normal use and development. So make foot health the style—your family's style this summer. Nothing could be smarter to wear than Ball-Band. See the complete line at your favorite shoe store.

The hidden message in this picture is that wearing these shoes will provide family fun and recreation.

Broad generalizations claim that these shoes are good for everyone.

For every foot of the Family—Every step of the way

PREMIER . . . an Arch-Gard shoe in black or brown for father and son.

ARCH-GARD*

GUARDS YOUR FEET AT ALL **3** VITAL POINTS

Cushions Metatarsal Arch

Cushions Long Arch

Cushions Heel Bone

The Ball-Band Arch-Gard firmly but gently supports foot muscles and bones in their most natural, comfortable position. It is scientifically "graded to size" in the last over which the shoes are made, so all three cushions are correctly placed for every member of the family.

The company makes scientific claims that are not proved.

ARCADIA . . . in blue and red for sister and the toddlers.

CROWN . . . an Arch-Gard Oxford in blue or white for every member of the family.

Ball-Band

MISHAWAKA, INDIANA
Look for the Red Ball in the store and on the sole of the shoe.

TRADE MARK

Reg. U. S. Pat. Off. 1901

It's amazing what you can learn from a twelve-year-old!

The picture is meant to persuade readers that even twelve-year-olds will enjoy this product.

Our twelve-year-old likes to pick her own clothes and does it mighty well. She's the one who picked NEOLITE for her shoes. "It'll save your money, Mummy!" she said. She was right. NEOLITE Soles outlast any sole I ever saw. But they offer more than wear for my shoes—and for her father's, too.

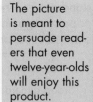

Comfort goes much further!
Yes, easy-going NEOLITE Soles give twice the wear of leather! And they need no *breaking-in*. They're flexible from the very start, yet they provide a firm platform for active feet. No matter how you look at it, NEOLITE is the perfect sole for *every* type of shoe, *every* member of the family!

INSIST ON GENUINE NEOLITE

The name is always plainly marked on the shank

"Store-Window Beauty" lasts longer when soles are NEOLITE! So light, so firm—this wonder sole is a joy to designers of many famous-make shoes. NEOLITE makes possible a new daintiness at the instep, beauty of finish and lasting good looks! NEOLITE Soles are *damp-proof*, too—won't let wet weather twist your shoes out of shape.

NEOLITE

NEOLITE, AN ELASTOMER-RESIN BLEND, T.M.—THE GOODYEAR TIRE & RUBBER COMPANY, AKRON, OHIO

SOLES

MAKE ANY SHOE A BETTER SHOE—ANY REPAIR JOB A BETTER JOB!

This statement is a broad generalization that uses loaded language.

Comparing Argumentative Texts

 1. Key Ideas and Details (a) How are the target audiences for Ball-Band shoes and Neolite Soles similar? **(b)** How are the two audiences different? **(c)** What **propaganda** techniques does each advertisement use? Cite specific examples.

Content-Area Vocabulary

2. (a) Use a dictionary to find definitions for the words *soles* and *platform* that differ from those given on page 512. **(b)** Then, write two sentences for each word: one showing the meaning as used in the advertisement, and the other showing a second meaning.

⏱ Timed Writing

Argumentative Text: Advertisement

Format and Audience
Your advertisement will be for radio. Therefore, it must not involve visuals. The prompt also tells you the audience for your writing.

Write a 30-second radio advertisement for a fictional brand of shoes that will compete with Ball-Band shoes. Appeal to the same audience as the Ball-Band ad. Include the name of your product and describe its positive features. Use at least two propaganda techniques in your advertisement. (25 minutes)

Academic Vocabulary
When you *describe* the features of something, you give information and details about it.

5-Minute Planner

Complete these steps before you begin to write:

1. Read the prompt. Look for highlighted key words.

2. Review the ad for Ball-Band shoes. Note the target audience. To whom are the words and images meant to appeal?

3. List claims you can make about your product, and determine which propaganda techniques will be most persuasive.

4. Name your product. Keep your target audience in mind.

5. Review the list of claims about your product. Narrow it to a few key points. Then, refer to that list as you draft your script.

Comparing Literary Works

Comparing Authors' Styles

An **author's style** is his or her usual way of writing. You can see an author's style in his or her use of the following elements:

- **Word choice or diction:** Authors can use words that are formal or informal, fancy or plain, technical or ordinary.

- **Arrangement of words:** Some authors prefer short sentences. Other authors write long and complicated sentences.

- **Emotion/Tone:** Authors often use words with strong connotations. A connotation is the feeling or emotion suggested by a word. A word's connotation helps the author express his or her tone, or attitude, toward a topic.

- **Figurative language:** Some authors use poetic language to present ideas in surprising ways. An author may, for example, use a comparison of unlike things or an exaggeration to make a point.

Analyzing an author's style can help you better understand the exact meaning of a text. "Letter From a Concentration Camp" is a letter written by a fictional character named Jimbo. "Letter to Scottie" was written by a father to his daughter. As you will see, the following letters reflect two very different styles. For each letter, use a chart like the one shown to note each author's style.

**Common Core
State Standards**

Reading Informational Text
4. Determine the meaning of words and phrases as they are used in a text, including figurative, connotative, and technical meanings.

Writing
2.a. Introduce a topic; organize ideas, concepts, and information, using strategies such as definition, classification, comparison/contrast, and cause/effect. *(Timed Writing)*

Word Choice	Emotion/Tone	Sentence Length	Figurative Language

www.PHLitOnline.com

- Vocabulary flashcards
- Interactive journals
- More about the authors

- Selection audio
- Interactive graphic organizers

What is important to *know?*

Writing About the Big Question

These two selections are letters written to somebody the author cares about who is far away. Complete this sentence starter.

Before reading letters like these, I would want to **know** _____ because_____ .

Meet the Authors

Yoshiko Uchida (1921–1992)

Author of "Letter From a Concentration Camp"

Yoshiko Uchida was born in California to parents who had emigrated from Japan. When Japan and the United States went to war during World War II, Uchida and her family were forced to live in a prison camp.

History Brought to Life As an adult, Uchida took pride in her heritage and decided to write works for children and adults. She dealt with her own wartime experience in two autobiographies as well as in fiction.

F. Scott Fitzgerald (1896–1940)

Author of "Letter to Scottie"

Francis Scott Key Fitzgerald was born in Minnesota. At age twenty-three, he published his first novel, *This Side of Paradise*, which became an instant success. Fitzgerald went on to write short stories, screenplays, and more novels.

The Personal Side Fitzgerald married and in 1921 had a daughter, Frances Scott Fitzgerald, whose nicknames were "Scottie" and "Pie." Because of her parents' travels, Scottie spent much of her youth in boarding schools. She was at camp when her father wrote her the following letter.

Letter From a
Concentration
Camp

Yoshiko Uchida

Background Although World War II had begun in 1939, the United States entered the war in December 1941, right after Japan attacked Pearl Harbor, a U.S. Navy base in Hawaii. President Franklin Roosevelt signed Executive Order 9066 in February 1942, moving people of Japanese heritage to internment camps—also called concentration camps—to make sure they did not aid the enemy. Yoshiko Uchida, who had to spend part of her youth in such a camp, created this letter, which is fictional.

Mailing Address: Barrack 16, Apartment 40
                     Tanforan Assembly Center
                     San Bruno, California
Actual Address: Stable 16, Horse stall 40
                     Tanforan Racetrack

May 6, 1942

Dear Hermie:

Here I am sitting on an army cot in a smelly old horse stall, where Mama, Bud, and I have to live for who knows how long. It's pouring rain, the wind's blowing in through all the cracks, and Mama looks like she wants to cry. I guess she misses Papa. Or maybe what got her down was that long, muddy walk along the racetrack to get to the mess hall for supper.

Anyway, now I know how it feels to stand in line at a soup kitchen with hundreds of hungry people. And that cold potato and weiner they gave me sure didn't make me feel much better. I'm still hungry, and I'd give you my last nickel if you appeared this minute with a big fat hamburger and a bagful of cookies.

You know what? It's like being in jail here—not being free to live in your own house, do what you want, or eat what you want. They've got barbed wire all around this racetrack and guard towers at each corner to make sure we can't get out. Doesn't that sound like a prison? It sure feels like one!

Author's Style
What language in this passage is informal?

Spiral Review
Figurative Language
Identify the idiom in the second paragraph. What does it reveal about Jimbo's state of mind?

Reading Check

What details about his surroundings make the letter writer feel as if he is in a prison?

◄ **Critical Viewing**
Based on the buildings, the faces of these families, and the items some are carrying, what might be happening in this picture? **[Infer]**

What I want to know is, What am I doing here anyway? Me—a genuine born-in-California citizen of the United States of America stuck behind barbed wire, just because I look like the enemy in Japan. And how come you're not in here too, with that German blood in your veins and a name like Herman Schnabel. We're at war with Germany too, aren't we? And with Italy? What about the people at Napoli Grocers?

My brother, Bud, says the US government made a terrible mistake that they'll **regret** someday. He says our leaders betrayed us and ignored the Constitution. But you know what I think? I think war makes people crazy. Why else would a smart man like President Franklin D. Roosevelt sign an executive order to force us Japanese Americans out of our homes and lock us up in concentration camps? Why else would the FBI take Papa off to a POW camp[1] just because he worked for a Japanese company? Papa—who loves America just as much as they do.

Hey, ask Mrs. Wilford what that was all about. I mean that stuff she taught us in sixth grade about the Bill of Rights and due process of law. If that means everybody can have a hearing before being thrown in prison, how come nobody gave us a hearing? I guess President Roosevelt forgot about the Constitution when he ordered us into concentration camps. I told you war makes people crazy!

---

1. **POW camp** prisoner-of-war camp, where persons captured in war are confined.

Well, Hermie, I gotta go now. Mama says we should get to the showers before the hot water runs out like it did when she went to do the laundry. Tomorrow she's getting up at 4:00 a.m. to beat the crowd. Can you imagine having to get up in the middle of the night and stand in line to wash your sheets and towels? By hand too! No luxuries like washing machines in this dump!

Hey, do me a favor? Go pet my dog, Rascal, for me. He's probably wondering why I had to leave him with Mrs. Harper next door. Tell him I'll be back to get him for sure. It's just that I don't know when. There's a rumor we're getting shipped to some desert—probably in Utah. But don't worry, when this stupid war is over, I'm coming home to California and nobody's ever going to kick me out again! You just wait and see! So long, Hermie.

Your pal,
Jimbo Kurasaki

Author's Style
What details of the author's style help reveal Jimbo's attitude toward his situation?

Critical Thinking

1. **Key Ideas and Details (a)** According to Jimbo, what does Bud think about holding Japanese Americans in the camps? **(b) Infer:** Why does Jimbo conclude that "war makes people crazy"?

Cite textual evidence to support your responses.

2. **Key Ideas and Details (a)** Why does Jimbo mention Mrs. Wilford's lessons about the Bill of Rights? **(b) Infer:** Why did the U.S. government deny Japanese Americans a hearing before sending them to camps?

3. **Key Ideas and Details (a)** Name some rights that Jimbo and his family have lost. **(b) Speculate:** When Jimbo is released from the camp, might his attitude toward those rights be different? Explain.

4. **Integration of Knowledge and Ideas (a)** How does the background given at the beginning of "Letter from a Concentration Camp" help the reader? **(b)** What other facts about this time in history would help you understand this fictional letter? *[Connect to the Big Question: What is important to know?]*

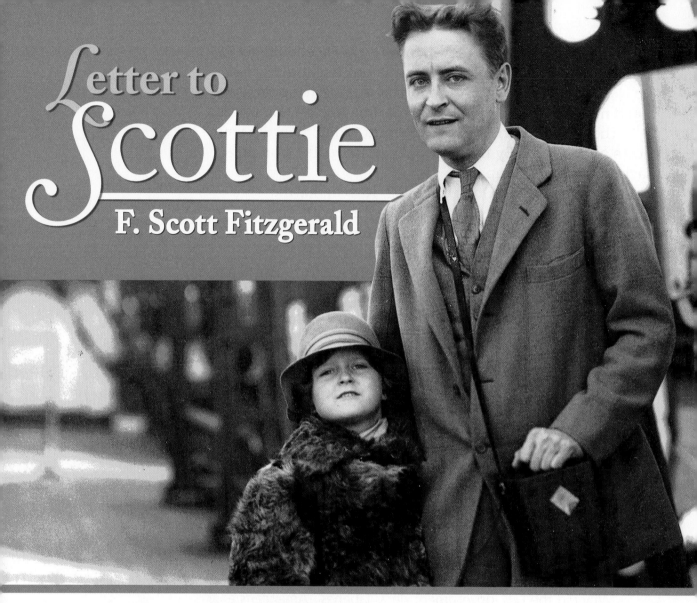

Letter to Scottie

F. Scott Fitzgerald

▲ **Critical Viewing**
What details in this photograph suggest that Fitzgerald and his daughter feel affection for each other? **[Analyze]**

Vocabulary
documentation
(däk´ yōō mən tā´ shən)
n. supporting evidence
misery (miz´ ər ē) n.
great sorrow

La Paix, Rodgers' Forge
Towson, Maryland

August 8, 1933

Dear Pie:
   I feel very strongly about you doing [your] duty. Would you give me a little more documentation about your reading in French? I am glad you are happy—but I never believe much in happiness. I never believe in misery either. Those are things you see on the stage or the screen or the printed page, they never really happen to you in life.

All I believe in in life is the rewards for virtue (according to your talents) and the *punishments* for not fulfilling your duties, which are doubly costly. If there is such a volume in the camp library, will you ask Mrs. Tyson to let you look up a sonnet of Shakespeare's in which the line occurs *"Lilies that fester smell far worse than weeds."*

Have had no thoughts today, life seems composed of getting up a *Saturday Evening Post*[1] story. I think of you, and always pleasantly; but if you call me "Pappy" again I am going to take the White Cat out and beat his bottom hard, *six times for every time you are impertinent.* Do you react to that?

I will arrange the camp bill.

Halfwit, I will conclude.

Things to worry about:

> Worry about courage
> Worry about cleanliness
> Worry about efficiency
> Worry about horsemanship
> Worry about . . .

Things not to worry about:

> Don't worry about popular opinion
> Don't worry about dolls
> Don't worry about the past
> Don't worry about the future
> Don't worry about growing up
> Don't worry about anybody getting ahead of you
> Don't worry about triumph
> Don't worry about failure unless it comes
>   through your own fault
> Don't worry about mosquitoes
> Don't worry about flies
> Don't worry about insects in general
> Don't worry about parents
> Don't worry about boys
> Don't worry about disappointments
> Don't worry about pleasures
> Don't worry about satisfactions

Things to think about:

> What am I really aiming at?

1. *Saturday Evening Post* a weekly magazine for which Fitzgerald wrote.

Author's Style
What makes this section of the letter straightforward and uncomplicated?

Author's Style
Is the author's style here humorous, serious, or both? Explain.

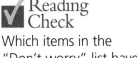
Reading Check
Which items in the "Don't worry" list have to do with competition?

Spiral Review
Figurative Language
Identify the metaphor in this section. What point is Fitzgerald making to his daughter?

How good am I really in comparison to my contemporaries in regard to:

(a) Scholarship

(b) Do I really understand about people and am I able to get along with them?

(c) Am I trying to make my body a useful instrument or am I neglecting it?

With dearest love,

[Daddy]

P.S. My come-back to your calling me Pappy is christening you by the word Egg, which implies that you belong to a very rudimentary state of life and that I could break you up and crack you open at my will and I think it would be a word that would hang on if I ever told it to your contemporaries. "Egg Fitzgerald." How would you like that to go through life with— "Eggie Fitzgerald" or "Bad Egg Fitzgerald" or any form that might occur to fertile minds? Try it once more and I swear I will hang it on you and it will be up to you to shake it off. Why borrow trouble?

Love anyhow.

Critical Thinking

Cite textual evidence to support your responses.

1. **Key Ideas and Details (a)** What is Scottie's nickname for her father? **(b) Infer:** How does he feel about this? How do you know?

2. **Key Ideas and Details (a)** How does Fitzgerald end the letter, just before he signs it? **(b) Speculate:** What kind of relationship do you think Fitzgerald had with his daughter?

3. **Key Ideas and Details (a)** Why does Fitzgerald advise his daughter not to worry about the past or the future? **(b) Take a Position:** Which item on the list of things to worry about is most important? Explain.

4. **Integration of Knowledge and Ideas (a)** Do you have to know who F. Scott Fitzgerald is in order to understand or appreciate this letter? **(b)** Do you think the advice in the letter is important? Why or why not? *[Connect to the Big Question: What is important to know?]*

Comparing Authors' Styles

© 1. Craft and Structure (a) In "Letter From a Concentration Camp," which words show informal word choice? **(b)** In "Letter to Scottie," which words show formal word choice?

© 2. Craft and Structure Describe the sentence style in each letter. Find an example sentence in each letter to support your answer.

© 3. Craft and Structure Which writer uses more figurative language? Explain.

© 4. Craft and Structure Complete a chart to show how each author's style suits each letter's purpose.

	Letter From a Concentration Camp	Letter to Scottie
Purpose		
Emotion/Tone		
Style Elements		

⏱ Timed Writing

Explanatory Text: Essay

Make connections between the texts by comparing and contrasting the authors' styles. In an essay, discuss the ways that the authors reveal their styles. **(30 minutes)**

5-Minute Planner

1. Read the prompt carefully and completely.

2. Gather your thoughts with answers to these questions:
   - Is the tone of each letter formal or informal?
   - What images does each author use to convey meaning?
   - What can you tell about the personalities of the writers—either real or fictional—from their writing?

3. Reread the prompt, and then draft your essay.

Writing Workshop

Common Core State Standards

Writing
1. Write arguments to support claims with clear reasons and relevant evidence.
1.a. Introduce claim(s) and organize the reasons and evidence clearly.
1.b. Support claim(s) with clear reasons and relevant evidence, using credible sources and demonstrating an understanding of the topic or text.

Write an Argument

Persuasion: Persuasive Essay

Defining the Form A **persuasive essay** argues the case for or against a particular position or urges readers to take a specific action. You might use elements of persuasive writing in speeches, advertisements, letters, and problem-solution essays.

Assignment Write a persuasive essay to convince readers to improve their lives in a specific way. Include these elements:

- ✔ *a clear thesis* or statement that presents a position on an issue that has at least two sides
- ✔ facts, examples, and reasons that *support the position*
- ✔ *powerful language* to appeal to a *specific audience*
- ✔ *evidence and arguments* to address readers' concerns
- ✔ *clear organization*, including an introduction, a body, and a strong conclusion
- ✔ *correct use of coordinating conjunctions*

To preview the criteria on which your persuasive essay may be judged, see the rubric on page 533.

 Writing Workshop: *Work in Progress*

Review the work you did on pages 487 and 509.

WRITE GUY
Jeff Anderson, M.Ed.

What Do You Notice?

Persuasion

The following passage is from Richard Durbin's persuasive speech "Preserving a Great American Symbol." Read it several times.

Mr. Speaker, I rise to condemn the desecration of a great American symbol. No, I am not referring to flagburning; I am referring to the baseball bat.

With a partner, discuss the qualities that make the sentence interesting and persuasive. For example, you may want to talk about the writer's use of word choice, style, and details. Now, think about ways you might use similar elements in your persuasive essay.

Reading-Writing Connection
To get the feel for persuasion, read the editorial "Preserving a Great American Symbol" on page 439.

Prewriting/Planning Strategies

Choose a two-sided topic. Select a topic that is important to you and that has two clear sides—one that you can support and one that you can oppose. Use these tips to zero in on an interesting topic:

- **Conduct a media review.** Think about the local issues in the news now. Look through the newspaper for stories, read letters to the editor, and watch and listen to local television and radio news programs to list all the topics that appeal to you. Then, choose one for your essay.

- **Organize a round table.** Gather classmates for a discussion of places and groups that are important to you. Think of issues that affect the locations and people you have listed. Jot down any ideas that interest you, and choose a topic.

Narrow your topic to a manageable size. Once you choose a topic, make sure it is not too big for a short persuasive essay. Use a graphic organizer like the one shown to narrow your topic.

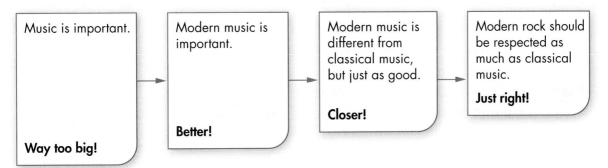

Music is important.

Way too big!

Modern music is important.

Better!

Modern music is different from classical music, but just as good.

Closer!

Modern rock should be respected as much as classical music.

Just right!

Build your argument. Plan how you will support your position with facts and strong details, and how you will answer any opposing points of view. Use these tips:

- **Collect evidence.** Identify facts, examples, statistics, quotations, and personal observations that support your position. Take notes on the sources of your information, because you need to credit any ideas or words that are not your own.

- **Anticipate counterarguments.** Look ahead to identify readers' questions and points of view that might differ from your position. Be prepared to include facts that will successfully address their questions and issues.

Drafting Strategies

Write a thesis statement. The evidence you have gathered will help support your position. Prepare a thesis statement—one sentence that names your issue and expresses your position.

Sample Thesis Statements

1. Our school should have recycling bins.

2. Young people should exercise twenty minutes every day.

Create a clear organization. Review the chart to organize your thoughts. Include your thesis in your introduction. Support your thesis statement in the body. Organize supporting information into paragraphs. Conclude with a restatement of your thesis.

Support each point. As you develop your evidence, be sure to support it fully.

- Find and use examples.
  Main idea: Vegetables are healthy snacks.
  Supporting example: Carrots are a source of Vitamin A.

- Use facts or statistics.
  Main idea: Rock music is often loud, but it is still music.
  Supporting fact: Rock follows a rhythmic pattern.

- Include quotations and expert opinions.
  Main idea: Our nation depends on volunteers.
  Supporting quotation: "Ask not what your country can do for you; ask what you can do for your country."
  —President John F. Kennedy

- Include personal observations to appeal to emotions.
  Main idea: Doctors agree that daily exercise is important.
  Supporting observation: I always feel better after jogging.

Maintain a formal style. Do not weaken your argument by using slang or informal language. Instead, use a formal, authoritative tone. Maintain that tone by using more difficult words and mixing in longer sentences with shorter ones.

Improve expression. Identify areas in your writing where you can clarify and improve your expression of ideas.

Target your audience. As always, keep your readers' ages and their knowledge about your topic in mind while writing.

Common Core State Standards

Writing

1.a. Introduce claim(s) and organize the reasons and evidence clearly.

1.b. Support claim(s) with clear reasons and relevant evidence, using credible sources and demonstrating an understanding of the topic or text.

1.d. Establish and maintain a formal style.

Language

1.e. Recognize variations from standard English in their own and others' writing and speaking, and identify and use strategies to improve expression in conventional language.

Introduction

Thesis statement

Body

Main point followed by facts, details, arguments, statistics, expert opinions. Explanations and evidence for the readers' concerns and counterarguments.

Conclusion

Summary of arguments. Strong restatement of position.

Writers on Writing

Zlata Filipović On Writing Persuasively

Zlata Filipović is the author of *Zlata's Diary* (p. 384).

Reading my diary inspired a large group of American high school students to write diaries about their life in a dangerous neighborhood of Los Angeles. Their book, published in 1999, became known as *The Freedom Writers Diary*. I was very moved by their project and wrote a foreword for their book, which is so full of enthusiasm about life and writing, and the power of both!

"My thoughts seem so much clearer when I write them down."
—Zlata Filipović

Professional Model:

from Foreword to *The Freedom Writers Diary*

Sometimes we suffer because of many things over which we have no control: the color of our skin, poverty, our religion, our family situation, war. It would be easy to become a victim of our circumstances and continue feeling sad, scared or angry; or instead, we could choose to deal with the injustice humanely and break the chains of negative thoughts and ~~actions~~ energies, . . . Writing about the things that happen to us allows us to look objectively at what's going on around us and turn a negative experience into something positive and useful. This process requires a lot of work, effort and greatness, but it is possible, and the Freedom Writers have proved it—they've chosen a difficult, but powerful, path. . . . I have heard people say that it is not what happens to us that matters, but how we deal with it. . . .

I connected problems of war with problems of racism or violence in what are considered peaceful countries to show that everywhere in the world people face difficulties.

I am fascinated by how people transform their experiences through writing, and by how powerful writing can be. Now I wish I had left in the word *actions*. It is more concrete than *energies*.

One always hears interesting quotes and ideas—they can all be an inspiration for writing and an effective way of making a point.

Revising Strategies

Revise to improve support. Review your draft to find places where you can strengthen the arguments that support your thesis. Follow these steps:

1. Underline your thesis statement.
2. Put a star next to each supporting point. Add more support if you have only one star.
3. Draw attention to a well-supported point by adding powerful language or a colorful comparison that helps readers connect one main point with another.
4. If you find a paragraph without support, review your prewriting notes and add support. If necessary, do additional research to find the support you need.
5. Review your conclusion to be sure that it flows logically from the argument you made in the body of your essay.

Revise to strengthen images and observations. Look for places you can add or improve an image or personal observation that illustrates your point. Use words that call specific pictures or sensory details to mind. Vivid language will appeal to your readers' emotions and help you persuade them to agree with you.

Common Core State Standards

Writing

1.b. Support claim(s) with clear reasons and relevant evidence, using credible sources and demonstrating an understanding of the topic or text.

1.c. Use words, phrases, and clauses to clarify the relationships among claim(s) and reasons.

1.e. Provide a concluding statement or section that follows from the argument presented.

5. With some guidance and support from peers and adults, develop and strengthen writing as needed by planning, editing, rewriting, or trying a new approach.

Language

1. Demonstrate command of the conventions of standard English grammar and usage when writing or speaking.

1.e. Recognize variations from standard English in their own and others' writing and speaking, and identify and use strategies to improve expression in conventional language.

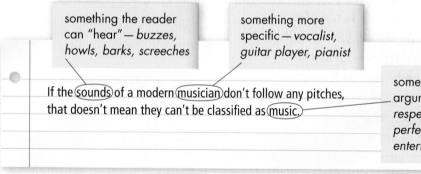

Peer Review

Ask a partner to identify places in your draft that spark emotional reactions, such as fear, pride, anger, or happiness. Consider adding more details to get the response you want. In addition, review each other's use of standard English. Suggest any necessary corrections.

Combining Sentences Using Coordinating Conjunctions

Coordinating conjunctions such as *and, but, or,* and *so* connect words or groups of words that are similar in form. They can connect nouns, phrases, or sentences.

Identifying Which Coordinating Conjunction to Use As the chart shows, each coordinating conjunction has its own distinct meaning and purpose. To join a pair of related sentences, first determine the relationship between the ideas in each sentence.

Coordinating Conjunction	Purpose	Use
and	to join similar or related ideas	I live in an apartment, **and** it is on the fourth floor.
but	to highlight difference or contrast	I like soccer, **but** my brother does not.
or	to show choices	You can have your lunch now, **or** you can wait for Molly.
so	to show cause and effect	I enjoy adventure stories, **so** I loved *Treasure Island*.

PH WRITING COACH

Further instruction and practice are available in *Prentice Hall Writing Coach*.

Using Coordinating Conjunctions Follow these steps:

1. **Identify the relationship between the sentences you wish to combine.**

2. **Choose a coordinating conjunction based on your purpose.**

3. **Join the two sentences using a comma and the coordinating conjunction you selected.** You may need to rephrase your sentences to make them work.

Grammar in Your Writing

Reread your persuasive essay, looking for short sentences that present related ideas. Then, use the rules and examples above to combine the sentences using coordinating conjunctions.

Student Model: Isaac Tetenbaum, Reseda, CA

Common Core State Standards

Language
2.b. Spell correctly.

Modern Rock Is Music, Too

Maybe you think Chopin is really cool—the blissful tones of the piano, played to serenade and mesmerize, the dazzling cadenzas and glistening high notes. For a change, though, why don't you pop in a modern rock CD? Contemporary music gets very little respect, yet most of the people who put it down haven't even listened to it. Modern rock deserves to be regarded and respected as music.

Music can be classified as any group of organized sounds. Yet while the roars of today's lead vocalists don't seem to make sense, even they are organized and related to the message of the song. Is it music? Yes. It follows a precise rhythmic pattern. It repeats. Just because howls from a modern vocalist don't follow any pitches doesn't mean they can't be classified as perfectly good music. You might not like the style, but you cannot deny it is music.

Once you've accepted rock as music, you might say all rock songs are in the same key—E. Just because the lowest string of the guitar is an E doesn't mean modern rock musicians continuously strum that string and open and end a tune with it. Nowadays, as new musicians experiment with different pitches, the common E of rock has almost disappeared.

In a technique called "dropping," guitarists and bassists of modern rock bands have been able to use lower pitches in their songs. In fact, a well-known modern guitarist has successfully created a seven-string guitar. Its seventh string has the default pitch of a B. Although you might have to listen a little harder to hear the evidence, the musicians of contemporary bands know their music. How else could they come up with "dropping" and the seven-string guitar?

I think anyone, even the most classical music lover, can appreciate today's sounds if given a chance. (Notice I didn't say love, just appreciate.) I listen to Chopin and modern rock. I respect both kinds of music because each one has its place. Chopin is like elegant figure skating—rock is like snowboarding. I feel free when I listen to my favorite rock group. Why don't you listen with me?

Isaac clearly establishes the two sides —those who like contemporary music and those who prefer classical. The last sentence in the introduction is the thesis.

The writer provides evidence that contemporary artists would be considered musical even by classical definitions.

Here, the writer admits that readers might think that all rock music is written in the same key—an argument he says is no longer true.

A powerful image helps readers understand Isaac's opinion.

Editing and Proofreading

Proofread to fix grammar, spelling, and punctuation errors.

Spelling Errors: Irregular Plurals Review these rules and examples, then double-check your work for spelling errors.

- Change the *f* to *v* and add *-es: elf, elves; wife, wives*
- Use the same spelling for words that have the same singular and plural forms: *one fish, two fish; one deer, two deer*
- Some words change vowel form to make them plural: *tooth, teeth; mouse, mice; goose, geese; foot, feet*

Publishing and Presenting

Consider one of the following ways to share your writing:

Deliver a speech. Use your persuasive composition as the basis for a speech that you give to your classmates.

Post your essay. Post your persuasive composition on a community bulletin board or online so that others can read it and discuss your position.

Reflecting on Your Writing

Writer's Journal Jot down your answer to this question:

How did your evidence change or deepen your view on the issue?

Rubric for Self-Assessment

Find evidence in your writing to address each category. Then, use the rating scale to grade your work.

Spiral Review

Earlier in the unit, you learned about **adverbs** (p. 486) and **conjunctions and interjections** (p. 508). Review your essay to be sure that you have used adverbs, conjunctions, and interjections correctly.

PH WRITING COACH

Further instruction and practice are available in *Prentice Hall Writing Coach.*

Criteria	Rating Scale				
	not very				*very*
Focus: How clearly is your position stated?	1	2	3	4	5
Organization: How organized are the introduction, body, and conclusion?	1	2	3	4	5
Support/Elaboration: How well are facts, statistics, examples, and reasons presented?	1	2	3	4	5
Style: How powerful are the images and language?	1	2	3	4	5
Conventions: How good is your grammar, especially your use of coordinating conjunctions?	1	2	3	4	5

Vocabulary Workshop

Words with Multiple Meanings

A **multiple-meaning word** is a word that has more than one basic definition. To determine the meaning intended in a sentence, look at the context—the words surrounding the word. This chart shows three different definitions and usages for the word *key*. Note how context clues suggest the meaning of *key* in each sentence.

Word	Use	Definition	Example Sentence
key	noun	a device used to open a lock	Use this **key** to unlock the door.
key	noun	a reef or low island	We paddled our boat out to the **key**.
key	adjective	important	The **key** point of the article is that tigers are an endangered species.

Practice A Use context and your prior knowledge to write the meaning of the italicized word in each sentence. Then, use a print or an online dictionary to verify, or confirm, the meanings.

1. **a.** The old chair was covered with *dust*.
   b. When you take the cookies out of the oven, *dust* them with powdered sugar.
2. **a.** Let's *watch* the news on television at six o'clock.
   b. Check your *watch* to see if we need to leave for home yet.
3. **a.** I think the *content* of that poem is beautiful.
   b. The applause made Mary feel *content* with her performance.
4. **a.** How many people were *present* at the meeting?
   b. I made a birthday *present* for my grandfather.

Common Core State Standards

Language

4. Determine or clarify the meaning of unknown and multiple-meaning words and phrases based on grade 6 reading and content, choosing flexibly from a range of strategies.

4.a. Use context as a clue to the meaning of a word or phrase.

4.c. Consult reference materials, both print and digital, to find the pronunciation of a word or determine or clarify its precise meaning or its part of speech.

4.d. Verify the preliminary determination of the meaning of a word or phrase.

Practice B For each word listed, write two sentences that use different meanings of the word. If necessary, look up the meanings in a dictionary.

1. bow
2. set
3. draft
4. cast
5. tip
6. cape
7. current
8. ruler

www.PHLitOnline.com
- Illustrated vocabulary words
- Interactive vocabulary games
- Vocabulary flashcards

Activity Look in a dictionary to find five words that have multiple meanings. Write each word on a separate notecard like the one shown. Fill in the left-hand column of the notecard based on one of the word's meanings. Fill in the right-hand column based on another of the word's meanings. Then, trade note cards with a partner. Discuss the different meanings and uses of the words that each of you found.

Use a dictionary to find the multiple meanings of these words:

1. pitcher
2. entry
3. hide
4. line
5. fast

Word: _____

Part of Speech:	Part of Speech:
Definition:	Definition:
Example Sentence:	Example Sentence:

Comprehension and Collaboration

Work with two or three classmates. Write a sentence for each of the following words, using two different meanings of the word in the same sentence. For example, "My brother can't *bear* to be without his teddy *bear*."

charge

hard

wave

Communications Workshop

Problem-Solution Proposal

A **problem-solution proposal** is a formal plan that suggests a course of action for solving a problem. The following strategies can help you present a convincing problem-solution proposal.

Learn the Skills

Use the following strategies to complete the activity on page 537.

Organize your ideas. First, identify the problem and make a list of its causes. Use statistics and examples to demonstrate these causes. Then, describe your proposed solution and list the reasons you think the solution will work. Add details that provide evidence for each point of your solution.

Establish connections and provide evidence. Use visual aids to show connections or provide evidence. For example, a bar graph or chart can show the connection between the problem you defined and the solution you are proposing. In the example shown, the bar graph illustrates the increase in accidents each year and provides support for the solution of installing a traffic light. Draw your visual aids or create them on a computer.

Plan your delivery. Practice your proposal and prepare any notes and visuals before your presentation so you do not forget your key points.

Remember your listener. Speak slowly so that your audience will be able to follow your presentation. Pause after you make an important point. To emphasize your main points, refer to your visuals and adjust your tone.

Use standard English. Your argument will be stronger if you use formal, correct language. As you speak, avoid slang and errors in grammar and usage.

Use eye contact and gestures. Make eye contact with members of the audience to keep them engaged, and use gestures to emphasize your points.

**Common Core
State Standards**

Speaking and Listening
4. Present claims and findings, sequencing ideas logically and using pertinent descriptions, facts, and details to accentuate main ideas or themes; use appropriate eye contact, adequate volume, and clear pronunciation.

Language
1.e. Recognize variations from standard English in their own and others' writing and speaking, and identify and use strategies to improve expression in conventional language.

Problem: Car accidents have increased each year.
Solution: Replace stop signs with traffic lights.

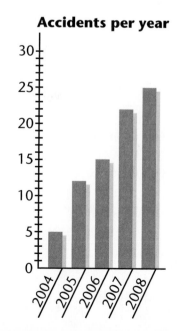

Accidents per year

Practice the Skills

Ⓒ Presentation of Knowledge and Ideas Use what you have learned in this workshop to complete the following activity.

ACTIVITY: Give a Problem-Solution Proposal

Find a problem and think of a solution for it. Then, follow the steps below.

- Make a list of causes.
- Use statistics and examples to demonstrate the causes.
- Organize your ideas around your solution.
- Use visual aids and evidence to support your solution.
- When delivering your proposal, make eye contact with the audience and use gestures.

Use a speaking guide like the one below to organize and plan your problem-solution proposal.

Speaking Guide

Problem: _____

Solution: _____

Supporting Points: _____

Visual Aids
Which visual aid will best support your solution? Briefly explain.

☐ graph   ☐ chart   ☐ table
☐ poster   ☐ diagram   ☐ video

Delivery of Presentation
Employ the following techniques when you present your proposal.

☐ eye contact   ☐ speaking rate
☐ volume level   ☐ clear enunciation
☐ natural gestures ☐ conventions of language

Ⓒ Comprehension and Collaboration Ask a classmate to evaluate your presentation. Discuss how well you communicated your ideas and how reasonable your solution is. Then, evaluate your classmate's proposal. Offer each other suggestions for improvement using proper conventions of language.

Cumulative Review

I. Reading Literature/Informational Text

Common Core
State Standards

RL.6.4, W.6.2.b, L.6.4.a
[For the full wording of the standards, see the standards chart in the front of your textbook.]

Directions: *Read the passage. Then, answer each question that follows.*

You work in the shadows. For weeks, or even years, you live in countries far from your home. Your assignments are top secret and dangerous. You carry fake documents—I.D. cards, a birth certificate, travel papers. You have a new name. You might wear a false nose or mustache and walk in a different way than usual. You might wear a coat with a button that is actually a lens for a hidden camera. If you are found out—if your <u>cover</u> is blown—you could lose your life. You are a spy for the CIA—the Central Intelligence Agency. Your job is to collect information for key government leaders.

For 25 years, Antonio Mendez was a master of disguise for the CIA. An accomplished artist, Mendez began his career at the agency by creating false documents for CIA agents. Later, he used his artistic skills to create disguises for agents, even for himself. The disguises allowed agents to hide their identities. Mendez eventually became chief of the agency's division of disguise.

Once, after ten days of disguise training in Washington, D.C., Mendez flew home to Denver. Before the flight home, he put on a pair of glasses and changed his hairline. His wife, waiting for him at the airport gate, did not recognize him as he walked past her. Perhaps his greatest feat was disguising diplomats as members of a Canadian film crew who were scouting locations for a movie. Mendez himself adopted an Irish accent and pretended to be the film's director.

Tony Mendez is now retired from the CIA. He lives with his family on a farm in Maryland. He has written two books about his life as a "disguise spy." He is a consultant for the International Spy Museum in Washington, D.C. Mendez sometimes misses the excitement of his former job. But he has returned to the work that landed him the CIA job in the first place: being an artist. The former master of the art of disguise is now a master of the art of painting.

1. Which of these words best describes the **author's tone** in the first paragraph of the passage?
   A. humorous
   B. serious
   C. playful
   D. confused

2. Which sentence from the passage uses **figurative language?**
   A. You work in the shadows.
   B. You have a new name.
   C. For 25 years, Antonio Mendez was a master of disguise for the CIA.
   D. Mendez sometimes misses the excitement of his former job.

3. Which of these words *best* describes the **author's attitude** toward Tony Mendez?
   A. fearful
   B. critical
   C. admiring
   D. disrespectful

4. Which of these phrases shows the *most* **formal word choice?**
   A. top secret and dangerous
   B. if your cover is blown
   C. lives with his family on a farm
   D. an accomplished artist

5. Which of these *best* describes the **mood** created in the last paragraph?
   A. scary
   B. sad
   C. upbeat
   D. threatening

6. Based on the ideas in the passage, which of these beliefs is most likely among the **author's influences?**
   A. Carrying fake documents is wrong.
   B. Most disguises are easy to detect.
   C. Most spy movies are unrealistic.
   D. CIA agents do important work.

7. Which characteristic listed below is *not* typical of biographical writing?
   A. It is a story about someone's life.
   B. Its purpose is to inform readers.
   C. It is told consistently from the third-person point of view.
   D. It is told consistently from the first-person point of view.

8. **Vocabulary** Which word is closest in meaning to the underlined word <u>cover</u> in this passage?
   A. close
   B. wrapper
   C. disguise
   D. report

 Timed Writing

9. In an essay, explain whether the **author's style** in this passage is formal or informal. **Support** your ideas with **details** from the text.

 **GO ON**

II. Reading Informational Text

Directions: *Read this speech. Then, answer each question that follows.*

Common Core State Standards

RI.6.2, RI.6.5; W.6.5; L.6.3
[For the full wording of the standards, see the standards chart in the front of your textbook.]

Do you ever wonder why students are lethargic after lunch, or why they cannot seem to pay attention in afternoon classes? This is most likely due to the foods students eat during lunch.

I believe that our school cafeteria needs healthier foods. If you look at the monthly menu, you will see that fried foods, pizza, and pasta dominate the daily specials. Although the daily specials are not our only options, the alternatives are soggy, wilting salads, bagels, or the fried chips, candy, and soda in the vending machines.

In the news, and in our health classes, we are lectured about eating well. Studies show that eating healthy food provides teens with the energy to succeed in school, along with a positive self-image. We are also informed of the growing obesity problem among children in America. This is quite evident here at Milton Middle School. So, why are we being tempted by battered onion rings, fatty nachos, and greasy fried chicken? Why can't we be tempted by fresh salad bars, grilled chicken sandwiches, and healthy soups? These healthier options teach us good habits and could save us from developing serious illnesses later in life.

If nutritious foods are served, every student in school will buy them, and you will see an increase in student achievement.

1. Which of these *best* summarizes the **author's conclusion** in paragraph 1?

   A. Students are lazy and tired.
   B. Eating lunch causes a lack of focus.
   C. Students eat foods that make them tired and unfocused.
   D. Teachers are annoyed after lunch.

2. Which **propaganda technique** does the writer use in the last sentence?

   A. The writer uses loaded language.
   B. The writer uses a broad generalization.
   C. The writer uses a hidden message.
   D. The writer uses emotional reasoning.

3. What **evidence** supports the author's conclusion about a healthy diet?

   A. The cafeteria serves fried food.
   B. Students are told they should eat well.
   C. Studies show that eating healthy food gives teens energy.
   D. Nachos are tempting.

4. Vocabulary Which word is closest in meaning to the underlined word lethargic?

   A. tired
   B. full
   C. hungry
   D. energetic

III. Writing and Language Conventions

Directions: *Read the passage, then answer each question.*

(1) Begin with two large, empty soda bottles. (2) Rinse each bottle well. (3) Next, tape a rubber washer to the top of one bottle, leaving the hole in the washer uncovered. (4) Use duct tape, which is strongest than most tapes. (5) Then fill that bottle three-fourths full of water. (6) Put the empty bottle upside down on top of the other bottle. (7) Tape the bottles tight together. (8) Next, turn the bottles over so that the bottle with water is on top. (9) Move the bottles quickly in big circles and put the bottom bottle on a table. (10) The water will swirl like a tornado.

1. Which title would be the *best* choice for this **how-to essay?**
   A. Bottoms Up
   B. Fun with Water
   C. Create a Stir
   D. Tornado in a Bottle

2. To correct an error in sentence 4, which **comparative adjective** should replace *strongest?*
   A. strong
   B. strongly
   C. stronger
   D. most strong

3. Which **materials** should be listed with these instructions?
   A. duct tape, washer, and scissors
   B. duct tape, washer, and bottles
   C. a measuring cup, washer, and duct tape
   D. a measuring cup, washer, and bottles

4. At what point in the instructions would a **diagram** be most helpful?
   A. after sentence 1
   B. after sentence 4
   C. after sentence 7
   D. after sentence 10

5. Which revision to sentence 7 corrects an error in the use of a **troublesome modifier?**
   A. Tape the bottles together tight.
   B. Tape the bottles tightly together.
   C. Tape the bottles tighter together.
   D. Tape the tighter bottles together.

6. Which **transition** word could the writer add to the beginning of sentence 9 to show **sequence?**
   A. First,
   B. Finally,
   C. Carefully,
   D. Quickly,

Performance Tasks

Directions: *Follow the instructions to complete the tasks below as required by your teacher.*
As you work on each task, incorporate both general academic vocabulary and literary terms you learned in this unit.

Common Core State Standards

RI.6.2, RI.6.4, RI.6.5, RI.6.8, RI.6.9;
W.6.2, W.6.4; SL.6.3, SL.6.4, SL.6.5,
SL.6.6
[For the full wording of the standards, see the standards chart in the front of your textbook.]

Writing

© Task 1: Informational Text [RI.6.6]
Determine the Author's Point of View

Write an essay in which you determine the author's point of view in a nonfiction text from this unit.

- Tell which work you chose and identify the topic it discusses.

- Explain the author's purpose and main idea by answering the question: What does this author want me to know or to do?

- Explain the point of view you think the author expresses in the text. Support your ideas by identifying any direct statements the author makes about his or her point of view.

- Further support your ideas by citing other details that show the author's point of view.

- In your conclusion, restate your explanation of the author's point of view.

© Task 2: Informational Text [RI.6.4, RI.6.5]
Analyze the Structure of a Text

Write an essay in which you analyze how a paragraph or section helps to develop ideas in a nonfiction work from this unit.

- Tell which work you chose and identify the paragraph or section you will examine.

- Explain why the paragraph you have chosen is important to the overall text and how it adds to the development of ideas.

- Determine the meanings of words and phrases as they are used in the paragraph. Identify the connotative, or associated meanings, of words and connect them to the ideas presented in the text. Explain why the author chose those particular words.

- Evaluate how well the author develops and structures his or her ideas in the work as a whole. Cite details to support your opinion.

© Task 3: Informational Text [RI.6.2]
Determine the Central Idea

Write an essay in which you determine the central idea of a nonfiction work from this unit.

- Explain which work you chose and provide a summary of the text. Do not include your opinions in the summary.

- State the central idea of the text in your own words. Then, explain how the central idea is developed in the work. Cite particular details from the beginning, middle, and end of the work that contribute to the development of the central idea.

Speaking and Listening

Task 4: Informational Text [RI.6.8; SL.6.6]

Trace and Evaluate an Argument

Write and present an essay in which you trace and evaluate the argument in a nonfiction work from this unit.

- Write an essay in which you explain the argument an author presents in a text.
- Trace the argument, showing how the author introduces, develops, and concludes it.
- Note specific claims, or separate ideas, that contribute to the overall argument.
- Include your evaluation of the argument, explaining whether it is logical and supported with strong evidence.
- Take turns orally presenting essays in a small group.
- Listen for slang or informal language in both your own and others' presentations. Discuss how to improve the use of formal language.
- Apply the feedback to revise your essay.

Task 5: Informational Text [RI.6.9; SL.6.4]

Compare Presentations of Events

Give an oral presentation of an essay in which you compare and contrast one author's presentation of events with that of another.

- Choose two nonfiction works from this unit written about the same subject.
- Compare and contrast one author's presentation of events with that of another. Use examples from the texts to support your analysis.

- Present your ideas in logical order, using specific details to support main ideas.
- As you speak, use appropriate eye contact. Speak clearly and loudly enough to be understood in a classroom setting.

Task 6: Informational Text [RI.6.4; SL.6.5]

Determine the Meaning of Connotative Language

Create and present a graphic that illustrates an example of connotative meaning in a work from this unit.

- Choose a work from the unit that includes striking word choices. Identify one word that is especially important to the author's ideas.
- Analyze the word's connotative meanings.
- Create a drawing or other graphic that illustrates the word's connotations.
- Write a paragraph to accompany your graphic in which you explain how the word's connotations suit the author's ideas.
- Present your graphic to the class.

What is important to know?
At the beginning of Unit 3, you wrote a response to the Big Question. Now that you have completed the unit, write a new response. Discuss how your initial ideas have expanded or changed. Cite specific examples from the literature in this unit, from other subject areas, and from your own life to support your ideas. Use Big Question vocabulary words (see p. 377) in your response.

Featured Titles

In this unit, you have read a variety of informational texts, including literary nonfiction. Continue to read on your own. Select works that you enjoy, but challenge yourself to explore new topics, new authors, and works of increasing depth and complexity. The titles suggested below will help you get started.

Informational Texts

Boy: Tales of Childhood

by Roald Dahl

Read this collection of funny—and true—stories to learn what Roald Dahl found important and fascinating in his own childhood. This **autobiography** shows that life can be just as comical and exciting as fiction.

Zlata's Diary: A Child's Life in Wartime Sarajevo

by Zlata Filipović

During the war in Bosnia and Herzegovina in the early 1990s, Zlata kept a **diary** recording the desperate situations her family faced in Sarajevo. Her diary provides an honest, unique view of what it is like to live during a war.

Discoveries: Digging for Answers

Build your knowledge in many subject areas as you read these **essays,** including "Searching for Pompeii," "Identifying Birds," "The Story of American Sign Language," and "The Measure of a Good Cook."

The Number Devil: A Mathematical Adventure

by Hans Magnus Enzensberger

Granta Books, 2000   EXEMPLAR TEXT

In this book, which is part math instruction and part good-humored **fantasy,** a boy who dislikes math dreams of meeting a number devil who teaches basic mathematical concepts in an entertaining way.

Adams on Adams

by John Adams   EXEMPLAR TEXT

Editor Paul M. Zall explores John Adams's own writings to present this founding father's life and worldview. This **autobiographical** collection includes Adams's "Letter on Thomas Jefferson."

Literature

A Wrinkle in Time

by Madeleine L'Engle

Square Fish, 2007   EXEMPLAR TEXT

In this **fantasy novel,** two children, along with a friend, set out on a quest through time and space to find their missing father. In their travels, they become part of a galactic battle between good and evil.

Preparing to Read Complex Texts

Attentive Reading As you read on your own, ask yourself questions about the text. The questions shown below and others that you ask as you read will help you learn and enjoy literature even more.

 **Common Core State Standards**

Reading Literature/Informational Text 10. By the end of the year, read and comprehend literature, including stories, dramas, and poems, and literary nonfiction in the grades 6–8 text complexity band proficiently, with scaffolding as needed at the high end of the range.

When reading literary nonfiction, ask yourself...

- Who is the author? Why did he or she write the work?
- Is the author writing about a personal experience or a topic he or she has studied? In either case, what are my expectations about the work?
- Are the ideas the author expresses important? Why or why not?
- Did the author live at a different time and place than the present? If so, how does that affect his or her choice of topic and attitude?
- Does the author express beliefs that are very different from mine? If so, how does that affect what I understand and feel about the text?
- Does any one idea seem more important than the others? Why?
- What can I learn from this work?

Ⓒ **Key Ideas and Details**

- Does the author organize ideas so that I can understand them? If not, what is unclear?
- Is the work interesting right from the start? If so, what has the author done to capture my interest? If not, why?
- Does the author give me a new way of looking at a topic? If so, how? If not, why?
- Is the author an expert on the topic? How do I know?
- Does the author use a variety of evidence that makes sense? If not, what is weak?
- Does the author use words in ways that are both interesting and clear? If so, are there any sections that I enjoy more than others? If not, why?

Ⓒ **Craft and Structure**

- Does the work seem believable? Why or why not?
- Do I agree or disagree with the author's arguments or ideas? Why or why not?
- Does this work remind me of others I have read? If so, in what ways?
- Does this work make me want to read more about this topic? Does it make me want to explore a related topic? Why or why not?

Ⓒ **Integration of Ideas**

Do we need words to *communicate* well?

PHLit
Online!
www.PHLitOnline.com

Hear It!
- Selection summary audio
- Selection audio
- BQ Tunes

See It!
- Author videos
- Big Question video
- Get Connected videos
- Background videos
- More about the authors
- Illustrated vocabulary words
- Vocabulary flashcards

Do It!
- Interactive journals
- Interactive graphic organizers
- Grammar tutorials
- Interactive vocabulary games
- Test practice

Do we need words to communicate well?

To **communicate** means to interact with others to promote understanding. Often, we use words to communicate our thoughts and feelings. However, we also use nonverbal communication methods that do not depend on words. An expression such as a smile or a frown can reveal your feelings. A gesture such as a wave or a nod can send a clear message, too.

Exploring the Big Question

Ⓒ **Collaboration: One-on-One Discussion** Start thinking about the Big Question by identifying various ways that we communicate with one another. List ways that people share thoughts and feelings. Describe examples of communicating information in the following situations:

- thanking someone for a gift
- asking for something you need or want
- persuading someone to change his or her mind
- sharing an important wish or dream
- listening to a friend share a difficult problem

   Share ideas with a partner. Highlight examples that use nonverbal communication. Which of these examples are *at least* as effective as using words?

Connecting to the Literature Each reading in this unit will give you additional insight into the Big Question.

PHLit Online!
www.PHLitOnline.com

- Big Question video
- Illustrated vocabulary words
- Interactive vocabulary games
- BQ Tunes

Learning Big Question Vocabulary

Acquire and Use Academic Vocabulary Academic vocabulary is the language you encounter in textbooks and on standardized tests. Review the definitions of these academic vocabulary words.

communicate (kə myoo´ ni kāt´) v. share thoughts or feelings, usually in words	**reveal** (ri vēl´) v. show; uncover
correspond (kôr´ ə spänd´) v. communicate with by letter; agree with	**symbolize** (sim´ bə liz´) v. stand for
quote (kwōt) v. use a speaker's or writer's words	**visual** (vizh´ oo əl) adj. able to be seen with the eyes

Use these words as you complete Big Question activities in this unit that involve reading, writing, speaking, and listening.

Gather Vocabulary Knowledge Additional Big Question words are listed below. Categorize the words by deciding whether you know each one well, know it a little bit, or do not know it at all.

connection	gesture	nonverbal
dialogue	language	share
expression	message	verbal

Then, do the following:

1. Write the definitions of the words you know.
2. If a word sounds familiar but you are not sure of its meaning, write down what you think the word means.
3. Then, using a print or an online dictionary, look up the meanings of the words you do not know or are not certain of. Write down their meanings.
4. Use all of the words in a brief paragraph about the various ways you communicate with others in your daily life.

Common Core State Standards

Speaking and Listening
1. Engage effectively in a range of collaborative discussions with diverse partners on grade 6 topics, texts, and issues, building on others' ideas and expressing their own clearly.

Language
6. Acquire and use accurately grade-appropriate general academic and domain-specific words and phrases; gather vocabulary knowledge when considering a word or phrase important to comprehension or expression.

Elements of Poetry

Poetry uses musical elements of language to help express thoughts and feelings.

Poetry is a type of literature in which the rhythms and sounds of words are as important as their definitions. When you read most poems, you can hear a **rhythm,** or beat. Other sound devices, such as **rhyme,** add to a poem's musical effect. Rhythm and sound help support a poem's meaning and shape its structure.

Structure Poems are arranged in **lines,** or groups of words, that help create rhythm and emphasis.

> **Example: Snowflake**
>
> A cold little star, spun from the sky,
> landed on the ground,
>   then vanished.

Poetry looks different from prose, or ordinary writing, because the lengths of individual lines in a poem may vary. In the example above, each of the snowflake's actions is presented on its own line.

The lines of a poem are arranged in units called stanzas. A **stanza** is a group of lines that work together to express a central idea. Like the paragraphs in an essay, the stanzas in a poem divide the text into logical parts.

Speaker When you read a poem, you can "hear" a voice speaking to you. The voice that narrates a poem is called the **speaker.** Like the narrator in a story, the speaker in a poem is an imaginary voice created by the poet. The speaker may present a unique point of view that is not necessarily the point of view of the poet.

Read the poem below, taking special note of its speaker and its structure. Notice the effects of these elements on the poem's meaning.

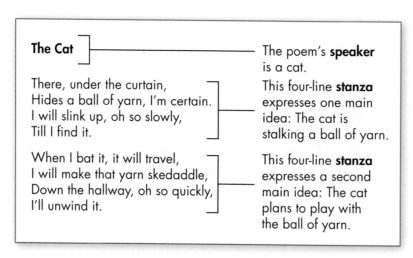

The Cat — The poem's **speaker** is a cat.

There, under the curtain,
Hides a ball of yarn, I'm certain.
I will slink up, oh so slowly,
Till I find it.

This four-line **stanza** expresses one main idea: The cat is stalking a ball of yarn.

When I bat it, it will travel,
I will make that yarn skedaddle,
Down the hallway, oh so quickly,
I'll unwind it.

This four-line **stanza** expresses a second main idea: The cat plans to play with the ball of yarn.

Sound Devices

Sound devices add a musical quality to poetry. Poets use the following devices to enhance a poem's mood and meaning.

Rhythm The rhythm of a poem is the beat created by its pattern of stressed and unstressed syllables. A stressed syllable is emphasized when it is spoken. An unstressed syllable is not emphasized. Rhythm can support meaning and make a poem memorable.

Read the following example aloud to hear its rhythm. Stressed syllables are printed in dark type.

> **Example:**
>
> The **anxious fans** shot **to** their **feet,**
> Their **faces filled** with **fear.**
> But **when** the **ball** swished
> **through** the **net,**
> They **cheered** a **migh**ty **cheer!**

In this poem, the regular rhythm is like the bouncing of a basketball. Not all poems have such a predictable rhythmic pattern, however. Poets may vary rhythms to emphasize certain words or to enhance meaning.

Rhyme is the repetition of sounds at the ends of words, as in *pool, rule,* and *fool.* As you read the following example, notice how rhyme connects ideas in the poem.

> **Example:**
>
> I was angry with my fr<u>iend</u>:
> I told my wrath, my wrath did <u>end</u>.
> I was angry with my f<u>oe</u>:
> I told it not, my wrath did <u>grow</u>.
> — from "The Poison Tree" by William Blake

The rhyming words *friend* and *end* create a connection between the first two lines of the poem. Together these lines state a sentence with a central idea. Likewise, rhyming words connect the next two lines, which state a second sentence and a new, but related, idea.

Repetition is the use of any element of language—a sound, word, phrase, or sentence—more than once.

Alliteration is the repetition of similar consonant sounds at the beginnings of words.

Onomatopoeia is the use of words to imitate sounds. In the poem below, examples of alliteration are highlighted in color and examples of onomatopoeia are underlined.

> **Example:**
>
> Outside, clouds curl before the storm.
> I snuggle inside, safe from the <u>whooshing</u> wind.
> I watch as the sky darkens,
> And put my hand to the cold window.

In This Section

Elements of Poetry

Analyzing Poetic Language

Analyzing Structure and Theme

Close Read: Determining Theme in Poetry
• Model Text
• Practice Text

After You Read

 Common Core State Standards

RL.6.4, RL.6.5, RL.6.6
[For the full wording of the standards, see the standards chart at the front of your textbook.]

Analyzing Poetic Language

Poets choose words carefully to express their ideas clearly and imaginatively.

Common Core State Standards

Reading Literature 4. Determine the meaning of words and phrases as they are used in a text, including figurative and connotative meanings; analyze the impact of a specific word choice on meaning and tone.

Connotation and Denotation A word can convey different kinds of meanings. One kind is the word's **denotation,** or dictionary definition. Another kind is the word's **connotation,** or the feelings and associations it evokes in people.

A word with positive connotations is associated with positive feelings and ideas. A word with negative connotations is associated with negative feelings and ideas. Think about the difference between the words *fragrance* and *odor*. Both words literally mean "smell." However, their connotative meanings are very different.

Meaning and Tone Tone is a writer's attitude toward his or her subject. A poem's **tone** can usually be described in one word, such as *joyful* or *lonely*. The connotations of the words in a poem can help convey its tone. Compare the following lines of poetry:

- They rolled over the swells until they slid ashore.
- They slammed over the waves until they hit land.

Both examples convey roughly the same information. However, in the first example, the words *rolled*, *swells*, and *slid* create a peaceful tone. In the second example, the words *slammed*, *waves*, and *hit* create an anxious tone.

Figurative Language Poets use **figurative language** to help readers see familiar ideas in fresh new ways. Figurative language is writing or speech that is not meant to be taken literally. Common types of figurative language are described below.

Types of Figurative Language

Simile compares two unlike things using the words *like* or *as*.

Example: The man was as gruff as a grizzly bear.

Metaphor compares two unlike things without using *like* or *as*.

Example: My aching feet were two bricks at the ends of my legs.

Personification gives human qualities to something that is not human.

Example: The flames of the campfire licked the night air.

Hyperbole is an extreme exaggeration.

Example: You've broken my heart into a million pieces!

Analyzing Structure and Theme

The words, lines, and stanzas of a poem work together to convey a **theme,** or message about life.

**Common Core
State Standards**

Reading Literature 5. Analyze how a particular sentence, chapter, scene, or stanza fits into the overall structure of a text and contributes to the development of the theme, setting, or plot.

Structure and Theme The **theme** of a poem is the message or insight about life that it conveys. Often, the structure of a poem contributes to its meaning. For example, each stanza may develop a central idea. Combining the central ideas of all the stanzas can lead you to the poem's theme.

As you read the following example, look for the theme of the poem.

> **Example: Waiting**
> The hands of the clock
> creep
> over
> the
> numbers
> until . . .
>
> The bell rings and sets me free.

Notice the different lengths of the poem's two stanzas. The first stanza has six lines, and the second stanza has only one. However, both stanzas contribute to the overall theme of the poem. In the first stanza, beginning with the second line, the poet puts one word on each line. This structure imitates the slow-ticking hands of a clock. The second stanza flows as one sentence. This suggests the speaker's relief upon hearing the bell. Together, the stanzas develop the theme of the poem: Time seems to move slowly when you are waiting for something you want.

Forms of Poetry Poetry comes in many different forms. Following are some of the common forms of poetry, which you will explore in this unit.

A **narrative** poem tells a story in verse. Narrative poetry has elements similar to those in short stories, such as plot and characters.

A **lyric** poem expresses the thoughts and feelings of a single speaker, often in highly musical verse.

A **concrete** poem is shaped to look like its subject. The poet arranges the lines to create a picture on the page.

A **haiku** is a Japanese form of poetry about nature, made up of three lines. The first and third lines have five syllables each. The second line has seven syllables.

A **limerick** is a humorous, rhyming five-line poem with a specific rhythm and pattern of rhyme.

A **free verse** poem does not have a strict structure, regular rhythm, or pattern of rhyme.

Close Read: Determining Theme in Poetry

The different elements of a poem work together to convey its theme.

The **theme** of a poem is its central message or insight. In most poems, the theme is not directly stated. Instead, it is suggested through the elements of the poem. To determine a poem's theme, look for patterns of meaning in the poem's elements. Notice what the images, figurative language, and main idea of each stanza have in common. Consider whether sound devices emphasize any key words, and analyze how the form of the poem helps support its meaning. Use the chart below as a guide.

Clues to Theme	
Poetic Structure • Lines of a poem are often grouped into stanzas. • Each stanza conveys a central idea.	**Word Choice and Tone** • Words with positive **connotations,** or associations, express a positive attitude, or **tone.** • Words with negative connotations express a negative tone.
Rhythm • Stressed and unstressed syllables create a pattern of beats. • Rhythm gives a poem a musical quality.	**Figurative Language** • A **simile** is a comparison that uses the word *like* or *as.* • A **metaphor** is a direct comparison that does not use *like* or *as.* • **Personification** gives human traits to things that are not human.
Sound Devices • **Repetition** is use of a word, phrase, line, or image more than once. • **Rhythm** is the repetition of sounds at the ends of words. • **Alliteration** is the repetition of consonant sounds at the beginnings of words. • **Onomatopoeia** is the use of words that imitate sounds.	**Sensory Language** • Sensory language creates images that appeal to one or more of the five senses. • These images help readers imagine the experiences described in poetry.

Model

About the Text As part of their traditions, the Navajo perform a nine-day ceremony called the Mountain Chant. During the ceremony, the shaman, or medicine man, performs many chants, including this one. The purposes of the ceremony are to cure diseases and to give thanks for abundant crops and rain, or—in a dry season—to ask for rain. The ceremony is usually celebrated in the winter, when there is less thunder and rain.

"Twelfth Song of Thunder" from the Navajo Mountain Chant

The voice that beautifies the land!
The voice above,
The voice of thunder
Within the dark cloud
5 Again and again it sounds,
The voice that beautifies the land.

The voice that beautifies the land!
The voice below,
The voice of the grasshopper
10 Among the plants
Again and again it sounds,
The voice that beautifies the land.

Sound Devices The speaker repeats this line and the word *voice* to celebrate the sounds of nature.

Figurative Language Throughout the poem, the poet uses personification to give elements of nature a human quality.

Sensory Language The description of the "dark cloud" appeals to the reader's sense of sight and helps set the scene.

Poetic Structures Each stanza presents different details about nature, but the stanzas work together to convey the poem's theme: Nature's beauty is far-reaching.

© EXEMPLAR TEXT

Independent Practice

About the Text The speakers in Gary Soto's poems often describe their experiences growing up in a Mexican American community in California. In "Oranges," Soto uses rich sensory language and surprising sound devices to paint a vivid picture in the reader's mind.

"Oranges" by Gary Soto

The first time I walked
With a girl, I was twelve,
Cold, and weighted down
With two oranges in my jacket.
5　December. Frost cracking
Beneath my steps, my breath
Before me, then gone,
As I walked toward
Her house, the one whose
10　Porch light burned yellow
Night and day, in any weather.
A dog barked at me, until
She came out pulling
At her gloves, face bright
15　With rouge[1]. I smiled,
Touched her shoulder, and led
Her down the street, across
A used car lot and a line
Of newly planted trees,
20　Until we were breathing
Before a drugstore. We
Entered, the tiny bell
Bringing a saleslady
Down a narrow aisle of goods.
25　I turned to the candies
Tiered[2] like bleachers,
And asked what she wanted—

Sensory Language To which senses do these lines appeal? What idea do they convey?

Word Choice and Tone How does the speaker feel about the girl? How can you tell?

Figurative Language Which type of figurative language does the poet use in these lines? What two things are being compared?

---

1. rouge (rōō zh) *n.* a reddish cosmetic used to color the cheeks.
2. tiered (tē r´d) *adj.* arranged in levels, one above another.

Light in her eyes, a smile
Starting at the corners
30 Of her mouth. I fingered
A nickel in my pocket,
And when she lifted a chocolate
That cost a dime,
I didn't say anything.
35 I took the nickel from
My pocket, then an orange,
And set them quietly on
The counter. When I looked up,
The lady's eyes met mine,
40 And held them, knowing
Very well what it was all
About.
            Outside,
A few cars hissing past,
45 Fog hanging like old
Coats between the trees.
I took my girl's hand
In mine for two blocks,
Then released it to let
50 Her unwrap the chocolate.
I peeled my orange
That was so bright against
The gray of December
That, from some distance,
55 Someone might have thought
I was making a fire in my hands.

Word Choice and Tone What tone does the speaker convey in these lines? Explain.

Poetic Structure The word "outside" indicates the beginning of a new stanza. What shift has occurred between the first and second stanza?

Sound Devices Which sound device does the poet use in this line?

Sensory Language How does the image presented in these lines sum up the poem and help convey a possible theme?

Independent Practice

About the Selection The speaker of "Ode to Family Photographs" fondly reflects on captured memories.

"Ode to Family Photographs" by Gary Soto

This is the pond, and these are my feet.
This is the rooster, and this is more of my feet.

Mamá was never good at pictures.

This is a statue of a famous general who lost an
    arm
5 And this is me with my head cut off.

This is a trash can chained to a gate,
This is my father with his eyes half-closed.

This is a photograph of my sister
And a giraffe looking over her
    shoulder.

10 This is our car's front bumper.
This is a bird with a pretzel in its
    beak.
This is my brother Pedro standing
    on one leg on a rock,
With a smear of chocolate on his
    face.

Mamá sneezed when she looked
15 *Behind the camera: the snapshots
    are blurry,*
*The angles dizzy as a spin on a
    merry-go-round.*

But we had fun when Mamá picked
    up the camera.
How can I tell?
Each of us laughing hard.
20 Can you see? I have candy in my
    mouth.

Tone How would you describe the tone of these lines?

Sound Devices What is the effect of the repeated phrase, "This is"?

Word Choice and Tone What can you tell about the speaker's family, based on the photos described in this stanza?

Figurative Language These lines are an example of which type of figurative language? What theme does this description suggest?

1. **Key Ideas and Details** **(a) Infer:** In "Oranges," why doesn't the speaker "say anything" when the girl picks out a chocolate that he can't afford? **(b) Explain:** Why does the speaker put the nickel and the orange on the counter?

2. **Key Ideas and Details** **(a)** What does the saleslady know about the boy that the girl does not know? **(b) Speculate:** How would the girl react if she knew what the saleslady knows?

3. **Key Ideas and Details** **(a)** The girl in "Oranges" is described as having "Light in her eyes." This description appeals to which of the reader's five senses? **(b) Interpret:** What does this detail tell you about the girl's feelings toward the speaker?

4. **Key Ideas and Details** **(a)** Based on the descriptions in "Ode to Family Photographs," how would you describe the speaker's mother as a photographer? **(b) Interpret:** How does the speaker feel about the photographs? How do you know?

5. **Craft and Structure** **(a) Analyze:** In "Ode to Family Photographs," what is the difference between the sentences in italics and the other lines? **(b) Analyze:** What is the difference between the last stanza and the rest of the poem?

6. **Craft and Structure** How are "Oranges" and "Ode to Family Photographs" similar? How are they different? Consider each poem's speaker, sound devices, structure, sensory language, and tone.

7. **Integration of Knowledge and Ideas (a)** Select one of the poems, and use the chart below to analyze examples of figurative language in it. In the first column, identify each example you find. In the second column, explain what the example means. In the third column, explain why it is important in helping you determine the poem's theme.

Example	What It Means	Why It Is Important

(b) Collaboration: Compare your chart with a partner's, and discuss your findings.

Leveled Texts

Build your skills and improve your comprehension of poetry with texts of increasing complexity.

The poems in **Poetry Collection 1** present a fearless child, a historic flight, and a dinosaur.

The poems in **Poetry Collection 2** explore loss, the value of bravery, and an odd meal.

Common Core State Standards

Meet these standards with the poems in either **Poetry Collection 1** (p. 564) or **Poetry Collection 2** (p. 572).

Reading Literature
4. Determine the meaning of words and phrases as they are used in the text, including figurative and connotative meanings; analyze the impact of a specific word choice on meaning and tone. *(Reading Skill: Context Clues; Literary Analysis: Rhythm and Rhyme)*

Spiral Review: RL.6.5

Writing
2. Write informative/explanatory texts to examine a topic and convey ideas, concepts, and information through the selection, organization, and analysis of relevant content.
2.b. Develop the content with relevant facts, definitions, concrete details, quotations, or other information and examples. **2.e.** Establish and maintain a formal style.

2.f. Provide a concluding statement or section that follows from the information or explanation presented. *(Writing: Letter to an Author)*

9. Draw evidence from literary or informational texts to support analysis, reflection, and research. *(Research and Technology: Illustrated Booklet)*

Language
1. Demonstrate command of the conventions of standard English grammar and usage when writing or speaking. *(Conventions: Simple and Compound Subjects)*

4.a. Use context as a clue to the meaning of a word or phrase. *(Reading Skill: Context Clues)*

Reading Skill: Context Clues

Context clues are found in the text surrounding an unfamiliar word. These clues help you determine the meaning of a word you may not know. Context clues may be explanations or words with the same meaning. To use context clues, **ask questions.**

- *Which nearby words restate, explain, or contrast with the word?*
- *What kind of word is it?*
- *What word can I use in place of the unfamiliar word?*
- *Does the new sentence I created make sense?*

Using the Strategy: Context Chart

As you read the poems in these collections, use a context chart like this one to help you find the meaning of unknown words.

Unfamiliar Word	Question	Answer	Meaning
stride	What kind of word?	It names a way you move to catch up.	"step"

PHLit Online!
www.PHLitOnline.com

Hear It!
- Selection summary audio
- Selection audio

See It!
- Get Connected video
- Background video
- More about the author
- Vocabulary flashcards

Do It!
- Interactive journals
- Interactive graphic organizers
- Self-test
- Internet activity
- Grammar tutorial
- Interactive vocabulary games

Literary Analysis: Rhythm and Rhyme

Rhythm and **rhyme** add a musical quality to poems.
- **Rhythm:** the sound pattern created by stressed and unstressed syllables.

     Jack and **Jill** went **up** the **hill**
     (4 stressed/3 unstressed)
- **Rhyme:** the repetition of sounds at the ends of words, such as *delight* and *excite*. Once a rhyme pattern, or *scheme,* is established, you come to expect rhymes.

Read the following poems aloud and listen to sound patterns like these to determine their effect. Listen for the ways in which the use of rhythm and rhyme adds layers of meaning. Also, think about how the poem's tone—the speaker's attitude—is created by these sound devices.

Do we need words to *communicate* well?

Writing About the Big Question

In "The Adventures of Isabel," Isabel communicates with action rather than words. The Wright brothers, on the other hand, use words to comfort and encourage each other. Use this sentence starter to help you develop your ideas about the Big Question.

> **Verbal** and **nonverbal communication** styles are effective in different kinds of situations because _____.

While You Read Look for examples of a variety of communication styles in these poems.

Vocabulary

Read each word and its definition. Decide whether you know the word well, know it a little bit, or do not know it at all. After you read, see how your knowledge of each word has increased.

- **ravenous** (rav´ ə nəs) *adj.* greedily hungry (p. 564) *The ravenous boys ate everything in sight.* ravenously *adv.* raven *n.*

- **cavernous** (kav´ ər nəs) *adj.* huge and hollow; like a cavern (p. 564) *We entered the cavernous room.* cavern *n.*

- **rancor** (raŋ´ kər) *n.* bitter hate or ill will (p. 565) *Rancor showed in his mean face.* rancorous *adj.* rancorously *adv.*

- **horrid** (hôr´ id) *adj.* shockingly dreadful; extremely unpleasant (p. 565) *The burned pudding was horrid.* horridly *adj.* horridness *n.*

- **inedible** (in ed´ ə bəl) *adj.* not fit to be eaten (p. 568) *Ice cream with chopped pickles is inedible!* inedibility *n.* edible *adj.*

- **minuscule** (min´ i skyōōl´) *adj.* very small; tiny (p. 568) *A minuscule ant was crawling along the leaf.*

Word Study

The **Latin root -min-** means "very small."

In "Ankylosaurus," a dinosaur is described as possessing a **minuscule,** or very small, mind.

Ogden Nash

(1902–1971)

Author of "Adventures of Isabel" (p. 564)

Ogden Nash, one of America's best-loved poets and humorists, threw away his first poetry attempt. Luckily, he pulled it out of the trash and sent it to *The New Yorker* magazine—which published it immediately! During his forty-year career, Nash wrote more than thirty poetry books.

Rosemary (1898–1962) and Stephen Vincent Benét

(1898–1943)

Authors of "Wilbur Wright and Orville Wright" (p. 566)

In 1933, this husband-and-wife team wrote a poetry collection called *A Book of Americans,* from which "Wilbur Wright and Orville Wright" is taken. Rosemary Benét was a frequent contributor to many important magazines. Stephen Vincent Benét won the Pulitzer Prize for Poetry—twice!

Jack Prelutsky

(b. 1944)

Author of "Ankylosaurus" (p. 568)

As a child, Jack Prelutsky was not a fan of poetry. As an adult, however, he decided to write some poems to accompany his drawings of imaginary creatures. Prelutsky soon published his first collection of poems. He went on to write many more books of humorous verse.

ADVENTURES OF
Isabel
Ogden Nash

Vocabulary

ravenous (rav´ ə nəs) *adj.* greedily hungry

cavernous (kav´ ər nəs) *adj.* huge and hollow; like a cavern

Isabel met an enormous bear,
Isabel, Isabel, didn't care;
The bear was hungry, the bear was ravenous,
The bear's big mouth was cruel and cavernous.
5 The bear said, Isabel, glad to meet you,
How do, Isabel, now I'll eat you!
Isabel, Isabel, didn't worry,
Isabel didn't scream or scurry.
She washed her hands and she straightened her
    hair up,
10 Then Isabel quietly ate the bear up.

Once in a night as black as pitch
Isabel met a wicked old witch.
The witch's face was cross and wrinkled,
The witch's gums with teeth were sprinkled.
15 Ho ho, Isabel! the old witch crowed,
I'll turn you into an ugly toad!
Isabel, Isabel, didn't worry,
Isabel didn't scream or scurry,
She showed no rage and she showed no rancor,
20 But she turned the witch into milk and drank her.

Isabel met a hideous giant,
Isabel continued self-reliant.
The giant was hairy, the giant was horrid,
He had one eye in the middle of his forehead.
25 Good morning Isabel, the giant said,
I'll grind your bones to make my bread.
Isabel, Isabel, didn't worry,
Isabel didn't scream or scurry.
She nibbled the zwieback that she always fed off,
30 And when it was gone, she cut the giant's head off.

Isabel met a troublesome doctor,
He punched and he poked till he really shocked her.
The doctor's talk was of coughs and chills
And the doctor's satchel bulged with pills.
35 The doctor said unto Isabel,
Swallow this, it will make you well.
Isabel, Isabel, didn't worry,
Isabel didn't scream or scurry.
She took those pills from the pill concocter,
40 And Isabel calmly cured the doctor.

Spiral Review
Structure What does this stanza add to your idea of how Isabel deals with fear?

Vocabulary
rancor (raṇ´ kər) *n.* bitter hate or ill will

horrid (hôr´ id) *adj.* shockingly dreadful; extremely unpleasant

Rhythm and Rhyme
What two-word rhymes are used in lines 29 and 30?

Context Clues
What clues help you understand that a satchel (line 34) is something that holds things?

Wilbur Wright AND Orville Wright

Rosemary and Stephen Vincent Benét

Said Orville Wright to Wilbur Wright,
"These birds are very trying.
I'm sick of hearing them cheep-cheep
About the fun of flying.

5 A bird has feathers, it is true.
That much I freely grant.
But, must that stop us, W?"
Said Wilbur Wright, "It shan't."

And so they built a glider, first,
10 And then they built another.
—There never were two brothers more
Devoted to each other.
They ran a dusty little shop

▼ **Critical Viewing**
The picture shows the Wright brothers flying the first power-driven, heavier-than-air machine in 1903, near Kitty Hawk, North Carolina. Compare this machine to today's airplanes. **[Compare]**

For bicycle-repairing,
15 And bought each other soda-pop
and praised each other's daring.

They glided here, they glided there,
They sometimes skinned their noses.
—For learning how to rule the air
20 Was not a bed of roses—
But each would murmur, afterward,
While patching up his bro,
"Are we discouraged, W?"
"Of course we are not, O!"

25 And finally, at Kitty Hawk
In Nineteen-Three (let's cheer it!)
The first real airplane really flew
With Orville there to steer it!
—And kingdoms may forget their kings
30 And dogs forget their bites,
But, not till Man forgets his wings,
Will men forget the Wrights.

▲ **Critical Viewing**
Based on this 1908 photo of Wilbur Wright, what words would you use to describe him? **[Analyze]**

Context Clues
How are *W* and *O* used here? What words would you use in their place?

Ankylosaurus

Jack Prelutsky

Clankity Clankity Clankity Clank!
Ankylosaurus was built like a tank,
its hide was a fortress as sturdy as steel,
it tended to be an inedible meal.

5 It was armored in front, it was armored behind,
there wasn't a thing on its minuscule mind,
it waddled about on its four stubby legs,
nibbling on plants with a mouthful of pegs.

Ankylosaurus was best left alone,
10 its tail was a cudgel of gristle and bone,
Clankity Clankity Clankity Clank!
Ankylosaurus was built like a tank.

Vocabulary
inedible (in ed´ ə bəl)
adj. not fit to be eaten
minuscule (min´ i
skyo͞ol´) *adj.* very
small; tiny

Rhythm and Rhyme
What is the pattern of
rhymes at the ends of
lines in each stanza?

Critical Thinking

Cite textual evidence to support your responses.

© **1. Key Ideas and Details (a) Support:** Describe Isabel's personality, using details from "Adventures of Isabel" to support your answer. **(b) Assess:** Is Isabel someone you would want as a friend? Explain.

© **2. Key Ideas and Details (a) Support:** What details in "Wilbur Wright and Orville Wright" reveal that the authors admire the Wright brothers? **(b) Evaluate:** Do you think the Wright brothers earned their fame? Explain.

© **3. Key Ideas and Details (a)** In "Ankylosaurus," what was Ankylosaurus built like? **(b) Analyze:** Which words help reinforce this image?

© **4. Craft and Structure (a)** How does the writer show the communication between the Wright Brothers in "Wilbur Wright and Orville Wright?" **(b) Evaluate:** Was their communication style effective? Explain. *[Connect to the Big Question: Do we need words to communicate well?]*

Reading Skill: Context Clues

1. For each of these lines explain how the italicized **context clues** help you find the meaning of the underlined word.

(a) These birds are very <u>trying</u>. I'm *sick of* hearing them.

(b) She *showed no rage*, and she *showed no* <u>rancor</u>.

Literary Analysis: Rhythm and Rhyme

© **2. Craft and Structure** How many stressed syllables are in this line of poetry? *They glided here, they glided there*

© **3. Craft and Structure** Complete a chart like the one shown to give examples of **rhyming** words each poet uses.

Poem	Rhyming Words		
"Adventures of Isabel"			
"Wilbur Wright…"			
"Ankylosaurus"	clank/tank		

© **4. Craft and Structure** How does each pair of words you listed in the chart affect the tone and meaning of the poem?

Vocabulary

© **Acquisition and Use** Write a sentence about each item. Use a word from the vocabulary list on page 562.

1. a person who has not eaten all day

2. a person who feels hatred

3. a dinner that has been burned

4. a movie character who behaves in a nasty, impolite way

5. a large cave you discover on a hike

6. a very small gift

Word Study Use the context of the sentence and what you know about the **Latin root -*min*-** to explain your answer.

1. Is a *minimart* similar to a department store?

2. Is *minimalist* art very complicated in design?

Word Study

The **Latin root -*min*-** means "very small."

Apply It Explain how the root -*min*- contributes to the meaning of these words. Consult a dictionary if necessary.

minimum

miniature

minimize

Do we need words to *communicate* well?

Writing About the Big Question

In "The Walrus and the Carpenter," the main characters fail to communicate their intentions to a group of young oysters. In "Life Doesn't Frighten Me," a girl insists that many scary things aren't scary at all. Use this sentence starter to develop your ideas about the Big Question.

Sometimes people do not use **language** to **share** their real thoughts and feelings because _____.

While You Read Look for hints that characters may not be stating their true intentions or feelings.

Vocabulary

Read each word and its definition. Decide whether you know the word well, know it a little bit, or do not know it at all. After you read, see how your knowledge of each word has increased.

- **deem** (dēm) *v.* hold as an opinion; judge (p. 573) *We deem it necessary to cancel due to snow.* *deemed v. deeming v.*

- **amid** (ə mid´) *prep.* in the middle of; surrounded by (p. 573) *I ate my lunch amid the other diners.* *admidst prep.*

- **pitiless** (pit´ ē lis) *adj.* without mercy (p. 573) *The pitiless crowd booed her off the stage.* *pity n. pitiful adj.*

- **beseech** (bē sēch´) *v.* beg (p. 577) *I beseech you to think about this.* *beseecher n. beseechingly adv.*

- **dismal** (diz´ məl) *adj.* causing gloom or misery (p. 579) *We were sad to hear the dismal news.* *dismally adv.*

- **sympathize** (sim´ pə thīz) *v.* share in a feeling; feel compassion (p. 580) *I sympathize with the girl who lost her dog.* *sympathizing v. sympathy n. empathy n.*

Word Study

The **Latin root -mal-** means "bad or evil."

In "The Walrus and the Carpenter," the two title characters do something **dismal**, or something that causes bad feelings.

Edgar Allan Poe

(1809–1849)

Author of "A Dream Within a Dream" (p. 572)

Edgar Allan Poe, one of America's best-known writers, led a troubled life. His father deserted him, his mother died before he was three, and his wife died young. Despite his problems, Poe produced a large body of work, including short stories, essays, and poems.

Maya Angelou

(b. 1928)

Author of "Life Doesn't Frighten Me" (p. 574)

Maya Angelou changed her childhood name (she was born Marguerite Johnson), and she has never stopped exploring who she is. In addition to being a poet and best-selling author, Angelou has been an educator, historian, actress, playwright, civil-rights activist, producer, and director.

Lewis Carroll

(1832–1898)

Author of "The Walrus and the Carpenter" (p. 576)

Lewis Carroll is the pen name of Englishman Charles Lutwidge Dodgson, a math professor. Carroll wrote two children's classics, *Alice's Adventures in Wonderland* (1865) and *Through the Looking Glass* (1872), which contains "The Walrus and the Carpenter."

A Dream Within a Dream

Edgar Allan Poe

Take this kiss upon the brow!
And, in parting from you now,
Thus much let me avow—
You are not wrong, who deem
5 That my days have been a dream;
Yet if hope has flown away
In a night, or in a day,
In a vision, or in none,
Is it therefore the less *gone*?
10 *All* that we see or seem
Is but a dream within a dream.
I stand amid the roar
Of a surf-tormented shore,
And I hold within my hand
15 Grains of the golden sand—
How few! yet how they creep
Through my fingers to the deep,
While I weep—while I weep!
O God! can I not grasp
20 Them with a tighter clasp?
O God! can I not save
One from the pitiless wave?
Is *all* that we see or seem
But a dream within a dream?

Life Doesn't Frighten Me

Maya Angelou

Rhythm and Rhyme
The poet uses lists of things to build rhythm and rhyme. What things does she list in the first stanza?

Shadows on the wall
Noises down the hall
Life doesn't frighten me at all
Bad dogs barking loud
5   Big ghosts in a cloud
Life doesn't frighten me at all.

Mean old Mother Goose
Lions on the loose
They don't frighten me at all
10   Dragons breathing flame
On my counterpane[1]
That doesn't frighten me at all.

Context Clues
What words help you understand the meaning of *shoo* in line 14? What does *shoo* mean?

I go boo
Make them shoo
15   I make fun
Way they run
I won't cry
So they fly
I just smile
20   They go wild
Life doesn't frighten me at all.

---

1. counterpane *n.* bedspread.

Tough guys in a fight
All alone at night
Life doesn't frighten me at all.

25 Panthers in the park
Strangers in the dark
No, they don't frighten me at all.

That new classroom where
Boys all pull my hair
30 (Kissy little girls
With their hair in curls)
They don't frighten me at all.

Don't show me frogs and snakes
And listen for my scream,
35 If I'm afraid at all
It's only in my dreams.

I've got a magic charm
That I keep up my sleeve,
I can walk the ocean floor
40 And never have to breathe.

Life doesn't frighten me at all
Not at all
Not at all.
Life doesn't frighten me at all.

Rhythm and Rhyme
What repeated words help create rhythm in this poem?

Spiral Review
Connotation What are the connotations of the phrase "Kissy little girls"? What does the phrase add to your idea of the speaker?

◀ **Critical Viewing**
What details show that this girl is confident and determined? **[Analyze]**

The Walrus and the Carpenter

Lewis Carroll

Context Clues
What words and phrases help you determine the meaning of the word *sulkily* in line 7? What does *sulkily* mean?

The sun was shining on the sea,
　　Shining with all his might:
He did his very best to make
　　The billows smooth and bright—
5　And this was odd, because it was
　　The middle of the night.

The moon was shining sulkily,
　　Because she thought the sun
Had got no business to be there
10　　After the day was done—
"It's very rude of him," she said,
　　"To come and spoil the fun!"

The sea was wet as wet could be,
　　The sands were dry as dry.
15　You could not see a cloud, because
　　No cloud was in the sky:
No birds were flying overhead—
　　There were no birds to fly.

The Walrus and the Carpenter
20   Were walking close at hand:
They wept like anything to see
        Such quantities of sand:
"If this were only cleared away,"
        They said, "it would be grand!"

25 "If seven maids with seven mops
        Swept it for half a year,
Do you suppose," the Walrus said,
        "That they could get it clear?"
"I doubt it," said the Carpenter,
30   And shed a bitter tear.

"O Oysters, come and walk with us!"
        The Walrus did beseech.
"A pleasant walk, a pleasant talk,
        Along the briny beach:
35 We cannot do with more than four,
        To give a hand to each."

The eldest Oyster looked at him,
        But never a word he said:
The eldest Oyster winked his eye,
40   And shook his heavy head—
Meaning to say he did not choose
        To leave the oyster-bed.

Vocabulary
beseech (bē sēch´) *v.*
beg

▼ **Critical Viewing**
In what way do the illustrations on pp. 576–580 reflect the feeling of the poem? **[Connect]**

Context Clues
What word does *frothy* describe in line 53? What actions help you know it means "churning or foamy"?

Rhythm and Rhyme
How many syllables should you pronounce in *conveniently* to keep the poem's rhythmic pattern?

But four young Oysters hurried up,
　　All eager for this treat:
45　Their coats were brushed, their faces washed,

　　Their shoes were clean and neat—
And this was odd, because, you know,
　　They hadn't any feet.
Four other Oysters followed them,
50　　And yet another four;
And thick and fast they came at last,
　　And more, and more, and more—
All hopping through the frothy waves,
　　And scrambling to the shore.

55　The Walrus and the Carpenter
　　Walked on a mile or so,
And then they rested on a rock
　　Conveniently low:
And all the little Oysters stood
60　　And waited in a row.

"The time has come," the Walrus said,
　　"To talk of many things:
Of shoes—and ships—and sealing wax—
　　Of cabbages—and kings—
65　And why the sea is boiling hot—
　　And whether pigs have wings."

"But wait a bit," the Oysters cried,
    "Before we have our chat;
For some of us are out of breath,
70   And all of us are fat!"
"No hurry!" said the Carpenter.
    They thanked him much for that.

"A loaf of bread," the Walrus said,
    "Is what we chiefly need:
75 Pepper and vinegar besides
    Are very good indeed—
Now, if you're ready, Oysters dear,
    We can begin to feed."

"But not on us!" the Oysters cried,
80   Turning a little blue.
"After such kindness, that would be
    A dismal thing to do!"
"The night is fine," the Walrus said.
    "Do you admire the view?"

85 "It was so kind of you to come!
    And you are very nice!"
The Carpenter said nothing but
    "Cut us another slice.
I wish you were not quite so deaf—
90   I've had to ask you twice!"

Rhythm and Rhyme
In each six-line stanza of this poem, which lines rhyme?

Vocabulary
dismal (diz´ məl) *adj.* causing gloom or misery

"It seems a shame," the Walrus said,
　　"To play them such a trick.
After we've brought them out so far,
　　And made them trot so quick!"
95　The Carpenter said nothing but
　　"The butter's spread too thick!"

"I weep for you," the Walrus said:
　　"I deeply sympathize."
With sobs and tears he sorted out
100　　Those of the largest size,
Holding his pocket-handkerchief
　　Before his streaming eyes.

"O Oysters," said the Carpenter,
　　"You've had a pleasant run!
105　Shall we be trotting home again?"
　　But answer came there none—
And this was scarcely odd, because
　　They'd eaten every one.

Vocabulary
sympathize (sim´ pə thīz) *v.* share in a feeling; feel compassion

Critical Thinking

© 1. Key Ideas and Details **(a) Analyze:** What is the speaker doing in lines 13–19 of "A Dream Within a Dream"? **(b) Connect:** How are these actions related to dreaming?

© 2. Key Ideas and Details **(a)** Name three things that do not frighten the speaker of "Life Doesn't Frighten Me." **(b) Infer:** Why does she smile at frightening things?

© 3. Key Ideas and Details **(a)** How does the "eldest Oyster" react to the Walrus and the Carpenter? **(b) Predict:** How does this oyster's reaction hint about future events?

© 4. Integration of Knowledge and Ideas **(a)** In "The Walrus and the Carpenter," how did the old oyster know to be wary of the Walrus and the Carpenter? **(b) Infer:** How might someone know that a situation is dangerous if no one has described the danger? *[Connect to the Big Question: Do we need words to communicate well?]*

Cite textual evidence to support your responses.

Reading Skill: Context Clues

1. For each of these lines, explain how the italicized **context clues** help you find the meaning of the underlined word.

(a) I stand amid the *roar* / of a <u>surf-tormented</u> *shore*

(b) "I *weep* for you," the Walrus said: / "I *deeply* <u>sympathize</u>."

Literary Analysis: Rhythm and Rhyme

2. Craft and Structure Count the stressed syllables:
"If seven maids with seven mops / Swept it for half a year"

3. Craft and Structure Complete a chart to give examples of **rhyming** words each poet uses.

Poem	Rhyming Words		
"A Dream Within a Dream"	brow/now/avow		
"Life Doesn't Frighten Me"			
"The Walrus and the Carpenter"			

4. Craft and Structure How does each pair of words you listed in the chart affect the tone and meaning of the poem?

Vocabulary

Acquisition and Use Write a sentence about each item using a word from the vocabulary list on page 570.

1. a person who wants his friends to help him move his sofa

2. a decision to award a prize

3. weather of drizzly rain and gray skies

4. someone who helps a little girl who fell down

5. a winning team against its struggling opponents

6. a beautiful toy in the middle of a junkyard

Word Study Use the context of the sentence and what you know about the **Latin root -mal-** to explain your answer.

1. If a plant is *maladapted* to its environment, will it grow?

2. If a bully's face showed *malice,* would you be frightened?

Word Study

The **Latin root -mal-** means "bad" or "evil."

Apply It Explain how the root -mal- contributes to the meaning of these words. Consult a dictionary if necessary.

malnourished
malodorous
malicious

Integrated Language Skills

Poetry Collections 1 and 2

Poetry Collection 1

Conventions: Simple and Compound Subjects

A sentence can contain a **simple** or a **compound subject**.

A **simple subject** is the person, place, or thing about which the sentence is written. A **compound subject** is made up of two or more nouns that share the same verb and are joined by conjunctions such as *and.* Most compound subjects take plural verb form.

Poetry Collection 2

Example	Simple subject
Ricardo skis every winter.	Ricardo
Example	**Compound Subject**
Ricardo and Pablo ski every winter.	Ricardo and Pablo

Practice A Identify the subject in each sentence and indicate whether it is a simple subject or a compound subject.

1. Isabel met an enormous bear.
2. An ankylosaurus is an inedible meal.
3. Wilbur and Orville built a glider.
4. The brothers pioneered flight.

© **Reading Application** Identify three subjects in the poem "Adventures of Isabel." In each case, explain whether the subject is simple or compound.

Practice B Revise these sentences where necessary to correct errors in agreement.

1. Steve and his friends enjoys Poe's poetry.
2. She and her mother are afraid of dogs.
3. Two frogs or one lizard cost six dollars.
4. The Walrus and the Carpenter were sneaky.
5. The oysters and the seashore was pure.

© **Writing Application** Use each of these compound subjects in a sentence with correct subject-verb agreement: **(a)** the sand and the waves **(b)** the sand or the waves **(c)** the carpenter or the walrus **(d)** oysters or clams **(e)** oysters and clams

PH **WRITING COACH** | Further instruction and practice are available in *Prentice Hall Writing Coach.*

Writing

 Explanatory Text One way to respond to literature is to write a **letter to an author**—even if you never mail it. Write a letter to one of the poets in the collection you read. Tell whether you like the poem and whether you would recommend it to others.

- Begin with your overall reaction to the poem.
- In several paragraphs, develop reasons and give examples. Establish and maintain a formal writing style.
- End with a brief conclusion that summarizes your ideas.
- Use the correct letter format. Review an example on page R27.

Grammar Application Review your use of simple and compound subjects in your letter.

Writing Workshop: *Work in Progress*

Prewriting for Exposition Scan newspapers, magazines, and news sites for stories that pose interesting problems. List the topics that interest you. Save your list in your portfolio.

 **Common Core State Standards**

L.6.1; W.6.2, W.6.2.b, W.6.2.e, W.6.2.f, W.6.9
[For the full wording of the standards, see page 560.]

Use this prewriting activity to prepare for the **Writing Workshop** on page 614.

Research and Technology

 Build and Present Knowledge Use library resources to find poems and stories to put in an **illustrated booklet.**

- If you read Poetry Collection 1, gather a selection of poems and stories about dinosaurs.
- If you read Poetry Collection 2, gather a selection of poems and stories written by Lewis Carroll.

Follow these steps to complete your assignment.

- Select poems and stories that you enjoy reading.
- Copy them into your booklet, leaving space for illustrations and annotations.
- Illustrate your booklet to capture the spirit of the writing.
- Prepare annotations to summarize selections and point out details for readers. Use these questions as a guide:

    How is the poem or story similar to or different from one of the poems I read in this book?

    How do the rhyme and rhythm in the poems I selected compare to those in the poems I read in this book?

www.PHLitOnline.com
- Interactive graphic organizers
- Grammar tutorial
- Interactive journals

Leveled Texts

Build your skills and improve your comprehension of poetry with texts of increasing complexity.

The poets represented in **Poetry Collection 3** use images of nature to express themselves.

The poems in **Poetry Collection 4** describe aspects of love, friendship, and the world.

Common Core State Standards

Meet these standards with either **Poetry Collection 3** (p. 588) or **Poetry Collection 4** (p. 594).

Reading Literature
4. Determine the meaning of words and phrases as they are used in a text, including figurative and connotative meanings; analyze the impact of a specific word choice on meaning and tone. *(Literary Analysis: Figurative Language)*

Spiral Review: RL.6.5
7. Compare and contrast the experience of reading a story, drama, or poem to listening to or viewing an audio, video, or live version of the text, including contrasting what they "see" and "hear" when reading the text to what they perceive when they listen or watch. *(Speaking and Listening: Dramatic Poetry Reading)*

Writing
3.d. Use precise words and phrases, relevant descriptive details, and sensory language to convey experiences and events. *(Writing: Poem)*

Speaking and Listening
6. Adapt speech to a variety of contexts and tasks, demonstrating command of formal English when indicated or appropriate. *(Speaking and Listening: Dramatic Poetry Reading)*

Language
3. Use knowledge of language and its conventions when writing, speaking, reading, or listening. *(Conventions: Sentence Types)*

4.a. Use context as a clue to the meaning of a word or phrase. *(Reading Skill: Context Clues)*

4.c. Consult reference materials, both print and digital, to find the pronunciation of a word or determine or clarify its precise meaning or its part of speech. *(Speaking and Listening: Dramatic Poetry Reading)*

Reading Skill: Context Clues

Details in a text that give you clues to a word's meaning are called **context clues. Reread and read ahead** to find context clues that clarify meanings of unfamiliar words as well as words with multiple meanings. This example shows how context clarifies the meaning of the multiple-meaning word *beat*.

Let the <u>rain</u> beat your <u>head with silver liquid drops</u>.

From the underlined context clues, you can figure out that "beat" is a verb, describing a gentle tap.

Literary Analysis: Figurative Language

Figurative language is language that is not meant to be taken literally. Authors use figurative language to state ideas in fresh ways. They may use one or more of the following types of figurative language:

- **Similes** compare two unlike things using *like* or *as*.
- **Metaphors** compare two unlike things by stating that one thing *is* another.
- **Personification** compares an object or animal to a human by giving the object or animal human characteristics.

Using the Strategy: Figurative Language Chart

Use a chart like this to unlock the meaning of figurative language in the poems that follow.

Figurative Language	Type	What the Language Does
a day as soft as silk	simile	compares weather to soft fabric to show that the weather is gentle

Do we need words to *communicate* well?

Writing About the Big Question

In Poetry Collection 3, you will notice that poets describe common things in uncommon ways. Use the following sentence starter to help you develop your ideas about the Big Question.

Poets make **connections** between common and uncommon things in order to _____.

While You Read Look for ways each poet communicates unusual ideas.

Vocabulary

Read each word and its definition. Decide whether you know the word well, know it a little bit, or do not know it at all. After you read, see how your knowledge of each word has increased.

- **crude** (krood) *adj.* lacking polish; not carefully made (p. 588) *I wrote a <u>crude</u> draft of the speech. cruder adj. crudest adj. crudely adv. crudeness n.*

- **soprano** (sə pran´ ō) *n.* a singer who can sing two octaves or more above middle C (p. 588) *People clapped when the <u>soprano</u> took a bow. sopranos n.*

- **stubby** (stub´ ē) *adj.* short and thick; bristly (p. 588) *Her fingers were short and <u>stubby</u>. stubbiest adj. stubbiness n.*

- **precious** (presh ´əs) *adj.* dear; beloved (p. 588) *The <u>precious</u> child was missing. preciously adv. preciousness n.*

- **thrives** (thrīvz) *v.* grows well (p. 588) *The orange tree <u>thrives</u> in a warm climate. thrive v. thrived v.*

Word Study

The **suffix -ness** means "state" or "condition of being."

The poem "Willow and Ginkgo" talks about the **preciousness** of the willow tree. This means that the willow tree has the condition of being precious, or beloved.

Eve Merriam

(1916–1992)

Author of "Simile: Willow and Ginkgo" (page 588)

Eve Merriam fell in love very early with the music of language. She wrote award-winning poetry for adults and children, and she also wrote and directed musical theater productions. Among her many books for young readers are *There Is No Rhyme for Silver, It Doesn't Always Have to Rhyme, Out Loud,* and *Rainbow Writing.*

Langston Hughes

(1902–1967)

Author of "April Rain Song" (page 589)

Award-winning poet, dramatist, and novelist Langston Hughes traveled to Africa and Europe as a young man before settling in Harlem in New York City. In the 1920s, he was one of the leaders of the Harlem Renaissance, a period in which African American writers, artists, and musicians produced brilliant works.

Emily Dickinson

(1830–1886)

Author of "Fame Is a Bee" (page 590)

After one year of college, Emily Dickinson was homesick and returned to her parents' house in Amherst, Massachusetts. For her remaining years, she seldom traveled or received guests. Dickinson read many books and wrote more than 1,700 poems, which form a kind of lifelong diary of her deepest thoughts. She is considered one of the leading voices of American poetry.

Simile: Willow and Ginkgo

Eve Merriam

© **Spiral Review**
Structure How does
the fourth stanza
expand on ideas of
the willow presented
earlier?

Figurative Language
What kind of figurative
language tells how the
ginkgo grows?

The willow is like an etching,[1]
Fine-lined against the sky.
The ginkgo is like a crude sketch,
Hardly worthy to be signed.

5 The willow's music is like a soprano,
Delicate and thin.
The ginkgo's tune is like a chorus
With everyone joining in.

The willow is sleek as a velvet-nosed calf;
10 The ginkgo is leathery as an old bull.
The willow's branches are like silken thread;
The ginkgo's like stubby rough wool.

The willow is like a nymph[2] with streaming hair;
Wherever it grows, there is green and gold and fair.
15 The willow dips to the water,
Protected and precious, like the king's favorite
    daughter.

The ginkgo forces its way through gray concrete;
Like a city child, it grows up in the street.
Thrust against the metal sky,
20 Somehow it survives and even thrives.

My eyes feast upon the willow,
But my heart goes to the ginkgo.

1. **etching** (ech´ iŋ) *n.* print of a drawing made on metal, glass, or wood.
2. **nymph** (nimf) *n.* goddess of nature, thought of as a beautiful maiden.

April Rain Song

Langston Hughes

Let the rain kiss you.
Let the rain beat upon your head with silver liquid drops.
Let the rain sing you a lullaby.

The rain makes still pools on the sidewalk.
5   The rain makes running pools in the gutter.
The rain plays a little sleep-song on our roof at night—

And I love the rain.

Context Clues
Which meaning of the word *running* does the poet use in line 5? How can you tell?

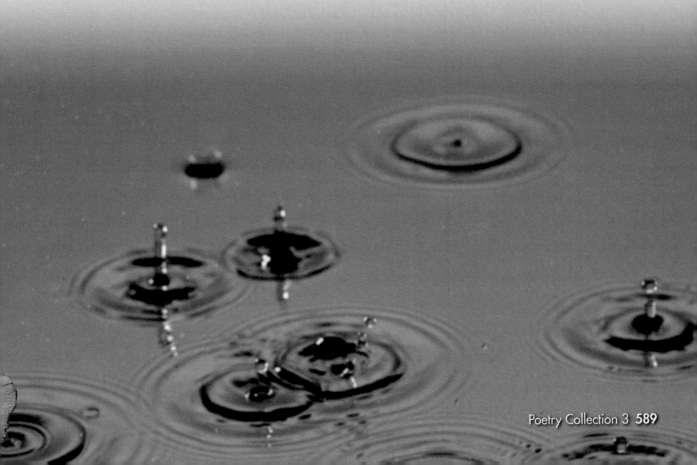

Fame Is a Bee

Emily Dickinson

Figurative Language
What type of figurative language is used to compare fame to a bee?

Fame is a bee.
It has a song—
It has a sting—
Ah, too, it has a wing.

Critical Thinking

Cite textual evidence to support your responses.

1. **Key Ideas and Details (a)** Merriam first compares the willow and the ginkgo to drawings. Name two other categories to which the poet compares both trees. **(b) Analyze:** What overall impression do you get of each tree?

2. **Key Ideas and Details (a)** In "April Rain Song," what kind of song does the rain sing? **(b) Infer:** What does the song tell you about the poet's feelings about rain? **(c) Speculate:** How would the poem be different if it were about the rain that comes with a hurricane?

3. **Key Ideas and Details (a) Interpret:** Fill out a three-column chart in response to the ideas in "Fame Is a Bee." In the first column, list the good things about fame. In the second, list the bad things about fame. **(b) Discuss:** Trade charts with a partner and discuss your responses. **(c) Respond:** In the third column of your chart, evaluate how your response has or has not changed based on your discussion.

4. **Integration of Knowledge and Ideas** In two of the poems in Poetry Collection 3, find examples of common things described in uncommon ways. Does this technique help poets to communicate their ideas effectively? Explain. *[Connect to the Big Question: Do we need words to communicate well?]*

After You Read
Poetry Collection 3

Simile: Willow and Ginkgo •
April Rain Song •
Fame Is a Bee

Reading Skill: Context Clues

1. In "Simile: Willow and Ginkgo," does the word *thin* (line 6) mean "skinny" or "fragile"? What **context clues** help you decide?

2. In "April Rain Song," what is the meaning of *pools* (line 4)? What context clues help you decide?

Literary Analysis: Figurative Language

Ⓒ **3. Craft and Structure** Find an example of each kind of **figurative language** in the poems in this collection. Fill in the following graphic organizer with your choices.

Title of Poem	Figurative Language	Example
	metaphor	
	personification	
	simile	

Ⓒ **4. Craft and Structure** How does the use of figurative language contribute to the **tone** of each poem?

Vocabulary

Ⓒ **Acquisition and Use** Answer each question, explaining your responses.

1. If an animal *thrives* in an environment, is it doing well?

2. Would you enter a *crude* drawing in an art contest?

3. Can a *soprano* hit the lowest notes?

4. Would you describe a long thin twig as *stubby*?

5. Is the fake diamond ring that you got for a dime *precious*?

Word Study Use what you know about the **suffix -*ness*** to explain your answer to each question.

1. Does *studiousness* result in good grades?

2. Would *playfulness* be a good quality in your best friend?

Word Study

The **suffix -*ness*** means "state" or "condition of being."

Apply It Explain how the suffix -*ness* contributes to the meaning of these words. Consult a dictionary if necessary.

moodiness
cleanliness
hopefulness

Do we need words to *communicate* well?

Writing About the Big Question

Poetry Collection 4 includes poems that convey the speakers' feelings about loved ones. You can let people know you care about them by using words or by your actions towards them. Use the following sentence starter to help you develop your ideas about the Big Question.

You can **reveal** your love of friends by _____.

While You Read Look for ways that the poets use language to **communicate** their feelings.

Vocabulary

Read each word and its definition. Decide whether you know the word well, know it a little bit, or do not know it at all. After you read, see how your knowledge of each word has increased.

- **sour** (sour) *adj.* having the sharp acid taste of lemon or vinegar. (p. 594) *The lemonade was too sour and needed more sugar.* sourly *adv.* soured *v.*

- **pleasant** (plez´ ənt) *adj.* agreeable; delightful (p. 595) *The sisters had a pleasant visit.* pleasantly *adv.* unpleasant *adj.*

- **billowing** (bil´ ō iŋ) *v.* filling with wind (p. 596) *The smoke was billowing out of the pipes.* billow *n.* billowed *v.*

- **accusers** (ə kyooz´ ərz) *n.* those who find fault or blame (p. 596) *My accusers pointed at me.* accuse *v.* accused *v.* accusation *n.*

- **plunging** (plunj´ iŋ) *v.* moving suddenly forward or downward (p. 596) *Grace was plunging the toy into the water.* plunge *v.* plunged *v.* plunger *n.*

Word Study

The **suffix -ant** means "state" or "condition of being."

In "The World Is Not a Pleasant Place to Be" the speaker tells of ways the world is not **pleasant** or in a pleasing state.

Sandra Cisneros

(b. 1954)

Author of "Abuelito Who" (page 594)

Sandra Cisneros was born in Chicago, but her family often traveled to Mexico to live with her grandfather, the abuelito in her poem "Abuelito Who." The frequent moves left Cisneros with few friends, but she remembers that she "retreated inside" herself, reading books and writing. She has won several awards for her poetry and short stories.

Nikki Giovanni

(b. 1943)

Author of "The World Is Not a Pleasant Place to Be" (page 595)

Born in Knoxville, Tennessee, Nikki Giovanni has become one of America's most popular poets. Her awards include the National Association for the Advancement of Colored People (NAACP) Image Award for Literature and the Langston Hughes Award for Distinguished Contributions to Arts and Letters. She is a college professor.

Theodore Roethke

(1908–1963)

Author of "Child on Top of a Greenhouse" (page 596)

Theodore Roethke was born and raised in Saginaw, Michigan, where his father and uncle grew and sold plants. As a child, Roethke spent hours in their greenhouse, which inspired the poem in this collection. In 1954, his book of poems, entitled *The Waking,* won a Pulitzer Prize.

Abuelito Who

Sandra Cisneros

Context Clues
What meaning of the word *watch* does the poet use in line 4?

Spiral Review
Structure How do lines 6 and 11 affect your picture of Abuelito?

Vocabulary
sour (sour) *adj.* having the sharp acid taste of lemon or vinegar

Figurative Language
What type of figurative language does the poet use to describe Abuelito in lines 14–19?

Abuelito[1] who throws coins like rain
and asks who loves him
who is dough and feathers
who is a watch and glass of water
5 whose hair is made of fur
is too sad to come downstairs today
who tells me in Spanish you are my diamond
who tells me in English you are my sky
whose little eyes are string
10 can't come out to play
sleeps in his little room all night and day
who used to laugh like the letter k
is sick
is a doorknob tied to a sour stick
15 is tired shut the door
doesn't live here anymore
is hiding underneath the bed
who talks to me inside my head
is blankets and spoons and big brown shoes
20 who snores up and down up and down up and down again
is the rain on the roof that falls like coins
asking who loves him
who loves him who?

---

1. Abuelito (ä bwā lē´ tō) *n.* in Spanish, an affectionate term for a grandfather.

The World Is Not a Pleasant Place to Be

Nikki Giovanni

the world is not a pleasant place
to be without
someone to hold and be held by

a river would stop
5   its flow if only
a stream were there
to receive it

an ocean would never laugh
if clouds weren't there
10   to kiss her tears

the world is not
a pleasant place to be without
someone

Vocabulary
pleasant (plez´ ənt) *adj.*
agreeable; delightful

Figurative Language
What type of figurative language is used in lines 8–10? What do you think the poet means?

Child on Top of a Greenhouse

Theodore Roethke

The wind billowing out the seat of my britches,
My feet crackling splinters of glass and dried putty,
The half-grown chrysanthemums staring up like accusers,
Up through the streaked glass, flashing with sunlight,
5　A few white clouds all rushing eastward,
A line of elms plunging and tossing like horses,
And everyone, everyone pointing up and shouting!

Critical Thinking

1. Key Ideas and Details **(a)** Whom is Cisneros's poem about? **(b) Connect:** Based on the descriptions of Abuelito, how does the speaker feel about him?

2. Key Ideas and Details **(a)** Fill out a three-column chart in response to the ideas in "The World Is Not a Pleasant Place to Be." In the first column, put good things about friends. In the second, discuss life without friends. **(b) Discuss:** Trade charts with a partner and discuss your responses. **(c) Respond:** In the third column of your chart, evaluate how your response to the poem has or has not changed based on your discussion.

3. Key Ideas and Details **(a)** Describe the weather in "Child on Top of a Greenhouse." **(b) Connect:** What feelings seem to be behind the speaker's words?

4. Integration of Knowledge and Ideas **(a)** What words does Cisneros use to convey the narrator's love for Abuelito? **(b)** In "Child on Top of a Greenhouse," how do you think the people referred to in the last line feel about the narrator? What do you think they are shouting? *[Connect to the Big Question: Do we need words to communicate well?]*

Cite textual evidence to support your responses.

After You Read
Poetry Collection 4

**Abuelito Who • The World Is
Not a Pleasant Place to Be •
Child on Top of a Greenhouse**

Reading Skill: Context Clues

1. In line 5 of "The World Is Not a Pleasant Place to Be," what is the meaning of *flow*? What **context clues** help you decide?

2. In "Child on Top of a Greenhouse," what does the word *seat* (line 1) mean? What context clues help you decide?

Literary Analysis: Figurative Language

3. Craft and Structure Find an example of each kind of **figurative language** in the poems in this collection. Fill in the following graphic organizer with your choices.

Title of Poem	Figurative Language	Example
	metaphor	
	personification	
	simile	

4. Craft and Structure How does the use of figurative language contribute to the **tone** of each poem?

Vocabulary

Acquisition and Use Explain your answers to the following questions.

1. If a sail is *billowing,* is it moving?

2. Should a person who is *plunging* into the deep end of a pool know how to swim?

3. Would you want to drink *sour* milk?

4. Are you *pleasant* after a sleepless night?

5. Does a thief thank his *accusers*?

Word Study Use the context of the sentence and what you know about the **suffix -*ant*** to explain your answers.

1. Is an *expectant* person waiting for something?

2. Is a *distant* relative part of your immediate family?

Word Study

The **suffix -*ant*** means "state" or "condition of being."

Apply It Explain how the suffix -*ant* contributes to the meaning of these words. Consult a dictionary if necessary.

vigilant
important
ignorant

Poetry Collections 3 and 4

Conventions: Sentence Types

Poetry Collection 3

Sentences can be classified according to what they do. This chart shows the four types of sentences.

Type of Sentence	Sample Sentence	Function	End Punctuation
Declarative	The sky is blue.	states an idea	period
Interrogative	What time is it?	asks a question	question mark
Imperative	Do not enter this room.	gives an order or direction	period or exclamation mark
Exclamatory	This is amazing!	expresses strong emotion	exclamation mark

Poetry Collection 4

When writing, always choose the sentence type appropriate to your meaning, and provide the appropriate end punctuation.

Practice A Add the correct punctuation to each sentence and tell what kind of sentence it is.

1. Do you like to sit under the willow tree or the ginkgo tree

2. I love the willow's thin, delicate branches

3. Fame has arrived at last

4. Don't slip on the puddles

Ⓒ **Speaking Application** In small groups, share your opinion about fame. Keep your audience interested by using each type of sentence at least once.

Practice B Identify each sentence type. Then, rewrite the sentence to convert it to another type of sentence.

1. I miss my Abuelito!

2. Abuelito asks, "Who loves me?"

3. The world is not a pleasant place to be.

4. Get down from the roof!

Ⓒ **Writing Application** Rewrite "The World Is Not a Pleasant Place to Be" in sentences, with traditional punctuation. Identify the sentence types you created. Then, change two into another form.

PH **WRITING COACH** Further instruction and practice are available in *Prentice Hall Writing Coach*.

Writing

 **Common Core State Standards**

L.3; W.3.d; L.4.c; RL.7; SL.6
[For the full wording of the standards, see page 584.]

ⓒ Poetry Write a **poem** using figurative language.

- Think about something that makes you happy—the beach on a sunny day, the stars twinkling in the dark sky, your favorite flavor of ice cream, or anything that comes to your mind.

- Use questions to think about your topic: *What qualities does this thing have? Can you compare the ocean to a roaring tiger? Do stars twinkle like your mother's eyes?* List ideas.

- Write your poem using precise descriptive language, fresh, unique comparisons, and figurative language. Experiment with rhyme and rhythm.

Grammar Application Include at least one sentence of each of the four types in your poem.

Writing Workshop: *Work in Progress*

Prewriting for Exposition Review your Topic List. Think about the problems you have listed. Choose one that you might be able to solve. Jot down some ideas for clearly explaining the problem and how you plan to solve it. Keep your Solution Strategy in your writing portfolio.

Use this prewriting activity to prepare for the **Writing Workshop** on page 614.

Speaking and Listening

ⓒ Presentation of Ideas Prepare a **dramatic poetry reading.** Select a poem you have read that is meaningful to you.

- First, be sure you know how to pronounce all the words in the poem. Use a dictionary to learn the pronunciations of unfamiliar words.

- Practice reading the poem aloud, using expression and pauses where appropriate. Enunciate clearly.

- Pay attention to the end-of-line punctuation.

- Vary volume and pitch to show emotion and to convey tone.

- Memorize your poem, and use gestures and body language to enhance your interpretation.

- Ask your classmates to silently read your poem.

- Now, present your dramatic poetry reading to the class.

- Discuss with classmates how reading the poem silently compared and contrasted with hearing it read aloud.

PHLit Online!
www.PHLitOnline.com

- Interactive graphic organizers
- Grammar tutorial
- Interactive journals

Test Practice: Reading

Context Clues

Fiction Selection

Directions: *Read the selection. Then, answer the questions.*

"The forecast for today calls for <u>record</u> high temperatures, Paul, so make sure you drink a lot of water," Mom said as she handed me a <u>gargantuan</u> water bottle instead of the normal-sized one I usually used.

I took the bottle from her. Mom was right. I would need the extra water because I would be sweating a lot today. I was going to sports camp, where I exerted myself all day playing basketball, football, baseball, and soccer on a shadeless field.

I had been excited about sports camp before the heat wave hit. Now, as I stood waiting for the bus with sweat pouring down my face, all I felt was <u>trepidation</u>.

1. What is the meaning of *record* in the context of this passage?
   A. reportedly
   B. musically
   C. to the greatest degree yet known
   D. over a long time

2. The underlined word *gargantuan* means—
   A. tiny
   B. refreshing
   C. huge
   D. cold

3. Which contrasting word or phrase provides the *best* clue to the meaning of *gargantuan*?
   A. handed me
   B. normal-sized
   C. drink
   D. a lot of water

4. Which word is the *best* replacement for *trepidation* in the last paragraph?
   A. nervousness
   B. anger
   C. tiredness
   D. heat

Writing for Assessment

Write a paragraph to continue the story about Paul going to sports camp during the heat wave. Include one of these words, and give context clues that help readers know what each word means.

sweltering *adj.* very hot

exhausted *adj.* extremely tired

Nonfiction Selection

Directions: *Read the selection. Then, answer the questions.*

When you exercise, drink plenty of water to keep your body <u>hydrated</u>. As you exercise, you sweat. The <u>perspiration</u> you wipe from your face and body is water that your body has lost. If you lose too much water, you become dehydrated. Even a very small water loss can make you sick. Some effects of dehydration are extreme exhaustion, dizziness, a feeling of weakness, and a dry mouth. Always, drink water before, during, and after exercise to <u>replenish</u> the water your body loses. Drinking water during activities and games will help you play your best.

1. The underlined word *hydrated* means—
   A. cool
   B. having enough water
   C. filled with oxygen
   D. clean and healthy

2. Which phrase is the *best* context clue to help you understand the meaning of *hydrated*?
   A. When you exercise
   B. drink plenty of water
   C. you sweat
   D. can make you sick

3. The context clue in this passage that helps you understand the meaning of *perspiration* is an example of—
   A. definition
   B. restatement
   C. contrast
   D. example

4. Which word is the *best* replacement for *replenish*?
   A. lose
   B. give
   C. replace
   D. expand

Writing for Assessment

Connecting Across Texts
Using facts you learned from the nonfiction passage, write a paragraph explaining why Paul needs his new water bottle. Use two of the underlined words on this page in your response. Give context clues so readers will understand the words.

PHLit Online!
www.PHLitOnline.com
- Online practice
- Instant feedback

Reading for Information

Analyzing Functional Texts

Instruction Manual

Contest Entry Form

Common Core State Standards

Reading Informational Text
5. Analyze how a particular sentence, paragraph, chapter, or section fits into the overall structure of a text and contributes to the development of the ideas.

Writing
4. Produce clear and coherent writing in which the development, organization, and style are appropriate to task, purpose, and audience. *(Timed Writing)*

Language
6. Acquire and use accurately grade-appropriate general academic and domain-specific words and phrases; gather vocabulary knowledge when considering a word or phrase important to comprehension or expression.

Reading Skill:
Follow Multiple-Step Instructions

When you read an instructional manual or a contest entry form, you must follow **multiple-step instructions** in order to complete a specific task. To follow instructions effectively, complete the steps in order. Note illustrations and insets that give further information about the steps. Use a checklist like the one shown.

Checklist for Following Multiple-Step Instructions

- ☐ Read all the requirements and instructions completely before starting to follow them.
- ☐ Look for clues such as bold type or capital letters that point out specific sections or important information.
- ☐ Take note of illustrations and other visual aids.
- ☐ Follow each step in the exact order given.
- ☐ Do not skip any steps.

Content-Area Vocabulary

These words appear in the selections that follow. You may also encounter them in other content-area texts.

- **vertical** (vʉrˊ tə kəl) *adj.* straight up and down; perpendicular to a level surface; upright

- **contestant** (kən testˊ ənt) *n.* person who takes part in a trial of skill to see who can win

ORIGAMI

by Rachel Katz

APATOSAURUS

Begin with a 9 inch by 12 inch piece of construction paper or an 8 ½ inch by 11 inch sheet of copy paper.

> The instructions tell what kind of paper you need to complete the project.

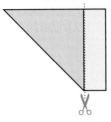

1 Place the rectangle sideways. Valley fold the left-hand side up to meet the top, thereby making a triangle.

2 Cut along the side of the triangle.

3 Save the rectangular piece of paper for the dinosaur's legs.

4 Open out the triangle into a square. Turn the square around to look like a diamond, making sure the existing fold-line is running horizontally across the paper.

Body

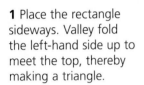
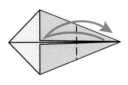
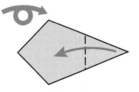

5 From the right-hand corner, valley fold the top and bottom sloping edges over to meet the middle fold-line, thereby making the kite base.

6 Valley fold the right-hand point over to meet the vertical edges. Press it flat and unfold it.

7 Turn the paper over. Valley fold the right-hand point over along the fold-line made in step 6.

8 Valley fold the point over back out toward the right.

> Numbered steps show the order in which instructions should be followed.

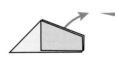
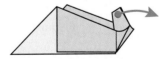

9 Valley fold the paper in half from bottom to top.

10 Reach inside the model and pull out the . . .

11 dinosaur's neck. Press it flat, into the position shown in step 12.

Illustrations help you check to see if you are completing the steps correctly.

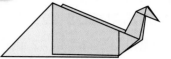

12 Reach inside the neck and pull out the . . .

13 Head. Press it flat, into the position shown, thereby completing the body.

Legs

1 Use the remaining rectangle. Fold bottom up to the top.

2 Unfold.

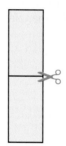

3 Cut in half along crease.

4 Fold in half.

5 Fold top down.

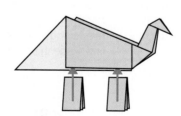

6 Staple as shown.

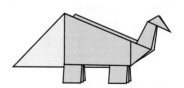

7 Here is the completed apatosaurus.

World of Escher Tessellation Contest

Now accepting New Entries for Contest 24

Tessellation is a combination of mathematics and artistic ability.

Do you have what it takes? Compete with entries from all over the world. See your work displayed on the Internet. Win prizes.

Each entry will be judged individually, and a winner will be announced. There will be prizes for each winner from our online store.

All winners will be included in our "Hall of Fame."

Rules

- Due to the number of great artworks entered, each entry will be pre-judged before being posted in the contest. This is to keep the quality of the voting at a maximum.

- Acceptable materials: watercolor; color pencils; pen & ink; marker; computer-generated.

- The symmetry art works of M.C. Escher should serve as the model for all entries.

- Entries may be scanned and e-mailed; or hard copies may be mailed to us (e-mail us for the address) and we will scan the image for you.

- Entries submitted by e-mail should conform with the Technical section below.

- Mailed in entries must be no larger than 8.5" x 11" with no matting or frames, we suggest making a color copy and submitting that copy.

- All entries received become the property of World of Escher, Inc. and will not be returned, unless such materials are provided at the cost of the entrant.

- World of Escher will not accept any copyrighted images. It is up to the contestant to verify copyright status.

- World of Escher will not market any images. We reserve the right to display the images in our gallery.

- All entries must be accompanied by the Contest Entry Form. These can be e-mailed in as attachments to the image, or affixed to the back of those entries that are mailed in.

- Decisions of the panel of judges are final.

- One entry per contestant.

Bold type highlights important requirements for contest entries.

Technical Requirements

For electronically submitted entries:

- Images must be in the .jpg format and must be attached via email. (We no longer accept files that are not in the .jpg format.)

- Image files will be converted, if necessary, by the World of Escher and no file will be larger than 100k bytes.

- The Contest Entry Form must be online or attached to the e-mail with the graphic.

Contest Entry Form

Contest Number: _____

Name of Tessellation: _____

Type of Tessellation: (check one) Computer _____ Hand _____

Age of Contestant: _____ Grade: _____

Name of Contestant: _____

Name of School: _____

Teacher's Name: _____

Mailing Address: _____

_____

For students, please use the school address

E-mail Address: _____ (required)
The teacher's address is fine for students.

By submitting this Contest Entry Form the contestant agrees:

1) the image is free from copyright restrictions.
2) that he/she has parental consent to submit his/her work.
3) that submission of his/her work grants World of Escher the right to display the work at World of Escher's discretion.

E-MAIL INSTRUCTIONS

To download the order form and send to World of Escher via e-mail:

1. Highlight this text and copy into your text editor.
2. Select Save or Save As to save the file to your disk.
3. Load the entry form into a text editor or word processor and fill it out.
4. Save the entry form to disk as an ASCII file.
5. E-mail to the Webmaster either as an attachment or in the body of the email message.
6. Be sure to attach your graphic file if sending via e-mail.

This section gives step-by-step instructions for submitting entries by e-mail.

Comparing Functional Texts

1. Key Ideas and Details (a) Explain how the section of the origami instructions that comes before the numbered steps can help readers. **(b)** Explain why the contest entry form presents "Rules" and "Technical Requirements" under separate headings. **(c)** Which text do you think has clearer **multiple-step instructions?** Explain.

Content-Area Vocabulary

2. Using a print or an online dictionary, find a word related to *contestant* and use both words in sentences that show their meaning.

⏱ Timed Writing

Functional Text: Set of Instructions

> **Format**
> The prompt directs you to write instructions. Therefore, you will need to describe a series of steps in a process, using sequence words, such as *first*, *next*, and *finally*.

Write a **set of instructions** for entering a contest. Provide at least five steps in your set of instructions and include diagrams or visuals, as necessary. Your writing should be brief, clear, and direct. You may refer to the contest entry form for ideas about formatting. (30 min)

> **Academic Vocabulary**
> When you *refer* to a document, you consult it and may use it as an example, but you do not copy directly from it.

5-Minute Planner

Complete these steps before you begin to write:

1. Read the prompt carefully. Look for key words. These will help you understand what you need to do.
2. Reread each section of the contest entry form. Jot down ideas about how to divide your own instructions into sections.
3. Create an outline showing how you will organize your instructions. Tell readers what materials they will need.
4. Refer to your outline and your notes as you begin your draft.

Comparing Imagery

An **image** is a word picture that appeals to one or more of the five senses of sight, hearing, smell, taste, and touch. Writers use descriptive language and sensory details to develop **imagery.**

- An image can appeal to more than one sense. For example, "soft carpet of yellow prairie flowers" appeals to both touch and sight.

- An image can create a feeling of movement. For example, "the autumn leaves floated to the ground" shows the reader *how* the leaves fell.

- Imagery helps writers express moods or emotions. Mood is the feeling that a poem creates in the reader. A poem can have many moods, including frightening, fanciful, thoughtful, and lonely.

In the poems "Dust of Snow" and "who knows if the moon's," each poet uses imagery to achieve a different effect. As you read each poem, use a chart such as the one below to record the picture the poem creates in your mind, the sense or senses each image appeals to, and the overall mood or emotion the poet communicates through imagery.

Poem title	Image	Sight	Hearing	Smell	Taste	Touch	Mood

**Common Core
State Standards**

Reading Literature
4. Determine the meaning of words and phrases as they are used in a text, including figurative and connotative meanings; analyze the impact of a specific word choice on meaning and tone.

Writing
2.a. Introduce a topic; organize ideas, concepts, and information, using strategies such as definition, classification, comparison/contrast, and cause/effect; include formatting, graphics, and multimedia when useful to aiding comprehension.
2.b. Develop the topic with relevant facts, definitions, concrete details, quotations, or other information and examples. *(Timed Writing)*

- Vocabulary flashcards
- Interactive journals
- More about the authors

- Selection audio
- Interactive graphic organizers

www.PHLitOnline.com

Do we need words to *communicate* well?

Writing About the Big Question

In these poems, the poets paint pictures with words. Complete this sentence starter to consider how other artists communicate.

> An idea or mood can be **expressed** through painting or photography when _____.

Meet the Authors

E.E. Cummings (1894–1962)

Author of "who knows if the moon's"

As a poet, E.E. Cummings experimented with punctuation, spelling, capitalization, and the arrangement of words on the page. For example, he often lowercased his name, and words in his poems that would normally be capitalized. His words in many poems seem to be scattered on a page. However, especially when read aloud, the "scattered" words create the effects Cummings wanted to achieve.

Painting Poems Edward Estlin Cummings was born in Cambridge, Massachusetts. Cummings studied painting, which perhaps explains why he became so interested in the visual effect of his poems.

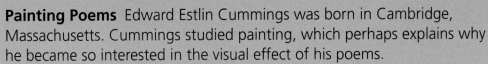

Robert Frost (1874–1963)

Author of "Dust of Snow"

Born in California, Robert Frost is often associated with New England. His family moved to Massachusetts when he was eleven, and he spent most of his life in the Northeast.

Slow Path to Fame Frost began writing poetry in high school. He kept writing while he worked as a farmer, mill worker, newspaper reporter, and teacher. Frost won four Pulitzer Prizes for his writing.

who knows if the moon's

E.E. CUMMINGS

who knows if the moon's
a balloon, coming out of a keen[1] city
in the sky—filled with pretty people?
(and if you and i should

5   get into it, if they
should take me and take you into their balloon,
why then
we'd go up higher with all the pretty people

than houses and *steeples* and clouds:
10   go sailing
away and away sailing into a keen
city which nobody's ever visited, where

always
        it's
15   Spring) and everyone's
in love and flowers pick themselves

---

1. keen (kēn) *adj.* slang for *good, fine.*

Imagery
What kind of movement does the balloon image suggest to you?

Vocabulary
steeples (stē´ pəlz) *n.* towers rising above churches or other structures

Critical Thinking

1. **Craft and Structure** Why do you think lines 13–15 are arranged differently from the other lines in the poem?

2. **Key Ideas and Details** Why might a place where everything is perfect be appealing to Cummings and his readers?

3. **Integration of Knowledge and Ideas** Identify an image in the poem and think about how you might capture it in a drawing. **(a)** What information do the words of the poem give you? What information is missing? **(b)** How could you fill in the missing information? **(c)** Describe or draw the picture you would make. **(d)** How are the idea and mood you convey similar to and different from the image in the poem? *[Connect to the Big Question: Do we need words to communicate well?]*

Cite textual evidence to support your responses.

Dust of Snow

Robert Frost

The way a crow
Shook down on me
The dust of snow
From a hemlock[1] tree

5   Has given my heart
A change of mood
And saved some part
Of a day I had rued.

Vocabulary
rued (rōōd) *v.*
regretted

1. **hemlock** (hem´ läk´) *n.* evergreen tree; member of the pine family.

Critical Thinking

© 1. **Key Ideas and Details (a)** What is the action that changes the speaker's mood? **(b) Classify:** Is this action planned or does it occur by chance? Explain.

© 2. **Key Ideas and Details (a)** Describe the change that the action brings about in the speaker. **(b) Analyze:** Why does the action have this effect? **(c) Generalize:** What lesson do you think the speaker learns from this experience?

© 3. **Key Ideas and Details** If such small, unexpected natural events happened every day, would they have the same impact on a person? Explain.

© 4. **Integration of Knowledge and Ideas (a)** Draw a quick sketch of an image like the one described in the poem. **(b)** What parts of the poem could you convey in your picture? **(c)** What parts of the poem are better conveyed in words? *[Connect to the Big Question: Do we need words to communicate well?]*

Cite textual evidence to support your responses.

Comparing Imagery

1. Craft and Structure (a) For each poem, choose an image and explain which senses the words appeal to. **(b)** Complete a graphic organizer like the one shown for each poem to analyze the poem's mood. In the center, write a word that describes the mood. Then, in the outer circles, list images, words, or phrases in the poem that help develop the mood.

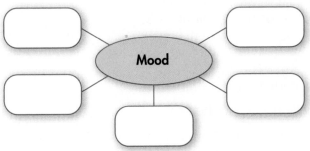

2. Key Ideas and Details In "who knows if the moon's," how does the imagery create a feeling of floating or weightlessness? List details that suggest this movement.

⏱ Timed Writing

Explanatory Text: Essay

Write an essay in which you draw conclusions about the role nature plays in each poem. In your writing, note which descriptive words or phrases contribute to the image of nature, and decide whether the image of nature is positive or negative. **(25 minutes)**

5-Minute Planner

1. Read the prompt carefully and completely.

2. Use these questions to help you get started:

   • In each poem, does nature play a central role, or is it a part of the background for the action?

   • What sensory language contributes to the images of nature?

   • Which words help you tell whether the images of nature are negative or positive?

3. Reread the prompt, and then draft your essay.

Writing Workshop

 **Common Core State Standards**

Writing

1. Write arguments to support claims with clear reasons and relevant evidence.

1.a. Introduce claim(s) and organize the reasons and evidence clearly.

1.b. Support claim(s) with clear reasons and relevant evidence, using credible sources and demonstrating an understanding of the topic or text.

Write an Argument

Argument: Problem-and-Solution Essay

Defining the Form In a **problem-and-solution essay,** the writer identifies and explains a problem and then proposes one or more possible solutions. The writer's goal is to persuade readers that the problem needs to be solved and that the proposed solution will solve the problem.

Assignment Think about a problem that affects your school, your community, or the world. Propose one or more solutions to the problem. Include these elements:

✔ an *introduction* to your topic

✔ a *thesis* stating the problem and your idea for a solution

✔ a *detailed explanation* of the situation surrounding the problem

✔ a *step-by-step description* of your proposed solution

✔ *persuasive evidence* that supports your proposed solution

✔ *consistent, logical organization*

✔ error-free writing, including *correct use of sentences*

To preview the criteria on which your essay may be judged, see the rubric on page 619.

 Writing Workshop: *Work in Progress*

Review the work you did on pages 583 and 599.

Prewriting/Planning Strategy

Gather details. Choose a topic you consider interesting and important. Gather details that clearly explain the problem as well as details that show why or how your solution will work.

Gathering Details
1. Gather statistics and examples of the problem.
2. Interview people to find out how they are affected by the problem.
3. Use the Internet to research how others have solved similar problems.
4. If possible, interview experts who can comment on your solution.

Support Your Ideas

Providing Support After you have explained the causes and effects of the problem and convinced your readers that it needs to be solved, your next step is to convince readers that your ideas for a solution will work. To do this, support your ideas with facts, details, examples, and explanations. You can get information from print sources such as magazines and newspapers, online sources, personal experience, or talking to experts. Ask yourself the following questions about each of your solutions:

- Is my solution practical? Can it really be done? If so, how?
- Has my solution ever been tried? If so, what was the result?
- Have experts considered my solution in the past? What did they say?
- What are the downsides of my solution? Why do I think it is a good solution?

Use a chart like this one for each of your proposed solutions to determine whether you have adequate support for your ideas. Here, an idea that solves the problem of students lacking adequate nutrition is examined.

Idea 1

Serve healthy food in the lunchroom.

Detail	Explanation	Fact	Example
A peanut butter and banana sandwich on whole-wheat bread, a slice of watermelon, and a glass of milk provide protein, complex carbohydrates, calcium, and potassium.	Studies show that students who get better nutrition at even one meal a day do better at school and get sick less often.	When other school districts switched over to healthier lunch menus, student grades improved and students were out sick less often.	Healthy food can be tasty. For example, a strawberry-yogurt fruit smoothie is loaded with nutrients and good taste.

Drafting Strategies

State your thesis. Begin your essay with a thesis that states the problem and your proposed solution. Make the problem clear by explaining the situation in the body of your essay. After you explain the problem, develop your solution with examples and details. In your conclusion, summarize why your solution will work.

Organize paragraphs to show cause and effect. As you present each step in your proposed solution, show the effect it will have on the problem or on the next step that needs to be taken. Finally, show the effects of your proposed solution. Add transition words such as *next*, *in addition*, or *after* to show the connections between the steps or parts of your solution.

Consider your audience. To achieve your overall purpose of persuading others to accept your proposed solution, keep your audience—your readers—in mind as you gather evidence and support. Choose details that will show how the problem and solution affects your audience. To make your argument more convincing, establish and maintain a formal style.

Common Core State Standards

Writing

1.c. Use words, phrases, and clauses to clarify the relationships among claim(s) and reasons.

1.d. Establish and maintain a formal style.

1.e. Provide a concluding statement or section that follows from the argument presented.

Revising Strategy

Revise for sentence structure. Review your essay to identify and correct **run-on sentences**. A **run-on sentence** is one in which two separate and complete thoughts are put together without a connecting word or punctuation mark. The following chart shows several ways to correct a run-on sentence.

> The traffic is terrible at the crossing of Main Street and Third Avenue I think something should be done about it.

Create Two Sentences	Use a Semicolon or a Connecting Word With a Comma	Make One of the Ideas Dependent on the Other One
The traffic is terrible at the crossing of Main Street and Third Avenue. I think something should be done about it.	The traffic is terrible at the crossing of Main Street and Third Avenue, and I think something should be done about it.	Because the traffic is terrible at the crossing of Main Street and Third Avenue, I think something should be done about it.

Revising for Strong, Functional Sentences

Make sure that each sentence in your essay serves the function it should and that each one has the correct end punctuation.

Identifying Errors in Sentence Functions and Punctuation

There are four types of sentences. Each type uses a specific punctuation mark. This chart provides a quick review.

Type of Sentence	Function	End Punctuation	Example(s)
declarative	makes a statement	period	Space travel may be available some day.
interrogative	asks a question	question mark	Would you like a vacation on Mars?
exclamatory	shows strong feelings	exclamation point	What a thrilling trip that would be!
imperative	gives an order or a direction	period or exclamation point	Please fasten your seat belt. Watch out!

PH WRITING COACH

Further instruction and practice are available in *Prentice Hall Writing Coach*.

Fixing Errors To find and fix errors related to sentence function and end punctuation, follow these steps:

1. Read each sentence that you have written.

2. Think about the function, or job, you want it to do.

3. Use the appropriate punctuation mark at the end of the sentence.

Grammar in Your Writing

Reread the draft of your essay. Carefully think about the function of each sentence. Then, use the rules and examples above to make sure that you have used the correct end punctuation.

Student Model: Shamus Cunningham, Dayton Beach, FL

 Common Core
State Standards

Language
2.b. Spell correctly.

Panther Problems

The Florida panther is one of our state's most interesting animals, but sadly, it is also one of the rarest. There are currently only about sixty panthers in Florida. Panther numbers don't grow because of shrinking panther habitat and increasing traffic in areas populated by panthers. To save panthers from extinction, we must make sure there is enough land set aside for panthers to live on and that they have safe ways to move through the areas in which they live.

A grown panther needs approximately 275 square miles to roam and hunt. If too many adult panthers occupy the same territory, they fight and injure or kill one another. In addition, panthers hunt other wild animals, such as deer, for food. To be a good habitat for a panther, an area must have prey animals for the panther to hunt. Because of development, the "wild" areas that panthers used to call home are now filled with houses and stores rather than food and hiding places. It is unlikely that development will suddenly stop or even slow down. Therefore, experts must plan ahead and set aside one or two large protected areas where panthers can live, rather than many smaller areas.

Loss of habitat isn't the only problem caused by development. More houses means more roads, and that means more problems for panthers. According to the Florida Game and Freshwater Fish Commission, 42% of panther deaths in a recent twenty-five-year period were road kills. Underpasses have been built to allow panthers and other animals to cross a territory without crossing a road. In an area known as Alligator Alley, one large underpass was built. Since then, there have been no reported killings of panthers by cars. The success of the underpass in this area shows that we can protect panthers without halting progress.

The two solutions suggested here would meet the needs of humans and panthers. The solutions are costly, but they have been proven effective, and they are the least disruptive to the human community. Saving the Florida panther is a complex issue, but if we put our heads together, I'm confident we will make the right decisions.

Shamus states his thesis in the first paragraph and suggests a two-step solution to the problem.

The problem is explained in more detail so that readers will understand the value of the proposed solution.

Transition words such as "because" and "therefore" show cause-and-effect relationships.

Each part of the problem and its solution is addressed in a separate paragraph. Statistics provide evidence that a solution is needed and that the proposed solution is the right one.

Editing and Proofreading

Proofread your draft to correct errors in spelling, grammar, and punctuation.

Focus on words with suffixes. Suffixes are word parts that are added to the ends of base words. To spell a word with a suffix, remember the following rules:

Suffixes that begin with a consonant *(-ful, -tion,-ly)*: Change final *y* to *i* in the base word, unless a vowel precedes the *y*.

Suffixes beginning with a vowel: Change final *y* to *i* in the base word, unless a vowel precedes the *y*. Usually, drop the final *e* in the base word.

Publishing and Presenting

Consider one of the following ways to share your writing:

Present a proposal. Use your problem-and-solution essay as the basis for a presentation.

Submit your paper for publication. Send a clean copy to your school paper or local newspaper. Include a cover letter.

Reflecting on Your Writing

Writer's Journal Jot down your answer to this question:

Who can implement the solutions proposed in your essay?

Rubric for Self-Assessment

Find evidence in your writing to address each category. Then, use the rating scale to grade your work.

Spiral Review
Earlier in the unit, you learned about **simple and compound subjects** (p. 582) and **sentence types** (p. 598). Check the punctuation of sentences in your essay and make sure that subjects are paired with the correct form of the verb.

Criteria	Rating Scale				
	not very				*very*
Focus: How clearly stated is the thesis statement?	1	2	3	4	5
Organization: How organized are the steps or parts of the solution?	1	2	3	4	5
Support/Elaboration: How strong and convincing is the support?	1	2	3	4	5
Style: How well did you use language to make your argument?	1	2	3	4	5
Conventions: How effectively are transitions used to connect ideas, and how consistently have you avoided run-on sentences?	1	2	3	4	5
Ideas: How well is your solution supported with convincing facts, details, examples, and explanations?	1	2	3	4	5

Leveled Texts

Build your skills and improve your comprehension of poetry with texts of increasing complexity.

The poems in **Poetry Collection 5** present everyday actions, scenes, and words in fresh, new ways.

The poets in **Poetry Collection 6** create meaning by using patterns of words, rhythm, and rhyme.

Common Core State Standards

Meet these standards with either **Poetry Collection 5** (p. 624) or **Poetry Collection 6** (p. 630).

Reading Literature
5. Analyze how a particular sentence, chapter, scene, or stanza fits into the overall structure of a text and contributes to the development of the theme, setting, or plot. *(Literary Analysis: Forms of Poetry)*

Spiral Review: RL.6.4

Writing
4. Produce clear and coherent writing in which the development, organization, and style are appropriate to task, purpose, and audience. *(Writing: Poem)*

6. Use technology, including the Internet, to produce and publish writing as well as to interact and collaborate with others; demonstrate sufficient command of keyboarding skills to type a minimum of three pages in a single sitting. *(Research and Technology: Presentation of a Poem)*

Language
3. Use knowledge of language and its conventions when writing, speaking, reading, or listening. *(Conventions: Subject Complements)*

6. Acquire and use accurately grade-appropriate general academic and domain-specific words and phrases; gather vocabulary knowledge when considering a word or phrase important to comprehension or expression. *(Vocabulary: Word Study)*

Reading Skill: Paraphrasing

Paraphrasing is restating an author's words in your own words. Paraphrasing difficult or confusing passages in a poem helps you identify the main idea and monitor your understanding. Use the following steps to help you:

- Stop and **reread** any difficult lines or passages.
- Identify unfamiliar words, find their meanings, and replace them with words that mean nearly the same thing.
- Restate the lines in your own words.
- Reread to see whether your paraphrase makes sense.

Use your paraphrases to help you identify the main idea or key emotion the poem conveys.

Using the Strategy: Paraphrase Chart

As you read the following poems, use a chart like the one shown to help you paraphrase complex lines.

Line	Unfamiliar Word(s)	Paraphrase
Afoot and lighthearted, I take to the open road.	afoot = on foot lighthearted = happy take to = start out on	On foot and happy, I start out on the road.

Literary Analysis: Forms of Poetry

Poets use **forms of poetry** suited to the meaning, images, and feelings they want to express. Here are three poetic forms:

- In a **concrete poem,** words are arranged in a shape that reflects the subject of the poem.
- A **haiku** is a Japanese verse form with three lines. Line 1 has five syllables, line 2 has seven, and line 3 has five.
- A **limerick** is a funny poem of five lines. Lines 1, 2, and 5 rhyme and have three beats, or stressed syllables. Lines 3 and 4 rhyme and have two beats.

Do we need words to *communicate* well?

Writing About the Big Question

A writer's toolbox always contains words, but poets use more than just words to communicate. Poets also use line length, rhyme, and rhythm to convey ideas. Use the following sentence starter to help you develop your ideas about the Big Question.

The **language** of poetry is unique because _____ .

While You Read Look for ways in which the poets use more than just words to communicate.

Vocabulary

Read each word and its definition. Decide whether you know the word well, know it a little bit, or do not know it at all. After you read, see how your knowledge of each word has increased.

- **skimming** (skim´ iŋ) *v.* gliding; moving swiftly and lightly over a surface (p. 625) *The boat was skimming over the lake. skim v. skimmed v.*

- **asphalt** (as´fôlt´) *n.* brown or black mixture of substances used to pave roads (p. 625) *The asphalt was hot on my bare feet.*

- **flee** (flē) *v.* run away as from danger (p. 626) *I will flee if they come after me. fleeing v. fled v.*

- **flaw** (flô) *n.* crack; defect (p. 626) *The leak was caused by a flaw in the ceiling. flawed adj. flawless adj.*

Word Study

The **Old English suffix** *-less* means "without" or "not able."

In the limerick, two insects go through a *flaw*, or crack, in a pipe. If the pipe had been **flawless**, it would have been perfect, without any cracks.

Matsuo Bashō

(1644–1694)

Author of Haiku (page 624)

Bashō was born into a family of Japanese landowners. When Bashō was twelve, his father died. Bashō then entered the service of a local lord and began to write poetry. He was an important developer of the haiku form and one of its greatest masters. Bashō wrote "An old silent pond" in the spring of 1686. He revised the poem several times, changing it from the past to the present tense, until he felt that it was right. The Japanese have built a monument near the place where Bashō is believed to have written this haiku.

Lillian Morrison

(b. 1917)

Author of "The Sidewalk Racer" (page 625)

As a child growing up in Jersey City, New Jersey, Lillian Morrison played street games and sports. The rhymes and chants she heard on the playground inspired her love of poetry. As an adult, Morrison spent nearly forty years working in the New York Public Library. She has written several books of poetry, including *The Sidewalk Racer and Other Poems of Sports and Motion*. Morrison has said, "I love rhythms, the body movement implicit in poetry, explicit in sports." Many of her poems, such as "The Sidewalk Racer," celebrate the human body in motion.

Haiku

Bashō

An old silent pond . . .
A frog jumps into the pond,
splash! Silence again.

The Sidewalk Racer
or On the Skateboard

Lillian Morrison

Skimming
an asphalt sea
I swerve, I curve, I
sway; I speed to whirring
5   sound an inch above the
ground; I'm the sailor
and the sail, I'm the
driver and the wheel
I'm the one and only
10   single engine
human auto
mobile.

Vocabulary
skimming (skim´ iŋ)
v. gliding; moving
swiftly and lightly
over a surface
asphalt (as´ fôlt´) n.
brown or black mix-
ture of substances
used to pave roads

◄ **Critical Viewing**
What words might
describe the spirit
of both this skate-
boarder and the
poem? **[Connect]**

Limerick Anonymous

Vocabulary
flee (flē) *v.* run away as from danger
flaw (flô) *n.* break; crack

A flea and a fly in a flue
Were caught, so what could they do?
    Said the fly, "Let us flee."
    "Let us fly," said the flea.
5 So they flew through a flaw in the flue.

Spiral Review
Word Choice Describe the tone of this limerick. How does word choice help to create this tone?

Cite textual evidence to support your responses.

Critical Thinking

1. **Key Ideas and Details** **(a)** Describe the setting of the haiku. **(b) Generalize:** What overall feeling does the haiku create? Explain.

2. **Key Ideas and Details** **(a) Interpret:** Which words and phrases help show motion in "The Sidewalk Racer"? **(b) Analyze:** How can the speaker be both "the sailor / and the sail"? **(c) Draw Conclusions:** Which image do you think most successfully conveys the sense of being on a skateboard? Explain.

3. **Key Ideas and Details** **(a)** What consonant sound is repeated in the limerick? **(b) Analyze:** How does this sound contribute to the humor in the poem?

4. **Integration of Knowledge and Ideas** The poems in this collection use few words to convey meaning. Would these poems be more effective if they were longer and used more words? Why or why not? *[Connect to the Big Question: Do we need words to communicate well?]*

Reading Skill: Paraphrasing

1. **(a)** Paraphrase the haiku by Bashō in your own words.
   (b) How does paraphrasing the haiku help you clarify
   your understanding of the poet's main ideas?
   (c) How does line length impact meaning in the haiku?

2. Paraphrase lines 6–12 of "The Sidewalk Racer."

3. How would you **paraphrase** lines 3–5 of the limerick?

Literary Analysis: Forms of Poetry

© 4. **Key Ideas and Details** **(a)** What image appears in each
   line of the **haiku?** Record answers in a web. **(b)** How does
   each line develop the scene in the poem?

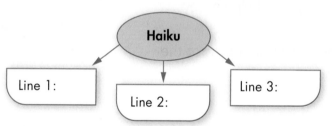

Haiku

Line 1:

Line 2:

Line 3:

© 5. **Craft and Structure** **(a)** Would "The Sidewalk Racer" be
   more effective if written in a different shape? Explain.

© 6. **Craft and Structure** Would it be possible to write a
   serious **limerick?** Explain.

Vocabulary

© **Acquisition and Use** Write a sentence that connects the
   situation in each item with a vocabulary word from page 622.

1. Milk dripped from a crack in the glass.

2. Jay watched as the birds glided across the nearby lake.

3. Suzy ran away when she heard a sound in the forest.

4. Jake ran after the ice cream truck, his bare feet burning.

Word Study Use context and what you know about the **Old
English suffix -less** to explain your answer to each question.

1. If you were *tireless*, would you need to rest?

2. If you were *restless*, would you fall asleep easily?

Word Study

The **Old English suffix
-less** means "without"
or "not able."

Apply It Explain how
the suffix -*less* contributes to the meaning of
these words. You may
consult a dictionary
if necessary.

relentless
clueless
reckless

Do we need words to *communicate* well?

Writing About the Big Question

Poets go beyond the meaning of words to convey their ideas. Haikus use patterns of syllables, limericks use rhythm and rhyme, and concrete poems use a visual arrangement of their words. Use the following sentence starter to help you develop your ideas about the Big Question.

> When **visual** images accompany text, they help convey meaning by _____.

While You Read Determine whether the visual forms of the poems affect their meanings.

Vocabulary

Read each word and its definition. Decide whether you know the word well, know it a little bit, or do not know it at all. After you read, see how your knowledge of each word has increased.

- **wintry** (win´ trē) *adj.* cold and snowy (p. 630) *The wind and snow of the <u>wintry</u> day gave me chills.* wintriness *n.* winter *n.*

- **howl** (houl) *v.* make a loud, sorrowful sound (p. 630) *The wolves <u>howl</u> every night.* howling *v.* howled *v.*

- **rage** (rāj) *n.* very strong anger (p. 630) *The red-faced man shook with <u>rage</u>.* raging *v.* enrage *v.* enraged *adj.*

- **fellow** (fel´ ō) *n.* man or boy (p. 632) *That <u>fellow</u> has his shirt on backwards.* fellowship *n.*

Word Study

The **suffix -ship** forms nouns. It means "all individuals in a certain category." It can also mean "the quality, condition, or state of being."

A *fellow* is a man or boy, and a **fellowship** is a friendly group of individuals.

Musō Soseki

(1275–1351)

Author of Haiku (page 630)

Musō Soseki made many important contributions to Japanese culture during his lifetime. He was a poet, scholar, and garden designer. He was also valued for his skills as an advisor to emperors and as a mediator during a period of civil wars in Japan. Soseki served as abbot, or head, of a Buddhist monastery. He was considered a great spiritual master and one of the most important religious leaders of his time. The haiku presented on the following page is one of a large body of poetry that Soseki wrote.

Haiku's Roots Haiku grew out of the "linked poem," or *renga*, tradition, which was popular in Japan in Soseki's day. Several poets would get together to compose a renga—short stanzas linked together to form one long poem. The renga eventually developed into the haiku form we know today, with its characteristic pattern of syllables and imagery.

Dorthi Charles

(b. 1960)

Author of "Concrete Cat" (page 631)

Dorthi Charles was a student when she wrote "Concrete Cat." Readers especially enjoy the creative way that Charles presents her subject. This poem is featured in the book *Knock at a Star: A Child's Introduction to Poetry*.

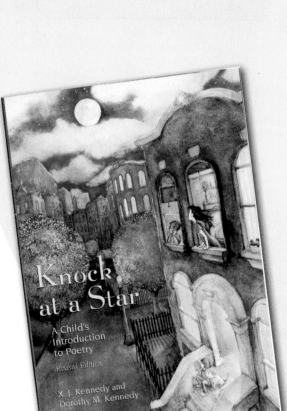

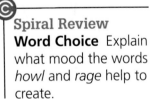

▲ **Critical Viewing**
What details in this
scene are similar to
the scene the poet
describes? **[Compare]**

Spiral Review
Word Choice Explain
what mood the words
howl and *rage* help to
create.

Vocabulary
wintry (win´ trē) *adj.*
cold and snowy,

howl (houl) *v.* make a
loud, sorrowful sound

rage (rāj) *n.* very
strong anger

Haiku
Musō Soseki

Over the wintry
forest, winds howl in a rage
with no leaves to blow.

Concrete Cat

Dorthi Charles

```
        A           A
      e   r       e   r

                          stripestripestripestripe t
      e Ye    e Ye                                   a
  whisker        whisker   stripestripestripe         i
                            stripestripestripestripe   l t a i l
  whisker  m   h  whisker   stripestripestripe
            o  t           stripestripestripe
            U
                    stripestripestripestripe


        paw paw        paw paw              ǝsnoɯ


  dishdish                      litterbox
                                litterbox
```

Limerick

Anonymous

There was a young fellow named Hall,
Who fell in the spring in the fall;
    'Twould have been a sad thing
    If he'd died in the spring,
5 But he didn't—he died in the fall.

Vocabulary
fellow (fel´ō) *n.* man or boy

Forms of Poetry
What are the stressed syllables in lines 1, 2, and 5?

▶ **Critical Viewing**
What part of the limerick does this image illustrate? **[Connect]**

Critical Thinking

Cite textual evidence to support your responses.

© **1. Key Ideas and Details (a)** What action does the haiku describe? **(b) Infer:** Why are there no leaves for the winds to blow?

© **2. Key Ideas and Details (a)** In the haiku, what emotion does the poet assign to the winds? **(b) Infer:** Why do you think the poet chose this emotion? **(c) Interpret:** What human character trait might the haiku be describing? Explain.

© **3. Craft and Structure (a)** What mood does the poet achieve through the use of form of "Concrete Cat"? **(b) Evaluate:** How well does the poet capture the essence of a cat? Explain.

© **4. Key Ideas and Details (a)** What incident is described in the limerick? **(b) Interpret:** What are the double meanings of *spring* and *fall* in the limerick? **(c) Analyze:** How do both meanings contribute to the humor in the limerick?

© **5. Integration of Knowledge and Ideas** Choose one poem in this collection and compare and contrast it with a different art form. Would the poem be as effective as art? Explain. *[Connect to the Big Question: Do we need words to communicate well?]*

Reading Skill: Paraphrasing

1. **(a) Paraphrase** the haiku by Soseki in your own words.
   (b) How does your paraphrase help clarify the main idea?

2. Review "Concrete Cat." In your own words, restate the meaning of the words that form the cat's head.

3. How would you **paraphrase** lines 1 and 2 of the limerick?

Literary Analysis: Forms of Poetry

4. **Key Ideas and Details (a)** What image appears in each line of the **haiku?** Record answers in a web. **(b)** How does each line develop the scene in the poem?

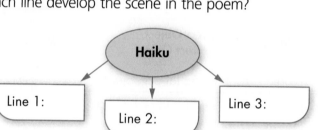

5. **Craft and Structure** Would "Concrete Cat" be more or less effective if it were written in a different shape? Explain.

6. **Craft and Structure** Could one write a serious **limerick?** Explain.

Vocabulary

Acquisition and Use Write a sentence that connects the situation in each item with a vocabulary word from page 628.

1. A young man walking to school

2. A woman who is angry about missing the bus

3. Wolves communicating with each other

4. A painting that shows snow covering the rooftops

Word Study Use context and what you know about the suffix **-ship** to explain your answer to each question.

1. Do you consider homework a *hardship*?

2. What is the value of true *friendship*?

Word Study

The **suffix -ship** forms nouns. It means "all individuals in a certain category." It can also mean "the quality, condition or state of being."

Apply It Explain how the suffix *-ship* contributes to the meaning of these words. You may consult a dictionary if necessary.

readership
professorship
penmanship

Integrated Language Skills

Poetry Collections 5 and 6

Conventions: Complements

Poetry Collection 5

In sentences with action verbs, a **direct object** is a noun or pronoun that receives the action of the verb and answers the question *Who?* or *What?* An **indirect object** names the person or thing to whom or for whom an action is done, and answers the question *To or for whom?* or *To or for what?* The indirect object appears between the verb and the direct object and is not part of a prepositional phrase.

Poetry Collection 6

Sentence	Question	Answer	Direct Object/ Indirect Object
Elsa baked bread.	Baked *what?*	*bread*	bread (direct object)
Mimi brought us a surprise.	Brought *what?* Brought *to whom?*	*surprise* *us*	surprise (direct object) us (indirect object)

Practice A Find the direct and indirect object in the following sentences. Not all sentences contain an indirect object. Then, rewrite each sentence with a different direct object.

1. John wrote Louisa a haiku.
2. The flea saw the flaw first.
3. The skateboard hit the ground.
4. The poem creates an image for me.

Ⓖ **Speaking Application** Choose an image in one of the poems. Discuss it with a partner, taking turns saying sentences about it that contain direct and indirect objects.

Practice B Use the following verbs to write sentences that contain direct and indirect objects.

1. give
2. bought
3. made
4. catch

Ⓖ **Writing Application** Using the italicized sentence as a model, write three sentences about communication. Identify the direct and indirect objects you use. *He told us a terrific story.*

PH WRITING COACH | Further instruction and practice are available in *Prentice Hall Writing Coach*.

Writing

 **Common Core State Standards**

L.6.3, L.6.6; W.6.4, W.6.6
[For the full wording of the standards, see page 620.]

⊚ Poetry Write your own haiku, limerick, or concrete **poem.**

- Brainstorm for a list of topics that inspire you. Think about nature, events from your daily life, an amusing incident, or something visual that you want to describe.

- Decide which of the three forms of poetry fits your topic.

- Write your poem. Choose the correct pattern for the poetry form. Use a visual layout if you are writing a concrete poem and humor and rhyming words if you are writing a limerick.

- Make copies of your poem for a small group of classmates. Read the poem aloud as they follow along.

Grammar Application Review your poem to be sure you have used indirect and direct objects correctly.

Writing Workshop: *Work in Progress*

Prewriting for Exposition For a comparison-and-contrast essay you may write, choose two examples of an object. For example, you might list two different shoes or two books. Describe each object's use and style. Save your list in your writing portfolio.

Use this prewriting activity to prepare for the **Writing Workshop** on page 668.

Research and Technology

⊚ Build and Present Knowledge Use a computer word processing program to develop and design a **presentation of a poem.**

- Choose a poem that you enjoyed reading.

- Type the poem exactly as it was written by the poet. You may have to set your margins extra wide to accommodate the poem's line breaks or use tabs to set off indented lines.

- Choose a font or style that is easy to read. Use a larger font size for the title.

- Proofread your poem. Don't forget to add the poet's name. Use "Anonymous" if the poet is unknown.

- Add pictures or illustrations to enhance the appearance of the poem.

- Post a copy of your poem as part of a class display.

PHLit Online!
www.PHLitOnline.com
- Interactive graphic organizers
- Grammar tutorial
- Interactive journals

Leveled Texts

Build your skills and improve your comprehension of poetry with texts of increasing complexity.

Poetry Collection 7 includes poems about an unwanted kitten, a natural wonder, and a circus parade.

Poetry Collection 8 contains a lullaby, a poem about self-acceptance, and a poem about the joys of snow.

Common Core State Standards

Meet these standards with either **Poetry Collection 7** (p. 640) or **Poetry Collection 8** (p. 648).

Reading Literature
4. Determine the meaning of words and phrases as they are used in a text, including figurative and connotative meanings; analyze the impact of a specific word choice on meaning and tone. *(Literary Analysis: Sound Devices)*

Writing
4. Produce clear and coherent writing in which the development, organization, and style are appropriate to task, purpose, and audience. *(Writing: Prose Description)*

6. Use technology, including the Internet, to produce and publish writing as well as to interact and collaborate with others; demonstrate sufficient command of keyboarding skills to type a minimum of three pages in a single sitting. *(Research and Technology: Résumé)*

Language
1. Demonstrate command of the conventions of standard English grammar and usage when writing or speaking. *(Conventions: Predicate Nouns and Predicate Adjectives)*

6. Acquire and use accurately grade-appropriate general academic and domain-specific words and phrases; gather vocabulary knowledge when considering a word or phrase important to comprehension or expression. *(Vocabulary: Word Study)*

Reading Skill: Paraphrasing

Paraphrasing is restating something in your own words. When you paraphrase text, you use simpler language to clarify its meaning. Before you paraphrase, **read original text fluently according to punctuation** to help you group words for meaning. When you read a poem aloud, do not automatically stop at the ends of lines. Instead, use the punctuation in the poem to decide where to pause. After you have read the poem aloud, create a paraphrase in which you capture its main idea.

Using the Strategy: Poetry Reading Guide

Use this chart to decide where to pause as you read.

Punctuation	How to Read
no punctuation	do not pause
comma (,)	slight pause
colon (:) semicolon (;) dash (—)	longer pause
period (.) question mark (?) exclamation point (!)	longest pause

Literary Analysis: Sound Devices

Tone, a writer's attitude toward his or her subject matter, is created through use of language. For example, a poem can have a humorous tone, created through the use of words such as *higgledy-piggledy.* The use of **sound devices** allows poets to develop tone, as well as to create musical effects and reinforce meaning. Sound devices commonly used in poetry include the following:

- **Repetition:** the repeated use of any element of language—a sound, word, phrase, or sentence—as in *of the people, by the people, for the people*
- **Alliteration:** the repetition of initial consonant sounds, such as the *b* sound in *big bad wolf*
- **Onomatopoeia:** the use of a word that sounds like what it means, such as *roar* or *buzz*

Do we need words to communicate well?

Writing About the Big Question

Poetry can make the ordinary—a kitten, a scene in nature, or a parade—seem extraordinary. Use this sentence starter to help develop your ideas about the Big Question.

When a poet writes about ordinary things he or she is **sharing,** we understand _____.

While You Read Focus on how each poet communicates ideas about ordinary things.

Vocabulary

Read each word and its definition. Decide whether you know the word well, know it a little bit, or do not know it at all. After you read, see how your knowledge of each word has increased.

- **cuddly** (kud´ lē) *adj.* having a quality which invites hugging or holding in one's arms (p. 641) *Sheryl slept with the <u>cuddly</u> teddy bear. cuddle v. cuddling v.*

- **gilded** (gild´ əd) *adj.* covered with gold or having a golden color (p. 643) *The king wore a <u>gilded</u> crown. gild v.*

- **leisurely** (lē´ zhər lē) *adj.* in an unhurried way (p. 643) *Steve took a <u>leisurely</u> stroll in the park. leisure n.*

- **hollowed** (häl´ ōd) *v.* created a hole or a space within (p. 644) *Mama <u>hollowed</u> the watermelon by scooping out all of the fruit. hollow adj. hollows v.*

- **dispersed** (di spʉrst´) *v.* distributed in many directions (p. 644) *The people on the float <u>dispersed</u> candy to the crowd. dispersing v. disperse v. dispersion n.*

- **sculpted** (sculpt´ əd) *v.* shaped or molded (p. 644) *The artist <u>sculpted</u> a figure out of clay. sculpture n. sculpting v. sculptor n.*

Word Study

The **suffix -ly** means "like," "characteristic of," or "in the manner of."

In "Parade," animals pass in a **leisurely** way, which means they walk in an unhurried manner. In "No Thank You," kittens are described as **cuddly,** or as having characteristics that invite cuddling or embracing.

Shel Silverstein

(1932–1999)

Author of "No Thank You" (p. 640)

Chicago-born Shel Silverstein was a talented poet, cartoonist, playwright, and songwriter. His popular poetry collections— *Where the Sidewalk Ends* and *A Light in the Attic*—show his imaginative sense of humor, which both children and adults enjoy. Silverstein also wrote the classic children's book *The Giving Tree.*

Rachel Field

(1894–1942)

Author of "Parade" (p. 642)

Rachel Field could not read until she was ten. This late reader, however, became a well-known writer of books for adults and children. She also became the first woman to receive a Newbery Medal, for her contribution to children's literature. One reason for her success as a writer was her "camera memory," which stored details such as those described in "Parade."

Octavio Paz

(1914–1998)

Author of "Wind and water and stone" (p. 644)

Although Mexican poet Octavio Paz (ok täv′ yō päs) lived in and visited many countries, he remained deeply committed to his Mexican heritage. In "Wind and water and stone," he captures a Mexican landscape and uses it to suggest how a culture changes and yet stays the same. In 1990, Paz received the Nobel Prize in Literature.

No Thank You

SHEL SILVERSTEIN

No I do not want a kitten,
No cute, cuddly kitty-poo,
No more long hair in my cornflakes,
No more midnight meowing mews.

5 No more scratchin', snarlin', spitters,
No more sofas clawed to shreds,
No more smell of kitty litter,
No more mousies in my bed.

No I will not take that kitten—
10 I've had lice and I've had fleas,
I've been scratched and sprayed and bitten,
I've developed allergies.

If you've got an ape, I'll take him,
If you have a lion, that's fine,
15 If you brought some walking bacon,
Leave him here, I'll treat him kind.

I have room for mice and gerbils,
I have beds for boars and bats,
But please, *please* take away that kitten—
20 Quick—'fore it becomes a cat.
Well . . . it is kind of cute at that.

Vocabulary
cuddly (kud´ lē) *adj.*
having a quality which
invites hugging or hold-
ing in one's arms

Sound Devices
What sound device is
used in lines 5 and 6?

Paraphrasing
How do the ellipsis
points (. . .) help you
understand the poet's
meaning?

PARADE

Rachel Field

Background "Parade" describes an old tradition—the circus parade. Before television and radio, the best way to advertise coming attractions was a march down Main Street featuring clowns, wild animals in cages, and a giant musical instrument called a calliope.

This is the day the circus comes
With blare of brass, with beating drums,
And clashing cymbals, and with roar
Of wild beasts never heard before
5 Within town limits. Spick and span
Will shine each gilded cage and van;
Cockades at every horse's head
Will nod, and riders dressed in red
Or blue trot by. There will be floats
10 In shapes like dragons, thrones and boats,
And clowns on stilts; freaks big and small,
Till leisurely and last of all
Camels and elephants will pass
Beneath our elms, along our grass.

Paraphrasing
In reading this poem aloud, would you stop or keep reading at the end of line 3? Explain.

Vocabulary
gilded (gild´ əd) *adj.* covered with gold or having a golden color
leisurely (lē´ zhər lē) *adv.* in an unhurried way

Wind and water and stone — *Octavio Paz*

Vocabulary
hollowed (häl´ ōd)
v. created a hole or
a space within

dispersed (di spʉrst´)
v. distributed in
many directions

sculpted (sculpt´ əd)
v. shaped or molded

Sound Devices
What effect is created
by the repetition of the
words in the fourth line
of each stanza?

The water hollowed the stone,
the wind dispersed the water,
the stone stopped the wind.
Water and wind and stone.

5 The wind sculpted the stone,
the stone is a cup of water,
the water runs off and is wind.
Stone and wind and water.

The wind sings in its turnings,
10 the water murmurs as it goes,
the motionless stone is quiet.
Wind and water and stone.

One is the other, and is neither:
among their empty names
15 they pass and disappear,
water and stone and wind.

Critical Thinking

1. Key Ideas and Details In "No Thank You," what are three reasons the speaker gives for not wanting another kitten?

2. Key Ideas and Details (a) What details in "Parade" describe the town? **(b) Infer:** What do these details suggest about the town?

Cite textual evidence to support your responses.

3. Key Ideas and Details According to "Wind and water and stone," what does each of the three natural elements do?

4. Integration of Knowledge and Ideas (a) Choose two images in the poems that make you think of something familiar in a new way. **(b)** For each image, explain what the poet communicates by making you think this way.
[Connect to the Big Question: Do we need words to communicate well?]

Reading Skill: Paraphrasing

1. Read "No Thank You" aloud. How does the punctuation help you understand the poem?

2. How does punctuation affect the pace or speed of "Parade"?

3. **(a) Paraphrase** the final stanza of "Wind and water and stone." **(b)** What ideas become clear after paraphrasing?

Literary Analysis: Sound Devices

© 4. **Craft and Structure** Complete a chart like the one shown by listing examples of **sound devices** in each poem.

	"No Thank You"	"Parade"	"Wind and water and stone"
repetition			
alliteration			
onomatopoeia			

© 5. **Craft and Structure** What **tone** is created through use of the sound devices in each poem?

Vocabulary

© **Acquisition and Use** Answer each question based on the meaning of the italicized word.

1. Where might you find people walking *leisurely*?

2. Why might a crowd have suddenly *dispersed*?

3. Why do children like *cuddly* toys?

4. What could you do with a *hollowed* stone?

5. Why are *gilded* ornaments used for decoration?

6. What things can be *sculpted* out of snow?

Word Study Use your knowledge of the **suffix -ly** to explain your answer to each question.

1. Does a student who listens *attentively* do well at school?

2. When you wait *impatiently* does time move quickly?

Word Study

The **suffix -ly** means "like," "characteristic of," or "in the manner of."

Apply It Explain how the suffix -ly contributes to the meaning of these words. Consult a dictionary if necessary.

neatly
respectfully
directly

Do we need words to *communicate* well?

Writing About the Big Question

The poems in Poetry Collection 8 all communicate experiences and feelings. Use this sentence starter to help you develop your ideas about the Big Question.

Reading about someone else's experiences helps readers feel a **connection** to _____.

While You Read Look for ways the poet expresses ideas through both format and word choice.

Vocabulary

Read each word and its definition. Decide whether you know the word well, know it a little bit, or do not know it at all. After you read, see how your knowledge of each word has increased.

- **thorny** (thôr´ nē) *adj.* prickly; full of thorns (p. 648) *The thorny bush was difficult to trim.* thornier *adj.* thorniest *adj.* thorn *n.*

- **nigh** (nī) *adj.* near (p. 648) *A chorus of birds signaled that dawn was nigh.*

- **hence** (hens) *adv.* away from this place (p. 648) *In Shakespeare's day, "Get thee hence!" meant "Go away!"* henceforth *adv.*

- **offense** (ə fens´) *n.* harmful act; violation of a law (p. 648) *Raul was punished for his offense.* offensive *adj.*

- **whirs** (wʉrz) *v.* flies or moves quickly with a buzzing sound (p. 650) *The fan whirs above my head all day.* whir *v.*

Word Study

The **suffix -y** forms adjectives that mean "having," "full of," or "characterized by."

In "The Fairies' Lullaby," the hedge-hogs are described as **thorny** because they have sharp, thorn-like quills.

William Shakespeare

(1564–1616)

Author of "The Fairies' Lullaby" (p. 648)

William Shakespeare is perhaps the most highly regarded writer in the English language. Born in the English town of Stratford-upon-Avon, Shakespeare went to London as a young man. There he began writing and acting in plays. He wrote at least thirty-seven plays and more than one hundred fifty poems. "The Fairies' Lullaby" is from the play *A Midsummer Night's Dream.*

Diana Chang

(b. 1934)

Author of "Saying Yes" (p. 649)

Diana Chang admits that she is "preoccupied" with identity and the way people search to understand who they are. She explores her Chinese American identity in her novels and poems. Chang's self-expression does not stop with her writing. She also paints and has exhibited her paintings in art galleries.

Gwendolyn Brooks

(1917–2000)

Author of "Cynthia in the Snow" (p. 650)

Gwendolyn Brooks wrote many poems about her neighbors in Chicago, the city she lived in most of her life. She started writing when she was seven and published her work in a well-known magazine as a teenager. In 1950, Brooks became the first African American writer to win a Pulitzer Prize.

The Fairies' Lullaby

from A Midsummer Night's Dream

William Shakespeare

Fairies. You spotted snakes with double tongue,
Thorny hedgehogs, be not seen.
Newts and blindworms,[1] do no wrong,
Come not near our fairy Queen.

5 **Chorus.** Philomel,[2] with melody
Sing in our sweet lullaby;
Lulla, lulla, lullaby, lulla, lulla, lullaby.
Never harm,
Nor spell, nor charm,
10 Come our lovely lady nigh.
So, good night, with lullaby.

Fairies. Weaving spiders, come not here.
Hence, you long-legged spinners, hence!
Beetles black, approach not near.
15 Worm nor snail do no offense.

Chorus. Philomel, with melody
Sing in our sweet lullaby;
Lulla, lulla, lullaby, lulla, lulla, lullaby.
Never harm,
20 Nor spell, nor charm,
Come our lovely lady nigh.
So, good night, with lullaby.

Paraphrasing
In reading aloud, why would you keep reading at the end of line 5? How would you paraphrase lines 5 and 6?

Vocabulary
thorny (thôr´ nē) *adj.* prickly; full of thorns
nigh (nī) *adj.* near
hence (hens) *adv.* away from this place
offense (ə fens´) *n.* harmful act; violation of a law

---

1. **newts** (nōōts) **and blindworms** *n.* newts are salamanders, which look like lizards but are related to frogs. Blindworms are legless lizards.
2. **Philomel** (fil´ ə mel´) *n.* nightingale.

Saying *Yes*

Diana Chang

"Are you Chinese?"
"Yes."

"American?"
"Yes."

5　"*Really* Chinese?"
"No . . . not quite."

"*Really* American?"
"Well, actually, you see . . ."

But I would rather say
10　yes.
Not neither-nor,
not maybe,
but both, and not only

The homes I've had,
15　the ways I am

I'd rather say it
twice,
yes.

▲ **Critical Viewing**
Do you think the poet, pictured here, likes what she sees in the mirror? Explain. **[Infer]**

Paraphrasing
How does the period after each use of the word *yes* help you understand the poem's meaning?

Cynthia in the Snow
Gwendolyn Brooks

Vocabulary

whirs (wʉrz) *v.* flies or moves quickly with a buzzing sound

Sound Devices

What sound device is at work in the words *SUSHES, hushes,* and *flitter-twitters?* What do these words express?

It SUSHES.
It hushes
The loudness in the road.
It flitter-twitters,
5 And laughs away from me.
It laughs a lovely whiteness,
And whitely whirs away,
To be
Some otherwhere,
10 Still white as milk or shirts.
So beautiful it hurts.

Critical Thinking

Cite textual evidence to support your responses.

© 1. **Key Ideas and Details** **(a)** Name all the creatures the fairies address in "The Fairies' Lullaby." **(b) Classify:** What do all these creatures have in common?

© 2. **Key Ideas and Details** **(a)** What questions are being asked of the speaker in "Saying Yes"? **(b) Infer:** Why might these questions make the speaker uncomfortable? **(c) Evaluate:** Does the speaker in "Saying Yes" have a good attitude toward her identity? Explain.

© 3. **Key Ideas and Details** **(a)** In "Cynthia in the Snow," what five things does the snow do? **(b) Analyze:** What is the speaker's overall reaction to the snow?

© 4. **Integration of Knowledge and Ideas** **(a)** In what way do the forms of the poems contribute to their meaning? **(b)** Which aspect of these poems—their form or word choice—has a greater impact on their meaning? Explain. *[Connect to the Big Question: Do we need words to communicate well?]*

Reading Skill: Paraphrasing

1. Read "Saying Yes" aloud. **(a)** How does the punctuation help you understand the poem? **(b) Paraphrase** the poem.

2. **(a)** In "The Fairies' Lullaby," after which words should the chorus pause? **(b)** Paraphrase the chorus's lines.

3. How does the punctuation affect the pace, or timing, of the words in "Cynthia in the Snow"?

Literary Analysis: Sound Devices

4. Craft and Structure Complete a chart like the one shown by listing examples of **sound devices** in each poem.

	"The Fairies' Lullaby"	"Saying Yes"	"Cynthia in the Snow"
repetition			
alliteration			
onomatopoeia			

5. Craft and Structure What **tone** is created through use of the sound devices in each poem?

Vocabulary

Acquisition and Use Answer each question based on the meaning of the italicized word.

1. What is an example of a child's minor *offense*?

2. Why would you say that something is *nigh*?

3. After Sarah picked up the *thorny* rose, what did she do?

4. Why might you tell someone to go *hence*?

5. What is an example of something that *whirs*?

Word Study Use context and what you know about the **suffix -y** to explain your answer to each question.

1. If a person is *thirsty*, what should he or she do?

2. When might a child's hands be *sticky*?

Word Study

The **suffix -y** forms adjectives that mean "having," "full of," or "characterized by."

Apply It Explain how the suffix -y contributes to the meaning of these words. Consult a dictionary if necessary.

wordy
grouchy
drowsy

Integrated Language Skills

Poetry Collections 7 and 8

Conventions: Predicate Nouns and Predicate Adjectives

Poetry Collection 7

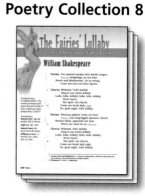

A **subject complement** is a noun, a pronoun, or an adjective that appears with a linking verb and tells something about the subject of the sentence. A **predicate noun** renames or identifies the subject of a sentence. A **predicate adjective** describes the subject of a sentence.

Poetry Collection 8

Predicate Noun	Predicate Adjective
Lucy is an excellent *doctor*.	Marc is *happy* with his classes.
Sparky is a loyal *dog*.	We were *relieved* to hear the news.
They were *spectators* at the event.	Our neighbor became *famous* after winning the contest.

Practice A Identify the predicate noun or predicate adjective in each sentence.

1. I am a kitten lover.
2. I am unsure about whether I want you to take this cat.
3. The stone is hollow.
4. The clowns are very funny.

⊙ Speaking Application Tell a partner about one of the poems you read, using at least one predicate adjective and one predicate noun in your description.

Practice B Identify the predicate noun or predicate adjective in each sentence. Then, rewrite each sentence replacing each predicate noun and predicate adjective.

1. The noisy rattlesnakes are scary.
2. Diana is Chinese American.
3. Diana is proud of her heritage.
4. The white snow is a gift from the sky.

⊙ Writing Application Write a description of the poem you liked best. Use at least two predicate adjectives and two predicate nouns in your description. Circle the predicate adjectives and the predicate nouns you use.

PH WRITING COACH Further instruction and practice are available in *Prentice Hall Writing Coach*.

Writing

 Common Core
State Standards

L.6.1; W.6.4, W.6.6
[For the full wording of the standards, see page 636.]

© **Description** Write a **prose description** inspired by one of the poems you read in Poetry Collection 7 or 8. Read it to the class.

- Select the poem you want to use as your subject.
- Jot down notes that capture the poem's images and feelings as well as your reactions to the poem.
- Use words that appeal to the senses of sight, sound, smell, taste, and touch.
- Write a paragraph that re-creates your impression of the poem.

Grammar Application Be sure to use predicate nouns and predicate adjectives correctly in your prose description.

Writing Workshop: *Work in Progress*

Prewriting for Exposition Choose a set of similar objects to analyze. In the outer circles of a Venn diagram, jot down notes about the differences you see between the objects you have chosen. In the overlapping middle section, write details about how the objects are alike. Save this Venn diagram in your writing portfolio.

Use this prewriting activity to prepare for the **Writing Workshop** on page 668.

Research and Technology

© **Build and Present Knowledge** A **résumé** is a specially formatted summary of information about a person's career and education. Prepare a résumé for one of the poets featured in Poetry Collection 7 or 8.

- Conduct research on the poet. Focus on specific categories such as schools attended, books written, awards won, and related jobs.
- Search online for examples of résumé formats. Look for writers' résumés to use as models.
- Write a résumé to showcase what you have learned about the poet. Organize your information, using the example resumes you found as a guide. Set categories such as *Education*, *Publishing History*, and *Honors*.
- Type your résumé using a word-processing program. Use tabs and settings in the program to correctly format the résumé.

PHLit
Online!
www.PHLitOnline.com
- Interactive graphic organizers
- Grammar tutorial
- Interactive journals

Test Practice: Reading

Paraphrasing

Fiction Selection

Directions: *Read the selection. Then, answer the questions.*

(1) On my visit with Aunt Lilly, she accompanied me to Coney Island in New York. (2) She suggested we ride the enormously popular Ferris wheel. (3) Initially, I enjoyed looking down and seeing the park spread out below us. (4) Higher and higher we rose into the air. (5) By the time we reached the top of the ride, I had squeezed my eyes shut and refused to open them until my feet touched the ground again.

1. An effective paraphrase—
   A. states the main points of the original work and changes point of view
   B. restates the ideas and maintains the point of view of the original work
   C. evaluates the main ideas in the original work
   D. compares the original work to a newer work

2. Which word or phrase might you choose to replace the word *accompanied* in paraphrase of sentence 1?
   A. drove
   B. went with
   C. treated
   D. raced

3. Which is the *best* paraphrase of sentence 4?
   A. We rose higher into the air.
   B. Up and up and up we went.
   C. The ride was designed to rise.
   D. The air was risen into by us.

4. Which is the *best* paraphrase for "I had squeezed my eyes shut," in sentence 5?
   A. I had shut my eyes.
   B. She had closed her eyes.
   C. I had closed my eyes tightly.
   D. She had closed her eyes tightly.

5. What main idea becomes clear through paraphrasing this passage?
   A. Amusement park rides are dangerous.
   B. Some people have never been to Coney Island.
   C. What is fun for some is scary for others.
   D. Relatives often take you to interesting places.

Writing for Assessment

Write a paraphrase of the passage above using words a second-grader could understand. In your paraphrase, try to stay true to the tone of the original text.

Nonfiction Selection

Directions: *Read the selection. Then, answer the questions.*

(1) Steeplechase Park in Coney Island, New York, was perhaps one of the most famous and beloved parks in history. (2) More than a century ago, in 1893, George Tilyou saw a Ferris wheel in Chicago and was immediately fascinated with it. (3) When he attempted to purchase the ride, he discovered that it had already been sold. (4) Undiscouraged, Tilyou hired the services of a steel company to build a Ferris wheel for him. (5) Tilyou's Ferris wheel ride opened in 1894. (6) In 1897, Tilyou opened Steeplechase Park, with its many rides and attractions. (7) Millions of visitors enjoyed the park for sixty-seven years until it closed forever in 1964.

1. Which is the *best* paraphrase of sentence 2?
   A. About one hundred years ago, George Tilyou saw a Ferris wheel and wanted one of his own right away.
   B. Tilyou fell in love with Ferris wheels at first sight.
   C. The first Ferris wheel was shown in Chicago in 1893.
   D. Immediately fascinated with amusement parks rides, George Tilyou decided to buy his own.

2. What synonyms for *famous* and *beloved* might you choose for a paraphrase of sentence 1?
   A. *adored* and *cherished*
   B. *adored* and *liked*
   C. *well-known* and *adored*
   D. *well-known* and *undervalued*

3. Which is the *best* paraphrase of sentence 4?
   A. Tilyou paid to have one built for him.
   B. Tilyou was determined to keep trying.
   C. Determined not to give up, Tilyou hired a company to build a Ferris wheel for him.
   D. A steel company was asked by Tilyou to build him a Ferris wheel.

Writing for Assessment

Connecting Across Texts
Mr. Tilyou and the narrator of the fiction passage have very different opinions of Ferris wheels. Write a short dialogue between Mr. Tilyou and the narrator in which they discuss their views. Paraphrase the information from both selections to create your dialogue.

PHLit
Online!
www.PHLitOnline.com
- Online practice
- Instant feedback

Reading for Information

Analyzing Functional Texts

Policies Document

Application

Common Core State Standards

Reading Informational Text
7. Integrate information presented in different media or formats as well as in words to develop a coherent understanding of a topic or issue.

Language
6. Acquire and use accurately grade-appropriate general academic and domain-specific words and phrases; gather vocabulary knowledge when considering a word or phrase important to comprehension or expression.

Reading Skill: Prepare Applications

When you **prepare applications,** you provide information requested by a group or organization that will make a decision based on that information. Common reasons to fill out an application include getting a public library card, opening a savings account at a bank, joining an athletic league, and getting a job.

Before filling out an application, read all policies and procedures so that you understand the rules and requirements. Then, use a check-list like the one shown to help you prepare your application correctly.

Checklist for Preparing Applications

- ☐ Have I read the entire application and followed all of the instructions step-by-step?
- ☐ Have I written or typed clearly?
- ☐ Have I checked the application for accuracy?
- ☐ Have I signed the application, if a signature is requested?
- ☐ Have I provided any additional materials requested?

Content-Area Vocabulary

These words appear in the selections that follow. You may also encounter them in other content-area texts.

- **eligible** (el´i jə bəl) *adj.* fit to be chosen; properly qualified
- **comply** (kəm plī´) *v.* obey a request or a command
- **violation** (vī´ə lā´ shən) *n.* act of breaking a law, rule, agreement, promise, or contract

Sara Hightower Regional Library System

Get Your Own Library Card

Provided you meet the following requirements we provide adult, youth, and non-resident cards. If you live in Georgia you are eligible for a library card with no fee.

Please note $10 in fines, fees, or lost materials prohibits borrowing on this card or any family member's card.

Adult Cards

Requirements (one or more of the following):

- ◆ Picture ID with current address
- ◆ Picture ID and mail with current address
- ◆ Picture ID from GA State Patrol
- ◆ Previous card on file
- ◆ Non-resident taxpayer must have receipt of payment of property tax paid in Floyd or Polk County
- ◆ Non-resident working in Floyd or Polk must have proof of employment
- ◆ Replacement - $2.00
- ◆ Damaged card - free

Youth Cards

Requirements:

- ◆ Be 0–17 years of age
- ◆ Be accompanied by parent(s)
- ◆ Guardian(s) must take full responsibility for all materials youth checks out
- ◆ Blank forms may be taken home (but parent must come back in with child and present identification or library card)

Non-Resident Cards

Requirements:

- ◆ Picture ID with current address
- ◆ Pay an annual $25 fee for library privileges (families may share one card)

Features:

- information about rules and/or regulations
- a description of requirements for membership or access
- text written for readers wishing to join an organization or use a service

These lists identify the types of documents an applicant must include with his or her application.

Features:
- statements regarding policies and procedures
- spaces for providing required information
- a line for the applicant's signature

SARA HIGHTOWER REGIONAL LIBRARY

CARD APPLICATION

LAST NAME	FIRST NAME	MIDDLE OR MAIDEN NAME
HOME PHONE	WORK OR CELL PHONE (OPTIONAL)	DATE OF BIRTH Year_____ Month_____ Day_____

MAILING ADDRESS				

CITY	COUNTY	STATE	ZIP CODE	Do you live within the city limits? (Circle One) YES NO
RESIDENCE ADDRESS (IF DIFFERENT FROM ABOVE)	CITY	STATE	ZIP CODE	

If you would like to be contacted for holds or overdue items by email, please list your email address.

Email:

I apply for the right to use the Library; agree to comply with all of the rules and regulations, and give immediate notice of any change of address.

I accept financial responsibility for all fines and/or damage to all Library materials, audiovisual materials and equipment beyond normal wear and tear, and I agree to pay the current replacement cost for any materials and/or equipment which is lost or damaged beyond use while checked out on my card. Failure to return items borrowed from a public library is considered a violation of Georgia state law.

Child Internet Permission:

☐ I give permission for my child to use the Internet access at the Library.

☐ I DO NOT give permission for my child to use the Internet access at the Library.

As the parent/guardian of this child 17 years old or younger, I am willing to allow him/her to borrow books from the Public Library. I will take responsibility to make good any damage or loss and overdue charges.

_____
Signature of Parent or Guardian

_____
Print Name

_____
Signature of Applicant

By signing on this line, the applicant agrees to the terms stated above.

_____
Date

Comparing Functional Texts

1. Key Ideas and Details (a) When you **prepare applications,** why is it important to first read the policies and/or instructions? **(b)** What kinds of information appear in the policies document but not on the application form?

Content-Area Vocabulary

2. Using all three vocabulary words from page 656, describe a situation in which someone who did not comply with rules might find him- or herself declared ineligible for a card or might lose library privileges.

Timed Writing

Functional Text: Write a How-to Guide

> **Format**
> The prompt directs you to write a *how-to guide.* Your writing needs to clearly lay out a series of steps.

Based on the texts you have read, write a **how-to guide** explaining the process and requirements for getting and using a library card. Integrate the information in both texts to present a comprehensive explanation of the topic. (20 minutes)

> **Academic Vocabulary**
> When you *integrate* information, you make connections between related ideas to provide a full picture.

5-Minute Planner

Complete these steps before you begin to write:

1. Read the prompt carefully. Look for key words like the ones highlighted to help you understand the assignment.

2. Reread the policies document and application. Jot down a list of steps involved in getting a library card. **TIP** To save time as you jot down your list of steps, use only short phrases, such as "Get application" and "Find proof of address."

3. Review your list to be sure that the steps are arranged in a logical order.

4. Refer to your list as you draft your how-to guide.

Comparing Sensory Language

Sensory language is writing or speech that appeals to one or more of the five senses—hearing, touch, taste, sight, and smell. It creates word pictures or **images** for the reader or listener.

Writers often use sensory language, imagery, and word choice to communicate a **theme** or insight into life. Look at these examples:

- *An icy wind blew in with a crackling moan.* (appeals to touch and hearing; may suggest nature's ferocity)

- *The old wooden stairs were splintery and worn.* (appeals to touch and sight; may suggest the difficulty of age)

The authors of the following selections use rich sensory language in their writing. However, each author uses a different form of writing to express ideas. One is an *essay,* or brief nonfiction work exploring a specific topic. The other is a *poem,* or work built from concise, rich, musical language. The form each writer chooses affects the way he or she communicates a theme.

- Essays use complete sentences, organized into paragraphs, that usually state ideas directly. Each paragraph expresses an idea that relates to the central idea, or theme.
  What essay readers do: The reader must tie the main ideas of paragraphs together to understand the central idea of the essay.

- Poems use fewer words and often communicate themes indirectly, through hints rather than direct statements.
  What poetry readers do: The reader must put images together to puzzle out the theme the poet is suggesting.

As you read these selections, record sensory language in a chart like the one shown. Notice the feelings that the words suggest to you and consider how the writer's choice of imagery, sensory language, and form help to convey a theme.

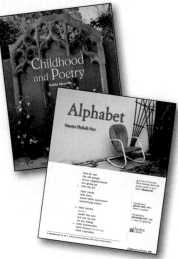

Common Core State Standards

Reading Literature

9. Compare and contrast texts in different forms or genres in terms of their approaches to similar themes and topics.

Writing

2.a. Introduce a topic; organize ideas, concepts, and information, using strategies such as definition, classification, comparison/contrast, and cause/effect. *(Timed Writing)*

Detail	Senses	Feeling

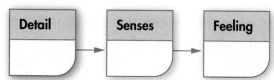
www.PHLitOnline.com

- Vocabulary flashcards
- Interactive journals
- More about the authors
- Selection audio
- Interactive graphic organizers

Writing About the Big Question

Both of these selections describe the emotional associations people build with treasured objects or places. Use this sentence starter to develop your ideas.

We can have wordless **connections** to places and memories because _____.

Meet the Authors

Pablo Neruda (1904–1973)

Author of "Childhood and Poetry"

Neruda's writing career was launched at the age of thirteen, when he began to write articles for a daily newspaper in Temuca, Chile. He published his first book of poems in 1923. By 1968, his complete works of poetry were contained in two volumes consisting of 3,237 pages.

Poet of the People Through his poetry, Neruda spoke out for peace and social justice. He gave a voice to poor workers who could not speak for themselves.

Naomi Shihab Nye (b. 1952)

Author of "Alphabet"

Naomi Shihab Nye was born to a Palestinian father and an American mother. She has lived in the United States and in the Middle East. Her writing—poetry, short stories, and children's books—draws on her heritage and world travel.

History and Home Nye has said she enjoys traveling because of "that luminous sense of being invisible . . . having no long, historical ties, simply being a drifting eye." Still, she says, ". . . after a while, I grow tired of that feeling and want to be somewhere where the trees are my personal friends again."

Childhood
and Poetry

Pablo Neruda

One time, investigating in the backyard of our house in Temuco [Chile] the tiny objects and minuscule beings of my world, I came upon a hole in one of the boards of the fence. I looked through the hole and saw a landscape like that behind our house, uncared for, and wild. I moved back a few steps, because I sensed vaguely that something was about to happen. All of a sudden a hand appeared—a tiny hand of a boy about my own age. By the time I came close again, the hand was gone, and in its place there was a marvelous white sheep.

The sheep's wool was faded. Its wheels had escaped. All of this only made it more authentic. I had never seen such a wonderful sheep. I looked back through the hole but the boy had disappeared. I went into the house and brought out a treasure of my own: a pinecone, opened, full of odor and resin,[1] which I adored. I set it down in the same spot and went off with the sheep.

I never saw either the hand or the boy again. And I have never again seen a sheep like that either. The toy I lost finally in a fire. But even now, in 1954, almost 50 years old, whenever I pass a toy shop, I look furtively into the window, but it's no use. They don't make sheep like that any more.

I have been a lucky man. To feel the intimacy of brothers is a marvelous thing in life. To feel the love of people whom we love is a fire that feeds our life. But to feel the affection that comes from those whom we do not know, from those unknown to us, who are watching over our sleep and solitude, over our dangers and our weaknesses—that is something still greater and more beautiful because it widens out the boundaries of our being, and unites all living things.

That exchange brought home to me for the first time a precious idea: that all of humanity is somehow together. That experience came to me again much later; this time it stood out strikingly against a background of trouble and persecution.

Vocabulary
vaguely (vāg´ lē)
adv. not clearly

Sensory Language
What sensory details help you see how the author feels about the toy sheep?

Vocabulary
furtively (fur´ tiv lē´)
adv. secretly; sneakily

persecution (pur´ sə kyōō´ shən) *n.* harassment meant to cause injury

Reading Check
Where did the author find a toy sheep?

---

1. resin (rez´ in) *n.* sticky substance, like sap, that oozes from some plants and trees.

Spiral Review
Word Choice Which words and phrases in this paragraph contribute to an elevated, or serious and dignified, tone?

It won't surprise you then that I attempted to give something resiny, earthlike, and fragrant in exchange for human brotherhood. Just as I once left the pinecone by the fence, I have since left my words on the door of so many people who were unknown to me, people in prison, or hunted, or alone.

That is the great lesson I learned in my childhood, in the backyard of a lonely house. Maybe it was nothing but a game two boys played who didn't know each other and wanted to pass to the other some good things of life. Yet maybe this small and mysterious exchange of gifts remained inside me also, deep and indestructible, giving my poetry light.

Critical Thinking

Cite textual evidence to support your responses.

1. **Key Ideas and Details (a)** Why does the narrator put a pinecone in the spot where the boy left the sheep? **(b) Draw Conclusions:** How did he feel about receiving the sheep? Support your answer with text details.

2. **Key Ideas and Details (a)** Why does the narrator say he has been a lucky man? **(b) Connect:** How does that sentiment—and bigger idea—relate to the story of the sheep?

3. **Key Ideas and Details (a) Speculate:** What do you think Neruda means when he says, "I have since left my words on the door of so many people"? **(b) Assess:** Can poetry be a gift? Explain.

4. **Integration of Knowledge and Ideas (a)** Was the communication between the two young boys meaningful, even without words? Explain. **(b)** How does Neruda connect his poetry to the sheep? *[Connect to the Big Question: Do we need words to communicate well?]*

Alphabet

Naomi Shihab Nye

One by one
the old people
of our neighborhood
are going up
5   into the air

their yards
still wear
small white narcissus[1]
sweetening winter

10   their stones
glisten
under the sun
but one by one
we are losing
15   their housecoats
their formal phrasings
their cupcakes

Vocabulary
glisten (glis´ ən) v. shine or sparkle
phrasings (frāz´ iŋz) n. ways of speaking

---

1. **narcissus** (när sis´ əs) n. heavily scented bulb plant with white or yellow flowers.

Spiral Review
Structure and Theme
What technique does Nye use in lines 18–19, 20–25, 26–28, and 29–30? How does this contribute to a theme of loss?

Sensory Language
How does the sensory phrase *rusted chairs* help the poet convey an insight about age?

When I string their names
on the long cord

20 when I think how
there is almost no one left
who remembers
what stood in that
brushy spot
25 ninety years ago

when I pass their yards
and the bare peach tree
bends a little
when I see their rusted chairs
30 sitting in the same spots

what will be forgotten
falls over me
like the sky
over our whole neighborhood

35 or the time my plane
circled high above our street
the roof of our house
dotting the tiniest
"i"

Critical Thinking

Cite textual evidence to support your responses.

1. **Key Ideas and Details (a)** What three things belonging to the old people does the speaker say "we are losing"? **(b) Infer:** Why might these three things hold special meaning for the speaker?

2. **Key Ideas and Details** How does the narrator feel about the loss of the old people? Explain your answer.

3. **Integration of Knowledge and Ideas (a)** What words does Nye use to tell you the old people have died? **(b)** Could Nye have conjured the images in the poem without words? Explain. *[Connect to the Big Question: Do we need words to communicate well?]*

Comparing Sensory Language

1. Key Ideas and Details (a) Which use of sensory language in "Childhood and Poetry" creates a vivid image? **(b)** What feelings or memories does the image evoke? **(c)** What theme do these words help the author convey about the power of poetry?

2. Key Ideas and Details (a) Which example of sensory language in "Alphabet" creates a vivid image for you? **(b)** What theme do these words help the author convey about a connection to neighbors and the past?

3. Key Ideas and Details On a chart like the one below, record the sensory images from each selection.

	Sight	Hearing	Touch	Taste	Smell
Childhood and Poetry					
Alphabet					

Timed Writing

Explanatory Text: Essay

In a brief essay, compare how the two authors explore the theme of connections between people. Consider the effect of the form each writer has chosen. **(40 minutes)**

5-Minute Planner

1. Read the prompt carefully and completely.

2. Consider these questions to get you started:

   • Which details concern connections between people?

   • What ideas or messages do those details suggest?

   • Does the writer use imagery to suggest his or her theme? In what way?

   • How does the form—essay or poem—affect the way meaning is conveyed?

3. Create an outline to organize your responses.

4. Reread the prompt, and then draft your essay.

Writing Workshop

 **Common Core State Standards**

Writing

2. Write informative/explanatory texts to examine a topic and convey ideas, concepts, and information through the selection, organization, and analysis of relevant content.

2.a. Introduce a topic; organize ideas, concepts, and information, using strategies such as definition, classification, comparison/contrast, and cause/effect; include formatting, graphics, and multimedia when useful to aiding comprehension.

Write an Informative Text

Exposition: Comparison-and-Contrast Essay

Defining the Form In a **comparison-and-contrast essay,** an author uses factual details to analyze similarities and differences between two or more subjects. You may use elements of a comparison and contrast essay in literary reviews, movie reviews, and comparisons.

Assignment Write a comparison-and-contrast essay in which you examine the similarities and differences between two subjects. Include these elements:

✔ *two or more subjects that are similar and different*

✔ an *organizational pattern* showing similarities and differences

✔ a *thesis*, or purpose, stated in a *strong opening paragraph*

✔ facts, descriptions, and examples that *support your assertions* of how the subjects are alike and how they are different

✔ a *well-supported conclusion* that wraps up your essay

✔ error-free writing, including *correct usage of compound complements*

To preview the criteria on which your comparison-and-contrast essay may be judged, see the rubric on page 675.

 Writing Workshop: *Work in Progress*

Review the work you did on pages 635 and 653.

WRITE GUY
Jeff Anderson, M.Ed.

What Do You Notice?

Descriptive Details

The following sentences are from Russell Baker's essay "Hard As Nails." Read them several times.

I hoped that wasn't the reason because he was the first newspaperman I ever knew, and I wanted him to be the real thing. Hard as nails.

With a partner, evaluate Baker's description. Discuss the ideas and images the words convey. Think of ways you can use descriptive details in your own essay.

Prewriting/Planning Strategies

Choose subjects that are similar and different in important ways. Use one of these strategies to find a topic:

Use a quicklist to choose your topic. Make a three-column chart. In the first column, jot down people, places, and things that are interesting to you. In the second column, list an adjective to describe each one. Then, in the third column, provide a detail about each. Review your list, looking for ideas that it suggests, such as two brands of frozen pizza or two sports you enjoy. Choose a pair of such ideas as your topic.

Use media flip-through to choose your topic. As you read a magazine or watch television, jot down pairs of related subjects such as issues in the news, television programs, or films. Review your notes, and choose the most interesting topic.

Narrow your topic. You could probably write an entire book comparing and contrasting Mexico and Spain. To make your broad topic more manageable, divide it into smaller subtopics. Then, choose one subtopic, such as Mexican and Spanish food, as the focus of your essay.

Organize details in a Venn diagram. Gather facts, descriptions, and examples that you can use to make comparisons and contrasts. Organize your details in a Venn diagram like the one shown. In the two outer sections, record details about how each subject is different. In the overlapping area, record similarities.

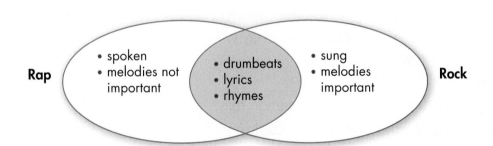

Rap
- spoken
- melodies not important

- drumbeats
- lyrics
- rhymes

- sung
- melodies important

Rock

Drafting Strategies

Follow an appropriate organizational pattern. Decide how you will organize your essay. Choose one of these patterns:

- **Block Method:** Present all the details about one subject first. Then, present all the details about the second subject. This method works well when you are writing about more than two things or are covering many different types of details.

- **Point-by-Point Method:** Discuss each aspect of your subjects in turn. For example, if you are comparing two types of dinosaurs, as shown in the chart, you could first discuss the diet of each one, then the size and mobility, and so on.

Block	Point by Point
1. Introduction	1. Introduction
2. Tyrannosaurus: diet, size, and mobility	2. Diet of tyrannosaurus vs. velociraptor
3. Velociraptor: diet, size, and mobility	3. Size and mobility of tyrannosaurus vs. velociraptor
4. Conclusion	4. Conclusion

Plan your introduction. Begin your essay with a strong introductory paragraph that does the following:

- introduces the subjects you are comparing and contrasting
- identifies the features or aspects you will discuss
- states a main idea about your subjects

Use specific details. The more you can pinpoint the similarities and differences, the more interesting and vibrant your essay will be. Compare the following examples.

> **General:** holiday meal

> **Concrete:** holiday breakfast of omelettes and cinnamon rolls

Use transitions. Use transitional words and phrases to signal that you are discussing either a similarity or a difference. Transitions that show similarity include *similarly, also, both,* and *like.* Transitions that show difference include *by contrast, unlike, on the other hand, but,* and *however.*

 Common Core State Standards

Writing

2.a. Introduce a topic; organize ideas, concepts, and information, using strategies such as definition, classification, comparison/contrast, and cause/effect; include formatting, graphics, and multimedia when useful to aiding comprehension.

2.b. Develop the topic with relevant facts, definitions, concrete details, quotations, or other information and examples.

2.c. Use appropriate transitions to clarify the relationships among ideas and concepts.

Gary Soto On Revising a Comparison

> Gary Soto is the author of "The Drive-In Movies" (p. 46), "Oranges" (p. 556), and "Ode to Family Photographs" (p. 558).

"The first sentence is always the scariest for me."
—Gary Soto

The type of writing known as comparison-and-contrast relates to something that we sometimes do naturally: look at others and compare them to ourselves. Perhaps the earliest example of that kind of comparison occurs between two siblings. In this paragraph, for instance, I compare myself with my older brother, Rick, and come up short, as usual. Below is the first draft with small revisions. I learned to write quickly and then go back to polish the writing.

Professional Model:

from *"My Brother and Me"*

My brother Rick is thirteen months older than I am and has always been at least a head taller. ~~Thus,~~ When we were kids, **therefore,** he cast a **much** larger shadow in the world. I was the tag-along kid who followed Rick because where he went was always cool. He seemed to be a lot stronger. When he shouldered a baseball bat, his swing was smooth. When I tried to do the same thing, I grunted through a strike. ~~Or if~~ **The few times** I did connect, the ball would dribble to~~ward~~ second base for an easy out. When ~~he~~ **Rick** went out for a pass during our front yard football games, the ball dropped sweetly into his outstretched arms. And me? With my mouth open, I juggled the ball ~~like~~ **as if** it ~~was~~ **were** three oranges tossed at me, concentrating intently before I dropped it.

I added *much* to subtly emphasize Rick's literal height advantage and the significant feeling of inferiority that I harbored.

The few times better indicates how poorly I played compared to Rick. I didn't scream, "Man, I was lousy all the time!"—which would have been an overstatement.

Naming my brother reminds the reader that I'm comparing Rick to Gary.

Revising Strategies

Common Core
State Standards

Writing

2.a. Introduce a topic; organize ideas, concepts, and information, using strategies such as definition, classification, comparison/contrast, and cause/effect; include formatting, graphics, and multimedia when useful to aiding comprehension.

2.b. Develop the topic with relevant facts, definitions, concrete details, quotations, or other information and examples.

Language

2.a. Use punctuation to set off nonrestrictive/parenthetical elements.

3. Use knowledge of language and its conventions when writing, speaking, reading, or listening.

Check organization and balance. Your essay should give equal space to each subject and should be organized consistently. To check the balance of your essay, take a moment to reread it.

- Use a red marker to underline or highlight all the features and details related to one subject. Use a yellow marker for the other subject.

- If one color dominates, add more features and details related to the other subject.

- If one color appears in large chunks, followed by other places where the colors seem to alternate, revise your organizational plan. For example, you may have made the mistake of starting with block organization and then switching to point-by-point organization.

Use a chart like the one below to help you figure out what features or details are missing from your essay.

	Subject #1	Subject #2
Point 1		
Point 2		
Point 3		
Point 4		

Check subject-verb agreement. Check your draft for correct subject-verb agreement. Make sure that sentences with singular subjects have singular verbs and that sentences with plural subjects have plural verbs.

Example: Unlike football, hockey **is** played on ice. (singular subject, singular verb)
Both football and hockey **are** fast-paced games. (plural subject, plural verb)

Peer Review

Have a classmate read your draft. Ask your reader to give you feedback about the organization and balance and to show you places where more information would improve your essay.

Revising Choppy Sentences

You can combine choppy sentences in your writing by using **compound complements**.

Understanding Complements **Complements** are words that are needed to complete the meaning of a sentence. Complements are dependent on the type of verb in the sentence. **Action verbs** take direct and indirect objects. **Linking verbs** take predicate adjectives and predicate nouns. (For more on complements, see page 652.)

> **PH** **WRITING COACH**
> Further instruction and practice are available in *Prentice Hall Writing Coach.*

Sentence Combining Using Complements This chart shows how combining complements can eliminate choppy sentences.

Complement	Choppy Sentences	Compound Complements
predicate adjective	Tennis is **fast-paced**. It is **fun**.	Tennis is fast-paced and fun.
predicate noun	One great sport is **tennis**. Another is **badminton.**	Two great sports are tennis and badminton.
direct object	Playing tennis well requires **equipment.** It requires **practice.**	Playing tennis well requires equipment and practice.
indirect object	Tennis gives **me** great exercise. It gives **Ed** exercise.	Tennis gives Ed and me exercise.

Punctuation Tip As you combine sentences, you may want to include interesting details that are not essential—details that may be omitted from a sentence without changing its basic meaning. Set off nonessential elements with commas, dashes, or parentheses.

Example: Tennis is fun—both to watch and to play.

Example: Tennis requires equipment (rackets, balls, and shoes) as well as practice.

Grammar in Your Writing
Reread the draft of your essay aloud. Listen for pairs of choppy sentences that compare or contrast your subjects. Then, use the rules and examples above to make the necessary corrections.

Student Model: Jessica Kursan, Franklin Lakes, NJ

Letters . . . Or Numbers?

Have you ever heard the saying, "You can't compare apples and oranges"? Well, I've done it, so I know it's possible. But I'm not here to compare apples and oranges. I'm here to compare something else: numbers and letters. Numbers and letters have so many unusual properties about them. They are probably two of the most difficult things to compare, but I'll tackle them anyway.

We'll start off with their differences. Numbers and letters have a lot of differences, obviously, but I'm only going to name a few. For one thing, letters are used to spell words, and numbers are used to, well, write numbers! Also, numbers go on forever, while letters stop at z, the twenty-sixth letter. No matter how many letters you have in your alphabet, whether it's Hebrew, Spanish, Greek, or anything else, it will always end somewhere. But numbers just keep right on going.

Also, letters can represent numbers, but not the other way around, unless you're a computer programmer. For example, you could have a list of instructions, and the steps could be labeled A, B, C, instead of 1, 2, 3. But you can't say that 586 spells car.

Numbers and letters have about as many similarities as they do differences, and they are just as simple. For one thing, words and numbers are both used in everyday speech. For example, you could say, "Mr. Johnson, may I walk your dog?" "But I have two dogs." Just the words themselves that you speak are made up of letters and numbers.

In addition, letters and numbers must be precise. This is tough to explain. Letters cannot just be arranged into any order. They have to spell out a real word. For example, you can't just grab a bunch of letters and stick them together because they look pretty. If you had a word like *sdlkhjiower*, what would it mean? Where would you use it? How would you pronounce it? None of these questions has a real answer because *sdlkhjiower* is not a real word. It's the same with numbers. You need to make sure your answer is precise. Also, you can't just say, "Well, I like 14, so I'm going to make 93 and 27 equal 14." That's not how it works. As with letters, you can't put numbers together just because they look good.

As you see, numbers and letters have many differences, but also many similarities. If you take the time, I'm sure you can find even more on your own.

Jessica's introduction grabs the reader's attention and identifies her topics for comparison.

The essay uses a point-by-point organization, first addressing differences and then addressing similarities.

Jessica uses examples to explain each point she presents.

A conclusion sums up Jessica's ideas and invites the reader to consider the topic further.

Editing and Proofreading

Revise to correct errors in grammar, spelling, and punctuation.

Focus on double comparisons. Comparison-and-contrast essays often contain comparative adjectives. Avoid using double comparisons. Never use -*er* or -*est* and *more* or *most* to form the comparative and superlative degrees in the same sentence.

Incorrect: The Great Dane was the *most biggest* dog in the show.

Correct: The Great Dane was the *biggest* dog in the show.

Spiral Review

Earlier in this unit, you learned about **direct and indirect objects** (p. 634) and **predicate nouns and predicate adjectives** (p. 652). Check your essay to be sure that you have used these complements correctly.

Publishing and Presenting

Consider one of the following ways to share your writing:

Create a picture essay. Find photographs to illustrate the similarities and differences you have discussed. Then, share your illustrated essay with classmates.

Make a recording. Practice reading your essay aloud a few times. Read slowly and clearly, emphasizing the strongest points. Then, record it and share it with a group of classmates.

Reflecting on Your Writing

Writer's Journal Jot down your answer to this question:

How has your writing changed your view on your topic?

Rubric for Self-Assessment

Find evidence in your writing to address each category. Then, use the rating scale to grade your work.

Criteria	Rating Scale not very / very
Focus: How clearly does the topic state how two or more subjects are alike and different?	1 2 3 4 5
Organization: How effectively are your points organized?	1 2 3 4 5
Support/Elaboration: How well do you use facts, descriptions, and examples to describe similarities and differences?	1 2 3 4 5
Style: How effective is your language in grabbing readers' interest?	1 2 3 4 5
Conventions: How correct is your grammar, especially your use of compound complements?	1 2 3 4 5

Vocabulary Workshop

Connotation and Denotation

A word's **denotation** is its definition. You can find denotations in a dictionary. The associations or feelings that a word suggests are called its **connotation.** Connotations can be positive, negative, or neutral. For example, the words *inexpensive, cheap,* and *economical* are synonyms that mean "low-priced." However, *cheap* suggests something that is poorly constructed. It has a negative connotation. *Economical* suggests something that saves money. It has a positive connotation. *Inexpensive* does not carry either positive or negative feelings. It has a neutral connotation.

 **Common Core State Standards**

Language

4.c. Consult reference materials, both print and digital, to find the pronunciation of a word or determine or clarify its precise meaning or its part of speech.

5. Demonstrate understanding of figurative language, word relationships, and nuances in word meanings.

5.c. Distinguish among the connotations (associations) of words with similar denotations (definitions).

Word	Denotation	Connotation	Example Sentence
unusual	not common or ordinary	not like others (neutral)	As birds, penguins are *unusual* in that they cannot fly.
exceptional		better than average (positive)	As birds, penguins are *exceptional* in that they cannot fly.
strange		different in an unwelcome way (negative)	As birds, penguins are *strange* in that they cannot fly.

Practice A Each of the following words has a positive, neutral, or negative connotation. For each word pair, identify which word has a more positive connotation. Use a dictionary if you need help checking a word's denotation.

1. bright, dazzling
2. argue, discuss
3. clever, sly
4. challenging, dangerous

Practice B Each of these verbs has a neutral connotation. Provide a synonym for each one using a dictionary or thesaurus if necessary. Then, label each of your synonyms *negative*, *positive*, or *neutral*. Finally, use five of your synonyms to write sentences that clearly show either a positive or a negative connotation.

1. ask
2. quiet
3. get
4. food
5. walk
6. car
7. laugh
8. curiosity
9. write
10. anticipate

Activity Each of the following words has a neutral connotation. Use a thesaurus to locate synonyms for each word. Find a synonym with a positive connotation and one with a negative connotation. Use a graphic organizer like this one to organize your synonyms. The first one has been completed as an example.

brave   warm   house   think   different

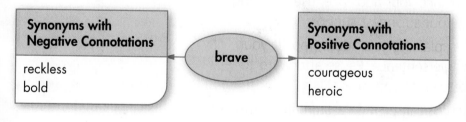

Synonyms with Negative Connotations	brave	Synonyms with Positive Connotations
reckless bold		courageous heroic

Comprehension and Collaboration
Work with a partner to list as many synonyms as you can for the word *talk*. Then classify the synonyms, analyzing their shades of meaning. Divide the words into groups to show whether they have *negative*, *positive*, or *neutral* connotations.

Communications Workshop

Delivering a Persuasive Speech

The purpose of a **persuasive speech** is to get an audience to think or act in a certain way. The speaker presents a claim, or argument, and uses strategies to convince the audience that his or her claim is right. The following strategies will help you deliver an effective persuasive speech.

Learn the Skills

Use these strategies to complete the activity on page 679.

Develop your argument. Select a topic that is important to you and that has two sides. Identify which side you support. Then, list the reasons you support that side.

Organize your ideas. Rank your reasons in order of importance. When you deliver your speech, save your most important reason for last.

Start strong. Begin with a startling comparison or an anecdote that will capture your audience's attention. Then, provide a clear statement of your position.

Make contact. Your audience will hear your presentation only once—make sure they hear each and every word.

- Speak loudly and slowly enough to be heard and understood.
- Make eye contact with your audience.
- Vary your volume and tone to emphasize key points.

Convince listeners. To convince your audience, use speaking strategies that will highlight your strongest support.

Repeat key points. After explaining your ideas, repeat your most important idea in a single sentence. Pause afterward to allow your listeners to process what you say.

Use visuals. A picture or chart can provide a dramatic illustration of a point you are making. Use your visuals to provide relevant evidence.

Common Core State Standards

Speaking and Listening
3. Delineate a speaker's argument and specific claims, distinguishing claims that are supported by reasons and evidence from claims that are not.
4. Present claims and findings, sequencing ideas logically and using pertinent descriptions, facts, and details to accentuate main ideas or themes; use appropriate eye contact, adequate volume, and clear pronunciation.
5. Include multimedia components and visual displays in presentations to clarify information.

Practice the Skills

© Presentation of Knowledge and Ideas Use what you've learned in this workshop to perform the following task.

ACTIVITY: Deliver a Persuasive Speech

Plan and deliver your speech to the class. Ask for feedback on how you can improve your delivery. Use a feedback form like the one shown. Remember the following points when you are delivering your speech:

- Engage listeners
- Make contact
- Repeat key points
- Use visuals

As your classmates deliver their persuasive speeches, consider whether they have been successful in convincing you to accept their views. Use the following form to evaluate their presentations.

Feedback Form for Persuasive Presentation

Rating System

Excellent	Average	Weak
+	✓	−

Content

___ Clear position

___ Clear attitude

___ Logical organization

___ Amount of strong evidence

Respond honestly to these questions:

What was the speaker's main claim?

What impact did the presentation have on you?

What question did the presentation raise for you?

On what point would you challenge the speaker?

Which claims were well supported with reasons and evidence? Which claims were not?

© Comprehension and Collaboration After you have delivered your speech, gather with a small group of classmates and discuss the feedback forms that you filled out for each other. As a group, discuss the class's most successful speeches and examine why they worked so well.

Cumulative Review

I. Reading Literature

Common Core
State Standards

RL.6.4; W.6.3.d; L.6.5, L.6.5.a
[For the full wording of the standards, see the standards chart in the front of your textbook.]

Directions: *Read the poem. Then, answer each question that follows.*

My Shadow
Robert Louis Stevenson

I have a little shadow that goes in and out with me,
And what can be the use of him is more than I can see.
He is very, very like me from the heels up to the head;
And I see him jump before me, when I jump into my bed.

5 The funniest thing about him is the way he likes to grow—
Not at all like proper children, which is always very slow;
For he sometimes shoots up taller like an india-rubber ball,
And he sometimes gets so little that there's none of him at all.

He hasn't got a notion of how children ought to play,
10 And can only make a fool of me in every sort of way.
He stays so close beside me, he's a coward you can see;
I'd think shame to stick to nursie as that shadow sticks to me!

One morning, very early, before the sun was up,
I rose and found the shining dew on every buttercup;
15 But my lazy little shadow, like an <u>errant</u> sleepy-head,
Had stayed at home behind me and was fast asleep in bed.

1. Which type of **figurative language** is used in the last stanza of the poem?

   A. simile
   B. metaphor
   C. personification
   D. figurative language is not used

2. Which of the following is an example of a **simile** in the poem?

   A. "He hasn't got a notion of how children ought to play"
   B. "He's a coward, you can see"
   C. "The funniest thing about him is the way he likes to grow"
   D. "For he sometimes shoots up taller like an india-rubber ball"

3. Which of the following describes the poem's **mood?**

   A. humorous
   B. lonely
   C. angry
   D. joyous

4. The **imagery** in this poem mostly appeals to which of the five senses?

   A. sight
   B. hearing
   C. touch
   D. sound

5. Which **sound device** is used in the phrase "But my lazy little shadow" in line 15?

   A. alliteration
   B. repetition
   C. onomatopoeia
   D. rhyme

6. Which of the following lines could replace line 3 without interrupting the **rhyme scheme?**

   A. He is very, very like me, he enjoys being free
   B. He is very, very like me, his cheeks a fiery red
   C. He is very, very like me from his head down to his heels
   D. He is very, very like me in every single way

7. To what does the speaker compare his shadow?

   A. a buttercup
   B. a child
   C. a nurse
   D. a fool

8. **Vocabulary** Which word is closest in meaning to the underlined word <u>errant?</u>

   A. loving
   B. obedient
   C. straying
   D. horrible

 Timed Writing

9. Write an essay or a poem. Use **personification** to describe a non-living object as though it were alive, the way Stevenson does in "My Shadow."

 GO ON

II. Reading Informational Text

Directions: *Read the application. Then, answer each question that follows.*

Common Core
State Standards

RI.6.2, RI.6.5; L.6.1
[For the full wording of the standards, see the standards chart in the front of your textbook.]

Application for Adventure Summer Camp

About our camp: Our summer program is for *students entering the 7th or 8th grades.* Applicants must be highly motivated and must see the value in helping others. An adventurous spirit is important because we will be hiking, kayaking, and camping. We will also spend time doing volunteer work in the community.

To apply for our camp: Answer the following questions. Type or print neatly. Provide one brief letter of reference from an adult who is not your parent. A second reference is optional.

No applications will be accepted after March 31.

(1) Name: _____   **(2)** Age: _____   **(3)** Entering grade: _____

(4) Address: _____

(5) Phone number: _____

(6) Hobbies: _____

(7) Why do you want to attend Adventure Camp? _____

(8) What skills make you a good **candidate** for Adventure Camp?

_____

(9) What type(s) of volunteer work would interest you most?

_____

---

1. Why does some information in the application appear in **italics?**

  A. to make the application easier to read

  B. to show that the information is important

  C. to make the application more interesting to look at

  D. to show that people do not have to read this information

2. What documents *must* an applicant send?

  A. application

  B. application and letter of reference

  C. application and two letters of reference

  D. application and birth certificate

3. All of the following could prevent an applicant from being accepted to the camp, *except*—

  A. The applicant is entering 6th grade.

  B. The applicant did not type her answers on the application.

  C. The applicant did not include any letters of reference.

  D. The applicant mailed her application on April 3.

III. Writing and Language Conventions

Directions: *Read the passage. Then, answer each question that follows.*

(1) Unfortunatly, six band students recently quit the band because they could not afford to buy or rent needed instruments. (2) Our school band is in desperate need of new instruments. (3) If everyone contributed a mere $5, we could purchase those six instruments. (4) Most of us spend $5 a week on snacks after school anyway. (5) We should stop buying snacks for just one week. (6) Music enriches the whole school, not just band students. (7) We must all work together to solve this problem.

1. Where should sentence 2 be placed to give better emphasis to the **main focus?**
   A. Before sentence 1
   B. Before sentence 4
   C. Before sentence 5
   D. Before sentence 7

2. Which of these sentences could *best* be added to help clarify the **problem?**
   A. The school usually supplies the instruments, but this year money is short.
   B. The students are unable to earn the money themselves.
   C. There are free snacks at school anyway.
   D. The band plays at a lot of school functions.

3. Which of the following **compound subjects** could best be substituted to clarify the subject in sentence 1?
   A. Four saxophone students
   B. Four saxophones and two oboes
   C. Three artists and three students
   D. Four saxophone students and two oboe students

4. How could the writer revise sentence 5 to make it an **imperative sentence?**
   A. Is it not possible to stop buying snacks for just one week?
   B. We will stop buying snacks for one week.
   C. We can stop buying snacks!
   D. Stop buying snacks for one week.

5. How could the writer revise sentence 7 to make it an **interrogative sentence?**
   A. We must work to solve this problem!
   B. Work together to solve this problem.
   C. Shouldn't we all work together to solve this problem?
   D. Working on this problem together will solve this problem.

6. Which word is misspelled in sentence 1?
   A. unfortunatly
   B. recently
   C. because
   D. afford

Performance Tasks

Directions: *Follow the instructions to complete the tasks below as required by your teacher.*

As you work on each task, incorporate both general academic vocabulary and literary terms you learned in this unit.

**Common Core
State Standards**

RL.6.4, RL.6.5, RL.6.7, RL.6.9; W.6.2, W.6.2.e, W.6.9.a; SL.6.1, SL.6.4, SL.6.5; L.6.5.a

[For the full wording of the standards, see the standards chart in the front of your textbook.]

Writing

Task 1: Literature [RL.6.4; L.6.5.a]

Analyze Figurative Language

Write an essay in which you analyze the figurative language used in a poem from this unit.

- Choose a poem that includes several examples of figurative language, such as simile, metaphor, or personification.

- Determine the meanings of the figurative phrases as they are used in the context of the poem. Analyze their impact on meaning and tone.

- If possible, use a word-processing program to type your essay and prepare it for publication.

Task 2: Literature [RL.6.5; W.6.2.e]

Analyze a Poem's Structure

Write an essay in which you analyze the structure of a poem from this unit.

- Choose a poem with three or more stanzas. Select one stanza to discuss.

- Explain which poem and stanza you chose to analyze.

- Discuss how your chosen stanza adds to the development of the poem. Explain specific images, figures of speech, emotions, or ideas it introduces that are important to the poem as a whole.

- Explain specific ways in which the stanza advances the key insight or theme of the poem.

- Establish and maintain a formal style. Choose words and phrases that convey your ideas precisely.

Task 3: Literature [RL.6.9; W.6.2]

Compare Themes in Different Genres

Write an essay in which you compare and contrast two works from this unit that represent different genres, or forms, but explore similar topics and themes.

- Explain which works you chose, the genre of each, and the topic they share.

- Briefly state the theme or meaning each work expresses.

- Identify similarities and differences in the way each work expresses its theme.

- Describe specific reasons that the two works express the themes differently. Consider whether the genre of the work is the reason for these differences.

- Support your ideas by citing specific details from both works.

Speaking and Listening

©Task 4: Literature [RL.6.4; SL.6.4]

Analyze Connotation

Give an oral presentation in which you analyze connotative meanings and their impact on tone in a poem from this unit.

- Determine the meanings of words and phrases as they are used in the poem. Explain their connotations—the shades of meaning they express.

- Analyze the impact that the connotative meanings of the words have on the tone of the poem. Explain how they affect the poem's overall meaning.

- Discuss how the tone of the poem would be affected if the poet had chosen words with similar definitions but different connotations.

- Present your ideas in logical order. Use details from the text to support your ideas.

©Task 5: Literature [RL.6.4; SL.6.5]

Analyze Sound Devices

Create a multimedia presentation in which you use visual and audio to enhance the sound devices used in a poem from this unit.

- Determine the purpose of the sound devices in your chosen poem, using evidence from the text to support your analysis.

- Prepare a multimedia presentation of the poem. Choose visuals, music, sound effects, or video that supports the author's use of sound devices in the poem and enhance your oral reading of it.

- Follow your oral reading with an explanation of your multimedia choices. Accurately use academic vocabulary in your explanation.

©Task 6: Literature [RL.6.7; SL.6.1, SL.6.4]

Compare Reading to Listening

Deliver an oral presentation in which you compare the experience of reading a poem from this unit with that of hearing the poem read aloud.

- With a partner, identify a poem you will discuss.

- Read the poem, and then listen to a recording of it. If no recording of the poem exists, read the poem aloud to each other.

- Take notes about your experiences, contrasting what you imagine and feel when reading with what you imagine and feel when listening.

- Organize and present your observations, sequencing them logically. Pronounce words clearly, both when speaking your own words and when reading the poem.

Do we need words to communicate well?

At the beginning of Unit 4, you wrote a response to the Big Question. Now that you have completed the unit, write a new response. Discuss how your initial ideas have expanded or changed. Cite specific examples from the literature in this unit, from other subject areas, and from your own life to support your ideas. Use Big Question vocabulary words (see p. 549) in your response.

Featured Titles

In this unit, you have read a wide variety of poems by many different poets. Continue to read on your own. Select works that you enjoy, but challenge yourself to explore new poets and works of increasing depth and complexity. The titles suggested below will help you get started.

Literature

The Fields of Praise: New and Selected Poems

by Marilyn Nelson
Louisiana State University Press, 1997

In this collection of **poems,** Nelson describes the struggles as well as the joys of the African American experience. In powerful language, she writes about faith, love, tragedy, heartbreak, and pride.

Fearless Fernie

by Gary Soto

This series of humorous **poems** tells the story of two sixth-grade boys who are very different but share the common bond of a lifelong friendship.

Acolytes

by Nikki Giovanni
William Morrow, 2007   **EXEMPLAR TEXT** ©

This inspiring collection of **poems** urges readers to remember the struggle for freedom, justice, and civil rights and honors men and women who have sacrificed to achieve equality.

Code Talker

by Joseph Bruchac
Speak, 2006

This **novel** tells the story of Ned Bega, who joins the Marines during World War II. He becomes one of the "code talkers," Navajo soldiers who used their own language as an unbreakable code and saved many American lives.

Informational Texts

A Short Walk Around the Pyramids and through the World of Art

by Philip Isaacson
Knopf Books for Young Readers   **EXEMPLAR TEXT** ©

This **nonfiction art book** takes the reader on a journey through the art world. More than 70 pictures of paintings, crafts, sculptures, architecture, and other works of art accompany Isaacson's lively discussion of art.

Restless Spirit: The Life and Work of Dorothea Lange

by Elizabeth Partridge

Dorothea Lange recorded a **photographic history** of people struggling through some of the most difficult periods in American history. The photographs in this book communicate a stirring portrait of ordinary people and of Lange herself.

Preparing to Read Complex Texts

Attentive Reading As you read on your own, ask yourself questions about the text. The questions shown below and others that you ask as you read will help you learn and enjoy literature even more.

Common Core State Standards

Reading Literature/Informational Text
10. By the end of the year, read and comprehend literature, including stories, dramas, and poems, and literary nonfiction in the grades 6–8 text complexity band proficiently, with scaffolding as needed at the high end of the range.

When reading poetry, ask yourself...

- Who is the speaker of the poem? What kind of person does the speaker seem to be? How do I know?
- What is the poem about?
- If the poem is telling a story, who are the characters, and what happens to them?
- Does any one line or section state the poem's theme, or meaning, directly? If so, what is that line or section?
- If there is no direct statement of a theme, what details help me to see the poem's deeper meaning?

Ⓒ Key Ideas and Details

- How does the poem look on the page? Is it long and rambling or short and concise? Does it have long or short lines?
- Does the poem have a formal structure, or is it free verse?
- How does the form affect how I read the poem?
- How many stanzas form this poem? What does each stanza tell me?
- Do I notice repetition, rhyme, or meter? Do I notice other sound effects? How do these elements affect how I read the poem?
- Even if I do not understand every word, do I like the way the poem sounds? Why or why not?
- Do any of the poet's word choices seem especially interesting or unusual? Why?
- What images do I notice? Do they create clear word-pictures in my mind? Why or why not?
- Would I like to read this poem aloud? Why or why not?

Ⓒ Craft and Structure

- Has the poem helped me understand its subject in a new way? If so, how?
- Does the poem remind me of others I have read? If so, how?
- In what ways is the poem different from others I have read?
- What information, ideas, or insights have I gained from reading this poem?
- Do I find the poem moving, funny, or mysterious? How does the poem make me feel?
- Would I like to read more poems by this poet? Why or why not?

Ⓒ Integration of Ideas

THE BIG **?** How do we decide *who* we are?

PHLit Online!
www.PHLitOnline.com

Hear It!
- Selection summary audio
- Selection audio
- BQ Tunes

See It!
- Author videos
- Big Question video
- Get Connected videos
- Background videos
- More about the authors
- Illustrated vocabulary words
- Vocabulary flashcards

Do It!
- Interactive journals
- Interactive graphic organizers
- Grammar tutorials
- Interactive vocabulary games
- Test practice

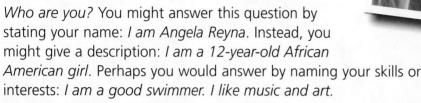
How do we decide *who* we are?

Who are you? You might answer this question by stating your name: *I am Angela Reyna*. Instead, you might give a description: *I am a 12-year-old African American girl*. Perhaps you would answer by naming your skills or interests: *I am a good swimmer. I like music and art.*

Many qualities make up who you are: your personality, your values, your hopes and dreams, and your experiences. Some of us may look alike, or we may have similar beliefs. In the end, however, each of us is unique.

How do we come to know exactly who we are?

Exploring the Big Question

© **Collaboration: One-on-One Discussion** Start thinking about the Big Question by identifying ways that help us learn about ourselves. Make a list of different situations that have revealed something about you or about another person. Make notes about what you can learn about yourself in each of the following situations:

- being in a contest or other type of competition
- making a mistake
- going to an unfamiliar place
- listening to what others say about you
- getting to know someone who is very different from you
- facing a difficult challenge

Share your examples with a partner. Talk about what each situation can teach a person about himself or herself. Use the Big Question Vocabulary in your discussion.

Connecting to the Literature Each reading in this unit will give you additional insight into the Big Question.

PHLit Online!
www.PHLitOnline.com
- Big Question video
- Illustrated vocabulary words
- Interactive vocabulary games
- BQ Tunes

Learning Big Question Vocabulary

© **Acquire and Use Academic Vocabulary** Academic vocabulary is the language you encounter in textbooks and on standardized tests. Review the definitions of these academic vocabulary words.

diverse (də vʉrs´) *adj.* many and different; from different backgrounds

perspective (pər spek´ tiv) *n.* point of view

reaction (rē´ ak´ shən) *n.* response to something said or done

reflect (ri flekt´) *v.* think or wonder about

respond (ri spänd´) *v.* answer or reply

similar (sim´ ə lər) *adj.* alike

unique (yo͞o nēk´) *adj.* one of a kind

Use these words as you complete Big Question activities in this unit that involve reading, writing, speaking, and listening.

© **Gather Vocabulary Knowledge** Additional Big Question words are listed below. Categorize the words by deciding whether you know each one well, know it a little bit, or do not know it at all.

appearance	expectations	personality
conscious	ideals	trend
custom	individuality	

Then, do the following:

1. Write the definitions of the words you know.
2. Consult a dictionary to confirm the meanings of the words whose definitions you wrote down. Revise your definitions if necessary.
3. Using a print or an online dictionary, look up the meanings of the words you are unsure of or do not know. Then, write the meanings.
4. Use all of the words in a brief paragraph about expressing individuality.

Common Core State Standards

Speaking and Listening
1. Engage effectively in a range of collaborative discussions with diverse partners on grade 6 topics, texts, and issues, building on others' ideas and expressing their own clearly.

Language
6. Acquire and use accurately grade-appropriate general academic and domain-specific words and phrases; gather vocabulary knowledge when considering a word or phrase important to comprehension or expression.

Elements of Drama

A drama is a story written to be performed by actors.

A **drama,** or play, is a story that is performed for an audience. You can read dramas, but they are really meant to be seen and heard. You can watch dramas on stage or on television, movie screens, or computer monitors.

In a drama, you meet **characters,** or fictional people. You watch their lives unfold in a particular **setting,** or time and place. Characters face a **conflict,** or problem, that moves them to act and react. The events that result form the **plot,** a series of actions that build to a **climax.** The climax is the plot's moment of greatest tension. After the climax, the action winds down. The conflict is settled—or left unsettled— in the **resolution,** or ending. Like most literary works, a drama expresses a **theme,** or insight about life.

The writer of a drama is called a **playwright** or **dramatist.** The written text of a drama is called a **script.** The script includes **dialogue,** or the words the actors speak. It may also include **stage directions** that describe the characters and setting.

Full-length dramas are divided into shorter sections, called **acts.** Each act may contain several **scenes.** A scene is like a little drama all by itself. It presents continuous action in a specific situation.

Elements of Drama	
Stage Directions	Stage directions are the playwright's instructions about how to perform the drama. They may include • details about the way the stage and characters should look; • instructions about where and how actors should move and speak; • details about other staging elements, such as scenery, lighting, sound, and costumes.
Dialogue	Conversation between characters is called dialogue. Through it, audiences learn about plot events and characters' feelings and actions.
Sets/Scenery	Sets and scenery are the constructions onstage that suggest the time and place of the action.
Props	Props are moveable items, such as books, coffee mugs, or newspapers. Actors use props to make their actions look realistic.
Acts and Scenes	Acts and scenes are units of action in dramas. Full-length dramas may have several acts, and each act may have several scenes.

Forms of Drama: Past and Present

The oldest surviving dramas come from the ancient Greeks, who divided drama into two types:

- **Comedies** have happy endings. Their humor often comes out of the dialogue and situations. Like modern comedies, ancient comedies entertained but sometimes also expressed serious ideas about human nature.
- **Tragedies** show the downfall of a great person, known as the **tragic hero,** brought down by a fault, or **tragic flaw,** in his or her nature. The ancient tragedies were meant to teach and inspire with stories of legendary figures.

The experience of watching a play in ancient Greece was different from that of today. In ancient Greece, plays were performed in huge, open theaters. Thousands of spectators sat on stone benches that formed a semicircle around the performance space. The actors were all men, and some played more than one role. Each actor wore a mask to indicate his character's gender, age, and social position.

The next important era for drama took place in England in the late 1500s and early 1600s. Then, many audiences attended plays by William Shakespeare— perhaps the greatest playwright of all time. They sat in an open-air wooden playhouse, not as large as the Greek theater. All characters were still played by men, but they used makeup instead of masks.

Shakespeare and other playwrights of his time wrote tragedies that followed the Greek form, as well as comedies with romantic themes.

Today, modern dramas present serious subjects that mix both comedy and tragedy. We can watch a drama with live actors on a stage or watch a performance in a movie theater. We can even watch dramas alone at home in front of our televisions or computers.

In This Section

Elements of Drama

Analyzing Dramatic Elements

Close Read: Story Development in Drama
- Model Text
- Practice Text

After You Read

 Common Core State Standards

RL.6.3, RL.6.5
[For the full wording of the standards, see the standards chart in the front of your textbook.]

Live Theater	Film/Movies	Television Drama	Radio Play
• performed live for an audience • follows a written play **script** • uses scenery and lighting for effect	• recorded on film or digitally and shown in theaters • follows a script called a **screenplay** • uses camera angles for effect	• recorded or performed live • follows a script called a **teleplay** • like film, uses camera angles for effect	• recorded or performed live • follows a script called a **radio play** • uses dialogue and sound effects

Analyzing Dramatic Elements

Most dramas focus on characters in conflict in order to express a theme.

Common Core
State Standards

Reading Literature 3. Describe how a particular story's or drama's plot unfolds in a series of episodes as well as how the characters respond or change as the plot moves toward a resolution.

Reading Literature 5. Analyze how a particular sentence, chapter, scene, or stanza fits into the overall structure of a text and contributes to the development of the theme, setting, or plot.

The action in a drama is conveyed through the spoken dialogue and physical actions of its characters. A drama's plot may be full of twists and turns and ups and downs. When you read or watch a drama, you get to go along for the ride.

Keys to Character While some plays feature a narrator who gives the audience important information, most plays do not. Instead, audiences learn about characters from what they say. Playwrights use dialogue to reveal their characters in several ways:

- Characters may speak their inner thoughts, feelings, and conflicts out loud.
- Conversations among characters can reveal their feelings and personality traits.
- Characters may talk about each other. The reader or audience must decide whether to accept such comments as truth.

Most dramatic dialogue takes the form of conversations between or among characters. Sometimes, however, one character holds the spotlight with a special kind of speech.

- A **monologue** is a long, uninterrupted speech spoken by a

character to other characters who remain silent. In a monologue, a character may reveal hidden feelings or may persuade another character to take action.

- A **soliloquy** is a speech a character delivers while alone. Sometimes the character speaks to the audience; sometimes only to himself or herself. Through a soliloquy, a character might explore an important question or make a decision.
- An **aside** is a comment made by a character to the audience. Other characters may be present, but an aside is not meant to be heard by anyone but the audience.

When you read a play, stage directions can provide important information about a character's feelings and personality. For example, in the following example, the stage direction (printed in italics) reveals that the character is tired and perhaps frustrated.

Example:

Angela: *(pausing wearily before speaking)* What do you mean by that?

Great plays feature interesting characters whose stories hold the audience or reader's attention. The best dramas feature **complex characters** who have strengths and weaknesses and experience a variety of emotions. Complex characters are often pulled in different directions because of the difficult situations that they face.

Conflict and Plot The problems, or conflicts, characters face are at the core of any drama. As characters respond to challenges and make decisions about how to solve conflicts, their feelings and behavior often change. These changes help move the plot from one event to another.

In drama, as in other types of literature, there are two main types of conflict. **External conflict** occurs between a character and an outside force, such as nature, society, or another character. **Internal conflict** occurs within the mind of a character. It arises when a character is torn between opposing feelings.

Type of Conflict	Examples
EXTERNAL CONFLICT *A character struggles against an outside force.*	• <u>Against nature</u>: A couple tries to climb a mountain. • <u>Against society</u>: A woman opposes a new city law. • <u>Against another character</u>: Two scientists claim the same discovery.
INTERNAL CONFLICT *A character struggles against himself or herself.*	• An artist seeks fame but compromises her ideals. • A man has to choose between telling the truth and protecting his brother.

Scenes, or Episodes The events of a play are often presented in separate, connected episodes, or scenes. Every scene has a purpose. It may introduce or change the setting. For example, a scene at a train station may be followed by a scene on a train. A scene may also introduce a character, show a character making a decision, or begin an action that will lead to other actions.

Theme in Drama All the elements of a drama work together to create an illusion of reality, which is known as the *dramatic effect*. Dramatic elements also work to express a **theme,** or central idea about life. The conflict, characters' actions, and the resolution, or outcome of the story, all point to a play's theme. Viewers or readers may interpret that theme in different ways. A strong interpretation will take into account all the play's elements.

Dramatic Subject	Possible Theme
A young girl learns that she can have a full life in spite of her blindness.	With determination, we can overcome limitations.
War forces a family to flee their home and move to a new country.	Political conflicts disrupt innocent people's lives. Still, people survive.

The better a drama is, the more audiences connect with the characters, their situation, and the play's theme. When it is most powerful and effective, drama allows audiences to make discoveries about their own lives by identifying with the imagined lives of others.

Close Read: Story Development in Drama

The elements of a drama help develop the story it presents.

As you read or watch a play, pay attention to the elements that help you understand the characters' feelings, thoughts, and behavior. Think about how each moment of the drama adds to your understanding of the conflict characters face. Also, notice how each scene adds important new information about the setting, plot, or theme.

Clues to Story Development in Drama

Plot

Plot is the sequence of events in a play. Look for details that reveal

- characters' conflicts, both external and internal;
- plot structure: points at which conflicts are introduced (exposition), developed (rising action), reach their greatest tension (climax), begin to be settled (falling action), and end (resolution).

Scenes

Each episode, or scene, is there for a reason. As you read, think about how each scene fits into the play as a whole. Consider whether a scene

- introduces a new character;
- begins or ends an action;
- introduces or changes a setting;
- changes the mood.

Characters and Conflict

Characters' conflicts can be external or internal. As you read, notice

- stage directions or dialogue that describes a character's feelings of anger or frustration;
- challenging situations or environments;

Stage Directions

Stage directions give information about characters and also tell how the drama is to be performed. As you read, pay attention to

- descriptions of how the stage should look;
- suggestions for lighting and sound effects;
- instructions about characters' movements, facial expressions, or tones of voice.

Setting

Setting is the time and place in which the action occurs. As you read, consider how the setting affects the characters and conflicts. Look for

- physical details in the setting that create a mood, atmosphere, or feeling;
- elements of the setting that cause conflicts or otherwise affect characters.

Dialogue

Dialogue carries the action and provides clues to characters' personalities. Look for dialogue that

- reveals a character's thoughts and feelings;
- suggests previous experiences;
- expresses external and internal conflicts;
- takes the form of a special speech, such as an aside, a monologue, or a soliloquy.

Model

About the Text This excerpt is from the play *Brighton Beach Memoirs* by Neil Simon. Simon is one of the world's most successful writers. His plays have been produced all over the world. Many, including *Brighton Beach Memoirs,* have been made into major feature films. One of his plays, *The Odd Couple,* was first a Broadway hit, then a popular movie, and finally the basis of a long-running TV series during the 1970s. Simon combines both comic and serious elements to tell engaging stories about funny, imperfect characters.

---

from *Brighton Beach Memoirs* by Neil Simon

STAN. *[half whisper]* Hey! Eugie!

EUGENE. Hi, Stan! *[to audience]* My brother, Stan. He's okay. You'll like him. *[to STAN]* What are you doing home so early?

STAN. *[looks around, lowers his voice]* Is Pop home yet?

EUGENE. No . . . Did you ask about the tickets?

STAN. What tickets?

EUGENE. For the Yankee game. You said your boss knew this guy who could get passes. You didn't ask him?

STAN. Me and my boss had other things to talk about. *[He sits on steps, his head down, almost in tears]* I'm in trouble, Eug. I mean really big trouble.

EUGENE. *[to audience]* This really shocked me. Because Stan is the kind of guy who could talk himself out of *any* kind of trouble. *[to STAN]* What kind of trouble?

STAN. . . . I got fired today!

EUGENE. *[shocked]* Fired? . . . You mean for good?

STAN. You don't get fired temporarily. It's permanent. It's a lifetime firing.

Dialogue Eugene introduces his brother, Stan, in an aside to the audience.

Stage Directions The stage directions describing Stan's body language give important clues about his feelings.

Characters and Conflict Stan's announcement introduces at least two external conflicts—one between Stan and his former boss, and another between Stan and his father.

Independent Practice

About the Text Joseph Bruchac (b. 1942), a professional storyteller, draws inspiration from the traditions of his ancestors, the Native American Abenaki people. *Gluskabe and Old Man Winter* is Bruchac's dramatization of a folk tale about a powerful hero, Gluskabe, and his wise old grandmother. Both characters frequently appear in Abenaki tales.

Gluskabe and Old Man Winter by Joseph Bruchac

CHARACTERS

Speaking Roles:	Non-speaking Roles:
NARRATOR	SUN
GLUSKABE	FLOWERS
GRANDMOTHER WOODCHUCK	PLANTS
HUMAN BEING	
OLD MAN WINTER	
FOUR OR MORE SUMMER LAND PEOPLE, including the leader	
FOUR CROWS	

Scene I: Gluskabe and Grandmother Woodchuck's Wigwam

GLUSKABE *and* GRANDMOTHER WOODCHUCK *sit inside with their blankets over their shoulders.*

NARRATOR: Long ago Gluskabe (gloo-SKAH-bey) lived with his grandmother, Woodchuck, who was old and very wise. Gluskabe's job was to help the people.

GLUSKABE: It is very cold this winter, Grandmother.

GRANDMOTHER WOODCHUCK: *Ni ya yo* (nee yah yo), Grandson. You are right!

GLUSKABE: The snow is very deep, Grandmother.

GRANDMOTHER WOODCHUCK: *Ni ya yo,* Grandson.

GLUSKABE: It has been winter for a very long time, Grandmother.

GRANDMOTHER WOODCHUCK: Ni ya yo, Grandson. But look, here comes one of those human beings who are our friends.

HUMAN BEING: *Kwai, Kwai, nidobak* (kwy kwy nee-DOH-bahk). Hello, my friends.

Setting What do you learn about the setting from the scene description and the stage direction?

Scenes What information does this scene provide so far about the characters and conflict they face?

Gluskabe and **Grandmother Woodchuck:** *Kwai, Kwai, nidoba* (kwy kwy nee-DOH-bah).

Human Being: Gluskabe, I have been sent by the other human beings to ask you for help. This winter has been too long. If it does not end soon, we will all die.

Gluskabe: I will do what I can. I will go to the wigwam of Old Man Winter. He has stayed here too long. I will ask him to go back to his home in the Winter Land to the north.

Grandmother Woodchuck: Be careful, Gluskabe.

Gluskabe: Don't worry, Grandmother. Winter cannot beat me.

Scene II: The Wigwam of Old Man Winter

Old Man Winter *sits in his wigwam, "warming" his hands over his fire made of ice. The four balls of summer are on one side of the stage.* **Gluskabe** *enters stage carrying his bag and stands to the side of the wigwam door. He taps on the wigwam.*

Old Man Winter: Who is there!

Gluskabe: It is Gluskabe.

Old Man Winter: Ah, come inside and sit by my fire.

Gluskabe *enters the wigwam.*

Gluskabe: The people are suffering. You must go back to your home in the Winter Land.

Old Man Winter: Oh, I must, eh? But tell me, do you like my fire?

Gluskabe: I do not like your fire. Your fire is not warm. It is cold.

Old Man Winter: Yes, my fire is made of ice. And so are you!

Old Man Winter *throws his white sheet over* **Gluskabe.** **Gluskabe** *falls down.* **Old Man Winter** *stands up.*

Old Man Winter: No one can defeat me!

Old Man Winter *pulls* **Gluskabe** *out of the lodge. Then he goes back inside and closes the door flap. The Sun comes out and shines on* **Gluskabe.** **Gluskabe** *sits up and looks at the Sun.*

Gluskabe: Ah, that was a good nap! But I am not going into Old Man Winter's lodge again until I talk with my grandmother.

Characters and Conflict What conflict is revealed by the exchange between Gluskabe and Old Man Winter? Is the conflict internal or external?

Stage Directions What actions are described in this stage direction? How might these actions affect Gluskabe's conflict with Old Man Winter?

Practice continued

GLUSKABE begins walking across the stage toward the four balls. GRANDMOTHER WOODCHUCK enters.

GRANDMOTHER WOODCHUCK: It is still winter, Gluskabe! Did Old Man Winter refuse to speak to you?

GLUSKABE: We spoke, but he did not listen. I will speak to him again; and I will make him listen. But tell me, Grandmother, where does the warm weather come from?

GRANDMOTHER WOODCHUCK: It is kept in the Summer Land.

GLUSKABE: I will go there and bring summer back here.

GRANDMOTHER WOODCHUCK: Grandson, the Summer Land people are strange people. Each of them has one eye. They are also greedy. They do not want to share the warm weather. It will be dangerous.

GLUSKABE: Why will it be dangerous?

GRANDMOTHER WOODCHUCK: The Summer Land people keep the summer in a big pot. They dance around it. Four giant crows guard the pot full of summer. Whenever a stranger tries to steal summer, those crows fly down and pull off his head!

GLUSKABE: Grandmother, I will go to the summer land. I will cover up one eye and look like the people there. And I will take these four balls of sinew with me.

GLUSKABE picks up the four balls, places them in his bag, and puts the bag over his shoulder.

Scene III: The Summer Land Village

The SUMMER LAND PEOPLE are dancing around the pot full of summer. They are singing a snake dance song, following their leader, who shakes a rattle in one hand. FOUR CROWS stand guard around the pot as the people dance.

SUMMER LAND PEOPLE: *Wee gai wah neh* (wee guy wah ney),

Wee gai wah neh,

Wee gai wah neh, wee gai wah neh,

Wee gai wah neh, wee gai wah neh,

Wee gai wah neh.

Plot What new complication to the plot does Grandmother Woodchuck's speech describe? How do you think Gluskabe will deal with it?

GLUSKABE enters, wearing an eye patch and carrying his bag with the balls in it.

GLUSKABE: *Kwai, kwai, nidobak!* Hello, my friends.

Everyone stops dancing. They gather around GLUSKABE.

LEADER OF THE SUMMER LAND PEOPLE: Who are you?

GLUSKABE: I am not a stranger. I am one of you. See, I have one eye.

SECOND SUMMER LAND PERSON: I do not remember you.

GLUSKABE: I have been gone a long time.

THIRD SUMMER LAND PERSON: He does have only one eye.

FOURTH SUMMER LAND PERSON: Let's welcome him back. Come join in our snake dance.

The singing and dancing begin again: "Wee gai wah neh," etc. GLUSKABE is at the end of the line as the dancers circle the pot full of summer. When GLUSKABE is close enough, he reaches in, grabs one of the summersticks, and breaks away, running back and forth.

LEADER OF THE SUMMER LAND PEOPLE: He has taken one of our summersticks!

SECOND SUMMER LAND PERSON: Someone stop him!

THIRD SUMMER LAND PERSON: Crows, catch him!

FOURTH SUMMER LAND PERSON: Pull off his head!

The CROWS swoop after GLUSKABE. He reaches into his pouch and pulls out one of the balls. As each CROW comes up to him, he ducks his head down and holds up the ball. The Crow grabs the ball. GLUSKABE keeps running, and pulls out another ball, repeating his actions until each of the Crows has grabbed a ball.

FIRST CROW: *Gah-gah!* I have his head.

SECOND CROW: *Gah-gah!* No, I have his head!

THIRD CROW: *Gah-gah!* Look, I have his head!

FOURTH CROW: *Gah-gah!* No, look—I have it too!

LEADER OF THE SUMMER LAND PEOPLE: How many heads did that stranger have?

Dialogue and Speeches What does this conversation reveal about the Summer Land People, in contrast to Gluskabe? What details helped you answer?

Practice continued

SECOND SUMMER LAND PERSON: He has tricked us. He got away.

Scene IV: *The Wigwam of Old Man Winter*

GLUSKABE *walks up to* ***OLD MAN WINTER'S*** *wigwam. He holds the summerstick in his hand and taps on the door.*

OLD MAN WINTER: Who is there!

GLUSKABE: It is Gluskabe.

OLD MAN WINTER: Ah, come inside and sit by my fire.

GLUSKABE *enters, sits, down, and places the summerstick in front of* ***OLD MAN WINTER.***

GLUSKABE: You must go back to your home in the Winter Land.

OLD MAN WINTER: Oh, I must, eh? But tell me, do you like my fire?

GLUSKABE: Your fire is no longer cold. It is getting warmer. Your wigwam is melting away. You are getting weaker.

OLD MAN WINTER: No one can defeat me!

GLUSKABE: Old Man, you are defeated. Warm weather has returned. Go back to your home in the north.

The blanket walls of ***OLD MAN WINTER'S*** *wigwam collapse.* ***OLD MAN WINTER'*** *stands up and walks away as swiftly as he can, crouching down as if getting smaller. People carrying the cutouts of the Sun, Flowers, and Plants come out and surround* ***GLUSKABE*** *as he sits there, smiling.*

NARRATOR: So Gluskabe defeated Old Man Winter. Because he brought only one small piece of summer, winter still returns each year. But, thanks to Gluskabe, spring always comes back again.

Setting How does the action here change the setting of the scene? How does this change signal the resolution of the conflict?

1. Key Ideas and Details (a) Infer: In the opening scene, what do you learn about the characters of Gluskabe and Grandmother Woodchuck? Explain. **(b) Interpret:** What signs do you see in this scene that Gluskabe will successfully help the people?

2. Key Ideas and Details (a) Cite: Identify details in the stage directions that establish the seasons at various points in the play. **(b) Analyze:** How are these changes in the setting connected to the main conflict in the play?

3. Key Ideas and Details Analyze: What relationship between human beings and nature is presented in the play? Cite details that support your answer.

4. Key Ideas and Details (a) What heroic qualities does Gluskabe show? How does Grandmother Woodchuck help him? **(b) Interpret:** What theme is suggested by the play?

5. Craft and Structure (a) What happens in each of the play's four scenes? **(b) Analyze:** Explain how these events form a plot with a conflict, rising action, climax, and resolution.

6. Integration of Knowledge and Ideas Many traditional tales explain an aspect of nature or show the values that the people of a culture find important. **(a) Interpret:** What aspect of nature does this play explain? **(b) Analyze:** What do you learn about the Abenaki people from this tale?

7. Integration of Knowledge and Ideas (a) In a chart like the one shown, list the actions of Old Man Winter and the Summer Land People. Then, list dialogue about these characters.

Character	Action of the Character	Dialogue About the Character
Old Man Winter	warms his hands over fire made of ice	**Grandmother Woodchuck:** "Be careful, Gluskabe."
Summer Land People	dance around the pot full of summer	**Grandmother Woodchuck:** "The Summer Land people are strange people."

(b) Collaborate: Share your chart with a partner. How has your understanding of the characters changed?

© Drama Selection

Build your skills and improve your comprehension of drama with texts of increasing complexity.

Read **The Phantom Tollbooth, Act I,** to join a boy named Milo on a fantastic journey.

© Common Core State Standards

Meet these standards with **The Phantom Tollbooth, Act I** (p. 708).

Reading Literature
2. Determine a theme or central idea of a text and how it is conveyed through particular details; provide a summary of the text distinct from personal opinions or judgments. *(Reading Skill: Summary)*

3. Describe how a particular story's or drama's plot unfolds in a series of episodes as well as how the characters respond or change as the plot moves toward a resolution. *(Literary Analysis: Spiral Review)*

5. Analyze how a particular sentence, chapter, scene, or stanza fits into the overall structure of a text and contributes to the development of the theme, setting, or plot. **6.** Explain how an author develops the point of view of the narrator or speaker in a text. *(Literary Analysis: Dialogue in Drama)*

Writing
4. Produce clear and coherent writing in which the development, organization, and style are appropriate to task, purpose, and audience. *(Writing: Summary)*

6. Use technology, including the Internet. **8.** Gather relevant information from multiple print and digital sources. *(Research and Technology: Multimedia Presentation)*

Speaking and Listening
5. Include multimedia components and visual displays in presentations to clarify information. *(Research and Technology: Multimedia Presentation)*

Language
1. Demonstrate command of the conventions of standard English grammar and usage when writing or speaking. *(Conventions: Prepositions and Appositives)*

2.a. Use punctuation to set off nonrestrictive/parenthetical elements.

Reading Skill: Summary

A **summary** restates the main ideas and most important points of a literary work. To summarize a drama, first **reread to identify main events.** Then, in your summary, include only major events that move the story forward. A summary should not include your personal opinions of the literary work. Present the events in the order in which they happened.

Using the Strategy: Events Chart

As you read, use a chart like the one shown to record the major events in Act I. Refer to your chart when you write a summary.

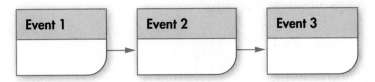

| Event 1 | Event 2 | Event 3 |

Literary Analysis: Dialogue in Drama

A **drama** is a story that is written to be performed. Like short stories, dramas have characters, a setting, and a plot that revolves around conflict. In dramas, however, these elements are developed mainly through **dialogue,** the words spoken by the characters. In the **script,** or written form of a drama, each character's name appears before his or her dialogue. Look at this example:

KATRINA. I can't believe you said that!

WALLACE. I was only kidding.

As you read this drama, look for ways that each character's point of view, or personality and beliefs, is developed through dialogue. Also, notice the way that the dialogue introduces conflict and moves the drama along.

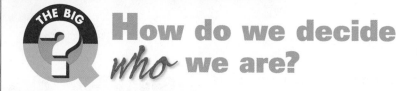

How do we decide *who* we are?

Writing About the Big Question

In *The Phantom Tollbooth*, Act I, Milo, a bored and unmotivated boy, receives an unexpected gift that leads him to discover an adventurous side of himself. Use this sentence starter to help you develop your ideas about the Big Question.

Experiences such as _____ can help people discover new aspects of their **personalities** because _____.

While You Read Notice the characters and situations that help Milo overcome boredom and find adventure and excitement.

Vocabulary

Read each word and its definition. Decide whether you know the word well, know it a little bit, or do not know it at all. After you read, see how your knowledge of each word has increased.

- **ignorance** (ig´ nə rəns) *n.* lack of knowledge, education, or experience (p. 708) *Babies are born in a state of total* <u>*ignorance*</u>. *ignorantly adv. ignorant adj. ignore v.*

- **precautionary** (pri kô´ shə ner´ ē) *adj.* done to prevent harm or danger (p. 710) *Locking the door is an important* <u>*precautionary*</u> *step against theft. precaution n. caution n.*

- **unethical** (un eth´ i kəl) *adj.* not conforming to the moral standards of a group (p. 713) *Taking that money without permission was* <u>*unethical*</u>. *ethic n.*

- **ferocious** (fə rō´ shəs) *adj.* wild and dangerous (p. 720) *Thank goodness the* <u>*ferocious*</u> *lion was in a cage.*

- **misapprehension** (mis´ ap rē hen´ shən) *n.* misunderstanding (p. 722) *She was under the* <u>*misapprehension*</u> *that snakes are slimy. misapprehend v. apprehend v.*

- **unabridged** (un´ ə brijd´) *adj.* complete; not shortened (p. 724) *I read the* <u>*unabridged*</u> *version of* Ivanhoe.

Word Study

The **Latin root -*eth*-** means "character" or "custom."

In this selection, Milo is told that to think in the land of the Doldrums is **unethical**, meaning that it shows poor character.

Meet
Susan Nanus

Author of

THE PHANTOM TOLLBOOTH

Susan Nanus has written many award-winning scripts for dramas, television mini-series, and movies. In 1997, she won the Writers Guild Award for best original script for the television drama *Harvest of Fire*.

Writing Adaptations Like other screenwriters, Nanus sometimes adapts, or reworks, novels to create screenplays for movies and scripts for stage plays. Her script for *The Phantom Tollbooth* was adapted from a novel by Norton Juster. Nanus lives and works in Los Angeles, California.

For a biography of Norton Juster, see page 747.

DID YOU KNOW?

Susan Nanus has earned several prizes for her writing, including the Christopher Award in 1988.

BACKGROUND FOR THE DRAMA

Descriptive Names

The names of these characters and places in *The Phantom Tollbooth* describe their qualities:

- The *Lethargarians* are sleepy characters who spend their days lounging around. Their name comes from the word *lethargy*, which means "sluggishness" or "lack of energy."

- *Digitopolis* is the place where all numbers come from. Its name is a combination of the word *digit*, which means "number," and the Greek root *-polis*, which means "city."

- *Dictionopolis* is the place where all words are born. Its name combines *diction*, which means "speech" or "language," with *-polis*.

THE PHANTOM TOLLBOOTH

Susan Nanus

based on the book by **Norton Juster**

CAST (in order of appearance)

- THE CLOCK
- MILO, a boy
- THE WHETHER MAN
- SIX LETHARGARIANS
- TOCK, THE WATCHDOG (same as the clock)
- AZAZ THE UNABRIDGED, KING OF DICTIONOPOLIS
- THE MATHEMAGICIAN, KING OF DIGITOPOLIS
- PRINCESS SWEET RHYME
- PRINCESS PURE REASON
- GATEKEEPER OF DICTIONOPOLIS

- THREE WORD MERCHANTS
- THE LETTERMAN (fourth word merchant)
- SPELLING BEE
- THE HUMBUG
- THE DUKE OF DEFINITION
- THE MINISTER OF MEANING
- THE EARL OF ESSENCE
- THE COUNT OF CONNOTATION
- THE UNDERSECRETARY OF UNDERSTANDING
- A PAGE

- KAKAFONOUS A.
- DISCHORD, DOCTOR OF DISSONANCE
- THE AWFUL DYNNE
- THE DODECAHEDRON
- MINERS OF THE NUMBERS MINE
- THE EVERPRESENT WORDSNATCHER
- THE TERRIBLE TRIVIUM
- THE DEMON OF INSINCERITY
- SENSES TAKER

THE SETS

1. MILO'S BEDROOM—with shelves, pennants, pictures on the wall, as well as suggestions of the characters of the Land of Wisdom.

2. THE ROAD TO THE LAND OF WISDOM— a forest, from which the Whether Man and the Lethargarians emerge.

3. DICTIONOPOLIS—a marketplace full of open air stalls as well as little shops. Letters and signs should abound.

4. DIGITOPOLIS—a dark, glittering place without trees or greenery, but full of shining rocks and cliffs, with hundreds of numbers shining everywhere.

5. THE LAND OF IGNORANCE—a gray, gloomy place full of cliffs and caves, with frightening faces. Different levels and heights should be suggested through one or two platforms or risers, with a set of stairs that lead to the castle in the air.

ACT 1 Scene i

[*The stage is completely dark and silent. Suddenly the sound of someone winding an alarm clock is heard, and after that, the sound of loud ticking is heard.*]

[*LIGHTS UP on the* CLOCK, *a huge alarm clock. The* CLOCK *reads 4:00. The lighting should make it appear that the* CLOCK *is suspended in mid-air (if possible). The* CLOCK *ticks for 30 seconds.*]

CLOCK. See that! Half a minute gone by. Seems like a long time when you're waiting for something to happen, doesn't it? Funny thing is, time can pass very slowly or very fast, and sometimes even both at once. The time now? Oh, a little after four, but what that means should depend on you. Too often, we do something simply because time tells us to. Time for school, time for bed, whoops, 12:00, time to be hungry. It can get a little silly, don't you think? Time is important, but it's what you do with it that makes it so. So my advice to you is to use it. Keep your eyes open and your ears perked. Otherwise it will pass before you know it, and you'll certainly have missed something!

Things have a habit of doing that, you know. Being here one minute and gone the next.

In the twinkling of an eye.

In a jiffy.

In a flash!

I know a girl who yawned and missed a whole summer vacation. And what about that caveman who took a nap one afternoon, and woke up to find himself completely alone. You see, while he was sleeping, someone had invented the wheel and everyone had moved to the suburbs. And then of course, there is Milo. [*LIGHTS UP to reveal* MILO's *Bedroom. The* CLOCK *appears to be on a shelf in the room of a young boy—a room filled with books, toys, games, maps, papers, pencils, a bed, a desk. There is a dartboard with numbers and the face of the* MATHEMAGICIAN, *a bedspread made from* KING AZAZ's *cloak, a kite looking like the spelling bee, a punching bag with the* HUMBUG's *face, as well as records, a television,*

Vocabulary
ignorance (igʹ nə rəns) *n.* lack of knowledge, education, or experience

Summary
How would you summarize the point Clock is making?

Reading Check
How do you know what characters and sets are in this play?

Turnpike Tollbooth

A turnpike is a road that people pay a fee, or toll, to use. Long ago, long spears called "pikes" barred the road. The pikes were turned aside only after travelers paid the toll. A tollbooth is the booth or gate at which tolls are collected. The first record of tolls being collected dates from about 2000 B.C., when tolls were collected on a Persian military road between Babylon and Syria.

Connect to the Literature

How might the tollbooth—an unusual gift—affect Milo's bored state of mind?

Vocabulary
precautionary (pri kô´ shə ner´ ē) *adj.* done to prevent harm or danger

---

a toy car, and a large box that is wrapped and has an envelope taped to the top. The sound of FOOTSTEPS *is heard, and then enter* MILO *dejectedly. He throws down his books and coat, flops into a chair, and sighs loudly.*] Who never knows what to do with himself—not just sometimes, but always. When he's in school, he wants to be out, and when he's out he wants to in. [*During the following speech,* MILO *examines various toys, tools, and other possessions in the room, trying them out and rejecting them.*] Wherever he is, he wants to be somewhere else—and when he gets there, so what. Everything is too much trouble or a waste of time. Books—he's already read them. Games—boring. T.V.—dumb. what's left? Another long, boring afternoon. Unless he bothers to notice a very large package that happened to arrive today.

MILO. [*Suddenly notices the package. He drags himself over to it, and disinterestedly reads the label.*] "For Milo, who has plenty of time." Well, that's true. [*Sighs and looks at it.*] No. [*Walks away.*] Well . . . [*Comes back. Rips open envelope and reads.*]

A VOICE. "One genuine turnpike tollbooth, easily assembled at home for use by those who have never traveled in lands beyond."

MILO. Beyond what? [*Continues reading.*]

A VOICE. "This package contains the following items:" [MILO *pulls the items out of the box and sets them up as they are mentioned.*] "One (1) genuine turnpike tollbooth to be erected according to directions. Three (3) precautionary signs to be used in a precautionary fashion. Assorted coins for paying tolls. One (1) map, strictly up to date, showing how to get from here to there. One (1) book of rules and traffic regulations which may not be bent or broken. Warning! Results are not guaranteed. If not perfectly satisfied, your wasted time will be refunded."

MILO. [*Skeptically.*] Come off it, who do you think you're kidding? [*Walks around and examines tollbooth.*] What am I supposed to do with this? [*The ticking of the* CLOCK *grows loud and impatient.*] Well . . . what else do I have to do. [MILO *gets into his toy car and drives up to the first sign.*]

VOICE. "HAVE YOUR DESTINATION IN MIND."

MILO. [*Pulls out the map.*] Now, let's see. That's funny. I never heard of any of these places. Well, it doesn't matter anyway. Dictionopolis. That's a weird name. I might as well go there. [*Begins to move, following map. Drives off.*]

CLOCK. See what I mean? You never know how things are going to get started. But when you're bored, what you need more than anything is a rude awakening.

[*The ALARM goes off very loudly as the stage darkens. The sound of the alarm is transformed into the honking of a car horn, and is then joined by the blasts, bleeps, roars and growls of heavy highway traffic. When the lights come up,* MILO's *bedroom is gone and we see a lonely road in the middle of nowhere.*]

Scene ii The Road to Dictionopolis

[*Enter* MILO *in his car.*]

MILO. This is weird! I don't recognize any of this scenery at all. [*A SIGN is held up before* MILO, *startling him.*] Huh? [*Reads.*] WELCOME TO EXPECTATIONS. INFORMATION, PREDICTIONS AND ADVICE CHEERFULLY OFFERED. PARK HERE AND BLOW HORN. [MILO *blows horn.*]

WHETHER MAN. [*A little man wearing a long coat and carrying an umbrella pops up from behind the sign that he was holding. He speaks very fast and excitedly.*] My, my, my, my, my, welcome, welcome, welcome, welcome to the Land of Expectations, Expectations, Expectations! We don't get many travelers these days; we certainly don't get many travelers. Now what can I do for you? I'm the Whether Man.

MILO. [*Referring to map.*] Uh . . . is this the right road to Dictionopolis?

Summary
Reread Scene i to identify and summarize the key events.

Dialogue in Drama
What do you learn about the Whether Man from his first speech?

✓ Reading Check
What is in the package Milo opens?

WHETHER MAN. Well now, well now, well now, I don't know of any wrong road to Dictionopolis, so if this road goes to Dictionopolis at all, it must be the right road, and if it doesn't, it must be the right road to somewhere else, because there are no wrong roads to anywhere. Do you think it will rain?

MILO. I thought you were the Weather Man.

WHETHER MAN. Oh, no, I'm the Whether Man, not the weather man. [*Pulls out a SIGN or opens a FLAP of his coat, which reads: "WHETHER."*] After all, it's more important to know whether there will be weather than what the weather will be.

MILO. What kind of place is Expectations?

Dialogue in Drama
What do you learn about the action from this dialogue between Milo and Whether Man?

WHETHER MAN. Good question, good question! Expectations is the place you must always go to before you get to where you are going. Of course, some people never go beyond Expectations, but my job is to hurry them along whether they like it or not. Now what else can I do for you? [*Opens his umbrella.*]

MILO. I think I can find my own way.

WHETHER MAN. Splendid, splendid, splendid! Whether or not you find your own way, you're bound to find some way. If you happen to find my way, please return it. I lost it years ago. I imagine by now it must be quite rusty. You did say it was going to rain, didn't you? [*Escorts* MILO *to the car under the open umbrella.*] I'm glad you made your own decision. I do so hate to make up my mind about anything, whether it's good or bad, up or down, rain or shine. Expect everything, I always say, and the unexpected never happens. Goodbye, goodbye, goodbye, good . . .

[*A loud CLAP of THUNDER is heard.*] Oh dear! [*He looks up at the sky, puts out his hand to feel for rain, and RUNS AWAY.* MILO *watches puzzledly and drives on.*]

Dialogue in Drama
How do Milo's words here move the plot along?

MILO. I'd better get out of Expectations, but fast. Talking to a guy like that all day would get me nowhere for sure. [*He tries to speed up, but finds instead that he is moving slower and slower.*] Oh, oh, now what? [*He can barely move. Behind* MILO, *the* LETHARGARIANS *begin* *to enter from all parts of the stage. They are dressed to blend in with the scenery and carry small pillows that look like rocks. Whenever they fall asleep, they rest on the pillows.]* Now I really am getting nowhere. I hope I didn't take a wrong turn. [*The car stops. He tries to start it. It won't move. He gets out and begins to tinker with it.*] I wonder where I am.

LETHARGARIAN 1. You're . . . in . . . the . . . Dol . . . drums . . . [MILO *looks around.*]

LETHARGARIAN 2. Yes . . . the . . . Dol . . . drums . . . [*A YAWN is heard.*]

MILO. [*Yelling.*] WHAT ARE THE DOLDRUMS?

LETHARGARIAN 3. The Doldrums, my friend, are where nothing ever happens and nothing ever changes. [*Parts of the Scenery stand up or Six People come out of the scenery colored in the same colors of the trees or the road. They move very slowly and as soon as they move, they stop to rest again.*] Allow me to introduce all of us. We are the Lethargarians at your service.

MILO. [*Uncertainly.*] Very pleased to meet you. I think I'm lost. Can you help me?

LETHARGARIAN 4. Don't say think. [*He yawns.*] It's against the law.

LETHARGARIAN 1. No one's allowed to think in the Doldrums. [*He falls asleep.*]

LETHARGARIAN 2. Don't you have a rule book? It's local ordinance 175389-J. [*He falls asleep.*]

MILO. [*Pulls out rule book and reads.*] Ordinance 175389-J: "It shall be unlawful, illegal and unethical to think, think of thinking, surmise, presume, reason, meditate or speculate while in the Doldrums. Anyone breaking this law shall be severely punished." That's a ridiculous law! Everybody thinks.

ALL THE LETHARGARIANS. We don't!

▼ **Critical Viewing**
What details in this picture show what the Lethargarians are like? **[Analyze]**

Vocabulary
unethical (un eth´ i kəl) *adj.* not conforming to the moral standards of a group

Reading Check
What are the Doldrums?

LETHARGARIAN 2. And most of the time, you don't, that's why you're here. You weren't thinking and you weren't paying attention either. People who don't pay attention often get stuck in the Doldrums. Face it, most of the time, you're just like us. [*Falls, snoring, to the ground.* MILO *laughs.*]

LETHARGARIAN 5. Stop that at once. Laughing is against the law. Don't you have a rule book? It's local ordinance 574381-W.

MILO. [*Opens rule book and reads.*] "In the Doldrums, laughter is frowned upon and smiling is permitted only on alternate Thursdays." Well, if you can't laugh or think, what can you do?

LETHARGARIAN 6. Anything as long as it's nothing, and everything as long as it isn't anything. There's lots to do. We have a very busy schedule . . .

LETHARGARIAN 1. At 8:00 we get up and then we spend from 8 to 9 daydreaming.

LETHARGARIAN 2. From 9:00 to 9:30 we take our early mid-morning nap . . .

LETHARGARIAN 3. From 9:30 to 10:30 we dawdle and delay . . .

LETHARGARIAN 4. From 10:30 to 11:30 we take our late early morning nap . . .

LETHARGARIAN 5. From 11:30 to 12:00 we bide our time and then we eat our lunch.

LETHARGARIAN 6. From 1:00 to 2:00 we linger and loiter . . .

LETHARGARIAN 1. From 2:00 to 2:30 we take our early afternoon nap . . .

LETHARGARIAN 2. From 2:30 to 3:30 we put off for tomorrow what we could have done today . . .

LETHARGARIAN 3. From 3:30 to 4:00 we take our early late afternoon nap . . .

LETHARGARIAN 4. From 4:00 to 5:00 we loaf and lounge until dinner . . .

LETHARGARIAN 5. From 6:00 to 7:00 we dilly-dally . . .

Dialogue in Drama
What does this dialogue reveal about the Doldrums?

Dialogue in Drama
Ellipsis points—three spaced periods—often indicate a pause or an unfinished thought. How does this punctuation help you understand the way the dialogue should be read?

Science Connection

Measuring Time

The Latin poet Ovid coined the phrase "Time flies." Through the ages, telling time has advanced from tracking shadows to measuring vibrations.

The quartz clock uses the vibrations of quartz crystal to generate an electric signal that drives the clock. Quartz powers digital watches.

Egyptian shadow clocks, or sundials, tell time by measuring the length or angle of a shadow on the dial as the sun moves across the sky.

3500 B.C.

Egyptian water clocks measured time by the flow of water through a small hole.

A.D. 100–1300

Chinese water clock towers, above, used water spilling from buckets to drive the wheels.

mid–1600s

This grandfather clock's weight-driven pendulum greatly improved timetelling accuracy.

1920s

1945

The atomic clock is the most accurate timepiece today. It tracks time by measuring movement between an atom's nucleus and surrounding electrons.

Connect to the Literature Do you think Milo is interested in keeping track of time? Explain.

LETHARGARIAN 6. From 7:00 to 8:00 we take our early evening nap and then for an hour before we go to bed, we waste time.

LETHARGARIAN 1. [*Yawning.*] You see, it's really quite strenuous doing nothing all day long, and so once a week, we take a holiday and go nowhere.

LETHARGARIAN 5. Which is just where we were going when you came along. Would you care to join us?

MILO. [*Yawning.*] That's where I seem to be going, anyway. [*Stretching.*] Tell me, does everyone here do nothing?

LETHARGARIAN 3. Everyone but the terrible watchdog. He's always sniffing around to see that nobody wastes time. A most unpleasant character.

MILO. The Watchdog?

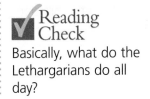

Reading Check

Basically, what do the Lethargarians do all day?

The Phantom Tollbooth, Act I **715**

LETHARGARIAN 6. THE WATCHDOG!

ALL THE LETHARGARIANS. [*Yelling at once.*] RUN! WAKE UP! RUN! HERE HE COMES! THE WATCHDOG! [*They all run off and ENTER a large dog with the head, feet, and tail of a dog, and the body of a clock, having the same face as the character* THE CLOCK.]

WATCHDOG. What are you doing here?

MILO. Nothing much. Just killing time. You see . . .

WATCHDOG. KILLING TIME! [*His ALARM RINGS in fury.*] It's bad enough wasting time without killing it. What are you doing in the Doldrums, anyway? Don't you have anywhere to go?

MILO. I think I was on my way to Dictionopolis when I got stuck here. Can you help me?

WATCHDOG. Help you! You've got to help yourself. I suppose you know why you got stuck.

MILO. I guess I just wasn't thinking.

WATCHDOG. Precisely. Now you're on your way.

MILO. I am?

WATCHDOG. Of course. Since you got here by not thinking, it seems reasonable that in order to get out, you must start thinking. Do you mind if I get in? I love automobile rides. [*He gets in. They wait.*] Well?

MILO. All right. I'll try. [*Screws up his face and thinks.*] Are we moving?

WATCHDOG. Not yet. Think harder.

MILO. I'm thinking as hard as I can.

WATCHDOG. Well, think just a little harder than that. Come on, you can do it.

MILO. All right, all right. . . . I'm thinking of all the planets in the solar system, and why water expands when it turns to ice, and all the words that begin with "q," and . . . [*The wheels begin to move.*] We're moving! We're moving!

WATCHDOG. Keep thinking.

Summary
Would you include the arrival of the Watchdog in a summary of this scene? Why or why not?

Spiral Review
Character How has Milo changed as a result of visiting the Lethargarians?

Dialogue in Drama
How does the dialogue between Milo and the Watchdog help you understand the problem here?

▲ **Critical Viewing**
Why is a clock part
of this character's
body? **[Connect]**

MILO. [*Thinking.*] How a steam engine works and how to
bake a pie and the difference between Fahrenheit and
Centigrade . . .

WATCHDOG. Dictionopolis, here we come.

MILO. Hey, Watchdog, are you coming along?

TOCK. You can call me Tock, and keep your eyes on the
road.

MILO. What kind of place is Dictionopolis, anyway?

TOCK. It's where all the words in the world come from. It
used to be a marvelous place, but ever since Rhyme and
Reason left, it hasn't been the same.

MILO. Rhyme and Reason?

TOCK. The two princesses. They used to settle all the arguments between their two brothers who rule over the

✓ Reading
Check
What does Milo think
about to get his car to
move?

Land of Wisdom. You see, Azaz is the king of Dictionopolis and the Mathemagician is the king of Digitopolis and they almost never see eye to eye on anything. It was the job of the Princesses Sweet Rhyme and Pure Reason to solve the differences between the two kings, and they always did so well that both sides usually went home feeling very satisfied. But then, one day, the kings had an argument to end all arguments. . . .

[*The LIGHTS DIM on* TOCK *and* MILO, *and come up on* KING AZAZ *of Dictionopolis on another part of the stage.* AZAZ *has a great stomach, a grey beard reaching to his waist, a small crown and a long robe with the letters of the alphabet written all over it.*]

AZAZ. Of course, I'll abide by the decision of Rhyme and Reason, though I have no doubt as to what it will be. They will choose words, of course. Everyone knows that words are more important than numbers any day of the week.

[*The* MATHEMAGICIAN *appears opposite* AZAZ. *The* MATHEMAGICIAN *wears a long flowing robe covered entirely with complex mathematical equations, and a tall pointed hat. He carries a long staff with a pencil point at one end and a large rubber eraser at the other.*]

MATHEMAGICIAN. That's what you think, Azaz. People wouldn't even know what day of the week it is without numbers. Haven't you ever looked at a calendar? Face it, Azaz. It's numbers that count.

AZAZ. Don't be ridiculous. [*To audience, as if leading a cheer.*] Let's hear it for WORDS!

MATHEMAGICIAN. [To audience, in the same manner.] Cast your vote for NUMBERS!

AZAZ. A, B, C's!

MATHEMAGICIAN. 1, 2, 3's! [*A FANFARE is heard.*]

AZAZ AND MATHEMAGICIAN. [*To each other.*] Quiet! Rhyme and Reason are about to announce their decision.

[RHYME *and* REASON *appear.*]

RHYME. Ladies and gentlemen, letters and numerals,

Summary
Briefly explain the argument between Azaz and the Mathemagician.

fractions and punctuation marks—may we have your attention, please. After careful consideration of the problem set before us by King Azaz of Dictionopolis [AZAZ *bows.*] and the Mathemagician of Digitopolis [MATHEMAGICIAN *raises his hands in a victory salute.*] we have come to the following conclusion:

REASON. Words and numbers are of equal value, for in the cloak of knowledge, one is the warp and the other is the woof.

RHYME. It is no more important to count the sands than it is to name the stars.

RHYME AND REASON. Therefore, let both kingdoms, Dictionopolis and Digitopolis, live in peace.

[*The sound of CHEERING is heard.*]

AZAZ. Boo! is what I say. Boo and Bah and Hiss!

MATHEMAGICIAN. What good are these girls if they can't even settle an argument in anyone's favor? I think I have come to a decision of my own.

AZAZ. So have I.

AZAZ AND MATHEMAGICIAN. [*To the* PRINCESSES.] You are hereby banished from this land to the Castle-in-the-Air. [*To each other.*] *And as for you, KEEP OUT OF MY WAY!* [*They stalk off in opposite directions.*]

[*During this time, the set has been changed to the Market Square of Dictionopolis. LIGHTS come UP on the deserted square.*]

TOCK. And ever since then, there has been neither Rhyme nor Reason in this kingdom. Words are misused and numbers are mismanaged. The argument between the two kings has divided everyone and the real value of both words and numbers has been forgotten. What a waste!

MILO. Why doesn't somebody rescue the Princesses and set everything straight again?

TOCK. That is easier said than done. The Castle-in-the-Air is very far from here, and the one path which leads to it is

Summary
Reread this section to summarize the events leading to Rhyme and Reason's banishment.

Reading Check

What conclusion do Reason and Rhyme reach?

Vocabulary
ferocious (fə rō´ shəs)
adj. wild and dangerous

guarded by ferocious demons. But hold on, here we are. [*A Man appears, carrying a Gate and a small Tollbooth.*]

GATEKEEPER. AHHHHREMMMM! This is Dictionopolis, a happy kingdom, advantageously located in the foothills of Confusion and caressed by gentle breezes from the Sea of Knowledge. Today, by royal proclamation, is Market Day. Have you come to buy or sell?

MILO. I beg your pardon?

GATEKEEPER. Buy or sell, buy or sell. Which is it? You must have come here for a reason.

MILO. Well, I . . .

GATEKEEPER. Come now, if you don't have a reason, you must at least have an explanation or certainly an excuse.

MILO. [*Meekly.*] Uh . . . no.

GATEKEEPER. [*Shaking his head.*] Very serious. You can't get in without a reason. [*Thoughtfully.*] Wait a minute. Maybe I have an old one you can use. [*Pulls out an old suitcase from the tollbooth and rummages through it.*] No . . . no . . . no . . . this won't do . . . hmmm . . .

MILO. [*To* TOCK.] What's he looking for? [TOCK *shrugs.*]

GATEKEEPER. Ah! This is fine. [*Pulls out a Medallion on a chain. Engraved in the Medallion is: "WHY NOT?"*] Why not. That's a good reason for almost anything . . . a bit used, perhaps, but still quite serviceable. There you are, sir. Now I can truly say: Welcome to Dictionopolis.

[*He opens the Gate and walks off.* CITIZENS *and* MERCHANTS *appear on all levels of the stage, and* MILO *and* TOCK *find themselves in the middle of a noisy marketplace. As some people buy and sell their wares, others hang a large banner which reads: WELCOME TO THE WORD MARKET.*]

MILO. Tock! Look!

MERCHANT 1. Hey-ya, hey-ya, hey-ya, step right up and take your pick. Juicy tempting words for sale. Get your fresh-picked "if's," "and's" and "but's"! Just take a look at these nice ripe "where's" and "when's."

Dialogue in Drama
What details does the Gatekeeper reveal about Dictionopolis?

MERCHANT 2. Step right up, step right up, fancy, best-quality words here for sale. Enrich your vocabulary and expand your speech with such elegant items as "quagmire," "flabbergast," or "upholstery."

MERCHANT 3. Words by the bag, buy them over here. Words by the bag for the more talkative customer. A pound of "happy's" at a very reasonable price . . . very useful for "Happy Birthday," "Happy New Year," "happy days," or "happy-go-lucky." Or how about a package of "good's," always handy for "good morning," "good afternoon," "good evening," and "goodbye."

MILO. I can't believe it. Did you ever see so many words?

TOCK. They're fine if you have something to say. [*They come to a Do-It-Yourself Bin.*]

MILO. [*To* MERCHANT 4 *at the bin.*] Excuse me, but what are these?

MERCHANT 4. These are for people who like to make up their own words. You can pick any assortment you like or buy a special box complete with all the letters and a book of instructions. Here, taste an "A." They're very good. [*He pops one into* MILO's *mouth.*]

MILO. [*Tastes it hesitantly.*] It's sweet! [*He eats it.*]

MERCHANT 4. I knew you'd like it. "A" is one of our best-sellers. All of them aren't that good, you know. The "Z," for instance—very dry and sawdusty. And the "X"? Tastes like a trunkful of stale air. But most of the others aren't bad at all. Here, try the "I."

MILO. [*Tasting.*] Cool! It tastes icy.

MERCHANT 4. [*To* TOCK.] How about the "C" for you? It's as crunchy as a bone. Most people are just too lazy to make their own words, but take it from me, not only is it more fun, but it's also *de*-lightful, [*Holds up a "D."*] *e*-lating, [*Holds up an "E."*] and extremely *u*seful! [*Holds up a "U."*]

MILO. But isn't it difficult? I'm not very good at making words.

> "Step right up, step right up, fancy, best-quality words here for sale."

Reading Check
What is sold in the Dictionopolis marketplace?

Summary
Would you include the scene in the Word Market in a summary of Scene ii? Why or why not?

Vocabulary
misapprehension
(mis´ ap rē hen´ shən)
n. misunderstanding

[*The* SPELLING BEE, *a large colorful bee, comes up from behind.*]

SPELLING BEE. Perhaps I can be of some assistance . . . a-s-s-i-s-t-a-n-c-e. [*The Three turn around and see him.*] Don't be alarmed . . . a-l-a-r-m-e-d. I am the Spelling Bee. I can spell anything. Anything. A-n-y-t-h-i-n-g. Try me. Try me.

MILO. [*Backing off,* TOCK *on his guard.*] Can you spell goodbye?

SPELLING BEE. Perhaps you are under the misapprehension . . . m-i-s-a-p-p-r-e-h-e-n-s-i-o-n that I am dangerous. Let me assure you that I am quite peaceful. Now, think of the most difficult word you can, and I'll spell it.

MILO. Uh . . . o.k. [*At this point,* MILO *may turn to the audience and ask them to help him choose a word or he may think of one on his own.*] How about . . . "Curiosity"?

SPELLING BEE. [*Winking.*] Let's see now . . . uh . . . how much time do I have?

MILO. Just ten seconds. Count them off, Tock.

SPELLING BEE. [*As* TOCK *counts.*] Oh dear, oh dear. [*Just at the last moment, quickly.*] C-u-r-i-o-s-i-t-y.

MERCHANT 4. Correct! [ALL *Cheer.*]

MILO. Can you spell anything?

SPELLING BEE. [*Proudly.*] Just about. You see, years ago, I was an ordinary bee minding my own business, smelling flowers all day, occasionally picking up part-time work in people's bonnets. Then one day, I realized that I'd never amount to anything without an education, so I decided that . . .

HUMBUG. [*Coming up in a booming voice.*] BALDERDASH! [*He wears a lavish coat, striped pants, checked vest, spats and a derby hat.*] Let me repeat . . . BALDERDASH! [*Swings his cane and clicks his heels in the air.*] Well, well, what have we here? Isn't someone going to introduce me to the little boy?

SPELLING BEE. [*Disdainfully.*] This is the Humbug. You can't trust a word he says.

HUMBUG. NONSENSE! Everyone can trust a Humbug. As I

was saying to the king just the other day . . .

SPELLING BEE. You've never met the king. [*To* MILO.] Don't believe a thing he tells you.

HUMBUG. Bosh, my boy, pure bosh. The Humbugs are an old and noble family, honorable to the core. Why, we fought in the Crusades with Richard the Lionhearted, crossed the Atlantic with Columbus, blazed trails with the pioneers. History is full of Humbugs.

SPELLING BEE. A very pretty speech . . . s-p-e-e-c-h. Now, why don't you go away? I was just advising the lad of the importance of proper spelling.

HUMBUG. BAH! As soon as you learn to spell one word, they ask you to spell another. You can never catch up, so why bother? [*Puts his arm around* MILO.] Take my advice, boy, and forget about it. As my great-great-great-grandfather George Washington Humbug used to say . . .

SPELLING BEE. You, sir, are an impostor i-m-p-o-s-t-o-r who can't even spell his own name!

HUMBUG. What? You dare to doubt my word? The word of a Humbug? The word of a Humbug who has direct access to the ear of a King? And the king shall hear of this, I promise you . . .

VOICE 1. Did someone call for the King?

VOICE 2. Did you mention the monarch?

VOICE 3. Speak of the sovereign?

VOICE 4. Entreat the Emperor?

▲ **Critical Viewing**
How does this picture of Spelling Bee compare with his description in the play? **[Compare]**

Dialogue in Drama
What does the dialogue between Humbug and Spelling Bee show about their relationship?

✓ Reading Check
What advice does Spelling Bee give Milo?

VOICE 5. Hail his highness?

[*Five tall, thin gentlemen regally dressed in silks and satins, plumed hats and buckled shoes appear as they speak.*]

MILO. Who are they?

SPELLING BEE. The King's advisors. Or in more formal terms, his cabinet.

MINISTER 1. Greetings!

MINISTER 2. Salutations!

MINISTER 3. Welcome!

MINISTER 4. Good Afternoon!

MINISTER 5. Hello!

MILO. Uh . . . Hi.

[*All the* MINISTERS, *from here on called by their numbers, unfold their scrolls and read in order.*]

Vocabulary
unabridged (un´ ə brijd´) *adj.* complete; not shortened

MINISTER 1. By the order of Azaz the Unabridged . . .

MINISTER 2. King of Dictionopolis . . .

MINISTER 3. Monarch of letters . . .

MINISTER 4. Emperor of phrases, sentences, and miscellaneous figures of speech . . .

MINISTER 5. We offer you the hospitality of our kingdom . . .

MINISTER 1. Country

MINISTER 2. Nation

MINISTER 3. State

MINISTER 4. Commonwealth

MINISTER 5. Realm

MINISTER 1. Empire

MINISTER 2. Palatinate

MINISTER 3. Principality.

Dialogue in Drama
How does the dialogue of the five ministers show the importance of words in Dictionopolis?

MILO. Do all those words mean the same thing?

MINISTER 1. Of course.

MINISTER 2. Certainly.

MINISTER 3. Precisely.

MINISTER 4. Exactly.

MINISTER 5. Yes.

MILO. Then why don't you use just one? Wouldn't that make a lot more sense?

MINISTER 1. Nonsense!

MINISTER 2. Ridiculous!

MINISTER 3. Fantastic!

MINISTER 4. Absurd!

MINISTER 5. Bosh!

MINISTER 1. We're not interested in making sense. It's not our job.

MINISTER 2. Besides, one word is as good as another, so why not use them all?

MINISTER 3. Then you don't have to choose which one is right.

MINISTER 4. Besides, if one is right, then ten are ten times as right.

MINISTER 5. Obviously, you don't know who we are.

[*Each presents himself and* MILO *acknowledges the introduction.*]

MINISTER 1. The Duke of Definition.

MINISTER 2. The Minister of Meaning.

MINISTER 3. The Earl of Essence.

MINISTER 4. The Count of Connotation.

MINISTER 5. The Undersecretary of Understanding.

ALL FIVE. And we have come to invite you to the Royal Banquet.

SPELLING BEE. The banquet! That's quite an honor, my boy. A real h-o-n-o-r.

HUMBUG. DON'T BE RIDICULOUS! Everybody goes to the Royal Banquet these days.

Summary
Briefly restate two ideas included in the ministers' welcome.

Reading
Check
What is the main responsibility of the ministers?

SPELLING BEE. [*To the* HUMBUG.] True, everybody does go. But some people are invited and others simply push their way in where they aren't wanted.

HUMBUG. HOW DARE YOU? You buzzing little upstart, I'll show you who's not wanted . . . [*Raises his cane threateningly.*]

SPELLING BEE. You just watch it! I'm warning w-a-r-n-i-n-g you! [*At that moment, an ear-shattering blast of TRUMPETS, entirely off-key, is heard, and a* PAGE *appears.*]

PAGE. King Azaz the Unabridged is about to begin the Royal banquet. All guests who do not appear promptly at the table will automatically lose their place. [*A huge Table is carried out with* KING AZAZ *sitting in a large chair, carried out at the head of the table.*]

AZAZ. Places. Everyone take your places. [*All the characters, including the* HUMBUG *and the* SPELLING BEE, *who forget their quarrel, rush to take their places at the table.* MILO *and* TOCK *sit near the king.* AZAZ *looks at* MILO.] And just who is this?

MILO. Your Highness, my name is Milo and this is Tock. Thank you very much for inviting us to your banquet, and I think your palace is beautiful!

MINISTER 1. Exquisite.

MINISTER 2. Lovely.

MINISTER 3. Handsome.

MINISTER 4. Pretty.

MINISTER 5. Charming.

AZAZ. SILENCE! Now tell me, young man, what can you do to entertain us? Sing songs? Tell stories? Juggle plates? Do tumbling tricks? Which is it?

MILO. I can't do any of those things.

AZAZ. What an ordinary little boy. Can't you do anything at all?

MILO. Well . . . I can count to a thousand.

AZAZ. AARGH, numbers! Never mention numbers here. Only

Dialogue in Drama How do these stage directions reinforce Azaz's words?

use them when we absolutely have to. Now, why don't we change the subject and have some dinner? Since you are the guest of honor, you may pick the menu.

MILO. Me? Well, uh . . . I'm not very hungry. Can we just have a light snack?

AZAZ. A light snack it shall be!

[*AZAZ claps his hands. Waiters rush in with covered trays. When they are uncovered, Shafts of Light pour out. The light may be created through the use of battery-operated flashlights which are secured in the trays and covered with a false bottom. The Guests help themselves.*]

HUMBUG. Not a very substantial meal. Maybe you can suggest something a little more filling.

MILO. Well, in that case, I think we ought to have a square meal . . .

AZAZ. [*Claps his hands.*] A square meal it is! [*Waiters serve trays of Colored Squares of all sizes. People serve themselves.*]

SPELLING BEE. These are awful. [*HUMBUG coughs and all the Guests do not care for the food.*]

AZAZ. [*Claps his hands and the trays are removed.*] Time for speeches. [*To MILO.*] You first.

MILO. [*Hesitantly.*] Your Majesty, ladies and gentlemen, I would like to take this opportunity to say that . . .

AZAZ. That's quite enough. Mustn't talk all day.

MILO. But I just started to . . .

AZAZ. NEXT!

HUMBUG. [*Quickly.*] Roast turkey, mashed potatoes, vanilla ice cream.

SPELLING BEE. Hamburgers, corn on the cob, chocolate pudding p-u-d-d-i-n-g. [*Each Guest names two dishes and a dessert.*]

AZAZ. [*The last.*] Pâté de foie gras, soupe à l'oignon, salade endives, fromage et fruits et demi-tasse. [*He claps his*

Dialogue in Drama
How do the dialogue and stage directions show that "a light snack" has different meanings for Milo and Azaz?

"Aargh, numbers! Never mention numbers here."

✓ Reading Check
What does Azaz forbid Milo to discuss?

hands. Waiters serve each Guest his Words.] Dig in. [*To* MILO.] Though I can't say I think much of your choice.

MILO. I didn't know I was going to have to eat my words.

AZAZ. Of course, of course, everybody here does. Your speech should have been in better taste.

MINISTER 1. Here, try some somersault. It improves the flavor.

MINISTER 2. Have a rigamarole. [*Offers breadbasket.*]

MINISTER 3. Or a ragamuffin.

MINISTER 4. Perhaps you'd care for a synonym bun.

MINISTER 5. Why not wait for your just desserts?

AZAZ. Ah yes, the dessert. We're having a special treat today . . . freshly made at the half-bakery.

MILO. The half-bakery?

AZAZ. Of course, the half-bakery! Where do you think half-baked ideas come from? Now, please don't interrupt. By royal command, the pastry chefs have . . .

MILO. What's a half-baked idea?

[AZAZ *gives up the idea of speaking as a cart is wheeled in and the Guests help themselves.*]

HUMBUG. They're very tasty, but they don't always agree with you. Here's a good one. [HUMBUG *hands one to* MILO.]

MILO. [*Reads.*] "The earth is flat."

SPELLING BEE. People swallowed that one for years. [*Picks up one and reads.*] "The moon is made of green cheese." Now, there's a half-baked idea.

[*Everyone chooses one and eats. They include:* "It Never Rains But Pours," "Night Air Is Bad Air," "Everything Happens for the Best," "Coffee Stunts Your Growth."]

AZAZ. And now for a few closing words. Attention! Let me have your attention! [*Everyone leaps up and Exits, except for* MILO, TOCK, *and the* HUMBUG.] Loyal subjects and friends, once again on this gala occasion, we have . . .

Dialogue in Drama
Identify one pun, or play on words, that adds humor to this dialogue.

Summary
Briefly summarize the events at the banquet.

MILO. Excuse me, but everybody left.

AZAZ. [*Sadly.*] I was hoping no one would notice. It happens every time.

HUMBUG. They're gone to dinner, and as soon as I finish this last bite, I shall join them.

MILO. That's ridiculous. How can they eat dinner right after a banquet?

AZAZ. SCANDALOUS! We'll put a stop to it at once. From now on, by royal command, everyone must eat dinner before the banquet.

MILO. But that's just as bad.

HUMBUG. Or just as good. Things which are equally bad are also equally good. Try to look at the bright side of things.

MILO. I don't know which side of anything to look at. Everything is so confusing, and all your words only make things worse.

AZAZ. How true. There must be something we can do about it.

HUMBUG. Pass a law.

AZAZ. We have almost as many laws as words.

HUMBUG. Offer a reward. [AZAZ *shakes his head and looks madder at each suggestion.*] Send for help? Drive a bargain? Pull the switch? Lower the boom? Toe the line?

[*As* AZAZ *continues to scowl, the* HUMBUG *loses confidence and finally gives up.*]

MILO. Maybe you should let Rhyme and Reason return.

AZAZ. How nice that would be. Even if they were a bother at times, things always went so well when they were here. But I'm afraid it can't be done.

HUMBUG. Certainly not. Can't be done.

MILO. Why not?

HUMBUG. [*Now siding with* MILO.] Why not, indeed?

AZAZ. Much too difficult.

> "Things which are equally bad are also equally good."

Reading Check

Why has everyone left the banquet?

HUMBUG. Of course, much too difficult.

MILO. You could, if you really wanted to.

HUMBUG. By all means, if you really wanted to, you could.

AZAZ. [*To* HUMBUG.] How?

MILO. [*Also to* HUMBUG.] Yeah, how?

HUMBUG. Why . . . uh, it's a simple task for a brave boy with a stout heart, a steadfast dog and a serviceable small automobile.

AZAZ. Go on.

HUMBUG. Well, all that he would have to do is cross the dangerous, unknown countryside between here and Digitopolis, where he would have to persuade the Mathemagician to release the Princesses, which we know to be impossible because the Mathemagician will never agree with Azaz about anything. Once achieving that, it's a simple matter of entering the Mountains of Ignorance from where no one has ever returned alive, an effortless climb up a two thousand foot stairway without railings in a high wind at night to the Castle-in-the-Air. After a pleasant chat with the Princesses, all that remains is a leisurely ride back through those chaotic crags where the frightening fiends have sworn to tear any intruder limb from limb and devour him down to his belt buckle. And finally after doing all that, a triumphal parade! If, of course, there is anything left to parade . . . followed by hot chocolate and cookies for everyone.

AZAZ. I never realized it would be so simple.

MILO. It sounds dangerous to me.

TOCK. And just who is supposed to make that journey?

AZAZ. A very good question. But there is one far more serious problem.

MILO. What's that?

AZAZ. I'm afraid I can't tell you that until you return.

MILO. But wait a minute, I didn't . . .

Dialogue in Drama
What major problem do Milo and Azaz discuss here?

AZAZ. Dictionopolis will always be grateful to you, my boy, and your dog. [AZAZ *pats* TOCK *and* MILO.]

TOCK. Now, just one moment, sire . . .

AZAZ. You will face many dangers on your journey, but fear not, for I can give you something for your protection. [AZAZ *gives* MILO *a box.*] In this box are the letters of the alphabet. With them you can form all the words you will ever need to help you overcome the obstacles that may stand in your path. All you must do is use them well and in the right places.

MILO. [*Miserably.*] Thanks a lot.

AZAZ. You will need a guide, of course, and since he knows the obstacles so well, the Humbug has cheerfully volunteered to accompany you.

HUMBUG. Now, see here . . . !

AZAZ. You will find him dependable, brave, resourceful and loyal.

HUMBUG. [*Flattered.*] Oh, your Majesty.

Dialogue in Drama
Based on these lines, how does Azaz feel about the power of words?

Reading
Check
What does Azaz give Milo for his journey?

MILO. I'm sure he'll be a great help. [*They approach the car.*]

TOCK. I hope so. It looks like we're going to need it.

[*The lights darken and the* KING *fades from view.*]

AZAZ. Good luck! Drive carefully! [*The three get into the car and begin to move. Suddenly a thunderously loud NOISE is heard. They slow down the car.*]

MILO. What was that?

TOCK. It came from up ahead.

HUMBUG. It's something terrible, I just know it. Oh, no. Something dreadful is going to happen to us. I can feel it in my bones. [*The NOISE is repeated. They all look at each other fearfully as the lights fade.*]

Summary
Reread Scene ii and summarize the main events.

Critical Thinking

© **1. Key Ideas and Details (a)** Who are Rhyme and Reason? **(b) Identify Cause and Effect:** What effect does their absence have on Dictionopolis?

© **2. Key Ideas and Details (a)** How does Humbug describe the journey that Milo must make? **(b) Predict:** In Act II, Milo will start his journey. What do you think it will be like? Give three details from Act I to support your answer.

© **3. Key Ideas and Details (a)** What does King Azaz give Milo? **(b) Hypothesize:** Describe a situation in which the gift might help Milo.

© **4. Integration of Knowledge and Ideas (a)** Compare and contrast Milo's personality at the beginning and end of Act I. **(b)** What has caused the change in Milo? *[Connect to the Big Question: How do we decide who we are?]*

Cite textual evidence to support your responses.

Reading Skill: Summary

1. (a) What events would you include in a **summary** of Act I?
(b) Explain why they are the most important events.

Literary Analysis: Dialogue in Drama

2. Key Ideas and Details Complete a chart like this one to explain what the **dialogue** reveals about a character, the setting, and an action. An example has been provided.

Dialogue	What It Suggests
MILO. Well, it doesn't matter anyway. Dictionopolis. That's a weird name. I might as well go there.	**Character:** Milo is bored. He doesn't care about anything.
GATEKEEPER. This is Dictionopolis, a happy kingdom, advantageously located in the foothills of Confusion and caressed by gentle breezes from the Sea of Knowledge.	**Setting:**
WATCHDOG. Do you mind if I get in? I love automobile rides.	**Action:**

Vocabulary

Acquisition and Use Write a vocabulary word from page 706 that fits with each of these word groups. Explain your answers.

1. growling, dangerous _____

2. confusion, disagreement _____

3. dullness, unawareness _____

4. immoral, dishonorable _____

5. carefully planned, safe _____

6. complete, entire _____

Word Study Use context and what you know about the **Latin root -eth-** to explain your answer to each question.

1. Is it *ethical* to take a book that does not belong to you?

2. Can an *ethicist* tell right from wrong?

Word Study

The **Latin root -eth-** means "character" or "custom."

Apply It Explain how the root -eth- contributes to the meaning of these words. Consult a dictionary if necessary.

ethnic

ethnicity

ethics

Integrated Language Skills

The Phantom Tollbooth, Act I

Conventions: Prepositions and Appositives

A **preposition** relates a noun or pronoun to another word in the sentence. Common prepositions are *on, by,* and *from.*

A **prepositional phrase** begins with a preposition and includes a noun or pronoun called the **object of the preposition.**

An **appositive** is a noun or pronoun that identifies or explains another noun or pronoun in the sentence.

An **appositive phrase** includes an appositive and its modifiers. Appositives can be set off by either commas or dashes.

Prepositions/<u>*Prepositional Phrases*</u>	*Appositives/*<u>*Appositive Phrases*</u>
Jenny stood <u>*between* the stage and the audience</u>.	Jenny, <u>a young *girl*</u>, stood between the stage and the audience.
<u>*After* the performance</u>, the audience clapped and cheered.	The audience, <u>a mostly young *crowd*</u>, clapped and cheered.

Practice A Rewrite each sentence, circling the preposition or prepositional phrase and underlining the object of the preposition.

1. Milo sat on his bed.
2. After school, Milo was bored.
3. In the play, the clock spoke.
4. Milo traveled to the land of Dictionopolis.

Ⓔ **Reading Application** Review the first act of *The Phantom Tollbooth* and identify at least three prepositional phrases.

Practice B Rewrite each sentence, circling the appositive or appositive phrase. Underline the noun or pronoun it identifies or explains.

1. Milo, a young boy, stared into space.
2. The Whether Man, a little man wearing a coat, was not a weather man.
3. Azaz, the king, had a banquet.
4. A dog with a clock for a body, the Watchdog, hopped into the car.

Ⓔ **Writing Application** Write three sentences based on *The Phantom Tollbooth,* Act I, containing appositive or prepositional phrases. Set off appositive phrases using either commas or dashes.

PH **WRITING COACH** | Further instruction and practice are available in *Prentice Hall Writing Coach.*

Writing

Common Core State Standards

L.6.1, L.6.2.a; W.6.4, W.6.6, W.6.8; SL.6.5
[For the full wording of the standards, see page 704.]

Informative Text Write a brief **summary** of *The Phantom Tollbooth*, Act I.

- Decide which events, characters, and ideas are important.
- Present events in the order in which they occur, giving your summary a beginning, a middle, and an end.
- Give enough information for readers to understand the main ideas and natural flow of the drama.
- Leave out unimportant details.

Grammar Application Be sure to use prepositions and appositives correctly in your summary.

Writing Workshop: *Work in Progress*

Prewriting for Response to Literature For a letter to an author that you might write, choose a literary work that you have read. Write down the name and author. Then, answer these questions: *What did you like or dislike about the work? Did it remind you of anything? Did it inspire you? Did it prompt a reaction in you?* Save your Response Sheet in your writing portfolio.

Use this prewriting activity to prepare for the **Writing Workshop** on page 738.

Research and Technology

Build and Present Knowledge Work with a small group to prepare and research a **multimedia presentation** on a topic related to drama. Because the audience for your presentation will be your class, choose your topic with your classmates' interests in mind. Possible topics: actors, theaters, stage sets, writers, comedy, or drama. Follow these suggestions to structure your presentation:

- Keep the background and interests of your audience in mind as you conduct your research, using online or print resources. Choose a topic your audience will find interesting.
- Include printouts, slides, photos, or drawings to illustrate the facts you present. Your illustrations should be lively to catch audience attention.
- Use other graphics, such as diagrams, timelines, and charts.
- Use audio aids, such as recordings and sound effects.

Deliver your presentation to the class.

PHLit Online!
www.PHLitOnline.com
- Interactive graphic organizers
- Grammar tutorial
- Interactive journals

Test Practice: Reading

Summarizing

Fiction Selection

Directions: *Read the selection. Then, answer the questions.*

Nicole's heart pounded in her chest as she waited outside the theater. Nicole's palms began to sweat. Mrs. Smith would be out any minute to call her name. She was next on the list of students waiting to try out for the leading role in the school play. She had rehearsed for hours the night before and had memorized all the lines perfectly. She just had to remember to deliver them properly. She remembered her mother's reassuring words of support as she left for school that morning. Nicole took a deep breath, dried her hands on her sweatshirt, and brushed her hair out of her eyes. Calmly and confidently, she walked out onto the stage when she heard Mrs. Smith call her name.

1. Which is the *most* important detail to include in a summary of this passage?
   A. Nicole was nervous.
   B. Nicole had to deliver her lines properly.
   C. Mrs. Smith would call her name soon.
   D. Nicole memorized all of her lines.

2. Which *best* completes this timeline?

Nicole rehearses	→	Nicole waits for Mrs. Smith to call her

   A. Nicole memorizes her lines
   B. Nicole gets the part
   C. Nicole's heart pounds
   D. Nicole tries out for the lead role

3. Which is the *best* summary of the selection?
   A. After rehearsing and memorizing her lines, Nicole tries out for a leading role in a play. Although she is nervous, she calmly auditions when the time comes.
   B. As Nicole waited nervously for her turn to try out for the play, she remembered her mother's support.
   C. Nicole memorized her lines but was nervous about her audition. She was grateful for her mother's support.
   D. Nicole was nervous about trying out for the school play. She rehearsed the night before and was ready.

Writing for Assessment

Reread the passage above to identify the main ideas. Then, write a short summary of the passage in your own words.

Nonfiction Selection

Directions: *Read the selection. Then, answer the questions.*

Drama has its roots in ancient Greece. In contrast to the elaborate staging and scenery used today, in ancient Greece there was little scenery, and only sunlight lit the stage. Tragedies were performed at religious festivals honoring the Greek god Dionysus. It was not uncommon for actors to travel to other countries to promote cultural identity. Performance competitions were held four times a year. Soon, comedies were added to these competitions and festivals. Participating in the competitions was a way to show loyalty to your state, and winners were richly rewarded.

Aristophanes is probably the best known Greek comic playwright. His plays were popular choices for these competitions and are still popular today.

1. What is the topic of this selection?
- **A.** origins of drama
- **B.** types of drama
- **C.** writers of drama
- **D.** characteristics of drama

2. Which detail is *most* important to include in a summary of the selection?
- **A.** Dionysus was honored at festivals.
- **B.** Aristophanes's plays are popular today.
- **C.** Comedies and tragedies were performed at religious festivals.
- **D.** Competitions were held four times a year.

3. Which detail would *not* belong in a summary of the selection?
- **A.** Drama began long ago in ancient Greece.
- **B.** Actors traveled to promote cultural identity.
- **C.** Festivals were held four times a year.
- **D.** Aristophanes's plays are still popular today.

Writing for Assessment

Connecting Across Texts
Actors like Nicole compete with other actors for parts, just as ancient Greek actors competed in festivals. Write a paragraph about a time you competed in an event. Reread what you wrote to identify the main ideas. Then, write one sentence that summarizes your paragraph.

PHLit
Online!
www.PHLitOnline.com
- Online practice
- Instant feedback

Writing Workshop

Write an Argument

Argument: Response to Literature

Defining the Form In a **response to literature,** the writer develops an argument that addresses one or more aspects of a literary work. One good way to respond to literature is to write *a letter to an author.* You might use elements of this form in movie reviews, book reviews, or critical responses.

Assignment Write a letter to a favorite author to share your response to his or her work. Include these elements:

✔ an *introduction* that identifies the work and summarizes your overall reaction

✔ an *interpretation* that *exhibits careful reading, understanding, and insight*

✔ *clear organizational format* in which you *support your arguments with reasons, examples, and relevant evidence from the text*

✔ elements of *formal business letters,* including a respectful tone

✔ error-free writing, including *correct use of participial phrases*

To preview the criteria on which your letter may be judged, see the rubric on page 743.

 Writing Workshop: *Work in Progress*

Review the work you did on page 735.

Prewriting/Planning Strategy

Use a hexagon. Choose a favorite work of literature. Then, use the six headings of a hexagon like the one shown to help you consider a variety of ideas. Gather details about the work under each heading. Review your ideas and choose one to present in your letter.

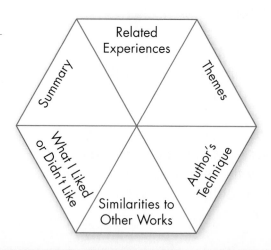

 Common Core State Standards

Writing

1. Write arguments to support claims with clear reasons and relevant evidence.

1.a. Introduce claim(s) and organize the reasons and evidence clearly.

1.b. Support claim(s) with clear reasons and relevant evidence, using credible sources and demonstrating an understanding of the topic or text.

1.c. Use words, phrases, and clauses to clarify the relationships among claim(s) and reasons.

9. Draw evidence from literary or informational texts to support analysis, reflection, and research.

Language

1.b. Use intensive pronouns.

4.c. Consult reference materials, both print and digital, to find the pronunciation of a word or determine or clarify its precise meaning or its part of speech.

Choose Your Words Carefully

Word Choice Precise, descriptive words make your ideas come across clearly and vividly. These tips will help you choose the best words to use in your letter to an author:

Choose specific words. Carefully chosen words will communicate precisely why an author's work is meaningful to you. Notice the differences in the following examples:

- **Example 1:** Your book, *Becoming an Astronaut*, was very interesting. I really liked it a lot. I read it many times. I may become an astronaut someday.

- **Example 2:** Thank you for changing my life and guiding me to explore an exciting career. Your amazing book, *Becoming an Astronaut*, has a permanent place on my bedside table, and I have read it six times so far.

The following word choices made the difference:

General Words	Specific Words
Interesting	Changed my life
I may become an astronaut	Explore an exciting career
Really liked it; read it many times	Read it six times

Choose precise words. A thesaurus is helpful when you need a specific word. For example, to tell an author that you thought her story was "very scary," follow these steps:

1. Look up the word *scary* in a thesaurus.

2. Jot down the entries in the thesaurus—you might find these words: *frightening, terrifying, creepy, hair-raising, shocking, disturbing,* and *alarming.*

3. Choose the word that conveys exactly what you want to say.

Use intensive pronouns. If you would like to add emphasis to one or more of your statements, use intensive pronouns. For example, you might write, *I,* **myself,** *have never been to the place you describe, but your details help me to picture it perfectly.* Place an intensive pronoun *after* its antecedent, as in the example above.

> **PH** **WRITING COACH**
>
> Further instruction and practice are available in *Prentice Hall Writing Coach.*

Drafting Strategies

Use standard business letter format. Include these elements:

- **Heading:** your address and the date of the letter
- **Inside address:** the name and address that show where the letter will be sent
- **Greeting:** an opening, including the recipient's name followed by a colon
- **Body:** text that explains and develops your message
- **Closing:** *Sincerely* or *Respectfully,* followed by a comma
- **Signature:** your full name—printed or typed—and your handwritten signature above it

In **block format,** each part of the letter begins at the left margin. In **modified block format,** the heading, the closing, and the signature are indented to the center of the page.

Justify your response. Elaborate on your general arguments with details from the literature. You can also elaborate by expressing ideas vividly through literary techniques such as metaphors, similes, and description, just like your author may use.

- **Instead of saying:** *The ending was sad and it made me cry.*
- **Say:** *When the brothers realized that they would never see each other again, I began to cry for their sorrow.*

Use a formal style. As you write, be careful to maintain a formal style. Avoid using slang or informal language, and adopt a respectful tone. Remember to address an author in the same way that you would want someone to address you.

Revising Strategies

Balance your introduction and conclusion. Your conclusion should be a restatement of the ideas in your first paragraph. The ideas throughout your letter should maintain the same focus. If the statements do not match, revise to improve the consistency of your ideas.

Add a quotation. Review the text to find quotations to support your arguments. This will add depth to your ideas.

Common Core State Standards

Writing
1.b. Support claim(s) with clear reasons and relevant evidence, using credible sources and demonstrating an understanding of the topic.
1.d. Establish and maintain a formal style.
1.e. Provide a concluding statement or section that follows from the argument presented.

Language
3.a. Vary sentence patterns for meaning, reader/listener interest, and style.

Block Format

Modified Block Format

Combining Sentences With Participial Phrases

A **participle** is a form of a verb that acts as an adjective. A **present participle** is the -*ing* form of a verb: *relaxing* or *catching*. A **past participle** is the past form of the verb: *relaxed* or *caught*.

A **participial phrase** combines a present or past participle with other words to make a phrase. The entire phrase acts as an adjective.

Example: *Catching the ball,* Damon threw it to home plate.
Relaxing after the game, Bill listened to music.
Caught in the rain, we got soaking wet.
Relaxed and happy, the children played quietly.

Using Participial Phrases Effectively You can often use a participial phrase to combine a pair of related sentences. Placing the participial phrase at the beginning of the new sentence will add variety to your sentence structure. Look at these examples:

Short Sentences	Combined
The lizard crawled slowly. It vanished into its burrow.	*Crawling slowly,* the lizard vanished into its burrow.

PH | WRITING COACH

Further instruction and practice are available in *Prentice Hall Writing Coach*.

Combining Sentences with Participial Phrases
Follow these steps to combine sentences:

1. **Look for pairs of short, related sentences.**

2. **Find the verb in each sentence of the pair.** Determine whether you can use one of these verbs, plus other words in the sentence, to form a participial phrase.

3. **Follow the examples to rewrite the sentence pair,** creating a stronger single sentence.

Grammar in Your Writing
Look for pairs of short, related sentences in your letter. Use the rules and examples above to revise using participial phrases.

Student Model: Jennifer Miller, Boise, ID

Common Core State Standards

Language
2. Demonstrate command of the conventions of standard English capitalization, punctuation, and spelling when writing.

Jennifer Miller
555 Any Street
Boise, Idaho 99009

October 4, 20–

Ms. Tamora Pierce
333 Any Avenue
New York, New York 10007

Dear Ms. Tamora Pierce:

In "The Circle Opens #2: Street Magic," I absolutely marvel at the simple words you can pull together to create the greatest adventure of all time. I love the impossible paths you lead me through. Your stories have no boundaries. You are able to think through the whole story and then add mysterious clues that lead up to the answer.

You've written so many books that follow into the next series. I enjoy how you build new characters and intermingle previous relationships to come up with an entirely new story line. Maybe your next series could be about Neal's second daughter who can foretell the future through drawing pictures. That would be exciting.

The passion and rhythm you put in your writing really sets the mood of the novel. Your characters turn into true living beings with feelings and emotion that are so deeply expressed that the reader feels them too. You have definitely captured the hearts of all who have read your books, including my 41-year-old dad. Thank you for putting everything into creating numerous novels that have expanded imagination beyond the outside world.

Sincerely,

Jennifer Miller

Jennifer writes her letter in block format.

The introduction identifies the work and makes it clear what Jennifer's feelings are about the author's writing.

To support her ideas, Jennifer mentions a character from the book.

The writer's conclusion balances her introduction.

Editing and Proofreading

Focus on capitalization. The following is a list of words that require capitalization. Use the list as a guide as you revise your draft.

- the first word in a sentence, a quotation (*She said, "Please leave."*), and the greeting and closing in a letter
- major words in titles of books, plays, movies, and television programs (*Letters from Rifka*)
- people's names and titles
- names of geographic locations and names of organizations

Spiral Review
Earlier in this unit, you learned about **prepositions** and **appositives** (p. 734). Check your letter to be sure you have used prepositions and appositives correctly.

Publishing and Presenting

Consider one of the following ways to share your writing:

Make a bulletin board display. Create a poster or other graphic display item, featuring biographical information about the author, a copy of your letter, and related artwork to showcase.

Send your letter. If you have chosen a living author, mail your letter to the author, in care of the publisher. Share your letter, and any response you receive, with your classmates.

Reflecting on Your Writing

Writer's Journal Jot down your answer to this question: *Which drafting strategy was most useful? Why?*

Rubric for Self-Assessment

Find evidence in your writing to address each category. Then, use the rating scale to grade your work.

Criteria	Rating Scale
	not very → *very*
Focus: How clearly do you state your reaction to the author's work?	1 2 3 4 5
Organization: How well do you organize your letter using standard business format? How clearly do you organize the body of your letter?	1 2 3 4 5
Support/Elaboration: How well do you use examples from the author's work to support your ideas?	1 2 3 4 5
Style: How formal and polite is the language?	1 2 3 4 5
Conventions: How correct is your grammar, especially your use of participial phrases?	1 2 3 4 5
Word Choice: Are your word choices specific and precise?	1 2 3 4 5

Drama Selection

Build your skills and improve your comprehension of drama with texts of increasing complexity.

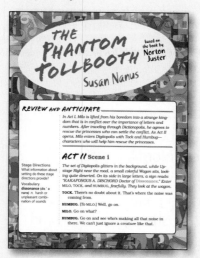

Read **The Phantom Tollbooth, Act II,** and accompany Milo as his journey continues.

Common Core State Standards

Meet these standards with **The Phantom Tollbooth, Act II** (p. 748).

Reading Literature
5. Analyze how a particular sentence, chapter, scene, or stanza fits into the overall structure of a text and contributes to the development of the theme, setting, or plot. *(Literary Analysis: Stage Directions)*

7. Compare and contrast the experience of reading a story, drama, or poem to listening to or viewing an audio, video, or live version of the text, including contrasting what they "see" and "hear" when reading the text to what they perceive when they listen or watch. *(Speaking and Listening: Group Discussion)*

Writing
1. Write arguments to support claims with clear reasons and relevant evidence. **1.a.** Introduce claim(s) and organize the reasons and evidence clearly. *(Writing: Review)*

Speaking and Listening
1.c. Pose and respond to specific questions with elaboration and detail by making comments

that contribute to the topic, text, or issue under discussion.

3. Delineate a speaker's argument and specific claims, distinguishing claims that are supported by reasons and evidence from claims that are not. *(Speaking and Listening: Group Discussion)*

Language
1. Demonstrate command of the conventions of standard English grammar and usage when writing or speaking. *(Writing: Review)*

3. Use knowledge of language and its conventions when writing, speaking, reading, or listening. *(Conventions: Gerunds and Gerund Phrases)*

6. Acquire and use accurately grade-appropriate general academic and domain-specific words and phrases; gather vocabulary knowledge when considering a word or phrase important to comprehension or expression. *(Vocabulary: Word Study)*

Reading Skill: Compare and Contrast

When you **compare** two things, you tell how they are alike. When you **contrast** two things, you tell how they are different. As you read drama, **picture the action** to compare and contrast characters, situations, and events. Pay attention to the dialogue and the descriptions of how characters speak and act.

Literary Analysis: Stage Directions

A **dramatic script** contains two main types of information. Lines of dialogue tell readers what the characters say. **Stage directions** are the words in a drama that the characters do not say. They tell performers how to move and speak. They also help readers picture the action, sounds, and scenery. Stage directions are usually printed in italics and set between brackets, as in this example.

> **CARLOS.** [*To* ISABEL.] Remember, don't make a sound! [*He tiptoes offstage.*]

Using the Strategy: Stage Directions Chart

As you read, use a chart like the one shown to record stage directions that help you picture the action and understand what the characters are thinking and feeling.

Stage Direction	What It Shows About the Character or Action

PHLit Online!
www.PHLitOnline.com

Hear It!
- Selection summary audio
- Selection audio

See It!
- Get Connected video
- Background video
- More about the author
- Vocabulary flashcards

Do It!
- Interactive journals
- Interactive graphic organizers
- Self-test
- Internet activity
- Grammar tutorial
- Interactive vocabulary games

How do we decide *who* we are?

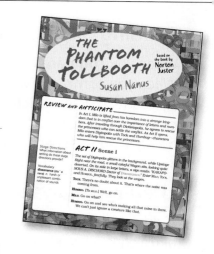

Writing About the Big Question

In Act II, Milo comes back from his adventure to find that he is not the same boy he used to be. Use this sentence starter to develop your ideas about the Big Question.

New experiences can give us a new **perspective** on _____ because _____.

While You Read Notice how Milo's imagination and interests are awakened by his experiences.

Vocabulary

Read each word and its definition. Decide whether you know the word well, know it a little bit, or do not know it at all. After you read, see how your knowledge of each word has increased.

- **dissonance** (dis′ ə nəns) *n.* harsh or unpleasant combination of sounds (p. 748) *Poorly tuned instruments create dissonance in an orchestra. dissonant adj.*

- **deficiency** (dē fish′ ən sē) *n.* shortage or lack (p. 750) *Eating a well-balanced diet will protect you against a vitamin deficiency. deficient adj.*

- **admonishing** (ad män′ ish iŋ) *adj.* disapproving (p. 754) *The librarian gave the noisy group an admonishing look.*

- **iridescent** (ir′ i des′ ənt) *adj.* showing different colors when seen from different angles (p. 757) *The peacock's iridescent feathers can appear either blue or green. iridescence n.*

- **malicious** (mə lish′ əs) *adj.* having or showing bad intentions (p. 765) *There was no truth to that malicious gossip. malice n. maliciously adv.*

- **transfixed** (trans fikst′) *v.* made motionless by horror or fascination (p. 767) *I sat still, transfixed by the scary movie. transfix v.*

Word Study

The **prefix *trans-*** means "across" or "through."

In *The Phantom Tollbooth*, Act II, Milo is **transfixed** by a soothing voice. It is as if he is fixed into place by a sharp object that is pierced through him.

Meet
Norton Juster
(b. 1929)

Author of

THE PHANTOM TOLLBOOTH

Norton Juster's first career was as an architect, designing buildings and other structures. He took up creative writing in his spare time "as a relaxation" from architecture. When he began writing *The Phantom Tollbooth*, the novel on which this drama is based, he thought it was just a short story for his own pleasure. Yet before long, Juster says, "it had created its own life, and I was hooked." The novel has been translated into several foreign languages and adapted for an animated film. Juster has even rewritten it as an opera!

A Pen Pal Although *The Phantom Tollbooth* was first published in 1961, Juster still gets fan mail from new readers. He tries to answer every letter.

For a biography of Susan Nanus, see page 707.

DID YOU KNOW?

Juster describes Tock as "the friend your mother wanted you to play with" and the Humbug as "the kind of kid your folks didn't want you to play with."

BACKGROUND FOR THE DRAMA

Words Versus Numbers

In *The Phantom Tollbooth*, Azaz and the Mathemagician cannot agree about which is more important—words or numbers. Without words, we would not be able to talk, read, write, or learn. Without numbers, on the other hand, we would not have money, maps, calendars, clocks, or schedules.

THE PHANTOM TOLLBOOTH

based on the book by **Norton Juster**

Susan Nanus

REVIEW AND ANTICIPATE

In Act I, Milo is lifted from his boredom into a strange kingdom that is in conflict over the importance of letters and numbers. After traveling through Dictionopolis, he agrees to rescue the princesses who can settle the conflict. As Act II opens, Milo enters Digitopolis with Tock and Humbug—characters who will help him rescue the princesses.

ACT II Scene i

Stage Directions
What information about setting do these stage directions provide?

Vocabulary
dissonance (dis´ ə nəns) *n.* harsh or unpleasant combination of sounds

The set of Digitopolis glitters in the background, while Upstage Right near the road, a small colorful Wagon sits, looking quite deserted. On its side in large letters, a sign reads: "KAKAFONOUS A. DISCHORD Doctor of Dissonance." Enter MILO, TOCK, and HUMBUG, *fearfully. They look at the wagon.*

TOCK. There's no doubt about it. That's where the noise was coming from.

HUMBUG. [*To* MILO.] Well, go on.

MILO. Go on what?

HUMBUG. Go on and see who's making all that noise in there. We can't just ignore a creature like that.

MILO. Creature? What kind of creature? Do you think he's dangerous?

HUMBUG. Go on, Milo. Knock on the door. We'll be right behind you.

MILO. O.K. Maybe he can tell us how much further it is to Digitopolis.

[MILO *tiptoes up to the wagon door and KNOCKS timidly. The moment he knocks, a terrible CRASH is heard inside the wagon, and* MILO *and the others jump back in fright. At the same time, the Door Flies Open, and from the dark interior, a Hoarse* VOICE *inquires.*]

VOICE. Have you ever heard a whole set of dishes dropped from the ceiling onto a hard stone floor? [*The Others are speechless with fright.* MILO *shakes his head.* VOICE *happily.*] Have you ever heard an ant wearing fur slippers walk across a thick wool carpet? [MILO *shakes his head again.*] Have you ever heard a blindfolded octopus unwrap a cellophane-covered bathtub? [MILO *shakes his head a third time.*] Ha! I knew it. [*He hops out, a little man, wearing a white coat, with a stethoscope around his neck, and a small mirror attached to his forehead, and with very huge ears, and a mortar and pestle in his hands. He stares at* MILO, TOCK *and* HUMBUG.] None of you looks well at all! Tsk, tsk, not at all. [*He opens the top or side of his Wagon, revealing a dusty interior resembling an old apothecary shop, with shelves lined with jars and boxes, a table, books, test tubes and bottles and measuring spoons.*]

MILO. [*Timidly.*] Are you a doctor?

DISCHORD. [VOICE.] I am KAKAFONOUS A. DISCHORD, DOCTOR OF DISSONANCE! [*Several small explosions and a grinding crash are heard.*]

HUMBUG. [*Stuttering with fear.*] What does the "A" stand for?

DISCHORD. AS LOUD AS POSSIBLE! [*Two screeches and a bump are heard.*] Now, step a little closer and stick out your tongues. [DISCHORD *examines them.*] Just as I expected. [*He opens a large dusty book and thumbs through the pages.*] You're all suffering from a severe lack of noise. [DISCHORD *begins running around, collecting bottles, reading the labels to himself as he goes along.*] "Loud

Stage Directions
What information about sound effects do you learn from these stage directions?

Reading Check
Why are Milo, Tock, and Humbug frightened?

Cries." "Soft Cries." "Bangs, Bongs, Swishes. Swooshes." "Snaps and Crackles." "Whistles and Gongs." "Squeeks, Squawks, and Miscellaneous Uproar." [*As he reads them off, he pours a little of each into a large glass beaker and stirs the mixture with a wooden spoon. The concoction smokes and bubbles.*] Be ready in just a moment.

MILO. [*Suspiciously.*] Just what kind of doctor are you?

DISCHORD. Well, you might say, I'm a specialist. I specialize in noises, from the loudest to the softest, and from the slightly annoying to the terribly unpleasant. For instance, have you ever heard a square-wheeled steamroller ride over a street full of hard-boiled eggs? [*Very loud CRUNCHING SOUNDS are heard.*]

MILO. [*Holding his ears.*] But who would want all those terrible noises?

DISCHORD. [*Surprised at the question.*] Everybody does. Why, I'm so busy I can hardly fill all the orders for noise pills, racket lotion, clamor salve and hubbub tonic. That's all people seem to want these days. Years ago, everyone wanted pleasant sounds and business was terrible. But then the cities were built and there was a great need for honking horns, screeching trains, clanging bells and all the rest of those wonderfully unpleasant sounds we use so much today. I've been working overtime ever since and my medicine here is in great demand. All you have to do is take one spoonful every day, and you'll never have to hear another beautiful sound again. Here, try some.

HUMBUG. [*Backing away.*] If it's all the same to you, I'd rather not.

MILO. I don't want to be cured of beautiful sounds.

TOCK. Besides, there's no such sickness as a lack of noise.

DISCHORD. How true. That's what makes it so difficult to cure. [*Takes a large glass bottle from the shelf.*] Very well, if you want to go all through life suffering from a noise **deficiency**, I'll just give this to Dynne for his lunch. [*Uncorks the bottle and pours the liquid into it. There is a rumbling and then a loud*

▼ **Critical Viewing**
What aspect of Dischord's appearance might lead you to guess that he is interested in sounds? **[Connect]**

Vocabulary
deficiency (dē fish´ ən sē) *n.* shortage or lack

explosion accompanied by smoke, out of which DYNNE, *a smog-like creature with yellow eyes and a frowning mouth, appears.*]

DYNNE. [*Smacking his lips.*] Ahhh, that was good, Master. I thought you'd never let me out. It was really cramped in there.

DISCHORD. This is my assistant, the awful Dynne. You must forgive his appearance, for he really doesn't have any.

MILO. What is a Dynne?

DISCHORD. You mean you've never heard of the awful Dynne? When you're playing in your room and making a great amount of noise, what do they tell you to stop?

MILO. That awful din.

DISCHORD. When the neighbors are playing their radio too loud late at night, what do you wish they'd turn down?

TOCK. That awful din.

DISCHORD. And when the street on your block is being repaired and the drills are working all day, what does everyone complain of?

HUMBUG. [*Brightly.*] The dreadful row.

DYNNE. The Dreadful Rauw was my grandfather. He perished in the great silence epidemic of 1712. I certainly can't understand why you don't like noise. Why, I heard an explosion last week that was so lovely, I groaned with appreciation for two days. [*He gives a loud groan at the memory.*]

DISCHORD. He's right, you know! Noise is the most valuable thing in the world.

MILO. King Azaz says words are.

DISCHORD. NONSENSE! Why, when a baby wants food, how does he ask?

DYNNE. [*Happily.*] He screams!

DISCHORD. And when a racing car wants gas?

DYNNE. [*Jumping for joy.*] It chokes!

Stage Directions
How does this stage direction help you imagine what Dynne is like?

Compare and Contrast
How are Dischord's opinions different from most people's regarding sounds?

Reading Check
What caused people to want noise and hubbub rather than pleasant sounds?

DISCHORD. And what happens to the dawn when a new day begins?

DYNNE. [*Delighted.*] It breaks!

DISCHORD. You see how simple it is? [*To* DYNNE.] Isn't it time for us to go?

MILO. Where to? Maybe we're going the same way.

Compare and Contrast
How are these rounds different from the daily rounds of people such as mail carriers?

DYNNE. I doubt it. [*Picking up empty sacks from the table.*] We're going on our collection rounds. Once a day, I travel throughout the kingdom and collect all the wonderfully horrible and beautifully unpleasant sounds I can find and bring them back to the doctor to use in his medicine.

DISCHORD. Where are you going?

MILO. To Digitopolis.

DISCHORD. Oh, there are a number of ways to get to Digitopolis, if you know how to follow directions. Just take a look at the sign at the fork in the road. Though why you'd ever want to go there, I'll never know.

MILO. We want to talk to the Mathemagician.

HUMBUG. About the release of the Princesses Rhyme and Reason.

Stage Directions
How do these stage directions help you understand what Dischord is doing?

DISCHORD. Rhyme and Reason? I remember them. Very nice girls, but a little too quiet for my taste. In fact, I've been meaning to send them something that Dynne brought home by mistake and which I have absolutely no use for. [*He rummages through the wagon.*] Ah, here it is . . . or maybe you'd like it for yourself. [*Hands* MILO *a Package.*]

MILO. What is it?

DISCHORD. The sounds of laughter. They're so unpleasant to hear, it's almost unbearable. All those giggles and snickers and happy shouts of joy, I don't know what Dynne was thinking of when he collected them. Here, take them to the Princesses or keep them for yourselves, I don't care. Well, time to move on. Goodbye now and good luck! [*He has shut the wagon by now and gets in. LOUD NOISES begin to erupt as* DYNNE *pulls the wagon offstage.*]

MILO. [*Calling after them.*] But wait! The fork in the road . . . you didn't tell us where it is . . .

TOCK. It's too late. He can't hear a thing.

HUMBUG. I could use a fork of my own, at the moment. And a knife and a spoon to go with it. All of a sudden, I feel very hungry.

MILO. So do I, but it's no use thinking about it. There won't be anything to eat until we reach Digitopolis. [*They get into the car.*]

HUMBUG. [*Rubbing his stomach.*] Well, the sooner the better is what I say. [*A SIGN suddenly appears.*]

> **DIGITOPOLIS**
> 5 Miles
> 1,600 Rods
> 8,800 Yards
> 26,400 Feet
> 316,800 Inches
> 633,600 Half Inches AND THEN SOME

◀ **Critical Viewing**
How are the different measurements on this sign related? **[Analyze]**

VOICE. [*A strange voice from nowhere.*] But which way will get you there sooner? That is the question.

TOCK. Did you hear something?

MILO. Look! The fork in the road and a signpost to Digitopolis! [*They read the Sign.*]

HUMBUG. Let's travel by miles, it's shorter.

MILO. Let's travel by half inches. It's quicker.

TOCK. But which road should we take? It must make a difference.

MILO. Do you think so?

TOCK. Well, I'm not sure, but . . .

HUMBUG. He could be right. On the other hand, he could also be wrong. Does it make a difference or not?

VOICE. Yes, indeed, indeed it does, certainly, my yes, it does make a difference.

✓ **Reading Check**
What does Dischord give to Milo, and why?

Stage Directions
Why would the information presented here be important to a group performing the play?

[*The* DODECAHEDRON *appears, a 12-sided figure with a different face on each side, and with all the edges labeled with a small letter and all the angles labeled with a large letter. He wears a beret and peers at the others with a serious face. He doffs his cap and recites:*]

DODECAHEDRON. *My angles are many.*
My sides are not few.
I'm the Dodecahedron.
Who are you?

MILO. What's a Dodecahedron?

DODECAHEDRON. [*Turning around slowly.*] See for yourself. A Dodecahedron is a mathematical shape with 12 faces. [*All his faces appear as he turns, each face with a different expression. He points to them.*] I usually use one at a time. It saves wear and tear. What are you called?

MILO. Milo.

DODECAHEDRON. That's an odd name. [*Changing his smiling face to a frowning one.*] And you have only one face.

MILO. [*Making sure it is still there.*] Is that bad?

DODECAHEDRON. You'll soon wear it out using it for everything. Is everyone with one face called Milo?

MILO. Oh, no. Some are called Billy or Jeffery or Sally or Lisa or lots of other things.

DODECAHEDRON. How confusing. Here everything is called exactly what it is. The triangles are called triangles, the circles are called circles, and even the same numbers have the same name. Can you imagine what would happen if we named all the twos Billy or Jeffery or Sally or Lisa or lots of other things? You'd have to say Robert plus John equals four, and if the fours were named Albert, things would be hopeless.

MILO. I never thought of it that way.

Vocabulary
admonishing (ad män´ ish iŋ) *adj.* disapproving

DODECAHEDRON. [*With an admonishing face.*] Then I suggest you begin at once, for in Digitopolis, everything is quite precise.

MILO. Then perhaps you can help us decide which road we should take.

DODECAHEDRON. [*Happily.*] By all means. There's nothing to it. [*As he talks, the three others try to solve the problem on a Large Blackboard that is wheeled onstage for the occasion.*] Now, if a small car carrying three people at 30 miles an hour for 10 minutes along a road 5 miles long at 11:35 in the morning starts at the same time as 3 people who have been traveling in a little automobile at 20 miles an hour for 15 minutes on another road exactly twice as long as half the distance of the other, while a dog, a bug, and a boy travel an equal distance in the same time or the same distance in an equal time along a third road in mid-October, then which one arrives first and which is the best way to go?

HUMBUG. Seventeen!

MILO. [*Still figuring frantically.*] I'm not sure, but . . .

DODECAHEDRON. You'll have to do better than that.

MILO. I'm not very good at problems.

DODECAHEDRON. What a shame. They're so very useful. Why, did you know that if a beaver 2 feet long with a tail a foot and a half long can build a dam 12 feet high and 6 feet wide in 2 days, all you would need to build Boulder Dam is a beaver 68 feet long with a 51 foot tail?

HUMBUG. [*Grumbling as his pencil snaps.*] Where would you find a beaver that big?

DODECAHEDRON. I don't know, but if you did, you'd certainly know what to do with him.

MILO. That's crazy.

DODECAHEDRON. That may be true, but it's completely accurate, and as long as the answer is right, who cares if the question is wrong?

TOCK. [*Who has been patiently doing the first problem.*] All three roads arrive at the same place at the same time.

DODECAHEDRON. Correct! And I'll take you there myself. [*The blackboard rolls off, and all four get into the car and drive off.*] Now you see how important problems are. If you hadn't done this one properly, you might have gone the wrong way.

Compare and Contrast
Based on his words and actions, how is Dodecahedron different from Milo and Humbug?

" ... as long as the answer is right, who cares if the question is wrong?"

Reading Check
Based on their responses to the problem Dodecahedron poses, who is best at mathematics: Milo, Tock, or Humbug?

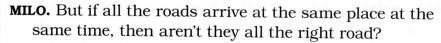

MILO. But if all the roads arrive at the same place at the same time, then aren't they all the right road?

DODECAHEDRON. [*Glaring from his upset face.*] Certainly not! They're all the wrong way! Just because you have a choice, it doesn't mean that any of them has to be right. [*Pointing in another direction.*] That's the way to Digitopolis and we'll be there any moment. [*Suddenly the lighting grows dimmer.*] In fact, we're here. Welcome to the Land of Numbers.

HUMBUG. [*Looking around at the barren landscape.*] It doesn't look very inviting.

MILO. Is this the place where numbers are made?

DODECAHEDRON. They're not made. You have to dig for them. Don't you know anything at all about numbers?

MILO. Well, I never really thought they were very important.

DODECAHEDRON. NOT IMPORTANT! Could you have tea for two without the 2? Or three blind mice without the 3? And how would you sail the seven seas without the 7?

MILO. All I meant was . . .

DODECAHEDRON. [*Continues shouting angrily.*] If you had high hopes, how would you know how high they were? And did you know that narrow escapes come in different widths? Would you travel the whole world wide without ever knowing how wide it was? And how could you do anything at long last without knowing how long the last was? Why, numbers are the most beautiful and valuable things in the world. Just follow me and I'll show you. [*He motions to them and pantomimes walking through rocky terrain with the others in tow. A Doorway similar to the Tollbooth appears and the* DODECAHEDRON *opens it and motions the others to follow him through.*] Come along, come along. I can't wait for you all day. [*They enter the doorway and the lights are dimmed very low, as to simulate the interior of a cave. The SOUNDS of scrapings and tapping, scuffling and digging are heard all around them. He hands them Helmets with flashlights attached.*] Put these on.

▼ **Critical Viewing**
Which qualities of Dodecahedron are the most interesting to you? Why? **[Respond]**

MILO. [*Whispering.*] Where are we going?

DODECAHEDRON. We're here. This is the numbers mine. [*LIGHTS UP A LITTLE, revealing Little Men digging and chopping, shoveling and scraping.*] Right this way and watch your step. [*His voice echoes and reverberates. Iridescent and glittery numbers seem to sparkle from everywhere.*]

MILO. [*Awed.*] Whose mine is it?

VOICE OF MATHEMAGICIAN. By the four million eight hundred and twenty-seven thousand six hundred and fifty-nine hairs on my head, it's mine, of course! [*ENTER the* MATHEMAGICIAN, *carrying his long staff which looks like a giant pencil.*]

HUMBUG. [*Already intimidated.*] It's a lovely mine, really it is.

MATHEMAGICIAN. [*Proudly.*] The biggest number mine in the kingdom.

MILO. [*Excitedly.*] Are there any precious stones in it?

MATHEMAGICIAN. Precious stones! [*Then softly.*] By the eight million two hundred and forty-seven thousand three hundred and twelve threads in my robe, I'll say there are. Look here. [*Reaches in a cart, pulls out a small object, polishes it vigorously and holds it to the light, where it sparkles.*]

MILO. But that's a five.

MATHEMAGICIAN. Exactly. As valuable a jewel as you'll find anywhere. Look at some of the others. [*Scoops up others and pours them into* MILO'S *arms. They include all numbers from 1 to 9 and an assortment of zeros.*]

DODECAHEDRON. We dig them and polish them right here, and then send them all over the world. Marvelous, aren't they?

TOCK. They are beautiful. [*He holds them up to compare them to the numbers on his clock body.*]

MILO. So that's where they come from. [*Looks at them and carefully hands them back, but drops a few which smash and break in half.*] Oh, I'm sorry!

Vocabulary
iridescent (ir´ ə des´ ənt) *adj.* showing different colors when seen from different angles

Stage Directions
What information do these stage directions provide about the action?

Reading Check
What do Dodecahedron and Mathemagician find exciting and valuable?

MATHEMAGICIAN. [*Scooping them up.*] Oh, don't worry about that. We use the broken ones for fractions. How about some lunch? [*Takes out a little whistle and blows it. Two miners rush in carrying an immense cauldron which is bubbling and steaming. The workers put down their tools and gather around to eat.*]

HUMBUG. That looks delicious! [TOCK *and* MILO *also look hungrily at the pot.*]

MATHEMAGICIAN. Perhaps you'd care for something to eat?

MILO. Oh, yes, sir!

TOCK. Thank you.

HUMBUG. [*Already eating.*] Ummm . . . delicious! [*All finish their bowls immediately.*]

MATHEMAGICIAN. Please have another portion. [*They eat and finish.* MATHEMAGICIAN *serves them again.*] Don't stop now. [*They finish.*] Come on, no need to be bashful. [*Serves them again.*]

MILO. [*To* TOCK *and* HUMBUG *as he finishes again.*] Do you want to hear something strange? Each one I eat makes me a little hungrier than before.

MATHEMAGICIAN. Do have some more. [*He serves them again. They eat frantically, until the* MATHEMAGICIAN *blows his whistle again and the pot is removed.*]

HUMBUG. [*Holding his stomach.*] Uggghhh! I think I'm starving.

MILO. Me, too, and I ate so much.

DODECAHEDRON. [*Wiping the gravy from several of his mouths.*] Yes, it was delicious, wasn't it? It's the specialty of the kingdom . . . subtraction stew.

▲ Critical Viewing
Which details in the picture suggest that this is Mathemagician?
[Analyze]

TOCK. [*Weak from hunger.*] I have more of an appetite than when I began.

MATHEMAGICIAN. Certainly, what did you expect? The more you eat, the hungrier you get, everyone knows that.

MILO. They do? Then how do you get enough?

MATHEMAGICIAN. Enough? Here in Digitopolis, we have our meals when we're full and eat until we're hungry. That way, when you don't have anything at all, you have more than enough. It's a very economical system. You must have been stuffed to have eaten so much.

DODECAHEDRON. It's completely logical. The more you want, the less you get, and the less you get, the more you have. Simple arithmetic, that's all. [TOCK, MILO *and* HUMBUG *look at him blankly.*] Now, look, suppose you had something and added nothing to it. What would you have?

MILO. The same.

DODECAHEDRON. Splendid! And suppose you had something and added less than nothing to it? What would you have then?

HUMBUG. Starvation! Oh, I'm so hungry.

DODECAHEDRON. Now, now, it's not as bad as all that. In a few hours, you'll be nice and full again . . . just in time for dinner.

MILO. But I only eat when I'm hungry.

MATHEMAGICIAN. [*Waving the eraser of his staff.*] What a curious idea. The next thing you'll have us believe is that you only sleep when you're tired.

[*The mine has disappeared as well as the Miners.*]

HUMBUG. Where did everyone go?

MATHEMAGICIAN. Oh, they're still in the mine. I often find that the best way to get from one place to another is to erase everything and start again. Please make yourself at home.

Compare and Contrast
How are the meals that characters eat in Digitopolis different from real-life meals?

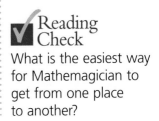

Reading Check
What is the easiest way for Mathemagician to get from one place to another?

[*They find themselves in a unique room, in which all the walls, tables, chairs, desks, cabinets and blackboards are labeled to show their heights, widths, depths and distances to and from each other. To one side is a gigantic notepad on an artist's easel, and from hooks and strings hang a collection of rulers, measures, weights and tapes, and all other measuring devices.*]

MILO. Do you always travel that way? [*He looks around in wonder.*]

MATHEMAGICIAN. No, indeed! [*He pulls a plumb line from a hook and walks.*] Most of the time I take the shortest distance between any two points. And of course, when I have to be in several places at once . . . [*He writes $3 \times 1 = 3$ on the notepad with his staff.*] I simply multiply. [THREE FIGURES *looking like the* MATHEMAGICIAN *appear on a platform above.*]

MILO. How did you do that?

MATHEMAGICIAN AND **THE THREE.** There's nothing to it, if you have a magic staff. [THE THREE FIGURES *cancel themselves out and disappear.*]

HUMBUG. That's nothing but a big pencil.

MATHEMAGICIAN. True enough, but once you learn to use it, there's no end to what you can do.

MILO. Can you make things disappear?

MATHEMAGICIAN. Just step a little closer and watch this. [*Shows them that there is nothing up his sleeve or in his hat. He writes:*]
$4 + 9 - 2 \times 16 + 1 = 3 \times 6 - 67 + 8 \times 2 - 3 + 26 - 1 - 34 + 3 - 7 + 2 - 5 =$ [*He looks up expectantly.*]

HUMBUG. Seventeen?

MILO. It all comes to zero.

MATHEMAGICIAN. Precisely. [*Makes a theatrical bow and rips off paper from notepad.*] Now, is there anything else you'd like to see? [*At this point, an appeal to the audience to see if anyone would like a problem solved.*]

MILO. Well . . . can you show me the biggest number there is?

MATHEMAGICIAN. Why, I'd be delighted. [*Opening a closet door.*] We keep it right here. It took four miners to dig it out. [*He shows them a huge "3" twice as high as the* **MATHEMAGICIAN.**]

MILO. No, that's not what I mean. Can you show me the longest number there is?

MATHEMAGICIAN. Sure. [*Opens another door.*] Here it is. It took three carts to carry it here. [*Door reveals an "8" that is as wide as the "3" was high.*]

MILO. No, no, that's not what I meant either. [*Looks helplessly at* TOCK.]

TOCK. I think what you would like to see is the number of the greatest possible magnitude.

MATHEMAGICIAN. Well, why didn't you say so? [*He busily measures them and all other things as he speaks, and marks it down.*] What's the greatest number you can think of? [*Here, an appeal can also be made to the audience or* MILO *may think of his own answers.*]

MILO. Uh . . . nine trillion, nine hundred and ninety-nine billion, nine hundred ninety-nine million, nine-hundred ninety-nine thousand, nine hundred and ninety-nine [*He puffs.*]

MATHEMAGICIAN. [*Writes that on the pad.*] Very good. Now add one to it. [MILO *or audience does.*] Now add one again. [MILO *or audience does so.*] Now add one again. Now add one again. Now add . . .

MILO. But when can I stop?

MATHEMAGICIAN. Never. Because the number you want is always at least one more than the number you have, and it's so large that if you started saying it yesterday, you wouldn't finish tomorrow.

HUMBUG. Where could you ever find a number so big?

MATHEMAGICIAN. In the same place they have the smallest number there is, and you know what that is?

Compare and Contrast
Based on Mathemagician's actions here, how does he see numbers differently from Milo?

Reading Check
What does Mathemagician teach Milo about numbers?

MILO. The smallest number . . . let's see . . . one one-millionth?

MATHEMAGICIAN. Almost. Now all you have to do is divide that in half and then divide that in half and then divide that in half and then divide that . . .

MILO. Doesn't that ever stop either?

MATHEMAGICIAN. How can it when you can always take half of what you have and divide it in half again? Look. [*Pointing offstage.*] You see that line?

MILO. You mean that long one out there?

MATHEMAGICIAN. That's it. Now, if you just follow that line forever, and when you reach the end, turn left, you will find the Land of Infinity. That's where the tallest, the shortest, the biggest, the smallest and the most and the least of everything are kept.

MILO. But how can you follow anything forever? You know, I get the feeling that everything in Digitopolis is very difficult.

MATHEMAGICIAN. But on the other hand, I think you'll find that the only thing you can do easily is be wrong, and that's hardly worth the effort.

MILO. But . . . what bothers me is . . . well, why is it that even when things are correct, they don't really seem to be right?

MATHEMAGICIAN. [*Grows sad and quiet.*] How true. It's been that way ever since Rhyme and Reason were banished. [*Sadness turns to fury.*] And all because of that stubborn wretch Azaz! It's all his fault.

MILO. Maybe if you discussed it with him . . .

MATHEMAGICIAN. He's just too unreasonable! Why just last month, I sent him a very friendly letter, which he never had the courtesy to answer. See for yourself. [*Puts the letter on the easel. The letter reads:*]

4738 1919,

667 394107 5841 62589 85371 14

39588 7190434 203 27689 57131 481206.

5864 98053,

62179875073

MILO. But maybe he doesn't understand numbers.

MATHEMAGICIAN. Nonsense! Everybody understands numbers. No matter what language you speak, they always mean the same thing. A seven is a seven everywhere in the world.

MILO. [*To* TOCK *and* HUMBUG.] Everyone is so sensitive about what he knows best.

TOCK. With your permission, sir, we'd like to rescue Rhyme and Reason.

MATHEMAGICIAN. Has Azaz agreed to it?

TOCK. Yes, sir.

MATHEMAGICIAN. THEN I DON'T! Ever since they've been banished, we've never agreed on anything, and we never will.

MILO. Never?

MATHEMAGICIAN. NEVER! And if you can prove otherwise, you have my permission to go.

MILO. Well then, with whatever Azaz agrees, you disagree.

MATHEMAGICIAN. Correct.

MILO. And with whatever Azaz disagrees, you agree.

MATHEMAGICIAN. [*Yawning, cleaning his nails.*] Also correct.

MILO. Then, each of you agrees that he will disagree with whatever each of you agrees with, and if you both disagree with the same thing, aren't you really in agreement?

MATHEMAGICIAN. I'VE BEEN TRICKED! [*Figures it over, but comes up with the same answer.*]

TOCK. And now may we go?

MATHEMAGICIAN. [*Nods weakly.*] It's a long and dangerous journey. Long before you find them, the demons will know you're there. Watch out for them, because if you

> " A seven is a seven everywhere in the world."

Stage Directions
What does this stage direction suggest about the Mathemagician's opinion of himself?

Reading Check
How does Milo outsmart Mathemagician?

ever come face to face, it will be too late. But there is one other obstacle even more serious than that.

MILO. [*Terrified.*] What is it?

MATHEMAGICIAN. I'm afraid I can't tell you until you return. But maybe I can give you something to help you out. [*Claps hands. ENTER the DODECAHEDRON, carrying something on a pillow. The MATHEMAGICIAN takes it.*] Here is your own magic staff. Use it well and there is nothing it can't do for you. [*Puts a small, gleaming pencil in MILO'S breast pocket.*]

HUMBUG. Are you sure you can't tell about that serious obstacle?

MATHEMAGICIAN. Only when you return. And now the Dodecahedron will escort you to the road that leads to the Castle-in-the-Air. Farewell, my friends, and good luck to you. [*They shake hands, say goodbye, and the DODECAHEDRON leads them off.*] Good luck to you! [*To himself.*] Because you're sure going to need it. [*He watches them through a telescope and marks down the calculations.*]

DODECAHEDRON. [*He re-enters.*] Well, they're on their way.

MATHEMAGICIAN. So I see. . . [DODECAHEDRON *stands waiting.*] Well, what is it?

DODECAHEDRON. I was just wondering myself, your Numbership. What actually is the serious obstacle you were talking about?

MATHEMAGICIAN. [*Looks at him in surprise.*] You mean you really don't know?

BLACKOUT

Scene ii The Land of Ignorance

LIGHTS UP on RHYME and REASON, in their castle, looking out two windows.

RHYME. *I'm worried sick, I must confess*
I wonder if they'll have success
All the others tried in vain,
And were never seen or heard again.

REASON. Now, Rhyme, there's no need to be so pessimistic.

Stage Directions
BLACKOUT means that all the lights focused on the stage are turned off. How does this add suspense here?

Stage Directions
What effect does the stage direction LIGHTS UP have on the action?

Milo, Tock, and Humbug have just as much chance of succeeding as they do of failing.

RHYME. *But the demons are so deadly smart*
They'll stuff your brain and fill your heart
With petty thoughts and selfish dreams
And trap you with their nasty schemes.

REASON. Now, Rhyme, be reasonable, won't you? And calm down, you always talk in couplets when you get nervous. Milo has learned a lot from his journey. I think he's a match for the demons and that he might soon be knocking at our door. Now come on, cheer up, won't you?

RHYME. I'll try.

[*LIGHTS FADE on the* PRINCESSES *and COME UP on the little Car, traveling slowly.*]

MILO. So this is the Land of Ignorance. It's so dark. I can hardly see a thing. Maybe we should wait until morning.

VOICE. They'll be mourning for you soon enough. [*They look up and see a large, soiled, ugly bird with a dangerous beak and a* malicious *expression.*]

MILO. I don't think you understand. We're looking for a place to spend the night.

BIRD. [*Shrieking.*] It's not yours to spend!

MILO. That doesn't make any sense, you see . . .

BIRD. Dollars or cents, it's still not yours to spend.

MILO. But I don't mean . . .

BIRD. Of course you're mean. Anybody who'd spend a night that doesn't belong to him is very mean.

TOCK. Must you interrupt like that?

BIRD. Naturally, it's my job. I take the words right out of your mouth. Haven't we met before? I'm the Everpresent Wordsnatcher.

MILO. Are you a demon?

BIRD. I'm afraid not. I've tried, but the best I can manage to be is a nuisance. [*Suddenly gets nervous as he looks beyond the three.*] And I don't have time to waste with you. [*Starts to leave.*]

Vocabulary
malicious (mə lish´ əs) *adj.* having or showing bad intentions

Compare and Contrast
How is the bird like other characters Milo meets?

Reading
Check
How does Reason reassure Rhyme?

TOCK. What is it? What's the matter?

MILO. Hey, don't leave. I wanted to ask you some questions. . . . Wait!

BIRD. Weight? Twenty-seven pounds. Bye-bye. [*Disappears.*]

MILO. Well, he was no help.

MAN. Perhaps I can be of some assistance to you? [*There appears a beautifully dressed man, very polished and clean.*] Hello, little boy. [*Shakes* MILO'S *hand.*] And how's the faithful dog? [*Pats* TOCK.] And who is this handsome creature? [*Tips his hat to* HUMBUG.]

HUMBUG. [*To others.*] What a pleasant surprise to meet someone so nice in a place like this.

MAN. But before I help you out, I wonder if first you could spare me a little of your time, and help me with a few small jobs?

HUMBUG. Why, certainly.

TOCK. Gladly.

MILO. Sure, we'd be happy to.

MAN. Splendid, for there are just three tasks. First, I would like to move this pile of sand from here to there. [*Indicates through pantomime a large pile of sand.*] But I'm afraid that all I have is this tiny tweezers. [*Hands it to* MILO, *who begins moving the sand one grain at a time.*] Second, I would like to empty this well and fill that other, but I have no bucket, so you'll have to use this eyedropper. [*Hands it to* TOCK, *who begins to work.*] And finally, I must have a hole in this cliff, and here is a needle to dig it. [HUMBUG *eagerly begins. The man leans against a tree and stares vacantly off into space. The* LIGHTS *indicate the passage of time.*]

MILO. You know something? I've been working steadily for a long time, now, and I don't feel the least bit tired or hungry. I could go right on the same way forever.

MAN. Maybe you will. [*He yawns.*]

MILO. [*Whispers to* TOCK.] Well, I wish I knew how long it was going to take.

Stage Directions
How do these stage directions move the action along?

TOCK. Why don't you use your magic staff and find out?

MILO. [*Takes out pencil and calculates. To* MAN.] Pardon me, sir, but it's going to take 837 years to finish these jobs.

MAN. Is that so? What a shame. Well then you'd better get on with them.

MILO. But . . . it hardly seems worthwhile.

MAN. WORTHWHILE! Of course they're not worthwhile. I wouldn't ask you to do anything that was worthwhile.

TOCK. Then why bother?

MAN. Because, my friends, what could be more important than doing unimportant things? If you stop to do enough of them, you'll never get where you are going. [*Laughs villainously.*]

MILO. [*Gasps.*] Oh, no, you must be . . .

MAN. Quite correct! I am the Terrible Trivium, demon of petty tasks and worthless jobs, ogre of wasted effort and monster of habit. [*They start to back away from him.*] Don't try to leave, there's so much to do, and you still have 837 years to go on the first job.

MILO. But why do unimportant things?

MAN. Think of all the trouble it saves. If you spend all your time doing only the easy and useless jobs, you'll never have time to worry about the important ones which are so difficult. [*Walks toward them whispering.*] Now do come and stay with me. We'll have such fun together. There are things to fill and things to empty, things to take away and things to bring back, things to pick up and things to put down . . . [*They are* transfixed *by his soothing voice. He is about to embrace them when a* VOICE *screams.*]

VOICE. Run! Run! [*They all wake up and run with the Trivium behind. As the voice continues to call out directions, they follow until they lose the Trivium.*] RUN! RUN! This way! This way! Over here! Over here! Up here! Down there! Quick, hurry up!

TOCK. [*Panting.*] I think we lost him.

Compare and Contrast
In what ways are Man and the Everpresent Wordsnatcher different?

Compare and Contrast
How is Terrible Trivium similar to the Lethargarians, who appear in Act I?

Vocabulary
transfixed (trans fikst´) *v.* made motionless by horror or fascination

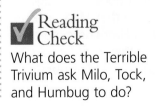
Reading Check
What does the Terrible Trivium ask Milo, Tock, and Humbug to do?

▲ Critical Viewing
How does this image show that Milo, Tock, and Humbug need one another in order to succeed? **[Connect]**

VOICE. Keep going straight! Keep going straight! Now step up! Now step up!

MILO. Look out! [*They all fall into a Trap.*] But he said "up!"

VOICE. Well, I hope you didn't expect to get anywhere by listening to me.

HUMBUG. We're in a deep pit! We'll never get out of here.

VOICE. That is quite an accurate evaluation of the situation.

MILO. [*Shouting angrily.*] Then why did you help us at all?

VOICE. Oh, I'd do as much for anybody. Bad advice is my specialty. [*A Little Furry Creature appears.*] I'm the demon of Insincerity. I don't mean what I say; I don't mean what I do; and I don't mean what I am.

MILO. Then why don't you go away and leave us alone!

INSINCERITY. (VOICE) Now, there's no need to get angry. You're a very clever boy and I have complete confidence in you. You can certainly climb out of that pit . . . come on, try. . .

MILO. I'm not listening to one word you say! You're just telling me what you think I'd like to hear, and not what is important.

INSINCERITY. Well, if that's the way you feel about it . . .

MILO. That's the way I feel about it. We will manage by ourselves without any unnecessary advice from you.

INSINCERITY. [*Stamping his foot.*] Well, all right for you! Most people listen to what I say, but if that's the way you feel, then I'll just go home. [*Exits in a huff.*]

HUMBUG. [*Who has been quivering with fright.*] And don't you ever come back! Well, I guess we showed him, didn't we?

MILO. You know something? This place is a lot more dangerous than I ever imagined.

TOCK. [*Who's been surveying the situation.*] I think I figured a way to get out. Here, hop on my back. [MILO *does so.*] Now, you, Humbug, on top of Milo. [*He does so.*] Now hook your umbrella onto that tree and hold on. [*They climb over* HUMBUG, *then pull him up.*]

HUMBUG. [*As they climb.*] Watch it! Watch it, now. Ow, be careful of my back! My back! Easy, easy . . . oh, this is so difficult. Aren't you finished yet?

TOCK. [*As he pulls up* HUMBUG.] There. Now, I'll lead for a while. Follow me, and we'll stay out of trouble. [*They walk and climb higher and higher.*]

HUMBUG. Can't we slow down a little?

TOCK. Something tells me we better reach the Castle-in-the-Air as soon as possible, and not stop to rest for a single moment. [*They speed up.*]

MILO. What is it, Tock? Did you see something?

TOCK. Just keep walking and don't look back.

MILO. You *did* see something!

HUMBUG. What is it? Another demon?

TOCK. Not just one, I'm afraid. If you want to see what I'm talking about, then turn around. [*They turn around. The stage darkens and hundreds of Yellow Gleaming Eyes can be seen.*]

HUMBUG. Good grief! Do you see how many there are? Hundreds! The Overbearing Know-it-all, the Gross Exaggeration, the Horrible Hopping Hindsight, . . . and look over there! The Triple Demons of Compromise! Let's get out of here! [*Starts to scurry.*] Hurry up, you two! Must you be so slow about everything?

MILO. Look! There it is, up ahead! The Castle-in-the-Air! [*They all run.*]

HUMBUG. They're gaining!

Compare and Contrast
How is the way these new creatures make their entrance different from the way other characters appear onstage?

Reading
Check
Why are Milo and the others running?

▼ **Critical Viewing**
Does this picture of
Senses Taker match the
image you formed as
you read his description
in the stage directions?
Explain. **[Compare
and Contrast]**

MILO. But there it is!

HUMBUG. I see it! I see it!

[*They reach the first step and are stopped by a little man in a frock coat, sleeping on a worn ledger. He has a long quill pen and a bottle of ink at his side. He is covered with ink stains over his clothes and wears spectacles.*]

TOCK. Shh! Be very careful. [*They try to step over him, but he wakes up.*]

SENSES TAKER. [*From sleeping position.*] Names? [*He sits up.*]

HUMBUG. Well, I . . .

SENSES TAKER. *NAMES?* [*He opens book and begins to write, splattering himself with ink.*]

HUMBUG. Uh . . . Humbug, Tock and this is Milo.

SENSES TAKER. Splendid, splendid. I haven't had an "M" in ages.

MILO. What do you want our names for? We're sort of in a hurry.

SENSES TAKER. Oh, this won't take long. I'm the official Senses Taker and I must have some information before I can take your sense. Now if you'll just tell me: [*Handing them a form to fill. Speaking slowly and deliberately.*] When you were born, where you were born, why you were born, how old you are now, how old you were then, how old you'll be in a little while . . .

MILO. I wish he'd hurry up. At this rate, the demons will be here before we know it!

SENSES TAKER. . . . Your mother's name, your father's name, where you live, how long you've lived there, the schools you've attended, the schools you haven't attended . . .

HUMBUG. I'm getting writer's cramp.

TOCK. I smell something very evil and it's getting stronger every second. [*To* SENSES TAKER.] May we go now?

SENSES TAKER. Just as soon as you tell me your height, your weight, the number of books you've read this year . . .

MILO. We have to go!

SENSES TAKER. All right, all right, I'll give you the short form. [*Pulls out a small piece of paper.*] Destination?

MILO. But we have to . . .

SENSES TAKER. *DESTINATION?*

MILO, TOCK AND **HUMBUG.** The Castle-in-the-Air! [*They throw down their papers and run past him up the first few stairs.*]

SENSES TAKER. Stop! I'm sure you'd rather see what I have to show you. [*Snaps his fingers; they freeze.*] A circus of your very own. [*CIRCUS MUSIC is heard.* MILO *seems to go into a trance.*] And wouldn't you enjoy this most wonderful smell? [TOCK *sniffs and goes into a trance.*] And here's something I know you'll enjoy hearing . . . [*To* HUMBUG. *The sound of CHEERS and APPLAUSE for* HUMBUG *is heard, and he goes into a trance.*] There we are. And now, I'll just sit back and let the demons catch up with you.

[MILO *accidentally drops his package of gifts. The Package of Laughter from* DR. DISCHORD *opens and the Sounds of Laughter are heard. After a moment,* MILO, TOCK *and* HUMBUG *join in laughing and the spells are broken.*]

MILO. There was no circus.

TOCK. There were no smells.

HUMBUG. The applause is gone.

SENSES TAKER. I warned you I was the Senses Taker. I'll steal your sense of Purpose, your sense of Duty, destroy your sense of Proportion—and but for one thing, you'd be helpless yet.

MILO. What's that?

Stage Directions
Without these stage directions, would you be able to picture the action here? Explain.

Reading Check
What happens to Senses Taker when Milo drops the Package of Laughter?

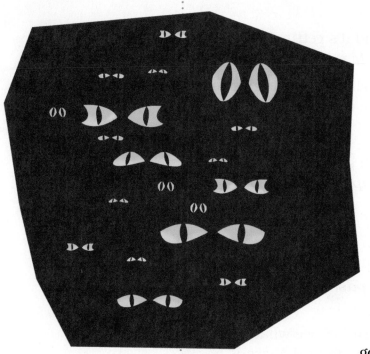

SENSES TAKER. As long as you have the sound of laughter, I cannot take your sense of Humor. Agh! That horrible sense of humor.

HUMBUG. HERE THEY COME! LET'S GET OUT OF HERE!

[*The demons appear in nasty slithering hordes, running through the audience and up onto the stage, trying to attack* TOCK, MILO *and* HUMBUG. *The three heroes run past the* SENSES TAKER *up the stairs toward the Castle-in-the-Air with the demons snarling behind them.*]

MILO. Don't look back! Just keep going! [*They reach the castle. The two princesses appear in the windows.*]

PRINCESSES. Hurry! Hurry! We've been expecting you.

MILO. You must be the Princesses. We've come to rescue you.

HUMBUG. And the demons are close behind!

TOCK. We should leave right away.

PRINCESSES. We're ready anytime you are.

MILO. Good, now if you'll just come out. But wait a minute—there's no door! How can we rescue you from the Castle-in-the-Air if there's no way to get in or out?

HUMBUG. Hurry, Milo! They're gaining on us.

REASON. Take your time, Milo, and think about it.

MILO. Ummm, all right . . . just give me a second or two. [*He thinks hard.*]

HUMBUG. I think I feel sick.

Compare and Contrast
Based on Milo's actions here, how has he changed since leaving his bedroom?

MILO. I've got it! Where's that package of presents? [*Opens the package of letters.*] Ah, here it is. [*Takes out the letters and sticks them on the door, spelling:*] E-N-T-R-A-N-C-E. Entrance. Now, let's see. [*Rummages through and spells in smaller letters:*] P-u-s-h. Push. [*He pushes and a* *door opens. The* PRINCESSES *come out of the castle. Slowly, the demons ascend the stairway.*]

HUMBUG. Oh, it's too late. They're coming up and there's no other way down!

MILO. Unless . . . [*Looks at* TOCK.] Well . . . Time flies, doesn't it?

TOCK. Quite often. Hold on, everyone, and I'll take you down.

HUMBUG. Can you carry us all?

TOCK. We'll soon find out. Ready or not, here we go! [*His alarm begins to ring. They jump off the platform and disappear. The demons, howling with rage, reach the top and find no one there. They see the* PRINCESSES *and the heroes running across the stage and bound down the stairs after them and into the audience. There is a mad chase scene until they reach the stage again.*]

HUMBUG. I'm exhausted! I can't run another step.

MILO. We can't stop now . . .

TOCK. Milo! Look out there! [*The armies of* AZAZ *and* MATHEMAGICIAN *appear at the back of the theater, with the Kings at their heads.*]

AZAZ. [*As they march toward the stage.*] Don't worry, Milo, we'll take over now.

MATHEMAGICIAN. Those demons may not know it, but their days are numbered!

SPELLING BEE. Charge! C-H-A-R-G-E! Charge! [*They rush at the demons and battle until the demons run off howling. Everyone cheers. The* FIVE MINISTERS OF AZAZ *appear and shake* MILO'S *hand.*]

MINISTER 1. Well done.

MINISTER 2. Fine job.

MINISTER 3. Good work!

MINISTER 4. Congratulations!

MINISTER 5. CHEERS! [*Everyone cheers again. A fanfare interrupts. A* PAGE *steps forward and reads from a large scroll:*]

Stage Directions
How do these stage directions help you know what the characters are feeling?

Reading Check
What does Milo do to get into the Castle-in-the-Air?

PAGE. *Henceforth, and forthwith,*
Let it be known by one and all,
That Rhyme and Reason
Reign once more in Wisdom.

[*The* PRINCESSES *bow gratefully and kiss their brothers, the* *Kings.*]

And furthermore,
The boy named Milo,
The dog known as Tock,
And the insect hereinafter referred to as the Humbug
Are hereby declared to be Heroes of the Realm.

[*All bow and salute the heroes.*]

MILO. But we never could have done it without a lot of help.

REASON. That may be true, but you had the courage to try, and what you can do is often a matter of what you *will* do.

AZAZ. That's why there was one very important thing about your quest we couldn't discuss until you returned.

MILO. I remember. What was it?

AZAZ. Very simple. It was impossible!

MATHEMAGICIAN. *Completely* impossible!

HUMBUG. Do you mean . . . ? [*Feeling faint.*] Oh . . . I think I need to sit down.

AZAZ. Yes, indeed, but if we'd told you then, you might not have gone.

Compare and Contrast
Do you think there are real-life situations in which Mathemagician's statement might hold true? Explain.

MATHEMAGICIAN. And, as you discovered, many things are possible just as long as you don't know they're impossible.

MILO. I think I understand.

RHYME. I'm afraid it's time to go now.

REASON. And you must say goodbye.

MILO. To everyone? [*Looks around at the crowd. To* TOCK *and* HUMBUG.] Can't you two come with me?

HUMBUG. I'm afraid not, old man. I'd like to, but I've arranged for a lecture tour which will keep me occupied for years.

TOCK. And they do need a watchdog here.

MILO. Well, O.K., then. [MILO *hugs the* HUMBUG.]

HUMBUG. [*Sadly.*] Oh, bah.

MILO. [*He hugs* TOCK, *and then faces everyone.*] Well, good-bye. We all spent so much time together, I know I'm going to miss you. [*To the* PRINCESSES.] I guess we would have reached you a lot sooner if I hadn't made so many mistakes.

REASON. You must never feel badly about making mistakes, Milo, as long as you take the trouble to learn from them. Very often you learn more by being wrong for the right reasons than you do by being right for the wrong ones.

MILO. But there's so much to learn.

RHYME. That's true, but it's not just learning that's important. It's learning what to do with what you learn and learning why you learn things that matters.

MILO. I think I know what you mean, Princess. At least, I hope I do. [*The car is rolled forward and* MILO *climbs in.*] Goodbye! Goodbye! I'll be back someday! I will! Anyway, I'll try. [*As* MILO *drives the set of the Land of Ignorance begins to move offstage.*]

AZAZ. Goodbye! Always remember. Words! Words! Words!

MATHEMAGICIAN. And numbers!

AZAZ. Now, don't tell me you think numbers are as important as words?

MATHEMAGICIAN. Is that so? Why I'll have you know . . . [*The set disappears, and* MILO *Room is seen onstage.*]

MILO. [*As he drives on.*] Oh, oh, I hope they don't start all over again. Because I don't think I'll have much time in the near future to help them out. [*The sound of loud ticking is heard.* MILO *finds himself in his room. He gets out of the car and looks around.*]

THE CLOCK. Did someone mention time?

Compare and Contrast
With which piece of advice—Reason's or Rhyme's—do you agree more? Explain.

© **Spiral Review**
Character How do the words "I think I know what you mean" indicate that Milo has grown and learned from his experiences?

MILO. Boy, I must have been gone for an awful long time. I wonder what time it is. [*Looks at clock.*] Five o'clock. I wonder what day it is. [*Looks at calendar.*] It's still today! I've only been gone for an hour! [*He continues to look at his calendar, and then begins to look at his books and toys and maps and chemistry set with great interest.*]

CLOCK. An hour. Sixty minutes. How long it really lasts depends on what you do with it. For some people, an hour seems to last forever. For others, just a moment, and so full of things to do.

MILO. [*Looks at clock.*] Six o'clock already?

CLOCK. In an instant. In a trice. Before you have time to blink. [*The stage goes black in less than no time at all.*]

Critical Thinking

Cite textual evidence to support your responses.

1. Key Ideas and Details (a) What does the Terrible Trivium want Milo, Tock, and Humbug to do? **(b) Deduce:** What will be the result if they follow his directions? **(c) Interpret:** What important lesson does Milo learn through his experience with the Terrible Trivium?

2. Key Ideas and Details (a) How is the Senses Taker's spell broken? **(b) Draw Conclusions:** What does Milo learn about humor from his encounter with the Senses Taker?

3. Key Ideas and Details Do you agree that the speed of time depends on what you are doing? Support your answer.

4. Integration of Knowledge and Ideas In your opinion, which of Milo's experiences will lead him to the most important new interest or hobby? Explain your answer. *[Connect to the Big Question: How do we decide who we are?]*

Reading Skill: Compare and Contrast

Create two Venn diagrams like the one shown. Then, use details from Act II to **compare** and **contrast** these characters:

1. Rhyme and Reason
2. Humbug and Tock

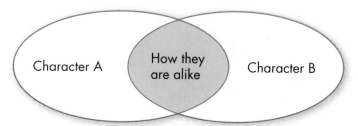

Character A | How they are alike | Character B

Literary Analysis: Stage Directions

Ⓒ 3. **Craft and Structure** **(a)** Describe one place in the play where **stage directions** are necessary for understanding the events. **(b)** Find one place in the play that has no stage directions. Write your own stage directions for that section of text.

Vocabulary

Ⓒ **Acquisition and Use** Write a sentence for each prompt. Use a vocabulary word from page 746 in each sentence.

1. a necktie that looks red or blue from different angles
2. the sounds that two yowling cats make
3. a child's unwillingness to turn off a video game
4. the act of spreading unkind gossip
5. a look that a baby sitter might give a rude child
6. a person's lack of enough vitamin C

Word Study Use context and what you know about the prefix **trans-** to explain your answers to these questions.

1. Is a *transcontinental* trip a short journey?
2. Can a person *transfer* money from one bank to another?

Word Study

The **prefix *trans-*** means "across" or "through."

Apply It Explain how the prefix *trans-* contributes to the meaning of these words. Consult a dictionary if necessary.

transform
transatlantic
transposition

Integrated Language Skills

The Phantom Tollbooth, Act II

Conventions: Gerunds and Gerund Phrases

A **gerund** is a verb form that ends in *-ing* and is used as a noun. A **gerund phrase** is a group of words containing a gerund and any modifiers or other words that relate to it.

Gerund	Gerund Phrase
Singing is fun.	*Singing that song* was fun. (Subject)
I enjoy *reading*.	I enjoy *reading about horses*. (Direct Object)

Gerunds are often confused with present participles, a kind of verb that ends in *-ing*. To identify a gerund, analyze the sentence and locate the verb. The verb describes what the subject does; the gerund names the activity taking place.

Practice A Rewrite each sentence, underlining the gerunds and gerund phrases.

1. Humbug and Milo finished eating the numbers.
2. Their traveling made them tired.
3. Understanding numbers is important!
4. In the Doldrums, thinking was strictly prohibited.
5. Dischord did not prevent them from making noise.

Ⓒ **Reading Application** Reread a section of Act II of *The Phantom Tollbooth* and write a paragraph about it using two gerunds and two gerund phrases. Underline the gerunds and gerund phrases.

Practice B Complete each sentence with a gerund or a gerund phrase.

1. Milo and Tock were planning on _____ the princesses.
2. Milo thinks _____ is quicker.
3. The Senses Taker was good at _____.
4. Milo and Tock kept _____ without slowing down.
5. King Azaz keeps _____ that words are important.

Ⓒ **Writing Application** Write two sets of sentences using the gerunds *learning, seeing,* and *counting*. In the first set, use these words as subjects. In the second set, use them as direct objects.

PH WRITING COACH | Further instruction and practice are available in *Prentice Hall Writing Coach*.

Writing

 **Common Core State Standards**

L.6.1, L.6.3, L.6.6; W.6.1, W.6.1.a; SL.6.1.c, SL.6.3
[For the full wording of the standards, see page 744.]

Ⓒ Argumentative Text Imagine you are a drama critic, and write a **review** of *The Phantom Tollbooth*. Follow these steps:

- Review Acts I and II. Take notes about the parts and characters you liked most and least.

- Begin your review by stating your overall opinion of the play. Then, logically organize the relevant examples from your notes to support your opinions and claims.

- Conclude by telling readers whether you recommend that they see this play.

Grammar Application Reread your writing to be sure you have used gerunds and gerund phrases correctly.

Writing Workshop: *Work in Progress*

Prewriting for Exposition To choose a topic for a cause-and-effect essay you may write, list five events in your personal history or your family's history. List a cause or a reason that each event occurred. Save this Cause List in your writing portfolio.

Use this prewriting activity to prepare for the **Writing Workshop** on page 800.

Speaking and Listening

Ⓒ Comprehension and Collaboration Now that you have read *The Phantom Tollbooth*, access the PHLitOnline audio version of the selection by going to www.phlitonline.com. As a class, listen to the audio version of the play. Then, hold a **group discussion** by forming small groups and talking about how the experience of reading the play was similar to and different from the experience of listening to it.

Use the following list of questions to guide your discussion. Choose a speaker to present your group's findings to the class.

- Did hearing different voices speak for different characters make the play easier to understand or seem more realistic?

- What was the effect of speakers' emphasizing certain words or phrases? Did the same words or phrases seem to require emphasis during your reading? Why or why not?

- Listen carefully to your classmates' arguments. Decide which claims are supported with strong evidence and reasons and which claims are not.

- Did listening to the play help you to imagine the action? Or were you better able to imagine the events and characters by reading about them? Explain your response.

PHLit Online!
www.PHLitOnline.com

- Interactive graphic organizers
- Grammar tutorial
- Interactive journals

Test Practice: Reading

Compare and Contrast

Fiction Selection

Directions: *Read the selection. Then, answer the questions.*

BEN: Did you like the play? The script was better than the book!

RYAN: I agree the script was well written, too, but the main character was annoying. Every time he came on stage I wanted to cover my ears or look away. And the singing was awful!

BEN: Ryan, you missed the whole point. The main actor was *supposed* to be annoying. That was his character. I thought the singing was pretty good.

RYAN: Well, maybe it was the musicians.

BEN: The music was prerecorded! What *did* you like about the play?

RYAN: We did have pretty good seats.

BEN: You're impossible!

1. What is the *main* detail on which Ben and Ryan disagree?
   A. where they were seated
   B. how well the play represents the book
   C. the play's reviews
   D. the singing in the play

2. What is one comparison that can be made between Ben and Ryan?
   A. They both enjoy going to the theater.
   B. They both want to see the play again.
   C. They both think the play was good.
   D. They both review plays.

3. Which statement *best* contrasts Ben's opinion with Ryan's opinion of the play?
   A. Both enjoyed the music, but Ryan did not like the main character.
   B. Both liked the play, but Ben did not like the music.
   C. Ryan did not like the music, but Ben liked the seats.
   D. They did not agree on anything about the play except they both thought it was well written.

Writing for Assessment

Write a paragraph comparing and contrasting the attitudes of Ben and Ryan. Use details from the passage to support your ideas.

Nonfiction Selection

Directions: *Read the selection. Then, answer the questions.*

Reviews of "The Phantom Tollbooth"

Reviewer 1: The production of "The Phantom Tollbooth" performed last night deserves four stars. The boy who played Milo beautifully interpreted the role and won the hearts of his audience. The set was beautifully constructed. Every detail Juster used in his book was accounted for on stage. The stage hands were kept busy changing these complicated sets.

Reviewer 2: Although Carl Masterson who played Milo performed well, the other actors gave poor performances. The actors were not equipped with microphones, making the play hard to follow. If the actors had better costumes and the staging was given more attention, their performance may have been better. I give this production 2 stars.

1. Comparing the two reviews, what is one detail both reviewers agree on?
  - **A.** The staging was good.
  - **B.** The actors gave good performances.
  - **C.** Masterson did a great job playing Milo.
  - **D.** Everybody worked hard creating the production.

2. On which detail do the two reviewers disagree?
  - **A.** the sound
  - **B.** the staging
  - **C.** the costumes
  - **D.** the actor who played Milo

3. What is the main difference between the two reviews?
  - **A.** The first reviewer focuses on the staging; the second reviewer does not mention the staging.
  - **B.** Reviewer 1 enjoyed the actor who played Milo; Reviewer 2 did not enjoy that actor.
  - **C.** Reviewer 1 is more positive in the review; Reviewer 2 is more negative.
  - **D.** There are no major differences.

Writing for Assessment

Connecting Across Texts

Think of a time you watched a movie, play, or TV show with another person. Write a paragraph comparing and contrasting your opinion with that of your companion. Focus your comparison on the same details that are compared in these passages.

PHLit Online!
www.PHLitOnline.com
- Online practice
- Instant feedback

Reading for Information

Analyzing Expository Text and Argument

Online News Article

Persuasive Article

**Common Core
State Standards**

Reading Informational Text
8. Trace and evaluate the argument and specific claims in a text, distinguishing claims that are supported by reasons and evidence from claims that are not.

9. Compare and contrast one author's presentation of events with that of another.

Writing
1. Write arguments to support claims with clear reasons and relevant evidence.

Language
6. Acquire and use accurately grade-appropriate general academic and domain-specific words and phrases; gather vocabulary knowledge when considering a word or phrase important to comprehension or expression.

Reading Skill: Evaluate Evidence

When you read informational and persuasive articles, it is important to **evaluate** the information being presented. In both types of texts, authors provide evidence and details to support their main ideas, claims, and conclusions. As you read, **determine the adequacy and appropriateness of evidence** using this checklist.

Checklist for Evaluating Evidence

- ❑ Does the author provide concrete evidence, such as facts, statistics, and expert opinions?
- ❑ Does the author identify the sources of his or her evidence?
- ❑ Can the author's evidence be verified?
- ❑ Does the author's evidence logically support his or her conclusions?

Look for differences and similarities in the way the authors present information about the same topic.

Content-Area Vocabulary

These words appear in the selections that follow. You may also encounter them in other content-area texts.

- **lunar** (loo´ nər) *adj.* related to the moon or the moon's surface
- **standardize** (stan´dər dīz´) *v.* make an accepted size, shape, quality, weight, or strength
- **practical** (prak´ti kəl) *adj.* of or belonging to all; concerning all

Features:
- informative title
- brief opener that states the main idea
- facts, statistics, and direct quotations that support main idea
- specialized and technical language
- text written for a general audience

NASA Finally Goes Metric

by *SPACE* Staff

When NASA returns astronauts to the moon, the mission will be measured in kilometers, not miles.

The agency has decided to use metric units for all operations on the lunar surface, according to a statement released today.

These brief opening paragraphs give the main idea.

The change will standardize parts and tools. It means Russian wrenches could be used to fix an air leak in a U.S.-built habitat. It will also make communications easier, such as when determining how far to send a rover for a science project.

NASA has ostensibly used the metric system since about 1990, the statement said, but English units are still employed on some missions, and a few projects use both. NASA uses both English and metric aboard the International Space Station.

The dual strategy led to the loss of the Mars Climate Orbiter robotic probe in 1999; a contractor provided thruster firing data in English units while NASA was calculating in metric.

The decision comes after a series of meetings between NASA and 13 other space agencies around the world, where metric measurements rule.

These paragraphs give information on the history behind the NASA decision.

This quotation provides an expert's facts and opinions to support the main idea.

"When we made the announcement at the meeting, the reps for the other space agencies all gave a little cheer," said Jeff Volosin, strategy development lead for NASA's Exploration Systems Mission Directorate. "I think NASA has been seen as maybe a bit stubborn by other space agencies in the past, so this was important as a gesture of our willingness to be cooperative when it comes to the Moon."

Informally, the space agencies have also discussed using Internet protocols for lunar communications, the statement said.

"That way, if some smaller space agency or some private company wants to get involved in something we're doing on the Moon, they can say, 'Hey, we already know how to do internet communications,'" Volosin said. "It lowers the barrier to entry."

Metric Metric
It's so nice, we'll say it twice!™

by *Metric Metric*

Goals of the Metric System

The Metric System Was Created Because:

In a nutshell, the metric system was created by French scientists at the request of the National Assembly of France. The National Assembly of France wanted a standardized system of weights and measures. The scientists, who were from the French Academy of Sciences, formed a commission who proposed a system of measurement that was both scientific in nature and simple to remember and use.

The system that was created became known as the metric system. Scientists named the meter, or the unit of length, after the Greek term *metron*, meaning "measure."

The Purpose and Goals of the Metric System Are:

- To make a universal system of measurement. The metric system is a neutral system that can be adopted around the globe.

- To make a system of measurement that can be replicated.

- To make a system of measurement that is easy to remember and use. The metric system is decimal. It only has seven units of measurement. It uses base 10 arithmetic. All of these factors seem to point to the metric system as being the logical choice for measurement.

- All of the prefixes for each type of measure are the same. *Kilo, hecto, deca, deci, centi, milli,* etc., are used to describe all units of measure in the metric system.

With all the information available comparing the different systems of measurement, switching to the metric system is the **practical** thing to do.

Benefits of the Metric System

For many years, there have been debates about the pros and cons of the metric system. No matter how many arguments or lengthy discussions stem from this debate of meter vs. foot, kilometer vs. mile and kilograms vs. pounds, there are many benefits of the metric system. Here are just a few:

1. The metric system has been adopted by most major countries around the world. By the mid-1970s, most countries had converted to the metric system or had plans to do so. When it comes to measurement, the United States is the only major country who has not adopted the metric system! Using the metric system just makes sense, in order to standardize measurement around the globe.

2. The metric system was created by scientists. When invented, it was designed to fit their needs, so it is a logical and exact system.

> This list contains facts that develop the argument.

3. The metric system was designed to be simple! When making measurements of all kinds, it is only necessary to know a few metric units! In all, there are only 7 base units in this system of measurement! Compared to the twenty base units found in the inch-pound system of measurement, it is much easier to remember. The metric system also follows the decimal number system, so each metric unit increases or decreases in size by 10.
(Ex. 1 meter = 10 decimeters; 1 decimeter = 10 centimeters; etc.)

Since there is no other system of measurement that matches the metric system in simplicity, it is the logical choice for use around the world.

> This sentence restates the authors' point of view.

Comparing Expository Text and Argument

1. Key Ideas and Details **(a)** Identify the main ideas of the news article and the claims in the persuasive article. **(b)** Compare and contrast the types of **evidence** and the authors' presentation of information.

Content-Area Vocabulary

2. (a) Look up the origin of the word *lunacy.* Using this information, explain how *lunar* and *lunacy* are related words. **(b)** Use the words *standardize* and *practical* correctly in a brief summary of the persuasive article.

Timed Writing

Argument: Evaluation

Format and Purpose
The prompt gives specific directions about what to write and what information to include in your response.

Write an essay evaluating whether the authors of "Metric Metric" used evidence that was appropriate and adequate to support their opinon about the metric system. State the authors' opinion, explain whether it was properly supported, and give examples from the text to illustrate your ideas. (30 minutes)

Academic Vocabulary
When evidence is *appropriate,* it is clearly and logically connected to the topic. When evidence is *adequate,* there is enough of it to fully cover the topic.

5-Minute Planner

Complete these steps before you begin to write:

1. Read the prompt carefully. Look for key words like the ones highlighted, which will help you understand the assignment.

2. Review the persuasive article "Metric Metric" to identify the authors' opinion of the metric system. Jot down notes about the evidence used to support the authors' opinion. After you have listed the evidence, reread passages that contain numbers, dates, or proper names to be sure your notes are accurate.

3. Look at your notes and weigh the evidence to determine whether the authors' opinion is well supported.

4. As you draft, decide which examples of evidence from your notes should be used to illustrate your ideas.

Comparing Author's Purpose Across Genres

An **author's purpose** is the main reason the author writes a work. It may be to inform, to entertain, to persuade, or to express emotions.

- To **inform,** an author gives factual information on a subject to educate his or her audience.

- To **persuade,** an author gives reasons, facts, and observations to try and sway his or her readers to share an opinion.

- To **entertain,** an author writes purely for the enjoyment of his or her audience.

Often, the genre, or specific form of writing, helps an author to meet a purpose. For example, to fulfill a purpose of informing, an author might choose to write an essay. To fulfill a purpose of entertaining, a short story, play, or humorous essay would be natural choices. Genre and purpose are usually closely related in informational texts, which are written to be used in a specific way.

The scene by Clark Gesner is from a musical comedy, and the article by Matthew MacDermid is a review of a production of that show. The two selections are related, but the writers use different genres and have different purposes for writing. As you read, use a chart like this one to note details that help you identify each author's unique purpose.

**Common Core
State Standards**

Reading Literature
9. Compare and contrast texts in different forms or genres in terms of their approaches to similar themes and topics.

Reading Informational Text
6. Determine an author's point of view or purpose in a text and explain how it is conveyed in the text.

Selection	Details	Author's Purpose
from *You're a Good Man, Charlie Brown*		
"Happiness is a Charming Charlie Brown at Orlando Rep"		

PHLit Online!
www.PHLitOnline.com

- Vocabulary flashcards
- Interactive journals
- More about the authors
- Selection audio
- Interactive graphic organizers

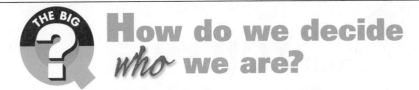

How do we decide *who* we are?

Writing About the Big Question

In the following scene from the play, Lucy learns how others see her. In a similar way, the drama review reports one critic's opinion of someone else's production. Use this sentence starter to help you develop your ideas.

> Someone else's comments on our **appearance** and **personality** can help us see _____.

Meet the Authors

Clark Gesner (1938–2002)

Dramatist of *You're a Good Man, Charlie Brown*

After graduating from Princeton University, Clark Gesner worked as a writer for the award-winning children's television shows *Captain Kangaroo* and *Sesame Street*. He wrote *You're a Good Man, Charlie Brown* because he loved Charles Schulz's comic strip.

Page to the Stage At first, Gesner did not intend *You're a Good Man, Charlie Brown* to become an actual show. Eventually, he sent a few scenes and songs to the cartoonist, who gave him permission to use his characters in the finished play. The production opened off-Broadway in 1967 and was immediately successful. It was revived in 1999, and has become one of the most frequently produced musical comedies in the United States.

Matthew MacDermid

Author of "Happiness is a Charming Charlie Brown at Orlando Rep"

Matthew MacDermid is a theater critic who reviews productions appearing in central Florida for *Talking Broadway*, an online theater resource. *Talking Broadway* provides current news about theater openings, revivals, and trends. It also provides a forum for interactive discussions on theatrical topics.

from You're a Good Man, Charlie Brown

Clark Gesner

Based on the comic strip *Peanuts* by Charles M. Schulz

▲ **Critical Viewing**
What do you already know about Charlie Brown and *Peanuts*? **[Use Prior Knowledge]**

SCHROEDER. I'm sorry to have to say it right to your face, Lucy, but it's true. You're a very crabby person. I know your crabbiness has probably become so natural to you now that you're not even aware when you're being crabby, but it's true just the same. You're a very crabby person and you're crabby to just about everyone you meet. (LUCY *remains silent—just barely*) Now I hope you don't mind my saying this, Lucy, and I hope you'll take it in the spirit that it's meant. I think we should all be open to any opportunity to learn more about ourselves. I think Socrates was very right when he said that one of the first rules for anyone in life is "Know thyself." (LUCY *has begun whistling quietly to herself*) Well, I guess I've said about enough. I hope I haven't offended you or anything. (*He makes an awkward exit*)

LUCY. (*Sits in silence, then shouts offstage at* SCHROEDER) Well, what's Socrates got to do with it anyway, huh? Who was *he* anyway? Did he ever get to be king, huh! Answer me that, did he ever get to be king! (*Suddenly to herself, a real question*) *Did* he ever get to be king? (*She shouts offstage, now a question*) Who was Socrates, anyway? (*She gives up the rampage and plunks herself down*) "Know thyself," hmph. (*She thinks a moment, then makes a silent resolution to herself, exits and quickly returns with a clipboard and pencil.* CHARLIE BROWN *and* SNOOPY *have entered, still with baseball equipment*)

CHARLIE BROWN. Hey, Snoopy, you want to help me get my arm back in shape? Watch out for this one, it's a new fastball.

LUCY. Excuse me a moment, Charlie Brown, but I was wondering if you'd mind answering a few questions.

CHARLIE BROWN. Not at all, Lucy. What kind of questions are they?

LUCY. Well, I'm conducting a survey to enable me to know myself better, and first of all I'd like to ask: on a scale of zero to one hundred, using a standard of fifty as average, seventy-five as above average and ninety as exceptional, where would you rate me with regards to crabbiness?

CHARLIE BROWN. (*Stands in silence for a moment, hesitating*) Well, Lucy, I . . .

LUCY. Your ballots need not be signed and all answers will be held in strictest confidence.

CHARLIE BROWN. Well still, Lucy, that's a very hard question to answer.

Author's Purpose
What does your reaction to Lucy's behavior here tell you about the author's purpose?

> You're a very crabby person and you're crabby to just about everyone you meet.

LUCY. You may have a few moments to think it over if you want, or we can come back to that question later.

CHARLIE BROWN. I think I'd like to come back to it, if you don't mind.

LUCY. Certainly. This next question deals with certain character traits you may have observed. Regarding personality, would you say that mine is *A* forceful, *B* pleasing, or *C* objectionable? Would that be *A*, *B*, or *C*? What would your answer be to that, Charlie Brown, forceful, pleasing or objectionable, which one would you say, hmm? Charlie Brown, hmm?

CHARLIE BROWN. Well, I guess I'd have to say forceful, Lucy, but . . .

LUCY. "Forceful." Well, we'll make a check mark at the letter *A* then. Now, would you rate my ability to get along with other people as poor, fair, good or excellent?

CHARLIE BROWN. I think that depends a lot on what you mean by "get along with other people."

LUCY. You know, make friends, sparkle in a crowd, that sort of thing.

CHARLIE BROWN. Do you have a place for abstention?

LUCY. Certainly, I'll just put a check mark at "None of the above." The next question deals with physical appearance. In referring to my beauty, would you say that I was "stunning," "mysterious," or "intoxicating"?

CHARLIE BROWN. (*Squirming*) Well, gee, I don't know, Lucy. You look just fine to me.

LUCY. (*Making a check on the page*) "Stunning." All right, Charlie Brown, I think we should get back to that first question. On a scale of zero to one hundred, using a standard of fifty as average, seventy-five as . . .

CHARLIE BROWN. (*Loud interruption*) I . . . (*quieter*) . . . remember the question, Lucy.

LUCY. Well?

CHARLIE BROWN. (*Tentatively*) Fifty-one?

Vocabulary
objectionable (əb jek´ shən ə bəl) *adj.* disagreeable

Vocabulary
tentatively (ten´ tə tiv lē) *adv.* in a hesitant way

LUCY. (*Noting it down*) Fifty-one is your crabbiness rating for me. Very well then, that about does it. Thank you very much for helping with this survey, Charlie Brown. Your cooperation has been greatly appreciated. (*She shakes hands with* CHARLIE BROWN)

CHARLIE BROWN. (*Flustered*) It was a pleasure, Lucy, any time. Come on, Snoopy.

LUCY. Oh, just a minute, there is one more question. Would you answer "Yes" or "No" to the question: "Is Lucy Van Pelt the sort of person that you would like to have as president of your club or civic organization?"

CHARLIE BROWN. Oh, yes, by all means, Lucy.

LUCY. (*Making note*) Yes. Well, thank you very much. That about does it, I think. (CHARLIE BROWN *exits, but* SNOOPY *pauses, turns, and strikes a dramatic "thumbs down" pose to* LUCY) WELL, WHO ASKED YOU! (SNOOPY *makes a hasty exit.* LUCY *stands center stage, figuring to herself on the clipboard and mumbling*) Now let's see. That's a fifty-one, "None of the above," and . . . (*She looks up*) Schroeder was right. I can already feel myself being filled with the glow of self-awareness. (PATTY *enters. She is heading for the other side of the stage, when* LUCY *stops her*) Oh, Patty, I'm conducting a survey and I wonder if . . .

PATTY. A hundred and ten, C, "Poor," "None of the above," "No," and what are you going to do about the dent you made in my bicycle! (PATTY *storms off.* LUCY *watches her go, then looks at the audience*)

LUCY. It's amazing how fast word of these surveys gets around. (LINUS *wanders in and plunks himself down in front of the TV.* LUCY *crosses to him, still figuring*)

LUCY. Oh, Linus, I'm glad you're here. I'm conducting a survey and there are a few questions I'd like to ask you.

LINUS. Sure, go ahead.

LUCY. The first question is: on a scale of zero to one hundred, with a standard of fifty as average, seventy-five as above average and ninety as exceptional, where would you rate me with regards to crabbiness?

Vocabulary
civic (siv´ ik) *adj.* representing a city or group of citizens

In referring to my beauty, would you say that I was "stunning," "mysterious," or "intoxicating"?

Spiral Review
Dialogue What does Patty's response show about her feelings for Lucy?

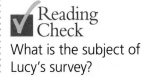
Reading Check
What is the subject of Lucy's survey?

LINUS. (*Slowly turns his head to look at her, then turns back to the TV*) You're my big sister.

LUCY. That's not the question.

LINUS. No, but that's the answer.

LUCY. Come on, Linus, answer the question.

LINUS. (*Getting up and facing* LUCY) Look, Lucy, I know very well that if I give any sort of honest answer to that question you're going to slug me.

LUCY. Linus. A survey that is not based on honest answers is like a house that is built on a foundation of sand. Would I be spending my time to conduct this survey if I didn't expect complete candor in all the responses? I promise not to slug you. Now what number would you give me as your crabbiness rating?

LINUS. (*After a few moments of interior struggle*) Ninety-five. (LUCY *sends a straight jab to his jaw which lays him out flat*)

Author's Purpose
What further details does the author provide here to help you understand his purpose?

LUCY. No decent person could be expected to keep her word with a rating over ninety. (*She stalks off, busily figuring away on her clipboard*) Now, I add these two columns and that gives me my answer. (*She figures energetically, then finally sits up with satisfaction*) There, it's all done. Now, let's see what we've got. (*She begins to scan the page. A look of trouble skims over her face. She rechecks the figures. Her eternal look of self-confidence wavers, then crumbles*) It's true. I'm a crabby person. I'm a very crabby person and everybody knows it. I've been spreading crabbiness wherever I go. I'm a supercrab. It's a wonder anyone will still talk to me. It's a wonder I have any friends at all—(*She looks at the figures on the paper*) or even associates. I've done nothing but make life miserable for everyone. I've done nothing but breed unhappiness and resentment. Where did I go wrong? How could I be so selfish? How could . . . (LINUS *has been listening. He comes and sits near her*)

LINUS. What's wrong, Lucy?

LUCY. Don't talk to me, Linus. I don't deserve to be spoken to. I don't deserve to breathe the air I breathe. I'm no good, Linus. I'm no good.

LINUS. That's not true, Lucy.

LUCY. Yes it is. I'm no good, and there's no reason at all why I should go on living on the face of this earth.

LINUS. Yes there is.

LUCY. Name one. Just tell me one single reason why I should still deserve to go on living on this planet.

LINUS. Well, for one thing, you have a little brother who loves you. (LUCY *looks at him. She is silent. Then she breaks into a great, sobbing "Wah!"*) Every now and then I say the right thing.

(LUCY *continues sobbing as she and* LINUS *exit. A brief musical interlude, a change of light, and* SCHROEDER *and* SALLY *come onstage*)

No decent person could be expected to keep her word with a rating over ninety.

Critical Thinking

1. **Key Ideas and Details (a)** What does Schroeder say that causes Lucy to develop the survey? **(b) Compare and Contrast:** How are Charlie Brown's answers different from Patty's responses? **(c) Interpret:** What do the different answers suggest about their contrasting feelings and personalities?

2. **Key Ideas and Details (a)** How does Snoopy react to Lucy? **(b) Infer:** What do Snoopy's gestures tell you about his feelings for Lucy?

3. **Key Ideas and Details (a)** Why is Linus afraid to tell Lucy the truth? **(b) Cause and Effect:** What happens when he tells the truth? **(c) Paraphrase:** Explain what Lucy means by the statement "No decent person could be expected to keep her word with a rating over ninety."

4. **Integration of Knowledge and Ideas (a)** What conclusion does Lucy draw about herself after the survey? **(b)** What does Linus say to try to change her mind? **(c)** What lesson might Lucy and the audience learn about "who we are"? Explain. *[Connect to the Big Question: How do we decide who we are?]*

Cite textual evidence to support your responses.

Happiness is a Charming Charlie Brown at Orlando Rep

David Hsieh, courtesy of www.reacttheatre.org

Matthew MacDermid

At the conclusion of *You're A Good Man, Charlie Brown*—the classic musical based on Charles M. Schulz's "Peanuts" comic strip—the well-known characters of Charlie Brown, Sally Brown, Lucy, Linus, Schroeder and Snoopy sing of the simple joys in life that bring them happiness. The melody by Clark M. Gesner, along with the charming lyrics (such as "playing the drum in your own school band" and "being alone every now and then") make for a rather touching moment, allowing children and adults of all ages to ponder where they find happiness. At the Orlando Repertory Theatre, which is opening its fourth season with the revised version of this long-running Off-Broadway hit, happiness is alive and evident in a wonderful production evoking the original script's charm and the contemporary flair of new orchestrations by Michael Gibson, as well as additional dialogue and music by Michael Mayer and Andrew Lippa, respectively.

Vocabulary
evoking (ē vōk´ iŋ)
v. calling forth

You're A Good Man, Charlie Brown is really a series of comic strip vignettes taken directly from Schulz's funny pages. Delightful musical numbers are added to comment on the situations, allowing charismatic performers to bring cartoon characters to three-dimensional life. The Rep's cast is an outstanding blend of fresh, wide-eyed professional talent headed by the outstanding Michael Swickard as Charlie Brown. His round eyes and round head perfectly embody the lovable loser constantly battling his affection for the little red headed girl across the school yard and his inability to properly fly a kite. Karla Sue Schultz, as Charlie's sister Sally, establishes youth, naivete and a terrific sense of humor backed by a great voice in sketches about jumping rope and coat-hanger sculptures. She is especially effective in one of Lippa's new numbers, "My New Philosophy." Ronald E. Hornsby's Schroeder has less showy material, even with the new number "Beethoven's Birthday," but does his best with what he is given.

However, three performers take their characters to a higher level, stealing the spotlight with every opportunity and even chewing a bit of the scenery along the way. Shannon Bilo is a wonder as Lucy, with a clarion belt and expert comic timing that seems to go for days. Mark Catlett is outstanding as her kid brother Linus, sucking his thumb and doing the tango with his blanket, all the while exuding the mind-numbing intelligence of such a youngster. And Chris Layton stops the show with his rousing Snoopy, channeling the showbiz legends of yesteryear (including Carol Channing) in his celebratory "Suppertime."

Technically, this production remains on par with its performers, a perfect blend of design excellence from Alvin DeLeon's scenery, Simone Smith's costumes, Sam Hazell's props, David M. Upton's lighting and James E. Cleveland's sound. Justin S. Fischer's musical direction is also terrific, with his five-piece band perfectly executing Gibson's fresh orchestrations.

Myles Thoroughgood's musical staging is character driven and lovely, providing each performer with a

Vocabulary
embody (em bäd´ē) *v.* give bodily form to; represent

Author's Purpose
What do you think the author's purpose is for writing this article?

✓ Reading Check
How does the critic feel about the overall production?

signature dance move that surfaces throughout. Jeffrey Revels' direction isn't quite up to the standard of everything else. While his work is mostly excellent, it is somewhat inconsistent, with several scene buttons falling flat and a couple that actually seem to bring the show to a halt. But what is good is great, and his decisions in casting have **abundantly** affected the success of his production.

The Orlando Repertory Theatre has produced one of their best productions to date with this *Charlie Brown*. It runs in the 328-seat Edyth Busch Theatre, in the Rep complex at 1001 E. Princeton Street in Orlando, through October 1st.

Cast:
Charlie Brown—Michael Swickard
Lucy—Shannon Bilo
Snoopy—Chris Layton
Linus—Mark Catlett
Sally—Karla Sue Schultz
Schroeder—Ronald E. Hornsby

Critical Thinking

1. **Key Ideas and Details (a)** How does the play relate to the comic strip? **(b) Interpret:** According to the review, what make this subject suitable for theater?

2. **Key Ideas and Details (a)** How are the author's opinions of each actor's performance similar? **(b) Contrast:** How are they different? **(c) Analyze:** Which actor seems to be his favorite? Explain.

Cite textual evidence to support your responses.

3. **Key Ideas and Details (a)** Which member of the production does the author criticize? **(b) Summarize:** What weaknesses does the author cite as part of his criticism?

4. **Integration of Knowledge and Ideas** If you were an actor in this production, how much value would you give to this review? Why? *[Connect to the Big Question: How do we decide who we are?]*

Comparing Author's Purpose

1. (a) What purpose did Clark Gesner have for writing his play *You're a Good Man, Charlie Brown*? **(b)** Explain what details helped you to decide the author's purpose.

2. (a) What purpose did Matthew MacDermid have for writing his article? **(b)** Explain how details in the article helped you to decide the author's purpose.

3. Complete a Venn diagram to show how the drama scene and the article are alike and different.

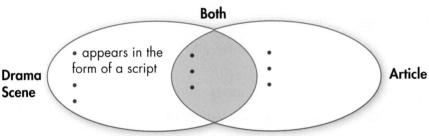

Both

Drama Scene

• appears in the form of a script
•
•

Article

⏱ Timed Writing

Explanatory Text: Essay

In an essay, compare and contrast each author's purpose for writing and the way in which each genre—play and review—presents its topic. Provide textual evidence to support your understanding. **(40 minutes)**

5-Minute Planner

1. Read the prompt carefully and completely. Consider these questions to get started.

- How does each selection convey ideas and information?
- What type of information does each author provide?
- What kind of audience is each genre—drama and play review—most likely to reach? Explain.

2. Use your graphic organizer on page 788 and your answers to the questions above to formulate a response.

3. Reread the prompt, and then draft your essay.

Writing Workshop

 **Common Core State Standards**

Writing
2. Write informative/explanatory texts to examine a topic and convey ideas, concepts, and information through the selection, organization, and analysis of relevant content.

Write an Explanatory Text

Exposition: Cause-and-Effect Essay

Defining the Form A **cause-and-effect essay** is a piece of expository writing that explains the reasons or the results for something that happens. You might use elements of this form in social studies reports, scientific lab reports, or news reports.

Assignment Write a cause-and-effect essay to explain the reasons leading to an event or situation and the results of that event or situation. Your essay should feature the following elements:

✔ a *thesis* that states the causes and effects of a situation

✔ facts and details that *support* the thesis statement

✔ an *organizational pattern* that emphasizes cause-and-effect relationships

✔ transitions that *make connections between ideas*

✔ error-free writing, including *correct usage of a variety of sentence patterns*

To preview the criteria on which your cause-and-effect essay may be judged, see the rubric on page 807.

 Writing Workshop: *Work in Progress*

Review the work you did on page 779.

WRITE GUY
Jeff Anderson, M.Ed.

What Do You Notice?

Cause and Effect

Read these sentences from Joseph Bruchac's play *Gluskabe and Old Man Winter* several times.

So Gluskabe defeated Old Man Winter. Because he brought only one small piece of summer, winter still returns each year. But, thanks to Gluskabe, spring always comes back again.

With a partner, discuss the qualities that make this passage a good model for cause and effect. Notice the writer's use of transitions and identify the cause and the effect. Then, jot down ways you can describe cause-and-effect relationships in your essay.

Prewriting/Planning Strategies

Brainstorm. In a group, discuss possible topics. You may wish to begin with a general idea such as "historical events" or a fill-in-the-blank exercise such as "What causes _____?" Review the results and choose an idea from the list as your topic.

Browse media sources. Look through the newspaper or a favorite magazine for topics that interest you. Circle key words or ideas and consider their causes or effects. Choose a topic based on what you find.

Use a topic web. Create a topic web like the one shown to help you evaluate and narrow your topic. First, write your topic inside a circle. Then, write connected ideas, or subtopics, inside circles surrounding your topic. Label each idea "cause" or "effect." When you have finished, review your completed web. To narrow your topic, focus on a single one of your subtopics.

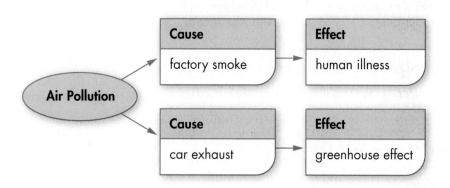

Use a T-chart in research. To find facts and examples that explain cause-and-effect relationships, you may need to conduct research. Use a T-chart to organize your ideas.

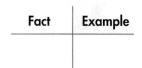

Drafting Strategies

Organize details. You may have identified a single cause and a single effect, or multiple causes for a single effect. This chart shows an example of a single cause with several effects. Select an organization for your essay from the following two common patterns.

- **Many Causes/Single Effect** If a number of unrelated events leads to a single result, focus one paragraph on each cause.
- **Single Cause/Many Effects** If one cause produces several effects, focus one paragraph on each effect.

**Common Core
State Standards**

Writing

2.a. Introduce a topic; organize ideas, concepts, and information, using strategies such as definition, classification, comparison/contrast, and cause/effect; include formatting, graphics, and multimedia when useful to aiding comprehension.

2.b. Develop the topic with relevant facts, definitions, concrete details, quotations, or other information and examples.

2.c. Use appropriate transitions to clarify the relationships among ideas and concepts.

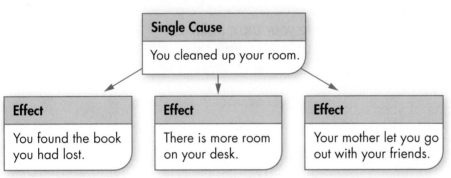

Focus your writing with a strong thesis statement. Consider the cause-and-effect relationship you will discuss. Using your notes, craft one sentence that states your main idea.

Example: If the city builds a new sports stadium, local businesses will get the benefit of increased sales.

Include enough information to build a link. Make sure that your sentences show readers exactly how the events or situations are linked in cause-and-effect relationships. Provide supporting details that are precise rather than vague.

Vague: If your skin is damaged, you are at risk for illness.

Clear: If you are fair-skinned and spend a lot of time in the sun without wearing sunscreen, you are more likely to get skin cancer.

Connect with transitions. Choose transitional words and phrases that make cause-and-effect relationships in your essay clear.

To show a cause: *Because* of the flood, many homes were damaged.

To show an effect: *As a result*, people have to rebuild.

Joseph Bruchac On Showing Causes and Effects

Joseph Bruchac is the author of
Gluskabe and Old Man Winter (p. 698).

This selection is from "Gluskabe and Dzidziz," my telling of a traditional Abenaki Indian tale. Gluskabe, a powerful hero, has just said that he can defeat anyone. But Dzidziz, the baby, turns out to be more than his match. By foolishly taking the baby's toy, Gluskabe causes several effects, including his own surrender. Cause-and-effect situations like this occur often in traditional tales, showing how our actions may have good—or bad—results.

"I'm a good writer but a great rewriter."
—Joseph Bruchac

Professional Model:

from "Gluskabe and Dzidziz"

Gluskabe bent closer. "Is that what gives you your power?" he said. ~~He decided to take it from the baby.~~ "Then I will take it from you." He ~~reached down and~~ pulled the leather turtle from the baby's hands. As soon as he did so the baby began to cry and scream. Gluskabe had never heard such a sound before. He ~~truly~~ thought it would break his ears and ~~so~~ he covered them with his hands.

~~Gluskabe told the baby to be silent.~~ "Be silent!" Gluskabe shouted, but Dzidziz did not stop screaming. Then Gluskabe tried singing to the baby. He sang a song ~~that was~~ powerful enough to calm the strong winds and quiet the most powerful storm. All around ^the Place of White Stone the winds stopped blowing and the waters became calm. But within the wigwam Dzidziz still screamed.

"You have won," Gluskabe shouted. "Here." He gave the leather turtle back to the baby. But Dzidziz was not yet ready to stop crying. . . .

I shorten as I revise. Taking out unnecessary words makes the causes and effects stand out more clearly.

I turned some narrative into dialogue. Characters talking for themselves seem more real than those just talked about.

I added "Place of the White Stone" to give a better sense of place.

In my first draft, I only called Dzidziz "the baby." In my revision, I introduced the Abenaki word for baby, "Dzidziz." This makes it feel more like an Abenaki Indian story.

Revising Strategies

Test for logical organization. Examine the connections between your paragraphs. Follow these steps to be sure the topic sentences or main ideas in each paragraph support the thesis of your essay.

1. Highlight the topic sentence of each paragraph.
2. Label each connection to the topic as *cause* or *effect*.
3. Read the topic sentences in the order in which they appear.
4. Reorder sentences or paragraphs for clarity.
5. Write a concluding statement that follows from the topic sentences of your essay.

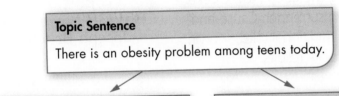

Topic Sentence

There is an obesity problem among teens today.

Cause

Teens watch too much television.

The diet of the average teen contains too much sugar.

Effect

Teen diabetes is on the rise.

Many teens have other health problems related to obesity.

Confirm the link. Make sure your essay describes events that are truly connected by cause and effect, not related only because one event happened after another.

Chronology:	We finished the dishes, then started our homework.
Cause and Effect:	I studied so hard for the test that I was able to do well.

Confirm accuracy. Compare your notes against your draft to ensure that your writing correctly reflects the facts.

Add graphics. Some cause-and-effect relationships are complicated for readers to grasp through words alone. Visual aids, such as diagrams or flowcharts, make complex processes easier to understand. Look for places to add graphics in your essay.

Peer Review

Share your essay with a partner. Ask your reader to tell you whether all of your cause-and-effect relationships are reliable, logical, and clearly explained.

 Common Core State Standards

Writing
2.a. Introduce a topic; organize ideas, concepts, and information, using strategies such as definition, classification, comparison/contrast, and cause/effect; include formatting, graphics, and multimedia when useful to aiding comprehension.
2.f. Provide a concluding statement or section that follows from the information or explanation presented.
5. With some guidance and support from peers and adults, develop and strengthen writing as needed by planning, revising, editing, rewriting, or trying a new approach.

Language
3.a. Vary sentence patterns for meaning, reader/listener interest, and style.

Combining Sentences for Variety

To add variety to your sentence patterns, include prepositional phrases, appositive phrases, or gerund phrases.

Type of Phrase	Its Use	Example
Prepositional phrase	• as an adjective • as an adverb	The boy **in the red jacket** is my brother. The book fell **off the table.**
Appositive Phrase	• as a noun phrase	Jim, **a 7-year old boy,** agreed.
Gerund phrase	• as a noun	I enjoy **playing the guitar.**

Combining Short Sentences These examples show how to use phrases to pack information into your sentences.

- **Using a Prepositional Phrase**

  Separate: The bus moved slowly. The road was wet.

  Combined: The bus moved slowly *along the wet road*.

- **Using an Appositive Phrase**

  Separate: Henry said he liked to take long walks.
                    Henry is an energetic 89-year-old man.

  Combined: Henry, an energetic 89-year-old man, said
                    he liked to take long walks.

- **Using a Gerund Phrase**

  Separate: Do not order beef. It would be a mistake.

  Combined: *Ordering beef* would be a mistake.

Fixing Choppy Sentences To improve a pattern of short sentences, follow these steps:

1. **Look for the relationship among ideas.** For example, one sentence might extend the idea of the other.

2. **Combine sentences to stress the connections among ideas.** Use prepositional, appositive, or gerund phrases for variety.

Grammar in Your Writing

Read your essay looking for pairs of short, related sentences. Using the examples as a guide, combine some for variety.

PH WRITING COACH

Further instruction and practice are available in *Prentice Hall Writing Coach*.

Don't Get Burned

Sunscreen should always be worn when you are out in the sun because the sun can be very dangerous to your skin. If your skin is exposed to the sun's ultraviolet rays without sunscreen, it will turn red, burn, and hurt. Many people believe that burning their skin is one step closer to their desire of getting a tan. They do not realize that both burning and tanning your skin can damage it. Once you burn or tan and the redness or color begins to fade, the damaged skin may begin to peel, leaving a new, unhealthy, thin, and sensitive layer of skin.

What you do to your skin as a child and as a young adult will affect your skin for your full life. Sunscreen can help. Doctors recommend that children apply sunscreen often and at least 30 minutes before going out in the sun. Adults, children, and young adults will benefit from using sunscreens with sun protection factor (SPF) numbers of 15 or more. The SPF numbers give some idea of how long you can stay out in the sun without burning. For example, an SPF of 15 should protect you for approximately 150 minutes—nearly two and a half hours—in the sun. While some sunscreens say they are waterproof, they do not give you total protection from water and sweat. As a result, it is also recommended that sunscreen be applied often.

Nobody's skin is immune to skin cancer. If your skin is damaged a lot by the sun during your childhood and adult years, your chances of getting skin cancer are greater than they are for people who have taken better steps toward protection. Some signs of skin cancer are leathery scab-like patches of skin that may be discolored, bleed, or burn. If you have been burned several times in a short period of time, you should be checked by a doctor because some forms of skin cancer cannot be detected.

So, think twice the next time you are at the beach or the pool without sunscreen, hoping to absorb the sun. Be careful and apply sunscreen to protect yourself from skin damage. Remember that even though a tan may look nice for a few days, it may cause you health problems and unhealthy-looking skin in the future.

Bryson begins by stating his thesis, the cause-and-effect relationship he will show.

Details about the sun's ability to damage the skin help support the writer's purpose.

The writer uses examples to make doctors' recommendations clear.

Each paragraph focuses on a cause or an effect related to Bryson's thesis.

Editing and Proofreading

Correct errors in grammar, spelling, and punctuation.

Focus on spelling. In words with multiple syllables, use a dictionary to help you spell the unstressed vowel sound. The sound, known as a *schwa*, is an open neutral sound like you hear in the words *a**go**, *ag**e**nt*, and *san**i**ty*. The *schwa* sound can be spelled with almost any vowel. In a dictionary, the *schwa* is represented with the symbol ə.

Spiral Review
Earlier in this unit, you learned about **gerunds and gerund phrases** (p. 778). As you review your cause-and-effect essay, be sure you have used gerunds correctly.

Publishing and Presenting

Consider one of the following ways to share your writing:

Make a movie proposal. Treat your cause-and-effect essay like a script for a short film. Create a storyboard that shows the images that you would choose.

Make an oral presentation. Read your essay aloud to classmates or family members. Then, invite questions and discussion.

Reflecting on Your Writing

Writer's Journal Jot down your answers to this question:

How do you view your topic differently now that you have analyzed its related causes and effects?

Rubric for Self-Assessment

Find evidence in your writing to address each category. Then, use the rating scale to grade your work.

Criteria	Rating Scale
	not very very
Focus: How clearly is your thesis on cause and effect stated?	1 2 3 4 5
Organization: How effective is your organization?	1 2 3 4 5
Support/Elaboration: How convincing are the facts and details used for support?	1 2 3 4 5
Style: How well are transitions used to connect ideas?	1 2 3 4 5
Conventions: How correct is your use of grammar, especially your use of phrases?	1 2 3 4 5

Vocabulary Workshop

Borrowed and Foreign Words

For hundreds of years, the English language has **borrowed** words from other cultures. You can use a dictionary to find their origins. For example, the dictionary entry for *gumbo* explains that the word comes from a Bantu name for the vegetable okra. Bantu is a language spoken in Africa. The English word *gumbo* refers to a type of soup that often contains okra. This chart shows the cultural influences of some borrowed words.

Common Core State Standards

Language
4.c. Consult reference materials, both print and digital, to find the pronunciation of a word or determine or clarify its precise meaning or its part of speech.

French and Italian	Spanish	Native American
European culture, fashion, art, and food: *ballet, violin, pizza*	American Southwest, landscape, lifestyle: *ranch, tornado, balcony*	North American wildlife and culture: *maize, moccasin, raccoon*

Practice A Find the following words in a dictionary. Tell the language from which each was borrowed.

1. violin   **3.** fiesta   **5.** camouflage

2. canyon   **4.** bok choy   **6.** banjo

Practice B The name of the Missouri River comes from the name of a group of Native Americans. Originally, their name meant "people of the big canoes." Many cities, rivers, and states have names with Native American roots. Some places, like the state of New Mexico and the region of New England, were named by settlers who came from foreign lands. Look up the following cities, rivers, and states in a dictionary. Identify the language from which each name came, and explain what the name originally meant.

Cities: San Antonio, Utica, Tampa, Des Moines

Rivers: Susquehanna, Rio Grande, Penobscot

States: Texas, Florida, California, Georgia

Activity Like pizza and gumbo, many popular American foods have come from other cultures. Use a dictionary to group these foods according to their origins: *quiche, spaghetti, noodle, taco, soufflé, zucchini, yam, cantaloupe, banana, strudel,* and *tangerine*. Record your answers in a chart like the one below.

Culture of Origin	Food
Africa	gumbo,
France	
Germany	
Italy	pizza,
Native Americans	
Spain and Latin America	

Then, prepare a dinner menu that contains foods from your chart. Include appetizers, entrées, desserts, and beverages on your menu. Try to include as many items from the chart as you can.

Comprehension and Collaboration

Work with a partner. Think of rivers, counties, cities, and parks in your home state. List at least five. Then use a dictionary or Internet sources to find the origins and original meanings of their names. When you are finished, share your results with classmates.

Communications Workshop

Identifying Tone, Mood, and Emotion

Common Core State Standards

Speaking and Listening
2. Interpret information presented in diverse media and formats and explain how it contributes to a topic, text, or issue under study.

Understanding oral communication involves being able to identify the speaker's tone, mood, and emotion.

- **Tone:** the speaker's attitude toward the subject
- **Mood**: the overall feeling of the presentation
- **Emotion:** the speaker's feelings

Learn the Skills

Use the strategies to complete the activity on page 811.

Identify the context. The context of a presentation often affects the speaker's tone, mood, and emotion. First, determine the speaker's purpose and audience. Then, identify the speaker's main idea. Imagine yourself in the place of the speaker. Consider how you would use tone, mood, and emotion to achieve your purpose.

Listen to tone of voice. In an oral presentation, a speaker conveys his or her attitude through tone of voice as well as through words. A serious speaker might speak slowly in a quiet voice. A speaker who is enthusiastically trying to persuade you might use a high-pitched voice and talk faster than in normal speech.

Consider content. The mood of a presentation is often a result of *what* is said, in addition to *how* it is said. The subject of a presentation often affects the audience's emotions.

Notice word choice. The specific words a speaker uses can indicate his or her attitude and emotion. A word's connotations, or the feelings that it suggests, are a clue to the speaker's emotions. Speakers also choose formal or informal language based on their audience and purpose.

Watch out for motion. A speaker's posture and gestures can communicate a positive or negative attitude toward his or her subject. Connect the speaker's body language to the mood and tone he or she is expressing.

Clue into expression. Facial expressions are clues to emotions. Smiles and frowns are meant to communicate feelings. Watch expressions to connect the speaker's feelings with his or her words.

Practice the Skills

Presentation of Knowledge and Ideas Use what you've learned in this workshop to perform the following task.

ACTIVITY: Evaluating a Speech

Listen to a presentation, such as a news broadcast, a television interview, or a political speech. Keep a chart like the one shown to record verbal and nonverbal clues to each speaker's tone, mood, and emotion. Answer the following questions as you evaluate the speakers.

- What is the content of the presentation?
- What tone, or attitude, does the speaker convey?
- How do specific word choices communicate attitude and emotion?
- How do gestures and expressions convey mood, tone, or emotion?

Context of Presentation

Speaker's Purpose ————————————————————————

Audience ————————————————————————————

Main Idea ————————————————————————————

Tone of Voice	**Motion**
_____ Energetic	_____ Energetic
_____ Flat	_____ Static
_____ Serious	_____ Aggressive
_____ Humorous	_____ Shy

Word Choice	**Expression**
_____ Positive Connotations	_____ Friendly
_____ Negative Connotations	_____ Hostile
_____ Formal	_____ Intense
_____ Informal	_____ Bland

Comprehension and Collaboration Meet in small groups to discuss your evaluations of presentations. How are they alike? How are they different? Examine how the content of the program affected your checklists. Discuss how this activity helped you to interpret how information is presented through mood, tone, and emotion.

Cumulative Review

 **Common Core**
State Standards

RL.6.3, RL.6.4, RL.6.5; W.6.2.b;
L.6.4.a; W.6.2
[For the full wording of the standards,
see the standards chart in the front of
your textbook.]

I. Reading Literature

Directions: *Read the play. Then, answer each question that follows.*

Scene 1: ELENI *and* ZACK, bored and restless, *sit on their front porch.*

ZACK: *[Angrily.]* I *told* Mom and Dad I didn't want to move! It's Saturday, and I don't have any friends to hang out with!

ELENI: *[Brightening.]* Hey, I've got a plan. Grab some of those pebbles. I'll get the checkerboard and spoons. Then, let's go to the park.

Scene II: ELENI *and* ZACK *sit at a picnic table in the park.* ELENI *opens the checkerboard and randomly places pebbles and spoons on it.*

ZACK: *[Looking confusedly at the game board.]* What game is *this*?

ELENI: *[Whispering.]* Just follow my lead. I see some kids our age.

ZACK: *[Looking* sheepish.*]* Oh, brother! What are you doing?!

As Tim and Sandra near the table, Eleni busily moves a few pebbles.

ELENI: *[Clapping her hands.]* Ah-HA! I scored a mudgy!

ZACK: *[Catching on.]* Oh yeah? Well how about this?! *[Zack covers one of the pebbles with a spoon.]* I just cancelled your mudgy!

TIM: *[Looking interested and friendly.]* Hi, I'm Tim and this is Sandra.

ELENI: *[Pretending* frustration *as she focuses on the game.]* Rats and grasshoppers! *[Then Eleni looks up and smiles.]* Oh—hi! I'm Eleni and this is Zack. He just hobbled my sprocket, but I can still win.

SANDRA: *[Shyly.]* Do you mind if we watch?

ELENI: *[Returning her concentration to the board.]* Not at all.

Zack moves some pebbles and a spoon around the board.

ZACK: *[Looking triumphant.]* ZANZIBAR!! *[Eleni looks defeated.]*

TIM: Uh, what game is that?

ELENI: It's called . . . um . . Zanzibar! *[Zack nods.]*

SANDRA: What's the point of the game?

ZACK: *[Smiling.]* The point is to make a couple of new friends. *[He winks knowingly at Eleni.]*

1. What is the purpose of the use of scenes in this **drama?**
   A. to show change in time and setting
   B. to show Zach's character growth
   C. to indicate various emotions
   D. to reveal setting

2. What main problem does the **dialogue** in this play reveal?
   A. Eleni and Zack did not want to move.
   B. Tim and Sandra do not understand the game that Eleni and Zack are playing.
   C. Zack does not understand what Eleni is doing when they go to the park.
   D. Eleni and Zack have not yet made friends in their new town.

3. Why do the **stage directions** in the play include descriptions such as *Brightening* and *Shyly*?
   A. so the actors will know how to move on the stage
   B. so the actors will know mood is being set
   C. so the actors will know how to react to one another
   D. so the actors will know how loudly to speak

4. According to the **stage directions**, where does the main part of the drama take place?
   A. at Eleni and Zack's house
   B. at Tim's house
   C. at a neighborhood park
   D. inside Eleni and Zack's house

5. Which of these would most likely serve as a prop in this **drama?**
   A. a bicycle tire
   B. a park swing set
   C. a book
   D. a game board

6. What happens in the **resolution** of the play?
   A. Zach and Eleni play a game.
   B. Zach and Eleni move to a new town.
   C. Eleni invents a new game.
   D. Zach and Eleni make new friends.

7. Which of these is most likely the **author's purpose** for writing this play?
   A. to entertain
   B. to persuade
   C. to inform
   D. to explain

8. **Vocabulary** Which word is closest in meaning to the underlined word <u>sheepish</u>?
   A. angry
   B. suspicious
   C. embarrassed
   D. confused

Timed Writing

9. In an essay, tell what the **dialogue** in this play reveals about either Eleni or Zack. Support your response with details from the play.

GO ON

II. Reading Informational Text

Directions: *Read this persuasive essay. Then, answer each question that follows.*

 **Common Core State Standards**

RI.6.1, RI.6.5; W.6.2.e; L.6.3, L.6.3.b
[For the full wording of the standards, see the standards chart in the front of your textbook.]

It is important that our school begin a recycling program. Our trash cans are brimming with bottles and cans that students carelessly toss away. The school community wastes thousands of pieces of paper every day, all of which is <u>discarded</u>. Recycling can reduce this waste. My family has reduced our waste by 30% by recycling.

Recycling has countless benefits for the school community and for the environment. Every ton of paper that is recycled will save 3.3 cubic yards of landfill space. Soda bottles can be turned into clothing or other useful items, instead of clogging landfills. Recycling will teach us all the value of working together to achieve a common goal. Some students have already voiced interest in this program.

Currently, this school has no environmental initiative in place. Our town's Department of Public Works is willing to donate recycling bins in our cafeteria for bottles and cans, and bins for paper recycling in each classroom. Once a week, a recycling truck will pick up the recyclables, just as the garbage truck comes to pick up the trash. That leaves the school community to place their paper, bottles, and cans in the appropriate bins, instead of the trash cans. This program will prove to have many benefits.

1. Which piece of **evidence** *best* supports the author's argument that recycling is beneficial?
   A. The school community will use less paper and fewer bottles.
   B. The new program will get all students involved.
   C. Recycling prevents waste from clogging landfills, which saves land.
   D. Recycling teaches valuable life lessons.

2. Which of the following pieces of evidence is *least* **appropriate?**
   A. Students want to start this recycling program.
   B. The author's family has reduced their waste by thirty percent.
   C. The garbage truck will still have to come and get their garbage.
   D. The Department of Public Works will help the school start a recycling program.

III. Writing and Language Conventions

Directions: *Read the letter. Then, answer each question.*

(1) Mr. Allan Reeves

(2) 13 Riverside Circle

(3) New York, New York 10007

(4) Dear Mr. Reeves:

   (5) I just finished your book *Common Denominators*. (6) I can't believe how awesome it was! (7) I read the story of the people lost at sea. (8) I was struck by their courage. (9) I wondered if I could survive such a frightening situation. (10) I hope you continue to write stories of courage and survival against the odds. (11) I think these stories inspire others. (12) I know they inspire me.

   (13) Sincerely yours,

   (14) Savion Miller

   (15) Savion Miller

1. What information is missing from the letter's **heading**?
   A. the purpose of the letter
   B. the sender's address and the date
   C. the sender's name
   D. the greeting

2. Which of the following **quotations from the author's work** would best support the idea in sentence 9?
   A. "I missed my family dearly and thought about them everyday."
   B. "We never gave up hope of rescue."
   C. "I can't tell you how relieved I was to see the rescue boat."
   D. "We did find many ways to entertain ourselves while waiting for a rescue."

3. How could the writer revise sentence 6 to have a more **formal tone?**
   A. I cannot believe how awesome it was.
   B. I will recommend this awesome book to all of my friends!
   C. I've read this awesome book six times.
   D. I really enjoyed this moving story of survival and hope.

4. Which of the following revisions best combines sentences 7 and 8 using a **participial phrase?**
   A. Reading the story of the people lost at sea, I was struck by their courage.
   B. I read the story of the people lost at sea, struck by their courage.
   C. Struck by their courage, I read the story of the people lost at sea.
   D. I read the story of the people lost at sea, and I was struck by their courage.

Performance Tasks

Directions: *Follow the instructions to complete the tasks below as required by your teacher.*
As you work on each task, incorporate both general academic vocabulary and literary terms you learned in this unit.

Common Core
State Standards

RL.6.2, RL.6.3, RL.6.5; RI.6.6; W.6.2; SL.6.1, SL.6.4; L.6.3, L.6.6
[For the full wording of the standards, see the standards chart in the front of your textbook.]

Writing

ⒸTask 1: Literature [RL.6.3; W.6.2]
Analyze Character

Write an essay in which you describe how a character in a drama changes as the plot unfolds.

- From one of the dramas in this unit, identify a character who changes from the beginning to the end of a play.

- Describe the points at which the character does something or learns something that contributes to the change.

- Compare the character at the beginning of the play to the character at the end of the play, and clearly state how the character changed.

- Use evidence from the play to support your analysis.

- Sum up with a conclusion that follows from the explanation you presented.

ⒸTask 2: Literature [RL.6.2; W.6.2]
Summarize

Write a summary of one of the dramatic selections in this unit and state the work's theme.

- Select the play excerpt or one of the acts that are included in this unit, and relate your selection in the form of a summary.

- Identify the major events in the selection, and determine why each of these events is important.

- State the theme of the selection. Your summary of important events and main points should lead to your statement of the theme and support it.

ⒸTask 3: Literature [RL.6.5; W.6.2]
Analyze a Scene

Write an essay in which you analyze how a particular scene fits into the overall structure of a play in this unit.

- Choose a scene that you consider to be significant.

- Explain how this scene functions in the play as a whole. For example, it might move the plot forward, introduce a problem, develop character, express part of the theme, or do some combination of these functions.

- Support your claims with evidence from the text.

- Maintain a consistent style and tone in your writing.

Speaking and Listening

ⓒ Task 4: Literature [RL.6.3; SL.6.4; L.6.3, L.6.6]

Analyze Plot Development

Give an oral presentation in which you analyze the plot of a play in this unit.

- Describe how the play's plot unfolds in episodes. Determine the conflict, climax, and resolution of the play.
- Visually display the key episodes in a plot diagram. You might draw a poster or create a brief slide show.
- Accurately use academic vocabulary in your presentation.

ⓒ Task 5: Literature [RL.6.5; SL.6.1]

Analyze Setting

Lead a small group discussion about the importance of setting in one of the dramatic selections from this unit.

- Come to the discussion prepared. Analyze the importance of setting in one of the plays from this unit. Consider whether or not the setting is part of the conflict and whether or not it helps to relate the theme. Create a list of questions to get the discussion started.
- During the discussion, pose more questions and respond to specific questions from members of your group. Use examples from the text to back up your ideas.
- At the end of the discussion, review the main points that your group made.

ⓒ Task 6: Informational Text [RI.6.6; SL.6.4]

Analyze Author's Purpose

Give an oral presentation analyzing an author's purpose in a nonfiction text.

- Select a nonfiction text from this unit and determine the author's purpose in writing it. For example, the author might be trying to persuade or to inform.
- Analyze the way in which the author's purpose is conveyed in the text. Use of evidence, reasoning, or persuasive language may point to the author's purpose.
- Include a visual display such as a graphic organizer to help present your information clearly.
- As you present, speak loudly enough to be heard well, and pronounce your words clearly.

THE BIG ?

How do we decide who we are?

At the beginning of Unit 5, you wrote a response to the Big Question. Now that you have completed the unit, write a new response. Discuss how your initial ideas have expanded or changed. Cite specific examples from the literature in this unit, from other subject areas, and from your own life to support your ideas. Use Big Question vocabulary words (see p. 691) in your response.

Featured Titles

In this unit, you have read a variety of dramatic works. Continue to read on your own. Select works that you enjoy, but challenge yourself to explore new playwrights and works of increasing depth and complexity. The titles suggested below will help you get started.

Literature

You're a Good Man, Charlie Brown
by Clark Gesner
Random House, Inc., 1967

This **musical comedy** is based on the hugely popular cartoon series *Peanuts* by Charles Schulz and features Snoopy, Lucy, Linus, and the gang.

James and the Giant Peach: A Play
by Roald Dahl

James goes on an adventure inside a giant peach in this **play** based on Dahl's beloved children's story. Complete with ideas for props and costumes, this play is one you could stage with your friends.

Seven Plays of Mystery and Suspense

This collection of **plays** will delight lovers of mystery and suspense stories. Expect to be on the edge of your seat as you read.

The Collected Poems of Langston Hughes
by Langston Hughes
Vintage, 1995   **EXEMPLAR TEXT**

This complete collection of Hughes's **poems** contains his life's work. Hughes celebrates African American life and shares the beauty of his language and the wisdom of his insights.

Informational Texts

Welcome to the Globe!
The Story of Shakespeare's Theatre
by Linda Martin

The Globe Theatre in London is where Shakespeare's plays were performed. This illustrated **nonfiction book** teaches the history of this famous theatre.

Small Things Considered:
Why There Is No Perfect Design
by Henry Petroski   **EXEMPLAR TEXT**

This **nonfiction book** explores the fascinating world of design. It includes the article "The Evolution of the Grocery Bag" and other essays that describe the thinking behind the design of everyday items such as telephone keypads and toothbrushes.

Preparing to Read Complex Texts

Attentive Reading As you read on your own, ask yourself questions about the text. The questions shown below and others that you ask as you read will help you learn and enjoy literature even more.

Common Core State Standards

Reading Literature/Informational Text 10. By the end of the year, read and comprehend literature, including stories, dramas, and poems, and literary nonfiction in the grades 6–8 text complexity band proficiently, with scaffolding as needed at the high end of the range.

When reading drama, ask yourself...

- Who is the main character? What struggles does this character face?

- What other characters are important? How do these characters relate to the main character?

- Where and when does the play take place? Do the time and place of the setting affect the characters? If so, how?

- Do the characters, settings, and events seem real? Why or why not?

- How does the play end? How does the ending make me feel?

- What theme or insight do I think the playwright is expressing? Do I find that theme to be important and true?

Key Ideas and Details

- Does the play have a narrator? If so, what information does the narrator provide?

- Does the playwright include background information? If so, how does this help me understand what I am reading?

- How many acts are in this play? What happens in each act?

- Does the dialogue sound like real speech? Are there specific passages that seem especially real? Are there any that seem false?

- What do the stage directions tell me about the ways characters move, speak, and feel? In what other ways do I learn about the characters?

- At what point in the play do I feel the most suspense? Why?

- What speech or passage in the play do I like the most? Why?

- Does the playwright seem to have a positive or a negative point of view? How do I think the playwright's point of view affects the story?

- Do I agree with the playwright's point of view? Why or why not?

Craft and Structure

- Does the play remind me of others I have read or seen? If so, how?

- In what ways is the play different from others I have read or seen?

- What new information or ideas have I gained from reading this play?

- What actors would I choose to play each role in this play?

- If I were to be in this play, what role would I want?

- Would I recommend this play to others? Why or why not?

Integration of Ideas

How much do our *communities* shape us?

Themes in Folk Literature

How much do our *communities* shape us?

The word **community** usually refers to a group of people who have common needs and interests. In fact, this word comes from a Latin word that means "common." People in a community may live near each other, or they may live far apart. One type of community is a neighborhood. Another can be an organization whose members live in different areas. People in communities often share languages and values. They may exchange information, support one another, and work together to solve problems. While individual members contribute to the shape of a community, the opposite is also true: a community can shape its members.

Exploring the Big Question

© **Collaboration: One-on-One Discussion** Start thinking about the Big Question by examining different types of communities. Briefly describe how the following groups are influenced by their communities:

- students in a classroom
- workers in a factory
- members of a sports team
- citizens of a town
- members of a choir or theater group

Share your lists and descriptions with a partner. Talk about your own experiences as a member of a community. Use the Big Question Vocabulary in your discussion.

Connecting to the Literature Each reading in this unit will give you additional insight into the Big Question.

PHLit Online!
www.PHLitOnline.com
- Big Question video
- Illustrated vocabulary words
- Interactive vocabulary games
- BQ Tunes

Learning Big Question Vocabulary

Acquire and Use Academic Vocabulary Academic vocabulary is the language you encounter in textbooks and on standardized tests. Review the definitions of these academic vocabulary words.

common (käm′ən) *adj.* ordinary; shared	**isolate** (ī′sə lāt′) *v.* set apart
influence (in′flōō əns) *v.* sway or persuade	**participation** (pär tis′ə pā′ shən) *n.* taking part in an event or activity
involve (in välv′) *v.* include	**support** (sə pôrt′) *v.* stand behind; back up

Use these words as you complete Big Question activities in this unit that involve reading, writing, speaking, and listening.

Gather Vocabulary Knowledge Additional Big Question words are listed below. Categorize the words by deciding whether you know each one well, know it a little bit, or do not know it at all.

belief	culture	group
community	family	history
connection	generation	values

Then, do the following:

1. Write the definitions of the words you know.

2. Consult a dictionary to confirm the meanings of the words whose definitions you wrote down. Revise your definition if necessary.

3. Using a print or an online dictionary, look up the meanings of the words you do not know. Then, write the meanings.

4. Write true or false statements about each word. For example, *Individuals sometimes have to stand up to pressures from a group. (true) People's values are always exactly the same as those of our neighbors. (false)*

5. Exchange your sentences with a partner to test each other on your knowledge of the words. Label each statement *true* or *false* and offer a brief explanation for each answer.

Common Core State Standards

Speaking and Listening
1. Engage effectively in a range of collaborative discussions with diverse partners on grade 6 topics, texts, and issues, building on others' ideas and expressing their own clearly.

Language
6. Acquire and use accurately grade-appropriate general academic and domain-specific words and phrases; gather vocabulary knowledge when considering a word or phrase important to comprehension or expression.

Elements of Folk Literature

Folk literature is a genre of writing that has its origins in the oral tradition.

The Oral Tradition Long before writing or books were invented, people told stories. These stories were passed along by word of mouth from one generation to the next. You may have experienced a similar sharing of stories among your family or friends. The passing along of stories is known as the **oral tradition.** Folk literature—including folk tales, fairy tales, fables, wise sayings, folk songs, legends, and myths—originated in the stories of the oral tradition.

Theme is the central message or insight in a literary work. The themes in folk literature have survived the test of time and place. This is because many themes in folk literature are universal.

Universal themes express ideas, values, and insights into human nature that people from different cultures and eras have found meaningful and important. For example, universal themes might warn of the dangers of greed or the value of kindness. Sometimes, the theme of a folk story is **culturally specific.** Such themes reflect the background, customs, and beliefs of a particular culture.

Purposes of Folk Literature The **purpose** of a literary work is the reason it is created. In folk literature, that purpose may be to teach a lesson, to explain something in nature, or simply to entertain. In folk literature, the purpose may be tied closely to the theme.

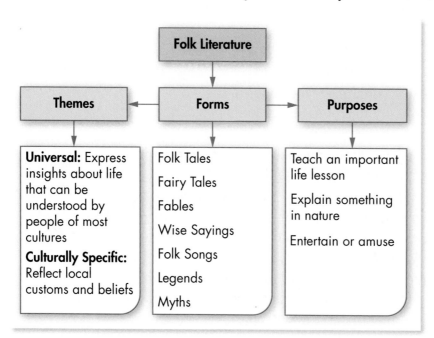

The Oral Tradition in Print

Once writing and books were invented, stories from the oral tradition were collected and put into print. Today, collections of folk literature are generally classified by type.

Folk and fairy tales are stories that often deal with heroes, adventure, magic, or romance. They were told not only to entertain but also to communicate the shared ideas of a culture.

Fables are brief stories or poems that teach lessons, or morals. These morals are usually stated directly at the ends of the fables. The main characters are often animals with human characteristics.

Wise sayings are clever statements that express a truth.

Folk songs present the ideas, values, feelings, and beliefs of a culture in musical form. With simple melodies and repeated lines, they tell stories of war, adventure, and romance.

Myths are fictional tales that explore the actions of gods and heroes or explain why things are a certain way in the natural world. Every ancient culture has its own **mythology.** The mythology of ancient Greece and Rome is known as **classical mythology.**

Legends are traditional, familiar stories about the past. Legends usually have some basis in fact. However, over time and through many retellings, the factual details have often been changed, making the legends more fiction than fact.

In This Section

Elements of Folk Literature

Determining Themes in Folk Literature

Analyzing Structure and Theme

Close Read: Story Development
• Model Text
• Practice Text

After You Read

 Common Core State Standards

RL.6.2
[For the full wording of the standards, see the standards chart in the front of your textbook.]

Characteristics of Folk Literature The different types of folk literature have many common characteristics.

Characteristic	Definition
Fantasy	writing that is highly imaginative and contains elements, such as magical creatures, not found in real life
Personification	type of figurative language in which a nonhuman subject is given human characteristics
Hyperbole	exaggeration or overstatement that is often used to create a comic effect
Irony	involves surprises, unexpected events, and interesting or amusing contradictions
Dialect	form of language spoken by people of a particular region or group

Determining Themes in Folk Literature

Works of folk literature express **themes**—central messages that provide insights into life and human nature.

Common Core State Standards

Reading Literature

2. Determine a theme or central idea of a text and how it is conveyed through particular details; provide a summary of the text distinct from personal opinions or judgments.

For modern readers, folk literature is a source of entertainment and insights. Elements of adventure, romance, and drama provide the entertainment. However, it is the themes—the deeper meanings of these stories—that provide insights into human nature.

Stated and Implied Theme Themes in folk literature are expressed in many different ways. In a fable, the theme is often stated at the end of the story as a moral, or lesson. Look at the following example.

Example: The Boy Who Cried Wolf

While watching his father's sheep, a boy decided to trick the local villagers. "Wolf! Wolf!" he cried, loud enough for all to hear. When the villagers ran to help him, they discovered that there was no wolf. The boy continued playing this trick for several days. Then one day, a wolf actually appeared. The boy cried, "Wolf! Wolf!" but the villagers thought the boy was playing his trick again. They ignored his pleas for help. As a result, the wolf ate the sheep.

Moral: If you always tell lies, no one will believe you when you tell the truth.

Not all themes in folk literature are so clearly stated, however. Sometimes, a theme is implied, or suggested. In these cases, readers must analyze the characters, setting, and events in the story to determine what the theme is.

Symbols and Theme A symbol is a person, place, or object that represents something beyond its literal meaning. For example, a mirror might symbolize vanity in a fairy tale or folk tale. As you read, pay attention to objects that seem to represent important ideas. Understanding the deeper meaning of a symbol can help you determine a story's theme.

Common Themes in Folk Literature
Here are some common themes in folk literature:

- Often, those who seem foolish are actually wise.
- Too much pride can lead to a fall.
- Wisdom comes through suffering.
- The virtues of kindness, generosity, and modesty are stronger than their opposites—cruelty, greed, and pride.
- An unappealing outward appearance may disguise a noble soul.

Analyzing Structure and Theme

Folk literature has several unique characteristics and structural devices that contribute to the development of theme. Keep these in mind as you read.

Simple Diction Diction is an author's choice of words, phrases, and sentence structure. The simple diction in much of folk literature is characterized by plain, common words, everyday language, and simple sentence construction. The use of simple diction helps convey theme in a way that people of all backgrounds can easily recognize and understand.

Repetition The repetition of events, lines of dialogue, descriptions, and sound patterns is a familiar element in folk literature. A **refrain,** often found in folk songs and poems, is the repetition of a phrase, line, or verse at regular intervals in the text. Repetition adds a pleasing rhythm to a story. In addition, it probably helped listeners and storytellers of the past remember the details of a story or song.

Patterns In folk literature, the story structure often follows a familiar and regular pattern. For example, many folk stories begin with simple phrases such as *Once upon a time...* or *Long ago, in a far-off land....* Another pattern often found in folk literature is the introduction of "threes"—for example, three characters or three events. The fairy tale "Rumpelstilskin" is a good example of the use of "threes."

> **Example: Rumpelstiltskin**
> - A young girl must spin <u>three</u> rooms of straw into gold.
> - She has <u>three</u> days to complete her task.
> - She gets <u>three</u> tries to guess the name of the odd little man who helps her.

Archetypes An **archetype** is an element that recurs regularly in literature and has similar meanings to people of different cultures and eras. Oral storytellers used archetypes to explore universal themes such as the dangers of greed and the importance of courage. Here are some common archetypes found in folk literature:

Common Archetypes in Folk Literature	
Plot	• dangerous journey • quest to prove one's honor • search for a valuable item
Characters	• enchanted princess • superhuman heroes and villains • trickster, or wise fool • talking animals
Ideas	• good vs. evil • magic in the normal world • hero or heroine aided by supernatural forces • evil disguised as good

Close Read: Story Development

All types of folk literature share common elements that help develop the story.

Each type of folk literature has its own unique qualities. However, all folk literature shares certain common elements. As you read, look for these elements. Compare stories to see how these elements move each story along.

Clues to Story Development in Folk Literature

Plot

Plot is the sequence of events in a story that revolves around a conflict, or problem. In folk literature, events in the plot often unfold quickly and predictably. As you read, notice

- the way events are presented in a logical sequence;
- the way the main character solves the conflict, often with the help of the gods or magic;
- the satisfying conclusion—for example, the hero receives a joyous welcome home or the prince and princess live happily ever after.

Characters

Characters in folk literature usually fit specific types. As you read, look for characters who

- have heroic traits, such as kindness, compassion, patience, and courage;
- are very good or very evil;
- have superhuman or magical qualities;
- are in disguise or are able to transform themselves.

Setting

As you read, consider how qualities of the setting affect story development, including

- magical or supernatural worlds;
- darkness and light;
- challenging landscapes, for example, rugged mountains, rushing rivers, or thick forests;
- weather, especially unexpected or unnaturally severe storms;
- the passage of time, especially when a character is racing the clock to complete a challenge.

Repetition/Patterns

Repetition and plot patterns in folk literature help unify a story and move it toward its conclusion. As you read, look for

- the repetition of dialogue, descriptions, and sound patterns;
- patterns of three;
- plot patterns, such as a hero's quest or a plan to outwit an enemy.

Theme

In folk literature, the theme, or central message, is often universal. As you read,

- look for a statement that expresses a moral or states a truth about life;
- think about lessons the characters learn or changes that characters undergo.

Model

About the Text This excerpt is from the book *Black Ships Before Troy: The Story of the "Iliad"* by Rosemary Sutcliff. The *Iliad* is an epic poem originally told by the Greek poet Homer. Homer lived sometime between the ninth and eighth centuries B.C. One of the greatest adventure stories of all time, the *Iliad* tells the story of the Trojan War and the fate of the hero Achilles.

from *Black Ships Before Troy: The Story of the "Iliad"* by Rosemary Sutcliff

In the high and far-off days when men were heroes and walked with the gods, Peleus, king of the Myrmidons, took for his wife a sea nymph called Thetis, Thetis of the Silver Feet. Many guests came to their wedding feast, and among the mortal guests came all the gods of high Olympus.

But as they sat feasting, one who had not been invited was suddenly in their midst: Eris, the goddess of discord, had been left out because wherever she went she took trouble with her; yet here she was, all the same, and in her blackest mood, to avenge the insult.

All she did—it seemed a small thing—was to toss down on the table a golden apple. Then she breathed upon the guests once, and vanished.

The apple lay gleaming among the piled fruits and the brimming wine cups; and bending close to look at it, everyone could see the words "To the fairest" traced on its side.

Then the three greatest of the goddesses each claimed that it was hers. Hera claimed it as wife to Zeus, the All-father, and queen of all the gods. Athene claimed that she had the better right, for the beauty of wisdom such as hers surpassed all else. Aphrodite only smiled, and asked who had a better claim to beauty's prize than the goddess of beauty herself.

They fell to arguing among themselves; the argument became a quarrel, and the quarrel grew more and more bitter, and each called upon the assembled guests to judge between them. But the other guests refused, for they knew well enough that, whichever goddess they chose to receive the golden apple, they would make enemies of the other two.

Setting The details describe a supernatural world of gods and goddesses. The events that follow could only happen in such a setting.

Characters The goddess Eris is an outcast, a familiar character type in folk literature. Though not invited to the feast, Eris appears anyway, seeking revenge. This sets the plot in motion.

Plot The use of an apple as a device to cause conflict recalls the story "Snow White," in which the evil queen tricks Snow White into eating a poisoned apple.

Theme The idea that it is dangerous to anger the gods is a familiar theme in classical mythology.

Ⓒ EXEMPLAR TEXT

Model continued

Setting This long passage of time could only occur in an exaggerated world of fantasy.

In the end, the three took the quarrel home with them to Olympus. The other gods took sides, some with one and some with another, and the ill will between them dragged on for a long while. More than long enough in the world of men for a child born when the quarrel first began, to grow to manhood and become a warrior or a herdsman. But the immortal gods do not know time as mortals know it.

Now on the northeast coast of the Aegean Sea, there was a city of men. Troy was its name, a great city surrounded by strong walls, and standing on a hill hard by the shore. It had grown rich on the tolls that its kings demanded from merchant ships passing up the nearby straits to the Black Sea cornlands and down again. Priam, who was now king, was lord of wide realms and long-maned horses, and he had many sons about his hearth. And when the quarrel about the golden apple was still raw and new, a last son was born to him and his wife Queen Hecuba, and they called him Paris.

There should have been great rejoicing, but while Hecuba still carried the babe within her, the soothsayers had foretold that she would give birth to a firebrand that should burn down Troy. And so, when he was born and named, the king bade a servant carry him out into the wilderness and leave him to die. The servant did as he was bid; but a herdsman searching for a missing calf found the babe and brought him up as his own.

The boy grew tall and strong and beautiful, the swiftest runner and the best archer in all the country around. So his boyhood passed among the oak woods and the high hill-pastures that rose toward Mount Ida. And there he met and fell in love with a wood nymph called Oenone, who loved him in return. She had the gift of being able to heal the wounds of mortal men, no matter how sorely they were hurt.

Among the oak woods they lived together and were happy—until one day the three jealous goddesses, still quarreling about the golden apple, chanced to look down from Olympus, and saw the beautiful young man herding his cattle on the slopes of Mount Ida.

They knew, for the gods know all things, that he was the son of Priam, king of Troy, though he himself did not know it yet; but the thought came to them that he would not know who they were, and therefore he would not be afraid to judge between them. They were growing somewhat weary of the argument by then.

So they tossed the apple down to him, and Paris put up his hands and caught it. After it the three came down, landing before him so lightly that their feet did not bend the mountain grasses, and bade him choose between them, which was the fairest and had best right to the prize he held in his hand.

First Athene, in her gleaming armor, fixed him with sword-gray eyes and promised him supreme wisdom if he would name her.

Then Hera, in her royal robes as queen of heaven, promised him vast wealth and power and honor if he awarded her the prize.

Lastly, Aphrodite drew near, her eyes as blue as deep-sea water, her hair like spun gold wreathed around her head, and, smiling honey-sweet, whispered that she would give him a wife as fair as herself if he tossed the apple to her.

And Paris forgot the other two with their offers of wisdom and power, forgot also, for that moment, dark-haired Oenome in the shadowed oak woods; and he gave the golden apple to Aphrodite.

Characters The three goddesses, who know everything that happens in the world, will use their magical powers to end their quarrel. This is a new development in the plot.

Plot Important events occur in the plot of a Greek myth when the gods and goddesses interact with humans. Here, Paris plays the familiar part of the human who is tricked, or used, by more powerful beings.

Independent Practice

About the Selection Julius Lester was inspired to write *Black Cowboy, Wild Horses* after reading a story about the legendary adventures of an ex-slave named Bob Lemmons. After slavery ended, Lemmons went to work as a cowboy on a ranch. There, he captured herds of wild horses all by himself, something no one else could do. He did it by making the horses believe he was one of them.

Black Cowboy, Wild Horses by Julius Lester

First Light. Bob Lemmons rode his horse slowly up the rise. When he reached the top, he stopped at the edge of the bluff. He looked down at the corral where the other cowboys were beginning the morning chores, then turned away and stared at the land stretching as wide as love in every direction. The sky was curved as if it were a lap on which the earth lay napping like a curled cat. High above, a hawk was suspended on cold threads of unseen winds. Far, far away, at what looked to be the edge of the world, land and sky kissed.

He guided Warrior, his black stallion, slowly down the bluff. When they reached the bottom, the horse reared, eager to run across the vastness of the plains until he reached forever. Bob smiled and patted him gently on the neck. "Easy. Easy," he whispered. "We'll have time for that. But not yet."

He let the horse trot for a while, then slowed him and began peering intently at the ground as if looking for the answer to a question he scarcely understood.

It was late afternoon when he saw them—the hoofprints of mustangs, the wild horses that lived on the plains. He stopped, dismounted, and walked around carefully until he had seen all the prints. Then he got down on his hands and knees to examine them more closely.

Some people learned from books. Bob had been a slave and never learned to read words. But he could look at the ground and read what animals had walked on it, their size and weight, when they had passed by, and where they were going. No one he knew could bring in mustangs by themselves, but Bob could make horses think he was one of them—because he was.

Setting What types of descriptions does the author use to convey the setting? What is the effect of these descriptions?

Character What does this description reveal about Bob? What technique does the author use to emphasize Bob's abilities?

He stood, reached into his saddlebag, took out an apple, and gave it to Warrior, who chewed with noisy enthusiasm. It was a herd of eight mares, a colt, and a stallion. They had passed there two days ago. He would see them soon. But he needed to smell of sun, moon, stars, and wind before the mustangs would accept him.

The sun went down and the chilly night air came quickly. Bob took the saddle, saddlebag, and blanket off Warrior. He was cold, but could not make a fire. The mustangs would smell the smoke in his clothes from miles away. He draped a thick blanket around himself, then took the cotton sack of dried fruit, beef jerky, and nuts from his saddlebag and ate. When he was done, he lay his head on his saddle and was quickly asleep. Warrior grazed in the tall, sweet grasses.

As soon as the sun's round shoulders came over the horizon, Bob awoke. He ate, filled his canteen, and saddling Warrior, rode away. All day he followed the tracks without hurrying.

Near dusk, clouds appeared, piled atop each other like mountains made of fear. Lightning flickered from within them like candle flames shivering in a breeze. Bob heard the faint but distinct rumbling of thunder. Suddenly lightning vaulted from cloud to cloud across the curved heavens.

Warrior reared, his front hooves pawing as if trying to knock the white streaks of fire from the night sky. Bob raced Warrior to a nearby ravine as the sky exploded sheets of light. And there, in the distance, beneath the ghostly light, Bob saw the herd of mustangs. As if sensing their presence, Warrior rose into the air once again, this time not challenging the heavens but almost in greeting. Bob thought he saw the mustang stallion rise in response as the earth shuddered from the sound of thunder.

Then the rain came as hard and stinging as remorse. Quickly Bob put on his poncho, and turning Warrior away from the wind and the rain, waited. The storm would pass soon. Or it wouldn't. There was nothing to do but wait.

Finally the rain slowed and then stopped. The clouds thinned, and there, high in the sky, the moon appeared as white as grief. Bob slept in the saddle while Warrior grazed on the wet grasses.

Patterns What is Bob's quest?

Setting How might the weather affect the development of the story?

Character What does Bob's reaction to the weather tell you about his attitude toward nature?

Practice continued

The sun rose into a clear sky and Bob was awake immediately. The storm would have washed away the tracks, but they had been going toward the big river. He would go there and wait.

By mid-afternoon he could see the ribbon of river shining in the distance. He stopped, needing only to be close enough to see the horses when they came to drink. Toward evening he saw a trail of rolling, dusty clouds.

In front was the mustang herd. As it reached the water, the stallion slowed and stopped. He looked around, his head raised, nostrils flared, smelling the air. He turned in Bob's direction and sniffed the air again.

Bob tensed. Had he come too close too soon? If the stallion smelled anything new, he and the herd would be gone and Bob would never find them again. The stallion seemed to be looking directly at him. Bob was too far away to be seen, but he did not even blink his eyes, afraid the stallion would hear the sound. Finally the stallion began drinking and the other horses followed. Bob let his breath out slowly. He had been accepted.

The next morning he crossed the river and picked up the herd's trail. He moved Warrior slowly, without sound, without dust. Soon he saw them grazing. He stopped. The horses did not notice him. After a while he moved forward, slowly, quietly. The stallion raised his head. Bob stopped.

When the stallion went back to grazing, Bob moved forward again. All day Bob watched the herd, moving only when it moved but always coming closer. The mustangs sensed his presence. They thought he was a horse. So did he.

The following morning Bob and Warrior walked into the herd. The stallion eyed them for a moment. Then, as if to test this newcomer, he led the herd off in a gallop. Bob lay flat across Warrior's back and moved with the herd. If anyone had been watching, they would not have noticed a man among the horses.

When the herd set out early the next day, it was moving slowly. If the horses had been going faster, it would not have happened.

The colt fell to the ground as if she had stepped into a hole and broken her leg. Bob and the horses heard the chilling sound of the

Plot Why is the stallion's reaction important to the outcome of Bob's quest?

Character What unique abilities enable Bob to track the horses successfully?

rattles. Rattlesnakes didn't always give a warning before they struck. Sometimes, when someone or something came too close, they bit with the fury of fear.

The horses whinnied and pranced nervously, smelling the snake and death among them. Bob saw the rattler, as beautiful as a necklace, sliding silently through the tall grasses. He made no move to kill it. Everything in nature had the right to protect itself, especially when it was afraid.

The stallion galloped to the colt. He pushed at her. The colt struggled to get up, but fell to her side, shivering and kicking feebly with her thin legs. Quickly she was dead.

Already vultures circled high in the sky. The mustangs milled aimlessly. The colt's mother whinnied, refusing to leave the side of her colt. The stallion wanted to move the herd from there, and pushed the mare with his head. She refused to budge, and he nipped her on the rump. She skittered away. Before she could return to the colt, the stallion bit her again, this time harder. She ran toward the herd. He bit her a third time, and the herd was off. As they galloped away, Bob looked back. The vultures were descending from the sky as gracefully as dusk.

It was time to take over the herd. The stallion would not have the heart to fight fiercely so soon after the death of the colt. Bob galloped Warrior to the front and wheeled around, forcing the stallion to stop quickly. The herd, confused, slowed and stopped also.

Bob raised Warrior to stand high on his back legs, fetlocks pawing and kicking the air. The stallion's eyes widened. He snorted and pawed the ground, surprised and uncertain. Bob charged at the stallion.

Both horses rose on hind legs, teeth bared as they kicked at each other. When they came down, Bob charged Warrior at the stallion again, pushing him backward. Bob rushed yet again.

The stallion neighed loudly, and nipped Warrior on the neck. Warrior snorted angrily, reared, and kicked out with his forelegs, striking the stallion on the nose. Still maintaining his balance, Warrior struck again and again. The mustang stallion cried out in pain. Warrior pushed hard against the stallion. The stallion lost his footing and fell to the earth.

Theme What central idea does Bob's reaction to the snake help develop?

Patterns What pattern does the author use in this passage to move the action of the story along?

Plot The clash between animals and humans is a common theme in the oral tradition. How is the conflict between Bob and the stallion important to the development of the story?

Practice continued

Warrior rose, neighing triumphantly, his front legs pawing as if seeking for the rungs on which he could climb a ladder into the sky.

The mustang scrambled to his feet, beaten. He snorted weakly. When Warrior made as if to attack again, the stallion turned, whinnied weakly, and trotted away.

Bob was now the herd's leader, but would they follow him? He rode slowly at first, then faster and faster. The mustangs followed as if being led on ropes.

Throughout that day and the next he rode with the horses. For Bob there was only the bulging of the horses' dark eyes, the quivering of their flesh, the rippling of muscles and bending of bones in their bodies. He was now sky and plains and grass and river and horse.

When his food was almost gone, Bob led the horses on one last ride, a dark surge of flesh flashing across the plains like black lightning. Toward evening he led the herd up the steep hillside, onto the bluff, and down the slope toward the big corral. The cowboys heard him coming and opened the corral gate. Bob led the herd, but at the last moment he swerved Warrior aside, and the mustangs flowed into the fenced enclosure. The cowboys leaped and shouted as they quickly closed the gate.

Bob rode away from them and back up to the bluff. He stopped and stared out onto the plains. Warrior reared and whinnied loudly.

"I know," Bob whispered. "I know. Maybe someday."

Maybe someday they would ride with the mustangs, ride to that forever place where land and sky kissed, and then ride on. Maybe someday.

Plot What problem has Bob solved? How does the ending compare to that of other stories about folk heroes you have read or heard?

Black Cowboy, Wild Horses

1. Key Ideas and Details (a) What examples does the story provide about Bob Lemmon's legendary ability? **(b) Infer:** What danger does Bob face in approaching the mustangs too soon?

2. Key Ideas and Details (a) Describe: How does Bob depend on Warrior? **(b) Compare:** Why does it seem that Warrior's goals or dreams are the same as Bob's goals?

3. Key Ideas and Details
(a) Summarize: What does Bob do after he leads the mustangs to the corral? **(b) Interpret:** What do his actions suggest about the life of a legendary hero?

4. Key Ideas and Details Analyze: What is the universal theme in this folk tale? Explain your answer, citing details from the story.

5. Integration of Knowledge and Ideas (a) Complete a diagram like the one shown by listing qualities about cowboy Bob that make him seem real and ones that exaggerate his abilities to make him seem like a **legend.**

Qualities of real cowboy Bob | Shared Qualities | Qualities of legendary cowboy Bob

(b) Collaborate: Discuss your chart with a classmate and explain how your understanding of Bob was confirmed or changed based on your discussion.

6. Key Ideas and Details Summarize: Write a brief summary of the story. Include the central ideas and key details, but do not include your own opinions or judgments.

© Leveled Texts

Build your skills and improve your comprehension of folk literature with texts of increasing complexity.

Read **"The Tiger Who Would Be King"** and **"The Ant and the Dove"** to see the difference between cooperation and conflict.

Read **"The Lion and the Bulls"** and **"A Crippled Boy"** to meet characters who use trickery to achieve their goals.

© Common Core State Standards

Meet these standards with either **"The Tiger Who Would Be King"** (p. 842) and **"The Ant and the Dove"** (p. 844) or **"The Lion and the Bulls"** (p. 848) and **"A Crippled Boy"** (p. 850).

Reading Literature

2. Determine a theme or central idea of a text and how it is conveyed through particular details. (*Literary Analysis: Fables*)

Writing

3.b. Use narrative techniques, such as dialogue, pacing, and description, to develop experiences, events, and/or characters. **3.c.** Use a variety of transition words, phrases, and clauses to convey sequence and signal shifts from time frame or setting to another. **3.e.** Provide a conclusion that follows from the narrated experiences or events. (*Writing: Fable*)

6. Use technology, including the Internet, to produce and publish writing. **7.** Conduct short research projects to answers question, drawing on several sources and refocusing the inquiry when appropriate. (*Speaking and Listening: Oral Report*)

Speaking and Listening

5. Include multimedia components and visual displays in presentations to clarify claims and findings and emphasize salient points. (*Speaking and Listening: Oral Report*)

Language

1. Demonstrate command of the conventions of standard English grammar and usage when writing or speaking. (*Conventions: Independent and Subordinate Clauses*)

4.b. Use common, grade-appropriate Greek or Latin affixes and roots as clues to the meaning of a word. (*Vocabulary: Word Study*)

Reading Skill: Cause and Effect

A **cause** is an event, action, or feeling that produces a result. The result is called an **effect.** Sometimes an effect is the result of a number of causes. To help you identify the relationship between an event and its causes, **reread** important passages in a literary work, looking for connections.

Using the Strategy: Cause-and-Effect Map

Use a chart like the one shown to record the events and actions that produce an effect.

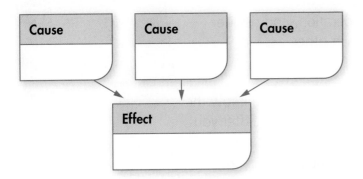

Literary Analysis: Fables and Folk Tales

Fables and **folk tales** are part of the oral tradition, in which stories and poems were passed from generation to generation by word of mouth.

- **Fables** are brief stories that teach a lesson or moral. They often feature animal characters.
- **Folk tales** often feature clever characters who get the best of their superiors. They may also have elements of magic and adventure.

Some fables and folk tales have **ironic,** or surprising, endings because they do not turn out as you expect. However, the twist ending helps you to see the **theme,** or message, the story conveys. As you read, notice how the setting, characters, and events introduce and develop the story's theme.

How much do our communities shape us?

Writing About the Big Question

These tales use animal characters to teach lessons about people struggling against each other and about people working together. Use these sentence starters to develop your ideas about the Big Question.

When members of a community cooperate and **support** one another, they can _____. When they work against each other, however, they can _____.

While You Read Look for signs of cooperation, and decide what the characters could do to help each other.

Vocabulary

Read each word and its definition. Decide whether you know the word well, know it a little bit, or do not know it at all. After you read, see how your knowledge of each word has increased.

- **prowled** (prould) *v.* moved around quietly and secretly (p. 842) *The coyote prowled the field in search of mice.* *prowl v. prowler n.*

- **inquired** (in kwīrd´) *v.* asked (p. 842) *I inquired about whether there would be a quiz.* *inquire v. inquiry n.*

- **repulse** (ri puls´) *v.* drive back; repel an attack (p. 843) *A skunk sprays its scent to repulse attackers.* *repulsive adj. repulsed v.*

- **monarch** (män´ ərk) *n.* single or sole ruler (p. 843) *The new monarch took power by force.* *monarchy n.*

- **startled** (stärt´ əld) *adj.* surprised (p. 844) *The balloon popped, and the startled baby cried.* *startle v.*

- **repaid** (ri pād´) *v.* did or gave in return (p. 844) *With his gift, Harry repaid me for my work.* *repay v. repays v. repayment n.*

Word Study

The **suffix -ment** means the "act," "art" or "process of." A word ending in -ment is usually a noun.

"The Ant and the Dove" is a story about the **repayment** of a favor, or the act of paying back a favor.

Meet the Authors

James Thurber (1894–1961)
Author of "The Tiger Who Would Be King"

James Thurber wrote for his high-school and college newspapers in his home state of Ohio. He also wrote plays and songs for Ohio State University's drama club and columns for his hometown newspaper, *The Columbus Dispatch*.

Amusing His Readers During World War I, Thurber left college to join the U.S. military. He soon left this serious position to pursue his love of laughter through writing and cartooning. Much of his early work appeared in *The New Yorker* magazine. Although failing eyesight forced him to give up drawing, Thurber kept making people laugh through his writing.

Leo Tolstoy (1828–1910)
Author of "The Ant and the Dove"

Born into a wealthy family in Russia, Leo Tolstoy inherited his family estate at age nineteen. By the time he was fifty, he had written some of the world's most famous novels, including *Anna Karenina* and *War and Peace*.

Famous, Yet Alone In midlife, Tolstoy began to reject his life of luxury. He surrendered the rights to many of his works and gave his property to his family. This world-famous writer died alone in a remote train station in Russia.

Did You Know?
James Thurber is often quoted as saying "It is better to know some of the questions than all of the answers."
Leo Tolstoy said: "Everyone thinks of changing the world, but no one thinks of changing himself."

The Tiger Who Would Be King

James Thurber

One morning the tiger woke up in the jungle and told his mate that he was king of beasts.

"Leo, the lion, is king of beasts," she said.

"We need a change," said the tiger. "The creatures are crying for a change."

The tigress listened but she could hear no crying, except that of her cubs.

"I'll be king of beasts by the time the moon rises," said the tiger. "It will be a yellow moon with black stripes, in my honor."

"Oh, sure," said the tigress as she went to look after her young, one of whom, a male, very like his father, had got an imaginary thorn in his paw.

The tiger prowled through the jungle till he came to the lion's den. "Come out," he roared, "and greet the king of beasts! The king is dead, long live the king!"

Inside the den, the lioness woke her mate. "The king is here to see you," she said.

"What king?" he inquired, sleepily.

"The king of beasts," she said.

"I am the king of beasts," roared Leo, and he charged out of the den to defend his crown against the pretender.

It was a terrible fight, and it lasted until the setting of the sun. All the animals of the jungle joined in, some taking the side of the tiger and others the side of the lion. Every creature from the aardvark to the zebra took part in the struggle to overthrow the lion or to repulse the tiger, and some did not know which they were fighting for, and some fought for both, and some fought whoever was nearest, and some fought for the sake of fighting.

"What are we fighting for?" someone asked the aardvark.

"The old order," said the aardvark.

"What are we dying for?" someone asked the zebra.

"The new order," said the zebra.

When the moon rose, fevered and gibbous,[1] it shone upon a jungle in which nothing stirred except a macaw[2] and a cockatoo,[3] screaming in horror. All the beasts were dead except the tiger, and his days were numbered and his time was ticking away. He was monarch of all he surveyed, but it didn't seem to mean anything.

MORAL:

You can't very well be king of beasts if there aren't any.

---

1. **gibbous** (gib´ əs) *adj.* more than half but less than completely illuminated.
2. **macaw** (mə kô´) *n.* bright-colored, harsh-voiced parrot of Central or South America.
3. **cockatoo** (kok´ ə tü´) *n.* crested parrot with white feathers tinged with yellow or pink.

LITERATURE IN CONTEXT

Language Connection

Allusions

James Thurber uses an allusion in his description of the tigress who attends to her male cub with an imaginary thorn in his paw. An *allusion* is a reference to a person, place, or thing in another artistic work. Thurber makes an allusion to the fable of the shepherd who boldly relieves the lion from the pain caused by the thorn in his paw. Later, when the shepherd is in danger, the lion remembers the shepherd's kindness and saves him.

Connect to Literature

Why does Thurber allude to the fable about the lion and the shepherd?

Vocabulary
repulse (ri puls´)
v. drive back;
repel an attack

monarch (män´ ərk)
n. single or sole ruler

Fables and Folk Tales
What conflict or problem does this fable address?

The Ant and the Dove

RUSSIAN FOLK TALE

Leo Tolstoy

A thirsty ant went to the stream to drink. Suddenly it got caught in a whirlpool and was almost carried away.

At that moment a dove was passing by with a twig in its beak. The dove dropped the twig for the tiny insect to grab hold of. So it was that the ant was saved.

A few days later a hunter was about to catch the dove in his net. When the ant saw what was happening, it walked right up to the man and bit him on the foot. Startled, the man dropped the net. And the dove, thinking that you never can tell how or when a kindness may be repaid, flew away.

Cite textual evidence to support your responses.

Critical Thinking

1. **Integration of Knowledge and Ideas (a)** Which two animals fight to rule in "The Tiger Who Would Be King"? **(b) Infer:** Some of the animals join the fight for the sake of fighting. What does this suggest about them? **(c) Apply:** What human qualities does Thurber show in these animals?

2. **Key Ideas and Details (a)** What does the dove in "The Ant and the Dove" do for the ant? **(b) Infer:** How does this action save the ant?

3. **Key Ideas and Details** Does "The Ant and the Dove" remind you of any other story or stories? Explain.

4. **Key Ideas and Details (a)** In the "Tiger Who Would Be King," what action in the community could have saved the animals? **(b)** Explain why the animals did not take that action. *[Connect to the Big Question: How much do our communities shape us?]*

Reading Skill: Cause and Effect

1. (a) In "The Tiger Who Would Be King," identify several **causes** of the fight in the jungle. **(b)** What is the **effect** of the fight?

2. What is the end **effect** of the dove's action in "The Ant and the Dove"?

Literary Analysis: Fables and Folk Tales

3. Key Ideas and Details Make a chart like the one shown to identify the elements of **fables** and **folk tales** in the two stories.

Title	Characters	Moral or Theme

4. Key Ideas and Details (a) What is **ironic,** or surprising, about the ending of "The Tiger Who Would Be King"? **(b)** What **theme** does it help to convey?

Vocabulary

Acquisition and Use Respond to each item based on your knowledge of the italicized words. Explain your answers.

1. Explain why a wolf might have *prowled* near a river.

2. Provide two reasons why garbage might *repulse* people.

3. Identify three things that a *startled* person might do.

4. Explain why you would have *inquired* about a friend's health.

5. If you have *repaid* a debt, do you still owe money?

6. Explain why the United States does not have a *monarch*.

Word Study Use context and what you know about the suffix **-ment** to explain your answer to each question.

1. When do you give your friends *encouragement*?

2. How do you get a *measurement*?

Word Study

The suffix **-ment** means the "act," "art," or "process of."

Apply It Explain how the suffix -*ment* contributes to the meaning of these words. Consult a dictionary if necessary.

argument
punishment
payment

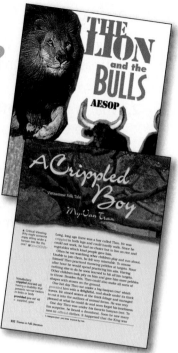

How much do our *communities* shape us?

Writing About the Big Question

In both of these tales, characters look for ways to achieve a goal. Use the following sentence starter to help you develop your ideas about the Big Question.

If a person achieves success by taking advantage of others in his or her **group,** the result can be_____.

While You Read Think about whether the actions of the characters in these stories put their **community** in danger.

Vocabulary

Read each word and its definition. Decide whether you know the word well, know it a little bit, or do not know it at all. After you read, see how your knowledge of each word has increased.

- **lure** (lo͞or) *v.* tempt or attract (p. 849) *The music will lure you to the party. luring v. lures v.*

- **slanderous** (slan´ dər əs) *adj.* including untrue and damaging statements (p. 849) *Do not believe her slanderous words. slander n. slanderer n.*

- **crippled** (krip´ əld) *adj.* having a disability that prevents normal motion in limbs or body (p. 850) *The accident left my dog physically crippled, but he is still as sharp as ever! crippling v.*

- **provided** (prə vīd´ əd) *v.* supplied; gave (p. 850) *A local restaurant provided food for the hungry. provide v. providing v. provision n.*

- **official** (ə fish´ əl) *adj.* formal; prescribed by an authority (p. 850) *The official boy scout uniform is sold here. officially adv. official n. office n.*

- **demonstrate** (dem´ ən strāt) *v.* show clearly; prove (p. 851) *Can you demonstrate the dance for us? demonstration n.*

Word Study

The **suffix -ous** means "having," "full of," or "characterized by." It usually indicates a word is an adjective.

In "The Lion and the Bulls," the Lion spreads **slanderous** rumors that are filled with damaging lies.

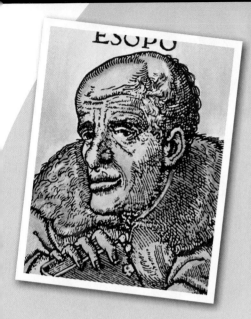

Aesop (ca. 620–560 B.C.)

Author of "The Lion and the Bulls"

Aesop's fables have been enjoyed for centuries. However, very little is known about the origin of these stories, including who actually wrote them.

A Man of Mystery According to tradition, Aesop was a Greek slave who lived on the island of Samos during the sixth century B.C. Some people believe that he defended criminals in court. Others believe that he was either an advisor or a riddle-solver for one of the Greek kings. The most widely held theory, however, is that Aesop was not an actual person. Because certain stories in ancient Greece were told over and over, people may have invented an imaginary author for them.

My-Van Tran (b. 1947)

Author of "A Crippled Boy"

My-Van Tran is from Saigon, now called Ho Chi Minh City, in Vietnam. Because of the Vietnam War, she left her native land and moved to Australia. However, she never abandoned her cultural heritage.

Supporting International Ties She received a medal from the Australian government for fostering Australian-Asian relations. Now at the University of South Australia, My-Van Tran teaches Asian studies and the history and politics of Asia.

Did You Know?

Aesop is said to be the author of "The Boy Who Cried Wolf," a story often told to caution children against lying.
My-Van Tran teaches Asian studies and the history and politics of Asia at the University of South Australia.

THE LION and the BULLS

AESOP

A lion often prowled about a pasture where three bulls grazed together. He had tried without success to lure one or the other of them to the edge of the pasture. He had even attempted a direct attack, only to see them form a ring so that from whatever direction he approached he was met by the horns of one of them.

Then a plan began to form in the lion's mind. Secretly he started spreading evil and slanderous reports of one bull against the other. The three bulls, distrustingly, began to avoid one another, and each withdrew to a different part of the pasture to graze. Of course, this was exactly what the lion wanted. One by one he fell upon the bulls, and so made easy prey of them all.

MORAL:
United we stand; divided we fall.

◄ **Critical Viewing**
Why might a lion sneak up on its prey, rather than attack it directly? **[Analyze]**

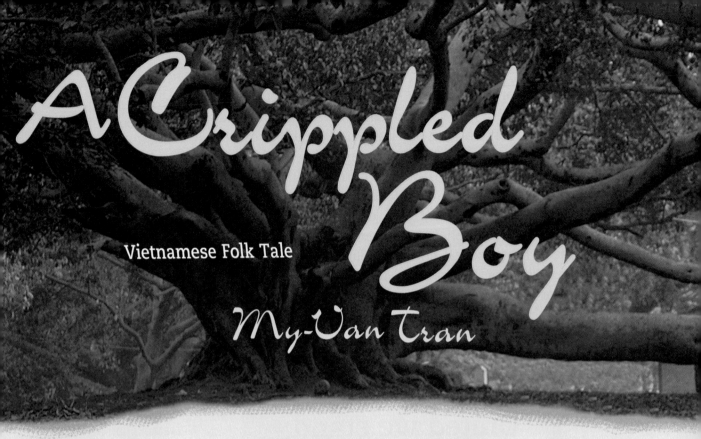

A Crippled Boy

Vietnamese Folk Tale

My-Van Tran

Vocabulary

crippled (krip´ əld) *adj.* having a disability that prevents normal motion in limbs or body

provided (prə vīd´ əd) *v.* supplied; gave

official (ə fish´ əl) *adj.* formal; prescribed by an authority

Long, long ago there was a boy called Theo. He was crippled in both legs and could hardly walk. Since he could not work, he had no choice but to live on rice and vegetables which kind people gave him.

Often he sat watching other children play and run about. Unable to join them, he felt very miserable. To amuse himself Theo practiced throwing pebbles at targets. Hour after hour he would spend practicing his aim. Having nothing else to do he soon learned to hit all his targets. Other children took pity on him and gave him more pebbles to throw. Besides this, Theo could also make all sorts of shapes with stones on the ground.

One hot day Theo sat under a big banyan tree[1] which provided him with a delightful, cool shade under its thick leaves. He aimed stones at the thick foliage and managed to cut it into the outlines of animal forms. He was very pleased at what he could do and soon forgot his loneliness.

One day Theo was under his favorite banyan tree. To his surprise, he heard a drumbeat. Soon he saw many men in official clothes. It happened that the King was

---

1. **banyan** (ban´ yən) **tree** tropical fig tree.

out for a country walk with some of his officials and was passing by Theo's tree.

The King's attention was caught by the unusual shadow of the tree. He stopped and was very surprised to see little crippled Theo sitting there all alone.

Theo was very frightened and tried to get away; but he could not crawl very far. The King asked Theo what he had been doing. Theo told the King his story.

Then the King asked Theo to demonstrate his skill at pebble throwing. Theo was happy to do so. The King was impressed and asked Theo to return with him to the palace where the King said:

"I have a little job for you to do." •

The following day, before the King had a meeting with his mandarins,[2] he ordered Theo to sit quietly behind a curtain. The King had ordered a few holes to be made in the curtain so that Theo could see what was going on.

---

2. **mandarins** (man´ də rinz) *n.* high-ranking officials and counselors.

▲ **Critical Viewing**
Why might some-one enjoy sitting under a banyan tree like this one?

Vocabulary
demonstrate (dem´ ən strāt) *v.* show clearly; prove

Cause and Effect
Reread to find out what effect the King hopes Theo's skill will have.

Spiral Review
Characters How are the characters in this story typical of folk tales?

"Most of my mandarins talk too much," the King explained. "They never bother to listen to me or let me finish my sentence. So if anybody opens his mouth to speak while I am talking, just throw a pebble into his mouth. This will teach him to shut up."

Sure enough, just as the meeting was about to start one mandarin opened his big mouth, ready to speak.

Oops! Something got into his mouth and he quickly closed it.

Another mandarin opened his mouth to speak but strangely enough he, too, shut his mouth without saying a word.

A miracle had happened. Throughout the whole meeting all the mandarins kept their silence.

For once the King could speak as much as he wanted without being interrupted. The King was extremely pleased with his success and the help that Theo had given him.

After that he always treasured Theo's presence and service. So Theo remained happily at the palace, no longer needing to beg for food and no longer always sitting alone under the banyan tree.

Critical Thinking

1. Key Ideas and Details (a) Speculate: In "The Lion and the Bulls," what kinds of lies do you think the lion tells the bulls? **(b) Infer:** Why are the bulls willing to believe the lion?

2. Integration of Knowledge and Ideas (a) Infer: What human qualities does Aesop show in the animals? **(b) Assess:** Is an animal fable more or less effective than one with human characters? Explain.

3. Key Ideas and Details (a) In "A Crippled Boy," why does Theo begin to throw stones? **(b) Analyze:** Name two ways in which Theo benefits from developing his talent.

4. Integration of Knowledge and Ideas How is the importance of a community working together—and *not* working together—reinforced in "The Lion and the Bulls"? *[Connect to the Big Question: How much do our communities shape us?]*

Cite textual evidence to support your responses.

Reading Skill: Cause and Effect

1. (a) In "The Lion and the Bulls," what **causes** the bulls to move away from one another? **(b)** What is the **effect**?

2. (a) In "A Crippled Boy," what events cause the King to invite Theo to live at the palace? **(b)** What effect does living at the palace have on Theo?

Literary Analysis: Fables and Folk Tales

3. Key Ideas and Details Make a chart like the one shown to identify the elements of **fables** and **folk tales** in the two stories.

Title	Characters	Moral or Theme

4. Integration of Knowledge and Ideas What is **ironic,** or surprising, about the ending of "A Crippled Boy"?

Vocabulary

Acquisition and Use Respond to each item based on your knowledge of the italicized words. Explain your responses.

1. Why do salespeople often *demonstrate* their products?

2. Why is lunch sometimes *provided* on field trips?

3. Why are *slanderous* comments considered bad?

4. Why might a *crippled* dog have trouble getting food?

5. How would you *lure* a runaway pet to you?

6. Describe an *official* uniform you have seen recently.

Word Study Use context and what you know about the **suffix -ous** to explain your answer to each question.

1. How would you expect a *mischievous* child to behave?

2. What makes you *courageous*?

Word Study

The **suffix -ous** means "having," "full of," or "characterized by."

Apply It Explain how the suffix -ous contributes to the meaning of these words. Consult a dictionary if necessary.

porous
contagious
odorous

Integrated Language Skills

The Tiger Who Would Be King • The Ant and the Dove • The Lion and the Bulls • A Crippled Boy

Conventions: Independent and Subordinate Clauses

A **clause** is a group of words with its own subject and verb.

An **independent clause** has a subject and a verb and can stand by itself as a complete sentence. A **subordinate clause** has a subject and a verb but cannot stand by itself as a complete sentence.

I hear you independent clause	because I hear you subordinate clause
please be there tomorrow independent clause	if you are there tomorrow subordinate clause
When I pick you up, we can talk. subordinate clause independent clause	

Practice A Add independent clauses to the subordinate clauses to make complete sentences.

1. when the tiger woke up
2. after the fight
3. before the tiger roared
4. in case you need a kindness

Reading Application Scan to find two independent clauses and one subordinate clause in "A Crippled Boy."

Practice B Add a subordinate clause to each of the following independent clauses to make a new sentence.

1. Three bulls grazed together.
2. The lion prowled.
3. The king wanted to hire Theo.
4. Theo threw a stone.

Writing Application Write a sentence in which you explain what you enjoyed about a fable or folk tale you read. In your sentence, use an independent clause and a subordinate clause.

PH WRITING COACH | Further instruction and practice are available in *Prentice Hall Writing Coach*.

Writing

Common Core State Standards

L.6.1; W.6.3.b, W.6.3.c, W.6.3.e, W.6.6, W.6.7; SL.6.5
[For the full wording of the standards, see page 838.]

Narrative Text Write a **fable** that teaches the same lesson as one of the stories you read. For your fable, you may create different characters and change the plot, but retain the moral.

- First decide on the lesson for your fable. Then, brainstorm for situations in which characters would learn that lesson.

- Use dialogue and description to develop characters. Pace the action. To slow the pace as you introduce scenes, use longer sentences and more details. To move faster and create tension, use short sentences.

- Use transitions to show a clear connection between the events that will lead to the lesson learned.

- Provide a moral at the end that logically follows from the events.

Grammar Application Review your fable to be sure that you have used subordinate clauses correctly.

Writing Workshop: *Work in Progress*

Prewriting for Research For a multimedia presentation you may develop, choose any idea from your writing portfolio to pursue. Plan one or two illustrations you might use and take notes or make sketches of what you might do. Save this Illustrations List in your writing portfolio.

Use this prewriting activity to prepare for the **Writing Workshop** on page 906.

Speaking and Listening

Presentation of Ideas Prepare an **oral report** on one of the authors whose work you have read here.

- Research the author's life using the Internet or print sources. Answer questions you have about the author's background and key published works. Add questions or change your focus, if needed, as your research develops.

- Take notes on key points you will want to share in your report. Then, compose an interesting oral presentation from your notes.

- Prepare visual aids such as pictures, timelines, and graphs to grab your audience's attention and to support your ideas.

- Practice delivering your presentation clearly. Use your voice to speak expressively, emphasizing key points. When you are ready, share your report with your class.

PHLit Online!
www.PHLitOnline.com

- Interactive graphic organizers
- Grammar tutorial
- Interactive journals

@ Leveled Texts

Build your skills and improve your comprehension of themes in folk literature with texts of increasing complexity.

Read the myth of **"Arachne"** to find out what happens when a young woman dares to challenge a goddess.

Read the Prologue from *The Whale Rider* to experience a legend that comes from the Maori people of New Zealand.

@ Common Core State Standards

Meet these standards with either **"Arachne"** (p. 860) or *Prologue from* **The Whale Rider** (p. 868).

Reading Literature

2. Determine a theme or central idea of a text and how it is conveyed through particular details *(Literary Analysis: Myths)*

5. Analyze how a particular sentence, chapter, scene, or stanza fits into the overall structure of a text and contributes to the development of the theme, setting, or plot. *(Reading Skill: Cause and Effect)*

Writing

2. Write informative/explanatory texts to examine a topic and convey ideas, concepts, and information through the selection, organization, and analysis of relevant content.

2.a. Introduce a topic; organize ideas, concepts, and information, using strategies such as definition, classification, comparison/contrast, and cause/effect.

2.d. Use precise language and domain-specific vocabulary

to inform about or explain the topic. **2.e.** Establish and maintain a formal style. *(Writing: Compare-and-Contrast Essay)*

8. Gather relevant information from multiple print and digital sources; assess the credibility of each source; and quote or paraphrase the data and conclusions of others while avoiding plagiarism and providing basic bibliographic information for sources. *(Research and Technology: Annotated Bibliography Entry)*

Language

3.a. Vary sentence patterns for meaning, reader/listener interest, and style. *(Conventions: Simple, Compound, and Complex Sentences)*

Reading Skill: Cause and Effect

A **cause** is an event, action, or emotion that makes something happen. An **effect** is what happens. When an effect occurs, it can then become the cause of another event. In most stories, the plot unfolds as a series of linked events—causes and effects—ordered into sentences, paragraphs, and scenes.

As you read, look for clue words such as *because, so,* and *as a result* that signal cause-and-effect relationships. Then, **ask questions** such as "What happened?" and "Why did this happen?" to help you follow the structure of cause-and-effect.

Literary Analysis: Myths

Myths are fictional tales that describe the actions of gods or heroes. Every culture has its own myths. A myth can do one or more of the following:

- Tell how the universe or a culture began
- Explain something in nature, such as thunder
- Express a **theme,** or insight—often one that emphasizes the importance of a value, such as honesty or bravery

The characters, plot, and imagery in a myth often provide a glimpse into the culture from which the myth came.

Using the Strategy: Myth Map

As you read, fill in a chart like the one shown to analyze the characteristics of myths.

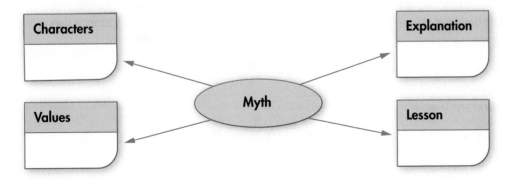

How much do our *communities* shape us?

Writing About the Big Question

Like many myths, "Arachne" teaches an important lesson. Use the following sentence starter to help you develop your ideas about the Big Question.

> Stories that are passed down from generation to generation within a community often teach about such **values** as

_____.

While You Read Look for details that lead Arachne to learn an important lesson that reflects the values of ancient Greek society.

Vocabulary

Read each word and its definition. Decide whether you know the word well, know it a little bit, or do not know it at all. After you read, see how your knowledge of each word has increased.

- **obscure** (əb skyoor´) *adj.* not well known (p. 860) *I have never heard of that obscure artist.* obscurity *n.* obscure *v.*

- **humble** (hum´ bəl) *adj.* modest; not proud (p. 860) *Mark is a smart but humble boy.* humbly *adv.* humbler *adj.*

- **mortal** (môr´ təl) *adj.* referring to humans, who eventually die (p. 862) *Mortal men cannot move mountains.* mortality *n.* immortal *adj.* immortality *n.*

- **indignantly** (in dig´ nənt lē) *adv.* in a way that expresses anger (p. 862) *Zoe indignantly demanded to speak to a manager about the restaurant's poor service.* indignant *adj.* dignity *n.*

- **obstinacy** (äb´ stə nə sē) *n.* stubbornness (p. 862) *The willful child was punished for her obstinacy.* obstinant *adj.* obstinantly *adv.*

- **strive** (strīv) *v.* struggle; compete (p. 863) *I will strive hard in the race.* striving *v.* strived *v.*

Word Study

The **Latin root -*mort*-** means "death."

Unlike a god or goddess, who does not die, Arachne was a **mortal**—a human being, who cannot live forever.

Meet
Olivia E. Coolidge
(1908–2006)

Author of
Arachne

Olivia Ensor Coolidge was born and educated in England and lived in both Europe and the United States. She taught English, Latin, and Greek, but she was best known as a writer.

Accuracy and Detail In addition to writing about subjects from classical mythology, such as the Trojan War, she wrote about colonial times in American history. Coolidge was known for the accuracy of her historical fiction and for her attention to detail.

DID YOU KNOW?

Coolidge said that she enjoyed writing about legends and myths because she felt that they express ancient values that are still important in the modern world.

BACKGROUND FOR THE MYTH

Spiders

Arachne is the name of the main character in this myth. *Arachnida* is the name of the class of creatures that includes spiders. Spiders live almost everywhere on the planet and are useful because they eat insect pests. The smallest spiders are anapids, which are no bigger than the head of a pin. The largest are tarantulas, some of which are as large as a dinner plate. Few spiders are harmful.

Arachne

Greek Myth

Olivia E. Coolidge

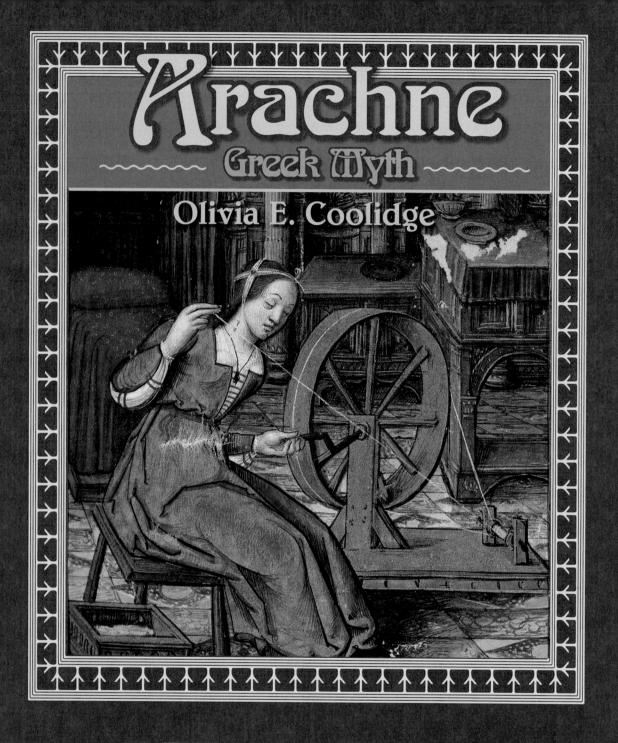

Arachne [ə rak´ nē] was a maiden who became famous throughout Greece, though she was neither wellborn nor beautiful and came from no great city. She lived in an obscure little village, and her father was a humble dyer of wool.

In this he was very skillful, producing many varied shades, while above all he was famous for the clear, bright scarlet which is made from shellfish, and which was the most glorious of all the colors used in ancient Greece. Even more skillful than her father was Arachne. It was her task to spin the fleecy wool into a fine, soft thread and to weave it into cloth on the high, standing loom within the cottage. Arachne was small and pale from much working. Her eyes were light and her hair was a dusty brown, yet she was quick and graceful, and her fingers, roughened as they were, went so fast that it was hard to follow their flickering movements. So soft and even was her thread, so fine her cloth, so gorgeous her embroidery, that soon her products were known all over Greece. No one had ever seen the like of them before.

At last Arachne's fame became so great that people used to come from far and wide to watch her working. Even the graceful nymphs[1] would steal in from stream or forest and peep shyly through the dark doorway, watching in wonder the white arms of Arachne as she stood at the loom and threw the shuttle from hand to hand between the hanging threads, or drew out the long wool, fine as a hair, from the distaff[2] as she sat spinning. "Surely Athene[3] herself must have taught her," people would murmur to one another. "Who else could know the secret of such marvelous skill?"

Arachne was used to being wondered at, and she was immensely proud of the skill that had brought so many to look on her. Praise was all she lived for, and it displeased her greatly that people should think anyone, even a goddess, could teach her anything. Therefore when she heard them murmur, she would stop her work and turn round indignantly to say, "With my own ten fingers I gained this skill, and by hard practice from early morning till night. I never had time to stand looking as you people do while another maiden worked. Nor if I had, would I give Athene credit because the girl was more skillful than I. As

Cause and Effect
What causes Arachne's work to be known all over Greece?

Spiral Review
Setting In this paragraph, what do you learn about the world of this story?

---

1. **nymphs** (nimfz) *n.* minor nature goddesses, represented as beautiful maidens living in rivers, trees, and mountains.
2. **distaff** (dis´taf´) *n.* stick on which flax or wool is wound for spinning.
3. **Athene** (ə thē´ nə) *n.* Greek goddess of wisdom, skills, and warfare.

for Athene's weaving, how could there be finer cloth or more beautiful embroidery than mine? If Athene herself were to come down and compete with me, she could do no better than I." •

One day when Arachne turned round with such words, an old woman answered her, a gray old woman, bent and very poor, who stood leaning on a staff and peering at Arachne amid the crowd of onlookers. "Reckless girl," she said, "how dare you claim to be equal to the immortal gods themselves? I am an old woman and have seen much. Take my advice and ask pardon of Athene for your words. Rest content with your fame of being the best spinner and weaver that mortal eyes have ever beheld."

"Stupid old woman," said Arachne indignantly, "who gave you a right to speak in this way to me? It is easy to see that you were never good for anything in your day, or you would not come here in poverty and rags to gaze at my skill. If Athene resents my words, let her answer them herself. I have challenged her to a contest, but she, of course, will not come. It is easy for the gods to avoid matching their skill with that of men."

At these words the old woman threw down her staff and stood erect. The wondering onlookers saw her grow tall and fair and stand clad in long robes of dazzling white. They were terribly afraid as they realized that they stood in the presence of Athene. Arachne herself flushed red for a moment, for she had never really believed that the goddess would hear her. Before the group that was gathered there she would not give in; so pressing her pale lips together in obstinacy and pride, she led the goddess to one of the great looms and set herself before the other. Without a word both began to thread the long woolen strands that hang from the rollers, and between which the shuttle[4] moves back and forth. Many skeins lay heaped beside

---

4. **shuttle** (shut´ əl) *n.* instrument used in weaving to carry thread back and forth.

them to use, bleached white, and gold, and scarlet, and other shades, varied as the rainbow. Arachne had never thought of giving credit for her success to her father's skill in dyeing, though in actual truth the colors were as remarkable as the cloth itself.

Soon there was no sound in the room but the breathing of the onlookers, the whirring of the shuttles, and the creaking of the wooden frames as each pressed the thread up into place or tightened the pegs by which the whole was held straight. The excited crowd in the doorway began to see that the skill of both in truth was very nearly equal, but that, however the cloth might turn out, the goddess was the quicker of the two. A pattern of many pictures was growing on her loom. There was a border of twined branches of the olive, Athene's favorite tree, while in the middle, figures began to appear. As they looked at the glowing colors, the spectators realized that Athene was weaving into her pattern a last warning to Arachne. The central figure was the goddess herself competing with Poseidon for possession of the city of Athens; but in the four corners were mortals who had tried to strive with gods and pictures of the awful fate that had overtaken them. The goddess ended a little before Arachne and stood back from her marvelous work to see what the maiden was doing. •

Never before had Arachne been matched against anyone whose skill was equal, or even nearly equal to her own. As she stole glances from time to time at Athene and saw the goddess working swiftly, calmly, and always a little faster than herself, she became angry instead of frightened, and an evil thought came into her head. Thus as Athene stepped back a pace to watch Arachne finishing her work, she saw that the maiden had taken for her design a pattern of scenes which showed evil or unworthy actions of the gods, how they had deceived fair maidens, resorted to trickery, and appeared on earth from time to time in the form of poor and humble people. When the goddess saw this insult glowing in bright colors on Arachne's loom, she did not wait while the cloth was

LITERATURE IN CONTEXT

Culture Connection

Athene

As goddess of wisdom and warfare, Athene was a key figure in Greek mythology. Athene protected her favorites, such as Odysseus and Heracles (or Hercules), and punished those who displeased her, including Arachne and Ajax, a famous Greek warrior. According to one story, the people of a major Greek city wanted to name their city after either Poseidon, the sea god, or Athene, depending on who gave them the more useful gift. Poseidon created horses, and Athene created olive trees. The gods judged Athene's gift more useful, so Athens was named for her. To honor Athene, the city built a great temple, called the Parthenon.

Connect to the Literature

Which of Athene's character traits does this myth illustrate?

Reading Check

Why is Arachne upset when people say Athene must have taught her to spin?

Myths
Why is Arachne's design disrespectful to the gods?

judged, but stepped forward, her gray eyes blazing with anger, and tore Arachne's work across. Then she struck Arachne across the face. Arachne stood there a moment, struggling with anger, fear, and pride. "I will not live under this insult," she cried, and seizing a rope from the wall, she made a noose and would have hanged herself.

The goddess touched the rope and touched the maiden. "Live on, wicked girl," she said. "Live on and spin, both you and your descendants. When men look at you they may remember that it is not wise to strive with Athene." At that the body of Arachne shriveled up, and her legs grew tiny, spindly, and distorted. There before the eyes of the spectators hung a little dusty brown spider on a slender thread.

Myths
What traits of spiders does this myth explain?

All spiders descend from Arachne, and as the Greeks watched them spinning their thread wonderfully fine, they remembered the contest with Athene and thought that it was not right for even the best of men to claim equality with the gods.

Critical Thinking

Cite textual evidence to support your responses.

© 1. **Key Ideas and Details** **(a)** What does Arachne value more than anything else? **(b) Interpret:** Why does Arachne refuse to accept the advice of the old woman? **(c) Analyze:** What character traits does Arachne reveal through her behavior?

© 2. **Key Ideas and Details** **(a)** What design does Athene weave? **(b) Infer:** What is Athene's original intention toward Arachne? **(c) Deduce:** What makes Athene angry?

© 3. **Key Ideas and Details** **(a) Take a Position:** Do you think that it was fair of Athene to turn Arachne into a spider? Explain. **(b) Discuss:** Share your response with a partner and decide together on a single answer to share with the class.

© 4. **Integration of Knowledge and Ideas** **(a)** In ancient Greece, what important life lesson might this myth have taught its audience? **(b)** What cultural value does the story, and its lesson, suggest? *[Connect to the Big Question: How much do our communities shape us?]*

Reading Skill: Cause and Effect

1. What is the **effect** of Arachne's skill as a weaver?

2. What **causes** Athene to visit Arachne?

3. Complete the chart to show causes and effects in "Arachne."

Causes	Effects
Arachne challenges Athene.	
	Arachne's design shows unworthy actions of the gods.
Athene touches the rope and touches Arachne.	

Literary Analysis: Myths

4. Key Ideas and Details What does this **myth** explain about spiders?

5. Integration of Knowledge and Ideas What beliefs and values about behavior are taught through the **theme** of this myth?

Vocabulary

Acquisition and Use Choose a word from the vocabulary list on page 858 to rewrite each sentence so that it has the opposite meaning.

1. The movie's main character had superhuman qualities.

2. Everyone in the class had heard of the famous novel.

3. Her agreeable nature makes her easy to get along with.

4. Mr. Vallone was a rich and famous tailor.

5. "No thank you," she said in a cheerful way.

6. The two brothers always tried help each other.

Word Study Use context and what you know about the **Latin root -mort-** to explain your answer to each question.

1. If an ancient Greek warrior received a *mortal* wound, would he recover?

2. How strongly embarrassed is someone who is *mortified?*

Word Study

The **Latin root -mort-** means "death."

Apply It Explain how the root -mort- contributes to the meaning of these words. Consult a dictionary if necessary.

immortal

mortician

mortuary

How much do our *communities* shape us?

Writing About the Big Question

Legends and myths are passed down through generations. They reveal the beliefs and ideas that are important to cultural communities. Use the following sentence starter to help you develop your ideas about the Big Question.

Ancient legends about a culture's values can **influence** modern people to _____ because _____.

While You Read Look for details about the gifts that the whale and its rider bring to the ancient Maori people—and to modern people.

Vocabulary

Read each word and its definition. Decide whether you know the word well, know it a little bit, or do not know it at all. After you read, see how your knowledge of each word has increased.

- **yearning** (yɐr´ niŋ) *n.* feeling of wanting something very much (p. 868) *I had a <u>yearning</u> for chocolate. yearn v.*

- **clatter** (klat´ ər) *n.* rattling sound (p. 869) *The plastic plates fell to the floor with a loud <u>clatter</u>. clattering adj.*

- **teemed** (tēmd) *v.* was full of (p. 869) *The garden <u>teemed</u> with butterflies. teem v. teeming v.*

- **reluctant** (ri luk´ tənt) *adj.* showing doubt or unwillingness (p. 870) *A picky eater is <u>reluctant</u> to try new foods. reluctance n. reluctantly adj.*

- **apex** (ā´ peks´) *n.* highest point (p. 870) *The lift took us to the <u>apex</u> of the mountain.*

- **splendor** (splen´ dər) *n.* great brightness (p. 871) *We admired the <u>splendor</u> of the setting sun. splendid adj. splendorous adj.*

Word Study

The **Latin root -splend-** means "shine."

When the whale rider first appears from the sea, his body dazzles with the silvery spray of water, and his eyes shine brightly with **splendor.**

Meet
Witi Ihimaera
(b. 1944)

Author of
Prologue from
The Whale Rider

Witi Ihimaera was raised in the Maori culture of New Zealand. He became interested in writing at an early age and recalls scribbling stories across a wall of his room at his family farm. After publishing his first book in 1972, Ihimaera served his country in the Ministry of Foreign Affairs in Australia, New York, and Washington, D.C.

Being a Maori Ihimaera is the first Maori to publish both a novel and a collection of short stories. He says that he sees writing as a way to express his experience of being a Maori. He continues to write and also lectures in the English department at Auckland University in New Zealand.

BACKGROUND FOR THE MYTH

Paikea

The prologue to *The Whale Rider* introduces a story based on the legend of Paikea. This legend comes from the Maori people of New Zealand. In the story, Kahutia Te Rangi is carried on the back of the whale Paikea to the shores of what is now called New Zealand's North Island. Kahutia Te Rangi then assumes the name of the whale and makes his home on the island.

DID YOU KNOW?

Ihimaera's book *The Whale Rider*, which he wrote in just three weeks in 1978, inspired the very successful movie *The Whale Rider* in 2002.

Prologue from The Whale Rider

Witi Ihimaera

In the old days, in the years that have gone before us, the land and sea felt a great emptiness, a yearning. The mountains were like a stairway to heaven, and the lush green rainforest was a rippling cloak of many colors. The sky was iridescent, swirling with the patterns of wind and clouds; sometimes it reflected the prisms of rainbow or southern aurora.[1] The sea was ever-changing, shimmering and seamless to the sky. This was the well at the bottom of the world, and when you looked into it you felt you could see to the end of forever.

---

1. **southern aurora** (ô rôr´ ə) *n.* streamers or arches of light appearing above Earth in the Southern Hemisphere.

This is not to say that the land and sea were without life, without vivacity. The tuatara, the ancient lizard with its third eye, was sentinel here, unblinking in the hot sun, watching and waiting to the east. The moa browsed in giant wingless herds across the southern island. Within the warm stomach of the rainforests, kiwi,[2] weka,[3] and the other birds foraged for *huhu* and similar succulent insects. The forests were loud with the clatter of tree bark, chatter of cicada, and murmur of fish-laden streams. Sometimes the forest grew suddenly quiet, and in wet bush could be heard the filigree of fairy laughter like a sparkling glissando.[4]

The sea, too, teemed with fish, but they also seemed to be waiting. They swam in brilliant shoals, like rains of glittering dust, throughout the greenstone depths—*hapuku, manga, kahawai, tamure, moki,* and *warehou*—herded by shark or *mango ururoa.* Sometimes from far off a white shape would be seen flying through the sea, but it would only be the serene flight of the *tarawhai,* the stingray with the spike on its tail.

Waiting. Waiting for the seeding. Waiting for the gifting. Waiting for the blessing to come. ●

Suddenly, looking up at the surface, the fish began to see the dark bellies of the canoes from the east. The first of the Ancients were coming, journeying from their island kingdom beyond the horizon. Then, after a period, canoes were seen to be returning to the east, making long cracks

---

2. **kiwi** (kē′ wē) *n.* small, flightless New Zealand bird.
3. **weka** (wā′ kä) *n.* flightless New Zealand wading bird.
4. **glissando** (gli sän′ dō) *n.* quick sliding up or down the musical scale.

Vocabulary
clatter (klat′ ər) *n.* rattling sound
teemed (tēmd) *v.* was full of

Cause and Effect
What effect do the arrival and departure of the Ancients have on the land and the sea?

Reading Check
What feeling did the land and sea have in the old days?

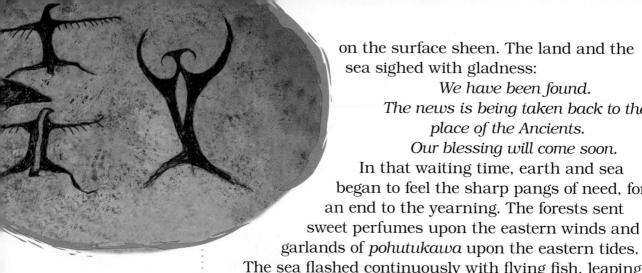

on the surface sheen. The land and the sea sighed with gladness:

> *We have been found.*
> *The news is being taken back to the place of the Ancients.*
> *Our blessing will come soon.*

In that waiting time, earth and sea began to feel the sharp pangs of need, for an end to the yearning. The forests sent sweet perfumes upon the eastern winds and garlands of *pohutukawa* upon the eastern tides.

The sea flashed continuously with flying fish, leaping high to look beyond the horizon and to be the first to announce the coming; in the shallows, the chameleon sea horses pranced at attention. The only reluctant ones were the fairy people, who retreated with their silver laughter to caves in glistening waterfalls.

The sun rose and set, rose and set. Then one day, at its noon apex, the first sighting was made. A spume on the horizon. A dark shape rising from the greenstone depths of the ocean, awesome, leviathan, breaching through the surface and hurling itself skyward before falling seaward again. Underwater the muted thunder boomed like a great door opening far away, and both sea and land trembled from the impact of that downward plunging. •

Suddenly the sea was filled with awesome singing, a song with eternity in it, a song to the land:

Vocabulary
reluctant (ri luk´ tənt) *adj.* showing doubt or unwillingness

apex (ā´ peks´) *n.* highest point

▼ **Critical Viewing**
What characteristics of whales might inspire people to develop myths about them? **[Speculate]**

You have called and I have come,
bearing the gift of the Gods.

The dark shape rising, rising again. A whale, gigantic. A sea monster. Just as it burst through the sea, a flying fish leaping high in its ecstasy saw water and air streaming like thunderous foam from that noble beast and knew, ah yes, that the time had come. For the sacred sign was on the monster, a swirling tattoo imprinted on the forehead.

Then the flying fish saw that astride the head, as it broke skyward, was a man. He was wondrous to look upon, the whale rider. The water streamed away from him and he opened his mouth to gasp in the cold air. His eyes were shining with splendor. His body dazzled with diamond spray. Upon that beast he looked like a small tattooed figurine, dark brown, glistening, and erect. He seemed, with all his strength, to be pulling the whale into the sky.

Rising, rising. And the man felt the power of the whale as it propelled itself from the sea. He saw far off the land long sought and now found, and he began to fling small spears seaward and landward on his magnificent journey toward the land.

Some of the spears in midflight turned into pigeons, which flew into the forests. Others, on landing in the sea, changed into eels. And the song in the sea drenched the air with ageless music, and land and sea opened themselves to him, the gift long waited for: *tangata*, man. With great gladness and thanksgiving, the man cried out to the land,

Spiral Review
Character What qualities common to mythic heroes does the whale rider have? Explain.

Vocabulary
splendor (splen´ dər)
n. great brightness

Myths
Do you think the whale rider is a mortal or a god? Explain.

Reading Check
Who emerges from the sea?

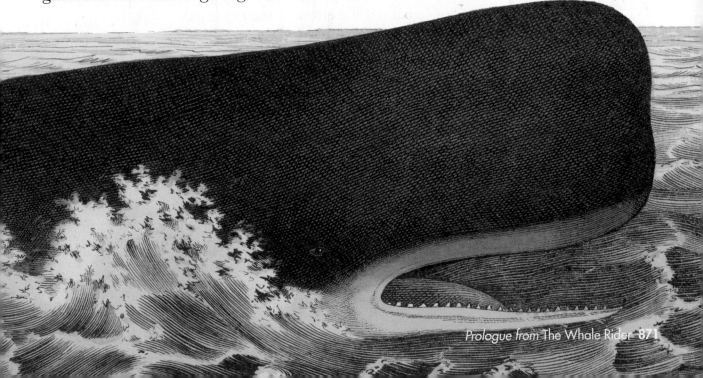

Karanga mai, karanga mai, karanga mai.

Call me. But there was one spear, so it is told, the last, that, when the whale rider tried to throw it, refused to leave his hand. Try as he might, the spear would not fly.

So the whale rider uttered a prayer over the wooden spear, saying, "Let this spear be planted in the years to come, for there are sufficient spear already implanted. Let this be the one to flower when the people are troubled and it is most needed."

And the spear then leaped from his hands with gladness and soared through the sky. It flew across a thousand years. When it hit the earth, it did not change but waited for another hundred and fifty years to pass until it was needed.

The flukes of the whale stroked majestically at the sky.

Hui e, haumi e, taiki e.

Let it be done.

Myths
What does this myth explain?

Critical Thinking

> Cite textual evidence to support your responses.

1. **Key Ideas and Details** **(a)** What emotions does the author give to the land and sea? **(b) Analyze:** What effect is created by giving human feelings to these nonhuman subjects?

2. **Key Ideas and Details** **(a)** What are the canoes described as doing? **(b) Infer:** Why are the land and sea excited about the arrival of the Ancients?

3. **Key Ideas and Details** **(a) Speculate:** Based on this prologue to the book, what do you think *The Whale Rider* will be about? **(b) Support:** What details support your response? **(c) Discuss:** Share your ideas with a partner and decide together on a single answer to share with the class.

4. **Integration of Knowledge and Ideas** **(a)** What gifts do the whale rider's spears bring? **(b)** What might these gifts suggest about the traditional values of the Maori people? **(c)** How might the last of these ancient spears be important to modern Maori people? *[Connect to the Big Question: How much do our communities shape us?]*

Reading Skill: Cause and Effect

1. What **causes** the land and sea to sigh with gladness?

2. What is the **effect** of the whale's jumping and plunging back into the sea?

3. Complete the chart to show causes and effects in the Prologue from *The Whale Rider.*

Causes	Effects
The land and sea feel a great emptiness.	
	Flying fish leap to look beyond the horizon.
The whale rider says a prayer over the last spear.	

Literary Analysis: Myths

4. Key Ideas and Details What does this **myth** explain in nature?

5. Integration of Knowledge and Ideas What values are taught through the **theme** of this myth?

Vocabulary

Acquisition and Use Choose a word from the vocabulary list on page 866 to rewrite each sentence so that it has the opposite meaning.

1. I am not wanting to jump into that cold water.

2. We were amazed by the dullness of the gold coins.

3. The horses' hoofs made no sound on the street.

4. He was looking forward to a trip to the dentist.

5. They hiked to the bottom of the mountain.

6. The sky was not filled with birds.

Word Study Use what you know about the **Latin root -splend-** to explain your answer to each question.

1. Would a rainy afternoon be *resplendent*?

2. Would a perfect test score be considered *splendid*?

Word Study

The **Latin root -splend-** means "to shine."

Apply It Explain how the root -*splend*- contributes to the meaning of these words. You may consult a dictionary if necessary.

resplendence
splendidly

Integrated Language Skills

Arachne • *Prologue from* The Whale Rider

Conventions:
Simple, Compound, and Complex Sentences

Sentences can be classified according to the number and kinds of their **clauses**—groups of words with their own subjects and verbs.

An **independent clause** can stand alone as a sentence. It expresses a complete thought. A **subordinate,** or **dependent,** clause cannot stand alone as a sentence. It does not express a complete thought. This chart shows how clauses are used to create the three types of sentence structures.

Simple Sentence	Compound Sentence	Complex Sentence
A single independent clause	Two or more independent clauses	One independent clause and one or more subordinate clauses
<u>The dog barked</u>. <u>He and I walked home</u>.	<u>Brad cooked the meal</u>, <u>Kai set the table</u>, and <u>I washed dishes</u>.	(Because the storm came,) <u>our game was postponed</u>.

Practice A Rewrite each sentence, underlining independent clauses and circling subordinate clauses. Tell what kind of sentence it is.

1. The father dyed wool, and the daughter spun it into thread.
2. Arachne answered the old woman.
3. After Athene finished her pattern, she stood back and watched Arachne.
4. Modern people will remember the lesson when they notice a spider.

ⓒ **Reading Application** Scan "Arachne" to find and record a simple, a compound, and a complex sentence.

Practice B Add to each group of words to make the kind of sentence indicated.

1. The land was beautiful before (complex)
2. The whale (simple)
3. The pigeons flew into the sky, and (compound)
4. The whale rider (complex)
5. The mountains were high (compound)

ⓒ **Writing Application** Write a brief summary of the selection you read. Include a simple, a compound, and a complex sentence. Circle each one.

PH WRITING COACH Further instruction and practice are available in *Prentice Hall Writing Coach*.

Writing

 **Common Core State Standards**

L.6.1; W.6.2, W.6.2.a, W.6.2.d, W.6.2.e, W.6.8
[For the full wording of the standards, see page 856.]

Explanatory Text Based on your reading of one of these myths, write a brief **compare-and-contrast essay.**

- If you read "Arachne," compare the difference between learning lessons from a myth and from your own experience.
- If you read the Prologue from *The Whale Rider*, compare the feelings the myth expresses with your own experience of waiting for something exciting to happen.

Choose an organizational structure, such as the block or point-by-point methods (see p. 670), to present your ideas clearly. Use language that expresses your meaning precisely and is appropriately formal for academic work. Support your ideas with examples from both the text and real life.

Grammar Application As you write, use different types of sentences, including simple, compound, and complex.

Writing Workshop: *Work in Progress*

Prewriting for Research Using the Illustrations List in your portfolio, decide on a topic. Write an explanation that tells why your chosen media best fits the topic. Save this Explanation in your writing portfolio.

Use this prewriting activity to prepare for the **Writing Workshop** on page 906.

Research and Technology

Build and Present Knowledge Find two reliable research sources that provide information about the values and culture of either ancient Greece or of the Maori people of New Zealand. Then write an **annotated bibliography entry** for each source.

- Use a library catalog or do a keyword search on the Internet to find reliable sources of information. Sources should be well-known for accuracy and recently published. A Web site should have an *.edu, .gov,* or *.org* at the end of the address.
- Write down publication information from two sources.
- Read each source. Paraphrase, or restate, key ideas in your own words. To avoid plagiarism, include publication information about all the sources you use.
- Write an annotated bibliography entry for each source. Include the publication information, your paraphrases, and an explanation of why the source is reliable and valuable.

PHLit Online!
www.PHLitOnline.com

- Interactive graphic organizers
- Grammar tutorial
- Interactive journals

Test Practice: Reading

Cause and Effect

Fiction Selection

Directions: *Read the selection. Then, answer the questions.*

Julia calls her brother, Todd, "the professor" because he tries to prove how much he knows. Sometimes, she gets annoyed because he knows so much. This morning, Julia woke to find her brother standing with a black garbage bag, a twist tie, and a long piece of string. Todd announced that he would teach Julia about hot-air balloons. Julia was skeptical, but curious, so she followed.

He moved the open bag through the cool air of the house. When the bag was full of air, Todd sealed it with the twist tie and tied the bag to a chair in the yard. The bag fell to the ground. Every hour or so, they checked on the bag. As the sun moved across the yard, the bag began to expand and rise. Julia was surprised.

"Told ya!" said her brother with a smirk.

1. Why does Julia call her brother "the professor"?
   A. He is a teacher at his sister's school.
   B. He likes to conduct experiments.
   C. He likes to shows off his knowledge.
   D. He asked Julia to call him by this name.

2. What causes Julia to join in the activity with her brother?
   A. She is curious.
   B. She is bored.
   C. She wants to be helpful.
   D. She will get credit at school.

3. Why is Julia surprised at the end of the story?
   A. The bag stays on the ground.
   B. The bag rises.
   C. The bag gets smaller.
   D. The bag floats into the clouds.

4. Which of these factors most likely causes the bag to rise?
   A. cool air
   B. wind currents
   C. loose string
   D. heat from the sun

Writing for Assessment

In a few sentences, explain what causes Julia to get annoyed with her brother. Use details from the passage to support your answer.

Nonfiction Selection

Directions: *Read the selection. Then, answer the questions.*

(1) When air is moving, we call it wind. (2) What makes the air move? (3) It moves because of uneven heating of the Earth's atmosphere. (4) The source of the heat is the sun. (5) The sun warms our planet's surface, which in turn warms its atmosphere. (6) Some parts of our planet get direct rays from the sun. (7) These places are warm most of the year. (8) Other parts of the planet get indirect rays and are colder. (9) Also, land warms up faster than water does. (10) For example, a forest warms up more quickly than a lake. (11) Warmed land and water give off heat at different rates. (12) Because it weighs less than cool air, warm air rises. (13) As a result, cooler air moves in to replace the warm air. (14) This moving air is wind.

1. Which cause-and-effect statement is true, according to the passage?
   A. Uneven heating of Earth's forests causes winds to blow.
   B. Cool air replacing rising warm air causes wind.
   C. Wind is caused by differences in the temperature of lakes.
   D. The sun's heat causes storms that make winds blow.

2. Which of these causes warming of Earth's atmosphere?
   A. indirect rays from the sun
   B. winds from forests and lakes
   C. warm air replacing cool air
   D. the heat of the sun

3. Which is the effect in sentence 12?
   A. because
   B. it weighs less than cool air
   C. cool air
   D. warm air rises

4. Which clue words signal a cause-and-effect relationship in sentence 13?
   A. as a result
   B. cooler air
   C. moves in
   D. to replace the warm air

Writing for Assessment

Connecting Across Texts
In a paragraph, explain what caused the bag of air to rise in the first passage. Use details from both passages to support your response.

www.PHLitOnline.com
- Online practice
- Instant feedback

Reading for Information

Analyzing Expository Texts

News Release

Encyclopedia Entry

Common Core State Standards

Reading Informational Text

2. Determine a central idea of a text and how it is conveyed through particular details; provide a summary of the text distinct from personal opinions or judgments.

5. Analyze how a particular sentence, paragraph, chapter, or section fits into the overall structure of a text and contributes to the development of the ideas.

9. Compare and contrast one author's presentation of events with that of another.

Language

4.b. Use common, grade-appropriate Greek or Latin affixes and roots as clues to the meaning of a word.

4.d. Verify the preliminary determination of the meaning of a word or phrase.

Reading Skill: Create Outlines

An **outline** is a list of main, or central, ideas, subtopics, and supporting details organized in a way that shows how the elements are related. You can use outlining as a study tool to help you recall information. Add notes to an outline to point out similarities and differences between the ideas in various sources. This will allow you to **connect main ideas across sources.** Use the outline structure below to take notes as you read.

```
I.  First Main Idea
     A.  First subtopic
          1.  supporting detail
          2.  supporting detail
     B.  Second subtopic
          1.  supporting detail
          2.  supporting detail
```

Content-Area Vocabulary

These words appear in the selections that follow. You may also encounter them in other content-area texts.

- **navigate** (nav´ə gāt) *v.* find the way; pilot
- **marine** (mə rēn´) *adj.* relating to the ocean or ocean life
- **meteorologists** (mē´tē ə räl´ə jists) *n.* scientists who study the atmosphere and weather

News Release

Features:
- current or breaking news
- text written for a general or a specific audience

Satellites and Sea Lions:
Working Together to Improve Ocean Models

NASA News Release
Updated 2/6/07

The best oceanographers in the world never studied at a university. Yet they know how to **navigate** expertly along oceanic fronts, the invisible boundaries between waters of different temperatures and densities. These ocean experts can find rich fishing in places and at depths that others would assume are barren. They regularly visit the most interesting and dynamic parts of the sea.

Sea lions, seals, sharks, tuna, and other top ocean predators share some of their experiences with human researchers, thanks to electronic tags. Besides tracking the animals, these sensors also collect oceanographic data, such as temperature and salinity. Scientists are beginning to incorporate this rich store of information into ocean models providing new insights into the inner workings of the ocean and the lives of its creatures.

"Our goal is to produce a three-dimensional model of the ocean," says oceanographer Dr. Yi Chao. Chao uses data from satellites, ships, buoys and floats to map the currents, heat content and different water densities beneath the ocean surface. When Chao heard Dr. Dan Costa, a professor of **marine** biology at the University of California, Santa Cruz, present some of his animal tagging data at a scientific meeting a few years ago, he

saw an opportunity to improve his ocean models. Costa recognized a chance to get a clearer picture of the place where his research subjects live. . . .

The research collaboration now includes Dr. Barbara Block, a professor of marine sciences at Stanford University, Palo Alto, Calif., and the scientists have added tagging data collected from tuna and sharks to their studies. Together with a group called TOPP, for Tagging of Pacific Pelagics, they are now working to expand the use of environmental and biological data collected by ocean inhabitants.

"We are at the forefront of knowing how animals use the ocean," says Costa. "But we want to understand the environment better. We still see the ocean primarily as

Note the details about the scientists' goals.

data sets have small errors, others much larger errors. Figuring out how to put these in our system is a challenge," he says. "But five years from now, we should be able to see the ocean the way a turtle sees it."

"As we are getting more data from the sea and improving our computer models," says Chao, "we should be able to make routine ocean forecasts, similar to what **meteorologists** have been doing in the past few decades. People who open the newspaper or turn on the TV in the morning will see the updated ocean forecast and make appropriate decisions as they plan their activities on the sea."

deep or shallow or near-shore or offshore. But just as there are different habitats on land, the ocean has fine-scale features that are very important to animals," he explains. "We want to be able to look at the ocean and say the equivalent of 'this is a grassland' or 'this is a forest.'"

In late January, Costa and his research group headed up the California coast to begin tagging elephant seals and collecting tags that were deployed last spring. The work is strictly regulated to ensure that the animals are protected from harm, and it requires a permit from the National Marine Fisheries Service. . . .

"Marine scientists have been tracking marine animals for years," says Chao. "It's an interesting challenge, though, to use the data. There are all sorts— from tuna, sharks, seals—you name it. Some of these

What is most important about using marine animals as ocean sensors is that the work benefits the animals, Costa explains. "Collaborations between biologists like Barbara Block and me and physical oceanographers like Yi are critical for understanding why the animals go where they go," he says, "as we need to know and understand the ocean physics and its relationship to climate processes. Further, the ability to understand how climate change is affecting the world oceans is not only of benefit to humans, but is vital for trying to figure out what is going to happen to habitats of marine animals."

This para graph lis details about the research benefit to animals.

California Sea Lions

This title clearly states the topic, or main idea.

Zalophus californianus
meaning of Latin name:
with crest and of California

DESCRIPTION: California sea lions are known for their intelligence, play-fulness, and noisy barking. Their color ranges from chocolate brown in males to a lighter, golden brown in females. Males may reach 1,000 lbs. (more often 850 lbs., or 390 kg) and seven feet (2.1 m) in length. Females grow to 220 lbs. (110 kg) and up to six feet (1.8 m) in length. They have a "dog-like" face, and at around five years of age, males develop a bony bump on top of their skull called a sagit-tal crest. The top of a male's head often gets lighter with age. These members of the otariid or walking seal family have external ear flaps and large flippers that they use to "walk" on land. The trained "seals" in zoos and aquariums are usu-ally California sea lions.

RANGE/HABITAT: California sea lions are found from Vancouver Island, British Columbia to the southern tip of Baja California in Mexico. They breed mainly on offshore islands, ranging from southern California's Channel Islands south to Mexico, although a few pups have been born on Año Nuevo

The text is organized into categories that can be useful in constructing your outline.

and the Farallon Islands in cen-tral California. There is a distinct population of California sea lions at the Galapagos Islands. A third population in the Sea of Japan became extinct, probably during World War II.

BEHAVIOR: California sea lions are very social animals, and groups often rest closely packed together at favored haul-out sites on land, or float together on the ocean's surface in "rafts." They are some-

times seen porpoising, or jumping out of the water, presumably to speed up their swimming. Sea lions have also been seen "surfing" breaking waves. California sea lions are opportunistic eaters, feeding on squid, octopus, herring, rockfish, mack-erel, and small sharks. In turn, sea lions are preyed upon by Orcas (killer whales) and great white sharks.

The author provides details under each boldface category heading.

MATING AND BREEDING: Most pups are born in June or July and weigh 13–20 lbs. (6–9 kg). They nurse for at least five to six months and sometimes over a year. Mothers recognize pups on crowded rookeries through smell, sight, and vocalizations. Pups also learn to recognize the vocalizations of their mothers. Breeding takes place a few weeks after birth. Males patrol territories and bark almost continuously during the breeding season.

STATUS: Their population is growing steadily, and California sea lions can be seen in many coastal spots such as Seal Rock or Pier 39 in San Francisco. The current population is approximately 200,000.

Comparing Expository Texts

© 1. Key Ideas and Details (a) How are the **main ideas** in the encyclopedia entry different from those in the news release? **(b)** Why might the main ideas be different? **(c)** Which are easier to **outline,** the main ideas and details in the news release or those in the encyclopedia? Explain.

Content-Area Vocabulary

2. (a) Explain how adding the suffixes *-ology, -ologist,* and *-oid* change the meaning of the word *meteor.* Use an online or print dictionary to verify each meaning. **(b)** Use each word in a sentence.

⏱ Timed Writing

Explanatory Text: Outline for an Essay

> **Format**
> The assignment is to create an outline and then write a brief essay. Be sure your essay follows the structure you set up in your outline.

Using information from both selections, create an outline for an essay discussing the California Sea Lion. Then, use your outline to write a brief essay. (35 minutes)

> **Academic Vocabulary**
> When you *discuss* a topic, you write about it in detail, taking into account different ideas or opinions.

5-Minute Planner

Complete these steps before you begin to write:

1. Read the prompt carefully and pay special attention to the highlighted words and notes.
2. Review both selections and jot down main ideas, subtopics, and supporting details.
3. Choose only the most important ideas and details from each text to include in your essay. Jot these down. **TIP** Be sure all the details you choose are related to your essay topic.
4. Organize your notes into an outline. List at least two subtopics. For each subtopic, list at least two supporting details. Then, use your outline as the structure for your essay.

Comparing Elements of Fantasy

Fantasy is imaginative writing that contains elements not found in real life. Many fantastic stories balance imagination with **realistic elements**—characters, events, or situations true to life. Realistic details help readers relate to an inventive, unusual, or whimsical story. Fantasy's blend of the impossible and the possible makes it an enjoyable genre. Use these questions to identify fantastic and realistic elements:

- Which elements of the story's setting could not exist in real life? Which elements could exist?

- Which elements of a character's behavior could not occur in real life? Which elements could occur?

- Which elements of the situation could not happen in real life? Which elements could happen?

Create a chart. Then, record fantastic and realistic elements.

Title:		
Element	**Fantastic or Realistic?**	**Why**

Fantasy and Theme Though works of fantasy are not realistic, they can convey serious **themes,** or insights into life and human nature. In "Mowgli's Brothers," for example, readers learn about the importance of belonging. In the excerpt from *James and the Giant Peach,* readers learn that communities can be imperfect but still valuable. The lessons are true even though the stories are not.

Fantasy elements can make a message stronger or highlight a story's lesson. Through the appeal of fantasy, the lessons reach readers effectively. As you read, think about each story's message and how the fantasy genre helps to make the message understandable.

**Common Core
State Standards**

Reading Literature
2. Determine a theme or central idea of a text and how it is conveyed through particular details.

Writing
2.a. Introduce a topic; organize ideas, concepts, and information, using strategies such as definition, classification, comparison/contrast, and cause/effect. *(Timed Writing)*

www.PHLitOnline.com

- Vocabulary flashcards
- Interactive journals
- More about the authors
- Selection audio
- Interactive graphic organizers

How much do our *communities* shape us?

Writing About the Big Question

In both of these stories, a boy enters an unknown community where out-of-the ordinary things happen. Use the following sentence starter to develop your ideas about the Big Question.

If a child is raised in an unusual **community**, he may learn_____.

Meet the Authors

Rudyard Kipling (1865–1936)

Author of "Mowgli's Brothers"

Rudyard Kipling was born in India to British parents. When he was very young, his Indian nurses told him folk tales that featured talking animals. These stories inspired the characters in many of Kipling's works, such as *The Jungle Book*, in which "Mowgli's Brothers" appears.

Award Winner As a boy, Kipling was sent to school in England. At age sixteen, he returned to India as a journalist. His work as a reporter, writer, and poet earned him the 1907 Nobel Prize.

Roald Dahl (1916–1990)

Author of *James and the Giant Peach*

As a boy growing up in Wales, Roald Dahl loved books and stories. When he was eight years old, he began keeping a diary, carefully hiding it from his sisters in a tin box tied to a high tree branch. Years later, Dahl began his formal writing career by describing his experiences in the Royal Air Force during World War II.

Encouraging Young Readers Dahl became interested in writing stories for children while making up bedtime stories for his daughters. That is how *James and the Giant Peach* came to be written. He believed strongly in the importance of reading. "I have a passion for teaching kids to become readers," he once said.

Mowgli's Brothers

Rudyard Kipling

Now Chil the Kite[1] brings home the night
　　That Mang the Bat sets free—
The herds are shut in byre[2] and hut
　　For loosed till dawn are we.
This is the hour of pride and power,
　　Talon and tush[3] and claw.
Oh hear the call!—Good hunting all
　　That keep the Jungle Law!
　　　　—Night-Song in the Jungle

---

1. **Kite** (kīt) *n.* bird of the hawk family.
2. **byre** (bīr) *n.* cow barn.
3. **tush** (tush) *n.* tusk.

It was seven o'clock of a very warm evening in the Seeonee hills[4] when Father Wolf woke up from his day's rest, scratched himself, yawned, and spread out his paws one after the other to get rid of the sleepy feeling in their tips. Mother Wolf lay with her big gray nose dropped across her four tumbling, squealing cubs, and the moon shone into the mouth of the cave where they all lived. "Augrh!" said Father Wolf, "it is time to hunt again"; and he was going to spring downhill when a little shadow with a bushy tail crossed the threshold and whined: "Good luck go with you, O Chief of the Wolves; and good luck and strong white teeth go with the noble children, that they may never forget the hungry in this world."

It was the jackal—Tabaqui the Dishlicker—and the wolves of India despise Tabaqui because he runs about making mischief, and telling tales, and eating rags and pieces of leather from the village rubbish-heaps. But they are afraid of him too, because Tabaqui, more than anyone else in the jungle, is apt to go mad, and then he forgets that he was ever afraid of anyone, and runs through the forest biting everything in his way. Even the tiger runs and hides when little Tabaqui goes mad, for madness is the most disgraceful thing that can overtake a wild creature. We call it hydrophobia, but they call it *dewanee*—the madness—and run.

"Enter, then, and look," said Father Wolf, stiffly; "but there is no food here."

"For a wolf, no," said Tabaqui; "but for so mean a person as myself a dry bone is a good feast. Who are we, the Gidur log [the jackal-people], to pick and choose?" He scuttled to the back of the cave, where he found the bone of a buck with some meat on it, and sat cracking the end merrily.

"All thanks for this good meal," he said, licking his lips. "How beautiful are the noble children! How large are their eyes! And so young too! Indeed, indeed, I might have remembered that the children of Kings are men from the beginning." •

Now, Tabaqui knew as well as anyone else that there is nothing so unlucky as to compliment children to their faces; and it pleases him to see Mother and Father Wolf look uncomfortable.

---

4. **Seeonee** (sē ōˊ nē) **hills** hills in central India.

Elements of Fantasy
What element of fantasy is introduced in this paragraph? Explain.

Elements of Fantasy
What is fantastic about Tabaqui's behavior? What is realistic about it?

✓ **Reading Check**
Why do the wolves despise Tabaqui?

Spiral Review
Folk Tale Although this story does not come from the oral tradition, what elements does it share with folk tales? Explain.

Tabaqui sat still, rejoicing in the mischief that he had made: then he said spitefully:

"Shere Khan, the Big One, has shifted his hunting-grounds. He will hunt among these hills for the next moon, so he has told me."

Shere Khan was the tiger who lived near the Waingunga River, twenty miles away.

"He has no right!" Father Wolf began angrily—"By the Law of the Jungle he has no right to change his quarters without due warning. He will frighten every head of game within ten miles, and I—I have to kill for two, these days."

"His mother did not call him Lungri [the Lame One] for nothing," said Mother Wolf, quietly. "He has been lame in one foot from his birth. That is why he has only killed cattle. Now the villagers of the Waingunga are angry with him, and he has come here to make our villagers angry. They will scour the Jungle for him when he is far away, and we and our children must run when the grass is set alight. Indeed, we are very grateful to Shere Khan!"

"Shall I tell him of your gratitude?" said Tabaqui.

"Out!" snapped Father Wolf. "Out and hunt with thy master. Thou hast done harm enough for one night."

"I go," said Tabaqui, quietly. "Ye can hear Shere Khan below in the thickets. I might have saved myself the message."

Father Wolf listened, and below in the valley that ran down to a little river, he heard the dry, angry, snarly, singsong whine of a tiger who has caught nothing and does not care if all the Jungle knows it.

"The fool!" said Father Wolf. "To begin a night's work with that noise! Does he think that our buck are like his fat Waingunga bullocks?"[5]

Elements of Fantasy
Do you think the behavior described in this paragraph is fantastic or realistic? Explain.

"H'sh! It is neither bullock nor buck he hunts tonight," said Mother Wolf. "It is Man." The whine had changed to a sort of humming purr that seemed to come from every quarter of the compass. It was the noise that bewilders woodcutters and gypsies sleeping in the open, and makes them run sometimes into the very mouth of the tiger.

"Man!" said Father Wolf, showing all his white teeth. "Faugh! Are there not enough beetles and frogs in the tanks

---

5. bullocks (bŏŏl′ əks) *n.* steers.

that he must eat Man and on our ground too!"

The Law of the Jungle, which never orders anything without a reason, forbids every beast to eat Man except when he is killing to show his children how to kill, and then he must hunt outside the hunting-grounds of his pack or tribe. The real reason for this is that man-killing means, sooner or later, the arrival of white men on elephants, with guns, and hundreds of brown men with gongs and rockets and torches. Then everybody in the jungle suffers. The reason the beasts give among themselves is that Man is the weakest and most defenseless of all living things, and it is unsportsmanlike to touch him. They say too—and it is true—that man-eaters become mangy,[6] and lose their teeth.

The purr grew louder, and ended in the full-throated "Aaarh!" of the tiger's charge.

Then there was a howl—an untigerish howl—from Shere Khan. "He has missed," said Mother Wolf. "What is it?"

Father Wolf ran out a few paces and heard Shere Khan muttering and mumbling savagely, as he tumbled about in the scrub.

"The fool has had no more sense than to jump at a woodcutter's campfire, and has burned his feet," said Father Wolf, with a grunt. "Tabaqui is with him."

"Something is coming up hill," said Mother Wolf, twitching one ear. "Get ready." •

The bushes rustled a little in the thicket, and Father Wolf dropped with his haunches under him, ready for his leap. Then, if you had been watching, you would have seen the most wonderful thing in the world—the wolf checked in mid-spring. He made his bound before he saw what it was he was jumping at, and then he tried to stop himself. The result was that he shot up straight into the air for four or five feet, landing almost where he left ground.

"Man!" he snapped. "A man's cub. Look!"

Directly in front of him, holding on by a low branch, stood a naked brown baby who could just walk—as soft and as dimpled a little atom[7] as ever came to a wolf's cave at night. He looked up into Father Wolf's face, and laughed.

"H'sh! It is neither bullock nor buck he hunts tonight," said Mother Wolf. "It is Man."

Elements of Fantasy
Do you think Father Wolf's behavior here could occur in real life? Why or why not?

Reading Check
Why does the Law of the Jungle generally forbid man-killing?

---

6. **mangy** (mān´ jē) *adj.* having mange, a skin disease of mammals that causes sores and loss of hair.

7. **atom** (at´ əm) *n.* tiny piece of matter.

"Is that a man's cub?" said Mother Wolf. "I have never seen one. Bring it here."

A wolf accustomed to moving his own cubs can, if necessary, mouth an egg without breaking it, and though Father Wolf's jaws closed right on the child's back not a tooth even scratched the skin, as he laid it down among the cubs.

"How little! How naked, and—how bold!" said Mother Wolf, softly. The baby was pushing his way between the cubs to get close to the warm hide. "Ahai! He is taking his meal with the others. And so this is a man's cub. Now, was there ever a wolf that could boast of a man's cub among her children?"

"I have heard now and again of such a thing, but never in our Pack or in my time," said Father Wolf. "He is altogether without hair, and I could kill him with a touch of my foot. But see, he looks up and is not afraid."

The moonlight was blocked out of the mouth of the cave, for Shere Khan's great square head and shoulders were thrust into the entrance. Tabaqui, behind him, was squeaking: "My lord, my lord, it went in here!"

"Shere Khan does us great honor," said Father Wolf, but his eyes were very angry. "What does Shere Khan need?"

"My quarry. A man's cub went this way," said Shere Khan. "Its parents have run off. Give it to me."

Shere Khan had jumped at a woodcutter's campfire, as Father Wolf had said, and was furious from the pain of his burned feet. But Father Wolf knew that the mouth of the cave was too narrow for a tiger to come in by. Even where he was, Shere Khan's shoulders and forepaws were cramped for want of room, as a man's would be if he tried to fight in a barrel.

"The Wolves are a free people," said Father Wolf. "They take orders from the Head of the Pack, and not from any striped cattle-killer. The man's cub is ours—to kill if we choose."

"Ye choose and ye do not choose! What talk is this of choosing? By the bull that I killed, am I to stand nosing into your dog's den for my fair dues? It is I, Shere Khan, who speak!"

The tiger's roar filled the cave with thunder. Mother Wolf shook herself clear of the cubs and sprang forward, her eyes, like two green moons in the darkness, facing the blazing eyes of Shere Khan.

Vocabulary
quarry (kwôr´ ē) *n.* prey; anything being hunted or pursued

"And it is I, Raksha [The Demon], who answer. The man's cub is mine, Lungri—mine to me! He shall not be killed. He shall live to run with the Pack and to hunt with the Pack; and in the end, look you, hunter of little naked cubs— frog-eater—fish-killer— he shall hunt thee! Now get hence, or by the Sambhur that I killed (I eat no starved cattle), back thou goest to thy mother, burned beast of the Jungle, lamer than ever thou camest into the world! Go!" •

Father Wolf looked on amazed. He had almost forgotten the days when he won Mother Wolf in fair fight from five other wolves, when she ran in the Pack and was not called The Demon for compliment's sake. Shere Khan might have faced Father Wolf, but he could not stand up against Mother Wolf, for he knew that where he was she had all the advantage of the ground, and would fight to the death. So he backed out of the cave-mouth growling, and when he was clear he shouted:

"Each dog barks in his own yard! We will see what the Pack will say to this fostering of man-cubs. The cub is mine, and to my teeth he will come in the end, O bush-tailed thieves!"

Mother Wolf threw herself down panting among the cubs, and Father Wolf said to her gravely:

"Shere Khan speaks this much truth. The cub must be shown to the Pack. Wilt thou still keep him, Mother?"

"Keep him!" she gasped. "He came naked, by night, alone and very hungry; yet he was not afraid! Look, he has pushed one of my babies to one side already. And that lame butcher would have killed him and would have run off to the Waingunga while the villagers here hunted through all our

▲ **Critical Viewing**
Do you think this tiger is friendly to humans? Why or why not? **[Speculate]**

Vocabulary
fostering (fôs´ tər iŋ) *n.* taking care of

Reading Check
How does Mother Wolf respond to Shere Kahn's demands?

lairs in revenge! Keep him? Assuredly I will keep him. Lie still, little frog. O thou Mowgli—for Mowgli the Frog I will call thee—the time will come when thou wilt hunt Shere Khan as he has hunted thee."

"But what will our Pack say?" said Father Wolf. The Law of the Jungle lays down very clearly that any wolf may, when he marries, withdraw from the Pack he belongs to; but as soon as his cubs are old enough to stand on their feet he must bring them to the Pack Council, which is generally held once a month at full moon, in order that the other wolves may identify them. After that inspection the cubs are free to run where they please, and until they have killed their first buck no excuse is accepted if a grown wolf of the Pack kills one of them. The punishment is death where the murderer can be found; and if you think for a minute you will see that this must be so. •

Father Wolf waited till his cubs could run a little, and then on the night of the Pack Meeting took them and Mowgli and Mother Wolf to the Council Rock—a hilltop covered with stones and boulders where a hundred wolves could hide. Akela, the great gray Lone Wolf, who led all the Pack by strength and cunning, lay out at full length on his rock, and below him sat forty or more wolves of every size and color, from badger-colored veterans who could handle a buck alone, to young black three-year-olds who thought they could. The Lone Wolf had led them for a year now. He had fallen twice into a wolf-trap in his youth, and once he had been beaten and left for dead; so he knew the manners and customs of men. There was very little talking at the Rock. The cubs tumbled over each other in the center of the circle where their mothers and fathers sat, and now and again a senior wolf would go quietly up to a cub, look at him carefully, and return to his place on noiseless feet. Sometimes a mother would push her cub far out into the moonlight, to be sure that he had not been overlooked. Akela from his rock would cry: "Ye know the Law—ye know the Law. Look well, O Wolves!" and the anxious mothers would take up the call: "Look—look well, O Wolves!"

At last—and Mother Wolf's neck-bristles lifted as the time came—Father Wolf pushed "Mowgli the Frog," as they called him, into the center, where he sat laughing and playing

Elements of Fantasy
What details about this meeting at Council Rock are realistic? What details are fantastic?

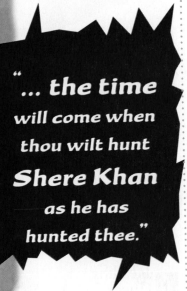

" ... the time will come when thou wilt hunt Shere Khan as he has hunted thee."

with some pebbles that glistened in the moonlight.

Akela never raised his head from his paws, but went on with the monotonous cry: "Look well!" A muffled roar came up from behind the rocks—the voice of Shere Khan crying: "The cub is mine. Give him to me. What have the Free People to do with a man's cub?" Akela never even twitched his ears: all he said was: "Look well, O Wolves! What have the Free People to do with the orders of any save the Free People? Look well!"

There was a chorus of deep growls, and a young wolf in his fourth year flung back Shere Khan's question to Akela: "What have the Free People to do with the man's cub?" Now the Law of the Jungle lays down that if there is any dispute as to the right of a cub to be accepted by the Pack, he must be spoken for by at least two members of the Pack who are not his father and mother.

"Who speaks for this cub?" said Akela. "Among the Free People who speaks?" There was no answer, and Mother Wolf got ready for what she knew would be her last fight, if things came to fighting.

Then the only other creature who is allowed at the Pack Council—Baloo, the sleepy brown bear who teaches the wolf cubs the Law of the Jungle: old Baloo, who can come and go where he pleases because he eats only nuts and roots and honey—rose up on his hind quarters and grunted.

"The man's cub—the man's cub?" he said. "I speak for the man's cub. There is no harm in a man's cub. I have no gift of words, but I speak the truth. Let him run with the Pack, and be entered with the others. I myself will teach him."

"We need yet another," said Akela. "Baloo has spoken, and he is our teacher for the young cubs. Who speaks besides Baloo?"

A black shadow dropped down into the circle. It was Bagheera the Black Panther, inky black all over, but with the panther marking showing up in certain lights like the pattern of watered silk. Everybody knew Bagheera, and nobody cared to cross his path; for he was as cunning as Tabaqui, as bold as the wild buffalo, and as reckless as the wounded elephant. But he had a voice as soft as wild honey dripping from a tree, and a skin softer than down.

"O Akela, and ye the Free People," he purred, "I have no

Vocabulary
monotonous
(mə nät´ n əs) *adj.*
unchanging

dispute (di spyo͞ot´) *n.*
argument; debate; quarrel

Elements of Fantasy
Does Baloo's speech in favor of keeping the child seem true to life or fantastic? Explain.

Reading Check
According to the Law of the Jungle, how must the Pack settle a dispute over accepting a cub?

right in your assembly; but the Law of the Jungle says that if there is a doubt which is not a killing matter in regard to a new cub, the life of that cub may be bought at a price. And the Law does not say who may or may not pay that price. Am I right?"

"Good! good!" said the young wolves, who are always hungry. "Listen to Bagheera. The cub can be bought for a price. It is the Law."

"Knowing that I have no right to speak here, I ask your leave."

"Speak then," cried twenty voices.

"To kill a naked cub is shame. Besides, he may make better sport for you when he is grown. Baloo has spoken in his behalf. Now to Baloo's word I will add one bull, and a fat one, newly killed, not half a mile from here, if ye will accept the man's cub according to the Law. Is it difficult?"

There was a clamor of scores of voices, saying: "What matter? He will die in the winter rains. He will scorch in the sun. What harm can a naked frog do us? Let him run with the Pack. Where is the bull, Bagheera? Let him be accepted." And then came Akela's deep bay, crying: "Look well—look well, O Wolves!"

Mowgli was still deeply interested in the pebbles, and he did not notice when the wolves came and looked at him one by one. At last they all went down the hill for the dead bull, and only Akela, Bagheera, Baloo, and Mowgli's own wolves were left. Shere Khan roared still in the night, for he was

▲ **Critical Viewing**
How do you think the other animals might behave toward a panther like the one shown? Explain.
[Speculate]

very angry that Mowgli had not been handed over to him.

"Ay, roar well," said Bagheera, under his whiskers; "for the time comes when this naked thing will make thee roar to another tune, or I know nothing of man."

"It was well done," said Akela. "Men and their cubs are very wise. He may be a help in time."

"Truly, a help in time of need; for none can hope to lead the Pack forever," said Bagheera.

Akela said nothing. He was thinking of the time that comes to every leader of every pack when his strength goes from him and he gets feebler and feebler till at last he is killed by the wolves and a new leader comes up—to be killed in his turn.

"Take him away," he said to Father Wolf, "and train him as befits one of the Free People."

And that is how Mowgli was entered into the Seeonee wolf-pack at the price of a bull and on Baloo's good word.

Elements of Fantasy
Which behavior described here is not likely to occur in real life?

Spiral Review
Theme How do Akela's thoughts suggest a possible theme?

Critical Thinking

1. Key Ideas and Details (a) How is Mowgli similar to the wolf cubs? How is he different? **(b) Analyze:** What qualities in Mowgli does Mother Wolf find appealing?

2. Key Ideas and Details (a) Who pays for Mowgli's life? **(b) Evaluate:** Are his reasons based on his own self-interest or on what is good for the pack? **(c) Support:** What examples from the story support your answer?

3. Key Ideas and Details (a) Describe how the wolves in the pack make decisions. **(b) Take a Position:** Do you think the process is effective? Explain.

4. Integration of Knowledge and Ideas "Mowgli's Brothers" takes place in a community that has many rules. **(a)** What is the purpose of the rules? **(b)** In what ways do the rules shape the actions of the characters? *[Connect to the Big Question: How much do our communities shape us?]*

Cite textual evidence to support your responses.

from

James and the Giant Peach

Roald Dahl

It was quite a large hole, the sort of thing an animal about the size of a fox might have made.

James knelt down in front of it and poked his head and shoulders inside.

He crawled in.

He kept on crawling.

This isn't just a hole, he thought excitedly. It's a tunnel!

The tunnel was damp and murky, and all around him there was the curious bittersweet smell of fresh peach. The floor was soggy under his knees, the walls were wet and sticky, and peach juice was dripping from the ceiling. James opened his mouth and caught some of it on his tongue. It tasted delicious.

He was crawling uphill now, as though the tunnel were leading straight toward the very center of the gigantic fruit. Every few seconds he paused and took a bite out of the wall. The peach flesh was sweet and juicy, and marvelously refreshing.

He crawled on for several more yards, and then suddenly—bang—the top of his head bumped into something extremely hard blocking his way. He glanced up. In front of him there was a solid wall that seemed at first as though it were made of wood. He touched it with his fingers. It certainly felt like wood, except that it was very jagged and full of deep grooves.

"Good heavens!" he said.

"I know what this is! I've come to the stone in the middle of the peach!" •

Then he noticed that there was a small door cut into the face of the peach stone. He gave a push. It swung open. He crawled through it, and before he had time to glance up and see where he was, he heard a voice saying, "Look who's here!" And another one said, "We've been waiting for you!"

James stopped and stared at the speakers, his face white with horror.

He started to stand up, but his knees were shaking so much he had to sit down again on the floor. He glanced behind him, thinking he could bolt back into the tunnel the way he had come, but the doorway had disappeared. There was now only a solid brown wall behind him.

◄ **Critical Viewing**
Which details of this picture are fantastic? Which are realistic? **[Analyze]**

Elements of Fantasy
Identify one fantastic element and one realistic element in this paragraph.

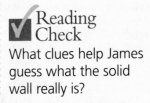
Reading Check
What clues help James guess what the solid wall really is?

from James and the Giant Peach **897**

Vocabulary
intently (in tent´ lē) *adv.*
with great attention
or determination

James's large frightened eyes traveled slowly around the room.

The creatures, some sitting on chairs, others reclining on a sofa, were all watching him **intently**.

Creatures?

Or were they insects?

An insect is usually something rather small, is it not? A grasshopper, for example, is an insect.

So what would you call it if you saw a grasshopper as large as a dog? As large as a large dog. You could hardly call that an insect, could you?

There was an Old-Green-Grasshopper as large as a large dog sitting on a stool directly across the room from James now.

And next to the Old-Green-Grasshopper, there was an enormous Spider.

And next to the Spider, there was a giant Ladybug with nine black spots on her scarlet shell.

Each of these three was squatting upon a magnificent chair.

On a sofa nearby, reclining comfortably in curled-up positions, there was a Centipede and an Earthworm.

On the floor over in the far corner, there was something thick and white that looked as though it might be a Silkworm. But it was sleeping soundly and nobody was paying any attention to it.

Every one of these "creatures" was at least as big as James himself, and in the strange greenish light that shone down from somewhere in the ceiling, they were absolutely terrifying to behold.

"I'm hungry!" the Spider announced suddenly, staring hard at James.

"I'm famished!" the Old-Green-Grasshopper said.

"So am I!" the Ladybug cried.

The Centipede sat up a little straighter on the sofa.

"Everyone's famished!" he said. "We need food!"

Four pairs of round black glassy eyes were all fixed upon James.

The Centipede made a wriggling movement with his body as though he were about to glide off the sofa—but he didn't.

There was a long pause—and a long silence.

The Spider (who happened to be a female spider) opened her mouth and ran a long black tongue delicately over her lips. "Aren't you hungry?" she asked suddenly, leaning forward and addressing herself to James. •

Poor James was backed up against the far wall, shivering with fright and much too terrified to answer.

"What's the matter with you?" the Old-Green-Grasshopper asked. "You look positively ill!"

"He looks as though he's going to faint any second," the Centipede said.

"Oh, my goodness, the poor thing!" the Ladybug cried. "I do believe he thinks it's him that we are wanting to eat!"

There was a roar of laughter from all sides.

"Oh dear, oh dear!" they said. "What an awful thought!"

"You mustn't be frightened," the Ladybug said kindly. "We wouldn't dream of hurting you. You are one of us now, didn't you know that? You are one of the crew. We're all in the same boat."

Elements of Fantasy
Identify one fantastic detail in this paragraph.

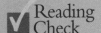

Spiral Review
Folk Tale How are the characters in this modern story similar to those in many folk tales? Explain.

Reading Check
Why do the creatures laugh at James's fright?

◄ **Critical Viewing**
What part of the story do you think this picture shows? **[Analyze]**

from James and the Giant Peach **899**

"We've been waiting for you all day long," the Old-Green-Grasshopper said. "We thought you were never going to turn up. I'm glad you made it."

"So cheer up, my boy, cheer up!" the Centipede said. "And meanwhile I wish you'd come over here and give me a hand with these boots. It takes me hours to get them all off by myself."

James decided that this was most certainly not a time to be disagreeable, so he crossed the room to where the Centipede was sitting and knelt down beside him.

"Thank you so much," the Centipede said. "You are very kind."

"You have a lot of boots," James murmured.

"I have a lot of legs," the Centipede answered proudly. "And a lot of feet. One hundred, to be exact."

"There he goes again!" the Earthworm cried, speaking for the first time. "He simply cannot stop telling lies about his legs! He doesn't have anything like a hundred of them! He's only got forty-two! The trouble is that most people don't bother to count them. They just take his word. And anyway, there is nothing marvelous, you know, Centipede, about having a lot of legs."

"Poor fellow," the Centipede said, whispering in James's ear. "He's blind. He can't see how splendid I look."

"In my opinion," the Earthworm said, "the really marvelous thing is to have no legs at all and to be able to walk just the same."

"You call that walking!" cried the Centipede. "You're a slitherer, that's all you are! You just slither along!"

"I glide," said the Earthworm primly.

"You are a slimy beast," answered the Centipede.

"I am not a slimy beast," the Earthworm said. "I am a useful and much loved creature. Ask any gardener you like. And as for you . . ."

"I am a pest!" the Centipede announced, grinning broadly and looking round the room for approval.

▲ **Critical Viewing**
Which characters are represented in this picture? **[Connect]**

"He is so proud of that," the Ladybug said, smiling at James. "Though for the life of me I cannot understand why."

"I am the only pest in this room!" cried the Centipede, still grinning away. "Unless you count Old-Green-Grasshopper over there. But he is long past it now. He is too old to be a pest any more."

The Old-Green-Grasshopper turned his huge black eyes upon the Centipede and gave him a withering look. "Young fellow," he said, speaking in a deep, slow, scornful voice, "I have never been a pest in my life. I am a musician."

"Hear, hear!" said the Ladybug.

"James," the Centipede said. "Your names is James, isn't it?"

✓ Reading Check
How do the Centipede and the Earthworm get along?

Vocabulary
colossal (kə läs´ əl) *adj.*
very large; huge

"Yes."

"Well, James, have you ever in your life seen such a marvelous colossal Centipede as me?"

"I certainly haven't," James answered. "How on earth did you get to be like that?"

"Very peculiar," the Centipede said. "Very, very peculiar indeed. Let me tell you what happened. I was messing about in the garden under the old peach tree and suddenly a funny little green thing came wriggling past my nose. Bright green it was, and extraordinarily beautiful, and it looked like some kind of a tiny stone or crystal . . ."

"Oh, but I know what that was!" cried James.

"It happened to me, too!" said the Ladybug.

"And me!" Miss Spider said. "Suddenly there were little green things everywhere! The soil was full of them!"

"I actually swallowed one!" the Earthworm declared proudly.

"So did I!" the Ladybug said.

"I swallowed three!" the Centipede cried. "But who's telling this story anyway? Don't interrupt!"

"It's too late to tell stories now," the Old-Green-Grasshopper announced. "It's time to go to sleep."

"I refuse to sleep in my boots!" the Centipede cried. "How many more are there to come off, James?"

"I think I've done about twenty so far," James told him.

"Then that leaves eighty to go," the Centipede said.

"Twenty-two, not eighty!" shrieked the Earthworm. "He's lying again."

The Centipede roared with laughter.

"Stop pulling the Earthworm's leg," the Ladybug said.

This sent the Centipede into hysterics. "Pulling his leg!" he cried, wriggling with glee and pointing at the Earthworm.

"Which leg am I pulling? You tell me that?"

James decided that he rather liked the Centipede. He was obviously a rascal, but what a change it was to hear somebody laughing once in a while. He had never heard Aunt Sponge or Aunt Spiker laughing aloud in all the time he had been with them.

"We really must get some sleep," the Old-Green-Grasshopper said. "We've got a tough day ahead of us tomorrow. So would you be kind enough, Miss Spider, to make the beds?" •

Elements of Fantasy
Which aspects of this good-natured teasing are realistic and which are fantastic?

A few minutes later, Miss Spider had made the first bed. It was hanging from the ceiling, suspended by a rope of threads at either end so that actually it looked more like a hammock than a bed. But it was a magnificent affair, and the stuff that it was made of shimmered like silk in the pale light.

"I do hope you'll find it comfortable," Miss Spider said to the Old-Green-Grasshopper. "I made it as soft and silky as I possibly could. I spun it with gossamer. That's a much better quality thread than the one I use for my own web."

"Thank you so much, my dear lady," the Old-Green-Grasshopper said, climbing into the hammock. "Ah, this is just what I needed. Good night, everybody. Good night."

Then Miss Spider spun the next hammock, and the Ladybug got in.

After that, she spun a long one for the Centipede, and an even longer one for the Earthworm.

"And how do you like your bed?" she said to James when it came to his turn. "Hard or soft?"

"I like it soft, thank you very much," James answered.

Elements of Fantasy
Would you call Miss Spider's bed-making behavior fantastic or realistic? Why?

Reading Check
How did the creatures get to be big?

"For goodness' sake stop staring round the room and get on with my boots!" the Centipede said. "You and I are never going to get any sleep at this rate! And kindly line them up neatly in pairs as you take them off. Don't just throw them over your shoulder."

James worked away frantically on the Centipede's boots. Each one had laces that had to be untied and loosened before it could be pulled off, and to make matters worse, all the laces were tied up in the most complicated knots that had to be unpicked with fingernails. It was just awful. It took about two hours. And by the time James had pulled off the last boot of all and had lined them up in a row on the floor—twenty-one pairs altogether—the Centipede was fast asleep.

Critical Thinking

1. **Key Ideas and Details** **(a)** What is James's first reaction when he encounters the creatures? **(b) Infer:** How does he interpret their actions and words at first?

2. **Key Ideas and Details** **(a)** What does the Centipede ask James to do? **(b) Infer:** What words would you use to describe the Centipede's personality? **(c) Analyze:** As a group, how do the creatures seem to get along? Give examples from the text to support your answer.

3. **Key Ideas and Details** **(a)** By bedtime, do you think James is beginning to like the creatures? Why or why not? **(b) Speculate:** What do you think will happen to James and his new friends? Why?

4. **Integration of Knowledge and Ideas** If James stays with the creatures for a year, how do you think his reaction to them might change? Explain. *[Connect to the Big Question: How much do our communities shape us?]*

Cite textual evidence to support your responses.

Comparing Elements of Fantasy

1. Integration of Knowledge and Ideas For each selection, complete a chart like the one shown to list the fantastic and realistic elements in each category.

Category	Fantastic Element	Realistic Element
Animals		
Human		
Setting		
Situation		

Timed Writing

Explanatory Text: Essay

In an essay, compare and contrast the use of fantastic and realistic elements in "Mowgli's Brothers" and in the excerpt from *James and the Giant Peach*. Use the information in your charts and the questions below to get started. **(30 minutes)**

5-Minute Planner

1. Read the prompt carefully and completely.

2. Organize your ideas by answering these questions:
   - In which story do the animals seem more realistic? Why?
   - Is the boy in either story fantastic in some way?
   - Which story's setting seems more realistic?
   - Could either situation happen in real life? Explain.
   - What might be the author's reason for including fantastic elements?
   - Do the fantasy elements of the story help readers understand the message of the story? Explain.

3. Reread the prompt, and then draft your essay.

Writing Workshop

Write an Informative Text

Research: Multimedia Report

Defining the Form A research report presents detailed, factual information about a subject. A **multimedia report** is a special type of research report. It presents information through a variety of media, including text, slides, videos, music, maps, charts, and art. You might use multimedia to enhance speeches, oral reports, or science fair projects.

Assignment Create a 15-minute multimedia report on a topic that you find interesting. Include these elements:

✔ a *topic* that you can cover effectively in the time allotted

✔ a *clearly stated main idea*

✔ *supportive facts, details, examples, and explanations*

✔ suitable *formatting*

✔ *ethical* and *effective* use of *media elements* that are appropriate for the *purpose, occasion,* and *audience*

✔ use of *technology* that *enhances communication*

✔ error-free writing, including use of *complete sentences*

To preview the criteria on which your work will be based, see the rubric on page 911.

 Writing Workshop: *Work in Progress*

Review the work you did on pages 855 and 875.

Prewriting/Planning Strategies

Interview yourself. Brainstorm to find a topic that interests you, that you know a little bit about, and that you want to learn more about. Complete a chart like the one shown.

Gather media. Conduct research to identify ways to present your topic,

What are my interests?	How much do I know?	What do I want to learn?

including but not limited to photos, maps, graphs, video demonstrations, charts, cartoons, and film clips.

 **Common Core State Standards**

Writing

2. Write informative/explanatory texts to examine a topic and convey ideas, concepts, and information through the selection, organization, and analysis of relevant content.

2.a. Introduce a topic; organize ideas, concepts, and information, using strategies such as definition, classification, comparison/contrast, and cause/effect; include formatting, graphics, and multimedia when useful to aiding comprehension.

6. Use technology, including the Internet, to produce and publish writing as well as to interact and collaborate with others; demonstrate sufficient command of keyboarding skills to type a minimum of three pages in a single sitting.

Language

3.b. Maintain consistency in style and tone.

Organizing Your Information

Consider the following ways to organize and present your ideas:

- Use **index cards** if your ideas include a lot of research. Write one idea on each card and color code by topic.
- Use a **timeline** to organize chronological events and to put events in a historical context.
- Use a **web** to organize details around a main point.
- Use a **story map** to lay out major events of the story you are telling. Use different shapes to identify different ideas.
- Use **graphs, charts, and tables** to compare and contrast information, or to visually show statistics or scientific facts.
- Use an **outline** to help you organize details, supporting evidence, and media aids.

Your information	Consider organizing by
1. Does your information work best in chronological order?	1. index cards, timeline, outline
2. Are some of your ideas more important than others?	2. web, index cards, outline
3. Is there a cause and effect relationship between your ideas?	3. chart, index cards, outline
4. Are you comparing and contrasting information?	4. graph, chart, index cards, outline
5. Are you telling a story?	5. story map, outline
6. Are you dealing with statistics or scientific findings?	6. graph, chart, table, outline

Use technology to help you organize. Word processing programs let you easily move information around as you figure out where it works best. Create a rough draft that shows your initial organizational plan. Focus your attention on producing a minimum of three pages in a single sitting. As you draft, you may revise your plan at any time.

Add elaboration. Add descriptive language to your ideas. Match graphics and illustrations to the text. Make sure that your tone, word choice, and mood are consistent and appropriate to your topic and audience.

Drafting Strategies

Write a script. Plan your presentation by writing a script. Include all words that you will speak and the directions that you will need to guide the media during your presentation. On the left side of a two-column chart, write the words of your script. On the right side, indicate sound effects, visuals, and other notes.

Plan your media needs. Read your draft, noting the media cited in the script. You will also need to complete these tasks:

- Draw pictures, make slides, or edit videos.
- Edit audio or other sound effects.
- Make charts and graphs.
- Copy or scan documents.

Consider the viewer. When you are creating slides with text, limit the number of words on each slide. Choose a suitable font. Use formatting tools like bullets or numbering to make your ideas readable.

Revising Strategies

Evaluate media. Review your draft to find places where adding media will improve the audience's understanding and enjoyment. Review your script and the multimedia elements that you have included. This chart presents the benefits of several commonly available types of media.

Types of Media	Effect on Presentation
Photos, pictures, illustrations, videos	Brings place or person to life; shows instead of telling; can improve viewer interest and enjoyment
Graphs, charts, maps, timelines	Clarifies information; provides visual organization to better present facts
Colorful graphics and backgrounds for text, fancy transitions, creative fonts, etc.	Can enhance presentation, but beware—too much dazzle can be distracting

Fine-tune your presentation. Rehearse your script until you are comfortable with the presentation. Where workable, identify smoother transitions to link your script to your media. Be sure any technology you use is in working condition and that you are able to use it easily and properly before you give your presentation.

Common Core State Standards

Writing

2.a. Include formatting, graphics, and multimedia when useful to aiding comprehension.

2.b. Develop the topic with relevant facts, definitions, concrete details, quotations, or other information and examples.

2.c. Use appropriate transitions to create cohesion and clarify the relationships among ideas and concepts.

6. Use technology, including the Internet, to produce and publish writing.

Speaking and Listening

5. Include multimedia components and visual displays in presentations to clarify information.

Revising Sentence Fragments

Sentence fragments can make your multimedia presentation difficult for your listeners to understand. A **sentence fragment** is a group of words that does not express a complete thought. To fix fragments, add more information to complete the idea.

Fragment: After I heard about the celebration.

Corrected: After I heard about the celebration, I started thinking about a gift.

Fragment: Although I got hurt when I fell.

Corrected: I really enjoyed the soccer game, although I got hurt when I fell.

Correcting Fragments Follow these steps to fix sentence errors in your writing.

1. Consider the complete idea you mean to convey.

2. Eliminate the fragment by either adding it to a nearby sentence or adding the necessary words to turn the incomplete phrase into a sentence. This chart shows several examples:

Changing Fragments into Sentences	
Fragment	**Complete Sentence**
Near the old clown.	The silly puppy flopped down *near the old clown*.
Taking a bow.	*Taking a bow*, the ringmaster had tears in his eyes.
To ask nicely.	She planned *to ask nicely* to go to the circus.

PH | **WRITING COACH**

Further instruction and practice are available in *Prentice Hall Writing Coach*.

Grammar in Your Writing

Choose three paragraphs in your draft. Read each set of words that is punctuated as a sentence. It may help to read these aloud, pausing after each period. Identify any sentence fragments and revise them by adding the necessary words and punctuation.

Student Model: David Papineau and Chris Casey, Indianapolis, IN

The Power of Numbers

Slide 1

Script: In this presentation, you will be shown the various uses of mathematics in a wide range of careers. You will also see some prime examples of what would happen if people did not know the fundamentals of mathematics in a real-life situation. So sit back and prepare to be amazed by . . .The Power of Numbers.

Visual: Blank screen (blues and greens). As the presentation begins, the following words appear letter by letter: The Power of Numbers

Sound: Typewriter

Sound: Explosion

> Math would be too broad a topic, but the writers have narrowed it to focus on how math is used in a variety of careers. Each slide will provide an example.

Slide 2

Script: A word of advice: Never go to a concert where the musicians can't add the fractions of the notes to get the correct beat count. If you do, though, you'd better have earplugs!

Visual: Violinist

Sound: Music played off tempo

> The best way to show the problems a "math-less musician" would have is to let the audience hear the results. The writers chose to include music that is played out of rhythm to support their point.

Slide 3

Script: The picture says it all. If you have a pilot who can't read graphs or make course calculations, you might find the plane way off course.

Visual: Snow-covered mountain top with an airplane flying near it

Sound: Airplane flying

> The use of a visual emphasizes the disastrous effects of a pilot's not knowing math.

[Slides 4–10 provide further examples developing the presentation's main idea.]

Slide 11

Script: So, now you've seen and heard a little bit about the power of numbers. Not only mathematicians need math in order to do a good job—musicians, pilots, store owners, and even chefs use some sort of math every day. A good grasp of math can help you in almost anything you choose to do!

Visual: Blank screens (reds and yellows). As the presentation closes, the following words appear letter by letter: The Power of Numbers

Sound: Explosion

Editing and Proofreading

Review your work to correct errors in spelling, grammar, and punctuation.

Focus on presentation materials. Mistakes look twice as bad when they are projected on a screen or printed on a handout. Check formatting and consistency, then make revised copies before your presentation.

Publishing and Presenting

Consider these possibilities for sharing your multimedia report:

Report to a small audience. With a small group, take turns presenting your multimedia reports and offering feedback.

Take it on the road. Take your report to a site outside of your school. Contact a local library, club, or retirement community that might be interested in your report.

Reflecting on Your Writing

Writer's Journal Jot down your answer to this question:

How might you use your skills in creating multimedia reports to enhance your participation in school clubs or after-school activities?

Rubric for Self-Assessment

Find evidence in your writing to address each category. Then use the rating scale to grade your work.

Spiral Review
Earlier in this unit, you learned about **independent** and **subordinate clauses** (p. 854) and **simple, compound,** and **complex sentences** (p. 874). Check your presentation to be sure that you have used clauses and different types of sentence structures correctly.

Criteria	Rating Scale
	not very / very
Focus: How clearly stated is your topic?	1 2 3 4 5
Organization: How clear is the method of organization?	1 2 3 4 5
Support/Elaboration: How well do you use a variety of media elements to provide support for the main ideas?	1 2 3 4 5
Style: How smooth are your transitions among media?	1 2 3 4 5
Conventions: How well have you corrected errors — including sentence fragments — in your material?	1 2 3 4 5
Ideas: How well were your ideas organized and presented in a logical sequence?	1 2 3 4 5

Leveled Texts

Build your skills and improve your comprehension of folk literature with texts of increasing complexity.

Read **"Why the Tortoise's Shell Is Not Smooth"** to learn what happens when a sneaky tortoise plays a trick.

Read **"He Lion, Bruh Bear, and Bruh Rabbit"** to find out how a clever rabbit deals with a threatening lion.

Common Core State Standards

Meet these standards with either **"Why the Tortoise's Shell Is Not Smooth"** (p. 916) or **"He Lion, Bruh Bear, and Bruh Rabbit"** (p. 924).

Reading Literature

4. Determine the meaning of words and phrases as they are used in a text, including figurative and connotative meanings; analyze the impact of a specific word choice on meaning and tone. *(Literary Analysis: Personification)*

Writing

4. Produce clear and coherent writing in which the development, organization, and style are appropriate to task, purpose, and audience. *(Writing: Invitation)*

Speaking and Listening

6. Adapt speech to a variety of contexts and tasks, demonstrating command of formal English when indicated or appropriate. *(Speaking and Listening: Dramatic Reading)*

Language

2. Demonstrate command of the conventions of standard English capitalization, punctuation, and spelling when writing. *(Conventions: Commas)*

5.a. Interpret figures of speech in context.

5.b. Use the relationship between particular words to better understand each of the words. *(Vocabulary: Analogy)*

6. Acquire and use accurately grade-appropriate general academic and domain-specific words and phrases; gather vocabulary knowledge when considering a word or phrase important to comprehension or expression. *(Vocabulary: Word Study)*

Reading Skill: Purpose for Reading

Your **purpose** for reading is the reason you read a text. Sometimes you choose a text based on a purpose you already have. Other times, you set a purpose based on the kind of text you are about to read. **Setting a purpose** helps you focus your reading. You might set a purpose to learn about a subject, to gain understanding, to take an action, or simply to be entertained.

Preview the text before you begin to read. Look at the title, the pictures, and the beginnings of paragraphs to get an idea about the focus of the work. This will help you set a purpose or decide whether the text will fit a purpose you already have.

Using the Strategy: Previewing Chart

Use a chart like this one to record details as you preview the text.

Text Details	What the Details Suggest About the Text
Title	
Pictures	
Beginnings of paragraphs	

Literary Analysis: Personification

Figurative language is language that is used imaginatively rather than literally. **Personification** is a type of figurative language in which a nonhuman subject is presented as if it had human qualities. In this example, *rain kisses her cheek*, the rain behaves like a person.

Personification is a common literary device that writers use to make text lively and interesting or to draw the reader's attention to an important point. In folk literature, personification is often used to give human qualities to animal characters. The actions of these animals can illustrate human traits, behavior, and problems in a humorous way. As you read, notice how personification adds interest and meaning to the story.

How much do our *communities* shape us?

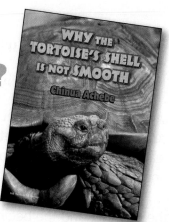

WHY THE TORTOISE'S SHELL IS NOT SMOOTH
Chinua Achebe

Writing About the Big Question

In "Why the Tortoise's Shell Is Not Smooth," a tortoise tricks some birds and leaves them hungry while he feasts. Use the following sentence starter to help you develop your ideas about the Big Question.

When an individual takes advantage of the members of his **community,** the **group** may respond by _____.

While You Read Notice the community rules Tortoise breaks, and look for clues that reveal the effects of his behavior.

Vocabulary

Read each word and its definition. Decide whether you know the word well, know it a little bit, or do not know it at all. After you read, see how your knowledge of each word has increased.

- **cunning** (kun´ iŋ) *n.* slyness; deception (p. 917) *Claire's <u>cunning</u> led to an argument. cunningly adv.*

- **famine** (fam´ in) *n.* shortage of food (p. 917) *There was a <u>famine</u> in Europe. famished adj.*

- **orator** (ôr´ ət ər) *n.* person who speaks well in public (p. 918) *His experience on the debate team made him an excellent <u>orator</u>. oration n. oratory n.*

- **custom** (kus´ təm) *n.* usual way of doing something; habit (p. 918) *Our family's <u>custom</u> was to eat dinner at eight. customary adj.*

- **eloquent** (el´ ə kwənt) *adj.* persuasive and expressive (p. 918) *We were moved by Grace's <u>eloquent</u> speech. eloquence n. eloquently adv.*

- **compound** (käm´ pound) *n.* grounds surrounded by buildings (p. 919) *The office <u>compound</u> was very large.*

Meet
Chinua Achebe
(b. 1930)

Author of

WHY THE TORTOISE'S SHELL IS NOT SMOOTH

Chinua Achebe likes to retell stories that originated in his native country of Nigeria many years ago. Achebe writes, "Our ancestors created their myths and legends and told their stories for a purpose. Any good story, any good novel, should have a message."

Achebe attended the local mission school where his father taught, and then went to University College in Ibadan, Nigeria. He later studied in London.

Acclaim and Resettlement Achebe became a professional writer and won acclaim with *Things Fall Apart,* his 1958 novel about changing times in Africa. He later wrote poetry, essays, fiction, and nonfiction and started a literary magazine. Achebe left Nigeria when the political climate there made it too dangerous to stay. He now lives in the United States.

BACKGROUND FOR THE FOLK TALE
The Oral Tradition

Folk tales are part of the oral tradition, which is the passing along of songs, stories, and poems by word of mouth. For example, "Why the Tortoise's Shell Is Not Smooth" was originally told orally. Many folk tales have now been preserved in written texts.

DID YOU KNOW?

In 2007, at the age of 76, Chinua Achebe won the International Man Booker prize for fiction. This award honors all of Achebe's works of fiction.

WHY THE TORTOISE'S SHELL IS NOT SMOOTH

Chinua Achebe

Low voices, broken now and again by singing, reached Okonkwo (ō kōn´ kwō) from his wives' huts as each woman and her children told folk stories. Ekwefi (e kwe´ fē) and her daughter, Ezinma (e zēn´ mä), sat on a mat on the floor. It was Ekwefi's turn to tell a story.

"Once upon a time," she began, "all the birds were invited to a feast in the sky. They were very happy and began to prepare themselves for the great day. They painted their bodies with red cam wood[1] and drew beautiful patterns on them with dye.

"Tortoise saw all these preparations and soon discovered what it all meant. Nothing that happened in the world of the animals ever escaped his notice; he was full of cunning. As soon as he heard of the great feast in the sky his throat began to itch at the very thought. There was a famine in those days and Tortoise had not eaten a good meal for two moons. His body rattled like a piece of dry stick in his empty shell. So he began to plan how he would go to the sky."

"But he had no wings," said Ezinma.

"Be patient," replied her mother. "That is the story. Tortoise had no wings, but he went to the birds and asked to be allowed to go with them.

"'We know you too well,' said the birds when they had heard him. 'You are full of cunning and you are ungrateful. If we allow you to come with us you will soon begin your mischief.'

" 'You do not know me,' said Tortoise. 'I am a changed man. I have learned that a man who makes trouble for others is also making it for himself.'

---

1. **red cam** (cam) **wood** hard West African wood that makes red dye.

Purpose for Reading
What purpose for reading does this story's title present?

Vocabulary
cunning (kun´ iŋ) *n.* slyness; deception
famine (fam´ in) *n.* shortage of food

Reading Check
Why is the tortoise hungry?

Why the Tortoise's Shell Is Not Smooth **917**

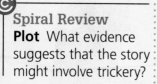

Spiral Review

Plot What evidence suggests that the story might involve trickery?

Vocabulary

orator (ôr´ ət ər) *n.* person who speaks well in public

custom (kus´ təm) *n.* usual way of doing something; habit

eloquent (el´ ə kwənt) *adj.* persuasive and expressive

"Tortoise had a sweet tongue, and within a short time all the birds agreed that he was a changed man, and they each gave him a feather, with which he made two wings.

"At last the great day came and Tortoise was the first to arrive at the meeting place. When all the birds had gathered together, they set off in a body. Tortoise was very happy as he flew among the birds, and he was soon chosen as the man to speak for the party because he was a great orator.

" 'There is one important thing which we must not forget,' he said as they flew on their way. 'When people are invited to a great feast like this, they take new names for the occasion. Our hosts in the sky will expect us to honor this age-old custom.'

"None of the birds had heard of this custom but they knew that Tortoise, in spite of his failings in other directions, was a widely traveled man who knew the customs of different peoples. And so they each took a new name. When they had all taken, Tortoise also took one. He was to be called *All of you.* •

"At last the party arrived in the sky and their hosts were very happy to see them. Tortoise stood up in his many-colored plumage and thanked them for their invitation. His speech was so eloquent that all the birds were glad they had brought him, and nodded their heads in approval of all he said. Their hosts took him as the king of the birds, especially as he looked somewhat different from the others.

"After kola nuts had been presented and eaten, the people of the sky set before their guests the most delectable dishes Tortoise had ever seen or dreamed of. The soup was brought out hot from the fire and in the very pot in which it had been cooked. It was full of meat and fish. Tortoise began to sniff aloud. There was pounded yam and also yam pottage[2] cooked with palm oil and fresh fish. There were also pots of palm wine. When everything had been set before the guests, one of the people of the sky came forward and tasted a little from each pot. He then invited the birds to eat. But Tortoise jumped to his feet and asked: 'For whom have you prepared this feast?'

---

2. **yam** (yam) **pottage** (pät´ ij) *n.* thick stew made of sweet potatoes.

"'For all of you,' replied the man.

"Tortoise turned to the birds and said: 'You remember that my name is *All of you*. The custom here is to serve the spokesman first and the others later. They will serve you when I have eaten.'

"He began to eat and the birds grumbled angrily. The people of the sky thought it must be their custom to leave all the food for their king. And so Tortoise ate the best part of the food and then drank two pots of palm wine, so that he was full of food and drink and his body grew fat enough to fill out his shell.

"The birds gathered round to eat what was left and to peck at the bones he had thrown all about the floor. Some of them were too angry to eat. They chose to fly home on an empty stomach. But before they left, each took back the feather he had lent to Tortoise. And there he stood in his hard shell full of food and wine but without any wings to fly home. He asked the birds to take a message for his wife, but they all refused. In the end Parrot, who had felt more angry than the others, suddenly changed his mind and agreed to take the message.

"'Tell my wife,' said Tortoise, 'to bring out all the soft things in my house and cover the compound with them so that I can jump down from the sky without very great danger.'

"Parrot promised to deliver the message, and then flew away. But when he reached Tortoise's house he told his wife to bring out all the hard things in the house.

Personification
What human qualities does Tortoise have?

Vocabulary
compound (käm´ pound) *n.* grounds surrounded by buildings

• "WHEN PEOPLE ARE INVITED TO A GREAT FEAST LIKE THIS, THEY TAKE NEW NAMES FOR THE OCCASION."

And so she brought out her husband's hoes, machetes, spears, guns, and even his cannon. Tortoise looked down from the sky and saw his wife bringing things out, but it was too far to see what they were. When all seemed ready he let himself go. He fell and fell and fell until he began to fear that he would never stop falling. And then like the sound of his cannon he crashed on the compound."

"Did he die?" asked Ezinma.

"No," replied Ekwefi. "His shell broke into pieces. But there was a great medicine man in the neighborhood. Tortoise's wife sent for him and he gathered all the bits of shell and stuck them together. That is why Tortoise's shell is not smooth."

Purpose for Reading
Did you achieve your purpose for reading this folk tale? Why or why not?

Critical Thinking

Cite textual evidence to support your responses.

1. **Key Ideas and Details** **(a)** Why does Tortoise want to go to the great feast? **(b) Infer:** Why do the birds not want to take him?

2. **Key Ideas and Details** **(a) Analyze:** Why do the birds decide to help Tortoise go to the feast? **(b) Deduce:** Why do they choose him to speak for the group? **(c) Assess:** How does Tortoise make use of this privilege?

3. **Key Ideas and Details** **(a) Interpret:** Explain how Tortoise's new name allows him to eat before the birds eat. **(b) Apply:** What lesson have the birds learned about Tortoise?

4. **Integration of Knowledge and Ideas** **(a)** What unwritten community rules did Tortoise break? Explain. **(b)** How do you think the birds will treat Tortoise after this incident? Explain. *[Connect to the Big Question: How much do our communities shape us?]*

Reading Skill: Purpose for Reading

1. (a) What was your **purpose for reading** this folk tale?
(b) How might your purpose be different if you were reading a nonfiction article about tortoises?

2. How well did previewing the title and pictures give you a sense of what the folk tale would be about? Explain.

Literary Analysis: Personification

© 3. Key Ideas and Details Complete a chart like the one shown to analyze one of the animal characters.

Character's Name:	
Animal Qualities:	Human Qualities:

© 4. Craft and Structure (a) Give three examples of **personification** in the description of Tortoise's character.
(b) What effect does the use of personification have on the story?

Vocabulary

© Acquisition and Use In an **analogy,** pairs of words share a relationship. Use a word from page 914 to complete each item.

1. *speech* is to *speaker* as *oration* is to _____

2. *tiresome* is to *boring* as *persuasive* is to _____

3. *hunger* is to *excess* as *gluttony* is to _____

4. *attractiveness* is to *beauty* as *craftiness* is to _____

5. *tree* is to *forest* as *building* is to _____

6. *future* is to *technology* as *past* is to _____

Word Study Use context and what you know about the **suffix -ary** to explain your answer to each question

1. Does a *cautionary* tale instruct you to be careful?

2. Would a *visionary* be a good inventor?

Word Study

The **suffix -ary** means "related to" or "connected with."

Apply It Explain how the suffix -ary contributes to the meaning of these words. Consult a dictionary if necessary.

primary
beneficiary
sanctuary

How much do our *communities* shape us?

Writing About the Big Question

In "He Lion, Bruh Bear, and Bruh Rabbit," a group of animals ask the wisest members of their community to help them solve a problem. Use the following sentence starter to help you develop your ideas about the Big Question.

It makes sense to **involve** a wise member of the **community** in a problem when _____.

While You Read Notice the ways the animals try to solve a problem and think about other ways the animals might find a solution.

Vocabulary

Read each word and its definition. Decide whether you know the word well, know it a little bit, or do not know it at all. After you read, see how your knowledge of each word has increased.

- **lair** (ler) *n.* den or resting place of a wild animal (p. 925) *The lion's lair was not big enough.*

- **cordial** (kôr´ jəl) *adj.* warm and friendly (p. 925) *We received a cordial welcome from our hosts.* *cordially adv.*

- **scrawny** (skrô´ nē) *adj.* very thin, skinny, and boney (p. 925) *The scrawny puppy looked hungry.* *scrawniness n. scrawnier adj.*

- **olden** (ōl´ dən) *adj.* old; ancient (p. 927) *That event took place centuries ago, in the olden days.* *old adj.*

- **thicket** (thik´ it) *n.* dense growth of shrubs or small trees (p. 927) *I knew George was somewhere behind the thicket.* *thicketed adj.*

- **peaceable** (pēs´ ə bəl) *adj.* harmonious; tranquil (p. 928) *There were peaceable demonstrators in front of the town municipal building.* *peace n. peaceful adj.*

Word Study

The **suffix -en** means "become," "cause to be," or "made of."

In this folk tale, a man is described as olden—he has come to be old.

Meet
Virginia Hamilton
(1936–2002)

Author of
HE LION, BRUH BEAR, AND BRUH RABBIT

Virginia Hamilton came from a family of storytellers who passed along tales of the family's experiences and heritage. Although she focused her writing mainly on African American subjects and characters, the themes in her books are meaningful to all people.

First Novel and More In 1967, Hamilton published her first novel, *Zeely,* to wide acclaim. Her next novel, *The House of Dies Drear,* published in 1968, was a modern mystery about a house on the Underground Railroad. During her writing career Hamilton collected and retold the tales she heard as a child. Some of her favorite stories are collected in *The People Could Fly: American Black Folktales.*

DID YOU KNOW?

Virginia Hamilton said, "I've been a writer all my life, since the time I was a child in grade school, when I first learned to scribble down sentences describing the pictures in my head."

BACKGROUND FOR THE FOLK TALE

Animal Characters

When they came to North America, enslaved Africans brought folk tales that had been passed down from generation to generation. Many of the tales involve animals, such as rabbits, bears, or turtles, with human characteristics. One popular character in many of these folk tales is the clever rabbit known as Bruh Rabbit.

HE LION, BRUH BEAR, AND BRUH RABBIT

Virginia Hamilton

▲ **Critical Viewing**
Why might a lion be used in a folk tale to represent someone with a high opinion of himself or herself?
[Draw Conclusions]

Purpose for Reading
Based on the title, what purpose might you set for reading this story?

Say that he Lion would get up each and every mornin. Stretch and walk around. He'd roar, "ME AND MYSELF, ME AND MYSELF," like that. Scare all the little animals so they were afraid to come outside in the sunshine. Afraid to go huntin or fishin or whatever the little animals wanted to do.

"What we gone do about it?" they asked one another. Squirrel leapin from branch to branch, just scared. Possum[1] playin dead, couldn't hardly move him.

He Lion just went on, stickin out his chest and roarin, "ME AND MYSELF, ME AND MYSELF."

The little animals held a sit-down talk, and one by one and two by two and all by all, they decide to go see Bruh[2]

---

1. **Possum** (päs´ əm) colloquial for "opossum," a small tree-dwelling mammal that pretends to be dead when it is trapped.
2. **Bruh** (bru) early African American dialect for "brother."

Bear and Bruh Rabbit. For they know that Bruh Bear been around. And Bruh Rabbit say he has, too.

So they went to Bruh Bear and Bruh Rabbit. Said, "We have some trouble. Old he Lion, him scarin everybody, roarin every mornin and all day, "ME AND MYSELF, ME AND MYSELF," like that.

"Why he Lion want to do that?" Bruh Bear said.

"Is that all he Lion have to say?" Bruh Rabbit asked.

"We don't know why, but that's all he Lion can tell us and we didn't ask him to tell us that," said the little animals. "And him scarin the children with it. And we wish him to stop it."

"Well, I'll go see him, talk to him. I've known he Lion a long kind of time," Bruh Bear said.

"I'll go with you," said Bruh Rabbit. "I've known he Lion most long as you."

That bear and that rabbit went off through the forest. They kept hearin somethin. Mumble, mumble. Couldn't make it out. They got farther in the forest. They heard it plain now. "ME AND MYSELF, ME AND MYSELF."

"Well, well, well," said Bruh Bear. He wasn't scared. He'd been around the whole forest, seen a lot.

"My, my, my," said Bruh Rabbit. He'd seen enough to know not to be afraid of an old he lion. Now old he lions could be dangerous, but you had to know how to handle them. •

The bear and the rabbit climbed up and up the cliff where he Lion had his lair. They found him. Kept their distance. He watchin them and they watchin him. Everybody actin cordial.

"Hear tell you are scarin everybody, all the little animals, with your roarin all the time," Bruh Rabbit said.

"I roars when I pleases," he Lion said.

"Well, might could you leave off the noise first thing in the mornin, so the little animals can get what they want to eat and drink?" asked Bruh Bear.

"Listen," said he Lion, and then he roared: "ME AND MYSELF, ME AND MYSELF. Nobody tell me what not to do," he said. "I'm the king of the forest, *me and myself.*"

"Better had let me tell you something," Bruh Rabbit said, "for I've seen Man, and I know him the real king of the forest."

He Lion was quiet awhile. He looked straight through that scrawny lil Rabbit like he was nothin atall. He looked at Bruh Bear and figured he'd talk to him.

Personification
What human qualities does Bruh Rabbit have?

Vocabulary
lair (ler) *n.* den or resting place of a wild animal

cordial (kôr´ jəl) *adj.* warm and friendly

scrawny (skrô´ nē) *adj.* very thin, skinny and bony

Reading Check
Why are the little animals afraid of the lion?

Spiral Review
Characters How does the author use dialogue to convey the characters of he Lion, Bruh Bear, and Bruh Rabbit?

"You, Bear, you been around," he Lion said.

"That's true," said old Bruh Bear. "I been about everywhere. I've been around the whole forest."

"Then you must know something," he Lion said.

"I know lots," said Bruh Bear, slow and quiet-like.

"Tell me what you know about Man," he Lion said. "He think him the king of the forest?"

"Well, now, I'll tell you," said Bruh Bear, "I been around, but I haven't ever come across Man that I know of. Couldn't tell you nothin about him."

So he Lion had to turn back to Bruh Rabbit. He didn't want to but he had to. "So what?" he said to that lil scrawny hare.

"Well, you got to come down from there if you want to see Man," Bruh Rabbit said. "Come down from there and I'll show you him."

He Lion thought a minute, an hour, and a whole day. Then, the next day, he came on down.

He roared just once, "ME AND MYSELF, ME AND MYSELF. Now," he said, "come show me Man."

So they set out. He Lion, Bruh Bear, and Bruh Rabbit. They go along and they go along, rangin the forest. Pretty soon, they come to a clearin. And playin in it is a little fellow about nine years old.

"Is that there Man?" asked he Lion.

▼ **Critical Viewing**
How well does this bear fit your image of Bruh Bear? Explain. **[Connect]**

"Why no, that one is called Will Be, but it sure is not Man," said Bruh Rabbit.

So they went along and they went along. Pretty soon, they come upon a shade tree. And sleepin under it is an old, olden fellow, about ninety years olden.

"There must lie Man," spoke he Lion. "I knew him wasn't gone be much."

"That's not Man," said Bruh Rabbit. "That fellow is Was Once. You'll know it when you see Man."

So they went on along. He Lion is gettin tired of strollin. So he roars, "ME AND MYSELF, ME AND MYSELF." Upsets Bear so that Bear doubles over and runs and climbs a tree.

"Come down from there," Bruh Rabbit tellin him. So after a while Bear comes down. He keepin his distance from he Lion, anyhow. And they set out some more. Goin along quiet and slow. •

In a little while they come to a road. And comin on way down the road, Bruh Rabbit sees Man comin. Man about twenty-one years old. Big and strong, with a big gun over his shoulder.

"There!" Bruh Rabbit says. "See there, he Lion? There's Man. You better go meet him."

"I will," says he Lion. And he sticks out his chest and he roars, "ME AND MYSELF, ME AND MYSELF." All the way to Man he's roarin proud, "ME AND MYSELF, ME AND MYSELF!"

"Come on, Bruh Bear, let's go!" Bruh Rabbit says.

"What for?" Bruh Bear wants to know.

"You better come on!" And Bruh Rabbit takes ahold of Bruh Bear and half drags him to a thicket. And there he makin the Bear hide with him.

For here comes Man. He sees old he Lion real good now. He drops to one knee and he takes aim with his big gun.

Old he Lion is roarin his head off: "ME AND MYSELF, ME AND MYSELF!"

The big gun goes off: PA-LOOOM!

He Lion falls back hard on his tail.

The gun goes off again. PA-LOOOM!

He Lion is flyin through the air. He lands in the thicket.

"Well, did you see Man?" asked Bruh Bear.

"I seen him," said he Lion. "Man spoken to me unkind, and got a great long stick him keepin on his shoulder. Then Man taken that stick down and him speakin real mean.

Personification
What human qualities does he Lion demonstrate here?

Reading Check
What two examples of man do the animals see first?

Thunderin at me and lightnin comin from that stick, awful bad. Made me sick. I had to turn around. And Man pointin that stick again and thunderin at me some more. So I come in here, cause it seem like him throwed some stickers at me each time it thunder, too."

"So you've met Man, and you know zactly what that kind of him is," says Bruh Rabbit.

"I surely do know that," he Lion said back.

Awhile after he Lion met Man, things were some better in the forest. Bruh Bear knew what Man looked like so he could keep out of his way. That rabbit always did know to keep out of Man's way. The little animals could go out in the mornin because he Lion was more peaceable. He didn't walk around roarin at the top of his voice all the time. And when he Lion did lift that voice of his, it was like, "Me and Myself and Man. Me and Myself and Man." Like that.

Wasn't too loud at all.

Vocabulary
peaceable (pēs´ ə bəl) *adj.* harmonious; tranquil

Critical Thinking

1. Key Ideas and Details (a) Why does he Lion want to see Man? **(b) Compare and Contrast:** Describe he Lion before and after he meets Man. **(c) Analyze Cause and Effect:** What causes the change in he Lion's attitude?

2. Integration of Knowledge and Ideas (a) Draw Conclusions: Based on he Lion's behavior, what lesson does this story appear to teach? **(b) Evaluate:** Does this lesson apply well to modern life? Explain.

3. Integration of Knowledge and Ideas (a) Why do the little animals go to Bruh Bear and Bruh Rabbit for help? Explain. **(b)** To whom do you go for help if a problem arises in your school community? Why might this person be able to solve a problem that the students cannot solve? *[Connect to the Big Question: How much do our communities shape us?]*

Cite textual evidence to support your responses.

Reading Skill: Purpose for Reading

1. (a) What was your **purpose for reading** this folk tale? **(b)** How might your purpose be different if you were reading a nonfiction article about animals in the wild?

2. How well did previewing the title and pictures give you a sense of what the folk tale would be about? Explain.

Literary Analysis: Personification

© **3. Key Ideas and Details** Complete a chart like the one shown to analyze one of the animal characters.

Character's Name:	
Animal Qualities:	Human Qualities:

© **4. Craft and Structure (a)** Give three examples of **personification** in the description of Bruh Rabbit. **(b)** What effect does the use of personification have on this story?

Vocabulary

© **Acquisition and Use** In an **analogy,** pairs of words or phrases share a relationship. Use a vocabulary word from page 922 to complete each analogy.

1. *home* is to *dwelling* as *den* is to _____

2. *rude* is to *polite* as *ill-mannered* is to _____

3. *shrub* is to *bush* as *growth of small trees* is to _____

4. *modern* is to *old* as *new* is to _____

5. *mean* is to *nice* as *violent* is to _____

6. *tall* is to *short* as *chubby* is to _____

Word Study Use context and what you know about the **suffix -en** to explain your answer to each question.

1. How can you tell if an item is *wooden*?

2. When does the sky *darken*?

Word Study

The **suffix -en** means "become," "cause to be," or "made of."

Apply It Explain how the suffix -en contributes to the meaning of these words. Consult a dictionary if necessary.

heighten
golden
strengthen

Integrated Language Skills

Why the Tortoise's Shell Is Not Smooth • He Lion, Bruh Bear, and Bruh Rabbit

Conventions: Commas

A **comma** is a punctuation mark used to separate words or groups of words.

Commas signal readers to pause. They also help prevent confusion in meaning. Use commas to separate three or more words or phrases in a series. Notice that a comma is placed after each word and each group of words, including the last word or group of words before the *and* in each sentence.

	Incorrect	Correct
word in a series	School supplies include pencils erasers notebooks and paper.	School supplies include pencils, erasers, notebooks, and paper.
phrases in a series	To find the library go up the stairs down the hallway and turn left at the double doors.	To find the library, go up the stairs, down the hallway, and turn left at the double doors.
phrases in a series	I went home studied for my science test ate dinner and went to bed.	I went home, studied for my science test, ate dinner, and went to bed.

Practice A Rewrite the sentences to take out incorrect commas and add correct commas.

1. The people sang, told folk stories and took care of the children.
2. The birds prepared themselves painted their bodies and drew patterns.
3. The Tortoise was a good, orator, a liar and a trickster.
4. Tortoise ate drank and grew fat.

© Reading Application Read a folk tale and identify a sentence in which commas are used to separate words or phrases in a series.

Practice B Complete these sentences, using commas with phrases or words in a series.

1. Lion got up every morning, _____.
2. Lion was scaring the _____.
3. The three humans that Lion saw were _____.
4. Man began to point his gun at he Lion, _____.

© Writing Application Write a summary of the tale you read. Include three sentences that use commas correctly with phrases or words in a series.

PH **WRITING COACH** Further instruction and practice are available in *Prentice Hall Writing Coach*.

Writing

 **Common Core State Standards**

L.6.6, L.6.2; W.6.4; SL.6.6
[For the full wording of the standards, see page 912.]

Narrative Text Write an **invitation** to either the feast in the sky in "Why the Tortoise's Shell Is Not Smooth" or the sit-down talk in "He Lion, Bruh Bear, and Bruh Rabbit." Decide on the best format for your invitation. For example, you may write a letter, create a card, or develop a poster. Follow these steps to include important information:

- Explain the purpose of the event.
- Include the date, time, and location of the event as well as directions.
- Ask your guests to let you know if they will be there.
- Include a phone number or an e-mail address for replies.

Grammar Application Use commas correctly in your invitation.

Writing Workshop: *Work in Progress*

Prewriting for Research Brainstorm for ideas for a research paper you may write. You can choose almost any topic that interests you, as long as you can locate information about it. Save your Possible Topics List in your writing portfolio.

Use this prewriting strategy to prepare for the **Writing Workshop** on page 988.

Speaking and Listening

Comprehension and Collaboration With a group, present a **dramatic reading.**

- If you read "He Lion, Bruh Bear, and Bruh Rabbit," act out the scene in which the characters search for Man.
- If you read "Why the Tortoise's Shell is Not Smooth," act out the scene in which Tortoise asks the birds if he can go with them to the feast.

Follow these steps to complete the assignment.

- Act out the parts of the characters using exact words from the folk tale.
- Use punctuation to help you read fluently and with appropriate pacing, intonation, and expression.
- Vary the volume and tone of your voice to show different levels of feeling. Use gestures to bring the words to life.
- Have classmates watch your dramatic reading and provide feedback. Then, practice and deliver it again.

PHLit Online!
www.PHLitOnline.com
- Interactive graphic organizers
- Grammar tutorial
- Interactive journals

Leveled Texts

Build your skills and improve your comprehension of folk literature with texts of increasing complexity.

Read **"The Three Wishes"** to meet a couple who have the opportunity to wish for anything they desire.

Read **"The Stone"** to find out what happens to a man who wishes to stay young forever.

Common Core State Standards

Meet these standards with either **"The Three Wishes"** (p. 936) or **"The Stone"** (p. 942).

Reading Literature
2. Determine a theme or central idea of a text and how it is conveyed through particular details; provide a summary of the text distinct from personal opinions or judgments. *(Literary Analysis: Universal Theme)*

Writing
4. Produce clear and coherent writing in which the development, organization, and style are appropriate to task, purpose, and audience. *(Writing: Plot Proposal)*

6. Use technology, including the Internet, to produce and publish writing. *(Research and Technology: Written and Visual Report)*

8. Gather relevant information from multiple print and digital sources. *(Research and Technology: Written and Visual Report)*

Speaking and Listening
1. Engage effectively in a range of collaborative discussions with diverse partners on grade 6 topics, texts, and issues, building on others' ideas and expressing their own clearly. *(Research and Technology: Written and Visual Report)*

Language
2. Demonstrate command of the conventions of standard English capitalization, punctuation, and spelling when writing. *(Conventions: Semicolons and Colons)*

6. Acquire and use accurately grade-appropriate general academic and domain-specific words and phrases; gather vocabulary knowledge when considering a word or phrase important to comprehension or expression. *(Vocabulary: Word Study)*

Reading Skill: Setting a Purpose

Setting a purpose for reading gives you a focus as you read. Once you have set your purpose, **adjust your reading rate** to help you accomplish that purpose.

- When you are reading to remember information, your reading rate should be slow and careful. Pause periodically to think about what you have read. Descriptive passages that are heavy with details should also be read slowly.

- When you are reading for enjoyment, you may decide to read more quickly. You may often choose to read dialogue quickly to imitate the flow of a conversation.

Keep your purpose in mind as you read. Then, after reading, determine whether you have successfully met your purpose.

Literary Analysis: Universal Theme

The theme of a literary work is its central idea or message about life and human nature. A **universal theme** is a message about life that is expressed regularly in many cultures and time periods. Examples of universal themes include the importance of courage, the power of love, and the danger of greed.

You can find the universal theme of a literary work by examining the story's conflict and the actions of the main character. In addition, notice the changes he or she undergoes and the effects of these changes.

Using the Strategy: Universal Theme Chart

As you read, use a chart like this one to help you determine the universal theme.

Character:	
How character changes	
Meaning of change	
Universal theme	

www.PHLitOnline.com

Hear It!
- Selection summary audio
- Selection audio

See It!
- Get Connected video
- Background video
- More about the author
- Vocabulary flashcards

Do It!
- Interactive journals
- Interactive graphic organizers
- Self-test
- Internet activity
- Grammar tutorial
- Interactive vocabulary games

How much do our *communities* shape us?

Writing About the Big Question

Different versions of "The Three Wishes" exist in cultures around the world. Use the following sentence starter to help you develop your ideas about the Big Question.

In many **cultures,** stories in which someone is granted three wishes are passed down through **generations** because these tales teach _____.

While You Read Think about the lesson the couple in this story learns from their experience with three wishes.

Vocabulary

Read each word and its definition. Decide whether you know the word well, know it a little bit, or do not know it at all. After you read, see how your knowledge of each word has increased.

- **scarcely** (skers´ lē) *adv.* hardly (p. 937) *I was scarcely finished with my homework when the telephone rang. scarce adj. scarcity n.*

- **embraced** (em brast´) *v.* clasped in the arms to show affection (p. 937) *Ana embraced her friends as she said goodbye. embrace v. embracing v.*

- **covetousness** (kuv´ ət əs nəs) *n.* enviousness; desire for what another has (p. 938) *His covetousness kept him from being satisfied with what he had. covet v.*

- **greed** (grēd) *n.* selfish desire for more (p. 938) *Robin's greed led her to take more than her share of the gifts. greedy adj. greedily adv.*

- **repentance** (ri pen´ təns) *n.* regret (p. 938) *She expressed her repentance in a sincere apology. repent v.*

Word Study

The **Latin root -pen-** means "punishment" or "pain."

In this folk tale, the main characters are rewarded for their **repentance,** or the pain they feel because of their wrongdoing.

Author of

The Three Wishes
Puerto Rican Folk Tale

Ricardo Alegría has been a leader in education, archaeology, and culture in his native Puerto Rico. Among other positions, Alegría served as the director of the Center for Advanced Studies of Puerto Rico and the Caribbean. On his 75th birthday, he was awarded the James Smithson Medal of the Smithsonian Institution for fifty years of contributions to arts and letters and to world culture.

DID YOU KNOW?

Alegría is considered a major figure in preserving the culture, values, Spanish language, and history of Puerto Rico's native people. He has said: "Culture is the way mankind expresses itself to live and live collectively."

BACKGROUND FOR THE FOLK TALE

Versions of Folk Tales

You may already know one or more versions of a "three wishes" tale. Because folk tales are passed on orally, they can "migrate" from one place to another. Each storyteller adds details based on personal experience or culture. After a number of tellings, a new version of the tale emerges.

The Three Wishes

Puerto Rican Folk Tale

Ricardo E. Alegría

▲ Critical Viewing
What details in this
picture match the
story's first few sen-
tences? [Connect]

Many years ago, there lived a woodsman and his wife.
They were very poor but very happy in their little house
in the forest. Poor as they were, they were always ready to
share what little they had with anyone who came to their
door. They loved each other very much and were quite
content with their life together. Each evening, before eating,
they gave thanks to God for their happiness.

One day, while the husband was working far off in the
woods, an old man came to the little house and said that
he had lost his way in the forest and had eaten nothing for
many days. The woodsman's wife had little to eat herself,
but, as was her custom, she gave a large portion of it to the
old man. After he had eaten everything she gave him, he
told the woman that he had been sent to test her and that,

as a reward for the kindness she and her husband showed to all who came to their house, they would be granted a special grace. This pleased the woman, and she asked what the special grace was.

The old man answered, "Beginning immediately, any three wishes you or your husband may wish will come true."

When she heard these words, the woman was overjoyed and exclaimed, "Oh, if my husband were only here to hear what you say!"

The last word had scarcely left her lips when the woodsman appeared in the little house with the ax still in his hands. The first wish had come true.

The woodsman couldn't understand it at all. How did it happen that he, who had been cutting wood in the forest, found himself here in his house? His wife explained it all as she embraced him. The woodsman just stood there, thinking over what his wife had said. He looked at the old man who stood quietly, too, saying nothing.

Suddenly he realized that his wife, without stopping to think, had used one of the three wishes, and he became very annoyed when he remembered all of the useful things she might have asked for with the first wish. For the first time, he became angry with his wife. The desire for riches had turned his head, and he scolded his wife, shouting at her, among other things, "It doesn't seem possible that you could be so stupid! You've wasted one of our wishes, and now we have only two left! May you grow ears of a donkey!"

He had no sooner said the words than his wife's ears began to grow, and they continued to grow until they changed into the pointed, furry ears of a donkey. •

When the woman put her hand up and felt them, she knew what had happened and began to cry. Her husband was very ashamed and sorry, indeed, for what he had done in his temper, and he went to his wife to comfort her.

The old man, who had stood by silently, now came to them and said, "Until now, you have known happiness together and have never quarreled with each other.

Setting a Purpose
At what rate would you read this part of the tale? Why?

Vocabulary
scarcely (skers´ lē) *adv.* hardly

embraced (em brāst´) *v.* clasped in the arms to show affection

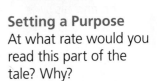

Reading Check
What conflict do the woodsman and his wife face?

Spiral Review
Plot How does the woodsman resolve the conflict he and his wife face?

Vocabulary
covetousness (kuv´ ət əs nəs) *n.* enviousness; desire for what another has

greed (grēd) *n.* a selfish desire for more

repentance (ri pen´ təns) *n.* regret

Nevertheless, the mere knowledge that you could have riches and power has changed you both. Remember, you have only one wish left. What do you want? Riches? Beautiful clothes? Servants? Power?"

The woodsman tightened his arm about his wife, looked at the old man, and said, "We want only the happiness and joy we knew before my wife grew donkey's ears."

No sooner had he said these words than the donkey ears disappeared. The woodsman and his wife fell upon their knees to ask forgiveness for having acted, if only for a moment, out of covetousness and greed. Then they gave thanks for all their happiness.

The old man left, but before going, he told them that they had undergone this test in order to learn that there can be happiness in poverty just as there can be unhappiness in riches. As a reward for their repentance, the old man said that he would bestow upon them the greatest happiness a married couple could know. Months later, a son was born to them. The family lived happily all the rest of their lives.

Critical Thinking

1. **Key Ideas and Details (a)** Describe the life of the woodsman and his wife before they make the three wishes. **(b) Draw Conclusions:** What does the old man's final action tell you about his values?

Cite textual evidence to support your responses.

2. **Key Ideas and Details (a)** How does the couple use the first two wishes? **(b) Compare and Contrast:** How does the behavior of the couple change after they are given the opportunity to make wishes? **(c) Analyze:** What does their changed behavior say about the consequences of greed?

3. **Key Ideas and Details** Do you think that the couple deserved to be rewarded for their repentance? Why or why not?

4. **Integration of Knowledge and Ideas (a)** What important lesson does this story teach? **(b)** Why do you think this lesson is included in the folk tales of many different cultures? *[Connect to the Big Question: How much do our communities shape us?]*

Reading Skill: Setting a Purpose

1. Choose two passages from the folk tale. In a chart like this one, tell your **reading rate** for each passage.

Passage	Reading Rate

2. Use the information in your chart to explain when and why you changed your reading rate as you read.

Literary Analysis: Universal Theme

3. Key Ideas and Details What message about life does the author suggest in the first paragraph of the folk tale?

4. Key Ideas and Details What **universal theme** is revealed in the story, just after the wife's donkey ears disappear?

5. Key Ideas and Details Which of the couple's actions best show the theme?

Vocabulary

Acquisition and Use Answer each question, using your knowledge of the italicized words. Explain your answer.

1. Would *greed* motivate a person to donate to charity?

2. If you *embraced* someone, did you show affection?

3. If you had *scarcely* enough food, would you share it?

4. If you repeat what you did wrong yesterday, can you say your *repentance* is complete?

5. If you feel *covetousness,* are you content?

Word Study Use context and what you know about the **Latin root -pen-** to explain your answer to each question

1. What is the purpose of our government's *penal* system?

2. Why would a person want to *repent*?

Word Study

The **Latin root -pen-** means "punishment" or "pain."

Apply It Explain how the root -pen- contributes to the meaning of these words. Consult a dictionary if necessary.
penitentiary
repentance
penalize

How much do our communities shape us?

Writing About the Big Question

In the story, a character's wish has a negative effect on his family and his farm. Use the following sentence starter to help you develop your ideas about the Big Question.

One person's actions can affect others in his **family** and **community** because _____.

While You Read Think about how Maibon's actions impact his family and his community.

Vocabulary

Read each word and its definition. Decide whether you know the word well, know it a little bit, or do not know it at all. After you read, see how your knowledge of each word has increased.

- **feeble** (fē´ bəl) *adj.* weak (p. 943) *The woman was feeble after so many days without food.* feebly *adv.* feebleness *n.*

- **vanished** (va´ nisht) *v.* disappeared (p. 945) *The magician vanished from sight in a cloud of smoke.* vanish *v.*

- **plight** (plīt) *n.* awkward, sad, or dangerous situation (p. 945) *Lisa's plight was our problem, too.*

- **jubilation** (joo´ bə lā´ shən) *n.* great joy; triumph (p. 947) *I could sense Frank's pure jubilation at winning the competition.* jubilated *v.* jubilant *adj.* jubilee *n.*

- **rue** (roo) *v.* feel sorrow or regret for something (p. 947) *Ralph will always rue the day he teased my little sister!* rueful *adj.*

- **sown** (sōn) *v.* planted; scattered with seeds (p. 948) *After having sown her garden, Polly rested.* sow *v.* sowing *v.*

Word Study

The **Latin root -van-** means "empty."

In this story, the stone **vanished**, or disappeared, leaving an empty space.

Meet
Lloyd Alexander
(1924–2007)

Author of
THE STONE

Lloyd Alexander's parents were shocked when he told them that he wanted to become a writer. "My family pleaded with me to forget literature and do something sensible, such as find some sort of useful work," he recalls.

Home of the Imagination Alexander eventually became a successful author, after working in a bank, serving in World War II, and writing for a magazine. He wrote stories and novels about an imaginary kingdom called Prydain. "The Stone" takes place in Prydain, where fantastic happenings are a part of everyday life.

BACKGROUND FOR THE STORY

Stories About Wishes

For generations, stories about wishes—like "The Stone"—have been told all over the world. Many of these stories are about the problems that arise when a wish is granted. The moral of such stories is that people should be happy with the lives they have. These stories are remembered and passed on because they teach about life.

DID YOU KNOW?

Alexander considered authors such as William Shakespeare, Charles Dickens, and Mark Twain his best writing teachers.

THE STONE

Lloyd Alexander

There was a cottager named Maibon, and one day he was driving down the road in his horse and cart when he saw an old man hobbling along, so frail and feeble he doubted the poor soul could go many more steps. Though Maibon offered to take him in the cart, the old man refused; and Maibon went his way home, shaking his head over such a pitiful sight, and said to his wife, Modrona:

"Ah, ah, what a sorry thing it is to have your bones creaking and cracking, and dim eyes, and dull wits. When I think this might come to me, too! A fine, strong-armed, sturdy-legged fellow like me? One day to go tottering, and have his teeth rattling in his head, and live on porridge, like a baby? There's no fate worse in all the world."

"There is," answered Modrona, "and that would be to have neither teeth nor porridge. Get on with you, Maibon, and stop borrowing trouble. Hoe your field or you'll have no crop to harvest, and no food for you, nor me, nor the little ones."

◀ **Critical Viewing**
What impression of old age is conveyed by this picture? **[Support]**

✓ Reading Check
Why is Maibon upset?

Setting a Purpose
At what rate would you read this descriptive passage? Why?

Sighing and grumbling, Maibon did as his wife bade him. Although the day was fair and cloudless, he took no pleasure in it. His ax-blade was notched, the wooden handle splintery; his saw had lost its edge; and his hoe, once shining new, had begun to rust. None of his tools, it seemed to him, cut or chopped or delved[1] as well as they once had done.

"They're as worn out as that old codger I saw on the road," Maibon said to himself. He squinted up at the sky. "Even the sun isn't as bright as it used to be, and doesn't warm me half as well. It's gone threadbare as my cloak. And no wonder, for it's been there longer than I can remember. Come to think of it, the moon's been looking a little wilted around the edges, too.

"As for me," went on Maibon, in dismay, "I'm in even a worse state. My appetite's faded, especially after meals. Mornings, when I wake, I can hardly keep myself from yawning. And at night, when I go to bed, my eyes are so heavy I can't hold them open. If that's the way things are now, the older I grow, the worse it will be!" •

In the midst of his complaining, Maibon glimpsed something bouncing and tossing back and forth beside a fallen tree in a corner of the field. Wondering if one of his piglets had squeezed out of the sty and gone rooting for

---

1. delved (delvd) v. dug.

acorns, Maibon hurried across the turf. Then he dropped his ax and gaped in astonishment.

There, struggling to free his leg which had been caught under the log, lay a short, thickset figure: a dwarf with red hair bristling in all directions beneath his round, close-fitting leather cap. At the sight of Maibon, the dwarf squeezed shut his bright red eyes and began holding his breath. After a moment, the dwarf's face went redder than his hair; his cheeks puffed out and soon turned purple. Then he opened one eye and blinked rapidly at Maibon, who was staring at him, speechless.

"What," snapped the dwarf, "you can still see me?"

"That I can," replied Maibon, more than ever puzzled, "and I can see very well you've got yourself tight as a wedge under that log, and all your kicking only makes it worse."

At this, the dwarf blew out his breath and shook his fists. "I can't do it!" he shouted. "No matter how I try! I can't make myself invisible! Everyone in my family can disappear—Poof! Gone! Vanished! But not me! Not Doli! Believe me, if I could have done, you never would have found me in such a plight. Worse luck! Well, come on. Don't stand there goggling like an idiot. Help me get loose!"

At this sharp command, Maibon began tugging and heaving at the log. Then he stopped, wrinkled his brow, and scratched his head, saying:

"Well, now, just a moment, friend. The way you look, and all your talk about turning yourself invisible—I'm thinking you might be one of the Fair Folk."

"Oh, clever!" Doli retorted. "Oh, brilliant! Great clodhopper! Giant beanpole! Of course I am! What else! Enough gabbling. Get a move on. My leg's going to sleep."

"If a man does the Fair Folk a good turn," cried Maibon, his excitement growing, "it's told they must do one for him."

"I knew sooner or later you'd come round to that," grumbled the dwarf. "That's the way of it with you ham-handed, heavy-footed oafs. Time was, you humans got along well with us. But nowadays, you no sooner see a Fair Folk than it's grab, grab, grab! Gobble, gobble, gobble! Grant my wish! Give me this, give me that! As if we had nothing better to do!

"Yes, I'll give you a favor," Doli went on. "That's the rule,

Vocabulary
vanished (va´ nisht) *v.* disappeared

plight (plīt) *n.* awkward, sad, or dangerous situation

Universal Theme
What problem does Maibon face?

Reading Check
What is unusual about Doli?

I'm obliged to. Now, get on with it."

Hearing this, Maibon pulled and pried and chopped away at the log as fast as he could, and soon freed the dwarf.

Doli heaved a sigh of relief, rubbed his shin, and cocked a red eye at Maibon, saying:

"All right. You've done your work, you'll have your reward. What do you want? Gold, I suppose. That's the usual. Jewels? Fine clothes? Take my advice, go for something practical. A hazelwood twig to help you find water if your well ever goes dry? An ax that never needs sharpening? A cook pot always brimming with food?"

"None of those!" cried Maibon. He bent down to the dwarf and whispered eagerly, "But I've heard tell that you Fair Folk have magic stones that can keep a man young forever. That's what I want. I claim one for my reward."

Universal Theme
Why is Doli frustrated by Maibon and other humans?

Doli snorted. "I might have known you'd pick something like that. As to be expected, you humans have it all muddled. There's nothing can make a man young again. That's even beyond the best of our skills. Those stones you're babbling about? Well, yes, there are such things. But greatly overrated. All they'll do is keep you from growing any older."

"Just as good!" Maibon exclaimed. "I want no more than that!"

Doli hesitated and frowned. "Ah—between the two of us, take the cook pot. Better all around. Those stones—we'd sooner not give them away. There's a difficulty—"

"Because you'd rather keep them for yourselves," Maibon broke in. "No, no, you shan't cheat me of my due. Don't put me off with excuses. I told you what I want, and that's what I'll have. Come, hand it over and not another word."

Doli shrugged and opened a leather pouch that hung from his belt. He spilled a number of brightly colored pebbles into his palm, picked out one of the larger stones, and handed it to Maibon. The dwarf then jumped up, took to his heels, raced across the field, and disappeared into a thicket. •

Laughing and crowing over his good fortune and his cleverness, Maibon hurried back to the cottage. There, he told his wife what had happened, and showed her the stone he had claimed from the Fair Folk.

"As I am now, so I'll always be!" Maibon declared, flexing his arms and thumping his chest. "A fine figure of a man! Oho, no gray beard and wrinkled brow for me!"

Instead of sharing her husband's jubilation, Modrona flung up her hands and burst out:

"Maibon, you're a greater fool than ever I supposed! And selfish into the bargain! You've turned down treasures! You didn't even ask that dwarf for so much as new jackets for the children! Nor a new apron for me! You could have had the roof mended. Or the walls plastered. No, a stone is what you ask for! A bit of rock no better than you'll dig up in the cow pasture!"

Crestfallen[2] and sheepish, Maibon began thinking his wife was right, and the dwarf had indeed given him no more than a common field stone.

"Eh, well, it's true," he stammered, "I feel no different than I did this morning, no better nor worse, but every way the same. That redheaded little wretch! He'll rue the day if I ever find him again!"

So saying, Maibon threw the stone into the fireplace. That night he grumbled his way to bed, dreaming revenge on the dishonest dwarf.

Next morning, after a restless night, he yawned, rubbed his eyes, and scratched his chin. Then he sat bolt upright in bed, patting his cheeks in amazement.

"My beard!" he cried, tumbling out and hurrying to tell his wife. "It hasn't grown! Not by a hair! Can it be the dwarf didn't cheat me after all?"

"Don't talk to me about beards," declared his wife as

Vocabulary
jubilation
(jōō′ bə lā′ shən) *n.* great joy; triumph

rue (rōō) *v.* Feel sorrow or regret for something

Setting a Purpose
How does your reading rate change when you read dialogue? Explain.

Reading Check
Why does Maibon's wife say he's a fool?

---

2. crestfallen (krest′ fôl′ ən) *adj.* made sad or humble; disheartened.

Maibon went to the fireplace, picked out the stone, and clutched it safely in both hands. "There's trouble enough in the chicken roost. Those eggs should have hatched by now, but the hen is still brooding on her nest."

"Let the chickens worry about that," answered Maibon. "Wife, don't you see what a grand thing's happened to me? I'm not a minute older than I was yesterday. Bless that generous-hearted dwarf!"

"Let me lay hands on him and I'll bless him," retorted Modrona. "That's all well and good for you. But what of me? You'll stay as you are, but I'll turn old and gray, and worn and wrinkled, and go doddering into my grave! And what of our little ones? They'll grow up and have children of their own. And grandchildren, and great-grandchildren. And you, younger than any of them. What a foolish sight you'll be!"

But Maibon, gleeful over his good luck, paid his wife no heed, and only tucked the stone deeper into his pocket. Next day, however, the eggs had still not hatched.

"And the cow!" Modrona cried. "She's long past due to calve, and no sign of a young one ready to be born!"

"Don't bother me with cows and chickens," replied Maibon. "They'll all come right, in time. As for time, I've got all the time in the world!"

Having no appetite for breakfast, Maibon went out into the field. Of all the seeds he had sown there, however, he was surprised to see not one had sprouted. The field, which by now should have been covered with green shoots, lay bare and empty. •

"Eh, things do seem a little late these days," Maibon said to himself. "Well, no hurry. It's that much less for me to do. The wheat isn't growing, but neither are the weeds."

Some days went by and still the eggs had not hatched, the cow had not calved, the wheat had not sprouted. And now Maibon saw that his apple tree showed no sign of even the smallest, greenest fruit.

"Maibon, it's the fault of that stone!" wailed his wife. "Get rid of the thing!"

"Nonsense," replied Maibon. "The season's slow, that's all."

Nevertheless, his wife kept at him and kept at him so much that Maibon at last, and very reluctantly, threw the stone out the cottage window. Not too far, though, for he

Vocabulary
sown (sōn) *v.* planted; scattered with seeds

▶ **Critical Viewing**
Find three details that suggest that the people in this picture lead a life similar to that of Maibon and his wife. **[Support]**

had it in the back of his mind to go later and find it again.

Next morning he had no need to go looking for it, for there was the stone sitting on the window ledge.

"You see?" said Maibon to his wife. "Here it is back again. So, it's a gift meant for me to keep."

"Maibon!" cried his wife. "Will you get rid of it! We've had nothing but trouble since you brought it into the house. Now the baby's fretting and fuming. Teething, poor little thing. But not a tooth to be seen! Maibon, that stone's bad luck and I want no part of it!"

Protesting it was none of his doing that the stone had come back, Maibon carried it into the vegetable patch. He dug a hole, not a very deep one, and put the stone into it.

Next day, there was the stone above ground, winking and glittering.

"Maibon!" cried his wife. "Once and for all, if you care for your family, get rid of that cursed thing!"

Seeing no other way to keep peace in the household, Maibon regretfully and unwillingly took the stone and threw it down the well, where it splashed into the water and sank from sight.

But that night, while he was trying vainly to sleep, there came such a rattling and clattering that Maibon clapped his hands over his ears, jumped out of bed, and went stumbling into the yard. At the well, the bucket was jiggling back and forth and up and down at the end of the rope;

✔ Reading Check
What is the stone doing to everything on Maibon's farm?

The Stone **949**

Literature Connection

Rocks and Roles

Stones play a role in many stories. For example, in Aesop's fable "The Crow and the Pitcher," a thirsty crow tries to drink from a pitcher, but the water is too far down for his beak to reach. After much thought, the crow solves his problem by dropping pebbles into the pitcher until the water rises enough that he can drink it. The moral: Necessity is the mother of invention.

In "The Stone," a rock causes problems rather than solving them when Maibon makes foolish choices.

Connect to the Literature

How might Maibon have used his stone wisely?

Setting a Purpose
At what rate would you read dialogue such as this? Why?

and in the bottom of the bucket was the stone.

Now Maibon began to be truly distressed, not only for the toothless baby, the calfless cow, the fruitless tree, and the hen sitting desperately on her eggs, but for himself as well.

"Nothing's moving along as it should," he groaned. "I can't tell one day from another. Nothing changes, there's nothing to look forward to, nothing to show for my work. Why sow if the seeds don't sprout? Why plant if there's never a harvest? Why eat if I don't get hungry? Why go to bed at night, or get up in the morning, or do anything at all? And the way it looks, so it will stay for ever and ever! I'll shrivel from boredom if nothing else!"

"Maibon," pleaded his wife, "for all our sakes, destroy the dreadful thing!"

Maibon tried now to pound the stone to dust with his heaviest mallet; but he could not so much as knock a chip from it. He put it against his grindstone without so much as scratching it. He set it on his anvil and belabored it with hammer and tongs, all to no avail.

At last he decided to bury the stone again, this time deeper than before. Picking up his shovel, he hurried to the field. But he suddenly halted and the shovel dropped from his hands. There, sitting cross-legged on a stump, was the dwarf. •

"You!" shouted Maibon, shaking his fist. "Cheat! Villain! Trickster! I did you a good turn, and see how you've repaid it!"

The dwarf blinked at the furious Maibon. "You mortals are an ungrateful crew. I gave you what you wanted."

"You should have warned me!" burst out Maibon.

"I did," Doli snapped back. "You wouldn't listen. No, you yapped and yammered, bound to have your way. I told you we didn't like to give away those stones. When you mortals get hold of one, you stay just as you are—but so does everything around you. Before you know it, you're mired in time like a rock in the mud. You take my advice.

Get rid of that stone as fast as you can."

"What do you think I've been trying to do?" blurted Maibon. "I've buried it, thrown it down the well, pounded it with a hammer—it keeps coming back to me!"

"That's because you really didn't want to give it up," Doli said. "In the back of your mind and the bottom of your heart, you didn't want to change along with the rest of the world. So long as you feel that way, the stone is yours."

"No, no!" cried Maibon. "I want no more of it. Whatever may happen, let it happen. That's better than nothing happening at all. I've had my share of being young, I'll take my share of being old. And when I come to the end of my days, at least I can say I've lived each one of them."

"If you mean that," answered Doli, "toss the stone onto the ground, right there at the stump. Then get home and be about your business."

© Spiral Review
Repetition What feeling is created by Maibon's repeated attempts to get rid of the stone?

Universal Theme
What message about change does Doli try to share with Maibon?

Maibon flung down the stone, spun around, and set off as fast as he could. When he dared at last to glance back over his shoulder, fearful the stone might be bouncing along at his heels, he saw no sign of it, nor of the redheaded dwarf.

Maibon gave a joyful cry, for at that same instant the fallow field was covered with green blades of wheat, the branches of the apple tree bent to the ground, so laden they were with fruit. He ran to the cottage, threw his arms around his wife and children, and told them the good news. The hen hatched her chicks, the cow bore her calf. And Maibon laughed with glee when he saw the first tooth in the baby's mouth.

Never again did Maibon meet any of the Fair Folk, and he was just as glad of it. He and his wife and children and grandchildren lived many years, and Maibon was proud of his white hair and long beard as he had been of his sturdy arms and legs.

"Stones are all right, in their way," said Maibon. "But the trouble with them is, they don't grow."

Critical Thinking

© 1. **Key Ideas and Details** **(a)** How does Maibon get the stone? **(b) Infer:** Why does Maibon choose the stone over other gifts?

© 2. **Key Ideas and Details** **(a)** What happens when Maibon tries to throw away the stone? **(b) Interpret:** Why can't Maibon get rid of the stone? **(c) Analyze:** What new belief finally allows Maibon to rid himself of the stone?

© 3. **Key Ideas and Details** Many messages in advertisements and on consumer products promote youthfulness. Do you think this is a good message? Why or why not?

© 4. **Integration of Knowledge and Ideas** **(a)** How might the stone have affected Maibon's neighbors if he had kept it? **(b)** Based on this story, what obligations do you think each individual has to his or her neighbors or community? Explain. *[Connect to the Big Question: How much do our communities shape us?]*

Cite textual evidence to support your responses.

Reading Skill: Setting a Purpose

1. Choose two passages from the folk tale. In a chart like this one, tell your **reading rate** for each passage.

Passage	Reading Rate

2. Use the information in your chart to explain when and why you changed your reading rate as you read.

Literary Analysis: Universal Theme

© **3. Key Ideas and Details** What lesson is Doli trying to teach Maibon when he says that the stones are greatly overrated?

© **4. Key Ideas and Details** What **universal theme** is revealed in the folk tale, just after Doli explains why the stone would not go away?

© **5. Key Ideas and Details** Which of Maibon's actions best shows the theme?

Vocabulary

© **Acquisition and Use** Using your knowledge of the italicized words, answer each question. Explain answers.

1. How could you solve a hungry person's *plight*?

2. Would you react with *jubilation* if you lost a contest?

3. Would you ask your *feeble* uncle to carry your suitcase?

4. Could you lend someone a book that has *vanished*?

5. Do you *rue* the day you met your best friend?

6. Can seeds be *sown* in the desert?

Word Study Use context and what you know about the **Latin root -van-** to explain your answer this question:

1. What are the dangers of having too much *vanity*?

2. How could the word *vain* be taken as an insult?

Word Study

The **Latin root -van-** means "empty."

Apply It Explain how the root -van- contributes to the meaning of these words. Consult a dictionary if necessary.

evanescence

vanquish

The Three Wishes • The Stone

Conventions: Semicolons and Colons

A **semicolon (;)** connects independent clauses that are connected in meaning. It also is used to separate items in a series if those items include commas or the word *and*.

A **colon (:)** is used after an independent clause to introduce a list of items, to show time, in the salutation of a business letter, and on warnings and labels.

Using Semicolons	Using Colons
The tomato is classified as a fruit; however, most people think of it as a vegetable.	You will need these items: a tent, boots, and a canteen.
I want to go to the Grand Canyon; my brother wants to see New York.	The train arrives at 4:55 P.M.
The recipe calls for two eggs, lightly beaten; a cup of flour, sifted; and one stick of butter, melted.	Warning: No swimming in this lake.

Practice A Correct each of the following sentences by adding colons or semicolons.

1. The woman had little to eat she gave most of it to the old man.

2. Please have the following pen, paper, and calculator.

3. The couple could have wished for good health gold, silver, and jewels or a long, happy life.

Reading Application Read or reread "The Stone." Identify an example of a semicolon used to connect independent clauses. Explain how the ideas in the clauses relate.

Practice B Rewrite the following sentences, correcting errors with colons and semicolons.

1. My appetite faded, especially after meals, I kept yawning, and I was tired.

2. It was late when he went to sleep he was not tired.

3. The couple wanted the following things, a child, riches, and good health.

Writing Application Expand the following sentence by adding a semicolon and a related clause. *Wishing often leads to trouble.*

PH WRITING COACH Further instruction and practice are available in *Prentice Hall Writing Coach*.

Writing

 **Common Core State Standards**

L.6.2, L.6.6; W.6.4, W.6.6, W.6.8; SL.6.1
[For the full wording of the standards, see page 932.]

© **Narrative Text** Write a **plot proposal**—a plan of story events—that illustrates the universal theme of "The Three Wishes" or "The Stone."

- Identify the universal theme your new story will convey.
- Brainstorm for a situation that illustrates the theme. Use your imagination and your own experience to develop an idea. Detail how the setting, characters, and plot will work together to reveal the theme.
- Write a brief description of the plot.
- When you finish writing, check to be sure that your proposal clearly illustrates the universal theme.

Grammar Application Use semicolons and colons correctly in your plot proposal.

Writing Workshop: *Work in Progress*

Prewriting for Research Choose a research topic from your Possible Topics. Choose one key word and build a word web. Save this Big Idea Web in your writing portfolio.

Use this prewriting activity to prepare for the **Writing Workshop** on page 988.

Research and Technology

© **Build and Present Knowledge** With a small group, prepare a **written and visual report** based on the folk tale you read.

- If you read "The Three Wishes," develop a report about the geographic features of Puerto Rico.
- If you read "The Stone," develop a report on human aging.

Follow these steps to complete the assignment:

- Decide what kind of research your group needs, then split the responsibilities among group members.
- Using the Internet, type keywords, such as "Puerto Rico geography" or "human aging process," into a Web browser to find information from multiple sources.
- Get together as a group to discuss what you have learned. Next, create an outline to organize your information.
- Decide how you will pair pictures with facts.
- Practice your presentation in your group before presenting to the rest of the class.

PHLit Online!
www.PHLitOnline.com
- Interactive graphic organizers
- Grammar tutorial
- Interactive journals

Test Practice: Reading

Purpose for Reading

Fiction Selection

Directions: *Read the selection. Then, answer the questions.*

A Sticky Situation: Dog Meets Porcupine

One bright day, Tom and Sultan set out for the woods near Tom's house. Sultan is a large dog full of lively curiosity. When Tom stopped to admire the view, Sultan trotted off. After a few minutes, Tom heard a loud yelp. He followed the sound until he found Sultan standing rigid and whimpering. The dog's face was bristling with porcupine quills. Tom picked up Sultan and carried him back to the house. Luckily, Tom is a doctor. He gave Sultan a shot to relax him. Then, working carefully, Tom broke each barbed quill and gently pulled it out. Sultan recovered. He remained curious, but he never went near a porcupine again.

1. What purpose for reading does the title suggest?
   A. to gain insight into an issue
   B. to explore two sides of an issue
   C. to be entertained
   D. to learn a new skill

2. Which of these would not be helpful in setting a purpose for reading?
   A. reading the title of the passage
   B. reading the first sentence of the passage
   C. noticing the writing style of the passage
   D. learning about the author's life

3. What is indicated by a preview of this passage?
   A. The text will focus on a relationship.
   B. The text will focus on a made-up story.
   C. The text will focus on a conflict.
   D. The text will focus on an interesting character.

4. You should read this passage at about the same rate as you would read
   A. a poem
   B. an encyclopedia article
   C. a short story
   D. a how-to manual

Writing for Assessment

In a few sentences, describe a photograph or illustration that could accompany the text to help a reader preview to set a purpose for reading this passage.

Nonfiction Selection

Directions: *Read the selection. Then, answer the questions.*

A Rodent Whose Name Means "Quill Pig"

What Is It and Where Does It Live? You may know this animal by its common name: porcupine. A porcupine is a prickly rodent found in many parts of the world. North American porcupines are tree-climbers who eat wood, fruit, and leaves.

What About Those Quills? A porcupine's quills protect it from enemies. The quills have needle-sharp tips and barbs, and usually lie flat in the porcupine's soft hair. When a porcupine is threatened, the quills stand up. You may have heard that a porcupine can shoot its quills at an enemy, but this is not true. The quills do come off easily, though, when they are touched. A porcupine can grow new quills. It is not unusual for a porcupine to have more than 30,000 quills.

1. Which of these is the most likely purpose for reading this passage?
  A. to be persuaded
  B. to be entertained
  C. to gain information
  D. to make a comparison

2. Which detail does not help you achieve your purpose for reading the passage?
  A. Porcupines are tree-climbers who eat wood, fruit, and leaves.
  B. When a porcupine is threatened, its quills stand up.
  C. You may have heard that a porcupine can shoot its quills.
  D. A porcupine can have more than 30,000 quills.

3. For what purpose might you preview this passage?
  A. to set a purpose for reading
  B. to learn all about porcupines
  C. to compare porcupines and rodents
  D. to learn about its publisher

4. For which sections of the passage would you slow your reading rate?
  A. the title
  B. the headings
  C. short, simple sentences
  D. complex sentences

Writing for Assessment

Connecting Across Texts
In a short paragraph, explain why you should use a different reading rate for each of these passages.

www.PHLitOnline.com
- Online practice
- Instant feedback

Reading for Information

Analyzing Expository and Functional Texts

Encyclopedia Entry

Street Map

**Common Core
State Standards**

Reading Informational Text
2. Determine a central idea of a text and how it is conveyed through particular details; provide a summary of the text distinct from personal opinions or judgments.

Language
4.b. Use common, grade-appropriate Greek or Latin affixes and roots as clues to the meaning of a word.
4.d. Verify the preliminary determination of the meaning of a word or phrase.

Reading Skill: Connect and Clarify Main Ideas

When you **connect and clarify main, or central, ideas,** you understand the links between information from multiple sources and related topics. For example, you can connect the main ideas given in a magazine article about camping with the main ideas in a "how-to" guide on pitching tents. In this lesson, you will read background information about how to use a map and apply your knowledge to correctly read a map.

Connecting Main Ideas	
Magazine Article "Camping"	• It is important to prepare for a safe trip. • You should know how to use equipment properly.
How-to Guide "Pitch a Tent"	• Be sure tent is in good condition. • Improper assembly can cause injury. • Assemble tent carefully, one piece at a time.
Connection	Two ways to stay safe on a camping trip are to check your tent's condition and learn how to safely and properly assemble it.

Content-Area Vocabulary

These words appear in the selections that follow. You may also encounter them in other content-area texts.

- **aeronautical** (er´ə nô´tə kəl) *adj.* related to the science of the design, manufacture, and operation of aircraft

- **contour maps** (kän´ to͞or´ maps) *n.* graphics that show the shapes and heights of land features in a certain area

- **scale** (skāl) *n.* proportion between the size of a plan, map, drawing, or model and the size of what it shows

Britannica Student Encyclopedia

How to Read a Road Map

> The main idea of the encyclopedia entry is presented here.

A globe is a small, round model of our round Earth, but maps of all or parts of the Earth are flat. Therefore only a globe can show distances, directions, and shapes as they really are. For most purposes, however, maps are more useful than globes. They can be larger and show more detail. They can be printed in books, such as in this encyclopedia. They can also be carried about easily, folded or rolled.

There are many kinds of maps and each kind tells a different story. For finding directions there are sea charts and aeronautical charts, railroad maps, road maps, and contour maps. Most common of all are the road maps used by automobile drivers.

When you unfold a road map, hold it so that you can read the words on it. North most likely will be at the top of the sheet, but you should check by looking for a direction arrow or a compass rose. If there is none, you can assume that north is at the top of the map.

If north is at the top, the right-hand edge is east, the left-hand edge is west, and south is at the bottom. When you spread a map on a table, turn it so that the map north is toward the north. Then the directions east and west on

your map will be east and west on the Earth. If you hang the map on a wall, try to hang it so that east is to the east as you face the map.

The mapmaker, like the architect, draws to scale. If he decides to make one inch (2.5 centimeters) represent 20 miles (32 kilometers), this must be true on every part of the map. If one inch represents 20 miles, one can easily figure the distance from point to point "as the crow flies." Since roads do not always follow a straight route, one must total the mileage shown on the map along the highways to calculate actual driving distance.

Many state road maps have separate maps of important cities. These maps are very small compared to the state map; but because they are drawn to a much larger scale, they can show streets, parks, and main buildings. The larger the scale, the more details a mapmaker can show.

> The information given here can be clarified by looking at a map of a city like the one shown on the next page.

Features:
- practical reference tool
- directions for cars, pedestrians, and cyclists
- community resources and sites

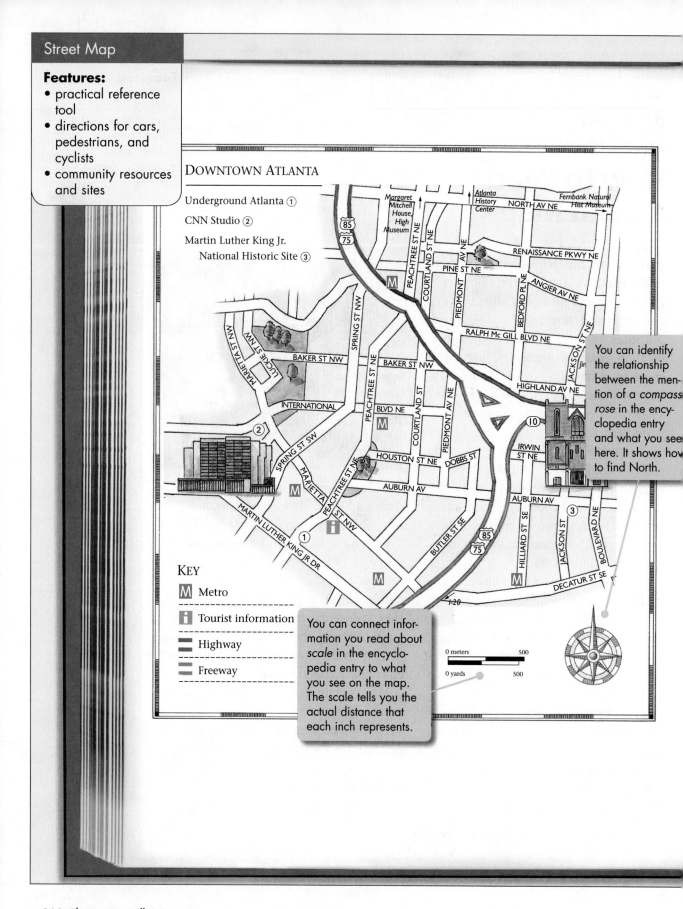

DOWNTOWN ATLANTA

Underground Atlanta ①

CNN Studio ②

Martin Luther King Jr.
   National Historic Site ③

KEY

M Metro

i Tourist information

Highway

Freeway

You can identify the relationship between the mention of a *compass rose* in the encyclopedia entry and what you see here. It shows how to find North.

You can connect information you read about *scale* in the encyclopedia entry to what you see on the map. The scale tells you the actual distance that each inch represents.

Comparing Expository and Functional Texts

1. Key Ideas and Details **(a)** State the central idea in the encyclopedia entry. **(b)** Write a summary of the text in which you explain the central idea and key details but do not express your opinion. **(c)** Explain how reading the encyclopedia entry with the street map helps you to **connect and clarify the main ideas**.

Content-Area Vocabulary

2. (a) The word *aeronautical* uses the Greek word part *aero-*, which means "air." Use your knowledge of *aero-* to define the following words: *aerodynamic, aerial.* **(b)** Use a dictionary to verify and, if necessary, correct your definitions.

Timed Writing

Explanatory Text: Write Directions

> **Audience**
> The assignment is to write directions for a classmate. Make sure to provide information that is easy to understand and follow.

> Review the encyclopedia entry for its main idea. Then, connect the information to write directions for a classmate who wants to walk from Underground Atlanta to the Martin Luther King Jr. Historic Site. Use the map of downtown Atlanta to write your directions. (25 minutes)

> **Academic Vocabulary**
> When you *review,* you look at something again to make sure you understand it. When you *connect* information from two sources, you identify relationships between ideas.

5-Minute Planner

Complete these steps before you begin to write:

1. Find the most important information in the encyclopedia entry. Then, find the starting and ending points on the Downtown Atlanta map.

2. Trace possible routes with a pencil to see which is the best route to follow. **TIP** When giving directions to others, use the simplest route with the fewest number of turns.

3. Assume that your classmate does not know Atlanta. Think of the best way to explain the route.

4. List the directions in steps, using north, south, east, or west to orient your friend.

Comparing Foreshadowing and Flashback

To develop exciting stories, writers may use a range of **plot techniques** and literary devices to tell the events in a story.

- **Foreshadowing** is the author's use of clues to hint at what might happen later in a story. For example, the description of a dark cloud in a story might foreshadow something bad that is about to happen. Foreshadowing helps build suspense, the quality that keeps you wondering what will happen next.

- A **flashback** is a scene that interrupts a story to describe an earlier event. Writers use flashback to show something about a character's past. For example, a flashback about a happy childhood journey might explain why an adult character loves to travel.

Plot Devices and Plot Structure Some plots move from the beginning to the end with no interruption. A diagram of such a plot would look like an orderly timeline. Devices such as flashback change a plot's structure by changing the sequence of events.

Flashback takes readers on a short trip to the past. Foreshadowing does not move the plot to the future, but it moves the reader's attention to possible future events. Foreshadowing also adds to a sense of completeness in a plot. First readers recognize a hint, then the event itself. Both devices can make the structure of a plot more interesting and more complex.

Compare the use of foreshadowing and flashback in "Lob's Girl" and "Jeremiah's Song" by using a chart such as the one shown.

Common Core State Standards

Reading Literature
5. Analyze how a particular sentence, chapter, scene, or stanza fits into the overall structure of a text and contributes to the development of the theme, setting, or plot.

Writing
2.a. Introduce a topic; organize ideas, concepts, and information, using strategies such as definition, classification, comparison/contrast, and cause/effect; include formatting, graphics, and multimedia when useful to aiding comprehension. *(Timed Writing)*

	Lob's Girl	Jeremiah's Song
Foreshadowing		
Flashback		

www.PHLitOnline.com

- Vocabulary flashcards
- Interactive journals
- More about the authors
- Selection audio
- Interactive graphic organizers

How much do our *communities* shape us?

Writing About the Big Question

The characters in both of these stories experience the death of someone dear to them. Use the following sentence starter to develop your ideas about the Big Question.

Living in a close **community** can help a person mourning a death because _____.

Meet the Authors

Joan Aiken (1924–2004)

Author of "Lob's Girl"

British author Joan Aiken began her writing career early—at the age of five! By her teens, she was a published author.

A Family of Writers Aiken's father was poet Conrad Aiken, and two of her sisters are professional writers. Fans of all ages enjoy reading her mysterious and unusual tales. Aiken once said, "Stories are like butterflies, which come fluttering out of nowhere, touch down for a brief instant, may be captured, may not, and then vanish into nowhere again."

Walter Dean Myers (b. 1937)

Author of "Jeremiah's Song"

By age five, Walter Dean Myers was reading a newspaper every day. In spite of this impressive start with words, Myers did not think that writing would be his career.

Writing From Life In his twenties, Myers won a writing contest. He has not stopped writing since—mostly about his heritage and his experiences growing up in Harlem, a part of New York City. Like the child in "Jeremiah's Song," Myers understands loss: He was three years old when his mother died.

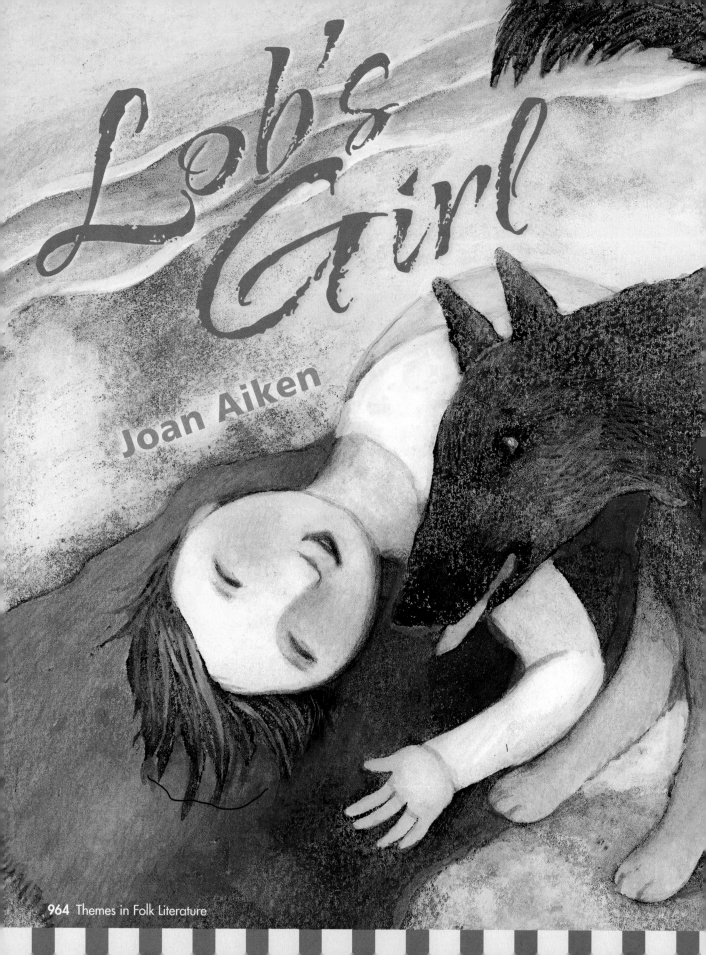

Lob's Girl

Joan Aiken

Some people choose their dogs, and some dogs choose their people. The Pengelly family had no say in the choosing of Lob; he came to them in the second way, and very decisively.

It began on the beach, the summer when Sandy was five, Don, her older brother, twelve, and the twins were three. Sandy was really Alexandra, because her grandmother had a beautiful picture of a queen in a diamond tiara and high collar of pearls. It hung by Granny Pearce's kitchen sink and was as familiar as the doormat. When Sandy was born everyone agreed that she was the living spit of the picture, and so she was called Alexandra and Sandy for short.

On this summer day she was lying peacefully reading a comic and not keeping an eye on the twins, who didn't need it because they were occupied in seeing which of them could wrap the most seaweed around the other one's legs. Father—Bert Pengelly—and Don were up on the Hard painting the bottom boards of the boat in which Father went fishing for pilchards. And Mother—Jean Pengelly—was getting ahead with making the Christmas puddings because she never felt easy in her mind if they weren't made and safely put away by the end of August. As usual, each member of the family was happily getting on with his or her own affairs. Little did they guess how soon this state of things would be changed by the large new member who was going to erupt into their midst.

Sandy rolled onto her back to make sure that the twins were not climbing on slippery rocks or getting cut off by the tide. At the same moment a large body struck her forcibly in the midriff and she was covered by flying sand. Instinctively she shut her eyes and felt the sand being wiped off her face by something that seemed like a warm, rough, damp flannel. She opened her eyes and looked. It was a tongue. Its owner was a large and bouncy young Alsatian, or German shepherd, with topaz eyes, black-tipped prick ears, a thick, soft coat, and a bushy black-tipped tail.

"*Lob!*" shouted a man farther up the beach. "Lob, come here!"

But Lob, as if trying to atone[1] for the surprise he had given her, went on licking the sand off Sandy's face,

---

1. **atone** (ə tōn´) *v.* make up for a wrong.

Vocabulary
decisively (dē sī´siv lē´)
adv. with determination

Foreshadowing and Flashback
Based on this hint that begins "Little did they guess," what do you think is going to happen in the story?

 **Reading Check**
How does Sandy meet Lob?

wagging his tail so hard while he kept on knocking up more clouds of sand. His owner, a gray-haired man with a limp, walked over as quickly as he could and seized him by the collar.

"I hope he didn't give you a fright?" the man said to Sandy. "He meant it in play—he's only young."

"Oh, no, I think he's *beautiful*." said Sandy truly. She picked up a bit of driftwood and threw it. Lob, whisking easily out of his master's grip, was after it like a sand-colored bullet. He came back with the stick, beaming, and gave it to Sandy. At the same time he gave himself, though no one else was aware of this at the time. But with Sandy, too, it was love at first sight, and when, after a lot more stick-throwing, she and the twins joined Father and Don to go home for tea, they cast many a backward glance at Lob being led firmly away by his master.

"I wish we could play with him every day." Tess sighed.

"Why can't we?" said Tim.

Sandy explained. "Because Mr. Dodsworth, who owns him, is from Liverpool, and he is only staying at the Fisherman's Arms till Saturday."

"Is Liverpool a long way off?"

"Right at the other end of England from Cornwall, I'm afraid."

It was a Cornish fishing village where the Pengelly family lived, with rocks and cliffs and a strip of beach and a little round harbor, and palm trees growing in the gardens of the little whitewashed stone houses. The village was approached by a narrow, steep, twisting hill-road, and guarded by a notice that said LOW GEAR FOR 1 ½ MILES, DANGEROUS TO CYCLISTS.

The Pengelly children went home to scones with Cornish cream and jam, thinking they had seen the last of Lob. But they were much mistaken. The whole family was

Foreshadowing and Flashback
What might this description of the road foreshadow?

▶ **Critical Viewing**
What details here are like the village described in the story? **[Connect]**

playing cards by the fire in the front room after supper when there was a loud thump and a crash of china in the kitchen.

"My Christmas puddings!" exclaimed Jean, and ran out.

"Did you put TNT in them, then?" her husband said.

But it was Lob, who, finding the front door shut, had gone around to the back and bounced in through the open kitchen window, where the puddings were cooling on the sill. Luckily only the smallest was knocked down and broken.

Lob stood on his hind legs and plastered Sandy's face with licks. Then he did the same for the twins, who shrieked with joy.

"Where does this friend of yours come from?" inquired Mr. Pengelly.

"He's staying at the Fisherman's Arms—I mean his owner is."

"Then he must go back there. Find a bit of string, Sandy, to tie to his collar."

"I wonder how he found his way here," Mrs. Pengelly said, when the reluctant Lob had been led whining away and Sandy had explained about their afternoon's game on the beach. "Fisherman's Arms is right around the other side of the harbor."

Lob's owner scolded him and thanked Mr. Pengelly for bringing him back. Jean Pengelly warned the children that they had better not encourage Lob any more if they met him on the beach, or it would only lead to more trouble. So they dutifully took no notice of him the next day until he spoiled their good **resolutions** by dashing up to them with joyful barks, wagging his tail so hard that he winded Tess and knocked Tim's legs from under him.

They had a happy day, playing on the sand.

The next day was Saturday. Sandy had found out that Mr. Dodsworth was to catch the half-past-nine train. She went out secretly, down to the station, nodded to Mr. Hoskins, the stationmaster, who wouldn't dream of charging any local for a platform ticket, and climbed up on the footbridge that led over the tracks. She didn't want to be seen, but she did want to see. She saw Mr. Dodsworth get on the train, accompanied by an unhappy-looking Lob with

"I wish we could play with him every day."

Vocabulary
resolutions
(rez´ ə lo͞o´ shənz) *n.* intentions; things decided

Reading Check
What causes the crash in the Pengellys' kitchen?

drooping ears and tail. Then she saw the train slide away
out of sight around the next headland, with a melancholy
wail that sounded like Lob's last good-bye.

Sandy wished she hadn't had the idea of coming to the
station. She walked home miserably, with her shoulders
hunched and her hands in her pockets. For the rest of the
day she was so cross and unlike herself that Tess and Tim
were quite surprised, and her mother gave her a dose of
senna.

A week passed. Then, one evening, Mrs. Pengelly and the
younger children were in the front room playing snakes
and ladders. Mr. Pengelly and Don had gone fishing on the
evening tide. If your father is a fisherman, he will never be
home at the same time from one week to the next.

Suddenly, history repeating itself, there was a crash
from the kitchen. Jean Pengelly leaped up, crying, "My
blackberry jelly!" She and the children had spent the
morning picking and the afternoon boiling fruit.

But Sandy was ahead of her mother. With flushed cheeks
and eyes like stars she had darted into the kitchen, where
she and Lob were hugging one another in a frenzy of joy.

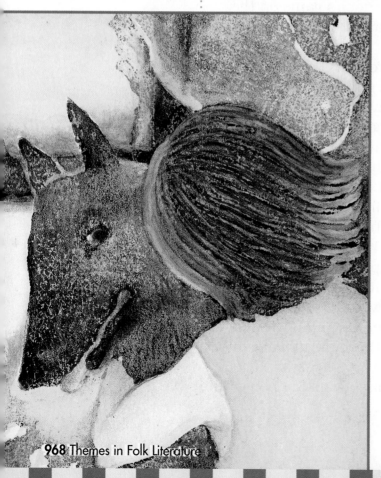

About a yard of his tongue was out,
and he was licking every part of her
that he could reach.

"Good heavens!" exclaimed Jean.
"How in the world did *he* get here?"

"He must have walked," said
Sandy. "Look at his feet."

They were worn, dusty, and tarry.
One had a cut on the pad.

"They ought to be bathed," said
Jean Pengelly. "Sandy, run a bowl of
warm water while I get disinfectant."

"What'll we do about him,
Mother?" said Sandy anxiously.

Mrs. Pengelly looked at her
daughter's pleading eyes and
sighed.

"He must go back to his owner, of
course," she said, making her voice
firm. "Your dad can get the address

from the Fisherman's tomorrow, and phone him or send a telegram. In the meantime he'd better have a long drink and a good meal."

Lob was very grateful for the drink and the meal, and made no objection to having his feet washed. Then he flopped down on the hearthrug and slept in front of the fire they had lit because it was a cold, wet evening, with his head on Sandy's feet. He was a very tired dog. He had walked all the way from Liverpool to Cornwall, which is more than four hundred miles.

The next day Mr. Pengelly phoned Lob's owner, and the following morning Mr. Dodsworth arrived off the night train, decidedly put out, to take his pet home. That parting was worse than the first. Lob whined, Don walked out of the house, the twins burst out crying, and Sandy crept up to her bedroom afterward and lay with her face pressed into the quilt, feeling as if she were bruised all over.

Jean Pengelly took them all into Plymouth to see the circus on the next day and the twins cheered up a little, but even the hour's ride in the train each way and the Liberty horses and performing seals could not cure Sandy's sore heart.

She need not have bothered, though. In ten days' time Lob was back—limping this time, with a torn ear and a patch missing out of his furry coat, as if he had met and tangled with an enemy or two in the course of his four-hundred-mile walk.

Bert Pengelly rang up Liverpool again. Mr. Dodsworth, when he answered, sounded weary. He said, "That dog has already cost me two days that I can't spare away from my work—plus endless time in police stations and drafting newspaper advertisements. I'm too old for these ups and downs. I think we'd better face the fact, Mr. Pengelly, that it's your family he wants to stay with—that is, if you want to have him."

Bert Pengelly gulped. He was not a rich man; and Lob was a pedigreed dog. He said cautiously, "How much would you be asking for him?"

"Good heavens, man, I'm not suggesting I'd sell him to you. You must have him as a gift. Think of the train fares I'll be saving. You'll be doing me a good turn."

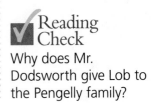

Reading Check

Why does Mr. Dodsworth give Lob to the Pengelly family?

"Is he a big eater?" Bert asked doubtfully.

By this time the children, breathless in the background listening to one side of this conversation, had realized what was in the wind and were dancing up and down with their hands clasped beseechingly.

"Oh, not for his size," Lob's owner assured Bert. "Two or three pounds of meat a day and some vegetables and gravy and biscuits—he does very well on that."

Alexandra's father looked over the telephone at his daughter's swimming eyes and trembling lips. He reached a decision. "Well, then, Mr. Dodsworth," he said briskly, "we'll accept your offer and thank you very much. The children will be overjoyed and you can be sure Lob has come to a good home. They'll look after him and see he gets enough exercise. But I can tell you," he ended firmly, "if he wants to settle in with us he'll have to learn to eat a lot of fish."

So that was how Lob came to live with the Pengelly family. Everybody loved him and he loved them all. But there was never any question who came first with him. He was Sandy's dog. He slept by her bed and followed her everywhere he was allowed.

Nine years went by, and each summer Mr. Dodsworth came back to stay at the Fisherman's Arms and call on his erstwhile dog. Lob always met him with recognition and dignified pleasure, accompanied him for a walk or two—but showed no signs of wishing to return to Liverpool. His place, he intimated,[2] was definitely with the Pengellys.

In the course of nine years Lob changed less than Sandy. As she went into her teens he became a little slower, a little stiffer, there was a touch of gray on his nose, but he was still a handsome dog. He and Sandy still loved one another devotedly.

One evening in October all the summer visitors had left, and the little fishing town looked empty and secretive. It was a wet, windy dusk. When the children came home from school—even the twins were at high school now, and Don was a full-fledged fisherman—Jean Pengelly said, "Sandy, your Aunt Rebecca says she's lonesome because Uncle Will Hoskins has gone out trawling, and she wants one of you to go and spend the evening with her. You go, dear; you can take your homework with you."

---

2. intimated (in´ tə māt´ əd) *v.* hinted; made known indirectly.

Sandy looked far from enthusiastic.

"Can I take Lob with me?"

"You know Aunt Becky doesn't really like dogs—Oh, very well." Mrs. Pengelly sighed. "I suppose she'll have to put up with him as well as you."

Reluctantly Sandy tidied herself, took her schoolbag, put on the damp raincoat she had just taken off, fastened Lob's lead to his collar, and set off to walk through the dusk to Aunt Becky's cottage, which was five minutes' climb up the steep hill.

The wind was howling through the shrouds of boats drawn up on the Hard.

Foreshadowing and Flashback
What do you think the descriptions in these paragraphs foreshadow?

"Put some cheerful music on, do," said Jean Pengelly to the nearest twin. "Anything to drown that wretched sound while I make your dad's supper." So Don, who had just come in, put on some rock music, loud. Which was why the Pengellys did not hear the truck hurtle down the hill and crash against the post office wall a few minutes later.

Dr. Travers was driving through Cornwall with his wife, taking a late holiday before patients began coming down with winter colds and flu. He saw the sign that said STEEP HILL. LOW GEAR FOR 1 ½ MILES. Dutifully he changed into second gear.

"We must be nearly there," said his wife, looking out of her window. "I noticed a sign on the coast road that said the Fisherman's Arms was two miles. What a narrow, dangerous hill! But the cottages are very pretty—Oh, Frank, stop, *stop*! There's a child, I'm sure it's a child—by the wall over there!"

Dr. Travers jammed on his brakes and brought the car to a stop. A little stream ran down by the road in a shallow stone culvert, and half in the water lay something that

▲ **Critical Viewing**
What elements of danger do you see in this picture? **[Analyze]**

 **Reading Check**
Where are Sandy and Lob going?

looked, in the dusk, like a pile of clothes—or was it the body of the child? Mrs. Travers was out of the car in a flash, but her husband was quicker.

"Don't touch her, Emily!" he said sharply. "She's been hit. Can't be more than a few minutes. Remember that truck that overtook us half a mile back, speeding like the devil? Here, quick, go into that cottage and phone for an ambulance. The girl's in a bad way. I'll stay here and do what I can to stop the bleeding. Don't waste a minute."

Doctors are expert at stopping dangerous bleeding, for they know the right places to press. This Dr. Travers was able to do, but he didn't dare do more; the girl was lying in a queerly crumpled heap, and he guessed she had a number of bones broken and that it would be highly dangerous to move her. He watched her with great concentration, wondering where the truck had got to and what other damage it had done.

Mrs. Travers was very quick. She had seen plenty of accident cases and knew the importance of speed. The first cottage she tried had a phone; in four minutes she was back, and in six an ambulance was wailing down the hill.

Its attendants lifted the child onto a stretcher as carefully as if she were made of fine thistledown. The ambulance sped off to Plymouth—for the local cottage hospital did not take serious accident cases—and Dr. Travers went down to the police station to report what he had done.

He found that the police already knew about the speeding truck—which had suffered from loss of brakes and ended up with its radiator halfway through the post-office wall. The driver was concussed and shocked, but the police thought he was the only person injured—until Dr. Travers told his tale.

At half-past nine that night Aunt Rebecca Hoskins was sitting by her fire thinking aggrieved[3] thoughts about the inconsiderateness of nieces who were asked to supper and never turned up, when she was startled by a neighbor, who burst in, exclaiming, "Have you heard about Sandy Pengelly, then, Mrs. Hoskins? Terrible thing, poor little soul, and they don't know if she's likely to live. Police have got the truck driver that hit her—ah, it didn't ought to be allowed,

---

3. **aggrieved** (ə grēvd´) adj. offended; wronged.

speeding through the place like that at umpty miles an hour, they ought to jail him for life—not that that'd be any comfort for poor Bert and Jean."

Horrified, Aunt Rebecca put on a coat and went down to her brother's house. She found the family with white shocked faces; Bert and Jean were about to drive off to the hospital where Sandy had been taken, and the twins were crying bitterly. Lob was nowhere to be seen. But Aunt Rebecca was not interested in dogs; she did not inquire about him.

"Thank the Lord you've come, Beck," said her brother. "Will you stay the night with Don and the twins? Don's out looking for Lob and heaven knows when we'll be back; we may get a bed with Jean's mother in Plymouth."

"Oh, if only I'd never invited the poor child," wailed Mrs. Hoskins. But Bert and Jean hardly heard her.

That night seemed to last forever. The twins cried themselves to sleep. Don came home very late and grim-faced. Bert and Jean sat in a waiting room of the Western Counties Hospital, but Sandy was unconscious, they were told, and she remained so. All that could be done for her was done. She was given transfusions to replace all the blood she had lost. The broken bones were set and put in slings and cradles.

"Is she a healthy girl? Has she a good constitution?" the emergency doctor asked.

"Aye, doctor, she is that," Bert said hoarsely. The lump in Jean's throat prevented her from answering; she merely nodded.

"Then she ought to have a chance. But I won't conceal from you that her condition is very serious, unless she shows signs of coming out from this coma."

But as hour succeeded hour, Sandy showed no signs of recovering consciousness. Her parents sat in the waiting room with haggard faces; sometimes one of them would go to telephone the family at home, or to try to get a little sleep at the home of Granny Pearce, not far away.

At noon next day Dr. and Mrs. Travers went to the Pengelly cottage to inquire how Sandy was doing, but the report was gloomy: "Still in a very serious condition."

Foreshadowing and Flashback
What clues in these paragraphs suggest that Lob may not be safe?

"She's been hit. Can't be more than a few minutes."

Reading Check
How does Sandy's family react to her condition?

Foreshadowing and Flashback

What do you learn about Sandy from the flashback in this paragraph?

The twins were miserably unhappy. They forgot that they had sometimes called their elder sister bossy and only remembered how often she had shared her pocket money with them, how she read to them and took them for picnics and helped with their homework. Now there was no Sandy, no Mother and Dad, Don went around with a gray, shuttered face, and worse still, there was no Lob.

The Western Counties Hospital is a large one, with dozens of different departments and five or six connected buildings, each with three or four entrances. By that afternoon it became noticeable that a dog seemed to have taken up position outside the hospital, with the fixed intention of getting in. Patiently he would try first one entrance and then another, all the way around, and then begin again. Sometimes he would get a little way inside, following a visitor, but animals were, of course, forbidden, and he was always kindly but firmly turned out again. Sometimes the guard at the main entrance gave him a pat or offered him a bit of sandwich—he looked so wet and beseeching and desperate. But he never ate the sandwich. No one seemed to own him or to know where he came from; Plymouth is a large city and he might have belonged to anybody.

At tea time Granny Pearce came through the pouring rain to bring a flask of hot tea with brandy in it to her daughter and son-in-law. Just as she reached the main entrance the guard was gently but forcibly shoving out a large, agitated, soaking-wet Alsatian dog.

"No, old fellow, you can *not* come in. Hospitals are for people, not for dogs."

Foreshadowing and Flashback

What do you think is foreshadowed when Granny Pearce recognizes the dog?

"Why, bless me," exclaimed old Mrs. Pearce. "That's Lob! Here, Lob, Lobby boy!"

Lob ran to her, whining. Mrs. Pearce walked up to the desk.

"I'm sorry, madam, you can't bring that dog in here," the guard said.

Mrs. Pearce was a very determined old lady. She looked the porter in the eye.

"Now, see here, young man. That dog has walked twenty miles from St. Killan to get to my granddaughter. Heaven knows how he knew she was here, but it's plain he knows. And he ought to have his rights! He ought to get to see her!"

Do you know," she went on, bristling, "that dog has walked the length of England—*twice*—to be with that girl? And you think you can keep him out with your fiddling rules and regulations?"

"I'll have to ask the medical officer," the guard said weakly.

"You do that, young man." Granny Pearce sat down in a determined manner, shutting her umbrella, and Lob sat patiently dripping at her feet. Every now and then he shook his head, as if to dislodge something heavy that was tied around his neck.

Presently a tired, thin, intelligent-looking man in a white coat came downstairs, with an impressive, silver-haired man in a dark suit, and there was a low-voiced discussion. Granny Pearce eyed them, biding her time.

"Frankly. . . not much to lose," said the older man. The man in the white coat approached Granny Pearce.

"It's strictly against every rule, but as it's such a serious case we are making an exception," he said to her quietly. "But only *outside* her bedroom door—and only for a moment or two."

Without a word, Granny Pearce rose and stumped upstairs. Lob followed close to her skirts, as if he knew his hope lay with her.

They waited in the green-floored corridor outside Sandy's room. The door was half shut. Bert and Jean were inside. Everything was terribly quiet. A nurse came out. The white-coated man asked her something and she shook her head. She had left the door ajar and through it could now be seen a high, narrow bed with a lot of gadgets around it. Sandy lay there, very flat under the covers, very still. Her head was turned away. All Lob's attention was riveted on the bed. He strained toward it, but Granny Pearce clasped his collar firmly.

"I've done a lot for you, my boy, now you behave yourself," she whispered grimly. Lob let out a faint whine, anxious and pleading.

Reading Check

How does Lob get into the hospital to see Sandy?

▲ **Critical Viewing**
What details of this final image reinforce the relationship between Sandy and Lob? **[Analyze]**

At the sound of that whine Sandy stirred just a little. She sighed and moved her head the least fraction. Lob whined again. And then Sandy turned her head right over. Her eyes opened, looking at the door.

"Lob?" she murmured—no more than a breath of sound. "Lobby, boy?"

The doctor by Granny Pearce drew a quick, sharp breath. Sandy moved her left arm—the one that was not broken—from below the covers and let her hand dangle down, feeling, as she always did in the mornings, for Lob's furry head. The doctor nodded slowly.

"All right," he whispered. "Let him go to the bedside. But keep a hold of him."

Granny Pearce and Lob moved to the bedside. Now she could see Bert and Jean, white-faced and shocked, on the far side of the bed. But she didn't look at them. She looked at the smile on her granddaughter's face as the groping fingers found Lob's wet ears and gently pulled them. "Good boy," whispered Sandy, and fell asleep again.

Granny Pearce led Lob out into the passage again. There she let go of him and he ran off swiftly down the stairs. She would have followed him, but Bert and Jean had come out into the passage, and she spoke to Bert fiercely.

"I don't know why you were so foolish as not to bring the dog before! Leaving him to find the way here himself—"

"But, Mother!" said Jean Pengelly. "That can't have been Lob. What a chance to take! Suppose Sandy hadn't—" She stopped, with her handkerchief pressed to her mouth.

"Not Lob? I've known that dog nine years! I suppose I ought to know my own granddaughter's dog?"

"Listen, Mother," said Bert. "Lob was killed by the same truck that hit Sandy. Don found him—when he went to look for Sandy's schoolbag. He was—he was dead. Ribs all smashed. No question of that. Don told me on the phone—he and Will Hoskins rowed a half mile out to sea and sank the dog with a lump of concrete tied to his collar. Poor old boy. Still—he was getting on. Couldn't have lasted forever."

"*Sank him at sea?* Then what—?"

Slowly old Mrs. Pearce, and then the other two, turned to look at the trail of dripping-wet footprints that led down the hospital stairs.

In the Pengellys' garden they have a stone, under the palm tree. It says: "Lob. Sandy's dog. Buried at sea."

Foreshadowing and Flashback
Why does the author include this flashback to an earlier event?

Spiral Review
Theme Is the message of this story *love conquers all*? Explain.

Critical Thinking

Cite textual evidence to support your responses.

1. **Key Ideas and Details (a)** How do Sandy and her family first meet Lob? **(b) Speculate:** Why does Lob travel more than 400 miles to the Pengellys' house? **(c) Analyze:** How does Sandy feel about Lob? Support your answer.

2. **Key Ideas and Details (a)** Why does Mr. Dodsworth give Lob to the Pengellys? **(b) Infer:** How do you think Mr. Dodsworth feels about giving the dog away? Explain.

3. **Key Ideas and Details (a)** What happens when Sandy goes to visit her aunt? **(b) Interpret:** How does Lob help Sandy at the hospital? **(c) Speculate:** What does Lob's mysterious return suggest about his bond with Sandy?

4. **Key Ideas and Details (a) Evaluate:** Why do you think the author chose to end the story in such an unusual way? **(b) Take a Position:** How important is the relationship between people and animals? Explain.

5. **Integration of Knowledge and Ideas** When Sandy gains consciousness, she will realize that Lob has died. **(a)** What might community members do for Sandy when she regains consciousness? **(b)** Will they be helpful? Explain. *[Connect to the Big Question: How much do our communities shape us?]*

Jeremiah's Song
Walter Dean Myers

I knowed my cousin Ellie was gonna be mad when Macon Smith come around to the house. She didn't have no use for Macon even when things was going right, and when Grandpa Jeremiah was fixing to die I just knowed she wasn't gonna be liking him hanging around. Grandpa Jeremiah raised Ellie after her folks died and they used to be real close. Then she got to go on to college and when she come back the first year she was different. She didn't want to hear all them stories he used to tell her anymore. Ellie said the stories wasn't true, and that's why she didn't want to hear them.

I didn't know if they was true or not. Tell the truth I didn't think much on it either way, but I liked to hear them stories. Grandpa Jeremiah said they wasn't stories anyway, they was songs.

"They the songs of my people," he used to say.

I didn't see how they was songs, not regular songs anyway. Every little thing we did down in Curry seemed to matter to Ellie that first summer she come home from college. You couldn't do nothin' that was gonna please her. She didn't even come to church much. 'Course she come on Sunday or everybody would have had a regular fit, but she didn't come on

▲ **Critical Viewing**
What kind of song do you think this man is playing? [Hypothesize]

Thursday nights and she didn't come on Saturday even though she used to sing in the gospel choir.

"I guess they teachin' her somethin' worthwhile up there at Greensboro," Grandpa Jeremiah said to Sister Todd. "I sure don't see what it is, though."

"You ain't never had no book learning, Jeremiah," Sister Todd shot back. She wiped at where a trickle of sweat made a little path through the white dusting powder she put on her chest to keep cool. "Them old ways you got ain't got nothing for these young folks."

"I guess you right," Grandpa Jeremiah said.

He said it but I could see he didn't like it none. He was a big man with a big head and had most all his hair even if it was white. All that summer, instead of sitting on the porch telling stories like he used to when I was real little, he would sit out there by himself while Ellie stayed in the house and watched the television or read a book. Sometimes I would think about asking him to tell me one of them stories he used to tell but they was too scary now that I didn't have nobody to sleep with but myself. I asked Ellie to sleep with me but she wouldn't.

"You're nine years old," she said, sounding real proper. "You're old enough to sleep alone."

I knew that. I just wanted her to sleep with me because I liked sleeping with her. Before she went off to college she used to put cocoa butter on her arms and face and it would smell real nice. When she come back from college she put something else on, but that smelled nice too.

It was right after Ellie went back to school that Grandpa Jeremiah had him a stroke and Macon started coming around. I think his mama probably made him come at first, but you could see he liked it. Macon had always been around, sitting over near the stuck window at church or going on the blueberry truck when we went picking down at Mister Gregory's place. For a long time he was just another kid, even though he was older'n me, but then, all of a sudden, he growed something fierce. I used to be up to his shoulder one time and then, before I could turn around good, I was only up to his shirt pocket. He changed too. When he used to just hang around with the other boys and play ball or shoot at birds he would laugh a lot. He didn't laugh so much anymore and I figured he was just about

Foreshadowing and Flashback
What do you learn about Ellie from this flashback?

Reading Check
Why does Grandpa Jeremiah raise Ellie?

grown. When Grandpa got sick he used to come around and help out with things around the house that was too hard for me to do. I mean, I could have done all the chores, but it would just take me longer.

When the work for the day was finished and the sows fed, Grandpa would kind of ease into one of his stories and Macon, he would sit and listen to them and be real interested. I didn't mind listening to the stories when Grandpa told them to Macon because he would be telling them in the middle of the afternoon and they would be past my mind by the time I had to go to bed.

Macon had an old guitar he used to mess with, too. He wasn't too bad on it, and sometimes Grandpa would tell him to play us a tune. He could play something he called "the Delta Blues" real good, but when Sister Todd or somebody from the church come around he'd play "Precious Lord" or "Just a Closer Walk With Thee."

Grandpa Jeremiah had been feeling poorly from that stroke, and one of his legs got a little drag to it. Just about the time Ellie come from school the next summer he was

Foreshadowing and Flashback
What clues here hint at a relationship developing between Macon and Grandpa Jeremiah?

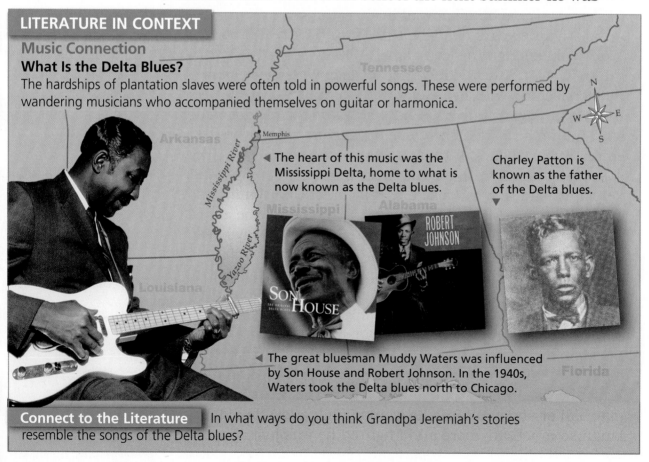

LITERATURE IN CONTEXT

Music Connection
What Is the Delta Blues?
The hardships of plantation slaves were often told in powerful songs. These were performed by wandering musicians who accompanied themselves on guitar or harmonica.

◀ The heart of this music was the Mississippi Delta, home to what is now known as the Delta blues.

Charley Patton is known as the father of the Delta blues. ▼

◀ The great bluesman Muddy Waters was influenced by Son House and Robert Johnson. In the 1940s, Waters took the Delta blues north to Chicago.

Connect to the Literature In what ways do you think Grandpa Jeremiah's stories resemble the songs of the Delta blues?

real sick. He was breathing loud so you could hear it even in the next room and he would stay in bed a lot even when there was something that needed doing or fixing.

"I don't think he's going to make it much longer," Dr. Crawford said. "The only thing I can do is to give him something for the pain."

"Are you sure of your diagnosis?" Ellie asked. She was sitting around the table with Sister Todd, Deacon Turner, and his little skinny yellow wife.

Dr. Crawford looked at Ellie like he was surprised to hear her talking. "Yes, I'm sure," he said. "He had tests a few weeks ago and his condition was bad then."

"How much time he got?" Sister Todd asked.

"Maybe a week or two at best," Dr. Crawford said.

When he said that, Deacon Turner's wife started crying and goin' on and I give her a hard look but she just went on. I was the one who loved Grandpa Jeremiah the most and she didn't hardly even know him so I didn't see why she was crying.

Everybody started tiptoeing around the house after that. They would go in and ask Grandpa Jeremiah if he was comfortable and stuff like that or take him some food or a cold glass of lemonade. Sister Todd come over and stayed with us. Mostly what she did is make supper and do a lot of praying, which was good because I figured that maybe God would do something to make Grandpa Jeremiah well. When she wasn't doing that she was piecing on a fancy quilt she was making for some white people in Wilmington.

Ellie, she went around asking everybody how they felt about Dr. Crawford and then she went into town and asked about the tests and things. Sister Jenkins asked her if she thought she knowed more than Dr. Crawford, and Ellie rolled her eyes at her, but Sister Jenkins was reading out her Bible and didn't make no notice of it.

Then Macon come over.

He had been away on what he called "a little piece of a job" and hadn't heard how bad off Grandpa Jeremiah was. When he come over he talked to Ellie and she told him what was going on and then he got him a soft drink from the refrigerator and sat out on the porch and before you know it he was crying.

You could look at his face and tell the difference between him sweating and the tears. The sweat was close against his skin and shiny and the tears come down fatter and more sparkly.

Vocabulary
diagnosis (dī əg nō′ sis) *n.* identification of a medical condition

Spiral Review
Theme How does the doctor's diagnosis affect the family? What does this suggest about the story's likely theme? Explain.

Reading Check
How does Macon help Grandpa Jeremiah?

Macon sat on the porch, without saying a word, until the sun went down and the crickets started chirping and carrying on. Then he went in to where Grandpa Jeremiah was and stayed in there for a long time.

Sister Todd was saying that Grandpa Jeremiah needed his rest and Ellie went in to see what Macon was doing. Then she come out real mad.

"He got Grandpa telling those old stories again," Ellie said. "I told him Grandpa needed his rest and for him not to be staying all night."

▲ **Critical Viewing**
Does this scene seem similar to the story's setting? Explain. **[Connect]**

Foreshadowing and Flashback
What does the description of Grandpa Jeremiah suggest about events to come?

He did leave soon, but bright and early the next morning Macon was back again. This time he brought his guitar with him and he went on in to Grandpa Jeremiah's room. I went in, too.

Grandpa Jeremiah's room smelled terrible. It was all closed up so no drafts could get on him and the whole room was smelled down with disinfect[1] and medicine. Grandpa Jeremiah lay propped up on the bed and he was so gray he looked scary. His hair wasn't combed down and his head on the pillow with his white hair sticking out was enough to send me flying if Macon hadn't been there. He was skinny, too. He looked like his skin got loose on his bones, and when he lifted his arms, it hung down like he was just wearing it instead of it being a part of him.

Macon sat slant-shouldered with his guitar across his lap. He was messin' with the guitar, not making any music, but just going over the strings as Grandpa talked.

"Old Carrie went around out back to where they kept the pigs penned up and she felt a cold wind across her face. . . ." Grandpa Jeremiah was telling the story about how a old woman out-tricked the Devil and got her son back. I had heard the story before, and I knew it was pretty

---

1. disinfect (dis´ in fect´) *n.* dialect, or regional language, for disinfectant, a substance that kills germs.

scary. "When she felt the cold breeze she didn't blink nary an eye, but looked straight ahead. . . ."

All the time Grandpa Jeremiah was talking I could see Macon fingering his guitar. I tried to imagine what it would be like if he was actually plucking the strings. I tried to fix my mind on that because I didn't like the way the story went with the old woman wrestling with the Devil.

We sat there for nearly all the afternoon until Ellie and Sister Todd come in and said that supper was ready. Me and Macon went out and ate some collard greens, ham hocks, and rice. Then Macon he went back in and listened to some more of Grandpa's stories until it was time for him to go home. I wasn't about to go in there and listen to no stories at night.

Dr. Crawford come around a few days later and said that Grandpa Jeremiah was doing a little better.

"You think the Good Lord gonna pull him through?" Sister Todd asked.

"I don't tell the Good Lord what He should or should not be doing," Dr. Crawford said, looking over at Sister Todd and at Ellie. "I just said that my patient seems to be doing okay for his condition."

"He been telling Macon all his stories," I said.

"Macon doesn't seem to understand that Grandpa Jeremiah needs his strength," Ellie said. "Now that he's improving, we don't want him to have a setback."

"No use in stopping him from telling his stories," Dr. Crawford said. "If it makes him feel good it's as good as any medicine I can give him."

I saw that this didn't set with Ellie, and when Dr. Crawford had left I asked her why.

"Dr. Crawford means well," she said, "but we have to get away from the kind of life that keeps us in the past."

She didn't say why we should be trying to get away from the stories and I really didn't care too much. All I knew was that when Macon was sitting in the room with Grandpa Jeremiah I wasn't nearly as scared as I used to be when it was just me and Ellie listening. I told that to Macon.

"You getting to be a big man, that's all," he said.

That was true. Me and Macon was getting to be good friends, too. I didn't even mind so much when he started being friends with Ellie later. It seemed kind of natural, almost like Macon was supposed to be there with us instead of just visiting.

Foreshadowing and Flashback
What does Macon's behavior suggest about what he might do later?

Reading Check
How does Macon react to Grandpa Jeremiah's illness?

Foreshadowing
and Flashback
What details here hint
that something pleasant
may lie ahead?

Grandpa wasn't getting no better, but he wasn't getting no worse, either.

"You liking Macon now?" I asked Ellie when we got to the middle of July. She was dishing out a plate of smothered chops for him and I hadn't even heard him ask for anything to eat.

"Macon's funny," Ellie said, not answering my question. "He's in there listening to all of those old stories like he's really interested in them. It's almost as if he and Grandpa Jeremiah are talking about something more than the stories, a secret language."

I didn't think I was supposed to say anything about that to Macon, but once, when Ellie, Sister Todd, and Macon were out on the porch shelling butter beans after Grandpa got tired and was resting, I went into his room and told him what Ellie had said.

"She said that?" Grandpa Jeremiah's face was skinny and old looking but his eyes looked like a baby's, they was so bright.

"Right there in the kitchen is where she said it," I said. "And I don't know what it mean but I was wondering about it."

"I didn't think she had any feeling for them stories," Grandpa Jeremiah said. "If she think we talking secrets, maybe she don't."

"I think she getting a feeling for Macon," I said,

"That's okay, too," Grandpa Jeremiah said. "They both young."

"Yeah, but them stories you be telling, Grandpa, they about old people who lived a long time ago," I said.

"What you got Grandpa?"

"You got you a bridge," Grandpa said. "And a meaning. Then when things get so hard you about to break, you can sneak across that bridge and see some folks who went before you and see how they didn't break. Some got bent and some got twisted and a few fell along the way, but they didn't break."

"Am I going to break, Grandpa?"

"You? As strong as you is?" Grandpa Jeremiah pushed himself up on his elbow and give me a look. "No way you going to break, boy. You gonna be strong as they come. One day you gonna tell all them stories I told you to your young'uns and they'll be as strong as you."

"Suppose I ain't got no stories, can I make some up?"

Foreshadowing
and Flashback
In what way are Grand-
pa Jeremiah's stories like
flashbacks?

"Sure you can, boy. You make 'em up and twist 'em around. Don't make no mind. Long as you got 'em."

"Is that what Macon is doing?" I asked. "Making up stories to play on his guitar?"

"He'll do with 'em what he see fit, I suppose," Grandpa Jeremiah said. "Can't ask more than that from a man."

It rained the first three days of August. It wasn't a hard rain but it rained anyway. The mailman said it was good for the crops over East but I didn't care about that so I didn't pay him no mind. What I did mind was when it rain like that the field mice come in and get in things like the flour bin and I always got the blame for leaving it open.

When the rain stopped I was pretty glad. Macon come over and sat with Grandpa and had something to eat with us. Sister Todd come over, too.

"How Grandpa doing?" Sister Todd asked. "They been asking about him in the church."

"He's doing all right," Ellie said.

"He's kind of quiet today," Macon said. "He was just talking about how the hogs needed breeding."

"He must have run out of stories to tell," Sister Todd said. "He'll be repeating on himself like my father used to do. That's the way I hear old folks get."

Everybody laughed at that because Sister Todd was pretty old, too. Maybe we was all happy because the sun was out after so much rain. When Sister Todd went in to take Grandpa Jeremiah a plate of potato salad with no mayonnaise like he liked it, she told him about how people was asking for him and he told her to tell them he was doing okay and to remember him in their prayers.

Sister Todd came over the next afternoon, too, with some rhubarb pie with cheese on it, which is my favorite pie. When she took a piece into Grandpa Jeremiah's room she come right out again and told Ellie to go fetch the Bible.

It was a hot day when they had the funeral. Mostly everybody was there. The church was hot as anything, even though they had the window open. Some yellowjackets flew in and buzzed around Sister Todd's niece and then around Deacon Turner's wife and settled right on her hat and stayed there until we all stood and sang "Soon-a Will Be Done."

Foreshadowing and Flashback
What event may be foreshadowed in Macon's description? Explain.

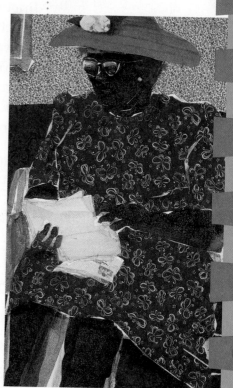

✓ **Reading Check**
How do Ellie's feelings for Macon change?

At the graveyard Macon played "Precious Lord" and I cried hard even though I told myself that I wasn't going to cry the way Ellie and Sister Todd was, but it was such a sad thing when we left and Grandpa Jeremiah was still out to the grave that I couldn't help it.

During the funeral and all, Macon kind of told everybody where to go and where to sit and which of the three cars to ride in. After it was over he come by the house and sat on the front porch and played on his guitar. Ellie was standing leaning against the rail and she was crying but it wasn't a hard crying. It was a soft crying, the kind that last inside of you for a long time.

Macon was playing a tune I hadn't heard before. I thought it might have been what he was working at when Grandpa Jeremiah was telling him those stories and I watched his fingers but I couldn't tell if it was or not. It wasn't nothing special, that tune Macon was playing, maybe halfway between them Delta blues he would do when Sister Todd wasn't around and something you would play at church. It was something different and something the same at the same time. I watched his fingers go over that guitar and figured I could learn that tune one day if I had a mind to.

Foreshadowing and Flashback
What event might this last sentence foreshadow?

Critical Thinking

> 1. **Key Ideas and Details (a)** What is Ellie's relationship to the narrator? **(b) Interpret:** Describe the narrator's feelings toward Ellie.
>
> 2. **Key Ideas and Details (a)** Why does Ellie not want Macon around Grandpa Jeremiah's house at first? **(b) Draw Conclusions:** How does the narrator feel toward Macon?
>
> 3. **Key Ideas and Details (a) Interpret:** What are Grandpa Jeremiah's "songs"? **(b) Take a Position:** Do you think songs and stories such as those Grandpa tells are important to future generations?
>
> 4. **Integration of Knowledge and Ideas (a)** What role does Macon play at the funeral for Grandpa? Is his role important? **(b)** Who do you suppose came to the funeral? Was their presence important? Explain. *[Connect to the Big Question: How much do our communities shape us?]*

Cite textual evidence to support your responses.

Comparing Foreshadowing and Flashback

© **1. Key Ideas and Details** Create a chart for each story. **(a)** In the left two columns, list clues in the story and the events they foreshadow. **(b)** In the right two columns, list flashbacks and tell what you learn from each one.

Foreshadowing		Flashback	
Clues ————————➤ Event		Detail ————————➤ Reveals	

© **2. Craft and Structure** Based on your charts, which writer makes more use of these plot devices? Explain.

🕐 Timed Writing

Explanatory Text: Essay

Compare and contrast the authors' use of foreshadowing and flashback in "Lob's Girl" and "Jeremiah's Song." In an essay, discuss the effects of these literary devices. **(30 minutes)**

5-Minute Planner

1. Read the prompt carefully and completely.

2. Review your charts for examples of foreshadowing and flashback in the stories.

3. Organize your thoughts by asking the following questions:

- Which story has more suspense, based on the use of foreshadowing?

- Which story's structure includes more flashbacks?

- What is the effect of the combination of foreshadowing and flashback on each story?

4. Select an organizational strategy that will suit your essay, such as block format or point-by-point organization.

5. Reread the prompt, and then draft your essay.

Writing Workshop

Common Core State Standards

Writing

2. Write informative/explanatory texts to examine a topic and convey ideas, concepts, and information through the selection, organization, and analysis of relevant content.

2.a. Introduce a topic; organize ideas, concepts, and information, using strategies such as definition, classification, comparison/contrast, and cause/effect; include formatting, graphics, and multimedia when useful to aiding comprehension.

2.b. Develop the topic with relevant facts, definitions, concrete details, quotations, or other information and examples.

7. Conduct short research projects to answer a question, drawing on several sources and refocusing the inquiry when appropriate.

8. Gather relevant information from multiple print and digital sources; assess the credibility of each source; and quote or paraphrase the data and conclusions of others while avoiding plagiarism and providing basic bibliographic information for sources.

Write an Informative Text

Research: Research Report

Defining the Form A **research report** presents facts and information gathered from credible sources and includes a bibliography that credits each source. You might use elements of this form in reports, articles, or speeches.

Assignment Write a research report to gain more knowledge about a topic that interests you. Include these elements:

- ✔ a *topic for inquiry* that is *narrow enough to cover thoroughly*
- ✔ a *strong introduction* that clearly defines the topic
- ✔ *facts, details, examples,* and *explanations* from a variety of *credible, authoritative sources* to support the main ideas
- ✔ information that is *accurate, relevant, valid,* and *current*
- ✔ a clear method of *organization*, including a *strong conclusion*
- ✔ a *bibliography* containing accurate and complete citations
- ✔ error-free grammar, including *proper punctuation* of citations

To preview the criteria on which your research report will be based, see the rubric on page 997.

 Writing Workshop: *Work in Progress*

Review the work you did on pages 931 and 955.

WRITE GUY
Jeff Anderson, M.Ed.

What Do You Notice?

Quotations

Read the following sentence from Patricia C. McKissack and Fredrick McKissack, Jr.'s expository essay "The Shutout."

Albigence Waldo, a surgeon with George Washington's troops at Valley Forge, wrote in his diary that soldiers were 'battling balls and running bases' in their free time.

With a partner, discuss what makes the introduction and the quotation effective. Together, list ways you might introduce quotations you gather and ways to give proper credit to your sources.

Prewriting/Planning Strategies

Browse to choose a topic. Browse through reference books at a library. For example, flip through an atlas, an almanac, or a volume of an encyclopedia. Jot down each person, place, object, or event that interests you. Then, scan your notes and circle any words or phrases that suggest a good topic.

Use a topic web. Make sure your topic is not too broad to cover effectively. Narrow your topic by using a topic web. Each row should contain smaller and smaller aspects of your general topic. The following topic web narrows the general topic "Ancient Rome" down to a specific building in ancient Rome.

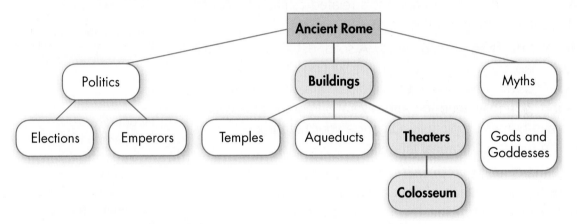

Take notes from a variety of sources. As part of your research, locate **primary sources**—firsthand or original accounts, such as interview transcripts and newspaper articles. In addition, find **secondary sources**—accounts that are not original, such as encyclopedia entries. As you gather facts, details, examples, and explanations, take careful notes, using a system of source cards and note cards.

- On each **source card,** record information about each source you use—title, author, publication date and place, and page numbers.

- On each **note card,** record information to use in your report. Use quotation marks when you copy words exactly, and indicate the page number on which the quotation appears. In most cases, use your own words to protect yourself from plagiarizing, or copying ideas, later.

Drafting Strategies

Use an outline to organize information. Group your notes by categories that break your topic into subtopics. For example, if you are writing about the Colosseum, you might use these topics in your outline:

- architecture
- construction
- events held
- spectators

Use Roman numerals (I, II, III) to number the subtopics and letters (A, B, C) to show details and facts related to each subtopic, as in the outline shown on this page.

Match your draft to your outline. A solid, detailed outline will serve as a map, guiding you through the writing of your draft. The headings with Roman numerals indicate main sections of your report. You may need to write several paragraphs to cover each Roman numeral topic fully. Organize your paragraphs around the topics with capital letters.

Support main ideas with facts. Using your outline, write sentences to express each of your main ideas. Then, refer to your note cards and provide support for your main ideas with facts, details, examples, and explanations that you gathered through your research.

Cite sources. To avoid **plagiarism**—presenting another's work as your own—you must include documentation every time you use another writer's ideas. As you draft, circle ideas that come from your sources. Use these tips to credit your research:

- For *paraphrased information* or facts that are not common knowledge, insert parentheses for the author's last name and the page number(s) from which the information came:

The Colosseum could hold 50,000 spectators (Smith 87–88).

- For a *direct quotation*, use quotation marks. After the end quotation mark, insert in parentheses the author's last name and the page number(s) from which the quotation came:

"It is the Romans' greatest work of architecture." (Smith 87).

Common Core State Standards

Writing

2.a. Introduce a topic; organize ideas, concepts, and information, using strategies such as definition, classification, comparison/contrast, and cause/effect; include formatting, graphics, and multimedia when useful to aiding comprehension.

2.b. Develop the topic with relevant facts, definitions, concrete details, quotations, or other information and examples.

8. Gather relevant information from multiple print and digital sources; assess the credibility of each source; and quote or paraphrase the data and conclusions of others while avoiding plagiarism and providing basic bibliographic information for sources.

I. Introduction
II. Architecture of Colosseum
  A. measurements
  B. building material
III. Construction of Colosseum
  A. beginning date
  B. workers
IV. Conclusion

Writers on Writing

Julius Lester On Writing Vivid Descriptions

Julius Lester is the author of *Black Cowboy, Wild Horses* (p. 832).

The writing of *Black Cowboy, Wild Horses* involved research. To make the story realistic and believable, I had to learn a lot about wild horses. How big was a herd? How was the herd organized? What did a herd do each day? Reading books about wild horses answered my questions. As you will see in the passage below, my research helped me write vivid descriptions.

". . . describe, not explain."
—Julius Lester

Professional Model:
from *Black Cowboy, Wild Horses*

The ~~next~~ ₍following₎ morning Bob ₍and Warrior₎ walked ~~his horse~~ into the herd. The stallion eyed ~~him~~ ₍them₎ for a moment. Then, as if to test this newcomer, ~~the stallion took~~ ₍he led the herd₎ off in a gallop. ~~Bob kicked his horse lightly and the romp was on.~~

~~He moved into the middle of the herd. He wanted to avoid the stallion's teeth. Stallions would sometimes gallop alongside a herd, biting a slow mare on the rump, ramming or bumping another who threatened to run separate from the group.~~

Bob lay flat across Warrior's back and moved with the herd. ₍If anyone had ₍been watching,₎ ~~seen the herd~~ they would not have noticed ~~the~~ ₍a₎ man among the horses. ~~in its midst, lying almost flat across his horse's back as if he had caught the wind and was going to ride it to where land and sky became one.~~

In the first sentence I changed "next morning" to "following morning" because I had used the phrase "next morning" two paragraphs before. It is important to keep the writing fresh, and one way to do this is by not repeating key words and phrases.

I cut this paragraph because the explanation slows the action of the story and I am just showing off the research I did. I used this fact about the stallion biting mares later in the story, where it fit the action.

I also cut a large section from the last paragraph because there was too much description. I liked the figure of speech about riding the wind. But a writer must take out even those elements he likes, if they detract from the story.

Revising Strategies

Check for effective paragraph structure. In a research report, most body paragraphs should be built according to this plan:

- a **topic sentence (T)** stating the paragraph's main idea
- a **restatement (R)** or elaboration of the topic sentence
- strong **illustrations (I),** including facts, examples, or details about the main idea

Review your draft. Label each of your sentences **T, R,** or **I.** If a paragraph contains a group of **I**'s, make sure that you have a strong **T** that they support. If you find a **T** by itself, add **I**'s to support it.

Revise for unity. In writing that has **unity,** everything comes together to form a complete, self-contained whole. Use the following checklist to assess your report's unity.

> **Unity Checklist**
>
> ✓ Every paragraph develops my thesis statement.
>
> ✓ All of my paragraphs contain topic sentences that support the thesis.
>
> ✓ I have eliminated any sentences that do not support my main idea.

Define technical terms and difficult words. While researching, you may have learned new words—either technical terms related to your topic or difficult words that were unfamiliar to you. Help your readers to understand and enjoy your report by adding context clues or definitions to make these words easier to understand.

Difficult: A popular show at the Roman Colosseum featured **gladiators.**

Defined: A popular show at the Roman Colosseum featured **gladiators,** trained fighters who often faced other men or even wild animals.

Create a bibliography or works-cited list. A "Works Cited" page provides readers with full bibliographic information on each source you cite. The author and page number within your report will lead your reader to the specific source in your bibliography page. Readers can use that information to read more about your topic. (For more information, see pages R34 and R35.)

Common Core State Standards

Writing

2.d. Use precise language and domain-specific vocabulary to inform about or explain the topic.

8. Gather relevant information from multiple print and digital sources; assess the credibility of each source; and quote or paraphrase the data and conclusions of others while avoiding plagiarism and providing basic bibliographic information for sources.

Language

1. Demonstrate command of the conventions of standard English grammar and usage when writing or speaking.

Punctuating Citations and Titles of Reference Works

Follow these guidelines for presenting the title of a work and the words of various sources in your research report:

- **Underlining and Italicizing** Underline or italicize the titles of long written works and the titles of periodicals.
- **Using Quotation Marks** Titles of short written works and Internet sites should be set off in quotation marks.

Including Direct Quotations A **direct quotation** conveys the exact words that another person wrote or said.

Underlined/Italicized	Quotation Marks
Title of a Book	Title of a Short Story
Title of a Play	Chapter From a Book
Title of a Long Poem	Title of a Short Poem
Title of a Magazine	Title of an Article
Title of a Newspaper	Title of a Web Site

PH WRITING COACH

Further instruction and practice are available in *Prentice Hall Writing Coach*.

- Introduce short quotations with a comma, setting them off with quotation marks, and follow with your own sentences.
- Introduce quotations that are five lines or longer with a colon. Set them off from your text by starting a new line and indenting the quotation. *Do not* use quotation marks.

Fixing Errors To find and fix errors involving quotation marks, underlining, and italics, follow these steps:

1. Check the quoted material you have used.

2. Make sure that the quotations are copied exactly from the source. Enclose these words in quotation marks.

3. Punctuate correctly. Follow the punctuation rules for the use of quotation marks and underlining or italicizing of titles.

Grammar in Your Writing

Reread the draft of your research report. Use the rules above to correct any mistakes in the punctuation of your citations.

Ice Ages

Ice ages occur every two hundred million years or so. An ice age is defined as a long period of cold where large amounts of water are trapped under ice. Although ice ages happened long ago, studying their causes and effects helps contemporary scientists understand geological conditions of the world today.

> The author defines her topic clearly in the highlighted sentence.

When an ice age does occur, ice covers much of the Earth. This ice forms when the climate changes. The polar regions become very cold and the temperatures drop everywhere else. The ice is trapped in enormous mountains of ice called glaciers. Glaciers can be as large as a continent in size. When the Earth's temperature warms up, the glaciers start to melt, forming rivers and lakes. Glaciers' tremendous weight and size can actually wear away mountains and valleys as the glaciers melt and move. The melting ice also raises ocean levels.

Southern extent of glacial ice 20,000 years ago

Landward limit of coastline in the past 5 million years

Location of coastline 20,000 years ago

Current location of coastline

300 MILES
400 KILOMETERS

Effects of Ice Age on Eastern Coastline of United States

> This map illustrates the writer's point that ice ages caused current conditions.

There are many different theories to explain why ice ages occur, but no one knows for sure. Many scientists agree that it is probably due to a combination of causes, including changes in the sun's intensity, the distance of the Earth from the sun, changes in ocean currents, the continental plates rubbing up against each other, and the varying amounts of carbon dioxide in the atmosphere (*PBS Nova* Web site "The Big Chill").

> Here the author presents factual information related to the possible causes of ice ages.

During the last ice age, or the Wisconsin Ice Age, people lived on the Earth. These people saw ice and snow all the time. It was never warm enough for it to melt, so it piled up. In summertime, women fished in chilly streams. The men hunted year-round.

The skeleton of one person who lived and hunted during this time was found by some hikers in 1901 in the European Alps. He had been buried in the ice for nearly 5,000 years. Nicknamed the "Iceman," scientists believe that perhaps he was suddenly caught by a blizzard or that he possibly ran out of food, became weak, and died.

Scientists were able to learn a lot about this ancient period from the leather clothes and animal skins he was wearing and the tools he was carrying (Roberts, p. 38).

Ice ages also affect life today. The ice sheets that formed weighed a huge amount. When the ice retreated, it left behind large rocks and other debris which otherwise would not be there. Also, without ice ages, large bodies of water like the Great Lakes simply wouldn't exist. We depend on these bodies of water every day for fresh drinking water, recreation, and shipping large quantities of materials.

Scientists discovered ice ages because of Louis Agassiz, a nineteenth-century scientist who is sometimes called the "Father of Glaciology." In Switzerland, he saw boulders of granite far from where any granite should be. He also noticed scrapes and grooves, or striae. He theorized that glaciers had caused all of these geologic features (University of California Museum of Paleontology Web page).

Many animals that are extinct now lived during the Ice Age. The saber-toothed tiger and the mastodon, an elephant-like animal, formerly lived in North America. They became extinct because of climate change and hunting. Other animals became extinct as well because they could not adapt to the way the Earth was changing.

Baron Gerard de Geer, a Swedish geologist, did pioneering work which esti-mated the end of the last ice age. In a similar way to the way we count

Elizabeth clearly and accurately cites her sources to show where she obtained a set of specific details.

In each section, Elizabeth explores a different aspect of the ice ages. Here she is explaining scientific discovery.

Writing
6. Demonstrate sufficient command of keyboarding skills to type a minimum of three pages in a single sitting.

tree rings to estimate a tree's age, De Geer used layers of sediment left by glacier's summer melts to calculate the history of the Ice Age. He did much of his work in Sweden, but he also visited areas that had been affected by glaciers in New England.

Thanks to scientists like De Geer and Agassiz, we know a great deal about that remote age when glaciers roamed the Earth. We can now estimate the history of ice ages and determine what features—valleys, inland seas, mountains, lakes, rocks—were caused, as you can see by the map displayed here of the Eastern United States. There is still a lot more to be discovered about the causes of ice ages, but one thing is clear: Glaciers had a powerful effect on the world as we know it today.

> The author restates the main idea that she presented in the introduction and supported in the body of the paper.

Bibliography

Department of Geosciences, University of Arizona. 10 Nov. 2000.
<http://www.geoarizona.edu/Antevs/degeer.html>.

History of the Universe. 11 Nov. 2000.
<http://www.historyoftheuniverse.com/iceage.html>.

Ice Age. Compton's Interactive Encyclopedia © The Learning Company, Inc. [CD-ROM] (1998).

Roberts, David. "The Iceman." *National Geographic Magazine*, June 1993: 37–49.

University of California Museum of Paleontology. 11 Nov. 2000.
<http://www.ucmp.berkeley.edu/history/agassiz.html>.

PBS Nova "The Big Chill." 10 Nov. 2000.
<http://www.pbs.org/wgbh/nova/ice/chill.html>.

> In her bibliography, Elizabeth cites all the sources used to research her paper.

Editing and Proofreading

Review your draft to correct errors in grammar, spelling, and punctuation.

Focus on accuracy. Check the names of the authors you quote and the names of the books, articles, or other sources you used. Demonstrate your keyboarding skills by typing your entire paper carefully and avoiding the introduction of errors.

Publishing and Presenting

Consider one of the following ways to share your writing.

Create a mini-lesson. Use your report as the basis for a short lesson on your topic. Plan a lesson that includes an activity related to the topic. Present your lesson to a group of classmates.

Offer your report to an organization. See if a local organization, club, or library would benefit from your research. Plan a presentation with visuals, such as posters, photographs, videos, or music, to accompany your presentation.

Reflecting on Your Writing

Writer's Journal Jot down your answer to this question:

What are some potential consequences for failing to give credit to a source?

Rubric for Self-Assessment

Find evidence in your writing to address each category. Then, use the rating scale to grade your work.

Spiral Review

Earlier in this unit, you learned about **commas** (p. 930) and **semicolons and colons** (p. 954). Reread your report to be sure you have used commas, semicolons, and colons correctly.

PH | WRITING COACH

Further instruction and practice are available in *Prentice Hall Writing Coach.*

Criteria	Rating Scale
	not very ———— very 1 2 3 4 5
Focus: How well defined is the topic?	1 2 3 4 5
Organization: How clear is the method of organization?	1 2 3 4 5
Support/Elaboration: How well have you used a variety of credible sources?	1 2 3 4 5
Style: How well do facts, details, examples, and explanations support the main idea?	1 2 3 4 5
Conventions: How accurate and complete are citations in the bibliography?	1 2 3 4 5

Vocabulary Workshop

Idioms

An **idiom** is an expression that has a different meaning from the literal meanings of the words it contains. For example, if a baseball game was postponed because it was "raining cats and dogs," it was postponed because it was raining very hard.

Some idioms are very common and easily understood. Others, however, can be confusing. Look for context clues in sentences that contain an idiom. For example, the sentence above contains the context clue that the game was "postponed." When you add your own background knowledge you can determine that a baseball game would be *postponed* if it was raining too hard to play.

Idioms usually develop in some specialized field where they originally make sense. Look at these common idioms and their sources:

Idiom	Source	Meaning
to watch like a hawk	wildlife	to look at something very closely
to hit the nail on the head	carpentry	to do or say something in exactly the right way
to be on an even keel	sailing	to be balanced, steady, and heading in the right direction

Common Core State Standards

Language
5. Interpret figures of speech in context.

Practice A Identify the idiom in each sentence.

1. We all worked like ants to finish the class art project.
2. Tom dropped the ball when he forgot to buy a gift for the party.
3. The members of the soccer team cut down on their snacks.
4. I think I might be coming down with a cold.
5. She let the cat out of the bag when she revealed the secret.

Practice B Identify the idiom in each sentence. Then, use context clues to figure out the meaning of the idiom. Restate the idiom in your own words.

1. I didn't want to apologize to my sister, but I had to face the music.
2. Kyle wanted to play a role he could sink his teeth into.
3. Leila was putting out fires all day at work until she came home and relaxed.
4. Mrs. Fine's grandchild was the apple of her eye.
5. When Gerald lost the chess match, he was fit to be tied.

Activity Think of three idioms you know. Then, using note-cards like the one shown, describe the source of each idiom. For example, your example may be an idiom that relates to an animal, nature, or a kind of food. Next, explain the meaning of each idiom. Finally, write a sentence using each idiom.

Idiom:

Source:

Meaning:

Example sentence:

Comprehension and Collaboration

With a partner, do online research to find idioms from another language, such as Spanish or Japanese. Try to find at least five examples. Share your findings with others in the class.

Communications Workshop

Oral Response to Literature

Common Core
State Standards

After you have read a literary work, you may be asked to deliver an **oral response to literature.** An oral response includes many of the characteristics of a written response. (See the Writing Workshop, pp. 264–269.)

Learn the Skills

The first step toward a successful oral response is to read carefully and thoughtfully to develop an interpretation.

Developing your response

- **Organize around clear ideas.** Organize your response around a number of clear ideas, premises, or images. Your introduction should include a thesis statement that expresses your interpretation of the work. The body of the speech should present clearly related and logically organized ideas. Conclude your response by restating your interpretation and sharing your opinion.

- **Create clear transitions among ideas.** Make sure your listeners can follow the flow of your ideas. To do so, use transitional words and phrases. Lead in to the use of examples with words and phrases like *for example, for instance, namely,* and *particularly.* Indicate emphasis with words like *above all* and *chiefly.*

- **Use examples and quotations from the text.** To develop your interpretation, use examples from the literature, including quotations, to support your opinion. Use visual aids to support your points.

Delivering your response

- **Use nonverbal elements.** Use nonverbal cues such as eye contact and hand gestures to help the audience follow your main ideas and to emphasize *salient,* or important, points.

- **Use effective rate, volume, and tone.** Use a strong, clear voice that can be heard in the back of the room. Speak slowly and enunciate every word. Do not be afraid to pause before reading a quotation or starting a new thought.

Speaking and Listening

1.c. Pose and respond to specific questions with elaboration and detail by making comments that contribute to the topic, text, or issue under discussion.

4. Present claims and findings, sequencing ideas logically and using pertinent descriptions, facts, and details to accentuate main ideas or themes; use appropriate eye contact, adequate volume, and clear pronunciation.

Practice the Skills

Ⓒ **Presentation of Knowledge and Ideas** Use what you have learned in this workshop to perform the following task.

> **ACTIVITY: Oral Response to Literature**
>
> Present an oral response to literature to your class. Follow the steps below.
> - Choose a work of literature on which to base your response
> - Organize your interpretation using the strategies in this workshop and the Writing Workshop on pages 264–269.
> - Present your response to the class.
> - Use the Speaking Guide below to deliver your response.

Use a Speaking Guide like the one below to organize and help you deliver your speech.

Speaking Guide

Preparing the response:

Novel, short story, or collection title: _____

Author: _____

Main points: _____

Supporting details: _____

Interpretation:

Delivering the response:
Before you present, practice these tips:
- ❑ Hold up the book in which the literary work appears.
- ❑ When reading a passage or a quotation, read directly from the work. Use sticky notes to mark pages before the presentation.
- ❑ Use props. Hold up an object mentioned in your presentation.

Speaking techniques:
- ❑ Employ eye contact and use natural gestures.
- ❑ Use an appropriate speaking rate and volume.
- ❑ Use a clear voice and enunciate your words.
- ❑ Use correct conventions of language.

Ⓒ **Comprehension and Collaboration** Evaluate and discuss a classmate's presentation. Listen to and interpret the verbal and nonverbal cues in the presentation. After paraphrasing the major ideas and supporting evidence, ask the speaker questions to clarify his or her purpose, perspective, or any other confusing points.

Cumulative Review

I. Reading Literature

Common Core
State Standards

RL.6.2, RL.6.4, RL.6.5; W.6.3, W.6.3.a;
L.6.4.a
[For the full wording of the standards,
see the standards chart in the front of
your textbook.]

Directions: *Read the passage. Then, answer each
question that follows.*

Papa Bird Touches the Sun

"If you eat too many worms, you will get a bellyache," Mama
Bird sternly warned Baby Bird. Papa Bird sat on his branch and
watched Baby hang his head in disappointment. But, when Mama
turned to do other things, Baby went right on eating worms.
Papa smiled. Baby would certainly have a bellyache tonight, but
that was all right. All lessons are learned in good time.

Papa closed his eyes and remembered his own youth. He had
been stubborn once, too—and determined. It was the sun and
not worms that had interested Papa when he was young. "I will
fly so high, I will touch the golden ball in the sky," he had announced
to his Mama one bright, sunny day. "You foolish child," she had
responded. "The sun is spiteful and mean. It will burn your glorious
feathers. Stay away from the sun!"

The elders caught Papa flying toward the golden ball more than
once, and each time they scolded him, saying that his mission was
foolish. But each time, Papa grew more determined. How could that
glorious shimmering ball in the sky be harmful? He would show
them all that they were wrong and he was right!

Papa came up with a plan. He would sneak away during the
Fabulous Feast, when all the other birds were too busy eating to
notice that he had gone. On the day of the Fabulous Feast, Papa
soared through the sky, filled with <u>anticipation</u>. He would finally
touch the golden ball and know its true nature for himself.

As he neared the sun, a terrible heat made Papa sweat and
brought tears to his eyes. But he could not give up. He was too
close. He flew on into the sweltering heat until the sun was right
there, within reach. Happily, he reached toward the sun with one
wing. Finally! But, then, all at once there was the awful burnt smell
and a pain on Papa's wing like he had never experienced.

Papa heard Mama calling the family for dinner. Mama and Papa
munched happily on their food, but Baby just sat clutching his belly.
Papa smiled. All lessons are learned in good time.

1. What type of story is "Papa Bird Touches the Sun"?
   A. a myth
   B. a biography
   C. a cause-and-effect essay
   D. a work of science fiction

2. Which of these is a **realistic element** of the story?
   A. Birds eat worms.
   B. Mother birds warn their young not to eat too much.
   C. The Fabulous Feast is an annual event.
   D. Birds can burn their wings if they fly too close to the sun.

3. Which of these is a **fantastic element** in the story?
   A. The sun is very hot.
   B. Mother birds care for their babies.
   C. Lessons can be learned through experience.
   D. The birds have a Fabulous Feast.

4. When Mama describes the sun as spiteful and mean, she is using—
   A. exaggeration.
   B. personification.
   C. a simile.
   D. a metaphor.

5. Which part of the story is told in a **flashback?**
   A. The first paragraph
   B. The first and last paragraphs
   C. The entire story
   D. The entire story, except for the first and last paragraphs

6. What event **foreshadows** the fact that Baby Bird gets a bellyache?
   A. Mama Bird sternly warns Baby Bird.
   B. Papa watches Baby hang his head.
   C. Mama turns to do other things.
   D. Baby keeps eating worms.

7. Twice during the story, Papa thinks, "All lessons are learned in good time." What does this thought suggest?
   A. a lesson
   B. a universal theme
   C. a main idea
   D. the topic sentence

8. **Vocabulary** Which word or phrase is the closest in meaning to the underlined word anticipation?
   A. stubbornness
   B. eagerness
   C. fear
   D. determination

 Timed Writing

Compose an original story that has the same **universal theme** as "Papa Bird Touches the Sun." Include both **realistic** and **fantastic elements.** At the end of the story, write a sentence that states the universal theme.

 GO ON

II. Reading Informational Text

Common Core
State Standards

RI.6.2, RI.6.5; W.6.5
[For the full wording of the standards, see the standards chart in the front of your textbook.]

Directions: *Read the excerpt from an online article. Then, answer each question that follows.*

To plan for a trip to Washington, D.C., Lucinda has prepared an outline of sites she wants to visits at the National Mall. She expects to learn and see many new things on this <u>enriching</u> trip.

I. Memorials and Monuments
- **A.** Lincoln Memorial
  - **1.** built in 1922 and pictured on pennies
  - **2.** 36 columns representing the states of the Union when Lincoln died
- **B.** Vietnam Veteran's Memorial
  - **1.** called "the wall"
  - **2.** inscribed with the names of about 58,000 American armed troops killed during the Vietnam War
- **C.** Washington Monument
  - **1.** 555.5-foot obelisk near east end of reflecting pool
  - **2.** designed by architect Robert Mills

II. Museums
- **A.** United States Holocaust Memorial Museum
  - **1.** newest and most visited site in the mall
  - **2.** remembers victims of the Holocaust
- **B.** Freer Gallery
  - **1.** museum of American and Asian Art
- **C.** Hirshorn Museum and Sculpture Garden
  - **1.** one of the best collections of modern art in the world
  - **2.** includes art by Edward Hopper and Georgia O'Keeffe
  - **3.** outside is a sculpture garden

1. According to Lucinda's **outline,** what is she most interested in visiting?
- **A.** museums, memorials, and monuments
- **B.** Washington, D.C.
- **C.** art museums
- **D.** areas with interesting architecture

2. What item could Lucinda add as II. D.?
- **A.** The Jefferson Memorial
- **B.** The United States Botanic Gardens
- **C.** The National Museum of American History
- **D.** The White House

3. What **other source of information** would **connect** to and **clarify the main ideas** of this outline?
- **A.** a travel guide that contains information about each place
- **B.** a street map of Washington, D.C.
- **C.** a tour guide who could take Lucinda to each place
- **D.** a U.S. history textbook

III. Writing and Language Conventions

Directions: *Read the following excerpt from a multimedia report. Then, answer each question that follows.*

Script for Multimedia Report: Maui

(1) **Visual:** photo of beach in Maui (2) Maui has 120 miles of coastline and over 30 miles of beaches. (3) It is the second largest of Hawaii's islands. (4) **Visual:** photo of Maui taken from the air. (5) The most interesting thing to do in Maui is hike up the Haleakala Crater. (6) The largest dormant volcano on earth. (7) At the top, the fog is very thick and it is surprisingly cold. (8) **Visual:** photo of crater (9) Becuase of Maui's diverse landscape, there are enough activities to keep anyone busy.

1. Which statement should the writer use to clearly state the **main idea** of this report?

A. Maui is a fun place to visit.

B. Haleakala Crater is the most interesting thing to see in Hawaii.

C. Maui is a beautiful island with interesting things to do.

D. Maui is an island in the Pacific Ocean.

2. What could this writer do to add variety to the multimedia aids and to support the **purpose?**

A. Use photos of more interesting subjects, such as people.

B. Show a map of the Haleakala Crater.

C. Include audio aids, such as music.

D. Include graphs, pie charts, and tables

3. Which **supporting detail** could best be added to this report?

A. a discussion of fun and interesting things to do in Maui

B. a step by step demonstration of how grass skirts are made

C. an in-depth look at the history of Hawaii

D. a comparison of Hawaiian and mainland music

4. What is the *best* method of fixing the fragment in sentence 6?

A. Add a verb to it.

B. Delete it.

C. Combine it with sentence 5.

D. Add a subject to it.

Performance Tasks

Directions: *Follow the instructions to complete the tasks below as required by your teacher.*

As you work on each task, incorporate both general academic vocabulary and literary terms you learned in this unit.

Common Core State Standards

RL.6.2, RL.6.3, RL.6.4, RL.6.5; W.6.1, W.6.2, W.6.9.a, W.6.9.b; SL.6.1, SL.6.4, SL.6.5, SL.6.6; L.6.1

[For the full wording of the standards, see the standards chart in the front of your textbook.]

Writing

Task 1: Literature [RL.6.5; W.6.2; W.6.9.a]
Analyze a Key Scene

Write an essay in which you analyze how a key scene in a literary work from this unit helps to communicate the work's theme.

- Identify and describe an important scene from the work. Explain why you chose this scene.

- State the overall theme of the work.

- Determine how this scene contributes to the development of the theme. Include details from the scene (for example, details about characters or cause and effect) that help readers understand the message of the work.

- Provide a conclusion that sums up your thinking.

Task 2: Literature [RL.6.3; L.6.1]
Analyze Plot Devices

Write an essay in which you analyze how a story's plot unfolds through the use of plot devices such as foreshadowing and flashback.

- Identify a work from the unit that includes a plot device such as foreshadowing or flashback.

- Discuss how the particular plot device helps the work's plot develop. Explain whether or not the plot device makes the work more effective, and why.

- Support your ideas with relevant evidence from the text.

- Make sure your sentences contain complete ideas. Correct any sentence fragments that you find.

Task 3: Literature [RL.6.2; W.6.9.a]
Evaluate Theme

Write an essay in which you evaluate the theme of a work from this unit that contains fantasy.

- State the theme of the work you selected.

- Explain how the expression of the theme is affected by the use of fantasy. Cite specifics from the work.

- Analyze the ways in which fantasy elements interact with realistic elements in the work.

- Use a formal writing style and tone.

- Sum up your analysis with a conclusion that follows from the explanation you presented.

Speaking and Listening

Task 4: Literature [RL.6.2; SL.6.4]

Oral Presentation

Deliver a presentation in which you analyze cause and effect in a literary work from this unit.

- Explain which work you chose and briefly summarize the story and theme.
- Explain why cause and effect plays a key role in the development of the story and its deeper meaning.
- Present your ideas to the class in an organized way. Use a visual display such as a graphic organizer to help communicate your ideas.
- Use appropriate eye contact, adequate volume, and clear pronunciation as you present.

Task 5: Literature [RL.6.4; SL.6.1]

Compare Uses of Personification

Lead a small group discussion in which you analyze and compare the portrayals of animal characters in one or more literary works from this unit.

- Come to the discussion prepared with general ideas about the reasons folk tales and legends often include animals with human qualities, as well as specific questions about at least two animal characters and their similarities and differences.
- Pose your questions and respond to ideas contributed by group members.
- Review the key ideas expressed by the group and state any new ideas you have arrived at during the discussion.

Task 6: Literature [RL.6.2; SL.6.4, SL.6.5]

Analyze Theme

Prepare and present an oral presentation in which you evaluate the theme of a work of literature from this unit.

- State the central idea or theme of the work you selected.
- Explain how the theme is conveyed through particular details in the work. Consider character, plot, setting, fantasy elements, and cultural details.
- In your presentation, use a logical organization. Sequence your ideas so that your audience can follow your reasoning easily.
- If you have the technology available, prepare a slideshow to accompany your oral presentation. Or, create a poster showing details relating to theme.

THE BIG ?

How much do our communities shape us?

At the beginning of Unit 6, you wrote a response to the Big Question. Now that you have completed the unit, write a new response. Discuss how your initial ideas have expanded or changed. Cite specific examples from the literature in this unit, from other subject areas, and from your own life to support your ideas. Use Big Question vocabulary words (see p. 823) in your response.

Featured Titles

In this unit, you have read a variety of literary works that originated in the oral tradition. Continue to read on your own. Select works that you enjoy, but challenge yourself to explore new writers and works of increasing depth and complexity. The titles suggested below will help you get started.

Literature

Black Ships Before Troy: The Story of the Iliad

by Rosemary Sutcliff

Laurel Leaf, 2005   EXEMPLAR TEXT

Sutcliff retells the grand **epic** of the Greeks' ten-year-long battle against the city of Troy in exciting and vivid detail. She breathes life into classical and mythical characters and also re-creates some of the brutal realities of battle.

Sleeping Ugly

by Jane Yolen

This funny **fairy tale** turns the original version upside down. Princess Miserella is beautiful but mean. Plain Jane is homely but sweet. To this pair of opposites, Jane Yolen adds a magical mix-up and an unsuspecting prince.

The Iron Ring

by Lloyd Alexander

When the young King Tamar loses his kingdom and its riches, he sets out on a journey to right his wrongs. In this **novel,** Tamar's community teaches him the value of honor, which he must regain.

Myths and Stories from the Americas

This collection of **myths** and **folk tales** includes stories of creation, tricksters, love, and adventure from North America, Hawaii, the Caribbean, Central America, and South America. Hear the voices of many cultures as you read these traditional selections.

This Big Sky

by Pat Mora

This book of fourteen **poems** combines Mora's vivid imagery with cut-paper collages to bring the awe-inspiring American Southwest to life for the reader.

Informational Texts

Discoveries: Finding Connections

This collection of **essays** explores the importance of communities in "The Maori Culture of New Zealand," "Natural Disasters," "The Delta Blues," and "Numbers: The Universal Language."

Understanding the Holy Land

by Mitch Frank

The Israeli-Palestinian conflict may be familiar to you, but how much do you really know? This **nonfiction book** explains why this conflict is important and how it affects the rest of the world.

Preparing to Read Complex Texts

Attentive Reading As you read on your own, ask yourself questions about the text. The questions shown below and others that you ask as you read will help you learn and enjoy literature even more.

 **Common Core State Standards**

Reading Literature/Informational Text
10. By the end of the year, read and comprehend literature, including stories, dramas, and poems, and literary nonfiction in the grades 6–8 text complexity band proficiently, with scaffolding as needed at the high end of the range.

When reading texts from the oral tradition, ask yourself...

- From what culture does this text come? What do I know about that culture?
- What type of text am I reading? For example, is it a myth, a legend, or a tall tale? What characters and events do I expect to find in this type of text?
- Does the text include the elements I expected? If not, how does it differ from what I expected?
- What elements of the culture do I see in the text? For example, do I notice beliefs, foods, or settings that have meaning for the people of this culture?
- Does the text teach a lesson or a moral? If so, is this a valuable lesson?

Ⓒ Key Ideas and Details

- Who is retelling or presenting this text? Do I think the author has changed the text from the original? If so, how?
- Does the text include characters and tell a story? If so, are the characters and plot interesting?
- What do I notice about the language used in the text? Which aspects seem similar to or different from the language used in modern texts?
- Does the text include symbols? If so, do they have a special meaning in the original culture of the text? Do they also have meaning in modern life?

Ⓒ Craft and Structure

- What does this text teach me about the culture from which it comes?
- What, if anything, does this text teach me about people in general?
- Does this text seem like others I have read or heard? Why or why not?
- Do I know of any modern versions of this text? How are they similar to or different from this one?
- If I were researching this culture for a report, would I include passages from this text? If so, what would those passages show?
- Do I enjoy reading this text and others like it? Why or why not?

Ⓒ Integration of Ideas

Resources

Glossary

Big Question vocabulary appears in **blue type**. High-utility Academic vocabulary is __underlined__.

A

abruptly (uh BRUHPT lee) *adv.* suddenly; unexpectedly

absent-minded (ab suhnt MYND uhd) *adj.* forgetful

accompanied (uh KUHM puh need) *v.* went along with; joined

accusers (uh KYOO zuhrz) *n.* those who find fault or blame

acquainted (uh KWAYNT uhd) *v.* know or become familiar with

admonishing (ad MON ihsh ihng) *adj.* disapproving

agonizing (AG uh nyz ihng) *v.* making great efforts or struggling; being in great pain

amid (uh MIHD) *prep.* in the middle of; surrounded by

anecdotes (AN ihk dohtz) *n.* short, entertaining tales

anxious (ANGK shuhs) *adj.* eager

anxiously (ANGK shuhs lee) *adv.* in a worried or uneasy way

apex (AY pehks) *n.* the highest point

appearance (uh PIHR uhns) *n.* how a person or thing looks

applications (AP luh KAY shuhnz) *n.* forms filled out to make a request

__argue__ (AHR gyoo) *v.* fight using words; debate

asphalt (AS fawlt) *n.* a brown or black mixture of substances used to pave roads

astray (uh STRAY) *adv.* away from the correct path

awed (awd) *adj.* filled with feelings of fear and wonder

B

barriers (BAR ee uhrz) *n.* something that makes progress difficult; obstacles

battle (BAT uhl) *n.* fight or major dispute

belief (bih LEEF) *n.* accepted idea

beseech (bih SEECH) *v.* beg

bewildered (bih WIHL duhrd) *v.* confused as by something complicated

billowing (BIHL oh ihng) *v.* a large swelling mass

bound (bownd) *v.* tied

C

catastrophe (kuh TAS truh fee) *n.* a disaster or misfortune

cavernous (KAV uhr nuhs) *adj.* huge and hollow; like a cavern

__challenge__ (CHAL uhnj) *n.* a dare; a calling into question

chaotic (kay OT ihk) *adj.* completely confused

charitable (CHAR uh tuh buhl) *adj.* kind and generous in giving help to others in need

choral (KAWR uhl) *adj.* relating to a singing group or choir

chorus (KAWR uhs) *n.* the sound produced by many voices singing or speaking at the same time

classified (KLAS uh fyd) *adj.* secret; available only to certain persons

clatter (KLAT uhr) *n.* rattling sound

coaxed (kohkst) *v.* persuaded by gentle urging or pleading

__common__ (KOM uhn) *adj.* ordinary or expected

__communicate__ (kuh MYOO nuh kayt) *v.* share thoughts or feelings, usually in words

community (kuh MYOO nuh tee) *n.* group of people living in a particular area

compete (kuhm PEET) *v.* contend; take part in a sport, game, or contest

composed (kuhm POHZD) *v.* made up of

compound (KOM pownd) *n.* an enclosed space with a building or a group of buildings

compulsion (kuhm PUHL shuhn) *n.* driving force

__concept__ (KON sehpt) *n.* general idea or notion

__conclude__ (kuhn KLOOD) *v.* to bring to a close; to end

condemnation (kon dehm NAY shuhn) *n.* an expression of strong disapproval

__confirm__ (kuhn FURM) *v.* support; show to be correct

confiscated (KON fihs kayt uhd) *v.* seized often by a governmental authority

connection (kuh NEHK shuhn) *n.* link or tie

conscious (KON shuhs) *adj.* awake or aware

consequently (KON suh kwehnt lee) *adv.* as a result

consoled (kuhn SOHLD) *v.* comforted

consumption (kuhn SUHMP shuhn) *n.* eating; drinking; using up

__convince__ (kuhn VIHNS) *v.* to persuade

cordial (KAWR juhl) *adj.* warm and friendly

correspond (kawr uh SPOND) *v.* agree with or be similar to

covetousness (KUHV uh tuhs ness) *n.* enviousness; wanting what another person has

craned (kraynd) *v.* stretched out for a better look

crippled (KRIHP uhld) *adj.* having a disability that prevents normal motion in a person's limbs or body

crude (krood) *adj.* lacking polish; not carefully made

cuddly (KUHD lee) *adj.* having a quality which invites hugging or holding in one's arms

culture (KUHL chuhr) *n.* collected customs of a group or community

cunning (KUHN ihng) *adj.* sly; crafty; deceptive

custody (KUHS tuh dee) *n.* protection or supervision

custom (KUHS tuhm) *n.* accepted practice

custom (KUHS tuhm) *n.* usual way of doing something; habit

D

decision (dih SIHZH uhn) *n.* choice; result of judging

declined (dih KLYND) *v.* refused

deem (deem) *v.* hold as an opinion; judge

defend (dih FEHND) *v.* guard from attack; protect

deficiency (dih FIHSH uhn see) *n.* shortage or lack

demented (dih MEHN tihd) *adj.* insane; mad

demise (dih MYZ) *n.* end of existence; death

demonstrate (DEHM uhn strayt) *v.* show clearly; prove

descendants (dih SEHN duhntz) *n.* a person's children, grandchildren, great grandchildren and so on

determine (dih TUR muhn) *v.* settle; reach a conclusion

devoured (dih VOWRD) *v.* ate hungrily or greedily

dialogue (DY uh lawg) *n.* conversation or exchange of words

dignity (DIHG nuh tee) *n.* being worthy of esteem or honor; proper pride and self respect

dilution (duh LOO shuhn) *n.* process of weakening by mixing with something else

dimensions (duh MEHN shuhnz) *n.* scope or importance

dismal (DIHZ muhl) *adj.* causing gloom or misery

dispersed (dihs PURST) *v.* distributed in many directions

dissonance (DIHS uh nuhns) *n.* harsh or unpleasant combination of sounds

distinguish (dihs TIHNG gwihsh) *v.* mark as different; set apart

distorted (dihs TAWRT uhd) *v.* twisted out of normal shape

distracted (dihs TRAKT uhd) *adj.* unable to concentrate

diverse (duh VURS) *adj.* many and different; from different backgrounds

diverse (duh VURS) *adj.* various; with differing characteristics

drone (drohn) *n.* continuous humming sound

E

eloquent (EHL uh kwuhnt) *adj.* vivid, persuasive and expressive

embedded (ehm BEHD ihd) *adj.* firmly fixed in surrounding material

embraced (ehm BRAYSD) *v.* hugged; clasped in the arms to show affection

emigrated (EHM uh grayt uhd) *v.* left one country to settle in another

endured (ehn DURD) *v.* suffered through

engulfing (ehn GUHLF ihng) *adj.* swallowing up; overwhelming

enroll (ehn ROHL) *v.* to place oneself on a register or list

enviously (EHN vee uhs lee) *adv.* with jealousy

equipped (ih KWIHPT) *v.* having what is needed

escorting (EHS kawrt ihng) *v.* going with as a companion

etiquette (EHT uh keht) *n.* acceptable social manners

evidence (EHV uh duhns) *n.* proof in support of a claim or statement

evident (EHV uh duhnt) *adj.* easy to see; very clear

evolved (ih VOLVD) *v.* grew gradually; developed

exact (ehg ZAKT) *v.* demand with force or authority

examine (ehg ZAM uhn) *v.* study in depth; look at closely

exhaust (ehg ZAWST) *v.* use up

exhausted (ehg ZAWST uhd) *adj.* very tired

expectations (EHKS pehk TAY shuhnz) *n.* feelings that something is about to happen

expression (ehk SPREHSH uhn) *n.* figure of speech

exuded (ehg ZOOD uhd) *v.* gave off; oozed

F

fact (fakt) *n.* idea or thought that is real or true

family (FAM uh lee) *n.* people related by blood or having a common ancestor

famine (FAM uhn) *n.* shortage of food

fantasy (FAN tuh see) *n.* idea or thought that is imagined or unreal

fascinated (FAS uh nayt uhd) *adj.* strongly attracted to something interesting or delightful

feeble (FEE buhl) *adj.* weak

fellow (FEHL oh) *n.* a man or boy

ferocious (fuh ROH shuhs) *adj.* wild and dangerous

fiction (FIHK shuhn) *n.* imagined or made-up thought or claim

flaw (flaw) *n.* crack; defect

flee (flee) *v.* to run away as from danger

flickering (FLIHK uhr ihng) *v.* burning unsteadily

fragments (FRAG muhntz) *n.* small, broken off parts

fragrant (FRAY gruhnt) *adj.* having a pleasant odor

frenzied (FREHN zeed) *adj.* acting in a wild, uncontrolled way

fulfilling (ful FIHL ihng) *v.* carrying out a promise; satisfying an obligation

G

game (gaym) *n.* contest; type of play in which there is usually one winner

generation (jehn uh RAY shuhn) *n.* people living at the same time and/or of about the same age

gesture (JEHS chuhr) *n.* motion of the hand or body to show or point

gilded (GIHLD uhd) *adj.* covered with gold or golden color

gnawing (NAW ihng) *v.* biting and cutting with teeth

greed (greed) *n.* a selfish desire for more than one's share of something

group (groop) *n.* collection or set, as of people

grudgingly (GRUHJ ihng lee) *adv.* in an unwilling or resentful way

guess (gehs) *n.* estimate based on little or no information

H

hence (hehns) *adv.* from this place or time

hereditary (huh REHD uh tehr ee) *adj.* a characteristic passed down from generation to generation

hesitated (HEHZ uh tayt uhd) *v.* stopped because of indecision

history (HIHS tuhr ee) *n.* record of past events

hollowed (HOL ohd) *v.* created a cavity or a space within

homey (HOHM ee) *adj.* comfortable; having a feeling of home

horrid (HAWR ihd) *adj.* shockingly dreadful; extremely unpleasant

howl (howl) *v.* make a loud, sorrowful sound

humble (HUHM buhl) *adj.* modest; not proud

I

ideals (y DEE uhlz) *n.* models or standards of excellence or perfection

idle (Y duhl) *adj.* not working or active; doing nothing

ignorance (IHG nuhr uhns) *n.* lack of knowledge, education, or experience

ignore (ihg NAWR) *v.* pay no attention to

imitate (IHM uh tayt) *v.* copy; mimic

immense (ih MEHNS) *adj.* huge

impatient (ihm PAY shuhnt) *adj.* feeling or showing annoyance because of delay

incessantly (ihn SEHS uhnt lee) *adv.* constantly; continuously

indignantly (ihn DIHG nuhnt lee) *adv.* expressing anger or scorn

individuality (ihn duh vihj u AL uh tee) *n.* way in which a person or thing stands apart or is different

inedible (ihn EHD uh buhl) *adj.* not fit to be eaten

inevitably (ihn EHV uh tuh blee) *adv.* unavoidably

infamous (IHN fuh muhs) *adj.* having a bad reputation

influence (IHN floo uhns) *v.* to sway or affect in some other way

inhabited (ihn HAB iht uhd) *adj.* lived in; occupied

inquired (ihn KWYRD) *v.* asked

inscribed (ihn SKRYBD) *v.* written on

instinctively (ihn STIHNGK tihv lee) *adv.* done automatically without thinking

integrate (IHN tuh grayt) *v.* remove all barriers and allow free association; bring together as a whole

intently (ihn TEHNT lee) *adv.* purposefully; earnestly

investigate (ihn VEHS tuh gayt) *v.* examine thoroughly, as an idea

involve (ihn VOLV) *v.* include

iridescent (ihr uh DEHS uhnt) *adj.* showing different colors when seen from different angles

irrational (ih RASH uh nuhl) *adj.* unreasonable

isolate (Y suh layt) *v.* set apart

issue (IHSH oo) *n.* problem or point on which there is disagreement

J

jubilation (joo buh LAY shuhn) *n.* great joy; triumph

judge (juhj) *v.* form an opinion of or pass judgment on

K

knowledge (NOL ihj) *n.* result of learning; awareness

L

lair (ler) *n.* den or resting place of a wild animal

language (LANG gwihj) *n.* form of communication between people

leisurely (LEE zhuhr lee) *adj.* in an unhurried way

liable (LY uh buhl) *adj.* likely to do something or to happen

limit (LIHM iht) *n.* as far as something can go; farthest extreme

lose (looz) *v.* to fail in a game or dispute

lure (lur) *v.* tempt or attract

M

malicious (muh LIHSH uhs) *adj.* having or showing evil intentions

mauled (mawld) *v.* badly injured by being attacked

measure (MEHZH uhr) *v.* place a value on

message (MEHS ihj) *n.* written or spoken communication

methods (MEHTH uhdz) *n.* ways of doing something

migrated (MY grayt uhd) *v.* moved from one place to another

miniscule (MIHN uh skyool) *adj.* very small; tiny

misapprehension (mihs ap rih HEHN shuhn) *n.* misunderstanding

mistook (mihs TUK) *v.* identified incorrectly; to misunderstand

mode (mohd) *n.* a way of acting, doing, or being

monarch (MON uhrk) *n.* the single or sole ruler of a state

mortal (MAWR tuhl) *adj.* referring to humans who eventually die

murmured (MUR muhrd) *v.* made a low, continuous sound

mystified (MIHS tuh fyd) *v.* perplexed; bewildered

N

narrow (NAR oh) *adj.* limited in extent, not wide

negotiate (nih GOH shee ayt) *v.* to settle or come to an agreement

nigh (ny) *adv.* near

nonverbal (nohn VUR buhl) *adj.* not involving or using words or speech

O

obscure (uhb SKYUR) *adj.* not well known

observant (uhb ZUR vuhnt) *adj.* quick to notice; alert; watchful

observe (uhb ZURV) *v.* notice or see

obstinacy (OB stuh nuh see) *n.* stubbornness

offense (uh FEHNS) *n.* harmful act; a violation of law

offensive (uh FEHN sihv) *adj.* unpleasant

official (uh FIHSH uhl) *adj.* formal; prescribed by an authority

olden (OHL duhn) *adj.* ancient; old

opinion (uh PIHN yuhn) *n.* personal view or belief

orator (AWR uh tuhr) *n.* a person who can speak well in public

P

participation (pahr tihs uh PAY shuhn) *n.* the act of taking part in an event or activity

peaceable (PEE suh buhl) *adj.* harmonious; tranquil

peculiar (pih KYOOL yuhr) *adj.* out of the ordinary; odd

persisted (puhr SIHST uhd) *v.* refused to give up

personality (pur suh NAL uh tee) *n.* the sum of behaviors and feelings that define an individual

perspective (puhr SPEHK tihv) *n.* point of view

petition (puh TIHSH uhn) *n.* document that people sign to express demands

pitiless (PIHT uh lihs) *adj.* without mercy

plagued (playgd) *v.* troubled or annoyed

pleaded (PLEED uhd) *v.* begged

pleasant (PLEHZ uhnt) *adj.* agreeable; delightful

plight (plyt) *n.* awkward, sad or dangerous situation

plunging (PLUHN jihng) *v.* moving suddenly forward or downward

precautionary (prih KAW shuh nehr ee) *adj.* done to prevent harm or danger

precious (PREHSH uhs) *adj.* dear; beloved

prejudiced (PREHJ uh dihst) *adj.* having unreasonable hostile feelings toward a racial, religious or other group

prelude (PREHL yood) *n.* introduction to a main event

prove (proov) *v.* establish the truth of, as in a claim or statement

provided (pruh VYD uhd) *v.* supplied; furnished

prowled (prowld) *v.* moved around quietly and secretly

pulsating (PUHL sayt ihng) *adj.* beating or throbbing rhythmically

purpose (PUR puhs) *n.* what something is used for

pursue (puhr SOO) *v.* be involved in; follow

pursuers (puhr SOO uhrz) *n.* those who follow in an effort to capture

Q

question (KWEHS chuhn) *v.* challenge the accuracy of; place in doubt

quote (kwoht) *v.* refer to the words of a source

R

rage (rayj) *n.* very strong anger

rancor (RANG kuhr) *n.* bitter hate or ill will

ravaged (RAV ihjd) *v.* violently destroyed; ruined

ravenous (RAV uh nuhs) *adj.* greedily hungry

reaction (ree AK shuhn) *n.* response or course of action taken in response to something said or done

realistic (ree uh LIHS tihk) *adj.* true to life; having to do with reality

recognize (REHK uhg nyz) *v.* know and remember

refer (rih FUR) *v.* point back to, as an authority or expert

reflect (rih FLEHKT) *v.* think about or consider

reflecting (rih FLEHKT ihng) *v.* thinking seriously

reluctant (rih LUHK tuhnt) *adj.* showing doubt or unwillingness

reluctantly (rih LUHK tuhnt lee) *adv.* unwillingly; unenthusiastically

repaid (rih PAYD) *v.* did or gave in return

repentance (rih PEHN tuhns) *n.* deep sorrow and regret; feeling of sorrow for wrongdoing

repulse (rih PUHLS) *v.* drive back; repel an attack

resident (REHZ uh duhnt) *adj.* living in a particular place

resist (rih ZIHST) *v.* to oppose actively; to refuse to give in

resolve (rih ZOLV) *v.* to settle or bring to an end

respond (rih SPOND) *v.* to reply or answer

retaliated (rih TAL ee ayt uhd) *v.* punished in return for an injury or wrong done

reunion (ree YOON yuhn) *n.* gathering of people who have been separated

reveal (rih VEEL) *v.* to show or uncover

revolution (rehv uh LOO shuhn) *n.* a complete or radical change of any kind

routine (roo TEEN) *n.* a customary or regular procedure

rue (roo) *v.* to be sorrowful or regretful

S

savoring (SAY vuhr ihng) *v.* enjoying; tasting with delight

scarce (skairs) *adj.* not enough to satisfy need

scarcely (SKAIRS lee) *adv.* hardly

scrawny (SKRAW nee) *adj.* very thin, skinny, and boney

sculpted (SKUHLPT uhd) *v.* shaped or molded

sensible (SEHN suh buhl) *adj.* logical; practical; intelligent

sentiment (SEHN tuh muhnt) *n.* a tender feeling or emotion

share (shair) *v.* to communicate with, such as an idea or experience

similar (SIHM uh luhr) *adj.* alike

skimming (SKIHM ihng) *v.* gliding; moving swiftly and lightly over a surface

slanderous (SLAN duhr uhs) *adj.* untrue and damaging statements

smugly (SMUHG lee) *adv.* in a way that shows satisfaction with oneself

soprano (suh PRAN oh) *n.* a singer who can sing two octaves or more above middle C

sour (sowr) *adj.* having the sharp acid taste of lemon or vinegar

source (sawrs) *n.* person or book that provides information

sown (sohn) *v.* scattered or planted seeds for growing

spasm (SPAZ uhm) *n.* sudden short burst of energy or activity

splendor (SPLEHN duhr) *n.* gorgeous appearance; magnificence

splendor (SPLEHN duhr) *n.* great brightness

startled (STAHR tuhld) *adj.* surprised

starvation (stahr VAY shuhn) *n.* a state of extreme hunger

striking (STRY kihng) *adj.* very noticeable or impressive; unusual

strive (stryv) *v.* struggle; compete

stubby (STUHB ee) *adj.* short and thick; bristly

study (STUHD ee) *n.* research or investigation into a claim

study (STUHD ee) *v.* to look into deeply

sublime (suh BLYM) *adj.* majestic; impressive because of great beauty

summit (SUHM iht) *n.* highest part

superb (su PURB) *adj.* extremely fine; excellent

support (suh PAWRT) *v.* to stand behind or back up

surmise (suhr MYZ) *v.* to infer without evidence; to guess

surplus (SUR pluhs) *adj.* an amount greater than what is needed

survival (suhr VY vuhl) *n.* the act of lasting or continuing to live

symbolize (SIHM buh lyz) *v.* to stand for

sympathize (SIHM puh thyz) *v.* to share in a feeling; to feel compassion

sympathy (SIHM puh thee) *n.* understanding and sharing another person's feelings

systematic (SIHS tuh MAT ihk) *adj.* orderly

T

teemed (teemd) *v.* was full of

temporarily (tehm puh REHR uh lee) *adv.* not permanently

test (tehst) *n.* method or process for proving or disproving a claim

thicket (THIHK iht) *n.* dense growth of shrubs or small trees

thorny (THAWR nee) *adj.* prickly; full of thorns

thrashing (THRASH ihng) *v.* wild moving

thrives (thryvz) *v.* grows well

timidly (TIHM ihd lee) *adv.* in a way that shows fear or shyness

trace (trays) *n.* mark left behind by something

transfixed (trans FIHKSD) *v.* made motionless

transport (trans PAWRT) *v.* carry from one place to another

traversed (TRAV uhrsd) *v.* went across

treacheries (TREHCH uhr eez) *n.* acts of betrayal

trend (trehnd) *n.* tendency or general direction

trespass (TREHS pahs) *v.* to go on another's land without permission

trotted (TROT uhd) *v.* a run by a four-legged animal in which the front foot

and the opposite hind foot lift at the same time

trudged (truhjd) *v.* walked as if tired or with effort

true (troo) *adj.* real; genuine

tyrant (TY ruhnt) *n.* a harsh cruel ruler

U

unbelievable (UHN bih LEE vuh buhl) *adj.* not likely; hard to accept as true

undulating (UHN juh layt ihng) *adj.* moving in waves, like a snake

unethical (uhn EHTH uh kuhl) *adj.* not conforming to moral standards or to the standards of a group

unique (yoo NEEK) *adj.* one of a kind

V

values (VAL yooz) *n.* beliefs of a person or group

vanish (VAN ihsh) *v.* disappear

verbal (VUR buhl) *adj.* involving or using words or speech

vigilance (VIHJ uh luhns) *n.* watchfulness

vigorously (VIHG uhr uhs lee) *adv.* forcefully or energetically

visual (VIHZH u uhl) *adj.* able to be seen or understood with the eyes

vow (vow) *n.* promise or pledge

W

whirs (hwurz) *v.* flies or moves quickly with a buzzing sound

win (wihn) *v.* to gain a victory or come out ahead

winced (wihnsd) *v.* drew back slightly as if in pain

wintry (WIHN tree) *adj.* being very cold, like winter weather

Y

yearning (YURN ihng) *n.* deep or anxious longing

Spanish Glossary

El vacabulario de Gran Pregunta aparece en **azul**. El vocabulario academico de alta utilidad está <u>subrayado</u>.

A

abruptly / súbitamente *adv.* repentinamente; inesperadamente

absent-minded / distraído *adj.* olvidadizo

accompanied / acompañó *v.* fue en compañía de otro; se unió; se juntó

accusers / acusadores *s.* personas que culpan

acquainted / conocer *v.* saber algo o familiarizarse con algo

admonishing / amonestado *adj.* desaprobado

agonizing / agonizando *v.* haciendo un gran esfuerzo o luchando; con mucho dolor

amid / entre *prep.* en el medio de; rodeado de

anecdotes / anécdotas *s.* relatos cortos y entretenidos

anxious / ansioso *adj.* deseoso

anxiously / ansiosamente *adv.* con preocupación o intranquilidad

apex / cumbre *s.* punto más alto

appearance / apariencia *s.* aspecto de una persona o cosa

applications / solicitudes *s.* formularios que se completan para hacer una petición

<u>**argue / discutir**</u> *v.* debate; desacuerdo verbal

asphalt / asfalto *s.* mezcla marrón o negra de sustancias que se usa para pavimentar carreteras

astray / descarriar *v.* alejar del camino correcto

awed / sobrecogido *adj.* con sentimientos de temor y asombro

B

barriers / barreras *s.* algo que dificulta el progreso; obstáculo

battle / lucha *s.* pelea; gran disputa

belief / creencia *s.* idea conforme

beseech / suplicar *v.* rogar

bewildered / desconcertado *adj.* confundido por algo complejo

billowing / hinchado *adj.* inflamado o inflado

bound / sujetó *v.* amarró

C

catastrophe / catástrofe *s.* desastre o desgracia

cavernous / cavernoso *adj.* enorme y hueco; como una caverna

<u>**challenge / desafío**</u> *s.* un reto; el acto de cuestionar

chaotic / caótico *adj.* completamente confuso

charitable / caritativo *adj.* que presta ayuda a los necesitados de una manera amable y generosa

choral / coral *adj.* relacionado con un grupo de cantantes o un coro

chorus / coro *s.* sonido que producen muchas voces al cantar o hablar al mismo tiempo

classified / clasificado *adj.* secreto; disponible solo para ciertas personas

clatter / traqueteo *s.* vibración

coaxed / convenció *v.* persuadió de manera sutil

<u>**common / común**</u> *adj.* ordinario; frecuente y esperado

<u>**communicate / comunicar**</u> *v.* compartir pensamientos o sentimientos, usualmente con palabras

community / comunidad *s.* grupo de personas que tienen un interés en común o que viven cerca el uno del otro

compete / competir *v.* contender; participar en un deporte, juego o concurso

composed / compuesto *adj.* formado por

compound / complejo residencial *s.* área que tiene una o varias edificaciones

compulsion / compulsión *s.* impulso irresistible

<u>**concept / concepto**</u> *s.* idea general o noción

<u>**conclude / concluir**</u> *v.* finalizar; terminar

condemnation / condena *s.* fuerte expresión de desaprobación

<u>**confirm / confirmar**</u> *v.* apoyar o corroborar

confiscated / confiscó *v.* embargó; acción que generalmente ejecuta el gobierno

connection / conección *s.* enlace o vínculo

conscious / conciente *adj.* que está despierto o tiene presente

consequently / consecuentemente *adv.* como resultado de

consoled / consoló *v.* alivió la pena

consumption / consumo *s.* uso alimentos o bebidas; utilización

<u>**convince / convencer**</u> *v.* persuadir; incitar a aceptar cierto punto de vista

cordial / cordial *adj.* afectuoso y amable

correspond / corresponder *v.* acordar en algo o asemejarse

covetousness / codicia *s.* envidia; deseo de tener lo que otra persona posee

craned / estiró *v.* se extendió para ver mejor

crippled / lisiado *adj.* persona que tiene una incapacidad física que previene el movimiento normal de los brazos y las piernas; el uso del equivalente en inglés de esta palabra para referirse a una persona es ofensivo

crude / crudo *adj.* sin pulir; hecho sin cuidado

cuddly / mimoso *adj.* que le encantan las caricias y los abrazos; muy afectuoso

culture / cultura *s.* conjunto de modos de vida y costumbres de un grupo o una comunidad

cunning / astuto *adj.* hábil; taimado; engañoso

custody / custodia *s.* protección o supervisión

custom / costumbre *s.* lo que se hace comúnmente

custom / costumbre *s.* manera común de hacer algo; hábito

D

decision / decisión *s.* elección; resultado de un juicio

declined / declinar *v.* rechazar

deem / considerar *v.* juzgar

defend / defender *v.* resguardar de un ataque; proteger

deficiency / deficiencia *s.* escasez o carencia

demented / demente *adj.* loco

demise / fallecimiento *s.* fin de la existencia; muerte

demonstrate / demostrar *v.* enseñar claramente; probar

descendants / descendientes *s.* hijos, nietos, bisnietos de una persona; generaciones que siguen a una persona

determine / determinar *v.* decidir; llegar a una conclusión

devoured / devoró *v.* comió con ansia o apresuradamente

dialogue / dialogar *s.* conversación; intercambio de palabras

dignity / dignidad *s.* cualidad de una persona que merece aprecio o trato con honor; comportamiento con orgullo y dándose a respetar

dilution / dilución *s.* proceso mediante el cual se diluyen los componentes mezclándolos

dimensions / dimensiones *s.* alcance o importancia

dismal / sombrío *adj.* que causa tristeza o melancolía

dispersed / dispersó *v.* distribuyó en varias direcciones

dissonance / disonancia *s.* conjunto desagradable de sonidos

distinguish / distinguir *v.* diferenciar; considerar por separado

distorted / distorsionó *adj.* torció de tal manera que cambia la forma original

distracted / distraído *adj.* que no se puede concentrar

diverse / diverso *adj.* en cantidad y variado; de orígenes diferentes

diverse / diverso *adj.* variado; con diferentes características

drone / zumbido *s.* sonido continuado y bronco

E

eloquent / elocuente *adj.* vívido, persuasivo y expresivo

embedded / incrustado *adj.* fijado fuertemente en otro material

embraced / abrazó *v.* rodeó con los brazos como muestra de afecto

emigrated / emigró *v.* se marchó de un país para establecerse en otro

endured / aguantó *v.* soportó una situación difícil

engulfing / arrollador *adj.* destructor; derribador; que puede sepultar

enroll / matricular *v.* inscribirse o registrarse

enviously / con envidia *adv.* con celos

equipped / equipado *adj.* con lo necesario

escorting / acompañar *v.* ir con otra persona

etiquette / etiqueta *s.* buenos modales que se debe tener en actos sociales

evidence / evidencia *s.* prueba que apoya una aseveración o argumento

evident / evidente *adj.* aparente; muy claro

evolved / evolucionó *v.* creció gradualmente; se desarrolló

exact / exigir *v.* pedir con fuerza y autoridad

examine / examinar *v.* estudiar a fondo; observar detenidamente

exhaust / agotar *v.* usar todo; terminar

exhausted / agotado *adj.* muy cansado

expectations / expectativas *s.* sensación de que algo está por ocurrir

expression / expresión *s.* figura retórica

exuded / exudar *v.* emitir; rezumar

F

fact / hecho *s.* idea o pensamiento real o verdadero

family / familia *s.* personas de relación consanguínea o que tienen un ancestro en común

famine / hambruna *s.* escasez de alimentos

fantasy / fantasía *s.* producto de la imaginación; ficción

fascinated / fascinado *adj.* atraído fuertemente a algo interesante o encantador

feeble / débil *adj.* flojo

fellow / tipo *s.* hombre o joven

ferocious / feroz *adj.* salvaje y peligroso

fiction / ficción *s.* lo inventado o imaginado

flaw / imperfección *s.* grieta; defecto

flee / huir *v.* alejarse apresuradamente del peligro, escaparse

flickering / parpadear *v.* titilar

fragments / fragmentos *s.* pequeños pedazos de algo

fragrant / fragante *adj.* que tiene un aroma agradable

frenzied / frenético *adj.* que actúa de manera alocada y desenfrenada

fulfilling / satisfacer *v.* cumplir con una promesa o con una obligación

G

game / juego *s.* concurso, tipo de diversión en el que usualmente hay un ganador

generation / generación *s.* personas que viven en en mismo período de tiempo y/o son de la misma edad

gesture / gesto *s.* movimiento de la mano o del cuerpo para demostrar o señalar

gilded / dorado *adj.* cubierto de oro o de color áureo

gnawing / morder *v.* apretar y cortar con los dientes

greed / codicia *s.* deseo egoísta de tener más de la porción establecida

group / grupo *s.* conjunto o agrupación, como de personas

grudgingly / a regañadientes *adv.* de mala gana o con resentimiento

guess / conjetura *s.* estimado basado en poca o ninguna información

H

hence / por lo tanto *adv.* desde ahora

hereditary / hereditario *adj.* característica que se pasa de generación a generación

hesitated / dudar *v.* detenerse por estar indeciso

history / historia *s.* récord de sucesos del pasado

hollowed / ahuecó *v.* abrió una cavidad o un espacio dentro de algo

homey / hogareño *adj.* cómodo; que genra el sentimiento de estar en el hogar

horrid / horrible *adj.* espantoso; muy desagradable

howl / aullar *v.* hacer un ruido alto y triste

humble / humilde *adj.* modesto; sin vanidad

I

ideals / ideales *s.* modelos o estándares de excelencia o perfección

idle / holgazán *adj.* ocioso, desocupado; que no trabaja; inactivo

ignorance / ignorancia *s.* falta de conocimiento, educación o experiencia

ignore / ignorar *v.* no prestar atención

imitate / imitar *v.* copiar; emular

immense / inmenso *adj.* enorme

impatient / impaciente *adj.* que siente o demuestra molestia por algún retraso

incessantly / sin cesar *adv.* constante; continuo

indignantly / con indignación *adv.* expresando ira o desprecio

individuality / individualidad *s.* forma en la que alguien o algo se diferencia de otros

inedible / incomible *adj.* que no se puede comer

inevitably / inevitablemente *adv.* que no se puede eludir

infamous / infame *adj.* que tiene mala reputación

influence / influencia *v.* poder o efecto sobre algo

inhabited / habitó *adj.* sitio donde se ha vivido, que ha sido ocupado

inquired / informado *v.* preguntado

inscribed / inscribir *v.* escribir o grabar en algún material

instinctively / instintivamente *adv.* automáticamente, sin pensar

integrate / integrar *v.* eliminar las barreras y permitir la libre asociación; unificar

intently / intencionadamente *adv.* seriamente, con atención

investigate / investigar *v.* examinar detenidamente, como una idea

involve / involucrar *v.* incluir

iridescent / iridiscente *adj.* que muestra colores distintos cuando se observa desde diferentes ángulos

irrational / irracional *adj.* que carece de razón

isolate / aislar *v.* considerar por separado

issue / asunto *s.* problema o punto en el que hay un desacuerdo

J

jubilation / júbilo *s.* gran alegría; triunfo

judge / juzgar *v.* formar una opinión o pronunciar juicio

K

knowledge / conocimiento *s.* el resultado del aprendizaje; tener presente

L

lair / guarida *s.* cueva o lugar donde guarecen los animales salvajes

language / lenguaje *s.* sistema de comunicación entre personas

leisurely / tranquilamente *adj.* sin apresuramiento

liable / responsable *adj.* que es probable que haga algo

limit / límite s. punto en el que no se puede seguir; extremo máximo

lose / perder v. fallar o fracasar en un juego o disputa

lure / atraer v. tentar o interesar

M

malicious / malicioso adj. que tiene o demuestra malas intenciones

mauled / magullar v. herir gravemente al atacar

measure / evaluar v. reconocer su valor

message / mensaje s. comunicación escrita o verbal

methods / métodos s. maneras de hacer las cosas

migrated / migró v. se fue de un lugar a otro

miniscule / minúsculo adj. muy pequeño; pequeñito

misapprehension / malentendido s. mala interpretación

mistook / equivocarse v. identificar incorrectamente; malentender

mode / modo s. manera de actuar o ser

monarch / monarca s. soberano de un estado

mortal / mortal adj. se refiere a seres que pueden morir

murmured / murmuró v. hizo un sonido bajo y continuo

mystified / desconcertó v. dejó perplejo; aturdió

N

narrow / estrecho adj. de extensión limitada; que no es ancho

negotiate / negociar v. decidir; llegar a un acuerdo

nigh / contiguo adv. cercano

nonverbal / no verbal adj. que no involucra o usa palabras o el habla

O

obscure / críptico adj. no muy conocido, oscuro, enigmático

observant / observador adj. que se da cuenta rápidamente; alerta; vigilante

observe / observar v. notar o ver

obstinacy / obstinación s. terquedad

offense / ofensa s. acto perjudicial; violación de la ley

offensive / ofensivo adj. desagradable

official / oficial adj. formal; dictado por una figura de la autoridad

olden / pasado adj. antiguo; viejo

opinion / opinión s. punto de vista personal o creencia

orator / orador s. persona que habla bien en público

P

participation / participación s. el acto de tomar parte en un evento o actividad

peaceable / grato adj. armonioso; tranquilo

peculiar / peculiar adj. fuera de lo normal; extraño

persisted / persistirse v. rehusarse a darse por vencido

personality / personalidad s. el conjunto de comportamientos y sentimientos que definen a un individuo

perspective / perspectiva s. punto de vista

petition / petición s. documento firmado para solicitar algo

pitiless / despiadado adj. sin piedad, cruel

plagued / asediar v. molestar o importunar a alguien sin descanso

pleaded / suplicó v. rogó

pleasant / placentero adj. agradable, apacible

plight / situación grave s. suceso muy extraño, triste o que puede causar peligro

plunging / desplomar v. caer repentinamente

precautionary / preventivo adj. algo que se hace para evitar daño o peligro

precious / precioso adj. muy querido; de mucho valor

prejudiced / prejuiciado adj. que tiene sentimientos hostiles e irracionales contra un grupo racial, religioso, etc.

prelude / preludio s. introducción a un evento

prove / probar v. establecer la veracidad de algo, como de una aseveración o argumento

provided / proveer v. suministrar; facilitar

prowled / rondar v. moverse por un lugar silenciosamente y en secreto

pulsating / pulsando v. latiendo o palpitando a cierto ritmo

purpose / propósito s. intención por la cual se usa algo

pursue / perseguir v. seguir; tratar de alcanzar algo

pursuers / perseguidores s. personas que buscan con el propósito de capturar

Q

question / cuestionar v. la precisión de algo; poner en duda

quote / citar v. relatar las palabras de una fuente de información

R

rage / rabia s. ira

rancor / rencor s. odio o mala voluntad

ravaged / devastó v. destruyó violentamente; arruinó

ravenous / hambriento adj. que tiene mucha hambre

reaction / reacción s. respuesta o acción que responde a algo dicho o hecho

realistic / realista adj. sensato; relacionado a la realidad

recognize / reconocer v. saber y recordar

refer / referir v. aludir a, como a una autoridad o a un experto

reflect / reflejar v. pensar en algo o considerar

reflecting / reflexionando v. pensando detenidamente

reluctant / reacio adj. que demuestra duda o poca voluntad para hacer algo

reluctantly / de mala gana adv. sin voluntad; sin entusiasmo

repaid / retribuyó v. hizo o dio a cambio de algo

repentance / remordimiento s. gran sentimiento de pena y arrepentimiento; sentimiento de pena por haber actuado incorrectamente

repulse / repeler v. rechazar un ataque obligando; alejar algo con fuerza

resident / residente adj. que vive en un lugar en particular

resist / resistir v. oponerse activamente; negarse a ceder

resolve / resolver v. decidir; finalizar

respond / responder v. replicar; contestar

retaliated / tomar represalias v. castigar por haber herido o por haber hecho una maldad

reunion / reunión s. congregación de personas que han estado separadas

reveal / revelar v. mostrar; descubrir

revolution / revolución s. cambio total o radical

routine / rutina s. proceso habitual o regular

rue / lamentar v. sufrir una pena o arrepentirse

S

savoring / saboreando v. degustando o apreciando con placer

scarce / escaso adj. insuficiente

scarcely / escasamente adv. difícilmente

scrawny / esquelético adj. muy delgado, flaco y huesudo

sculpted / esculpió v. dio forma o moldeó

sensible / sensato adj. lógico; práctico; inteligente

sentiment / sensación s. ternura o emoción

share / compartir v. comunicar una idea o experiencia

similar / similar adj. semejante

skimming / rasar v. deslizarse; moverse rápida y ligeramente por una superficie

slanderous / calumnioso adj. que contiene argumentos falsos y perjudiciales

smugly / presuntuoso adv. se refiere a las personas que muestran extrema satisfacción consigo mismas

soprano / soprano s. persona que puede cantar dos octavos o más por encima del do central

sour / ácido adj. con el sabor fuerte y ácido de limón o vinagre

source / fuente s. persona o texto que provee información

sown / sembró v. regó o plantó semillas

spasm / arranque s. ímpetu de energía o inicio repentino de una actividad

splendor / esplendor s. belleza impresionante; magnificencia

splendor / resplandor s. brillo intenso

startled / sobresaltado adj. sorprendido

starvation / inanición s. falta extrema de alimento

striking / destacado adj. muy notable o impresionante; inusual

strive / esforzarse v. luchar; competir

stubby / regordete adj. bajo y grueso

study / estudiar v. examinar; observar a fondo

study / estudio s. búsqueda o investigación de un tema

sublime / sublime adj. mejestuoso; impresionante por su belleza

summit / cumbre s. la parte más alta

superb / espléndido adj. extremadamente fino; excelente

support / apoyar v. basar; fundar

surmise / presumir v. inferir sin evidencia; figurarse

surplus / excedente adj. cantidad mayor a la que se necesita

survival / supervivencia s. lo que perdura o continua viviendo

symbolize / simbolizar v. atribuir; representar

sympathize / compadecer v. compartir un sentimiento; sentir compasión

sympathy / compasión s. comprensión de los sentimientos de otra persona

systematic / sistemático adj. ordenado

T

teemed / repleto v. lleno de

temporarily / temporalmente adv. por algún tiempo, pero no de manera permanente

test / prueba s. método o proceso de probar o desmentir una aseveración

thicket / matorral s. terreno denso de arbustos y pequeños árboles

thorny / espinoso adj. lleno de espinas

thrashing / golpear v. mover de manera repentina y violenta un cuerpo contra otro

thrives / prosperar v. crecer muy bien

timidly / tímidamente adv. con temor o modestia

trace / rastro *s.* huella que deja algo o alguien a su paso

transfixed / paralizar *v.* detener el movimiento

transport / transportar *v.* llevar de un lugar a otro

traversed / atravesó *v.* cruzó

treacheries / traiciones *s.* actos desleales

trend / tendencia *s.* inclinacion o dirección en general

trespass / entrar sin autorización *v.* pasar a territorio ajeno sin permiso

trotted / trotar *v.* manera de correr de un animal cuadrúpedo en la cual la pata delantera y la pata trasera opuesta se usan al mismo tiempo

trudged / marchar fatigosamente *v.* caminar de manera cansada o con mucho esfuerzo

true / cierto *adj.* real; auténtico

tyrant / tirano *s.* gobernador cruel y severo

U

unbelievable / increíble *adj.* que no es probable; difícil de aceptar como cierto

undulating / ondulado *adj.* que se mueve en oleadas, como una serpiente

unethical / poco ético *adj.* que no respeta los estándares morales o los de un grupo

unique / único *adj.* sin otro de su especie

V

values / valores *s.* creencias de una persona o grupo

vanish / desvanecer *v.* desaparecer

verbal / verbal *adj.* que involucra o usa palabras o el habla

vigilance / vigilancia *s.* supervisión

vigorously / vigorosamente *adv.* con fuerza o energía

visual / visual *adj.* que se puede ver o entender por medio de la vista

vow / juramento *s.* promesa o compromiso

W

whirs / runrunear *v.* que vuela o se mueve rápidamente emitiendo un zumbido

win / ganar *v.* vencer; terminar por delante

winced / retorcer *v.* moverse por causa de dolor

wintry / invernal *adj.* muy frío, como el clima de invierno

Y

yearning / anhelo *s.* deseo profundo o ansioso

Literary Terms

ALLITERATION *Alliteration* is the repetition of initial consonant sounds. Writers use alliteration to draw attention to certain words or ideas, to imitate sounds, and to create musical effects.

ALLUSION An *allusion* is a reference to a well-known person, event, place, literary work, or work of art. Understanding what a literary work is saying often depends on recognizing its allusions and the meanings they suggest.

ANALOGY An *analogy* makes a comparison between two or more things that are similar in some ways but otherwise unalike.

ANECDOTE An *anecdote* is a brief story about an interesting, amusing, or strange event. Writers tell anecdotes to entertain or to make a point.

ANTAGONIST An *antagonist* is a character or a force in conflict with a main character, or protagonist.

See *Conflict* and *Protagonist.*

ARGUMENT See *Persuasion.*

ATMOSPHERE *Atmosphere,* or *mood,* is the feeling created in the reader by a literary work or passage.

AUTHOR'S INFLUENCES An *author's influences* are things that affect his or her writing. These factors include the author's time and place of birth and cultural background, as well as world events that took place during the author's lifetime.

AUTHOR'S STYLE *Style* is an author's typical way of writing. Many factors determine an author's style, including diction; tone; use of characteristic elements such as figurative language, dialect, rhyme, meter, or rhythmic devices; typical grammatical structures and patterns; typical sentence length; and typical methods of organization.

AUTOBIOGRAPHY An *autobiography* is the story of the writer's own life, told by the writer. Autobiographical writing may tell about the person's whole life or only a part of it.

Because autobiographies are about real people and events, they are a form of nonfiction. Most autobiographies are written in the first person.

See *Biography, Nonfiction,* and *Point of View.*

BIOGRAPHY A *biography* is a form of nonfiction in which a writer tells the life story of another person. Most biographies are written about famous or admirable people. Although biographies are nonfiction, the most effective ones share the qualities of good narrative writing.

See *Autobiography* and *Nonfiction.*

CHARACTER A *character* is a person or an animal that takes part in the action of a literary work. The main, or *major,* character is the most important character in a story, poem, or play. A *minor* character is one who takes part in the action but is not the focus of attention.

Characters are sometimes classified as flat or round. A *flat character* is one-sided and often stereotypical. A *round character,* on the other hand, is fully developed and exhibits many traits—often both faults and virtues. Characters can also be classified as dynamic or static. A *dynamic character* is one who changes or grows during the course of the work. A *static character* is one who does not change.

See *Characterization, Hero/Heroine,* and *Motive.*

CHARACTERIZATION *Characterization* is the act of creating and developing a character. Authors use two major methods of characterization—*direct* and *indirect.* When using *direct* characterization, a writer states the *character's traits,* or characteristics.

When describing a character *indirectly,* a writer depends on the reader to draw conclusions about the character's traits. Sometimes the writer tells what other participants in the story say and think about the character.

See *Character* and *Motive.*

CHARACTER TRAITS *Character traits* are the qualities, attitudes, and values that a character has or displays—for example, dependability, intelligence, selfishness, or stubbornness.

CLIMAX The *climax,* also called the turning point, is the high point in the action of the plot. It is the moment of greatest tension, when the outcome of the plot hangs in the balance.

See *Plot.*

COMEDY A *comedy* is a literary work, especially a play, that is light, is often humorous or satirical, and ends happily. Comedies frequently depict ordinary characters faced with temporary difficulties and conflicts. Types of comedy include *romantic comedy,* which involves problems between lovers, and the *comedy of manners,* which satirically challenges social customs of a society.

CONCRETE POEM A *concrete poem* is one with a shape that suggests its subject. The poet arranges the letters, punctuation, and lines to create an image, or picture, on the page.

CONFLICT A *conflict* is a struggle between opposing forces. Conflict is one of the most important elements of stories, novels, and plays because it causes the action. There are two kinds of conflict: external and internal. An *external conflict* is one in which a character struggles against some outside force, such as another person. Another kind of external conflict may occur between a character and some force in nature.

An *internal conflict* takes place within the mind of a character. The character struggles to make a decision, take an action, or overcome a feeling.

See *Plot.*

CONNOTATIONS The *connotation* of a word is the set of ideas associated with it in addition to its explicit meaning. The connotation of a word can be personal, based on individual experiences. More often, cultural connotations—those recognizable by most people in a group—determine a writer's word choices.

See also *Denotation.*

DENOTATION The *denotation* of a word is its dictionary meaning, independent of other associations that the word may have. The denotation of the word *lake,* for example, is "an inland body of water." "Vacation spot" and "place where the fishing is good" are connotations of the word *lake.*

See also *Connotation.*

DESCRIPTION A *description* is a portrait, in words, of a person, place, or object. Descriptive writing uses images that appeal to the five senses—sight, hearing, touch, taste, and smell.

See *Image.*

DEVELOPMENT See *Plot.*

DIALECT *Dialect* is the form of a language spoken by people in a particular region or group. Dialects differ in pronunciation, grammar, and word choice. The English language is divided into many dialects. British English differs from American English.

DIALOGUE A *dialogue* is a conversation between characters. In poems, novels, and short stories, dialogue is usually set off by quotation marks to indicate a speaker's exact words.

In a play, dialogue follows the names of the characters, and no quotation marks are used.

DRAMA A *drama* is a story written to be performed by actors. Although a drama is meant to be performed, one can also read the script, or written version, and imagine the action. The *script* of a drama is made up of dialogue and stage directions. The *dialogue* is the words spoken by the actors. The *stage directions,* usually printed in italics, tell how the actors should look, move, and speak. They also describe the setting, sound effects, and lighting.

Dramas are often divided into parts called *acts.*

The acts are often divided into smaller parts called *scenes.*

DYNAMIC CHARACTER See *Character.*

ESSAY An *essay* is a short nonfiction work about a particular subject. Most essays have a single major focus and a clear introduction, body, and conclusion.

There are many types of essays. An *informal essay* uses casual, conversational language. A *historical essay* gives facts, explanations, and insights about historical events. An *expository essay* explains an idea by breaking it down. A *narrative essay* tells a story about a real-life experience. An *informational essay* explains a process. A *persuasive essay* offers an opinion and supports it.

See *Exposition, Narration,* and *Persuasion.*

EXPOSITION In the plot of a story or a drama, the *exposition,* or introduction, is the part of the work that introduces the characters, setting, and basic situation.

See *Plot.*

EXPOSITORY WRITING *Expository writing* is writing that explains or informs.

EXTENDED METAPHOR In an *extended metaphor,* as in a regular metaphor, a subject is spoken or written of as though it were something else. However, extended metaphor differs from regular metaphor in that several connected comparisons are made.

See *Metaphor.*

EXTERNAL CONFLICT See *Conflict.*

FABLE A *fable* is a brief story or poem, usually with animal characters, that teaches a lesson, or moral. The moral is usually stated at the end of the fable.

See *Irony* and *Moral.*

FANTASY A *fantasy* is highly imaginative writing that contains elements not found in real life. Examples of fantasy include stories that involve supernatural elements, stories that resemble fairy tales, stories that deal with imaginary places and creatures, and science-fiction stories.

See *Science Fiction.*

FICTION *Fiction* is prose writing that tells about imaginary characters and events. Short stories and novels are works of fiction. Some writers base their fiction on actual events and people, adding invented characters, dialogue, settings, and plots. Other writers rely on imagination alone.

See *Narration, Nonfiction,* and *Prose.*

FIGURATIVE LANGUAGE *Figurative language* is writing or speech that is not meant to be taken literally. The many types of figurative language are known as *figures of speech.* Common figures of speech include metaphor, personification, and simile. Writers use figurative language to state ideas in vivid and imaginative ways.

See *Metaphor, Personification, Simile,* and *Symbol.*

FIGURE OF SPEECH See *Figurative Language.*

FLASHBACK A *flashback* is a scene within a story that interrupts the sequence of events to relate events that occurred in the past.

FLAT CHARACTER See *Character.*

FOLK TALE A *folk tale* is a story composed orally and then passed from person to person by word of mouth. Folk tales originated among people who could neither read nor write. These people entertained one another by telling stories aloud—often dealing with heroes, adventure, magic, or romance. Eventually, modern scholars collected these stories and wrote them down.

Folk tales reflect the cultural beliefs and environments from which they come.

See *Fable, Legend, Myth,* and *Oral Tradition.*

FOOT See *Meter.*

FORESHADOWING *Foreshadowing* is the author's use of clues to hint at what might happen later in the story. Writers use foreshadowing to build their readers' expectations and to create suspense.

FREE VERSE *Free verse* is poetry not written in a regular, rhythmical pattern, or meter. The poet is free to write lines of any length or with any number of stresses, or beats. Free verse is therefore less constraining than *metrical verse,* in which every line must have a certain length and a certain number of stresses.

See *Meter.*

GENRE A *genre* is a division or type of literature. Literature is commonly divided into three major genres: poetry, prose, and drama. Each major genre is, in turn, divided into lesser genres, as follows:

1. *Poetry:* lyric poetry, concrete poetry, dramatic poetry, narrative poetry, epic poetry

2. *Prose:* fiction (novels and short stories) and nonfiction (biography, autobiography, letters, essays, and reports)

3. *Drama:* serious drama and tragedy, comic drama, melodrama, and farce

See *Drama, Poetry,* and *Prose.*

HAIKU The *haiku* is a three-line Japanese verse form. The first and third lines of a haiku each have five syllables. The second line has seven syllables. A writer of haiku uses images to create a single, vivid picture, generally of a scene from nature.

HERO/HEROINE A *hero* or *heroine* is a character whose actions are inspiring, or noble. Often heroes and heroines struggle to overcome the obstacles and problems that stand in their way. Note that the term *hero* was originally used only for male characters, while heroic female characters were always called *heroines.* However, it is now acceptable to use *hero* to refer to females as well as to males.

HISTORICAL FICTION In *historical fiction,* real events, places, or people are incorporated into a fictional or made-up story.

IMAGERY See *Images.*

IMAGES *Images* are words or phrases that appeal to one or more of the five senses. Writers use images to describe how their subjects look, sound, feel, taste, and smell. Poets often paint images, or word pictures, that appeal to your senses. These pictures help you experience the poem fully.

INTERNAL CONFLICT See *Conflict.*

IRONY *Irony* is a contradiction between what happens and what is expected. The three main types of irony are *situational irony, verbal irony,* and *dramatic irony.*

JOURNAL A *journal* is a daily, or periodic, account of events and the writer's thoughts and feelings about those events. Personal journals are not normally written for publication, but sometimes they do get published later with permission from the author or the author's family.

LEGEND A *legend* is a widely told story about the past—one that may or may not have a foundation in fact. Every culture has its own legends—its familiar, traditional stories.

See *Folk Tale, Myth,* and *Oral Tradition.*

LETTERS A *letter* is a written communication from one person to another. In personal letters, the writer shares information and his or her thoughts and feelings with one other person or group. Although letters are not normally written for publication, they sometimes do get published later with the permission of the author or the author's family.

LIMERICK A *limerick* is a humorous, rhyming, five-line poem with a specific meter and rhyme scheme. Most limericks have three strong stresses in lines 1, 2, and 5 and two strong stresses in lines 3 and 4. Most follow the rhyme scheme *aabba.*

LYRIC POEM A *lyric poem* is a highly musical verse that expresses the observations and feelings of a single speaker. It creates a single, unified impression.

MAIN CHARACTER See *Character.*

MEDIA ACCOUNTS *Media accounts* are reports, explanations, opinions, or descriptions written for television, radio, newspapers, and magazines. While some media accounts report only facts, others include the writer's thoughts and reflections.

METAPHOR A *metaphor* is a figure of speech in which something is described as though it were something else. A metaphor, like a simile, works by pointing out a similarity between two unlike things.

See *Extended Metaphor* and *Simile.*

METER The *meter* of a poem is its rhythmical pattern. This pattern is determined by the number of *stresses,* or beats, in each line. To describe the meter of a poem, read it while emphasizing the beats in each line. Then, mark the stressed and unstressed syllables, as follows:

M̆y fáth | ĕr wás | th̆e fírst | t̆o héar |

As you can see, each strong stress is marked with a slanted line (´) and each unstressed syllable with a horseshoe symbol (˘). The weak and strong stresses are then divided by vertical lines (|) into groups called *feet.*

MINOR CHARACTER See *Character.*

MOOD See *Atmosphere.*

MORAL A *moral* is a lesson taught by a literary work. A fable usually ends with a moral that is directly stated. A poem, novel, short story, or essay often suggests a moral that is not directly stated. The moral must be drawn by the reader, based on other elements in the work.

See *Fable.*

MOTIVATION See *Motive.*

MOTIVE A *motive* is a reason that explains or partially explains a character's thoughts, feelings, actions, or speech. Writers try to make their characters' motives, or motivations, as clear as possible. If the motives of a main character are not clear, then the character will not be believable.

Characters are often motivated by needs, such as food and shelter. They are also motivated by feelings, such as fear, love, and pride. Motives may be obvious or hidden.

MYTH A *myth* is a fictional tale that explains the actions of gods or heroes or the origins of elements of nature. Myths are part of the oral tradition. They are composed orally and then passed from generation to generation by word of mouth. Every ancient culture has its own mythology, or collection of myths. Greek and Roman myths are known collectively as *classical mythology.*

See *Oral Tradition.*

NARRATION *Narration* is writing that tells a story. The act of telling a story is also called narration. Each piece is a *narrative.* A story told in fiction, nonfiction, poetry, or even in drama is called a narrative.

See *Narrative, Narrative Poem,* and *Narrator.*

NARRATIVE A *narrative* is a story. A narrative can be either fiction or nonfiction. Novels and short stories are types of fictional narratives. Biographies and autobiographies are nonfiction narratives. Poems that tell stories are also narratives.

See *Narration* and *Narrative Poem.*

NARRATIVE POEM A *narrative poem* is a story told in verse. Narrative poems often have all the elements of short stories, including characters, conflict, and plot.

NARRATOR A *narrator* is a speaker or a character who tells a story. The narrator's perspective is the way he or she sees things. A *third-person narrator* is one who stands outside the action and speaks about it. A *first-person narrator* is one who tells a story and participates in its action.

See *Point of View.*

NONFICTION *Nonfiction* is prose writing that presents and explains ideas or that tells about real people, places, objects, or events. Autobiographies, biographies, essays, reports, letters, memos, and newspaper articles are all types of nonfiction.

See *Fiction.*

NOVEL A *novel* is a long work of fiction. Novels contain such elements as characters, plot, conflict, and setting. The writer of novels, or novelist, develops these elements. In addition to its main plot, a novel may contain one or more subplots, or independent, related stories. A novel may also have several themes.

See *Fiction* and *Short Story.*

NOVELLA A fiction work that is longer than a short story but shorter than a novel.

ONOMATOPOEIA *Onomatopoeia* is the use of words that imitate sounds. *Crash, buzz, screech, hiss, neigh, jingle,* and *cluck* are examples of onomatopoeia. *Chickadee, towhee,* and *whippoorwill* are onomatopoeic names of birds.

Onomatopoeia can help put the reader in the activity of a poem.

ORAL TRADITION *Oral tradition* is the passing of songs, stories, and poems from generation to generation by word of mouth. Folk songs, folk tales, legends, and myths all come from the oral tradition. No one knows who first created these stories and poems.

See *Folk Tale, Legend,* and *Myth.*

OXYMORON An *oxymoron* (pl. *oxymora*) is a figure of speech that links two opposite or contradictory words, to point out an idea or situation that seems contradictory or inconsistent but on closer inspection turns out to be somehow true.

PERSONIFICATION *Personification* is a type of figurative language in which a nonhuman subject is given human characteristics.

PERSPECTIVE See *Narrator* and *Point of View.*

PERSUASION *Persuasion* is used in writing or speech that attempts to convince the reader or listener to adopt a particular opinion or course of action. Newspaper editorials and letters to the editor use persuasion. So do advertisements and campaign speeches given by political candidates. An *argument* is a logical way of presenting a belief, conclusion, or stance. A good argument is supported with reasoning and evidence.

See *Essay.*

PLAYWRIGHT A *playwright* is a person who writes plays. William Shakespeare is regarded as the greatest playwright in English literature.

PLOT *Plot* is the sequence of events in which each event results from a previous one and causes the next. In most novels, dramas, short stories, and narrative poems, the plot involves both characters and a central conflict. The plot usually begins with an exposition that introduces the setting, the characters, and the basic situation. This is followed by the *inciting incident,* which introduces the central conflict. The conflict then increases during the *development* until it reaches a high point of interest or suspense, the *climax.* The climax is followed by the *falling action,* or end, of the central conflict. Any events that occur during the *falling action* make up the *resolution,* or *denouement.*

Some plots do not have all of these parts. Some stories begin with the inciting incident and end with the resolution.

See *Conflict.*

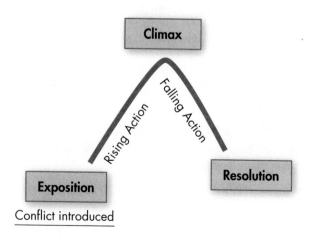

Conflict introduced

POETRY *Poetry* is one of the three major types of literature, the others being prose and drama. Most poems make use of highly concise, musical, and emotionally charged language. Many also make use of imagery, figurative lan-

guage, and special devices of sound such as rhyme. Major types of poetry include lyric poetry, narrative poetry, and concrete poetry.

See *Concrete Poem, Genre, Lyric Poem,* and *Narrative Poem.*

POINT OF VIEW *Point of view* is the perspective, or vantage point, from which a story is told. The storyteller is either a narrator outside the story or a character in the story. *First-person point of view* describes a story told by a character who uses the first-person pronoun "I."

The two kinds of *third-person point of view,* limited and omniscient, are called "third person" because the narrator uses third-person pronouns such as "he" and "she" to refer to the characters. There is no "I" telling the story.

In stories told from the *omniscient third-person point of view,* the narrator knows and tells about what each character feels and thinks.

In stories told from the *limited third-person point of view,* the narrator relates the inner thoughts and feelings of only one character, and everything is viewed from this character's perspective.

See *Narrator.*

PROBLEM See *Conflict.*

PROSE *Prose* is the ordinary form of written language. Most writing that is not poetry, drama, or song is considered prose. Prose is one of the major genres of literature and occurs in two forms—fiction and nonfiction.

See *Fiction, Genre,* and *Nonfiction.*

PROTAGONIST The *protagonist* is the main character in a literary work. Often, the protagonist is a person, but sometimes it can be an animal.

See *Antagonist* and *Character.*

REFRAIN A *refrain* is a regularly repeated line or group of lines in a poem or a song.

REPETITION *Repetition* is the use, more than once, of any element of language—a sound, word, phrase, clause, or sentence. Repetition is used in both prose and poetry.

See *Alliteration, Meter, Plot, Rhyme,* and *Rhyme Scheme.*

RESOLUTION The *resolution* is the outcome of the conflict in a plot.

See *Plot.*

RHYME *Rhyme* is the repetition of sounds at the ends of words. Poets use rhyme to lend a songlike quality to their verses and to emphasize certain words and ideas. Many traditional poems contain **end rhymes,** or rhyming words at the ends of lines.

Another common device is the use of **internal rhymes,** or rhyming words within lines. Internal rhyme also emphasizes the flowing nature of a poem.

See *Rhyme Scheme.*

RHYME SCHEME A *rhyme scheme* is a regular pattern of rhyming words in a poem. To indicate the rhyme scheme of a poem, one uses lowercase letters. Each rhyme is assigned a different letter, as follows in the first stanza of "Dust of Snow" by Robert Frost:

The way a crow	*a*
Shook down on me	*b*
The dust of snow	*a*
From a hemlock tree	*b*

Thus, the stanza has the rhyme scheme *abab.*

RHYTHM *Rhythm* is the pattern of stressed and unstressed syllables in spoken or written language.

See *Meter.*

ROUND CHARACTER See *Character.*

SCENE A *scene* is a section of uninterrupted action in the act of a drama.

See *Drama.*

SCIENCE FICTION *Science fiction* combines elements of fiction and fantasy with scientific fact. Many science-fiction stories are set in the future.

SENSORY LANGUAGE *Sensory language* is writing or speech that appeals to one or more of the five senses.

See *Images.*

SETTING The *setting* of a literary work is the time and place of the action. The setting includes all the details of a place and time—the year, the time of day, even the weather. The place may be a specific country, state, region, community, neighborhood, building, institution, or home. Details such as dialects, clothing, customs, and modes of transportation are often used to establish setting. In most stories, the setting serves as a backdrop—a context in which the characters interact. Setting can also help create a feeling, or atmosphere.

See *Atmosphere.*

SHORT STORY A *short story* is a brief work of fiction. Like a novel, a short story presents a sequence of events, or plot. The plot usually deals with a central conflict faced by a main character, or protagonist. The events in a short story usually communicate a message about life or human nature. This message, or central idea, is the story's theme.

See *Conflict, Plot,* and *Theme.*

SIMILE A *simile* is a figure of speech that uses *like* or *as* to make a direct comparison between two unlike ideas. Everyday speech often contains similes, such as "pale as a ghost," "good as gold," "spread like wildfire," and "clever as a fox."

SPEAKER The *speaker* is the imaginary voice a poet uses when writing a poem. The speaker is the character who tells the poem. This character, or voice, often is not identified by name. There can be important differences between the poet and the poem's speaker.

See *Narrator.*

STAGE DIRECTIONS *Stage directions* are notes included in a drama to describe how the work is to be performed or staged. Stage directions are usually printed in italics and enclosed within parentheses or brackets. Some stage directions describe the movements, costumes, emotional states, and ways of speaking of the characters.

STAGING *Staging* includes the setting, lighting, costumes, special effects, music, dance, and so on that go into putting on a stage performance of a drama.

See *Drama.*

STANZA A *stanza* is a group of lines of poetry that are usually similar in length and pattern and are separated by spaces. A stanza is like a paragraph of poetry—it states and develops a single main idea.

STATIC CHARACTER See *Character.*

SURPRISE ENDING A *surprise ending* is a conclusion that is unexpected. The reader has certain expectations about the ending based on details in the story. Often, a surprise ending is **foreshadowed,** or subtly hinted at, in the course of the work.

See *Foreshadowing* and *Plot.*

SUSPENSE *Suspense* is a feeling of anxious uncertainty about the outcome of events in a literary work. Writers create suspense by raising questions in the minds of their readers.

SYMBOL A *symbol* is anything that stands for or represents something else. Symbols are common in everyday life. A dove with an olive branch in its beak is a symbol of peace. A blindfolded woman holding a balanced scale is a symbol of justice. A crown is a symbol of a king's status and authority.

SYMBOLISM *Symbolism* is the use of symbols. Symbolism plays an important role in many different types of literature. It can highlight certain elements the author wishes to emphasize and also add levels of meaning.

THEME The *theme* is a central message, concern, or purpose in a literary work. A theme can usually be expressed as a generalization, or a general statement, about human beings or about life. The theme of a work is not a summary of its plot. The theme is the writer's central idea.

Although a theme may be stated directly in the text, it is more often presented indirectly. When the theme is stated indirectly, or implied, the reader must figure out what the theme is by looking carefully at what the work reveals about people or about life.

TONE The *tone* of a literary work is the writer's attitude toward his or her audience and subject. The tone can often be described by a single adjective, such as *formal* or *informal, serious* or *playful, bitter,* or *ironic.* Factors that contribute to the tone are word choice, sentence structure, line length, rhyme, rhythm, and repetition.

TRAGEDY A *tragedy* is a work of literature, especially a play, that results in a catastrophe for the main character. In ancient Greek drama, the main character is always a significant person—a king or a hero—and the cause of the tragedy is a tragic flaw, or weakness, in his or her character. In modern drama, the main character can be an ordinary person, and the cause of the tragedy can be some evil in society itself. The purpose of tragedy is not only to arouse fear and pity in the audience but also, in some cases, to convey a sense of the grandeur and nobility of the human spirit.

TURNING POINT See *Climax.*

UNIVERSAL THEME A *universal theme* is a message about life that is expressed regularly in many different cultures and time periods. Folk tales, epics, and romances often address universal themes like the importance of courage, the power of love, or the danger of greed.

Tips for Literature Circles

As you read and study literature, discussions with other readers can help you understand and enjoy what you have read. Use the following tips.

- ## Understand the purpose of your discussion

  Your purpose when you discuss literature is to broaden your understanding of a work by testing your own ideas and hearing the ideas of others. Keep your comments focused on the literature you are discussing. Starting with one focus question will help to keep your discussion on track.

- ## Communicate effectively

  Effective communication requires thinking before speaking. Plan the points that you want to make and decide how you will express them. Organize these points in logical order and use details from the work to support your ideas. Jot down informal notes to help keep your ideas focused.

  Remember to speak clearly, pronouncing words slowly and carefully. Also, listen attentively when others are speaking, and avoid interrupting.

- ## Consider other ideas and interpretations

  A work of literature can generate a wide variety of responses in different readers. Be open to the idea that many interpretations can be valid. To support your own ideas, point to the events, descriptions, characters, or other literary elements in the work that led to your interpretation. To consider someone else's ideas, decide whether details in the work support the interpretation he or she presents. Be sure to convey your criticism of the ideas of others in a respectful and supportive manner.

- ## Ask questions

  Ask questions to clarify your understanding of another reader's ideas. You can also use questions to call attention to possible areas of confusion, to points that are open to debate, or to errors in the speaker's points. To move a discussion forward, summarize and evaluate conclusions reached by the group members.

  When you meet with a group to discuss literature, use a chart like the one shown to analyze the discussion.

Work Being Discussed:	
Focus Question:	
Your Response:	Another Student's Response:
Supporting Evidence:	Supporting Evidence:

Tips for Improving Reading Fluency

When you were younger, you learned to read. Then, you read to expand your experiences or for pure enjoyment. Now, you are expected to read to learn. As you progress in school, you are given more and more material to read. The tips on these pages will help you improve your reading fluency, or your ability to read easily, smoothly, and expressively.

Keeping Your Concentration

One common problem that readers face is the loss of concentration. When you are reading an assignment, you might find yourself rereading the same sentence several times without really understanding it. The first step in changing this behavior is to notice that you do it. Becoming an active, aware reader will help you get the most from your assignments. Practice using these strategies:

- Cover what you have already read with a note card as you go along. Then, you will not be able to reread without noticing that you are doing it.

- Set a purpose for reading beyond just completing the assignment. Then, read actively by pausing to ask yourself questions about the material as you read.

- Use the Reading Strategy instruction and notes that appear with each selection in this textbook.

- Stop reading after a specified period of time (for example, 5 minutes) and summarize what you have read. To help you with this strategy, use the Reading Check questions that appear with each selection in this textbook. Reread to find any answers you do not know.

Reading Phrases

Fluent readers read phrases rather than individual words. Reading this way will speed up your reading and improve your comprehension. Here are some useful ideas:

- Experts recommend rereading as a strategy to increase fluency. Choose a passage of text that is neither too hard nor too easy. Read the same passage aloud several times until you can read it smoothly. When you can read the passage fluently, pick another passage and keep practicing.

- Read aloud into a tape recorder. Then, listen to the recording, noting your accuracy, pacing, and expression. You can also read aloud and share feedback with a partner.

- Use *Hear It!* Prentice Hall Literature Audio program CDs to hear the selections read aloud. Read along silently in your textbook, noticing how the reader uses his or her voice and emphasizes certain words and phrases.

Understanding Key Vocabulary

If you do not understand some of the words in an assignment, you may miss out on important concepts. Therefore, it is helpful to keep a dictionary nearby when you are reading. Follow these steps:

- Before you begin reading, scan the text for unfamiliar words or terms. Find out what those words mean before you begin reading.

- Use context—the surrounding words, phrases, and sentences—to help you determine the meanings of unfamiliar words.

- If you are unable to understand the meaning through context, refer to the dictionary.

Paying Attention to Punctuation

When you read, pay attention to punctuation. Commas, periods, exclamation points, semicolons, and colons tell you when to pause or stop. They also indicate relationships between groups of words. When you recognize these relationships you will read with greater understanding and expression. Look at the chart below

Punctuation Mark	Meaning
comma	brief pause
period	pause at the end of a thought
exclamation point	pause that indicates emphasis
semicolon	pause between related but distinct thoughts
colon	pause before giving explanation or examples

Using the Reading Fluency Checklist

Use the checklist below each time you read a selection in this textbook. In your Language Arts journal or notebook, note which skills you need to work on and chart your progress each week.

Reading Fluency Checklist
☐ Preview the text to check for difficult or unfamiliar words.
☐ Practice reading aloud.
☐ Read according to punctuation.
☐ Break down long sentences into the subject and its meaning.
☐ Read groups of words for meaning rather than reading single words.
☐ Read with expression (change your tone of voice to add meaning to the word).

Reading is a skill that can be improved with practice. The key to improving your fluency is to read. The more you read, the better your reading will become.

Types of Writing

Good writing can be a powerful tool used for many purposes. Writing can allow you to defend something you believe in or show how much you know about a subject. Writing can also help you share what you have experienced, imagined, thought, and felt. The three main types of writing are argument, informative/explanatory, and narrative.

Argument

When you think of the word *argument*, you might think of a disagreement between two people, but an argument is more than that. An argument is a logical way of presenting a belief, conclusion, or stance. A good argument is supported with reasoning and evidence.

Argument writing can be used for many purposes, such as to change a reader's point of view or opinion or to bring about an action or a response from a reader.

There are three main purposes for writing a formal argument:

- to change the reader's mind
- to convince the reader to accept what is written
- to motivate the reader to take action, based on what is written

The following are some types of argument writing:

Advertisements An advertisement is a planned message meant to be seen, heard, or read. It attempts to persuade an audience to buy a product or service, accept an idea, or support a cause. Advertisements may appear in print, online, or in broadcast form.

Several common types of advertisements are public service announcements, billboards, merchandise ads, service ads, and political campaign literature.

Persuasive Essay A persuasive essay presents a position on an issue, urges readers to accept that position, and may encourage a specific action. An effective persuasive essay

- Explores an issue of importance to the writer
- Addresses an issue that is arguable
- Uses facts, examples, statistics, or personal experiences to support a position
- Tries to influence the audience through appeals to the readers' knowledge, experiences, or emotions
- Uses clear organization to present a logical argument

Forms of persuasion include editorials, position papers, persuasive speeches, grant proposals, advertisements, and debates.

Informative/Explanatory

Informative/explanatory writing should rely on facts to inform or explain. Informative/explanatory writing serves some closely related purposes: to increase readers' knowledge of a subject, to help readers better understand a procedure or process, or to provide readers with an enhanced comprehension of a concept. It should also feature a clear introduction, body, and conclusion. The following are some examples of informative/explanatory writing:

Cause-and-Effect Essay A cause-and-effect essay examines the relationship between events, explaining how one event or situation causes another. A successful cause-and-effect essay includes

- A discussion of a cause, event, or condition that produces a specific result
- An explanation of an effect, outcome, or result
- Evidence and examples to support the relationship between cause and effect
- A logical organization that makes the explanation clear

Comparison-and-Contrast Essay A comparison-and-contrast essay analyzes the similarities and differences between or among two or more things. An effective comparison-and-contrast essay

- Identifies a purpose for comparison and contrast
- Identifies similarities and differences between or among two or more things, people, places, or ideas
- Gives factual details about the subjects
- Uses an organizational plan suited to the topic and purpose

Descriptive Writing Descriptive writing creates a vivid picture of a person, place, thing, or event. Most descriptive writing includes

- Sensory details—sights, sounds, smells, tastes, and physical sensations
- Vivid, precise language
- Figurative language or comparisons

- Adjectives and adverbs that paint a word picture

- An organization suited to the subject

Types of descriptive writing include descriptions of ideas, observations, travel brochures, physical descriptions, functional descriptions, remembrances, and character sketches.

Problem-and-Solution Essay A problem-and-solution essay describes a problem and offers one or more solutions to it. It describes a clear set of steps to achieve a result. An effective problem-and-solution essay includes

- A clear statement of the problem, with its causes and effects summarized for the reader

- The most important aspects of the problem

- A proposal of at least one realistic solution

- Facts, statistics, data, or expert testimony to support the solution

- A clear organization that makes the relationship between problem and solution obvious

Research Writing Research writing is based on information gathered from outside sources. A research paper—a focused study of a topic—helps writers explore and connect ideas, make discoveries, and share their findings with an audience. An effective research paper

- Focuses on a specific, narrow topic, which is usually summarized in a thesis statement

- Presents relevant information from a wide variety of sources

- Uses a clear organization that includes an introduction, body, and conclusion

- Includes a bibliography or works-cited list that identifies the sources from which the information was drawn

Other types of writing that depend on accurate and insightful research include multimedia presentations, statistical reports, annotated bibliographies, and experiment journals.

Workplace Writing Workplace writing is probably the format you will use most after you finish school. In general, workplace writing is fact-based and meant to communicate specific information in a structured format. Effective workplace writing

- Communicates information concisely

- Includes details that provide necessary information and anticipate potential questions

- Is error-free and neatly presented

Common types of workplace writing include business letters, memorandums, résumés, forms, and applications.

Narrative

Narrative writing conveys experience, either real or imaginary, and uses time to provide structure. It can be used to inform, instruct, persuade, or entertain. Whenever writers tell a of story, they are using narrative writing. Most types of narrative writing share certain elements, such as characters, a setting, a sequence of events, and, often, a theme. The following are some types of narration:

Autobiographical Writing Autobiographical writing tells a true story about an important period, experience, or relationship in the writer's life. Effective autobiographical writing includes

- A series of events that involve the writer as the main character

- Details, thoughts, feelings, and insights from the writer's perspective

- A conflict or an event that affects the writer

- A logical organization that tells the story clearly

- Insights that the writer gained from the experience

Types of autobiographical writing include autobiographical sketches, personal narratives, reflective essays, eyewitness accounts, and memoirs.

Short Story A short story is a brief, creative narrative. Most short stories include

- Details that establish the setting in time and place

- A main character who undergoes a change or learns something during the course of the story

- A conflict or a problem to be introduced, developed, and resolved

- A plot, the series of events that make up the action of the story

- A theme or message about life

Types of short stories include realistic stories, fantasies, historical narratives, mysteries, thrillers, science-fiction stories, and adventure stories.

Writing Friendly Letters

Writing Friendly Letters

A friendly letter is much less formal than a business letter. It is a letter to a friend, a family member, or anyone with whom the writer wants to communicate in a personal, friendly way. Most friendly letters are made up of five parts:

- ✔ the heading
- ✔ the salutation, or greeting
- ✔ the body
- ✔ the closing
- ✔ the signature

The purpose of a friendly letter is often one of the following:

- ✔ to share personal news and feelings
- ✔ to send or to answer an invitation
- ✔ to express thanks

Model Friendly Letter

In this friendly letter, Betsy thanks her grandparents for a birthday present and gives them some news about her life.

---

11 Old Farm Road
Topsham, Maine 04011

April 14, 20—

> The **heading** includes the writer's address and the date on which he or she wrote the letter.

Dear Grandma and Grandpa,

Thank you for the sweater you sent me for my birthday. It fits perfectly, and I love the color. I wore my new sweater to the carnival at school last weekend and got lots of compliments.

The weather here has been cool but sunny. Mom thinks that "real" spring will never come. I can't wait until it's warm enough to go swimming.

School is going fairly well. I really like my Social Studies class. We are learning about the U.S. Constitution, and I think it's very interesting. Maybe I will be a lawyer when I grow up.

When are you coming out to visit us? We haven't seen you since Thanksgiving. You can stay in my room when you come. I'll be happy to sleep on the couch. (The TV is in that room!!)

Well, thanks again and hope all is well with you.

Love,

Betsy

> The **body** is the main part of the letter and contains the basic message.

> Some common **closings** for personal letters include "Best wishes," "Love," "Sincerely," and "Yours truly."

Writing Business Letters

Formatting Business Letters

Business letters follow one of several acceptable formats. In **block format,** each part of the letter begins at the left margin. A double space is used between paragraphs. In **modified block format,** some parts of the letter are indented to the center of the page. No matter which format is used, all letters in business format have a heading, an inside address, a salutation or greeting, a body, a closing, and a signature. These parts are shown and annotated on the model business letter below, formatted in modified block style.

Model Business Letter

In this letter, Yolanda Dodson uses modified block format to request information.

Students for a Cleaner Planet
c/o Memorial High School
333 Veteran's Drive
Denver, CO 80211

January 25, 20—

Steven Wilson, Director
Resource Recovery Really Works
300 Oak Street
Denver, CO 80216

Dear Mr. Wilson:

Memorial High School would like to start a branch of your successful recycling program. We share your commitment to reclaiming as much reusable material as we can. Because your program has been successful in other neighborhoods, we're sure that it can work in our community. Our school includes grades 9–12 and has about 800 students.

Would you send us some information about your community recycling program? For example, we need to know what materials can be recycled and how we can implement the program.

At least fifty students have already expressed an interest in getting involved, so I know we'll have the people power to make the program work. Please help us get started.

Thank you in advance for your time and consideration.

Sincerely,

Yolanda Dodson

Yolanda Dodson

The **heading** shows the writer's address and organization (if any) and the date.

The **inside address** indicates where the letter will be sent.

A **salutation** is punctuated by a colon. When the specific addressee is not known, use a general greeting such as "To whom it may concern:"

The **body** of the letter states the writer's purpose. In this case, the writer requests information.

The **closing** "Sincerely" is common, but "Yours truly" or "Respectfully yours" are also acceptable. To end the letter, the writer types her name and provides a **signature.**

21st-Century Skills

New technology has created many new ways to communicate. Today, it is easy to contribute information to the Internet and send a variety of messages to friends far and near. You can also share your ideas through photos, illustrations, video, and sound recordings. *21st-Century Skills* gives you an overview of some ways you can use today's technology to create, share, and find information. Here are the topics you will find in this section.

- ✔ Blogs
- ✔ Social Networking
- ✔ Widgets and Feeds
- ✔ Multimedia Elements
- ✔ Podcasts
- ✔ Wikis

BLOGS

A **blog** is a common form of online writing. The word *blog* is a contraction of *Web log*. Most blogs include a series of entries known as *posts*. The posts appear in a single column and are displayed in reverse chronological order. That means that the most recent post is at the top of the page. As you scroll down, you will find earlier posts.

Blogs have become increasingly popular. Researchers estimate that 75,000 new blogs are launched every day. Blog authors are often called *bloggers*. They can use their personal sites to share ideas, songs, videos, photos, and other media. People who read blogs can often post their responses with a comments feature found in each new post.

Because blogs are designed so that they are easy to update, bloggers can post new messages as often as they like, often daily. For some people blogs become a public journal or diary, in which they share their thoughts about daily events.

Types of Blogs

Not all blogs are the same. Many blogs have a single author, but others are group projects. These are some common types of blog:

- ✔ Personal blogs often have a general focus. Bloggers post their thoughts on any topic they find interesting in their daily lives.

- ✔ Topical blogs focus on a specific theme, such as movie reviews, political news, class assignments, or health-care opportunities.

Web Safety

Always be aware that information you post on the Internet can be read by everyone with access to that page. Once you post a picture or text, it can be saved on someone else's computer, even if you later remove it.

Using the Internet safely means keeping personal information personal. Never include your address (e-mail or real), last name, or telephone numbers. Avoid mentioning places you can be frequently found. Never give out passwords you use to access other Web sites and do not respond to e-mails from people you do not know.

Anatomy of a Blog

Here are some of the features you can include in a blog.

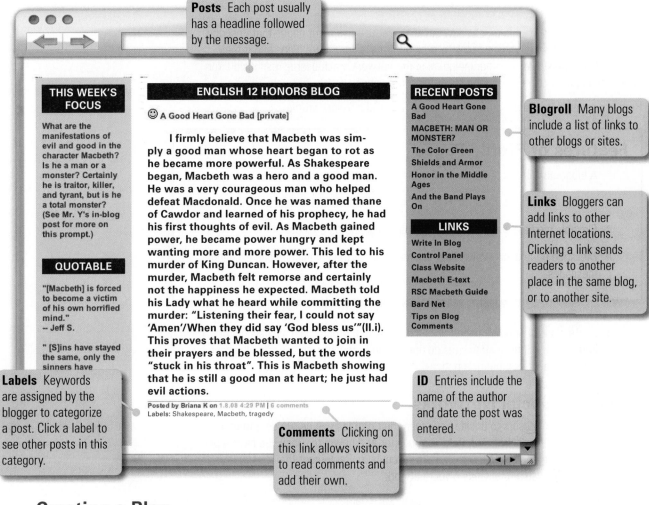

Posts Each post usually has a headline followed by the message.

THIS WEEK'S FOCUS

What are the manifestations of evil and good in the character Macbeth? Is he a man or a monster? Certainly he is traitor, killer, and tyrant, but is he a total monster? (See Mr. Y's in-blog post for more on this prompt.)

QUOTABLE

"[Macbeth] is forced to become a victim of his own horrified mind."
-- Jeff S.

" [S]ins have stayed the same, only the sinners have

ENGLISH 12 HONORS BLOG

☺ A Good Heart Gone Bad [private]

I firmly believe that Macbeth was simply a good man whose heart began to rot as he became more powerful. As Shakespeare began, Macbeth was a hero and a good man. He was a very courageous man who helped defeat Macdonald. Once he was named thane of Cawdor and learned of his prophecy, he had his first thoughts of evil. As Macbeth gained power, he became power hungry and kept wanting more and more power. This led to his murder of King Duncan. However, after the murder, Macbeth felt remorse and certainly not the happiness he expected. Macbeth told his Lady what he heard while committing the murder: "Listening their fear, I could not say 'Amen'/When they did say 'God bless us'"(II.i). This proves that Macbeth wanted to join in their prayers and be blessed, but the words "stuck in his throat". This is Macbeth showing that he is still a good man at heart; he just had evil actions.

Posted by Briana K on 1.8.08 4:29 PM | 6 comments
Labels: Shakespeare, Macbeth, tragedy

RECENT POSTS
A Good Heart Gone Bad
MACBETH: MAN OR MONSTER?
The Color Green
Shields and Armor
Honor in the Middle Ages
And the Band Plays On

LINKS
Write In Blog
Control Panel
Class Website
Macbeth E-text
RSC Macbeth Guide
Bard Net
Tips on Blog Comments

Blogroll Many blogs include a list of links to other blogs or sites.

Links Bloggers can add links to other Internet locations. Clicking a link sends readers to another place in the same blog, or to another site.

Labels Keywords are assigned by the blogger to categorize a post. Click a label to see other posts in this category.

Comments Clicking on this link allows visitors to read comments and add their own.

ID Entries include the name of the author and date the post was entered.

Creating a Blog

Keep these hints and strategies in mind to help you create an interesting and fair blog:

- ✔ Focus each blog entry on a single topic.

- ✔ Vary the length of your posts. Sometimes, all you need is a line or two to share a quick thought. Other posts will be much longer.

- ✔ Choose font colors and styles that can be read easily.

- ✔ Many people scan blogs rather than read them closely. You can make your main ideas pop out by using clear or clever headlines and boldfacing key terms.

- ✔ Give credit to other people's work and ideas. State the names of people whose ideas you are quoting or add a link to take readers to that person's blog or site.

- ✔ If you post comments, try to make them brief and polite.

SOCIAL NETWORKING

Social networking means any interaction between members of an online community. People can exchange many different kinds of information, from text and voice messages to video images.

Many social network communities allow users to create permanent pages that describe themselves. Users create home pages to express themselves, share ideas about their lives, and post messages to other members in the network. Each user is responsible for adding and updating the content on his or her profile page.

Here are some features you are likely to find on a social network profile:

Features of Profile Pages

- A biographical description, including photographs and artwork.

- Lists of favorite things, such as books, movies, music, and fashions.

- Playable media elements such as videos and sound recordings.

- Message boards, or "walls" in which members of the community can exchange messages.

You can create a social network page for an individual or a group, such as a school or special interest club. Many hosting sites do not charge to register, so you can also have fun by creating a page for a pet or a fictional character.

Privacy in Social Networks

Social networks allow users to decide how open their profiles will be. Be sure to read introductory information carefully before you register at a new site. Once you have a personal profile page, monitor your privacy settings regularly. Remember that any information you post will be available to anyone in your network.

Users often post messages anonymously or using false names, or *pseudonyms*. People can also post using someone else's name. Judge all information on the net critically. Do not assume that you know who posted some information simply because you recognize the name of the post author. The rapid speed of communication on the Internet can make it easy to jump to conclusions—be careful to avoid this trap.

Tips for Sending Effective Messages

Technology makes it easy to share ideas quickly, but writing for the Internet poses some special challenges, as well. The writing style for blogs and social networks is often very conversational. In blog posts and comments, instant messages, and e-mails, writers often express themselves very quickly, using relaxed language, short sentences, and abbreviations. However, in a conversation, we get a lot of information from a speaker's tone of voice and body language. On the Internet, those clues are missing. As a result, Internet writers often use italics or bracketed labels to indicate emotions. Another alternative is using *emoticons*—strings of characters that give visual clues to indicate emotion:

:-)	smile (happy)	:-(	frown (unhappy)	;-)	wink (light sarcasm)

Use these strategies to communicate effectively when using the Internet:

✔ Reread your messages. Before you click *Send,* read your message through and make sure that your tone will be clear to the reader.

✔ Do not jump to conclusions—ask for clarification first. Make sure you really understand what someone is saying before you respond.

✔ Use abbreviations your reader will understand.

WIDGETS AND FEEDS

A **widget** is a small application that performs a specific task. You might find widgets that give weather predictions, offer dictionary definitions or translations, provide entertainment such as games, or present a daily word, photograph, or quotation.

A **feed** is a special kind of widget. It displays headlines taken from the latest content on a specific media source. Clicking on the headline will take you to the full article.

Many social network communities and other Web sites allow you to personalize your home page by adding widgets and feeds.

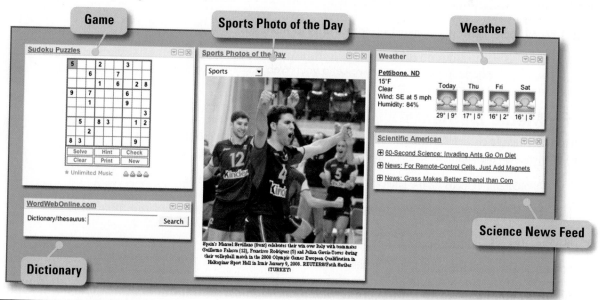

MULTIMEDIA ELEMENTS

One of the great advantages of communicating on the Internet is that you are not limited to using text only. When you create a Web profile or blog, you can share your ideas using a wide variety of media. In addition to widgets and feeds (see page R31), these media elements can make your Internet communication more entertaining and useful.

Graphics

Graphics	
Photographs	You can post photos taken by digital cameras.
Illustrations	Artwork can be created using computer software. You can also use a scanner to post a digital image of a drawing or sketch.
Charts, Graphs, and Maps	Charts and graphs can make statistical information clear. Use spreadsheet software to create these elements. Use Internet sites to find maps of specific places.

Video

Video	
Live Action	Digital video can be recorded by a camera or recorded from another media source.
Animation	Animated videos can also be created using software.

Sound

Sound	
Music	Many social network communities make it easy to share your favorite music with people who visit your page.
Voice	Use a microphone to add your own voice to your Web page.

Editing Media Elements

You can use software to customize media elements. Open source software is free and available to anyone on the Internet. Here are some things you can do with software:

- ✔ Crop a photograph to focus on the subject or brighten an image that is too dark.
- ✔ Transform a drawing's appearance from flat to three-dimensional.
- ✔ Insert a "You Are Here" arrow on a map.
- ✔ Edit a video or sound file to shorten its running time.
- ✔ Add background music or sound effects to a video.

PODCASTS

A **podcast** is a digital audio or video recording of a program that is made available on the Internet. Users can replay the podcast on a computer, or download it and replay it on a personal audio player. You might think of podcasts as radio or television programs that you create yourself. They can be embedded on a Web site or fed to a Web page through a podcast widget.

Creating an Effective Podcast

To make a podcast, you will need a recording device, such as a microphone or digital video camera, as well as editing software. Open source editing software is widely available and free of charge. Most audio podcasts are converted into the MP3 format. Here are some tips for creating a podcast that is clear and entertaining:

- ✔ Listen to several podcasts by different authors to get a feeling for the medium. Make a list of features and styles you like and also those you want to avoid.

- ✔ Test your microphone to find the best recording distance. Stand close enough to the microphone so that your voice sounds full, but not so close that you create an echo.

- ✔ Create an outline that shows your estimated timing for each element.

- ✔ Be prepared before you record. Rehearse, but do not create a script. Podcasts are best when they have a natural, easy flow.

- ✔ Talk directly to your listeners. Slow down enough so they can understand you.

- ✔ Use software to edit your podcast before publishing it. You can edit out mistakes or add additional elements.

WIKIS

A **wiki** is a collaborative Web site that lets visitors create, add, remove, and edit content. The term comes from the Hawaiian phrase *wiki wiki,* which means "quick." Web users at a wiki are both the readers and the writers of the site. Some wikis are open to contributions from anyone. Others require visitors to register before they can edit the content.

All of the text in these collaborative Web sites was written by people who use the site. Articles are constantly changing, as visitors find and correct errors and improve texts.

Wikis have both advantages and disadvantages as sources of information. They are valuable open forums for the exchange of ideas. The unique collaborative writing process allows entries to change over time. However, entries can also be modified incorrectly. Careless or malicious users can delete good content and add inappropriate or inaccurate information.

You can change the information on a wiki, but be sure your information is correct and clear before you add it. Wikis keep track of all changes, so your work will be recorded and can be evaluated by other users.

Citing Sources and Preparing Manuscript

Proofreading and Preparing Manuscript

Before preparing a final copy, proofread your manuscript. The chart shows the standard symbols for marking corrections to be made.

Proofreading Symbols	
Insert	∧
delete	ℱ
close space	⌒
new paragraph	¶
add comma	⋏
add period	⊙
transpose (switch)	∿
change to cap	a̲
change to lowercase	A̸

- Choose a standard, easy-to-read font.
- Type or print on one side of unlined 8 1/2" x 11" paper.
- Set the margins for the side, top, and bottom of your paper at approximately one inch. Most word-processing programs have a default setting that is appropriate.
- Double-space the document.
- Indent the first line of each paragraph.
- Number the pages in the upper right corner.

Follow your teacher's directions for formatting formal research papers. Most papers will have the following features:

- Title page
- Table of Contents or Outline
- Works-Cited List

Avoiding Plagiarism

Whether you are presenting a formal research paper or an opinion paper on a current event, you must be careful to give credit for any ideas or opinions that are not your own. Presenting someone else's ideas, research, or opinion as your own—even if you have phrased it in different words—is *plagiarism,* the equivalent of academic stealing, or fraud.

Do not use the ideas or research of others in place of your own. Read from several sources to draw your own conclusions and form your own opinions. Incorporate the ideas and research of others to support your points. Credit the source of the following types of support:

- Statistics
- Direct quotations
- Indirectly quoted statements of opinions
- Conclusions presented by an expert
- Facts available in only one or two sources

Crediting Sources

When you credit a source, you acknowledge where you found your information and you give your readers the details necessary for locating the source themselves. Within the body of the paper, you provide a short citation, a footnote number linked to a footnote, or an endnote number linked to an endnote reference. These brief references show the page numbers on which you found the information. Prepare a reference list at the end of the paper to provide full bibliographic information on your sources. These are two common types of reference lists:

- A bibliography provides a listing of all the resources you consulted during your research.
- A works-cited list indicates the works you have referenced in your paper.

The chart on the next page shows the Modern Language Association format for crediting sources. This is the most common format for papers written in the content areas in middle school and high school. Unless instructed otherwise by your teacher, use this format for crediting sources.

MLA Style for Listing Sources

Book with one author	Pyles, Thomas. *The Origins and Development of the English Language.* 2nd ed. New York: Harcourt Brace Jovanovich, Inc., 1971.
Book with two or three authors	McCrum, Robert, William Cran, and Robert MacNeil. *The Story of English.* New York: Penguin Books, 1987.
Book with an editor	Truth, Sojourner. *Narrative of Sojourner Truth.* Ed. Margaret Washington. New York: Vintage Books, 1993.
Book with more than three authors or editors	Donald, Robert B., et al. *Writing Clear Essays.* Upper Saddle River, NJ: Prentice Hall, Inc., 1996.
Single work from an anthology	Hawthorne, Nathaniel. "Young Goodman Brown." *Literature: An Introduction to Reading and Writing.* Ed, Edgar V. Roberts and Henry E. Jacobs. Upper Saddle River, NJ: Prentice Hall, Inc., 1998. 376–385. [Indicate pages for the entire selection.]
Introduction in a published edition	Washington, Margaret. Introduction. *Narrative of Sojourner, Truth.* By Sojourner Truth. Ed. Margaret Washington. New York: Vintage Books, 1993, pp. v–xi.
Signed article in a weekly magazine	Wallace, C. (2000, February 14). A Vodacious Deal. *Time,* 155, 63.
Signed article in a monthly magazine	Gustaitis, Joseph. "The Sticky History of Chewing Gum." *American History* Oct. 1998: 30–38.
Unsigned editorial or story	"Selective Silence." Editorial. *Wall Street Journal* 11 Feb. 2000: A14. [If the editorial or story is signed, begin with the author's name.]
Signed pamphlet or brochure	[Treat the pamphlet as though it were a book.]
Pamphlet with no author, publisher, or date	*Are You at Risk of Heart Attack?* n.p. n.d. [n.p. n.d. indicates that there is no known publisher or date.]
Filmstrips, slide programs, videocassettes, DVDs, and other audiovisual media	*The Diary of Anne Frank.* Dir. George Stevens. Perf. Millie Perkins, Shelly Winters, Joseph Schildkraut, Lou Jacobi, and Richard Beymer. Twentieth Century Fox, 1959.
Radio or television program transcript	"The First Immortal Generation." *Ockam's Razor.* Host Robyn Williams. Guest Damien Broderick. National Public Radio. 23 May 1999. Transcript.
Internet	"Fun Facts About Gum." NACGM site. National Association of Chewing Gum Manufacturers. 19 Dec. 1999 <http://www.nacgm.org/consumer/funfacts.html> [Indicate the date you accessed the information. Content and addresses at Web sites change frequently.]
Newspaper	Thurow, Roger. "South Africans Who Fought for Sanctions Now Scrap for Investors." *Wall Street Journal* 11 Feb. 2000: A1+ [For a multipage article, write only the first page number on which it appears, followed by a plus sign.]
Personal interview	Smith, Jane. Personal interview. 10 Feb. 2000.
CD (with multiple publishers)	Simms, James, ed. *Romeo and Juliet.* By William Shakespeare. CD-ROM. Oxford: Attica Cybernetics Ltd.; London: BBC Education; London: HarperCollins Publishers, 1995.
Signed article from an encyclopedia	Askeland, Donald R. (1991). "Welding." *World Book Encyclopedia.* 1991 ed.

Guide to Rubrics

What is a rubric?

A rubric is a tool, often in the form of a chart or a grid, that helps you assess your work. Rubrics are particularly helpful for writing and speaking assignments.

To help you or others assess, or evaluate, your work, a rubric offers several specific criteria to be applied to your work. Then the rubric helps you or an evaluator indicate your range of success or failure according to those specific criteria. Rubrics are often used to evaluate writing for standardized tests.

Using a rubric will save you time, focus your learning, and improve the work you do. When you know what the rubric will be before you begin writing a persuasive essay, for example, as you write you will be aware of specific criteria that are important in that kind of an essay. As you evaluate the essay before giving it to your teacher, you will focus on the specific areas that your teacher wants you to master—or on areas that you know present challenges for you. Instead of searching through your work randomly for any way to improve it or correct its errors, you will have a clear and helpful focus on specific criteria.

How are rubrics constructed?

Rubrics can be constructed in several different ways.

- Your teacher may assign a rubric for a specific assignment.

- Your teacher may direct you to a rubric in your text-book.

- Your teacher and your class may construct a rubric for a particular assignment together.

- You and your classmates may construct a rubric together.

- You may create your own rubric with criteria you want to evaluate in your work.

How will a rubric help me?

A rubric will help you assess your work on a scale. Scales vary from rubric to rubric but usually range from 6 to 1, 5 to 1, or 4 to 1, with 6, 5, or 4 being the highest score and 1 being the lowest. If someone else is using the rubric to assess your work, the rubric will give your evaluator a clear range within which to place your work. If you are using the rubric yourself, it will help you make improvements to your work.

What are the types of rubrics?

- A **holistic rubric** has general criteria that can apply to a variety of assignments. See p. R29 for an example of a holistic rubric.

- An **analytic rubric** is specific to a particular assignment. The criteria for evaluation address the specific issues important in that assignment. See p. R28 for examples of analytic rubrics.

Sample Analytic Rubrics

Rubric With a 4-point Scale

The following analytic rubric is an example of a rubric to assess a persuasive essay.
It will help you evaluate focus, organization, support/elaboration, and style/convention.

	Focus	Organization	Support/Elaboration	Style/Convention
4	Demonstrates highly effective word choice; clearly focused on task.	Uses clear, consistent organizational strategy.	Provides convincing, well-elaborated reasons to support the position.	Incorporates transitions; includes very few mechanical errors.
3	Demonstrates good word choice; stays focused on persuasive task.	Uses clear organizational strategy with occasional inconsistencies.	Provides two or more moderately elaborated reasons to support the position.	Incorporates some transitions; includes few mechanical errors.
2	Shows some good word choices; minimally stays focused on persuasive task.	Uses inconsistent organizational strategy; presentation is not logical.	Provides several reasons, but few are elaborated; only one elaborated reason.	Incorporates few transitions; includes many mechanical errors.
1	Shows lack of attention to persuasive task.	Demonstrates lack of organizational strategy.	Provides no specific reasons or does not elaborate.	Does not connect ideas; includes many mechanical errors.

Rubric With a 6-point Scale

The following analytic rubric is an example of a rubric to assess a persuasive essay.
It will help you evaluate presentation, position, evidence, and arguments.

	Presentation	Position	Evidence	Arguments
6	Essay clearly and effectively addresses an issue with more than one side.	Essay clearly states a supportable position on the issue.	All evidence is logically organized, well presented, and supports the position.	All reader concerns and counterarguments are effectively addressed.
5	Most of essay addresses an issue that has more than one side.	Essay clearly states a position on the issue.	Most evidence is logically organized, well presented, and supports the position.	Most reader concerns and counterarguments are effectively addressed.
4	Essay adequately addresses issue that has more than one side.	Essay adequately states a position on the issue.	Many parts of evidence support the position; some evidence is out of order.	Many reader concerns and counterarguments are adequately addressed.
3	Essay addresses issue with two sides but does not present second side clearly.	Essay states a position on the issue, but the position is difficult to support.	Some evidence supports the position, but some evidence is out of order.	Some reader concerns and counterarguments are addressed.
2	Essay addresses issue with two sides but does not present second side.	Essay states a position on the issue, but the position is not supportable.	Not much evidence supports the position, and what is included is out of order.	A few reader concerns and counterarguments are addressed.
1	Essay does not address issue with more than one side.	Essay does not state a position on the issue.	No evidence supports the position.	No reader concerns or counterarguments are addressed.

Sample Holistic Rubric

Holistic rubrics such as this one are sometimes used to assess writing assignments on standardized tests. Notice that the criteria for evaluation are focus, organization, support, and use of conventions.

Points	Criteria
6 Points	• The writing is strongly focused and shows fresh insight into the writing task. • The writing is marked by a sense of completeness and coherence and is organized with a logical progression of ideas. • A main idea is fully developed, and support is specific and substantial. • A mature command of the language is evident, and the writing may employ characteristic creative writing strategies. • Sentence structure is varied, and writing is free of all but purposefully used fragments. • Virtually no errors in writing conventions appear.
5 Points	• The writing is clearly focused on the task. • The writing is well organized and has a logical progression of ideas, though there may be occasional lapses. • A main idea is well developed and supported with relevant detail. • Sentence structure is varied, and the writing is free of fragments, except when used purposefully. • Writing conventions are followed correctly.
4 Points	• The writing is clearly focused on the task, but extraneous material may intrude at times. • Clear organizational pattern is present, though lapses may occur. • A main idea is adequately supported, but development may be uneven. • Sentence structure is generally fragment free but shows little variation. • Writing conventions are generally followed correctly.
3 Points	• Writing is generally focused on the task, but extraneous material may intrude at times. • An organizational pattern is evident, but writing may lack a logical progression of ideas. • Support for the main idea is generally present but is sometimes illogical. • Sentence structure is generally free of fragments, but there is almost no variation. • The work generally demonstrates a knowledge of writing conventions, with occasional misspellings.
2 Points	• The writing is related to the task but generally lacks focus. • There is little evidence of organizational pattern, and there is little sense of cohesion. • Support for the main idea is generally inadequate, illogical, or absent. • Sentence structure is unvaried, and serious errors may occur. • Errors in writing conventions and spellings are frequent.
1 Point	• The writing may have little connection to the task and is generally unfocused. • There has been little attempt at organization or development. • The paper seems fragmented, with no clear main idea. • Sentence structure is unvaried, and serious errors appear. • Poor word choice and poor command of the language obscure meaning. • Errors in writing conventions and spelling are frequent.
Unscorable	The paper is considered unscorable if: • The response is unrelated to the task or is simply a rewording of the prompt. • The response has been copied from a published work. • The student did not write a response. • The response is illegible. • The words in the response are arranged with no meaning. • There is an insufficient amount of writing to score.

Student Model

Persuasive Writing

This persuasive essay, which would receive a top score according to a persuasive rubric, is a response to the following writing prompt, or assignment:

Most young people today spend more than 5 hours a day watching television. Many adults worry about the effects on youth of seeing too much television violence. Write a persuasive piece in which you argue against or defend the effects of television watching on young people. Be sure to include examples to support your views.

Until the television was invented, families spent their time doing different activities. Now most families stay home and watch TV. Watching TV risks the family's health, reduces the children's study time, and is a bad influence on young minds. Watching television can be harmful.

The writer clearly states a position in the first paragraph.

The most important reason why watching TV is bad is that the viewers get less exercise. For example, instead of watching their favorite show, people could get exercise for 30 minutes. If people spent less time watching TV and more time exercising, then they could have healthier bodies. My mother told me a story about a man who died of a heart attack because he was out of shape from watching television all the time. Obviously, watching TV put a person's health in danger.

Each paragraph provides details that support the writer's main point.

Furthermore, watching television reduces childern's study time. For example, children would spend more time studying if they didn't watch television. If students spent more time studying at home, then they would make better grades at school. Last week I had a major test in science, but I didn't study because I started watching a movie. I was not prepared for the test and my grade reflected my lack of studying. Indeed, watching television is bad because it can hurt a student's grades.

Finally, watching TV can be a bad influence on children. For example, some TV shows have inappropriate language and too much violence. If children watch programs that use bad language and show violence, then they may start repeating these actions because they think the behavior is "cool." In fact, it has been proven that children copy what they see on TV. Clearly, watching TV is bad for children and its affects children's behavior.

In conclusion, watching television is a bad influence for these reasons: It reduces people's exercise time and students' study time and it shows children inappropriate behavior. Therefore, people should take control of their lives and stop allowing television to harm them.

The conclusion restates the writer's position.

Grammar, Usage, and Mechanics Handbook

Parts of Speech

Nouns A **noun** is the name of a person, place, or thing. A **common noun** names any one of a class of people, places, or things. A **proper noun** names a specific person, place, or thing.

Pronouns A **pronoun** is a word that stands for a noun or for a word that takes the place of a noun. A **personal pronoun** refers to (1) the person speaking, (2) the person spoken to, or (3) the person, place, or thing spoken about.

	Singular	*Plural*
First Person	I, me, my, mine	we, us, our, ours
Second Person	you, your, yours	you, your, yours
Third Person	he, him, his, she, her, hers, it, its	they, them, their, theirs

A **reflexive pronoun** is a word that ends in self or selves and names the person or thing receiving the action when that person or thing is the same as the one performing the action.

A **demonstrative pronoun** directs attention to a specific person, place, or thing.

These are the juiciest pears I have ever tasted.

An **interrogative pronoun** is used to begin a question.

Who is the author of "Jeremiah's Song"?

An **indefinite pronoun** refers to a person, place, or thing, often without specifying which one.

Everyone bought something.

Verbs A **verb** is a word that expresses time while showing an action, a condition, or the fact that something exists. An **action verb** indicates the action of someone or something. A **linking verb** connects the subject of a sentence with a noun or a pronoun that renames or describes the subject. A **helping verb** can be added to another verb to make a single verb phrase.

Adjectives An **adjective** describes a noun or a pronoun or gives a noun or a pronoun a more specific meaning. Adjectives answer the questions *what kind, which one, how many,* or *how much.*

The articles the, a, and an are adjectives. An is used before a word beginning with a vowel sound.

A noun may sometimes be used as an adjective.

family home   *science* fiction

A **proper adjective** is (1) a proper noun used as an adjective or (2) an adjective formed from a proper noun. When this, that, these, or those appears immediately before a noun, that word is functioning as a **demonstrative adjective.**

Adverbs An **adverb** modifies a verb, an adjective, or another adverb. Adverbs answer the questions *where, when, in what way,* or *to what extent.*

Prepositions A **preposition** relates a noun or a pronoun following it to another word in the sentence.

Conjunctions A **conjunction** connects other words or groups of words. A **coordinating conjunction** connects similar kinds or groups of words. **Correlative conjunctions** are used in pairs to connect similar words or groups of words.

both Granpa *and* Grandma   *neither* they *nor I*

A **Subordinating conjunctions** is a word used to join two complete ideas by making one of the ideas dependent on the other.

Interjections An interjection is a word that expresses feeling or emotion and functions independently of a sentence.

Phrases, Clauses, and Sentences

Sentences A **sentence** is a group of words with two main parts: a complete subject and a complete predicate. Together, these parts express a complete thought.

A **fragment** is a group of words that does not express a complete thought.

Subject The **subject** of a sentence is the word or group of words that tells whom or what the sentence is about. The **simple subject** is the essential noun, pronoun, or group of words acting as a noun that cannot be left out of the complete subject. A **complete subject** is the simple subject plus any modifiers.

A **compound subject** is two or more subjects that have the same verb and are joined by a conjunction.

Neither the horse nor the driver looked tired.

Predicate The **predicate** of a sentence is the verb or verb phrase that tells what the complete subject of the sentence does or is. The **simple predicate** is the essential verb or verb phrase that cannot be left out of the complete predicate. A **complete predicate** is the simple predicate plus any modifiers or complements.

Pony express riders carried packages more than 2,000 miles.

A **compound predicate** is two or more verbs that have the same subject and are joined by a conjunction.

She *sneezed and coughed* throughout the trip.

Complement A **complement** is a word or group of words that completes the meaning of the predicate of a sentence. Five different kinds of complements can be found in English sentences: *direct objects, indirect objects, objective complements, predicate nominatives,* and *predicate adjectives.*

A **direct object** is a noun, pronoun, or group of words acting as a noun that receives the action of a transitive verb.

We watched the *liftoff.*

An **indirect object** is a noun, pronoun, or group of words that appears with a direct object and names the person or thing that something is given to or done for.

He sold the *family* a mirror.

An **objective complement** is an adjective or noun that appears with a direct object and describes or renames it.

I called Meg my *friend.*

A **subject complement** is a noun, pronoun, or adjective that appears with a linking verb and tells something about the subject. A subject complement may be a *predicate nominative* or a *predicate adjective.*

A **predicate nominative** is a noun or pronoun that appears with a linking verb and renames, identifies, or explains the subject.

Kiglo was the *leader.*

A **predicate adjective** is an adjective that appears with a linking verb and describes the subject of a sentence.

Roko became *tired.*

Sentence Types A **simple sentence** consists of a single independent clause. A **compound sentence** consists of two or more independent clauses joined by a comma and a coordinating conjunction or by a semicolon. A **complex sentence** consists of one independent clause and one or more subordinate clauses. A **compound-complex sentence** consists of two or more independent clauses and one or more subordinate clauses. A **declarative sentence** states an idea and ends with a period. **Interrogative Sentence** An interrogative sentence asks a question and ends with a question mark. An **imperative sentence** gives an order or a direction and ends with either a period or an exclamation mark. An **exclamatory sentence** conveys a strong emotion and ends with an exclamation mark.

Phrases A **phrase** is a group of words, without a subject and a verb, that functions in a sentence as one part of speech. A **prepositional phrase** is a group of words that includes a preposition and a noun or a pronoun that is the object of the preposition. An **adjective phrase** is a prepositional phrase that modifies a noun or a pronoun by telling what kind or which one. An **adverb phrase** is a prepositional phrase that modifies a verb, an adjective, or an adverb by pointing out *where, when, in what manner,* or *to what extent.* An **appositive phrase** is a noun or a pronoun with modifiers, placed next to a noun or a pronoun to add information and details. A **participial phrase** is a participle modified by an adjective or an adverb phrase or accompanied by a complement. The entire phrase acts as an adjective.

Running at top speed, he soon caught up with them.

An **infinitive phrase** is an infinitive with modifiers, complements, or a subject, all acting together as a single part of speech.

At first I was too busy enjoying my food *to notice how the guests were doing.*

Gerunds A **gerund** is a noun formed from the present participle of a verb ending in *–ing.* Like other nouns, gerunds can be used as subjects, direct objects, predicate nouns, and objects of prepositions.

Gerund Phrases A **gerund phrase** is a gerund with modifiers or a complement, all acting together as a noun.

Clauses A **clause** is a group of words with its own subject and verb. An **independent clause** can stand by itself as a complete sentence.

A **subordinate clause** has a subject and a verb but cannot stand by itself as a complete sentence; it can only be part of a sentence.

"Although it was late"

Using Verbs, Pronouns, and Modifiers

Principal Parts A **verb** has **four principal parts:** the *present,* the *present participle,* the *past,* and the *past participle.* Regular verbs form the past and past participle by adding -ed to the present form.

Irregular verbs form the past and past participle by changing form rather than by adding -ed.

Verb Tense A **verb tense** tells whether the time of an action or condition is in the past, the present, or the future. Every verb has six tenses: *present, past, future, present perfect, past perfect,* and *future perfect.* The **present tense** shows actions that happen in the present. The **past tense** shows actions that have already happened. The **future tense** shows actions that will happen. The **present perfect tense** shows actions that begin in the past and continue to the present. The **past perfect tense** shows a past action or condition that ended before another past action. The **future perfect tense** shows a future action or condition that will have ended before another begins.

Pronoun Case The **case** of a pronoun is the form it takes to show its use in a sentence. There are three pronoun cases: *nominative, objective,* and *possessive.* The **nominative case** is used to name or rename the subject of the sentence. The nominative case pronouns are *I, you, he, she, it, we, you, they.* The **objective case** is used as the direct object, indirect object, or object of a preposition. The objective case pronouns are *me, you, him, her, it, us, you, them.* The **possessive case** is used to show ownership. The possessive pronouns are *my, your, his, her, its, our, their, mine, yours, his, hers, its, ours, theirs.*

Subject-Verb Agreement To make a subject and a verb agree, make sure that both are singular or both are plural. Two or more singular subjects joined by *or* or *nor* must have a singular verb. When singular and plural subjects are joined by *or* or *nor,* the verb must agree with the closest subject.

Pronoun-Antecedent Agreement Pronouns must agree with their antecedents in number and gender. Use singular pronouns with singular antecedents and plural pronouns with plural antecedents. Many errors in pronoun-antecedent agreement occur when a plural pronoun is used to refer to a singular antecedent for which the gender is not specified.

Incorrect: Everyone did their best.

Correct: Everyone did his or her best.

The following indefinite pronouns are singular: *anybody, anyone, each, either, everybody, everyone, neither, nobody, no one, one, somebody, someone.*

The following indefinite pronouns are plural: *both, few, many, several.*

The following indefinite pronouns may be either singular or plural: *all, any, most, none, some.*

Modifiers The **comparative** and **superlative** degrees of most adjectives and adverbs of one or two syllables can be formed in either of two ways: Use *–er* or *more* to form a comparative degree and *–est* or *most* to form the superlative degree of most one- and two-syllable modifiers.

More and *most* can also be used to form the comparative and superlative degrees of most one- and two- syllable modifiers. These words should not be used when the result sounds awkward, as in "A greyhound *is more* fast than a beagle."

Glossary of Common Usage

accept, except: *Accept* is a verb that means "to receive" or "to agree to." *Except* is a preposition that means "other than" or "leaving out." Do not confuse these two words.

affect, effect: *Affect* is normally a verb meaning "to influence" or "to bring about a change in." *Effect* is usually a noun, meaning "result."

among, between: *Among* is usually used with three or more items. *Between* is generally used with only two items.

bad, badly: Use the predicate adjective *bad* after linking verbs such as *feel, look,* and *seem.* Use *badly* whenever an adverb is required.

beside, besides: *Beside* means "at the side of" or "close to." *Besides* means "in addition to."

can, may: The verb *can* generally refers to the ability to do something. The verb *may* generally refers to permission to do something.

different from, different than: *Different from* is generally preferred over *different than.*

farther, further: Use *farther* when you refer to distance. Use *further* when you mean "to a greater degree or extent" or "additional."

fewer, less: Use *fewer* for things that can be counted. Use *less* for amounts or quantities that cannot be counted.

good, well: Use the predicate adjective *good* after linking verbs such as *feel, look, smell, taste,* and *seem.* Use well whenever you need an adverb.

its, it's: The word *its* with no apostrophe is a possessive pronoun. The word *it's* is a contraction for *it is.* Do not confuse the possessive pronoun *its* with the contraction *it's,* standing for "it is" or "it has."

lay, lie: Do not confuse these verbs. *Lay* is a transitive verb meaning "to set or put something down." Its principal parts are *lay, laying, laid, laid. Lie* is an intransitive verb meaning "to recline." Its principal parts are *lie, lying, lay, lain.*

like, as: *Like* is a preposition that usually means "similar to" or "in the same way as." *Like* should always be followed by an object. Do not use *like* before a subject and a verb. Use *as* or *that* instead.

of, have: Do not use *of* in place of have after auxiliary verbs like *would, could, should, may, might,* or *must.*

raise, rise: *Raise* is a transitive verb that usually takes a direct object. *Rise* is intransitive and never takes a direct object.

set, sit: *Set* is a transitive verb meaning "to put (something) in a certain place." Its principal parts are s*et, setting, set, set. Sit* is an intransitive verb meaning "to be seated." Its principal parts are *sit, sitting, sat, sat.*

than, then: The conjunction *than* is used to connect the two parts of a comparison. Do not confuse *than* with the adverb *then,* which usually refers to time.

that, which, who: Use the relative pronoun *that* to refer to things or people. Use *which* only for things and *who* only for people.

when, where, why: Do not use *when, where,* or *why* directly after a linking verb such as *is.* Reword the sentence.

Faulty: Suspense is when an author increases the reader's tension.

Revised: An author uses suspense to increase the reader's tension.

who, whom: In formal writing, remember to use *who* only as a subject in clauses and sentences and *whom* only as an object.

Capitalization and Punctuation

Capitalization

1. Capitalize the first word of a sentence.
2. Capitalize all proper nouns and adjectives.
3. Capitalize a person's title when it is followed by the person's name or when it is used in direct address.
4. Capitalize titles showing family relationships when they refer to a specific person, unless they are preceded by a possessive noun or pronoun.
5. Capitalize the first word and all other key words in the titles of books, periodicals, poems, stories, plays, paintings, and other works of art.
6. Capitalize the first word and all nouns in letter salutations and the first word in letter closings.

Punctuation

End Marks

1. Use a **period** to end a declarative sentence, an imperative sentence, and most abbreviations.
2. Use a **question mark** to end a direct question or an incomplete question in which the rest of the question is understood.
3. Use an **exclamation mark** after a statement showing strong emotion, an urgent imperative sentence, or an interjection expressing strong emotion.

Commas

1. Use a comma before the conjunction to separate two independent clauses in a compound sentence.
2. Use commas to separate three or more words, phrases, or clauses in a series.
3. Use commas to separate adjectives of equal rank. Do not use commas to separate adjectives that must stay in a specific order.
4. Use a comma after an introductory word, phrase, or clause.
5. Use commas to set off parenthetical and nonessential expressions.
6. Use commas with places and dates made up of two or more parts.
7. Use commas after items in addresses, after the salutation in a personal letter, after the closing in all letters, and in numbers of more than three digits.

Semicolons

1. Use a semicolon to join independent clauses that are not already joined by a conjunction.
2. Use a semicolon to join independent clauses or items in a series that already contain commas.

Colons

1. Use a colon before a list of items following an independent clause.
2. Use a colon in numbers giving the time, in salutations in business letters, and in labels used to signal important ideas.

Quotation Marks

1. A **direct quotation** represents a person's exact speech or thoughts and is enclosed in quotation marks.
2. An **indirect quotation** reports only the general meaning of what a person said or thought and does not require quotation marks.
3. Always place a comma or a period inside the final quotation mark of a direct quotation.
4. Place a question mark or an exclamation mark inside the final quotation mark if the end mark is part of the quotation; if it is not part of the quotation, place it outside the final quotation mark.

Titles

1. Underline or italicize the titles of long written works, movies, television and radio shows, lengthy works of music, paintings, and sculptures.
2. Use quotation marks around the titles of short written works, episodes in a series, songs, and titles of works mentioned as parts of collections.

Hyphens

1. Use a **hyphen** with certain numbers, after certain prefixes, with two or more words used as one word, and with a compound modifier that comes before a noun.

Apostrophes

1. Add an **apostrophe** and s to show the possessive case of most singular nouns.
2. Add an apostrophe to show the possessive case of plural nouns ending in *s* and *es*.
3. Add an apostrophe and s to show the possessive case of plural nouns that do not end in *s* or *es*.
4. Use an apostrophe in a contraction to indicate the position of the missing letter or letters.

Index of Skills

Boldface numbers indicate pages where terms are defined.

Literary Analysis

Acts (drama), **692**

Address, **379**

Advertisement, 379, R24

Alliteration, 551, 554, **637**, **R13**

Allusion, **R13**

Analogy, **921**, **R13**

Analytic rubric, **R36**

Anecdote, 131, 381, 382, **R13**
  diary, 388, 389

Antagonist, **R13**

Archetype, **827**

Argument, lxviii–lxxiii, 110, 418, 435, 438, 526, 530, 542, 738, 740, 744, 779, 782
  elements, lxviii
  informational text, lxix
  rhetorical devices and persuasive techniques, lxx
  speech, lxxi

Aside, **694**

Assembly instructions, **5**

Atmosphere, **R13**

Author's influences, **469**, 477, 483, 485, **R13**

Author's perspective, 93, 98, 99, 101, 106, 107, 378, 380

Author's point of view, 378, 380, 382
  diary, 387

Author's purpose, **7**, 378, **380**, 382, **395**, 403, **788**, 791, 794, 797, 799
  biography, 383
  diary, 386, 392
  folk literature, 824
  nonfiction, 408

Author's purpose, Test Practice, 436

Author's style, **516**, 525, **R13**

Autobiographical narrative, **154**, **395**, 403, 415

Autobiographical writing, **379**, **R2**

Autobiography, 5, **379**, **444**, 461, **R13**

Bandwagon/anti-bandwagon approach, **lxx**

Bibliography, **R34**

Biography, 5, **444**, 461, **R13**

Block format (letter), **740**

Blogs, **R28**, **R29**

Body (letter), **740**

Brochure, **5**

Cause, **839**, 845, 853, **857**, 865, 873

Central idea, 4, **7**. See also Main idea
  letter, 17
  speech, 19
  stated and implied, 16

Character, 4, **8**, **178**, 181, 206, 208, 209, 210, 215, 692, **694**, 696, 698, 828, 857, **R13**
  drama, **692**, 694, 695, 696, 697, 699
  fiction, 8
  folk literature, 828, 829, 831, 832, 833, 834
  short story, 10, 12, 13, 15, **178**, **182**

Character map, **189**

Character motives, **178**, **250**, 263, **R17**

Character traits, **178**, 181, **182**, **189**, **250**, **R13**
  short story, **181**, **182**, 183, 184, 185

Characterization, 178, **181**, 182, 196, 201, **R13**
  direct/indirect, **181**, **189**, 194, 203, 215

Chronological organization, **156**

Claim (assertion), lxviii

Climax, **21**, 29, 39, **156**, **179**, **356**, 692, **R13**

Closing (letter), **740**

Comedy, **692**, **R14**

Comparison, **16**
  speech, 19

Comparison of works, **R25**

Conclusions, **271**

Concrete poem, **553**, **621**, 627, 633, **R14**

Conflict, 4, **8**, 12, **21**, 29, 39, **178**, **179**, 180, 181, 182, 222, 224, 226, 228, 229, 235, 236, 356, 692, 695, 696, 703, **R14**
  chart, 231, 362
  drama, **692**, 695, 696, 697, 699
  external/internal, **178**, **180**, **219**, 239, **695**, 696, **R15**, **R16**
  short story, 9, 10, 11, 12, 13, 14, 178, 180, 181, 182, 183, 184

Connotation, 380, 382, 552, **678**, 679, **R14**
  diary, 386

Context clues, 581, **585**, 591, 597

Creative writing, **R25**

Cultural context, **824**

Denotation, 552, **678**, **R14**

Denouement, **179**

Description, **R14**, **R24**
  letter, 17
  short story, 10, 14
  speech, 18

Descriptive writing, **86**, **R24**

Details
  important/unimportant, 495, 506, 507
  key, **469**, 477, 482, 485

Development. See Plot

Development of ideas, **382**
  diary, 390

Dialect, **825**, **R14**

Dialogue, **692**, 696, 702, 703, **705**, 711, 712, 714, 716, 720, 722, 723, 724, 727, 728, 730, 731, 733, **R14**
  drama, 696, 697, 701

Diaries and journals, 5, **379**, **R16**

Diction, 827

Direct characterization, **181**

Drama, **692**, **R14**, **R18**, **R25**. See also Dialogue; Stage directions
  elements, **692**, 693, 694, 703
  forms of, **693**
  script, 692, **705**, 745
  staging, **R19**

Dramatist, **692**

Dynamic character, **R13**

Editorial, **379**

Effect, **839**, 845, 853, **857**, 865, 873

Emotion. See Tone/emotion

Emotional appeal, **lxx**

Endorsement, **lxx**

Essay, 5, **379**, **419**, **R14**
  cause-and-effect, **800**, **R24**
  comparison-and-contrast, **668**, **R24**
  descriptive, **86**
  expository, **379**, **419**, 425, 430, 431, 433
  how-to, **462**
  narrative, **379**, **395**, 400, 403, 407, 410, 413, 415
  persuasive, **379**, **526**
  problem-and-solution, **614**, **825**, **R25**
  reflective, **379**

Events chart, **705**

Examples, **16**, **382**
  biography, 383

Explanatory writing, **R24–R25**

Exposition, **21**, **179**, **R15**

Expository essay, **379**

Expository writing, **356**, 419, **R15**

Extended metaphor, **R15**

Fable, **825**, **839**, 845, **R15**

Fable elements chart, 853

Reading for Information

Reading Skills

Writing Strategies

Index of Features

Boldface numbers indicate pages where terms are defined.

Index of Authors and Titles

Notes: Page numbers in *italics* refer to biographical information; nonfiction appears in red. For a complete listing of the informational texts in this program, please see page **xxxii**.

Acknowledgments

Grateful acknowledgment is made to the following for copyrighted material:

English—Language Arts Content Standards for California Public Schools reproduced by permission, California Department of Education, CD Press, 1430 N Street, Suite 3207, Sacramento, CA 95814.

Airmont Publishing Company, Inc. "Water" by Helen Keller from *The Story of My Life.* Copyright © 1965 by Airmont Publishing Company, Inc. Used by permission of Airmont Publishing Company, Inc.

Ricardo E. Alegría "The Three Wishes" selected and adapted by Ricardo E. Alegría from *The Three Wishes: A Collection of Puerto Rican Folktales.* Copyright © 1969 by Ricardo E. Alegría. Used by permission of Ricardo E. Alegría.

American Red Cross National Headquarters "Red Cross Helps Florida Residents Recover From Tornadoes" by Arindam Mukherjee, December 29, 2006 posted on *www.redcross.org.* Used by permission courtesy of the American National Red Cross. All rights reserved in all countries.

ASPCA ASPCA Animaland from *http://www.aspca.org.* Copyright © 2007 by The American Society for the Prevention of Cruelty to Animals. Used by permission.

The Associated Press "Rescuers to Carry Oxygen Masks for Pets" from *www.postcrescent.com.* Copyright © 2007 The Associated Press. Used with permission. All rights reserved.

Atheneum Books for Young Readers, an imprint of Simon & Schuster "Stray" by Cynthia Rylant from *Every Living Thing.* Copyright © 1985 by Cynthia Rylant. Used by permission of Atheneum Books for Young Readers, an imprint of Simon & Schuster Children's Publishing Division.

The Bancroft Library, Administrative Offices "Letter from a Concentration Camp" by Yoshiko Uchida from *The Big Book For Peace.* Text copyright © 1990 by Yoshiko Uchida. Courtesy of the Bancroft Library University of California, Berkeley. Used with permission.

Bantam Doubleday Dell Publishing "Black Ships Before Troy: The Story of The Iliad" by Rosemary Sutcliff from *Delacorte Press.* Copyright © 1993 by Frances Lincoln Limited.

Susan Bergholz Literary Services "Abuelito Who" by Sandra Cisneros from *My Wicked Wicked Ways.* Copyright © 1987 by Sandra Cisneros. Published by Third Woman Press and in hardcover by Alfred A. Knopf. Used by permission of Third Woman Press and Susan Bergholz Literary Services, New York. "Names/Nombres" by Julia Alvarez from *Nuestro, March, 1985.* Copyright © 1985 by Julia Alvarez. First published in *Nuestro. March, 1985.* "Something to Declare" (Introduction) by Julia Alvarez. Copyright © 1998 by Julia Alvarez. From *Something To Declare,* published by Plume, an imprint of Penguin Group (USA), in 1999 and originally in hardcover by Algonquin Books of Chapel Hill. "Eleven" from *Woman Hollering Creek* by Sandra Cisneros. Copyright © 1991 by Sandra Cisneros. Published by Vintage Books, a division of Random House, Inc., New York and originally in hardcover by Random House, Inc. Used by permission of Susan Bergholz Literary Services, New York, NY and Lamy, NM. All rights reserved.

Robert Bly "Friends All of Us" from *Childhood and Poetry* by Pablo Neruda. Reprinted from *Neruda and Vallejo: Selected Poems,* by Robert Bly, Beacon Press, Boston, 1993. Used by permission.

BOA Editions, Ltd. c/o The Permissions Company "Alphabet" by Naomi Shihab Nye from *Fuel.* Copyright © 1998 by Naomi Shihab Nye. All rights reserved. Used by permission of BOA Editions Ltd., www.boaeditions.org.

Georges Borchardt, Inc. "Dragon, Dragon" from *Dragon, Dragon And Other Tales* by John Gardner. Copyright © 1975 by Boskydell Artists, Ltd. Used by permission of Georges Borchardt, Inc., for the Estate of John Gardner.

Brandt & Hochman Literary Agents, Inc. "Wilbur Wright and Orville Wright" by Stephen Vincent Benét, from *A Book of Americans* by Rosemary and Stephen Vincent Benét. Copyright © 1933 by Rosemary and Stephen Vincent Benét. Copyright © renewed 1961 by Rosemary Carr Benét. "Lob's Girl" from *A Whisper in the Night* by Joan Aiken. Delacorte Press. Copyright © 1984 by Joan Aiken Enterprises, Ltd. Used by permission of Brandt & Hochman Literary Agents, Inc.

John Brewton, George M. Blackburn & Lorraine A. Blackburn "Limerick (Accidents--More or Less Fatal)" from *Laughable Limericks.* Copyright © 1965 by Sara and John E. Brewton. Used by permission of Brewton, Blackburn and Blackburn.

Brooks Permissions "Cynthia In the Snow" from *Bronzeville Boys and Girls* by Gwendolyn Brooks. Copyright © 1956 by Gwendolyn Brooks. Used by consent of Brooks Permissions.

Curtis Brown Ltd. From *The Pigman & Me (Learning the Rules)* by Paul Zindel. Copyright © 1992 by Paul Zindel. First published by HarperCollins. "Adventures of Isabel" by Ogden Nash from *Parents Keep Out.* Originally published by *Nash's Pall Mall Magazine.* Copyright © 1936 by Ogden Nash. All rights reserved. "Greyling" by Jane Yolen from *Greyling: A Picture Story from the Islands.* Copyright © 1968, 1996 by Jane Yolen. First published by Penguin Putnam. Used by permission of Curtis Brown, Ltd.

Diana Chang (Diana C. Herrmann) "Saying Yes" by Diana Chang. Copyright by Diana Chang. Used by permission of the author.

Chronicle Books "Oranges" from *New and Selected Poems* by Gary Soto. Copyright © 1995 by Gary Soto. Visit www.chroniclebooks.com. Used with permission of Chronicle Books LLC, San Francisco.

Clarion Books, a division of Houghton Mifflin "A Backwoods Boy" from *Lincoln: A Photobiography.* Copyright © 1987 by Russell Freedman. Used by permission of Clarion Books/Houghton Mifflin Company. All rights reserved.

Ruth Cohen Literary Agency, Inc. "The All-American Slurp" by Lensey Namioka, copyright © 1987, from *Visions,* ed. by Donald R. Gallo. Used by permission of Lensey Namioka. All rights reserved by the Author.

Don Congdon Associates, Inc. "The Sound of Summer Running" by Ray Bradbury from *The Saturday Evening Post, 2/18/56.* Copyright © 1956 by the Curtis Publishing Company, copyright © renewed 1984 by Ray Bradbury. "Hard As Nails" from *The Good Times* by

Russell Baker. Copyright © 1989 by Russell Baker. Used by permission of Don Congdon Associates, Inc.

Gary N. DaSilva Excerpt from *Brighton Beach Memoirs* by Neil Simon from *McGraw Hill Glencoe*, copyright © 1984 by Neil Simon.

Dell Publishing, a division of Random House, Inc. "Jeremiah's Song" by Walter Dean Myers, from *Visions* by Donald R. Gallo, Editor, copyright © 1987 by Donald R. Gallo. "The Tail" Copyright © 1992 by Joyce Hansen from *Funny You Should Ask* by David Gale, Editor. Used by permission of Dell Publishing, a division of Random House, Inc.

Dial Books for Young Readers, a division of Penguin Young Readers Group *Black Cowboy, Wild Horses* written by Julius Lester and illustrated by Jerry Pinkney. Text copyright © 1998 by Julius Lester. Illustrations copyright © 1998 by Jerry Pinkney. "Gluskabe and Old Man Winter: Abenaki" by Joseph Bruchac from *Pushing Up the Sky*. Copyright © 2000 by Joseph Bruchac, text. Used by permission of Dial Books for Young Readers, A Division of Penguin Young Readers Group, A Member of Penguin Group (USA).

Doubleday, a division of Random House, Inc. "Child on Top of a Greenhouse" by Theodore Roethke from *The Collected Poems of Theodore Roethke*, copyright © 1946 by Editorial Publications, Inc. "The Fun They Had" from *Isaac Asimov: The Complete Stories of Vol. I*, by Isaac Asimov, copyright © 1957 by Isaac Asimov. Used by permission of Doubleday, a division of Random House, Inc.

Dover Publications, Inc. "Rendezvous with Despair" by Thomas E. Dewey from *The World's Great Speeches*, copyright © 1958, 1973 by Dover Publications, Inc.

Encyclopaedia Britannica "How to Read a Road Map" from *Britannica Student Encyclopaedia Online www.britannica.com/ebi/article-199642*. Copyright © 2007 Encyclopaedia Brittanica, Inc. Used with permission from Britannica Student Encyclopedia.

Paul S. Eriksson "My Papa, Mark Twain" by Susy Clemens from *Small Voices* by Josef and Dorothy Berger. Copyright © 1966 by Josef and Dorothy Berger in arrangement with Paul S. Eriksson, Publisher. Used by permission.

Jean Grasso Fitzpatrick "The Ant and the Dove" by Leo Tolstoy from *Fables and Folktales Adapted from Tolstoy*. Translated by Jean Grasso Fitzpatrick. Used with permission.

Florida Fish and Wildlife Conservation Commission Manatee Decal Art Contest from *http://myfwc.com/manatee/decals/contest2007.htm*. Copyright © 2007 Florida Fish and Wildlife Conservation Commission. Used by permission.

Samuel French, Inc. "The Phantom Tollbooth" from *The Phantom Tollbooth: A Children's Play in Two Acts* by Susan Nanus and Norton Juster. Copyright © 1977 by Susan Nanus and Norton Juster. Used by permission of Samuel French, Inc. All rights reserved. CAUTION: Professionals and amateurs are hereby warned that "The Phantom Tollbooth," being fully protected under the copyright laws of the United States of America, the British Commonwealth countries, including Canada, and the other countries of the Copyright Union, is subject to royalty. All rights, including professional, amateur, motion picture, recitation, lecturing, public reading, radio, television and cable broadcasting, and the rights of translation into foreign languages, are strictly reserved. Any inquiry regarding the avail-

ability of performance rights, or the purchase of individual copies of the authorized acting edition, must be directed to Samuel French, Inc., 45 West 25th Street, NY, NY 10010 with other locations in Hollywood and Toronto, Canada.

Greenwillow Books, a division of HarperCollins "Ankylosaurus" by Jack Prelutsky from *Tyrannosaurus Was a Beast*. Text copyright © 1988 by Jack Prelutsky. Used by permission of HarperCollins Publishers.

Harcourt, Inc. "Ode to Family Photographs" from *Neighborhood Odes*, copyright © 1992 by Gary Soto. Used by permission of Harcourt, Inc.

Harcourt Education Limited "Why the Tortoise's Shell Is Not Smooth" by Chinua Achebe from *Things Fall Apart*. Copyright © 1959 by Chinua Achebe. Used with permission of Harcourt Education.

HarperCollins Publishers, Inc. "No Thank You" by Shel Silverstein from *Falling Up*. Copyright © 1996 by Shel Silverstein. All rights reserved. "Zlateh the Goat" by Isaac Bashevis Singer from *Zlateh the Goat and Other Stories*. Text copyright © 1966 by Isaac Bashevis Singer, copyright © renewed 1994 by Alma Singer. Art copyright © 1966 by Maurice Sendak, copyright © renewed 1994 by Maurice Sendak. "The Homecoming" by Laurence Yep from *The Rainbow People*. Copyright © 1989 by Laurence Yep. From *The Wounded Wolf* by Jean Craighead George. Text copyright © 1978 by Jean Craighead George. Used by permission of HarperCollins Publishers. "Langston Terrace" by Eloise Greenfield, from *Childtimes: A Three-Generation Memoir*, copyright © 1979 by Eloise Greenfield and Lessie Jones Little. "Aaron's Gift" from *The Witch of Fourth Street and Other Stories* by Myron Levoy. Text copyright © 1972 by Myron Levoy.

Harper's Magazine "Preserving a Great American Symbol," (originally titled "Desecrating America") by Richard Durbin from *Harper's Magazine, October 1989, p.32*. Copyright © 1989 by *Harper's Magazine*. All rights reserved. Reproduced from the October issue by special permission.

Harvard University Press "Fame Is a Bee" (#1763) by Emily Dickinson is used by permission of the publishers and the Trustees of Amherst College from *The Poems of Emily Dickinson*, Thomas H. Johnson, editor, Cambridge, Mass.: The Belknap Press of Harvard University Press, Copyright © 1951, 1955, 1979, 1983 by the President and Fellows of Harvard College.

Sara Hightower Regional Library System Sara Hightower Regional Library Systems Card Policies and Application from *http://www.romelibrary.org/card.htm*. Copyright © 2007 Sara Hightower Regional Library System. Used by permission.

The Barbara Hogenson Agency, Inc. "The Tiger Who Would Be King" by James Thurber, from *Further Fables for Our Time*. Copyright © 1956 James Thurber. Copyright © renewed 1984 by Rosemary A. Thurber. Used by arrangement with Rosemary A. Thurber and The Barbara Hogenson Agency, Inc.

Henry Holt and Company, Inc. "Dust of Snow" by Robert Frost from *The Poetry of Robert Frost* edited by Edward Connery Lathem. Copyright © 1923, 1969 by Henry Holt & Company. Copyright © 1951 by Robert Frost. "The Stone" from *The Foundling And Other Tales Of Prydain* by Lloyd Alexander. Copyright © 1973, 2002 by Lloyd Alexander. Used by permission of Henry Holt and Company, LLC.

Marian Reiner, Literary Agent "Haiku ("An old silent pond...")" by Matsuo Basho translated by Harry Behn from *Cricket Songs: Japanese Haiku*. Copyright © 1964 by Harry Behn; Copyright © renewed 1992 Prescott Behn, Pamela Behn Adam and Peter Behn. "Haiku ("Over the wintry")" by Muso Soseki translated by Harry Behn from *Cricket Songs: Japanese Haiku*. Copyright © 1964 Harry Behn. Copyright renewed © 1992 by Prescott Behn, Pamela Behn Adam, and Peter Behn. Used by permission of Marian Reiner.

The Sacramento Bee "The Journey by Land" from *The Great American Gold Rush* by Rhoda Blumberg, *The Gold Rush* by Liza Ketchum, *The California Gold Rush*, published by American Heritage, *The California Gold Rush* by Elizabeth Van Steenwyk, *Hunting for Gold* by William Downie, *Sea Routes to the Gold Fields* by Oscar Lewis, *If You Traveled West in a Covered Wagon* by Ellen Levine, *The East Indiamen* by Russell Miller, Steve and Eric Chrissman of the National Nautical Heritage Society.

San Francisco Chronicle "O'Neil Belongs Inside this Hall" by Scott Ostler from *http://sfgate.com/*. Copyright © 2006 by San Francisco Chronicle. Used by permission of San Francisco Chronicle via Copyright Clearance Center.

San Francisco Public Library San Francisco Public Library Card Policies and Application from *http://sfpl.lib.ca.us/services/librarycard.htm*. Copyright © 2002-2006 by San Francisco Public Library. Used by permission.

Sarasota County Library Sarasota County Library Card Services, Policies, and Application from *http://suncat.co.sarasota.fl.us/services/librarycard.aspx*. Copyright © 2007 Sarasota County Library. Used by permission.

Scholastic Inc. "The Shutout" from *Black Diamond: The Story Of The Negro Baseball Leagues* by Patricia C. McKissack and Fredrick McKissack, Jr. Copyright © 1994 by Patricia C. McKissack and Fredrick McKissack, Jr. "Why Monkeys Live in Trees" from *How Many Spots Does A Leopard Have? And Other Tales* by Julius Lester. Copyright © 1989 by Julius Lester. Reproduced by permission of Scholastic Inc.

Scovil Chichak Galen Literary Agency, Inc. "Feathered Friend" from *The Other Side Of the Sky* by Arthur C. Clarke. Copyright © 1958 by Arthur C. Clarke. Used by permission of the author and the author's agents, Scovil Chichak Galen Literary Agency, Inc.

Scribner, a division of Simon & Schuster "Letter to Scottie" by F. Scott Fitzgerald, from *F. Scott Fitzgerald: A Life in Letters*, edited by Matthey J. Bruccoli. Used by permission of Scribner, an imprint of Simon & Schuster Adult Publishing Group. Copyright © 1994 by The Trustees under Agreement dated July 3, 1975. Created by Frances Scott Fitzgerald Smith.

Simon & Schuster Books for Young Readers "Parade" used by the permission of Simon & Schuster Books for Young Readers, an imprint of Simon & Schuster Children's Publishing Division from *Branches Green* by Rachel Field. Copyright © 1934 Macmillan Publishing Company; copyright © renewed 1962 by Arthur S. Pederson.

St. Martin's Press "The Market Square Dog" from *James Herriot's Treasury for Children* by James Herriot. Copyright © 1989 James Herriot. Used by permission of St. Martin's Press, LLC.

William Strauss, Director, The Cappies "You're a Good Man, Charlie Brown at Robert E. Lee (High School)" by Brianna Sonnefeld from *www.cappies.com/nca/news/reviews/06-07/le.htm*. Copyright © 2005 The Cappies, Inc., All Rights Reserved. Used by permission.

Talkin' Broadway "Happiness is a Charming Charlie Brown at Orlando Rep "by Matthew MacDermid from *www.talkinbroadway.com*. Copyright © TalkinBroadway.com, a project of www.TalkinBroadway.org, Inc. Used by permission.

Thorgate, LLC "Metric Metric: It's so nice, we say it twice!™" from *www.metricmetric.com*. Copyright © 2007 Metric Metric. Used by permission.

Dr. My-Van Tran "A Crippled Boy" from *Folk Tales from Indochina* by Dr. My-Van Tran. First published in 1987. Copyright © Vietnamese Language and Culture Publications and Tran My-Van. Used by permission.

University of Nebraska Press "The Old Woman Who Lived With the Wolves" reprinted from *Stories Of The Sioux* by Luther Standing Bear. Used by permission of the University of Nebraska Press. Copyright © 1934 by Luther Standing Bear. Copyright © renewed 1961 by May M. Jones.

University Press of New England "The Drive-In Movies" from *A Summer Life* copyright © 1990 by University Press of New England, Hanover, NH. Used by permission.

Viking Penguin, Inc. "La lena buena," (retitled) pages 113-144 from *Places Left Unfinished At The Time Of Creation* by John Phillip Santos, copyright © 1999 by John Phillip Santos. From *Zlata's Diary* by Zlata Filipovic from *Zlata's Life: A Child's Life in Sarajevo*. Translated by Christina Pribichevich-zoric. Copyright © 1994 Editions Robert Laffont/Fixot. Used by permission of Viking Penguin, a division of Penguin Group (USA) Inc.

Villard Books, a division of Random House, Inc. "The Lady and the Spider" from *All I Really Need to Know I Learned In Kindergarten* by Robert L. Fulghum. Copyright © 1986, 1988 by Robert L. Fulghum. Used by permission of Villard Books, a division of Random House, Inc.

World Book, Inc. From "Tornado" by Howard B. Bluestein from *World Book Reference Center*. Copyright © 2007. World Book, Inc. Used by permission of publisher. *www.worldbookonline.com*.

World of Escher "World of Escher Tessallation Contest" from *www.worldofescher.com/contest*. Copyright © 1995-2007 WorldofEscher.com. All rights reserved. Used by permission.

Jane Yolen "My Heart is in the Highlands" by Jane Yolen from *My Heart Is In The Highlands*. Copyright © Jane Yolen.

Note: Every effort has been made to locate the copyright owner of material reproduced in this component. Omissions brought to our attention will be corrected in subsequent editions.

Credits

Photo Credits

xlviii Suzanne Tucker/Shutterstock **Grade 6 Unit 1 9:** Bkgrnd. JeremyWalker/Getty Images; **9:** Inset. © James Gritz; **10-11:** b. Evelyn Macduff/Getty Images; **12:** Jeremy Walker/Getty Images; **12:** l. Jeremy Walker/Getty Images; **13:** l. © Moodboard/ CORBIS; **14:** Photo 24/Brand X Pictures/Jupiter Images; **14-15:** © Brand X Pictures; **17:** l. Silver Burdett Ginn; **17:** r. Silver Burdett Ginn; **23:** t. Courtesy of Cynthia Rylant; **23:** b. © Lew Robertson/CORBIS; **24:** Bkgrnd. © narvikk/istockphoto. com; **24:** Inset. © Lew Robertson/CORBIS; **26:** © GK Hart/Vikki Hart; **27:** © Ciaran Griffin; **28:** © Lew Robertson/CORBIS; **31:** t. Prentice Hall; **31:** b. istockphoto.com/maten; **32:** Christie's Images/CORBIS; **34:** The Art Archive/Free Library of Philadelphia/Album/Joseph Martin; **36:** The Granger Collection, New York; **37:** The Art Archive / Free library Philadelphia; **38:** istockphoto.com/maten; **45:** t. Courtesy of the Author; **45:** Randy Faris/CORBIS; **46-47:** Randy Faris/CORBIS; **47:** Car Culture/ CORBIS; **48-49:** t. Marcela Brasse/istockphoto.com; **48:** Orlando/ Hulton Archive/Getty Images, Inc; **50:** l. istockphoto.com; **50:** r. Valerie Loiseleux/istockphoto.com; **53:** t. Julian Calder/CORBIS; **53:** Copyright © 1992 by James Herriot and Ruth Brown. From James Herriot's *Treasury for Children* by James Herriot, illustrated by Ruth Brown and Peter Barrett. Reprinted by permission of St. Martin's Press, LLC; **55:** t. Copyright © 1992 by James Herriot and Ruth Brown. From James Herriot's *Treasury for Children* by James Herriot, illustrated by Ruth Brown and Peter Barrett. Reprinted by permission of St. Martin's Press, LLC; **56:** Copyright © 1992 by James Herriot and Ruth Brown. From James Herriot's *Treasury for Children* by James Herriot, illustrated by Ruth Brown and Peter Barrett. Reprinted by permission of St. Martin's Press, LLC; **57:** Copyright © 1992 by James Herriot and Ruth Brown. From James Herriot's *Treasury for Children* by James Herriot, illustrated by Ruth Brown and Peter Barrett. Reprinted by permission of St. Martin's Press, LLC; **58:** l. Copyright © 1992 by James Herriot and Ruth Brown. From James Herriot's *Treasury for Children* by James Herriot, illustrated by Ruth Brown and Peter Barrett. Reprinted by permission of St. Martin's Press, LLC; **58:** r. Copyright © 1992 by James Herriot and Ruth Brown. From James Herriot's *Treasury for Children* by James Herriot, illustrated by Ruth Brown and Peter Barrett. Reprinted by permission of St. Martin's Press, LLC; **59:** Copyright © 1992 by James Herriot and Ruth Brown. From James Herriot's *Treasury for Children* by James Herriot, illustrated by Ruth Brown and Peter Barrett. Reprinted by permission of St. Martin's Press, LLC; **60:** Copyright © 1992 by James Herriot and Ruth Brown. From James Herriot's *Treasury for Children* by James Herriot, illustrated by Ruth Brown and Peter Barrett. Reprinted by permission of St. Martin's Press, LLC; **67:** tl. istockphoto.com; **67:** ml. BRIAN J. SKERRY/National Geographic Image Collection; **68:** istockphoto.com; **69:** © Don Hammond/Design Pics/CORBIS; **70:** © Michael Newman / PhotoEdit; **73:** r. Prentice Hall; **73:** l. Courtesy Susan Quinlan; **82:** r. Peter Anderson/© Dorling Kindersley; **82:** tl. Cyril Laubscher/© Dorling Kindersley; **82:** tm. Geoff Dann/© Dorling Kindersley; **82:** ml. Colin Keates ©Dorling Kindersley, Courtesy of the Natural History Museum, London; **82:** bl. Frank Greenway/© Dorling Kindersley; **82:** m. © Dorling Kindersley; **82:** bm. ©Geoff Dann/ Dorling Kindersley; **95:** t. The Mark Twain House, Hartford, CT; **98:** Inset. Bettmann/CORBIS; **99:** The Granger Collection, New York; **103:** Bettmann/CORBIS; **113:** t. Photo: © Daniel Cima; **120:** Collage (detail), 1992, Juan Sanchez, Courtesy of Juan Sanchez and Guarighen, Inc., NYC; **121:** b. AP/Wide World Photos; **124:** © Kathryn Bell istockphoto.com; **125:** © Sharon Dominick istockphoto.com; **126:** John McNally/PhotoLibrary.com; **126-127:** l. George McCarthy/CORBIS; **128:** m. © Elena Kalistratova istockphoto.com; **128:** l. © Marguerite Voisey istockphoto.com; **141:** t. AP/Wide World Photos; **142:** © Helen Vaughn/ Superstock; **146:** Images.com/CORBIS; **149:** Inset. Peter Byron/PhotoEdit; **150:** Michael Newman/PhotoEdit; **172:** (TL) AP/Wide World Photos, (BR) Photo by Charles Barry/Santa Clara University

GRADE 6 UNIT 2 180: PEANUTS reprinted by permission of United Feature Syndicate, Inc.; **184:** ©Still Picture/Peter Arnold, Inc.; **191:** t. Photo by Austin V. Hansen, Jr. Courtesy of the author; **191:** b. Photodisc; **192:** Bkgrnd. istockphoto.com; **192:** tm. © Push Pictures/ CORBIS; **193:** b. Photodisc; **195:** b. © Sean Justice/CORBIS; **195:** t. © Push Pictures/CORBIS; **197:** istockphoto.com/jubrancoelho; **198:** CORBIS Digital Stock; **201:** b. © Push Pictures/CORBIS; **202:** r. Photodisc; **202:** bl. Photodisc; **202:** tl. © Push Pictures/CORBIS; **202:** tl. © Push Pictures/CORBIS; **205:** t. ©Joel Gardner; **221:** t. Robert Maass/CORBIS; **221:** b. istockphoto.com/ PaulMaguire; **223:** from "Zlateh the Goat and Other Stories" by Isaac Bashevis Singer, illustrations by Maurice Sendak © 1966, HarperCollins Publishers, Inc.; **225:** from "Zlateh the Goat and Other Stories" by Isaac Bashevis Singer, illustrations by Maurice Sendak © 1966, HarperCollins, Publishers, Inc.; **227:** from "Zlateh the Goat and Other Stories" by Isaac Bashevis Singer, illustra-tions by Maurice Sendak © 1966, HarperCollins, Publishers, Inc.; **230:** from "Zlateh the Goat and Other Stories" by Isaac Bashevis Singer, illustrations by Maurice Sendak © 1966, HarperCollins, Publishers, Inc.; **233:** t. Bettmann/CORBIS; **234:** *Time to Hunt,* John Newcomb/SuperStock; **236:** r. The Granger Collection, New York; **236:** l. Bettmann/CORBIS; **245:** t. Archives Charmet; **245:** m. Private Collection, Archives Charmet / The Bridgeman Art Library International; **245:** b. Private Collection, The Stapleton Collection/The Bridgeman Art Library International; **246:** tl. Private Collection, Archives Charmet/The Bridgeman Art Library International; **246:** tr. Private Collection, Archives Charmet / The Bridgeman Art Library International; **246:** b. Private Collection, Archives Charmet/The Bridgeman Art Library International; **247:** b. Richard Bonson/© Dorling Kindersley; **248:** t. David Sutherland/Photo Researchers, Inc.; **248:** b. The Art Archive/Egyptian Museum Cairo / Gianni Dagli Orti; **251:** b. Didi Cutler; **251:** t. gezette.de Buro fur Fotografie; **252:** *Daddy's Girl,* 1992, Carlton Murrell, Courtesy of the artist, photo by John Lei/Omni-Photo Communications, Inc.; **255:** *Biking for Fun,* 1992, Carlton Murrell, Courtesy of the artist, photo by John Lei/Omni-Photo Communications, Inc.; **258:** *Mother, I Love to Ride,* 1992, Carlton Murrell, Courtesy of the artist, photo by John Lei/Omni-Photo Communications, Inc.; **260:** t. **273:** t. Photo by Charles Barry. Copyright Santa Clara University; **281:** © Bill Aron/PhotoEdit; **285:** t. Courtesy of the author. Photo by Don Perkins.; **286:** Stephane Jorisch; **290:** Stephane Jorisch; **290:** tl. Stephane Jorisch; **291:** Stephane Jorisch; **292:** Stephane Jorisch; **294-295:** Stephane Jorisch; **296:** Stephane Jorish; **303:** t. Bettmann/CORBIS; **304:** The Granger Collection, New York; **308:** b. Getty Images; **309:** r. Corel Professional Photos CD-ROM™; **317:** t. Prentice Hall; **323:** Underwood & Underwood/CORBIS; **335:** CORBIS; **336:** ©Bettmann/CORBIS; **343:** b. AP/Wide World Photos; **372:** (CR) © Julian Calder/Corbis

GRADE 6 UNIT 3 379: t. The Granger Collection, New York; **380:** CALVIN AND HOBBES © 1992 Watterson. Reprinted with permission of UNIVERSAL PRESS SYNDICATE. All rights reserved. **383:** Boulat Alexandra/Sipa; **384:** Boulat Alexandra/Sipa; **387:** Boulat Alexandra/Sipa **389:** Boulat Alexandra/Sipa; **390:** Boulat Alexandra/Sipa; **392:** Boulat Alexandra/Sipa; **397:** t. Bettmann/CORBIS; **398:** *The Goosegirl,* c.1866 (oil on canvas), Millet, Jean-Francois (1814-75) / © Tokyo Fuji Art Museum, Tokyo, Japan, / The Bridgeman Art Library International; **399:** tl. Time & Life Pictures/Getty Images/Walter Sanders/Stringer; **400:** bl. Getty Images/Museum of the City of New York/Contributor; **401:** Photolibrary. com /Peter Fogg; **405:** t. Yvonne Hemsey/Getty Images; **406:** ©Anthony Potter Collections/Archive Photos; **406-407:** border. The Granger Collection, New York; **406:** Bkgrnd. Peter Hansen/istockphoto.com; **410:** ©Levick/Archive Photos; **412:** AP/Wide World Photos; **414:** mr. © SuperStock, Inc. / SuperStock; **421:** t. Seth Resnick/CORBIS; **421:** b. Getty Images, Inc; **422:** t. Bettmann/CORBIS; **423:** Bettmann/CORBIS; **427:** b. Courtesy of the author; **428:** National Baseball Library and Archive, Cooperstown, N.Y.; **429:** AP/Wide World Photos/Gene J. Puskar;

431: National Baseball Library and Archive, Cooperstown, N.Y.; 439: AP/Wide World Photos; 441: Rich Pilling/MLB Photos/Getty Images; 445: t. Copyright© by Julia Alvarez/Bill Eichner. Reprinted by permission of Susan Bergholz Literary Services, NY. All Rights reserved.; 448: Bettmann/CORBIS; 450: © Bettmann/CORBIS; 452: The Granger Collection, New York; 454: The Granger Collection, New York; 455: b. Courtesy of the Library of Congress; 455: b. Courtesy of the Library of Congress; 455: b. Copyright © North Wind/North Wind Picture Archives - - All rights reserved.; 457: The Granger Collection, New York; 458: ml. © SuperStock, Inc. / SuperStock; 474: l. Steve & Dave Maslowski/Photo Researchers, Inc.; 474: r. David M. Dennis/Animals Animals; 479: t. Courtesy Eloise Greenfield; 479: b. Used by permission of HarperCollins Publishers; 481: CORBIS; 491: t. Photo: Mike Minehan, Berlin; 492-493: t. Getty Images/David McNew/Staff; 497: t. Harper Collins; 497: b. Getty Images; 498: Getty Images, Inc; 501: Michael Grimm / Getty Images, Inc.; 505: Frank Siteman; 513: Image of The Advertising Archive; 514: The Advertising Archive Ltd./The Picture Desk; 517: t. NO CREDIT NECESSARY; 517: b. Bettmann/CORBIS; 518-519: CORBIS; 520: Bettmann/CORBIS; 522: Culver Pictures, Inc.; 526: Bonnie Kamin/PhotoEdit Inc.; 529: Prentice Hall; 544: (CR) Library of Congress

Grade 6 Unit 4 551: ©Images.com/CORBIS; 552: LUCKY COW © 2003 Mark Pett. Dist. by UNIVERSAL PRESS SYNDICATE. Reprinted with permission. All rights reserved.; 555: Three Fruit, Ashton Hinrichs/SuperStock; 557: Patrik Giardino/CORBIS; 557: Getty Images; 559: Patrik Giardino/CORBIS; 563: t. UPI/CORBIS-Bettmann; 563: b. No credit necessary; 566: b. The Granger Collection, New York; 566-567: Bkgrnd. Kathleen Brown/CORBIS; 567: Inset. Bettmann/CORBIS; 571: t. The Granger Collection, New York; 571: l. The Granger Collection, New York; 571: m. Getty Images; 575: ©Jeffery A. Salter; 576-577: Illustrations copyright © 1998 by Jane Breskin Zalben from The Walrus and the Carpenter. Published by Caroline House, Boyds Mills Press, Inc. Reprinted by permission.; 578-579: Illustrations copyright © 1998 by Jane Breskin Zalben from The Walrus and the Carpenter. Published by Caroline House, Boyds Mills Press, Inc. Reprinted by permission.; 587: t. Photo by Bachrach; 587: m. Getty Images; 587: b. Amherst College Archives and Special Collections, by permission of the Trustees of Amherst College; 593: t. AP/Wide World Photos; 593: m. ©Jan Cobb; 593: b. Bentley Historical Library; 594: Ezra Davenport, 1929, Clarence Holbrook Carter, Oil on canvas, Courtesy of the artist; 595: NASA; 596: Charles Neal/SuperStock; 605: Chris Newbert/Minden Pictures; 606:Richard Hackett/omniphoto.com; 609: b. Dimitri Kessel/Life Magazine; 609: t. AP/Wide World Photos; 612: David Macias/Photo Researchers, Inc.; 623: t. The Granger Collection, New York; 623: Isidro Rodriguez. Used by permission of Marian Reiner for the author; 624: Moodboard/CORBIS; 629: t. Christie's Images/CORBIS; 629: b. ©1999 Little Brown & Co. Illustration ©1999 Karen Lee Baker; 630: Christie's Images/CORBIS; 632: HarperCollins; 639: t. AP/Wide World Photos; 640: © 1996 EVIL EYE MUSIC, INC. Used by permission of HarperCollins Publishers; 644: © Frank Krahmer/zefa/CORBIS; 647: t. William Shakespeare, (detail), attributed to John Taylor, by courtesy of the National Portrait Gallery, London; 647: Photo by George Wallace; 647: ©Nancy Crampton; 648:Blue Lantern Studio/CORBIS; 649: University of Washington Press. Photo by Gordon Robotham; 650: CORBIS; 657: Photodisc/GettyImages; 661: b. ©1998 James McGoon; 661: t. AP/Wide World Photos; 662: © Harpur Garden Library/CORBIS; 665: Jim Vecchi/CORBIS; 668: Jonathan Nourok/PhotoEdit Inc.; 686: (BL) Jan Cobb Photography Ltd.

Grade 6 Unit 5 693: t. ©Getty Images; 694: ZIGGY © 1998 ZIGGY AND FRIENDS, INC. Reprinted with permission of UNIVERSAL PRESS SYNDICATE. All rights reserved.; 695: ©Getty Images; 697: Rights and Permissions will be adding acknowledgement in their section; 698: border. © Danny Lehman/CORBIS; 700: border. © Danny Lehman/CORBIS; 701: Rights and Permissions will be adding acknowledgement in their section; 702: Rights and Permissions will be adding acknowledgement in their section; 702: border. © Danny Lehman/CORBIS;

710: Getty Images; 713: "illustrations" by Jules Fieffer, copyright © 1961 by Jules Feiffer. Copyright renewed 1989 by Jules Feiffer, from The Phantom Tollbooth by Norton Juster illustrated by Jules Feiffer. Used with permission of Random House Children's Books, a division of Random House, Inc.; 715: "illustrations" by Jules Feiffer, copyright © 1961 by Jules Feiffer. Copyright renewed 1989 by Jules Feiffer, from The Phantom Tollbooth by Norton Juster illustrated by Jules Feiffer. Used with permission of Random House Children's Books, a division of Random House, Inc.; 715: 2. John Woodcock/© Dorling Kindersley; 715: 3. HIP/Art Resource, NY; 715: 4. Réunion des Musées Nationaux/Art Resource, NY; 715: 5. Mike Dunning/© Dorling Kindersley; 717: "illustrations" by Jules Feiffer, copyright © 1961 by Jules Feiffer. Copyright renewed 1989 by Jules Feiffer, from The Phantom Tollbooth by Norton Juster illustrated by Jules Feiffer. Used with permission of Random House Children's Books, a division of Random House, Inc.; 747: t. Photo, John Martin; 760: Getty Images; 784: Audio Visual Archives at the John F. Kennedy Library; 785: Andy Crawfod/© Dorling Kindersley; 786: David Frazier Photolibrary/Photo Researchers, Inc.; 789: t. © United Feature Syndicate, Inc.; 790: © United Feature Syndicate, Inc.; 796: David Hsieh/The Repertory Actors Theatre; 800: Royalty-Free/CORBIS; 803: Prentice Hall

Grade 6 Unit 6 825: t. Adolf Fenyes/SuperStock; 826:Reprinted with the permission of Bob Thaves and the Cartoonist Group. All rights reserved.; 827: The Granger Collection, New York; 829: Rights and Permissions will include acknowledgement in their section; 830: Rights and Permissions will include acknowledgement in their section; 832: Corel Professional Photos CD-ROM™; 834-835: Rights and Permissions will include acknowledgement in their section; 836: Rights and Permissions will include acknowledgement in their section; 841: b. L. N. Tolstoi, I. E. Repin, Sovfoto/Eastfoto; 841: t. Bettmann/CORBIS; 847: The Granger Collection, New York; 847: b. Courtesy of Dr. My-Van Tran; 859: t. Courtesy, Houghton Mifflin Company; 863: Mimmo Jodice/CORBIS; 867: t. Photo by Godfrey Boehnke, Courtesy of the University of Auckland; 885: t. Betmann/CORBIS; 885: b. Rights and Permissions will include credit line in their Acknowledgments section; 891: Walt Disney Pictures/Photofest; 896: Walt Disney Pictures/Photofest; 898:Walt Disney Pictures/Photofest; 900: Walt Disney Pictures/Photofest; 901: Walt Disney Pictures/Photofest; 903: Walt Disney Pictures/Photofest; 915: t. Reuters Pictures; 923: t. Prentice Hall; 935: t. Courtesy of the author; 941: t. Alexander Limont; 941: © SuperStock, Inc. / SuperStock 900-128723-A-P22B; 942-943: © SuperStock, Inc. / SuperStock 128727-A-P22J; 943: © SuperStock, Inc. / SuperStock 900-128724-A-P22B; 946: Fairy Art Museum, Tokyo, Japan/The Bridgeman Art Library, London/New York; 949: © SuperStock, Inc. / SuperStock 900-128723-A-P22B; 951: b. © SuperStock, Inc. / SuperStock 900-128730-A-P22J; 952: CORBIS; 961: Bob Krist/CORBIS; 962: Arun Pottirayil /© Dorling Kindersley; 963: t. No Credit Necessary; 963: b. Miriam Berkley; 980: b. Terry Cryer/CORBIS; 980: r. Getty Images; 980: ml. Courtesy of Columbia Records; 980: mr. Courtesy of Columbia Records; 988: Tony Freeman//PhotoEdit Inc.; 991: Prentice Hall; 1008: (CR) Cheron Bayna/Pat Mora

Staff Credits

The people who made up the Pearson Prentice Hall Literature team—representing design, editorial, editorial services, education technology, manufacturing and inventory planning, market research, marketing services, planning and budgeting, product planning, production services, project office, publishing processes, and rights and permissions—are listed below. Boldface type denotes the core team members.

Tobey Antao, Margaret Antonini, Rosalyn Arcilla, Penny Baker, James Ryan Bannon, Stephan Barth, **Tricia Battipede,** Krista Baudo, Rachel Beckman, Julie Berger, Lawrence Berkowitz, Melissa Biezin, **Suzanne Biron,** Rick Blount, **Marcela Boos, Betsy Bostwick,** Kay Bosworth, Jeff Bradley, Andrea Brescia, Susan Brorein, Lois Brown, **Pam Carey,** Lisa Carrillo, **Geoffrey Cassar,** Patty Cavuoto, Doria Ceraso, Jennifer Ciccone, Jaime Cohen,

Rebecca Cottingham, Joe Cucchiara, Jason Cuoco, **Alan Dalgleish**, **Karen Edmonds**, **Irene Ehrmann**, Stephen Eldridge, Amy Fleming, Dorothea Fox, Steve Frankel, Cindy Frederick, Philip Fried, Diane Fristachi, Phillip Gagler, **Pamela Gallo**, Husain Gatlin, **Elaine Goldman**, Elizabeth Good, John Guild, Phil Hadad, Patricia Hade, Monduane Harris, Brian Hawkes, Jennifer B. Heart, Martha Heller, John Hill, Beth Hyslip, Mary Jean Jones, Grace Kang, Nathan Kinney, Roxanne Knoll, **Kate Krimsky**, Monisha Kumar, Jill Kushner, Sue Langan, Melisa Leong, Susan Levine, Dave Liston, **Mary Luthi**, **George Lychock**, **Gregory Lynch**, **Joan Mazzeo**, **Sandra McGloster**, Eve Melnechuk, Kathleen Mercandetti, Salita Mehta, Artur Mkrtchyan, Karyn Mueller, Alison Muff, Christine Mulcahy, Kenneth Myett, Elizabeth Nemeth, Stefano Nese, Carrie O'Connor, April Okano, Kim Ortell, Sonia Pap, Raymond Parenteau, Dominique Pickens, Linda Punskovsky, **Sheila Ramsay**, Maureen Raymond, Mairead Reddin, **Erin Rehill-Seker**, **Renee Roberts**, **Laura Ross**, Bryan Salacki, Sharon Schultz, Jennifer Serra, **Melissa Shustyk**, Rose Sievers, Christy Singer, Yvonne Stecky, **Cynthia Summers**, Steve Thomas, Merle Uuesoo, Roberta Warshaw, Patricia Williams, Daniela Velez

Additional Credits

Lydie Bemba, Victoria Blades, Denise Data, Rachel Drice, Eleanor Kostyk, Jill Little, Loraine Machlin, Evan Marx, Marilyn McCarthy, Patrick O'Keefe, Shelia M. Smith, Lucia Tirondola, Laura Vivenzio, Linda Waldman, Angel Weyant